Periodic Table of Elements

Representative elements: Groups 1–2 and 13–18 · Transition elements: Groups 3–12

Alkali metals: Group 1 · Alkaline earth metals: Group 2 · Halogens: Group 17 · Noble gases: Group 18

Period number	1 Group 1A	2 Group 2A	3 3B	4 4B	5 5B	6 6B	7 7B	8 8B	9 8B	10 8B	11 1B	12 2B	13 Group 3A	14 Group 4A	15 Group 5A	16 Group 6A	17 Group 7A	18 Group 8A
1	1 H 1.008																	2 He 4.003
2	3 Li 6.941	4 Be 9.012											5 B 10.81	6 C 12.01	7 N 14.01	8 O 16.00	9 F 19.00	10 Ne 20.18
3	11 Na 22.99	12 Mg 24.31											13 Al 26.98	14 Si 28.09	15 P 30.97	16 S 32.07	17 Cl 35.45	18 Ar 39.95
4	19 K 39.10	20 Ca 40.08	21 Sc 44.96	22 Ti 47.87	23 V 50.94	24 Cr 52.00	25 Mn 54.94	26 Fe 55.85	27 Co 58.93	28 Ni 58.69	29 Cu 63.55	30 Zn 65.41	31 Ga 69.72	32 Ge 72.64	33 As 74.92	34 Se 78.96	35 Br 79.90	36 Kr 83.80
5	37 Rb 85.47	38 Sr 87.62	39 Y 88.91	40 Zr 91.22	41 Nb 92.91	42 Mo 95.94	43 Tc (99)	44 Ru 101.1	45 Rh 102.9	46 Pd 106.4	47 Ag 107.9	48 Cd 112.4	49 In 114.8	50 Sn 118.7	51 Sb 121.8	52 Te 127.6	53 I 126.9	54 Xe 131.3
6	55 Cs 132.9	56 Ba 137.3	57* La 138.9	72 Hf 178.5	73 Ta 180.9	74 W 183.8	75 Re 186.2	76 Os 190.2	77 Ir 192.2	78 Pt 195.1	79 Au 197.0	80 Hg 200.6	81 Tl 204.4	82 Pb 207.2	83 Bi 209.0	84 Po (209)	85 At (210)	86 Rn (222)
7	87 Fr (223)	88 Ra (226)	89† Ac (227)	104 Rf (261)	105 Db (262)	106 Sg (266)	107 Bh (264)	108 Hs (265)	109 Mt (266)	110 Ds (271)	111 Rg (272)	112 Cn (285)	113 — (284)	114 Fl (289)	115 — (288)	116 Lv (293)	117 — (293)	118 — (294)

*Lanthanides	58 Ce 140.1	59 Pr 140.9	60 Nd 144.2	61 Pm (145)	62 Sm 150.4	63 Eu 152.0	64 Gd 157.3	65 Tb 158.9	66 Dy 162.5	67 Ho 164.9	68 Er 167.3	69 Tm 168.9	70 Yb 173.0	71 Lu 175.0
†Actinides	90 Th 232.0	91 Pa 231.0	92 U 238.0	93 Np (237)	94 Pu (244)	95 Am (243)	96 Cm (247)	97 Bk (247)	98 Cf (251)	99 Es (252)	100 Fm (257)	101 Md (258)	102 No (259)	103 Lr (262)

Metals · Metalloids · Nonmetals

Atomic Masses of the Elements

Name	Symbol	Atomic Number	Atomic Mass[a]	Name	Symbol	Atomic Number	Atomic Mass[a]
Actinium	Ac	89	(227)[b]	Mendelevium	Md	101	(258)
Aluminum	Al	13	26.98	Mercury	Hg	80	200.6
Americium	Am	95	(243)	Molybdenum	Mo	42	95.94
Antimony	Sb	51	121.8	Neodymium	Nd	60	144.2
Argon	Ar	18	39.95	Neon	Ne	10	20.18
Arsenic	As	33	74.92	Neptunium	Np	93	(237)
Astatine	At	85	(210)	Nickel	Ni	28	58.69
Barium	Ba	56	137.3	Niobium	Nb	41	92.91
Berkelium	Bk	97	(247)	Nitrogen	N	7	14.01
Beryllium	Be	4	9.012	Nobelium	No	102	(259)
Bismuth	Bi	83	209.0	Osmium	Os	76	190.2
Bohrium	Bh	107	(264)	Oxygen	O	8	16.00
Boron	B	5	10.81	Palladium	Pd	46	106.4
Bromine	Br	35	79.90	Phosphorus	P	15	30.97
Cadmium	Cd	48	112.4	Platinum	Pt	78	195.1
Calcium	Ca	20	40.08	Plutonium	Pu	94	(244)
Californium	Cf	98	(251)	Polonium	Po	84	(209)
Carbon	C	6	12.01	Potassium	K	19	39.10
Cerium	Ce	58	140.1	Praseodymium	Pr	59	140.9
Cesium	Cs	55	132.9	Promethium	Pm	61	(145)
Chlorine	Cl	17	35.45	Protactinium	Pa	91	231.0
Chromium	Cr	24	52.00	Radium	Ra	88	(226)
Cobalt	Co	27	58.93	Radon	Rn	86	(222)
Copernicium	Cn	112	(285)	Rhenium	Re	75	186.2
Copper	Cu	29	63.55	Rhodium	Rh	45	102.9
Curium	Cm	96	(247)	Roentgenium	Rg	111	(272)
Darmstadtium	Ds	110	(271)	Rubidium	Rb	37	85.47
Dubnium	Db	105	(262)	Ruthenium	Ru	44	101.1
Dysprosium	Dy	66	162.5	Rutherfordium	Rf	104	(261)
Einsteinium	Es	99	(252)	Samarium	Sm	62	150.4
Erbium	Er	68	167.3	Scandium	Sc	21	44.96
Europium	Eu	63	152.0	Seaborgium	Sg	106	(266)
Fermium	Fm	100	(257)	Selenium	Se	34	78.96
Flerovium	Fl	114	(289)	Silicon	Si	14	28.09
Fluorine	F	9	19.00	Silver	Ag	47	107.9
Francium	Fr	87	(223)	Sodium	Na	11	22.99
Gadolinium	Gd	64	157.3	Strontium	Sr	38	87.62
Gallium	Ga	31	69.72	Sulfur	S	16	32.07
Germanium	Ge	32	72.64	Tantalum	Ta	73	180.9
Gold	Au	79	197.0	Technetium	Tc	43	(99)
Hafnium	Hf	72	178.5	Tellurium	Te	52	127.6
Hassium	Hs	108	(265)	Terbium	Tb	65	158.9
Helium	He	2	4.003	Thallium	Tl	81	204.4
Holmium	Ho	67	164.9	Thorium	Th	90	232.0
Hydrogen	H	1	1.008	Thulium	Tm	69	168.9
Indium	In	49	114.8	Tin	Sn	50	118.7
Iodine	I	53	126.9	Titanium	Ti	22	47.87
Iridium	Ir	77	192.2	Tungsten	W	74	183.8
Iron	Fe	26	55.85	Uranium	U	92	238.0
Krypton	Kr	36	83.80	Vanadium	V	23	50.94
Lanthanum	La	57	138.9	Xenon	Xe	54	131.3
Lawrencium	Lr	103	(262)	Ytterbium	Yb	70	173.0
Lead	Pb	82	207.2	Yttrium	Y	39	88.91
Lithium	Li	3	6.941	Zinc	Zn	30	65.41
Livermorium	Lv	116	(293)	Zirconium	Zr	40	91.22
Lutetium	Lu	71	175.0	—	—	113	(284)
Magnesium	Mg	12	24.31	—	—	115	(288)
Manganese	Mn	25	54.94	—	—	117	(293)
Meitnerium	Mt	109	(268)	—	—	118	(294)

[a]Values for atomic masses are given to four significant figures.
[b]Values in parentheses are the mass number of an important radioactive isotope.

BASIC CHEMISTRY

BASIC CHEMISTRY

Fourth Edition

KAREN C. TIMBERLAKE
WILLIAM TIMBERLAKE

PEARSON

Boston Columbus Indianapolis New York San Francisco Upper Saddle River
Amsterdam Cape Town Dubai London Madrid Milan Munich Paris Montréal Toronto
Delhi Mexico City São Paulo Sydney Hong Kong Seoul Singapore Taipei Tokyo

Editor in Chief: Adam Jaworski
Senior Marketing Manager: Jonathan Cottrell
Project Editor: Jessica Moro
Assistant Editor: Coleen Morrison
Editorial Assistant: Fran Falk
Marketing Assistant: Nicola Houston
Executive Editorial Media Producer: Deb Perry
Media Project Manager: Shannon Kong
Managing Editor, Chemistry and Geosciences: Gina M. Cheselka
Senior Production Project Manager: Beth Sweeten
Production Management: Andrea Stefanowicz, PreMediaGlobal
Compositor: PreMediaGlobal
Illustrator: Imagineering
Image Lead: Maya Melenchuk
Photo Researcher: Eric Schrader
Text Permissions Manager: Alison Bruckner
Text Permissions Researcher: Jillian Santos, PreMediaGlobal
Design Manager: Derek Bacchus
Interior Designer: Riezebos Holzbaur Design
Cover Designer: Riezebos Holzbaur Design
Operations Specialist: Jeffrey Sargent
Cover Image Credit: Kenneth Libbrecht / Photo Researchers, Inc.

Credits and acknowledgments borrowed from other sources and reproduced, with permission, in this textbook appear on pp. C-1 to C-4.

Library of Congress Cataloging-in-Publication Data

Timberlake, Karen C.
Basic chemistry.—Fourth edition/Karen Timberlake, Los Angeles Valley College,
William Timberlake, Los Angeles Harbor College.
pages cm.
ISBN-13: 978-0-321-80928-5
ISBN-10: 0-321-80928-9
1. Chemistry—Textbooks. I. Timberlake, William E. II. Title.
QD31.3.T54 2014
540—dc23

2012031269

4 5 6 7 8 9 10—**V011**—16 15 14

ISBN-10: 0-13-310022-7;
ISBN-13: 978-0-13-310022-8 (High School Binding)

Brief Contents

Table of Contents

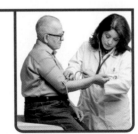

1 Chemistry in Our Lives 1

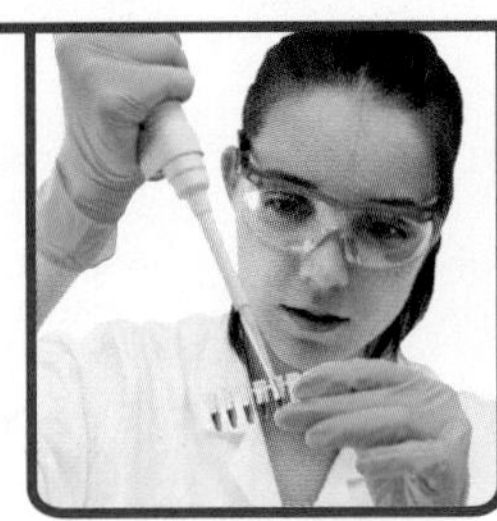

2 Measurements 24

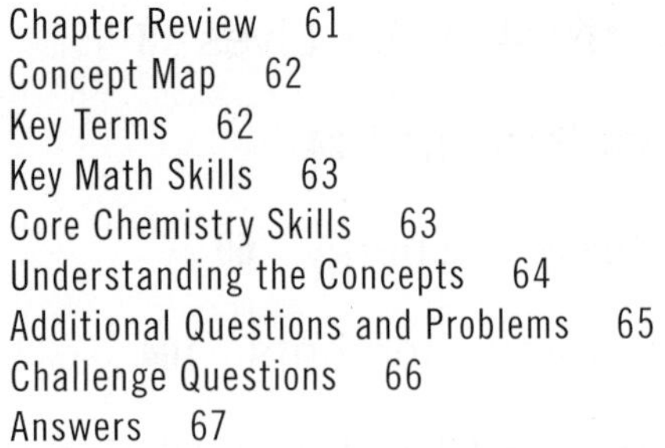

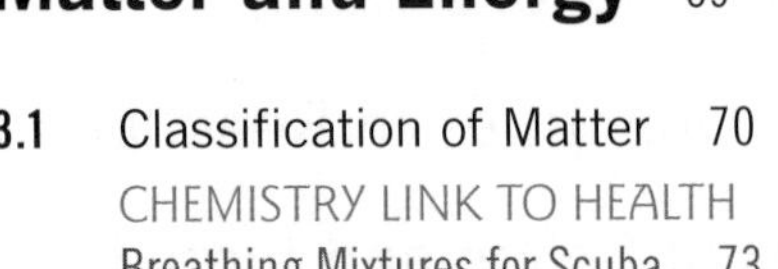

3 Matter and Energy 69

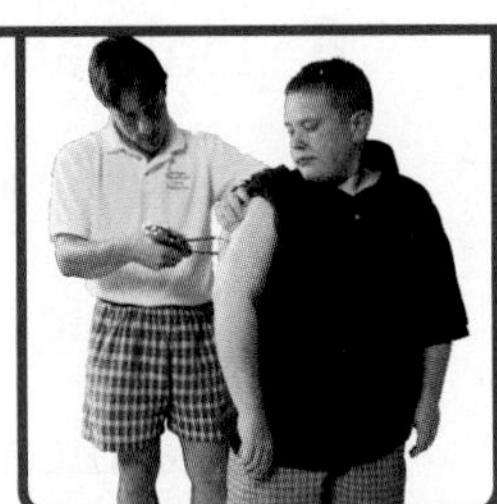

4 Atoms and Elements 104

5 Electronic Structure and Periodic Trends 133

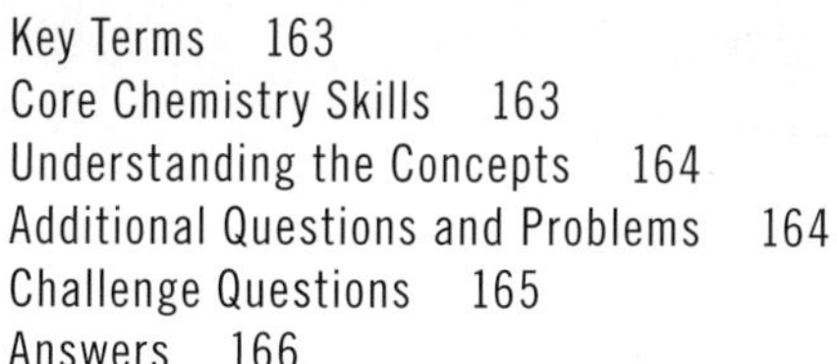

6 Ionic and Molecular Compounds 168

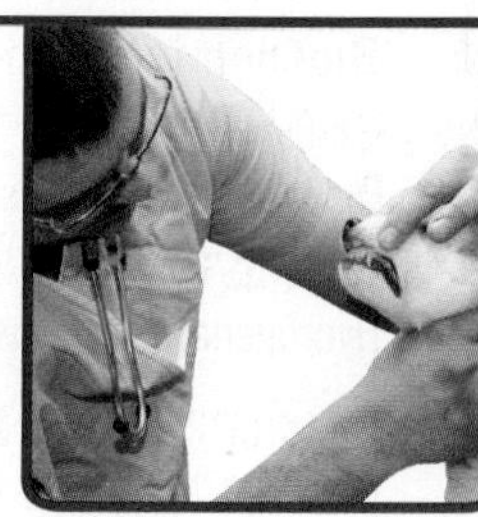

7 Chemical Quantities 207

8 Chemical Reactions 239

9 Chemical Quantities in Reactions 279

10 Properties of Solids and Liquids 306

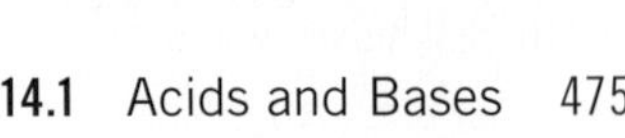

14 Acids and Bases 473

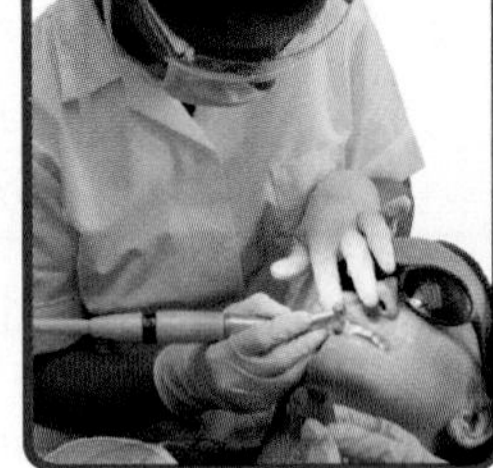

15 Oxidation and Reduction 521

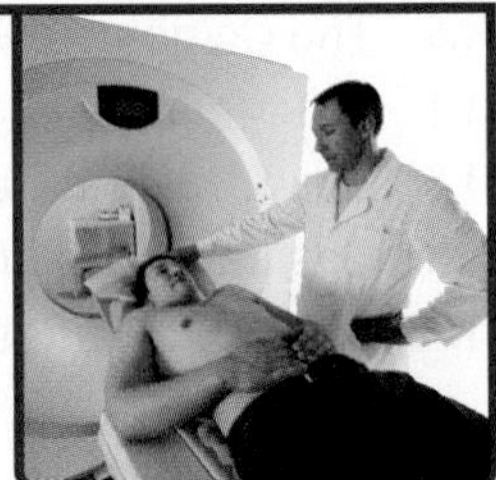

16 Nuclear Chemistry 559

17
Organic Chemistry 594

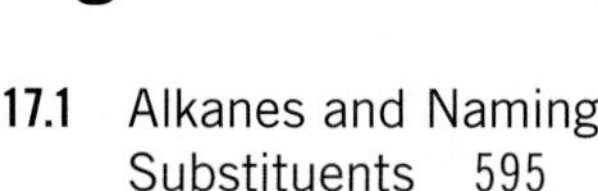

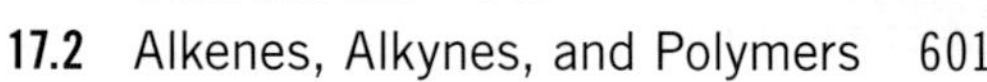

18
Biochemistry 637

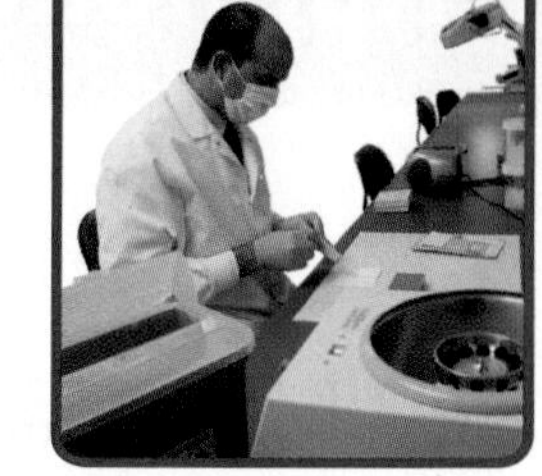

Applications and Activities

Key Math Skills

Core Chemistry Skills

Guide to Problem Solving

Preface

Welcome to the fourth edition of *Basic Chemistry*. The main objective in writing this text is to make the study of chemistry an engaging and positive experience for you by relating the structure and behavior of matter to real life. This new edition introduces more problem-solving strategies, including math remediation, new concept checks, more problem-solving guides, new Analyze the Problem features, conceptual and challenge problems, and new sets of combined problems.

It is our goal to help you become a critical thinker by understanding scientific concepts that will form a basis for making important decisions about issues concerning health and the environment. Thus, we have utilized materials that

- help you to learn and enjoy chemistry
- develop problem-solving skills that lead to success in your chemistry course
- promote learning and success in your chosen career

New to This Fourth Edition

New and updated features have been added throughout this fourth edition, including the following:

- **NEW! Chapter Openers** provide timely examples and engaging, topical issues of the chemistry that is part of contemporary professions.
- **NEW! Integrated math remediation** includes new Key Math Skills that review basic math relevant to chemistry throughout the text concluding with a Key Math Skills review at the end of each chapter with examples.
- **NEW! Core Chemistry Skills** icons identify the key chemical principles in each chapter that are required for successfully learning chemistry. A Core Chemistry Skills review at the end of each chapter summarizes and gives examples.
- **NEW! Chapter Readiness** at the beginning of each chapter lists the Key Math Skills and Core Chemistry Skills from the previous chapters that provide the foundation for new chemistry principles in the current chapter.
- **NEW! Analyze the Problem features** that are now included in the solutions of the Sample Problems to strengthen critical-thinking skills illustrate the breakdown of a word problem into the components required to solve it.
- **UPDATED! Combining Ideas** features offer sets of integrated problems that test students' understanding by integrating topics from two or more previous chapters.
- **UPDATED! End-of-Chapter Problems** based on reviewer feedback and MasteringChemistry® metadata ensure a range of difficulty levels, while added section references make homework and review more efficient for students.
- **NEW! Chemistry Link to Health boxes**, "Brachytherapy," "Polycyclic Aromatic Hydrocarbons (PAHs)," and "Breathing Mixtures for Scuba," have been added.
- **NEW! Chemistry Link to the Environment boxes**, "Energy-Saving Fluorescent Bulbs," "Vanilla," and "Pheromones in Insect Communication," have been added.
- **NEW! Guides to Problem Solving** have been added.
- **UPDATED! Chapter Reviews** now include bulleted lists and thumbnail art samples related to the content of each section.

Chapter-by-Chapter Organization and Changes to the Fourth Edition

In each textbook we write, we consider it essential to relate every chemical concept to real-life issues of health and environment. Because a chemistry course may be taught in different time frames, it may be difficult to cover all the chapters in this text. However, each chapter is a complete package, which allows some chapters to be skipped or the order of presentation to be changed. In this edition, we have incorporated many topics of organic chemistry from Chapter 17 and some of biochemistry from Chapter 18 into the early chapters of the text to integrate general chemistry with organic chemistry.

Chapter 1, Chemistry in Our Lives, introduces the concepts of chemicals and chemistry, discusses the scientific method in everyday terms, and guides students in developing a study plan for learning chemistry.

- New chapter-opening features the work and career of a forensic scientist.
- A new section, "Learning Chemistry: Key Math Skills," reviews basic math required in chemistry, such as place values, positive and negative numbers, percentages, solving equations, and interpreting a line graph.

Chapter 2, Measurements, looks at measurement and emphasizes the need to understand numerical relationships of the metric system. An explanation of scientific notation and working with a calculator is included in the chapter.

- New chapter-opening features the work and career of a registered nurse.
- New Guide to Writing a Number in Scientific Notation was added.
- New material was added that illustrates how to count significant figures in equalities and in conversion factors used in a problem setup.
- New photos that were added include the standard kilogram, mass of a nickel, and a virus.
- The number of parts in multiple-part questions in *MasteringChemistry* was reduced when time needed for students to complete them exceeded 15 minutes.

Chapter 3, Matter and Energy, classifies matter and states of matter, describes temperature measurement, and discusses energy and its measurement. Physical and chemical changes and physical and chemical properties are now discussed in more depth. The section on forms of energy has been deleted. The feature Combining Ideas utilizing concepts from Chapters 1, 2, and 3 follows as an interchapter problem set.

- New chapter-opening features the work and career of a dietitian.
- New Guide to Calculating Temperature was added.
- New problems were added to complete matched sets of problems.
- The effect of the high specific heat of water on coastal cities compared to inland cities was added.
- New Guide to Calculating Specific Heat was added.
- New Guide to Calculating Energy from a Food was added.
- Problems with high difficulty in *MasteringChemistry* were rewritten to identify data and needed answers.

Chapter 4, Atoms and Elements, looks at elements, atoms, subatomic particles, atomic numbers, and mass numbers. Using the naturally occurring isotopes and abundances, atomic mass is calculated.

- New chapter-opening now features the chemistry utilized by a farmer and farming as a career.
- Number of elements now given as 118.
- Table 4.1 was expanded to include the symbols of the elements listed.
- Symbols of the elements Copernicium, Cn (112), Fl (114), and Lv (116) were added to the periodic table of elements.
- "Chemistry Link to Industry: Many Forms of Carbon" was moved into Section 4.1, "Elements and Symbols."
- Photo upgrades through Chapter 4 improve the visual representations of concepts.
- Updated art for the nuclei of the three naturally occurring magnesium isotopes now shows them as three different shades of blue.
- New analogy for the weighted average of bowling balls now introduces concepts of weighted average for atomic mass of an element.
- Table 4.8 now includes the "most prevalent isotopes."
- Isotopes and percent abundances of thallium and rubidium are now included in atomic mass calculations.
- Questions and Problems in *MasteringChemistry* that had high difficulty for students were rewritten.

Chapter 5, Electronic Structure and Periodic Trends, uses the electromagnetic spectrum to explain atomic spectra and develop the concept of energy levels and sublevels. Electrons in sublevels and orbitals are represented using orbital diagrams and electron configurations. Periodic properties of elements, including atomic radius and ionization energy, are related to their valence electrons. Section 5.4 is now titled "Orbital Diagrams and Electron Configurations." Section 5.6 is now titled "Trends in Periodic Properties." Small periodic tables have been added to Section 5.6 to illustrate the trends of periodic properties.

- The new chapter opener features engineers working in the field of materials science.
- Peaks and dips of a wave are now described as crests and troughs.
- The wave equation is now solved for wavelength or for frequency.
- New Guide to Using the Wave Equation was added.
- New Guide to Drawing Orbital Diagrams was added.
- The discussion on electron energy levels was rewritten, and an updated illustration of energy levels was added.
- New diagrams of the *d* orbitals have been added to the representations of *s* and *p* orbitals.
- A discussion of metallic character has been added to Section 5.6, "Trends in Periodic Properties."
- A new summary of the properties for valence electrons, atomic size, ionization energy, and metallic character from top to bottom of a group and going from left to right across a period was added to Section 5.6, "Trends in Periodic Properties."

Chapter 6, Ionic and Molecular Compounds, describes how atoms form ionic and covalent bonds. Chemical formulas are written, and ionic compounds—including those with polyatomic ions—and molecular compounds are named. An introduction to the three-dimensional shape of carbon molecules provides a basis for the shape of organic and biochemical compounds. Organic chemistry is introduced with the properties of inorganic and organic compounds and condensed structural formulas of alkanes. Section 6.1 is now titled "Ions: Transfer of Electrons," 6.2 is titled "Writing Formulas for Ionic

Compounds," 6.3 is titled "Naming Ionic Compounds," and 6.5 is titled "Molecular Compounds: Sharing Electrons."

- New chapter-opening features the work and career of a pharmacist.
- "Ions: Transfer of Electrons" has been rewritten to emphasize the stability of the electron configuration of a noble gas.
- New art comparing the particles and bonding of ionic compounds and molecular compounds has been added.
- New flowchart for Naming Chemical Compounds in Section 6.5 shows naming patterns for ionic and molecular compounds and includes naming alkanes.
- New Guide to Writing Formulas with Polyatomic Ions was added.
- New Concept Check, "Electron-Dot Formulas," was added.
- New Concept Checks include the names and formulas of ionic and covalent compounds.
- "Organic Compounds" and "Names and Formulas of Alkanes" are labeled as Extended Topics.
- Representations of methane and ethane have been updated to emphasize the tetrahedral shape.
- The skeletal formulas of alkanes have been added to the types of formulas for drawing alkanes.

Chapter 7, Chemical Quantities, discusses Avogadro's number, the mole, and molar masses of compounds, which are used in calculations to determine the mass or number of particles in a quantity of a substance. The mass percent composition of a compound is calculated and used to determine its empirical and molecular formula. Combining Ideas from Chapters 4, 5, 6, and 7 follows as an interchapter problem set.

- The chapter opener describes the work and career of a veterinarian.
- The periodic table in Section 7.2 now includes symbols of Fl (114) and Lv (116).
- New Concept Check 7.4, "Calculating Mass Percent from Experimental Data," was added.
- New Guide to Calculating Moles was added.
- New Guide to Calculating Mass Percent Composition was added.

Chapter 8, Chemical Reactions, looks at the interaction of atoms and molecules in chemical reactions. Chemical equations are balanced and organized into combination, decomposition, single replacement, double replacement, and combustion reactions. Section 8.4, "Functional Groups and Reactions of Organic Compounds," and Section 8.5, "Biochemical Compounds," are now Extended Topics, which classify compounds according to their structures to predict their properties and reactions. The Chemistry Link to Health features, "Amines in Health and Medicine" and "Omega-3 Fatty Acids in Fish Oils," and the Chemistry Link to Industry feature, "Hydrogenation of Unsaturated Fats," are included in Chapter 8.

- The chapter opener describes the work and career of an exercise physiologist.
- Section 8.3, "Types of Reactions," now includes combustion reactions and balancing equations for combustion reactions.
- Chemistry Links to Health were added, including "Hand Sanitizers and Ethanol," "Polycyclic Aromatic Hydrocarbons (PAHs) (moved from Chapter 17)," and "Salicylic Acid from the Willow Tree (moved from Chapter 14)," and a new Chemistry Link to the Environment, "Pheromones in Insect Communication," was also added.
- Section 8.5 is now titled "Biochemical Compounds: Extended Topic," which discusses functional groups in carbohydrates, lipids, and proteins.

Chapter 9, Chemical Quantities in Reactions, describes the mole and mass relationships among the reactants and products and provides calculations of limiting reactants and percent yields. A section on "Energy in Chemical Reactions" completes the chapter.

- A new chapter opener describes the work and career of an environmental scientist.
- Mole and mass relationships among the reactants and products are examined along with calculations of percent yield and limiting reactants.
- A new diagram illustrates the process of changing grams of one substance to the grams of another substance.
- New diagrams illustrate the change in energy level of reactants and products for exothermic reactions and for endothermic reactions.

Chapter 10, Properties of Solids and Liquids, introduces electron-dot formulas for molecules and ions with single and multiple bonds as well as resonance structures. Electronegativity leads to a discussion of the polarity of bonds and molecules. Electron-dot formulas and VSEPR theory illustrate covalent bonding and the three-dimensional shapes of molecules and ions. The attractive forces between particles and their impact on states of matter and changes of state are described. Combining Ideas from Chapters 8, 9, and 10 follows as an interchapter problem set.

- A new chapter opener describes the work and career of a histologist.
- New illustrations of molecular models provide visual representations of three-dimensional structures.
- New wedge–dash notation for tetrahedral structures and trigonal pyramidal structures was added.
- The Heating Curve, Figure 10.6, for water has been updated.

- Ethanol, acetic acid, and acetone have been added to heat calculations.
- Heat equation for combining energy calculations is reviewed.
- A new Guide to Determination of Polarity of a Molecule has been added.
- The Guide to Calculations Using Heat of Fusion/Vaporization was rewritten.
- Table 10.6, Comparison of Bonding and Attractive Forces, has been updated.
- A new diagram of unsymmetrical distribution of electrons in nonpolar molecules to give weak dispersion force attractions was added.
- Sublimation was moved to the end of the chapter.

Chapter 11, Gases, describes the properties of a gas and calculates changes in gases using the gas laws and the ideal gas law. The amounts of gases required or produced in chemical reactions are calculated.

- A new chapter opener describes the work and career of a respiratory therapist.
- A table of initial and final gas conditions now includes the factors that remain constant.
- A new Guide to Calculating the Molar Mass of a Gas has been added.
- Several GPS Steps have been rewritten.

Chapter 12, Solutions, describes solutions, saturation and solubility, concentrations, and colligative properties. The volumes and molarities of solutions are used in calculations of reactants and products in chemical reactions, as well as dilutions and titrations. Section 12.4 is now titled "Concentration of Solutions" and Section 12.5 is now titled "Dilution and Chemical Reactions in Solution." Section 12.6, "Properties of Solutions," discusses the properties of solutions and the impact of particle concentration on the boiling point, freezing point, and osmotic pressure.

- A new chapter opener describes the work and career of a dialysis nurse.
- Sections on "Formation of Solutions" and "Electrolytes" have been rewritten for improved clarity.
- New photos added include rock candy made from a saturated sugar solution, vanilla extract and lemon extract, and the Alaska Upis beetle, which produces its own biological antifreeze.
- A new Table 12.7 summarizes percent concentration and molarity and their units.
- A new Guide to Calculating Molality was added.
- A new Guide to Using Molality was added.
- New material on using molality to calculate freezing point depression and boiling point elevation was added.
- New problems were added to provide matched sets of problems.

Chapter 13, Reaction Rates and Chemical Equilibrium, looks at the rates of reactions and the equilibrium condition when forward and reverse rates for a reaction become equal. Equilibrium expressions for reactions are written, and equilibrium constants are calculated. Using equilibrium constants, reactions are evaluated to determine whether stress causes the equilibrium to shift in the direction of the reactants or the products. Le Châtelier's principle is used to evaluate the impact on concentrations when a stress is placed on the equilibrium system. The equilibrium of dissolving and crystallizing in saturated solutions is evaluated using solubility product constants.

- A new chapter opener describes the work and career of a chemical oceanographer.
- Enzymes in laundry detergents are discussed as examples of catalysts in everyday products.
- Art in Figures 13.8 and 13.9 has been updated.
- A new diagram of analogy of water in tanks reaching equilibrium has been added.
- A new Figure 13.11 has been added, illustrating the effect of concentration changes on equilibrium.
- Updated diagrams illustrate the decrease of reactants and increase of products to reach equilibrium.
- Guides to Writing the Equilibrium Constant Expression, Calculating the K_c Value, Using the Equilibrium Constant, Calculating K_{sp}, and Calculating Molar Solubility from K_{sp} have been updated and rewritten.
- Art on the effect of adding a common ion of Mg^{2+} or CO_3^{2-} to a solution of $MgCO_3$ has been updated.
- New photos of slightly soluble salts, including calcium oxalate, calcium carbonate, and cadmium sulfide, have been added.

Chapter 14, Acids and Bases, discusses acids and bases and their strengths, conjugate acid–base pairs, the dissociation of weak acids and bases and water, pH and pOH, and buffers. Acid–base titration uses the neutralization reactions between acids and bases to calculate quantities of acid in a sample. Section 14.9, "Acid–Base Properties of Salt Solutions," has been deleted. Combining Ideas from Chapters 11, 12, 13, and 14 follows as an interchapter problem set.

- A new chapter opener describes the work and career of a clinical laboratory technician.
- Three-dimensional models of sulfuric acid, bicarbonate, carbonic acid, formate, and formic acid were added.
- Table 14.4, Relative Strengths of Acids and Bases, was moved to Section 14.3, "Strengths of Acids and Bases."
- A new Guide to Writing Conjugate Acid–Base Pairs has been added.
- New material on diprotic acids has been added.
- New art on weak acid hydrofluoric acid was added.

- New material and art on gastric cells and the production of HCl has been added to Chemistry Link to Health, "Stomach Acid, HCl."
- New photos of calcium hydroxide and information about its use in the food industry, dentistry, and preparation of corn kernels for hominy were added.
- Guides to Calculating $[H_3O^+]$ and $[OH^-]$ in Aqueous Solutions and Calculating pH of an Aqueous Solution have been rewritten.
- A new Guide Calculating $[H_3O^+]$ from pH was added.
- A new photo of sodium bicarbonate reacting with acetic acid has been added to chemical reactions of acids and bases.

Chapter 15, Oxidation and Reduction, looks at the characteristics of oxidation and reduction reactions. Oxidation numbers are assigned to the atoms in elements, molecules, and ions to determine the components that lose electrons during oxidation and gain electrons during reduction. The half-reaction method is utilized to balance oxidation–reduction reactions. The production of electrical energy in voltaic cells and the requirement of electrical energy in electrolytic cells are diagrammed using half-cells. The activity series is used to determine the spontaneous direction of an oxidation–reduction reaction.

- A new chapter opener describes the work and career of a dentist.
- A new Guide to Using Oxidation Numbers has been added.
- Oxidation–reduction equations are now balanced using half-reactions in acidic or basic solutions.
- The Guide to Balancing Redox Equations Using Half-Reactions was rewritten.
- Section 15.4, which is titled "Electrical Energy from Oxidation–Reduction Reactions," now begins with the Activity Series followed by Voltaic Cells.
- The section "Oxidation of Alcohols" is now an Extended Topic at the end of the chapter and includes the oxidation of alcohol in the body.

Chapter 16, Nuclear Chemistry, looks at the type of radioactive particles that are emitted from the nuclei of radioactive atoms. Equations are written and balanced for both naturally occurring radioactivity and artificially produced radioactivity. The half-lives of radioisotopes are discussed, and the amount of time for a sample to decay is calculated. Radioisotopes important in the field of nuclear medicine are described. Combining Ideas from Chapters 15 and 16 follows as an interchapter problem set.

- The new chapter opener describes the work and career of a radiologist.
- A new Sample Problem, Dating Using Half-Lives, now calculates time elapsed for a bone sample.
- New photos include a smoke detector and bone in a skeleton used in carbon dating.

Chapter 17, Organic Chemistry, discusses each family of organic compounds, thus forming a basis for understanding the biomolecules of living systems. In this fourth edition, topics such as functional groups, reactions of organic compounds, and naming organic acids are now included in earlier chapters on naming molecular compounds and chemical reactions. This organic chapter is now streamlined with an emphasis on naming and drawing formulas of organic compounds from alkanes with substituents to amines and amides.

- A new chapter opener describes the work and career of a firefighter.
- The skeletal formula for carbon chains has been added.
- Drawing a skeletal formula has been added to Sample Problem 17.2 along with drawing condensed structural formulas.
- A new Guide to Naming Aromatic Compounds has been added.
- Skeletal structures are now included as compounds in Questions and Problems.
- A table of the IUPAC and common names of selected carboxylic acids was added.
- New illustrations for naming esters were added.

Chapter 18, Biochemistry, looks at the chemical structures and reactions of chemicals that occur in living systems. We focus on four types of biomolecules—carbohydrates, lipids, proteins, and nucleic acids—as well as their biochemical reactions. The shape of proteins is related to the activity and regulation of enzyme activity. A discussion of the genetic code and protein synthesis completes the chapter. Combining Ideas from Chapters 17 and 18 follows as an interchapter problem set.

- A new chapter opener describes the work and career of a forensic toxicologist.
- An updated graph of blood glucose levels with time has replaced the previous graph.
- New monosaccharide open-chain structures have been added to Questions and Problems for Carbohydrates.
- The term Haworth Structures is now used for the term cyclic structures for monosaccharides, disaccharides, and polysaccharides.
- The Guide to Drawing Haworth Structures has been rewritten.
- Art added to the introduction of lipids distinguishes between the structures of fatty acids, waxes, triacylglycerols, and steroids.

- Table 18.2 has been expanded and includes more examples of common fatty acids as well as their skeletal formulas.
- New art and ball-and-stick models of *cis*-2-butene and *trans*-2-butene have been added.
- New material on some typical waxes and their condensed structural formulas has been added.
- New art illustrating triacylglycerols has been added.
- New art for the olestra molecule has been added.
- New art for a steroid and cholesterol has been added.
- New art for amino acids and ionized amino acids has been added.
- New single letter abbreviations for amino acids have been added.
- New art for the ribbon models of proteins has been added.
- New energy diagram for carbonic anhydrase and the active site in an enzyme has been added.
- New art for the induced-fit model of enzyme action has been added.

Program Components

Basic Chemistry, Fourth Edition, provides an integrated teaching and learning package of support material for both students and teachers.

For Students

The following resources are available for purchase.

The **Study Guide for *Basic Chemistry*, Fourth Edition,** by Karen Timberlake is keyed to the learning goals in the text and designed to promote active learning through a variety of exercises with answers as well as practice tests. The **Study Guide** also contains complete solutions to odd-numbered problems.

Laboratory Manual by Karen Timberlake This best-selling lab manual coordinates 35 experiments with the topics in *Basic Chemistry*, Fourth Edition, and uses new terms during the lab and explores chemical concepts. Laboratory investigations develop skills of manipulating equipment, reporting data, solving problems, making calculations, and drawing conclusions. These labs are also available within Pearson Custom Library, which gives teachers the power to create a custom text by selecting content from our course-specific collections.

For Teachers

Most of the teacher supplements and resources for this text are available electronically to qualified adopters on the Instructor Resource Center (IRC). Upon adoption or to preview, please go to **www.PearsonSchool.com/Access_Request** and select Instructor Resource Center. You will be required to complete a brief one-time registration subject to verification of educator status. Upon verification, access information and instructions will be sent to you via e-mail. Once logged into the IRC, enter your text ISBN in the **Search our Catalog** box to locate your resources.

Instructor Solutions Manual Prepared by Mark Quirie, this manual highlights chapter topics. It contains complete solution setups and answers to all the problems in the text. (Available in print)

Instructor's Resource Materials for *Basic Chemistry*, Fourth Edition This resource includes all the art, photos, and tables from the book in JPG format for use in classroom projection or when creating study materials and tests. In addition, teachers can access the PowerPoint™ lecture outlines, featuring over 2000 slides. Also available are downloadable files of the *Instructor Solutions Manual* and a set of "clicker questions" designed for use with classroom-response systems. (Download only)

TestGen Test Bank Prepared by William Timberlake, this resource includes more than 1600 questions in multiple-choice, matching, true/false, and short-answer format. (Download only)

Online Instructor Manual for Laboratory Manual This manual contains answers to report pages for the *Laboratory Manual*. (Download only)

For Students and Teachers

MasteringChemistry® The most advanced, most widely used online chemistry tutorial and homework program is available for the fourth edition of Basic Chemistry. MasteringChemistry®, with Pearson eText, utilizes the Socratic method to coach students through problem-solving techniques, offering hints and simpler questions on request to help students learn, not just practice. New tutorials have been created to guide students through the most challenging Basic Chemistry topics and help them make connections between chemical concepts.

Teachers can create online assignments for their students by choosing from a wide range of items, including end-of-chapter problems and research-enhanced tutorials. Assignments are automatically graded with up-to-date diagnostic information, helping teachers pinpoint where students struggle either individually or as a class as a whole.

Upon textbook purchase, students and teachers are granted access to MasteringChemistry. High school teachers can obtain preview or adoption access for MasteringChemisty in one of the following ways:

Preview Access

- Teachers can request preview access online by visiting **PearsonSchool.com/Access_Request**, using Option 2. Preview Access information will be sent to the teacher via e-mail.

Adoption Access

- With the purchase of this program, a Pearson Adoption Access Card, with codes and complete instructions, will be delivered with your textbook purchase. (ISBN 0130343919)
- Ask your sales representative for an Adoption Access Code Card (ISBN: 0130343919)
  OR
- Visit **PearsonSchool.com/Access_Request** using Option 3. Adoption access information will be sent to the teacher via e-mail.

Students, ask your teacher for access.

Acknowledgments

The preparation of a new text is a continuous effort of many people. As in our work on other textbooks, we are thankful for the support, encouragement, and dedication of many people who put in hours of tireless effort to produce a high-quality book that provides an outstanding learning package. The editorial team at Pearson Publishing has done an exceptional job. We want to thank, Adam Jaworski, editor in chief, who supported our vision of this fourth edition and the development of new math remediation strategies with Chapter Readiness, Key Math Skills, and Core Chemistry Skills, which appear throughout the chapter along with their reviews at the end of each chapter and with the new Analyze the Problem feature that clarifies the components of a word problem for problem solving. We also appreciate the addition of new Concept Checks, more Guides to Problem Solving, new Chemistry Links to Health, Chemistry Link to History, Chemistry Link to Industry, and Chemistry Link to the Environment boxes, and new problems in Understanding the Concepts and Combining Ideas.

We much appreciate all the wonderful work of Jessica Moro, project editor, who was like an angel encouraging us at each step, while skillfully coordinating reviews, art, web site materials, and all the things it takes to make a book come together. We appreciate the work of Beth Sweeten, project manager, and Andrea Stefanowicz of PreMediaGlobal, who brilliantly coordinated all phases of the manuscript to the final pages of a beautiful book. Thanks to Mark Quirie, manuscript and accuracy reviewer, and Betty Pessagno, copy editor, who precisely analyzed and edited the initial and final manuscripts and pages to make sure the words and problems were correct to help students learn chemistry. Their keen eyes and thoughtful comments were extremely helpful in the development of this text.

We are especially proud of the art program in this text, which lends beauty and understanding to chemistry. We would like to thank Connie Long and Derek Bacchus, art director and book designer, whose creative ideas provided the outstanding design for the cover and pages of the book. Eric Schrader, photo researcher, was invaluable in researching and selecting vivid photos for the text so that students can see the beauty of chemistry. Thanks also to *Bio-Rad Laboratories* for their courtesy and use of *KnowItAll ChemWindows*, drawing software that helped us produce chemical structures for the manuscript. The macro-to-micro illustrations designed by Production Solutions and Precision Graphics give students visual impressions of the atomic and molecular organization of everyday things and are a fantastic learning tool. We want to thank Martha Ghent for the hours spent proofreading all the pages. We also appreciate all the hard work put in by the marketing team in the field and Jonathan Cottrell, marketing manager.

We are extremely grateful to an incredible group of peers for their careful assessment of all the new ideas for the text; for their suggested additions, corrections, changes, and deletions; and for providing an incredible amount of feedback about improvements for the book. In addition, we appreciate the time scientists took to let us take photos and discuss their work with them. We admire and appreciate every one of you.

If you would like to share your experience with chemistry, or have questions and comments about this text, we would appreciate hearing from you.

Karen and Bill Timberlake
Email: khemist@aol.com

Reviewers

Fourth Edition Reviewers

Edward Alexander
San Diego Mesa College

Kristen Casey
Anne Arundel Community College

James Falender
Central Michigan University

Tamara Hanna
Texas Tech University

Shawn Korman
Rio Salado Community College

Robin Lasey
Arkansas Tech University

Lynda Nelson
University of Arkansas Fort Smith

Mary Repaske
Cincinnati State Technical and Community College

Mitchell Robertson
Southwestern Illinois College

Alan Sherman
Middlesex County College

Trent Vorlicek
Minnesota State University-Mankato

Joy Walker
Truman College

Marie Wolff
Joliet Junior College

Regina Zibuck
Wayne State University

Accuracy Reviewer

Mark Quirie
Algonquin College

Previous Edition Reviewers

Maher Atteya
Georgia Perimeter College

Pamela Goodman
Moraine Valley Community College

David Nachman
Mesa Community College

MaryKay Orgill
University of Nevada, Las Vegas

Mark Quirie
Algonquin College

Ben Rutherford
Washington State Community College

About the Author

KAREN TIMBERLAKE is Professor Emerita of Chemistry at Los Angeles Valley College, where she taught chemistry for allied health and preparatory chemistry for 36 years. She received her bachelor's degree in chemistry from the University of Washington and her master's degree in biochemistry from the University of California at Los Angeles.

Professor Timberlake has been writing chemistry textbooks for 40 years. During that time, her name has become associated with the strategic use of pedagogical tools that promote student success in chemistry and the application of chemistry to real-life situations. More than one million students have learned chemistry using texts, laboratory manuals, and study guides written by Karen Timberlake. In addition to ***Basic Chemistry,* Fourth Edition,** she is also the author of ***Chemistry: An Introduction to General, Organic, and Biological Chemistry,* Eleventh Edition,** and ***General, Organic, and Biological Chemistry: Structures of Life,* Fourth Edition.**

Professor Timberlake belongs to numerous scientific and educational organizations including the American Chemical Society (ACS) and the National Science Teachers Association (NSTA). She was the Western Regional Winner of Excellence in College Chemistry Teaching Award given by the Chemical Manufacturers Association. She received the McGuffey Award in Physical Sciences from the Textbook Authors Association for her textbook ***Chemistry: An Introduction to General, Organic, and Biological Chemistry,* Eighth Edition.** She received the "Texty" Textbook Excellence Award from the Textbook Authors Association for the first edition of ***Basic Chemistry.*** She has participated in education grants for science teaching including the Los Angeles Collaborative for Teaching Excellence (LACTE) and a Title III grant at her college. She speaks at conferences and educational meetings on the use of student-centered teaching methods in chemistry to promote the learning success of students.

Her husband, William Timberlake, who is the coauthor of this text, is Professor Emeritus of Chemistry at Los Angeles Harbor College, where he taught preparatory and organic chemistry for 36 years. He received his bachelor's degree in chemistry from Carnegie Mellon University and his master's degree in organic chemistry from the University of California at Los Angeles. When the Professors Timberlake are not writing textbooks, they relax by hiking, traveling, trying new restaurants, cooking, playing tennis, and taking care of their grandchildren, Daniel and Emily.

DEDICATION

We dedicate this book to

- Our son, John, daughter-in-law, Cindy, grandson, Daniel, and granddaughter, Emily, for the precious things in life
- The wonderful students over many years whose hard work and commitment always motivated us and put purpose in our writing

Students learn chemistry using real-world examples

"Discovery consists of seeing what everybody has seen and thinking what nobody has thought."
—Albert Szent-Györgyi

Feature	Description	Benefit	Page
NEW! Chapter Opener	Chapters begin with **stories** involving careers in fields such as nursing, dentistry, agriculture, engineering, exercise physiology, and veterinary sciences.	Shows you how health professionals use chemistry every day	69
UPDATED! Chemistry Link to Health	**Chemistry Links to Health** apply chemical concepts to relevant topics of health and medicine such as weight loss and weight gain, trans fats, anabolic steroids, alcohol abuse, blood buffers, kidney dialysis, and cancer.	Provides you with connections that illustrate the importance of understanding chemistry in real life health and medical situations	259
Chemistry Links to the Environment	**Chemistry Links to the Environment** relate chemistry to environmental topics such as global warming, radon in our homes, acid rain, and pheromones.	Helps you extend your understanding of the impact of chemistry on the environment	56
Chemistry Links to Industry and Chemistry Link to History	**Chemistry Links to Industry** describe industrial and commercial applications while **Chemistry Links to History** describe the historical development of chemical ideas.	Helps you understand the importance of chemistry in industry and history	106, 4
UPDATED! Macro-to-Micro Art	**Macro-to-Micro Art** utilizes photographs and drawings to illustrate the atomic structure of chemical phenomena.	Helps you connect the world of atoms and molecules to the macroscopic world	245

Engage students in the world of chemistry

"I never teach my pupils; I only attempt to provide the conditions in which they can learn."
—Albert Einstein

Feature	Description	Benefit	Page
Learning Goals LEARNING GOAL *Write the symbols for the simple ions of the representative elements.*	**Learning Goals** at the beginning and end of each section identify the key concepts for that section and provide a roadmap for your study.	Helps you focus your studying by emphasizing what is most important in each section	169
Writing Style **8.5 Biochemical Compounds: Extended Topic** Biochemical compounds are organic compounds that are found in living things. Biochemical processes and reactions are part of every cell from which we derive energy and cellular components. Our diets are rich with biochemical compounds including carbohydrates, lipids, and proteins. All of the biochemical compounds are very large molecules, but each contains the same functional groups that are present in organic compounds.	Timberlake's accessible **writing style** is based on careful development of chemical concepts suited to the skills and backgrounds of students in preparatory chemistry.	Helps you understand new terms and chemical concepts	263
UPDATED! Concept Maps CONCEPT MAP MATTER AND ENERGY	**Concept Maps** at the end of each chapter show how all the key concepts fit together.	Encourages learning by providing a **visual** guide to the interrelationship among all the concepts in each chapter	96
NEW! Key Math Skills KEY MATH SKILL *Identifying Place Values*	**Key Math Skills** provide practice problems related to basic math.	Helps you master the basic quantitative skills to succeed in preparatory chemistry	12
NEW! Core Chemistry Skills CORE CHEMISTRY SKILL *Counting Significant Figures*	**Core Chemistry Skills** provide content crucial to problem-solving strategies related to chemistry.	Helps you master the basic problem-solving skills needed to succeed in chemistry	33
UPDATED! Art Program	The **art program** is beautifully rendered, pedagogically effective, and includes questions with all the figures.	Helps you think critically using photos and illustrations	498
UPDATED! Chapter Reviews CHAPTER REVIEW 2.1 Units of Measurement *LEARNING GOAL: Write the names and abbreviations for the metric or SI units used in measurements of length, volume, mass, temperature, and time.* • In science, physical quantities are described in units of the metric or International System of Units (SI). • Some important units are meter (m) for length, liter (L) for volume, gram (g) and kilogram (kg) for mass, degree Celsius (°C) and Kelvin (K) for temperature, and second (s) for time.	The **Chapter Reviews** include Learning Goals and new visual thumbnails to summarize the key points in each section.	Helps you determine your mastery of the chapter concepts and study for your tests	61

Many tools show students how to solve problems

"The whole art of teaching is only the art of awakening the natural curiosity of young minds."
—Anatole France

Feature	Description	Benefit	Page
UPDATED! Guides to Problem Solving (GPS)	**Guides to Problem Solving (GPS)** illustrate the steps needed to solve problems.	Visually guides you step-by-step through each problem-solving strategy	31
End-of-Section Questions and Problems	**Questions** and **Problems** are placed at the end of each section. Problems are paired and the Answers to the odd-numbered problems are given at the end of each chapter.	Encourages you to become involved immediately in the process of problem solving	34
UPDATED! Concept Checks	**Concept Checks** that transition from conceptual ideas to problem-solving strategies are placed throughout each chapter.	Allows you to check your understanding of new chemical terms and ideas as they are introduced in the chapter	88
UPDATED! Sample Problems with Study Checks	**Sample Problems** illustrate worked-out solutions with step-by-step explanations and required calculations. **Study Checks** associated with each Sample Problem allow you to check your problem-solving strategies.	Provides the intermediate steps to guide you successfully through each type of problem	214
NEW! Analyze the Problems	**Analyze the Problems** feature now included in Sample Problem Solutions convert information in a word problem into components for problem solving.	Helps you identify and utilize the components within a word problem to set up a solution strategy	214
UPDATED! Understanding the Concepts 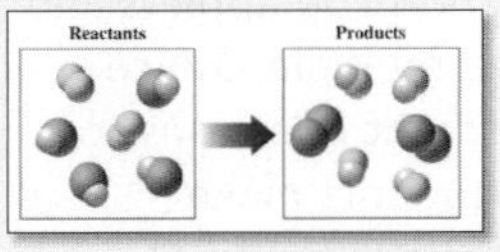	**Understanding the Concepts** are questions with visual representations placed at the end of each chapter.	Builds an understanding of newly learned chemical concepts	273
UPDATED! Additional Questions and Problems	**Additional Questions and Problems** at the end of chapter provide further study and application of the topics from the entire chapter.	Promotes critical thinking	275
Challenge Questions	**Challenge Questions** at the end of each chapter provide complex questions.	Promotes critical thinking, group work, and cooperative learning environments	276
UPDATED! Combining Ideas 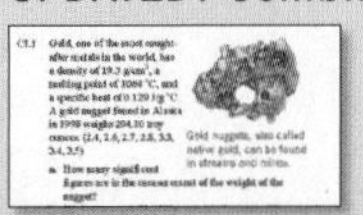	**Combining Ideas** are sets of integrated problems that are placed after every 2–4 chapters.	Tests your understanding of the concepts from previous chapters by integrating topics	102

MasteringChemistry® for Students

The Mastering platform is the most effective and widely used online homework, tutorial, and assessment system for the sciences. The Mastering system motivates students to learn outside of class and arrive prepared.

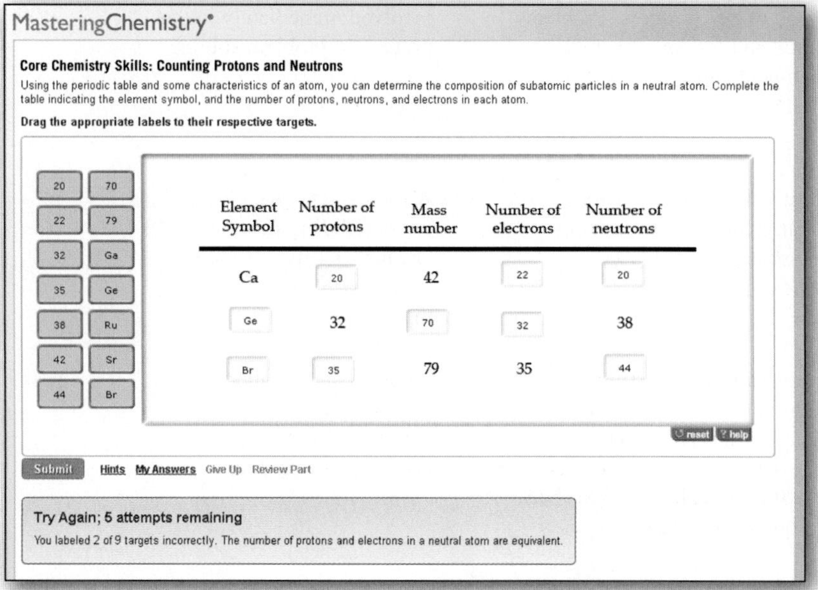

NEW! Key Math Skills and Core Chemistry Skills Tutorials

Key Math Skills and Core Chemistry Skills Tutorials provide assignable practice problems related to the in-text feature boxes, ensuring that students master the basic quantitative and science skills they need to succeed in the course.

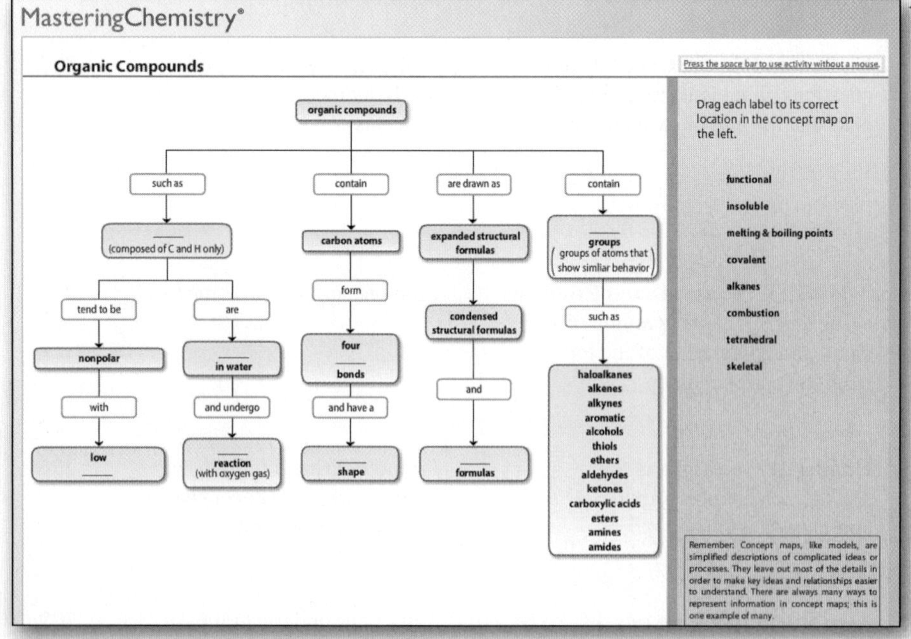

NEW! Concept Map Quizzes

Concept Map Quizzes use drag-and-drop applets and related multiple-choice assessment questions to help students make connections between important concepts within each chapter.

MasteringChemistry promotes interactivity and active learning in Basic Chemistry. Research shows that Mastering's immediate feedback and tutorial assistance help students understand and master concepts and skills in chemistry—allowing them to retain more knowledge and perform better in this course and beyond.

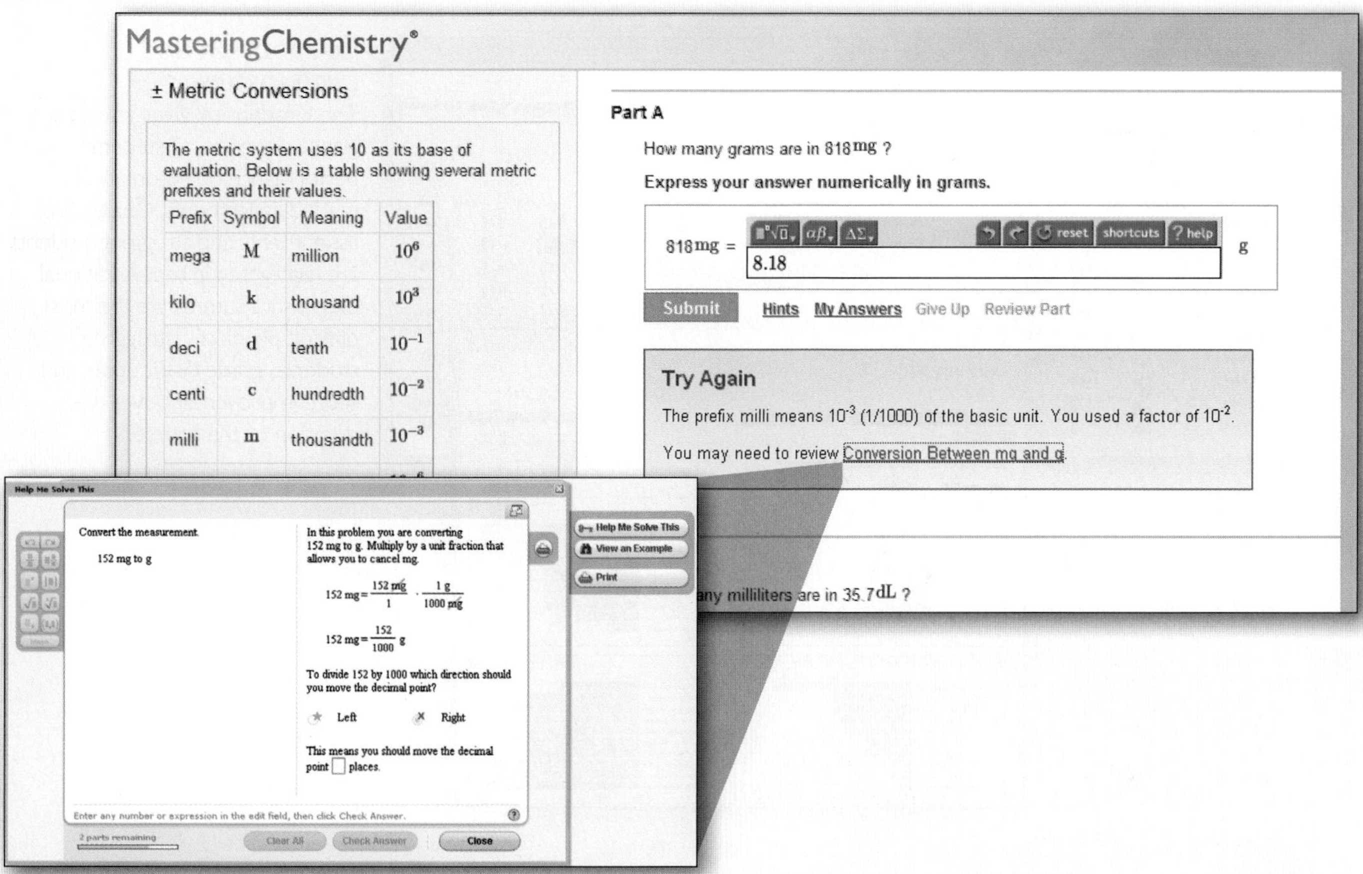

▲ **Math Remediation**

MasteringChemistry offers a variety of math remediation options for students to brush up on required quantitative skills. The Mathematics Review chapter contains practice tutorials covering key math topics in the course. A new Math Remediation Quiz provides a comprehensive set of review questions with links to additional algorithmically generated practice problems in MathXL. Select tutorials also contain Math Remediation Links to additional MathXL® questions.

End-of-Chapter Questions and Problems

A high percentage of the text's end-of-chapter questions and problems are now easily assignable within MasteringChemistry. The overall number of algorithmic and randomized problems has also been increased for this edition.

Access to MasteringChemistry with Pearson eText comes with the purchase of *Basic Chemistry.* Students—ask your teacher for information.

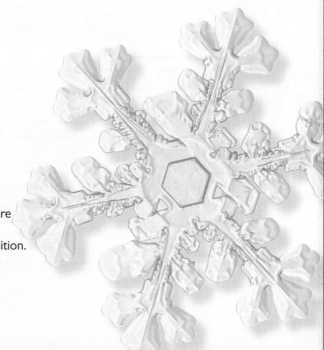

MasteringChemistry® for Teachers

With the Mastering gradebook and diagnostics, you'll be better informed about your students' progress than ever before. Mastering captures the step-by-step work of every student—including wrong answers submitted, hints requested, and time taken at each step of an assigned problem.

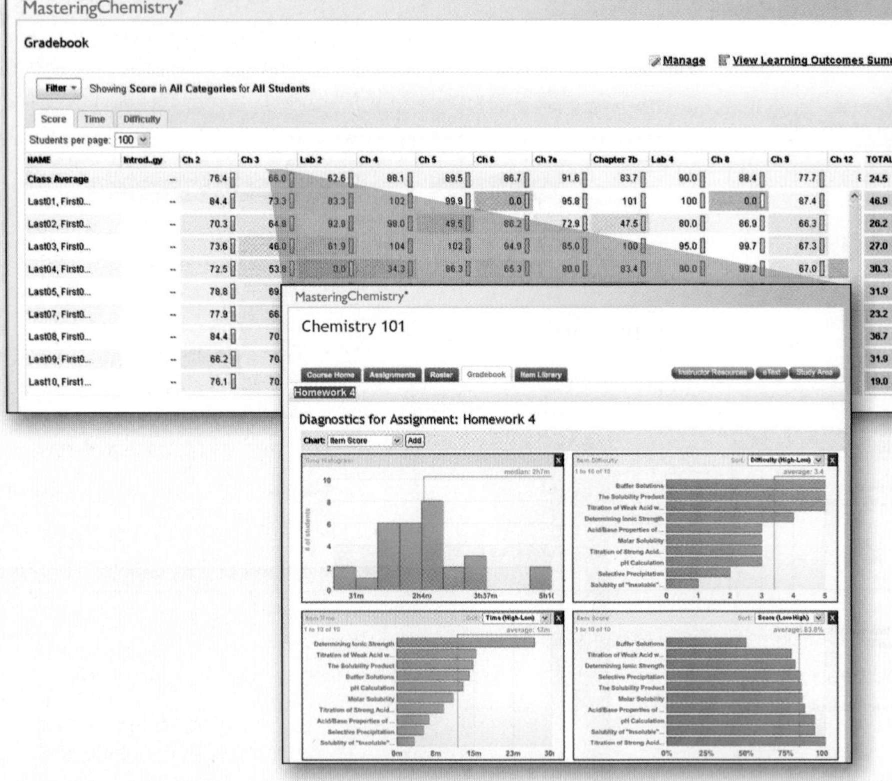

Gradebook and Diagnostics

The Gradebook gives you an at-a-glance overview of student performance on automatically graded assignments. Challenging assignments and struggling students are highlighted in red. Additional diagnostics summarize the most difficult problems, struggling students, grade distribution, and score improvement over the duration of the course.

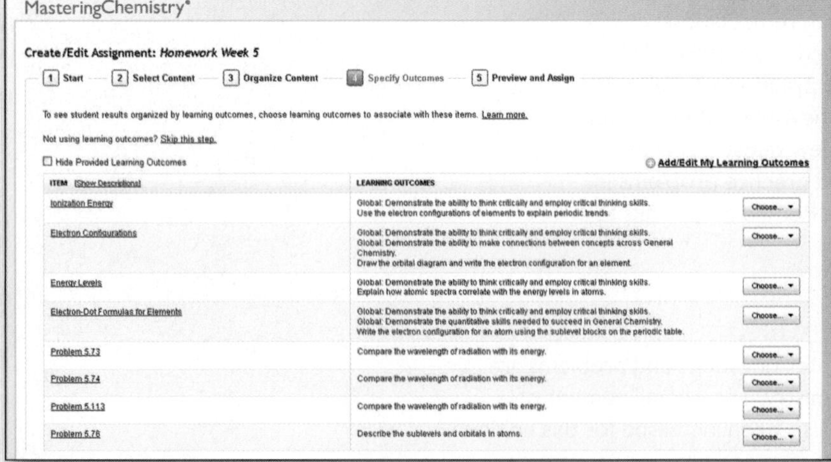

NEW! Learning Outcomes

Let Mastering do the work in tracking student performance against your learning outcomes:

- Add your own or use the publisher-provided learning outcomes.
- View class performance against the specified learning outcomes.
- Export results to a spreadsheet that you can further customize.

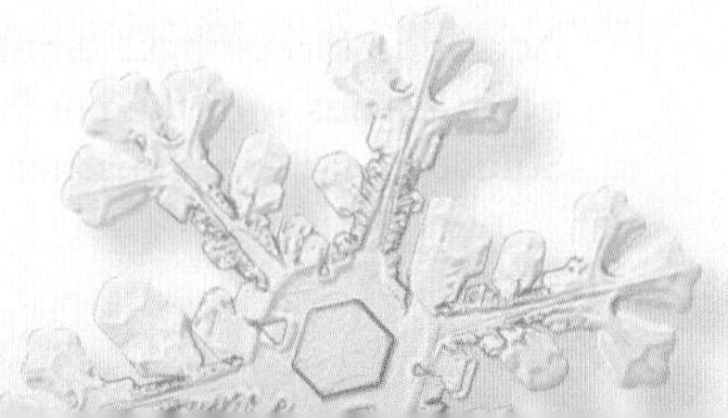

Mastering provides a rich and flexible set of course materials to get you started quickly, including homework, tutorial, and assessment tools that you can use as is or customize to fit your needs.

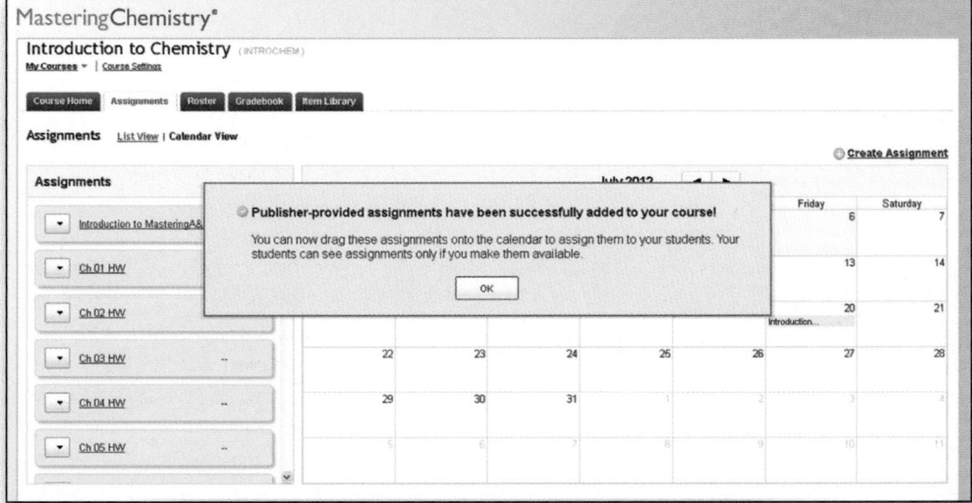

NEW! Calendar Features

The Course Home default page now features a **Calendar View** displaying upcoming assignments and due dates.

- Teachers can schedule assignments by dragging and dropping the assignment onto a date in the calendar. If the due date of an assignment needs to change, teachers can drag the assignment to the new due date and change the "available from and to dates" accordingly.
- The calendar view gives students a syllabus-style overview of due dates, making it easy to see all assignments due in a given month.

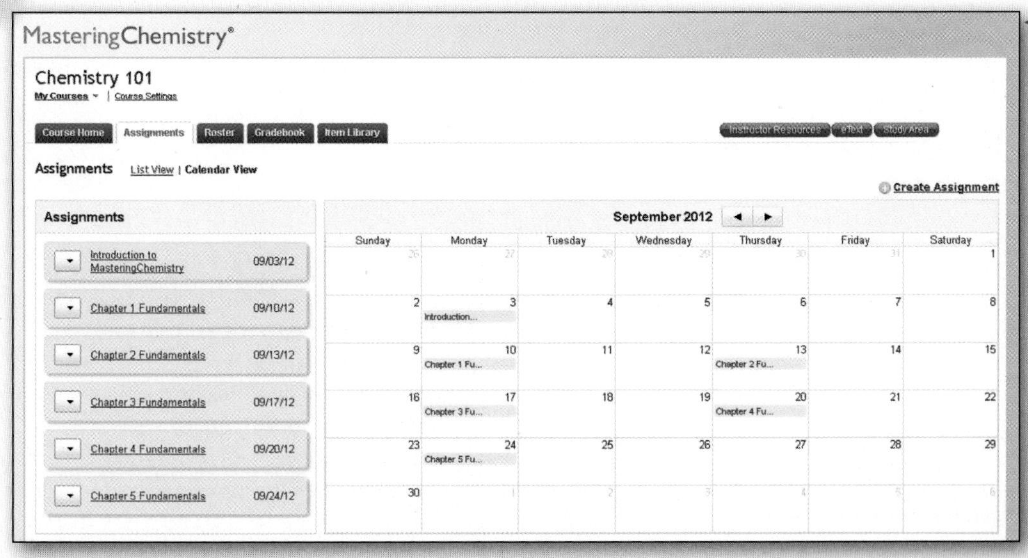

NEW! Publisher Assignments

When creating a course, teachers now have the option of copying a complete set of pre-built assignments for each chapter pulled from the Mastering item library, containing end-of-chapter questions, tutorials, reading quiz questions, and media activities.

Student and teacher access to MasteringChemistry with Pearson eText comes with the purchase of this text. For teacher preview or adoption access information see page xix.

Chemistry in Our Lives 1

LOOKING AHEAD

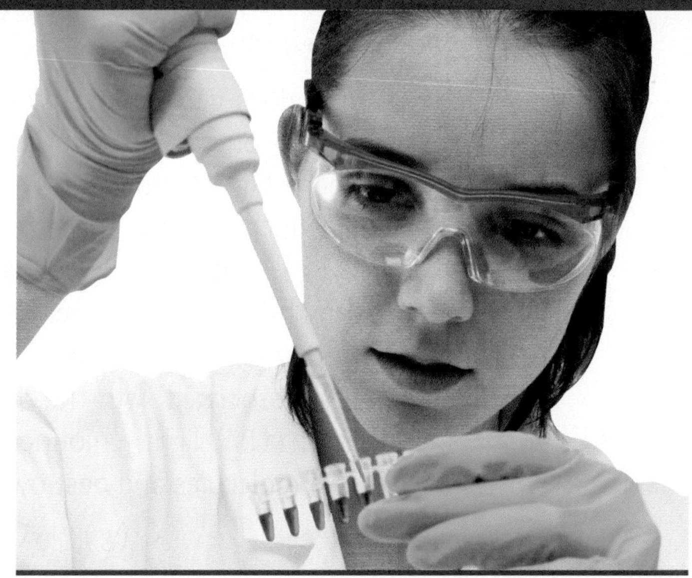

Sarah works as a forensic scientist where she applies scientific procedures to evidence from law enforcement agencies. Such evidence may include blood, hair, or fiber from clothing found at a crime scene. At work, she analyzes blood for the presence of drugs, poisons, and alcohol. She prepares tissues for typing factors and for DNA analysis. Her lab partner Mark is working on matching characteristics of a bullet to a firearm found at a crime scene. He is also using fingerprinting techniques to identify the victim of a crime.

A female victim is found dead in her home. The police suspect that she was murdered, so samples of her blood and stomach contents are sent to Sarah. Using a variety of qualitative and quantitative tests, Sarah finds traces of ethylene glycol. The qualitative tests show that ethylene glycol is present, while the quantitative tests indicate the amount of ethylene glycol the victim has in her system. Sarah determines that the victim was poisoned when she ingested ethylene glycol placed in an alcoholic beverage. Since the initial symptoms of ethylene glycol poisoning are similar to being intoxicated, the victim was unaware of the poisoning.

The alcohol in beverages undergoes oxidation reactions to other compounds that are eliminated by the body. When ethylene glycol is oxidized, the products can cause renal failure and may be toxic to the body.

Career: Forensic Scientist

Most forensic scientists work in crime laboratories that are part of city or county legal systems where they analyze bodily fluids and tissue samples collected by crime scene investigators. In analyzing these samples, a forensic scientist identifies the presence or absence of specific chemicals within the body to help solve the criminal case. Some of the chemicals they look for include alcohol, illegal or prescription drugs, poisons, arson debris, metals, and various gases such as carbon monoxide. In order to identify these substances, a variety of chemical instruments and highly specific methodologies are used. A forensic scientist also analyzes samples from criminal suspects, athletes, and potential employees. They also work on cases involving environmental contamination and animal samples for wildlife crimes. A forensic scientist usually has a bachelor's degree that includes courses in math, chemistry, and biology.

Now that you are in a chemistry class, you may be wondering what you will be learning. What questions in science have you been curious about? Perhaps you are interested in how smog is formed, what causes ozone depletion, how nails form rust, or how aspirin relieves a headache. Just like you, chemists are curious about the world we live in.

- How does car exhaust produce the smog that hangs over our cities? One component of car exhaust is nitrogen oxide (NO), which forms in car engines where high temperatures convert nitrogen gas (N_2) and oxygen gas (O_2) to NO. In chemistry, these reactions are written in the form of equations such as $N_2(g) + O_2(g) \longrightarrow 2NO(g)$.
- Why has the ozone layer been depleted in certain parts of the atmosphere? During the 1970s, scientists discovered that substances called chlorofluorocarbons (CFCs) were associated with the depletion of ozone. As CFCs are broken down by ultraviolet (UV) light, chlorine (Cl) is released that causes the breakdown of ozone (O_3) molecules and destroys the ozone layer.

$$Cl(g) + O_3(g) \longrightarrow ClO(g) + O_2(g)$$

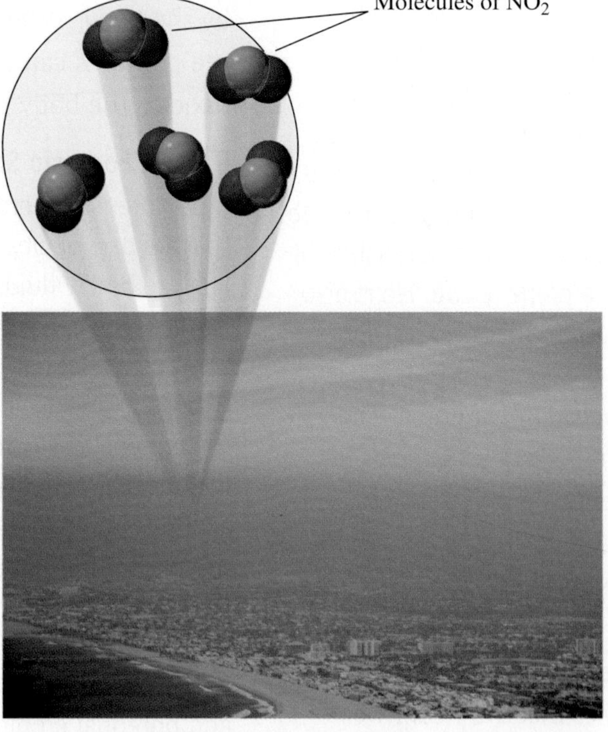

The chemical reaction of NO with oxygen in the air forms NO_2, which produces the reddish brown color of smog.

- Why does aspirin relieve a headache? When a part of the body is injured, substances called prostaglandins are produced, which cause inflammation and pain. Aspirin acts to block the production of prostaglandins, thereby reducing inflammation, pain, and fever.

Chemists perform many different kinds of research. Some design new fuels and more efficient ways to use them. Researchers in the medical field develop new treatments for diabetes, genetic defects, cancer, AIDS, and other diseases. Researchers in the environmental field study the ways in which human development impacts the environment and develop processes that help reduce environmental degradation. For the researcher in the laboratory, the physician in the dialysis unit, the environmental chemist, or the agricultural scientist, chemistry plays a central role in understanding problems, assessing possible solutions, and making important decisions.

A geochemist collects newly erupted lava samples from Kilauea Volcano, Hawaii.

CHAPTER READINESS

Key Math Skills

- Identifying Place Values (1.4A)
- Using Positive and Negative Numbers in Calculations (1.4B)
- Calculating a Percentage (1.4C)
- Solving Equations (1.4D)
- Interpreting a Line Graph (1.4E)

1.1 Chemistry and Chemicals

LEARNING GOAL

Define the term chemistry and identify substances as chemicals.

Chemistry is the study of the composition, structure, properties, and reactions of matter. *Matter* is another word for all the substances that make up our world. Perhaps you imagine that chemistry takes place only in a laboratory where a chemist is working in a white coat and goggles. Actually, chemistry happens all around you every day and has an impact on everything you use and do. You are doing chemistry when you cook food, add bleach to your laundry, or start your car. A chemical reaction has taken place when silver tarnishes or an antacid tablet fizzes when dropped into water. Plants grow because chemical reactions convert carbon dioxide, water, and energy to carbohydrates. Chemical reactions take place when you digest food and break it down into substances that you need for energy and health.

Branches of Chemistry

The field of chemistry is divided into several branches. General chemistry is the study of the composition, properties, and reactions of matter. Organic chemistry is the study of substances that contain the element carbon. Biological chemistry is the study of the chemical reactions that take place in biological systems.

Today chemistry is often combined with other sciences, such as geology and physics, to form cross-disciplines such as geochemistry and physical chemistry. Geochemistry is the study of the chemical composition of ores, soils, and minerals of the surface of the Earth and other planets. Physical chemistry is the study of the physical nature of chemical systems, including energy changes.

Antacid tablets undergo a chemical reaction when dropped into water.

Chemistry Link to History

EARLY CHEMISTS: THE ALCHEMISTS

For many centuries, chemists have studied changes in matter. From the time of the ancient Greeks to about the sixteenth century, early scientists, called alchemists, described matter in terms of four components of nature: earth, air, fire, and water. These components had the qualities of hot, cold, wet, or dry. By the eighth century, alchemists believed that they could rearrange these qualities to change metals such as copper and lead into gold and silver. They searched for an unknown substance called a *philosopher's stone*, which they thought would turn metals into gold as well as prolong youth and postpone death. Although these efforts failed, the alchemists did provide information on the processes and chemical reactions involved in the extraction of metals from ores. During the many centuries that alchemy flourished, alchemists made observations of matter and identified the properties of many substances. They also designed some of the first laboratory equipment and developed early laboratory procedures.

The alchemist Paracelsus (1493–1541) thought that alchemy should be about preparing new medicines, not about producing gold. Using observation and experimentation, he proposed that a healthy body was regulated by a series of chemical processes that could be unbalanced by certain chemical compounds and rebalanced by using minerals and medicines. For example, he determined that inhaled dust, not underground spirits, caused lung disease in miners. He also thought that goiter was a problem caused by contaminated water, and he treated syphilis with compounds of mercury. His opinion of medicines was that the right dose makes the difference between a poison and a cure. Today this idea is part of the risk–benefit assessment of medicine. Paracelsus changed alchemy in ways that helped to establish modern medicine and chemistry.

Alchemists in the Middle Ages developed laboratory procedures.

Swiss alchemist Paracelsus (1493–1541) believed that chemicals and minerals could be used as medicines.

Chemicals

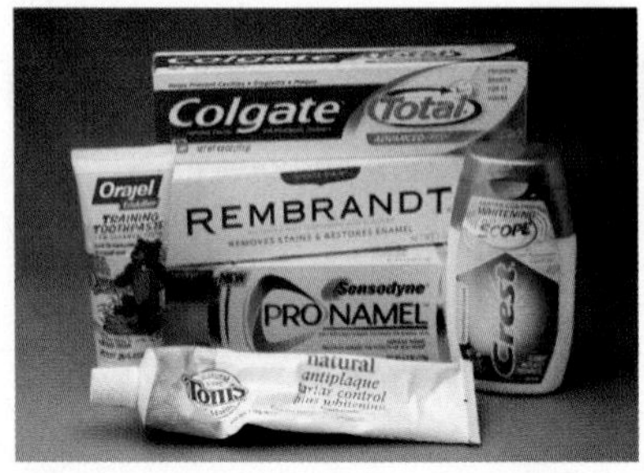

Toothpaste is a combination of many chemicals.

A **chemical** is a substance that always has the same composition and properties wherever it is found. All the things you see around you are composed of one or more chemicals. Chemical processes take place in chemistry laboratories, manufacturing plants, and pharmaceutical labs as well as every day in nature and in our bodies. Often the terms *chemical* and *substance* are used interchangeably to describe a specific type of matter.

Every day, you use products containing substances that were developed and prepared by chemists. Soaps and shampoos contain chemicals that remove oils on your skin and scalp. When you brush your teeth, the substances in toothpaste clean your teeth, prevent plaque formation, and stop tooth decay. Some of the chemicals used to make toothpaste are listed in Table 1.1.

TABLE 1.1 Chemicals Commonly Used in Toothpaste

Chemical	Function
Calcium carbonate	Used as an abrasive to remove plaque
Sorbitol	Prevents loss of water and hardening of toothpaste
Sodium lauryl sulfate	Used to loosen plaque
Titanium dioxide	Makes toothpaste white and opaque
Triclosan	Inhibits bacteria that cause plaque and gum disease
Sodium fluorophosphate	Prevents formation of cavities by strengthening tooth enamel with fluoride
Methyl salicylate	Gives toothpaste a pleasant wintergreen flavor

In cosmetics and lotions, chemicals are used to moisturize, prevent deterioration of the product, fight bacteria, and thicken the product. Your clothes may be made of natural materials such as cotton or synthetic substances such as nylon or polyester. Perhaps you wear a ring or watch made of gold, silver, or platinum. Your breakfast cereal is probably fortified with iron, calcium, and phosphorus, while the milk you drink is enriched with vitamins A and D. Antioxidants are chemicals added to food to prevent it from spoiling. Some of the chemicals you may encounter when you cook in the kitchen are shown in Figure 1.1.

FIGURE 1.1 Many of the items found in a kitchen are chemicals or products of chemical reactions.
Q What are some other chemicals found in a kitchen?

CONCEPT CHECK 1.1 Chemicals

Why is the copper in a copper wire an example of a chemical?

ANSWER

Copper has the same composition and properties wherever it is found. Thus, copper is a chemical.

SAMPLE PROBLEM 1.1 Everyday Chemicals

Identify the chemical in each of the following statements:

a. Soda cans are made from aluminum.
b. Salt (sodium chloride) is used to preserve meat and fish.
c. Sugar (sucrose) is used as a sweetener.

SOLUTION

a. aluminum **b.** salt (sodium chloride) **c.** sugar (sucrose)

STUDY CHECK 1.1

Which of the following are chemicals?

a. iron **b.** tin **c.** a low temperature **d.** water

The answers to all of the *Study Checks* can be found at the end of each chapter.

QUESTIONS AND PROBLEMS

1.1 Chemistry and Chemicals

LEARNING GOAL: *Define the term chemistry and identify substances as chemicals.*

In every chapter, odd-numbered exercises in the *Questions and Problems* are paired with even-numbered exercises. The answers for the magenta, odd-numbered *Questions and Problems* are given at the end of this chapter. The complete solutions to the odd-numbered *Questions and Problems* are in the *Student Solutions Manual*.

1.1 Write a one-sentence definition for each of the following:
a. chemistry **b.** chemical

1.2 Ask two of your friends (not in this class) to define the terms in Problem 1.1. Do their answers agree with the definitions you provided?

1.3 Obtain a bottle of multivitamins and read the list of ingredients. What are four chemicals from the list?

1.4 Obtain a box of breakfast cereal and read the list of ingredients. What are four chemicals from the list?

1.5 Read the labels on some items found in your medicine cabinet. What are the names of some chemicals contained in those items?

1.6 Read the labels on products used to wash and clean your car. What are the names of some chemicals contained in those products?

1.7 Pesticides are chemicals. Give one advantage and one disadvantage of using pesticides.

1.8 Sugar is a chemical. Give one advantage and one disadvantage of eating sugar.

LEARNING GOAL

Describe the activities that are part of the scientific method.

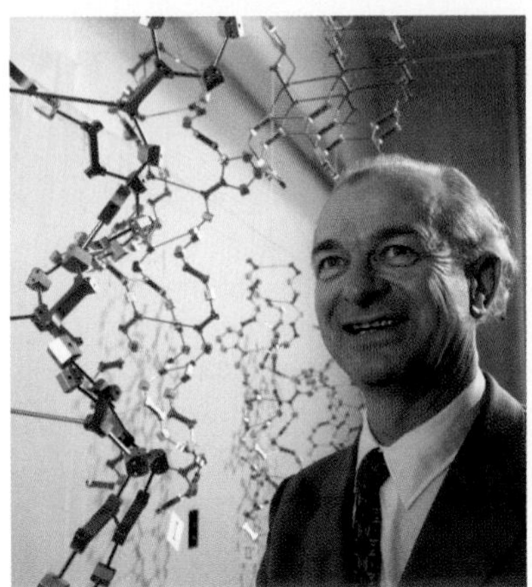

Linus Pauling won the Nobel Prize in chemistry in 1954.

Students make observations in the chemistry laboratory.

1.2 Scientific Method: Thinking Like a Scientist

When you were very young, you explored the things around you by touching and tasting. As you grew, you asked questions about the world in which you live. What is lightning? Where does a rainbow come from? Why is water blue? As an adult, you may have wondered how antibiotics work or why vitamins are important to your health. Every day, you ask questions and seek answers to organize and make sense of the world around you.

When the late Nobel Laureate Linus Pauling described his student life in Oregon, he recalled that he read many books on chemistry, mineralogy, and physics. "I mulled over the properties of materials: why are some substances colored and others not, why are some minerals or inorganic compounds hard and others soft?" He said, "I was building up this tremendous background of empirical knowledge and at the same time asking a great number of questions." Linus Pauling won two Nobel Prizes: the first, in 1954, was in chemistry for his work on the nature of chemical bonds and the determination of the structures of complex substances; the second, in 1962, was the Peace Prize.

Scientific Method

Although the process of trying to understand nature is unique to each scientist, a set of general principles, called the **scientific method**, helps to describe how a scientist thinks.

1. **Observations.** The first step in the scientific method is to observe, describe, and measure an event in nature. Observations based on measurements are called *data.*
2. **Hypothesis.** After sufficient data are collected, a *hypothesis* is proposed, which states a possible interpretation of the observations. The hypothesis must be stated in a way that it can be tested by experiments.
3. **Experiments.** Experiments are tests that determine the validity of the hypothesis. Often, many experiments are performed to test the hypothesis, and a large amount of information is collected. Many experiments are needed to support the original hypothesis. However, if just one experiment produces a different result than predicted by the hypothesis, a modified hypothesis must be proposed. Then new experiments are conducted to test the new hypothesis.
4. **Theory.** When experiments are repeated by many scientists with consistent results, the hypothesis may be confirmed. Consequently, that hypothesis may become a *theory.* Even then, a theory continues to be tested and, based on new experimental results, may need to be modified or replaced. Then the cycle of the scientific method begins again with the proposal of a new hypothesis.

Scientific Method

Observations

Hypothesis

Theory modified if additional experiments do not support it.

Hypothesis changed if experiments do not support it.

Experiments

Theory

The scientific method develops a theory using observations, hypotheses, and experiments.

Using the Scientific Method in Everyday Life

You may be surprised to realize that you use the scientific method in your everyday life. Suppose you visit a friend in her home. Soon after you arrive, your eyes start to itch and you begin to sneeze. Then you observe that your friend has a new cat. Perhaps you ask yourself why you are sneezing and you form the hypothesis that you are allergic to cats. To test your hypothesis, you leave your friend's home. If the sneezing stops, perhaps your hypothesis is correct. You test your hypothesis further by visiting another friend who also has a cat. If you start to sneeze again, your experimental results support your hypothesis that you are allergic to cats. However, if you continue sneezing after you leave your friend's home, your hypothesis is not supported. Now you need to form a new hypothesis, which could be that you have a cold.

Through observation you may determine that you are allergic to cat hair and dander.

CONCEPT CHECK 1.2 Scientific Method

Identify each of the following as an observation (O), a hypothesis (H), or an experiment (E):

a. Drinking coffee at night keeps me awake.
b. If I stop drinking coffee in the afternoon, I will be able to sleep at night.
c. I will try drinking coffee only in the morning.

ANSWER

a. Describing what happens when I drink coffee is an observation (O).
b. Describing what may happen if I stop drinking coffee in the afternoon is a hypothesis (H).
c. Changing the time for drinking coffee is an experiment (E).

SAMPLE PROBLEM 1.2 Scientific Method

Identify each of the following statements as an observation (O) or a hypothesis (H):

a. A silver tray turns a dull gray color when left uncovered.
b. North of the equator, it is warmer in summer than in winter.
c. Ice cubes float in water because they are less dense.

SOLUTION

a. observation (O)
b. observation (O)
c. hypothesis (H)

STUDY CHECK 1.2

The following statements are found in a student's notebook. Identify each of the following as an observation (O), a hypothesis (H), or an experiment (E):

a. "Today I placed two tomato seedlings in the garden, and two more in a closet. I will give all the plants the same amount of water and fertilizer."
b. "After 50 days, the tomato plants in the garden are 3 ft high with green leaves. The plants in the closet are 8 in. tall and yellow."
c. "Tomato plants need sunlight to grow."

A silver tray tarnishes when exposed to the air.

Tomato plants grow faster when placed in the sun.

Chemistry Link to the Environment

DDT—GOOD PESTICIDE, BAD PESTICIDE

DDT (**D**ichloro**d**iphenyl**t**richloroethane) was once one of the most commonly used pesticides. DDT is an example of organic compounds, which typically are composed of the elements of carbon (C) and hydrogen (H). In a molecule of DDT, there are 14 carbon atoms and 9 hydrogen atoms, as well as 5 chlorine atoms. The hydrocarbon portion makes DDT insoluble in water, and the Cl atoms make DDT difficult to break down.

Although DDT was first synthesized in 1874, it was not used as an insecticide until 1939. Before DDT was widely used, insect-borne diseases such as malaria and typhus were rampant in many parts of the world. Paul Müller, who discovered that DDT was an effective pesticide, was recognized for saving many lives and received the Nobel Prize in Physiology or Medicine in 1948. DDT was considered the ideal pesticide because it was toxic to many insects, had a low toxicity to humans and animals, and was inexpensive to prepare.

In the United States, DDT was used extensively in homes as well as on crops, such as cotton and soybeans. Because of its stable chemical structure, DDT did not break down quickly in the environment, which meant that it did not have to be applied as often. At first, everyone was pleased with DDT as crop yields increased and diseases such as malaria and typhus were controlled.

DDT... FOR CONTROL OF HOUSEHOLD PESTS

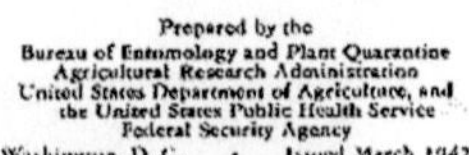

Prepared by the
Bureau of Entomology and Plant Quarantine
Agricultural Research Administration
United States Department of Agriculture, and
the United States Public Health Service
Federal Security Agency
Washington, D. C. • Issued March 1947

A 1947 advertisement recommends the household use of DDT.

However, by the early 1950s, problems attributed to DDT began to surface. Insects were becoming more resistant to the pesticide. At the same time, the public was increasingly concerned about the long-term impact of a substance that could remain in the environment for many years. The metabolic systems of humans and animals cannot break down DDT, which is soluble in fats but not in water and is stored in the fatty tissues of the body. Although the concentration of DDT applied to crops was very low, runoff containing DDT reached the oceans, where the DDT was absorbed by fish.

When birds such as the Brown Pelicans in Florida and California consumed fish contaminated with DDT, the amount of calcium in their eggshells was significantly reduced. As a result, incubating eggs cracked open early, causing offspring to die. Due to this difficulty with reproduction, the populations of birds such as the Brown Pelican dropped significantly and they became endangered.

The Brown Pelican was once an endangered species due to the use of DDT.

By 1972, DDT was banned in the United States. Since then, the population of Brown Pelicans has increased, and they are no longer considered endangered. Today new types of pesticides, which are more water-soluble and break down faster in the environment, have replaced the long-lasting pesticides such as DDT. However, these new pesticides are much more toxic to humans.

A field is sprayed with pesticide.

QUESTIONS AND PROBLEMS

1.2 Scientific Method: Thinking Like a Scientist

LEARNING GOAL: *Describe the activities that are part of the scientific method.*

1.9 Define each of the following terms of the scientific method:
a. hypothesis **b.** experiment
c. theory **d.** observation

1.10 Identify each of the following activities in the scientific method as an observation (O), a hypothesis (H), an experiment (E), or a theory (T):
a. Formulate a possible explanation for your experimental results.
b. Collect data.

c. Design an experimental plan that will give new information about a problem.
d. State a generalized summary of your experimental results.

1.11 Identify each activity, **a–f**, as an observation (O), a hypothesis (H), an experiment (E), or a theory (T).
At a popular restaurant, where Chang is the head chef, the following occurred:
a. Chang determined that sales of the house salad had dropped.
b. Chang decided that the house salad needed a new dressing.
c. In a taste test, Chang prepared four bowls of lettuce, each with a new dressing: sesame seed, olive oil and balsamic vinegar, creamy Italian, and blue cheese.
d. The tasters rated the sesame seed salad dressing as the favorite.
e. After two weeks, Chang noted that the orders for the house salad with the new sesame seed dressing had doubled.
f. Chang decided that the sesame seed dressing improved the sales of the house salad because the sesame seed dressing enhanced the taste.

Customers rated the sesame seed dressing as the best.

1.12 Identify each activity, **a–f**, as an observation (O), a hypothesis (H), an experiment (E), or a theory (T).
Lucia wants to develop a process for dyeing shirts so that the color will not fade when the shirt is washed. She proceeds with the following activities:
a. Lucia notices that the dye in a design fades when the shirt is washed.
b. Lucia decides that the dye needs something to help it combine with the fabric.
c. She places a spot of dye on each of four shirts and then places each one separately in water, salt water, vinegar, and baking soda and water.
d. After one hour, all the shirts are removed and washed with a detergent.
e. Lucia notices that the dye has faded on the shirts in water, salt water, and baking soda, while the dye did not fade on the shirt soaked in vinegar.
f. Lucia thinks that the vinegar binds with the dye so it does not fade when the shirt is washed.

1.3 Learning Chemistry: A Study Plan

LEARNING GOAL

Develop a study plan for learning chemistry.

Here you are taking chemistry, perhaps for the first time. Whatever your reasons for choosing to study chemistry, you can look forward to learning many new and exciting ideas.

Features in This Text Help You Study Chemistry

This text has been designed with study features to complement your individual learning style. On the inside of the front cover is a periodic table of the elements. On the inside of the back cover are tables that summarize useful information needed throughout your study of chemistry. Each chapter begins with *Looking Ahead*, which outlines the topics in the chapter. At the end of the text, there is a comprehensive *Glossary and Index*, which lists and defines key terms used in the text. *Key Math Skills* that will be helpful to your understanding of chemical calculations are reviewed. *Core Chemistry Skills* that are critical to learning chemistry are indicated by icons in the margin, and summarized at the end of each chapter. In the *Chapter Readiness* list at the beginning of every chapter, the *Key Math Skills* and *Core Chemistry Skills* from previous chapters related to the current chapter concepts are highlighted for your review.

Before you begin reading, obtain an overview of a chapter by reviewing the topics in *Looking Ahead*. As you prepare to read a section of the chapter, look at the section title and turn it into a question. For example, for Section 1.1, "Chemistry and Chemicals," you could ask "What is chemistry?" or "What are chemicals?". Throughout each chapter, you will find *Concept Checks* that will help you understand key ideas. When you come to a *Sample Problem*, take the time to work it through and compare your solution to the one provided. Then try the associated *Study Check*. Many *Sample Problems* are accompanied by a *Guide to Problem Solving* (*GPS*), which gives the steps needed to work the problem. In some *Sample Problems*, an *Analyze the Problem* feature shows how to organize the data in the word problem to obtain a solution. At the end of each chapter section, you will find a set of *Questions and Problems* that allows you to apply problem solving immediately to the new concepts.

Analyze the Problem	Given	Need
	165 lb	kilograms

Throughout each chapter, boxes titled "Chemistry Link to Health," "Chemistry Link to History," "Chemistry Link to Industry," and "Chemistry Link to the Environment" help you connect the chemical concepts you are learning to real-life situations. Many of the figures and diagrams use macro-to-micro illustrations to depict the atomic level of organization of ordinary objects. These visual models illustrate the concepts described in the text and allow you to "see" the world in a microscopic way.

At the end of each chapter, you will find several study aids that complete the chapter. *Chapter Reviews* provide a summary and *Concept Maps* show the connections between important topics. The *Key Terms*, which are in boldface type within the chapter, are listed with their definitions. *Understanding the Concepts*, a set of questions that use art and models, helps you visualize concepts. *Additional Questions and Problems* and *Challenge Problems* provide additional exercises to test your understanding of the topics in the chapter. The problems are paired, which means that each of the odd-numbered problems is matched to the following even-numbered problem. The answers to all the *Study Checks*, as well as the answers to all the odd-numbered problems are provided at the end of the chapter. If the answers provided match your answers, you most likely understand the topic; if not, you need to study the section again.

After some chapters, problem sets called *Combining Ideas* test your ability to solve problems containing material from more than one chapter.

Using Active Learning

A student who is an active learner continually interacts with the chemical ideas while reading the text, working problems, and attending lectures. Let's see how this is done.

As you read and practice problem solving, you remain actively involved in studying, which enhances the learning process. In this way, you learn small bits of information at a time and establish the necessary foundation for understanding the next section. You may also note questions you have about the reading to discuss with your professor or laboratory instructor. Table 1.2 summarizes these steps for active learning. The time you spend in a lecture is also a useful learning time. By keeping track of the class schedule and reading the assigned material before a lecture, you become aware of the new terms and concepts you need to learn. Some questions that occur during your reading may be answered during the lecture. If not, you can ask your professor for further clarification.

TABLE 1.2 Steps in Active Learning

1. Read each *Learning Goal* for an overview of the material.
2. Form a question from the title of the section you are going to read.
3. Read the section, looking for answers to your question.
4. Self-test by working *Concept Checks*, *Sample Problems*, and *Study Checks*.
5. Complete the *Questions and Problems* that follow that section, and check the answers for the magenta odd-numbered problems.
6. Proceed to the next section and repeat the steps.

Studying in a group can be beneficial to learning.

Many students find that studying with a group can be beneficial to learning. In a group, students motivate each other to study, fill in gaps, and correct misunderstandings by teaching and learning together. Studying alone does not allow the process of peer correction. In a group, you can cover the ideas more thoroughly as you discuss the reading and problem solve with other students. You may find that it is easier to retain new material and new ideas if you study in short sessions throughout the week rather than all at once. Waiting to study until the night before an exam does not give you time to understand concepts and practice problem solving.

Making a Study Plan

As you embark on your journey into the world of chemistry, think about your approach to studying and learning chemistry. You might consider some of the ideas in the following list. Check those ideas that will help you successfully learn chemistry. Commit to them now. *Your* success depends on *you*.

My study plan for learning chemistry will include the following:

________ reading the chapter before lecture

________ going to lecture

________ reviewing the *Learning Goals*

________ keeping a problem notebook

_______ reading the text as an active learner
_______ working the *Questions and Problems* following each section and checking answers at the end of the chapter
_______ being an active learner in lecture
_______ organizing a study group
_______ seeing the professor during office hours
_______ reviewing *Key Math Skills* and *Core Chemistry Skills*
_______ attending review sessions
_______ organizing my own review sessions
_______ studying as often as I can

Students discuss a chemistry problem with their professor during office hours.

CONCEPT CHECK 1.3 A Study Plan for Chemistry

What are some advantages to studying in a group?

ANSWER

In a group, students motivate and support each other, fill in gaps, and correct misunderstandings. Ideas are discussed while reading and problem solving together.

SAMPLE PROBLEM 1.3 A Study Plan for Learning Chemistry

Which of the following activities would you include in your study plan for learning chemistry successfully?

a. skipping lecture
b. forming a study group
c. keeping a problem notebook
d. waiting to study until the night before the exam
e. becoming an active learner

SOLUTION

Your success in chemistry can be improved by

b. forming a study group
c. keeping a problem notebook
e. becoming an active learner

STUDY CHECK 1.3

Which of the following will help you learn chemistry?

a. skipping review sessions
b. working assigned problems
c. attending the professor's office hours
d. staying up all night before an exam
e. reading the assignment before a lecture

QUESTIONS AND PROBLEMS

1.3 Learning Chemistry: A Study Plan

LEARNING GOAL: *Develop a study plan for learning chemistry.*

1.13 What are four things you can do to help yourself to succeed in chemistry?

1.14 What are four things that would make it difficult for you to learn chemistry?

1.15 A student in your class asks you for advice on learning chemistry. Which of the following might you suggest?
a. Form a study group.
b. Skip a lecture.
c. Visit the professor during office hours.
d. Wait until the night before an exam to study.
e. Become an active learner.

1.16 A student in your class asks you for advice on learning chemistry. Which of the following might you suggest?
a. Do the assigned problems.
b. Don't read the text; it's never on the test.
c. Attend review sessions.
d. Read the assignment before a lecture.
e. Keep a problem notebook.

LEARNING GOAL

Review math concepts used in chemistry: place values, positive and negative numbers, percentages, solving equations, and interpreting line graphs.

1.4 Learning Chemistry: Key Math Skills

During your study of chemistry, you will work many problems that involve numbers. You will need various math skills and operations. We will review some of the key math skills that are particularly important for chemistry. As we move through the chapters, we will also reference the key math skills as they apply.

KEY MATH SKILL

Identifying Place Values

A. Identifying Place Values

For any number, we can identify the *place value* for each of the digits in that number. These place values have names such as the ones place (first place to the left of the decimal point) or the tens place (second place to the left of the decimal point). Let's look first at the place values for a number without a decimal point.

2518

Digit	Place Value
2	thousands
5	hundreds
1	tens
8	ones

Now we look at a number that has a decimal point. We identify place values such as the tenths place (first place to the right of the decimal point) and hundredths place (second place to the right of the decimal place).

6.407

Digit	Place Value
6	ones
4	ten**ths**
0	hundred**ths**
7	thousand**ths**

Note that place values ending with the suffix *ths* refer to the decimal places to the right of the decimal point.

CONCEPT CHECK 1.4 Place Values

Identify the place value for each of the digits in the number 825.10.

Digit	Place Value
8	
2	
5	
1	
0	

ANSWER

Digit	Place Value
8	hundreds
2	tens
5	ones
1	tenths
0	hundredths

B. Using Positive and Negative Numbers in Calculations

KEY MATH SKILL

Using Positive and Negative Numbers in Calculations

A *positive number* is any number that is greater than zero and has a positive sign $(+)$. Often the positive sign is understood and not written in front of the number. For example, the number $+8$ can also be written as 8. A *negative number* is any number that is less than zero and is written with a negative sign $(-)$. For example, a negative eight is written as -8.

Multiplication and Division of Positive and Negative Numbers

When two positive numbers or two negative numbers are multiplied, the answer is positive $(+)$.

$$2 \times 3 = +6$$
$$(-2) \times (-3) = +6$$

When a positive number and a negative number are multiplied, the answer is negative $(-)$.

$$2 \times (-3) = -6$$
$$(-2) \times 3 = -6$$

The rules for the division of positive and negative numbers are the same as the rules for multiplication. When two positive numbers or two negative numbers are divided, the answer is positive $(+)$.

$$\frac{6}{3} = 2 \qquad \frac{-6}{-3} = 2$$

When a positive number and a negative number are divided, the answer is negative $(-)$.

$$\frac{-6}{3} = -2 \qquad \frac{6}{-3} = -2$$

Addition of Positive and Negative Numbers

When positive numbers are added, the sign of the answer is positive.

$3 + 4 = 7$ The $+$ sign $(+7)$ is understood.

When negative numbers are added, the sign of the answer is negative.

$$(-3) + (-4) = -7$$

When a positive number and a negative number are added, the smaller number is subtracted from the larger number, and the result has the same sign as the larger number.

$$12 + (-15) = -3$$

Subtraction of Positive and Negative Numbers

When two numbers are subtracted, change the sign of the number to be subtracted.

$$12 - \mathbf{(+5)} = 12 \mathbf{- 5} = 7$$
$$12 - \mathbf{(-5)} = 12 \mathbf{+ 5} = 17$$
$$-12 - \mathbf{(-5)} = -12 \mathbf{+ 5} = -7$$
$$-12 - \mathbf{(+5)} = -12 \mathbf{- 5} = -17$$

KEY MATH SKILL

Calculating a Percentage

C. Calculating a Percentage

To determine a percent, divide the parts by the total (whole) and multiply by 100%. For example, if there are 8 chemistry books on a shelf that has a total of 32 books, what is the percent of chemistry books?

$$\frac{\text{8 chemistry books}}{\text{32 total books}} \times 100\% = 25\% \text{ chemistry books}$$

When a value is described as a percent (%), it represents the number of parts of an item in 100 of those items. If the percent of red balls is 5%, it means there are 5 red balls in every 100 balls. If the percent of blue balls is 50%, there are 50 blue balls in every 100 balls.

$$5\% \text{ red balls} = \frac{\text{5 red balls}}{\text{100 balls}} \qquad 50\% \text{ blue balls} = \frac{\text{50 blue balls}}{\text{100 balls}}$$

CONCEPT CHECK 1.5 Percentage

If you eat 3 pieces (parts) of a pizza that contained 6 pieces (whole), what percent of the pizza did you eat?

ANSWER

We can calculate the percentage as

$$\frac{\text{3 pieces of pizza}}{\text{6 pieces of pizza}} \times 100\% = 50\%$$

If you eat 3 pieces (parts) of a pizza that contained 6 pieces (whole), you ate 50% of that pizza.

Percentages as Decimals

If you are given a percent such as 25%, it can be converted to a decimal.

1. Write the percent value over 100. $\quad \frac{25}{100}$
2. Express the fraction as a decimal number. $\quad 0.25$

KEY MATH SKILL

Solving Equations

D. Solving Equations

In chemistry, we use equations that express the relationship between certain variables. Let's look at how we would solve for x in the following equation:

$$2x + 8 = 14$$

Our overall goal is to rearrange the items in the equation to obtain x on one side.

1. *Place all like terms on one side.* The numbers 8 and 14 are like terms. To remove the 8 from the left side of the equation, we subtract 8. To keep a balance, we need to subtract 8 from the 14 on the other side.

$$2x + \cancel{8} - \cancel{8} = 14 - 8$$
$$2x = 6$$

2. *Isolate the variable you need to solve for.* In this problem, we obtain x by dividing both sides of the equation by 2. The value of x is the result when 6 is divided by 2.

$$\frac{\cancel{2}x}{\cancel{2}} = \frac{6}{2}$$
$$x = 3$$

3. *Check your answer.* Check your answer by substituting your value for x back into the original equation.

$2(3) + 8 = 6 + 8 = 14$ Your answer $x = 3$ is correct.

Summary: To solve an equation for a particular variable, be sure you perform the same mathematical operations on *both* sides of the equation.

If you eliminate a symbol or number by subtracting, you need to subtract that same symbol or number on the opposite side.

If you eliminate a symbol or number by adding, you need to add that same symbol or number on the opposite side.

If you cancel a symbol or number by dividing, you need to divide both sides by that same symbol or number.

If you cancel a symbol or number by multiplying, you need to multiply both sides by that same symbol or number.

When we work with temperature, we may need to convert between degrees Celsius and degrees Fahrenheit using the following equation:

$$T_F = 1.8T_C + 32$$

To obtain the equation for converting degrees Fahrenheit to degrees Celsius, we subtract 32 from both sides.

$$T_F = 1.8T_C + 32$$
$$T_F - 32 = 1.8T_C + \cancel{32} - \cancel{32}$$
$$T_F - 32 = 1.8T_C$$

To obtain T_C by itself, we divide both sides by 1.8.

$$\frac{T_F - 32}{1.8} = \frac{\cancel{1.8}T_C}{\cancel{1.8}} = T_C$$

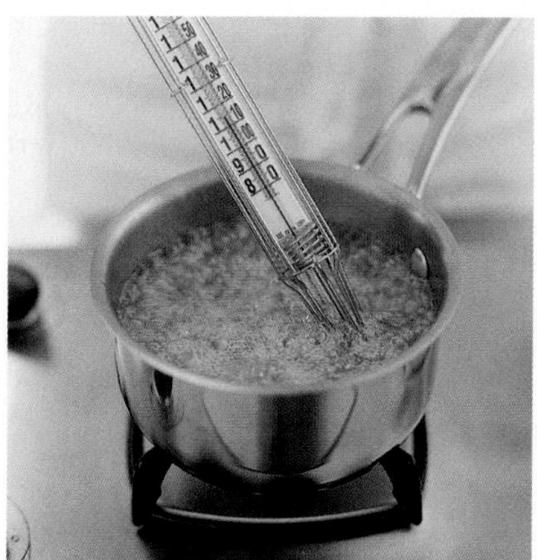

Temperatures are measured in degrees Fahrenheit and Celsius.

CONCEPT CHECK 1.6 Solving Equations

Solve each of the following equations for the specified variable:

a. $P_1V_1 = P_2V_2$; solve for V_2
b. $q = m \times \Delta T \times SH$; solve for m

ANSWER

a. $P_1V_1 = P_2V_2$

To solve for V_2, divide both sides by the symbol P_2.

$$\frac{P_1V_1}{P_2} = \frac{\cancel{P_2}V_2}{\cancel{P_2}}$$

$$V_2 = \frac{P_1V_1}{P_2}$$

b. $q = m \times \Delta T \times SH$

To solve for m, divide both sides by the symbols ΔT and SH.

$$\frac{q}{\Delta T \times SH} = \frac{m \times \cancel{\Delta T} \times \cancel{SH}}{\cancel{\Delta T} \times \cancel{SH}}$$

$$m = \frac{q}{\Delta T \times SH}$$

KEY MATH SKILL

Interpreting a Line Graph

E. Interpreting a Line Graph

A line graph represents the relationship between two variables. These quantities are plotted along two perpendicular axes, which are the x axis (horizontal) and y axis (vertical).

Example

In the following graph, the volume of a gas in a balloon is plotted against its temperature.

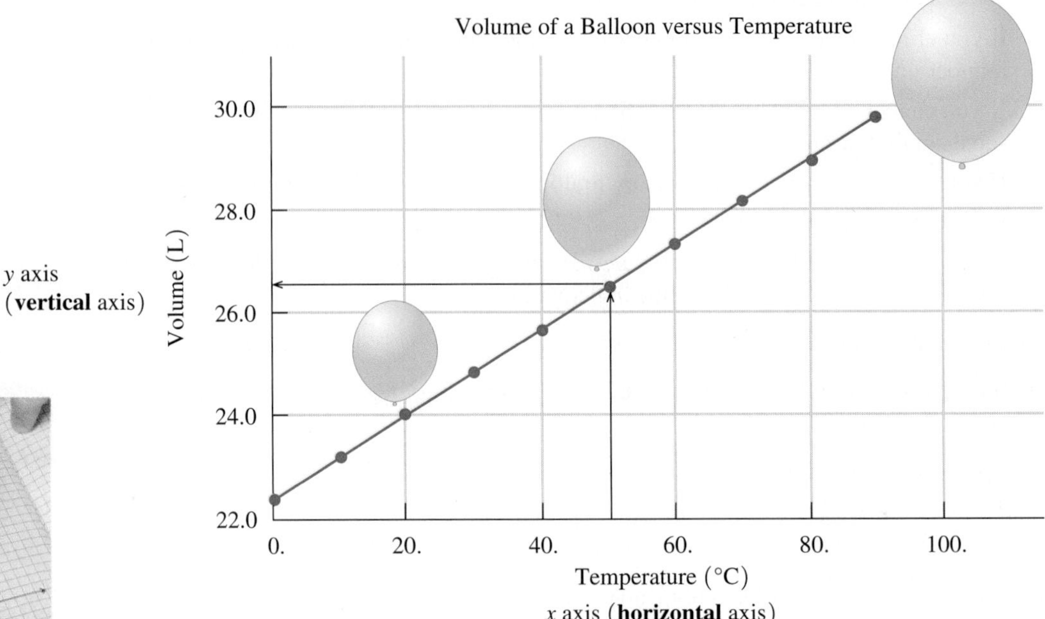

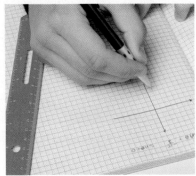

A line graph shows the relationship between two variables.

Title

Look at the title. What does it tell us about the graph? The title indicates that the volume of a balloon was measured at different temperatures.

Vertical Axis

Look at the label and the numbers on the vertical (y) axis. The label indicates that the volume of the balloon was measured in liters. The numbers, which are chosen to include the low and high measurements of the volume of the gas, are evenly spaced from 22.0 L to 30.0 L.

Horizontal Axis

The label on the horizontal (x) axis indicates that the temperature of the balloon was measured in degrees Celsius (°C). The numbers are measurements of the Celsius temperature, which are evenly spaced from 0. °C to 100. °C.

Points on the Graph

Each point on the graph represents a volume in liters that was measured at a specific temperature. When these points are connected, a straight line is obtained.

Interpreting the Line Graph

From the line graph, we see that the volume of the gas increases as the temperature of the gas increases. This is called a *direct relationship*. Now we use the line graph to determine the volume at various temperatures. For example, suppose we want to know the volume of the gas at 50. °C. We would start by finding 50. °C on the x axis and then drawing a line up to the line graph. From there, we would draw a horizontal line that intersects the y axis and read the volume value where the line crosses the y axis.

CONCEPT CHECK 1.7 Interpreting a Line Graph

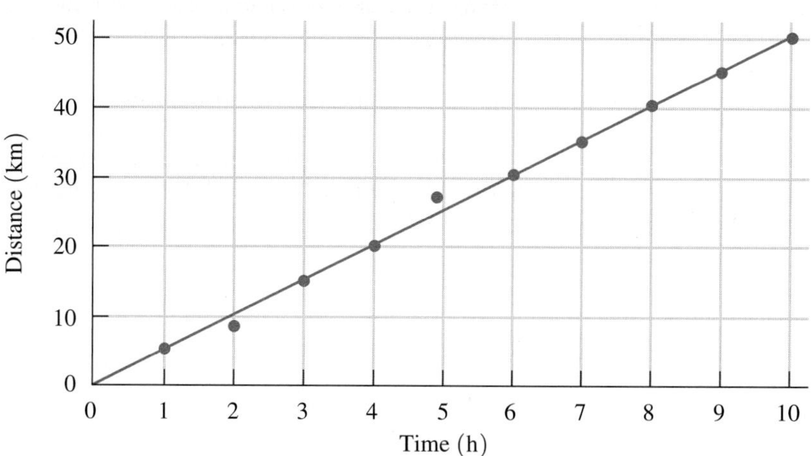

In this line graph, the distance traveled by a bicycle rider was measured for 10 h.

a. What is measured on the vertical axis?
b. What is the range of values on the vertical axis?
c. What is measured on the horizontal axis?
d. What is the range of values on the horizontal axis?
e. Does the distance increase or decrease with an increase in time?
f. What distance, in kilometers, did the bicycle rider cover in 6 h?
g. How many hours did the bicycle rider need to cover a distance of 15 km?

ANSWER

a. distance, in kilometers
b. 0 km to 50 km
c. time, in hours
d. 0 h to 10 h
e. increase
f. 30 km
g. 3 h

QUESTIONS AND PROBLEMS

1.4 Learning Chemistry: Key Math Skills

LEARNING GOAL: *Review math concepts used in chemistry: place values, positive and negative numbers, percentages, solving equations, and interpreting line graphs.*

1.17 What is the place value for the bold digit?
a. 7.32**8**8
b. 1**6**.1234
c. 4**6**75.99

1.18 What is the place value for the bold digit?
a. 97.**5**689
b. **3**75.88
c. 46.1**0**00

1.19 Solve each of the following:
a. $15 - (-8) =$ _______
b. $-8 + (-22) =$ _______
c. $4 \times (-2) + 6 =$ _______

1.20 Solve each of the following:
a. $-11 - (-9) =$ _______
b. $34 + (-55) =$ _______
c. $\frac{-56}{8} =$ _______

1.21 **a.** A test has 25 questions. If a student has 21 answers correct, what percent of the questions was correct? Express your answer to the ones place.
b. An alloy contains 56 g of pure silver and 22 g of pure copper. What is the percent silver in the alloy? Express your answer to the ones place.
c. A collection of coins contains 11 nickels, 5 quarters, and 7 dimes. What is the percent of dimes in the collection? Express your answer to the ones place.

1.22 **a.** A test has 35 questions. If a student has 29 answers correct, what percent was correct? Express your answer to the ones place.
b. An alloy contains 67 g of pure gold and 35 g of pure zinc. What is the percent zinc in the alloy? Express your answer to the ones place.
c. A collection of coins contains 15 pennies, 14 dimes, and 6 quarters. What is the percent of pennies in the collection? Express your answer to the ones place.

1.23 Solve each of the following for a:
a. $4a + 4 = 40$
b. $\frac{a}{6} = 7$

1.24 Solve each of the following for b:

a. $2b + 7 = b + 10$

b. $3b - 4 = 24 - b$

Use the following line graph for Questions 1.25 and 1.26:

Time for Cooling of Tea versus Temperature

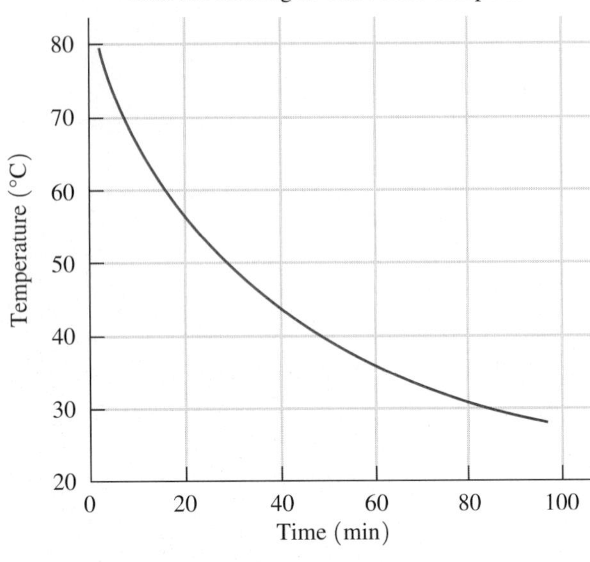

1.25 **a.** What does the title indicate about the graph?

b. What is measured on the vertical axis?

c. What is the range of values on the vertical axis?

d. Does the temperature increase or decrease with an increase in time?

1.26 **a.** What is measured on the horizontal axis?

b. What is the range of values on the horizontal axis?

c. What is the temperature of the tea after 20 min?

d. How many minutes were needed to reach a temperature of 45 °C?

CHAPTER REVIEW

1.1 Chemistry and Chemicals

LEARNING GOAL: *Define the term chemistry and identify substances as chemicals.*

- Chemistry is the study of the composition, structure, properties, and reactions of matter.
- A chemical is any substance that always has the same composition and properties wherever it is found.

1.2 Scientific Method: Thinking Like a Scientist

LEARNING GOAL: *Describe the activities that are part of the scientific method.*

- The scientific method is a process of explaining natural phenomena beginning with making observations, forming a hypothesis, and performing experiments.
- A theory may be proposed when repeated experimental results by many scientists support the hypothesis.

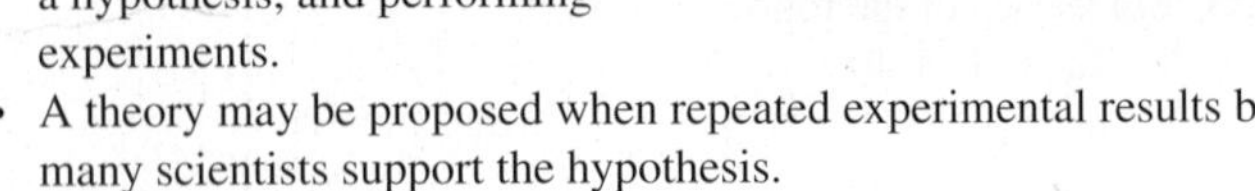

1.3 Learning Chemistry: A Study Plan

LEARNING GOAL: *Develop a study plan for learning chemistry.*

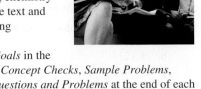

- A study plan for learning chemistry utilizes the features in the text and develops an active learning approach to study.
- By using the *Learning Goals* in the chapter and working the *Concept Checks*, *Sample Problems*, *Study Checks*, and the *Questions and Problems* at the end of each section, you can successfully learn the concepts of chemistry.

1.4 Learning Chemistry: Key Math Skills

LEARNING GOAL: *Review math concepts used in chemistry: place values, positive and negative numbers, percentages, solving equations, and interpreting line graphs.*

- Solving chemistry problems involves a number of math skills: determining place values, using positive and negative numbers, using percentages, solving algebraic equations, and interpreting graphs.

CONCEPT MAP

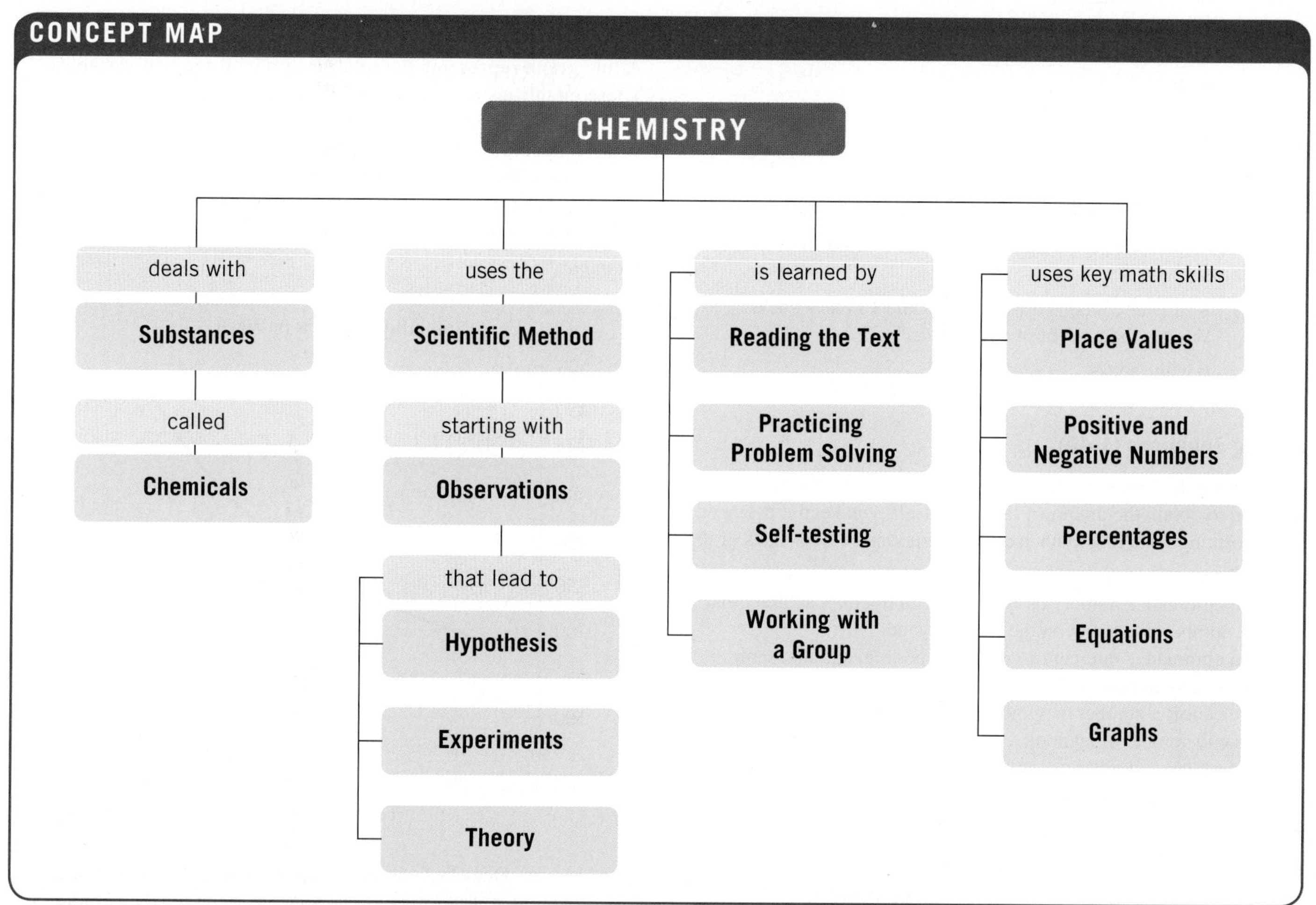

KEY TERMS

chemical A substance that has the same composition and properties wherever it is found.

chemistry The study of the composition, structure, properties, and reactions of matter.

experiment A procedure that tests the validity of a hypothesis.

hypothesis An unverified explanation of a natural phenomenon.

observation Information determined by noting and recording a natural phenomenon.

scientific method The process of making observations, proposing a hypothesis, testing the hypothesis, and developing a theory that explains a natural event.

theory An explanation of an observation that has been validated by repeated experiments that support a hypothesis.

KEY MATH SKILLS

The chapter section containing each Key Math Skill is shown in parentheses at the end of each heading.

Identifying Place Values (1.4A)

- The place value identifies the numerical value of each digit in a number.

Example: Identify the place values for each of the digits in the number 456.78.

Answer:

Digit	Place Value
4	hundreds
5	tens
6	ones
7	tenths
8	hundredths

Using Positive and Negative Numbers in Calculations (1.4B)

- A *positive number* is any number that is greater than zero and has a positive sign $(+)$. A *negative number* is any number that is less than zero and is written with a negative sign $(-)$.
- When two positive numbers are added, multiplied, or divided, the answer is positive.
- When two negative numbers are multiplied or divided, the answer is positive.
- When a positive and a negative number are multiplied or divided, the answer is negative.
- When a positive and a negative number are added, the smaller number is subtracted from the larger number and the result has the same sign as the larger number.
- When two numbers are subtracted, change the sign of the number to be subtracted.

Example: Solve each of the following:

a. $-8 - 14 =$ ______

b. $6 \times (-3) =$ ______

Answer: **a.** $-8 - 14 = -22$

b. $6 \times (-3) = -18$

Calculating a Percentage (1.4C)

- A percentage is the part divided by the total (whole) multiplied by 100%.

Example: A drawer contains 6 white socks and 18 black socks. What is the percent of white socks?

Answer: $\frac{6 \text{ white socks}}{24 \text{ total socks}} \times 100\% = 25\%$ white socks

Solving Equations (1.4D)

An equation in chemistry often contains an unknown. To rearrange an equation to obtain the unknown factor by itself, you keep it balanced by performing matching mathematical operations on both sides of the equation.

- If you eliminate a number or symbol by subtracting, subtract that same number or symbol on the opposite side.
- If you eliminate a number or symbol by adding, add that same number or symbol on the opposite side.
- If you cancel a number or symbol by dividing, divide both sides by that same number or symbol.
- If you cancel a number or symbol by multiplying, multiply both sides by that same number or symbol.

Example: Solve the equation for a: $3a - 8 = 28$

Answer: *Add 8 to both sides* $3a - \cancel{8} + \cancel{8} = 28 + 8$

$3a = 36$

Divide both sides by 3 $\frac{\cancel{3}a}{\cancel{3}} = \frac{36}{3}$

$a = 12$

Interpreting a Line Graph (1.4E)

A line graph represents the relationship between two variables. These quantities are plotted along two perpendicular axes, which are the x axis (horizontal) and y axis (vertical). The title indicates the components of the x and y axes. Numbers on the x and y axes show the range of values of the variables. The line graph shows the relationship between the component on the y axis and that on the x axis.

Example:

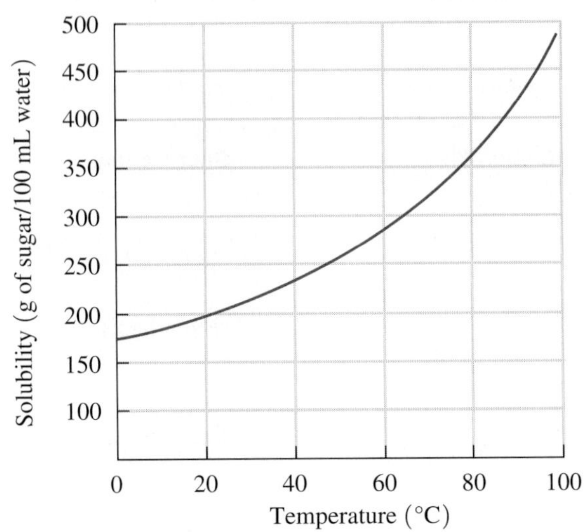

a. Does the amount of sugar that dissolves in 100 mL of water increase or decrease when the temperature increases?

b. How many grams of sugar dissolve in 100 mL of water at 70 °C?

c. At what temperature (°C) will 275 g of sugar dissolve in 100 mL of water?

Answer: **a.** increase

b. 320 g

c. 55 °C

UNDERSTANDING THE CONCEPTS

The chapter sections to review are shown in parentheses at the end of each question.

1.27 A "chemical-free" shampoo includes the following ingredients: water, cocomide, glycerin, and citric acid. Is the shampoo truly "chemical-free"? (1.1)

1.28 A "chemical-free" sunscreen includes the following ingredients: titanium dioxide, vitamin E, and vitamin C. Is the sunscreen truly "chemical-free"? (1.1)

1.29 According to Sherlock Holmes, "One must follow the rules of scientific inquiry, gathering, observing, and testing data, then formulating, modifying, and rejecting hypotheses, until only one remains." Did Sherlock use the scientific method? Why or why not? (1.2)

Sherlock Holmes is a fictional detective in novels written by Arthur Conan Doyle.

1.30 In *A Scandal in Bohemia*, Sherlock Holmes receives a mysterious note. He states, "I have no data yet. It is a capital mistake to theorize before one has data. Insensibly one begins to twist facts to suit theories, instead of theories to suit facts." What do you think Sherlock meant? (1.2)

1.31 Classify each of the following statements as an observation (O) or a hypothesis (H): (1.2)

a. Aluminum melts at 660 °C.

b. Dinosaurs became extinct when a large meteorite struck Earth and caused a huge dust cloud that severely decreased the amount of light reaching Earth.

c. The 100-yard dash was run in 9.8 seconds.

Aluminum melts at 660 °C.

1.32 Classify each of the following statements as an observation (O) or a hypothesis (H): (1.2)

a. Analysis of 10 ceramic dishes showed that four dishes contained lead levels that exceeded federal safety standards.

b. Marble statues undergo corrosion in acid rain.

c. Statues corrode in acid rain because the acidity is sufficient to dissolve calcium carbonate, the major substance of marble.

1.33 For each of the following, indicate if the answer has a positive or negative sign: (1.4)

a. Two negative numbers are added.

b. A positive and negative number are multiplied.

1.34 For each of the following, indicate if the answer has a positive or negative sign: (1.4)

a. A negative number is subtracted from a positive number.

b. Two negative numbers are divided.

ADDITIONAL QUESTIONS AND PROBLEMS

1.35 Why does the scientific method include a hypothesis? (1.2)

1.36 Why is experimentation an important part of the scientific method? (1.2)

1.37 Select the correct phrase(s) to complete the following statement: If experimental results do not support your hypothesis, you should (1.2)

a. pretend that the experimental results support your hypothesis.

b. write another hypothesis.

c. do more experiments.

1.38 Select the correct phrase(s) to complete the following statement: A hypothesis becomes a theory when (1.2)

a. one experiment proves the hypothesis.

b. many experiments by many scientists validate the hypothesis.

c. you decide to call it a theory.

1.39 Which of the following will help you develop a successful study plan? (1.3)

a. Skip lecture and just read the text.

b. Work the *Sample Problems* as you go through a chapter.

c. Go to your professor's office hours.

d. Read through the chapter, but work the problems later.

1.40 Which of the following will help you develop a successful study plan? (1.3)

a. Study all night before the exam.

b. Form a study group and discuss the problems together.

c. Work problems in a notebook for easy reference.

d. Copy the answers to homework from a friend.

1.41 Solve each of the following: (1.4)

a. $4 \times (-8) =$ ______

b. $-12 - 48 =$ ______

c. $\frac{-168}{-4} =$ ______

1.42 Solve each of the following: (1.4)

a. $-95 - (-11) =$ ______

b. $\frac{152}{-19} =$ ______

c. $4 - 56 =$ ______

1.43 A bag of gumdrops contains 16 orange gumdrops, 8 yellow gumdrops, and 16 black gumdrops. (1.4)

a. What is the percent of yellow gumdrops?

b. What is the percent of black gumdrops?

1.44 On the first chemistry test, 12 students got As, 18 students got Bs, and 20 students got Cs. (1.4)

a. What is the percent of students who received Bs? Express your answer to the ones place.

b. What is the percent of students who received Cs? Express your answer to the ones place.

CHALLENGE QUESTIONS

The following groups of questions are related to the topics in this chapter. However, they do not all follow the chapter order, and they require you to combine concepts and skills from several sections. These questions will help you increase your critical thinking skills and prepare for your next exam.

1.45 Classify each of the following as an observation (O), a hypothesis (H), or an experiment (E): (1.2)
a. The bicycle tire is flat.
b. If I add air to the bicycle tire, it will expand to the proper size.
c. When I added air to the bicycle tire, it was still flat.
d. The bicycle tire must have a leak in it.

1.46 Classify each of the following as an observation (O), a hypothesis (H), or an experiment (E): (1.2)
a. A big log in the fire does not burn well.
b. If I chop the log into smaller wood pieces, it will burn better.
c. The small wood pieces burn brighter and make a hotter fire.
d. The small wood pieces are used up faster than burning the big log.

1.47 Solve each of the following for x: (1.4)
a. $2x + 5 = 41$
b. $\frac{5x}{3} = 40$

1.48 Solve each of the following for z: (1.4)
a. $3z - (-6) = 12$
b. $\frac{4z}{-12} = -8$

Use the following graph for Problems 1.49 and 1.50:

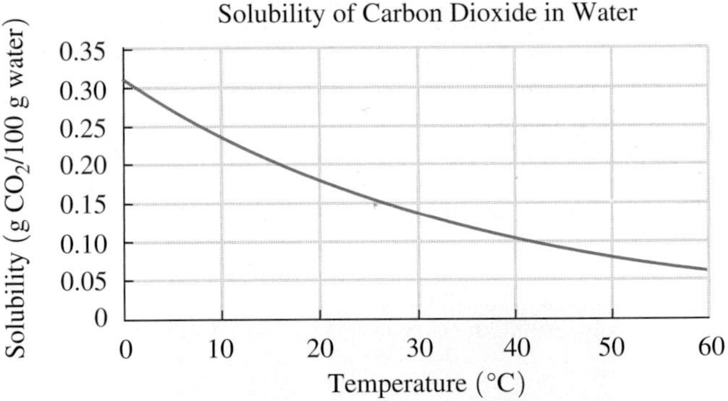

1.49 **a.** What does the title indicate about the graph? (1.4)
b. What is measured on the vertical axis?
c. What is the range of values on the vertical axis?
d. Does the solubility of carbon dioxide increase or decrease with an increase in temperature?

1.50 **a.** What is measured on the horizontal axis? (1.4)
b. What is the range of values on the horizontal axis?
c. What is the solubility of carbon dioxide in water at 25 °C?
d. At what temperature does carbon dioxide have a solubility of 0.2 g/100 g water?

ANSWERS

Answers to Study Checks

1.1 a, b, and **d**

1.2 **a.** experiment (E)
b. observation (O)
c. hypothesis (H)

1.3 b, c, and **e**

Answers to Selected Questions and Problems

1.1 **a.** Chemistry is the study of the composition, structure, properties, and reactions of matter.
b. A chemical is a substance that has the same composition and properties wherever it is found.

1.3 Many chemicals are listed on a vitamin bottle such as vitamin A, vitamin B_3, vitamin B_{12}, vitamin C, and folic acid.

1.5 Typical items found in a medicine cabinet and some of the chemicals they contain are as follows:

Antacid tablets: calcium carbonate, cellulose, starch, stearic acid, silicon dioxide
Mouthwash: water, alcohol, thymol, glycerol, sodium benzoate, benzoic acid
Cough suppressant: menthol, beta-carotene, sucrose, glucose

1.7 An advantage of a pesticide is that it gets rid of insects that bite or damage crops. A disadvantage is that a pesticide can destroy beneficial insects or be retained in a crop that is eventually eaten by animals or humans.

1.9 **a.** A hypothesis proposes a possible explanation for a natural phenomenon.
b. An experiment is a procedure that tests the validity of a hypothesis.
c. A theory is a hypothesis that has been validated many times by many scientists.
d. An observation is a description or measurement of a natural phenomenon.

1.11 **a.** observation (O) **b.** hypothesis (H)
c. experiment (E) **d.** observation (O)
e. observation (O) **f.** theory (T)

1.13 There are several things you can do that will help you successfully learn chemistry, including forming a study group, going to lecture, working *Sample Problems* and *Study Checks*, working *Questions and Problems* and checking answers, reading the assignment ahead of class, and keeping a problem notebook.

1.15 a, c, and **e**

1.17 **a.** thousandths **b.** ones **c.** hundreds

1.19 a. 23 **b.** −30 **c.** −2

1.21 a. 84% **b.** 72% **c.** 30%

1.23 a. 9 **b.** 42

1.25 a. The graph shows the relationship between the temperature of a cup of tea and time.
b. temperature, in °C
c. 20 °C to 80 °C
d. decrease

1.27 No. All of the ingredients are chemicals.

1.29 Yes. Sherlock's investigation includes making observations (gathering data), formulating a hypothesis, testing the hypothesis, and modifying it until one of the hypotheses is validated.

1.31 a. observation (O) **b.** hypothesis (H)
c. observation (O)

1.33 a. negative **b.** negative

1.35 A hypothesis, which is a possible explanation for an observation, can be tested with experiments.

1.37 **b** and **c**

1.39 **b** and **c**

1.41 a. −32 **b.** −60 **c.** 42

1.43 a. 20% **b.** 40%

1.45 a. observation (O) **b.** hypothesis (H)
c. experiment (E) **d.** hypothesis (H)

1.47 a. 18 **b.** 24

1.49 a. The graph shows the relationship between the solubility of carbon dioxide in water and temperature.
b. solubility of carbon dioxide (g CO_2/100 g water)
c. 0 to 0.35 g of CO_2/100 g of water
d. decrease

2 Measurements

LOOKING AHEAD

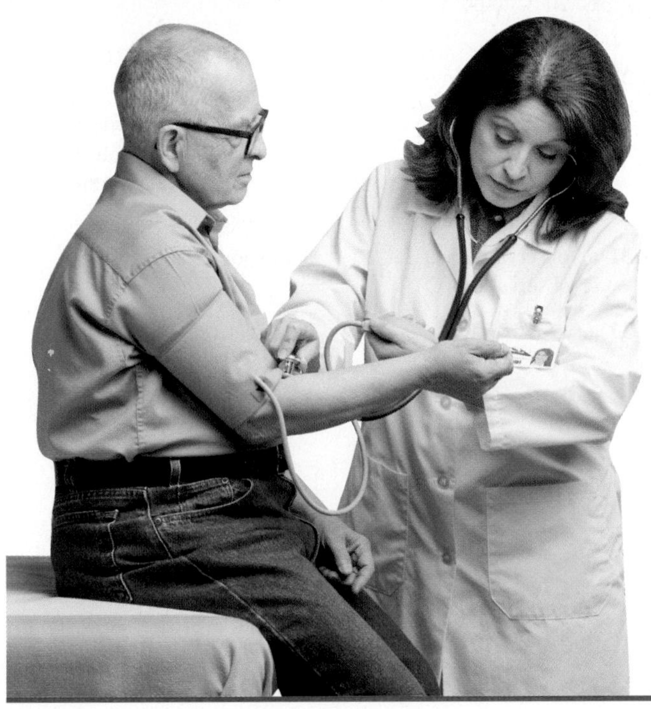

During the past few months, Greg has been experiencing an increased number of headaches, and frequently feels dizzy and nauseous. He goes to his doctor's office where the registered nurse completes the initial part of the exam by recording several measurements: weight 88.5 kg, height 190.5 cm, temperature 37.2 °C, and blood pressure at 155/95. A normal blood pressure is 120/80 or below.

When Greg sees his doctor, he is diagnosed as having high blood pressure (hypertension). The doctor prescribes 80 mg of Inderal (propranolol), which is used to treat hypertension and is to be taken once a day. The registered nurse fills the prescription at the pharmacy.

Two weeks later, Greg visits his doctor again, who determines that his blood pressure is now 152/90. The doctor increases the dosage of Inderal to 160 mg, once daily. The registered nurse informs Greg that he needs to increase his daily dosage to 2 tablets.

Career: Registered Nurse

In addition to assisting physicians, registered nurses work to promote patient health, and prevent and treat disease. They provide patient care and help patients cope with illness. They take measurements such as a patient's weight, height, temperature, and blood pressure; make conversions; and calculate drug dosage rates. Registered nurses also maintain detailed medical records of patient symptoms, prescribed medications, and any reactions.

Chemistry and measurements are an important part of our everyday lives. Levels of toxic materials in the air, soil, and water are discussed in our newspapers. We read about radon gas in our homes, holes in the ozone layer, trans fatty acids, and climate change. Understanding chemistry and measurement helps us make proper choices about our world.

Think about your day. You probably took some measurements. Perhaps you checked your weight by stepping on a bathroom scale. If you made some rice for dinner, you added 2 cups of water to 1 cup of rice. If you did not feel well, you may have taken your temperature. Whenever you take a measurement, you use a measuring device such as a balance, a measuring cup, or a thermometer. Over the years, you have learned to read the markings on each device to take a correct measurement.

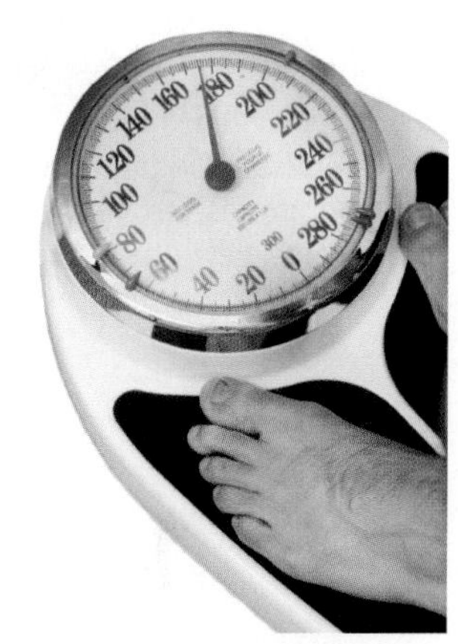
Your weight on a bathroom scale is a measurement.

Scientists measure the amounts of the materials that make up everything in our universe. An engineer determines the amount of metal in an alloy or the volume of seawater flowing through a desalination plant. A physician orders laboratory tests to measure substances in the blood such as glucose or cholesterol. An environmental chemist measures the levels of pollutants such as lead and carbon monoxide in our soil and atmosphere.

By learning about measurement, you develop skills for solving problems and how to work with numbers in chemistry. An understanding of measurement is essential to evaluate our health and surroundings.

CHAPTER READINESS*

Key Math Skills

- Identifying Place Values **(1.4A)**

*This Key Math Skill from the previous chapter is listed here for your review as you proceed to the new material in this chapter.

2.1 Units of Measurement

LEARNING GOAL

Write the names and abbreviations for the metric or SI units used in measurements of length, volume, mass, temperature, and time.

Suppose you walked 1.3 mi to campus today carrying a backpack that weighs 26 lb. The temperature was 72 °F. Perhaps you weigh 128 lb and your height is 65 in. These measurements and units may seem familiar to you because they are stated in the U.S. system of measurement. However, in chemistry, we use the *metric system* in making our measurements. Using the metric system, you walked 2.1 km to campus carrying a backpack that has a mass of 12 kg, when the temperature was 22 °C. You have a mass of 58.2 kg and a height of 165 cm.

Scientists throughout the world use the **metric system** of measurement. The **International System of Units (SI)** or Système International is the official system of measurement throughout the world except for the United States. In chemistry, we use metric and SI units for length, volume, mass, temperature, and time (see Table 2.1).

Chemists working in research laboratories test new products and develop new pharmaceuticals.

TABLE 2.1 Units of Measurement and Their Abbreviations

Measurement	Metric	SI
Length	meter (m)	meter (m)
Volume	liter (L)	cubic meter (m^3)
Mass	gram (g)	kilogram (kg)
Temperature	degree Celsius (°C)	kelvin (K)
Time	second (s)	second (s)

Length

The metric and SI unit of length is the **meter (m)**. A meter is 39.37 in., which makes it slightly longer than a yard (1.094 yd). The **centimeter (cm)**, a smaller unit of length, is commonly used in chemistry and is about equal to the width of your little finger. For comparison, there are 2.54 cm in 1 in. (see Figure 2.1). Some useful relationships between different units for length follow:

1 m = 1.094 yd
1 m = 39.37 in.
1 m = 100 cm
2.54 cm = 1 in.

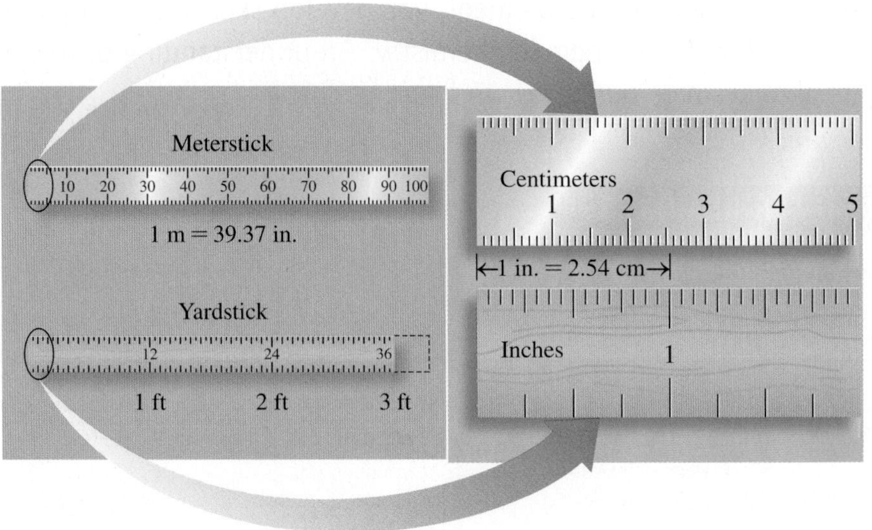

FIGURE 2.1 Length in the metric (SI) system is based on the meter, which is slightly longer than a yard.

Q How many centimeters are in a length of 1 inch?

Volume

Volume (*V*) is the amount of space a substance occupies. The SI unit of volume, the **cubic meter (m^3)** is the volume of a cube that has sides that measure 1 m in length. In a laboratory or a hospital, the cubic meter is too large for practical use. Instead, chemists work with metric units of volume that are smaller and more convenient, such as the **liter (L)** and **milliliter (mL)**. The volume of 1 mL is the same as 1 cm^3. A liter is slightly larger than a quart (1 L = 1.057 qt) and contains 1000 mL, as shown in Figure 2.2. A cubic meter is the same volume as 1000 L. Some useful relationships between different units for volume follow:

1 m^3 = 1000 L
1 L = 1000 mL
1 mL = 1 cm^3
1 L = 1.057 qt
946.3 mL = 1 qt

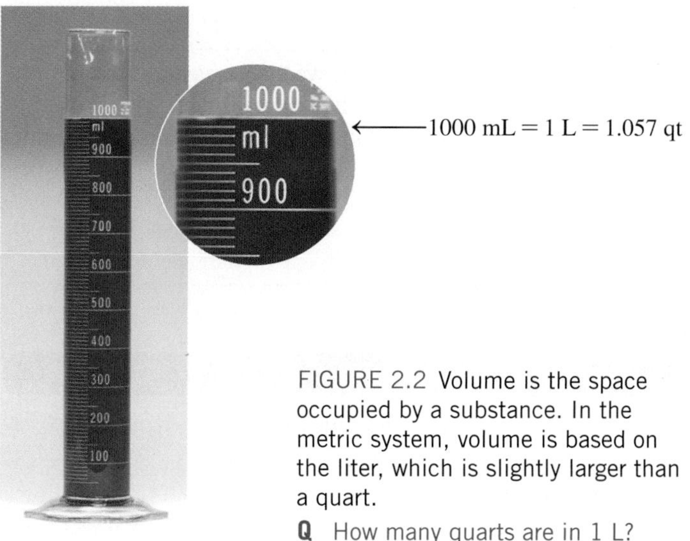

FIGURE 2.2 Volume is the space occupied by a substance. In the metric system, volume is based on the liter, which is slightly larger than a quart.

Q How many quarts are in 1 L?

The standard kilogram for the United States is stored at the National Institute of Standards and Technology (NIST).

Mass

The **mass** of an object is a measure of the quantity of material it contains. The SI unit of mass, the **kilogram (kg)**, is used for larger masses, such as body mass. The standard for mass, the international prototype kilogram (IPK), is a cylinder that is made of a platinum–iridium alloy. In the metric system, the unit for mass is the **gram (g)**, which is used for smaller masses. There are 1000 g in one kilogram. In comparison to the U.S. system, the mass of 1 kg is equivalent to 2.205 lb, and 453.6 g is equal to one pound. Some useful relationships between different units for mass follow:

$$1 \text{ kg} = 1000 \text{ g}$$
$$1 \text{ kg} = 2.205 \text{ lb}$$
$$453.6 \text{ g} = 1 \text{ lb}$$

You may be more familiar with the term *weight* than with the word *mass*. Weight is a measure of the gravitational pull on an object. On Earth, an astronaut with a mass of 75.0 kg has a weight of 165 lb. On the Moon, where the gravitational pull is one-sixth that of Earth, the astronaut would weigh 27.5 lb. However, the mass of the astronaut, 75.0 kg, is the same on the Moon as on Earth. Scientists measure mass rather than weight because mass does not depend on gravity.

In a chemistry laboratory, an electronic balance is used to measure the mass of a substance in grams (see Figure 2.3).

FIGURE 2.3 On an electronic balance, the digital readout gives the mass of a nickel, which is 5.01 g.

Q What would be the mass of 10 nickels?

Temperature

Temperature tells us how hot something is, and how cold it is outside, or it helps us determine if we have a fever. In the metric system, temperature is measured in degrees Celsius. On the **Celsius (°C) temperature scale**, water freezes at 0 °C and boils at 100 °C, while on the Fahrenheit (°F) scale, water freezes at 32 °F and boils at 212 °F (see Figure 2.4). In the SI system, temperature is measured using the **Kelvin (K) temperature scale**, on which the lowest temperature is 0 K. A unit on the Kelvin scale is called a kelvin (K) and is not written with a degree sign.

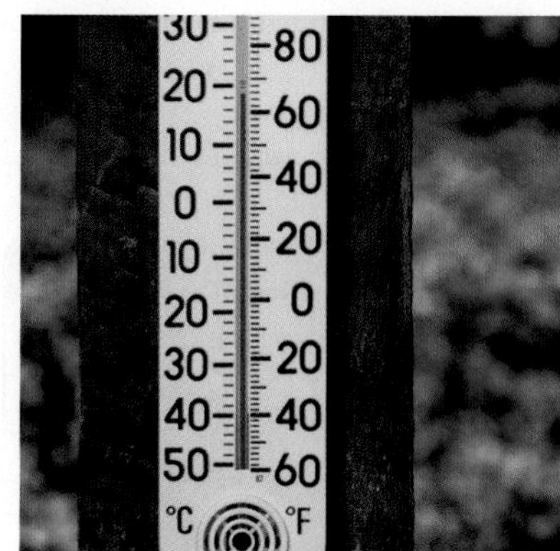

FIGURE 2.4 A thermometer is used to determine temperature.

Q What kinds of temperature readings have you made today?

A stopwatch is used to measure the time of a race.

Time

The SI and metric unit of time is the **second (s)**. However, we also measure time in units such as years (y), days, hours (h), or minutes (min). The standard device now used to determine a second is an atomic clock. Some useful relationships between different units for time follow:

$$1 \text{ day} = 24 \text{ h}$$
$$1 \text{ h} = 60 \text{ min}$$
$$1 \text{ min} = 60 \text{ s}$$

CONCEPT CHECK 2.1 Units of Measurement

State the type of measurement indicated in each of the following:

a. 45.6 g **b.** 1.85 m^3
c. 14 cm **d.** 45 °C

ANSWER

a. A gram is a unit of mass.
b. A cubic meter is a unit of volume.
c. A centimeter is a unit of length.
d. A degree Celsius is a unit of temperature.

QUESTIONS AND PROBLEMS

2.1 Units of Measurement

LEARNING GOAL: *Write the names and abbreviations for the metric or SI units used in measurements of length, volume, mass, temperature, and time.*

2.1 State the name of the unit and the type of measurement for each of the following:
a. 4.8 m **b.** 325 g **c.** 1.5 L
d. 480 s **e.** 28 °C

2.2 State the name of the unit and the type of measurement for each of the following:
a. 85 mL **b.** 36 cm **c.** 14 kg
d. 35 g **e.** 373 K

2.3 State the name of the unit in each of the following, and identify that unit as a metric/SI unit or not:
a. 5.5 mL **b.** 45 kg **c.** 16 in.
d. 25 s **e.** 22 °C

2.4 State the name of the unit in each of the following, and identify that unit as a metric/SI unit or not:
a. 8 m^3 **b.** 245 K **c.** 45 °F
d. 125 L **e.** 125 g

2.5 Give the abbreviation for each of the following:
a. gram **b.** liter
c. degree Celsius **d.** pound
e. second

2.6 Give the abbreviation for each of the following:
a. kilogram **b.** kelvin
c. quart **d.** meter
e. cubic meter

LEARNING GOAL

Write a number in scientific notation.

2.2 Scientific Notation

In chemistry, we use numbers that are very large and very small. We might measure something as tiny as the width of a human hair, which is about 0.000 008 m. Or perhaps we want to count the number of hairs on the average human scalp, which is about 100 000 hairs (see Figure 2.5). In this text, we add spaces between sets of three digits when it helps make the places easier to count. However, we will see that it is more convenient to write large and small numbers in *scientific notation.*

Item	Standard Number	Scientific Notation
Width of a human hair	0.000 008 m	8×10^{-6} m
Hairs on a human scalp	100 000 hairs	1×10^{5} hairs

FIGURE 2.5 Humans have an average of 1×10^5 hairs on their scalps. Each hair is about 8×10^{-6} m wide.

Q Why are large and small numbers written in scientific notation?

Writing a Number in Scientific Notation

KEY MATH SKILL 

Using Scientific Notation

A number written in **scientific notation** consists of three parts: a coefficient, a power of 10, and a unit of measurement. For example, 2400 m is written in scientific notation as 2.4×10^3 m. The coefficient is 2.4, and the value 10^3 shows the power of 10 is 3, while the unit is meter (m). The coefficient was obtained by moving the decimal point to the left to give a number that was at least 1 but less than 10. Because we moved the decimal point three places to the left, the power of 10 is a positive 3, which is written as 10^3. When a number greater than 1 is converted to scientific notation, the power of 10 is positive.

$$2400.\text{ m} = 2.4 \times 10^3 \text{ m}$$

← 3 places; Coefficient; Power of ten; Unit

When a number less than 1 is written in scientific notation, the power of 10 is a negative number. For example, the number 0.000 86 g is written in scientific notation by moving the decimal point to give a coefficient of 8.6. Because the decimal point was moved four places to the right, the power of 10 becomes a negative 4, written as 10^{-4}.

$$0.00086 \text{ g} = 8.6 \times 10^{-4} \text{ g}$$

4 places →; Coefficient; Power of ten; Unit

Table 2.2 gives examples of numbers written as positive and negative powers of 10. The powers of 10 are a way of keeping track of the decimal point in the decimal number. Table 2.3 gives several examples of writing measurements in scientific notation.

TABLE 2.2 Some Powers of 10

Number	Multiples of 10	Scientific Notation	
1000	$10 \times 10 \times 10$	1×10^3	Some positive powers of 10
100	10×10	1×10^2	
10	10	1×10^1	
1	0	1×10^0	
0.1	$\frac{1}{10}$	1×10^{-1}	Some negative powers of 10
0.01	$\frac{1}{10} \times \frac{1}{10} = \frac{1}{100}$	1×10^{-2}	
0.001	$\frac{1}{10} \times \frac{1}{10} \times \frac{1}{10} = \frac{1}{1000}$	1×10^{-3}	

TABLE 2.3 Some Measurements Written in Scientific Notation

Measured Quantity	Measurement	Scientific Notation
Volume of gasoline used in the United States each year	550 000 000 000 L	5.5×10^{11} L
Diameter of Earth	12 800 000 m	1.28×10^{7} m
Time for light to travel from the Sun to Earth	500 s	5×10^{2} s
Mass of a typical human	68 kg	6.8×10^{1} kg
Mass of a hummingbird	0.002 kg	2×10^{-3} kg
Diameter of a chickenpox (*varicella zoster*) virus	0.000 000 3 m	3×10^{-7} m
Mass of bacterium (mycoplasma)	0.000 000 000 000 000 000 1 kg	1×10^{-19} kg

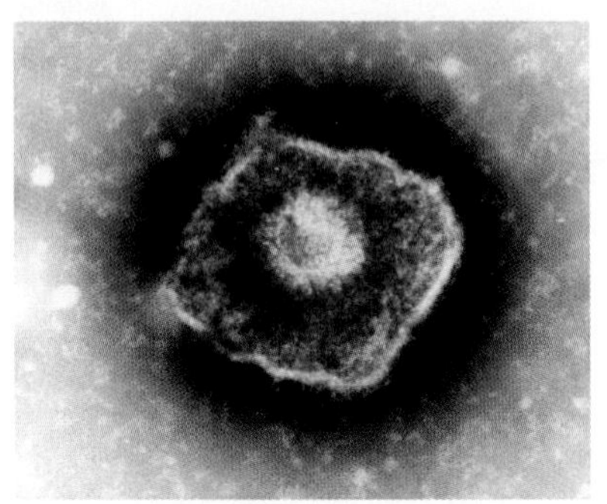

A chickenpox virus has a diameter of 3×10^{-7} m.

Scientific Notation and Calculators

You can enter a number written in scientific notation on many calculators using the EE or EXP key. After you enter the coefficient, press the EXP (or EE) key and enter the power (exponent), because the EXP function key already includes the ×10 value. To enter a negative power, you press the plus/minus (+/−) key or the minus (−) key, depending on your calculator. As you work through these problems, read the instruction manual for your particular calculator to determine the proper sequence for using keys.

Number to Enter	Method	Calculator Display
4×10^{6}	4 EXP (EE) 6	4 06 or 4^{06} or 4 E06
2.5×10^{-4}	2.5 EXP (EE) +/− 4	2.5−04 or 2.5^{-04} or 2.5E−04

When a calculator display appears in scientific notation, it is shown as a number that is more than 1 but less than 10, followed by a space and the power (exponent). To express this in scientific notation, write the coefficient, followed by ×10, and an exponent as the power of 10.

Calculator Display	Expressed in Scientific Notation
7.52 04 or 7.52^{04} or 7.52 E04	7.52×10^{4}
5.8−02 or 5.8^{-02} or 5.8E−02	5.8×10^{-2}

On many scientific calculators, a number is converted into scientific notation using the appropriate keys. For example, the number 0.000 52 is entered, followed by pressing the 2nd or 3rd function key and the SCI key. The scientific notation appears in the calculator display as a coefficient and the power of 10.

0.000 52 [2nd or 3rd function key] [SCI] = 5.2−04 or 5.2^{-04} or 5.2E−04 = 5.2×10^{-4}

Key Key Calculator display

SAMPLE PROBLEM 2.1 Scientific Notation

Write each of the following in scientific notation:

a. 3500 g **b.** 0.000 016 L

SOLUTION

a. 3500 g

Step 1 **Move the decimal point to obtain a coefficient that is at least 1 but less than 10.** For a number greater than 1, the decimal point is moved to the left three places to give a coefficient of 3.5.

Step 2 **Express the number of places moved as a power of 10.** When the decimal point is moved to the left, the power of 10 is positive. Moving the decimal point three places to the left gives a power of 3, written as 10^3.

Step 3 **Write the product of the coefficient multiplied by the power of 10 with the unit.**

$$3.5 \times 10^3 \text{ g}$$

b. 0.000 016 L

Step 1 **Move the decimal point to obtain a coefficient that is at least 1 but less than 10.** For a number less than 1, the decimal point is moved to the right five places to give a coefficient of 1.6.

Step 2 **Express the number of places moved as a power of 10.** When the decimal point is moved to the right, the power of 10 is negative. Moving the decimal point five places to the right gives a power of negative 5, written as 10^{-5}.

Step 3 **Write the product of the coefficient multiplied by the power of 10 with the unit.**

$$1.6 \times 10^{-5} \text{ L}$$

STUDY CHECK 2.1

Write each of the following in scientific notation:

a. 425 000 m
b. 0.000 000 8 g

Guide to Writing a Number in Scientific Notation

1. Move the decimal point to obtain a coefficient that is at least 1 but less than 10.
2. Express the number of places moved as a power of 10.
3. Write the product of the coefficient multiplied by the power of 10 with the unit.

Converting Scientific Notation to a Standard Number

When a number written in scientific notation has a positive power of 10, the standard number is obtained by moving the decimal point to the right for the same number of places as the power of 10. Placeholder zeros are used, as needed, to give additional places.

$$4.3 \times 10^2 \text{ L} = 4.30 \text{ L} = 430 \text{ L}$$

For a number with a negative power of 10, the standard number is obtained by moving the decimal point to the left for the same number of places as the power of 10. Placeholder zeros are added in front of the coefficient as needed.

$$2.5 \times 10^{-5} \text{ s} = 0000025 \text{ s} = 0.000\,025 \text{ s}$$

SAMPLE PROBLEM 2.2 Writing Scientific Notation as a Standard Number

Write each of the following as a standard number:

a. 7.2×10^{-3} m **b.** 2.4×10^5 g

SOLUTION

a. To write the standard number for an exponential number with a negative power of 10, move the decimal point to the left (in front of 7.2) the same number of places (three) as the power of 10. Add placeholder zeros before the coefficient as needed.

$$7.2 \times 10^{-3} \text{ m} = 0007.2 \text{ m} = 0.0072 \text{ m}$$

b. To write the standard number for an exponential number with a positive power of 10, move the decimal point to the right (after 2.4) the same number of places (five) as the power of 10. Add placeholder zeros following the coefficient as needed.

$$2.4 \times 10^5 \text{ g} = 2.40000 \text{ g} = 240\,000 \text{ g}$$

STUDY CHECK 2.2

Write 7.25×10^{-4} s as a standard number.

QUESTIONS AND PROBLEMS

2.2 Scientific Notation

LEARNING GOAL: *Write a number in scientific notation.*

2.7 Write each of the following in scientific notation:
a. 55 000 m **b.** 480 g **c.** 0.000 005 cm
d. 0.000 14 s **e.** 0.007 85 L **f.** 670 000 kg

2.8 Write each of the following in scientific notation:
a. 180 000 000 g **b.** 0.000 06 m
c. 750 000 g **d.** 0.15 mL
e. 0.024 s **f.** 1500 m^3

2.9 In each of the following pairs, which number is larger?
a. 7.2×10^3 cm or 4.2×10^3 cm
b. 4.5×10^{-4} kg or 3.2×10^{-2} kg
c. 1×10^4 L or 1×10^{-4} L
d. 0.000 52 m or 6.8×10^{-2} m

2.10 In each of the following pairs, which number is smaller?
a. 4.9×10^{-3} s or 5.5×10^{-9} s
b. 1500 kg or 3.4×10^2 kg
c. 0.000 000 41 m or 5.0×10^2 m
d. 2.5×10^5 g or 4.0×10^5 g

2.11 Write each of the following as a standard number:
a. 1.2×10^4 s
b. 8.25×10^{-2} kg
c. 4×10^6 g
d. 5.8×10^{-3} m^3

2.12 Write each of the following as a standard number:
a. 3.6×10^{-5} L
b. 8.75×10^4 cm
c. 3×10^{-2} mL
d. 2.12×10^5 kg

LEARNING GOAL

Identify a number as measured or exact; determine the number of significant figures in a measured number.

2.3 Measured Numbers and Significant Figures

When you make a measurement, you use some type of measuring device. For example, you may use a meterstick to measure your height, a scale to check your weight, or a thermometer to take your temperature.

Measured Numbers

Measured numbers are the numbers you obtain when you measure a quantity using a measuring tool. Suppose you are going to measure the lengths of the objects in Figure 2.6. You would select a metric ruler that may have lines marked in 1-cm divisions or perhaps in divisions of 0.1 cm. To report the length of an object, you observe the numerical values of the marked lines at the end of the object. Finally, you *estimate* by visually dividing the space between the smallest marked lines. This estimated number is the final digit that is reported for a measured number.

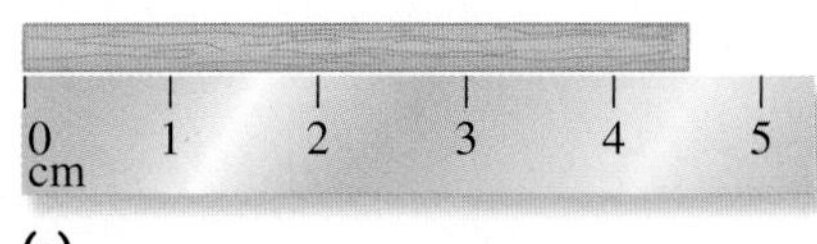

(a)

(b)

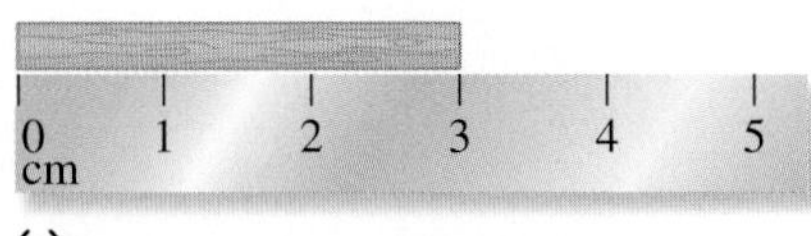

(c)

FIGURE 2.6 The lengths of the rectangular objects are measured as **(a)** 4.5 cm and **(b)** 4.55 cm.

Q What is the length of the object in (c)?

For example, in Figure 2.6a, the end of the object is between the marks for 4 cm and 5 cm. Thus you know that its length is more than 4 cm but less than 5 cm. Now you could estimate that the end is halfway between 4 cm and 5 cm and report its length as 4.5 cm. However, another student might estimate the length of this object as 4.4 cm because people do not estimate the same way. Therefore, there is always some uncertainty about the estimated number in every measurement.

The metric ruler shown in Figure 2.6b is marked at every 0.1 cm. With this ruler, you can now estimate the value of the hundredths place (0.01 cm). Now you could estimate that the length of the object is between 4.5 and 4.6 cm. Perhaps you report its length as 4.55 cm, while another student may report its length as 4.56 cm. Both results are acceptable.

In Figure 2.6c, the end of the object appears to line up with the 3-cm mark. Because the divisions are marked in units of 1 cm, the estimated digit in the tenths place (0.1 cm) is 0. The reported measurement for length is reported as 3.0 cm, not 3. This means that the uncertainty of the measurement (the last digit) is in the tenths place (0.1 cm). *There is always uncertainty in every measurement.*

Significant Figures

In a *measured number*, the **significant figures (SFs)** are all the digits including the estimated digit. All *nonzero* numbers are counted as significant figures. However, a zero may or may not be significant, depending on its position in the number. Table 2.4 gives the rules and examples for counting significant figures.

TABLE 2.4 Significant Figures in Measured Numbers

Rule	Measured Number	Number of Significant Figures
1. A number is a *significant figure* if it is		
a. not a zero	4.5 g	2
	122.35 m	5
b. one or more zeros between nonzero digits	205 m	3
	5.008 kg	4
c. one or more zeros at the end of a decimal number	50. L	2
	25.0 °C	3
	16.00 g	4
d. in the coefficient of a number written in scientific notation	4.8×10^5 kg	2
	5.70×10^{-3} m	3
2. A zero is *not significant* if it is		
a. at the beginning of a decimal number	0.0004 s	1
	0.075 cm	2
b. used as a placeholder in a large number without a decimal point	850 000 m	2
	1 250 000 g	3

CORE CHEMISTRY SKILL 

Counting Significant Figures

Scientific Notation and Significant Zeros

When one or more zeros in a large number are significant, they are shown clearly by writing the number in scientific notation. For example, if the first zero in the measurement 500 m is significant, but the second zero is not, the measurement is written as 5.0×10^2 m. In this text, we will place a decimal point after a significant zero at the end of a number. For example, if a measurement is written as 500. g, the decimal point after the second zero indicates that *both zeros* are significant. To show this more clearly, we can write it as 5.00×10^2 g. We will assume that zeros at the end of large standard numbers without a decimal point are not significant. Therefore, we write 400 000 g as 4×10^5 g, which has only one significant figure.

CONCEPT CHECK 2.2 Significant Zeros

Identify the zeros as significant or not significant in each of the following measured numbers:

a. 0.000 250 m **b.** 70.040 g **c.** 1 020 000 L

ANSWER

a. The zeros preceding the first nonzero digit of 2 are not significant. The zero in the last decimal place following the 5 is significant.
b. Zeros between nonzero digits or at the end of decimal numbers are significant. All zeros in 70.040 g are significant.
c. Zeros between nonzero digits are significant. Zeros at the end of a large number with no decimal point are placeholders but not significant. The zero between 1 and 2 is significant, but the four zeros following the 2 are not significant.

Exact Numbers

Exact numbers *are those numbers obtained by counting items or using a definition that compares two units in the same measuring system.* Suppose a friend asks you how many classes you are taking this term. You would answer by counting the number of classes. It is not necessary for you to use any type of measuring tool. Suppose you are asked to state the number of seconds in 1 minute. Without using any measuring device, you would give the definition: 60 seconds is 1 minute. *Exact numbers are not measured, do not have a*

The number of baseballs is counted, which means 2 is an exact number.

limited number of significant figures, and do not affect the number of significant figures in a calculated answer (see Table 2.5).

TABLE 2.5 Examples of Some Exact Numbers

Counted Numbers	Defined Equalities	
Items	**Metric System**	**U.S. System**
8 doughnuts	1 L = 1000 mL	1 ft = 12 in.
2 baseballs	1 m = 100 cm	1 qt = 4 cups
5 capsules	1 kg = 1000 g	1 lb = 16 oz

CONCEPT CHECK 2.3 Significant Figures

Identify each of the following numbers as measured or exact and give the number of significant figures (SFs) in each of the measured numbers:

a. 42.2 g
b. 3 eggs
c. 5.0×10^{-3} cm
d. 1 kg = 1000 g

ANSWER

a. The mass of 42.2 g is a measured number because it is obtained with a measuring tool. There are three SFs in 42.2 g because nonzero digits are always significant.
b. The value of 3 eggs is an exact number because it is obtained by counting rather than using a measuring tool.
c. The length of 5.0×10^{-3} cm is a measured number because it is obtained with a measuring tool. There are two SFs in 5.0×10^{-3} cm because all the numbers in the coefficient of a number written in scientific notation are significant.
d. The masses of 1 kg and 1000 g are both exact numbers because the relationship 1 kg = 1000 g is a definition in the metric system of measurement.

QUESTIONS AND PROBLEMS

2.3 Measured Numbers and Significant Figures

LEARNING GOAL: *Identify a number as measured or exact; determine the number of significant figures in a measured number.*

2.13 What is the estimated digit in each of the following measured numbers?
a. 8.6 m **b.** 45.25 g **c.** 29 °C

2.14 What is the estimated digit in each of the following measured numbers?
a. 125.04 g **b.** 5.057 m **c.** 525.8 °C

2.15 Identify the number(s) in each of the following as measured or exact:
a. A person weighs 67.5 kg.
b. The basket holds 8 apples.
c. In the metric system, 1 m is equal to 1000 mm.
d. The distance from Denver, Colorado, to Houston, Texas, is 1720 km.

2.16 Identify the number(s) in each of the following as measured or exact:
a. There are 31 students in the laboratory.
b. The oldest-known flower lived 1.2×10^8 y ago.
c. The largest gem ever found, an aquamarine, has a mass of 104 kg.
d. A laboratory test shows a blood cholesterol level of 184 mg/dL.

2.17 Identify the measured number(s), if any, in each of the following pairs of numbers:
a. 3 hamburgers and 6 oz of hamburger
b. 1 table and 4 chairs
c. 0.75 lb of grapes and 350 g of butter
d. 60 s = 1 min

2.18 Identify the measured number(s), if any, in each of the following pairs of numbers:
a. 5 pizzas and 50.0 g of cheese
b. 6 nickels and 16 g of nickel
c. 3 onions and 3 lb of onions
d. 5 miles and 5 cars

2.19 Indicate the significant zeros, if any, in each of the following and give a reason:
a. 0.0038 m **b.** 5.04 cm **c.** 800. L
d. 3.0×10^{-3} kg **e.** 85 000 g

2.20 Indicate the significant zeros, if any, in each of the following and give a reason:
a. 20.05 °C **b.** 5.00 m **c.** 0.000 02 L
d. 120 000 y **e.** 8.05×10^2 g

2.21 How many significant figures are in each of the following?
a. 11.005 kg **b.** 0.000 32 m^3 **c.** 36 000 000 m
d. 1.80×10^4 g **e.** 0.8250 L **f.** 30.0 °C

2.22 How many significant figures are in each of the following?
a. 20.60 mL **b.** 1036.48 g **c.** 4.00 m
d. 20.8 °C **e.** 60 800 000 kg **f.** 5.0×10^{-3} L

2.23 Identify the measurement in each of the following pairs that contains more significant figures:
a. 11.0 m and 11.00 m
b. 405 K and 405.0 K
c. 0.0120 s and 12 000 s
d. 2500 mL and 2.50×10^{-2} mL

2.24 Identify the measurement in each of the following pairs that contains more significant figures:
a. 28.33 g and 2.8×10^{-3} g
b. 0.0250 m and 0.2005 m
c. 150 000 s and 1.50×10^4 s
d. 3.8×10^{-2} L and 3.80×10^5 L

2.25 Write each of the following in scientific notation with two significant figures:
a. 5000 L **b.** 30 000 g
c. 100 000 m **d.** 0.000 25 cm

2.26 Write each of the following in scientific notation with two significant figures:
a. 5 100 000 g **b.** 26 000 s
c. 40 000 m **d.** 0.000 820 kg

2.4 Significant Figures in Calculations

LEARNING GOAL

Adjust calculated answers to give the correct number of significant figures.

In the sciences, we measure many things: the length of a bacterium, the volume of a gas sample, the temperature of a reaction mixture, or the mass of iron in a sample. The numbers obtained from these types of measurements are often used in calculations. The number of significant figures in the measured numbers determines the number of significant figures in the calculated answer.

Using a calculator will help you perform calculations faster. However, calculators cannot think for you. It is up to you to enter the numbers correctly, press the correct function keys, and give an answer with the correct number of significant figures.

Rounding Off

CORE CHEMISTRY SKILL 

Rounding Off

Suppose you decide to buy carpeting for a room that measures 5.52 m by 3.58 m. Each measurement of length has three significant figures because the measuring tape limits your estimated place to 0.01 m. To determine how much carpeting you need, you would calculate the area of the room by multiplying 5.52 times 3.58. If you used a calculator, the display shows the numbers 19.7616. However, this display has too many numbers, which is the result of the multiplication process. Because each of the original measurements has three significant figures, the display numbers of 19.7616 must be *rounded off* to three significant figures, 19.8. Therefore, you can order carpeting that will cover an area of 19.8 m^2 (square meters).

Each time you use a calculator, it is important to look at the original measurements and determine the number of significant figures that can be used for the answer. You can use the following rules to round off the numbers in a calculator display:

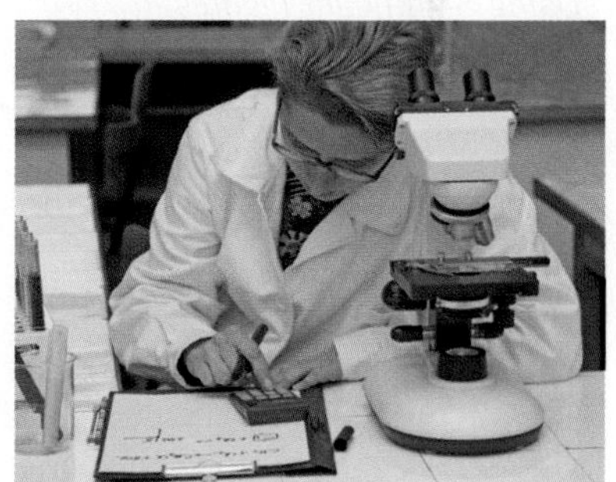

A technician uses a calculator in the laboratory.

Rules for Rounding Off

1. If the first digit to be dropped is *4 or less*, then it and all following digits are simply dropped from the number.
2. If the first digit to be dropped is *5 or greater*, then the last retained digit is increased by 1.

Number to Round off	Three Significant Figures	Two Significant Figures
8.4234	8.42 (drop 34)	8.4 (drop 234)
14.780	14.8 (drop 80, increase the last retained digit by 1)	15 (drop 780, increase the last retained digit by 1)
3256	3260* (drop 6, increase the last retained digit by 1, add 0) (3.26×10^3)	3300* (drop 56, increase the last retained digit by 1, add 00) (3.3×10^3)

*The value of a large number is retained by using placeholder zeros to replace dropped digits.

SAMPLE PROBLEM 2.3 Rounding Off

Round off each of the following numbers to three significant figures:

a. 35.7823 m **b.** 0.002 621 7 L **c.** 3.8268×10^3 g

SOLUTION

a. To round off 35.7823 m to three significant figures, drop the numbers 823 and increase the last retained digit by 1 to give 35.8 m.

b. To round off 0.002 621 7 L to three significant figures, drop the numbers 17 to give 0.002 62 L.

c. To round off 3.8268×10^3 g to three significant figures, drop the numbers 68 and increase the last retained digit by 1 to give 3.83×10^3 g.

STUDY CHECK 2.3

Round off each of the numbers in Sample Problem 2.3 to two significant figures.

A calculator is helpful in working problems and doing calculations faster.

Multiplication and Division with Measured Numbers

In multiplication or division, the final answer is written so that it has the same number of significant figures (SFs) as the measurement with the fewest SFs. Some examples of rounding off numbers from multiplication and division follow:

Example 1

Multiply the following measured numbers: 24.65×0.67

24.65	⊠	0.67	⊟	16.5155	⟶	17
Four SFs		Two SFs		Calculator display		Final answer, rounded off to two SFs

Because the calculator display has more digits than the significant figures in the measured numbers allow, we need to round off. Using the measurement that has the fewer number (two) of significant figures, 0.67, we round off the calculator display to two significant figures.

CORE CHEMISTRY SKILL

Using Significant Figures in Calculations

Example 2

Perform the following operations with measured numbers:

$$\frac{2.85}{0.3741 \times 1.50}$$

A problem with multiple steps is worked on a calculator by dividing the number in the numerator by each of the numbers in the denominator.

2.85	÷	0.3741	÷	1.50	=	5.0788559	⟶	5.08
Three SFs		Four SFs		Three SFs		Calculator display		Three SFs

The calculator display is rounded off to give an answer with three significant figures, 5.08.

Adding Significant Zeros

Sometimes a calculator display consists of a small whole number. Then we add one or more significant zeros to the calculator display to obtain the correct number of significant figures. For example, suppose the calculator display is 4, but you used measurements that have three significant numbers. Then two significant zeros are *added* to give 4.00 as the correct answer.

$\frac{8.00}{2.00}$ =	4.	⟶	4.00
Three SFs	Calculator display		Final answer, two zeros added to give three SFs

SAMPLE PROBLEM 2.4 Significant Figures in Multiplication and Division

Perform the following calculations of measured numbers. Give each answer with the correct number of significant figures.

a. $\dfrac{2.075}{(8.42)(0.0045)}$ **b.** $\dfrac{2.0 \times 6.00}{4.00}$

SOLUTION

a. 2.075 ÷ 8.42 ÷ 0.0045 = 54.76378992 ⟶ 55

Four SFs, Three SFs, Two SFs; Calculator display; Final answer, rounded off to two SFs

b. 2.0 × 6.00 ÷ 4.00 = 3. ⟶ 3.0

Two SFs, Three SFs, Three SFs; Calculator display; Final answer, one significant zero added to give two SFs

STUDY CHECK 2.4

Perform the following calculations of measured numbers and give the answers with the correct number of significant figures:

a. 45.26 × 0.010 88 **b.** $\dfrac{4.0 \times 8.00}{16}$

Addition and Subtraction with Measured Numbers

In addition or subtraction, the final answer is written so that it has the same number of decimal places as the measurement having the fewest decimal places. Some examples of addition and subtraction follow:

Example 3

Add:

2.367	Thousandths place
+ 34.1	Tenths place
36.467	Calculator display
36.5	Answer, rounded off to tenths place

Example 4

Subtract:

255	Ones place
− 175.65	Hundredths place
79.35	Calculator display
79	Answer, rounded off to the ones place

When numbers are added or subtracted to give an answer ending in zero, that zero does not appear after the decimal point in the calculator display. For example, 14.5 g − 2.5 g = 12.0 g. However, when you do the subtraction on your calculator, the calculator display shows 12. The correct answer, 12.0 g, is obtained by placing a significant zero after the decimal point.

Example 5

Subtract:

14.5 g	Tenths place
− 2.5 g	Tenths place
12.	Calculator display
12.0 g	Answer, zero written after the decimal point to give a digit in the tenths place

SAMPLE PROBLEM 2.5 Significant Figures in Addition and Subtraction

Perform the following calculations and give the answers with the correct number of decimal places:

a. 104.45 mL + 0.838 mL + 46 mL **b.** 153.247 g − 14.82 g

SOLUTION

a.

104.45 mL	Hundredths place
0.838 mL	Thousandths place
⊕ 46 mL	Ones place
151 mL	Answer, rounded off to the ones place

b.

153.247 g	Thousandths place
⊖ 14.82 g	Hundredths place
138.43 g	Answer, rounded off to hundredths place

STUDY CHECK 2.5

Perform the following calculations and give the answers with the correct number of decimal places:

a. 82.45 g + 1.245 g + 0.000 56 g **b.** 4.259 L − 3.8 L
c. 0.385 m + 12.5 m − 5.85 m

QUESTIONS AND PROBLEMS

2.4 Significant Figures in Calculations

LEARNING GOAL: *Adjust calculated answers to give the correct number of significant figures.*

2.27 Why do we usually round off the calculator display of a calculation that includes measured numbers?

2.28 Why do we sometimes add a zero to a number in a calculator display of a calculation that includes measured numbers?

2.29 Round off each of the following measurements to three significant figures:
a. 1.854 kg **b.** 88.0238 L **c.** 0.004 738 265 cm
d. 8807 m **e.** 1.8329×10^3 s

2.30 Round off each of the measurements in Problem 2.29 to two significant figures.

2.31 Round off or add zeros to each of the following to give an answer with three significant figures:
a. 56.855 m **b.** 0.002 282 g
c. 11 527 s **d.** 8.1 L

2.32 Round off or add zeros to each of the following to give an answer with two significant figures:
a. 3.2805 m **b.** 1.855×10^2 g
c. 0.002 341 mL **d.** 2 L

2.33 Perform each of the following calculations, and give an answer with the correct number of significant figures:
a. 45.7×0.034 **b.** $0.002\,78 \times 5$
c. $\dfrac{34.56}{1.25}$ **d.** $\dfrac{(0.2465)(25)}{1.78}$
e. $(2.8 \times 10^4)(5.05 \times 10^{-6})$
f. $\dfrac{(3.45 \times 10^{-2})(1.8 \times 10^5)}{(8 \times 10^3)}$

2.34 Perform each of the following calculations, and give an answer with the correct number of significant figures:
a. 400×185 **b.** $\dfrac{2.40}{(4)(125)}$
c. $0.825 \times 3.6 \times 5.1$ **d.** $\dfrac{(3.5)(0.261)}{(8.24)(20.0)}$
e. $\dfrac{(5 \times 10^{-5})(1.05 \times 10^4)}{(8.24 \times 10^{-8})}$
f. $\dfrac{(4.25 \times 10^2)(2.56 \times 10^{-3})}{(2.245 \times 10^{-3})(56.5)}$

2.35 Perform each of the following calculations, and give an answer with the correct number of decimal places:
a. 45.48 cm + 8.057 cm **b.** 23.45 g + 104.1 g + 0.025 g
c. 145.675 mL − 24.2 mL **d.** 1.08 L − 0.585 L

2.36 Perform each of the following calculations, and give an answer with the correct number of decimal places:
a. 5.08 g + 25.1 g
b. 85.66 cm + 104.10 cm + 0.025 cm
c. 24.568 mL − 14.25 mL **d.** 0.2654 L − 0.2585 L

LEARNING GOAL

Use the numerical values of prefixes to write a metric equality.

2.5 Prefixes and Equalities

In the metric and SI systems of units, a **prefix** attached to any unit increases or decreases its size by some factor of 10. Table 2.6 lists some of the SI and metric prefixes, their symbols, and their numerical values.

CORE CHEMISTRY SKILL 

Using Prefixes

The prefix *centi* is like cents in a dollar. One cent would be a *centidollar*, or 0.01 of a dollar. That also means that one dollar is the same as 100 cents. The prefix *deci* is like the value of a dime to a dollar. One dime would be a *decidollar*, or 0.1 of a dollar. That also means that one dollar has the same value as 10 dimes.

The relationship of a prefix to a unit can be expressed by replacing the prefix with its numerical value. For example, when the prefix *kilo* in kilometer is replaced with its value of 1000, we find that a kilometer is equal to 1000 m. Other examples follow:

1 **kilo**meter (1 km) = **1000** meters ($1000 \text{ m} = 10^3 \text{ m}$)
1 **kilo**liter (1 kL) = **1000** liters ($1000 \text{ L} = 10^3 \text{ L}$)
1 **kilo**gram (1 kg) = **1000** grams ($1000 \text{ g} = 10^3 \text{ g}$)

CONCEPT CHECK 2.4 Prefix Values

Fill in the blanks with the correct prefix:

a. 1000 g = 1 ____ g **b.** 0.01 m = 1 ____ m **c.** 1×10^6 L = 1 ____ L

ANSWER

a. The prefix for 1000 is *kilo*; 1000 g = 1 kg
b. The prefix for 0.01 is *centi*; 0.01 m = 1 cm
c. The prefix for 1×10^6 is *mega*; 1×10^6 L = 1 ML

TABLE 2.6 Metric and SI Prefixes

Prefix	Symbol	Numerical Value	Scientific Notation	Equality
Prefixes That Increase the Size of the Unit				
peta	P	1 000 000 000 000 000	10^{15}	$1 \text{ Pg} = 1 \times 10^{15} \text{ g}$ $1 \text{ g} = 1 \times 10^{-15} \text{ Pg}$
tera	T	1 000 000 000 000	10^{12}	$1 \text{ Ts} = 1 \times 10^{12} \text{ s}$ $1 \text{ s} = 1 \times 10^{-12} \text{ Ts}$
giga	G	1 000 000 000	10^{9}	$1 \text{ Gm} = 1 \times 10^{9} \text{ m}$ $1 \text{ m} = 1 \times 10^{-9} \text{ Gm}$
mega	M	1 000 000	10^{6}	$1 \text{ Mg} = 1 \times 10^{6} \text{ g}$ $1 \text{ g} = 1 \times 10^{-6} \text{ Mg}$
kilo	k	1 000	10^{3}	$1 \text{ km} = 1 \times 10^{3} \text{ m}$ $1 \text{ m} = 1 \times 10^{-3} \text{ km}$
Prefixes That Decrease the Size of the Unit				
deci	d	0.1	10^{-1}	$1 \text{ dL} = 1 \times 10^{-1} \text{ L}$ $1 \text{ L} = 10 \text{ dL}$
centi	c	0.01	10^{-2}	$1 \text{ cm} = 1 \times 10^{-2} \text{ m}$ $1 \text{ m} = 100 \text{ cm}$
milli	m	0.001	10^{-3}	$1 \text{ ms} = 1 \times 10^{-3} \text{ s}$ $1 \text{ s} = 1 \times 10^{3} \text{ ms}$
micro	μ	0.000 001	10^{-6}	$1 \mu\text{g} = 1 \times 10^{-6} \text{ g}$ $1 \text{ g} = 1 \times 10^{6} \mu\text{g}$
nano	n	0.000 000 001	10^{-9}	$1 \text{ nm} = 1 \times 10^{-9} \text{ m}$ $1 \text{ m} = 1 \times 10^{9} \text{ nm}$
pico	p	0.000 000 000 001	10^{-12}	$1 \text{ ps} = 1 \times 10^{-12} \text{ s}$ $1 \text{ s} = 1 \times 10^{12} \text{ ps}$
femto	f	0.000 000 000 000 001	10^{-15}	$1 \text{ fs} = 1 \times 10^{-15} \text{ s}$ $1 \text{ s} = 1 \times 10^{15} \text{ fs}$

A 1 terabyte hard disk drive stores 10^{12} bytes of information.

SAMPLE PROBLEM 2.6 Using Prefixes

The storage capacity for a hard-disk drive (HDD) is specified using prefixes: megabyte (MB), gigabyte (GB), or terabyte (TB). Indicate the storage capacity in bytes for each of the following hard-disk drives. Suggest a reason for describing an HDD storage capacity in megabytes, gigabytes, or terabytes.

a. 5 MB **b.** 6.4 GB

SOLUTION

a. The prefix *mega* (M) in MB is equal to 1 000 000 or 1×10^6 bytes. Thus, 5 megabytes (MB) is equal to 5 000 000 (5×10^6) bytes.

b. The prefix *giga* (G) in GB is equal to 1 000 000 000 or 1×10^9 bytes. Thus, 6.4 GB is equal to 6 400 000 000 (6.4×10^9) bytes.

Expressing HDD capacity in megabytes, gigabytes, or terabytes gives a more reasonable number to work with than a number with many zeros or a large power of 10.

STUDY CHECK 2.6

A hard drive has a storage capacity of 2.0 TB. How many bytes can be stored?

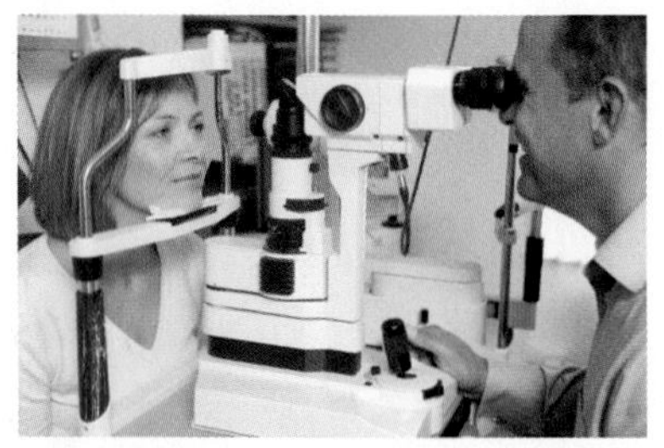

Using a retinal camera, an ophthalmologist photographs the retina of an eye.

Measuring Length

An ophthalmologist may measure the retina of the eye in centimeters (cm), whereas a surgeon may need to know the length of a nerve in millimeters (mm). When the prefix *centi* is used with the unit meter, it becomes centimeter, a length that is one-hundredth of a meter (0.01 m). When the prefix *milli* is used with the unit meter, it becomes millimeter, a length that is one-thousandth of a meter (0.001 m). There are 100 cm and 1000 mm in a meter (see Figure 2.7).

An **equality** shows the relationship between two units that measure the same quantity. For example, we know that 1 m is the same length as 100 cm. Then the equality for this relationship is written as 1 m = 100 cm. *In any equality, we show both the number and unit for each quantity.*

First Quantity			**Second Quantity**	
1	m	=	100	cm
↑	↑		↑	↑
Number +	unit		Number +	unit

This example of an equality shows the relationship between meters and centimeters.

Other examples of equalities between different metric units of length follow:

$$1\text{ m} = 100\text{ cm} = 1 \times 10^2\text{ cm}$$
$$1\text{ m} = 1000\text{ mm} = 1 \times 10^3\text{ mm}$$
$$1\text{ cm} = 10\text{ mm} = 1 \times 10^1\text{ mm}$$

Some metric units for length are compared in Figure 2.7.

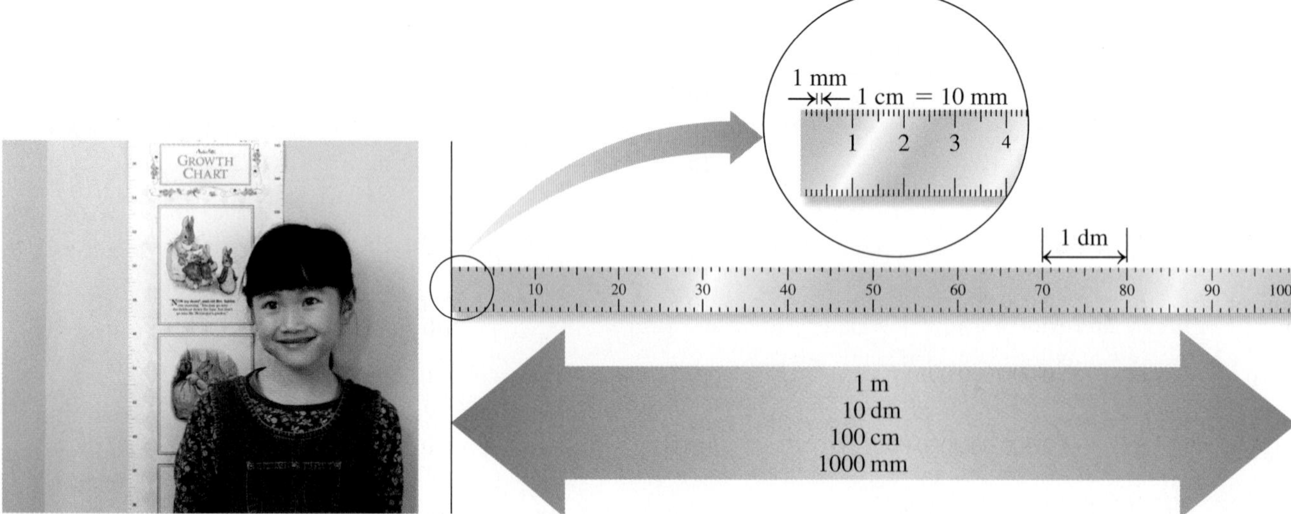

FIGURE 2.7 The metric length of 1 m is the same length as 10 dm, 100 cm, and 1000 mm.

Q How many millimeters (mm) are in 1 cm?

Measuring Volume

A volume of 1 L or smaller is common in the laboratory. When a liter is divided into 10 equal parts, each is a deciliter (dL). There are 10 dL in 1 L.

When a liter is divided into a thousand parts, each is a milliliter (mL). In a 1-L container of soda, there are 1000 mL of soda. Other examples of equalities between different metric units of volume follow:

$$1\ \text{L} = 10\ \text{dL} = 1 \times 10^1\ \text{dL}$$
$$1\ \text{L} = 1000\ \text{mL} = 1 \times 10^3\ \text{mL}$$
$$1\ \text{dL} = 100\ \text{mL} = 1 \times 10^2\ \text{mL}$$

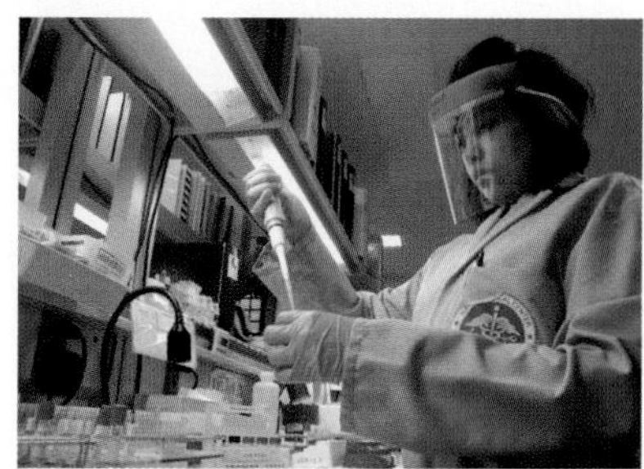

A laboratory technician transfers small volumes using a micropipette.

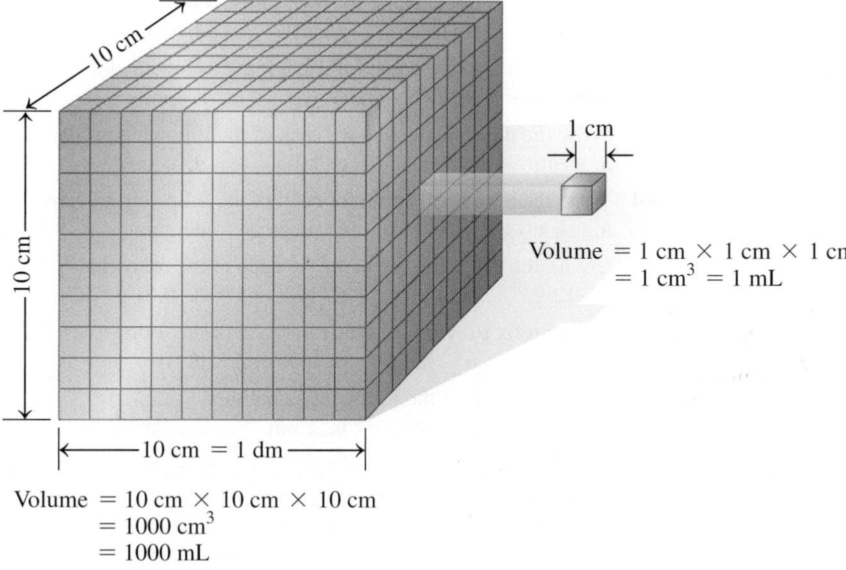
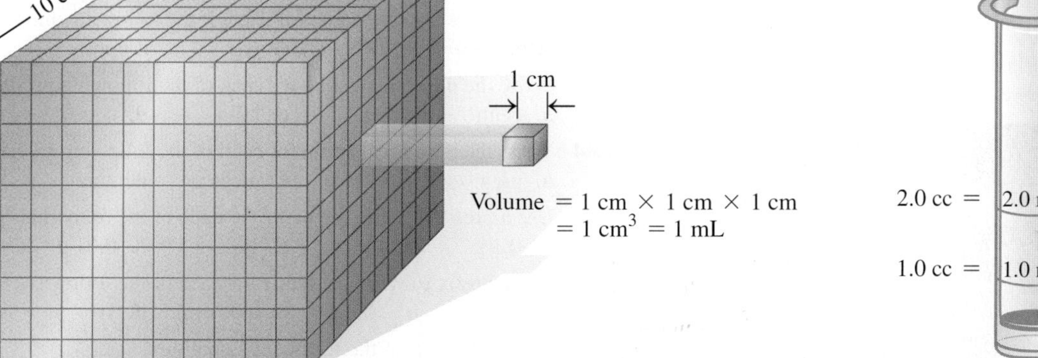

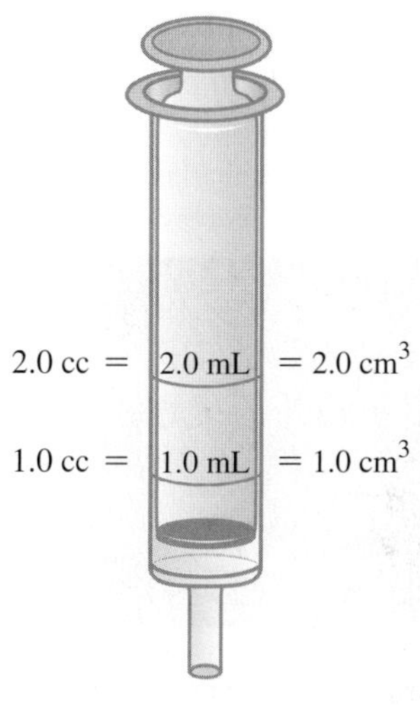

FIGURE 2.8 A cube measuring 10 cm on each side has a volume of 1000 cm^3, or 1 L; a cube measuring 1 cm on each side has a volume of 1 cm^3 (cc) or 1 mL.

Q What is the relationship between a milliliter (mL) and a cubic centimeter (cm^3)?

The **cubic centimeter (cm^3 or cc)** is the volume of a cube whose dimensions are 1 cm on each side. A cubic centimeter has the same volume as a milliliter, and the units are often used interchangeably.

$$1\ \text{cm}^3 = 1\ \text{cc} = 1\ \text{mL}$$

When you see *1 cm*, you are reading about length; when you see *1 cc* or *1 cm^3* or *1 mL*, you are reading about volume. A comparison of units of volume is illustrated in Figure 2.8.

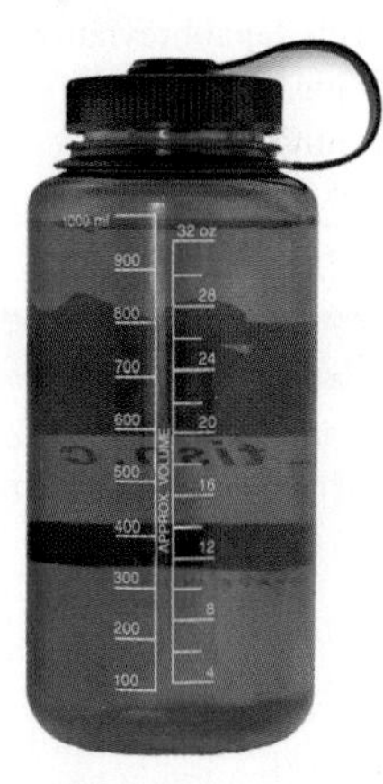

A 1-liter water bottle contains 1000 mL.

Measuring Mass

When you go to the doctor for a physical examination, your mass is recorded in kilograms, whereas the results of your laboratory tests are reported in grams, milligrams (mg), or micrograms (μg). A kilogram is equal to 1000 g. As an equality, this is written as 1 kg = 1000 g. One gram represents the same mass as 1000 mg, and 1 mg equals 1000 μg. Some examples of equalities between different metric units of mass follow:

$$1\ \text{kg} = 1000\ \text{g} = 1 \times 10^3\ \text{g}$$
$$1\ \text{g} = 1000\ \text{mg} = 1 \times 10^3\ \text{mg}$$
$$1\ \text{mg} = 1000\ \mu\text{g} = 1 \times 10^3\ \mu\text{g}$$

CONCEPT CHECK 2.5 Writing Metric Relationships

Complete the following list of metric equalities:

a. 1 L = _____ dL
b. 1 kg = _____ g
c. 1 cm = _____ m
d. 1 cm^3 = _____ mL

ANSWER

a. 10 dL **b.** 1000 g **c.** 0.01 m **d.** 1 mL

QUESTIONS AND PROBLEMS

2.5 Prefixes and Equalities

LEARNING GOAL: *Use the numerical values of prefixes to write a metric equality.*

2.37 The speedometer is marked in both km/h and mi/h. What is the meaning of each abbreviation?

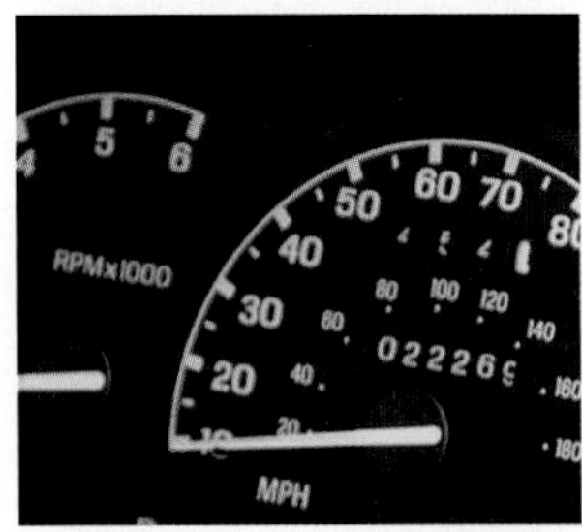

2.38 In a French car, the odometer reads 2250. What units would this be? What units would it be if this were an odometer in a car made for the United States?

2.39 Write the abbreviation for each of the following units:
a. milligram **b.** deciliter
c. kilometer **d.** femtogram

2.40 Write the abbreviation for each of the following units:
a. gigagram **b.** megameter
c. microliter **d.** nanosecond

2.41 Write the complete name for each of the following units:
a. cL **b.** kg **c.** ms **d.** Gm

2.42 Write the complete name for each of the following units:
a. dL **b.** Ts **c.** μg **d.** pm

2.43 Write the numerical value for each of the following prefixes:
a. centi **b.** tera **c.** milli **d.** deci

2.44 Write the numerical value for each of the following prefixes:
a. giga **b.** micro **c.** mega **d.** nano

2.45 Use a prefix to write the name for each of the following:
a. 0.1 g **b.** 10^{-6} g **c.** 1000 g **d.** 0.01 g

2.46 Use a prefix to write the name for each of the following:
a. 10^9 m **b.** 10^6 m **c.** 0.001 m **d.** 10^{-12} m

2.47 Complete each of the following equalities:
a. 1 m = _____ cm **b.** 1 nm = _____ m
c. 1 mm = _____ m **d.** 1 L = _____ mL

2.48 Complete each of the following equalities:
a. 1 Mg = _____ g **b.** 1 μL = _____ L
c. 1 g = _____ kg **d.** 1 g = _____ mg

2.49 For each of the following pairs, which is the larger unit?
a. milligram or kilogram **b.** milliliter or microliter
c. cm or pm **d.** kL or dL

2.50 For each of the following pairs, which is the smaller unit?
a. mg or g **b.** centimeter or millimeter
c. mm or μm **d.** mL or dL

LEARNING GOAL

Write a conversion factor for two units that describe the same quantity.

CORE CHEMISTRY SKILL

Writing Conversion Factors from Equalities

2.6 Writing Conversion Factors

Many problems in chemistry, engineering, and medicine require you to change from one unit to another unit. For example, suppose you spent 2.0 h on your homework, and someone asked you how many minutes that was. You would answer 120 min. You must have multiplied 2.0 h × 60 min/h because you knew that one hour is equal to 60 minutes (1 h = 60 min). The relationship between the units, hours and minutes, is called an *equality*, which means they both measure the same quantity. When you expressed 2.0 h as 120 min, you did not change the amount of time. You changed only the unit of measurement used to express the time. *Any equality can be written as fractions called* **conversion factors** *with one of the quantities in the numerator and the other quantity in the denominator.* Be sure to include the units when you write the conversion factors. Two conversion factors are always possible from any equality.

Two Conversion Factors for the Equality 60 min = 1 h

$$\frac{\text{Numerator}}{\text{Denominator}} \quad \begin{matrix}\longrightarrow \\ \longrightarrow\end{matrix} \quad \frac{60\text{ min}}{1\text{ h}} \quad \text{and} \quad \frac{1\text{ h}}{60\text{ min}}$$

These conversion factors are read as "60 minutes per 1 hour" and "1 hour per 60 minutes." The term *per* means "divide." The relationship may also be written as 60 min/h. Some

TABLE 2.7 Some Common Equalities

Quantity	Metric (SI)	U.S.	Metric–U.S.
Length	1 km = 1000 m 1 m = 1000 mm 1 cm = 10 mm	1 ft = 12 in. 1 yd = 3 ft 1 mi = 5280 ft	2.54 cm = 1 in. (exact) 1 m = 39.37 in. 1 km = 0.6214 mi
Volume	1 L = 1000 mL 1 dL = 100 mL 1 mL = 1 cm^3	1 qt = 4 cups 1 qt = 2 pt 1 gal = 4 qt	1 L = 1.057 qt 946.3 mL = 1 qt
Mass	1 kg = 1000 g 1 g = 1000 mg	1 lb = 16 oz	1 kg = 2.205 lb 453.6 g = 1 lb
Time	1 h = 60 min 1 min = 60 s		

common relationships are given in Table 2.7. It is important that the equality you select to form a conversion factor is an actual relationship between the two units.

The numbers in any equality between two metric units or between two U.S. system units are obtained by definition. Because numbers in a definition are exact, they are not used to determine significant figures. For example, the equality of 1 g = 1000 mg is defined, which means that both of the numbers 1 and 1000 are exact. *However, when an equality consists of a metric unit and a U.S. unit, one of the numbers in the equality is obtained by measurement and counts toward the significant figures in the answer.* For example, the equality of 1 lb = 453.6 g is obtained by measuring the grams in exactly 1 lb. In this equality, the measured quantity 453.6 g has four significant figures, whereas the 1 is exact. An exception is the relationship of 1 in. = 2.54 cm where 2.54 has been defined as exact.

Metric Conversion Factors

We can write conversion factors for any of the metric relationships. For example, from the equality for meters and centimeters, we can write the following factors:

Metric Equality	Conversion Factors
1 m = 100 cm	$\frac{100\text{ cm}}{1\text{ m}}$ and $\frac{1\text{ m}}{100\text{ cm}}$

Both of these conversion factors represent the same equality; one is just the inverse of the other. *The usefulness of conversion factors is enhanced by the fact that we can turn a conversion factor over and use its inverse.* The number 100 and 1 in this equality and its conversion factors are both *exact* numbers.

CONCEPT CHECK 2.6 **Conversion Factors**

Identify one or more correct conversion factors for the equality of gigagrams and grams.

a. $\frac{1\text{ Gg}}{1 \times 10^{9}\text{ g}}$ **b.** $\frac{1 \times 10^{-9}\text{ g}}{1\text{ Gg}}$ **c.** $\frac{1 \times 10^{9}\text{ Gg}}{1\text{ g}}$ **d.** $\frac{1 \times 10^{9}\text{ g}}{1\text{ Gg}}$

ANSWER

Using Table 2.6 prefixes, we can write the equality for gigagrams and grams as 1 Gg = 1×10^9 g. Answers **a** and **d** are correctly written conversion factors that represent this equality.

Metric–U.S. System Conversion Factors

Suppose you need to convert from pounds, a unit in the U.S. system, to kilograms in the metric (or SI) system. A relationship you could use is

1 kg = 2.205 lb

FIGURE 2.9 In the United States, the contents of many packaged foods are listed in both U.S. and metric units.

Q What are some advantages of using the metric system?

The corresponding conversion factors would be

$$\frac{2.205 \text{ lb}}{1 \text{ kg}} \quad \text{and} \quad \frac{1 \text{ kg}}{2.205 \text{ lb}}$$

In the metric–U.S. equality, the number in 2.205 lb is obtained from the measurement of exactly 1 kg.

Figure 2.9 illustrates the contents of some packaged foods in both U.S. and metric units.

CONCEPT CHECK 2.7 Writing Conversion Factors from Equalities

Write an equality and its conversion factors, and state whether the numbers are exact or measured for each of the following:

a. millimeters and meters **b.** quarts and milliliters

ANSWER

Equality	Conversion Factors	Exact or Measured Quantities
a. 1 m = 1000 mm	$\frac{1000 \text{ mm}}{1 \text{ m}}$ and $\frac{1 \text{ m}}{1000 \text{ mm}}$	In the definition of a metric equality, both 1 m and 1000 mm are exact quantities.
b. 1 qt = 946.3 mL	$\frac{946.3 \text{ mL}}{1 \text{ qt}}$ and $\frac{1 \text{ qt}}{946.3 \text{ mL}}$	In a metric–U.S. equality, the 1 qt is exact and the 946.3 mL is measured (four significant figures).

Conversion Factors with Powers

Sometimes we use a conversion factor that is squared or cubed. This is the case when we need to calculate an area or a volume.

Distance = length
Area = length × length = length^2
Volume = length × length × length = length^3

Suppose you want to write the equality and the conversion factors for the relationship between an area in square centimeters and in square meters. To square the equality 1 m = 100 cm, we square both the number and the unit on each side.

Equality: 1 m = 100 cm
Area: $(1 \text{ m})^2 = (100 \text{ cm})^2$ or $1 \text{ m}^2 = (100)^2 \text{ cm}^2$

From the new equality, we can write two conversion factors as follows:

$$\text{Conversion factors: } \frac{(1 \text{ m})^2}{(100 \text{ cm})^2} \quad \text{and} \quad \frac{(100 \text{ cm})^2}{(1 \text{ m})^2}$$

In the following example, we show that the equality 1 in. = 2.54 cm can be squared to give area or can be cubed to give volume. *Both the number and the unit must be squared or cubed.*

Measurement	Equality	Conversion Factors
Length	1 in. = 2.54 cm	$\frac{1 \text{ in.}}{2.54 \text{ cm}}$ and $\frac{2.54 \text{ cm}}{1 \text{ in.}}$
Area	$(1 \text{ in.})^2 = (2.54 \text{ cm})^2$ $(1 \text{ in.})^2 = (2.54)^2 \text{ cm}^2 = 6.45 \text{ cm}^2$	$\frac{(1 \text{ in.})^2}{(2.54 \text{ cm})^2}$ and $\frac{(2.54 \text{ cm})^2}{(1 \text{ in.})^2}$
Volume	$(1 \text{ in.})^3 = (2.54 \text{ cm})^3$ $(1 \text{ in.})^3 = (2.54)^3 \text{ cm}^3 = 16.4 \text{ cm}^3$	$\frac{(1 \text{ in.})^3}{(2.54 \text{ cm})^3}$ and $\frac{(2.54 \text{ cm})^3}{(1 \text{ in.})^3}$

SAMPLE PROBLEM 2.7 Writing Conversion Factors

Write the equality and its conversion factors for the relationship between the following pairs of units:

a. milligrams and grams
b. quarts and liters
c. square inches and square feet

SOLUTION

Equality	Conversion Factors
a. $1\ \text{g} = 1000\ \text{mg}$	$\dfrac{1\ \text{g}}{1000\ \text{mg}}$ and $\dfrac{1000\ \text{mg}}{1\ \text{g}}$
b. $1\ \text{L} = 1.057\ \text{qt}$	$\dfrac{1\ \text{L}}{1.057\ \text{qt}}$ and $\dfrac{1.057\ \text{qt}}{1\ \text{L}}$
c. $(1\ \text{ft})^2 = (12\ \text{in.})^2 = 144\ \text{in.}^2$	$\dfrac{(1\ \text{ft})^2}{(12\ \text{in.})^2}$ and $\dfrac{(12\ \text{in.})^2}{(1\ \text{ft})^2}$

STUDY CHECK 2.7

A zeptosecond (zs) is a very small quantity of time. As an equality, it is written

$$1\ \text{zs} = 1 \times 10^{-21}\ \text{s}$$

Write the conversion factors for this equality.

Equalities and Conversion Factors Stated Within a Problem

An equality may also be stated within a problem that applies only to that problem. For example, the cost of 1 kg of oranges or the speed of a car in kilometers per hour would be specific relationships for that problem only. However, it is possible to identify these relationships within a problem and to write corresponding conversion factors.

From each of the following statements, we can write an equality, and its conversion factors, and identify each number as exact or give its significant figures:

1. The motorcycle was traveling at a speed of 85 km/h.

Equality	Conversion Factors	Significant Figures or Exact
$85\ \text{km} = 1\ \text{h}$	$\dfrac{85\ \text{km}}{1\ \text{h}}$ and $\dfrac{1\ \text{h}}{85\ \text{km}}$	The 85 km is measured: It has two significant figures. The 1 in 1 h is exact.

2. One tablet contains 500 mg of vitamin C.

Equality	Conversion Factors	Significant Figures or Exact
1 tablet = 500 mg of vitamin C	$\dfrac{500\ \text{mg vitamin C}}{1\ \text{tablet}}$ and $\dfrac{1\ \text{tablet}}{500\ \text{mg vitamin C}}$	The 500 mg is measured: It has one significant figure. The 1 in 1 tablet is exact.

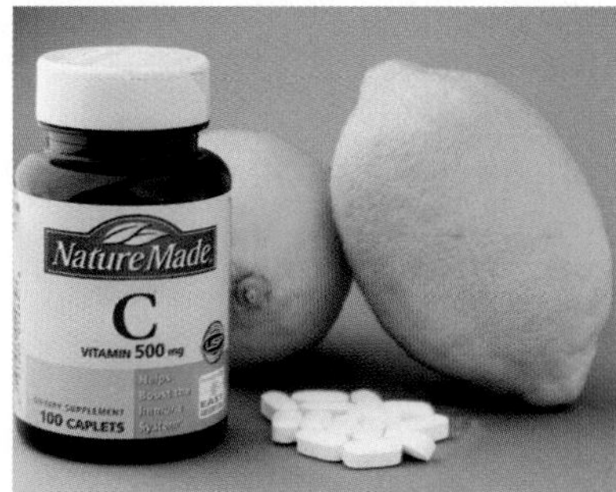

Vitamin C, an antioxidant needed by the body, is found in fruits such as lemons.

Conversion Factors from a Percentage, ppm, and ppb

A percent (%) is written as a conversion factor by choosing a unit and expressing the numerical relationship of the parts of this unit to 100 parts of the whole. For example, a person might have 18% body fat by mass (see Figure 2.10). The percent quantity can be written as 18 mass

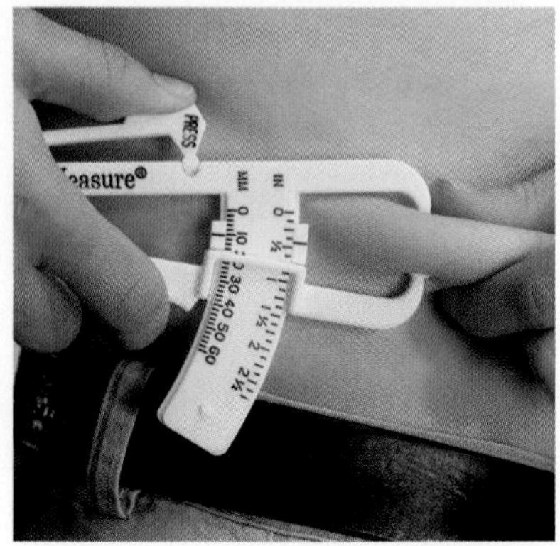

FIGURE 2.10 The thickness (mm) of the skin fold at the waist is used to determine the percent of body fat.

Q What is the percent body fat of an athlete with a body mass of 120 kg and 18 kg of body fat?

units of body fat in every 100 mass units of body mass. Different mass units, such as grams (g), kilograms (kg), or pounds (lb) can be used, but both units in the factor must be the same.

Equality	Conversion Factors	Significant Figures or Exact
18 kg of body fat = 100 kg of body mass	$\frac{100 \text{ kg body mass}}{18 \text{ kg body fat}}$ and $\frac{18 \text{ kg body fat}}{100 \text{ kg body mass}}$	The 18 kg is measured: It has two significant figures. The 100 in 100 kg is exact.

When scientists want to indicate very small ratios, they use numerical relationships called *parts per million* (ppm) or *parts per billion* (ppb). The ratio of parts per million is the same as the milligrams of a substance per kilogram (mg/kg). The ratio of parts per billion equals the micrograms per kilogram (μg/kg).

Ratio	Units
parts per million (ppm)	milligrams per kilogram (mg/kg)
parts per billion (ppb)	micrograms per kilogram (μg/kg)

For example, the maximum amount of lead that is allowed by the Food and Drug Administration (FDA) in glazed pottery bowls is 2 ppm, which is 2 mg/kg.

Equality	Conversion Factors	Significant Figures or Exact
2 mg of lead = 1 kg of glaze	$\frac{2 \text{ mg lead}}{1 \text{ kg glaze}}$ and $\frac{1 \text{ kg glaze}}{2 \text{ mg lead}}$	The 2 mg is measured: It has one significant figure. The 1 in 1 kg is exact.

SAMPLE PROBLEM 2.8 Conversion Factors Stated in a Problem

Write the equality and its corresponding conversion factors, and identify each number as exact or give its significant figures for each of the following statements:

a. There are 325 mg of aspirin in 1 tablet.
b. One kilogram of bananas costs $1.25 at the grocery store.
c. The EPA has set the maximum level for mercury in tuna at 0.5 ppm.

SOLUTION

a. There are 325 mg of aspirin in 1 tablet.

Equality	Conversion Factors	Significant Figures or Exact
325 mg of aspirin = 1 tablet	$\frac{325 \text{ mg aspirin}}{1 \text{ tablet}}$ and $\frac{1 \text{ tablet}}{325 \text{ mg aspirin}}$	The 325 mg is measured: It has three significant figures. The 1 in 1 tablet is exact.

b. One kilogram of bananas costs $1.25 at the grocery store.

Equality	Conversion Factors	Significant Figures or Exact
1 kg of bananas = $1.25	$\frac{\$1.25}{1 \text{ kg bananas}}$ and $\frac{1 \text{ kg bananas}}{\$1.25}$	The $1.25 is measured: It has three significant figures. The 1 in 1 kg is exact.

c. The EPA has set the maximum level for mercury in tuna at 0.5 ppm.

Equality	Conversion Factors	Significant Figures or Exact
0.5 mg of mercury = 1 kg of tuna	$\frac{0.5\text{ mg mercury}}{1\text{ kg tuna}}$ and $\frac{1\text{ kg tuna}}{0.5\text{ mg mercury}}$	The 0.5 mg is measured: It has one significant figure. The 1 in 1 kg is exact.

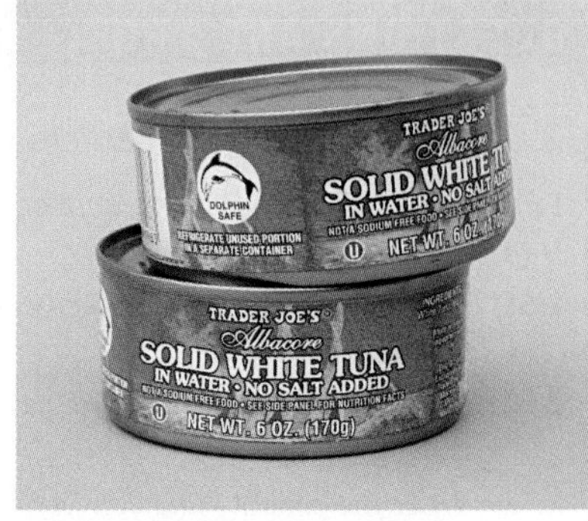

The maximum amount of mercury allowed in tuna is 0.5 ppm.

STUDY CHECK 2.8

Write the equality and its corresponding conversion factors, and identify each number as exact or give its number of significant figures for each of the following:

a. A cyclist in the Tour de France bicycle race rides at an average speed of 62.2 km/h.
b. The permissible level of arsenic in water is 10 ppb.

Chemistry Link to Health

TOXICOLOGY AND RISK–BENEFIT ASSESSMENT

Every day, we make choices about what we do or what we eat, often without thinking about the risks associated with these choices. We are aware of the risks of cancer from smoking, and we know there is a greater risk of having an accident if we cross a street where there is no light or crosswalk.

A basic concept of toxicology is the statement of Paracelsus that the right dose is the difference between a poison and a cure. To evaluate the level of danger from various substances, natural or synthetic, a risk assessment is made by exposing laboratory animals to the substances and monitoring the effects. Often, doses very much greater than humans might ordinarily encounter are given to the test animals.

Many hazardous chemicals or substances have been identified by these tests. One measure of toxicity is the LD_{50} or "lethal dose," which is the concentration of the substance that causes death in 50% of the test animals. A dose is typically measured in ppm (mg/kg) of body mass or ppb (μg/kg).

Other evaluations need to be made, but it is easy to compare LD_{50} values. Parathion, a pesticide, with an LD_{50} of 3 ppm, would be highly toxic. That means that 3 mg of parathion per kg of body mass would be fatal to half of the test animals. Table salt (sodium chloride) with an LD_{50} of 3750 ppm has a much lower toxicity. You would need to ingest a huge amount of salt before any toxic effect would be observed. However, increased salt intake may increase renal and blood pressure disorders. Although the risk to animals based on dose can be evaluated in the laboratory, it is more difficult to determine the impact in the environment since there is a difference between continuous exposure and a single, large dose of the substance.

Table 2.8 lists some LD_{50} values and compares substances in order of increasing toxicity.

The LD_{50} of caffeine is 192 ppm.

TABLE 2.8 Some LD_{50} Values for Substances Tested in Rats

Substance	LD_{50} (ppm)
Table sugar	29 700
Boric acid	5140
Baking soda	4220
Table salt	3750
Ethanol	2080
Aspirin	1100
Caffeine	192
DDT	113
Dichlorvos (pesticide strips)	56
Sodium cyanide	6
Parathion	3

QUESTIONS AND PROBLEMS

2.6 Writing Conversion Factors

LEARNING GOAL: *Write a conversion factor for two units that describe the same quantity.*

2.51 Why can two conversion factors be written for an equality like 1 m = 100 cm?

2.52 How can you check that you have written the correct conversion factors for an equality?

2.53 Write the equality and conversion factors for each of the following pairs of units:
- **a.** centimeters and meters
- **b.** grams and nanograms
- **c.** kiloliters and liters
- **d.** seconds and milliseconds
- **e.** cubic meters and cubic centimeters

2.54 Write the equality and conversion factors for each of the following pairs of units:
- **a.** centimeters and inches
- **b.** pounds and kilograms
- **c.** pounds and grams
- **d.** quarts and milliliters
- **e.** square centimeters and square inches

2.55 Write the equality and conversion factors, and identify the numbers as exact or give the number of significant figures for each of the following:
- **a.** One yard is 3 ft.
- **b.** One kilogram is 2.205 lb.
- **c.** One minute is 60 s.
- **d.** A car travels 27 mi on 1 gal of gasoline.
- **e.** Silicon makes up 48% of the Earth's crust.

2.56 Write the equality and conversion factors, and identify the numbers as exact or give the number of significant figures for each of the following:
- **a.** One liter is 1.057 qt.
- **b.** At the store, lemons are $1.29 per lb.
- **c.** There are 7 days in 1 week.
- **d.** One deciliter contains 100 mL.
- **e.** An 18-carat gold ring contains 75% gold by mass.

2.57 Write the equality and conversion factors, and identify the numbers as exact or give the number of significant figures for each of the following:
- **a.** A bee flies at an average speed of 3.5 m/s.
- **b.** One milliliter of gasoline has a mass of 0.74 g.
- **c.** An automobile traveled 46.0 km on 1 gal of gasoline.
- **d.** Sterling silver is 93% by mass silver.
- **e.** The pesticide level in plums was 29 ppb.

2.58 Write the equality and conversion factors, and identify the numbers as exact or give the number of significant figures for each of the following:
- **a.** The highway gas mileage was 28 mi/gal.
- **b.** There are 20 drops in 1 mL of water.
- **c.** The nitrate level in well water was 32 ppm.
- **d.** A DVD contains 17 GB of information.
- **e.** One capsule of fish oil contains 360 mg of omega-3-fatty acids.

LEARNING GOAL

Use conversion factors to change from one unit to another.

CORE CHEMISTRY SKILL

Using Conversion Factors

2.7 Problem Solving Using Unit Conversion

The process of problem solving in chemistry often requires the conversion of a given quantity in one unit to a needed quantity that has a different unit. We will show the problem-solving process by analyzing the problem to

- identify the given unit and the needed unit
- write a plan that converts the given unit to the needed unit
- identify one or more conversion factors that cancel units and provide the needed unit
- set up a calculation

Suppose you need to convert 18.2 mm to meters. By separating the problem into units, you would identify the given as millimeters and the needed as meters.

Given: 18.2 mm **Need:** meters

Now write a plan that will convert the given unit to the needed unit

millimeters (Given) → Conversion factor → meters (Need)

Now look for the connection between millimeters and meters. From Table 2.6, use the equality that relates meters and millimeters, which is 1 m = 1000 mm. From this equality, write two conversion factors. *Be sure to include the units in all the quantities of the conversion factors.*

$$1\ \text{m} = 1000\ \text{mm} \qquad \frac{1\ \text{m}}{1000\ \text{mm}} \text{ and } \frac{1000\ \text{mm}}{1\ \text{m}}$$

Equality — Conversion Factors

To set up the calculation, select the conversion factor that cancels the given unit, which is millimeter. Complete the calculation and round off to give the needed answer with the correct number of significant figures.

millimeters → Conversion factor → meters

$$18.2\ \cancel{\text{mm}} \times \frac{1\ \text{m}}{1000\ \cancel{\text{mm}}} = 0.0182\ \text{m}$$

CONCEPT CHECK 2.8 Units Needed in Conversion Factors

Suppose you are asked to convert 14.5 cm to inches.

a. Identify the given and needed units as metric or U.S.

b. Suppose you write the following plan:

centimeters → Factor → inches

Select the correct type of factor (**1**, **2**, or **3**) to set up the calculation.

(1) Metric factor **(2)** U.S. factor **(3)** Metric–U.S. factor

c. Which of the following factor (**1**, **2**, or **3**) would you use in the setup for the following calculation?

14.5 cm × Factor = inches

(1) $\frac{2.54\ \text{in.}}{1\ \text{cm}}$ **(2)** $\frac{1\ \text{in.}}{2.54\ \text{cm}}$ **(3)** $\frac{2.54\ \text{cm}}{1\ \text{in.}}$

ANSWER

a. 14.5 cm is a metric unit of length, whereas inches is a U.S. unit of length.

b. (**3**) A metric–U.S. factor converts from a metric unit of length to a U.S. unit of length.

centimeters → Metric–U.S. factor → inches

c. (**2**) The correct equality is 1 in. = 2.54 cm. The factor with 2.54 cm in the denominator is used to cancel cm. The 1 in. in the numerator is the correct unit needed for the answer.

$$14.5\ \cancel{\text{cm}} \times \frac{1\ \text{in.}}{2.54\ \cancel{\text{cm}}} = 5.71\ \text{in. (rounded off to three SFs)}$$

Sample Problem 2.9 illustrates the steps in the problem-solving process using conversion factors.

SAMPLE PROBLEM 2.9 Problem Solving Using Conversion Factors

In radiological imaging such as PET or CT scans, dosages of pharmaceuticals are based on body mass. If a person weighs 165 lb, what is that body mass in kilograms?

SOLUTION

Step 1 **State the given and needed quantities.**

Analyze the Problem	Given	Need
	165 lb	kilograms

Guide to Problem Solving Using Conversion Factors

1 State the given and needed quantities.

2 Write a plan to convert the given unit to the needed unit.

3 State the equalities and conversion factors.

4 Set up the problem to cancel units and calculate the answer.

Step 2 **Write a plan to convert the given unit to the needed unit.** From the given and needed units in our Analyze the Problem, we can now determine that we need a U.S.–metric factor that converts from pounds to kilograms. Using Table 2.7, we find a U.S.–metric factor of 2.205 lb = 1 kg.

pounds → U.S.–Metric factor → kilograms

Step 3 **State the equalities and conversion factors.**

$$2.205 \text{ lb} = 1 \text{ kg}$$

$$\frac{2.205 \text{ lb}}{1 \text{ kg}} \quad \text{and} \quad \frac{1 \text{ kg}}{2.205 \text{ lb}}$$

Step 4 **Set up the problem to cancel units and calculate the answer.** Write the given, 165 lb, and multiply by the conversion factor that has lb in the denominator (bottom number) to cancel lb in the given.

Unit for answer goes here

$$165 \cancel{\text{lb}} \times \frac{1 \text{ kg}}{2.205 \cancel{\text{lb}}} = 74.8 \text{ kg}$$

Given unit — Conversion factor (cancels given unit) — Answer (needed unit)

Look at how the units cancel. The given unit lb cancels out, and the needed unit kg is the one that remains in the numerator (top number). *The unit that you want in the answer is the one that remains after the other units have canceled out.* This is a helpful way to check that a problem is set up properly.

$$\cancel{\text{lb}} \times \frac{\text{kg}}{\cancel{\text{lb}}} = \text{kg} \quad \text{Unit needed for answer}$$

The calculator display gives the numerical part of the answer, which is rounded off to give a final answer with the correct number of significant figures (SFs).

165	×	Exact $\frac{1}{2.205}$	=	165	÷	2.205	=	74.82993197	=	74.8
Three SFs		Four SFs		Three SFs		Four SFs		Calculator display		Three SFs (rounded off)

When the value of 74.8 is combined with the unit, kg, the final answer of 74.8 kg is obtained. *An answer to a numerical problem always contains both a number and a unit.*

STUDY CHECK 2.9

A can of orange juice concentrate contains 0.36 qt. What is the volume of juice in milliliters?

Using Two or More Conversion Factors

In problem solving, two or more conversion factors are often needed to complete the change of units. In setting up these problems, one factor follows the other. Each factor is arranged to cancel the preceding unit until the needed unit is obtained. Once the problem is set up to cancel units, the calculations can be done without writing intermediate values. This process is worth practicing until you understand unit cancellation, the steps on the calculator, and rounding off. In this text, the final answer will be based on obtaining a final calculator display and rounding off (or adding zeros) to give the correct number of significant figures.

CONCEPT CHECK 2.9 Canceling Units

Fill in the missing conversion factor (numbers and units) in the following setup, show the canceled units, and give the correct answer:

$$0.350\ \text{L} \times \frac{\_\_\square}{\_\_\square} \times \frac{0.480\ \text{g}}{1\ \text{mL}} = \_\_\_\_\_\_$$

ANSWER

In the conversion factor, the unit of L is placed in the denominator to cancel the given L. The unit of mL is in the numerator to cancel mL in the denominator of the last conversion factor. The metric equality for L and mL is 1 L = 1000 mL. The unit g that remains is the unit of the final answer.

$$0.350\ \cancel{\text{L}} \times \frac{1000\ \cancel{\text{mL}}}{1\ \cancel{\text{L}}} \times \frac{0.480\ \text{g}}{1\ \cancel{\text{mL}}} = 168\ \text{g}$$

SAMPLE PROBLEM 2.10 Problem Solving Using Two Conversion Factors

During a volcanic eruption on Mauna Loa, the lava flowed at a rate of 33 m/min. At this rate, what distance, in kilometers, will the lava travel in 45 min?

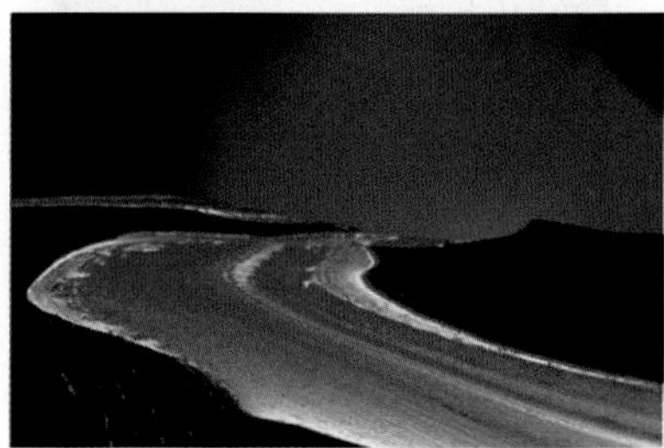

Lava flows from an eruption of Mauna Loa volcano, Hawaii.

SOLUTION

Step 1 State the given and needed quantities.

	Given	Need
Analyze the Problem	45 min 33 m/min	kilometers

Step 2 Write a plan to convert the given unit to the needed unit.

minutes → Rate factor → meters → Metric factor → kilometers

Step 3 State the equalities and conversion factors. The rate of lava flow (33 m/min) is used as an equality as well as the metric equality for meters and kilometers. Then conversion factors can be written for both.

1 min = 33 m

$$\frac{1\ \text{min}}{33\ \text{m}} \text{ and } \frac{33\ \text{m}}{1\ \text{min}}$$

1 km = 1000 m

$$\frac{1\ \text{km}}{1000\ \text{m}} \text{ and } \frac{1000\ \text{m}}{1\ \text{km}}$$

Step 4 Set up the problem to cancel units and calculate the answer.

$$45\ \cancel{\text{min}} \times \frac{33\ \cancel{\text{m}}}{1\ \cancel{\text{min}}} \times \frac{1\ \text{km}}{1000\ \cancel{\text{m}}}$$

The calculation is done as follows:

45 ⊠ 33 ÷ 1000 = 1.485

Calculator display

Because there are two significant figures in the measured quantities, we write the needed answer with two significant figures, 1.5, and the unit km to give the final answer, 1.5 km.

$$\underset{\text{Two SFs}}{45\ \cancel{\text{min}}} \times \overset{\text{Two SFs}}{\underset{\text{Exact}}{\frac{33\ \cancel{\text{m}}}{1\ \cancel{\text{min}}}}} \times \overset{\text{Exact}}{\underset{\text{Exact}}{\frac{1\ \text{km}}{1000\ \cancel{\text{m}}}}} = \underset{\text{Two SFs}}{1.5\ \text{km}}$$

STUDY CHECK 2.10

How many hours are required for the lava to flow a distance of 5.0 km?

SAMPLE PROBLEM 2.11 Using a Percent As a Conversion Factor

Molten bronze is poured into molds.

Bronze is 80.0% by mass copper and 20.0% by mass tin. A sculptor is preparing to cast a figure that requires 1.75 lb of bronze. How many kilograms of copper are needed for the bronze figure?

SOLUTION

Step 1 State the given and needed quantities.

Analyze the Problem	Given	Need
	1.75 lb of bronze 80.0% by mass copper	kilograms of copper

Step 2 Write a plan to convert the given unit to the needed unit.

pounds of bronze → U.S.–Metric factor → kilograms of bronze → Percent factor → kilograms of copper

Step 3 State the equalities and conversion factors.

$$1\ \text{kg of bronze} = 2.205\ \text{lb of bronze}$$
$$\frac{1\ \text{kg bronze}}{2.205\ \text{lb bronze}} \text{ and } \frac{2.205\ \text{lb bronze}}{1\ \text{kg bronze}}$$

$$100\ \text{kg of bronze} = 80.0\ \text{kg of copper}$$
$$\frac{80.0\ \text{kg copper}}{100\ \text{kg bronze}} \text{ and } \frac{100\ \text{kg bronze}}{80.0\ \text{kg copper}}$$

Step 4 Set up the problem to cancel units and calculate the answer.

$$\underset{\text{Three SFs}}{1.75\ \cancel{\text{lb bronze}}} \times \overset{\text{Exact}}{\underset{\text{Four SFs}}{\frac{1\ \cancel{\text{kg bronze}}}{2.205\ \cancel{\text{lb bronze}}}}} \times \overset{\text{Three SFs}}{\underset{\text{Exact}}{\frac{80.0\ \text{kg copper}}{100\ \cancel{\text{kg bronze}}}}} = \underset{\text{Three SFs}}{0.635\ \text{kg of copper}}$$

You could set up this problem in a different way by using the following relationships and conversion factors:

$$1\ \text{lb} = 453.6\ \text{g}$$
$$\frac{1\ \text{lb}}{453.6\ \text{g}} \text{ and } \frac{453.6\ \text{g}}{1\ \text{lb}}$$

$$100\ \text{g of bronze} = 80.0\ \text{g of copper}$$
$$\frac{80.0\ \text{g copper}}{100\ \text{g bronze}} \text{ and } \frac{100\ \text{g bronze}}{80.0\ \text{g copper}}$$

$$1\ \text{kg} = 1000\ \text{g}$$
$$\frac{1\ \text{kg}}{1000\ \text{g}} \text{ and } \frac{1000\ \text{g}}{1\ \text{kg}}$$

Then the setup would appear as follows:

$$\underset{\text{Three SFs}}{1.75\ \cancel{\text{lb bronze}}} \times \underset{\text{Exact}}{\overset{\text{Four SFs}}{\frac{453.6\ \cancel{\text{g bronze}}}{1\ \cancel{\text{lb bronze}}}}} \times \underset{\text{Exact}}{\overset{\text{Three SFs}}{\frac{80.0\ \cancel{\text{g copper}}}{100\ \cancel{\text{g bronze}}}}} \times \underset{\text{Exact}}{\overset{\text{Exact}}{\frac{1\ \text{kg copper}}{1000\ \cancel{\text{g copper}}}}} = \underset{\text{Three SFs}}{0.635\ \text{kg of copper}}$$

STUDY CHECK 2.11

Uncooked lean ground beef can contain up to 22% fat by mass. How many grams of fat would be contained in 0.25 lb of ground beef?

QUESTIONS AND PROBLEMS

2.7 Problem Solving Using Unit Conversion

LEARNING GOAL: *Use conversion factors to change from one unit to another.*

2.59 When you convert one unit to another, how do you know which unit of the conversion factor to place in the denominator?

2.60 When you convert one unit to another, how do you know which unit of the conversion factor to place in the numerator?

2.61 Perform each of the following conversions using metric conversion factors:
- **a.** 44.2 mL to liters
- **b.** 8.65 m to nanometers
- **c.** 5.2×10^8 g to megagrams
- **d.** 0.72 ks to milliseconds

2.62 Perform each of the following conversions using metric conversion factors:
- **a.** 4.82×10^{-5} L to picoliters
- **b.** 575.2 dm to kilometers
- **c.** 5×10^{-4} kg to micrograms
- **d.** 6.4×10^{10} ps to seconds

2.63 Perform each of the following conversions using metric and U.S. conversion factors:
- **a.** 3.428 lb to kilograms
- **b.** 1.6 m to inches
- **c.** 4.2 L to quarts
- **d.** 0.672 ft to millimeters

2.64 Perform each of the following conversions using metric and U.S. conversion factors:
- **a.** 0.21 lb to grams
- **b.** 11.6 in. to centimeters
- **c.** 0.15 qt to milliliters
- **d.** 35.41 kg to pounds

2.65 Use metric conversion factors to solve each of the following problems:
- **a.** The height of a student is 175 cm. How tall is the student in meters?
- **b.** A cooler has a volume of 5500 mL. What is the capacity of the cooler in liters?
- **c.** A hummingbird has a mass of 0.0055 kg. What is the mass, in grams, of the hummingbird?
- **d.** A balloon has a volume of 350 cm^3. What is the volume in m^3?

2.66 Use metric conversion factors to solve each of the following problems:
- **a.** The daily requirement of phosphorus is 800 mg. How many grams of phosphorus are needed?
- **b.** A glass of orange juice contains 0.85 dL of juice. How many milliliters of orange juice are in the glass?
- **c.** A package of chocolate instant pudding contains 2840 mg of sodium. How many grams of sodium are in the pudding?
- **d.** A park has an area of 150 000 m^2. What is the area in km^2?

2.67 Solve each of the following problems using one or more conversion factors (see Table 2.7):
- **a.** A container holds 0.750 qt of liquid. How many milliliters of lemonade will it hold?
- **b.** In England, a person is weighed in stones. If one stone is 14.0 lb, what is the mass, in kilograms, of a person who weighs 11.8 stones?
- **c.** The femur, or thighbone, is the longest bone in the body. In a 6-ft-tall person, the femur is 19.5 in. long. What is the length of that femur in millimeters?
- **d.** How many inches thick is an arterial wall that measures 0.50 μm?

2.68 Solve each of the following problems using one or more conversion factors (see Table 2.7):
- **a.** You need 4.0 oz of a steroid ointment. If there are 16 oz in 1 lb, how many grams of ointment does the pharmacist need to prepare?
- **b.** During surgery, a person receives 5.0 pt of plasma. How many milliliters of plasma were given?
- **c.** Solar flares containing hot gases can rise to 120 000 mi above the surface of the Sun. What is that distance in kilometers?
- **d.** A filled gas tank contains 18.5 gal of fuel. If a car uses 46.0 L, how many gallons of fuel remain in the tank?

2.69 The singles portion of a tennis court is 27.0 ft wide and 78.0 ft long (see diagram).

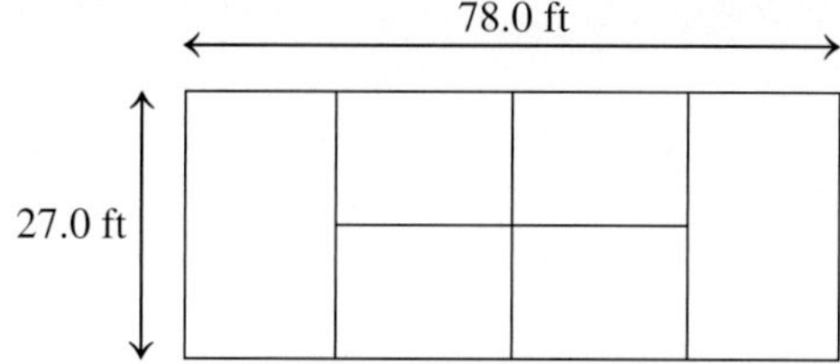

a. What is the length of the court in meters?
b. What is the area of the court in square meters (m^2)?
c. If a serve is measured at 185 km/h, how many seconds does it take for the tennis ball to travel the length of the court?
d. How many liters of paint are needed to paint the court if 1 gal of paint covers 150 ft^2?

2.70 A football field is 160. ft wide and 300. ft long between goal lines (see diagram).

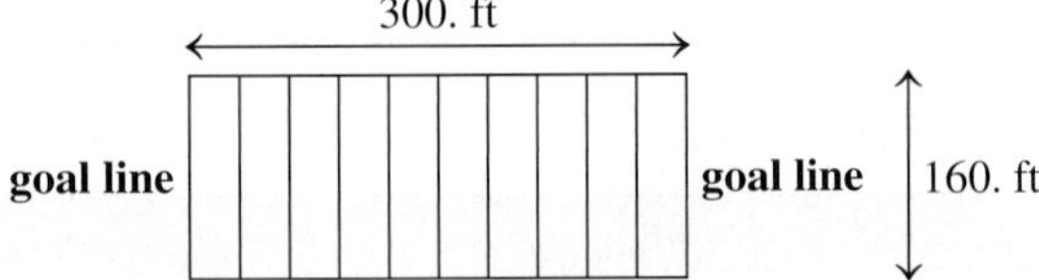

a. What distance, in meters, does a player run if he catches the ball on his own goal line and scores a touchdown?
b. If a player catches the football and runs 45 yd, how many meters will he gain?
c. How many square meters of Astroturf are required to completely cover the playing field?
d. If a player runs at a speed of 36 km/h, how many seconds does it take to run from the 50-yd line to the 20-yd line?

2.71 a. Oxygen (O) makes up 46.7% by mass of Earth's crust. How many grams of oxygen are present if a sample of the crust has a mass of 325 g?
b. Magnesium (Mg) makes up 2.1% by mass of Earth's crust. How many grams of magnesium are present if a sample of the crust has a mass of 1.25 g?
c. A plant fertilizer contains 15% by mass nitrogen (N). In a container of soluble plant food, there are 10.0 oz of fertilizer. How many grams of nitrogen are in the container?

Agricultural fertilizers applied to a field provide nitrogen for plant growth.

d. In a candy factory, the nutty chocolate bars contain 22.0% by mass pecans. If 5.0 kg of pecans were used for candy last Tuesday, how many pounds of nutty chocolate bars were made?

2.72 a. Water is 11.2% by mass hydrogen (H). How many kilograms of water would contain 5.0 g of hydrogen?
b. Water is 88.8% by mass oxygen. How many grams of water would contain 2.25 kg of oxygen?
c. Blueberry fiber cakes contain 51% dietary fiber. If a package with a net weight of 12 oz contains six cakes, how many grams of fiber are in each cake?
d. A jar of crunchy peanut butter contains 1.43 kg of peanut butter. If you use 8.0% of the peanut butter for a sandwich, how many ounces of peanut butter did you take out of the container?

LEARNING GOAL

Calculate the density of a substance; use the density to calculate the mass or volume of a substance.

2.8 Density

Density is a physical property of matter that compares the mass of a substance to its volume. Every substance has a unique density, which distinguishes it from other substances. Density is used in chemistry in many ways. Density can be used to identify a specific substance. Density is also used to predict if an object will sink or float in a liquid or in the air. *If an object is less dense than a liquid, the object floats when placed in the liquid.* In Figure 2.11, the lead object sinks in water because the density of lead is greater than the density of water. However, the cork floats in water because the density of cork is less than that of water.

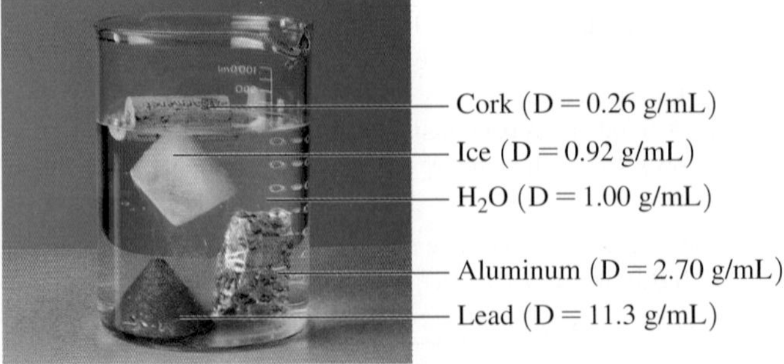

FIGURE 2.11 Objects that sink in water are more dense than water; objects that float are less dense.

Q An ice cube floats in water and a piece of aluminum sinks. Why?

Calculating Density

Once the mass and volume of a substance are measured, we can place them in a relationship called the *density expression*:

$$\text{Density} = \frac{\text{mass of substance}}{\text{volume of substance}}$$

In substances with high densities, the particles tend to be close together, whereas in substances with low densities, the particles are farther apart. Thus, metals such as gold and lead have higher densities because their atoms are close and tightly packed in small volumes, whereas gases have very low densities because their atoms are far apart in large volumes.

In the metric system, the densities of solids and liquids are usually expressed as grams per cubic centimeter (g/cm^3) or grams per milliliter (g/mL). The density of a gas is usually stated as grams per liter (g/L). Table 2.9 gives the densities of some common substances.

TABLE 2.9 Densities of Some Common Substances

Solids (at 25 °C)	Density (g/cm^3 or g/mL)	Liquids (at 25 °C)	Density (g/mL)	Gases (at 0 °C, 1 atm)	Density (g/L)
Cork	0.26	Gasoline	0.74	Hydrogen	0.090
Ice (at 0 °C)	0.92	Ethanol	0.785	Helium	0.179
Sugar	1.59	Olive oil	0.92	Methane	0.714
Salt (NaCl)	2.16	Water (at 4 °C)	1.00	Neon	0.902
Aluminum	2.70	Milk	1.04	Nitrogen	1.25
Diamond	3.52	Mercury	13.6	Air (dry)	1.29
Iron	7.86			Oxygen	1.43
Copper	8.92			Carbon dioxide	1.96
Silver	10.5				
Lead	11.3				
Gold	19.3				

CONCEPT CHECK 2.10 Density

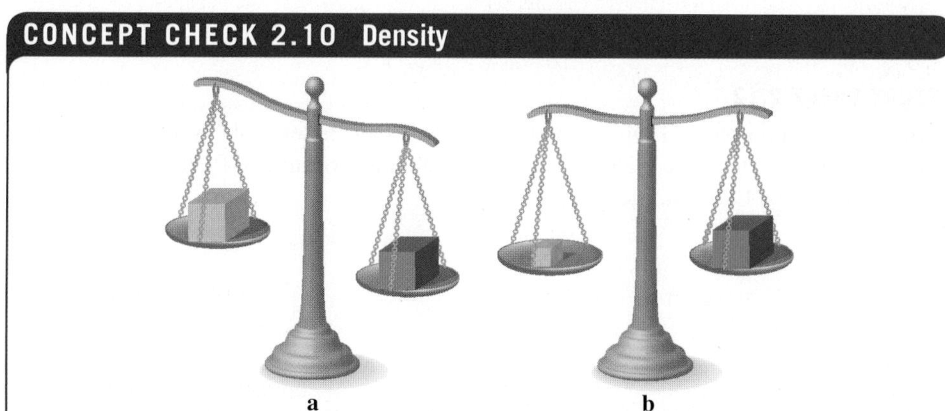

a. In diagram **a**, the gray cube has a density of 4.5 g/cm^3. Is the density of the green cube the same, lower than, or higher than that of the gray cube?

b. In diagram **b**, the gray cube has a density of 4.5 g/cm^3. Is the density of the green cube the same, lower than, or higher than that of the gray cube?

ANSWER

a. The green cube has the same volume as the gray cube. However, the green cube has a larger mass on the scale, which means that its mass/volume ratio is larger. Thus, the density of the green cube is higher than the density of the gray cube.

b. The green cube has the same mass as the gray cube. However, the green cube has a larger volume, which means that its mass/volume ratio is smaller. Thus, the density of the green cube is lower than the density of the gray cube.

Guide to Calculating Density

1. State the given and needed quantities.
2. Write the density expression.
3. Express mass in grams and volume in milliliters (mL) or cm^3.
4. Substitute mass and volume into the density expression and calculate the density.

SAMPLE PROBLEM 2.12 Calculating Density

High-density lipoprotein (HDL) is a type of cholesterol, sometimes called "good cholesterol," that is measured in a routine blood test. If a 0.258-g sample of HDL has a volume of 0.215 cm^3, what is the density of the HDL sample?

SOLUTION

Step 1 State the given and needed quantities.

Analyze the Problem	Given	Need
	0.258 g of HDL 0.215 cm^3	density (g/cm^3) of HDL

Step 2 Write the density expression.

$$\text{Density} = \frac{\text{mass of substance}}{\text{volume of substance}}$$

Step 3 Express mass in grams and volume in cm^3.

Mass of HDL sample = 0.258 g
Volume of HDL sample = 0.215 cm^3

Step 4 Substitute mass and volume into the density expression and calculate the density.

$$\text{Density} = \frac{\overset{\text{Three SFs}}{0.258\text{ g}}}{\underset{\text{Three SFs}}{0.215\text{ cm}^3}} = \frac{1.20\text{ g}}{1\text{ cm}^3} = \underset{\text{Three SFs}}{1.20\text{ g/cm}^3}$$

STUDY CHECK 2.12

Low-density lipoprotein (LDL), sometimes called "bad cholesterol," is also measured in a routine blood test. If a 0.380-g sample of LDL has a volume of 0.362 cm^3, what is the density of the LDL sample?

Chemistry Link to the Environment

DENSITY OF CRUDE OIL

Crude oil (also called petroleum or fossil fuel) is oil that has not been processed and comes up from underneath the ground. The most typical compounds found in crude oil are hydrocarbons, which are compounds composed of the elements carbon and hydrogen. Crude oil may be transported by trucks, pipelines, or ships to oil refineries, where it is separated into compounds mostly used for energy. Because the crude oil typically has a density of about 0.8 g/mL, it is less dense than water (1.00 g/mL). When there is an oil spill in the ocean, the crude oil does not mix with water and thus forms a thin layer about one millimeter thick on the surface, which spreads over a large area of the ocean.

In April 2010, an explosion on an oil-drilling rig in the Gulf of Mexico caused the largest oil spill in U.S. history. At its maximum, an estimated 10 million liters of oil was leaked every day. Other major oil spills occurred in Queensland, Australia (2009), the coast

In an oil spill, crude oil spreads out to form a thin layer on top of the ocean surface.

of Wales (1996), the Shetland Islands (1993), and Alaska (the *Exxon Valdez*), in 1989. If the crude oil reaches land, there can be considerable damage to beaches, shellfish, fish, birds, and wildlife habitats.

When animals such as birds are covered with oil, they must be cleaned quickly because ingestion of the hydrocarbons when they try to clean themselves is fatal. Cleanup of oil spills includes mechanical, chemical, and microbiological methods. A boom may be placed around the ship to contain the leaking oil until it can be removed. Boats called skimmers then scoop up the oil and place it in tanks. In a chemical method, a substance that attracts oil is used to pick it up and then the oil is scraped off into recovery tanks. Certain bacteria that ingest oil are used to break it down into less harmful products.

Density of Solids

The density of a solid is calculated from its mass and volume. When a solid is completely submerged, it displaces a volume of water that is equal to the volume of the solid. In Figure 2.12, the water level rises from 35.5 mL to 45.0 mL after the zinc object is added. Because the object displaced 9.5 mL (45.0 mL − 35.5 mL) of water, the zinc object has a volume of 9.5 mL. The density of the zinc is calculated as follows:

$$\text{Density} = \frac{68.60 \text{ g Zn}}{9.5 \text{ mL}} = 7.2 \text{ g/mL}$$

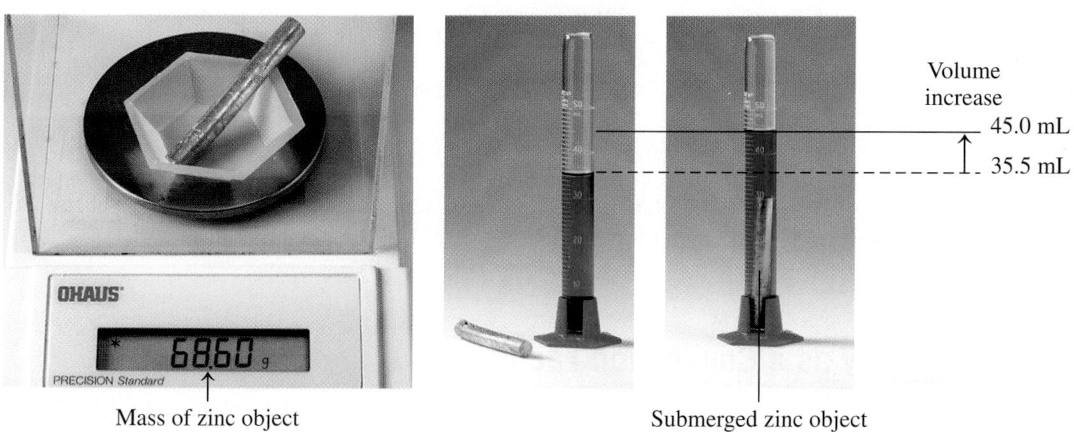

FIGURE 2.12 The density of a solid can be determined by volume displacement because a submerged object displaces a volume of water equal to its own volume.

Q How is the volume of the zinc object determined?

SAMPLE PROBLEM 2.13 Using Volume Displacement to Calculate Density

A lead weight used in the belt of a scuba diver has a mass of 226 g. When the weight is carefully placed in a large graduated cylinder containing 200.0 cm^3 of water, the water level rises to 220.0 cm^3. What is the density of the lead weight (g/cm^3)?

SOLUTION

Step 1 State the given and needed quantities.

	Given	Need
Analyze the Problem	226 g of lead water level + lead = 220.0 cm^3 water level (initial) = 200.0 cm^3	density (g/cm^3) of lead

Lead weights in a belt counteract the buoyancy of a scuba diver.

Step 2 **Write the density expression.**

$$\text{Density} = \frac{\text{mass of substance}}{\text{volume of substance}}$$

Step 3 **Express mass in grams and volume in cm^3.**

$$\text{Mass of lead weight} = 226 \text{ g}$$

The volume of the lead weight is equal to the volume of water it displaced, which is calculated as follows:

Water level after object submerged	=	220.0 cm^3
Water level before object submerged	=	−200.0 cm^3
Water level displaced (volume of lead)	=	20.0 cm^3

Step 4 **Substitute mass and volume into the density expression and calculate the density.** Be sure to use the volume of water displaced and *not* the initial volume of water.

$$\text{Density} = \frac{\overset{\text{Three SFs}}{226 \text{ g}}}{\underset{\text{Three SFs}}{20.0 \text{ cm}^3}} = \underset{\text{Three SFs}}{11.3 \text{ g/cm}^3}$$

STUDY CHECK 2.13

A total of 0.500 lb of glass marbles is added to 425 mL of water. The water level rises to a volume of 528 mL. What is the density (g/cm^3) of the glass marbles?

A sample of milk has a density of 1.04 g/mL.

CORE CHEMISTRY SKILL

Using Density as a Conversion Factor

Density as a Conversion Factor

Density can be used as a conversion factor. For example, if the volume and the density of a sample are known, the mass in grams of the sample can be calculated as shown in Sample Problem 2.14.

SAMPLE PROBLEM 2.14 Problem Solving Using Density

If the density of milk is 1.04 g/mL, how many grams of milk are in 0.50 qt?

SOLUTION

Step 1 **State the given and needed quantities.**

Analyze the Problem	Given	Need
	0.50 qt of milk density of milk = 1.04 g/L	grams of milk

Step 2 **Write a plan to calculate the needed quantity.**

quarts → U.S.–Metric factor → liters → Metric factor → milliliters → Density factor → grams

Step 3 **Write equalities and their conversion factors, including density.**

$$1 \text{ L} = 1.057 \text{ qt} \qquad \frac{1 \text{ L}}{1.057 \text{ qt}} \text{ and } \frac{1.057 \text{ qt}}{1 \text{ L}}$$

$$1 \text{ L} = 1000 \text{ mL} \qquad \frac{1 \text{ L}}{1000 \text{ mL}} \text{ and } \frac{1000 \text{ mL}}{1 \text{ L}}$$

$$1 \text{ mL} = 1.04 \text{ g} \qquad \frac{1 \text{ mL}}{1.04 \text{ g}} \text{ and } \frac{1.04 \text{ g}}{1 \text{ mL}}$$

Guide to Using Density

1. State the given and needed quantities.
2. Write a plan to calculate the needed quantity.
3. Write equalities and their conversion factors, including density.
4. Set up the problem to calculate the needed quantity.

Step 4 **Set up the problem to calculate the needed quantity.**

$$\underset{\text{Two SFs}}{0.50\ \cancel{qt}} \times \underset{\text{Four SFs}}{\overset{\text{Exact}}{\frac{1\ \cancel{L}}{1.057\ \cancel{qt}}}} \times \underset{\text{Exact}}{\overset{\text{Exact}}{\frac{1000\ \cancel{mL}}{1\ \cancel{L}}}} \times \underset{\text{Exact}}{\overset{\text{Three SFs}}{\frac{1.04\ g}{1\ \cancel{mL}}}} = \underset{\text{Two SFs}}{490\ g\ (4.9 \times 10^2\ g)}$$

Maple syrup is produced by boiling the sap from sugar maple trees.

STUDY CHECK 2.14

The density of maple syrup is 1.33 g/mL. A bottle of maple syrup contains 740 mL of syrup. What is the mass of the syrup?

Chemistry Link to Health

BONE DENSITY

The density of our bones determines their health and strength. Our bones are constantly gaining and losing minerals such as calcium, magnesium, and phosphate. In childhood, bones form at a faster rate than they break down. As we age, the breakdown of bone occurs more rapidly than new bone forms. As the loss of bone minerals increases, bones begin to thin, causing a decrease in mass and density. Thinner bones lack strength, which increases the risk of fracture. Hormonal changes, disease, and certain medications can also contribute to the thinning of bone. Eventually, a condition of severe thinning of bone known as *osteoporosis* may occur. *Scanning electron micrographs* (SEMs) show (**a**) normal bone and (**b**) bone in osteoporosis due to loss of bone minerals.

Bone density is often determined by passing low-dose X-rays through the narrow part at the top of the femur (hip) and the spine (**c**). These locations are where fractures are more likely to occur, especially as we age. Bones with high density will block more of the X-rays compared to bones that are less dense. The results of a bone density test are compared to those of a healthy young adult as well as to other people of the same age.

Recommendations to improve bone strength include supplements of calcium and vitamin D. Weight-bearing exercise such as walking and lifting weights can also improve muscle strength, which in turn increases bone strength.

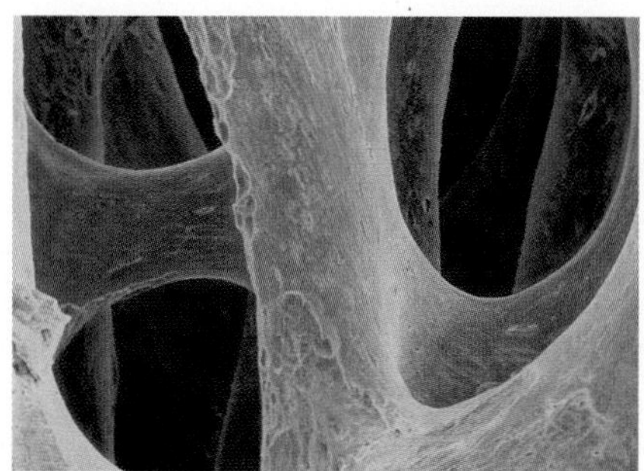

(**a**) Normal bone

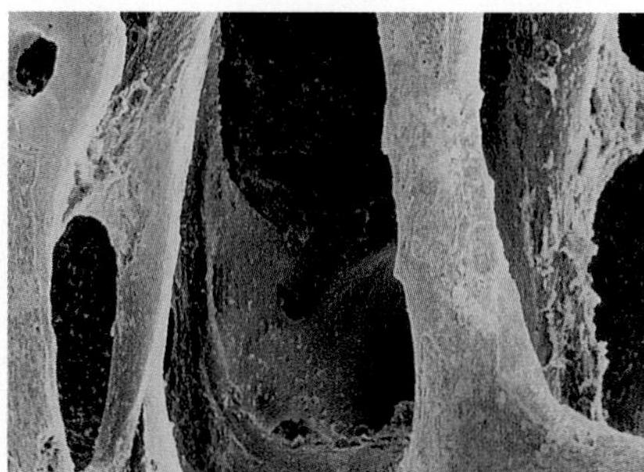

(**b**) Bone with osteoporosis

(**c**) Viewing a low-dose X-ray of the spine

QUESTIONS AND PROBLEMS

2.8 Density

LEARNING GOAL: *Calculate the density of a substance; use the density to calculate the mass or volume of a substance.*

2.73 In an old trunk, you find a piece of metal that you think may be aluminum, silver, or lead. In a lab, you find it has a mass of 217 g and a volume of 19.2 cm^3. Using Table 2.9, what is the metal you found?

2.74 Suppose you have two 100-mL graduated cylinders. In each cylinder, there is 40.0 mL of water. You also have two cubes: one is lead, and the other is aluminum. Each cube measures 2.0 cm on each side. After you carefully lower each cube into the water of its own cylinder, what will the new water level be in each of the cylinders?

2.75 Determine the density (g/mL) for each of the following:
a. A 20.0-mL sample of a salt solution that has a mass of 24.0 g.
b. A cube of butter weighs 0.250 lb and has a volume of 130.3 mL.
c. A gem has a mass of 4.50 g. When the gem is placed in a graduated cylinder containing 12.00 mL of water, the water level rises to 13.45 mL.

2.76 Determine the density (g/mL) for each of the following:
a. The fluid in a car battery has a volume of 125 mL and a mass of 155 g.
b. A plastic material weighs 2.68 lb and has a volume of 3.5 L.
c. A 5.00-mL urine sample from a person suffering from diabetes mellitus has a mass of 5.025 g.

2.77 Determine the density (g/mL) for each of the following:
a. A lightweight head on a golf club is made of titanium. If the volume of a sample of titanium is 114 cm^3 and the mass is 514.1 g, what is the density of titanium?

Lightweight heads on golf clubs are made of titanium.

b. A syrup is added to an empty container with a mass of 115.25 g. When 0.100 pt of syrup is added, the total mass of the container and syrup is 182.48 g. (1 qt = 2 pt)

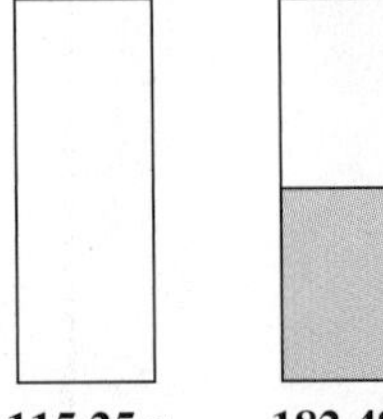

c. A block of aluminum metal has a volume of 3.15 L and a mass of 8.51 kg. What is the density of the aluminum?

2.78 Determine the density (g/mL) for each of the following:
a. An ebony carving has a mass of 275 g and a volume of 207 cm^3.
b. A 14.3-cm^3 sample of tin has a mass of 0.104 kg.
c. A bottle of acetone (fingernail polish remover) contains 55.0 mL of acetone. If the acetone has a mass of 43.5 g, what is the density of acetone?

2.79 Use the density values in Table 2.9 to solve each of the following problems:
a. How many liters of ethanol contain 1.50 kg of ethanol?
b. How many grams of mercury are present in a barometer that holds 6.5 mL of mercury?
c. A sculptor has prepared a mold for casting a silver figure. The figure has a volume of 225 cm^3. How many ounces of silver are needed in the preparation of the silver figure?

2.80 Use the density values in Table 2.9 to solve each of the following problems:
a. A graduated cylinder contains 18.0 mL of water. What is the new water level, in milliliters, after 35.6 g of silver metal is submerged in the water?
b. A thermometer containing 8.3 g of mercury has broken. What volume, in cubic centimeters, of mercury spilled?
c. A fish tank holds 35 gal of water. How many kilograms of water are in the fish tank?

2.81 Use the density values in Table 2.9 to solve each of the following problems:
a. What is the mass, in grams, of a cube of copper that has a volume of 74.1 cm^3?
b. How many kilograms of gasoline fill a 12.0-gal gas tank?
c. What is the volume, in cm^3, of an ice cube that has a mass of 27 g?

2.82 Use the density values in Table 2.9 to solve each of the following problems:
a. If a bottle of olive oil contains 1.2 kg of olive oil, what is the volume, in milliliters, of the olive oil?
b. A cannon ball made of iron has a volume of 115 cm^3. What is the mass, in kilograms, of the cannon ball?
c. A balloon filled with helium has a volume of 7.3 L. What is the mass, in grams, of helium in the balloon?

CHAPTER REVIEW

2.1 Units of Measurement

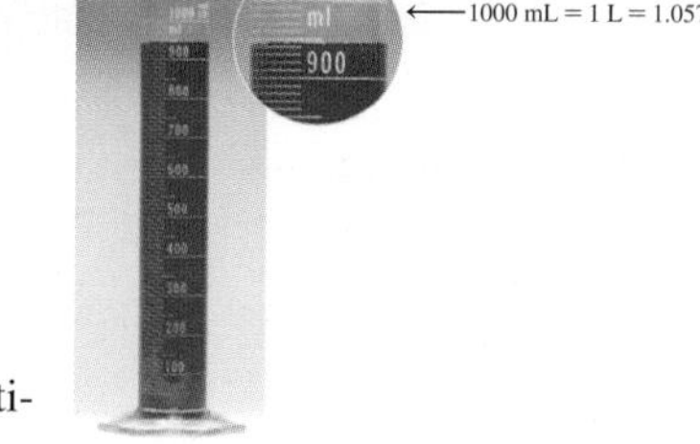

LEARNING GOAL: *Write the names and abbreviations for the metric or SI units used in measurements of length, volume, mass, temperature, and time.*

- In science, physical quantities are described in units of the metric or International System of Units (SI).
- Some important units are meter (m) for length, liter (L) for volume, gram (g) and kilogram (kg) for mass, degree Celsius (°C) and Kelvin (K) for temperature, and second (s) for time.

2.2 Scientific Notation

1×10^5 hairs

8×10^{-6} m

LEARNING GOAL: *Write a number in scientific notation.*

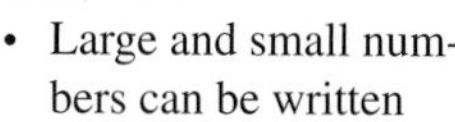

- Large and small numbers can be written using scientific notation in which the decimal point is moved to give a coefficient of at least 1 but less than 10, and the number of decimal places moved is shown as a power of 10.

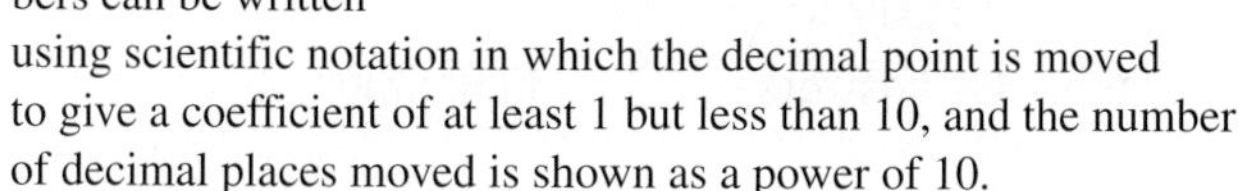

- A number greater than 1 will have a positive power of 10, while a number less than 1 will have a negative power of 10.

2.3 Measured Numbers and Significant Figures

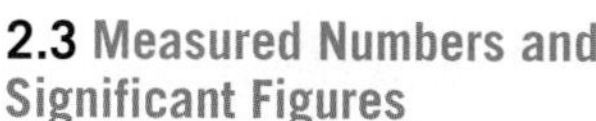

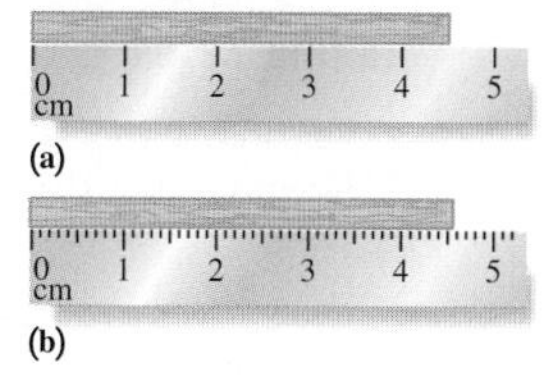

LEARNING GOAL: *Identify a number as measured or exact; determine the number of significant figures in a measured number.*

- A measured number is any number obtained by using a measuring device.
- An exact number is obtained by counting items or from a definition; no measuring device is needed.
- Significant figures are the numbers reported in a measurement including the estimated digit.
- Zeros in front of a decimal number or at the end of a nondecimal number are not significant.

2.4 Significant Figures in Calculations

LEARNING GOAL: *Adjust calculated answers to give the correct number of significant figures.*

- In multiplication and division, the final answer is written so that it has the same number of significant figures as the measurement with the fewest significant figures.
- In addition and subtraction, the final answer is written so that it has the same number of decimal places as the measurement with the fewest decimal places.

2.5 Prefixes and Equalities

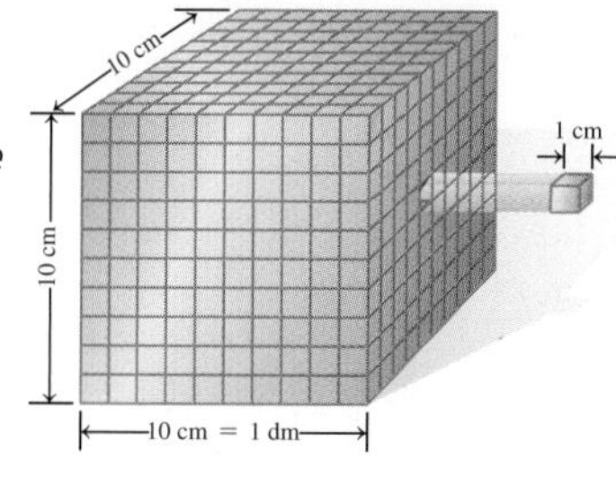

LEARNING GOAL: *Use the numerical values of prefixes to write a metric equality.*

- A prefix placed in front of a metric or SI unit changes the size of the unit by factors of 10.
- Prefixes such as *centi*, *milli*, and *micro* provide smaller units; prefixes such as *kilo*, *mega*, and *tera* provide larger units.
- An equality shows the relationship between two units that measure the same quantity of length, volume, mass, or time.
- Examples of metric equalities are: 1 m = 100 cm, 1 L = 1000 mL, 1 kg = 1000 g, and 1 min = 60 s.

2.6 Writing Conversion Factors

LEARNING GOAL: *Write a conversion factor for two units that describe the same quantity.*

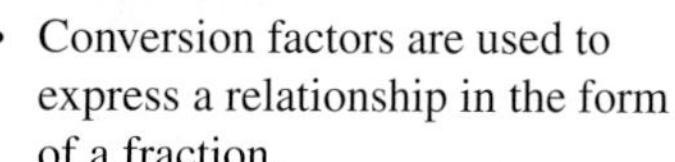

- Conversion factors are used to express a relationship in the form of a fraction.
- Two conversion factors can be written for any relationship in the metric or U.S. system.
- A percentage is written as a conversion factor by expressing matching units as the parts in 100 parts of the whole.
- Extremely small percentage values are written as parts per million (ppm) or parts per billion (ppb).

2.7 Problem Solving Using Unit Conversion

LEARNING GOAL: *Use conversion factors to change from one unit to another.*

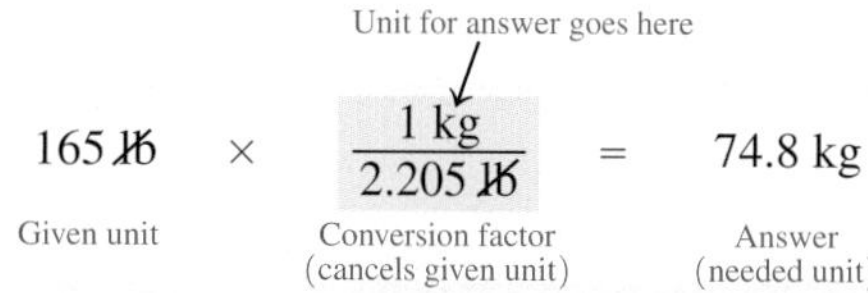

- Conversion factors are useful when changing a quantity expressed in one unit to a quantity expressed in another unit.
- In the problem-solving process, a given unit is multiplied by one or more conversion factors that cancel units until the needed answer is obtained.

2.8 Density

LEARNING GOAL: *Calculate the density of a substance; use the density to calculate the mass or volume of a substance.*

- The density of a substance is a ratio of its mass to its volume, usually g/mL or g/cm^3.
- The units of density can be used to write conversion factors that convert between the mass and volume of a substance.

CONCEPT MAP

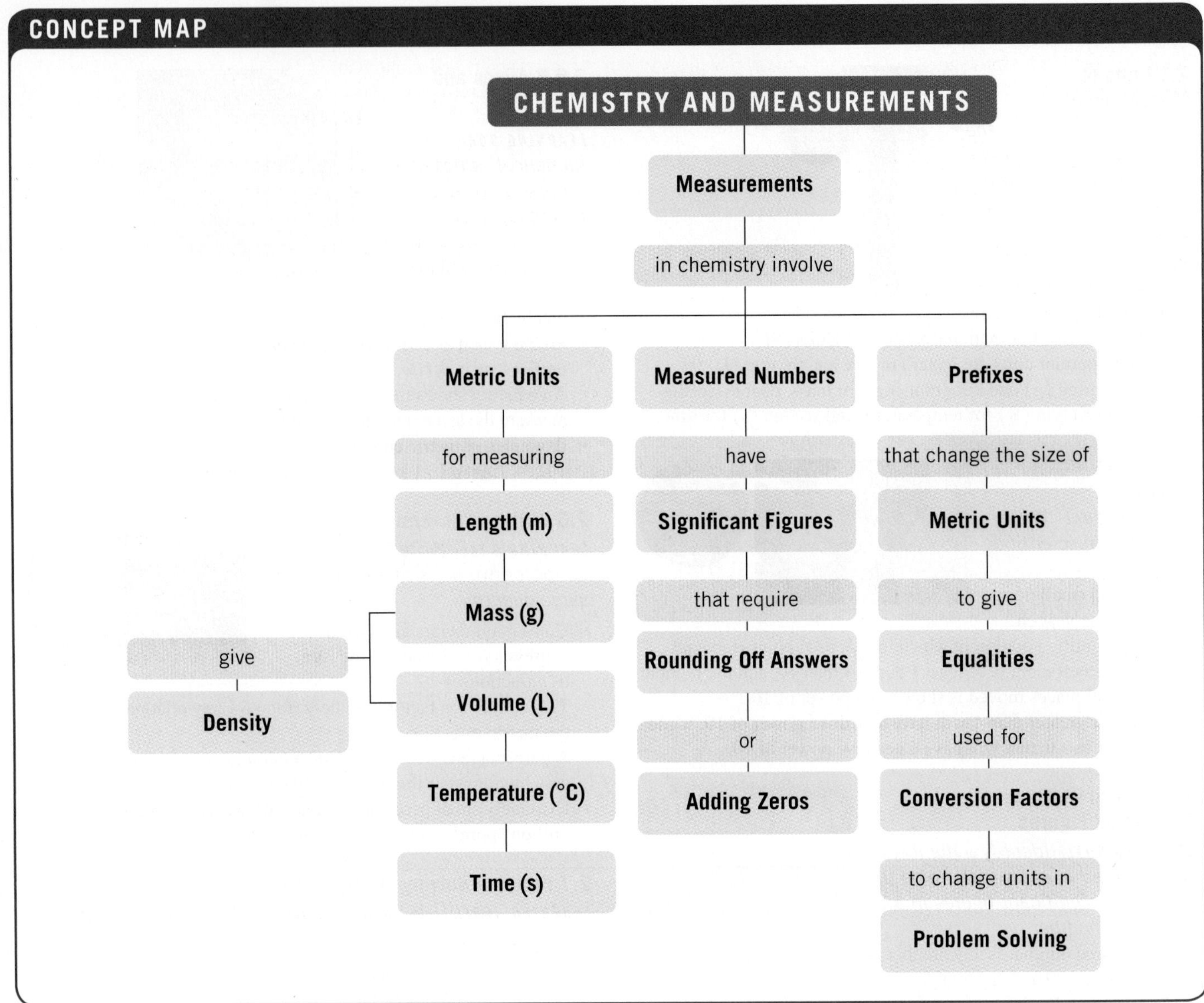

KEY TERMS

Celsius (°C) temperature scale A temperature scale on which water has a freezing point of 0 °C and a boiling point of 100 °C.

centimeter (cm) A unit of length in the metric system; there are 2.54 cm in 1 in.

conversion factor A ratio in which the numerator and denominator are quantities from an equality or given relationship. For example, the conversion factors for the relationship 1 kg = 2.205 lb are written as:

$$\frac{2.205 \text{ lb}}{1 \text{ kg}} \quad \text{and} \quad \frac{1 \text{ kg}}{2.205 \text{ lb}}$$

cubic centimeter (cm^3, cc) The volume of a cube that has 1-cm sides; 1 cm^3 is equal to 1 mL.

cubic meter (m^3) The SI unit of volume; the volume of a cube with sides that measure 1 m.

density The relationship of the mass of an object to its volume, expressed as grams per cubic centimeter (g/cm^3), grams per milliliter (g/mL), or grams per liter (g/L).

equality A relationship between two units that measure the same quantity.

exact number A number obtained by counting or definition.

gram (g) The metric unit used in measurements of mass.

International System of Units (SI) An international system of units that modifies the metric system.

Kelvin (K) temperature scale A temperature scale on which the lowest possible temperature is 0 K, which makes the freezing point of water 273 K and the boiling point of water 373 K.

kilogram (kg) A metric mass of 1000 g, equal to 2.205 lb. The kilogram is the SI standard unit of mass.
liter (L) A metric unit for volume that is slightly larger than a quart.
mass A measure of the quantity of material in an object.
measured number A number obtained when a quantity is determined by using a measuring device.
meter (m) A metric unit for length that is slightly longer than a yard. The meter is the SI standard unit of length.
metric system A system of measurement used by scientists and in most countries of the world.
milliliter (mL) A metric unit of volume equal to one-thousandth of a liter (0.001 L).
prefix The part of the name of a metric unit that precedes the base unit and specifies the size of the measurement. All prefixes are related on a decimal scale.
scientific notation A form of writing large and small numbers using a coefficient that is greater than 1 but less than 10, followed by a power of 10.
second (s) The standard unit of time in both the SI and metric systems.
SI See International System of Units (SI).
significant figures (SFs) The numbers recorded in a measurement.
temperature An indicator of the hotness or coldness of an object.
volume (*V*) The amount of space occupied by a substance.

KEY MATH SKILLS

The chapter section containing each Key Math Skill is shown in parentheses at the end of each heading.

Using Scientific Notation (2.2)

A number is written in scientific notation by:

- Moving the decimal point to obtain a coefficient that is at least 1 but less than 10.
- Expressing the number of places moved as a power of 10. The power of 10 is positive if the decimal point moved to the left, negative if the decimal point moved to the right.
- A number written in scientific notation consists of three parts: a coefficient, a power of 10, and a unit of measurement.

Example: Write the number 28 000 g in scientific notation.

Answer: Moving the decimal point four places to the left gives a coefficient of 2.8 and a positive power of 10 of 10^4. The number 28 000 g written in scientific notation is 2.8×10^4 g.

Example: Write the standard number for 3.6×10^{-4} cm.

Answer: The negative power of 10, 10^{-4}, indicates that the decimal point needs to move four places to the left to give 0.00036 cm.

CORE CHEMISTRY SKILLS

The chapter section containing each Core Chemistry Skill is shown in parentheses at the end of each heading.

Counting Significant Figures (2.3)

The significant figures are all the *measured* numbers including the last, estimated digit:

- All nonzero digits
- Zeros between nonzero digits
- Zeros within a decimal number
- All digits in a coefficient of a number written in scientific notation

An *exact* number is obtained from counting or a definition and has no effect on the number of significant figures in the final answer.

Example: State the number of significant figures in each of the following:

0.003045 mm	*Answer*:	four SFs
15 000 m		two SFs
45.067 kg		five SFs
5.30×10^3 g		three SFs
2 cans of soda		exact

Rounding Off (2.4)

Calculator displays are rounded off to give the correct number of significant figures.

- If the first digit to be dropped is *4 or less*, then it and all following digits are simply dropped from the number.
- If the first digit to be dropped is *5 or greater*, then the last retained digit of the number is increased by 1.

One or more significant zeros are added when the calculator display has fewer digits than the needed number of significant figures.

Example: Round off each of the following to three significant figures:

3.60892 L	*Answer*:	3.61 L
0.003 870 298 m		0.00387 m
6 g		6.00 g

Using Significant Figures in Calculations (2.4)

- In multiplication or division, the final answer is written so that it has the same number of significant figures as the measurement with the fewest significant figures (SFs).
- In addition or subtraction, the final answer is written so that it has the same number of decimal places as the measurement having the fewest decimal places.

Perform the following calculations using measured numbers and give answers with the correct number of SFs:

Example: 4.05 m × 0.6078 m

Answer: 2.46159 rounded off to 2.46 m^2 (three SFs)

Example: $\frac{4.50 \text{ g}}{3.27 \text{ mL}}$

Answer: 1.376 146 789 rounded off to 1.38 g/mL (three SFs)

Example: 0.758 g + 3.10 g

Answer: 3.858 rounded off to 3.86 g (hundredths place)

Example: 13.538 km – 8.6 km

Answer: 4.938 rounded off to 4.9 km (tenths place)

Using Prefixes (2.5)

- In the metric and SI systems of units, a prefix attached to any unit increases or decreases its size by some factor of 10.
- When the prefix *centi* is used with the unit meter, it becomes centimeter, a length that is one-hundredth of a meter (0.01 m).
- When the prefix *milli* is used with the unit meter, it becomes millimeter, a length that is one-thousandth of a meter (0.001 m).

Example: Complete the following statements with the correct prefix symbol:

a. 1000 m = 1 ____ m **b.** 0.01 g = 1 ____ g

Answer:

a. 1000 m = 1 km **b.** 0.01 g = 1 cg

Writing Conversion Factors from Equalities (2.6)

- A conversion factor allows you to change from one unit to another.
- Two conversion factors can be written for any equality in the metric, U.S., or metric–U.S. systems of measurement.
- Two conversion factors can be written for a relationship stated within a problem, a percentage (%), parts per million (ppm) expressed as mg/kg, and parts per billion (ppb) expressed as μg/kg.

Example: Write two conversion factors for the equality 1 L = 1000 mL.

Answer: $\frac{1000\text{ mL}}{1\text{ L}}$ and $\frac{1\text{ L}}{1000\text{ mL}}$

Example: Express 2 ppm of arsenic in liver as an equality and conversion factors.

Answer: 2 mg of arsenic = 1 kg of liver.

$\frac{2\text{ mg arsenic}}{1\text{ kg liver}}$ and $\frac{1\text{ kg liver}}{2\text{ mg arsenic}}$

Using Conversion Factors (2.7)

In problem solving, conversion factors are used to cancel the given unit and to provide the needed unit for the answer.

- State the given and needed quantities.
- Write a plan to convert the given unit to the needed unit.
- State the equalities and conversion factors.
- Set up problem to cancel units and calculate the answer.

Example: A computer chip has a width of 0.75 in. What is that distance in millimeters?

Answer:

Equalities: 1 in. = 2.54 cm; 1 cm = 10 mm

Conversion Factors: $\frac{2.54\text{ cm}}{1\text{ in.}}$ and $\frac{1\text{ in.}}{2.54\text{ cm}}$; $\frac{10\text{ mm}}{1\text{ cm}}$ and $\frac{1\text{ cm}}{10\text{ mm}}$

Problem Setup: $0.75\ \cancel{\text{in.}} \times \frac{2.54\ \cancel{\text{cm}}}{1\ \cancel{\text{in.}}} \times \frac{10\text{ mm}}{1\ \cancel{\text{cm}}} = 19\text{ mm}$

Using Density as a Conversion Factor (2.8)

Density is an equality of mass and volume for a substance, which is written as the *density expression*:

$$\text{Density} = \frac{\text{mass of substance}}{\text{volume of substance}}$$

Density is useful as a conversion factor to convert between mass and volume.

Example: The element tungsten used in lightbulb filaments has a density of 19.3 g/cm^3. What is the volume, in cm^3, of 250 g of tungsten?

Answer:

Equality: 1 cm^3 = 19.3 g

Conversion Factors: $\frac{19.3\text{ g}}{1\text{ cm}^3}$ and $\frac{1\text{ cm}^3}{19.3\text{ g}}$

Problem Setup: $250\ \cancel{\text{g}} \times \frac{1\text{ cm}^3}{19.3\ \cancel{\text{g}}} = 13\text{ cm}^3$

UNDERSTANDING THE CONCEPTS

The chapter sections to review are shown in parentheses at the end of each question.

2.83 Indicate if each of the following is an exact number or a measured number: (2.3)

a. number of legs
b. height of table
c. number of chairs at the table
d. area of tabletop

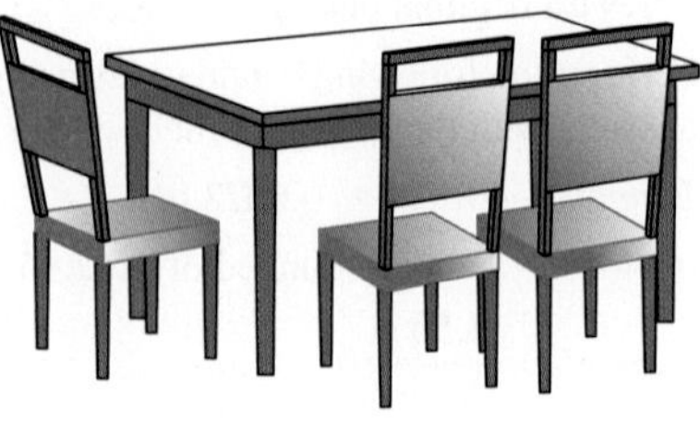

2.84 State the temperature on each of the Celsius thermometers to the correct number of significant figures: (2.3)

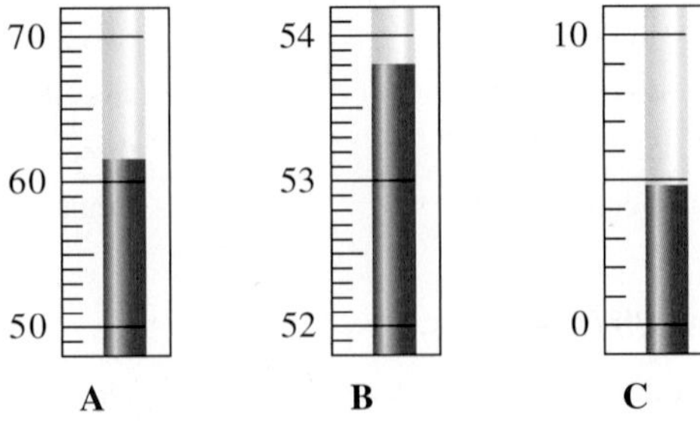

2.85 The length of this rug is 38.4 in. and the width is 24.2 in. (2.3)

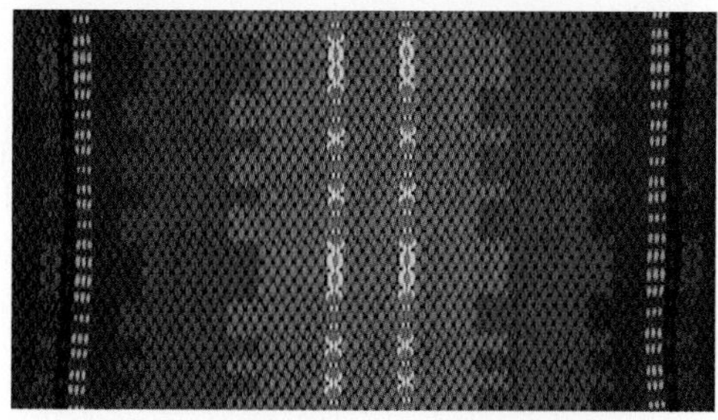

a. What is the length of this rug measured in centimeters?
b. What is the width of this rug measured in centimeters?
c. How many significant figures are in the length measurement?
d. Calculate the area of the rug, in cm^2, to the correct number of significant figures.

2.86 Measure the length of each of the objects in diagrams (**a**), (**b**), and (**c**) using the metric ruler shown. Indicate the number of significant figures for each and the estimated digit for each. (2.3)

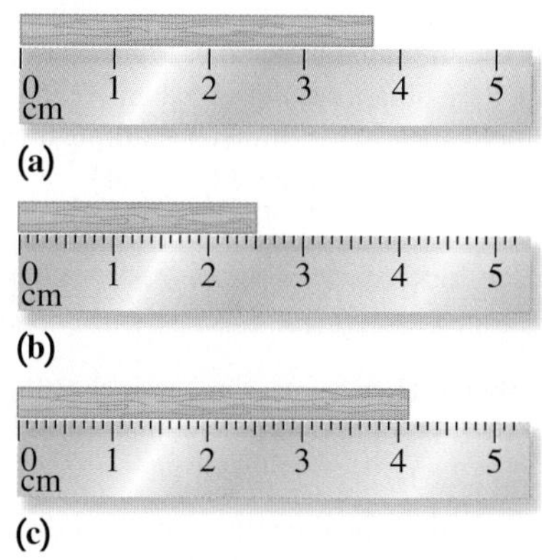

2.87 What is the density of the solid object that is weighed and submerged in water? (2.8)

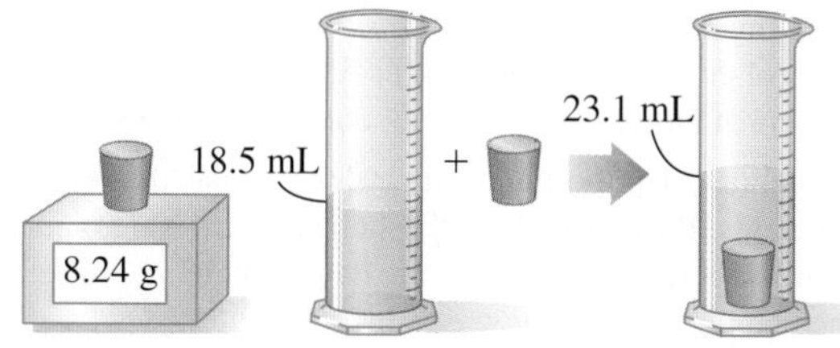

2.88 Each of the following diagrams represents a container of water and a cube. Some cubes float while others sink. Match diagrams **1**, **2**, **3**, or **4** with one of the following descriptions and explain your choices: (2.8)
a. The cube has a greater density than water.
b. The cube has a density that is 0.60–0.80 g/mL.
c. The cube has a density that is one-half the density of water.
d. The cube has the same density as water.

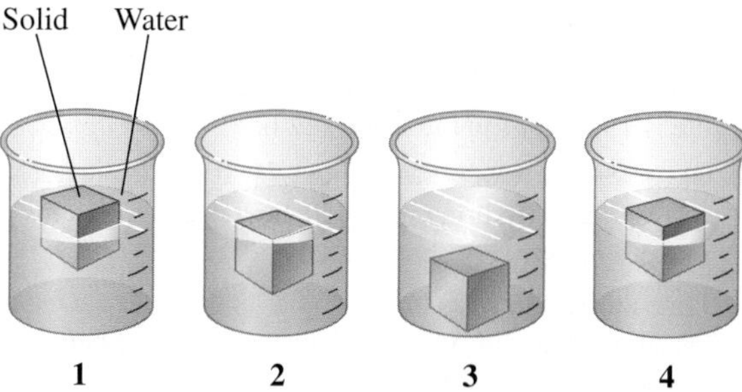

2.89 A graduated cylinder contains three liquids **A**, **B**, and **C**, which have different densities and do not mix: mercury (D = 13.6 g/mL), vegetable oil (D = 0.92 g/mL), and water (D = 1.00 g/mL). Identify the liquids **A**, **B**, and **C** in the cylinder. (2.8)

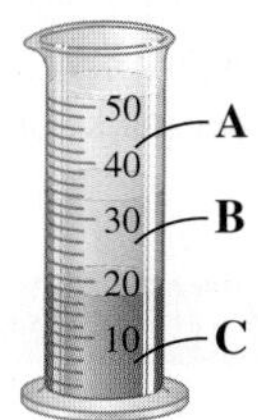

2.90 The solids **A**, **B**, and **C** are made of aluminum, gold, or silver. If each has a mass of 10.0 g, what is the identity of each? (2.8)

Density of aluminum = 2.70 g/mL
Density of gold = 19.3 g/mL
Density of silver = 10.5 g/mL

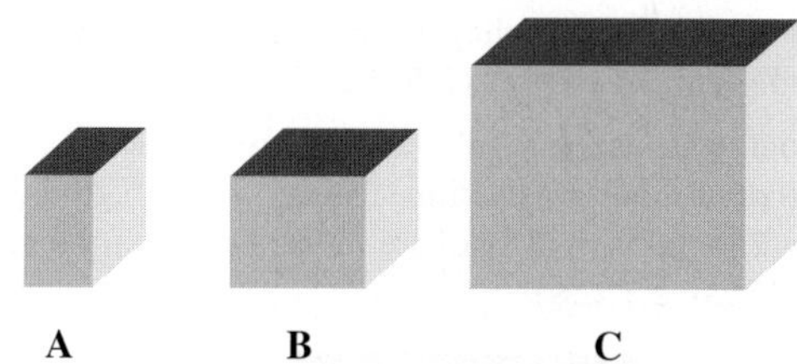

ADDITIONAL QUESTIONS AND PROBLEMS

2.91 Round off or add zeros to the following calculated answers to give a final answer with three significant figures: (2.3)
a. 0.000 012 58 L
b. 3.528×10^2 kg
c. 125 111 m^3
d. 58.703 m

2.92 Round off or add zeros to the following calculated answers to give a final answer with two significant figures: (2.3)
a. 0.004 mL
b. 34 677 g
c. 4.393 cm
d. 1.74×10^3 ms

2.93 What is the total mass, in grams, of a dessert containing 137.25 g of vanilla ice cream, 84 g of fudge sauce, and 43.7 g of nuts? (2.4)

2.94 A fish company delivers 22 kg of salmon, 5.5 kg of crab, and 3.48 kg of oysters to your seafood restaurant. What is the total mass, in kilograms, of the seafood? (2.4)

2.95 During a workout at the gym, you set the treadmill at a pace of 55.0 m/min. How many minutes will you walk if you cover a distance of 7500 ft? (2.6, 2.7)

2.96 The distance between two cities is 1700 km. How long will it take, in h, to drive from one city to the other if your average speed is 63 mi/h? (2.6, 2.7)

2.97 Bill's recipe for onion soup calls for 4.0 lb of thinly sliced onions. If an onion has an average mass of 115 g, how many onions does Bill need? (2.6, 2.7)

2.98 An aquarium store unit requires 75 000 mL of water. How many gallons of water are needed? (2.6, 2.7)

2.99 In Mexico, avocados are 48 pesos per kilogram. What is the cost, in cents, of an avocado that weighs 0.45 lb if the exchange rate is 13.0 pesos to the dollar? (2.6, 2.7)

2.100 The price of 1 lb of potatoes is \$1.75. If all the potatoes sold today at the store bring in \$1420, how many kilograms of potatoes did grocery shoppers buy? (2.6, 2.7)

2.101 Some athletes have as little as 3.0% body fat. If such a person has a body mass of 65 kg, how many pounds of body fat does that person have? (2.6, 2.7)

2.102 A typical adult body contains 55% water. If a person has a mass of 65 kg, how many pounds of water does she have in her body? (2.6, 2.7)

2.103 Sterling silver is 92.5% silver by mass with a density of 10.3 g/cm^3. If a cube of sterling silver has a volume of 27.0 cm^3, how many ounces of pure silver are present? (2.6, 2.7, 2.8)

2.104 Celeste's diet restricts her intake of protein to 24 g per day. (2.6, 2.7)

a. If she eats an 8.0-oz burger that is 15.0% protein, has she exceeded her protein limit for the day?

b. How many ounces of a burger would be allowed by her diet?

2.105 If a recycling center collects 1254 aluminum cans and there are 22 aluminum cans in 1 lb, what volume, in liters, of aluminum was collected (see Table 2.9)? (2.6, 2.7, 2.8)

2.106 What is the volume, in quarts, of 1.35 kg of ethanol (C_2H_6O) (see Table 2.9)? (2.6, 2.7, 2.8)

2.107 The water level in a graduated cylinder initially at 215 mL rises to 285 mL after a piece of lead is submerged. What is the mass, in grams, of the lead (see Table 2.9)? (2.6, 2.7, 2.8)

2.108 An object has a mass of 3.15 oz. When it is submerged in a graduated cylinder initially containing 325.2 mL of water, the water level rises to 442.5 mL. What is the density (g/mL) of the object? (2.8)

2.109 A balance measures mass to 0.001 g. If you determine the mass of an object that weighs about 30 g, would you record the mass as 30 g, 32 g, 32.1 g, or 32.075 g? Explain your choice by writing one or two complete sentences that describe your thinking. (2.3, 2.4)

2.110 When three students use the same meterstick to measure the length of a paperclip, they obtain results of 5.8 cm, 5.75 cm, and 5.76 cm. If the meterstick has millimeter markings, what are some reasons for the different values? (2.3, 2.4)

CHALLENGE QUESTIONS

The following groups of questions are related to the topics in this chapter. However, they do not all follow the chapter order, and they require you to combine concepts and skills from several sections. These questions will help you increase your critical thinking skills and prepare for your next exam.

2.111 A sunscreen preparation contains 2.50% by mass benzyl salicylate. If a tube contains 4.0 oz of sunscreen, how many kilograms of benzyl salicylate are needed to manufacture 325 tubes of sunscreen? (2.6, 2.7)

2.112 A mouthwash is 21.6% alcohol by mass. If each bottle contains 0.358 pt of mouthwash with a density of 0.876 g/mL, how many kilograms of alcohol are in 180 bottles of the mouthwash? (2.6, 2.7, 2.8)

A mouthwash may contain over 20% alcohol.

2.113 A package of aluminum foil is 66.7 yd long, 12 in. wide, and 0.000 30 in. thick. If aluminum has a density of 2.70 g/cm^3, what is the mass, in grams, of the foil? (2.6, 2.7, 2.8)

2.114 In the manufacturing of computer chips, cylinders of silicon are cut into thin wafers that are 3.00 in. in diameter and have a mass of 1.50 g of silicon. How thick (mm) is each wafer if silicon has a density of 2.33 g/cm^3? (The volume of a cylinder is $V = \pi r^2 h$) (2.6, 2.7, 2.8)

2.115 For a 180-lb person, calculate the quantity of each of the following that must be ingested to provide the LD_{50} for caffeine given in Table 2.8: (2.6, 2.7)

a. cups of coffee if one cup is 12 fluid ounces and there is 100. mg of caffeine per 6 fl oz of drip-brewed coffee

b. cans of cola if one can contains 50. mg of caffeine

c. tablets of No-Doz if one tablet contains 100. mg of caffeine

2.116 The label on a 1-pt bottle of mineral water lists the following components. If the density is the same as pure water and you drink three bottles of water in one day, how many milligrams of each component will you obtain? (2.6, 2.7, 2.8)

a. calcium 28 ppm

b. fluoride 0.08 ppm

c. magnesium 12 ppm

d. potassium 3.2 ppm

e. sodium 15 ppm

2.117 How many cubic centimeters (cm^3) of olive oil have the same mass as 1.00 L of gasoline (see Table 2.9)? (2.8)

2.118 In liposuction, a doctor removes fat deposits from a person's body. If body fat has a density of 0.94 g/mL and 3.0 L of fat is removed, how many pounds of fat were removed from the patient? (2.8)

2.119 A graduated cylinder contains 155 mL of water. A 15.0-g piece of iron and a 20.0-g piece of lead are added. What is the new water level in the cylinder (see Table 2.9)? (2.8)

2.120 A 50.0-g silver object and a 50.0-g gold object are both added to 75.5 mL of water contained in a graduated cylinder. What is the new water level in the cylinder (see Table 2.9)? (2.8)

ANSWERS

Answers to Study Checks

2.1 a. 4.25×10^5 m **b.** 8×10^{-7} g

2.2 0.000 725 s

2.3 a. 36 m **b.** 0.0026 L **c.** 3.8×10^3 g

2.4 a. 0.4924 **b.** 2.0

2.5 a. 83.70 g **b.** 0.5 L **c.** 7.0 m

2.6 2.0×10^{12} bytes

2.7 $\frac{1 \text{ zs}}{1 \times 10^{-21} \text{ s}}$ and $\frac{1 \times 10^{-21} \text{ s}}{1 \text{ zs}}$

2.8 a. 1 h = 62.2 km; $\frac{1 \text{ h}}{62.2 \text{ km}}$ and $\frac{62.2 \text{ km}}{1 \text{ h}}$

62.2 is measured and has three significant figures; 1 is exact.

b. 1 kg of water = 10 μg of arsenic; $\frac{10\ \mu\text{g arsenic}}{1 \text{ kg water}}$ and $\frac{1 \text{ kg water}}{10\ \mu\text{g arsenic}}$

10 is measured and has one significant figure; 1 is exact.

2.9 340 mL

2.10 2.5 h

2.11 25 g of fat

2.12 1.05 g/cm^3

2.13 2.2 g/cm^3

2.14 980 g of syrup

Answers to Selected Questions and Problems

2.1 a. meter, length **b.** gram, mass
c. liter, volume **d.** second, time
e. degree Celsius, temperature

2.3 a. milliliter, metric **b.** kilogram, metric/SI
c. inch, not metric/SI **d.** second, metric/SI
e. degree Celsius, metric

2.5 a. g **b.** L **c.** °C **d.** lb **e.** s

2.7 a. 5.5×10^4 m **b.** 4.8×10^2 g
c. 5×10^{-6} cm **d.** 1.4×10^{-4} s
e. 7.85×10^{-3} L **f.** 6.7×10^5 kg

2.9 a. 7.2×10^3 cm **b.** 3.2×10^{-2} kg
c. 1×10^4 L **d.** 6.8×10^{-2} m

2.11 a. 12 000 s **b.** 0.0825 kg
c. 4 000 000 g **d.** 0.0058 m^3

2.13 a. the 6 (0.6) in the tenths place
b. the 5 (0.05) in the hundredths place
c. the 9 in the ones place

2.15 a. measured **b.** exact
c. exact **d.** measured

2.17 a. 6 oz of hamburger
b. none (counting numbers are exact)
c. 0.75 lb, 350 g
d. none (definitions are exact)

2.19 a. Zeros preceding the first nonzero digit are not significant.
b. Zeros between nonzero digits are significant.
c. Zeros after the first nonzero digit in a decimal number are significant.
d. Zeros in the coefficient of a number in scientific notation are significant.
e. Zeros in a large number without a decimal point are not significant.

2.21 a. five SFs **b.** two SFs **c.** two SFs
d. three SFs **e.** four SFs **f.** three SFs

2.23 a. 11.00 m **b.** 405.0 K
c. 0.0120 s **d.** 2.50×10^{-2} mL

2.25 a. 5.0×10^3 L **b.** 3.0×10^4 g
c. 1.0×10^5 m **d.** 2.5×10^{-4} cm

2.27 The significant figures in the measurements used in a calculation are usually fewer than the number of figures in the calculator display, which requires rounding off.

2.29 a. 1.85 kg **b.** 88.0 L
c. 0.004 74 cm **d.** 8810 m
e. 1.83×10^3 s

2.31 a. 56.9 m **b.** 0.002 28 g
c. 11 500 s (1.15×10^4 s) **d.** 8.10 L

2.33 a. 1.6 **b.** 0.01 **c.** 27.6
d. 3.5 **e.** 1.4×10^{-1} (0.14) **f.** 8×10^{-1} (0.8)

2.35 a. 53.54 cm **b.** 127.6 g
c. 121.5 mL **d.** 0.50 L

2.37 km/h is kilometers per hour; mi/h is miles per hour.

2.39 a. mg **b.** dL **c.** km **d.** fg

2.41 a. centiliter **b.** kilogram
c. millisecond **d.** gigameter

2.43 a. 0.01 **b.** 10^{12} **c.** 0.001 **d.** 0.1

2.45 a. decigram **b.** microgram
c. kilogram **d.** centigram

2.47 a. 100 cm **b.** 10^{-9} m
c. 0.001 m **d.** 1000 mL

2.49 a. kilogram **b.** milliliter
c. cm **d.** kL

2.51 A conversion factor can be inverted to give a second conversion factor.

2.53 a. 1 m = 100 cm; $\frac{100 \text{ cm}}{1 \text{ m}}$ and $\frac{1 \text{ m}}{100 \text{ cm}}$

b. 1 g = 1×10^9 ng; $\frac{1 \text{ g}}{1 \times 10^9 \text{ ng}}$ and $\frac{1 \times 10^9 \text{ ng}}{1 \text{ g}}$

c. 1 kL = 1000 L; $\frac{1000 \text{ L}}{1 \text{ kL}}$ and $\frac{1 \text{ kL}}{1000 \text{ L}}$

d. 1 s = 1000 ms; $\frac{1000 \text{ ms}}{1 \text{ s}}$ and $\frac{1 \text{ s}}{1000 \text{ ms}}$

e. $(1 \text{ m})^3 = (100 \text{ cm})^3$; $\frac{(100 \text{ cm})^3}{(1 \text{ m})^3}$ and $\frac{(1 \text{ m})^3}{(100 \text{ cm})^3}$

2.55 **a.** 1 yd = 3 ft; $\frac{3\text{ ft}}{1\text{ yd}}$ and $\frac{1\text{ yd}}{3\text{ ft}}$
Both of the numbers 1 and 3 are exact (U.S. definition).

b. 1 kg = 2.205 lb; $\frac{2.205\text{ lb}}{1\text{ kg}}$ and $\frac{1\text{ kg}}{2.205\text{ lb}}$
The number 1 is exact, and the number 2.205 is measured and has four SFs.

c. 1 min = 60 s; $\frac{60\text{ s}}{1\text{ min}}$ and $\frac{1\text{ min}}{60\text{ s}}$
Both of the numbers 1 and 60 are exact (metric definition).

d. 1 gal = 27 mi; $\frac{1\text{ gal}}{27\text{ mi}}$ and $\frac{27\text{ mi}}{1\text{ gal}}$
The number 1 is exact, and the number 27 is measured and has two SFs.

e. 48 g of silicon = 100 g of crust;
$\frac{48\text{ g of silicon}}{100\text{ g of crust}}$ and $\frac{100\text{ g of crust}}{48\text{ g of silicon}}$
The number 100 is exact, and the number 48 is measured and has two SFs.

2.57 **a.** 3.5 m = 1 s; $\frac{3.5\text{ m}}{1\text{ s}}$ and $\frac{1\text{ s}}{3.5\text{ m}}$
The number 1 is exact; the number 3.5 is measured and has two SFs.

b. 0.74 g = 1 mL; $\frac{0.74\text{ g}}{1\text{ mL}}$ and $\frac{1\text{ mL}}{0.74\text{ g}}$
The number 1 is exact; the number 0.74 is measured and has two SFs.

c. 46.0 km = 1 gal; $\frac{46.0\text{ km}}{1\text{ gal}}$ and $\frac{1\text{ gal}}{46.0\text{ km}}$
The number 1 is exact; the number 46.0 is measured and has three SFs.

d. 93 g of silver = 100 g of sterling;
$\frac{93\text{ g silver}}{100\text{ g sterling}}$ and $\frac{100\text{ g sterling}}{93\text{ g silver}}$
The number 100 is exact; the number 93 is measured and has two SFs.

e. 29 μg of pesticide = 1 kg of plums
$\frac{29\ \mu\text{g pesticide}}{1\text{ kg}}$ and $\frac{1\text{ kg}}{29\ \mu\text{g pesticide}}$
The number 1 is exact; the number 29 is measured and has two SFs.

2.59 The unit in the denominator must cancel with the preceding unit in the numerator.

2.61 **a.** 0.0442 L **b.** 8.65×10^9 nm
c. 5.2×10^2 Mg **d.** 7.2×10^5 ms

2.63 **a.** 1.555 kg **b.** 63 in.
c. 4.4 qt **d.** 205 mm

2.65 **a.** 1.75 m **b.** 5.5 L
c. 5.5 g **d.** 3.5×10^{-4} m^3

2.67 **a.** 710. mL **b.** 74.9 kg
c. 495 mm **d.** 2.0×10^{-5} in.

2.69 **a.** 23.8 m **b.** 196 m^2
c. 0.463 s **d.** 53 L of paint

2.71 **a.** 152 g of oxygen **b.** 0.026 g of magnesium
c. 43 g of nitrogen **d.** 50. lb of chocolate bars

2.73 lead, 11.3 g/cm^3

2.75 **a.** 1.20 g/mL **b.** 0.870 g/mL **c.** 3.10 g/mL

2.77 **a.** 4.51 g/mL **b.** 1.42 g/mL **c.** 2.70 g/mL

2.79 **a.** 1.91 L of ethanol **b.** 88 g of mercury
c. 83.3 oz of silver

2.81 **a.** 661 g **b.** 34 kg **c.** 29 cm^3

2.83 **a.** exact **b.** measured **c.** exact **d.** measured

2.85 **a.** length = 97.5 cm **b.** width = 61.5 cm
c. 3 significant figures **d.** 6.00×10^3 cm^2

2.87 1.8 g/mL

2.89 A is vegetable oil, B is water, and C is mercury.

2.91 **a.** 1.26×10^{-5} L **b.** 3.53×10^2 kg
c. 1.25×10^5 m^3 **d.** 58.7 m

2.93 265 g

2.95 42 min

2.97 16 onions

2.99 75 cents

2.101 4.3 lb of body fat

2.103 9.07 oz of pure silver

2.105 9.57 L

2.107 790 g

2.109 Because the balance can measure mass to 0.001 g, the mass should be given to 0.001 g. You should record the mass of the object as 32.075 g.

2.111 0.92 kg

2.113 3.8×10^2 g of aluminum

2.115 **a.** 78 cups
b. 310 cans
c. 160 tablets

2.117 8.0×10^2 cm^3

2.119 159 mL

Matter and Energy 3

LOOKING AHEAD

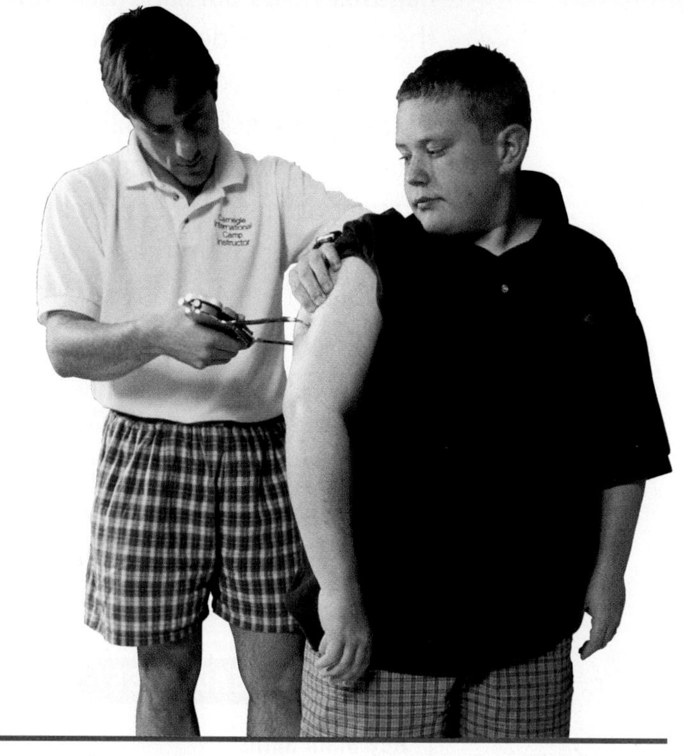

Charles is 13 years old and overweight for his age. His doctor is worried that Charles is at risk for type 2 diabetes and advises his mother to make an appointment with a dietitian. Daniel, a dietitian, explains to them that choosing the appropriate foods is important to living a healthy lifestyle, losing weight, and preventing or managing diabetes.

Daniel also explains that food contains potential or stored energy, and different foods contain different amounts of potential energy. For instance, carbohydrates contain 4 kcal/g while fats contain 9 kcal/g. He then explains that diets high in fat require more exercise to burn the fats, as they contain more potential energy. Daniel encourages Charles and his mother to include whole grains, fruits, and vegetables in their diet instead of foods high in fat. They also discuss food labels and the fact that smaller serving sizes of healthy foods are necessary in order to lose weight. Before leaving, Charles and his mother are given a menu for the following two weeks, as well as a diary to keep track of what, and how much, they actually consume.

Career: Dietitian

Dietitians specialize in helping individuals learn about good nutrition and the need for a balanced diet. This requires them to understand biochemical processes, the importance of vitamins, and food labels, as well as the differences between carbohydrates, fats, and proteins in terms of their energy value and how they are metabolized. Dietitians work in a variety of environments including hospitals, nursing homes, school cafeterias, and public health clinics. In these environments, they create specialized diets for individuals diagnosed with a specific disease, or create meal plans for those in a nursing home.

Every day, we see a variety of materials with many different shapes and forms. To a scientist, all of this material is *matter*. Matter is everywhere around us: the orange juice we had for breakfast, the water we put in the coffeemaker, the plastic bag that holds our sandwich, our toothbrush and toothpaste, the oxygen we inhale, and the carbon dioxide we exhale.

When we look around, we see that matter takes the physical form of a solid, a liquid, or a gas. Water is a familiar example that we routinely observe in all three states. In the solid state, water can be an ice cube or a snowflake. It is a liquid when it comes out of a faucet or fills a pool. Water forms a gas, or vapor, when it evaporates from wet clothes or boils in a pan. In these examples, water changes state by losing or gaining energy. For example, energy is added to melt ice cubes and to boil water in a teakettle. Conversely, energy is removed to freeze liquid water in an ice-cube tray and to condense water vapor to liquid droplets.

Almost everything we do involves energy. We use energy when we heat water, cook food, turn on lights, walk, study, use a washing machine, or drive our cars. Of course, that energy has to come from something. In our bodies, the food we eat provides us with energy. Energy from burning fossil fuels or the Sun is used to heat a home or water for a pool.

CHAPTER READINESS*

Key Math Skills

- Using Positive and Negative Numbers in Calculations (1.4B)
- Solving Equations (1.4D)

Core Chemistry Skills

- Counting Significant Figures (2.3)
- Rounding Off (2.4)
- Using Significant Figures in Calculations (2.4)
- Writing Conversion Factors from Equalities (2.6)
- Using Conversion Factors (2.7)

*These Key Math Skills and the Core Chemistry Skills from previous chapters are listed here for your review as you proceed to the new material in this chapter.

LEARNING GOAL

Classify examples of matter as pure substances or mixtures.

3.1 Classification of Matter

Matter is anything that has mass and occupies space. Matter makes up all things we use, such as water, wood, plates, plastic bags, clothes, and shoes. The different types of matter are classified by their composition.

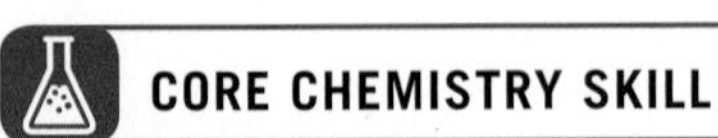

Classifying Matter

Pure Substances: Elements and Compounds

A **pure substance** is matter that has a fixed or constant composition. There are two kinds of pure substances: elements and compounds. An **element**, the simplest type of a pure substance, is composed of only one type of material, such as silver, iron, or aluminum. Every element is composed of *atoms*, which are extremely tiny particles that make up each type of matter. Silver is composed of silver atoms, iron of iron atoms, and aluminum of aluminum atoms. A full list of the elements is found on the inside front cover of this text.

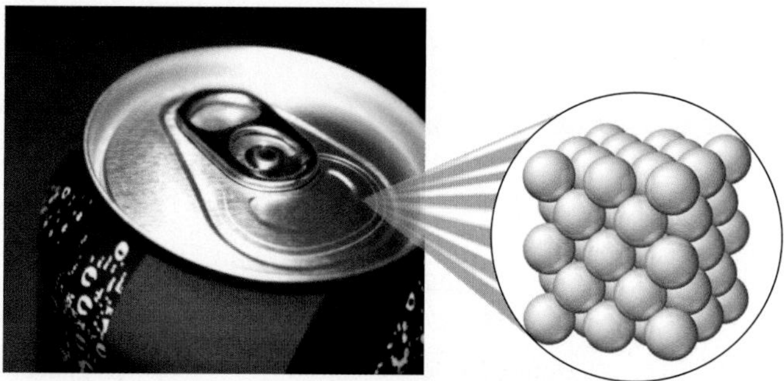

An aluminum can consists of many atoms of aluminum.

A molecule of water, H_2O, consists of two atoms of hydrogen (white) for every one atom of oxygen (red).

A **compound** is also a pure substance, but it consists of two or more elements chemically combined in the same proportion. In compounds, the atoms are held together by attractions called *bonds*, which form small groups of atoms called molecules. For example, a molecule of the compound water has two hydrogen atoms for every one oxygen atom, and is represented by the formula H_2O. This means that water found anywhere always has the same composition of H_2O. Another compound that consists of a combination of hydrogen and oxygen is hydrogen peroxide. However, it consists of two hydrogen atoms for every two oxygen atoms, and is represented by the formula H_2O_2. Thus, water (H_2O) and hydrogen peroxide (H_2O_2) are different compounds that have different properties.

Pure substances that are compounds can be broken down by chemical processes into their elements. They cannot be broken down through physical methods such as boiling or sifting. For example, the compound in ordinary table salt, NaCl, is chemically broken down into the elements sodium and chlorine as seen in Figure 3.1. Elements cannot be broken down further.

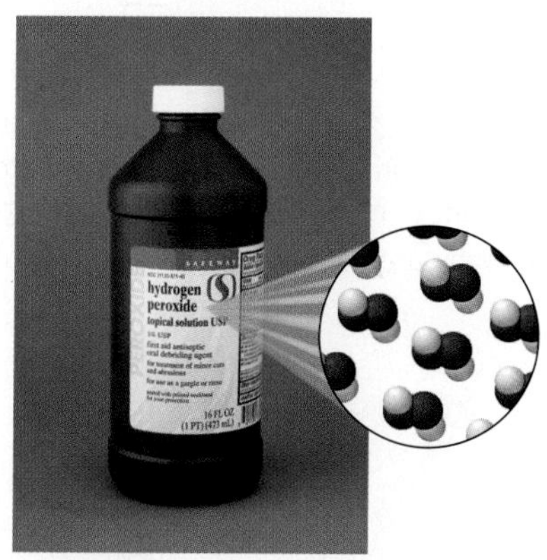

A molecule of hydrogen peroxide, H_2O_2, consists of two atoms of hydrogen (white) for every two atoms of oxygen (red).

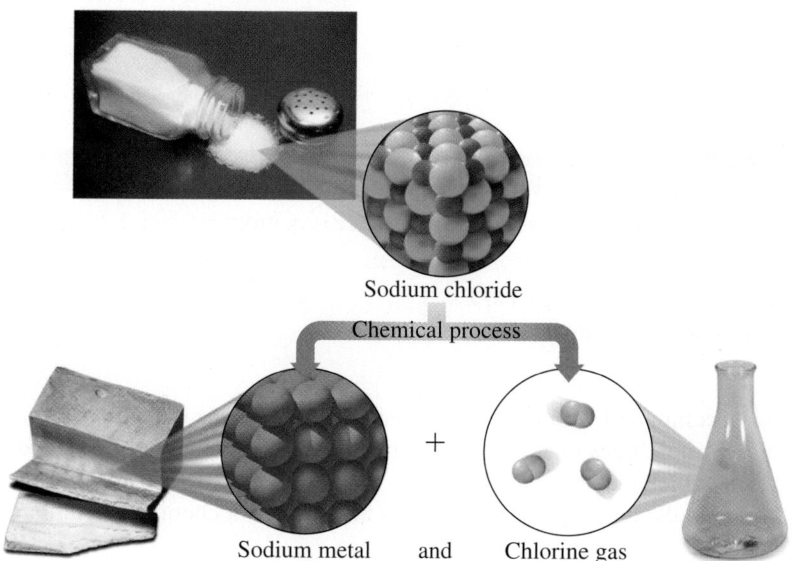

FIGURE 3.1 The decomposition of salt, NaCl, produces the elements sodium and chlorine.

Q How do elements and compounds differ?

Mixtures

In a **mixture**, two or more different substances are physically mixed, but not chemically combined. Much of the matter in our everyday lives consists of mixtures (see Figure 3.2). The air we breathe is a mixture of mostly oxygen and nitrogen gases. The steel in buildings and railroad tracks is a mixture of iron, nickel, carbon, and chromium. The brass in doorknobs and fixtures is a mixture of zinc and copper. Different types of brass have different properties, depending on the ratio of copper to zinc. Tea, coffee, and ocean water are mixtures, too. Unlike compounds, the proportions of the substances in a mixture are

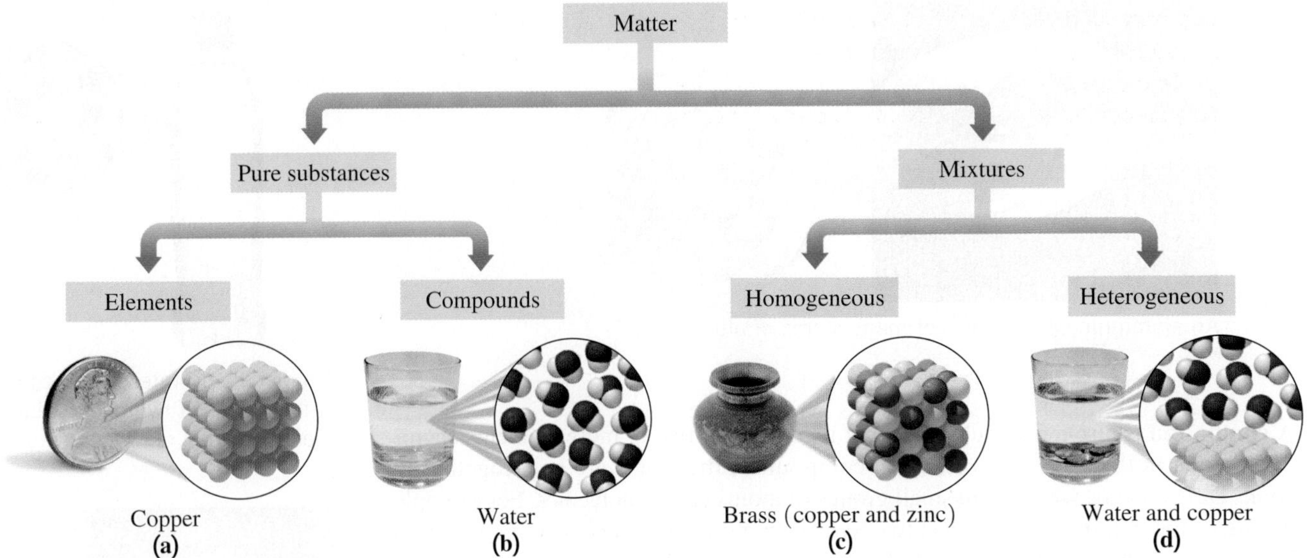

FIGURE 3.2 Matter is organized by its components: elements, compounds, and mixtures. **(a)** The element copper consists of copper atoms. **(b)** The compound water consists of H_2O molecules. **(c)** Brass is a homogeneous mixture of copper and zinc atoms. **(d)** Copper metal in water is a heterogeneous mixture of Cu atoms and H_2O molecules.

Q Why are copper and water pure substances, but brass is a mixture?

not consistent but can vary. For example, two sugar–water mixtures may look the same, but the one with the higher ratio of sugar to water would taste sweeter.

Physical processes can be used to separate mixtures because there are no chemical interactions between the components. For example, different coins, such as nickels, dimes, and quarters, can be separated by size; iron particles mixed with sand can be picked up with a magnet; and water is separated from cooked spaghetti by using a strainer (see Figure 3.3).

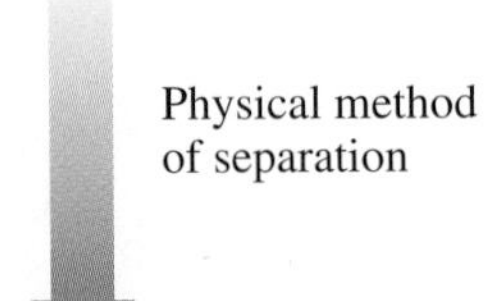

FIGURE 3.3 A mixture of spaghetti and water is separated using a strainer, a physical method of separation.

Q Why can physical methods be used to separate mixtures but not compounds?

CONCEPT CHECK 3.1 Pure Substances and Mixtures

Classify each of the following as a pure substance or a mixture:

a. sugar in a sugar bowl
b. nickels and dimes in a piggy bank
c. coffee with milk and sugar

ANSWER

a. Sugar is a compound with one type of matter, which makes it a pure substance.
b. The nickels and dimes in a piggy bank are physically mixed, but not chemically combined, which makes them a mixture.
c. The coffee, milk, and sugar are physically mixed but not chemically combined, which makes it a mixture.

Types of Mixtures

Mixtures are classified further. In a *homogeneous mixture*, also called a *solution*, the composition of the substances in the mixture is uniform. Examples of familiar homogeneous mixtures are air, which contains oxygen and nitrogen gases; and seawater, a solution of salt and water.

In a *heterogeneous mixture*, the components are visible and do not have a uniform composition throughout the sample. For example, a mixture of oil and water is heterogeneous because the oil floats on the surface of the water. Other examples of heterogeneous mixtures are a cookie with raisins and pulp in orange juice.

In the chemistry laboratory, mixtures are separated by various methods. Solids are separated from liquids by *filtration*, which involves pouring a mixture through a filter paper set in a funnel. In *chromatography*, different components of a liquid mixture separate as they move at different rates up the surface of a piece of paper.

(a)

(b)

(a) A mixture of a liquid and a solid is separated by filtration. **(b)** Different substances are separated as they travel at different rates up the surface of chromatography paper.

Chemistry Link to Health

BREATHING MIXTURES FOR SCUBA

The air we breathe is composed mostly of the gases oxygen (21%) and nitrogen (79%). The homogeneous breathing mixtures used by scuba divers differ from the air we breathe, depending on the depth of the dive. For example, a breathing mixture known as Nitrox contains more oxygen gas (up to 32%) and less nitrogen gas (68%) than air. A breathing mixture with less nitrogen gas decreases the risk of *nitrogen narcosis*, which causes mental confusion and is associated with breathing regular air while diving. Another breathing mixture, Heliox, contains oxygen and helium, which is typically used for diving to more than 200 ft. By replacing nitrogen with helium, nitrogen narcosis does not occur. However, at dive depths over 300 ft, helium is associated with severe shaking and body temperature drop.

A breathing mixture used for dives to over 400 ft is Trimix, which contains oxygen, helium, and some nitrogen. The addition of some nitrogen lessens the problem of shaking that comes with breathing high levels of helium. Heliox and Trimix are used only by professional, military, or highly trained divers.

A Nitrox mixture is used to fill scuba tanks.

SAMPLE PROBLEM 3.1 Classifying Mixtures

Classify each of the following as a pure substance (element or compound) or a mixture (homogeneous or heterogeneous):

a. copper in copper wire
b. a chocolate-chip cookie
c. Nitrox, a combination of oxygen and nitrogen used to fill scuba tanks

Oil and water do not form a mixture.

SOLUTION

a. Copper is an element, which is a pure substance.
b. A chocolate-chip cookie does not have a uniform composition, which makes it a heterogeneous mixture.
c. The gases oxygen and nitrogen have a uniform composition in Nitrox, which makes it a homogeneous mixture.

STUDY CHECK 3.1

A salad dressing is prepared with oil, vinegar, and chunks of blue cheese. Is this a homogeneous or heterogeneous mixture?

QUESTIONS AND PROBLEMS

3.1 Classification of Matter

LEARNING GOAL: *Classify examples of matter as pure substances or mixtures.*

3.1 Classify each of the following as a pure substance or a mixture:
a. baking soda ($NaHCO_3$)
b. a blueberry muffin
c. ice (H_2O)
d. zinc (Zn)
e. Trimix (oxygen, nitrogen, and helium) in a scuba tank

3.2 Classify each of the following as a pure substance or a mixture:
a. a soft drink
b. propane (C_3H_8)
c. a cheese sandwich
d. an iron (Fe) nail
e. salt substitute (KCl)

3.3 Classify each of the following pure substances as an element or a compound:
a. a silicon (Si) chip
b. hydrogen peroxide (H_2O_2)
c. oxygen (O_2)
d. rust (Fe_2O_3)
e. methane (CH_4) in natural gas

3.4 Classify each of the following pure substances as an element or a compound:
a. helium gas (He)
b. mercury (Hg) in a thermometer
c. sugar ($C_{12}H_{22}O_{11}$)
d. sulfur (S)
e. lye (NaOH)

3.5 Classify each of the following mixtures as homogeneous or heterogeneous:
a. vegetable soup
b. seawater
c. tea
d. tea with ice and lemon slices
e. fruit salad

3.6 Classify each of the following mixtures as homogeneous or heterogeneous:
a. nonfat milk
b. chocolate-chip ice cream
c. gasoline
d. peanut butter sandwich
e. cranberry juice

LEARNING GOAL

Identify the states and the physical and chemical properties of matter.

3.2 States and Properties of Matter

On Earth, matter exists in one of three **states of matter**: solids, liquids, and gases. A **solid**, such as a pebble or a baseball, has a definite shape and volume. You can probably recognize several solids within your reach right now, such as books, pencils, or a computer mouse. In a solid, strong attractive forces hold particles such as atoms or molecules close together. The particles in a solid are arranged in such a rigid pattern, their only movement is to vibrate slowly in their fixed positions. For many solids, their rigid structures form crystal such as that seen in amethyst.

Amethyst, a solid, is a purple form of quartz (SiO_2).

A **liquid** has a definite volume but not a definite shape. In a liquid, the particles move slowly in random directions but are sufficiently attracted to each other to maintain a definite volume, although not a rigid structure. Thus, when water, oil, or vinegar is poured from one container to another, the liquid maintains its own volume but takes the shape of the new container.

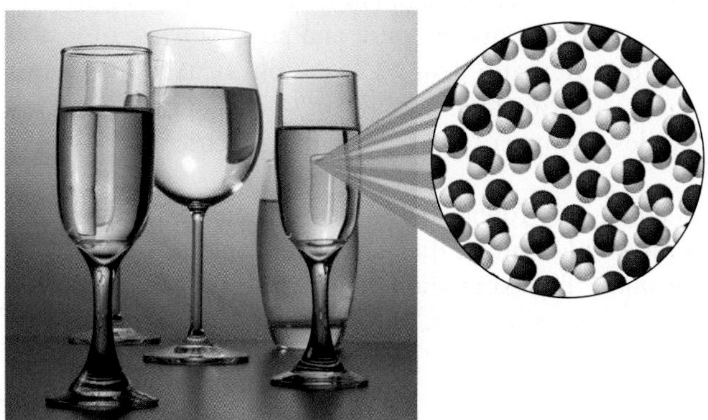
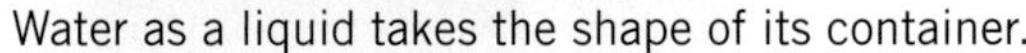

Water as a liquid takes the shape of its container.

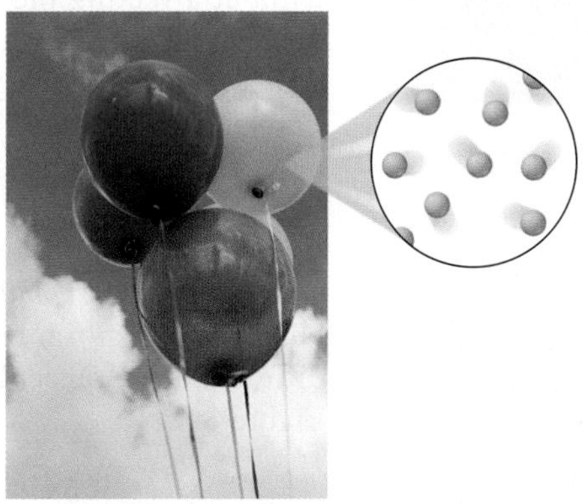

A gas takes the shape and volume of its container.

A **gas** does not have a definite shape or volume. In a gas, the particles are far apart, have little attraction to each other, and move at high speeds, taking the shape and volume of their container. When you inflate a bicycle tire, the air, which is a gas, fills the entire volume of the tire. The propane gas in a tank fills the entire volume of the tank. Table 3.1 compares the three states of matter.

TABLE 3.1 A Comparison of Solids, Liquids, and Gases

Characteristic	Solid	Liquid	Gas
Shape	Has a definite shape	Takes the shape of the container	Takes the shape of the container
Volume	Has a definite volume	Has a definite volume	Fills the volume of the container
Arrangement of particles	Fixed, very close	Random, close	Random, far apart
Interaction between particles	Very strong	Strong	Essentially none
Movement of particles	Very slow	Moderate	Very fast
Examples	Ice, salt, iron	Water, oil, vinegar	Water vapor, helium, air

CONCEPT CHECK 3.2 States of Matter

Identify the state(s) of matter described for a substance in each of the following:

a. no change in volume when placed in a different container
b. has an especially low density
c. shape depends on its container
d. has a definite shape and volume

ANSWER

a. Both a solid and a liquid have their own volume that does not depend on the volume of their container.
b. In a gas, the particles are far apart, which gives a small mass per volume, or a very low density.
c. Both a liquid and a gas take the shape of their containers.
d. A solid has a rigid arrangement of particles that gives it a definite shape and volume.

CORE CHEMISTRY SKILL 

Identifying Physical and Chemical Changes

Copper, used in cookware, is a good conductor of heat.

TABLE 3.2 Some Physical Properties of Copper

Color	Reddish orange
Odor	Odorless
Melting point	1083 °C
Boiling point	2567 °C
State at 25 °C	Solid
Luster	Shiny
Conduction of electricity	Excellent
Conduction of heat	Excellent

Physical Properties and Physical Changes

One way to describe matter is to observe its physical properties. If you were asked to describe yourself, you might list characteristics such as the color of your eyes and skin or the length, color, and texture of your hair.

Physical properties are those characteristics that can be observed or measured without affecting the identity of a substance. In chemistry, typical physical properties include the shape, color, melting point, boiling point, and physical state of a substance. For example, you might observe that a penny has the physical properties of a round shape, an orange-red color, a solid state, and a shiny luster. Table 3.2 gives more examples of physical properties of copper found in pennies, electrical wiring, and copper pans.

Water is a substance that is commonly found in all three states: solid, liquid, and gas. When matter undergoes a **physical change**, its state or its appearance changes, but its composition remains the same. The solid state of water—snow or ice—has a different appearance than its liquid or gaseous state, but all three states are water (see Figure 3.4).

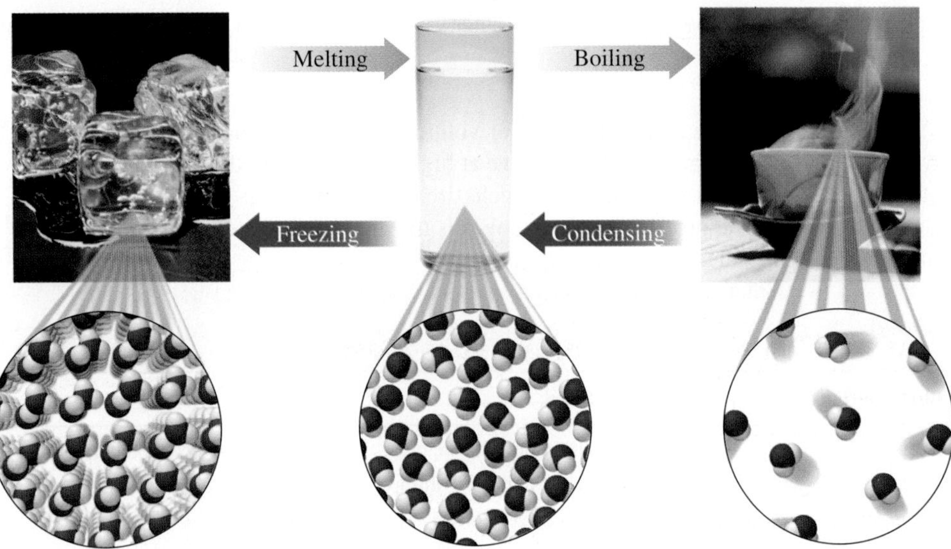

FIGURE 3.4 Water exists in an ice cube as a solid, water as a liquid, and water vapor as a gas.

Q In what state of matter does water have a definite volume but not a definite shape?

Salt crystals form as water evaporates from seawater.

In a physical change, a gold ingot is hammered to form gold leaf.

The physical appearance of a substance can change in other ways, too. Suppose that you dissolved some salt in water. In the solution, you would no longer see the salt but you could taste it. However, you could re-form the salt crystals by heating the mixture and evaporating the water. In a physical change, there are no new substances produced.

Table 3.3 gives more examples of physical changes.

TABLE 3.3 Examples of Some Physical Changes

Type of Physical Change	Example
Change of state	Boiling water
	Freezing of liquid water to solid water (ice)
Change of appearance	Dissolving sugar in water
Change of shape	Hammering a gold ingot into shiny gold leaf
	Drawing copper into thin copper wire
Change of size	Cutting paper into tiny pieces for confetti
	Grinding pepper into smaller particles

Chemical Properties and Chemical Changes

Chemical properties are those that describe the ability of a substance to change into a new substance. When a **chemical change** takes place, the original substance is converted into a new substance, which has different physical and chemical properties. For example, the rusting or corrosion of a metal such as iron is a chemical property. In the rain, an iron (Fe) nail reacts with oxygen (O_2) to form rust (Fe_2O_3). A chemical change has taken place: rust is a new substance with new physical and chemical properties. Table 3.4 gives examples of some chemical changes.

TABLE 3.4 Examples of Some Chemical Changes

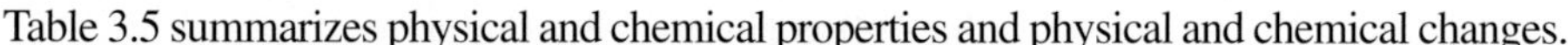

Type of Chemical Change	Change in Chemical Properties
Tarnishing silver	Shiny, silver metal reacts in air to produce a black, grainy coating.
Burning wood	A piece of pine burns with a bright flame, producing heat, ashes, carbon dioxide, and water vapor.
Caramelizing sugar	At high temperatures, white, granular sugar changes to a smooth, caramel-colored substance.
Forming rust	Iron, which is gray and shiny, combines with oxygen to form orange-red rust.

Flan has a topping of caramelized sugar.

Table 3.5 summarizes physical and chemical properties and physical and chemical changes.

TABLE 3.5 Summary of Physical and Chemical Properties and Changes

	Physical	Chemical
Property	A characteristic of a substance such as color, shape, odor, luster, size, melting point, and density.	A characteristic that indicates the ability of a substance to form another substance: paper can burn, iron can rust, silver can tarnish.
Change	A change in a physical property that retains the identity of the substance: a change of state, a change in size, or a change in shape.	A change in which the original substance is converted to one or more new substances: paper burns, iron rusts, silver tarnishes.

CONCEPT CHECK 3.3 Physical and Chemical Properties

Classify each of the following as a physical or chemical property:

a. Gasoline is a liquid at room temperature.
b. Gasoline burns in air.
c. Gasoline has a pungent odor.

ANSWER

a. A liquid is a state of matter, which makes it a physical property.
b. When gasoline burns, it changes to different substances with new properties, which is a chemical property.
c. The odor of gasoline is a physical property.

SAMPLE PROBLEM 3.2 Physical and Chemical Changes

Classify each of the following as a physical or chemical change:

a. An ice cube melts to form liquid water.
b. An enzyme breaks down the lactose in milk.
c. Garlic is chopped into small pieces.

SOLUTION

a. A physical change occurs when the ice cube changes state from solid to liquid.
b. A chemical change occurs when an enzyme breaks down lactose into simpler substances.
c. A physical change occurs when the size of an object changes.

STUDY CHECK 3.2

Which of the following are chemical changes?

a. Gas bubbles form when baking powder is placed in vinegar.
b. A log is chopped for firewood.
c. A log is burned in a fireplace.

QUESTIONS AND PROBLEMS

3.2 States and Properties of Matter

LEARNING GOAL: *Identify the states and the physical and chemical properties of matter.*

3.7 Indicate whether each of the following describes a gas, a liquid, or a solid:
a. This substance has no definite volume or shape.
b. The particles in a substance do not interact with each other.
c. The particles in a substance are held in a rigid structure.

3.8 Indicate whether each of the following describes a gas, a liquid, or a solid:
a. This substance has a definite volume but takes the shape of its container.
b. The particles in a substance are very far apart.
c. This substance occupies the entire volume of the container.

3.9 Describe each of the following properties as physical or chemical:
a. Chromium is a steel-gray solid.
b. Hydrogen reacts readily with oxygen.
c. Nitrogen freezes at −210 °C.
d. Milk will sour when left in a warm room.
e. Butane gas in an igniter burns in oxygen.

3.10 Describe each of the following properties as physical or chemical:
a. Neon is a colorless gas at room temperature.
b. Apple slices turn brown when they are exposed to air.
c. Phosphorus will ignite when exposed to air.
d. At room temperature, mercury is a liquid.
e. Propane gas is compressed to a liquid for placement in a small cylinder.

3.11 What type of change, physical or chemical, takes place in each of the following?
a. Water vapor condenses to form rain.
b. Cesium metal reacts explosively with water.
c. Gold melts at 1064 °C.
d. A puzzle is cut into 1000 pieces.
e. Cheese is grated on top of pasta.

3.12 What type of change, physical or chemical, takes place in each of the following?
a. Gold is hammered into thin sheets.
b. A silver pin tarnishes in the air.
c. A tree is cut into boards at a saw mill.
d. Food is digested.
e. A chocolate bar melts.

3.13 Describe each property of the element fluorine as physical or chemical.
a. is highly reactive
b. is a gas at room temperature
c. has a pale, yellow color
d. will explode in the presence of hydrogen
e. has a melting point of −220 °C

3.14 Describe each property of the element zirconium as physical or chemical.
a. melts at 1852 °C
b. is resistant to corrosion
c. has a grayish white color
d. ignites spontaneously in air when finely divided
e. is a shiny metal

LEARNING GOAL

Given a temperature, calculate a corresponding value on another temperature scale.

3.3 Temperature

Temperatures in science are measured and reported in *Celsius* (°*C*) units. On the Celsius scale, the reference points are the freezing point of water, defined as 0 °C, and the boiling point, 100 °C. In the United States, everyday temperatures are commonly reported in *Fahrenheit* (°*F*) units. On the Fahrenheit scale, pure water freezes at exactly 32 °F and boils at exactly 212 °F. A typical room temperature of 22 °C would be the same as 72 °F. Normal human body temperature is 37.0 °C, which is the same temperature as 98.6 °F.

On the Celsius and Fahrenheit temperature scales, the temperature difference between freezing and boiling is divided into smaller units called *degrees*. On the Celsius scale, there are 100 degrees Celsius between the freezing and boiling points of water. On the Fahrenheit scale, there are 180 degrees Fahrenheit between the freezing and boiling points of water. That makes a degree Celsius almost twice the size of a degree Fahrenheit: 1 °C = 1.8 °F (see Figure 3.5).

$$180 \text{ Fahrenheit degrees} = 100 \text{ Celsius degrees}$$

$$\frac{180 \text{ Fahrenheit degrees}}{100 \text{ Celsius degrees}} = \frac{1.8\,^\circ\text{F}}{1\,^\circ\text{C}}$$

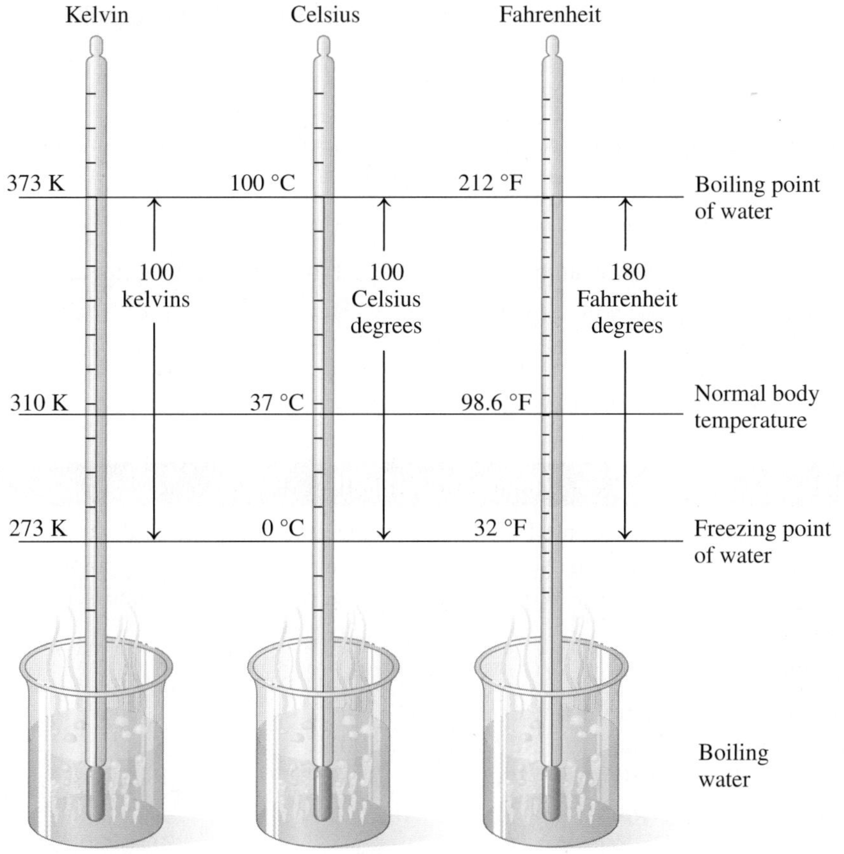

Kelvin Celsius Fahrenheit

373 K 100 °C 212 °F Boiling point of water

100 kelvins 100 Celsius degrees 180 Fahrenheit degrees

310 K 37 °C 98.6 °F Normal body temperature

273 K 0 °C 32 °F Freezing point of water

Boiling water

FIGURE 3.5 A comparison of the Fahrenheit, Celsius, and Kelvin temperature scales between the freezing and boiling points of water.

Q What is the difference in the freezing points of water on the Celsius and Fahrenheit temperature scales?

We can write a temperature equation that relates a Fahrenheit temperature and its corresponding Celsius temperature. In this equation, the Celsius temperature (T_C) is multiplied by 1.8 to change °C to °F. The Fahrenheit temperature (T_F) is obtained by adding 32, which adjusts the Celsius freezing point, 0 °C, to the Fahrenheit freezing point, 32 °F. The values, 1.8 and 32, used in the temperature equation are exact numbers and are not used to determine significant figures in the answer.

CORE CHEMISTRY SKILL 

Converting between Temperature Scales

$$T_F = \frac{1.8\ °F(T_C)}{1\ °C} + 32 \quad \text{or} \quad T_F = 1.8(T_C) + 32$$

Temperature equation to obtain degrees Fahrenheit

Changes °C to °F — Adjusts freezing point

To convert from Fahrenheit to Celsius, the temperature equation is rearranged to solve for T_C. First, we subtract 32 from both sides since we must apply the same operation to both sides of the equation.

$$T_F - 32 = 1.8(T_C) + \cancel{32} - \cancel{32}$$

$$T_F - 32 = 1.8(T_C)$$

Second, we solve the equation for T_C by dividing both sides by 1.8.

$$\frac{T_F - 32}{1.8} = \frac{\cancel{1.8}(T_C)}{\cancel{1.8}}$$

$$\frac{T_F - 32}{1.8} = T_C$$

Temperature equation to obtain degrees Celsius

Scientists have learned that the coldest temperature possible is −273 °C (more precisely −273.15 °C). On the *Kelvin* scale, this temperature, called *absolute zero*, has the value of 0 K. Temperature units on the Kelvin scale are called kelvins (K); *no degree symbol is used.* Because there is no lower temperature, the Kelvin scale has no negative temperature values. Between the freezing point of water, 273 K, and its boiling point, 373 K, there are 100 kelvins, which makes a kelvin equal to a Celsius degree.

$$1\text{ K} = 1\text{ °C}$$

We can write an equation that relates a Celsius temperature to its corresponding Kelvin temperature by adding 273 to the Celsius temperature.

$$T_K = T_C + 273$$ Temperature equation to obtain kelvins

To calculate a Celsius temperature, 273 is subtracted from the Kelvin temperature:

$$T_K - 273 = T_C + \cancel{273} - \cancel{273}$$
$$T_K - 273 = T_C$$
$$T_C = T_K - 273$$ Temperature equation to obtain degrees Celsius

CONCEPT CHECK 3.4 Temperature Scales

In 1730, before France adopted the Celsius scale, a temperature scale known as the Réaumur (°Ré) scale was in use that set the freezing point and boiling points of water at 0 degrees and 80 degrees. Write an equation that relates the Réaumur scale and the Celsius scale.

ANSWER

Freezing point: Réaumur 0 °Ré Celsius 0 °C
Boiling point: Réaumur 80 °Ré Celsius 100 °C
Degrees relationship: 80 °Ré = 100 °C or 8 °Ré/10 °C = 0.8 °Ré/1 °C

$$T_R = T_C \times \frac{0.8\text{ °Ré}}{1\text{ °C}} = 0.8\,T_C$$

No adjustment is needed for the freezing point because both temperature scales have a freezing point of water at 0°.

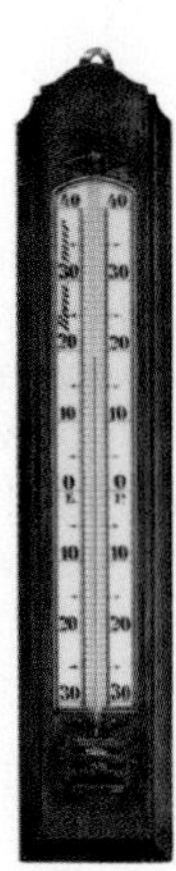

A Réaumur thermometer measures temperature in degrees Réaumur.

SAMPLE PROBLEM 3.3 Converting from Celsius to Fahrenheit

During the winter, the thermostat in a room is set at 21 °C. To what temperature, in Fahrenheit degrees, should you set the thermostat?

SOLUTION

Step 1 **State the given and needed quantities.**

Analyze the Problem	Given	Need
	21 °C	*T* in degrees Fahrenheit

Step 2 **Write a temperature equation.**

$$T_F = 1.8(T_C) + 32$$

Step 3 **Substitute in the known values and calculate the new temperature.** In the temperature equation, *the values of 1.8 and 32 are exact numbers.* The answer is reported using significant figure rules.

$$T_F = 1.8(21) + 32$$ 1.8 is exact; 32 is exact

$$T_F = 38 + 32$$
$$= 70.\text{°F}$$ Answer to the ones place

Guide to Calculating Temperature

1. State the given and needed quantities.
2. Write a temperature equation.
3. Substitute in the known values and calculate the new temperature.

STUDY CHECK 3.3

In the process of making ice cream, rock salt is added to chill the ice cream mixture. If the temperature drops to −11 °C, what is the temperature in degrees Fahrenheit?

SAMPLE PROBLEM 3.4 Converting from Fahrenheit to Celsius

In a type of cancer treatment called *thermotherapy*, temperatures as high as 113 °F are used to destroy cancer cells. What is that temperature in degrees Celsius?

SOLUTION

Step 1 State the given and needed quantities.

Analyze the Problem	Given	Need
	113 °F	*T* in degrees Celsius

Step 2 Write a temperature equation.

$$T_C = \frac{T_F - 32}{1.8}$$

Step 3 Substitute in the known values and calculate the new temperature.

$$T_C = \frac{(113 - 32)}{1.8} \quad \text{32 is exact; 1.8 is exact}$$

$$= \frac{81}{1.8} = 45\ °C \quad \text{Answer to the ones place}$$

STUDY CHECK 3.4

A child has a temperature of 103.6 °F. What is this temperature on a Celsius thermometer?

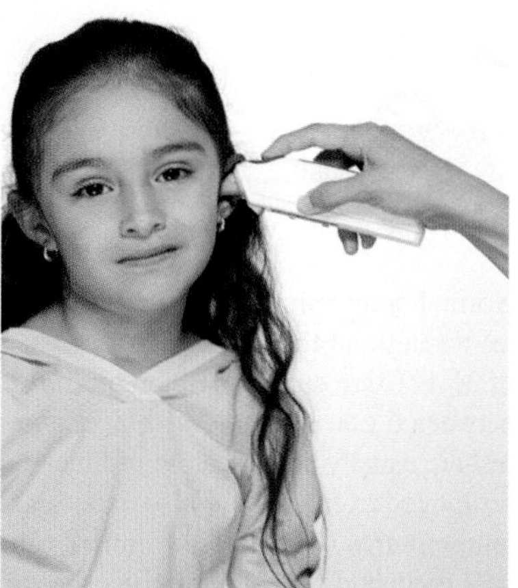

A digital ear thermometer is used to measure body temperature.

Table 3.6 gives a comparison of some temperatures on the three temperature scales.

TABLE 3.6 Comparison of Temperatures

Example	Fahrenheit (°F)	Celsius (°C)	Kelvin (K)
Sun	9937	5503	5776
A hot oven	450	232	505
A desert	120	49	322
A high fever	104	40	313
Room temperature	70	21	294
Water freezes	32	0	273
An Alaska winter	−66	−54	219
Helium boils	−452	−269	4
Absolute zero	−459	−273	0

SAMPLE PROBLEM 3.5 Converting from Celsius to Kelvin

A dermatologist may use cryogenic liquid nitrogen at −196 °C to remove skin lesions and some skin cancers. What is the temperature, in kelvins, of the liquid nitrogen?

SOLUTION

Step 1 State the given and needed quantities.

Analyze the Problem	Given	Need
	−196 °C	*T* in kelvins

Step 2 Write a temperature equation.

$$T_K = T_C + 273$$

Step 3 **Substitute in the known values and calculate the new temperature.**

$$T_K = -196 + 273$$
$$= 77\text{ K} \quad \text{Answer to the ones place}$$

STUDY CHECK 3.5

On the planet Mercury, the average night temperature is 13 K and the average day temperature is 683 K. What are these temperatures in degrees Celsius?

Chemistry Link to Health

VARIATION IN BODY TEMPERATURE

Normal body temperature is considered to be 37.0 °C, although it varies throughout the day and from person to person. Oral temperatures of 36.1 °C are common in the morning and climb to a high of 37.2 °C between 6 P.M. and 10 P.M. Temperatures above 37.2 °C for a person at rest are usually an indication of illness. Individuals who are involved in prolonged exercise may also experience elevated temperatures. Body temperatures of marathon runners can range from 39 °C to 41 °C as heat production during exercise exceeds the body's ability to lose heat.

Changes of more than 3.5 °C from the normal body temperature begin to interfere with bodily functions. Body temperatures above 41 °C, *hyperthermia*, can lead to convulsions, particularly in children, which may cause permanent brain damage. Heatstroke occurs above 41.1 °C. Sweat production stops, and the skin becomes hot and dry. The pulse rate is elevated, and respiration becomes weak and rapid. The person can become lethargic and lapse into a coma. Damage to internal organs is a major concern, and treatment, which must be immediate, may involve immersing the person in an ice-water bath.

At the low temperature extreme of *hypothermia*, body temperature can drop as low as 28.5 °C. The person may appear cold and pale and have an irregular heartbeat. Unconsciousness can occur if the body temperature drops below 26.7 °C. Respiration becomes slow and shallow, and oxygenation of the tissues decreases. Treatment involves providing oxygen and increasing blood volume with glucose and saline fluids. Injecting warm fluids (37.0 °C) into the peritoneal cavity may restore the internal temperature.

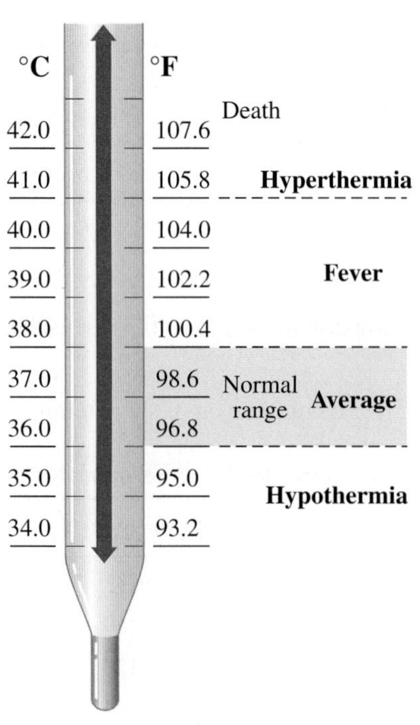

QUESTIONS AND PROBLEMS

3.3 Temperature

LEARNING GOAL: *Given a temperature, calculate a corresponding value on another temperature scale.*

3.15 Your friend who is visiting from Canada just took her temperature. When it reads 99.8, she becomes concerned that she is quite ill. How would you explain this temperature to your friend?

3.16 You have a friend who is using a recipe for flan from a Mexican cookbook. You notice that he set your oven temperature at 175 °F. What would you advise him to do?

3.17 Perform the following temperature conversions:
a. 37.0 °C = _____ °F
b. 65.3 °F = _____ °C
c. −27 °C = _____ K
d. 224 K = _____ °C
e. 15 °F = _____ °C

3.18 Perform the following temperature conversions:
a. 25 °C = _____ °F
b. 155 °C = _____ °F
c. −25 °F = _____ °C
d. 62 °C = _____ K
e. 145 °C = _____ K

3.19 **a.** A person with hyperthermia has a temperature of 106 °F. What does this read on a Celsius thermometer?
b. Because high fevers can cause convulsions in children, the doctor wants to be called if a child's temperature goes over 40.0 °C. Should the doctor be called if a child has a temperature of 103 °F?

3.20 **a.** Water is heated to 145 °F. What is the temperature of the hot water in degrees Celsius?
b. During extreme hypothermia, a boy's temperature dropped to 20.6 °C. What was his temperature in degrees Fahrenheit?

3.4 Energy

LEARNING GOAL

Identify energy as potential or kinetic; convert between units of energy.

When you are running, walking, dancing, or thinking, you are using energy to do **work**, any activity that requires energy. In fact, **energy** is defined as the ability to do work. Suppose you are climbing a steep hill and you become too tired to go on. At that moment, you do not have sufficient energy to do any more work. Now suppose you sit down and have lunch. In a while, you will have obtained energy from the food, and you will be able to do more work and complete the climb.

Kinetic and Potential Energy

Energy can be classified as kinetic or potential energy. **Kinetic energy** is the energy of motion. Any object that is moving has kinetic energy. **Potential energy** is determined by the position of an object or by the chemical composition of a substance. A boulder resting on top of a mountain has potential energy because of its location. If the boulder rolls down the mountain, the potential energy becomes kinetic energy. Water in a reservoir behind a dam has potential energy. When the water goes over the dam and falls to the stream below, its potential energy is converted to kinetic energy. Foods and fossil fuels have potential energy in their molecules. When you digest food or burn gasoline in your car, potential energy is converted to kinetic energy to do work.

Water at the top of the dam stores potential energy. When the water flows over the dam, potential energy is converted to kinetic energy.

CONCEPT CHECK 3.5 Potential and Kinetic Energy

Identify each of the following as an example of potential or kinetic energy:

a. gasoline **b.** skating **c.** candy bar

ANSWER

a. Gasoline is burned to provide energy and heat; it contains potential energy in its molecules.

b. A skater uses energy to move; skating is kinetic energy (energy of motion).

c. A candy bar has potential energy. When digested, its components provide energy for the body to do work.

Heat and Units of Energy

Heat is associated with the motion of particles. A frozen pizza feels cold because heat flows from your hand into the pizza. The faster the particles move, the greater the heat or thermal energy of the substance. In the frozen pizza, the particles are moving very slowly. As heat is added and the pizza becomes warmer, the motions of the particles in the pizza increase. Eventually, the particles have enough energy to make the pizza hot and ready to eat.

Units of Energy

The SI unit of energy and work is the **joule (J)** (pronounced "jewel"). The joule is a small amount of energy, so scientists often use the kilojoule (kJ), 1000 joules. When you heat water for one cup of tea, you use about 75 000 J or 75 kJ of heat. Table 3.7 shows a comparison of energy in joules for several energy sources.

TABLE 3.7 A Comparison of Energy for Various Resources

Energy in Joules

Energy in Joules	Resource
10^{27}	
	Energy radiated by Sun per second (10^{26})
10^{24}	
	World reserves of fossil fuel (10^{23})
10^{21}	
	Energy consumption for one year in US (10^{20})
10^{18}	
	Solar energy reaching the Earth per second (10^{17})
10^{15}	
10^{12}	
	Energy use per person in one year in US (10^{11})
10^{9}	
	Energy from one gallon of gasoline (10^{8})
10^{6}	Energy from one serving of pasta, a doughnut, or needed to bicycle one hour (10^{6})
10^{3}	Energy used to sleep one hour (10^{5})
10^{0}	

CORE CHEMISTRY SKILL

Using Energy Units

You may be more familiar with the unit **calorie (cal)**, from the Latin *caloric*, meaning "heat." The calorie was originally defined as the amount of energy (heat) needed to raise the temperature of 1 g of water by 1 °C. Now one calorie is defined as exactly 4.184 J. This equality can also be written as a conversion factor:

$$1 \text{ cal} = 4.184 \text{ J (exact)} \qquad \frac{4.184 \text{ J}}{1 \text{ cal}} \text{ and } \frac{1 \text{ cal}}{4.184 \text{ J}}$$

One *kilocalorie* (kcal) is equal to 1000 calories, and one *kilojoule* (kJ) is 1000 joules.

$$1 \text{ kcal} = 1000 \text{ cal}$$
$$1 \text{ kJ} = 1000 \text{ J}$$

SAMPLE PROBLEM 3.6 Energy Units

When 1.0 g of diesel fuel burns in a diesel car engine, 48 000 J are released. What is this energy in calories?

SOLUTION

Step 1 State the given and needed quantities.

Analyze the Problem	Given	Need
	48 000 J	calories

Step 2 Write a plan to convert the given unit to the needed unit.

joules → Energy factor → calories

Step 3 State the equalities and conversion factors.

$$1 \text{ cal} = 4.184 \text{ J}$$
$$\frac{1 \text{ cal}}{4.184 \text{ J}} \text{ and } \frac{4.184 \text{ J}}{1 \text{ cal}}$$

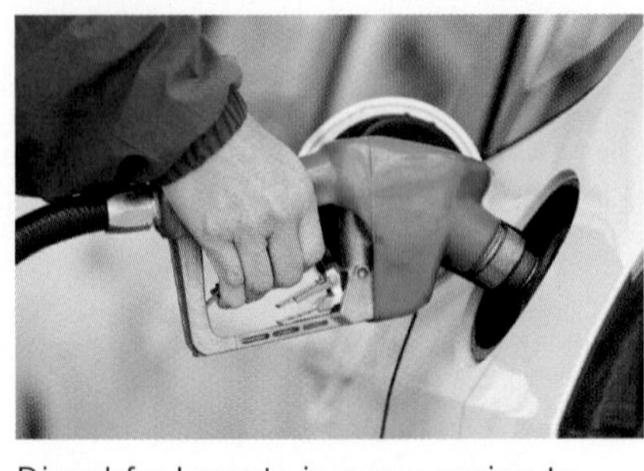

Diesel fuel reacts in a car engine to produce energy.

Step 4 **Set up the problem to calculate the needed quantity.**

$$\underset{\text{Two SFs}}{48\,000\,\cancel{J}} \times \underset{\text{Exact}}{\overset{\text{Exact}}{\frac{1\text{ cal}}{4.184\,\cancel{J}}}} = \underset{\text{Two SFs}}{11\,000\ (1.1 \times 10^4)\text{ cal}}$$

STUDY CHECK 3.6

The burning of 1.0 g of coal produces 8.4 kcal. How many kilojoules are produced?

QUESTIONS AND PROBLEMS

3.4 Energy

LEARNING GOAL: *Identify energy as potential or kinetic; convert between units of energy.*

3.21 Discuss the changes in the potential and kinetic energy of a roller-coaster ride as the roller coaster climbs to the top and goes down the other side.

3.22 Discuss the changes in the potential and kinetic energy of a ski jumper taking the elevator to the top of the jump and going down the ramp.

3.23 Indicate whether each of the following statements describes potential or kinetic energy:
a. water at the top of a waterfall
b. kicking a ball
c. the energy in a lump of coal
d. a skier at the top of a hill

3.24 Indicate whether each of the following statements describes potential or kinetic energy:
a. the energy in your food
b. a tightly wound spring
c. an earthquake
d. a car speeding down the freeway

3.25 The energy needed to keep a 75-watt lightbulb burning for 1.0 h is 270 kJ. Calculate the energy required to keep the lightbulb burning for 3.0 h in each of the following energy units:
a. joules **b.** kilocalories

3.26 A person uses 750 kcal on a long hike. Calculate the energy used for the hike in each of the following energy units:
a. joules **b.** kilojoules

3.27 Convert each of the following energy units:
a. 3500 cal to kcal **b.** 415 J to cal
c. 28 cal to J **d.** 4.5 kJ to cal

3.28 Convert each of the following energy units:
a. 8.1 kcal to cal **b.** 325 J to kJ
c. 2550 cal to kJ **d.** 2.50 kcal to J

3.5 Specific Heat

LEARNING GOAL

Use specific heat to calculate heat loss or gain, temperature change, or mass of a sample.

Every substance has its own characteristic ability to absorb heat. When you bake a potato, you place it in a hot oven. If you are cooking pasta, you add the pasta to boiling water. You already know that adding heat to water increases its temperature until it boils. Certain substances absorb more heat than others to reach a certain temperature.

CORE CHEMISTRY SKILL 

Calculating Specific Heat

The energy requirements for different substances are described in terms of a physical property called *specific heat*. The **specific heat (*SH*)** for a substance is defined as the amount of heat (q), in joules (or calories), needed to change the temperature of exactly 1 g of a substance by exactly 1 °C. To calculate the specific heat of a substance, we measure the heat (q) in joules (J), the mass (m) in grams, and the temperature change, which is written as ΔT. The symbol delta (Δ) means "change in." For example, the specific heat for water is 4.184 J/g °C.

$$SH = \frac{q}{m \times \Delta T} = \frac{\text{J}}{\text{g °C}} \qquad SH \text{ of } H_2O(l) = \frac{4.184\text{ J}}{\text{g °C}}$$

Symbol	Meaning	Unit
SH	specific heat	$\frac{\text{J}}{\text{g °C}}$
q	heat	joules (J)
m	mass	grams (g)
ΔT	change in temperature	degrees Celsius (°C)

If we look at Table 3.8, we see that 1 g of water requires 4.184 J to increase its temperature by 1 °C. Water has a large specific heat that is about five times the specific heat of aluminum. Aluminum has a specific heat that is about twice that of copper. Therefore, 4.184 J will increase the temperature of 1 g of water by 1 °C, whereas the same amount of heat (4.184 J) will increase the temperature of 1 g of aluminum by about 5 °C and 1 g of copper by about 10 °C. The low specific heats of aluminum and copper mean they transfer heat efficiently, which makes them useful in cookware.

TABLE 3.8 Specific Heats of Some Substances

	Substance	Specific Heat (J/g °C)
Elements	Aluminum, Al(*s*)	0.897
	Copper, Cu(*s*)	0.385
	Gold, Au(*s*)	0.129
	Iron, Fe(*s*)	0.452
	Silver, Ag(*s*)	0.235
	Titanium, Ti(*s*)	0.523
Compounds	Ammonia, $NH_3(g)$	2.04
	Ethanol, $C_2H_5OH(l)$	2.46
	Sodium chloride, NaCl(*s*)	0.864
	Water, $H_2O(l)$	4.184
	Water, $H_2O(s)$	2.03

The high specific heat of water keeps temperatures more moderate in summer and winter.

The high specific heat of liquid water has a major impact on the temperatures in a coastal city compared to an inland city. A large mass of water near a coastal city can absorb or release five times the energy absorbed or released by the same mass of rock near an inland city. This means that in the summer a body of water absorbs large quantities of heat, which cools a coastal city, and then in the winter that same body of water releases large quantities of heat, which provides warmer temperatures. A similar effect happens with our bodies, which contain 70% by mass water. Water in the body absorbs or releases large quantities of heat in order to maintain an almost constant body temperature.

CONCEPT CHECK 3.6 Specific Heat

Samples of aluminum, gold, and iron, each with a mass of 10.0 g, absorb the same amount of heat. If the three samples have the same initial temperature, which one will attain the highest final temperature? Explain.

ANSWER

Because gold has the lowest specific heat of the three metals, the absorption of the same amount of heat will cause a larger increase in the temperature of gold than for aluminum or iron.

SAMPLE PROBLEM 3.7 Calculating Specific Heat

What is the specific heat, in J/g °C, of lead if 57.0 J raises the temperature of 35.6 g of lead by 12.5 °C?

SOLUTION

Step 1 State the given and needed quantities.

	Given	Need
Analyze the Problem	$q = 57.0$ J $m = 35.6$ g of lead $\Delta T = 12.5$ °C	*SH* of lead (J/g °C)

Step 2 **Write the relationship for specific heat.** The specific heat (SH) is calculated by dividing the heat (q) by the mass (m) and by the temperature change (ΔT).

$$SH = \frac{\text{heat}}{\text{mass} \quad \Delta T} = \frac{q}{m \quad \Delta T}$$

Step 3 **Set up the problem to calculate the specific heat.**

$$SH = \frac{\overset{\text{Three SFs}}{57.0 \text{ J}}}{\underset{\text{Three SFs}}{35.6 \text{ g}} \quad \underset{\text{Three SFs}}{12.5 \text{ °C}}} = \frac{0.128 \text{ J}}{\text{g °C}} \quad \text{Three SFs}$$

STUDY CHECK 3.7

What is the specific heat, in J/g °C, of sodium if 123 J is needed to raise the temperature of 4.00 g of sodium by 25.0 °C?

Guide to Calculating Specific Heat

1. State the given and needed quantities.
2. Write the relationship for specific heat.
3. Set up the problem to calculate the specific heat.

Heat Equation from Specific Heat

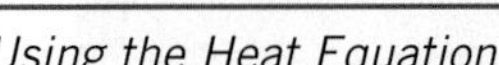

CORE CHEMISTRY SKILL

Using the Heat Equation

It is often helpful to know the quantity of heat (q) absorbed or lost by a substance. The *heat equation* is derived from the specific heat relationship, when we multiply both sides by m and ΔT.

$$SH = \frac{q}{m \times \Delta T}$$

$$m \times \Delta T \times SH = \frac{q}{\cancel{m} \times \cancel{\Delta T}} \times \cancel{m} \times \cancel{\Delta T}$$

Now we can write the heat equation as

$$q = m \times \Delta T \times SH$$

The heat lost or gained, in joules, is obtained when the units of grams and °C in the numerator cancel grams and °C in the denominator of specific heat in the heat equation.

$$\text{J} = \cancel{\text{g}} \times \cancel{\text{°C}} \times \frac{\text{J}}{\cancel{\text{g}} \, \cancel{\text{°C}}}$$

SAMPLE PROBLEM 3.8 Calculating Heat with Temperature Increase

How many joules are absorbed by 45.2 g of aluminum (Al) if its temperature rises from 12.5 °C to 76.8 °C (see Table 3.8)?

SOLUTION

Step 1 **State the given and needed quantities.**

	Given	Need
Analyze the Problem	45.2 g of aluminum SH for aluminum = 0.897 J/g °C $T_{initial}$ = 12.5 °C; T_{final} = 76.8 °C	joules (J) absorbed by aluminum

Step 2 **Calculate the temperature change (ΔT).**

$$\Delta T = 76.8 \text{ °C} - 12.5 \text{ °C} = 64.3 \text{ °C}$$

Step 3 **Write the heat equation.**

$$q = m \times \Delta T \times SH$$

Guide to Calculations Using Specific Heat

1. State the given and needed quantities.
2. Calculate the temperature change (ΔT).
3. Write the heat equation.
4. Substitute in the given values and solve, making sure units cancel.

The copper on a pan conducts heat rapidly to the food in the pan.

Step 4 **Substitute in the given values and solve, making sure units cancel.**

$$q = \underset{\text{Three SFs}}{45.2\,\cancel{g}} \times \underset{\text{Three SFs}}{64.3\,\cancel{^\circ C}} \times \overset{\text{Three SFs}}{\frac{0.897\text{ J}}{\cancel{g}\,\cancel{^\circ C}}} = \underset{\text{Three SFs}}{2.61 \times 10^3\text{ J}}$$

STUDY CHECK 3.8

Some cooking pans have a layer of copper on the bottom. How many kilojoules are needed to raise the temperature of 125 g of copper from 22 °C to 325 °C (see Table 3.8)?

SAMPLE PROBLEM 3.9 Calculating Heat Loss

A 225-g sample of hot tea cools from 74.6 °C to 22.4 °C. How much heat, in kilojoules, is lost, assuming that tea has the same specific heat as water?

SOLUTION

Step 1 **State the given and needed quantities.**

	Given	Need
Analyze the Problem	225 g of tea *SH* for tea (water) = 4.184 J/g °C $T_{initial}$ = 74.6 °C; T_{final} = 22.4 °C	*q* in kilojoules

Equality/Conversion Factors

$$1\text{ kJ} = 1000\text{ J}$$

$$\frac{1000\text{ J}}{1\text{ kJ}} \text{ and } \frac{1\text{ kJ}}{1000\text{ J}}$$

Step 2 **Calculate the temperature change.**

$$\Delta T = 74.6\text{ °C} - 22.4\text{ °C} = 52.2\text{ °C}$$

Step 3 **Write the heat equation.**

$$q = m \times \Delta T \times SH$$

Step 4 **Substitute the given values and solve, making sure units cancel.**

$$q = \underset{\text{Three SFs}}{225\,\cancel{g}} \times \underset{\text{Three SFs}}{52.2\,\cancel{^\circ C}} \times \overset{\text{Four SFs}}{\underset{\text{Three SFs}}{\frac{4.184\,\cancel{J}}{\cancel{g}\,\cancel{^\circ C}}}} \times \overset{\text{Exact}}{\underset{\text{Exact}}{\frac{1\text{ kJ}}{1000\,\cancel{J}}}} = 49.1\text{ kJ} \quad \text{Three SFs}$$

Hot tea cools by losing heat energy.

STUDY CHECK 3.9

How much heat, in joules, is lost when 15.5 g of gold cools from 215 °C to 35 °C (see Table 3.8)?

CONCEPT CHECK 3.7 Solving the Heat Equation for Mass

Solve the following heat equation for mass:

$$q = m \times \Delta T \times SH$$

ANSWER

To solve for mass, we divide both sides of the equation by ΔT and *SH*.

$$\frac{q}{\Delta T \times SH} = \frac{m \times \cancel{\Delta T} \times \cancel{SH}}{\cancel{\Delta T} \times \cancel{SH}}$$

$$m = \frac{q}{\Delta T \times SH}$$

SAMPLE PROBLEM 3.10 Using the Heat Equation

When 655 J is added to a sample of ethanol, its temperature rises from 18.2 °C to 32.8 °C. What is the mass, in grams, of the ethanol sample (see Table 3.8)?

SOLUTION

Step 1 **State the given and needed quantities.**

	Given	Need
Analyze the Problem	$q = 655$ J $T_{initial} = 18.2$ °C; $T_{final} = 32.8$ °C *SH* for ethanol = 2.46 J/g °C	*m* of ethanol in grams

Step 2 **Calculate the temperature change.**

$$\Delta T = 32.8\ °C - 18.2\ °C = 14.6\ °C$$

Step 3 **Write the heat equation.**

$$q = m \times \Delta T \times SH$$

As shown in Concept Check 3.7, the heat equation is solved for mass (m) when the heat is divided by the temperature change and the specific heat.

$$m = \frac{q}{\Delta T \ SH}$$

Step 4 **Substitute in the given values and solve, making sure units cancel.**

$$m = \frac{\overset{\text{Three SFs}}{655\ \cancel{J}}}{\underset{\text{Three SFs}}{14.6\ \cancel{°C}}\ \underset{\text{Three SFs}}{\dfrac{2.46\ \cancel{J}}{g\ \cancel{°C}}}}$$

$$m = 18.2\ g \quad \text{Three SFs}$$

STUDY CHECK 3.10

When 8.81 kJ is absorbed by a piece of iron, its temperature rises from 15 °C to 122 °C. What is its mass, in grams (see Table 3.8)?

Chemistry Link to the Environment

CARBON DIOXIDE AND GLOBAL WARMING

Earth's climate is a product of interactions between sunlight, the atmosphere, and the oceans. The Sun provides us with energy in the form of solar radiation. Some of this radiation is reflected back into space. The rest is absorbed by the clouds, atmospheric gases including carbon dioxide, and Earth's surface. For millions of years, concentrations of carbon dioxide (CO_2) have fluctuated. However, in the past 100 years, the amount of carbon dioxide (CO_2) gas in our atmosphere has increased significantly. From the years 1000 to 1800, the atmospheric carbon dioxide averaged 280 ppm. But since the beginning of the Industrial Revolution in 1800, the level of atmospheric carbon dioxide has risen from about 280 ppm to about 390 ppm in 2011, a 40% increase.

As the atmospheric CO_2 levels increase, more solar radiation is trapped, which raises the temperature at Earth's surface. Some scientists have estimated that if the carbon dioxide level doubles from its level before the Industrial Revolution, the average temperature globally could increase by 2.0 °C to 4.4 °C. Although this seems to be a small temperature change, it could have dramatic impact worldwide. Even now, glaciers and snow cover in much of the world have diminished. Ice sheets in Antarctica and Greenland are melting rapidly and breaking apart. Although no one knows for sure how rapidly the ice in the polar regions is melting, this accelerating change will contribute to a rise in sea level. In the twentieth century, the sea level rose 15 to 23 cm, and some scientists predict the sea level will rise 1 m in this century. Such an increase will have a major impact on coastal areas.

Until recently, the carbon dioxide level was maintained as algae in the oceans, and trees in the forests utilized the carbon dioxide.

However, the ability of these and other forms of plant life to absorb carbon dioxide is not keeping up with the increase in carbon dioxide. Most scientists agree that the primary source of the increase of carbon dioxide is the burning of fossil fuels such as gasoline, coal, and natural gas. The cutting and burning of trees in the rain forests (deforestation) also reduces the amount of carbon dioxide removed from the atmosphere.

Worldwide efforts are being made to reduce the carbon dioxide produced by burning fossil fuels that heat our homes, run our cars, and provide energy for industries. Scientists are exploring ways to provide alternative energy sources and to reduce the effects of deforestation. Meanwhile, we can reduce energy use in our homes by using appliances that are more energy efficient, such as replacing incandescent light bulbs with fluorescent lights. Such an effort worldwide will reduce the possible impact of global warming and at the same time save our fuel resources.

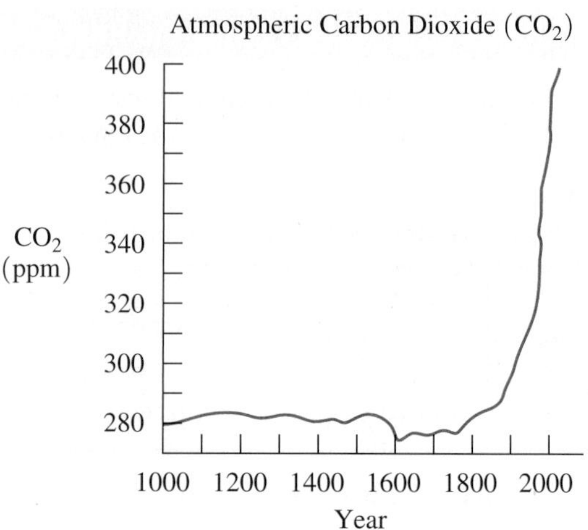

Atmospheric carbon dioxide levels are shown for the years from 1000 C.E. to 2010 C.E.

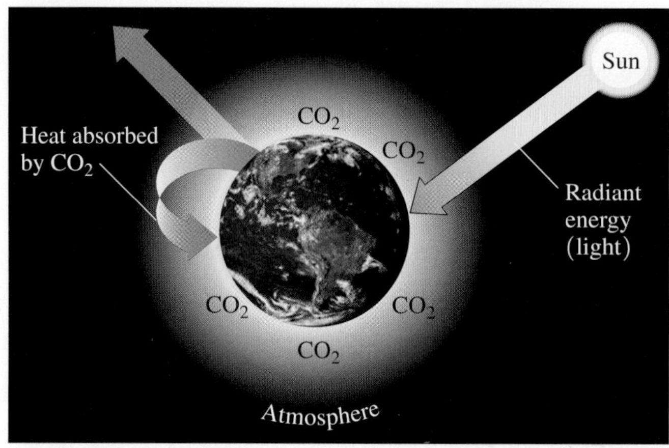

Heat from the Sun is trapped by the CO_2 layer in the atmosphere.

QUESTIONS AND PROBLEMS

3.5 Specific Heat

LEARNING GOAL: *Use specific heat to calculate heat loss or gain, temperature change, or mass of a sample.*

3.29 If the same amount of heat is supplied to samples of 10.0 g each of aluminum, iron, and copper all at 15.0 °C, which sample would reach the highest temperature (see Table 3.8)?

3.30 Substances A and B are the same mass and at the same initial temperature. When the same amount of heat is added to each, the final temperature of A is 75 °C and B is 35 °C. What does this tell you about the specific heats of A and B?

3.31 Calculate the specific heat (J/g °C) for each of the following:

a. a 13.5-g sample of zinc (Zn) heated from 24.2 °C to 83.6 °C that absorbs 312 J of heat

b. a 48.2-g sample of a metal that absorbs 345 J with a temperature increase from 35.0 °C to 57.9 °C

3.32 Calculate the specific heat (J/g °C) for each of the following:

a. an 18.5-g sample of tin (Sn) that absorbs 183 J of heat when its temperature increases from 35.0 °C to 78.6 °C

b. a 22.5-g sample of a metal that absorbs 645 J when its temperature increases from 36.2 °C to 92.0 °C

3.33 Use the heat equation to calculate the energy, in joules, for each of the following (see Table 3.8):

a. required to heat 25.0 g of water, H_2O, from 12.5 °C to 25.7 °C

b. required to heat 38.0 g of copper (Cu) from 122 °C to 246 °C

3.34 Use the heat equation to calculate the energy, in joules, for each of the following (see Table 3.8):

a. required to heat 5.25 g of water, H_2O, from 5.5 °C to 64.8 °C

b. required to heat 10.0 g of silver (Ag) from 112 °C to 275 °C

3.35 Use the heat equation to calculate the energy, in joules, for each of the following (see Table 3.8):
a. lost when 15.0 g of ethanol, C_2H_5OH, cools from 60.5 °C to −42.0 °C
b. lost when 125 g of iron (Fe) cools from 118 °C to 55 °C

3.36 Use the heat equation to calculate the energy, in joules, for each of the following (see Table 3.8):
a. lost when 75.0 g of water, H_2O, cools from 86.4 °C to 2.1 °C
b. lost when 18.0 g of gold (Au) cools from 224 °C to 118 °C

3.37 Calculate the mass, in grams, for each of the following using Table 3.8:
a. a sample of gold (Au) that absorbs 225 J to increase its temperature from 15.0 °C to 47.0 °C
b. a sample of iron (Fe) that loses 8.40 kJ when its temperature decreases from 168.0 °C to 82.0 °C

3.38 Calculate the mass, in grams, for each of the following using Table 3.8:
a. a sample of water, H_2O, that absorbs 8250 J when its temperature increases from 18.4 °C to 92.6 °C
b. a sample of silver (Ag) that loses 3.22 kJ when its temperature decreases from 145 °C to 24 °C

3.39 Calculate the mass, in grams, for each of the following using Table 3.8:
a. a sample of aluminum (Al) that absorbs 8.80 kJ when heated from 12.5 °C to 26.8 °C
b. a sample of titanium (Ti) that loses 14 200 J when it cools from 185 °C to 42 °C

3.40 Calculate the mass, in grams, for each of the following using Table 3.8:
a. a sample of aluminum (Al) that absorbs 1650 J when its temperature increases from 65 °C to 187 °C
b. an iron (Fe) bar that loses 2.52 kJ when its temperature decreases from 252 °C to 75 °C

3.41 Calculate the change in temperature (ΔT) for each of the following using Table 3.8:
a. 20.0 g of iron (Fe) that absorbs 1580 J
b. 150.0 g of water, H_2O, that absorbs 7.10 kJ

3.42 Calculate the change in temperature (ΔT) for each of the following using Table 3.8:
a. 115 g of copper (Cu) that loses 2.45 kJ
b. 22.0 g of silver (Ag) that loses 625 J

3.43 Calculate the change in temperature (ΔT) for each of the following using Table 3.8:
a. 85.0 g of gold (Au) that absorbs 7680 J
b. 50.0 g of copper (Cu) that absorbs 6.75 kJ

3.44 Calculate the change in temperature (ΔT) for each of the following using Table 3.8:
a. 0.650 kg of water, H_2O, that loses 5.48 kJ
b. 35.0 g of silver (Ag) that loses 472 J

3.6 Energy and Nutrition

LEARNING GOAL

Use the energy values to calculate the kilojoules (kJ) or kilocalories (kcal) in a food.

The food we eat provides energy to do work in the body, which includes the growth and repair of cells. Carbohydrates are the primary fuel for the body, but if carbohydrate reserves are exhausted, fats and then proteins are used for energy.

For many years in the field of nutrition, the energy from food was measured as Calories or kilocalories. The nutritional unit *Calorie*, *Cal* (with an uppercase C), is the same as 1000 cal, or 1 kcal. The international unit, kilojoule (kJ), is becoming more prevalent. A typical diet of 2100 Cal (kcal) is the same as an 8800 kJ diet.

$$1 \text{ Cal} = 1 \text{ kcal} = 1000 \text{ cal}$$

$$1 \text{ Cal} = 4.184 \text{ kJ} = 4184 \text{ J}$$

Energy Values for Foods

In the nutrition laboratory, foods are burned in a *calorimeter* to determine their *energy value* (kJ/g or kcal/g). A sample of food is placed in a steel container called a calorimeter filled with oxygen with a measured amount of water that fills the surrounding chamber. The food sample is ignited, releasing heat that increases the temperature of the water. From the mass of the food and water as well as the temperature increase, the energy value for the food is calculated. We will assume that the energy absorbed by the calorimeter is negligible.

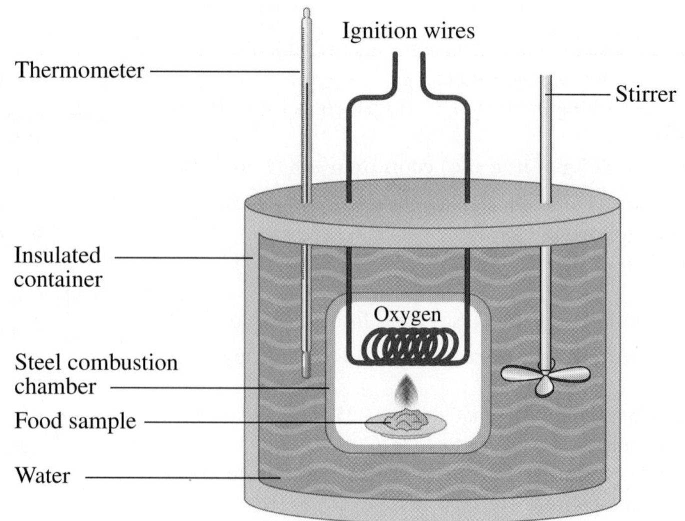

Heat released from burning a food sample in a calorimeter is used to determine the energy value of the food.

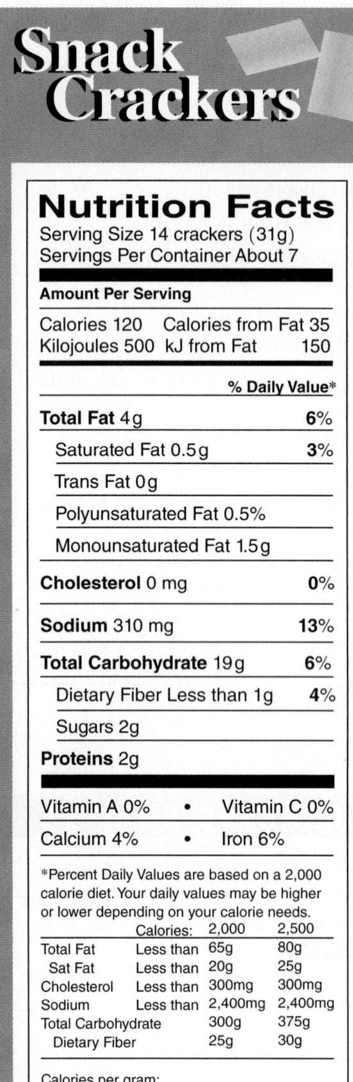

On the labels of packaged foods, the nutrition facts include the total Calories and kilojoules, and the grams of carbohydrate, fat, and protein per serving.

CONCEPT CHECK 3.8 Energy Values for Food

When 5.5 g of pasta is burned in a calorimeter, 22 Cal of heat is released.

a. What is the energy value for pasta, in kcal/g?

b. If this nutrition laboratory were in Italy, what is the energy value in kJ/g for the pasta?

ANSWER

Using the equality of 1 Cal = 1 kcal, we can calculate the energy values, in kcal/g and kJ/g for the pasta.

a. $$\frac{22\ \cancel{\text{Cal}}}{5.5\ \text{g}} \times \frac{1\ \text{kcal}}{1\ \cancel{\text{Cal}}} = 4.0\ \text{kcal/g}$$

b. $$\frac{22\ \cancel{\text{Cal}}}{5.5\ \text{g}} \times \frac{4.184\ \text{kJ}}{1\ \cancel{\text{Cal}}} = 17\ \text{kJ/g}$$

The **energy values** for foods, in kJ/g and kcal/g, have been determined for each food type: carbohydrate, fat, and protein (see Table 3.9).

TABLE 3.9 Energy Values for the Three Food Types

Food Type	kJ/g	kcal/g
Carbohydrate	17	4
Fat	38	9
Protein	17	4

We can use the energy values in Table 3.9 to calculate the energy from a food type when its mass is known, and the total energy of a food when the mass of each food type is known.

$$\text{kilojoules} = \cancel{\text{g}} \times \frac{\text{kJ}}{\cancel{\text{g}}} \qquad \text{kilocalories} = \cancel{\text{g}} \times \frac{\text{kcal}}{\cancel{\text{g}}}$$

The general composition and energy of some foods are given in Table 3.10.

TABLE 3.10 General Composition and Energy of Some Foods

Food	Carbohydrate (g)	Fat (g)	Protein (g)	Energy*
Banana, 1 medium	26	0	1	460 kJ (110 kcal)
Beef, ground, 3 oz	0	14	22	910 kJ (220 kcal)
Carrots, raw, 1 cup	11	0	1	200 kJ (50 kcal)
Chicken, no skin, 3 oz	0	3	20	460 kJ (110 kcal)
Egg, 1 large	0	6	6	330 kJ (80 kcal)
Milk, 4% fat, 1 cup	12	9	9	700 kJ (170 kcal)
Milk, nonfat, 1 cup	12	0	9	360 kJ (90 kcal)
Potato, baked	23	0	3	440 kJ (100 kcal)
Salmon, 3 oz	0	5	16	460 kJ (110 kcal)
Steak, 3 oz	0	27	19	1350 kJ (320 kcal)

*Energy values are rounded off to the tens place.

SAMPLE PROBLEM 3.11 Energy from a Food

At a fast-food restaurant, a hamburger contains 37 g of carbohydrate, 19 g of fat, and 23 g of protein. What is the energy from each food type and the total energy, in kilocalories, for the hamburger? Round off the kilocalories for each food type to the tens place.

SOLUTION

Step 1 State the given and needed quantities.

Analyze the Problem	Given	Need
	carbohydrate, 37 g fat, 19 g protein, 23 g	kilocalories for each food type, total number of kilocalories

Step 2 Use the energy value for each food type and calculate the kJ or kcal rounded off to the tens place. Using the energy values for carbohydrate, fat, and protein (see Table 3.9), we can calculate the energy for each type of food.

Food Type	Mass	Energy Value	Energy
Carbohydrate	$37\ \cancel{g}$	$\times \dfrac{4\text{ kcal}}{1\ \cancel{g}} =$	150 kcal
Fat	$19\ \cancel{g}$	$\times \dfrac{9\text{ kcal}}{1\ \cancel{g}} =$	170 kcal
Protein	$23\ \cancel{g}$	$\times \dfrac{4\text{ kcal}}{1\ \cancel{g}} =$	90 kcal

Step 3 Add the energy for each food type to give the total energy from the food.

$$\text{Total energy} = 150\text{ kcal} + 170\text{ kcal} + 90\text{ kcal} = 410\text{ kcal}$$

STUDY CHECK 3.11

Suppose your breakfast consisted of a 1-oz (28 g) serving of oat-bran hot cereal with half a cup of whole milk. The breakfast contains 22 g of carbohydrate, 7 g of fat, and 10 g of protein.

a. What is the energy, in kilojoules, from each food type? Round off the kilojoules for each food type to the tens place.
b. What is the total energy, in kilojoules, from your breakfast?

Guide to Calculating the Energy from a Food

1. State the given and needed quantities.
2. Use the energy value for each food type and calculate the kJ or kcal rounded off to the tens place.
3. Add the energy for each food type to give the total energy from the food.

Chemistry Link to Health

LOSING AND GAINING WEIGHT

The number of kilojoules or kilocalories needed in the daily diet of an adult depends on gender, age, and level of physical activity. Some typical levels of energy needs are given in Table 3.11.

A person gains weight when food intake exceeds energy output. The amount of food a person eats is regulated by the hunger center in the hypothalamus, which is located in the brain. Food intake is normally proportional to the nutrient stores in the body. If these nutrient stores are low, you feel hungry; if they are high, you do not feel like eating.

A person loses weight when food intake is less than energy output. Many diet products contain cellulose, which has no nutritive value but provides bulk and makes you feel full. Some diet drugs depress the hunger center and must be used with caution, because they excite the nervous system and elevate blood pressure. Because muscular exercise is an important way to expend energy, an increase in daily exercise aids weight loss. Table 3.12 lists some activities and the amount of energy they require.

TABLE 3.11 Typical Energy Requirements for Adults

Gender	Age	Moderately Active kJ (kcal)	Highly Active kJ (kcal)
Female	19–30	8800 (2100)	10 000 (2400)
	31–50	8400 (2000)	9200 (2200)
Male	19–30	11 300 (2700)	12 600 (3000)
	31–50	10 500 (2500)	12 100 (2900)

TABLE 3.12 Energy Expended by a 70.0-kg (154-lb) Adult

Activity	Energy (kJ/h)	Energy (kcal/h)
Sleeping	250	60
Sitting	420	100
Walking	840	200
Swimming	2100	500
Running	3100	750

One hour of swimming requires 2100 kJ of energy.

QUESTIONS AND PROBLEMS

3.6 Energy and Nutrition

LEARNING GOAL: *Use the energy values to calculate the kilojoules (kJ) or kilocalories (kcal) in a food.*

3.45 Using the following data, determine the kilojoules for each food burned in a calorimeter:
- **a.** one stalk of celery that heats 505 g of water from 25.2 °C to 35.7 °C
- **b.** a waffle that heats 4980 g of water from 20.6 °C to 62.4 °C

3.46 Using the following data, determine the kilojoules for each food burned in a calorimeter:
- **a.** one cup of popcorn that changes the temperature of 1250 g of water from 25.5 °C to 50.8 °C
- **b.** a sample of butter that produces energy to increase the temperature of 357 g of water from 22.7 °C to 38.8 °C

3.47 Using the energy values for food (see Table 3.9), determine each of the following (round off the answers in kilojoules or kilocalories to the tens place):
- **a.** the total kilojoules and kilocalories for 1 cup of orange juice that contains 26 g of carbohydrate, 2 g of protein, and no fat
- **b.** the grams of carbohydrate in one apple if the apple has no fat and no protein and provides 72 kcal of energy

3.48 Using the energy values for food (see Table 3.9), determine each of the following (round off the answers in kilojoules or kilocalories to the tens place):
- **a.** the total kilojoules and kilocalories in 2 tablespoons of crunchy peanut butter that contains 6 g of carbohydrate, 16 g of fat, and 7 g of protein
- **b.** the grams of protein in 1 cup of soup that provides 110 kcal with 9 g of carbohydrate and 7 g of fat

3.49 Using the energy values for food (see Table 3.9), determine the total kilojoules and kilocalories from each of the following (round off the answers in kilojoules or kilocalories to the tens place):
- **a.** 1 tablespoon of vegetable oil, which contains 14 g of fat and no carbohydrate or protein
- **b.** a diet that consists of 68 g of carbohydrate, 9 g of fat, and 150 g of protein

3.50 Using the energy values for food (see Table 3.9), determine the total kilojoules and kilocalories from each of the following (round off the answers in kilojoules or kilocalories to the tens place):
- **a.** one can of cola if it has 40. g of carbohydrate and no fat or protein
- **b.** one cup of clam chowder that contains 16 g of carbohydrate, 12 g of fat, and 9 g of protein

CHAPTER REVIEW

3.1 Classification of Matter

LEARNING GOAL: *Classify examples of matter as pure substances or mixtures.*

- Matter is anything that has mass and occupies space.
- Matter is classified as pure substances or mixtures.
- Pure substances, which are elements or compounds, have fixed compositions, and mixtures have variable compositions.
- The substances in mixtures can be separated using physical methods.

3.2 States and Properties of Matter

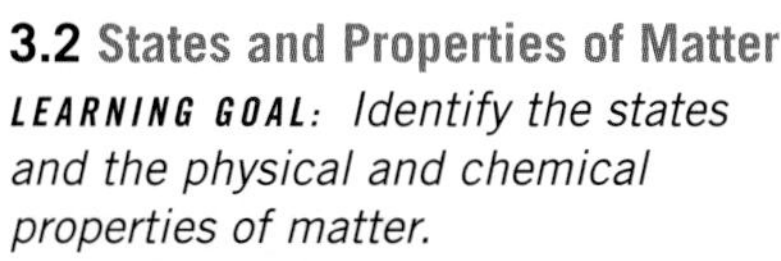

LEARNING GOAL: *Identify the states and the physical and chemical properties of matter.*

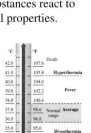

- The three states of matter are solid, liquid, and gas.
- A physical property is a characteristic of a substance in which the identity of the substance does not change.
- A physical change occurs when physical properties change, but not the composition of the substance.
- A chemical property indicates the ability of a substance to change into another substance.
- A chemical change occurs when one or more substances react to form a substance with new physical and chemical properties.

3.3 Temperature

LEARNING GOAL: *Given a temperature, calculate a corresponding value on another temperature scale.*

- In science, temperature is measured in degrees Celsius (°C) or kelvins (K).
- On the Celsius scale, there are 100 units between the freezing point of water (0 °C) and the boiling point (100 °C).
- On the Fahrenheit scale, there are 180 units between the freezing point of water (32 °F) and the boiling point (212 °F).
- A Fahrenheit temperature is related to its Celsius temperature by the equation $T_F = 1.8T_C + 32$.
- The SI unit, kelvin, is related to the Celsius temperature by the equation $T_K = T_C + 273$.

3.4 Energy

LEARNING GOAL: *Identify energy as potential or kinetic; convert between units of energy.*

- Energy is the ability to do work.
- Potential energy is stored energy; kinetic energy is the energy of motion.
- Common units of energy are the calorie (cal), kilocalorie (kcal), joule (J), and kilojoule (kJ).

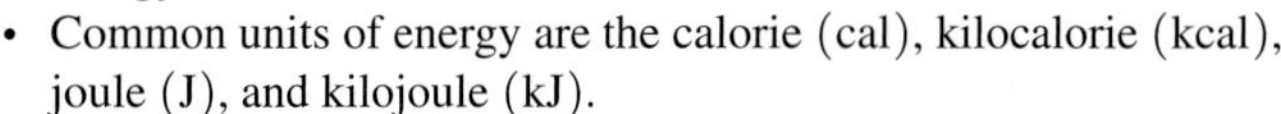

- One calorie is equal to 4.184 J.

3.5 Specific Heat

LEARNING GOAL: *Use specific heat to calculate heat loss or gain, temperature change, or mass of a sample.*

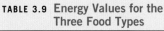

- Specific heat is the amount of energy required to raise the temperature of exactly 1 g of a substance by exactly 1 °C.
- The heat lost or gained by a substance is determined by multiplying its mass, the temperature change, and its specific heat.

3.6 Energy and Nutrition

LEARNING GOAL: *Use the energy values to calculate the kilojoules (kJ) or kilocalories (kcal) in a food.*

TABLE 3.9 Energy Values for the Three Food Types

Food Type	kJ/g	kcal/g
Carbohydrate	17	4
Fat	38	9
Protein	17	4

- The nutritional Calorie is the same amount of energy as 1 kcal or 1000 calories.
- The energy of a food is the sum of kilojoules or kilocalories from carbohydrate, fat, and protein.

CONCEPT MAP

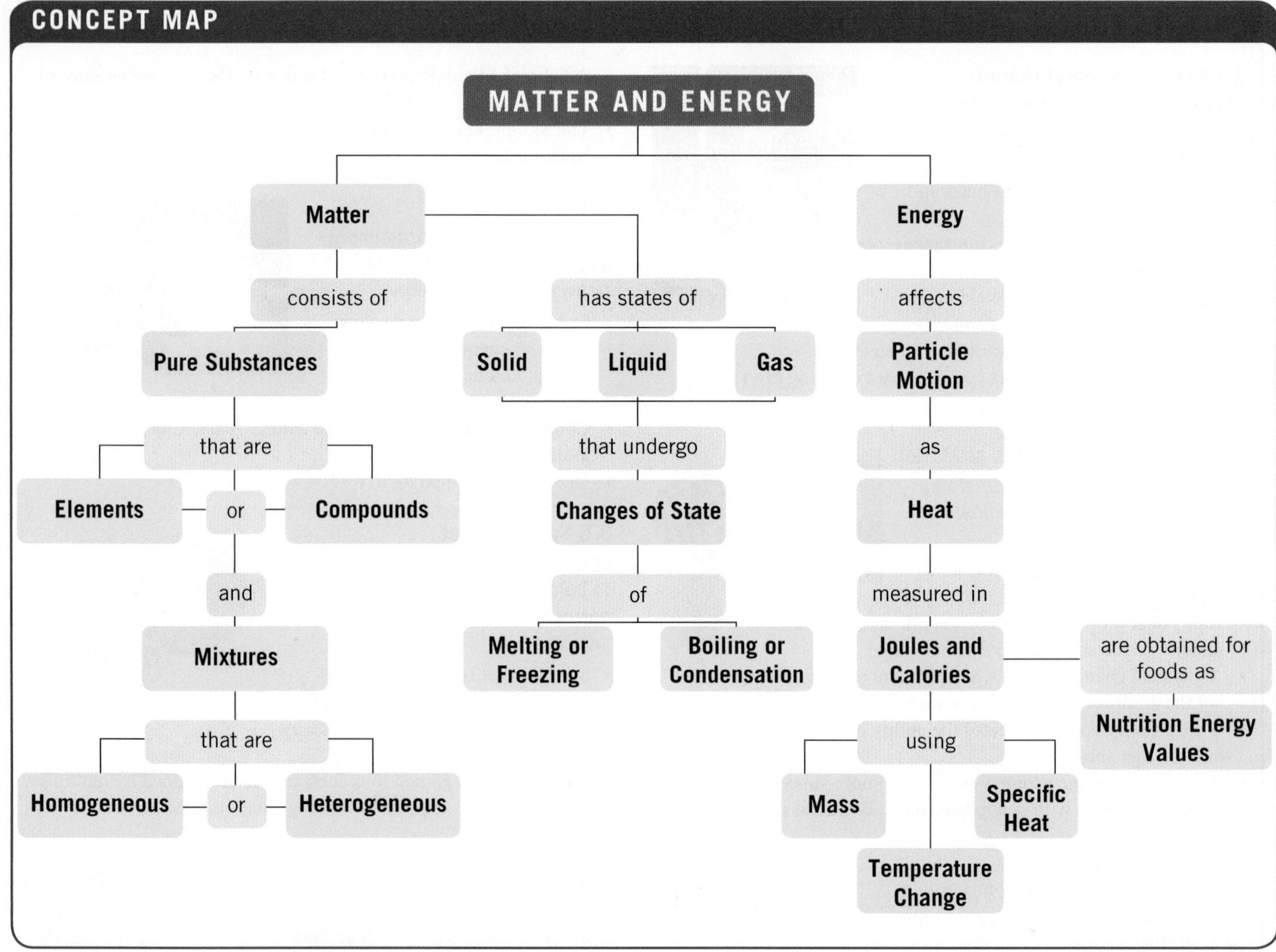

KEY TERMS

calorie (cal) The amount of heat energy that raises the temperature of exactly 1 g of water by exactly 1 °C; 1 calorie = 4.184 J.

chemical change A change during which the original substance is converted into a new substance that has a different composition and new chemical and physical properties.

chemical properties The properties that indicate the ability of a substance to change into a new substance.

compound A pure substance consisting of two or more elements, with a definite composition, that can be broken down into simpler substances only by chemical methods.

element A pure substance containing only one type of matter, which cannot be broken down by chemical methods.

energy The ability to do work.

energy value The kilocalories obtained per gram of the three food types: carbohydrate, fat, and protein.

gas A state of matter that does not have a definite shape or volume.

heat The energy associated with the motion of particles that flows from a hotter to a colder object.

joule (J) The SI unit of heat energy; 4.184 J = 1 cal.

kinetic energy A type of energy that is required for actively doing work; energy of motion.

liquid A state of matter that takes the shape of the container but has a definite volume.

matter The material that makes up a substance and has mass and occupies space.

mixture The physical combination of two or more substances that does not change the identities of the mixed substances.

physical change A change in which the physical properties of a substance change without any change in its identity.

physical properties The properties that can be observed or measured without affecting the identity of a substance.

potential energy A type of energy related to position or composition of a substance.

pure substance A type of matter composed of elements and compounds that has a definite composition.

solid A state of matter that has its own shape and volume.

specific heat (*SH*) A quantity of heat that changes the temperature of exactly 1 g of a substance by exactly 1 °C.

states of matter Three forms of matter: solid, liquid, and gas.

work An activity that requires energy.

CORE CHEMISTRY SKILLS

The chapter containing each Core Chemistry Skill is shown in parentheses at the end of each heading.

Classifying Matter (3.1)

- A pure substance is matter that has a fixed or constant composition.
- An element, the simplest type of a pure substance, is composed of only one type of matter, such as silver, iron, or aluminum.
- A compound is also a pure substance, but it consists of two or more elements chemically combined in the same proportion.
- In a *homogeneous mixture*, also called a *solution*, the composition of the substances in the mixture is uniform.
- In a *heterogeneous mixture*, the components are visible and do not have a uniform composition throughout the sample.

Example: Classify each of the following as a pure substance (element or compound) or a mixture (homogeneous or heterogeneous):

a. iron in a nail
b. black coffee
c. carbon dioxide, a greenhouse gas

Answer: **a.** Iron is a pure substance, which is an element.
b. Black coffee contains different substances with uniform composition, which makes it a homogeneous mixture.
c. The gas carbon dioxide, which is a pure substance that contains two elements, is a compound.

Identifying Physical and Chemical Changes (3.2)

- When matter undergoes a physical change, its state or its appearance changes, but its composition remains the same.
- When a chemical change takes place, the original substance is converted into a new substance, which has different physical and chemical properties.

Example: Classify each of the following as a physical or chemical property:

a. Helium in a balloon is a gas.
b. Methane, in natural gas, burns.
c. Hydrogen sulfide smells like rotten eggs.

Answer: **a.** A gas is a state of matter, which makes it a physical property.
b. When methane burns, it changes to different substances with new properties, which is a chemical property.
c. The odor of hydrogen sulfide is a physical property.

Converting between Temperature Scales (3.3)

- The temperature equation $T_F = 1.8T_C + 32$ is used to convert from Celsius to Fahrenheit and can be rearranged to convert from Fahrenheit to Celsius.
- The temperature equation $T_K = T_C + 273$ is used to convert from Celsius to Kelvin and can be rearranged to convert from Kelvin to Celsius.

Example: Convert 75.0 °C to degrees Fahrenheit.

Answer: $T_F = 1.8T_C + 32$

$T_F = 1.8(75.0) + 32 = 135 + 32$

$= 167\ °\text{F}$

Example: Convert 355 K to degrees Celsius.

Answer: $T_K = T_C + 273$

To solve the equation for T_C, subtract 273 from both sides.

$T_K - 273 = T_C + \cancel{273} - \cancel{273}$

$T_C = T_K - 273$

$T_C = 355 - 273$

$= 82\ °\text{C}$

Using Energy Units (3.4)

- Equalities for energy units include 1 cal = 4.184 J, 1 kcal = 1000 cal, and 1 kJ = 1000 J.
- Each equality for energy units can be written as two conversion factors:

$$\frac{4.184\ \text{J}}{1\ \text{cal}} \text{ and } \frac{1\ \text{cal}}{4.184\ \text{J}};\quad \frac{1000\ \text{cal}}{1\ \text{kcal}} \text{ and } \frac{1\ \text{kcal}}{1000\ \text{cal}};\quad \frac{1000\ \text{J}}{1\ \text{kJ}} \text{ and } \frac{1\ \text{kJ}}{1000\ \text{J}}$$

- The energy unit conversion factors are used to cancel given units of energy and to obtain the needed unit of energy.

Example: Convert 45 000 J to kilocalories.

Answer: Using the conversion factors above, we start with the given 45 000 J and convert it to kilocalories.

$$45\ 000\ \cancel{\text{J}} \times \frac{1\ \cancel{\text{cal}}}{4.184\ \cancel{\text{J}}} \times \frac{1\ \text{kcal}}{1000\ \cancel{\text{cal}}} = 11\ \text{kcal}$$

Calculating Specific Heat (3.5)

- Specific heat (SH) is the amount of heat (q) that raises the temperature of 1 g of a substance by 1°C.

$$SH = \frac{q}{m \times \Delta T} = \frac{\text{J}}{\text{g °C}}$$

- To calculate specific heat, the heat lost or gained is divided by the mass of the substance and the change in temperature (ΔT).

Example: Calculate the specific heat, in J/g °C, for a 4.0-g sample of tin that absorbs 66 J when heated from 125 °C to 197 °C.

Answer: $q = 66\ \text{J} \quad m = 4.0\ \text{g} \quad \Delta T = 197\ °\text{C} - 125\ °\text{C} = 72\ °\text{C}$

$$SH = \frac{q}{m \times \Delta T} = \frac{66\ \text{J}}{4.0\ \text{g} \times 72\ °\text{C}} = \frac{0.23\ \text{J}}{\text{g °C}}$$

Using the Heat Equation (3.5)

- The quantity of heat (q) absorbed or lost by a substance is calculated using the heat equation.

  $q = m \times \Delta T \times SH$

- Heat, in joules, is obtained when the specific heat of a substance in J/g °C is used.
- To cancel, the unit grams is used for mass, and the unit °C is used for temperature change.

Example: How many joules are required to heat 5.25 g of titanium from 85.5 °C to 132.5 °C?

Answer: $m = 5.25$ g, $\Delta T = 132.5\ °\text{C} - 85.5\ °\text{C} = 47.0\ °\text{C}$

SH for titanium = 0.523 J/g °C

The known values are substituted into the heat equation making sure units cancel.

$$q = m \times \Delta T \times SH = 5.25\ \cancel{\text{g}} \times 47.0\ \cancel{°\text{C}} \times \frac{0.523\ \text{J}}{\cancel{\text{g}}\ \cancel{°\text{C}}} = 129\ \text{J}$$

UNDERSTANDING THE CONCEPTS

The chapter sections to review are shown in parentheses at the end of each question.

3.51 Identify each of the following as an element, compound, or mixture: (3.1)

a.

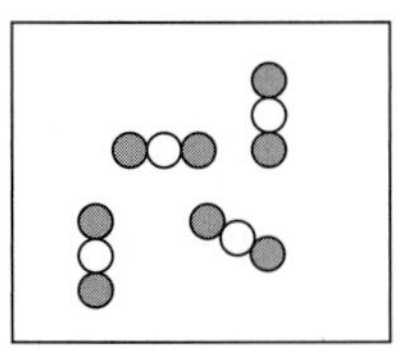

b.

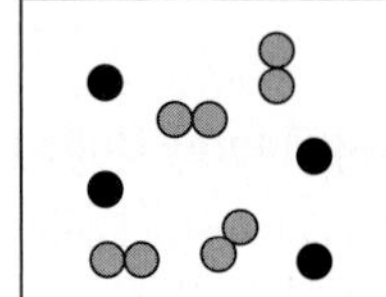

c.

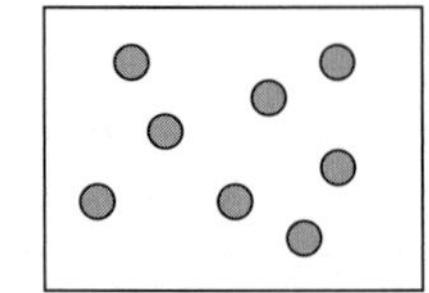

3.52 Which diagram illustrates a homogeneous mixture? Explain your choice. Which diagrams illustrate heterogeneous mixtures? Explain your choice. (3.1)

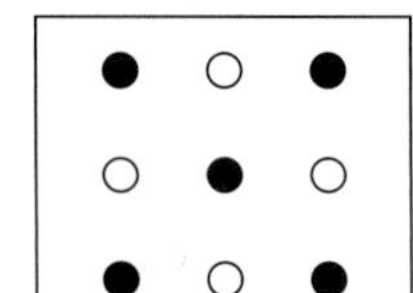

a.

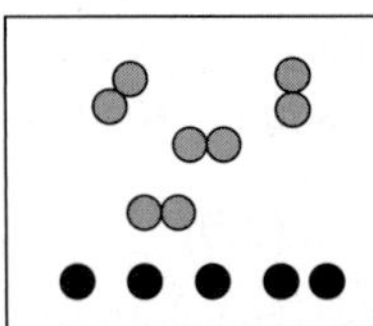

b.

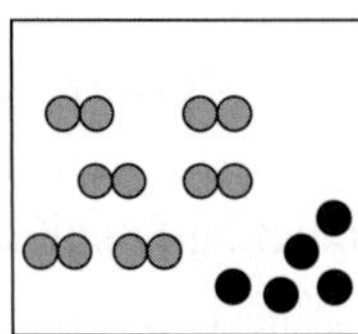

c.

3.53 Classify each of the following as a homogeneous mixture or heterogeneous mixture: (3.1)

a. lemon-flavored water **b.** stuffed mushrooms
c. eye drops

3.54 Classify each of the following as a homogeneous mixture or heterogeneous mixture: (3.1)

a. ketchup **b.** tortilla soup **c.** hard-boiled egg

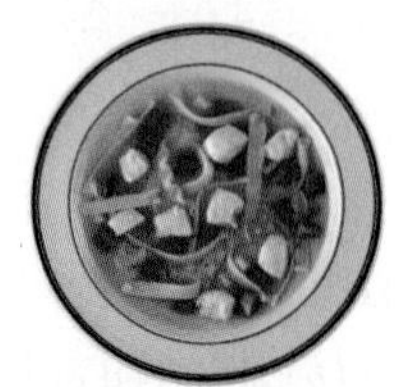

3.55 Compost can be made at home from grass clippings, some kitchen scraps, and dry leaves. As microbes break down organic matter, heat is generated and the compost can reach a temperature of 155 °F, which kills most pathogens. What is this temperature in Celsius degrees? (3.3)

Compost produced from decayed plant material is used to enrich the soil.

3.56 After a week, biochemical reactions in compost slow, and the temperature drops to 45 °C. The dark brown organic-rich mixture is ready for use in the garden. What is this temperature in Fahrenheit degrees? In kelvins? (3.3)

3.57 Calculate the energy to heat two cubes (gold and aluminum) each with a volume of 10.0 cm^3 from 15 °C to 25 °C. Refer to Tables 2.9 and 3.8. (3.5)

3.58 Calculate the energy to heat two cubes (silver and copper), each with a volume of 10.0 cm^3 from 15 °C to 25 °C. Refer to Tables 2.9 and 3.8. (3.5)

3.59 A 70.0-kg person had a quarter-pound cheeseburger, french fries, and a chocolate shake. (3.6)

Item	Carbohydrate (g)	Fat (g)	Protein (g)
Cheeseburger	46	40.	47
French fries	47	16	4
Chocolate shake	76	10.	10.

a. Using Table 3.9, calculate the total kilocalories for each food type in this meal (round off the kilocalories to the tens place).

b. Determine the total kilocalories for the meal (round off to the tens place).

c. Using Table 3.12, determine the number of hours of sleeping needed to burn off the kilocalories in this meal.

d. Using Table 3.12, determine the number of hours of running needed to burn off the kilocalories in this meal.

3.60 For lunch, your friend, who has a mass of 70.0 kg, has a slice of pizza, a cola soft drink, and ice cream. (3.6)

Item	Carbohydrate (g)	Fat (g)	Protein (g)
Pizza	29	10.	13
Cola	51	0	0
Ice cream	44	28	8

a. Using Table 3.9, calculate the total kilocalories for each food type in this meal (round off the kilocalories to the tens place).
b. Determine the total kilocalories for the meal (round off to the tens place).
c. Using Table 3.12, determine the number of hours of sitting needed to burn off the kilocalories in this meal.
d. Using Table 3.12, determine the number of hours of swimming needed to burn off the kilocalories in this meal.

ADDITIONAL QUESTIONS AND PROBLEMS

3.61 Classify each of the following as an element, a compound, or a mixture: (3.1)
a. carbon in pencils
b. carbon dioxide (CO_2) we exhale
c. orange juice

3.62 Classify each of the following as an element, a compound, or a mixture: (3.1)
a. neon gas in lights
b. a salad dressing of oil and vinegar
c. sodium hypochlorite (NaOCl) in bleach

3.63 Classify each of the following mixtures as homogeneous or heterogeneous: (3.1)
a. hot fudge sundae **b.** herbal tea
c. vegetable oil

3.64 Classify each of the following mixtures as homogeneous or heterogeneous: (3.1)
a. water and sand **b.** mustard
c. blue ink

3.65 Identify each of the following as solid, liquid, or gas: (3.2)
a. vitamin tablets in a bottle **b.** helium in a balloon
c. milk in a bottle **d.** the air you breathe
e. charcoal briquettes on a barbecue

3.66 Identify each of the following as solid, liquid, or gas: (3.2)
a. popcorn in a bag **b.** water in a garden hose
c. a computer mouse **d.** air in a tire
e. hot tea in a teacup

3.67 Identify each of the following as a physical or chemical property: (3.2)
a. Gold is shiny.
b. Gold melts at 1064 °C.
c. Gold is a good conductor of electricity.
d. When gold reacts with yellow sulfur, a black sulfide compound forms.

3.68 Identify each of the following as a physical or chemical property: (3.2)
a. A candle is 10 in. high and 2 in. in diameter.
b. A candle burns.
c. The wax of a candle softens on a hot day.
d. A candle is blue.

3.69 Identify each of the following as a physical or chemical change: (3.2)
a. A plant grows a new leaf.
b. Chocolate is melted for a dessert.
c. Wood is chopped for the fireplace.
d. Wood burns in a woodstove.

3.70 Identify each of the following as a physical or chemical change: (3.2)
a. Short hair grows until it is long.
b. Carrots are grated for use in a salad.
c. Malt undergoes fermentation to make beer.
d. A copper pipe reacts with air and turns green.

3.71 Calculate each of the following temperatures in degrees Celsius and kelvins: (3.3)
a. The highest recorded temperature in the continental United States was 134 °F in Death Valley, California, on July 10, 1913.
b. The lowest recorded temperature in the continental United States was −69.7 °F in Rodgers Pass, Montana, on January 20, 1954.

3.72 Calculate each of the following temperatures in kelvins and degrees Fahrenheit: (3.3)
a. The highest recorded temperature in the world was 58.0 °C in El Azizia, Libya, on September 13, 1922.
b. The lowest recorded temperature in the world was −89.2 °C in Vostok, Antarctica, on July 21, 1983.

3.73 What is −15 °F in degrees Celsius and in kelvins? (3.3)

3.74 The highest recorded body temperature that a person has survived is 46.5 °C. Calculate that temperature in degrees Fahrenheit and in kelvins. (3.3)

3.75 If you want to lose 1 lb of "body fat," which is 15% water, how many kilocalories do you need to expend? (3.6)

3.76 Calculate the Cal (kcal) in 1 cup of whole milk that contains 12 g of carbohydrate, 9 g of fat, and 9 g of protein. (3.6)

On a sunny day, the sand gets hot but the water stays cool.

3.77 On a hot day, the beach sand gets hot but the water stays cool. Would you predict that the specific heat of sand is higher or lower than that of water? Explain. (3.5)

3.78 On a hot sunny day, you get out of the swimming pool and sit in a metal chair, which is very hot. Would you predict that the specific heat of the metal is higher or lower than that of water? Explain. (3.5)

3.79 A hot-water bottle contains 725 g of water at 65 °C. If the water cools to body temperature (37 °C), how many kilojoules of heat could be transferred to sore muscles? (3.5)

3.80 A large bottle containing 883 g of water at 4 °C is removed from the refrigerator. How many kilojoules are absorbed to warm the water to room temperature of 27 °C? (3.5)

3.81 A 0.50-g sample of vegetable oil is placed in a calorimeter. When the sample is burned, 18.9 kJ is given off. What is the energy value (kcal/g) for the oil? (3.6)

3.82 A 1.3-g sample of rice is placed in a calorimeter. When the sample is burned, 22 kJ is given off. What is the energy value (kcal/g) for the rice? (3.6)

CHALLENGE QUESTIONS

The following groups of questions are related to the topics in this chapter. However, they do not all follow the chapter order, and they require you to combine concepts and skills from several sections. These questions will help you increase your critical thinking skills and prepare for your next exam.

3.83 A 25.0-g sample of a metal at 98.0 °C is placed in 50.0 g of water at 18.0 °C. If the final temperature of the metal and water is 27.4 °C, what is the specific heat, in J/g °C, of the metal? (3.5)

3.84 A 125-g piece of metal is heated to 288 °C and dropped into 85.0 g of water at 26.0 °C. If the final temperature of the water and metal is 58.0 °C, what is the specific heat of the metal (J/g °C)? (3.5)

3.85 When a 0.66-g sample of olive oil is burned in a calorimeter, the heat released increases the temperature of 370 g of water from 22.7 °C to 38.8 °C. What is the energy value for the olive oil in kJ/g and kcal/g? (3.5, 3.6)

3.86 When 1.0 g of gasoline burns, 11 500 cal of energy are given off. If the density of gasoline is 0.74 g/mL, how many kilocalories of energy are obtained from 1.5 gal of gasoline? (3.5)

3.87 A piece of copper metal (specific heat 0.385 J/g °C) at 86.0 °C is placed in 50.0 g of water at 16.0 °C. The metal and water come to the same temperature of 24.0 °C. What was the mass of the piece of copper? (3.5)

3.88 Copper is sometimes coated on the bottom surface of cooking pans. Copper has a specific heat of 0.385 J/g °C. A 25.0-g sample of copper heated to 85.0 °C is dropped into water at an initial temperature of 14.0 °C. If the final temperature reached by the copper and water is 36.0 °C, how many grams of water are present? (3.5)

ANSWERS

Answers to Study Checks

3.1 This is a heterogeneous mixture because it does not have a uniform composition.

3.2 **a** and **c** are chemical changes.

3.3 12 °F

3.4 39.8 °C

3.5 night, −260. °C; day, 410. °C

3.6 35 kJ

3.7 *SH* = 1.23 J/g °C

3.8 14.6 kJ

3.9 360. J

3.10 182 g of iron

3.11 **a.** carbohydrate 370 kJ, fat 270 kJ, and protein 170 kJ
b. 810 kJ

Answers to Selected Questions and Problems

3.1 **a.** pure substance **b.** mixture
c. pure substance **d.** pure substance
e. mixture

3.3 **a.** element **b.** compound
c. element **d.** compound
e. compound

3.5 **a.** heterogeneous **b.** homogeneous
c. homogeneous **d.** heterogeneous
e. heterogeneous

3.7 **a.** gas **b.** gas **c.** solid

3.9 **a.** physical property **b.** chemical property **c.** physical property
d. chemical property **e.** chemical property

3.11 **a.** physical change **b.** chemical change **c.** physical change
d. physical change **e.** physical change

3.13 **a.** chemical property **b.** physical property **c.** physical property
d. chemical property **e.** physical property

3.15 In the United States, we still use the Fahrenheit temperature scale. In °F, normal body temperature is 98.6. On the Celsius scale, her temperature would be 37.7 °C, a mild fever.

3.17 **a.** 98.6 °F **b.** 18.5 °C **c.** 246 K
d. −49 °C **e.** −9.4 °C

3.19 **a.** 41 °C
b. No. The temperature is equivalent to 39 °C.

3.21 When the car is at the top of the ramp, it has its maximum potential energy. As it descends, potential energy changes to kinetic energy. At the bottom, all the energy is kinetic.

3.23 **a.** potential **b.** kinetic
c. potential **d.** potential

3.25 **a.** 8.1×10^5 J **b.** 190 kcal

3.27 **a.** 3.5 kcal **b.** 99.2 cal
c. 120 J **d.** 1100 cal

3.29 Copper, which has the lowest specific heat, would reach the highest temperature.

3.31 **a.** 0.389 J/g °C **b.** 0.313 J/g °C

3.33 **a.** 1380 J **b.** 1810 J

3.35 **a.** 3780 J **b.** 3600 J

3.37 **a.** 54.5 g **b.** 216 g

3.39 **a.** 686 g **b.** 190. g

3.41 **a.** 175 °C **b.** 11.3 °C

3.43 **a.** 700. °C **b.** 351 °C

3.45 **a.** 22.2 kJ **b.** 871 kJ

3.47 **a.** 470 kJ; 110 kcal **b.** 18 g of carbohydrate

3.49 **a.** 530 kJ; 130 kcal **b.** 4050 kJ; 950 kcal

3.51 **a.** compound **b.** mixture **c.** element

3.53 **a.** homogeneous **b.** heterogeneous
c. homogeneous

3.55 68.3 °C

3.57 gold 250 J or 60. cal; aluminum 240 J or 58 cal

3.59 **a.** carbohydrate 680 kcal; fat 590 kcal; protein 240 kcal
b. 1510 kcal **c.** 25 h **d.** 2.0 h

3.61 **a.** element **b.** compound **c.** mixture

3.63 **a.** heterogeneous **b.** homogeneous
c. homogeneous

3.65 **a.** solid **b.** gas **c.** liquid
d. gas **e.** solid

3.67 **a.** physical property **b.** physical property
c. physical property **d.** chemical property

3.69 **a.** chemical change **b.** physical change
c. physical change **d.** chemical change

3.71 **a.** 56.7 °C, 330. K **b.** −56.5 °C, 217 K

3.73 −26 °C, 247 K

3.75 3500 kcal

3.77 The same amount of heat causes a greater temperature change in the sand than in the water, thus sand must have a lower specific heat than that of water.

3.79 85 kJ

3.81 9.0 kcal/g

3.83 1.1 J/g °C

3.85 38 kJ/g; 9.0 kcal/g

3.87 70. g of copper

Combining Ideas from Chapters 1 to 3

The chapter sections to review are shown in parentheses at the end of each question.

CI.1 Gold, one of the most sought-after metals in the world, has a density of 19.3 g/cm^3, a melting point of 1064 °C, and a specific heat of 0.129 J/g °C. A gold nugget found in Alaska in 1998 weighs 294.10 troy ounces. (2.4, 2.6, 2.7, 2.8, 3.3, 3.4, 3.5)

Gold nuggets, also called native gold, can be found in streams and mines.

a. How many significant figures are in the measurement of the weight of the nugget?

b. If 1 troy ounce is 31.1035 g, what is the mass of the nugget in grams? In kilograms?

c. If the nugget were pure gold, what would its volume be in cm^3?

d. If the gold nugget were hammered into a foil with a thickness of 0.0035 in., what would be the area of the foil in m^2?

e. What is the melting point of gold in degrees Fahrenheit and kelvins?

f. How many kilojoules are required to raise the temperature of the nugget from 63 °F to 85 °F?

CI.2 The mileage for a motorcycle with a fuel-tank capacity of 22 L is 35 mi/gal. The density of gasoline is 0.74 g/mL. (2.4, 2.6, 2.7, 2.8, 3.4, 3.5)

a. How long can a trip, in kilometers, be made on one full tank of gasoline?

b. If the price of gasoline is \$3.59/gal, what would be the cost of fuel for the trip?

c. If the average speed during the trip is 44 mi/h, how many hours will it take to reach the destination?

d. What is the mass, in grams, of the fuel in the tank?

e. When 1.0 g of gasoline burns, 47 kJ of energy is released. How many kilojoules are produced when the fuel in one full tank is burned?

When 1.0 g of gasoline is burned, 47 kJ of energy is released.

CI.3

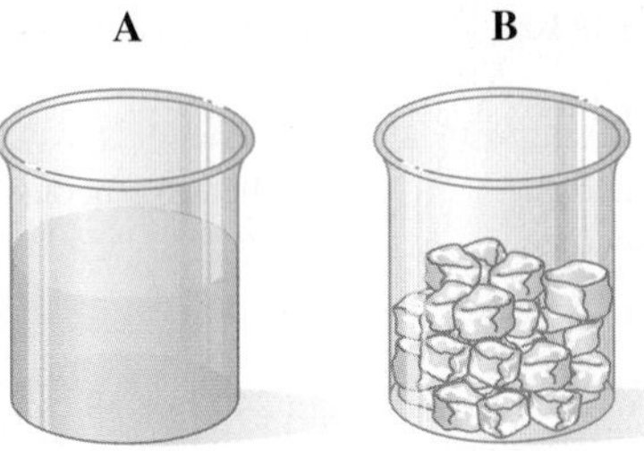

Answer the following questions for the water samples **A** and **B** shown in the diagrams: (3.1, 3.2)

a. In which sample (**A** or **B**) does the water have its own shape?

b. Which diagram (**1** or **2** or **3**) represents the arrangement of particles in water sample **A**?

c. Which diagram (**1** or **2** or **3**) represents the arrangement of particles in water sample **B**?

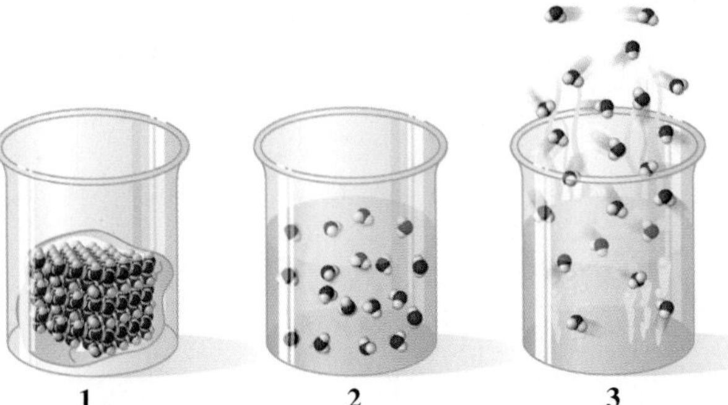

Answer the following for diagrams **1**, **2**, and **3**: (3.2, 3.3)

d. The state of matter indicated in diagram **1** is a _________; in diagram **2**, it is a _________; and in diagram **3**, it is a _________.

e. The motion of the particles is slowest in diagram _________.

f. The arrangement of particles is farthest apart in diagram _________.

g. The particles fill the volume of the container in diagram _________.

h. If the water in diagram **2** has a mass of 19 g and a temperature of 45 °C, how much heat, in kilojoules, is removed to cool the liquid to 0 °C?

CI.4 The label of a black cherry almond energy bar with a mass of 68 g lists the "nutrition facts" as 39 g of carbohydrate, 5 g of fat, and 10. g of protein. (3.4, 3.5)

a. Using the energy values of carbohydrates, fats, and proteins (see Table 3.9), what are the kilocalories (Calories) for the black cherry almond bar? (Round off answers for each food type to the tens place.)

b. What are the kilojoules for the black cherry almond bar? (Round off answers for each food type to the tens place.)

c. If you obtain 160 kJ, how many grams of the black cherry almond bar did you eat?

d. If you are walking and using energy at a rate of 840 kJ/h, how many minutes will you need to walk to expend the energy from two black cherry almond bars (see Table 3.12)?

An energy bar contains carbohydrate, fat, and protein.

CI.5 In one box, there are 75 iron nails weighing 0.250 lb. The density of iron is 7.86 g/cm^3. The specific heat of iron is 0.452 J/g °C. (2.5, 2.7, 2.8, 3.5)

a. What is the volume, in cm^3, of the iron nails in the box?

b. If 30 nails are added to a graduated cylinder containing 17.6 mL of water, what is the new level of water in the cylinder?

c. How much heat, in joules, must be added to the nails in the box to raise their temperature from 16 °C to 125 °C?

d. If all the iron nails at 55.0 °C are added to 325 g of water at 4.0 °C, what will be the final temperature (°C) of the nails and water?

Nails made of iron have a density of 7.86 g/cm^3.

CI.6 A hot tub with a surface area of 25 ft^2 is filled with water to a depth of 28 in. *Hint*: Volume is calculated as area × height ($V = A \times h$). (2.5, 2.7, 2.8, 3.5)

a. What is the volume, in liters, of water in the tub?

b. What is the mass, in kilograms, of water it contains?

c. How many kilojoules are needed to heat the water from 62 °F to 105 °F?

d. If the hot-tub heater provides 5900 kJ/min, how long, in minutes, will it take to heat the water in the hot tub from 62 °F to 105 °F?

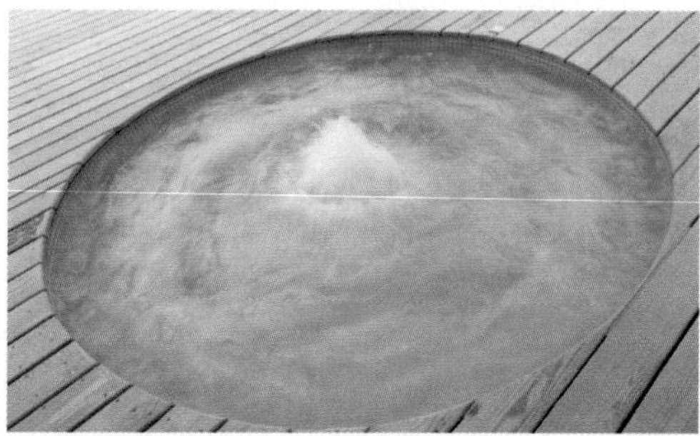
A hot tub filled with water is heated to 105 °F.

ANSWERS

CI.1
a. 5 significant figures
b. 9147.5 g, 9.1475 kg
c. 474 cm^3
d. 5.3 m^2
e. 1947 °F, 1337 K
f. 14 kJ

CI.3
a. **B**
b. **A** is represented by diagram **2**.
c. **B** is represented by diagram **1**.
d. solid, liquid, gas
e. diagram **1**
f. diagram **3**
g. diagram **3**
h. 3.6 kJ

CI.5
a. 14.4 cm^3
b. 23.4 mL
c. 5590 J
d. 5.8 °C

4 Atoms and Elements

LOOKING AHEAD

John is preparing for the next growing season as he decides how much of each crop should be planted and their location on his farm. Part of this decision is determined by the quality of the soil including the pH, the amount of moisture, and the nutrient content in the soil. He begins by sampling the soil and performing a few chemical tests on the soil. John determines that several of his fields need additional fertilizer before the crops can be planted.

John considers several different types of fertilizers as each supplies different nutrients to the soil to help increase crop production. Plants need three basic elements for plant growth. These elements are potassium, nitrogen, and phosphorus. Potassium (K on the periodic table) is a metal, while nitrogen (N) and phosphorus (P) are nonmetals. Fertilizers may also contain several other elements including calcium (Ca), magnesium (Mg), and sulfur (S). John applies a fertilizer containing a mixture of all of these elements to his soil and plans to re-check the soil nutrient content in a few days.

Career: Farmer

Farming involves much more than growing crops and raising animals. Farmers must understand how to perform chemical tests and how to apply fertilizer to soil and pesticides or herbicides to crops. Pesticides are chemicals used to kill insects that could destroy the crop, while herbicides are chemicals used to kill weeds that would compete for the crop's water and nutrient supply. This requires knowledge of how these chemicals work, their safety, effectiveness, and their storage. In using this information, farmers are able to grow crops that produce a higher yield, greater nutritional value, and better taste.

All matter is composed of *elements*, of which there are 118 different kinds. Of these, 88 elements occur naturally and make all the substances in our world. Many elements are already familiar to you. Perhaps you use aluminum in the form of foil or drink soft drinks from aluminum cans. You may have a ring or necklace made of gold, or silver, or perhaps platinum. If you play tennis or golf, then you may have noticed that your racket or clubs may be made from the elements titanium or carbon. In our bodies, calcium and phosphorus form the structure of bones and teeth, iron and copper are needed in the formation of red blood cells, and iodine is required for the proper functioning of the thyroid.

The correct amounts of certain elements are crucial to the proper growth and health of our bodies. Low levels of iron can lead to anemia, while low levels of iodine can cause hypothyroidism and goiter. Laboratory tests are used to confirm that elements such as iron, copper, zinc, or iodine are within normal ranges in our bodies.

CHAPTER READINESS*

Key Math Skills

- Using Positive and Negative Numbers in Calculations (1.4B)
- Calculating a Percentage (1.4C)

Core Chemistry Skills

- Counting Significant Figures (2.3)
- Rounding Off (2.4)
- Using Significant Figures in Calculations (2.4)

*These Key Math Skills and the Core Chemistry Skills from previous chapters are listed here for your review as you proceed to the new material in this chapter.

4.1 Elements and Symbols

LEARNING GOAL

Given the name of an element, write its correct symbol; from the symbol, write the correct name.

Elements are pure substances from which all other things are built. As we discussed, elements cannot be broken down into simpler substances. Over the centuries, elements have been named for planets, mythological figures, colors, minerals, geographic locations, and famous people. Some sources of names of elements are listed in Table 4.1. The names and symbols of all the elements are found on the inside cover of this text.

TABLE 4.1 Some Elements, Symbols, and Source of Names

Element	Symbol	Source of Name
Uranium	U	The planet Uranus
Titanium	Ti	Titans (mythology)
Chlorine	Cl	*Chloros*: "greenish yellow" (Greek)
Iodine	I	*Ioeides*: "violet" (Greek)
Magnesium	Mg	Magnesia, a mineral
Californium	Cf	California
Curium	Cm	Marie and Pierre Curie
Copernicium	Cn	Nicolaus Copernicus

One-Letter Symbols		Two-Letter Symbols	
C	Carbon	Co	Cobalt
S	Sulfur	Si	Silicon
N	Nitrogen	Ne	Neon
I	Iodine	Ni	Nickel

Chemical Symbols

Chemical symbols are one- or two-letter abbreviations for the names of the elements. Only the first letter of an element's symbol is capitalized. If the symbol has a second letter, it is lowercase so that we know when a different element is indicated. If two letters are capitalized, they represent the symbols of two different elements. For example, the element cobalt has the symbol Co. However, the two capital letters CO specify two elements, carbon (C) and oxygen (O).

Chemistry Link to Industry

MANY FORMS OF CARBON

Carbon has the symbol C. However, its atoms can be arranged in different ways to give several different substances. Two forms of carbon—diamond and graphite—have been known since prehistoric times. A diamond is transparent and harder than any other substance, whereas graphite is black and soft. In diamond, carbon atoms are arranged in a rigid structure, while in graphite the carbon atoms are arranged in hexagonal rings which form planes that slide over each other. Graphite is used as pencil lead, as lubricants, and in the manufacture of carbon fibers used to make lightweight golf clubs and tennis rackets.

Two other forms of carbon have been discovered more recently. In the form called *Buckminsterfullerene*, or *buckyball* (named after R. Buckminster Fuller, who popularized the geodesic dome), 60 carbon atoms are arranged as rings of 5 and 6 atoms to give a spherical cage-like structure. When a fullerene structure is stretched out, it produces a cylinder with a diameter of only a few nanometers, called a *nanotube*. Practical uses for buckyballs and nanotubes have not yet been developed, but it is hopeful that they can be used in lightweight structural materials, heat conductors, computer parts, and medicine.

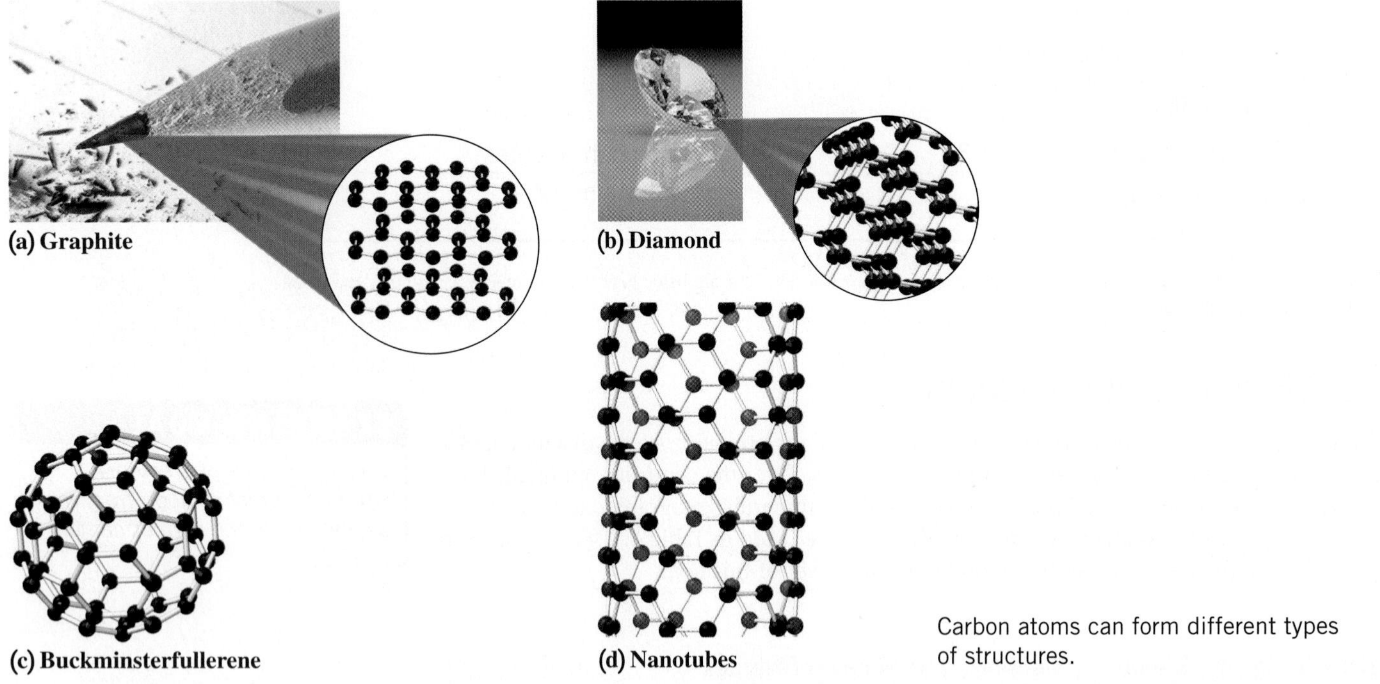

Carbon atoms can form different types of structures.

Although most of the symbols use letters from the current names, some are derived from their ancient names. For example, Na, the symbol for sodium, comes from the Latin word *natrium.* The symbol for iron, Fe, is derived from the Latin name *ferrum.* Table 4.2 lists the names and symbols of some common elements. Learning their names and symbols will greatly help your learning of chemistry.

TABLE 4.2 Names and Symbols of Some Common Elements

Name*	Symbol	Name*	Symbol	Name*	Symbol
Aluminum	Al	Gold (*aurum*)	Au	Phosphorus	P
Argon	Ar	Helium	He	Platinum	Pt
Arsenic	As	Hydrogen	H	Potassium (*kalium*)	K
Barium	Ba	Iodine	I	Radium	Ra
Boron	B	Iron (*ferrum*)	Fe	Silicon	Si
Bromine	Br	Lead (*plumbum*)	Pb	Silver (*argentum*)	Ag
Cadmium	Cd	Lithium	Li	Sodium (*natrium*)	Na
Calcium	Ca	Magnesium	Mg	Strontium	Sr
Carbon	C	Manganese	Mn	Sulfur	S
Chlorine	Cl	Mercury (*hydrargyrum*)	Hg	Tin (*stannum*)	Sn
Chromium	Cr	Neon	Ne	Titanium	Ti
Cobalt	Co	Nickel	Ni	Uranium	U
Copper (*cuprum*)	Cu	Nitrogen	N	Zinc	Zn
Fluorine	F	Oxygen	O		

*Names given in parentheses are ancient Latin or Greek words from which the symbols are derived.

Aluminum

Carbon

Silver

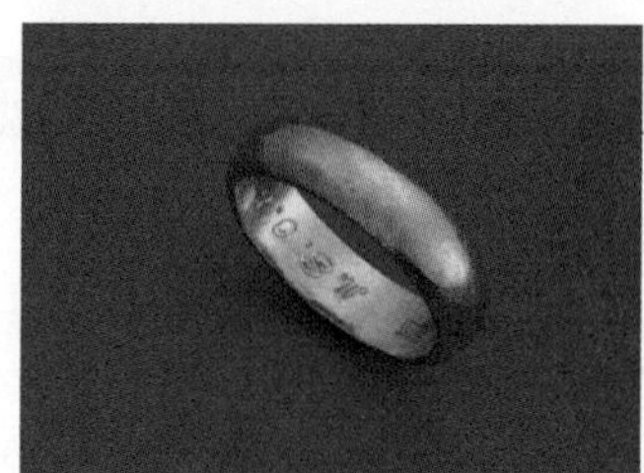

Gold

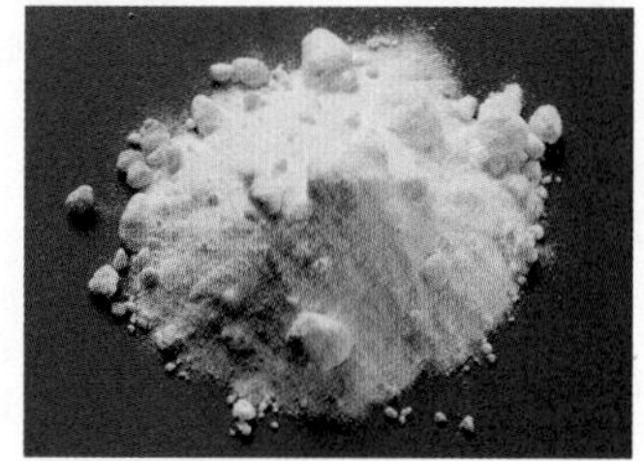

Sulfur

CONCEPT CHECK 4.1 Symbols of the Elements

The symbol for carbon is C, and the symbol for sulfur is S. However, the symbol for cesium is Cs, not CS. Why?

ANSWER

When the symbol for an element has two letters, the first letter is capitalized, but the second letter is lowercase. If both letters are capitalized, such as in CS, two elements—carbon and sulfur—are indicated.

SAMPLE PROBLEM 4.1 Writing Chemical Symbols

What are the chemical symbols for the following elements?

a. nickel **b.** nitrogen **c.** neon

SOLUTION

a. Ni **b.** N **c.** Ne

STUDY CHECK 4.1

What are the chemical symbols for the elements silicon, sulfur, and silver?

SAMPLE PROBLEM 4.2 Names and Symbols of Chemical Elements

Give the name of the element that corresponds to each of the following chemical symbols:

a. Zn **b.** K **c.** H **d.** Fe

SOLUTION

a. zinc **b.** potassium **c.** hydrogen **d.** iron

STUDY CHECK 4.2

What are the names of the elements with the chemical symbols Mg, Al, and F?

Chemistry Link to Health

MERCURY

Mercury is a silvery, shiny transition element that is a liquid at room temperature. Mercury can enter the body through inhaled mercury vapor, contact with the skin, or foods or water contaminated with mercury. In the body, mercury destroys proteins and disrupts cell function. Long-term exposure to mercury can damage the brain and kidneys, cause mental retardation, and decrease physical development. Blood, urine, and hair samples are used to test for mercury.

In both freshwater and seawater, bacteria convert mercury into toxic methylmercury, which attacks the central nervous system (CNS). Because fish absorb methylmercury, we are exposed to mercury by consuming mercury-contaminated fish. The Food and Drug Administration (FDA) has set a maximum level of one part mercury per million parts seafood (1 ppm), which is the same as 1 mg of mercury in every kilogram of seafood. Fish higher in the food chain, such as swordfish, tuna, and shark, can have such high levels of mercury that the Environmental Protection Agency (EPA) recommends they be consumed no more than once a week.

One of the worst incidents of mercury poisoning occurred in Minamata and Niigata, Japan, in 1950. At that time, the ocean was polluted with high levels of mercury from industrial wastes. Because fish were a major food in the diet, more than 2000 people were affected with mercury poisoning and many died or developed neural damage. In the United States, between 1988 and 1997, the use of mercury decreased by 75% when mercury was banned from paint and pesticides, and regulated in batteries and other products. Certain batteries and compact fluorescent light bulbs (CFL) contain mercury, and instructions for their safe disposal should be followed.

This mercury fountain, housed in glass, was designed by Alexander Calder for the 1937 World's Fair in Paris.

QUESTIONS AND PROBLEMS

4.1 Elements and Symbols

LEARNING GOAL: *Given the name of an element, write its correct symbol; from the symbol, write the correct name.*

4.1 Write the symbols for the following elements:
a. copper **b.** platinum **c.** calcium
d. manganese **e.** iron **f.** barium
g. lead **h.** strontium

4.2 Write the symbols for the following elements:
a. oxygen **b.** lithium **c.** uranium
d. titanium **e.** hydrogen **f.** chromium
g. tin **h.** gold

4.3 Write the name of the element for each symbol.
a. C **b.** Cl **c.** I **d.** Hg
e. Ag **f.** Ar **g.** B **h.** Ni

4.4 Write the name of the element for each symbol.
a. He **b.** P **c.** Na **d.** As
e. Ca **f.** Br **g.** Cd **h.** Si

4.5 What elements are represented by the symbols in each of the following substances?
a. table salt, $NaCl$
b. plaster casts, $CaSO_4$
c. Demerol, $C_{15}H_{22}ClNO_2$
d. pigment, $BaCrO_4$

4.6 What elements are represented by the symbols in each of the following substances?
a. fireworks, KNO_3
b. dental cement, $Zn_3(PO_4)_2$
c. antacid, $Mg(OH)_2$
d. manufacture of aluminum, AlF_3

LEARNING GOAL

Use the periodic table to identify the group and the period of an element; identify the element as a metal, a nonmetal, or a metalloid.

4.2 The Periodic Table

As more elements were discovered, it became necessary to organize them into some type of classification system. By the late 1800s, scientists recognized that certain elements looked alike and behaved much the same way. In 1872, a Russian chemist, Dmitri Mendeleev, arranged the 60 elements known at that time into groups with similar properties and placed them in order of increasing atomic masses. Today this arrangement of 118 elements is known as the **periodic table** (see Figure 4.1).

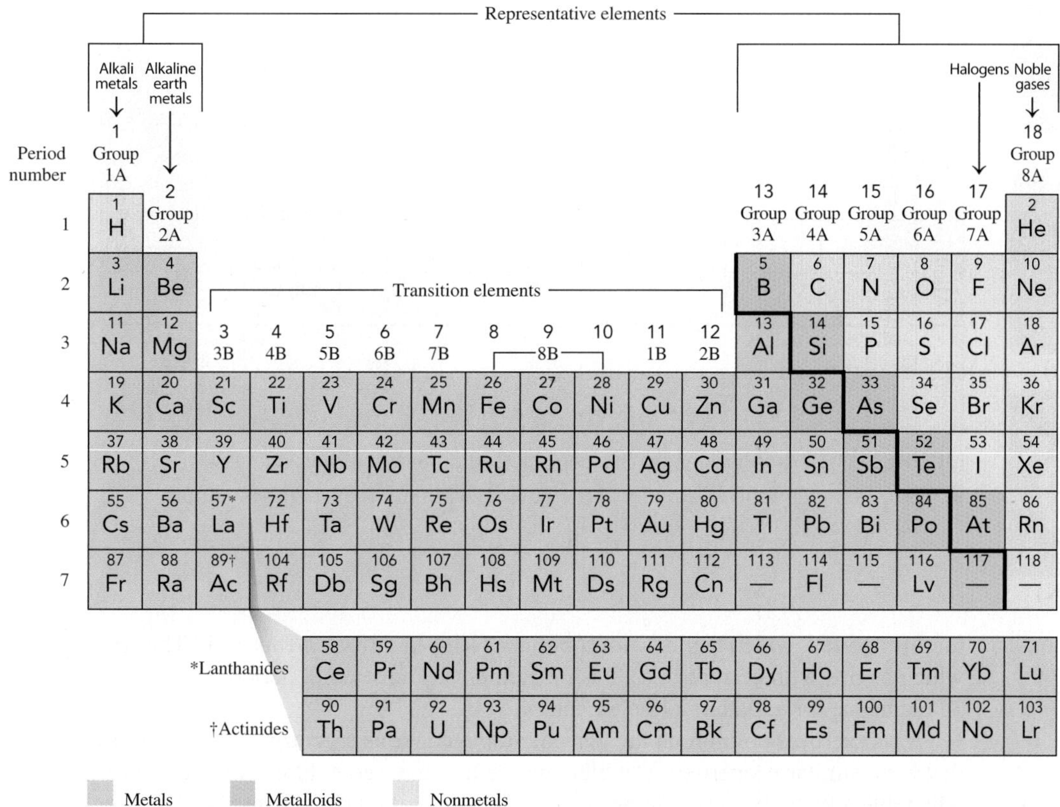

FIGURE 4.1 On the periodic table, groups are the elements arranged as vertical columns, and periods are the elements in each horizontal row.

Q What is the symbol of the element in Group 1A (1), Period 3?

Periods and Groups

Each horizontal row in the periodic table is a **period** (see Figure 4.2). The periods are counted from the top of the table as Period 1 to Period 7. The first period contains two elements: hydrogen (H) and helium (He). The second period contains eight elements: lithium (Li), beryllium (Be), boron (B), carbon (C), nitrogen (N), oxygen (O), fluorine (F), and neon (Ne). The third period also contains eight elements, beginning with sodium (Na) and ending with argon (Ar). The fourth period, which begins with potassium (K), and

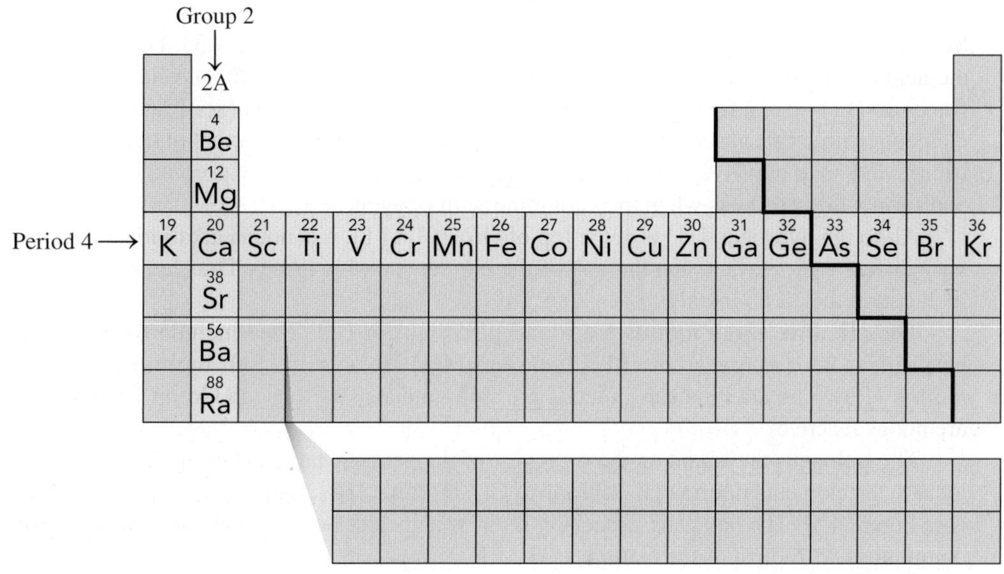

FIGURE 4.2 On the periodic table, each vertical column represents a group of elements, and each horizontal row of elements represents a period.

Q Are the elements Si, P, and S part of a group or a period?

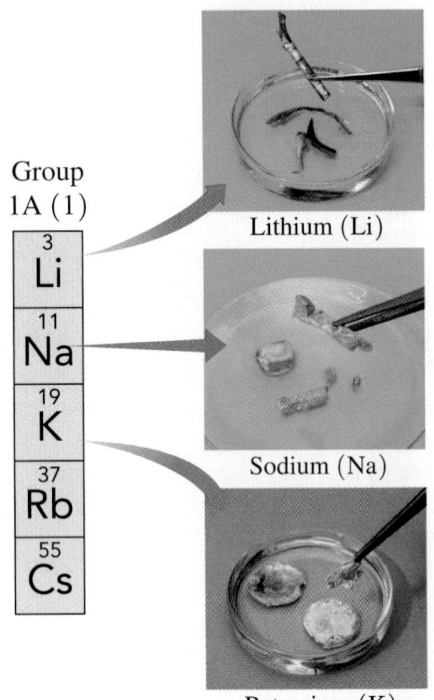

FIGURE 4.4 Lithium (Li), sodium (Na), and potassium (K) are some alkali metals from Group 1A (1).

Q What physical properties do these alkali metals have in common?

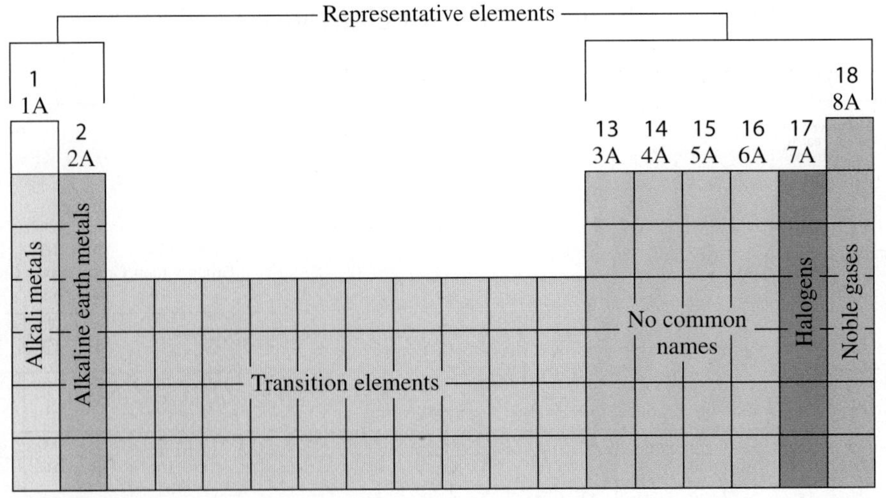

FIGURE 4.3 Certain groups on the periodic table have common names.

Q What is the common name for the group of elements that includes helium and argon?

the fifth period, which begins with rubidium (Rb), has 18 elements each. The sixth period, which begins with cesium (Cs), has 32 elements. The seventh period as of today contains 32 elements, for a total of 118 elements.

Each vertical column on the periodic table contains a **group** (or family) of elements that have similar properties. The elements in the first two columns on the left of the periodic table and the last six columns on the right are called the **representative elements**.

A **group number** is written at the top of each vertical column (group) in the periodic table. For many years, the representative elements have had group numbers 1A–8A. In the center of the periodic table is a block of elements known as the **transition elements**, which have had group numbers followed by the letter "B." A newer system assigns numbers of 1–18 to all of the groups going left to right across the periodic table. Because both systems are currently in use, they are both shown on the periodic table in this text and are included in our discussions of elements and group numbers. The two rows of 14 elements called the lanthanides and actinides (or the inner transition elements), which are part of Periods 6 and 7, are placed at the bottom of the periodic table to allow it to fit on a page.

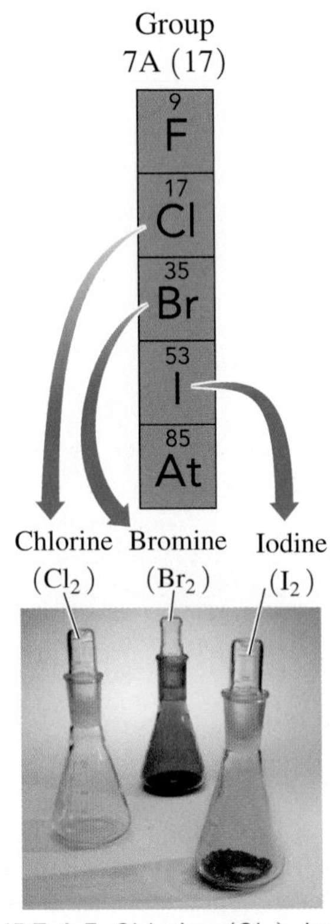

FIGURE 4.5 Chlorine (Cl_2), bromine (Br_2), and iodine (I_2) are halogens from Group 7A (17).

Q What elements are in the halogen group?

Names of Groups

Several groups in the periodic table have special names (see Figure 4.3). Group 1A (1) elements—lithium (Li), sodium (Na), potassium (K), rubidium (Rb), cesium (Cs), and francium (Fr)—are a family of elements known as the **alkali metals** (see Figure 4.4). The elements within this group are soft, shiny metals that are good conductors of heat and electricity, and have relatively low melting points. Alkali metals react vigorously with water and form white products when they combine with oxygen.

Although hydrogen (H) is at the top of Group 1A (1), it is not an alkali metal and has very different properties than the rest of the elements in this group. Thus hydrogen is not included in the alkali metals.

The **alkaline earth metals** are found in Group 2A (2). They include the elements beryllium (Be), magnesium (Mg), calcium (Ca), strontium (Sr), barium (Ba), and radium (Ra). The alkaline earth metals are shiny metals like those in Group 1A, but they are not as reactive.

The **halogens** are found on the right side of the periodic table in Group 7A (17). They include the elements fluorine (F), chlorine (Cl), bromine (Br), iodine (I), and astatine (At) (see Figure 4.5). The halogens, especially fluorine and chlorine, are highly reactive and form compounds with most of the elements.

The **noble gases** are found in Group 8A (18). They include helium (He), neon (Ne), argon (Ar), krypton (Kr), xenon (Xe), and radon (Rn). They are quite unreactive and are seldom found in combination with other elements.

SAMPLE PROBLEM 4.3 Group and Period Numbers of Some Elements

Give the group and period numbers for each of the following elements and identify each as a representative or a transition element:

a. manganese **b.** barium **c.** gold

SOLUTION

a. Manganese (Mn) in Group 7B (7) and Period 4 is a transition element.
b. Barium (Ba) in Group 2A (2) and Period 6 is a representative element.
c. Gold (Au) in Group 1B (11) and Period 6 is a transition element.

STUDY CHECK 4.3

Strontium is an element that gives a brilliant red color to fireworks.

a. In what group is strontium found?
b. What is the name of this chemical family?
c. In what period is strontium found?

Strontium provides the red color in fireworks.

Metals, Nonmetals, and Metalloids

The heavy zigzag line on the periodic table separates the *metals* and the *nonmetals*. *Except for hydrogen*, the metals are to the left of the line with the nonmetals to the right (see Figure 4.6). In general, most **metals** are shiny solids, such as copper (Cu), gold (Au), and silver (Ag). Metals can be shaped into wires (ductile) or hammered into a flat sheet (malleable). Metals are good conductors of heat and electricity. They usually melt at higher temperatures than nonmetals. All of the metals are solids at room temperature, except for mercury (Hg), which is a liquid.

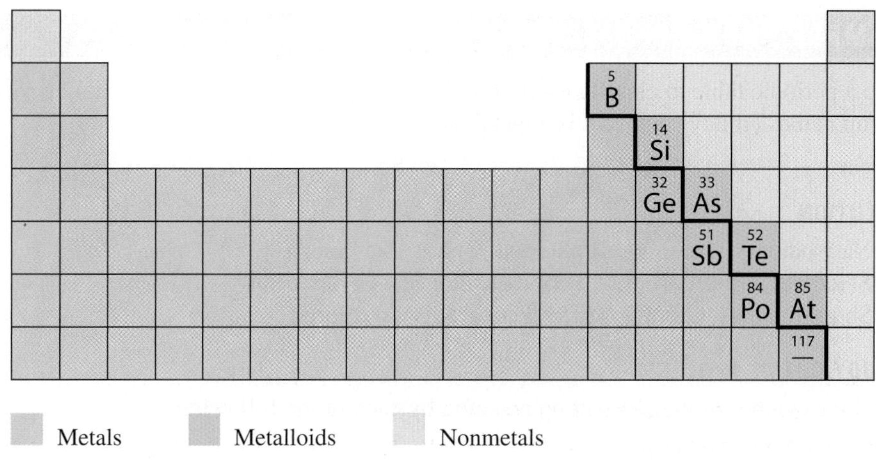

FIGURE 4.6 Along the heavy zigzag line on the periodic table that separates the metals and nonmetals are metalloids that exhibit characteristics of both metals and nonmetals.

Q On which side of the heavy zigzag line are the nonmetals located?

Nonmetals are not especially shiny, malleable, or ductile, and they are often poor conductors of heat and electricity. They typically have low melting points and low densities. Some examples of nonmetals are hydrogen (H), carbon (C), nitrogen (N), oxygen (O), chlorine (Cl), and sulfur (S).

Except for aluminum, the elements located along the heavy zigzag line are **metalloids**: B, Si, Ge, As, Sb, Te, Po, and At. Metalloids exhibit some properties that are typical of the metals, and other properties that are characteristic of the nonmetals. For example, metalloids are better conductors of heat and electricity than the nonmetals, but not as good as the metals. The metalloids are semiconductors because they can be modified to function as conductors or insulators. Table 4.3 compares some characteristics of silver, a metal, with those of antimony, a metalloid, and sulfur, a nonmetal.

A silver cup is shiny, antimony is a blue-gray solid, and sulfur is a dull, yellow color.

TABLE 4.3 Some Characteristics of a Metal, a Metalloid, and a Nonmetal

Silver (Ag)	Antimony (Sb)	Sulfur (S)
Metal	Metalloid	Nonmetal
Shiny	Blue-gray, shiny	Dull, yellow
Extremely ductile	Brittle	Brittle
Can be hammered into sheets (malleable)	Shatters when hammered	Shatters when hammered
Good conductor of heat and electricity	Poor conductor of heat and electricity	Poor conductor of heat and electricity
Used in coins, jewelry, tableware	Used to harden lead, color glass and plastics	Used in gunpowder, rubber, fungicides
Density 10.5 g/mL	Density 6.7 g/mL	Density 2.1 g/mL
Melting point 962 °C	Melting point 630 °C	Melting point 113 °C

CONCEPT CHECK 4.2 Groups and Periods on the Periodic Table

Consider the elements aluminum, silicon, and phosphorus.

a. In what group and period are they found?
b. Identify each as a metal, a nonmetal, or a metalloid.

ANSWER

a. They are all found in Period 3. Aluminum is in Group 3A (13), silicon is in Group 4A (14), and phosphorus is in Group 5A (15).
b. Aluminum is a metal, phosphorus is a nonmetal, and silicon is a metalloid.

SAMPLE PROBLEM 4.4 Metals, Nonmetals, and Metalloids

Use a periodic table to classify each of the following elements by its group and period, group names (if any), and if it is a metal, a nonmetal, or a metalloid:

a. Na **b.** I **c.** Sb

SOLUTION

a. Na (sodium), Group 1A (1), Period 3, is an alkali metal.
b. I (iodine), Group 7A (17), Period 5, halogen, is a nonmetal.
c. Sb (antimony), Group 5A (15), Period 5, is a metalloid.

STUDY CHECK 4.4

Give the symbol of the element represented by each of the following:

a. Group 5A (15), Period 4
b. a noble gas in Period 6
c. a metalloid in Period 2

Chemistry Link to Health

ELEMENTS ESSENTIAL TO HEALTH

Of all the elements, only about 20 are essential for the well-being and survival of the human body. Of those, four elements—oxygen, carbon, hydrogen, and nitrogen—which are representative elements located in Period 1 and Period 2 on the periodic table, make up 96% of our body mass. Most of the food in our daily diet provides these elements, which are found in carbohydrates, fats, and proteins. Most of the hydrogen and oxygen is found in water, which makes up 55–60% of our body mass.

The *macrominerals*—Ca, P, K, Cl, S, Na, and Mg—are representative elements located in Period 3 and Period 4 of the periodic table. They are involved in the formation of bones and teeth, maintenance of heart and blood vessels, muscle contractions, nerve impulses, acid–base balance of body fluids, and regulation of cellular metabolism. The macrominerals are present in lower amounts than the major elements, so smaller amounts are required in our daily diets.

The other essential elements, called *microminerals* or *trace elements*, are mostly transition elements in Period 4, along with Mo and I in Period 5. They are present in the human body in very small amounts, some less than 100 mg. In recent years, the detection of such small amounts has improved so that researchers can more easily identify the roles of trace elements. Some trace elements, such as arsenic, chromium, and selenium, are toxic at high levels in the body but are still required by the body. Other elements, such as tin and nickel, are thought to be essential, but their metabolic role has not yet been determined. Some examples and the amounts present in a 60-kg person are listed in Table 4.4.

TABLE 4.4 Typical Amounts of Essential Elements in a 60-kg Adult

Element	Quantity	Function
Major Elements		
Oxygen (O)	39 kg	Building block of biomolecules and water (H_2O)
Carbon (C)	11 kg	Building block of organic and biomolecules
Hydrogen (H)	6 kg	Component of biomolecules, water (H_2O), and pH of body fluids, stomach acid (HCl)
Nitrogen (N)	1.5 kg	Component of proteins and nucleic acids
Macrominerals		
Calcium (Ca)	1000 g	Needed for bone and teeth, muscle contraction, nerve impulses
Phosphorus (P)	600 g	Needed for bone and teeth, nucleic acids, ATP
Potassium (K)	120 g	Most prevalent positive ion (K^+) in cells, muscle contraction, nerve impulses
Chlorine (Cl)	100 g	Most prevalent negative ion (Cl^-) in fluids outside cells, stomach acid (HCl)
Sulfur (S)	86 g	Component of proteins, liver, vitamin B_1, insulin
Sodium (Na)	60 g	Most prevalent positive ion (Na^+) in fluids outside cells, water balance, functions in muscle contraction, nerve impulses
Magnesium (Mg)	36 g	Component of bone, required for metabolic reactions
Microminerals (trace elements)		
Iron (Fe)	3600 mg	Component of oxygen carrier hemoglobin
Silicon (Si)	3000 mg	Needed for growth and maintenance of bone and teeth, tendons and ligaments, hair and skin
Zinc (Zn)	2000 mg	Used in metabolic reactions in cells, DNA synthesis, growth of bone, teeth, connective tissue, immune system
Copper (Cu)	240 mg	Needed for blood vessels, blood pressure, immune system
Manganese (Mn)	60 mg	Needed for bone growth, blood clotting, necessary for metabolic reactions
Iodine (I)	20 mg	Needed for proper thyroid function
Molybdenum (Mo)	12 mg	Needed to process Fe and N from diets
Arsenic (As)	3 mg	Needed for growth and reproduction
Chromium (Cr)	3 mg	Needed for maintenance of blood sugar levels, synthesis of biomolecules
Cobalt (Co)	3 mg	Component of vitamin B_{12}, red blood cells
Selenium (Se)	2 mg	Used in the immune system, health of heart and pancreas
Vanadium (V)	2 mg	Needed in the formation of bone and teeth, energy from food

	1 Group 1A	2 Group 2A	3 3B	4 4B	5 5B	6 6B	7 7B	8 8B	9 8B	10 8B	11 1B	12 2B	13 Group 3A	14 Group 4A	15 Group 5A	16 Group 6A	17 Group 7A	18 Group 8A
1	1 H																	2 He
2	3 Li	4 Be											5 B	6 C	7 N	8 O	9 F	10 Ne
3	11 Na	12 Mg											13 Al	14 Si	15 P	16 S	17 Cl	18 Ar
4	19 K	20 Ca	21 Sc	22 Ti	23 V	24 Cr	25 Mn	26 Fe	27 Co	28 Ni	29 Cu	30 Zn	31 Ga	32 Ge	33 As	34 Se	35 Br	36 Kr
5	37 Rb	38 Sr	39 Y	40 Zr	41 Nb	42 Mo	43 Tc	44 Ru	45 Rh	46 Pd	47 Ag	48 Cd	49 In	50 Sn	51 Sb	52 Te	53 I	54 Xe
6	55 Cs	56 Ba	57* La	72 Hf	73 Ta	74 W	75 Re	76 Os	77 Ir	78 Pt	79 Au	80 Hg	81 Tl	82 Pb	83 Bi	84 Po	85 At	86 Rn
7	87 Fr	88 Ra	89† Ac	104 Rf	105 Db	106 Sg	107 Bh	108 Hs	109 Mt	110 Ds	111 Rg	112 Cn	113 —	114 Fl	115 —	116 Lv	117 —	118 —

Major elements in the human body Macrominerals Microminerals (trace elements)

QUESTIONS AND PROBLEMS

4.2 The Periodic Table

LEARNING GOAL: *Use the periodic table to identify the group and the period of an element: identify the element as a metal, a nonmetal, or a metalloid.*

4.7 Identify the group or period number described by each of the following:

a. contains the elements C, N, and O
b. begins with helium
c. contains the alkali metals
d. is the period with neon

4.8 Identify the group or period number described by each of the following:

a. contains Na, K, and Rb
b. is the period with Li
c. contains the noble gases
d. contains F, Cl, Br, and I

4.9 Classify each of the following as an alkali metal, alkaline earth metal, transition element, halogen, or noble gas:

a. Ca **b.** Fe **c.** Xe
d. K **e.** Cl

4.10 Classify each of the following as an alkali metal, alkaline earth metal, transition element, halogen, or noble gas:

a. Ne **b.** Mg **c.** Cu
d. Br **e.** Ba

4.11 Give the symbol of the element described by each of the following:

a. Group 4A (14), Period 2
b. a noble gas in Period 1
c. an alkali metal in Period 3
d. Group 2A (2), Period 4
e. Group 3A (13), Period 3

4.12 Give the symbol of the element described by each of the following:

a. an alkaline earth metal in Period 2
b. Group 5A (15), Period 3
c. a noble gas in Period 4
d. a halogen in Period 5
e. Group 4A (14), Period 4

4.13 Identify each of the following elements as a metal, a nonmetal, or a metalloid:

a. calcium
b. sulfur
c. a shiny element
d. an element that is a gas at room temperature
e. located in Group 8A (18)
f. bromine
g. boron
h. silver

4.14 Identify each of the following elements as a metal, a nonmetal, or a metalloid:

a. located in Group 2A (2)
b. a good conductor of electricity
c. chlorine
d. silicon
e. an element that is not shiny
f. oxygen
g. nitrogen
h. tin

4.3 The Atom

LEARNING GOAL

Describe the electrical charge and location in an atom for a proton, a neutron, and an electron.

All the elements listed on the periodic table are made up of atoms. As we discussed, an **atom** is the smallest particle of an element. Imagine that you are tearing a piece of aluminum foil into smaller and smaller pieces. Now imagine that you have a microscopic piece so small that it cannot be divided any further. Then you would have a single atom of aluminum.

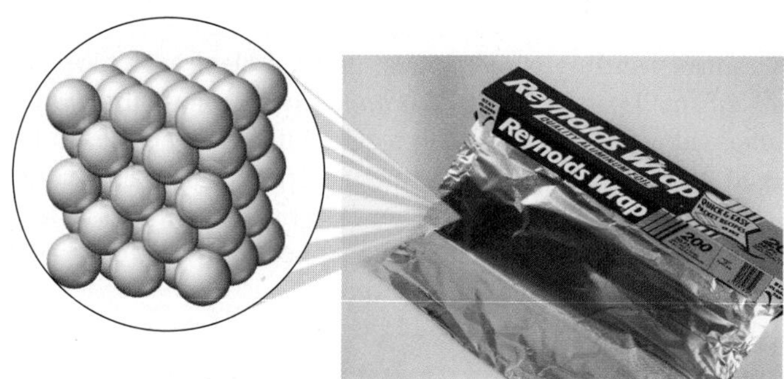

Aluminum foil consists of atoms of aluminum.

The concept of the atom is relatively recent. Although the Greek philosophers in 500 B.C.E. reasoned that everything must contain minute particles they called *atomos*, the idea of atoms did not become a scientific theory until 1808. Then John Dalton (1766–1844) developed an atomic theory that proposed that atoms were responsible for the combinations of elements found in compounds.

Dalton's Atomic Theory

1. All matter is made up of tiny particles called atoms.
2. All atoms of a given element are identical to one another and different from atoms of other elements.
3. Atoms of two or more different elements combine to form compounds. A particular compound is always made up of the same kinds of atoms and the same number of each kind of atom.
4. A chemical reaction involves the rearrangement, separation, or combination of atoms. Atoms are never created or destroyed during a chemical reaction.

Dalton's atomic theory formed the basis of current atomic theory, although we have modified some of Dalton's statements. We now know that atoms of the same element are not completely identical to each other and consist of even smaller particles. However, an atom is still the smallest particle of any element.

Although atoms are the building blocks of everything we see around us, we cannot see an atom or even a billion atoms with the naked eye. However, when billions and billions of atoms are packed together, the characteristics of each atom are added to those of the next until we can see the characteristics we associate with the element. For example, a small piece of the shiny element we call nickel consists of many, many nickel atoms. A special kind of microscope called a *scanning tunneling microscope* (STM) produces images of individual atoms (see Figure 4.7).

FIGURE 4.7 Images of nickel atoms are produced when nickel is magnified millions of times by a scanning tunneling microscope (STM).

Q Why is a microscope with extremely high magnification needed to see atoms?

Electrical Charges in an Atom

By the end of the 1800s, experiments with electricity showed that atoms were not solid spheres but were composed of even smaller bits of matter, called **subatomic particles**, three of which are the *proton*, *neutron*, and *electron*. Two of these subatomic particles were discovered because they have electrical charges.

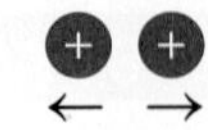

Positive charges repel

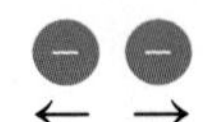

Negative charges repel

Unlike charges attract

FIGURE 4.8 Like charges repel, and unlike charges attract.

Q Why are the electrons attracted to the protons in the nucleus of an atom?

An electrical charge can be positive or negative. Experiments show that like charges repel, or push away from each other. When you brush your hair on a dry day, electrical charges that are alike build up on the brush and in your hair. As a result, your hair flies away from the brush. Opposite or unlike charges attract. The crackle of clothes taken from the clothes dryer indicates the presence of electrical charges. The clinginess of the clothing results from the attraction of opposite, unlike charges (see Figure 4.8).

Structure of the Atom

In 1897, J. J. Thomson, an English physicist, applied electricity to a glass tube, which produced streams of small particles called *cathode rays*. Because these rays were attracted to a positively charged electrode, Thomson realized that the particles in the rays must be negatively charged. In further experiments, these particles called **electrons** were found to be much smaller than the atom and to have an extremely small mass. Because atoms are neutral, scientists soon discovered that atoms contained positively charged particles called **protons** that were much heavier than the electrons.

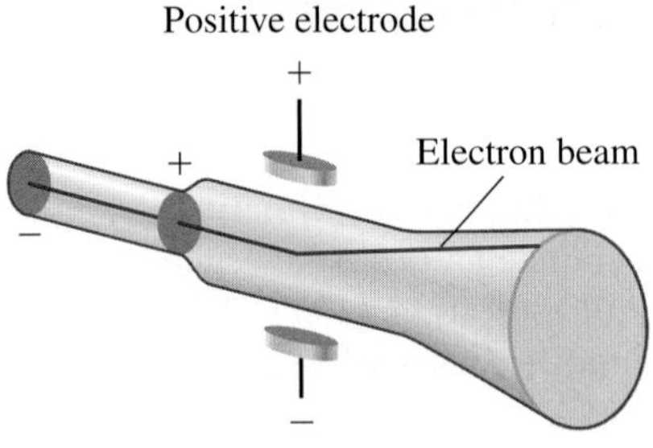

Negatively charged cathode rays (electrons) are attracted to the positive electrode.

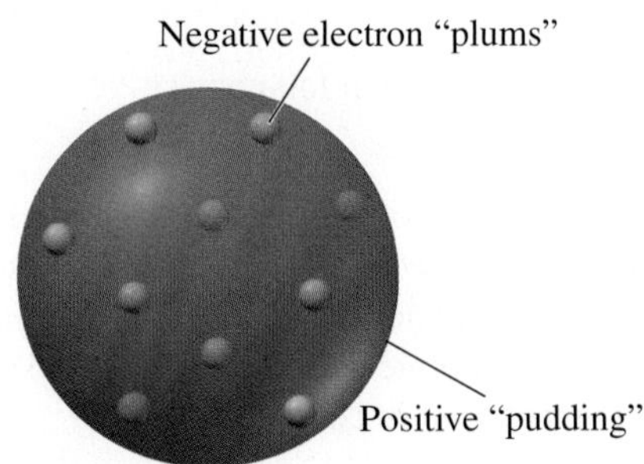

Thomson's "plum-pudding" model had protons and electrons scattered throughout the atom.

Thomson proposed a "plum-pudding" model for the atom in which the electrons (negative) were randomly distributed in a positively charged cloud like "plums in a pudding" or "chocolate chips in a cookie." In 1911, Ernest Rutherford worked with Thomson to test this model. In Rutherford's experiment, positively charged particles were aimed at a thin sheet of gold foil (see Figure 4.9). If the Thomson model were correct, the particles would travel in straight paths through the gold foil. Rutherford was greatly surprised to find that some of the particles were deflected slightly as they passed through the gold foil, and a few particles were deflected so much that they went back in the opposite direction.

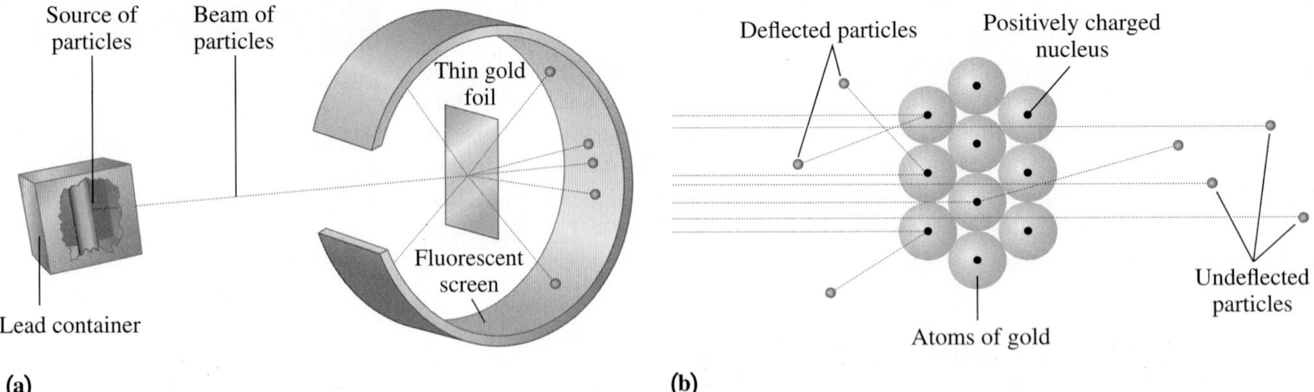

FIGURE 4.9 **(a)** Positive particles are aimed at a piece of gold foil. **(b)** Particles that come close to the atomic nuclei are deflected from their straight path.

Q Why are some particles deflected while most pass through the gold foil undeflected?

From his gold-foil experiments, Rutherford realized that the protons must be contained in a small, positively charged region at the center of the atom, which he called the **nucleus**. He proposed that the electrons in the atom occupy the space surrounding the nucleus through which most of the particles traveled undisturbed. Only the particles that came near this dense, positive center were deflected. If an atom were the size of a football stadium, the nucleus would be about the size of a golf ball placed in the center of the field.

Scientists knew that the nucleus was heavier than the mass of the protons, so they looked for another subatomic particle. Eventually, James Chadwick, in 1932, discovered that the nucleus also contained a particle called a **neutron**, which is neutral. Thus, the masses of the protons and neutrons in the nucleus determine its mass (see Figure 4.10).

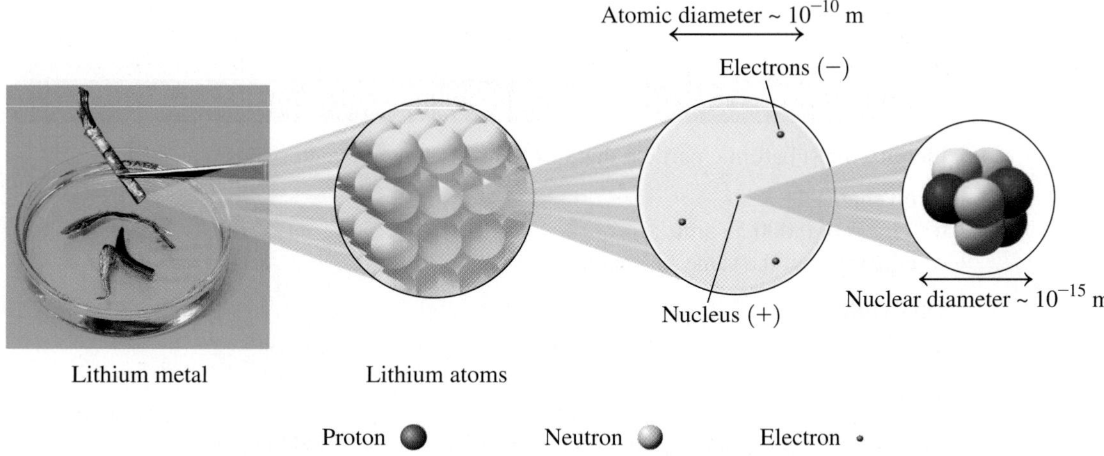

FIGURE 4.10 In an atom, the protons and neutrons that make up almost all the mass of the atom are packed into the tiny volume of the nucleus. The rapidly moving electrons (negative charge) surround the nucleus and account for the large volume of the atom.

Q Why can we say that an atom is mostly empty space?

Mass of the Atom

All the subatomic particles are extremely small compared with the things you see around you. One proton has a mass of 1.673×10^{-24} g, and the neutron is about the same. The mass of the electron is 9.110×10^{-28} g, which is much less than either a proton or neutron. Because the masses of subatomic particles are so small, chemists use a unit called an **atomic mass unit (amu)**. An amu is defined as one-twelfth of the mass of the carbon atom with 6 protons and 6 neutrons, a standard with which the mass of every other atom is compared. In biology, the atomic mass unit is called a *Dalton* (Da) in honor of John Dalton. On the amu scale, the proton and neutron each have a mass of about 1 amu. Because the electron mass is so small, it is usually ignored in atomic mass calculations. Table 4.5 summarizes some information about the subatomic particles in an atom.

TABLE 4.5 Subatomic Particles in the Atom

Particle	Symbol	Electrical Charge	Mass (g)	Mass (amu)	Location in Atom
Proton	p or p^+	1+	1.673×10^{-24}	1.007	Nucleus
Neutron	n or n^0	0	1.675×10^{-24}	1.008	Nucleus
Electron	e^-	1−	9.110×10^{-28}	0.000 55	Outside nucleus

CONCEPT CHECK 4.3 Subatomic Particles

Is each of the following statements *true* or *false*? If false, correct the statement.

a. Protons are heavier than electrons.
b. Protons are attracted to neutrons.
c. Electrons are so small that they have no electrical charge.
d. The nucleus contains all the protons and neutrons of an atom.

ANSWER

a. True
b. False; protons are attracted to electrons.
c. False; electrons have a 1− charge.
d. True

SAMPLE PROBLEM 4.4 Identifying Subatomic Particles

Identify the subatomic particle that has the following characteristics:

a. no charge
b. a mass of 0.000 55 amu
c. a mass about the same as a neutron

SOLUTION

a. neutron **b.** electron **c.** proton

STUDY CHECK 4.5

Is the following statement *true* or *false*? If false, correct the statement.
The nucleus occupies a large volume in an atom.

QUESTIONS AND PROBLEMS

4.3 The Atom

LEARNING GOAL: *Describe the electrical charge and location in an atom for a proton, a neutron, and an electron.*

4.15 Identify each of the following as describing a proton, a neutron, or an electron:
a. has the smallest mass
b. carries a 1+ charge
c. is found outside the nucleus
d. is electrically neutral

4.16 Identify each of the following as describing a proton, a neutron, or an electron:
a. has a mass about the same as a proton
b. is found in the nucleus
c. is attracted to the protons
d. has a 1− charge

4.17 What did Rutherford determine about the structure of the atom from his gold-foil experiment?

4.18 How did Thomson determine that the electrons have a negative charge?

4.19 Is each of the following statements *true* or *false*?
a. A proton and an electron have opposite charges.
b. The nucleus contains most of the mass of an atom.
c. Electrons repel each other.
d. An electron is attracted to a neutron.

4.20 Is each of the following statements *true* or *false*?
a. A proton is attracted to an electron.
b. A neutron has twice the mass of a proton.
c. Neutrons repel each other.
d. Electrons and neutrons have opposite charges.

4.21 On a dry day, your hair flies away when you brush it. How would you explain this?

4.22 Sometimes clothes cling together when removed from a dryer. What kinds of charges are on the clothes?

LEARNING GOAL

Given the atomic number and the mass number of an atom, state the number of protons, neutrons, and electrons.

4.4 Atomic Number and Mass Number

All of the atoms of the same element always have the same number of protons. This feature distinguishes atoms of one element from atoms of all the other elements.

Atomic Number

CORE CHEMISTRY SKILL

Counting Protons and Neutrons

The **atomic number** of an element is equal to the number of protons in every atom of that element. The atomic number is the whole number that appears above the symbol of each element on the periodic table.

Atomic number = number of protons in an atom

The periodic table on the inside front cover of this text shows the elements in order of atomic number from 1 to 118. We can use an atomic number to identify the number of protons in an atom of any element. For example, a lithium atom, with atomic number 3, has 3 protons. Every lithium atom has 3 and only 3 protons. Any atom with 3 protons is always a lithium atom. In the same way, we determine that a carbon atom, with atomic number 6, has 6 protons. Every carbon atom has 6 protons, and any atom with 6 protons is carbon; every copper atom, with atomic number 29, has 29 protons and any atom with 29 protons is copper.

An atom is electrically neutral. That means that the number of protons in an atom is equal to the number of electrons, which gives every atom an overall electrical charge of zero. Thus, for any atom, the atomic number also gives the number of electrons.

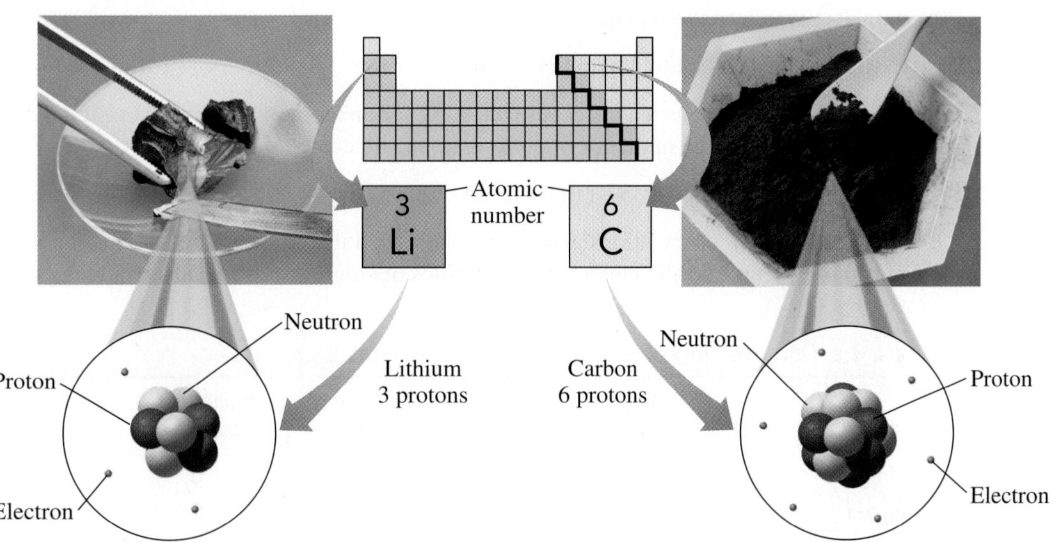

All atoms of lithium (left) contain 3 protons, and all atoms of carbon (right) contain 6 protons.

SAMPLE PROBLEM 4.6 Atomic Number, Protons, and Electrons

Using the periodic table, state the atomic number, number of protons, and number of electrons for the atoms of each of the following elements:

a. nitrogen **b.** magnesium **c.** bromine

SOLUTION

Analyze the Problem	Atomic Number	Number of Protons	Number of Electrons
	shown above the element symbol on the periodic table	equal to atomic number	equal to number of protons

a. On the periodic table, the atomic number for nitrogen (N) is 7. Thus, nitrogen atoms contain 7 protons and 7 electrons.

b. On the periodic table, the atomic number for magnesium (Mg) is 12. Thus, magnesium atoms contain 12 protons and 12 electrons.

c. On the periodic table, the atomic number for bromine (Br) is 35. Thus, bromine atoms contain 35 protons and 35 electrons.

STUDY CHECK 4.6

Consider an atom that has 79 electrons.

a. How many protons are in its nucleus?
b. What is its atomic number?
c. What is its name, and what is its symbol?

Mass Number

We now know that the protons and neutrons determine the mass of the nucleus. Thus, for a single atom, we assign a **mass number**, which is the total number of protons and neutrons in its nucleus. However, the mass number does not appear on the periodic table because it applies to single atoms only.

$$\text{Mass number} = \text{number of protons} + \text{number of neutrons in a nucleus}$$

For example, the nucleus of a single oxygen atom that contains 8 protons and 8 neutrons has a mass number of 16. If the nucleus of a single iron atom contains 26 protons and 32 neutrons, it would have a mass number of 58.

If we are given the mass number of an atom and its atomic number, we can calculate the number of neutrons in its nucleus.

$$\text{Number of neutrons in a nucleus} = \text{mass number} - \text{number of protons}$$

For example, if we are given a mass number of 37 for an atom of chlorine (atomic number 17), we can calculate the number of neutrons in its nucleus.

$$\text{Number of neutrons} = 37\ (\text{mass number}) - 17\ (\text{protons}) = 20\ \text{neutrons}$$

Table 4.6 illustrates these relationships between atomic number, mass number, and the number of protons, neutrons, and electrons in examples of single atoms for different elements.

TABLE 4.6 Composition of Some Atoms of Different Elements

Element	Symbol	Atomic Number	Mass Number	Number of Protons	Number of Neutrons	Number of Electrons
Hydrogen	H	1	1	1	0	1
Nitrogen	N	7	14	7	7	7
Oxygen	O	8	16	16	8	8
Chlorine	Cl	17	37	17	20	17
Iron	Fe	26	58	26	32	26
Gold	Au	79	197	79	118	79

CONCEPT CHECK 4.4 Subatomic Particles in Atoms

An atom of silver has a mass number of 109.

a. How many protons are in the nucleus?
b. How many neutrons are in the nucleus?
c. How many electrons are in the atom?

ANSWER

a. Silver (Ag), with atomic number 47, has 47 protons.
b. The number of neutrons is calculated by subtracting the number of protons from the mass number.

$$109 - 47 = 62 \text{ neutrons for an atom of Ag with a mass number of } 109$$

c. In a neutral atom, the number of electrons is equal to the number of protons. An atom of silver with 47 protons has 47 electrons.

SAMPLE PROBLEM 4.7 Calculating Numbers of Protons, Neutrons, and Electrons

For an atom of zinc that has a mass number of 68, determine the following:

a. the number of protons **b.** the number of neutrons
c. the number of electrons

SOLUTION

Analyze the Problem	Element	Atomic Number	Mass Number	Number of Protons	Number of Neutrons	Number of Electrons
	Zinc (Zn)	30 (periodic table)	68	equal to atomic number	mass number − number of protons	equal to number of protons

a. Zinc (Zn), with an atomic number of 30, has 30 protons.
b. The number of neutrons in this atom is found by subtracting the number of protons (atomic number) from the mass number.

$$\text{Mass number} - \text{atomic number} = \text{number of neutrons}$$
$$68 - 30 = 38$$

c. Because the zinc atom is neutral, the number of electrons is equal to the number of protons. A zinc atom has 30 electrons.

STUDY CHECK 4.7

How many neutrons are in the nucleus of a bromine atom that has a mass number of 80?

QUESTIONS AND PROBLEMS

4.4 Atomic Number and Mass Number

LEARNING GOAL: *Given the atomic number and the mass number of an atom, state the number of protons, neutrons, and electrons.*

4.23 Would you use atomic number, mass number, or both to obtain the following?
a. number of protons in an atom
b. number of neutrons in an atom
c. number of particles in the nucleus
d. number of electrons in a neutral atom

4.24 Identify the type of subatomic particles described by each of the following:
a. atomic number
b. mass number
c. mass number − atomic number
d. mass number + atomic number

4.25 Write the name and symbol of the element with each of the following atomic numbers:
a. 3 **b.** 9 **c.** 20 **d.** 30
e. 10 **f.** 14 **g.** 53 **h.** 8

4.26 Write the name and symbol of the element with each of the following atomic numbers:
a. 1 **b.** 11 **c.** 19 **d.** 82
e. 35 **f.** 47 **g.** 15 **h.** 2

4.27 How many protons and electrons are there in a neutral atom of each of the following?
a. argon **b.** manganese
c. iodine **d.** cadmium

4.28 How many protons and electrons are there in a neutral atom of each of the following?
a. carbon **b.** fluorine
c. tin **d.** nickel

4.29 Complete the following table for a neutral atom of each element:

Name of the Element	Symbol	Atomic Number	Mass Number	Number of Protons	Number of Neutrons	Number of Electrons
	Al		27			
		12			12	
Potassium					20	
				16	15	
			56			26

4.30 Complete the following table for a neutral atom of each element:

Name of the Element	Symbol	Atomic Number	Mass Number	Number of Protons	Number of Neutrons	Number of Electrons
	N		15			
Calcium			42			
				38	50	
		14			16	
		56	138			

LEARNING GOAL

Give the number of protons, electrons, and neutrons in one or more of the isotopes of an element; calculate the atomic mass of an element using the percent abundance and mass of its naturally occurring isotopes.

CORE CHEMISTRY SKILL

Writing Atomic Symbols for Isotopes

4.5 Isotopes and Atomic Mass

We have seen that all atoms of the same element have the same number of protons and electrons. However, the atoms of any one element are not entirely identical because the atoms of most elements have different numbers of neutrons. When a sample of an element consists of two or more atoms with differing numbers of neutrons, those atoms are called *isotopes*.

Atoms and Isotopes

Isotopes are atoms of the same element that have the same atomic number but different numbers of neutrons. For example, all atoms of the element magnesium (Mg) have an atomic number of 12. Thus every magnesium atom always has 12 protons. However, some naturally occurring magnesium atoms have 12 neutrons, others have 13 neutrons, and still others have 14 neutrons. The different numbers of neutrons give the magnesium atoms different mass numbers but do not change their chemical behavior. The three isotopes of magnesium have the same atomic number but different mass numbers.

To distinguish between the different isotopes of an element, we write an **atomic symbol** for a particular isotope with its mass number in the upper left corner and its atomic number in the lower left corner.

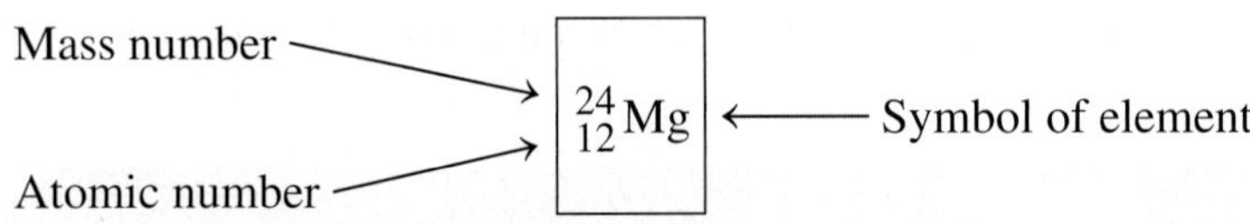

Atomic symbol for an isotope of magnesium, Mg-24

An isotope may be referred to by its name or symbol, followed by the mass number, such as magnesium-24 or Mg-24. Magnesium has three naturally occurring isotopes, as shown in Table 4.7.

TABLE 4.7 Isotopes of Magnesium

Atomic Symbol	$^{24}_{12}Mg$	$^{25}_{12}Mg$	$^{26}_{12}Mg$
Name	Mg-24	Mg-25	Mg-26
Number of Protons	12	12	12
Number of Electrons	12	12	12
Mass Number	**24**	**25**	**26**
Number of Neutrons	**12**	**13**	**14**
Mass of Isotope (amu)	**23.99**	**24.99**	**25.98**
% Abundance	78.70	10.13	11.17

SAMPLE PROBLEM 4.8 Identifying Protons and Neutrons in Isotopes

The element neon has three naturally occurring isotopes: Ne-20, Ne-21, and Ne-22. State the number of protons and neutrons in these stable isotopes of neon.

a. $^{20}_{10}Ne$ **b.** $^{21}_{10}Ne$ **c.** $^{22}_{10}Ne$

SOLUTION

Analyze the Problem	Atomic Number	Mass Number	Number of Protons	Number of Neutrons
	number in lower left corner	number in upper left corner	equal to atomic number	equal to mass number − number of protons

In the atomic symbol, the mass number is shown in the upper left corner of the symbol, and the atomic number is shown in the lower left corner of the symbol. Thus, each isotope of Ne, atomic number 10, has 10 protons. The number of neutrons is found by subtracting the number of protons (10) from the mass number of each isotope.

Isotope	Atomic Number	Mass Number	Number of Protons	Number of Neutrons
a. $^{20}_{10}Ne$	10	20	10	$20 - 10 = 10$
b. $^{21}_{10}Ne$	10	21	10	$21 - 10 = 11$
c. $^{22}_{10}Ne$	10	22	10	$22 - 10 = 12$

STUDY CHECK 4.8

Write an atomic symbol for each of the following isotopes:

a. a nitrogen atom with 8 neutrons
b. an atom with 35 protons and 46 neutrons
c. an atom with mass number 27 and 13 neutrons

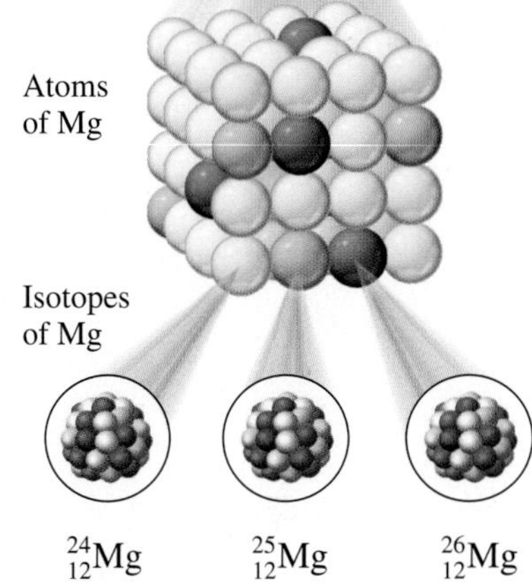

The nuclei of the three naturally occurring magnesium isotopes have the same number of protons but different numbers of neutrons.

Atomic Mass

In laboratory work, a chemist generally uses samples with many atoms that contain all the different isotopes of an element. Because each kind of isotope has a different mass, chemists have calculated an **atomic mass** for an "average atom," which is a *weighted average* of the masses of all the naturally occurring isotopes of that element. On the periodic table, the atomic mass is the number including decimal places that is shown below the symbol of each element. Most of the elements consist of two or more isotopes, which is one reason that the atomic masses on the periodic table are seldom whole numbers.

Weighted Average Analogy

To understand how the atomic mass as a weighted average for a group of isotopes is calculated, we will use an analogy of bowling balls with different weights. Suppose that a bowling alley has ordered 5 bowling balls for children that weigh 8 lb each and 20 bowling balls for adults that weigh 14 lb each. In this group of bowling balls, there are more 14-lb balls than 8-lb balls. The abundance of the 14-lb balls is 80.% (20/25), and the abundance of the 8-lb balls is 20.% (5/25). Now we can calculate a weighted average for the "average" bowling ball using the weight and percent abundance of the two types of bowling balls.

The weighted average of 8-lb and 14-lb bowling balls is calculated using their percent abundance.

	Weight		Percent Abundance		Weight from Each Type
14-lb bowling balls	14 lb	$\times$	$\frac{80.}{100}$	=	11.2 lb
8-lb bowling balls	8 lb	$\times$	$\frac{20.}{100}$	=	1.6 lb
			Weighted average of a bowling ball	=	12.8 lb
			"Atomic mass" of a bowling ball	=	12.8 lb

Calculating Atomic Mass Using Isotopes

To calculate the atomic mass of an element, we need to know the mass of each isotope and the percent abundance of each isotope, which are determined experimentally. For example, a large sample of naturally occurring chlorine consists of 75.76% of ${}^{35}_{17}Cl$ atoms and 24.24% of ${}^{37}_{17}Cl$ atoms. The atomic mass can then be calculated as a weighted average from the percent abundance of each isotope and its mass: the isotope ${}^{35}_{17}Cl$ has a mass of 34.97 amu, and the isotope ${}^{37}_{17}Cl$ has a mass of 36.97 amu.

$$\text{Atomic mass of Cl} = \underbrace{\text{mass of } {}^{35}_{17}\text{Cl} \times \frac{{}^{35}_{17}\text{Cl}\%}{100\%}}_{\text{mass from } {}^{35}_{17}\text{Cl}} + \underbrace{\text{mass of } {}^{37}_{17}\text{Cl} \times \frac{{}^{37}_{17}\text{Cl}\%}{100\%}}_{\text{mass from } {}^{37}_{17}\text{Cl}}$$

Isotope	Mass (amu)	$\times$	Abundance (%)	=	Contribution to Average Cl Atom
${}^{35}_{17}Cl$	34.97	$\times$	$\frac{75.76}{100}$	=	26.49 amu
${}^{37}_{17}Cl$	36.97	$\times$	$\frac{24.24}{100}$	=	8.962 amu
			Atomic mass of Cl	=	35.45 amu (weighted average mass)

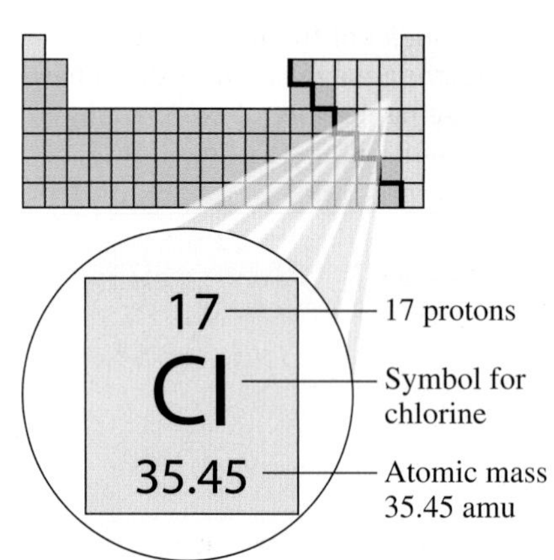

The atomic mass of 35.45 amu is the weighted average mass of a sample of Cl atoms, although no individual Cl atom actually has this mass. An atomic mass of 35.45, which is closer to the mass number of Cl-35, also indicates there is a higher percentage of ${}^{35}_{17}Cl$ atoms in the chlorine sample. In fact, there are about three atoms of ${}^{35}_{17}Cl$ for every one atom of ${}^{37}_{17}Cl$ in a sample of chlorine atoms.

Table 4.8 lists the naturally occurring isotopes of selected elements and their atomic mass, along with their most prevalent isotopes.

TABLE 4.8 The Atomic Mass of Some Elements

Element	Stable Isotopes	Atomic Mass (Weighted Average)	Most Prevalent Isotope
Lithium	${}^{6}_{3}Li$, ${}^{7}_{3}Li$	6.941 amu	${}^{7}_{3}Li$
Carbon	${}^{12}_{6}C$, ${}^{13}_{6}C$, ${}^{14}_{6}C$	12.01 amu	${}^{12}_{6}C$
Oxygen	${}^{16}_{8}O$, ${}^{17}_{8}O$, ${}^{18}_{8}O$	16.00 amu	${}^{16}_{8}O$
Fluorine	${}^{19}_{9}F$	19.00 amu	${}^{19}_{9}F$
Sulfur	${}^{32}_{16}S$, ${}^{33}_{16}S$, ${}^{34}_{16}S$, ${}^{36}_{16}S$	32.07 amu	${}^{32}_{16}S$
Copper	${}^{63}_{29}Cu$, ${}^{65}_{29}Cu$	63.55 amu	${}^{63}_{29}Cu$

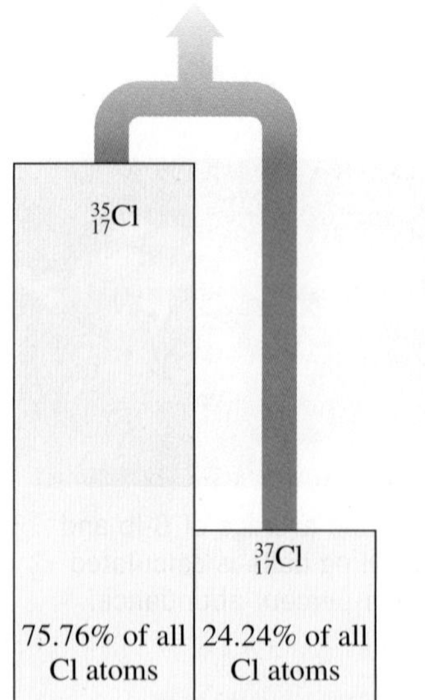

Chlorine, with two naturally occurring isotopes, has an atomic mass of 35.45.

CONCEPT CHECK 4.5 Average Atomic Mass

Neon consists of three naturally occurring isotopes: ${}^{20}_{10}Ne$, ${}^{21}_{10}Ne$, and ${}^{22}_{10}Ne$. Using the atomic mass on the periodic table, which isotope of neon is the most prevalent?

ANSWER

Using the periodic table, we find that the atomic mass for all the naturally occurring isotopes of neon is 20.18 amu. Because its mass number is very close to the atomic mass, the isotope ${}^{20}_{10}Ne$ must be the most prevalent isotope in a neon sample.

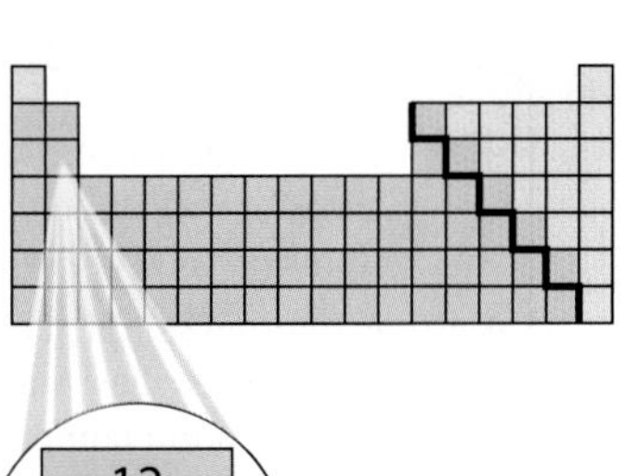

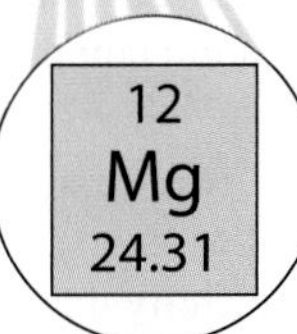

SAMPLE PROBLEM 4.9 Calculating Atomic Mass

Using Table 4.7, calculate the atomic mass for magnesium.

SOLUTION

To determine atomic mass, calculate the contribution of each isotope to the total atomic mass, by multiplying the mass of each of the isotopes by its percent abundance/100 and adding the results.

$$\text{Atomic mass} = \text{mass of isotope 1} \times \text{\% abundance/100 isotope 1} + \text{mass of isotope 2} \times \text{\% abundance/100 isotope 2} + \ldots$$

Isotope	Mass (amu)	×	Abundance (%)	=	Contribution to Average Mg Atom
$^{24}_{12}Mg$	23.99	×	$\frac{78.70}{100}$	=	18.88 amu
$^{25}_{12}Mg$	24.99	×	$\frac{10.13}{100}$	=	2.531 amu
$^{26}_{12}Mg$	25.98	×	$\frac{11.17}{100}$	=	2.902 amu
			Atomic mass of Mg	=	24.31 amu (weighted average mass)

STUDY CHECK 4.9

There are two naturally occurring isotopes of boron. The isotope $^{10}_{5}B$ has a mass of 10.01 amu with a percent abundance of 19.80%, and $^{11}_{5}B$ has a mass of 11.01 amu with a percent abundance of 80.20%. What is the atomic mass of boron?

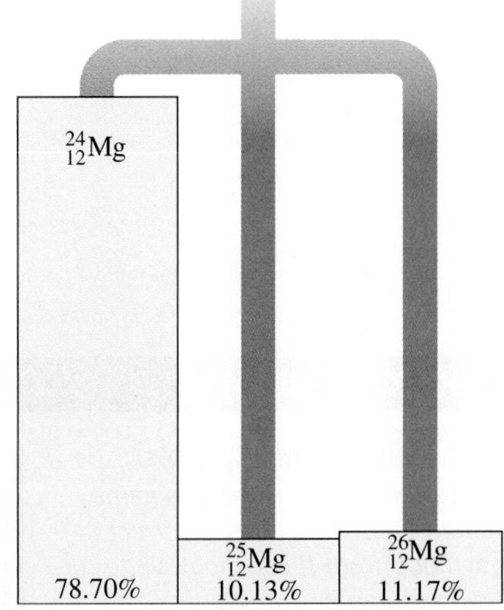

Magnesium, with three naturally occurring isotopes, has an atomic mass of 24.31.

QUESTIONS AND PROBLEMS

4.5 Isotopes and Atomic Mass

LEARNING GOAL: *Give the number of protons, electrons, and neutrons in one or more of the isotopes of an element; calculate the atomic mass of an element using the percent abundance and mass of its naturally occurring isotopes.*

4.31 What are the numbers of protons, neutrons, and electrons in the following isotopes?
a. $^{89}_{38}Sr$ **b.** $^{52}_{24}Cr$ **c.** $^{34}_{16}S$ **d.** $^{81}_{35}Br$

4.32 What are the numbers of protons, neutrons, and electrons in the following isotopes?
a. $^{2}_{1}H$ **b.** $^{14}_{7}N$ **c.** $^{26}_{14}Si$ **d.** $^{70}_{30}Zn$

4.33 Write the atomic symbols for isotopes with the following characteristics:
a. 15 protons and 16 neutrons
b. 35 protons and 45 neutrons
c. 50 electrons and 72 neutrons
d. a chlorine atom with 18 neutrons
e. a mercury atom with 122 neutrons

4.34 Write the atomic symbols for isotopes with the following characteristics:
a. an oxygen atom with 10 neutrons
b. 4 protons and 5 neutrons
c. 25 electrons and 28 neutrons
d. a mass number of 24 and 13 neutrons
e. a nickel atom with 32 neutrons

4.35 Argon has three naturally occurring isotopes, with mass numbers 36, 38, and 40.
a. Write the atomic symbol for each of these atoms.
b. How are these isotopes alike?
c. How are they different?
d. Why is the atomic mass of argon listed on the periodic table not a whole number?
e. Which isotope is the most prevalent in a sample of argon?

4.36 Strontium has four naturally occurring isotopes, with mass numbers 84, 86, 87, and 88.
a. Write the atomic symbol for each of these atoms.
b. How are these isotopes alike?
c. How are they different?
d. Why is the atomic mass of strontium listed on the periodic table not a whole number?
e. Which isotope is the most prevalent in a sample of strontium?

4.37 What is the difference between the mass of an isotope and the atomic mass of an element?

4.38 What is the difference between the mass number and the atomic mass of an element?

4.39 Copper consists of two isotopes, $^{63}_{29}Cu$ and $^{65}_{29}Cu$. If the atomic mass for copper on the periodic table is 63.55, are there more atoms of $^{63}_{29}Cu$ or $^{65}_{29}Cu$ in a sample of copper?

4.40 A fluorine sample consists of only one type of atom, $^{19}_{9}F$, which has a mass of 19.00 amu. How would the mass of a $^{19}_{9}F$ atom compare to the atomic mass listed on the periodic table?

4.41 There are two naturally occurring isotopes of thallium: $^{203}_{81}Tl$ and $^{205}_{81}Tl$. Use the atomic mass of neon listed on the periodic table to identify the most prevalent isotope.

4.42 Zinc consists of five naturally occurring isotopes: $^{64}_{30}Zn$, $^{66}_{30}Zn$, $^{67}_{30}Zn$, $^{68}_{30}Zn$, and $^{70}_{30}Zn$. None of these isotopes has the atomic mass of 65.41 listed for zinc on the periodic table. Explain.

4.43 Two isotopes of gallium are naturally occurring, with $^{69}_{31}Ga$ at 60.11% (68.93 amu) and $^{71}_{31}Ga$ at 39.89% (70.92 amu). What is the atomic mass of gallium?

4.44 Two isotopes of rubidium occur naturally, $^{85}_{37}Rb$ at 72.17% (84.91 amu) and $^{87}_{37}Rb$ at 27.83% (86.91 amu). What is the atomic mass of rubidium?

CHAPTER REVIEW

4.1 Elements and Symbols

LEARNING GOAL: *Given the name of an element, write its correct symbol; from the symbol, write the correct name.*

- Elements are the primary substances of matter.
- Chemical symbols are one- or two-letter abbreviations of the names of the elements.

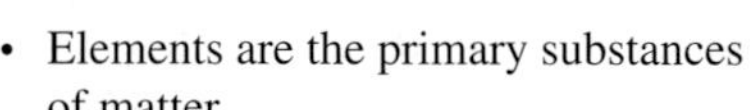

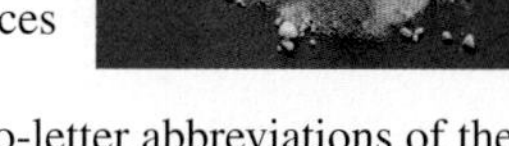

4.2 The Periodic Table

LEARNING GOAL: *Use the periodic table to identify the group and the period of an element; identify the element as a metal, a nonmetal, or a metalloid.*

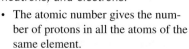

- The periodic table is an arrangement of the elements by increasing atomic number.
- A horizontal row is called a *period*. A vertical column on the periodic table containing elements with similar properties is called a *group*.
- Elements in Group 1A (1) are called the *alkali metals*; Group 2A (2), the *alkaline earth metals*; Group 7A (17), the *halogens*; and Group 8A (18), the *noble gases*.
- On the periodic table, *metals* are located on the left of the heavy zigzag line, and *nonmetals* are to the right of the heavy zigzag line.
- Except for aluminum, elements located along the heavy zigzag line are called *metalloids*.

4.3 The Atom

LEARNING GOAL: *Describe the electrical charge and location in an atom for a proton, a neutron, and an electron.*

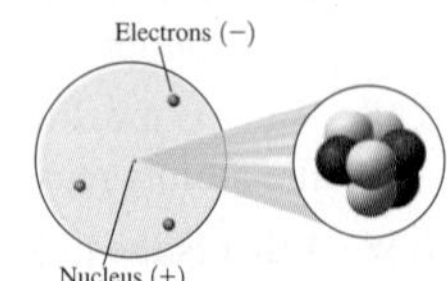

- An atom is the smallest particle that retains the characteristics of an element.
- Atoms are composed of three types of subatomic particles.
- Protons have a positive charge (+), electrons carry a negative charge (−), and neutrons are electrically neutral.
- The protons and neutrons are found in the tiny, dense nucleus; electrons are located outside the nucleus.

4.4 Atomic Number and Mass Number

LEARNING GOAL: *Given the atomic number and the mass number of an atom, state the number of protons, neutrons, and electrons.*

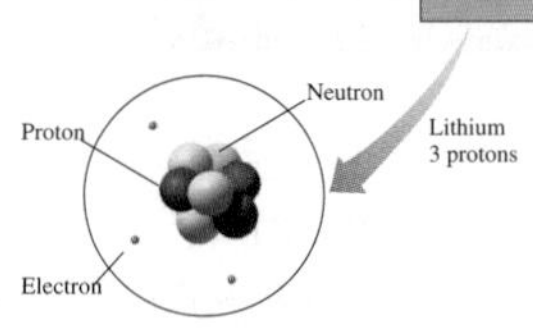

- The atomic number gives the number of protons in all the atoms of the same element.
- In a neutral atom, the number of protons and electrons is equal.
- The mass number is the total number of protons and neutrons in an atom.

4.5 Isotopes and Atomic Mass

LEARNING GOAL: *Give the number of protons, electrons, and neutrons in one or more of the isotopes of an element; calculate the atomic mass of an element using the percent abundance and mass of its naturally occurring isotopes.*

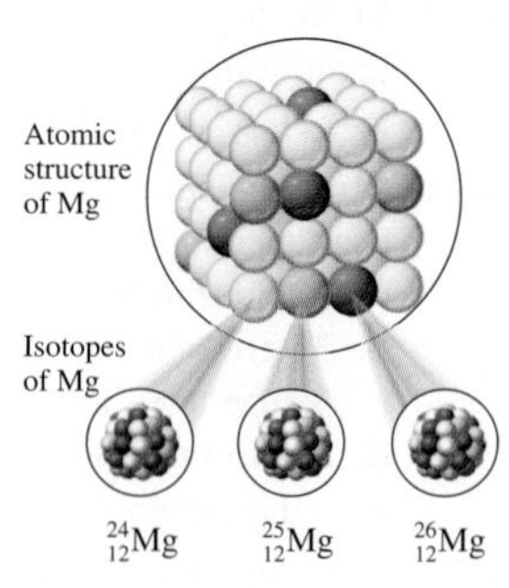

- Atoms that have the same number of protons but different numbers of neutrons are called *isotopes*.
- The atomic mass of an element is the weighted average mass of all the isotopes in a naturally occurring sample of that element.

CONCEPT MAP

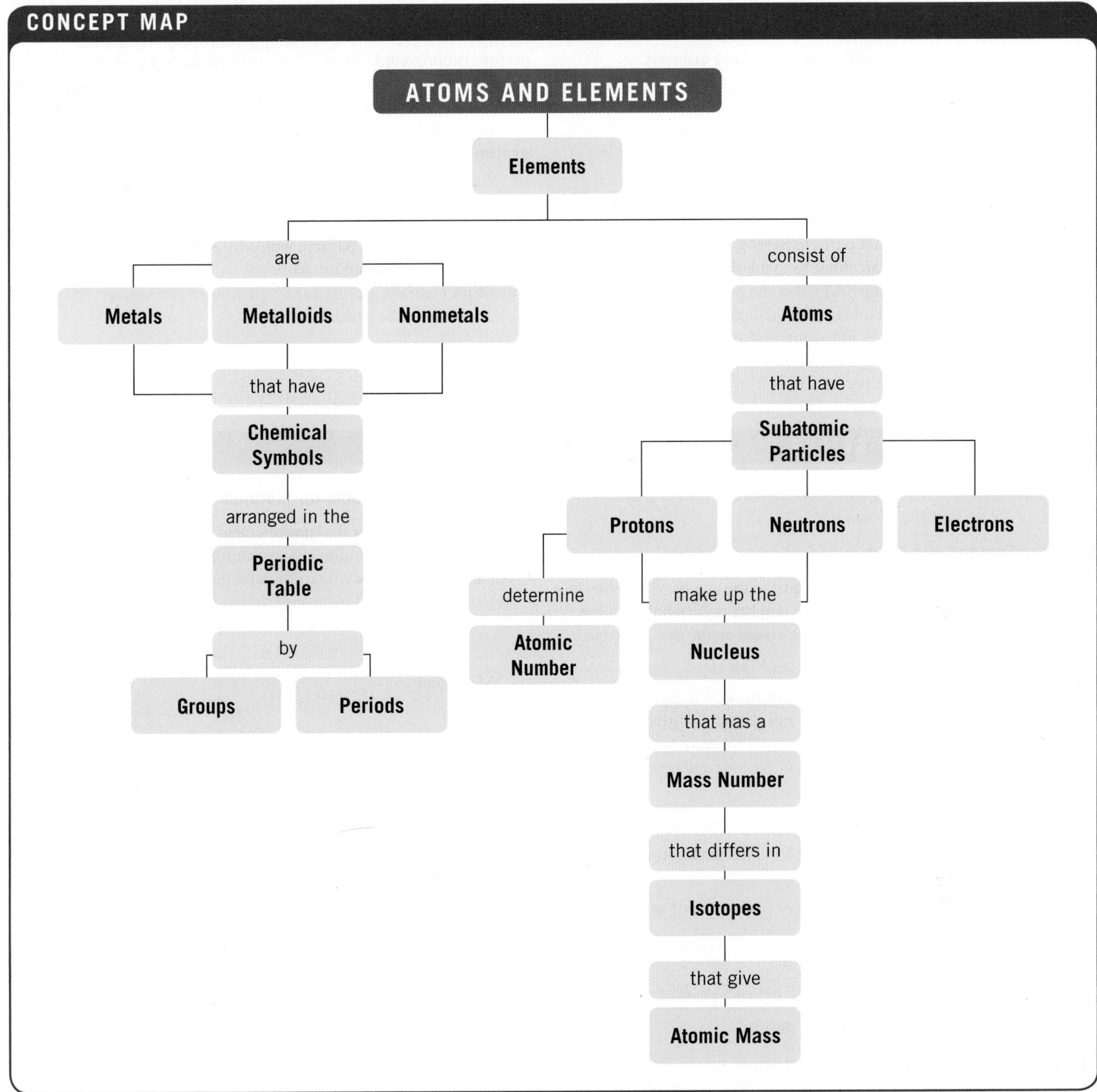

KEY TERMS

alkali metals Elements of Group 1A (1) except hydrogen; these are soft, shiny metals.

alkaline earth metals Group 2A (2) elements.

atom The smallest particle of an element that retains the characteristics of the element.

atomic mass The weighted average mass of all the naturally occurring isotopes of an element.

atomic mass unit (amu) A small mass unit used to describe the mass of very small particles such as atoms and subatomic particles; 1 amu is equal to one-twelfth the mass of a carbon-12 atom.

atomic number A number that is equal to the number of protons in an atom.

atomic symbol An abbreviation used to indicate the mass number and atomic number of an isotope.

chemical symbol An abbreviation that represents the name of an element.

electron A negatively charged subatomic particle having a very small mass that is usually ignored in mass calculations; its symbol is e^-.

group A vertical column in the periodic table that contains elements having similar physical and chemical properties.

group number A number that appears at the top of each vertical column (group) on the periodic tables.

halogens Group 7A (17) elements of fluorine, chlorine, bromine, iodine, and astatine.

isotope An atom that differs only in mass number from another atom of the same element. Isotopes have the same atomic number (number of protons) but different numbers of neutrons.

mass number The total number of protons and neutrons in the nucleus of an atom.

metal An element that is shiny, malleable, ductile, and a good conductor of heat and electricity. The metals are located to the left of the heavy zigzag line on the periodic table.

metalloid Elements with properties of both metals and nonmetals located along the heavy zigzag line on the periodic table.

neutron A neutral subatomic particle having a mass of 1 amu and found in the nucleus of an atom; its symbol is n or n^0.

noble gas An element in Group 8A (18) of the periodic table, generally unreactive and seldom found in combination with other elements.

nonmetal An element that is not shiny and is a poor conductor of heat and electricity. The nonmetals are located to the right of the heavy zigzag line on the periodic table.

nucleus The compact, very dense center of an atom, containing the protons and neutrons of the atom.

period A horizontal row of elements in the periodic table.

periodic table An arrangement of elements by increasing atomic number such that elements having similar chemical behavior are grouped in vertical columns.

proton A positively charged subatomic particle having a mass of 1 amu and found in the nucleus of an atom; its symbol is p or p^+.

representative element An element found in Groups 1A (1) through 8A (18) excluding B groups (3–12) of the periodic table.

subatomic particle A particle within an atom; protons, neutrons, and electrons are subatomic particles.

transition element An element located between Groups 2A (2) and 3A (13) on the periodic table.

CORE CHEMISTRY SKILLS

The chapter section containing each Core Chemistry Skill is shown in parentheses at the end of each heading.

Counting Protons and Neutrons (4.4)

- The atomic number of an element is equal to the number of protons in every atom of that element. The atomic number is the whole number that appears above the symbol of each element on the periodic table.

  Atomic number = number of protons in an atom

- Because atoms are neutral, the number of protons is equal to the number of electrons. Thus, the atomic number gives the number of electrons.
- The mass number is the total number of protons and neutrons in the nucleus of an atom.

  Mass number = number of protons + number of neutrons

- The number of neutrons is calculated from the mass number and atomic number.

  Number of neutrons = mass number − number of protons

Example: Calculate the number of protons and neutrons in a krypton atom with a mass number of 80.

Answer:

Element	Atomic Number	Mass Number	Number of Protons	Number of Neutrons	Number of Electrons
Kr	36	80	36	equal to mass number − number of protons $80 - 36 = 44$	36

Writing Atomic Symbols for Isotopes (4.5)

- Isotopes are atoms of the same element that have the same atomic number but different numbers of neutrons.
- An atomic symbol is written for a particular isotope with its mass number (protons and neutrons) shown in the upper left corner and its atomic number (protons) shown in the lower left corner.

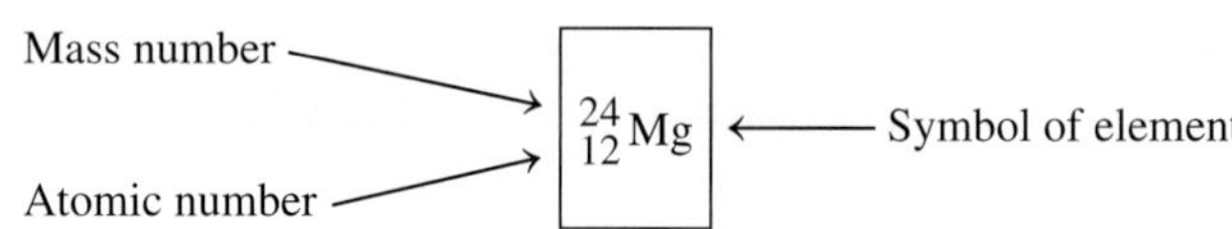

Example: Calculate the number of protons and neutrons in the cadmium isotope $^{112}_{48}Cd$.

Answer:

Isotope	Atomic Number	Mass Number	Number of Protons	Number of Neutrons
$^{112}_{48}Cd$	number (48) in lower left corner	number (112) in upper left corner	equal to atomic number (48)	equal to mass number − number of protons $112 - 48 = 64$

UNDERSTANDING THE CONCEPTS

The chapter sections to review are shown in parentheses at the end of each question.

4.45 According to Dalton's atomic theory, are each of the following *true* or *false*? If false, correct the statement. (4.3)

a. Atoms of an element are identical to atoms of other elements.

b. Every element is made of atoms.

c. Atoms of two different elements combine to form compounds.

d. In a chemical reaction, some atoms disappear and new atoms appear.

4.46 Use Rutherford's gold-foil experiment to answer each of the following: (4.3)

a. What did Rutherford expect to happen when he aimed particles at the gold foil?

b. How did the results differ from what he expected?
c. How did he use the results to propose a new model of the atom?

4.47 Match the subatomic particles (**1–3**) to each of the descriptions below: (4.3)
1. protons **2.** neutrons **3.** electrons
a. atomic mass **b.** atomic number
c. positive charge **d.** negative charge
e. mass number – atomic number

4.48 Match the subatomic particles (**1–3**) to each of the descriptions below: (4.3)
1. protons **2.** neutrons **3.** electrons
a. mass number **b.** surround the nucleus
c. nucleus **d.** charge of 0
e. equal to number of electrons

4.49 Consider the following atoms in which X represents the chemical symbol of the element: (4.4, 4.5)

$^{16}_{8}X$ $^{16}_{9}X$ $^{18}_{10}X$ $^{17}_{8}X$ $^{18}_{8}X$

a. What atoms have the same number of protons?
b. Which atoms are isotopes? Of what element?
c. Which atoms have the same mass number?
d. What atoms have the same number of neutrons?

4.50 For each of the following, write the symbol and name for X and the number of protons and neutrons. Which are isotopes of each other? (4.4, 4.5)
a. $^{124}_{47}X$ **b.** $^{116}_{49}X$ **c.** $^{116}_{50}X$
d. $^{124}_{50}X$ **e.** $^{116}_{48}X$

4.51 Indicate if the atoms in each pair have the same number of protons, neutrons, or electrons. (4.4, 4.5)
a. $^{37}_{17}Cl$, $^{38}_{18}Ar$ **b.** $^{36}_{16}S$, $^{34}_{16}S$
c. $^{79}_{34}Se$, $^{81}_{35}Br$ **d.** $^{40}_{18}Ar$, $^{39}_{17}Cl$

4.52 Complete the following table for the three naturally occurring isotopes of silicon, the major component in computer chips: (4.5)

	Isotope		
	$^{28}_{14}Si$	$^{29}_{14}Si$	$^{30}_{14}Si$
Atomic Number			
Mass Number			
Number of Protons			
Number of Neutrons			
Number of Electrons			

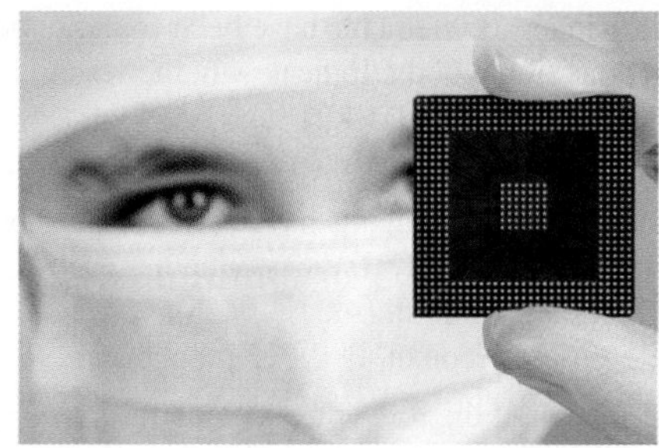

Computer chips consist primarily of the element silicon.

4.53 For each representation of a nucleus **A–E**, write the atomic symbol and determine which ones are isotopes. (4.4, 4.5)
Proton ●
Neutron ●

A **B** **C** **D** **E**

4.54 Identify the element represented by each nucleus **A–E** in Problem 4.53 as a metal, a nonmetal, or a metalloid. (4.2, 4.3, 4.4)

4.55 Provide the following information: (4.2, 4.3, 4.4)
a. the atomic number and symbol of the lightest alkali metal
b. the atomic number and symbol of the heaviest noble gas
c. the atomic mass and symbol of the alkaline earth metal in Period 3
d. the atomic mass and symbol of the halogen with the fewest electrons

4.56 Provide the following information: (4.2, 4.3, 4.4)
a. the atomic number and symbol of the heaviest metalloid in Group 4A (14)
b. the atomic number and symbol of the element in Group 5A (15), Period 6
c. the atomic mass and symbol of the alkali metal in Period 4
d. the metalloid in Group 3A (13)

ADDITIONAL QUESTIONS AND PROBLEMS

4.57 Why is Co the symbol for cobalt, not CO? (4.1)

4.58 Which of the following is correct? Write the correct symbol if needed. (4.1)
a. copper, Cp **b.** silicon, SI
c. iron, Fe **d.** fluorine, Fl
e. potassium, P **f.** sodium, Na
g. gold, Au **h.** lead, PB

4.59 Give the group and period numbers for each of the following elements: (4.1, 4.2)
a. bromine **b.** argon
c. lithium **d.** radium

4.60 Give the group and period numbers for each of the following elements: (4.1, 4.2)
a. potassium **b.** phosphorus
c. carbon **d.** neon

4.61 The following trace elements have been found to be crucial to the functions of the body. Indicate whether each is a metal, a nonmetal, or a metalloid. (4.2)
a. copper **b.** selenium **c.** arsenic **d.** chromium

4.62 The following trace elements have been found to be crucial to the functions of the body. Indicate whether each is a metal, a nonmetal, or a metalloid. (4.2)
a. zinc **b.** cobalt **c.** manganese **d.** iodine

4.63 Indicate if each of the following statements is *true* or *false*. If false, correct the statement. (4.3)
a. The proton is a negatively charged particle.
b. The neutron is 2000 times as heavy as a proton.
c. The atomic mass unit is based on a carbon atom with 6 protons and 6 neutrons.
d. The nucleus is the largest part of the atom.
e. The electrons are located outside the nucleus.

4.64 Indicate if each of the following statements is *true* or *false*. If false, correct the statement. (4.3)
a. The neutron is electrically neutral.
b. Most of the mass of an atom is due to the protons and neutrons.
c. The charge of an electron is equal, but opposite, to the charge of a neutron.
d. The proton and the electron have about the same mass.
e. The mass number is the number of protons.

4.65 Complete the following statements: (4.3)
a. The atomic number gives the number of __________ in the nucleus.
b. In an atom, the number of electrons is equal to the number of __________ .
c. Sodium and potassium are examples of elements called __________ .

4.66 Complete the following statements: (4.3)
a. The number of protons and neutrons in an atom is the __________ number.
b. The elements in Group 7A (17) are called the __________ .
c. Elements that are shiny and conduct heat are called __________ .

4.67 Write the name and symbol of the element with the following atomic number: (4.4)
a. 28 **b.** 56 **c.** 88
d. 33 **e.** 50 **f.** 55

4.68 Write the name and symbol of the element with the following atomic number: (4.4)
a. 22 **b.** 48 **c.** 26
d. 54 **e.** 78 **f.** 83

4.69 Give the number of protons and electrons in neutral atoms of each of the following: (4.4)
a. Mn **b.** phosphorus **c.** Sr
d. Co **e.** uranium

4.70 Give the number of protons and electrons in neutral atoms of each of the following: (4.4)
a. chromium **b.** Cs **c.** copper
d. chlorine **e.** Cd

4.71 For the following atoms, determine the number of protons, neutrons, and electrons: (4.4)
a. $^{114}_{48}Cd$ **b.** $^{98}_{43}Tc$ **c.** $^{199}_{79}Au$
d. $^{222}_{86}Rn$ **e.** $^{136}_{54}Xe$

4.72 For the following atoms, determine the number of protons, neutrons, and electrons: (4.4)
a. $^{202}_{80}Hg$ **b.** $^{127}_{53}I$ **c.** $^{75}_{35}Br$
d. $^{133}_{55}Cs$ **e.** $^{195}_{78}Pt$

4.73 Write the atomic symbol for each of the following: (4.5)
a. an atom with 4 protons and 5 neutrons
b. an atom with 12 protons and 14 neutrons
c. a calcium atom with a mass number of 46
d. an atom with 30 electrons and 40 neutrons

4.74 Write the atomic symbol for each of the following: (4.5)
a. an aluminum atom with 14 neutrons
b. an atom with atomic number 26 and 32 neutrons
c. a strontium atom with 50 neutrons
d. an atom with a mass number of 72 and atomic number 33

4.75 Complete the following table: (4.5)

Name	Atomic Symbol	Number of Protons	Number of Neutrons	Number of Electrons
	$^{80}_{34}Se$			
		28	34	
Magnesium			14	
	$^{220}_{86}Rn$			

4.76 Complete the following table: (4.5)

Name	Atomic Symbol	Number of Protons	Number of Neutrons	Number of Electrons
Potassium			22	
	$^{51}_{23}V$			
		48	64	
Cobalt			32	

4.77 The most prevalent isotope of gold is Au-197. (4.5)
a. How many protons, neutrons, and electrons are in this isotope?
b. What is the atomic symbol of another isotope of gold with 116 neutrons?
c. What is the atomic symbol of an atom with an atomic number of 78 and 116 neutrons?

4.78 Cadmium, atomic number 48, consists of eight naturally occurring isotopes. Do you expect any of the isotopes to have the atomic mass listed on the periodic table for cadmium? Explain. (4.5)

CHALLENGE QUESTIONS

The following groups of questions are related to the topics in this chapter. However, they do not all follow the chapter order, and they require you to combine concepts and skills from several sections. These questions will help you increase your critical thinking skills and prepare for your next exam.

4.79 The most prevalent isotope of lead is $^{208}_{82}Pb$. (4.5)
a. How many protons, neutrons, and electrons are in $^{208}_{82}Pb$?
b. What is the atomic symbol of another isotope of lead with 132 neutrons?
c. What is the name and atomic symbol of an atom with the same mass number as in part **b** and 131 neutrons?

4.80 The most prevalent isotope of silver is $^{107}_{47}Ag$. (4.5)
a. How many protons, neutrons, and electrons are in $^{107}_{47}Ag$?
b. What is the atomic symbol of an isotope of silver with 62 neutrons?
c. What is the name and atomic symbol of another atom with the same mass number as in part **b** and 61 neutrons?

4.81 Lead consists of four naturally occurring isotopes. Calculate the atomic mass of lead. (4.5)

Isotope	Mass (amu)	Abundance (%)
$^{204}_{82}Pb$	204.0	1.40
$^{206}_{82}Pb$	206.0	24.10
$^{207}_{82}Pb$	207.0	22.10
$^{208}_{82}Pb$	208.0	52.40

4.82 Silicon has three naturally occurring isotopes. Calculate the atomic mass of silicon. (4.5)

Isotope	Mass (amu)	Abundance (%)
$^{28}_{14}Si$	27.98	92.23
$^{29}_{14}Si$	28.98	4.68
$^{30}_{14}Si$	29.97	3.09

4.83 Indium (In) has two naturally occurring isotopes: In-113 and In-115. If In-113 has a 4.30 % abundance and a mass of 112.9 amu, and In-115 has a 95.70% abundance and a mass of 114.9 amu, what is the atomic mass of indium? (4.5)

4.84 Antimony (Sb) has two naturally occurring isotopes: Sb-121 and Sb-123. If Sb-121 has a 57.21% abundance and a mass of 120.9 amu, and Sb-123 has a 42.79% abundance and a mass of 122.9 amu, what is the atomic mass of antimony? (4.5)

4.85 If the diameter of a sodium atom is 3.14×10^{-8} cm, how many sodium atoms would fit along a line exactly 1 in. long? (4.3)

4.86 A lead atom has a mass of 3.4×10^{-22} g. How many lead atoms are in a cube of lead that has a volume of 2.00 cm^3 if the density of lead is 11.3 g/cm^3? (4.3)

ANSWERS

Answers to Study Checks

4.1 Si, S, and Ag

4.2 magnesium, aluminum, and fluorine

4.3 **a.** Strontium is in Group 2A (2).
b. This is the alkaline earth metals.
c. Strontium is in Period 5.

4.4 **a.** As **b.** Rn **c.** B

4.5 False; most of the volume of an atom is outside the nucleus.

4.6 **a.** 79 protons **b.** 79 **c.** gold, Au

4.7 45 neutrons

4.8 **a.** $^{15}_{7}N$ **b.** $^{81}_{35}Br$ **c.** $^{27}_{14}Si$

4.9 10.81 amu

Answers to Selected Questions and Problems

4.1 **a.** Cu **b.** Pt **c.** Ca
d. Mn **e.** Fe **f.** Ba
g. Pb **h.** Sr

4.3 **a.** carbon **b.** chlorine **c.** iodine
d. mercury **e.** silver **f.** argon
g. boron **h.** nickel

4.5 **a.** sodium, chlorine
b. calcium, sulfur, oxygen
c. carbon, hydrogen, chlorine, nitrogen, oxygen
d. barium, chromium, oxygen

4.7 **a.** Period 2 **b.** Group 8A (18)
c. Group 1A (1) **d.** Period 2

4.9 **a.** alkaline earth metal **b.** transition element
c. noble gas **d.** alkali metal
e. halogen

4.11 **a.** C **b.** He **c.** Na
d. Ca **e.** Al

4.13 **a.** metal **b.** nonmetal **c.** metal
d. nonmetal **e.** nonmetal **f.** nonmetal
g. metalloid **h.** metal

4.15 **a.** electron **b.** proton
c. electron **d.** neutron

4.17 Rutherford determined that an atom contains a small, compact nucleus that is positively charged.

4.19 **a**, **b**, and **c** are true, but **d** is false.

4.21 In the process of brushing your hair, strands of hair become charged with like charges that repel each other.

4.23 **a.** atomic number **b.** both
c. mass number **d.** atomic number

4.25 **a.** lithium, Li **b.** fluorine, F
c. calcium, Ca **d.** zinc, Zn
e. neon, Ne **f.** silicon, Si
g. iodine, I **h.** oxygen, O

4.27 **a.** 18 protons and 18 electrons
b. 25 protons and 25 electrons
c. 53 protons and 53 electrons
d. 48 protons and 48 electrons

4.29

Name of the Element	Symbol	Atomic Number	Mass Number	Number of Protons	Number of Neutrons	Number of Electrons
Aluminum	Al	13	27	13	14	13
Magnesium	Mg	12	24	12	12	12
Potassium	K	19	39	19	20	19
Sulfur	S	16	31	16	15	16
Iron	Fe	26	56	26	30	26

4.31 **a.** 38 protons, 51 neutrons, 38 electrons
b. 24 protons, 28 neutrons, 24 electrons
c. 16 protons, 18 neutrons, 16 electrons
d. 35 protons, 46 neutrons, 35 electrons

4.33 **a.** $^{31}_{15}P$ **b.** $^{80}_{35}Br$ **c.** $^{122}_{50}Sn$
d. $^{35}_{17}Cl$ **e.** $^{202}_{80}Hg$

4.35 **a.** $^{36}_{18}Ar$, $^{38}_{18}Ar$, $^{40}_{18}Ar$
b. They all have the same number of protons and electrons.
c. They have different numbers of neutrons, which gives them different mass numbers.
d. The atomic mass of Ar listed on the periodic table is the weighted average atomic mass of all the naturally occurring isotopes.
e. The isotope Ar-40 is most prevalent because its mass is closest to the atomic mass on the periodic table.

4.37 The mass of an isotope is the mass of an individual atom. The atomic mass is the weighted average of all the naturally occurring isotopes of that element.

4.39 Since the atomic mass of copper is closer to 63 amu, there are more atoms of $^{63}_{29}Cu$.

4.41 Since the atomic mass of thallium is 204.4 amu, the most prevalent isotope is $^{205}_{81}Tl$.

4.43 69.72 amu

4.45 **a.** False; all atoms of a given element are identical to one another and different from atoms of other elements.
b. True
c. True
d. False; atoms are never created or destroyed during a chemical reaction.

4.47 **a.** 1 and 2 **b.** 1 **c.** 1
d. 3 **e.** 2

4.49 **a.** $^{16}_{8}X$, $^{17}_{8}X$, $^{18}_{8}X$ all have eight protons.
b. $^{16}_{8}X$, $^{17}_{8}X$, $^{18}_{8}X$ all are isotopes of oxygen.
c. $^{16}_{8}X$ and $^{16}_{9}X$ have mass numbers of 16, whereas $^{18}_{8}X$ and $^{18}_{10}X$ have mass numbers of 18.
d. $^{16}_{8}X$ and $^{18}_{10}X$ both have eight neutrons.

4.51 **a.** Both have 20 neutrons.
b. Both have 16 protons and 16 electrons.
c. None are the same.
d. Both have 22 neutrons.

4.53 **a.** $^{9}_{4}Be$ **b.** $^{11}_{5}B$ **c.** $^{13}_{6}C$
d. $^{10}_{5}B$ **e.** $^{12}_{6}C$
b and **d** are isotopes of boron; **c** and **e** are isotopes of carbon.

4.55 **a.** 3, Li **b.** 86, Rn
c. 24.31 amu, Mg **d.** 19.00 amu, F

4.57 The first letter of a symbol is a capital, but a second letter is lowercase. The symbol Co is for cobalt, but the symbols in CO are for carbon and oxygen.

4.59 **a.** Group 7A (17), Period 4 **b.** Group 8A (18), Period 3
c. Group 1A (1), Period 2 **d.** Group 2A (2), Period 7

4.61 **a.** metal **b.** nonmetal
c. metalloid **d.** metal

4.63 **a.** False; the proton is a positively charged particle.
b. False; the neutron has about the same mass as the proton.
c. True
d. False; the nucleus is the small, dense core of the atom.
e. True

4.65 **a.** protons **b.** protons
c. alkali metals

4.67 **a.** nickel, Ni **b.** barium, Ba
c. radium, Ra **d.** arsenic, As
e. tin, Sn **f.** cesium, Cs

4.69 **a.** 25 protons, 25 electrons **b.** 15 protons, 15 electrons
c. 38 protons, 38 electrons **d.** 27 protons, 27 electrons
e. 92 protons, 92 electrons

4.71 **a.** 48 protons, 66 neutrons, 48 electrons
b. 43 protons, 55 neutrons, 43 electrons
c. 79 protons, 120 neutrons, 79 electrons
d. 86 protons, 136 neutrons, 86 electrons
e. 54 protons, 82 neutrons, 54 electrons

4.73 **a.** $^{9}_{4}Be$ **b.** $^{26}_{12}Mg$ **c.** $^{46}_{20}Ca$
d. $^{70}_{30}Zn$

4.75

Name	Atomic Symbol	Number of Protons	Number of Neutrons	Number of Electrons
Selenium	$^{80}_{34}Se$	34	46	34
Nickel	$^{62}_{28}Ni$	28	34	28
Magnesium	$^{26}_{12}Mg$	12	14	12
Radon	$^{220}_{86}Rn$	86	134	86

4.77 **a.** 79 protons, 118 neutrons, 79 electrons
b. $^{195}_{79}Au$
c. $^{194}_{78}Pt$

4.79 **a.** 82 protons, 126 neutrons, 82 electrons
b. $^{214}_{82}Pb$
c. $^{214}_{83}Bi$, bismuth

4.81 207.2 amu

4.83 114.8 amu

4.85 8.09×10^{7} atoms of Na

Electronic Structure and Periodic Trends 5

LOOKING AHEAD

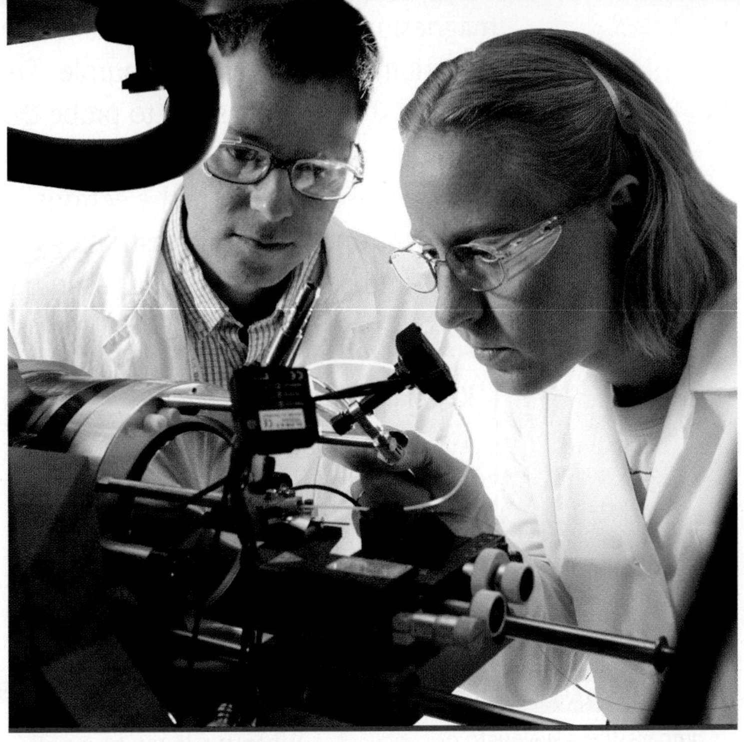

Robert and Jennifer work in the materials science department of a research laboratory. As materials engineers they deal with developing and testing various materials that are used in the manufacturing of consumer goods like computer chips, television sets, golf clubs, and snow skis. These engineers create new materials out of metals, ceramics, plastics, semiconductors, and combinations of materials called composites, which are needed for mechanical, chemical, and electrical industries. Often materials engineers study materials at an atomic level to learn how to improve the characteristics of materials.

In their research, Robert and Jennifer are working with some of the elements in Groups 3A (13), 4A (14), and 5A (15) of the periodic table. These elements such as silicon have properties that make them good semiconductors. A microchip requires growing a single crystal of a semiconductor such as pure silicon. When small amounts of impurities are added to the crystalline structure, holes form through which electrons can travel with little obstruction. Microchips are manufactured for use in computers, cell phones, satellites, televisions, calculators, GPS, and many other devices. Robert and Jennifer are working on new, more complex microchips that will offer new applications.

Career: Engineer

A bachelor's degree in engineering is required for most entry-level jobs. Engineering is a broad area with many specific disciplines including bioinformatics, civil engineering, systems engineering, electrical engineering, mechanical engineering, and software engineering. Engineers use mathematics and the principles of chemistry and other sciences to solve technical problems. Engineers also try to connect new scientific developments to practical applications that meet people's needs.

When sunlight passes through a prism or raindrops, the light bends at different angles and separates into the many colors we see in a rainbow. Similar colors are also seen when certain elements are heated. You see this effect during a fireworks display. Lithium and strontium make red colors in fireworks, sodium gives yellow, magnesium is used for white, barium makes a green color, copper is blue, and mixtures of strontium and copper make purple. The energy emitted from an atom such as visible light is a tool that scientists use to probe the behavior of electrons in atoms. Eventually work by physicists and chemists revealed that electrons behave both as particles and light waves.

We will also learn that electrons are arranged in different energy levels within atoms. The electrons in the highest energy level, called *valence electrons*, relate groups of elements and determine similarities in their physical and chemical behavior.

CHAPTER READINESS*

Key Math Skills

- Solving Equations (1.4D)
- Using Scientific Notation (2.2)

Core Chemistry Skills

- Using Prefixes (2.5)

*These Key Math Skills and the Core Chemistry Skills from previous chapters are listed here for your review as you proceed to the new material in this chapter.

LEARNING GOAL

Compare the wavelength of radiation with its frequency.

5.1 Electromagnetic Radiation

When we listen to a radio, use a microwave oven, turn on a light, see the colors of a rainbow, or have an X-ray taken, we are experiencing various forms of **electromagnetic radiation**. All of these types of electromagnetic radiation, including light, consist of particles that move as waves of energy.

Wavelength and Frequency

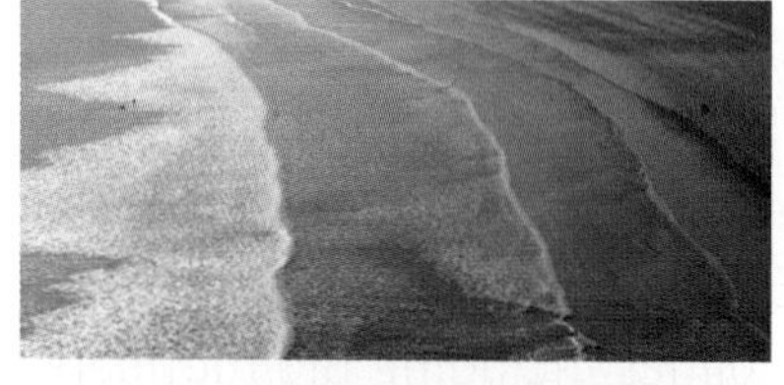

The wavelength is the distance between adjacent crests or troughs in a wave.

You are probably familiar with the action of waves in the ocean. If you were at a beach, you might notice that the water in each wave rises and falls as the wave comes in to shore. The highest point on the wave is called a *crest*, whereas the lowest point is a *trough*. On a calm day, there might be long distances between crests or troughs. However, if there is a storm with a lot of energy, the crests or troughs are much closer together.

The waves of electromagnetic radiation also have crests and troughs. The **wavelength** (symbol λ, lambda) is the distance from a crest or trough in the wave to the next crest or trough in the wave (see Figure 5.1). In some types of radiation, the crests or troughs are far apart, while in others, they are close together.

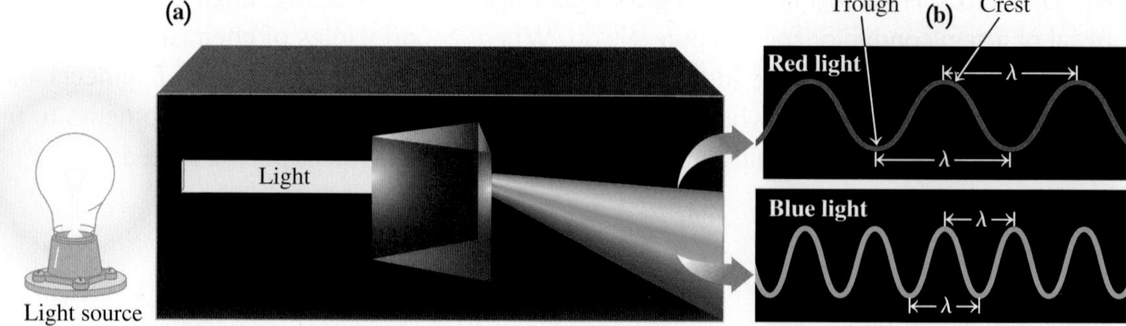

FIGURE 5.1 **(a)** Light passing through a prism is separated into a spectrum of colors we see in a rainbow. **(b)** The wavelength (λ) is the distance from a crest or trough on a wave to the next crest or trough.

Q How does the wavelength of red light compare to that of blue light?

The **frequency** (symbol ν, nu) is the number of times the crests of a wave pass a point in 1 s. The frequency is measured in hertz (Hz), which is equal to cycles/s or s^{-1}. All electromagnetic radiation travels at the speed of light (c), which is 3.00×10^8 m/s. Mathematically, the *wave equation* expresses the relationship of the speed of light (m/s) to wavelength (m) and frequency (s^{-1}).

$c = \lambda\nu$ Wave equation

$$\text{Speed of light } (c) = 3.00 \times 10^8 \text{ m/s} = \text{wavelength } (\lambda) \times \text{frequency } (\nu)$$
$$= 3.00 \times 10^8 \text{ ms}^{-1} = \text{wavelength (m)} \times \text{frequency } (\text{s}^{-1})$$

The speed of light is about a million times faster than the speed of sound, which is the reason we see lightning before we hear thunder during a storm.

Electromagnetic Spectrum

The **electromagnetic spectrum** is an arrangement of different types of electromagnetic radiation from longest wavelength to shortest wavelength or from lowest energy to highest energy. The wave equation for the speed of light (c) shows that the relationship of wavelength (λ) and frequency (ν) is inversely proportional.

$$c = \lambda\nu$$

As the wavelength decreases, the frequency increases. Or as the wavelength increases, the frequency decreases. Because the speed of light is constant, we can solve the wave equation to calculate the wavelength or frequency if we know the value of the other.

To solve the wave equation algebraically for frequency ν, we divide each side of the equation by the wavelength λ.

$$\frac{c}{\lambda} = \frac{\cancel{\lambda}\nu}{\cancel{\lambda}} = \nu \quad \text{or} \quad \nu = \frac{c}{\lambda}$$

To solve the wave equation algebraically for wavelength λ, we divide each side of the equation by the frequency ν.

$$\frac{c}{\nu} = \frac{\lambda\cancel{\nu}}{\cancel{\nu}} = \lambda \quad \text{or} \quad \lambda = \frac{c}{\nu}$$

Scientists have shown that energy is proportional to frequency, which means that energy is also inversely proportional to the wavelength. Thus, as the wavelength of radiation increases, the frequency and therefore the energy decrease.

At one end of the electromagnetic spectrum are radiations with long wavelengths such as *radio waves* that are used for AM and FM radio bands, cellular phones, and TV signals. The wavelength of a typical AM radio wave can be as long as a football field. *Microwaves* have shorter wavelengths and higher frequencies than radio waves. *Infrared radiation* (IR) is responsible for the heat we feel from sunlight and the infrared lamps used to warm food in restaurants. When we change the volume or the station on a TV set, we use a remote control to send infrared impulses to the receiver in the TV. Wireless technology uses radiation with higher frequencies than infrared to connect many electronic devices, including mobile and cell phones and laptops (see Figure 5.2).

Visible light with wavelengths from 700 to 400 nm is the only light our eyes can detect. Red light has the longest wavelength at 700 nm; orange is about 600 nm; green is about 500 nm; and violet at 400 nm has the shortest wavelength of visible light. We see objects as different colors because the objects reflect only certain wavelengths, which are absorbed by our eyes.

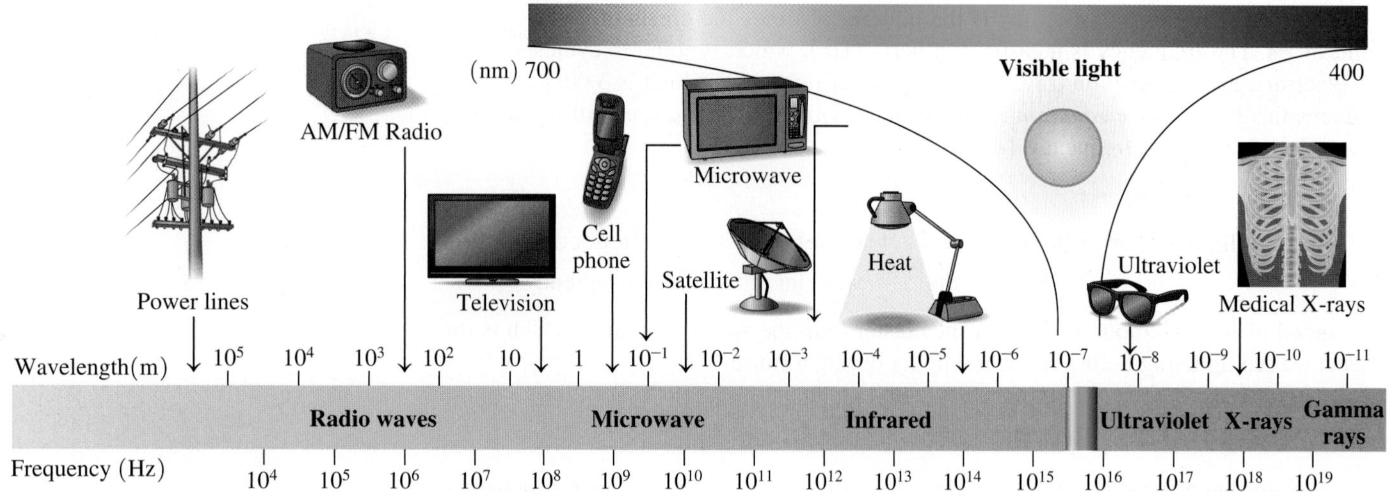

FIGURE 5.2 The electromagnetic spectrum shows the arrangement of wavelengths of electromagnetic radiation. The visible portion consists of wavelengths from 700 nm to 400 nm.

Q How does the wavelength of ultraviolet light compare to that of a microwave?

Ultraviolet (UV) light has shorter wavelengths and higher frequencies than violet light of the visible range. The UV radiation in sunlight can cause serious sunburn, which may lead to skin cancer. While some UV light from the Sun is blocked by the ozone layer, the cosmetic industry has developed sunscreens to prevent the absorption of UV light by the skin. *X-rays* have shorter wavelengths than ultraviolet light, which means they have some of the highest frequencies. X-rays can pass through soft substances but not metals or bone, which allows us to see images of the bones and teeth in the body.

CONCEPT CHECK 5.1 The Electromagnetic Spectrum

1. Arrange the following in order of decreasing wavelengths: X-rays, ultraviolet light, FM radio waves, and microwaves.
2. Visible light contains colors from red to violet.
   a. What color has the shortest wavelength?
   b. What color has the lowest frequency?

ANSWER

1. The electromagnetic radiation with the longest wavelength is FM radio waves, then microwaves, followed by ultraviolet light, and then X-rays, which have the shortest wavelengths.
2. The shortest wavelengths are in the blue-violet range of visible light; the longest wavelengths are in the red range.
   a. Violet light has the shortest wavelength.
   b. Red light has the longest wavelength. Because frequency is inversely related to wavelength, red light would also have the lowest frequency.

Chemistry Link to Health

BIOLOGICAL REACTIONS TO UV LIGHT

Our everyday life depends on sunlight, but exposure to sunlight can have damaging effects on living cells, and too much exposure can even cause their death. Light energy, especially ultraviolet (UV), excites electrons and may lead to unwanted chemical reactions. The list of damaging effects of sunlight includes sunburn; wrinkling and premature aging of the skin; changes in the DNA of the cells, which can lead to skin cancer; inflammation of the eyes; and cataracts.

Some drugs, like the acne medications Accutane and Retin-A, as well as antibiotics, diuretics, sulfonamides, and estrogen, make the skin extremely sensitive to light.

High-energy radiation is the most damaging biologically. Most of the radiation in this range is absorbed in the epidermis of the skin. The degree to which radiation is absorbed depends on the thickness of the epidermis, the hydration of the skin, the amount of pigments and proteins of the skin, and the arrangement of the blood vessels. In light-skinned people, 85–90% of the radiation is absorbed by the epidermis, with the rest reaching the lower dermis layer. In dark-skinned people, 90–95% of the radiation is absorbed by the epidermis, with a smaller percentage reaching the dermis. However, medicine does take advantage of the beneficial effect of sunlight. Phototherapy can be used to treat certain skin conditions, including psoriasis, eczema, and dermatitis. In the treatment of psoriasis, for example, oral drugs are given to make the skin more photosensitive; then exposure to UV radiation follows. Low-energy radiation is used to break down bilirubin in neonatal jaundice. Sunlight is also a factor in stimulating the immune system.

In a disorder called Seasonal Affective Disorder, or SAD, people experience mood swings and depression during the winter. Some research suggests that SAD is the result of a decrease in serotonin, or an increase in melatonin, when there are fewer hours of sunlight. One treatment for SAD is therapy using bright light provided by a lamp called a light box. A daily exposure to intense light for 30–60 min seems to reduce symptoms of SAD.

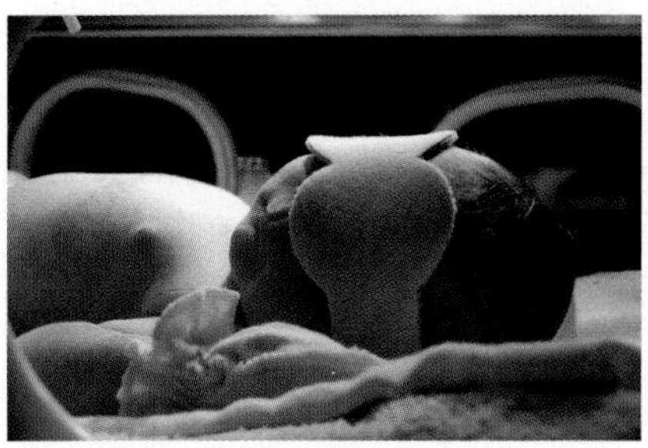

Babies with neonatal jaundice are treated with UV light.

SAMPLE PROBLEM 5.1 Frequency and Wavelength

A student uses a microwave oven to make popcorn. If the frequency of the electromagnetic radiation in a microwave is 2.5×10^9 Hz, what is the wavelength, in meters, of the microwave radiation?

A microwave oven uses microwave radiation to heat food.

SOLUTION

Step 1 State the given and needed quantities.

Analyze the Problem	Given	Need
	$\nu = 2.5 \times 10^9$ Hz $= 2.5 \times 10^9\ s^{-1}$	wavelength in meters

Step 2 Solve the wave equation for the needed quantity.

$$\lambda = \frac{c}{\nu}$$

Step 3 Substitute the known quantities into the wave equation and calculate the needed quantity. We calculate the wavelength by substituting in the speed of light (3.00×10^8 m/s or $3.00 \times 10^8\ ms^{-1}$) and the frequency in s^{-1}.

$$\lambda = \frac{3.00 \times 10^8\ m\cancel{s^{-1}}}{2.5 \times 10^9\ \cancel{s^{-1}}} = 1.2 \times 10^{-1}\ m$$

STUDY CHECK 5.1

Sunglasses with UV protection block UV light of 400 nm. What is that frequency, in hertz, of the UV light?

Guide to Using the Wave Equation

1. State the given and needed quantities.
2. Solve the wave equation for the needed quantity.
3. Substitute the known quantities into the wave equation and calculate the needed quantity.

QUESTIONS AND PROBLEMS

5.1 Electromagnetic Radiation

LEARNING GOAL: *Compare the wavelength of radiation with its frequency.*

5.1 What is meant by the wavelength of UV light?

5.2 How are the wavelength and frequency of light related?

5.3 What is the difference between "white" light and blue or red light?

5.4 Why can we use X-rays, but not radio waves or microwaves, to give an image of bones and teeth?

5.5 An AM radio station broadcasts news at 650 kHz. What is the frequency of this AM radio wave in hertz?

5.6 An FM radio station broadcasts news at 98.0 MHz. What is the frequency of this radio wave in hertz?

5.7 If orange light has a wavelength of 6.3×10^{-5} cm, what is its wavelength in meters and nanometers?

5.8 A wavelength of 850 nm is used for fiber-optic transmission. What is its wavelength in meters?

5.9 Which type of electromagnetic radiation, ultraviolet light, microwaves, or X-rays has the longest wavelengths?

5.10 Of radio waves, infrared light, and UV light, which has the shortest wavelengths?

5.11 Place the following types of electromagnetic radiation in order of increasing wavelengths: the blue color in a rainbow, X-rays, and microwaves from an oven.

5.12 Place the following types of electromagnetic radiation in order of decreasing wavelengths: FM radio station, red color in neon lights, and cell phone.

5.13 Place the following types of electromagnetic radiation in order of increasing frequencies: TV signal, X-rays, and microwaves.

5.14 Place the following types of electromagnetic radiation in order of decreasing frequencies: AM music station, UV radiation from the Sun, and infrared radiation from a heat lamp.

LEARNING GOAL

Explain how atomic spectra correlate with the energy levels in atoms.

5.2 Atomic Spectra and Energy Levels

When the white light from the Sun or a lightbulb is passed through a prism or raindrops, it produces a *continuous spectrum*, like a rainbow. When atoms of elements are heated, they also produce light. At night, you may have seen the yellow color of sodium streetlamps or the red color of neon lights.

A rainbow forms when light passes through water droplets.

Photons

The light emitted when atoms are heated is a stream of particles called **photons**. Each photon is a packet of energy also known as a *quantum*. All photons travel at the speed of light as a wave of energy. We say that photons have both particle and wave characteristics. The energy of a photon is directly proportional to its frequency. Thus, high-frequency photons have high energy and short wavelengths, whereas low-frequency photons have low energy and long wavelengths.

Photons play an important role in our modern world, particularly in the use of lasers, which use a narrow range of wavelengths. For example, lasers use photons of a single frequency to read pits on compact discs (CDs) and digital versatile discs (DVDs) or to scan bar codes on labels when we buy groceries. A CD is read by a laser with a wavelength of 780 nm. The newer DVDs are read by a blue laser with a wavelength of 405 nm, hence the name Blu-ray. The shorter wavelength allows a smaller pit size on the disc, which means that the disc has a greater storage capacity. In hospitals, high-energy photons are used in treatments to reach tumors within the tissues without damaging the surrounding tissue.

Colors are produced when electricity excites electrons in noble gases.

CONCEPT CHECK 5.2 Energy, Frequency, and Wavelengths of Photons

Compare the energy, frequency, and wavelength of photons of gamma radiation and green light.

ANSWER

The energy of a photon is directly related to its frequency and inversely related to its wavelength. Thus, a photon of gamma radiation has higher energy and higher frequency but a shorter wavelength than a photon of green light.

Atomic Spectra

When the light emitted from heated elements is passed through a prism, it does not produce a continuous spectrum. Instead, an **atomic spectrum** is produced that consists of lines of different colors separated by dark areas (see Figure 5.3). This separation of colors

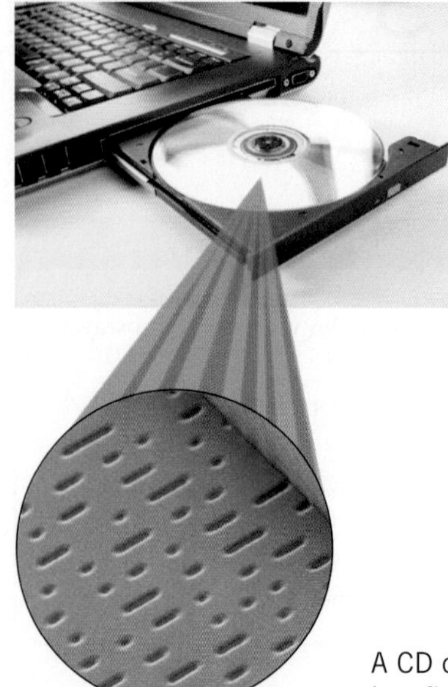

A CD or DVD is read when light from a laser is reflected from the pits on the surface.

QUESTIONS AND PROBLEMS

5.2 Atomic Spectra and Energy Levels

LEARNING GOAL: *Explain how atomic spectra correlate with the energy levels in atoms.*

5.15 What feature of an atomic spectrum indicates that the energy emitted by heating an element is not continuous?

5.16 How can we explain the distinct lines that appear in an atomic spectrum?

5.17 Electrons can jump to higher energy levels when they ______ (absorb/emit) a photon.

5.18 Electrons drop to lower energy levels when they ______ (absorb/emit) a photon.

5.19 Identify the type of photon in each pair with the greater energy.

a. green light or yellow light
b. red light or blue light

5.20 Identify the type of photon in each pair with the greater energy.

a. orange light or violet light
b. infrared light or ultraviolet light

5.3 Sublevels and Orbitals

LEARNING GOAL

Describe the sublevels and orbitals in atoms.

We have seen that the protons and neutrons are contained in the small, dense nucleus of an atom. However, it is the electrons within the atoms that determine the physical and chemical properties of the elements. Therefore, we will look at the arrangement of electrons within the large volume of space surrounding the nucleus.

There is a limit to the number of electrons allowed in each energy level. Only a few electrons can occupy the lower energy levels, while more electrons can be accommodated in higher energy levels. The maximum number of electrons allowed in any energy level is calculated using the formula $2n^2$ (two times the square of the principal quantum number). Table 5.1 shows the maximum number of electrons allowed in the first four energy levels.

TABLE 5.1 Maximum Number of Electrons Allowed in Energy Levels 1–4

Energy Level (n)	1	2	3	4
$2n^2$	$2(1)^2$	$2(2)^2$	$2(3)^2$	$2(4)^2$
Maximum Number of Electrons	2	8	18	32

Sublevels

Each of the energy levels consists of one or more **sublevels**, in which electrons with identical energy are found. The sublevels are identified by the letters *s*, *p*, *d*, and *f*. The number of sublevels within an energy level is equal to the principal quantum number, *n*. For example, the first energy level ($n = 1$) has only one sublevel, 1*s*. The second energy level ($n = 2$) has two sublevels, 2*s* and 2*p*. The third energy level ($n = 3$) has three sublevels, 3*s*, 3*p*, and 3*d*. The fourth energy level ($n = 4$) has four sublevels, 4*s*, 4*p*, 4*d*, and 4*f*. Energy levels $n = 5$, $n = 6$, and $n = 7$ also have as many sublevels as the value of *n*, but only *s*, *p*, *d*, and *f* sublevels are needed to hold the electrons in atoms of the 118 known elements (see Figure 5.5).

FIGURE 5.5 The number of sublevels in an energy level is the same as the principal quantum number, *n*.

Q How many sublevels are in the $n = 5$ energy level?

Within each energy level, the *s* sublevel has the lowest energy. If there are additional sublevels, the *p* sublevel has the next lowest energy, then the *d* sublevel, and finally the *f* sublevel.

Order of Increasing Energy of Sublevels in an Energy Level

$s < p < d < f$

Lowest Energy ⟶ Highest Energy

CONCEPT CHECK 5.3 Energy Levels and Sublevels

Complete the following table with the energy level and sublevels:

Energy Level (*n*)	Sublevels			
	s	*p*	*d*	*f*
			4*d*	
1				
	2*s*			
		3*p*		

ANSWER

The number of sublevels is equal to the principal quantum number, *n*. The available sublevels begin with the lowest energy *s*, followed by *p*, *d*, and *f*. For the $n = 1$ energy level, there is one sublevel 1*s*. For the $n = 2$ energy level, there are two sublevels 2*s* and 2*p*. For the $n = 3$ energy level, there are three sublevels 3*s*, 3*p*, and 3*d*. For the $n = 4$ energy level, there are four sublevels 4*s*, 4*p*, 4*d*, and 4*f*.

Energy Level (*n*)	Sublevels			
	s	*p*	*d*	*f*
4	4*s*	4*p*	4*d*	4*f*
1	1*s*			
2	2*s*	2*p*		
3	3*s*	3*p*	3*d*	

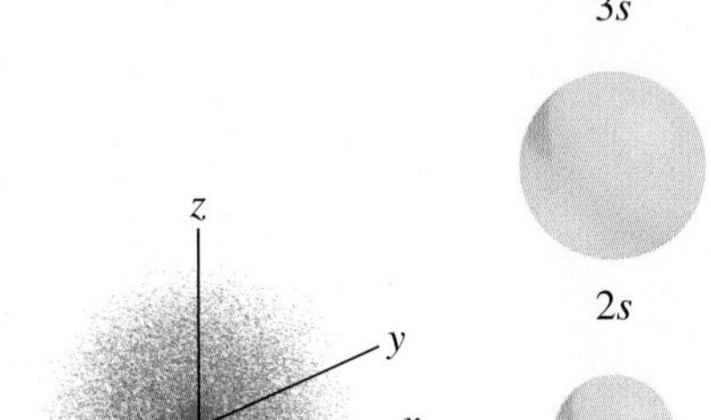

FIGURE 5.6 **(a)** The electron cloud of an *s* orbital represents the highest probability of finding an *s* electron. **(b)** The *s* orbitals are shown as spheres. The sizes of the *s* orbitals increase because they contain electrons at higher energy levels.

Q Is the probability high or low of finding an *s* electron outside an *s* orbital?

Orbitals

There is no way to know the exact location of an electron in an atom. Instead, scientists describe the location of an electron in terms of probability. The **orbital** is the three-dimensional volume in which electrons have the highest probability of being found.

As an analogy, imagine that you could draw a circle with a 100-m radius around your chemistry classroom. There is a high probability of finding you within that circle when your chemistry class is in session. But once in a while, you may be outside that circle because you were sick or your car did not start.

Shapes of Orbitals

Each type of orbital has a unique three-dimensional shape. Electrons in an *s* orbital are most likely found in a region with a spherical shape. Imagine that you take a picture of the location of an electron in an *s* orbital every second for an hour. When all these pictures are overlaid, the result, called a probability density, would look like the electron cloud shown in Figure 5.6a. For convenience, we draw this electron cloud as a sphere called an *s* orbital. There is one *s* orbital for every energy level starting with $n = 1$. For example, in

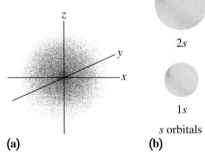

the first, second, and third energy levels there are *s* orbitals designated as 1*s*, 2*s*, and 3*s*. As the principal quantum number increases, there is an increase in the size of the *s* orbitals, although the shape is the same (see Figure 5.6b).

The orbitals occupied by *p*, *d*, and *f* electrons have three-dimensional shapes different from those of the *s* electrons. There are three *p* orbitals, starting with $n = 2$. Each *p* orbital has two lobes like a balloon tied in the middle. The three *p* orbitals are arranged in three perpendicular directions, along the *x*, *y*, and *z* axes around the nucleus (see Figure 5.7). As with *s* orbitals, the shape of *p* orbitals is the same, but the volume increases at higher energy levels.

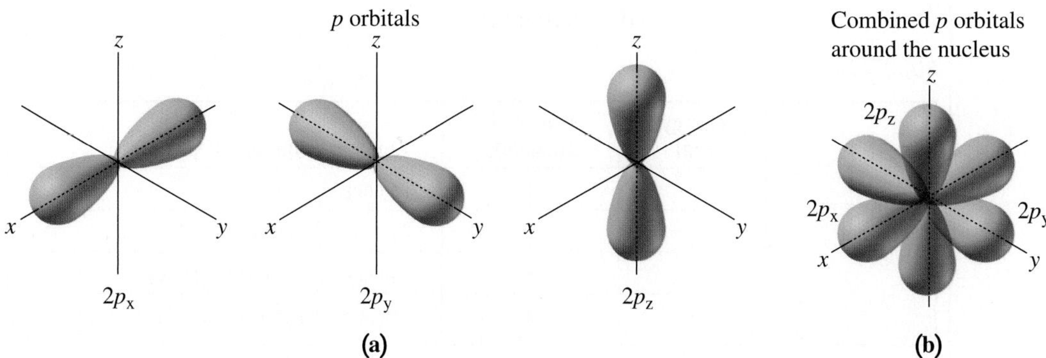

FIGURE 5.7 A *p* orbital has two regions of high probability, which gives a "dumb-bell" shape. **(a)** Each *p* orbital is aligned along a different axis from the other *p* orbitals. **(b)** All three *p* orbitals are shown around the nucleus.

Q What are some similarities and differences of the *p* orbitals in the $n = 3$ energy level?

In summary, the $n = 2$ energy level, which has 2*s* and 2*p* sublevels, consists of one *s* orbital and three *p* orbitals.

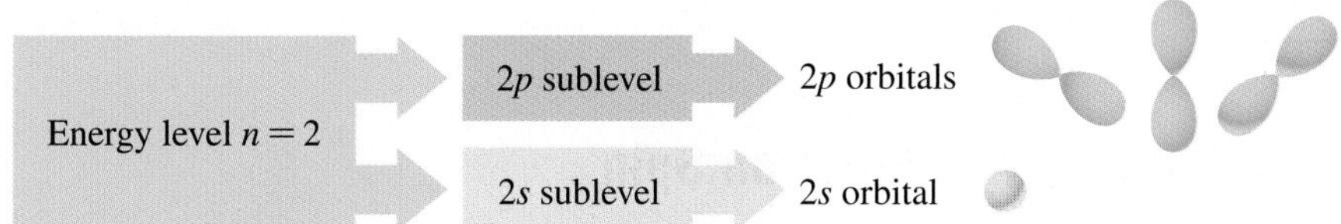

Energy level $n = 2$ consists of one 2*s* orbital and three 2*p* orbitals.

Energy level $n = 3$ consists of three sublevels *s*, *p*, and *d*. The *d* sublevels contain five *d* orbitals (see Figure 5.8).

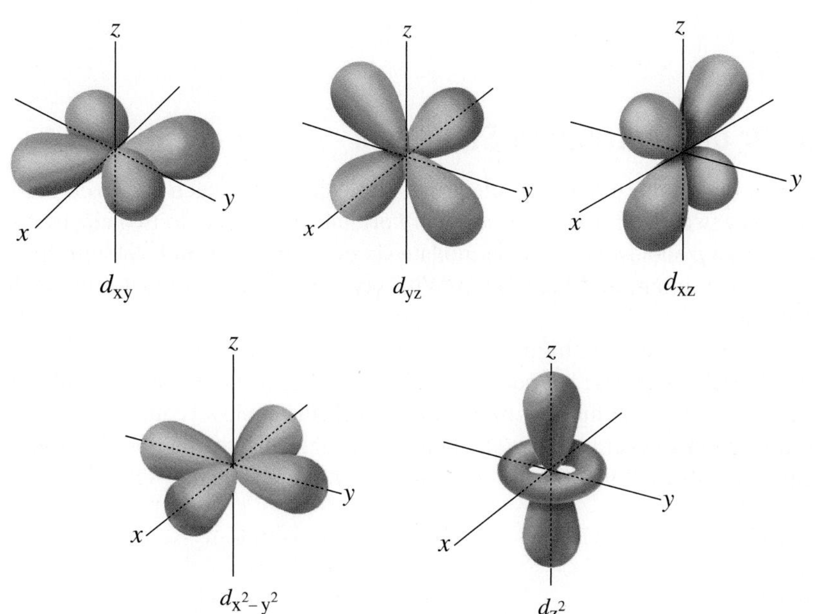

FIGURE 5.8 Four of the five *d* orbitals consist of four lobes that are aligned along or between different axes. One *d* orbital consists of two lobes and a doughnut-shaped ring around its center.

Q How many orbitals are there in the 5*d* sublevel?

Energy level $n = 4$ consists of four sublevels *s*, *p*, *d*, and *f*. In the *f* sublevel, there are seven *f* orbitals. The shapes of *f* orbitals are complex and so we have not included them in this text.

SAMPLE PROBLEM 5.3 Energy Levels, Sublevels, and Orbitals

Indicate the type and number of orbitals in each of the following energy levels or sublevels:

a. 3*p* sublevel **b.** $n = 2$
c. $n = 3$ **d.** 4*d* sublevel

SOLUTION

	Energy Level	Number of Sublevels	Types and Number of Orbitals
Analyze the Problem	1	1	1*s* (one)
	2	2	2*s* (one) 2*p* (three)
	3	3	3*s* (one) 3*p* (three) 3*d* (five)
	4	4	4*s* (one) 4*p* (three) 4*d* (five) 4*f* (seven)

a. The 3*p* sublevel contains three 3*p* orbitals.
b. The $n = 2$ energy level consists of one 2*s* and three 2*p* orbitals.
c. The $n = 3$ energy level consists of one 3*s*, three 3*p*, and five 3*d* orbitals.
d. The 4*d* sublevel contains five 4*d* orbitals.

STUDY CHECK 5.3

What is similar and what is different for 1*s*, 2*s*, and 3*s* orbitals?

Orbital Capacity and Electron Spin

The *Pauli exclusion principle* states that each orbital can hold a maximum of two electrons. According to a useful model for electron behavior, an electron is seen as spinning on its axis, which generates a magnetic field. When two electrons are in the same orbital, they will repel each other unless their magnetic fields cancel. This happens only when the two electrons spin in opposite directions. We can represent the spins of the electrons in the same orbital with one arrow pointing up and the other pointing down.

Electron spinning counterclockwise   Electron spinning clockwise

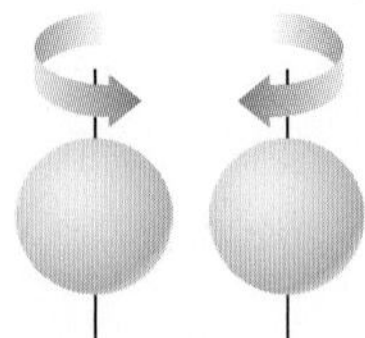

Opposite spins of electrons in an orbital

An orbital can hold up to two electrons with opposite spins.

Number of Electrons in Sublevels

There is a maximum number of electrons that can occupy each sublevel. An *s* sublevel holds one or two electrons. Because each *p* orbital can hold up to two electrons, the three *p* orbitals in a *p* sublevel can accommodate six electrons. A *d* sublevel with five *d* orbitals can hold a maximum of 10 electrons. With seven *f* orbitals, an *f* sublevel can hold up to 14 electrons.

As mentioned earlier, higher energy levels such as $n = 5$, 6, and 7 would have 5, 6, and 7 sublevels, but those beyond sublevel *f* are not utilized by the atoms of the elements known today. The total number of electrons in all the sublevels adds up to give the electrons allowed in an energy level. The number of sublevels, the number of orbitals, and the maximum number of electrons for energy levels 1–4 are shown in Table 5.2.

TABLE 5.2 Electron Capacity in Sublevels for Energy Levels 1–4

Energy Level (n)	Number of Sublevels	Type of Sublevel	Number of Orbitals	Maximum Number of Electrons	Total Electrons ($2n^2$)
4	4	$4f$	7	14	32
		$4d$	5	10	
		$4p$	3	6	
		$4s$	1	2	
3	3	$3d$	5	10	18
		$3p$	3	6	
		$3s$	1	2	
2	2	$2p$	3	6	8
		$2s$	1	2	
1	1	$1s$	1	2	2

QUESTIONS AND PROBLEMS

5.3 Sublevels and Orbitals

LEARNING GOAL: *Describe the sublevels and orbitals in atoms.*

5.21 Describe the shape of each of the following orbitals:
a. $1s$ **b.** $2p$ **c.** $5s$

5.22 Describe the shape of each of the following orbitals:
a. $3p$ **b.** $6s$ **c.** $4p$

5.23 Match statements **1–3** with **a–d**:
1. They have the same shape.
2. The maximum number of electrons is the same.
3. They are in the same energy level.

a. $1s$ and $2s$ orbitals **b.** $3s$ and $3p$ sublevels
c. $3p$ and $4p$ sublevels **d.** three $3p$ orbitals

5.24 Match statements **1–3** with **a–d**:
1. They have the same shape.
2. The maximum number of electrons is the same.
3. They are in the same energy level.

a. $5s$ and $6s$ orbitals **b.** $3p$ and $4p$ orbitals
c. $3s$ and $4s$ sublevels **d.** $2s$ and $2p$ orbitals

5.25 Indicate the number of each in the following:
a. orbitals in the $3d$ sublevel
b. sublevels in the $n = 1$ energy level
c. orbitals in the $6s$ sublevel
d. orbitals in the $n = 3$ energy level

5.26 Indicate the number of each in the following:
a. orbitals in the $n = 2$ energy level
b. sublevels in the $n = 4$ energy level
c. orbitals in the $5f$ sublevel
d. orbitals in the $6p$ sublevel

5.27 Indicate the maximum number of electrons in the following:
a. $2p$ orbital
b. $3p$ sublevel
c. $n = 4$ energy level
d. $5d$ sublevel

5.28 Indicate the maximum number of electrons in the following:
a. $3s$ sublevel
b. $4p$ orbital
c. $n = 3$ energy level
d. $4f$ sublevel

5.4 Orbital Diagrams and Electron Configurations

LEARNING GOAL

Draw the orbital diagram and write the electron configuration for an element.

We can now look at how electrons are arranged in the orbitals within an atom. An **orbital diagram** shows the placement of the electrons in the orbitals in order of increasing energy (Figure 5.9). In this energy diagram, we see that the electrons in the $1s$ orbital have the lowest energy level. The energy level is higher for the $2s$ orbital and is even higher for the $2p$ orbitals.

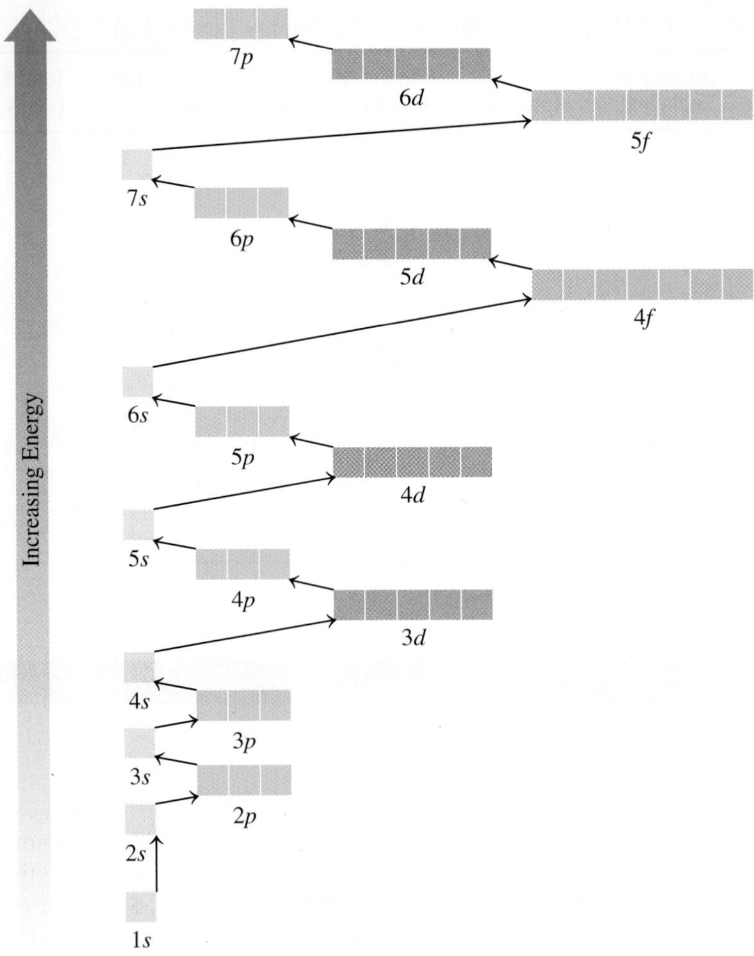

FIGURE 5.9 The orbitals in an atom fill in order of increasing energy beginning with 1*s*.

Q Why do 3*d* orbitals fill after the 4*s* orbital?

We can begin our discussion of electron configuration by using orbital diagrams in which boxes represent the orbitals. Any orbital can have a maximum of two electrons.

To draw an orbital diagram, the lowest energy orbitals are filled first. For example, we can draw the orbital diagram for carbon. The atomic number of carbon is 6, which means that a carbon atom has six electrons. The first two electrons go into the 1*s* orbital; the next two electrons go into the 2*s* orbital. In the orbital diagram, the two electrons in the 1*s* and 2*s* orbitals are shown with opposite spins; the first arrow is up and the second is down. The last two electrons in carbon begin to fill the 2*p* sublevel, which has the next lowest energy. However, there are three 2*p* orbitals of equal energy. Because the negatively charged electrons repel each other, they are placed in separate 2*p* orbitals. With few exceptions (which will be noted later in this chapter) lower energy sublevels are filled first, and then the "building" of electrons continues to the next lowest energy sublevel that is available until all the electrons are placed.

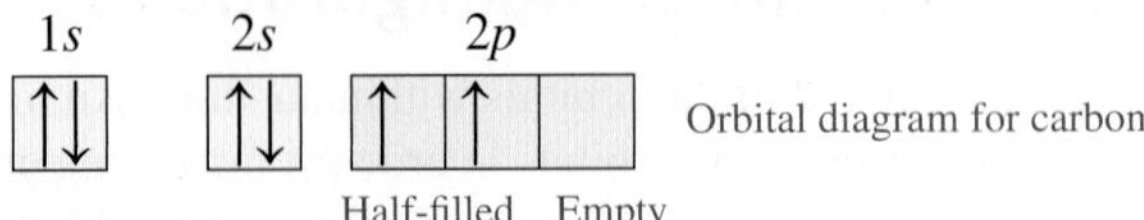

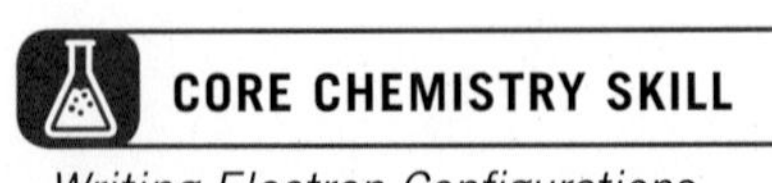

Writing Electron Configurations

Electron Configurations

Chemists use a notation called the **electron configuration** to indicate the placement of the electrons of an atom in order of increasing energy. The electron configuration is written with the lowest energy sublevel first, followed by the next lowest energy sublevel. The number of electrons in each sublevel is shown as a superscript.

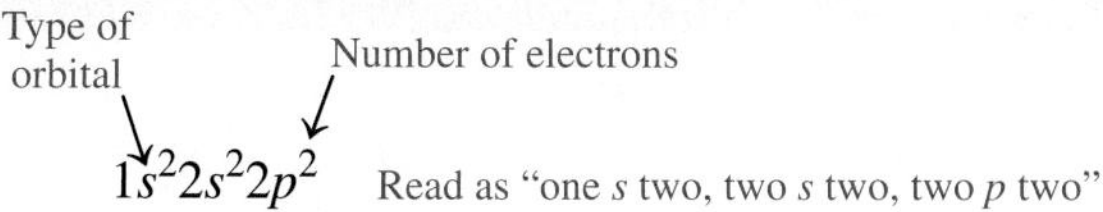

Period 1: Hydrogen and Helium

We will draw orbital diagrams and write electron configurations for the elements H and He in Period 1. The 1*s* orbital (which is the 1*s* sublevel) is written first because it has the lowest energy. Hydrogen has one electron in the 1*s* sublevel; helium has two. In the orbital diagram, the electrons for helium are shown as arrows pointing in opposite directions.

Element	Atomic Number	Orbital Diagram	Electron Configuration
		1*s*	
H	1	[↑]	$1s^1$
He	2	[↑↓]	$1s^2$

Period 2: Lithium to Neon

Period 2 begins with lithium, which has three electrons. The first two electrons fill the 1*s* orbital, while the third electron goes into the 2*s* orbital, the sublevel with the next lowest energy. In beryllium, another electron is added to complete the 2*s* orbital. The next six electrons are used to fill the 2*p* orbitals. The electrons are added one at a time from boron to nitrogen, which gives three half-filled 2*p* orbitals. Because orbitals in the same sublevel are equal in energy, there is less repulsion when electrons are placed in separate orbitals.

From oxygen to neon, the remaining three electrons are paired up using opposite spins to complete the 2*p* sublevel. In writing the electron configurations for the elements in Period 2, begin with the 1*s* orbital followed by the 2*s* and then the 2*p* orbitals.

An electron configuration can also be written in an *abbreviated configuration*. The electron configuration of the preceding noble gas is replaced by writing its element symbol inside square brackets. For example, the electron configuration for lithium, $1s^22s^1$, can be abbreviated as [He]$2s^1$ where [He] replaces $1s^2$.

Element	Atomic Number	Orbital Diagram 1*s*	2*s*	2*p*	Electron Configuration	Abbreviated Electron Configuration
Li	3	[↑↓]	[↑]		$1s^22s^1$	[He]$2s^1$
Be	4	[↑↓]	[↑↓]		$1s^22s^2$	[He]$2s^2$
B	5	[↑↓]	[↑↓]	[↑][ ][ ]	$1s^22s^22p^1$	[He]$2s^22p^1$
C	6	[↑↓]	[↑↓]	[↑][↑][ ]	$1s^22s^22p^2$	[He]$2s^22p^2$
				Unpaired electrons		
N	7	[↑↓]	[↑↓]	[↑][↑][↑]	$1s^22s^22p^3$	[He]$2s^22p^3$
O	8	[↑↓]	[↑↓]	[↑↓][↑][↑]	$1s^22s^22p^4$	[He]$2s^22p^4$
F	9	[↑↓]	[↑↓]	[↑↓][↑↓][↑]	$1s^22s^22p^5$	[He]$2s^22p^5$
Ne	10	[↑↓]	[↑↓]	[↑↓][↑↓][↑↓]	$1s^22s^22p^6$	[He]$2s^22p^6$

Guide to Drawing Orbital Diagrams

1. Draw boxes to represent the occupied orbitals.
2. Place a pair of electrons with opposite spins in each filled orbital.
3. Place remaining electrons in the last occupied sublevel in separate orbitals.

SAMPLE PROBLEM 5.4 Drawing Orbital Diagrams

Draw the orbital diagram for nitrogen.

SOLUTION

Step 1 **Draw boxes to represent the occupied orbitals.** Nitrogen has atomic number 7, which means it has seven electrons. For the orbital diagram, we draw boxes to represent the 1*s*, 2*s*, and 2*p* orbitals.

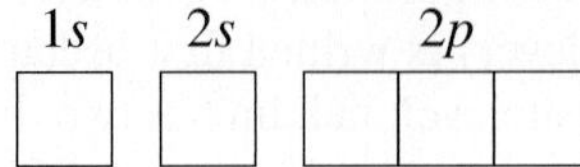

Step 2 **Place a pair of electrons with opposite spins in each filled orbital.** First, we place a pair of electrons with opposite spins in both the 1*s* and 2*s* orbitals.

1*s*	2*s*	2*p*		
↑↓	↑↓			

Step 3 **Place remaining electrons in the last occupied sublevel in separate orbitals.** Then we place the three remaining electrons in three separate 2*p* orbitals with arrows drawn in the same direction.

1*s*	2*s*	2*p*		
↑↓	↑↓	↑	↑	↑

Orbital diagram for nitrogen (N)

STUDY CHECK 5.4

Draw the orbital diagram for fluorine.

Electron configuration of magnesium

Period 3: Sodium to Argon

In Period 3, electrons enter the orbitals of the 3*s* and 3*p* sublevels, but not the 3*d* sublevel. We notice that the elements sodium to argon, which are directly below the elements lithium to neon in Period 2, have a similar pattern of filling their *s* and *p* orbitals. In sodium and magnesium, one and two electrons go into the 3*s* orbital. The electrons for aluminum, silicon, and phosphorus go into separate 3*p* orbitals. The remaining electrons in sulfur, chlorine, and argon are paired up (opposite spins) with the electrons already in the 3*p* orbitals. For the abbreviated electron configurations of Period 3, the symbol [Ne] replaces $1s^22s^22p^6$.

Element	Atomic Number	Orbital Diagram (3*s* and 3*p* orbitals only) 3*s* 3*p*	Electron Configuration	Abbreviated Electron Configuration
Na	11	[Ne] [↑] [ ][ ][ ]	$1s^22s^22p^63s^1$	$[Ne]3s^1$
Mg	12	[Ne] [↑↓] [ ][ ][ ]	$1s^22s^22p^63s^2$	$[Ne]3s^2$
Al	13	[Ne] [↑↓] [↑][ ][ ]	$1s^22s^22p^63s^23p^1$	$[Ne]3s^23p^1$
Si	14	[Ne] [↑↓] [↑][↑][ ]	$1s^22s^22p^63s^23p^2$	$[Ne]3s^23p^2$
P	15	[Ne] [↑↓] [↑][↑][↑]	$1s^22s^22p^63s^23p^3$	$[Ne]3s^23p^3$
S	16	[Ne] [↑↓] [↑↓][↑][↑]	$1s^22s^22p^63s^23p^4$	$[Ne]3s^23p^4$
Cl	17	[Ne] [↑↓] [↑↓][↑↓][↑]	$1s^22s^22p^63s^23p^5$	$[Ne]3s^23p^5$
Ar	18	[Ne] [↑↓] [↑↓][↑↓][↑↓]	$1s^22s^22p^63s^23p^6$	$[Ne]3s^23p^6$

SAMPLE PROBLEM 5.5 Orbital Diagrams and Electron Configurations

For the element silicon, draw or write each of the following:

a. orbital diagram **b.** abbreviated orbital diagram
c. electron configuration **d.** abbreviated electron configuration

SOLUTION

	Element	Atomic Number	Orbital Diagram	Abbreviated Orbital Diagram	Electron Configuration	Abbreviated Electron Configuration
Analyze the Problem	Silicon (Si)	14	Use the order of filling, placing two electrons in each orbital, and single electrons in the highest energy level.	Use the symbol of the preceding noble gas followed by the remaining electrons.	List the sublevels in order of filling.	Substitute the symbol of the preceding noble gas followed by the remaining electrons.

a. Starting with the 1*s* orbital, add paired electrons with opposite spins up to 3*s*. Then we place the last two electrons in separate 3*p* orbitals with parallel spins.

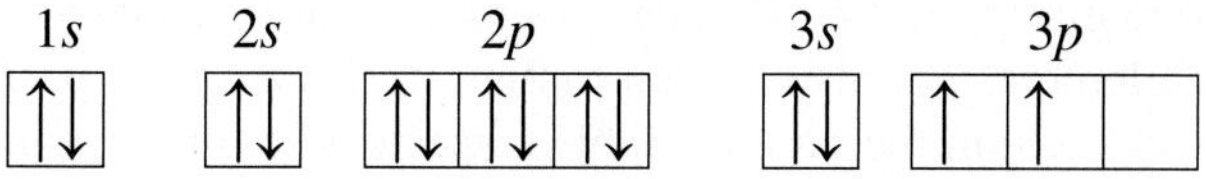

1*s*	2*s*	2*p*	3*s*	3*p*
[↑↓]	[↑↓]	[↑↓][↑↓][↑↓]	[↑↓]	[↑][↑][ ]

Complete orbital diagram for Si

b. For silicon, the preceding noble gas is neon. In the abbreviated orbital diagram, the orbitals 1*s*, 2*s*, and 2*p* are replaced by [Ne].

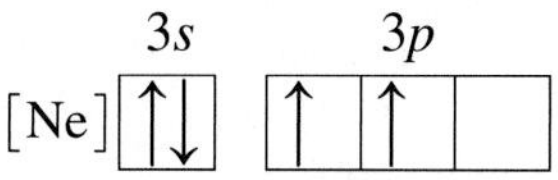

	3*s*	3*p*
[Ne]	[↑↓]	[↑][↑][ ]

Abbreviated orbital diagram for Si

c. The electron configuration shows the electrons that fill the sublevels in order of increasing energy. The first 10 electrons in silicon would complete the sublevels in Periods 1 and 2: $1s^2$, $2s^2$, and $2p^6$. In Period 3, two electrons go into the 3*s* sublevel, and the remaining two electrons go into the 3*p* sublevel.

$1s^22s^22p^63s^23p^2$ Electron configuration for Si

d. For silicon, the preceding noble gas is neon. To write the abbreviated electron configuration for silicon, we replace $1s^22s^22p^6$ with [Ne].

$[\text{Ne}]3s^23p^2$ Abbreviated electron configuration for Si

STUDY CHECK 5.5

Write the complete and abbreviated electron configurations for sulfur.

QUESTIONS AND PROBLEMS

5.4 Orbital Diagrams and Electron Configurations

LEARNING GOAL: *Draw the orbital diagram and write the electron configuration for an element.*

5.29 Compare the terms *electron configuration* and *abbreviated electron configuration*.

5.30 Compare the terms *orbital diagram* and *electron configuration*.

5.31 Draw the orbital diagram for each of the following:
a. boron **b.** aluminum
c. phosphorus **d.** argon

5.32 Draw the orbital diagram for each of the following:
a. fluorine **b.** sulfur
c. magnesium **d.** beryllium

5.33 Write a complete electron configuration for each of the following:
a. boron **b.** sodium
c. lithium **d.** magnesium

5.34 Write a complete electron configuration for each of the following:
a. nitrogen **b.** chlorine
c. oxygen **d.** neon

5.35 Write an abbreviated electron configuration for each of the following:
a. carbon **b.** silicon
c. phosphorus **d.** fluorine

5.36 Write an abbreviated electron configuration for each of the following:
a. magnesium **b.** oxygen
c. sulfur **d.** nitrogen

5.37 Give the symbol of the element with each of the following electron or abbreviated electron configurations:
a. $1s^22s^1$ **b.** $1s^22s^22p^63s^23p^4$
c. $[Ne]3s^23p^2$ **d.** $[He]2s^22p^5$

5.38 Give the symbol of the element with each of the following electron or abbreviated electron configurations:
a. $1s^22s^22p^4$ **b.** $[Ne]3s^2$
c. $1s^22s^22p^63s^23p^6$ **d.** $[Ne]3s^23p^1$

5.39 Give the symbol of the element that meets the following conditions:
a. has three electrons in the $n = 3$ energy level
b. has two $2p$ electrons
c. completes the $3p$ sublevel
d. completes the $2s$ sublevel

5.40 Give the symbol of the element that meets the following conditions:
a. has five electrons in the $3p$ sublevel
b. has four $2p$ electrons
c. completes the $3s$ sublevel
d. has one electron in the $3s$ sublevel

LEARNING GOAL

Write the electron configuration for an atom using the sublevel blocks on the periodic table.

5.5 Electron Configurations and the Periodic Table

Up to now, we have written electron configurations using their energy level diagrams. As configurations involve more energy levels, this can become tedious. However, the electron configurations of the elements are also related to their position on the periodic table. Different sections or blocks within the periodic table correspond to the *s*, *p*, *d*, and *f* sublevels (see Figure 5.10). Therefore, we can "build" the electron configurations of atoms by reading the periodic table in order of increasing atomic number.

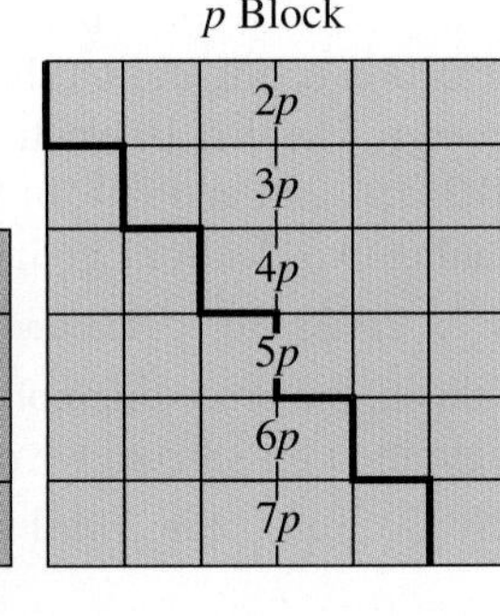

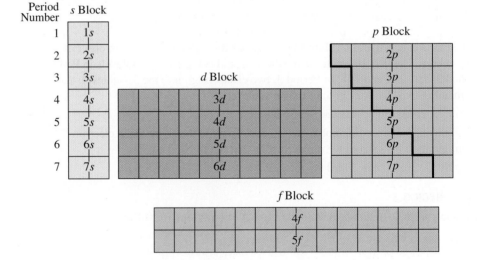

FIGURE 5.10 Electron configurations follow the order of occupied sublevels on the periodic table.

Q If neon is in Group 8A (18), Period 2, how many electrons are in the 1*s*, 2*s*, and 2*p* sublevels of neon?

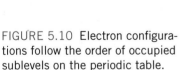

CORE CHEMISTRY SKILL

Using the Periodic Table to Write Electron Configurations

Blocks on the Periodic Table

1. The ***s* block** includes hydrogen and helium as well as the elements in Group 1A (1) and Group 2A (2). This means that the final one or two electrons in the elements of the *s* block are located in an *s* orbital. The period number indicates the particular *s* orbital that is filling: 1*s*, 2*s*, and so on.
2. The ***p* block** consists of the elements in Group 3A (13) to Group 8A (18). There are six *p* block elements in each period because three *p* orbitals can hold up to six electrons. The period number indicates the particular *p* sublevel that is filling: 2*p*, 3*p*, and so on.

3. The ***d* block**, containing the transition elements, first appears after calcium (atomic number 20). There are 10 elements in each period of the *d* block because five *d* orbitals can hold up to 10 electrons. The particular *d* sublevel is one less $(n - 1)$ than the period number. For example, in Period 4, the *d* block is the 3*d* sublevel. In Period 5, the *d* block is the 4*d* sublevel.
4. The ***f* block**, the inner transition elements, are the two rows at the bottom of the periodic table. There are 14 elements in each *f* block because seven *f* orbitals can hold up to 14 electrons. Elements that have atomic numbers higher than 57 (La) have electrons in the 4*f* block. The particular *f* sublevel is two less $(n - 2)$ than the period number. For example, in Period 6, the *f* block is the 4*f* sublevel. In Period 7, the *f* block is the 5*f* sublevel.

CONCEPT CHECK 5.4 Electron Filling of Sublevel Blocks

Identify the sublevel block that is involved when electrons are filling the following sets of elements:

a. Going across the periodic table from Al to Ar
b. Going across the periodic table from Cs to Ba
c. Going across the periodic table from Sc to Zn

ANSWER

a. Period 3 consists of a 3*s* block followed by the elements filling the 3*p* block going from Al to Ar.
b. Period 6 begins with the 6*s* block filling with the elements Cs and Ba.
c. Period 4 consists of K and Ca in the 4*s* block followed by the elements filling the 3*d* block going from Sc to Zn.

Electron Configurations Using the Periodic Table

Now we can write electron configurations using the sublevel blocks on the periodic table. As before, each configuration begins at H. But now we move across the table from left to right, writing down each sublevel block we come to until we reach the element for which we are writing an electron configuration. We will show how to write the electron configuration for chlorine (atomic number 17) from the sublevel blocks on the periodic table in Sample Problem 5.6.

CONCEPT CHECK 5.5 Electron Configurations Using Sublevel Blocks

Give the symbol and name of the element with each of the following electron configurations:

a. $1s^22s^22p^5$ **b.** $1s^22s^22p^63s^23p^64s^23d^{10}4p^2$
c. $[Ar]4s^23d^6$ **d.** $[Kr]5s^24d^{10}5p^5$

ANSWER

a. In the *p* block, Period 2, the fifth element across is F, fluorine.
b. In the *p* block, Period 4, the second element across is Ge, germanium.
c. In the *d* block, Period 4, the sixth element across is Fe, iron.
d. In the *p* block, Period 5, the fifth element across is I, iodine.

SAMPLE PROBLEM 5.6 Using the Sublevel Blocks to Write Electron Configurations

Use the sublevel blocks on the periodic table to write the electron configuration for chlorine.

SOLUTION

Step 1 **Locate the element on the periodic table.** Chlorine (atomic number 17) is in Group 7A (17) and Period 3.

Guide to Writing Electron Configurations Using Sublevel Blocks

1 Locate the element on the periodic table.

2 Write the filled sublevels in order, going across each period.

3 Complete the configuration by counting the electrons in the last occupied sublevel block.

Step 2 **Write the filled sublevels in order, going across each period.**

Period	Sublevel Block Filling	Sublevel Block Notation (filled)
1	1*s* (H → He)	$1s^2$
2	2*s* (Li → Be) and 2*p* (B → Ne)	$2s^22p^6$
3	3*s* (Na → Mg)	$3s^2$

Step 3 **Complete the configuration by counting the electrons in the last occupied sublevel block.** Because chlorine is the fifth element in the 3*p* block, there are five electrons in the 3*p* sublevel.

Period	Sublevel Block Filling	Sublevel Block Notation
3	3*p* (Al → Cl)	$3p^5$

The electron configuration for chlorine (Cl) is: $1s^22s^22p^63s^23p^5$.

STUDY CHECK 5.6

Use the sublevel blocks on the periodic table to write the electron configuration for germanium.

Period 4

Up to Period 4, the filling of the sublevels has progressed in order. However, if we look at the sublevel blocks in Period 4, we see that the 4*s* sublevel fills before the 3*d* sublevel. This occurs because the electrons in the 4*s* sublevel have slightly lower energy than the electrons in the 3*d* sublevel. This order occurs again in Period 5 when the 5*s* sublevel fills before the 4*d* sublevel and again in Period 6 when the 6*s* fills before the 5*d*.

At the beginning of Period 4, the electrons in potassium (19) and calcium (20) go into the 4*s* sublevel. In scandium, the next electron added after the 4*s* sublevel is filled goes into the 3*d* block. The 3*d* block continues to fill until it is complete with 10 electrons at zinc (30). Once the 3*d* block is complete, the next six electrons, gallium to krypton, go into the 4*p* block.

Element	Atomic Number	Electron Configuration	Abbreviated Electron Configuration
4*s* Block			
K	19	$1s^22s^22p^63s^23p^64s^1$	$[Ar]4s^1$
Ca	20	$1s^22s^22p^63s^23p^64s^2$	$[Ar]4s^2$
3*d* Block			
Sc	21	$1s^22s^22p^63s^23p^64s^23d^1$	$[Ar]4s^23d^1$
Ti	22	$1s^22s^22p^63s^23p^64s^23d^2$	$[Ar]4s^23d^2$
V	23	$1s^22s^22p^63s^23p^64s^23d^3$	$[Ar]4s^23d^3$
Cr*	24	$1s^22s^22p^63s^23p^64s^13d^5$	$[Ar]4s^13d^5$ (half-filled *d* sublevel is stable)
Mn	25	$1s^22s^22p^63s^23p^64s^23d^5$	$[Ar]4s^23d^5$
Fe	26	$1s^22s^22p^63s^23p^64s^23d^6$	$[Ar]4s^23d^6$
Co	27	$1s^22s^22p^63s^23p^64s^23d^7$	$[Ar]4s^23d^7$
Ni	28	$1s^22s^22p^63s^23p^64s^23d^8$	$[Ar]4s^23d^8$
Cu*	29	$1s^22s^22p^63s^23p^64s^13d^{10}$	$[Ar]4s^13d^{10}$ (filled *d* sublevel is stable)
Zn	30	$1s^22s^22p^63s^23p^64s^23d^{10}$	$[Ar]4s^23d^{10}$

Element	Atomic Number	Electron Configuration	Abbreviated Electron Configuration
4*p* Block			
Ga	31	$1s^22s^22p^63s^23p^64s^23d^{10}4p^1$	$[Ar]4s^23d^{10}4p^1$
Ge	32	$1s^22s^22p^63s^23p^64s^23d^{10}4p^2$	$[Ar]4s^23d^{10}4p^2$
As	33	$1s^22s^22p^63s^23p^64s^23d^{10}4p^3$	$[Ar]4s^23d^{10}4p^3$
Se	34	$1s^22s^22p^63s^23p^64s^23d^{10}4p^4$	$[Ar]4s^23d^{10}4p^4$
Br	35	$1s^22s^22p^63s^23p^64s^23d^{10}4p^5$	$[Ar]4s^23d^{10}4p^5$
Kr	36	$1s^22s^22p^63s^23p^64s^23d^{10}4p^6$	$[Ar]4s^23d^{10}4p^6$

*Exceptions to the order of filling.

SAMPLE PROBLEM 5.7 Using Sublevel Blocks to Write Electron Configurations

Use the sublevel blocks on the periodic table to write the electron configuration for selenium.

SOLUTION

Step 1 **Locate the element on the periodic table.** Selenium is in Period 4 and Group 6A (16), which is in a *p* block.

Step 2 **Write the filled sublevels in order, going across each period.**

Period	Sublevel Block Filling	Sublevel Block Notation (filled)
1	1*s* (H → He)	$1s^2$
2	2*s* (Li → Be) and 2*p* (B → Ne)	$2s^22p^6$
3	3*s* (Na → Mg) and 3*p* (Al → Ar)	$3s^23p^6$
4	4*s* (K → Ca) and 3*d* (Sc → Zn)	$4s^23d^{10}$

Step 3 **Complete the configuration by counting the electrons in the last occupied sublevel block.** Because selenium is the fourth element in the 4*p* block, there are four electrons to place in the 4*p* sublevel.

Period	Sublevel Block Filling	Sublevel Block Notation
4	4*p* (Ga → Se)	$4p^4$

The electron configuration for selenium (Se) is: $1s^22s^22p^63s^23p^64s^23d^{10}4p^4$.

STUDY CHECK 5.7

Use the sublevel blocks on the periodic table to write the electron configuration for tin.

Some Exceptions in Sublevel Block Order

Within the filling of the 3*d* sublevel, exceptions occur for chromium and copper. In Cr and Cu, the 3*d* sublevel is close to being a half-filled or filled sublevel, which is particularly stable. Thus, the electron configuration for chromium has only one electron in the 4*s* and five electrons in the 3*d* sublevel to give the added stability of a half-filled *d* sublevel. This is shown in the abbreviated orbital diagram for chromium:

	4*s*	3*d* (half-filled)	4*p*
[Ar]	↑	↑ ↑ ↑ ↑ ↑	(empty) (empty) (empty)

Abbreviated orbital diagram for chromium

A similar exception occurs when copper achieves a stable, filled 3*d* sublevel with 10 electrons and only one electron in the 4*s* orbital. This is shown in the abbreviated orbital diagram for copper:

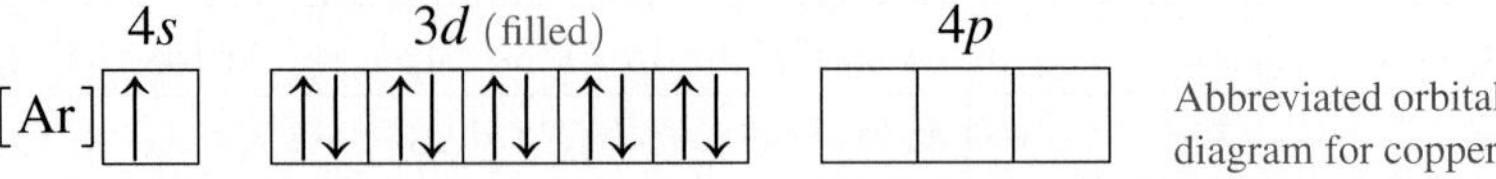

Abbreviated orbital diagram for copper

After the 4*s* and 3*d* sublevels are completed, the 4*p* sublevel fills as expected from gallium to krypton, the noble gas that completes Period 4. There are also exceptions in filling for the higher *d* and *f* electron sublevels, some caused by the added stability of half-filled shells and others where the cause is not known.

QUESTIONS AND PROBLEMS

5.5 Electron Configurations and the Periodic Table

LEARNING GOAL: *Write the electron configuration for an atom using the sublevel blocks on the periodic table.*

5.41 Use the sublevel blocks on the periodic table to write a complete electron configuration for an atom of each of the following:
a. arsenic **b.** iron
c. indium **d.** iodine

5.42 Use the sublevel blocks on the periodic table to write a complete electron configuration for an atom of each of the following:
a. calcium **b.** cobalt
c. gallium **d.** cadmium

5.43 Use the sublevel blocks on the periodic table to write an abbreviated electron configuration for an atom of each of the following:
a. titanium **b.** bromine
c. barium **d.** lead

5.44 Use the sublevel blocks on the periodic table to write an abbreviated electron configuration for an atom of each of the following:
a. nickel **b.** arsenic
c. tin **d.** cesium

5.45 Use the periodic table to give the symbol of the element with each of the following electron configurations:
a. $1s^22s^22p^63s^23p^3$
b. $1s^22s^22p^63s^23p^64s^23d^7$
c. $[Ar]4s^23d^{10}$
d. $[Xe]6s^24f^{14}5d^{10}6p^3$

5.46 Use the periodic table to give the symbol of the element with each of the following electron configurations:
a. $1s^22s^22p^63s^23p^64s^23d^8$
b. $[Kr]5s^24d^{10}5p^4$
c. $1s^22s^22p^63s^23p^64s^23d^{10}4p^2$
d. $[Ar]4s^23d^{10}4p^5$

5.47 Use the periodic table to give the symbol of the element that meets the following conditions:
a. has three electrons in the $n = 4$ energy level
b. has three 2*p* electrons
c. completes the 5*p* sublevel
d. has two electrons in the 4*d* sublevel

5.48 Use the periodic table to give the symbol of the element that meets the following conditions:
a. has five electrons in the $n = 3$ energy level
b. has one electron in the 6*p* sublevel
c. completes the 7*s* sublevel
d. has four 5*p* electrons

5.49 Use the periodic table to give the number of electrons in the indicated sublevels for the following:
a. 3*d* in zinc **b.** 2*p* in sodium
c. 4*p* in arsenic **d.** 5*s* in rubidium

5.50 Use the periodic table to give the number of electrons in the indicated sublevels for the following:
a. 3*d* in manganese **b.** 5*p* in antimony
c. 6*p* in lead **d.** 3*s* in magnesium

LEARNING GOAL

Use the electron configurations of elements to explain the trends in periodic properties.

CORE CHEMISTRY SKILL

Identifying Trends in Periodic Properties

5.6 Trends in Periodic Properties

The electron configurations of atoms are an important factor in the physical and chemical properties of the elements and in the properties of the compounds that they form. In this section, we will look at the *valence electrons* in atoms, the trends in *atomic size*, *ionization energy*, and *metallic character*. Going across a period, there is a pattern of regular change in these properties from one group to the next. Known as *periodic properties*, each property increases or decreases across a period, and then the trend is repeated in each successive period. We can use the seasonal changes in temperatures as an analogy for periodic properties. In the winter, temperatures are cold and become warmer in the spring. By summer, the outdoor temperatures are hot but begin to cool in the fall. By winter, we expect cold temperatures again as the pattern of decreasing and increasing temperatures repeats for another year.

Group Number and Valence Electrons

The chemical properties of representative elements are mostly due to the **valence electrons**, which are the electrons in the outermost energy level. These valence electrons occupy the *s* and *p* sublevels with the highest principal quantum number *n*. The group numbers indicate the number of valence (outer) electrons for the elements in each vertical column. For example, the elements in Group 1A (1), such as lithium, sodium, and potassium, all have one electron in an *s* orbital. Looking at the sublevel block, we can represent the valence electron in the alkali metals of Group 1A (1) as ns^1. All the elements in Group 2A (2), the alkaline earth metals, have two valence electrons, ns^2. The halogens in Group 7A (17) have seven valence electrons, ns^2np^5.

We can see the repetition of the outermost *s* and *p* electrons for the representative elements for Periods 1 to 4 in Table 5.3. Helium is included in Group 8A (18) because it is a noble gas, but it has only two electrons in its complete energy level.

TABLE 5.3 Valence Electron Configuration for Representative Elements in Periods 1–4

1A (1)	2A (2)	3A (13)	4A (14)	5A (15)	6A (16)	7A (17)	8A (18)
1 H $1s^1$							2 He $1s^2$
3 Li $2s^1$	4 Be $2s^2$	5 B $2s^22p^1$	6 C $2s^22p^2$	7 N $2s^22p^3$	8 O $2s^22p^4$	9 F $2s^22p^5$	10 Ne $2s^22p^6$
11 Na $3s^1$	12 Mg $3s^2$	13 Al $3s^23p^1$	14 Si $3s^23p^2$	15 P $3s^23p^3$	16 S $3s^23p^4$	17 Cl $3s^23p^5$	18 Ar $3s^23p^6$
19 K $4s^1$	20 Ca $4s^2$	31 Ga $4s^24p^1$	32 Ge $4s^24p^2$	33 As $4s^24p^3$	34 Se $4s^24p^4$	35 Br $4s^24p^5$	36 Kr $4s^24p^6$

CONCEPT CHECK 5.6 Valence Electrons

Identify the number of valence electrons in an atom of each of the following:

a. P **b.** Ba **c.** F **d.** B

ANSWER

a. On the periodic table P appears in Group 5A (15); P has five valence electrons.
b. On the periodic table Ba appears in Group 2A (2); Ba has two valence electrons.
c. On the periodic table F appears in Group 7A (17); F has seven valence electrons.
d. On the periodic table B appears in Group 3A (13); B has three valence electrons.

SAMPLE PROBLEM 5.8 Using Group Numbers

Using the periodic table, write the group number, the period, and the valence electron configuration for the following:

a. calcium **b.** iodine **c.** lead

SOLUTION

The valence electrons are the outermost *s* and *p* electrons. Although there may be electrons in the *d* or *f* sublevels, they are not valence electrons.

a. Calcium is in Group 2A (2), Period 4. It has a valence electron configuration of $4s^2$.
b. Iodine is in Group 7A (17), Period 5. It has a valence electron configuration of $5s^25p^5$.
c. Lead is in Group 4A (14), Period 6. It has a valence electron configuration of $6s^26p^2$.

STUDY CHECK 5.8

What are the group numbers, the periods, and the valence electron configurations for sulfur and strontium?

CORE CHEMISTRY SKILL

Drawing Electron-Dot Symbols

Electron-Dot Symbols

An **electron-dot symbol** is a convenient way to represent the valence electrons, which are shown as dots placed on the sides, top, or bottom of the symbol for the element. One to four valence electrons are arranged as single dots. When there are five to eight electrons, one or more electrons are paired. Any of the following would be an acceptable electron-dot symbol for magnesium, which has two valence electrons:

Electron-Dot Symbols for Magnesium

Ṁg· Ṁg̣ ·Ṁg ·Mg· Mg̣· ·Ṁg

Electron-dot symbols for selected elements are given in Table 5.4.

Increasing Number of Valence Electrons →

TABLE 5.4 Electron-Dot Symbols for Selected Elements in Periods 1–4

	Group Number							
	1A (1)	2A (2)	3A (13)	4A (14)	5A (15)	6A (16)	7A (17)	8A (18)
Number of Valence Electrons	1	2	3	4	5	6	7	8*
Electron-Dot Symbol	H·							He:
	Li·	Ḃe·	·Ḃ·	·Ċ·	·N̈·	·Ö:	·F̤̈:	:N̤̈e:
	Na·	Ṁg·	·Ȧl·	·Ṡi̤·	·P̈·	·S̤̈:	·C̤̈l:	:Ä̤r:
	K·	Ċa·	·Ġa·	·Ġe̤·	·Ä̤s·	·S̤̈e:	·B̤̈r:	:K̤̈r:

* Helium (He) is stable with 2 valence electrons.

SAMPLE PROBLEM 5.9 Drawing Electron-Dot Symbols

Draw the electron-dot symbol for each of the following:

a. bromine
b. aluminum

SOLUTION

a. The electron-dot symbol for bromine, which is in Group 7A (17), has seven valence electrons. Thus, three pairs of dots and one single dot are drawn on the sides of the Br symbol.

·B̤̈r:

b. The electron-dot symbol for aluminum, which is in Group 3A (13), has three valence electrons drawn as single dots on the sides of the Al symbol.

·Ȧl·

STUDY CHECK 5.9

What is the electron-dot symbol for phosphorus?

Atomic Size

The **atomic size** of an atom is determined by the distance of the valence electrons from the nucleus. For each group of representative elements, the atomic size *increases* going from the top to the bottom because the outermost electrons in each energy level are farther from the nucleus. For example, in Group 1A (1), Li has a valence electron in energy level 2; Na has a valence electron in energy level 3; and K has a valence electron in energy level 4. This means that a K atom is larger than a Na atom and a Na atom is larger than a Li atom (see Figure 5.11).

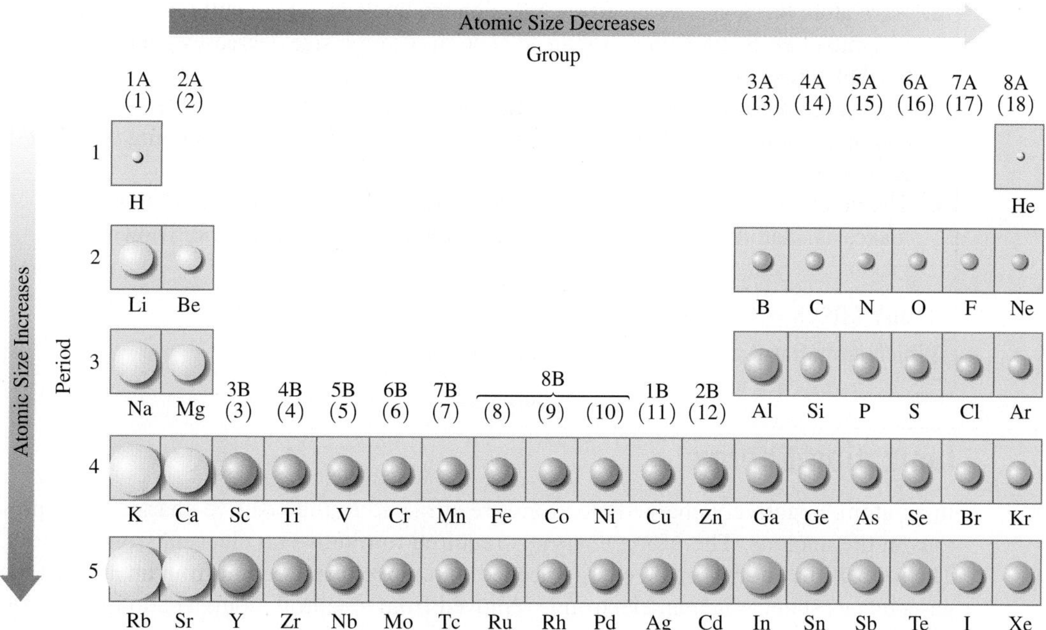

FIGURE 5.11 The atomic size increases going down a group but decreases going from left to right across a period.

Q Why does the atomic size increase going down a group?

The atomic size of representative elements is affected by the attractive forces of the protons in the nucleus on the electrons in the outermost level. For the elements going across a period, the increase in the number of protons in the nucleus increases the positive charge of the nucleus. As a result, the electrons are pulled closer to the nucleus, which means that the atomic size of representative elements decreases going from left to right across a period.

The size of atoms of transition elements within the same period changes only slightly because electrons are filling *d* orbitals rather than the outermost energy level. Because the increase in nuclear charge is canceled by an increase in *d* electrons, the attraction of the valence electrons by the nucleus remains about the same. Because there is little change in the nuclear attraction for the valence electrons, the atomic size remains relatively constant for the transition elements.

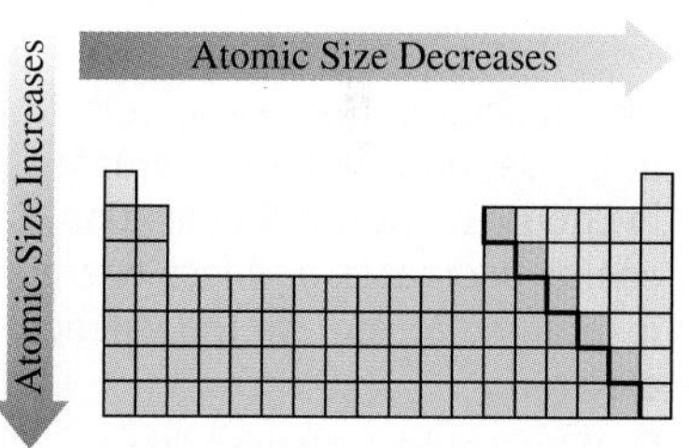

Atomic size increases going down a group and decreases going from left to right across a period.

CONCEPT CHECK 5.7 Atomic Size

Why is a phosphorus atom larger than a nitrogen atom but smaller than a silicon atom?

ANSWER

A phosphorus atom is larger than a nitrogen atom because phosphorus has valence electrons in a higher energy level, which is farther from the nucleus. A phosphorus atom has one more proton than a silicon atom; therefore, the nucleus in phosphorus has a stronger attraction for the valence electrons, which decreases its size compared to a silicon atom.

SAMPLE PROBLEM 5.10 Size of Atoms

Identify the smaller atom in each of the following pairs:

a. N or F **b.** K or Kr **c.** Ca and Sr

SOLUTION

a. An F atom has a greater positive charge on the nucleus, which pulls electrons closer, and makes an F atom smaller than an N atom. Atomic size decreases going from left to right across a period.

b. A Kr atom has a greater positive charge on the nucleus, which pulls electrons closer, and makes a Kr atom smaller than a K atom. Atomic size decreases going from left to right across a period.

c. The outer electrons in a Ca atom are closer to the nucleus than in a Sr atom, which makes a Ca atom smaller than a Sr atom. Atomic size increases going down a group.

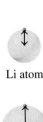

STUDY CHECK 5.10

Which atom has the largest atomic size, P, As, or Se?

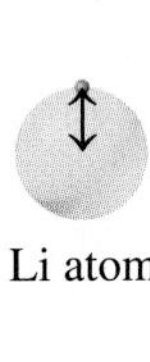

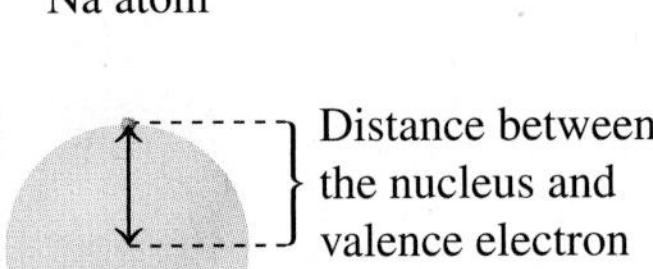

FIGURE 5.12 As the distance from the nucleus to the valence electron in Li, Na, and K atoms increases in Group 1A (1), the ionization energy decreases and less energy is required to remove the valence electron.

Q Why would Cs have a lower ionization energy than K?

Ionization Energy

In an atom, negatively charged electrons are attracted to the positive charge of the protons in the nucleus. Therefore, energy is required to remove an electron from an atom. The **ionization energy** is the energy needed to remove one electron from an atom in the gaseous (g) state. When an electron is removed from a neutral atom, a cation with a 1+ charge is formed.

$$Na(g) + \text{energy (ionization)} \longrightarrow Na^{+}(g) + e^{-}$$

1s	2s	2p	3s		1s	2s	2p	3s	
↑↓	↑↓	↑↓ ↑↓ ↑↓	↑		↑↓	↑↓	↑↓ ↑↓ ↑↓		+ ↑

The attraction of a nucleus for the outermost electrons decreases as those electrons are farther from the nucleus. Thus the ionization energy decreases going down a group (see Figure 5.12). However, going across a period from left to right, the positive charge of the nucleus increases because there is an increase in the number of protons. Thus the ionization energy increases going from left to right across the periodic table.

In summary, the ionization energy is low for the metals and high for the nonmetals. The high ionization energies of the noble gases indicate that their electron configurations are especially stable.

CONCEPT CHECK 5.8 Ionization

An atom of magnesium has the electron configuration $1s^22s^22p^63s^2$.

When a magnesium atom ionizes to form a magnesium ion Mg^{2+}, which electrons are lost?

a. the $1s$ electrons **b.** the $2s$ electrons
c. the $2p$ electrons **d.** the $3s$ electrons

ANSWER

d. When a magnesium atom Mg ionizes to form Mg^{2+}, it loses the two valence electrons, which are the outermost $3s$ electrons.

SAMPLE PROBLEM 5.11 Ionization Energy

Indicate the element in each pair that has the higher ionization energy and explain your choice.

a. K or Na **b.** Mg or Cl **c.** F or N

SOLUTION

a. Na. In Na, an electron is removed from a sublevel closer to the nucleus, which requires a higher ionization energy for Na compared with K.

b. Cl. The increased nuclear charge of Cl increases the attraction for the valence electrons, which requires a higher ionization energy for Cl compared to Mg.

c. F. The increased nuclear charge of F increases the attraction for the valence electrons, which requires a higher ionization energy for F compared to N.

STUDY CHECK 5.11

Arrange Sn, Sr, and I in order of increasing ionization energy.

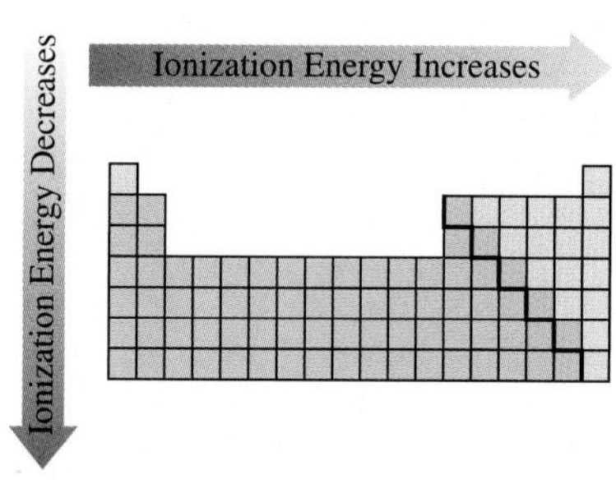

Ionization energy decreases going down a group and increases going from left to right across a period.

Metallic Character

In Section 4.2, we identified elements as metals, nonmetals, and metalloids. An element that has **metallic character** is an element that loses valence electrons easily. Metallic character is more prevalent in the elements (metals) on the left side of the periodic table and decreases going from left to right across a period. The elements (nonmetals) on the right side of the periodic table do not easily lose electrons, which means they are less metallic. Most of the metalloids between the metals and nonmetals tend to lose electrons, but not as easily as the metals. Thus, in Period 3, sodium, which loses electrons most easily, would be the most metallic. Going across from left to right in Period 3, metallic character decreases to argon, which has the least metallic character.

For elements in the same group of representative elements, metallic character increases going from top to bottom. Atoms at the bottom of any group have more electron levels, which makes it easier to lose electrons. Thus, the elements at the bottom of a group on the periodic table have lower ionization energy and are more metallic compared to the elements at the top.

A summary of the trends in periodic properties we have discussed is given in Table 5.5.

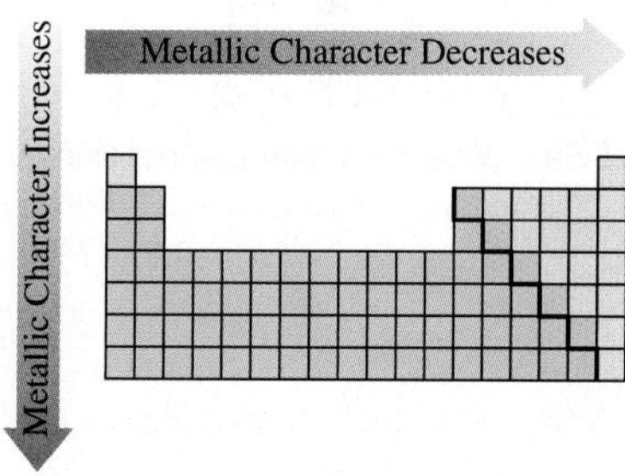

Metallic character increases going down a group and decreases going from left to right across a period.

TABLE 5.5 Summary of Trends in Periodic Properties of Representative Elements

Periodic Property	Top to Bottom within a Group	Left to Right across a Period
Valence Electrons	Remains the same	Increases
Atomic Size	Increases due to the increase in the number of energy levels	Decreases as the number of protons increases, which strengthens the attraction of the nucleus for the valence electrons, and pulls them closer to the nucleus
Ionization Energy	Decreases because the valence electrons are easier to remove when they are farther from the nucleus	Increases as the increase in the number of protons strengthens the attraction of the nucleus for the valence electrons, and more energy is needed to remove an electron
Metallic Character	Increases because the valence electrons are easier to remove when they are farther from the nucleus	Decreases as the number of protons increases, which strengthens the attraction of the nucleus for the valence electrons, and makes it more difficult to remove a valence electron

CONCEPT CHECK 5.9 Metallic Character

Identify the element that has more metallic character in each of the following pairs:

a. Mg or Al **b.** Na or K

ANSWER

a. Mg is more metallic than Al because metallic character decreases going from left to right across a period.

b. K is more metallic than Na because metallic character increases going down a group.

QUESTIONS AND PROBLEMS

5.6 Trends in Periodic Properties

LEARNING GOAL: *Use the electron configurations of elements to explain the trends in periodic properties.*

5.51 What do the group numbers from 1A to 8A for the elements indicate about electron configurations of those elements?

5.52 What is similar and what is different about the valence electrons of the elements in a group?

5.53 Write the group number using both A/B and 1–18 notations for elements that have the following outer electron configuration:
Example: $3s^2 3p^1$ 3A (13)
a. $2s^2$ **b.** $3s^2 3p^3$
c. $4s^2 3d^5$ **d.** $5s^2 4d^{10} 5p^4$

5.54 Write the group number using both A/B and 1–18 notations for elements that have the following outer electron configuration:
Example: $3s^2 3p^1$ 3A (13)
a. $4s^2 3d^{10} 4p^5$ **b.** $4s^1$
c. $4s^2 3d^8$ **d.** $5s^2 4d^{10} 5p^2$

5.55 Write the valence electron configuration for each of the following:
Example: $ns^2 np^4$
a. alkali metals **b.** Group 4A
c. Group 17 **d.** Group 5A

5.56 Write the valence electron configuration for each of the following:
Example: $ns^2 np^4$
a. halogens **b.** Group 6A
c. Group 13 **d.** alkaline earth metals

5.57 Indicate the number of valence electrons in each of the following:
a. aluminum **b.** Group 5A
c. barium **d.** F, Cl, Br, and I

5.58 Indicate the number of valence electrons in each of the following:
a. Li, Na, K, Rb, and Cs **b.** Se
c. C, Si, Ge, Sn, and Pb **d.** Group 8A

5.59 Write the group number and electron-dot symbol for each of the following elements:
a. sulfur **b.** nitrogen
c. calcium **d.** sodium
e. gallium

5.60 Write the group number and electron-dot symbol for each of the following elements:
a. carbon **b.** oxygen
c. argon **d.** lithium
e. chlorine

5.61 Select the larger atom in each pair.
a. Na or Cl **b.** Na or Rb
c. Na or Mg **d.** Rb or I

5.62 Select the larger atom in each pair.
a. S or Ar **b.** S or O
c. S or K **d.** S or Mg

5.63 Place the elements in each set in order of decreasing atomic size.
a. Al, Si, Mg **b.** Cl, Br, I
c. Sb, Sr, I **d.** P, Si, Na

5.64 Place the elements in each set in order of decreasing atomic size.
a. Cl, S, P **b.** Ge, Si, C
c. Ba, Ca, Sr **d.** S, O, Se

5.65 Select the element in each pair with the higher ionization energy.
a. Br or I **b.** Mg or Sr
c. Si or P **d.** I or Xe

5.66 Select the element in each pair with the higher ionization energy.
a. O or Ne **b.** K or Br
c. Ca or Ba **d.** N or Ne

5.67 Arrange each set of elements in order of increasing ionization energy.
a. F, Cl, Br **b.** Na, Cl, Al
c. Na, K, Cs **d.** As, Ca, Br

5.68 Arrange each set of elements in order of increasing ionization energy.
a. O, N, C **b.** S, P, Cl
c. P, As, N **d.** Al, Si, P

5.69 Place the following in order of decreasing metallic character:
Br, Ge, Ca, Ga

5.70 Place the following in order of increasing metallic character:
Na, P, Al, Ar

5.71 Fill in each of the following blanks using *higher* or *lower*, *more* or *less*: Sr has a __________ ionization energy and is __________ metallic than Sb.

5.72 Fill in each of the following blanks using *higher* or *lower*, *more* or *less*: N has a __________ ionization energy and is __________ metallic than As.

5.73 Complete each of the following statements **a–d** using **1**, **2**, or **3**:
1. decreases **2.** increases **3.** remains the same
Going down Group 6A (16),
a. the ionization energy __________
b. the atomic size __________
c. the metallic character __________
d. the number of valence electrons __________

5.74 Complete each of the following statements **a–d** using **1**, **2**, or **3**:
1. decreases **2.** increases **3.** remains the same

Going from left to right across Period 3,
a. the ionization energy ____________
b. the atomic size ____________
c. the metallic character ____________
d. the number of valence electrons ____________

5.75 Which statements completed with **a–e** will be *true* and which will be *false*?

In Period 2, an atom of N compared to an atom of Li has a larger (greater)
a. atomic size
b. ionization energy
c. number of protons
d. metallic character
e. number of valence electrons

5.76 Which statements completed with **a–e** will be *true* and which will be *false*?

In Group 4A (14), an atom of C compared to an atom of Sn has a larger (greater)
a. atomic size
b. ionization energy
c. number of protons
d. metallic character
e. number of valence electrons

CHAPTER REVIEW

5.1 Electromagnetic Radiation

LEARNING GOAL: *Compare the wavelength of radiation with its frequency.*

- Electromagnetic radiation such as radio waves and visible light is energy that travels at the speed of light.
- Each particular type of radiation has a specific wavelength and frequency.
- A wavelength (symbol λ, lambda) is the distance between a crest in a wave and the next crest on that wave.
- The frequency (symbol ν, nu) is the number of waves that pass a certain point in 1 s.
- All electromagnetic radiation travels at the speed of light (c), which is 3.00×10^8 m/s.
- Mathematically, the relationship of the speed of light, wavelength, and frequency is expressed as $c = \lambda\nu$.
- Long-wavelength radiation has low frequencies, while short-wavelength radiation has high frequencies.
- Radiation with a high frequency has high energy.

5.2 Atomic Spectra and Energy Levels

LEARNING GOAL: *Explain how atomic spectra correlate with the energy levels in atoms.*

- The atomic spectra of elements are related to the specific energy levels occupied by electrons.
- Light consists of photons, which are particles of a specific energy or *quanta*.
- When an electron absorbs a photon of a particular energy, it attains a higher energy level. When an electron drops to a lower energy level, a photon of a particular energy is emitted.
- Each element has its own unique atomic spectrum.

5.3 Sublevels and Orbitals

LEARNING GOAL: *Describe the sublevels and orbitals in atoms.*

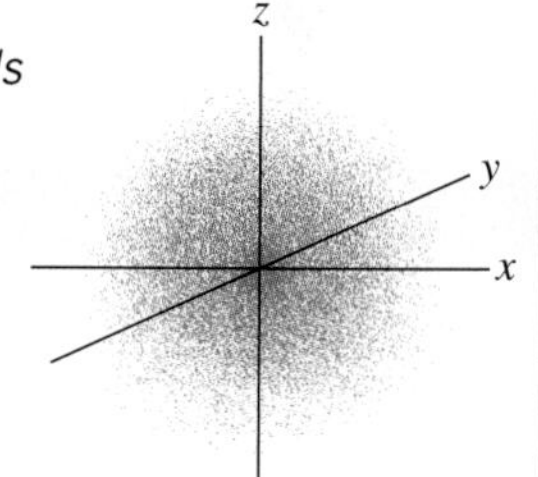

- An orbital is a region around the nucleus where an electron with a specific energy is most likely to be found.
- Each orbital holds a maximum of two electrons, which must have opposite spins.
- In each energy level (n), electrons occupy orbitals of identical energy within sublevels.
- An s sublevel contains one s orbital, a p sublevel contains three p orbitals, a d sublevel contains five d orbitals, and an f sublevel contains seven f orbitals.
- Each type of orbital has a unique shape.

5.4 Orbital Diagrams and Electron Configurations

LEARNING GOAL: *Draw the orbital diagram and write the electron configuration for an element.*

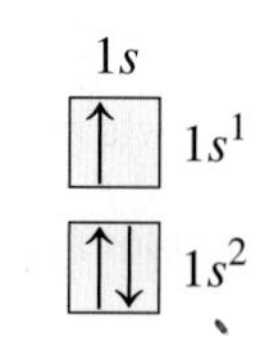

- Within a sublevel, electrons enter orbitals in the same energy level one at a time until all the orbitals are half-filled.
- Additional electrons enter with opposite spins until the orbitals in that sublevel are filled with two electrons each.
- The orbital diagram for an element such as silicon shows the orbitals that are occupied by paired and unpaired electrons:

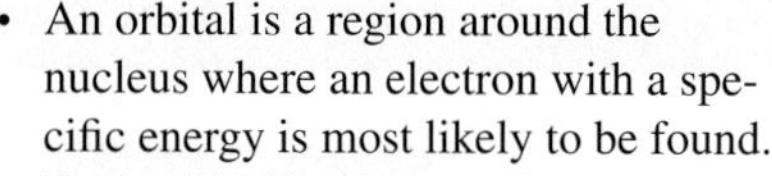
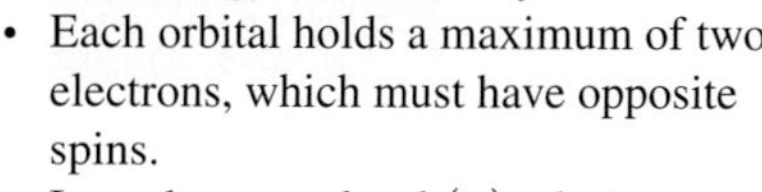

- The electron configuration for an element such as silicon shows the number of electrons in each sublevel: $1s^22s^22p^63s^23p^2$.
- An abbreviated electron configuration for an element such as silicon places the symbol of a noble gas in brackets to represent the filled sublevels: $[Ne]3s^23p^2$.

5.5 Electron Configurations and the Periodic Table

LEARNING GOAL: *Write the electron configuration for an atom using the sublevel blocks on the periodic table.*

- The periodic table consists of *s*, *p*, *d*, and *f* sublevel blocks.
- An electron configuration can be written following the order of the sublevel blocks on the periodic table.
- Beginning with 1*s*, an electron configuration is obtained by writing the sublevel blocks in order going across each period on the periodic table until the element is reached.

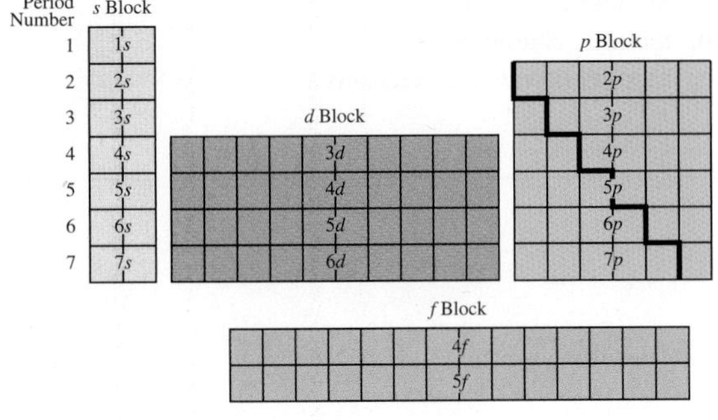

5.6 Trends in Periodic Properties

LEARNING GOAL: *Use the electron configurations of elements to explain the trends in periodic properties.*

Li atom

Na atom

K atom

Distance between the nucleus and valence electron

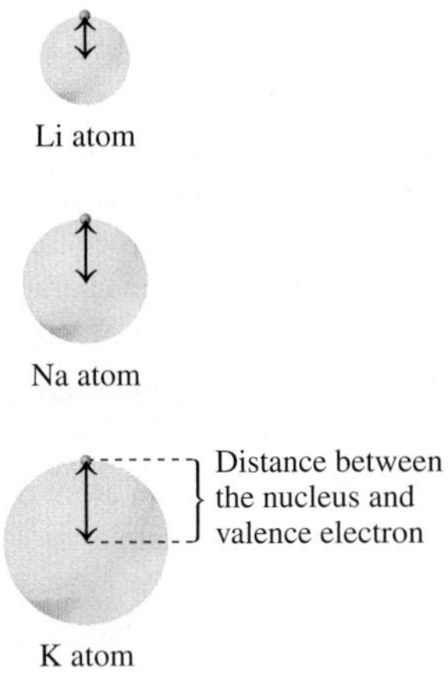

- The properties of elements are related to the valence electrons of the atoms.
- With only a few exceptions, each group of elements has the same arrangement of valence electrons differing only in the energy level.
- Valence electrons are represented as dots around the symbol of the element.
- The size of an atom increases going down a group and decreases going from left to right across a period.
- The energy required to remove a valence electron is the ionization energy, which decreases going down a group, and generally increases going from left to right across a period.
- The metallic character of an element increases going down a group and decreases going from left to right across a period.

CONCEPT MAP

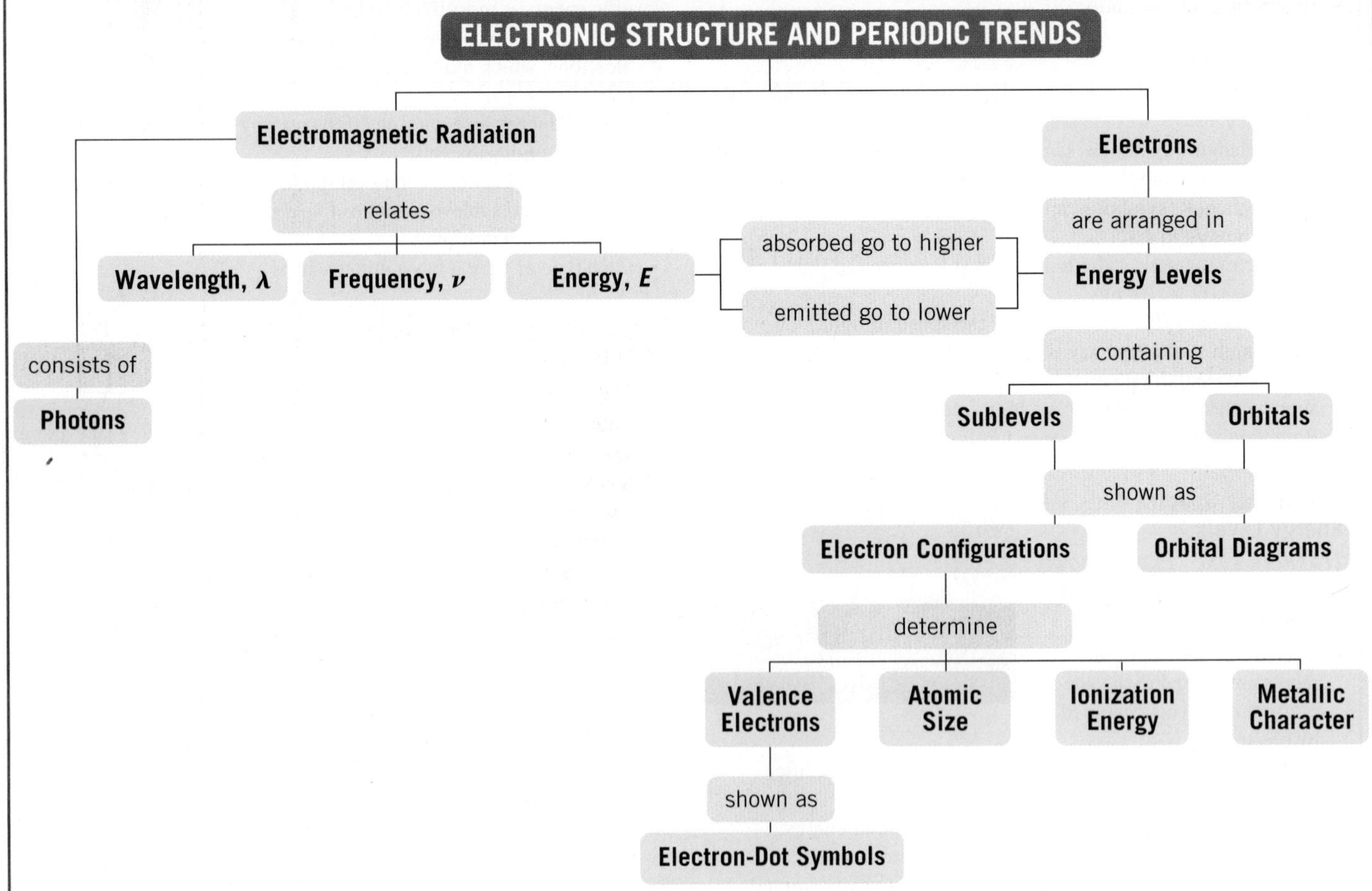

ELECTRONIC STRUCTURE AND PERIODIC TRENDS

- **Electromagnetic Radiation**
  - relates **Wavelength, λ**, **Frequency, ν**, **Energy, *E***
  - consists of **Photons**
- **Electrons**
  - are arranged in **Energy Levels** (absorbed go to higher / emitted go to lower — **Energy, *E***)
  - containing **Sublevels** and **Orbitals**
    - shown as **Electron Configurations** and **Orbital Diagrams**
    - **Electron Configurations** determine **Valence Electrons**, **Atomic Size**, **Ionization Energy**, **Metallic Character**
      - **Valence Electrons** shown as **Electron-Dot Symbols**

KEY TERMS

atomic size The distance between the outermost electrons and the nucleus.

atomic spectrum A series of lines specific for each element produced by photons emitted by electrons dropping to lower energy levels.

***d* block** The 10 elements in Groups 3B (3) to 2B (12) in which electrons fill the five *d* orbitals.

electromagnetic radiation Forms of energy such as visible light, microwaves, radio waves, infrared, ultraviolet light, and X-rays that travel as waves at the speed of light.

electromagnetic spectrum The arrangement of types of radiation from long wavelengths to short wavelengths.

electron configuration A list of the number of electrons in each sublevel within an atom, arranged by increasing energy.

electron-dot symbol The representation of an atom that shows valence electrons as dots around the symbol of the element.

energy level A group of electrons with similar energy.

***f* block** The 14 elements in the rows at the bottom of the periodic table in which electrons fill the seven 4*f* and 5*f* orbitals.

frequency The number of times the crests of a wave pass a point in 1 s.

ionization energy The energy needed to remove the least tightly bound electron from the outermost energy level of an atom.

metallic character A measure of how easily an element loses a valence electron.

orbital The region around the nucleus of an atom where electrons of certain energy are most likely to be found: *s* orbitals are spherical; *p* orbitals have two lobes.

orbital diagram A diagram that shows the distribution of electrons in the orbitals of the energy levels.

***p* block** The elements in Groups 3A (13) to 8A (18) in which electrons fill the *p* orbitals.

photon The smallest particle of light.

principal quantum number (*n*) The number ($n = 1, n = 2, \ldots$) assigned to an energy level.

***s* block** The elements in Groups 1A (1) and 2A (2) in which electrons fill the *s* orbitals.

sublevel A group of orbitals of equal energy within energy levels. The number of sublevels in each energy level is the same as the principal quantum number (*n*).

valence electrons The electrons in the highest energy level of an atom.

wavelength The distance between adjacent crests in a wave.

CORE CHEMISTRY SKILLS

The chapter section containing each Core Chemistry Skill is shown in parentheses at the end of each heading.

Writing Electron Configurations (5.4)

- The electron configuration for an atom specifies the energy levels and sublevels occupied by the electrons of an atom.
- An electron configuration is written starting with the lowest energy sublevel, followed by the next lowest energy sublevel.
- The number of electrons in each sublevel is shown as a superscript.

Example: Write the electron configuration for palladium.

Answer: Palladium has atomic number 46, which means it has 46 protons and 46 electrons.

$$1s^22s^22p^63s^23p^64s^23d^{10}4p^65s^24d^8$$

Using the Periodic Table to Write Electron Configurations (5.5)

- An electron configuration corresponds to the location of an element on the periodic table, where different blocks within the periodic table are identified as the *s*, *p*, *d*, and *f* sublevels.

Example: Use the periodic table to write the electron configuration of sulfur.

Answer: Sulfur (atomic number 16) is in Group 6A (16) and Period 3.

Period	Sublevel Block Filling	Sublevel Block Notation (filled)
1	$1s$ (H $\rightarrow$ He)	$1s^2$
2	$2s$ (Li $\rightarrow$ Be) and $2p$ (B $\rightarrow$ Ne)	$2s^22p^6$
3	$3s$ (Na $\rightarrow$ Mg) $3p$ (Al $\rightarrow$ S)	$3s^2$ $3p^4$

The electron configuration for sulfur (S) is: $1s^22s^22p^63s^23p^4$.

Identifying Trends in Periodic Properties (5.6)

- The size of an atom increases going down a group and decreases going from left to right across a period.
- The ionization energy decreases going down a group and increases going from left to right across a period.
- The metallic character of an element increases going down a group and decreases going from left to right across a period.

Example: For Mg, P, and Cl, identify which has the

a. largest atomic size
b. highest ionization energy
c. greatest metallic character

Answer: **a.** Mg **b.** Cl **c.** Mg

Drawing Electron-Dot Symbols (5.6)

- The valence electrons are the electrons in the *s* and *p* sublevels with the highest principal quantum number *n*.
- The number of valence electrons is the same as the group number of the representative elements.
- An electron-dot symbol represents the number of valence electrons shown as dots placed around the symbol for the element.

Example: Give the group number and number of valence electrons, and draw the electron-dot symbol for each of the following:

a. Rb **b.** Se **c.** Xe

Answer: **a.** Group 1A (1), one valence electron, Rb·
b. Group 6A (16), six valence electrons, ·$\ddot{\text{Se}}$:
c. Group 8A (18), eight valence electrons, :$\ddot{\text{Xe}}$:

UNDERSTANDING THE CONCEPTS

The chapter sections to review are shown in parentheses at the end of each question.

Use the following diagram for Problems 5.77 and 5.78:

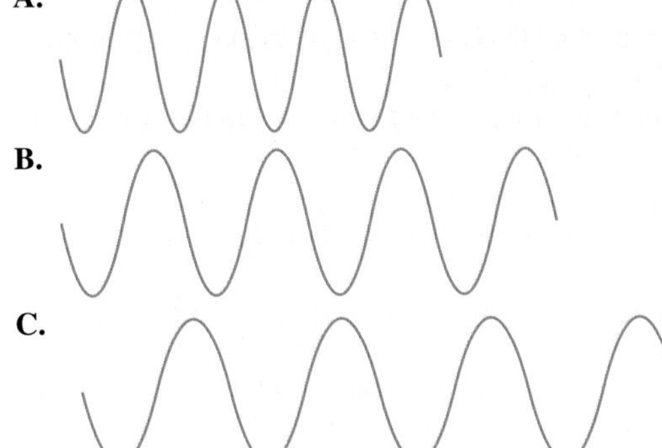

5.77 Select diagram **A**, **B**, or **C** that (5.1)
 a. has the longest wavelength
 b. has the shortest wavelength
 c. has the highest frequency
 d. has the lowest frequency

5.78 Select diagram **A**, **B**, or **C** that (5.1)
 a. has the highest energy
 b. has the lowest energy
 c. would represent blue light
 d. would represent red light

5.79 Match the following with an *s* or *p* orbital: (5.3)

a. **b.** **c.**

5.80 Match the following with *s* or *p* orbitals: (5.3)
 a. two lobes
 b. spherical shape
 c. found in $n = 1$
 d. found in $n = 3$

5.81 Indicate whether or not the following orbital diagrams are possible and explain. When possible, indicate the element it represents. (5.4)

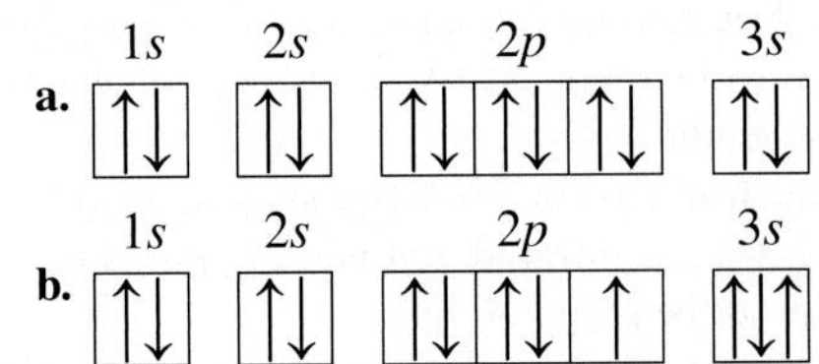

5.82 Indicate whether or not the following abbreviated orbital diagrams are possible and explain. When possible, indicate the element it represents. (5.4)

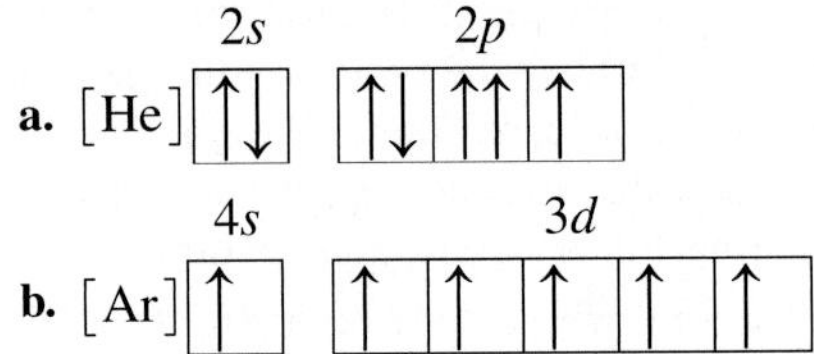

5.83 Match the spheres represented with atoms of Li, Na, K, and Rb. (5.6)

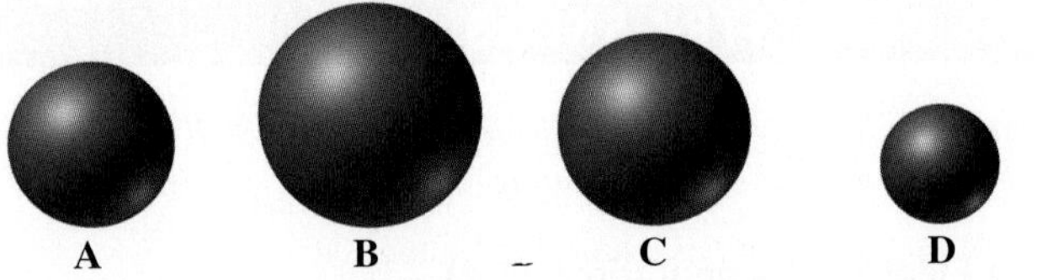

5.84 Match the spheres represented with atoms of K, Ge, Ca, and Kr. (5.6)

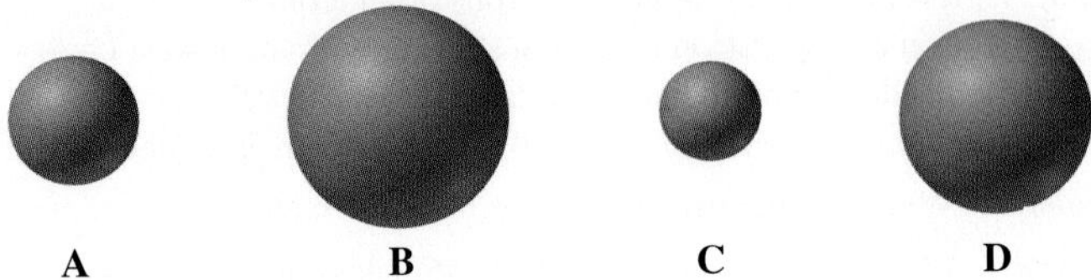

ADDITIONAL QUESTIONS AND PROBLEMS

5.85 What is the difference between a continuous spectrum and an atomic spectrum? (5.1)

5.86 Why does a neon sign give off red light? (5.1)

5.87 What is the Pauli exclusion principle? (5.3)

5.88 Why would there be five unpaired electrons in a *d* sublevel but no paired electrons? (5.3)

5.89 Which of the following orbitals are possible in an atom: 4*p*, 2*d*, 3*f*, and 5*f*? (5.3)

5.90 Which of the following orbitals are possible in an atom: 1*p*, 4*f*, 6*s*, and 4*d*? (5.3)

5.91 **a.** What electron sublevel starts to fill after completion of the 3*s* sublevel? (5.4)
 b. What electron sublevel starts to fill after completion of the 4*p* sublevel?
 c. What electron sublevel starts to fill after completion of the 3*d* sublevel?
 d. What electron sublevel starts to fill after completion of the 3*p* sublevel?

5.92 **a.** What electron sublevel starts to fill after completion of the 5*s* sublevel? (5.4)
 b. What electron sublevel starts to fill after completion of the 4*d* sublevel?
 c. What electron sublevel starts to fill after completion of the 4*f* sublevel?
 d. What electron sublevel starts to fill after completion of the 5*p* sublevel?

5.93 **a.** How many $3d$ electrons are in Fe? (5.4)
b. How many $5p$ electrons are in Ba?
c. How many $4d$ electrons are in I?
d. How many $7s$ electrons are in Ra?

5.94 **a.** How many $4d$ electrons are in Cd? (5.4)
b. How many $4p$ electrons are in Br?
c. How many $6p$ electrons are in Bi?
d. How many $4s$ electrons are in Zn?

5.95 What do the elements Ca, Sr, and Ba have in common in terms of their electron configuration? Where are they located on the periodic table? (5.4, 5.5)

5.96 What do the elements O, S, and Se have in common in terms of their electron configuration? Where are they located on the periodic table? (5.4, 5.5)

5.97 Consider three elements with the following abbreviated electron configurations: (5.4, 5.5, 5.6)

$X = [Ar]4s^2$ $Y = [Ne]3s^23p^4$ $Z = [Ar]4s^23d^{10}4p^4$

a. Identify each element as a metal, nonmetal, or metalloid.
b. Which element has the largest atomic size?
c. Which element has the highest ionization energy?
d. Which element has the smallest atomic size?

5.98 Consider three elements with the following abbreviated electron configurations: (5.4, 5.5, 5.6)

$X = [Ar]4s^23d^5$ $Y = [Ar]4s^23d^{10}4p^1$ $Z = [Ar]4s^23d^{10}4p^6$

a. Identify each element as a metal, nonmetal, or metalloid.
b. Which element has the smallest atomic size?
c. Which element has the highest ionization energy?
d. Which element has a half-filled sublevel?

5.99 Name the element that corresponds to each of the following: (5.4, 5.5, 5.6)
a. $1s^22s^22p^63s^23p^3$
b. alkali metal with the smallest atomic size
c. $[Kr]5s^24d^{10}$
d. Group 5A (15) element with the highest ionization energy
e. Period 3 element with the largest atomic size

5.100 Name the element that corresponds to each of the following: (5.4, 5.5, 5.6)
a. $1s^22s^22p^63s^23p^64s^13d^5$
b. $[Xe]6s^24f^{14}5d^{10}6p^5$
c. halogen with the highest ionization energy
d. Group 2A (2) element with the lowest ionization energy
e. Period 4 element with the smallest atomic size

5.101 Why is the ionization energy of Ca higher than that of K but lower than that of Mg? (5.6)

5.102 Why is the ionization energy of Br lower than that of Cl but higher than that of Se? (5.6)

5.103 Select the more metallic element in each pair. (5.6)
a. As or Sb **b.** Sn or Sb **c.** Cl or P **d.** O or P

5.104 Select the more metallic element in each pair. (5.6)
a. Sn or As **b.** Cl or I **c.** Ca or Ba **d.** Ba or Hg

5.105 Of the elements Na, P, Cl, and F, which (5.6)
a. is a metal?
b. has the largest atomic size?
c. has the highest ionization energy?
d. loses an electron most easily?
e. is found in Group 7A (17), Period 3?
f. has the least metallic character?

5.106 Of the elements K, Ca, Br, Kr, which (5.6)
a. is a noble gas?
b. has the smallest atomic size?
c. has the lowest ionization energy?
d. has the most metallic character?
e. requires the most energy to remove an electron?
f. is found in Group 2A (2), Period 4?

5.107 Write the abbreviated electron configuration and group number for each of the following elements: (5.4)
a. Si **b.** Se **c.** Mn **d.** Sb

5.108 Write the abbreviated electron configuration and group number for each of the following elements: (5.4)
a. Br **b.** Rh **c.** Tc **d.** Ra

CHALLENGE QUESTIONS

5.109 Give the symbol of the element that has the (5.6)
a. smallest atomic size in Group 6A (16)
b. smallest atomic size in Period 3
c. highest ionization energy in Group 3A (13)
d. lowest ionization energy in Period 3
e. abbreviated electron configuration $[Kr]5s^24d^6$

5.110 Give the symbol of the element that has the (5.6)
a. largest atomic size in Period 5
b. largest atomic size in Group 2A (2)
c. highest ionization energy in Group 8A (18)
d. lowest ionization energy in Period 2
e. abbreviated electron configuration $[Kr]5s^24d^{10}5p^2$

5.111 Compare the speed, wavelength, and frequency of ultraviolet light and microwaves. (5.1)

5.112 Radio waves, which travel at the speed of light, are used to communicate with satellites in space. If a message from flight control requires 170 s to reach a satellite, how far, in kilometers, is the satellite from Earth? (5.1)

Global Positioning Satellites (GPS) in orbit transmit microwaves to receivers for navigation and mapmaking.

5.113 How do scientists explain the colored lines observed in the spectra of heated atoms? (5.2)

5.114 Even though H has only one electron, there are many lines in the atomic spectrum of H. Explain. (5.2)

5.115 What is meant by an energy level, a sublevel, and an orbital? (5.3)

5.116 In some periodic tables, H is placed in Group 1A (1). In other periodic tables, H is also placed in Group 7A (17). Why? (5.4, 5.5)

5.117 Compare F, S, and Cl in terms of atomic size and ionization energy. (5.6)

5.118 Compare K, Cs, and Li in terms of atomic size and ionization energy. (5.6)

ANSWERS

Answers to Study Checks

5.1 8×10^{14} Hz

5.2 Because the spectra of elements consisted of only discrete, separated lines, scientists concluded that electrons occupied only certain energy levels in the atom.

5.3 The 1*s*, 2*s*, and 3*s* orbitals are all spherical, but they increase in volume because the electron is most likely to be found farther from the nucleus for higher energy levels.

5.4 1*s* 2*s* 2*p*

[↑↓] [↑↓] [↑↓|↑↓|↑]

5.5 $1s^22s^22p^63s^23p^64s^23d^{10}4p^65s^24d^{10}5p^3$

$[Kr]5s^24d^{10}5p^3$

5.6 $1s^22s^22p^63s^23p^64s^23d^{10}4p^2$

5.7 $1s^22s^22p^63s^23p^64s^23d^{10}4p^65s^24d^{10}5p^2$

5.8 Sulfur in Group 6A (16), Period 3, and has a $3s^23p^4$ valence electron configuration.
Strontium in Group 2A (2), Period 5, and has a $5s^2$ valence electron configuration.

5.9 $\cdot\ddot{\text{P}}\cdot$ (P with five dots)

5.10 As has the largest atomic size.

5.11 Ionization energy increases going from left to right across a period: Sr is lowest, Sn is higher, and I is the highest of this group.

Answers to Selected Questions and Problems

5.1 The wavelength of UV light is the distance between crests of the wave.

5.3 White light has all the colors of the spectrum, including red and blue light.

5.5 6.5×10^5 Hz

5.7 6.3×10^{-7} m; 630 nm

5.9 Microwaves have a longer wavelength than ultraviolet light or X-rays.

5.11 Order of increasing wavelengths: X-rays, blue light, microwaves.

5.13 Order of increasing frequencies: TV, microwaves, X-rays

5.15 Atomic spectra consist of a series of lines separated by dark sections, indicating that the energy emitted by the elements is not continuous.

5.17 absorb

5.19 The photon with greater energy is
a. green light **b.** blue light

5.21 **a.** spherical **b.** two lobes **c.** spherical

5.23 **a.** **1** and **2** **b.** **3**
c. **1** and **2** **d.** **1**, **2**, and **3**

5.25 **a.** There are five orbitals in the 3*d* sublevel.
b. There is one sublevel in the $n = 1$ energy level.
c. There is one orbital in the 6*s* sublevel.
d. There are nine orbitals in the $n = 3$ energy level.

5.27 **a.** There is a maximum of two electrons in a 2*p* orbital.
b. There is a maximum of six electrons in the 3*p* sublevel.
c. There is a maximum of 32 electrons in the $n = 4$ energy level.
d. There is a maximum of 10 electrons in the 5*d* sublevel.

5.29 The electron configuration shows the number of electrons in each sublevel of an atom. The abbreviated electron configuration uses the symbol of the preceding noble gas to show completed sublevels.

5.31

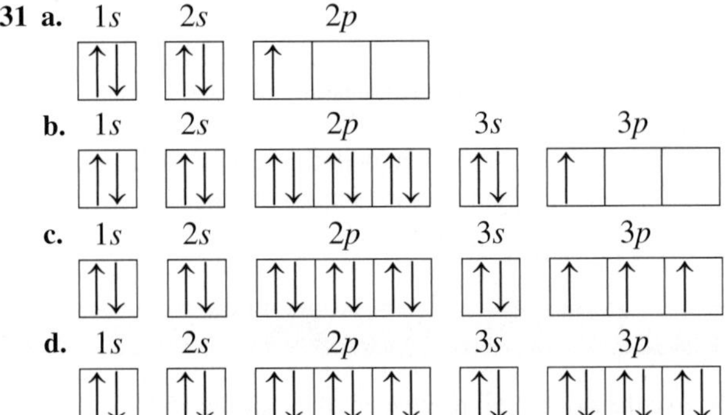

5.33 **a.** $1s^22s^22p^1$
b. $1s^22s^22p^63s^1$
c. $1s^22s^1$
d. $1s^22s^22p^63s^2$

5.35 **a.** $[He]2s^22p^2$ **b.** $[Ne]3s^23p^2$
c. $[Ne]3s^23p^3$ **d.** $[He]2s^22p^5$

5.37 **a.** Li **b.** S **c.** Si **d.** F

5.39 **a.** Al **b.** C **c.** Ar **d.** Be

5.41 **a.** $1s^22s^22p^63s^23p^64s^23d^{10}4p^3$
b. $1s^22s^22p^63s^23p^64s^23d^6$
c. $1s^22s^22p^63s^23p^64s^23d^{10}4p^65s^24d^{10}5p^1$
d. $1s^22s^22p^63s^23p^64s^23d^{10}4p^65s^24d^{10}5p^5$

5.43 **a.** $[Ar]4s^23d^2$ **b.** $[Ar]4s^23d^{10}4p^5$
c. $[Xe]6s^2$ **d.** $[Xe]6s^24f^{14}5d^{10}6p^2$

5.45 **a.** P **b.** Co **c.** Zn **d.** Bi

5.47 **a.** Ga **b.** N **c.** Xe **d.** Zr

5.49 **a.** 10 **b.** 6 **c.** 3 **d.** 1

5.51 The group numbers 1A–8A indicate the number of valence electrons from 1 to 8.

5.53 **a.** 2A (2) **b.** 5A (15) **c.** 7B (7) **d.** 6A (16)

5.55 **a.** ns^1 **b.** ns^2np^2 **c.** ns^2np^5 **d.** ns^2np^3

5.57 **a.** 3 **b.** 5 **c.** 2 **d.** 7

5.59 **a.** Sulfur is in Group 6A (16); ·S̤̈:
b. Nitrogen is in Group 5A (15); ·N̤̈·
c. Calcium is in Group 2A (2); Ċa·
d. Sodium is in Group 1A (1); Na·
e. Gallium is in Group 3A (13); ·Ġa·

5.61 **a.** Na **b.** Rb **c.** Na **d.** Rb

5.63 **a.** Mg, Al, Si **b.** I, Br, Cl
c. Sr, Sb, I **d.** Na, Si, P

5.65 **a.** Br **b.** Mg **c.** P **d.** Xe

5.67 **a.** Br, Cl, F **b.** Na, Al, Cl
c. Cs, K, Na **d.** Ca, As, Br

5.69 Ca, Ga, Ge, Br

5.71 lower, more

5.73 **a.** **1.** decreases
b. **2.** increases
c. **2.** increases
d. **3.** remains the same

5.75 **a.** false **b.** true **c.** true **d.** false **e.** true

5.77 **a.** **C** has the longest wavelength.
b. **A** has the shortest wavelength.
c. **A** has the highest frequency.
d. **C** has the lowest frequency.

5.79 **a.** *p* **b.** *s* **c.** *p*

5.81 **a.** This is possible. This element is magnesium.
b. Not possible. The 2*p* sublevel would fill before the 3*s*, and only two electrons are allowed in an *s* orbital.

5.83 Li is **D**, Na is **A**, K is **C**, and Rb is **B**.

5.85 A continuous spectrum from white light contains wavelengths of all energies. Atomic spectra are line spectra in which a series of lines corresponds to energy emitted when electrons drop from a higher energy level to a lower level.

5.87 The Pauli exclusion principle states that two electrons in the same orbital must have opposite spins.

5.89 A 4*p* orbital is possible because the $n = 4$ energy level has four sublevels, including a *p* sublevel. A 2*d* orbital is not possible because the $n = 2$ energy level has only *s* and *p* sublevels. There are no 3*f* orbitals because only *s*, *p*, and *d* sublevels are allowed for the $n = 3$ energy level. A 5*f* sublevel is possible in the $n = 5$ energy level because five sublevels are allowed, including an *f* sublevel.

5.91 **a.** 3*p* **b.** 5*s* **c.** 4*p* **d.** 4*s*

5.93 **a.** 6 **b.** 6 **c.** 10 **d.** 2

5.95 Ca, Sr, and Ba all have two valence electrons, ns^2, which place them in Group 2A (2).

5.97 **a.** X is a metal; Y and Z are nonmetals.
b. X has the largest atomic size.
c. Y has the highest ionization energy.
d. Y has the smallest atomic size.

5.99 **a.** phosphorus **b.** lithium (H is a nonmetal)
c. cadmium **d.** nitrogen
e. sodium

5.101 Calcium has a greater number of protons than K. The least tightly bound electron in Ca is farther from the nucleus than in Mg and needs less energy to remove.

5.103 **a.** Sb **b.** Sn **c.** P **d.** P

5.105 **a.** Na **b.** Na **c.** F
d. Na **e.** Cl **f.** F

5.107 **a.** $[Ne]3s^23p^2$; Group 4A (14)
b. $[Ar]4s^23d^{10}4p^4$; Group 6A (16)
c. $[Ar]4s^23d^5$; Group 7B (7)
d. $[Kr]5s^24d^{10}5p^3$; Group 5A (15)

5.109 **a.** O **b.** Ar **c.** B
d. Na **e.** Ru

5.111 Ultraviolet light and microwaves both travel at the same speed: 3.00×10^8 m/s. The wavelength of ultraviolet light is shorter than the wavelength of microwaves, and the frequency of ultraviolet light is higher than the frequency of microwaves.

5.113 The series of lines separated by dark sections in atomic spectra indicate that the energy emitted by the elements is not continuous and that electrons are moving between discrete energy levels.

5.115 The energy level contains all the electrons with similar energy. A sublevel contains electrons with the same energy, while an orbital is the region around the nucleus where electrons of a certain energy are most likely to be found.

5.117 S has a larger atomic size than Cl; Cl is larger than F: S > Cl > F. F has a higher ionization energy than Cl; Cl has a higher ionization energy than S: F > Cl > S.

6 Ionic and Molecular Compounds

LOOKING AHEAD

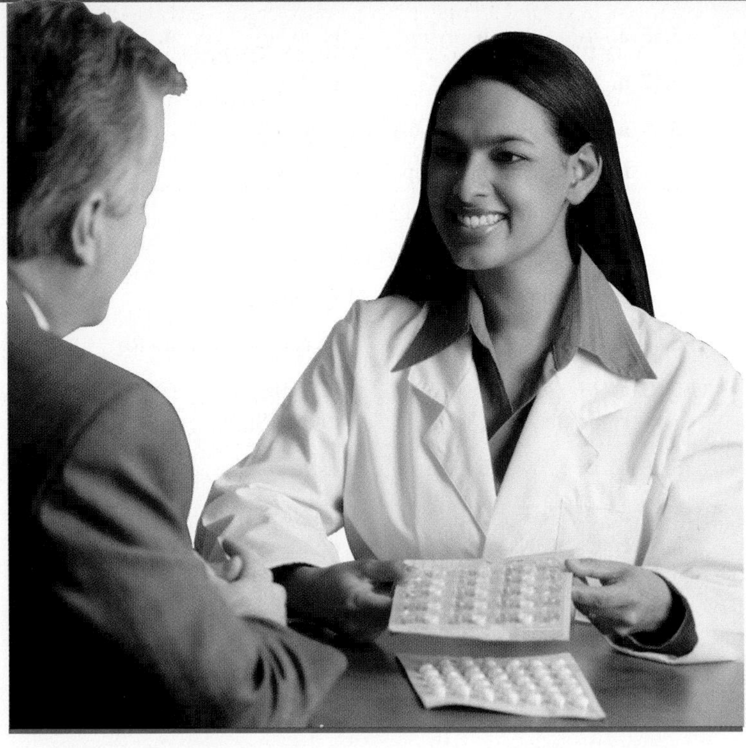

Sarah, a pharmacist, is working at a local drug store. A customer asks Sarah about the effects of aspirin, as his doctor has recommended that he take a low-dose aspirin (81 mg) every day to prevent heart attack or stroke.

Sarah informs her customer that aspirin is acetylsalicylic acid and has the chemical formula, $C_9H_8O_4$. Aspirin is a molecular compound, often referred to as an organic molecule because it contains the nonmetals carbon (C), hydrogen (H), and oxygen (O). Sarah shows her customer the chemical structure of aspirin, and explains that aspirin is used to relieve minor pains, to reduce inflammation and fever, and to slow blood clotting. Some potential side effects of aspirin may include heartburn, upset stomach, nausea, and an increased risk of a stomach ulcer.

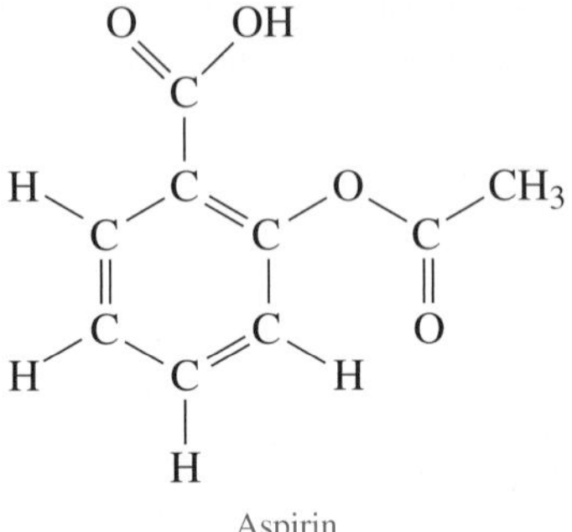

Aspirin

Career: Pharmacist

Pharmacists work in hospitals, pharmacies, clinics, research, and long-term care facilities where they are responsible for the preparation and distribution of pharmaceutical medications based on a doctor's orders. They obtain the proper medication, and also calculate, measure, and label the patient's medication. Pharmacists advise customers and health care practitioners on the selection of both prescription and over-the-counter drugs, proper dosages, and geriatric considerations, as well as possible side effects and interactions. They may also administer vaccinations, prepare sterile intravenous solutions, and advise customers about health, diet, and home medical equipment. Pharmacists also prepare insurance claims, and create and maintain patient records.

In nature, atoms of almost all the elements on the periodic table are found in combination with other atoms. Only the atoms of the noble gases—He, Ne, Ar, Kr, Xe, and Rn—do not combine in nature with other atoms. A compound is composed of two or more elements with a definite composition.

Compounds may be ionic or molecular. In an *ionic compound*, one or more electrons are transferred from metals to nonmetals, which form positive and negative ions. The attraction between these ions is called an *ionic bond*. We utilize ionic compounds every day including salt, NaCl, and baking soda, $NaHCO_3$. Milk of magnesia, $Mg(OH)_2$, or calcium carbonate, $CaCO_3$, may be taken to settle an upset stomach. In a mineral supplement, iron may be present as iron(II) sulfate, $FeSO_4$, iodine as potassium iodide, KI, and manganese as manganese(II) sulfate, $MnSO_4$. Some sunscreens contain zinc oxide, ZnO, and tin(II) fluoride, SnF_2, in toothpaste provides fluoride to help prevent tooth decay.

Small amounts of metals cause the different colors of gemstones.

Precious and semiprecious gemstones are examples of ionic compounds called minerals that are cut and polished to make jewelry. For example, sapphires and rubies are made of aluminum oxide, Al_2O_3. Impurities of chromium make rubies red, and iron and titanium make sapphires blue.

A *molecular compound* consists of two or more nonmetals that share one or more valence electrons. The resulting molecules are held together by *covalent bonds*. There are many more molecular compounds than there are ionic ones. For example, a molecule of water, H_2O, consists of two atoms of hydrogen and one atom of oxygen. When you have iced tea, perhaps you add molecules of table sugar, $C_{12}H_{22}O_{11}$.

Molecular compounds consisting of mostly carbon and hydrogen are known as *organic* compounds. Familiar examples include propane, C_3H_8, butane, C_4H_{10}, and ethyl alcohol, C_2H_6O. Your food contains much bigger *organic molecules*, known as *biomolecules*, such as the polysaccharide starch, which contains many covalent bonds between atoms of carbon, hydrogen, and oxygen.

CHAPTER READINESS*

Key Math Skills

- Using Positive and Negative Numbers in Calculations (1.4B)
- Solving Equations (1.4D)

Core Chemistry Skills

- Writing Electron Configurations (5.4)
- Drawing Electron-Dot Symbols (5.6)

*These Key Math Skills and Core Chemistry Skills from previous chapters are listed here for your review as you proceed to the new material in this chapter.

6.1 Ions: Transfer of Electrons

LEARNING GOAL

Write the symbols for the simple ions of the representative elements.

Most of the elements, except the noble gases, are found in nature combined as compounds. The noble gases are so stable that they form compounds only under extreme conditions. One explanation for their stability is they have a filled valence electron energy level.

Compounds form when electrons are transferred or shared to give stable electron configurations to the atoms. In the formation of either an *ionic bond* or a *covalent bond*, atoms lose, gain, or share valence electrons to acquire an octet of eight valence electrons. This tendency of atoms to attain a stable electron configuration is known as the **octet rule** and provides a key to our understanding of the ways in which atoms bond and form compounds. A few elements achieve the stability of helium with two valence electrons. However, we do not use the octet rule with transition elements.

Ionic bonds occur when the valence electrons of atoms of a metal are transferred to atoms of nonmetals. For example, sodium atoms lose electrons and chlorine atoms gain electrons to form the ionic compound NaCl. *Covalent bonds* form when atoms of nonmetals share valence electrons. In the molecular compounds H_2O and C_3H_8, atoms share electrons.

Type of Compound	Ionic	Molecular	
Particles	Ions	Molecules	
Bonding	Ionic bonds	Covalent bonds	
Examples	Na^+ Cl^- ions	H_2O molecules	C_3H_8 molecules

Chemistry Link to Industry

SOME USES FOR NOBLE GASES

Noble gases may be used when it is necessary to have a substance that is unreactive. Scuba divers normally use a pressurized mixture of nitrogen and oxygen gases for breathing under water. However, when the air mixture is used at depths where pressure is high, the nitrogen gas is absorbed into the blood, where it can cause mental disorientation. To avoid *nitrogen narcosis*, a breathing mixture of oxygen and helium may be substituted (see *Breathing Mixtures for Scuba* in Section 3.1). The diver still obtains the necessary oxygen, but the unreactive helium that dissolves in the blood does not cause mental disorientation. However, its lower density does change the vibrations of the vocal cords, and the diver will sound like Donald Duck.

Helium is also used to fill blimps and balloons. When dirigibles were first designed, they were filled with hydrogen, a very light gas. However, when they came in contact with any type of spark or heating source, they exploded violently because of the extreme reactivity of hydrogen gas with oxygen present in the air. Today blimps are filled with unreactive helium gas, which presents no danger of explosion.

Lighting tubes are generally filled with a noble gas such as neon or argon. While the electrically heated filaments that produce the light get very hot, the surrounding noble gases do not react with the hot filament. If heated in air, the elements that constitute the filament will quickly burn out when oxygen is present.

The helium in a blimp is much less dense than air, which allows the blimp to fly above the ground.

CORE CHEMISTRY SKILL

Writing Positive and Negative Ions

Positive Ions: Loss of Electrons

In ionic bonding, **ions**, which have electrical charges, form when atoms lose or gain electrons to form a stable electron configuration. Because the ionization energies of metals of Groups 1A (1), 2A (2), and 3A (13) are low, metal atoms readily lose their valence electrons. In doing so, they form ions with positive charges. For example, when a sodium atom loses its single valence electron, the remaining electrons have a stable electron configuration. By losing an electron, sodium has 10 negatively charged electrons instead of 11. Because there are still 11 positively charged protons in its nucleus, the atom is no longer neutral. It is now a sodium ion with a positive electrical charge, called an **ionic charge**, of 1+.

$$\text{Ionic charge} = \text{Charge of protons} + \text{Charge of electrons}$$
$$1+ = (11+) \qquad + (10-)$$

In the symbol for the sodium ion, the ionic charge of 1+ is written in the upper right-hand corner, Na^+, where the 1 is understood. The sodium ion is smaller than the sodium atom because the ion has lost its outermost electron from the third energy level. The positively charged ions of metals are called **cations** (pronounced *cat-eye-uns*) and use the name of the element.

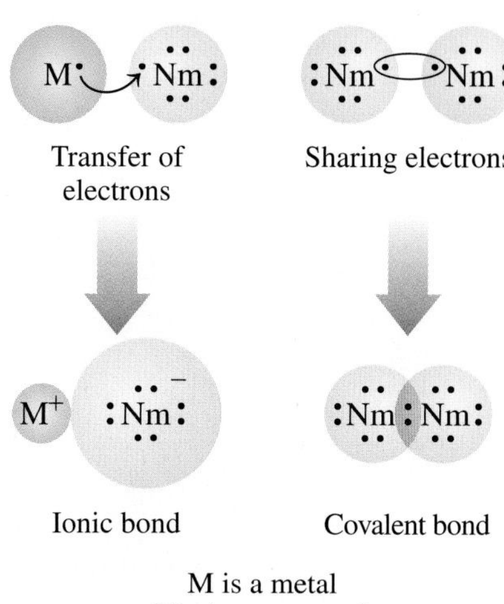

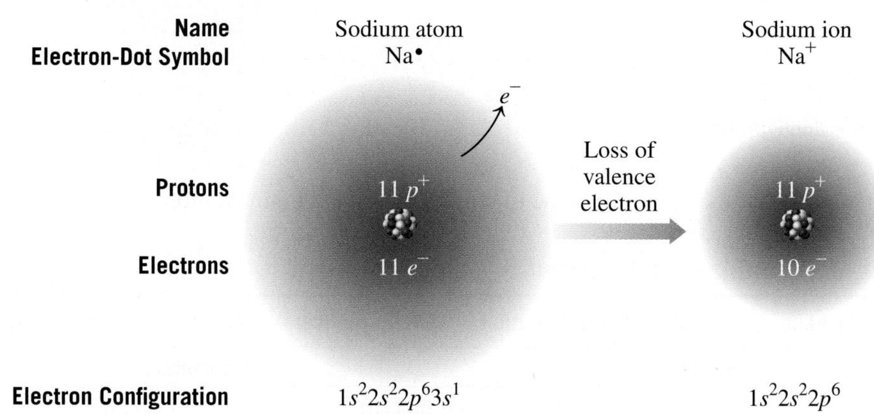

Magnesium, a metal in Group 2A (2), obtains a stable electron configuration by losing two valence electrons to form a magnesium ion with a 2+ ionic charge, Mg^{2+}. The magnesium ion is smaller than the magnesium atom because the outermost electrons in the third energy level were removed. The octet in the magnesium ion is made up of electrons that fill its second energy level.

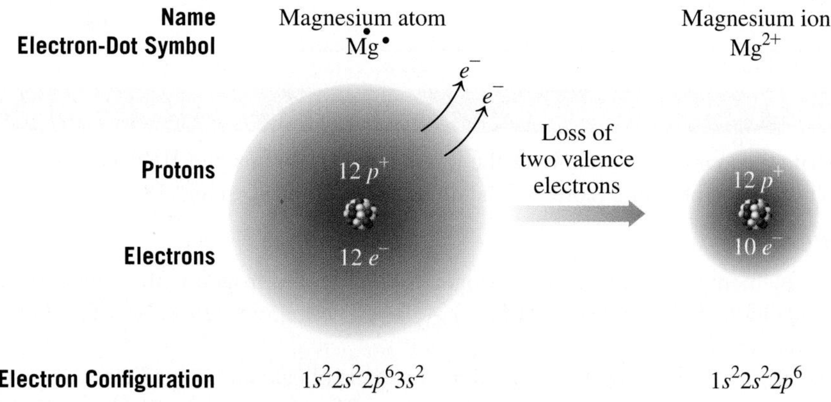

Negative Ions: Gain of Electrons

The ionization energy of a nonmetal atom in Groups 5A (15), 6A (16), and 7A (17) is high. Rather than lose electrons to form ions, a nonmetal atom gains one or more electrons to obtain a stable electron configuration. For example, an atom of chlorine with seven valence electrons gains one electron to form an octet. Because it now has 18 electrons and 17 protons, the chlorine atom is no longer neutral. It becomes a chloride ion with an ionic charge of 1−, which is written as Cl^-, with the 1 understood.

$$\text{Ionic charge} = \text{Charge of protons} + \text{Charge of electrons}$$
$$1- \quad = \quad (17+) \quad + \quad (18-)$$

A negatively charged ion, called an **anion** (pronounced *an-eye-un*), is named by using the first syllable of its element name followed by *ide*. The chloride ion is larger than the chlorine atom because the ion has an additional electron, which completes its outermost energy level.

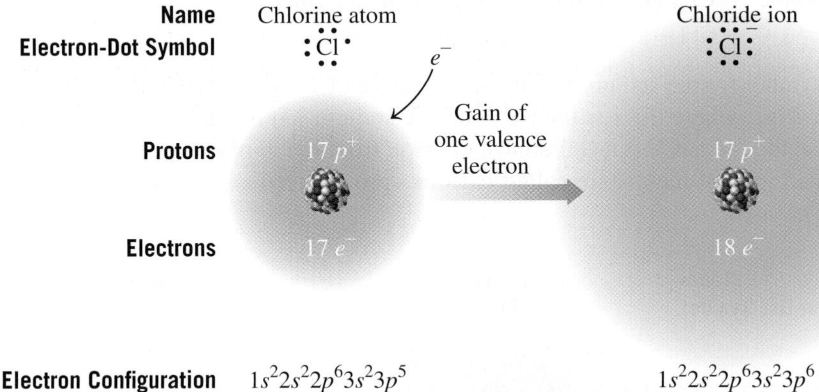

Table 6.1 lists the names of some important metal and nonmetal ions.

TABLE 6.1 Formulas and Names of Some Common Ions

Group Number	Cation	Name of Cation	Group Number	Anion	Name of Anion
	Metals			**Nonmetals**	
1A (1)	Li^+	Lithium	**5A (15)**	N^{3-}	Nitride
	Na^+	Sodium		P^{3-}	Phosphide
	K^+	Potassium	**6A (16)**	O^{2-}	Oxide
2A (2)	Mg^{2+}	Magnesium		S^{2-}	Sulfide
	Ca^{2+}	Calcium	**7A (17)**	F^-	Fluoride
	Ba^{2+}	Barium		Cl^-	Chloride
3A (13)	Al^{3+}	Aluminum		Br^-	Bromide
				I^-	Iodide

CONCEPT CHECK 6.1 Ions

a. Write the symbol and name for the ion that has 7 protons and 10 electrons.
b. Write the symbol and name for the ion that has 20 protons and 18 electrons.

ANSWER

a. The element with 7 protons is nitrogen. In an ion of nitrogen with 10 electrons, the ionic charge is 3−, $(7+) + (10-) = 3-$. The ion, written as N^{3-}, is called the *nitride* ion.
b. The element with 20 protons is calcium. In an ion of calcium with 18 electrons, the ionic charge is 2+, $(20+) + (18-) = 2+$. The ion, written as Ca^{2+}, is called the *calcium* ion.

CONCEPT CHECK 6.2 Ions: Protons and Electrons

How many protons and electrons are in each of the following ions?

a. S^{2-} **b.** Al^{3+}

ANSWER

a. The element S has atomic number 16, which means it has 16 protons. Using the ionic charge and the charge of protons, we can solve for the charge of electrons.

Ionic charge = Charge of protons + Charge of electrons

Solve for the charge of electrons

Ionic charge	−	Charge of protons	=	Charge of electrons
2−	−	(16+)	=	18−

Since each electron has a 1− charge, there must be 18 electrons.

b. The element Al has atomic number 13, which means it has 13 protons. Using the ionic charge and the charge of protons, we can solve for the charge of electrons.

Ionic charge = Charge of protons + Charge of electrons

Solve for the charge of electrons

Ionic charge	−	Charge of protons	=	Charge of electrons
3+	−	(13+)	=	10−

Since each electron has a 1− charge, there must be 10 electrons.

Ionic Charges from Group Numbers

In ionic compounds, representative elements usually lose or gain electrons to give eight valence electrons like their nearest noble gas (or two for helium). We can use the group numbers in the periodic table to determine the charges for the ions of the representative elements. The elements in Group 1A (1) lose one electron to form ions with a 1+ charge. The atoms of the elements in Group 2A (2) lose two electrons to form ions with a 2+ charge. The atoms of the elements in Group 3A (13) lose three electrons to form ions with a 3+ charge. In this text, we do not use the group numbers of the transition elements to determine their ionic charges.

In ionic compounds, the atoms of the nonmetals in Group 7A (17) gain one electron to form ions with a 1− charge. The atoms of the elements in Group 6A (16) gain two electrons to form ions with a 2− charge. The atoms of the elements in Group 5A (15) typically gain three electrons to form ions with a 3− charge.

The nonmetals of Group 4A (14) do not typically form ions, although the metals Sn and Pb lose electrons to form positive ions. Table 6.2 lists the ionic charges for some common ions of representative elements.

TABLE 6.2 Examples of Common Ions and Their Nearest Noble Gases

		Metals Lose Valence Electrons			Nonmetals Gain Valence Electrons				
Noble Gases		1A (1)	2A (2)	3A (13)	5A (15)	6A (16)	7A (17)		Noble Gases
He	⇦	Li^+							
Ne	⇦	Na^+	Mg^{2+}	Al^{3+}	N^{3-}	O^{2-}	F^-	⇨	Ne
Ar	⇦	K^+	Ca^{2+}		P^{3-}	S^{2-}	Cl^-	⇨	Ar
Kr	⇦	Rb^+	Sr^{2+}				Br^-	⇨	Kr
Xe	⇦	Cs^+	Ba^{2+}				I^-	⇨	Xe

SAMPLE PROBLEM 6.1 Writing Positive and Negative Ions

Consider the elements aluminum and oxygen.

a. Identify each as a metal or a nonmetal.
b. State the number of valence electrons for each.
c. State the number of electrons that must be lost or gained for each to achieve an octet.
d. Write the symbol and name for each resulting ion, including its ionic charge.
e. Write the electron configuration for each ion.

SOLUTION

Aluminum	Oxygen
a. metal	nonmetal
b. three valence electrons	six valence electrons
c. loses 3 e^-	gains 2 e^-
d. Al^{3+}, aluminum ion $(13+) + (10-) = 3+$	O^{2-}, oxide ion $(8+) + (10-) = 2-$
e. $1s^22s^22p^6$	$1s^22s^22p^6$

STUDY CHECK 6.1

For the element potassium, answer each of the following:

a. Identify potassium as a metal or a nonmetal.
b. State the number of valence electrons for potassium.
c. State the number of electrons that must be lost or gained for potassium to achieve an octet.
d. Write the symbol and name for the resulting ion, including its ionic charge.
e. Write the electron configuration for the ion.

Chemistry Link to Health

SOME IMPORTANT IONS IN THE BODY

Several ions in body fluids have important physiological and metabolic functions. Some of them are listed in Table 6.3. Foods such as bananas, milk, cheese, and potatoes provide ions that are important in regulating body functions.

Milk, cheese, and potatoes provide ions for the body.

TABLE 6.3 Ions in the Body

Ion	Occurrence	Function	Source	Result of Too Little	Result of Too Much
Na^+	Principal cation outside the cell	Regulates and controls body fluids	Salt, cheese, pickles, potato chips, pretzels	Hyponatremia, anxiety, diarrhea, circulatory failure, decrease in body fluid	Hypernatremia, little urine, thirst, edema
K^+	Principal cation inside the cell	Regulates body fluids and cellular functions	Bananas, orange juice, milk, prunes, potatoes	Hypokalemia (hypopotassemia), lethargy, muscle weakness, failure of neurological impulses	Hyperkalemia (hyperpotassemia), irritability, nausea, little urine, cardiac arrest
Ca^{2+}	Cation outside the cell; 90% of calcium in the body in bone as $Ca_3(PO_4)_2$ or $CaCO_3$	Major cation of bone; needed for muscle contraction	Milk, yogurt, cheese, greens, spinach	Hypocalcemia, tingling fingertips, muscle cramps, osteoporosis	Hypercalcemia, relaxed muscles, kidney stones, deep bone pain
Mg^{2+}	Cation outside the cell; 50% of magnesium in the body in bone structure	Essential for certain enzymes, muscles, nerve control	Widely distributed (part of chlorophyll of all green plants), nuts, whole grains	Disorientation, hypertension, tremors, slow pulse	Drowsiness
Cl^-	Principal anion outside the cell	Gastric juice, regulation of body fluids	Salt	Same as for Na^+	Same as for Na^+

QUESTIONS AND PROBLEMS

6.1 Ions: Transfer of Electrons

LEARNING GOAL: *Write the symbols for the simple ions of the representative elements.*

6.1 State the number of electrons that are lost by atoms of each of the following to obtain a stable electron configuration:
a. Li **b.** Ca
c. Ga **d.** Cs

6.2 State the number of electrons that are gained by atoms of each of the following to obtain a stable electron configuration:
a. Cl **b.** S
c. N **d.** I

6.3 Write the electron configuration for each of the following ions:
a. Li^{+} **b.** Mg^{2+}
c. Ga^{3+} **d.** P^{3-}

6.4 Write the electron configuration for each of the following ions:
a. Na^{+} **b.** Sr^{2+}
c. S^{2-} **d.** Sn^{4+}

6.5 State the number of electrons lost or gained when the following elements form ions:
a. Sr
b. P
c. Group 7A (17)
d. Na

6.6 State the number of electrons lost or gained when the following elements form ions:
a. Br
b. Group 2A (2)
c. F
d. Rb

6.7 Write the symbols for the ions with the following number of protons and electrons:
a. 3 protons, 2 electrons
b. 53 protons, 54 electrons
c. 38 protons, 36 electrons
d. 26 protons, 23 electrons

6.8 Write the symbols for the ions with the following number of protons and electrons:
a. 30 protons, 28 electrons
b. 9 protons, 10 electrons
c. 82 protons, 78 electrons
d. 15 protons, 18 electrons

6.9 How many protons and electrons are in each of the following ions?
a. O^{2-} **b.** K^{+}
c. Br^{-} **d.** S^{2-}

6.10 How many protons and electrons are in each of the following ions?
a. P^{3-} **b.** F^{-}
c. Au^{3+} **d.** Cs^{+}

6.11 Write the symbol for the ion of each of the following:
a. chlorine
b. barium
c. aluminum
d. selenium

6.12 Write the symbol for the ion of each of the following:
a. fluorine
b. calcium
c. sodium
d. nitrogen

6.2 Writing Formulas for Ionic Compounds

LEARNING GOAL

Using charge balance, write the correct formula for an ionic compound.

Ionic compounds consist of positive and negative ions. The ions are held together by strong electrical attractions between the opposite charges, called **ionic bonds**. The positive ions are formed by *metals* losing electrons, and the negative ions are formed when *nonmetals* gain electrons. Even though noble gases are nonmetals, they already have stable electron configurations and do not form compounds.

Properties of Ionic Compounds

The physical and chemical properties of an ionic compound such as NaCl are very different from those of the original elements. For example, the original elements of NaCl were sodium, which is a soft, shiny metal, and chlorine, which is a yellow-green poisonous gas. However, when they react and form positive and negative ions, they produce ordinary table salt, NaCl, a hard, white, crystalline substance that is important in our diet.

In a crystal of NaCl, the larger Cl^{-} ions are arranged in a three-dimensional structure in which the smaller Na^{+} ions occupy the spaces between the Cl^{-} ions (see Figure 6.1). In this crystal, every Na^{+} ion is surrounded by six Cl^{-} ions, and every Cl^{-} ion is surrounded by six Na^{+} ions. Thus, there are many strong attractions between oppositely charged ions, which account for the high melting points of ionic compounds. For example, NaCl has a melting point of 801 °C. At room temperature, ionic compounds are solids.

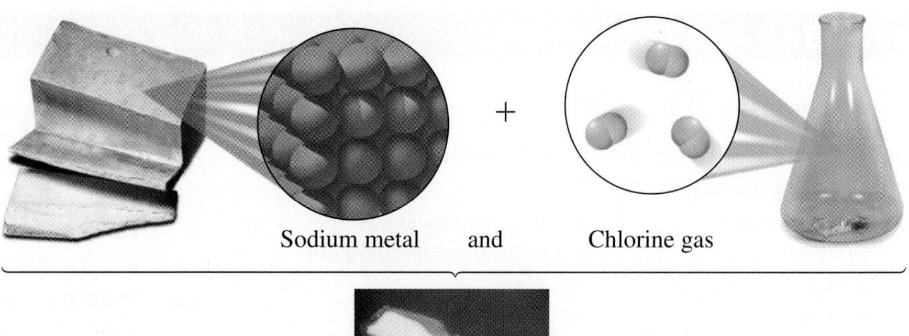

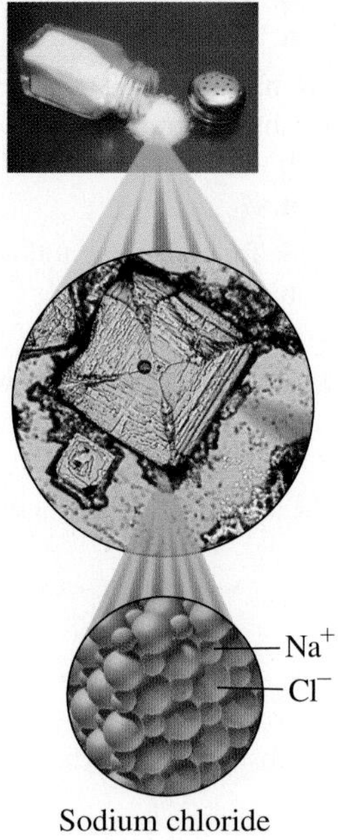

FIGURE 6.1 The elements sodium and chlorine react to form the ionic compound sodium chloride, the compound that makes up table salt. The magnification of NaCl crystals shows the arrangement of Na^+ ions and Cl^- ions in a crystal of NaCl.

Q What is the type of bonding between Na^+ and Cl^- ions in NaCl?

Chemical Formulas of Ionic Compounds

The **chemical formula** of a compound represents the symbols and subscripts in the lowest whole-number ratio of the atoms or ions. In the formula of an ionic compound, the sum of the ionic charges is always zero. *Thus, the total amount of positive charge is equal to the total amount of negative charge.* For example, to achieve a stable electron configuration, a Na atom (metal) loses its one valence electron to form Na^+, and one Cl atom (nonmetal) gains one electron to form a Cl^- ion. The formula NaCl indicates that the compound has charge balance because there is one sodium ion, Na^+, for every chloride ion, Cl^-. Although the ions have charges, they are not shown in the formula, NaCl, of the compound.

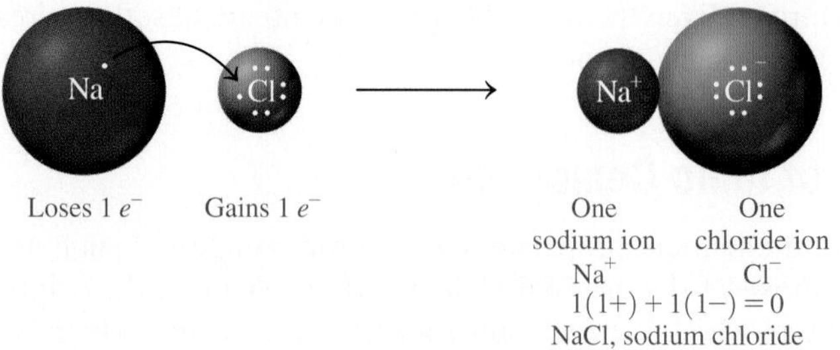

Subscripts in Formulas

Consider a compound of magnesium and chlorine. To achieve a stable electron configuration, a Mg atom (metal) loses its two valence electrons to form Mg^{2+}. Two Cl atoms (nonmetals) each gain one electron to form two Cl^- ions. The two Cl^- ions are needed to balance the positive charge of Mg^{2+}. This gives the formula $MgCl_2$, magnesium chloride, in which the subscript 2 shows that two Cl^- ions are needed for charge balance.

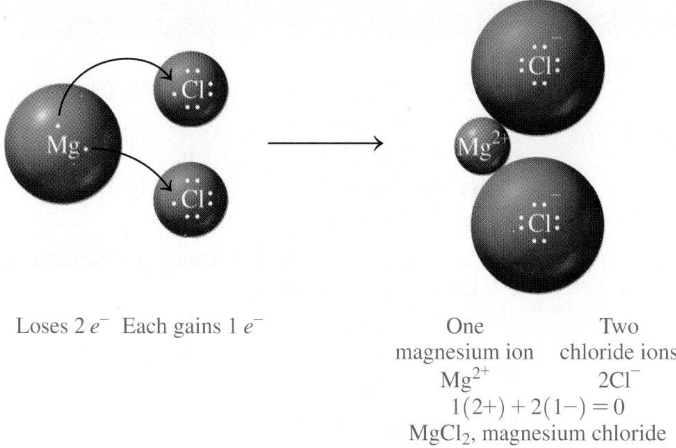

Writing Ionic Formulas from Ionic Charges

Writing Ionic Formulas

The subscripts in the formula of an ionic compound represent the number of positive and negative ions that give an overall charge of zero. Thus, we can now write a formula directly from the ionic charges of the positive and negative ions. In the formula of an ionic compound, the cation from a metal is written first, followed by the anion from a nonmetal. Suppose we wish to write the formula for the ionic compound containing Na^+ and S^{2-} ions. To balance the ionic charge of the S^{2-} ion, we show two Na^+ ions by using a subscript 2 in the formula. This gives the formula Na_2S, which has an overall charge of zero. When there is no subscript for a symbol such as the S in Na_2S, it is assumed to be 1. The group of ions that has the lowest ratio of the ions in an ionic compound is called a *formula unit*.

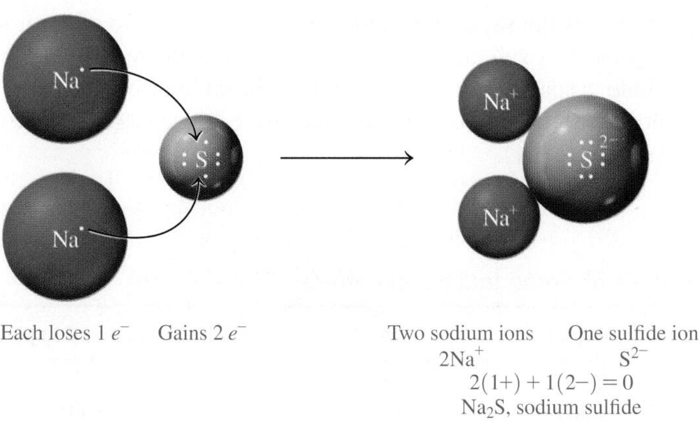

CONCEPT CHECK 6.3 Writing Formulas from Ionic Charges

Determine the ionic charges and write the formula for the ionic compound formed when lithium and nitrogen react.

ANSWER

Lithium, which is a metal in Group 1A (1) forms Li^+; nitrogen, which is a nonmetal in Group 5A (15), forms N^{3-}. The charge of 3− for N^{3-} is balanced by three Li^+ ions.

$$3(1+) + (3-) = 0$$

Writing the cation (positive ion) first and the anion (negative ion) second gives the formula Li_3N.

QUESTIONS AND PROBLEMS

6.2 Writing Formulas for Ionic Compounds

LEARNING GOAL: *Using charge balance, write the correct formula for an ionic compound.*

6.13 Which of the following pairs of elements are likely to form ionic compounds?
a. lithium and chlorine
b. oxygen and bromine
c. potassium and oxygen
d. sodium and neon
e. sodium and magnesium
f. nitrogen and fluorine

6.14 Which of the following pairs of elements are likely to form ionic compounds?
a. helium and oxygen
b. magnesium and chlorine
c. chlorine and bromine
d. potassium and sulfur
e. sodium and potassium
f. nitrogen and iodine

6.15 Write the correct ionic formula for the compound formed between the following:
a. Na^+ and O^{2-}
b. Al^{3+} and Br^-
c. Ba^{2+} and N^{3-}
d. Mg^{2+} and F^-
e. Al^{3+} and S^{2-}

6.16 Write the correct ionic formula for the compound formed between the following:
a. Al^{3+} and Cl^-
b. Ca^{2+} and S^{2-}
c. Li^+ and S^{2-}
d. Rb^+ and P^{3-}
e. Cs^+ and I^-

6.17 Write the symbols for the ions and the correct formula for the ionic compound formed by each of the following:
a. potassium and sulfur
b. sodium and nitrogen
c. aluminum and iodine
d. gallium and oxygen

6.18 Write the symbols for the ions and the correct formula for the ionic compound formed by each of the following:
a. calcium and chlorine
b. rubidium and bromine
c. sodium and phosphorus
d. magnesium and oxygen

LEARNING GOAL

Given the formula of an ionic compound, write the correct name; given the name of an ionic compound, write the correct formula.

CORE CHEMISTRY SKILL

Naming Ionic Compounds

Guide to Naming Ionic Compounds with Metals That Form a Single Ion

1. Identify the cation and anion.
2. Name the cation by its element name.
3. Name the anion by using the first syllable of its element name followed by *ide*.
4. Write the name for the cation first and the name for the anion second.

6.3 Naming Ionic Compounds

In the name of an ionic compound made up of two elements, the name of the metal ion, which is written first, is the same as its element name. The name of the nonmetal ion is obtained by using the first syllable of its element name followed by *ide*. In the name of any ionic compound, a space separates the name of the cation from the name of the anion. Subscripts are not used; they are understood because of the charge balance of the ions in the compound (see Table 6.4).

TABLE 6.4 Names of Some Ionic Compounds

Compound	Cation	Anion	Name of Ionic Compound
KI	K^+ Potassium	I^- Iodide	Potassium iodide
$MgBr_2$	Mg^{2+} Magnesium	Br^- Bromide	Magnesium bromide
Al_2O_3	Al^{3+} Aluminum	O^{2-} Oxide	Aluminum oxide

SAMPLE PROBLEM 6.2 Naming Ionic Compounds

Write the name for the ionic compound Mg_3N_2.

SOLUTION

Step 1 **Identify the cation and anion.** The cation from Group 2A (2) is Mg^{2+}, and the anion from Group 5A (15) is N^{3-}.

Step 2 **Name the cation by its element name.** The cation Mg^{2+} is magnesium.

Step 3 **Name the anion by using the first syllable of its element name followed by *ide*.** The anion N^{3-} is nitride.

Step 4 **Write the name for the cation first and the name for the anion second.** Mg_3N_2 is magnesium nitride.

STUDY CHECK 6.2

Name the compound Ga_2S_3.

Metals with Variable Charges

We have seen that the charge of an ion of a representative element can be obtained from its group number. However, it is not as easy to determine the charge of a transition element because they typically form two or more positive ions. The transition elements can lose *s* electrons from their highest energy level as well as *d* electrons. This is also true for metals of representative elements in Groups 4A (14) and 5A (15), such as Pb, Sn, and Bi.

In some ionic compounds, iron is in the Fe^{2+} form; but in other compounds, it has the Fe^{3+} form. Copper also forms two different ions: Cu^+ and Cu^{2+}. When a metal can form two or more ions, it has a *variable charge*. Thus, for these metals, we cannot predict the ionic charge from the group number.

For metals that form two or more different ions, a naming system is needed to identify the particular cation. Then a Roman numeral that is equal to the ionic charge is placed in parentheses immediately after the name of the metal. For example, Fe^{2+} is named iron(II), and Fe^{3+} is named iron(III). Table 6.5 lists the ions of some metals that produce two or more ions.

TABLE 6.5 Some Metals That Form More Than One Positive Ion

Element	Ions	Name of Ion	Element	Ions	Name of Ion
Bismuth	Bi^{3+}	Bismuth(III)	Lead	Pb^{2+}	Lead(II)
	Bi^{5+}	Bismuth(V)		Pb^{4+}	Lead(IV)
Chromium	Cr^{2+}	Chromium(II)	Manganese	Mn^{2+}	Manganese(II)
	Cr^{3+}	Chromium(III)		Mn^{3+}	Manganese(III)
Cobalt	Co^{2+}	Cobalt(II)	Mercury	Hg_2^{2+}	Mercury(I)*
	Co^{3+}	Cobalt(III)		Hg^{2+}	Mercury(II)
Copper	Cu^{+}	Copper(I)	Nickel	Ni^{2+}	Nickel(II)
	Cu^{2+}	Copper(II)		Ni^{3+}	Nickel(III)
Gold	Au^{+}	Gold(I)	Tin	Sn^{2+}	Tin(II)
	Au^{3+}	Gold(III)		Sn^{4+}	Tin(IV)
Iron	Fe^{2+}	Iron(II)			
	Fe^{3+}	Iron(III)			

*Mercury(I) ions form pairs with a 2+ charge.

Figure 6.2 shows some ions and their location on the periodic table. The transition elements form more than one positive ion except for zinc (Zn^{2+}), cadmium (Cd^{2+}), and silver (Ag^+), which form only one ion. Thus, no Roman numerals are used with zinc, cadmium, and silver when naming their cations. Metals in Groups 4A (14) and 5A (15) also form more than one positive ion. For example, lead and tin in Group 4A (14) form cations with charges of 2+ and 4+, and bismuth in Group 5A (15) forms cations with charges of 3+ and 5+.

1 Group 1A	2 Group 2A	3 3B	4 4B	5 5B	6 6B	7 7B	8 8B	9 8B	10 8B	11 1B	12 2B	13 Group 3A	14 Group 4A	15 Group 5A	16 Group 6A	17 Group 7A	18 Group 8A
H^+																	
Li^+														N^{3-}	O^{2-}	F^-	
Na^+	Mg^{2+}											Al^{3+}		P^{3-}	S^{2-}	Cl^-	
K^+	Ca^{2+}				Cr^{2+} Cr^{3+}	Mn^{2+} Mn^{3+}	Fe^{2+} Fe^{3+}	Co^{2+} Co^{3+}	Ni^{2+} Ni^{3+}	Cu^+ Cu^{2+}	Zn^{2+}					Br^-	
Rb^+	Sr^{2+}									Ag^+	Cd^{2+}		Sn^{2+} Sn^{4+}			I^-	
Cs^+	Ba^{2+}									Au^+ Au^{3+}	Hg_2^{2+} Hg^{2+}		Pb^{2+} Pb^{4+}	Bi^{3+} Bi^{5+}			

Metals Metalloids Nonmetals

FIGURE 6.2 On the periodic table, positive ions are produced from metals and negative ions are produced from nonmetals.

Q What are the possible ions of calcium, copper, and oxygen?

When you name an ionic compound, you need to determine if the metal forms two or more ions. If it is a transition element, except for zinc, cadmium, or silver, you will need to write a Roman numeral in parentheses after its name to show its ionic charge. The calculation of ionic charge depends on the negative charge of the anions in the formula as shown in Sample Problem 6.3.

Guide to Naming Ionic Compounds with Variable Charge Metals

1. Determine the charge of the cation from the anion.
2. Name the cation by its element name, and use a Roman numeral in parentheses for the charge.
3. Name the anion by using the first syllable of its element name followed by *ide.*
4. Write the name for the cation first and the name for the anion second.

SAMPLE PROBLEM 6.3 Naming Ionic Compounds with Variable Charge Metal Ions

Antifouling paint contains Cu_2O, which prevents the growth of barnacles and algae on the bottom of boats. What is the name of Cu_2O?

SOLUTION

Step 1 Determine the charge of the cation from the anion.

	Metal	Nonmetal
Formula	Cu_2O	
Elements	Copper (Cu)	Oxygen (O)
Groups	Transition element	6A (16)
Ions	Cu?	O^{2-}
Charge Balance	2Cu? +	(2−) = 0
	$\frac{\cancel{2}\text{Cu?}}{\cancel{2}} = \frac{\cancel{2}+}{\cancel{2}} = 1+$	
Ions	Cu^+	O^{2-}

Step 2 Name the cation by its element name, and use a Roman numeral in parentheses for the charge. copper(I)

Step 3 Name the anion by using the first syllable of its element name followed by *ide*. oxide

Step 4 **Write the name for the cation first and the name for the anion second.** copper(I) oxide

STUDY CHECK 6.3

Write the name for the compound with the formula Mn_2S_3.

Table 6.6 lists the names of some ionic compounds in which the transition elements and metals from Group 4A (14) have more than one positive ion.

TABLE 6.6 Some Ionic Compounds of Metals That Form Two Kinds of Positive Ions

Compound	Systematic Name
$FeCl_2$	Iron(II) chloride
Fe_2O_3	Iron(III) oxide
Cu_3P	Copper(I) phosphide
$CuBr_2$	Copper(II) bromide
$SnCl_2$	Tin(II) chloride
SnS_2	Tin(IV) sulfide

Writing Formulas from the Name of an Ionic Compound

The formula for an ionic compound is written from the first part of the name that describes the metal ion including its charge, and the second part that specifies the nonmetal ion. Subscripts are added as needed to balance the charge. The steps for writing a formula from the name of an ionic compound are shown in Sample Problem 6.4.

SAMPLE PROBLEM 6.4 Writing Formulas for Ionic Compounds

Write the formula for iron(III) chloride.

SOLUTION

Step 1 **Identify the cation and anion.** The Roman numeral (III) indicates that the charge of the iron ion is 3+, Fe^{3+}.

Analyze the Problem	Type of Ion	Cation	Anion
	Name	iron(III)	chloride
	Group	transition element	7A (17)
	Symbol of Ion	Fe^{3+}	Cl^-

Step 2 **Balance the charges.**

Fe^{3+} Cl^-

Cl^-

Cl^-

$$1(3+) + 3(1-) = 0$$

Becomes a subscript in the formula

Step 3 **Write the formula, cation first, using subscripts from the charge balance.**

$FeCl_3$

STUDY CHECK 6.4

The pigment chrome oxide green contains chromium(III) oxide. Write the correct formula for chromium(III) oxide.

Guide to Writing Formulas from the Name of an Ionic Compound

1 Identify the cation and anion.

2 Balance the charges.

3 Write the formula, cation first, using subscripts from the charge balance.

The pigment chrome oxide green contains chromium(III) oxide.

QUESTIONS AND PROBLEMS

6.3 Naming Ionic Compounds

LEARNING GOAL: *Given the formula for an ionic compound, write the correct name; given the name of an ionic compound, write the correct formula.*

6.19 Write the name for each of the following ionic compounds:
a. Al_2O_3 **b.** Cs_2S **c.** Na_2O
d. Mg_3P_2 **e.** KI **f.** BaF_2

6.20 Write the name for each of the following ionic compounds:
a. $MgCl_2$ **b.** K_3P **c.** Li_2S
d. CsF **e.** MgO **f.** $SrBr_2$

6.21 Why is a Roman numeral placed after the name of the ions of most transition elements?

6.22 The compound $CaCl_2$ is named calcium chloride; the compound $CuCl_2$ is named copper(II) chloride. Explain why a Roman numeral is used in one name but not in the other.

6.23 Write the name for each of the following ions (include the Roman numeral when necessary):
a. Fe^{2+} **b.** Cu^{2+} **c.** Zn^{2+}
d. Pb^{4+} **e.** Cr^{3+} **f.** Mn^{2+}

6.24 Write the name for each of the following ions (include the Roman numeral when necessary):
a. Ag^{+} **b.** Cu^{+} **c.** Bi^{3+}
d. Sn^{2+} **e.** Au^{3+} **f.** Ni^{2+}

6.25 Write the name for each of the following ionic compounds:
a. $SnCl_2$ **b.** FeO **c.** Cu_2S
d. CuS **e.** $CdBr_2$ **f.** $HgCl_2$

6.26 Write the name for each of the following ionic compounds:
a. Ag_3P **b.** PbS **c.** SnO_2
d. $MnCl_3$ **e.** Bi_2O_3 **f.** CoS

6.27 Write the symbol for the cation in each of the following ionic compounds:
a. $AuCl_3$ **b.** CrO
c. PbI_4 **d.** $SnCl_2$

6.28 Write the symbol for the cation in each of the following ionic compounds:
a. $FeCl_2$ **b.** Fe_2O_3
c. Bi_2S_3 **d.** AlP

6.29 Write the formula for each of the following ionic compounds:
a. magnesium chloride
b. sodium sulfide
c. copper(I) oxide
d. zinc phosphide
e. gold(III) nitride
f. cobalt(III) fluoride

6.30 Write the formula for each of the following ionic compounds:
a. nickel(III) oxide
b. bismuth(V) fluoride
c. tin(IV) chloride
d. silver sulfide
e. copper(II) iodide
f. potassium nitride

6.31 Write the formula for each of the following ionic compounds:
a. cobalt(III) chloride
b. lead(IV) oxide
c. silver iodide
d. calcium nitride
e. copper(I) phosphide
f. chromium(II) chloride

6.32 Write the formula for each of the following ionic compounds:
a. zinc bromide
b. iron(III) sulfide
c. manganese(IV) oxide
d. chromium(III) iodide
e. lithium nitride
f. gold(I) oxide

LEARNING GOAL

Write the name and formula for an ionic compound containing a polyatomic ion.

6.4 Polyatomic Ions

An ionic compound may also contain a polyatomic ion as one of its cations or anions. A **polyatomic ion** is a group of covalently bonded atoms that has an overall ionic charge. Most polyatomic ions consist of a nonmetal such as phosphorus, sulfur, carbon, or nitrogen covalently bonded to oxygen atoms.

Almost all the polyatomic ions are anions with charges of 1−, 2−, or 3−. Only one common polyatomic ion, NH_4^+, has a positive charge. Some models of common polyatomic ions are shown in Figure 6.3.

Plaster molding
$CaSO_4$

Ca^{2+} SO_4^{2-}
Sulfate ion

Fertilizer
NH_4NO_3

NH_4^+
Ammonium ion

NO_3^-
Nitrate ion

FIGURE 6.3 Many products contain polyatomic ions, which are groups of atoms that have an ionic charge.

Q What is the charge of a sulfate ion?

Naming Polyatomic Ions

The names of the most common negatively charged polyatomic ions end in *ate* such as nitrate and sulfate. When a related ion has one less oxygen atom, the *ite* ending is used for its name such as nitrite and sulfite. Recognizing these endings will help you identify polyatomic ions in the names of compounds. The hydroxide ion (OH^-) and cyanide ion (CN^-) are exceptions to this naming pattern.

By learning the formulas, charges, and names of the polyatomic ions shown in bold type in Table 6.7, you can derive the related ions. Note that the *ate* and *ite* ions of a particular nonmetal have the same ionic charge. For example, the sulfate ion is SO_4^{2-}, and the sulfite ion, which has one less oxygen atom, is SO_3^{2-}. Phosphate and phosphite ions each have a 3− charge; nitrate and nitrite each have a 1− charge. The elements in Group 7A (17) form four different polyatomic ions with oxygen. Prefixes are added to the names, and the ending is changed to distinguish among these ions, The prefix *per* is used for the polyatomic ion that has one more oxygen atom than the *ate* form. The ending *ate* is changed to *ite* for the ion with one less oxygen. The prefix *hypo* is used for the polyatomic ion that has one less oxygen than the *ite* form. For example, each of the polyatomic ions of chlorine—perchlorate, chlorate, chlorite, and hypochlorite—has a 1− charge.

The formula of hydrogen carbonate, or *bicarbonate*, is written by placing a hydrogen in front of the polyatomic ion formula for carbonate (CO_3^{2-}), and the charge is decreased from 2− to 1− to give HCO_3^-.

$$H^+ + CO_3^{2-} = HCO_3^-$$

TABLE 6.7 Names and Formulas of Some Common Polyatomic Ions

Nonmetal	Formula of Ion*	Name of Ion
Hydrogen	OH^-	Hydroxide
Nitrogen	NH_4^+	Ammonium
	$\mathbf{NO_3^-}$	**Nitrate**
	NO_2^-	Nitrite
Chlorine	ClO_4^-	Perchlorate
	$\mathbf{ClO_3^-}$	**Chlorate**
	ClO_2^-	Chlorite
	ClO^-	Hypochlorite
Carbon	$\mathbf{CO_3^{2-}}$	**Carbonate**
	HCO_3^-	Hydrogen carbonate (or bicarbonate)
	CN^-	Cyanide
	$C_2H_3O_2^-$	Acetate
	SCN^-	Thiocyanate
Sulfur	$\mathbf{SO_4^{2-}}$	**Sulfate**
	HSO_4^-	Hydrogen sulfate (or bisulfate)
	SO_3^{2-}	Sulfite
	HSO_3^-	Hydrogen sulfite (or bisulfite)
Phosphorus	$\mathbf{PO_4^{3-}}$	**Phosphate**
	HPO_4^{2-}	Hydrogen phosphate
	$H_2PO_4^-$	Dihydrogen phosphate
	PO_3^{3-}	Phosphite
Chromium	$\mathbf{CrO_4^{2-}}$	**Chromate**
	$Cr_2O_7^{2-}$	Dichromate
Manganese	MnO_4^-	Permanganate

*Formulas and names in bold show the most common polyatomic ion for that element.

Writing Formulas for Compounds Containing Polyatomic Ions

No polyatomic ion exists by itself. Like any ion, a polyatomic ion must be associated with ions of opposite charge. The bonding between polyatomic ions and other ions is one of electrical attraction. For example, the compound sodium chlorite consists of sodium ions (Na^+) and chlorite ions (ClO_2^-) held together by ionic bonds.

Sodium chlorite is used in the processing and bleaching of pulp from wood fibers and recycled cardboard.

To write correct formulas for compounds containing polyatomic ions, we follow the same rules of charge balance that we used for writing the formulas of simple ionic compounds. The total negative and positive charges must equal zero. For example, consider the formula for a compound containing sodium ions and chlorite ions. The ions are written as

Na^+	ClO_2^-
Sodium ion	Chlorite ion

$$(1+) + (1-) = 0$$

Because one ion of each balances the charge, the formula is written as

$NaClO_2$
Sodium chlorite

When more than one polyatomic ion is needed for charge balance, parentheses are used to enclose the formula of the ion. A subscript is written outside the closing parenthesis of the polyatomic ion to indicate the number needed for charge balance. The formula for magnesium nitrate contains the magnesium ion and the polyatomic nitrate ion.

Mg^{2+}	NO_3^-
Magnesium ion	Nitrate ion

To balance the positive charge of 2+ on the magnesium ion, two nitrate ions are needed. In the formula of the compound, parentheses are placed around the nitrate ion, and the subscript 2 is written outside the closing parenthesis.

Mg^{2+} NO_3^- NO_3^-

$$(2+) + 2(1-) = 0$$

Magnesium nitrate
$Mg(NO_3)_2$

Parentheses enclose the formula of the nitrate ion

Subscript outside the parenthesis indicates the use of two nitrate ions

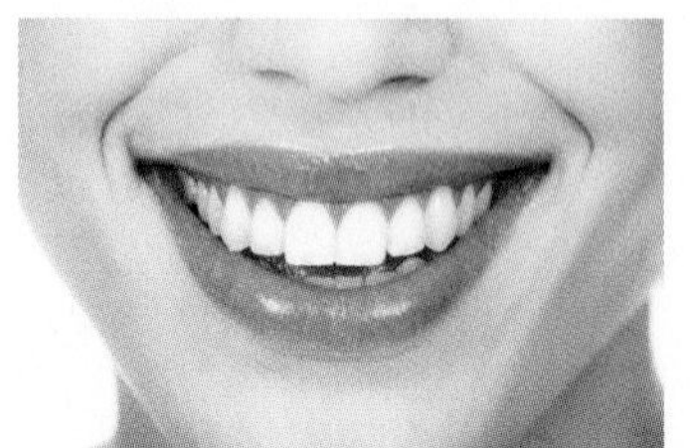
The mineral substance in teeth contains phosphate and hydroxide ions.

CONCEPT CHECK 6.4 Polyatomic Ions in Bones and Teeth

Bones and teeth contain a mineral substance called hydroxyapatite, $Ca_{10}(PO_4)_6(OH)_2$, a solid. What polyatomic ions are contained in the mineral substance of bone and teeth?

ANSWER

The polyatomic ions, which contain atoms of two or more elements, are phosphate (PO_4^{3-}) ions and hydroxide (OH^-) ions.

Guide to Writing Formulas with Polyatomic Ions

1. Identify the cation and polyatomic ion (anion).
2. Balance the charges.
3. Write the formula, cation first, using the subscripts from charge balance.

SAMPLE PROBLEM 6.5 Writing Formulas Containing Polyatomic Ions

Write the formula for aluminum bicarbonate.

SOLUTION

Step 1 Identify the cation and polyatomic ion (anion).

Cation	Polyatomic Ion (anion)
Al^{3+}	HCO_3^-

Step 2 Balance the charges.

Al^{3+} HCO_3^- HCO_3^- HCO_3^-

$$\mathbf{1}(3+) + \mathbf{3}(1-) = 0$$

Becomes a subscript in the formula

Step 3 **Write the formula, cation first, using the subscripts from charge balance.** The formula for the compound is written by enclosing the formula of the bicarbonate ion, HCO_3^-, in parentheses and writing the subscript 3 outside the right parenthesis.

$$Al(HCO_3)_3$$

STUDY CHECK 6.5

Write the formula for a compound containing ammonium ions and phosphate ions.

Naming Ionic Compounds Containing Polyatomic Ions

When naming ionic compounds containing polyatomic ions, we write the positive ion, usually a metal, first, and then we write the name of the polyatomic ion. It is important that you learn to recognize the polyatomic ion in the formula and name it correctly. As with other ionic compounds, no prefixes are used.

Na_2SO_4	$FePO_4$	$Al_2(CO_3)_3$
$Na_2\boxed{SO_4}$	$Fe\boxed{PO_4}$	$Al_2(\boxed{CO_3})_3$
Sodium sulfate	Iron(III) phosphate	Aluminum carbonate

Table 6.8 lists the formulas and names of some ionic compounds that include polyatomic ions and also gives their uses in medicine and industry.

TABLE 6.8 Some Compounds That Contain Polyatomic Ions

Formula	Name	Use
$BaSO_4$	Barium sulfate	Contrast medium for X-rays
$CaCO_3$	Calcium carbonate	Antacid, calcium supplement
$CaSO_3$	Calcium sulfite	Preservative in cider and fruit juices
$CaSO_4$	Calcium sulfate	Plaster casts
$AgNO_3$	Silver nitrate	Topical anti-infective
$NaHCO_3$	Sodium bicarbonate *or* Sodium hydrogen carbonate	Antacid
$Zn_3(PO_4)_2$	Zinc phosphate	Dental cements
$FePO_4$	Iron(III) phosphate	Food and bread enrichment
K_2CO_3	Potassium carbonate	Alkalizer, diuretic
$Al_2(SO_4)_3$	Aluminum sulfate	Antiperspirant, anti-infective
$AlPO_4$	Aluminum phosphate	Antacid
$MgSO_4$	Magnesium sulfate	Cathartic, Epsom salts

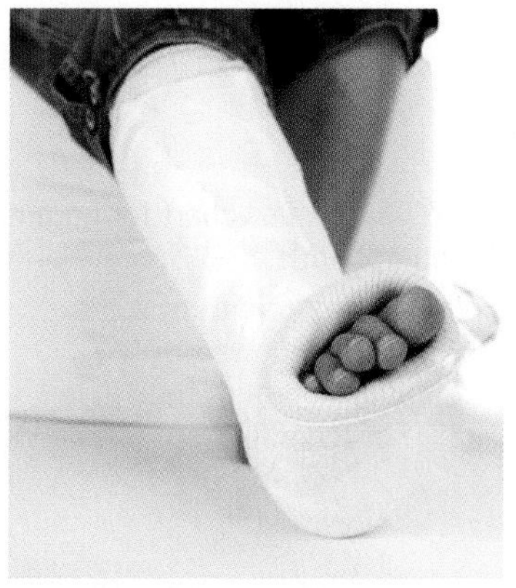

A plaster cast made of $CaSO_4$ immobilizes a broken leg.

Guide to Naming Ionic Compounds with Polyatomic Ions

1 Identify the cation and polyatomic ion (anion).

2 Name the cation using a Roman numeral, if needed.

3 Name the polyatomic ion.

4 Write the name for the compound, cation first and the polyatomic ion second.

SAMPLE PROBLEM 6.6 Naming Compounds Containing Polyatomic Ions

Name the following ionic compounds:

a. $KClO_3$
b. $Mn(OH)_2$

SOLUTION

We can name compounds with polyatomic ions by separating the compound into a cation and an anion, which is usually the polyatomic ion.

	Step 1		Step 2	Step 3	Step 4
Formula	Cation	Anion	Name of Cation	Name of Anion	Name of Compound
a. $KClO_3$	K^+	ClO_3^-	Potassium ion	Chlorate ion	Potassium chlorate
b. $Mn(OH)_2$	Mn^{2+}	OH^-	Manganese(II) ion	Hydroxide ion	Manganese(II) hydroxide

STUDY CHECK 6.6

What is the name of $Ca_3(PO_4)_2$, which is used to replenish calcium?

Summary of Naming Ionic Compounds

Throughout this chapter, we have examined strategies for naming ionic compounds. Now we can summarize the rules, as illustrated in Figure 6.4. In general, ionic compounds that have two elements are named by stating the first element, followed by the second element with an *ide* ending. For ionic compounds, it is necessary to determine whether the metal can form more than one positive ion; if so, a Roman numeral following the name of the metal indicates the particular ionic charge. Ionic compounds with three or more elements include some type of polyatomic ion. They are named by ionic rules but usually have an *ate* or *ite* ending when the polyatomic ion has a negative charge.

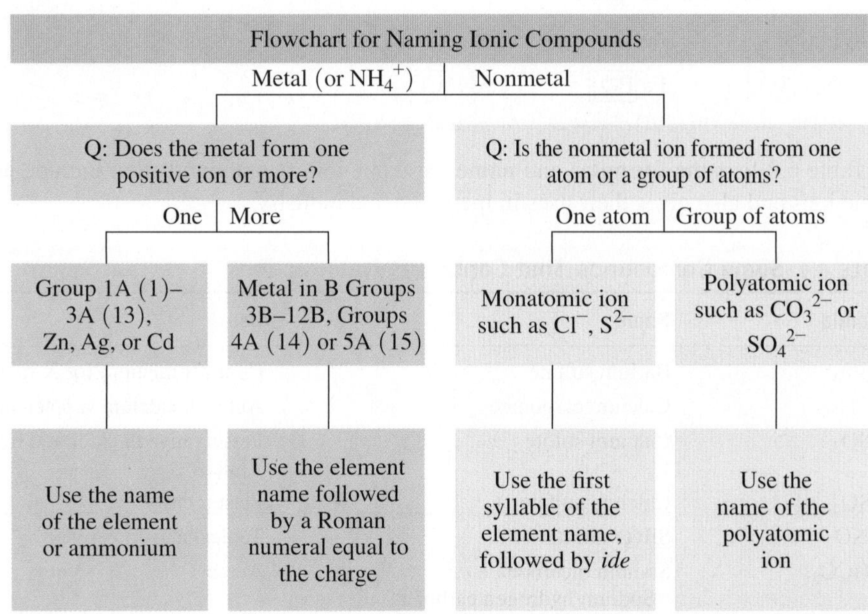

FIGURE 6.4 A flowchart for naming ionic compounds.

Q Why are the names of some metal ions followed by a Roman numeral in the name of a compound?

SAMPLE PROBLEM 6.7 Naming Ionic Compounds

Name the following ionic compounds:

a. Na_3P
b. $CuSO_4$
c. $Cr(ClO)_3$

SOLUTION

	Step 1		Step 2	Step 3	Step 4
Formula	**Cation**	**Anion**	**Name of Cation**	**Name of Anion**	**Name of Compound**
a. Na_3P	Na^+	P^{3-}	Sodium ion	Phosphide ion	Sodium phosphide
b. $CuSO_4$	Cu^{2+}	SO_4^{2-}	Copper(II) ion	Sulfate ion	Copper(II) sulfate
c. $Cr(ClO)_3$	Cr^{3+}	ClO^-	Chromium(III) ion	Hypochlorite ion	Chromium(III) hypochlorite

STUDY CHECK 6.7

What is the name of $Fe(NO_3)_2$?

QUESTIONS AND PROBLEMS

6.4 Polyatomic Ions

LEARNING GOAL: *Write the name and formula for an ionic compound containing a polyatomic ion.*

6.33 Write the formula including the charge for the following polyatomic ions:
a. bicarbonate **b.** ammonium
c. phosphate **d.** hydrogen sulfate
e. hypochlorite

6.34 Write the formula including the charge for the following polyatomic ions:
a. nitrite **b.** sulfite
c. hydroxide **d.** phosphite
e. acetate

6.35 Name the following polyatomic ions:
a. SO_4^{2-} **b.** CO_3^{2-} **c.** PO_4^{3-}
d. NO_3^- **e.** ClO_4^-

6.36 Name the following polyatomic ions:
a. OH^- **b.** HSO_3^- **c.** CN^-
d. NO_2^- **e.** CrO_4^{2-}

6.37 Complete the following table with the formula and name of the compound that forms between each pair of ions:

	NO_2^-	CO_3^{2-}	HSO_4^-	PO_4^{3-}
Li^+				
Cu^{2+}				
Ba^{2+}				

6.38 Complete the following table with the formula and name of the compound that forms between each pair of ions:

	NO_3^-	HCO_3^-	SO_3^{2-}	HPO_4^{2-}
NH_4^+				
Al^{3+}				
Pb^{4+}				

6.39 Write the formula for the polyatomic ion in each of the following and name each compound:
a. Na_2CO_3 **b.** NH_4Cl **c.** Na_3PO_3
d. $Mn(NO_2)_2$ **e.** $FeSO_3$ **f.** $KC_2H_3O_2$

6.40 Write the formula for the polyatomic ion in each of the following and name each compound:
a. KOH **b.** $NaNO_3$ **c.** Au_2CO_3
d. $NaHCO_3$ **e.** $BaSO_4$ **f.** $Ca(ClO)_2$

6.41 Write the correct formula for each of the following ionic compounds:
a. barium hydroxide **b.** sodium hydrogen sulfite
c. iron(II) nitrate **d.** zinc phosphate
e. iron(III) carbonate

6.42 Write the correct formula for each of the following ionic compounds:
a. aluminum chlorate **b.** ammonium oxide
c. magnesium bicarbonate **d.** sodium nitrite
e. copper(I) sulfate

6.43 Name each of the following ionic compounds:
a. $Al_2(SO_4)_3$, antiperspirant
b. $Mg_3(PO_4)_2$, antacid
c. Cr_2O_3, green pigment
d. Na_3PO_4, laxative
e. $(NH_4)_2SO_4$, fertilizer
f. Bi_2S_3, found in bismuth ore

6.44 Name each of the following ionic compounds:
a. $Co_3(PO_4)_2$, violet pigment
b. $CaCO_3$, antacid
c. $FeSO_4$, iron supplement in vitamins
d. $MgSO_4$, Epsom salts
e. Cu_2O, fungicide
f. SnF_2, tooth decay preventative

6.5 Molecular Compounds: Sharing Electrons

LEARNING GOAL

Given the formula of a molecular compound, write its correct name; given the name of a molecular compound, write its formula.

A **molecular compound** contains two or more nonmetals that form *covalent bonds*. Because nonmetals have high ionization energies, valence electrons are shared by nonmetal atoms to achieve stability. When atoms share electrons, the bond is a **covalent bond**. When two or more atoms share electrons, they form a **molecule**.

Formation of a Hydrogen Molecule

The simplest molecule is hydrogen, H_2. When two H atoms are far apart, there are no attractions between them. As the H atoms move closer, the positive charge of each nucleus attracts the electron of the other atom. This attraction, which is greater than the repulsion between the valence electrons, pulls the atoms closer until they share a pair of valence electrons (see Figure 6.5). The result is called a *covalent bond*, in which each H atom has a stable electron configuration. The atoms bonded in H_2 are more stable than two individual H atoms.

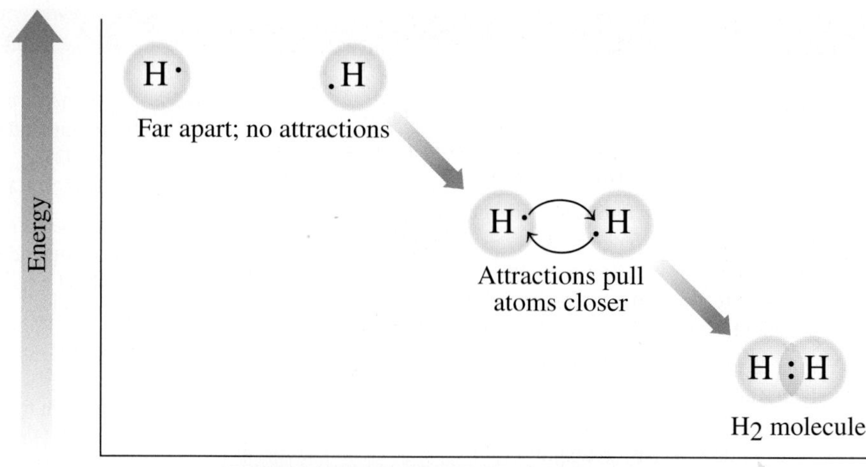

FIGURE 6.5 A covalent bond forms as H atoms move close together to share electrons.

Q What determines the attraction between two H atoms?

Electron-Dot Formulas of Molecular Compounds

The valence electrons in molecular compounds are shown using an *electron-dot formula*, also called a Lewis structure. The shared electrons, or **bonding pairs**, are shown as two dots or a single line between atoms. The nonbonding pairs of electrons, or **lone pairs**, are placed on the outside. For example, a fluorine molecule (F_2) consists of two fluorine atoms, Group 7A (17), each with seven valence electrons. In the F_2 molecule, each F atom achieves an octet by sharing its unpaired valence electron.

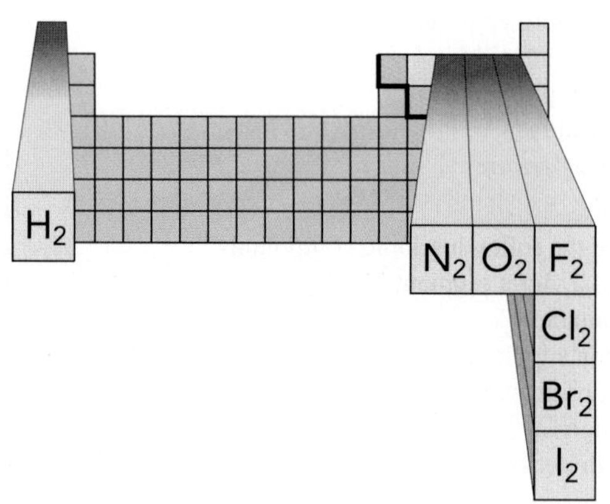

The elements hydrogen, nitrogen, oxygen, fluorine, chlorine, bromine, and iodine exist as diatomic molecules.

A lone pair

A bonding pair

:F· + ·F: ⟶ :F:F: :F—F: = F_2

Electrons to share

A shared pair of electrons

A covalent bond

A fluorine molecule

TABLE 6.9 Elements That Exist as Diatomic Molecules

Diatomic Molecule	Name
H_2	Hydrogen
N_2	Nitrogen
O_2	Oxygen
F_2	Fluorine
Cl_2	Chlorine
Br_2	Bromine
I_2	Iodine

Hydrogen (H_2) and fluorine (F_2) are examples of nonmetals whose natural state is *diatomic*; that is, they contain two like atoms. The elements that exist as diatomic molecules are listed in Table 6.9.

Sharing Electrons Between Atoms of Different Elements

Methane, a component of natural gas, is a compound of carbon and hydrogen. By sharing electrons, each carbon atom forms four bonds, and each hydrogen atom forms one bond. The carbon atom obtains an octet, and each hydrogen atom is complete with two shared electrons. As seen in Table 6.10, the electron-dot formula for methane is drawn with the carbon atom as the center atom with the hydrogen atoms on each of the sides. The bonding pairs of electrons, which are single covalent bonds, may also be shown as single lines between the carbon atom and each of the hydrogen atoms. Table 6.10 gives the formulas of some molecular compounds for Period 2 elements.

TABLE 6.10 Electron-Dot Formulas for Some Molecular Compounds

CH_4	NH_3	H_2O
Electron-Dot Formulas		
H H:C:H H	H:N̈:H H	:Ö:H H
Formulas Using Bonds and Electron Dots		
H | H—C—H | H	H—N̈—H | H	:Ö—H | H
Molecular Models		

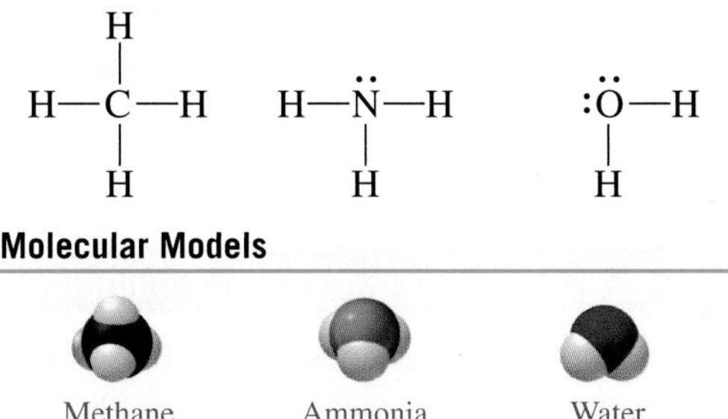

Methane molecule	Ammonia molecule	Water molecule

Nonmetals form molecular compounds.

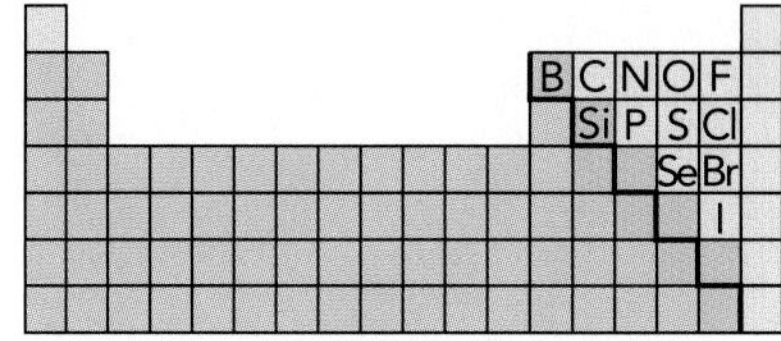

Examples: CO_2, SF_2, PCl_3, CH_4

The number of covalent bonds that a nonmetal atom forms is usually equal to the number of electrons it needs to acquire a stable electron configuration.

CONCEPT CHECK 6.5 Electron-Dot Formulas

State the number of valence electrons, bonding pairs, and lone pairs in each of the following electron-dot formulas:

a. H:F̤̈:

b. :S̤̈:F̤̈:
:F̤̈:

ANSWER

a. eight valence electrons, one bonding pair and three lone pairs
b. 20 valence electrons, two bonding pairs and eight lone pairs

Names and Formulas of Molecular Compounds

CORE CHEMISTRY SKILL 

Writing the Names and Formulas for Molecular Compounds

When naming a molecular compound, the first nonmetal in the formula is named by its element name; the second nonmetal is named using the first syllable of its element name, followed by *ide*. When a subscript indicates two or more atoms of an element, a prefix is shown in front of its name. Table 6.11 lists prefixes used in naming molecular compounds.

The names of molecular compounds use prefixes because it is possible for atoms of two nonmetals to form two or more different compounds. For example, atoms of carbon and oxygen form carbon monoxide (CO) and carbon dioxide (CO_2), in which the number of atoms of oxygen in each compound is indicated by the prefixes *mono* or *di* in their names.

When the vowels *o* and *o* or *a* and *o* appear together, the first vowel is omitted, as in carbon monoxide. In the name of a molecular compound, the prefix *mono* is usually omitted, as in NO, nitrogen oxide. Traditionally, however, CO is named carbon monoxide. Table 6.12 lists the formulas, names, and commercial uses of some common molecular compounds.

TABLE 6.11 Prefixes Used in Naming Molecular Compounds

1	mono	6	hexa
2	di	7	hepta
3	tri	8	octa
4	tetra	9	nona
5	penta	10	deca

TABLE 6.12 Some Common Molecular Compounds

Formula	Name	Commercial Uses
CS_2	Carbon disulfide	Manufacture of rayon
CO_2	Carbon dioxide	Carbonation of beverages, fire extinguishers, propellant in aerosols, dry ice
NO	Nitrogen oxide	Stabilizer
N_2O	Dinitrogen oxide	Inhaled anesthetic, "laughing gas"
SiO_2	Silicon dioxide	Manufacturer of glass
SO_2	Sulfur dioxide	Preserving fruits, vegetables; disinfectant in wineries; bleaching textiles
SF_6	Sulfur hexafluoride	Electrical circuits (insulation)

CONCEPT CHECK 6.6 Naming Molecular Compounds

Why is it that the name of the molecular compound BrCl, bromine chloride, does not include a prefix, but the name of the molecular compound OCl_2, oxygen dichloride, does?

ANSWER

When a molecular formula has one atom of each element, the prefix (mono) is not used in the name. Thus, the name of BrCl is bromine chloride. However, two or more atoms of an element are indicated by using a prefix. Thus, the name of the molecular compound OCl_2 contains the prefix *di*, oxygen dichloride.

SAMPLE PROBLEM 6.8 Naming Molecular Compounds

Name the molecular compound NCl_3.

SOLUTION

Analyze the Problem	Symbol of Element	N	Cl
	Name	nitrogen	chloride
	Subscript	1	3
	Prefix	none	tri

Step 1 **Name the first nonmetal by its element name.** In NCl_3, the first nonmetal (N) is nitrogen.

Step 2 **Name the second nonmetal by using the first syllable of its element name followed by *ide*.** The second nonmetal (Cl) is chloride.

Step 3 **Add prefixes to indicate the number of atoms (subscripts).** Because there is one nitrogen atom, no prefix is needed. The subscript 3 for the Cl atoms is written as the prefix *tri*. The name of NCl_3 is nitrogen trichloride.

STUDY CHECK 6.8

Write the name for each of the following molecular compounds:

a. $SiBr_4$ **b.** Br_2O

Guide to Naming Molecular Compounds

1. Name the first nonmetal by its element name.
2. Name the second nonmetal by using the first syllable of its element name followed by *ide*.
3. Add prefixes to indicate the number of atoms (subscripts).

Writing Formulas from the Names of Molecular Compounds

In the name of a molecular compound, the names of two nonmetals are given, along with prefixes for the number of atoms of each. To write the formula from the name, we use the symbol for each element and a subscript when a prefix indicates two or more atoms, as shown in Sample Problem 6.9.

SAMPLE PROBLEM 6.9 Writing Formulas for Molecular Compounds

Write the formula for the molecular compound diboron trioxide.

SOLUTION

Analyze the Problem	Name	Diboron	Trioxide
	Symbol of Element	B	O
	Subscript	2 (from *di*)	3 (from *tri*)

Step 1 **Write the symbols in the order of the elements in the name.** In this molecular compound of two nonmetals, the first nonmetal is boron (B), and the second nonmetal is oxygen (O).

B O

Step 2 **Write any prefixes as subscripts.** The prefix *di* in *di*boron indicates that there are two atoms of boron, shown as a subscript 2 in the formula. The prefix *tri* in *tri*oxide indicates that there are three atoms of oxygen, shown as a subscript 3 in the formula.

B_2O_3

STUDY CHECK 6.9

What is the molecular formula of iodine heptafluoride?

Guide to Writing Formulas for Molecular Compounds

1. Write the symbols in the order of the elements in the name.
2. Write any prefixes as subscripts.

Summary of Naming Ionic and Molecular Compounds

We have examined strategies for naming ionic and molecular compounds. In general, compounds that have two elements are named by stating the first element name, followed by the second element with an *ide* ending. If the first element is a metal, the compound is usually ionic; if the first element is a nonmetal, the compound is usually molecular. For ionic compounds, it is necessary to determine whether the metal can form more than one type of positive ion; if so, a Roman numeral following the name of the metal indicates the particular ionic charge. One exception is the ammonium ion, NH_4^+, which is written first as a positively charged polyatomic ion. Ionic compounds that have three or more elements include some type of polyatomic ion. They are named by rules for ionic compounds but have an *ate* or *ite* ending when the polyatomic ion has a negative charge.

In naming molecular compounds having two elements, prefixes are used to indicate the number of atoms of each nonmetal in a formula. Organic compounds of C and H, such as CH_4 and C_2H_6, use a different system of naming that we will discuss in the next section. A flowchart for naming the various types of compounds is shown in Figure 6.6.

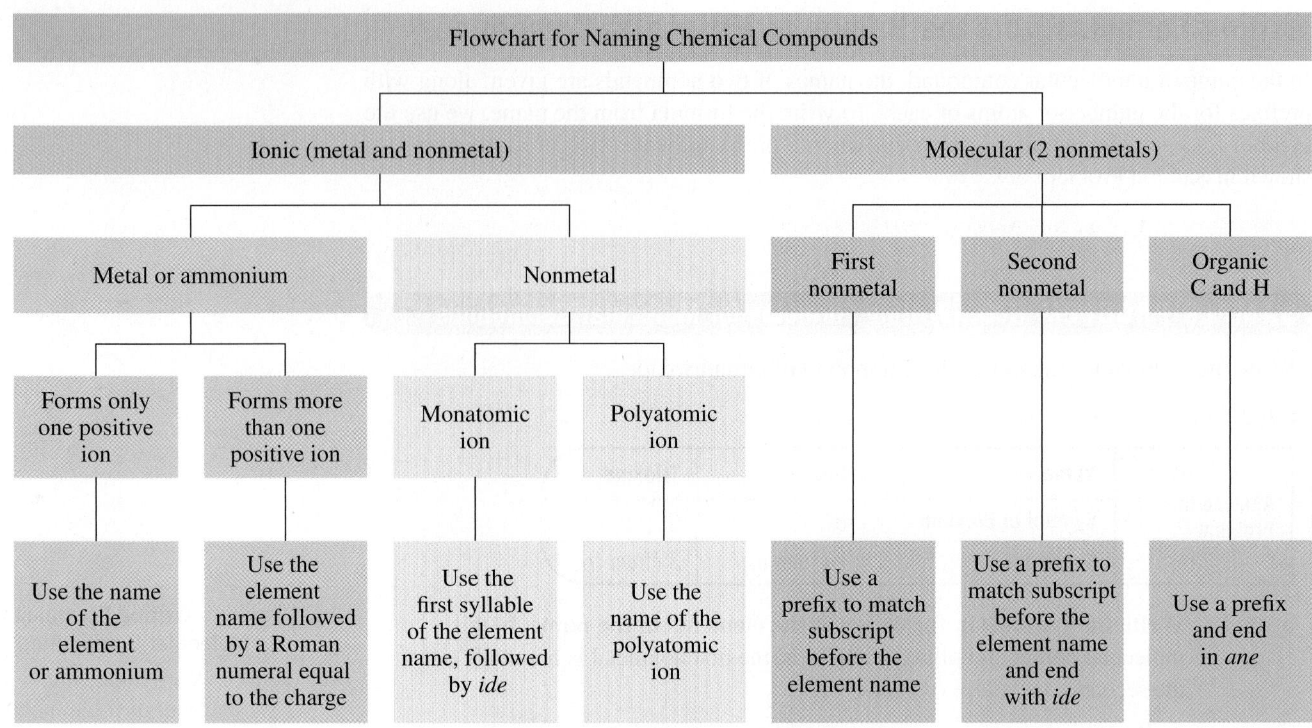

FIGURE 6.6 A flowchart for naming ionic and molecular compounds including organic compounds.

Q Why is sodium sulfide an ionic compound and sulfur hexafluoride a molecular compound?

CONCEPT CHECK 6.7 Naming Ionic and Molecular Compounds

Identify each of the following as an ionic or molecular compound and give its name:

a. Ca_3N_2 **b.** Cu_3PO_4 **c.** SO_3

ANSWER

a. Ca_3N_2, consisting of a metal and a nonmetal, is an ionic compound. As a representative metal in Group 2A (2), Ca forms a calcium ion, Ca^{2+}. Nitrogen, as a representative element in Group 5A (15), forms a nitride ion, N^{3-}. Writing the name for the cation followed by the name for the anion gives the name calcium nitride.

b. Cu_3PO_4, consisting of a cation of a transition element and a polyatomic phosphate anion, PO_4^{3-}, is an ionic compound. As a transition element, Cu forms more than one ion. In this formula, the 3− charge of PO_4^{3-} is balanced by three copper (1+) ions, Cu^+, named copper(I). In the name, a Roman numeral written after the metal name, copper(I), specifies the 1+ charge. The compound is named copper(I) phosphate.

c. SO_3 consists of two nonmetals, which indicates that it is a molecular compound. The first element, S, is *sulfur* (no prefix is needed). The second element, O, *oxide*, has a subscript 3, which requires the prefix *tri* in the name. The compound is named sulfur trioxide.

QUESTIONS AND PROBLEMS

6.5 Molecular Compounds: Sharing Electrons

LEARNING GOAL: *Given the formula of a molecular compound, write its correct name; given the name of a molecular compound, write its formula.*

6.45 What elements on the periodic table are most likely to form molecular compounds?

6.46 How does the bond that forms between Na and Cl differ from the bond that forms between N and Cl?

6.47 State the number of valence electrons, bonding pairs, and lone pairs in each of the following electron-dot formulas:

a. H:H **b.** H:B̤̈r: **c.** :B̤̈r:B̤̈r:

6.48 State the number of valence electrons, bonding pairs, and lone pairs in each of the following electron-dot formulas:

a. H:Ö: (with H above O) **b.** H:N̤̈:H (with H below N) **c.** :B̤̈r:Ö:B̤̈r:

6.49 Name each of the following molecular compounds:
a. PBr_3 **b.** CBr_4 **c.** SiO_2
d. HF **e.** NI_3

6.50 Name each of the following molecular compounds:
a. CS_2 **b.** P_2O_5 **c.** Cl_2O
d. PCl_3 **e.** CO

6.51 Name each of the following molecular compounds:
a. N_2O_3 **b.** NCl_3 **c.** $SiBr_4$
d. PCl_5 **e.** N_2S_3

6.52 Name each of the following molecular compounds:
a. SiF_4 **b.** IBr_3 **c.** CO_2
d. SO_2 **e.** N_2O

6.53 Write the formula for each of the following molecular compounds:
a. carbon tetrachloride
b. carbon monoxide
c. phosphorus trichloride
d. dinitrogen tetroxide

6.54 Write the formula for each of the following molecular compounds:
a. sulfur dioxide
b. silicon tetrachloride
c. iodine trichloride
d. dinitrogen oxide

6.55 Write the formula for each of the following molecular compounds:
a. oxygen difluoride
b. boron trifluoride
c. dinitrogen trioxide
d. sulfur hexafluoride

6.56 Write the formula for each of the following molecular compounds:
a. sulfur dibromide
b. carbon disulfide
c. tetraphosphorus hexoxide
d. dinitrogen pentoxide

6.57 Name each of the following ionic or molecular compounds:
a. $AlCl_3$ **b.** B_2O_3 **c.** N_2O_4
d. $Sn(NO_3)_2$ **e.** $Cu(ClO_2)_2$

6.58 Name each of the following ionic or molecular compounds:
a. BrF_3 **b.** $Mg(BrO)_2$ **c.** SiI_4
d. $NiSO_4$ **e.** Fe_2S_3

6.6 Organic Compounds: Extended Topic

LEARNING GOAL

Identify the properties characteristic of organic and inorganic compounds.

The element carbon has a special role because many carbon atoms can bond together to give a vast array of molecular compounds. **Organic compounds** always contain carbon and hydrogen, and sometimes oxygen, sulfur, nitrogen, phosphorus, or a halogen. We find organic compounds in many common products we use every day, such as gasoline, medicine, shampoos, plastics, and perfumes. The food we eat is composed of organic compounds such as carbohydrates, fats, and proteins that supply us with fuel for energy and the carbon atoms needed to build and repair the cells of our bodies.

Although many organic compounds occur in nature, chemists have synthesized even more. The cotton, wool, or silk in your clothes contains naturally occurring organic compounds, whereas materials such as polyester, nylon, or plastic have been synthesized. Learning about the structures and reactions of organic compounds will provide you with a foundation for understanding the more complex molecules of biochemistry.

Vegetable oil, an organic compound, is not soluble in water.

The formulas of organic compounds are written with carbon first, followed by hydrogen, and any other elements. Organic compounds typically have low melting and boiling points, are not soluble in water, and are less dense than water. For example, vegetable oil, which is a mixture of organic compounds, does not dissolve in water but floats on top. Many organic compounds undergo combustion and burn vigorously in air.

By contrast, many inorganic compounds have high melting and boiling points. Inorganic compounds that are ionic are usually soluble in water, and most do not burn in air. Table 6.13 contrasts some of the properties associated with organic and inorganic compounds, such as propane, C_3H_8, and sodium chloride, NaCl.

TABLE 6.13 Some Properties of Organic and Inorganic Compounds

Property	Organic	Example: C_3H_8	Inorganic	Example: NaCl
Elements	C and H	C and H	Most metals and nonmetals	Na and Cl
Bonding	Mostly covalent	Covalent (4 bonds to each C)	Mostly ionic	Ionic
Type of Compound	Molecular	Molecular	Mostly ionic	Ionic
Melting Point	Usually low	−188 °C	Usually high	801 °C
Boiling Point	Usually low	−42 °C	Usually high	1413 °C
Flammability	High	Burns in air	Low	Does not burn
Solubility in Water	Not usually soluble	No	Most are soluble	Yes

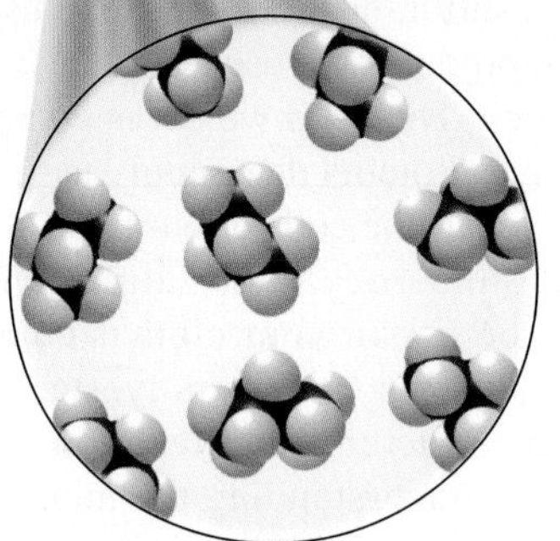

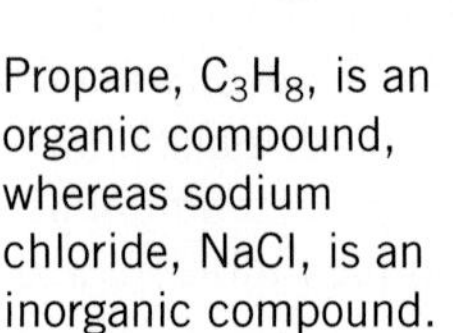

Propane, C_3H_8, is an organic compound, whereas sodium chloride, NaCl, is an inorganic compound.

CONCEPT CHECK 6.8 Properties of Organic Compounds

Identify each of the following properties as more typical of an organic or inorganic compound:

a. is not soluble in water
b. has a high melting point
c. burns in air

ANSWER

a. an organic compound
b. an inorganic compound
c. an organic compound

Bonding in Organic Compounds

Hydrocarbons, as the name suggests, are organic compounds that consist of only carbon and hydrogen. In the simplest hydrocarbon, methane (CH_4), the carbon atom forms an octet by sharing four valence electrons with four hydrogen atoms. In the electron-dot formula, each shared pair of electrons represents a single covalent bond. In organic molecules, every carbon atom has four bonds. A hydrocarbon is referred to as a *saturated hydrocarbon* when all of the bonds in the molecules are single bonds. An **expanded structural formula** is drawn when we show the bonds between all of the atoms.

The Tetrahedral Structure of Carbon

In methane, CH_4, the covalent bonds from carbon to hydrogen are directed to the corners of a tetrahedron. This gives the lowest amount of repulsion between the H atoms. This three-dimensional structure of methane can be illustrated as a ball-and-stick model. The expanded structural formula is a two-dimensional representation in which the bonds from carbon to each hydrogen atom are shown.

H
H:C:H
H
(a)

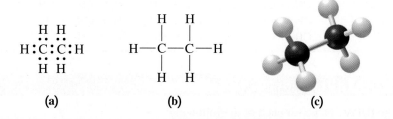

H
H—C—H
H
(b)

(c)

Two-dimensional and three-dimensional representations of methane, CH_4: **(a)** electron-dot formula, **(b)** expanded structural formula, and **(c)** ball-and-stick model.

In ethane, C_2H_6, two carbon atoms are attached and each carbon atom is also bonded to three hydrogen atoms.

H H
H:C:C:H
H H
(a)

H H
H—C—C—H
H H
(b)

(c)

Two-dimensional and three-dimensional representations of ethane, C_2H_6: **(a)** electron-dot formula, **(b)** expanded structural formula, and **(c)** ball-and-stick model.

QUESTIONS AND PROBLEMS

6.6 Organic Compounds: Extended Topic

LEARNING GOAL: *Identify the properties characteristic of organic and inorganic compounds.*

6.59 Identify the following as formulas of organic or inorganic compounds:
a. KCl **b.** C_4H_{10} **c.** C_2H_6O
d. H_2SO_4 **e.** $CaCl_2$ **f.** C_3H_7Cl

6.60 Identify the following as formulas of organic or inorganic compounds:
a. $C_6H_{12}O_6$ **b.** K_3PO_4 **c.** I_2
d. C_4H_9Br **e.** $C_{10}H_{22}$ **f.** CH_4

6.61 Identify the following properties as most typical of organic or inorganic compounds:
a. is soluble in water
b. has a low boiling point
c. contains carbon and hydrogen
d. has ionic bonds

6.62 Identify the following properties as most typical of organic or inorganic compounds:
a. contains Li and F
b. is a gas at room temperature
c. has covalent bonds
d. produces ions in water

6.63 Match the following physical and chemical properties with the compounds ethane, C_2H_6, or sodium bromide, NaBr:
a. boils at −89 °C
b. burns vigorously in air
c. is a solid at 250 °C
d. dissolves in water

6.64 Match the following physical and chemical properties with the compounds cyclohexane, C_6H_{12}, or calcium nitrate, $Ca(NO_3)_2$:
a. melts at 500 °C
b. insoluble in water
c. does not burn in air
d. is a liquid at room temperature

6.7 Names and Formulas of Alkanes: Extended Topic

LEARNING GOAL

Write the IUPAC name and draw the condensed structural formula for an alkane.

More than 90% of the compounds in the world are organic compounds. This large number of carbon compounds is possible because the covalent bond between carbon atoms (C—C) is very strong, allowing carbon atoms to form long, stable chains. To help us study this large group of compounds, we organize them into classes that have similar structures and chemical properties.

CORE CHEMISTRY SKILL

Naming and Drawing Alkanes

The **alkanes** are a class of hydrocarbons in which the atoms are connected by single bonds. One of the most common uses of alkanes is as fuels. Methane, used in gas heaters and gas cooktops, is an alkane with one carbon atom. The alkanes ethane, propane, and butane contain two, three, and four carbon atoms, respectively, connected in a row or a *continuous* chain. As we can see, all the names for alkanes end in *ane*. Such names are part of the **IUPAC** (International Union of Pure and Applied Chemistry) **system** used by chemists to name organic compounds. Alkanes with five or more carbon atoms in a chain are named using the prefixes *pent* (5), *hex* (6), *hept* (7), *oct* (8), *non* (9), and *dec* (10) (see Table 6.14).

TABLE 6.14 IUPAC Names of the First 10 Alkanes

Number of Carbon Atoms	Prefix	Name	Molecular Formula	Condensed Structural Formula
1	Meth	Methane	CH_4	CH_4
2	Eth	Ethane	C_2H_6	CH_3-CH_3
3	Prop	Propane	C_3H_8	$CH_3-CH_2-CH_3$
4	But	Butane	C_4H_{10}	$CH_3-CH_2-CH_2-CH_3$
5	Pent	Pentane	C_5H_{12}	$CH_3-CH_2-CH_2-CH_2-CH_3$
6	Hex	Hexane	C_6H_{14}	$CH_3-CH_2-CH_2-CH_2-CH_2-CH_3$
7	Hept	Heptane	C_7H_{16}	$CH_3-CH_2-CH_2-CH_2-CH_2-CH_2-CH_3$
8	Oct	Octane	C_8H_{18}	$CH_3-CH_2-CH_2-CH_2-CH_2-CH_2-CH_2-CH_3$
9	Non	Nonane	C_9H_{20}	$CH_3-CH_2-CH_2-CH_2-CH_2-CH_2-CH_2-CH_2-CH_3$
10	Dec	Decane	$C_{10}H_{22}$	$CH_3-CH_2-CH_2-CH_2-CH_2-CH_2-CH_2-CH_2-CH_2-CH_3$

SAMPLE PROBLEM 6.10 Naming Alkanes

Write the IUPAC name for each of the following:

a. $CH_3-CH_2-CH_3$

b. C_6H_{14}

SOLUTION

a. A chain of three carbon atoms and eight hydrogen atoms is propane.

b. A chain with six carbon atoms and 14 hydrogen atoms is hexane.

STUDY CHECK 6.10

What is the IUPAC name of C_8H_{18}?

Condensed Structural Formulas

In a **condensed structural formula**, each carbon atom and its attached hydrogen atoms are written as a group. A subscript indicates the number of hydrogen atoms bonded to each carbon atom.

$$\underset{\text{Expanded}}{\mathrm{H-\overset{\displaystyle H}{\underset{\displaystyle H}{\overset{|}{\underset{|}{C}}}}-}} \;=\; \underset{\text{Condensed}}{CH_3-} \qquad \underset{\text{Expanded}}{\mathrm{-\overset{\displaystyle H}{\underset{\displaystyle H}{\overset{|}{\underset{|}{C}}}}-}} \;=\; \underset{\text{Condensed}}{-CH_2-}$$

By contrast, the *molecular formula* gives the total number of carbon atoms and hydrogen atoms but does not indicate the arrangement of the atoms in the molecule.

When a molecule consists of a chain of three or more carbon atoms, the carbon atoms do not lie in a straight line. Rather, they are arranged in a zigzag pattern, which is seen in the ball-and-stick model of hexane.

A simplified structure called the *skeletal formula* is a carbon skeleton in which carbon atoms are represented as the end of each line or as corners in a zigzag pattern. The hydrogen atoms are not shown, but each carbon is understood to have bonds to four atoms, including hydrogen.

Alkane Name Hexane
Molecular Formula C_6H_{14}
Ball-and-Stick Model

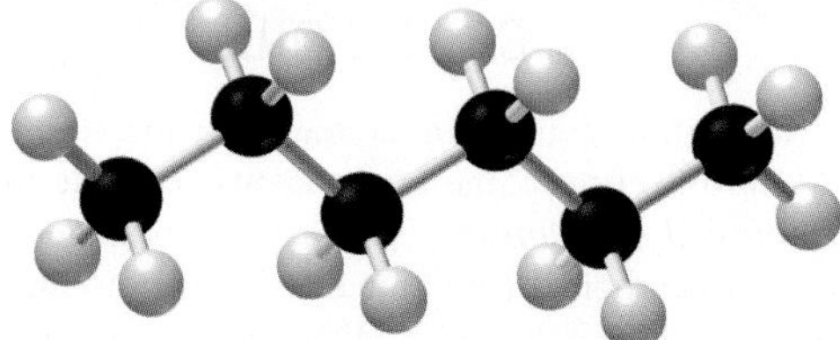

Expanded Structural Formula

```
    H   H   H   H   H   H
    |   |   |   |   |   |
H — C — C — C — C — C — C — H
    |   |   |   |   |   |
    H   H   H   H   H   H
```

Condensed Structural Formulas

```
     CH2     CH2     CH3
    /   \   /   \   /
 CH3     CH2     CH2
```

$CH_3-CH_2-CH_2-CH_2-CH_2-CH_3$

Skeletal Formula

A hexane molecule can be represented in several ways: molecular formula, ball-and-stick model, expanded structural formula, condensed structural formula, and skeletal formula.

CONCEPT CHECK 6.9 Drawing Expanded and Condensed Structural Formulas for Alkanes

Draw the expanded structural formula, condensed structural formula, and skeletal formula for butane.

ANSWER

A molecule of butane, C_4H_{10}, has four carbon atoms in a row. In the expanded structural formula, the four carbon atoms are connected to each other and to hydrogen atoms with single bonds to give each carbon atom a total of four bonds. In the condensed structural formula, the carbon and hydrogen atoms on the ends are written as CH_3- and the carbon and hydrogen atoms in the middle are written as $-CH_2-$. The skeletal formula shows the carbon skeleton as a zigzag line where the ends and corners represent C atoms.

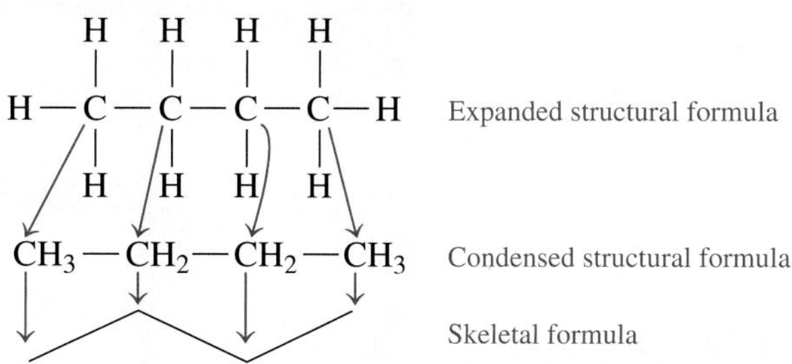

Properties of Alkanes

Many types of alkanes are the components of fuels that power our cars and oil that heats our homes. The first four alkanes—methane, ethane, propane, and butane—are gases at room temperature and are widely used as heating fuels.

Alkanes with 5–8 carbon atoms (pentane, hexane, heptane, and octane) are liquids at room temperature. They are highly volatile, which makes them useful in fuels such as gasoline.

Liquid alkanes with 9–17 carbon atoms have higher boiling points and are found in kerosene, diesel, and jet fuels. Motor oil is a mixture of liquid hydrocarbons and is used to lubricate the internal components of engines. Mineral oil is a mixture of liquid hydrocarbons and is used as a laxative and a lubricant. Alkanes with 18 or more carbon atoms are waxy solids at room temperature. Known as paraffins, these compounds are used in waxy coatings for fruits and vegetables to retain moisture, inhibit mold growth, and enhance appearance. Petrolatum, or Vaseline, is a semisolid mixture of liquid hydrocarbons with more than 25 carbon atoms used in ointments and cosmetics and as a lubricant.

The solid alkanes that make up waxy coatings on fruits and vegetables help to retain moisture, inhibit mold, and enhance appearance.

Chemistry Link to Industry

CRUDE OIL

Crude oil, or petroleum, contains a wide variety of hydrocarbons. At an oil refinery, the components in crude oil are separated by *fractional distillation*, a process that removes groups or fractions of hydrocarbons by continually heating the mixture to higher temperatures (see Table 6.15). Fractions containing alkanes with longer carbon chains require higher temperatures before they reach their boiling temperature and form gases. The gases are removed and passed through a distillation column where they cool and condense back to liquids. The major use of crude oil is to obtain gasoline. To increase the production of gasoline, heating oils are broken down using specialized catalysts to give the lower-weight alkanes.

TABLE 6.15 Typical Alkane Mixtures Obtained by Distillation of Crude Oil

Distillation Temperatures (°C)	Number of Carbon Atoms	Product
Below 30	1–4	Natural gas
30–200	5–12	Gasoline
200–250	12–16	Kerosene, jet fuel
250–350	16–18	Diesel fuel, heating oil
350–450	18–25	Lubricating oil
Nonvolatile residue	Over 25	Asphalt, tar

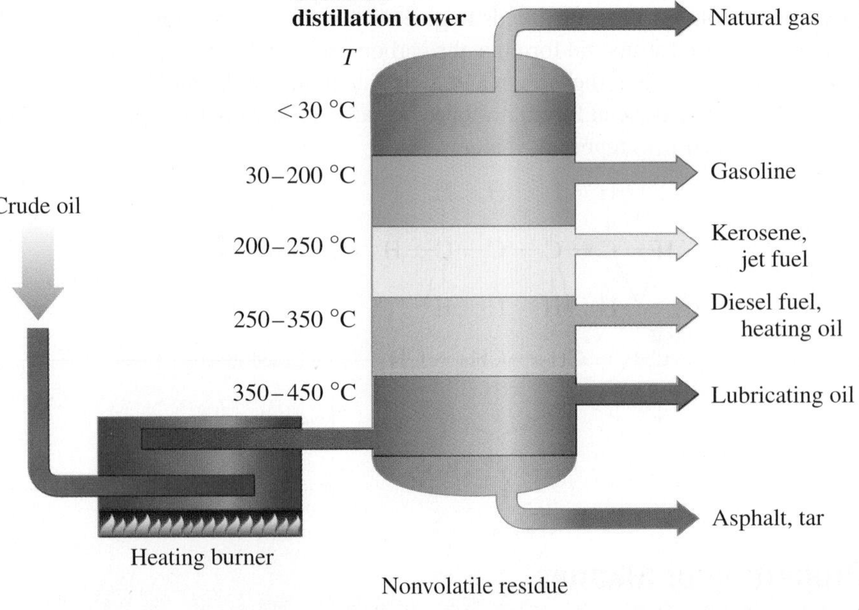

QUESTIONS AND PROBLEMS

6.7 Names and Formulas of Alkanes: Extended Topic

LEARNING GOAL: *Write the IUPAC name and draw the condensed structural formula for an alkane.*

6.65 Write the IUPAC name for each of the following alkanes:

a. $CH_3-CH_2-CH_2-CH_2-CH_3$
b. CH_3-CH_3
c. $CH_3-CH_2-CH_2-CH_2-CH_2-CH_3$

6.66 Write the IUPAC name for each of the following alkanes:

a. CH_4
b. $CH_3-CH_2-CH_2-CH_3$
c. $CH_3-CH_2-CH_2-CH_2-CH_2-CH_2-CH_3$

6.67 Draw the condensed structural formula for each of the following:

a. methane **b.** ethane **c.** pentane

6.68 Draw the condensed structural formula for each of the following:

a. propane **b.** hexane **c.** octane

6.69 Heptane, used as a solvent for rubber cement, has a density of 0.68 g/mL and boils at 98 °C.

a. What is the molecular formula of heptane?
b. Draw the condensed structural formula and the skeletal formula for heptane.
c. Is heptane a solid, liquid, or gas at room temperature?
d. Is heptane soluble in water?
e. Will heptane float or sink in water?

6.70 Nonane, a component of kerosene, has a density of 0.72 g/mL and boils at 151 °C.

a. What is the molecular formula of nonane?
b. Draw the condensed structural formula and the skeletal formula for nonane.
c. Is nonane a solid, liquid, or gas at room temperature?
d. Is nonane soluble in water?
e. Will nonane float or sink in water?

CHAPTER REVIEW

6.1 Ions: Transfer of Electrons

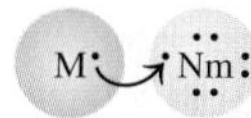

Transfer of electrons

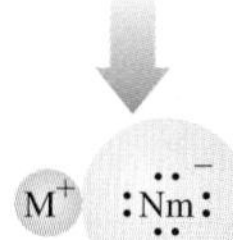

Ionic bond

LEARNING GOAL: *Write the symbols for the simple ions of the representative elements.*

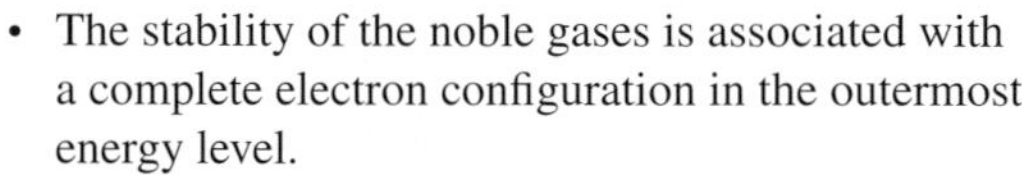

- The stability of the noble gases is associated with a complete electron configuration in the outermost energy level.

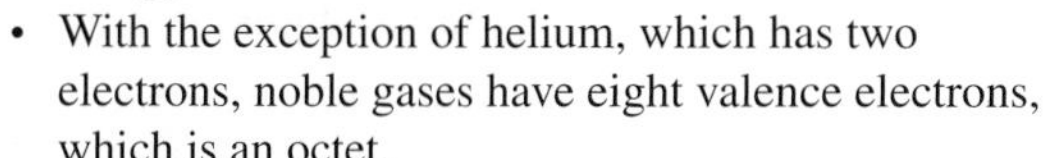

- With the exception of helium, which has two electrons, noble gases have eight valence electrons, which is an octet.

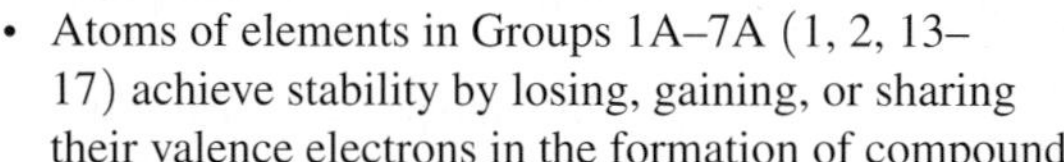

- Atoms of elements in Groups 1A–7A (1, 2, 13–17) achieve stability by losing, gaining, or sharing their valence electrons in the formation of compounds.

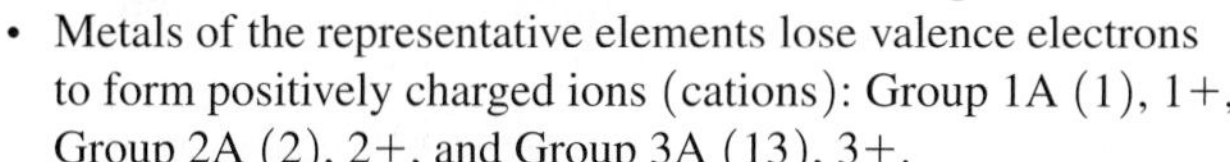

- Metals of the representative elements lose valence electrons to form positively charged ions (cations): Group 1A (1), 1+, Group 2A (2), 2+, and Group 3A (13), 3+.
- When reacting with metals, nonmetals gain electrons to form octets and form negatively charged ions (anions): Groups 5A (15), 3−, 6A (16), 2−, and 7A (17), 1−.

6.2 Writing Formulas for Ionic Compounds

LEARNING GOAL: *Using charge balance, write the correct formula for an ionic compound.*

- The total positive and negative ionic charge is balanced in the formula of an ionic compound.
- Charge balance in a formula is achieved by using subscripts after each symbol so that the overall charge is zero.

Sodium chloride

6.3 Naming Ionic Compounds

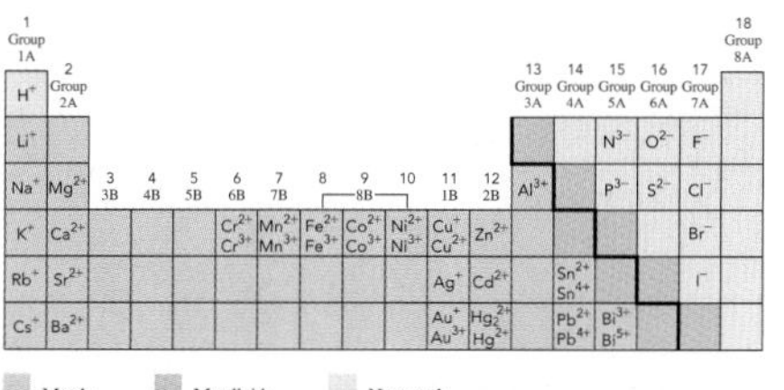

LEARNING GOAL: *Given the formula of an ionic compound, write the correct name; given the name of an ionic compound, write the correct formula.*

- In naming ionic compounds, the positive ion is given first, followed by the name of the negative ion.
- The names of ionic compounds containing two elements end with *ide*.
- Except for Ag, Cd, and Zn, transition elements form cations with two or more ionic charges.
- The charge of the cation is determined from the total negative charge in the formula and included as a Roman numeral immediately following the name of the metal.

6.4 Polyatomic Ions

LEARNING GOAL: *Write the name and formula for an ionic compound containing a polyatomic ion.*

- A polyatomic ion is a covalently bonded group of atoms with an electrical charge; for example, the carbonate ion has the formula CO_3^{2-}.
- Most polyatomic ions have names that end with *ate* or *ite*.
- Most polyatomic ions contain a nonmetal and one or more oxygen atoms.
- The ammonium ion, NH_4^+, is a positive polyatomic ion.
- When more than one polyatomic ion is used for charge balance, parentheses enclose the formula of the polyatomic ion.

6.5 Molecular Compounds: Sharing Electrons

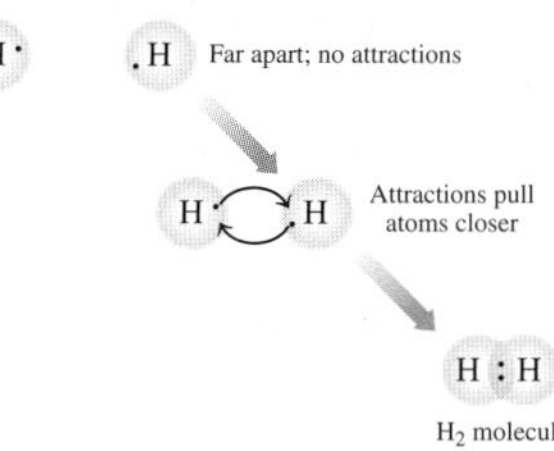

LEARNING GOAL: *Given the formula of a molecular compound, write its correct name; given the name of a molecular compound, write its formula.*

- In a covalent bond, atoms of nonmetals share valence electrons such that each atom has a stable electron configuration.
- The first nonmetal in a molecular compound uses its element name; the second nonmetal uses the first syllable of its element name followed by *ide*.
- The name of a molecular compound with two different atoms uses prefixes to indicate the subscripts in the formula.

6.6 Organic Compounds: Extended Topic

LEARNING GOAL: *Identify the properties characteristic of organic and inorganic compounds.*

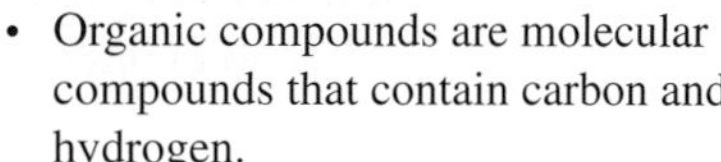

- Organic compounds are molecular compounds that contain carbon and hydrogen.

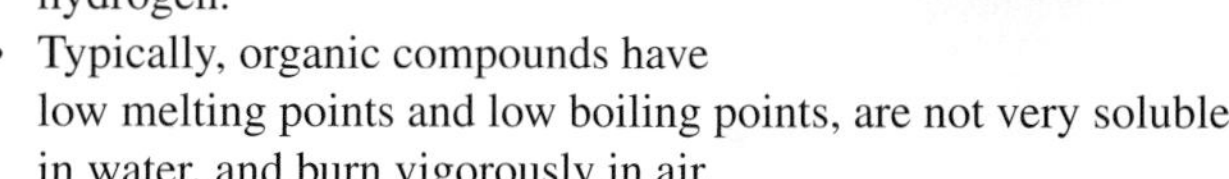

- Typically, organic compounds have low melting points and low boiling points, are not very soluble in water, and burn vigorously in air.
- In contrast, typical inorganic compounds are ionic compounds, have high melting and boiling points, are usually soluble in water, and do not burn in air.
- In organic compounds, carbon atoms share four valence electrons to form four covalent bonds.
- In the simplest organic molecule, methane, CH_4, the four hydrogen atoms bonded to the carbon atom are in the corners of a tetrahedron.

6.7 Names and Formulas of Alkanes: Extended Topic

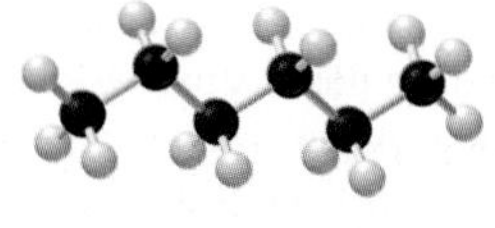

LEARNING GOAL: *Write the IUPAC name and draw the condensed structural formula for an alkane.*

- Alkanes are hydrocarbons that have only C—C single bonds.
- In the expanded structural formula, a separate line is drawn for every bonded atom.
- A condensed structural formula depicts each carbon atom and the number of attached hydrogen atoms.
- A skeletal formula shows the carbon atoms at the corners and ends of a zigzag chain.
- The IUPAC name of an alkane indicates the number of carbon atoms and ends in *ane*.

CONCEPT MAP

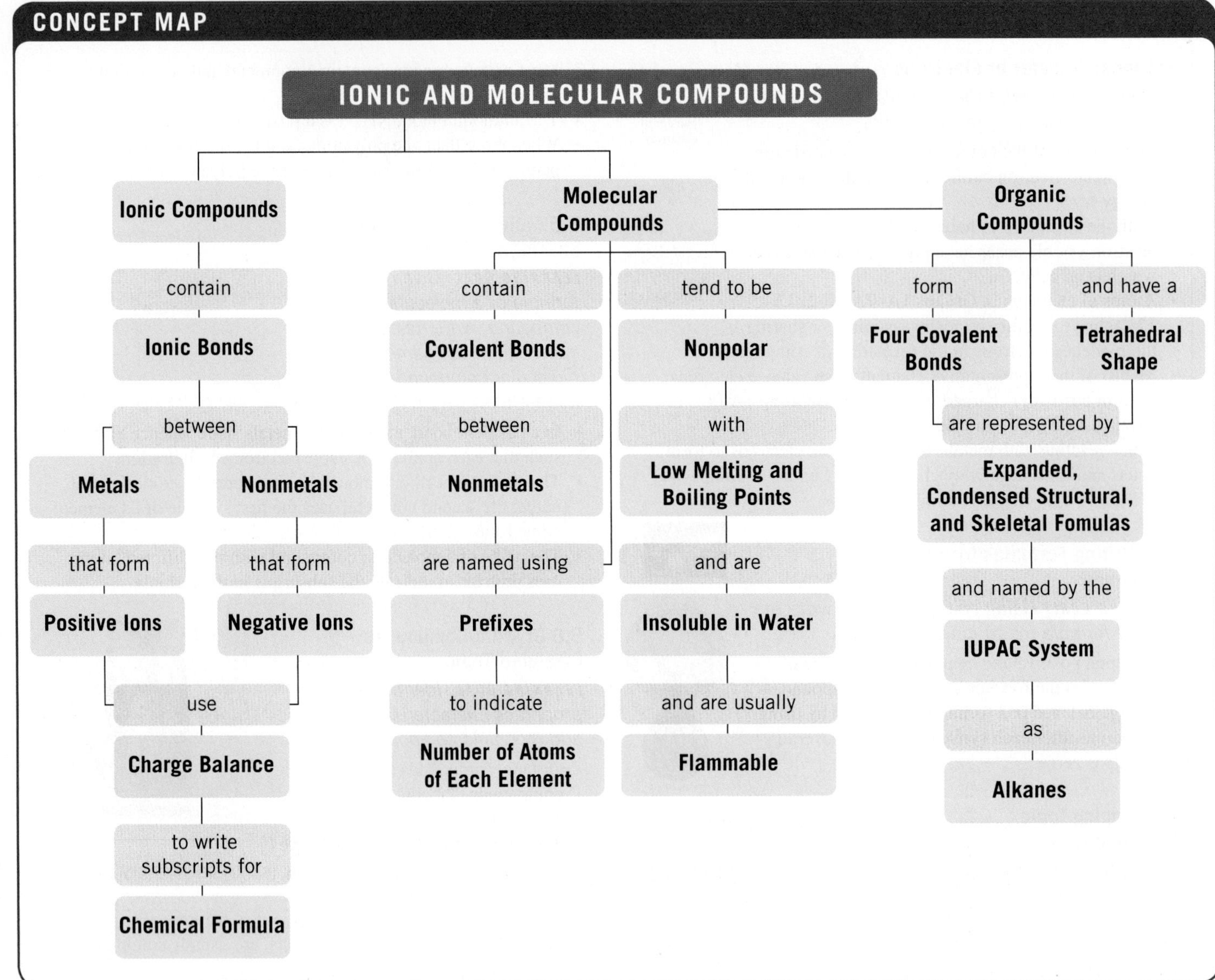

KEY TERMS

alkanes Hydrocarbons containing only single bonds between carbon atoms.

anion A negatively charged ion.

bonding pair A pair of electrons shared between two atoms.

cation A positively charged ion.

chemical formula The symbols and subscripts that represent the lowest whole-number ratio of atoms or ions in a compound.

condensed structural formula A structural formula that shows the arrangement of the carbon atoms in a molecule but groups each carbon atom with its bonded hydrogen atoms.

covalent bond A sharing of valence electrons by atoms.

expanded structural formula A type of structural formula that shows the arrangement of the atoms by drawing each bond between carbon atoms or between carbon and hydrogen.

hydrocarbons Organic compounds consisting of only carbon and hydrogen.

ion An atom or a group of atoms having an electrical charge because of a loss or gain of electrons.

ionic bond The attraction between oppositely charged ions.

ionic charge The difference between the number of protons (positive) and the number of electrons (negative), written in the upper right corner of the symbol for the ion.

ionic compound A compound of positive and negative ions held together by ionic bonds.

IUPAC system A system for naming organic compounds determined by the International Union of Pure and Applied Chemistry.

lone pair Electrons in a molecule that are not shared in a bond but complete the octet for an element.

molecular compound A combination of atoms in which noble gas configurations are attained by electron sharing.

molecule The smallest unit of two or more atoms held together by covalent bonds.

octet rule Representative elements react with other elements to produce a noble gas configuration with eight valence electrons.

organic compounds Compounds of carbon that have covalent bonds with properties that include low melting and boiling points, insolubility in water, and flammability.

polyatomic ion A group of covalently bonded atoms that has an overall electrical charge.

CORE CHEMISTRY SKILLS

The chapter section containing each Core Chemistry Skill is shown in parentheses at the end of each heading.

Writing Positive and Negative Ions (6.1)

- In the formation of an ionic bond, atoms of a metal lose and atoms of a nonmetal gain valence electrons to acquire a stable electron configuration, usually eight valence electrons.
- This tendency of atoms to attain a stable electron configuration is known as the octet rule.

Example: State the number of electrons lost or gained by atoms and the ion formed for each of the following to obtain a stable electron configuration:

a. Br **b.** Ca **c.** S

Answer: **a.** Br atoms will gain one electron to achieve a stable electron configuration, Br^-.
b. Ca atoms will lose two electrons to achieve a stable electron configuration, Ca^{2+}.
c. S atoms will gain two electrons to achieve a stable electron configuration, S^{2-}.

Writing Ionic Formulas (6.2, 6.4)

- The chemical formula of a compound represents the lowest whole-number ratio of the atoms or ions.
- In the chemical formula of an ionic compound, the sum of the positive and negative charges is always zero.
- Thus, in a chemical formula of an ionic compound, the total positive charge is equal to the total negative charge.

Example: Write the formula for magnesium phosphate.

Answer: Magnesium phosphate is an ionic compound that contains the ions Mg^{2+} and PO_4^{3-}.
Using charge balance, we determine the number(s) of each type of ion.

$$3(2+) + 2(3-) = 0$$

$3Mg^{2+}$ and $2PO_4^{3-}$ gives the formula: $Mg_3(PO_4)_2$

Naming Ionic Compounds (6.3, 6.4)

- In the name of an ionic compound made up of two elements, the name of the metal ion, which is written first, is the same as its element name.
- For metals that form two or more different ions, a Roman numeral that is equal to the ionic charge is placed in parentheses immediately after the name of the metal.
- The name of a nonmetal ion is obtained by using the first syllable of its element name followed by *ide.*
- The name of a polyatomic ion usually ends in *ate* or *ite*.

Example: What is the name for $PbSO_4$?

Answer: This compound contains the polyatomic ion SO_4^{2-}, which is sulfate with a 2− charge.
For charge balance, the positive ion must have a charge of 2+.

$$Pb? + (2-) = 0; \quad Pb = 2+$$

Because lead can form two different positive ions, a Roman numeral II is used in the name of the compound: lead(II) sulfate.

Writing the Names and Formulas for Molecular Compounds (6.5)

- When naming a molecular compound, the first nonmetal in the formula is named by its element name; the second nonmetal is named using the first syllable of its element name, followed by *ide*.
- When a subscript indicates two or more atoms of an element, a prefix is shown in front of its name.
- To write the molecular formula from the name, we use the symbol for each element and a subscript when a prefix indicates two or more atoms.

Example: Name the molecular compound BrF_5.

Answer: Two nonmetals share electrons and form a molecular compound. Br (first nonmetal) is bromine; F (second nonmetal) is fluoride. In the name for a molecular compound, prefixes indicate the subscripts in the formulas. The subscript 1 is understood for Br. The subscript 5 for fluoride is written with the prefix *penta*. The name is bromine pentafluoride.

Naming and Drawing Alkanes (6.7)

- The alkanes ethane, propane, and butane contain two, three, and four carbon atoms, respectively, connected in a row or a *continuous* chain.
- Alkanes with five or more carbon atoms in a chain are named using the prefixes *pent* (5), *hex* (6), *hept* (7), *oct* (8), *non* (9), and *dec* (10).
- In the condensed structural formula, the carbon and hydrogen atoms on the ends are written as $CH_3—$ and the carbon and hydrogen atoms in the middle are written as $—CH_2—$.

Example: **a.** What is the name of $CH_3—CH_2—CH_2—CH_3$?
b. Draw the condensed structural formula for pentane.

Answer: **a.** An alkane with a four-carbon chain is named with the prefix *but* followed by *ane*, which is butane.
b. Pentane is an alkane with a five-carbon chain. The carbon atoms on the ends are attached to 3 H atoms each, and the carbon atoms in the middle are attached to 2 H each. $CH_3—CH_2—CH_2—CH_2—CH_3$

UNDERSTANDING THE CONCEPTS

The chapter sections to review are shown in parentheses at the end of each question.

6.71 **a.** How does the octet rule explain the formation of a calcium ion? (6.1)
b. What is the electron configuration of the calcium ion?
c. Why are Group 1A (1) and Group 2A (2) elements found in many compounds but not Group 8A (18) elements?

6.72 **a.** How does the octet rule explain the formation of a sulfide ion? (6.1)
b. What is the electron configuration of the sulfide ion?
c. Why are Group 6A (16) elements found in many compounds but not Group 8A (18) elements?

6.73 Identify each of the following atoms or ions: (6.1)

a.	**b.**	**c.**	**d.**
18 e^-	8 e^-	28 e^-	23 e^-
15 p^+	8 p^+	30 p^+	26 p^+
16 n	8 n	35 n	28 n

6.74 Identify each of the following atoms or ions: (6.1)

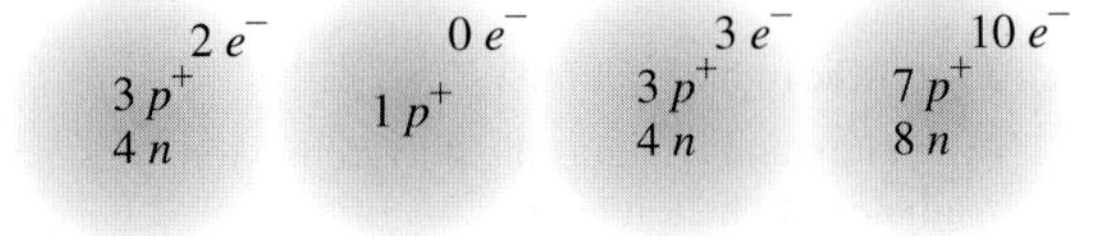

a.	b.	c.	d.
$2\,e^-$, $3\,p^+$, $4\,n$	$0\,e^-$, $1\,p^+$	$3\,e^-$, $3\,p^+$, $4\,n$	$10\,e^-$, $7\,p^+$, $8\,n$

6.75 Identify each of the following ions: (6.1)

a. 35 protons and 36 electrons
b. 47 protons and 46 electrons
c. 50 protons and 46 electrons

6.76 Identify each of the following ions: (6.1)

a. 28 protons and 26 electrons
b. 82 protons and 78 electrons
c. 34 protons and 36 electrons

6.77 Consider the following electron-dot symbols of representative elements X and Y: (6.1, 6.2)

X· and ·Ÿ·

a. What are the group numbers of X and Y?
b. Will a compound of X and Y be ionic or molecular?
c. What ions would be formed by X and Y?
d. What would be the formula of a compound of X and Y?
e. What would be the formula of a compound of X and chlorine?
f. What would be the formula of a compound of Y and sodium?
g. Is the compound in part **f** ionic or molecular?

6.78 Consider the following electron-dot symbols of representative elements X and Y: (6.1, 6.2)

·X· and ·Ÿ·

a. What are the group numbers of X and Y?
b. Will a compound of X and Y be ionic or molecular?
c. What ions would be formed by X and Y?
d. What would be the formula of a compound of X and Y?
e. What would be the formula of a compound of X and chlorine?
f. What would be the formula of a compound of Y and potassium?
g. Is the compound in part **f** ionic or molecular?

6.79 Use the period number and the electron-dot symbols in the following table to determine the elements and the formula and name of the ionic compound formed: (6.1, 6.2, 6.3)

Period	Electron-Dot Symbols	Elements	Formula of Compound	Name of Compound
2	X· and ·Ÿ·			
4	Ẋ· and :Ÿ·			
4	·Ẋ· and :Ÿ·			

6.80 Use the period number and the electron-dot symbols in the following table to determine the elements and the formula and name of the ionic compound formed: (6.1, 6.2, 6.3)

Period	Electron-Dot Symbols	Elements	Formula of Compound	Name of Compound
3	Ẋ· and ·Ÿ·			
3	·Ẋ· and :Ÿ·			
5	Ẋ· and :Ÿ·			

6.81 Write the ions, formulas, and names for the ionic compounds using the electron configuration of the elements. (6.1, 6.2, 6.3)

Electron Configurations		Symbols of Ions			
Metal	**Nonmetal**	**Cation**	**Anion**	**Formula of Compound**	**Name of Compound**
$1s^22s^22p^63s^2$	$1s^22s^22p^3$				
$1s^22s^22p^63s^23p^64s^1$	$1s^22s^22p^4$				
$1s^22s^22p^63s^23p^1$	$1s^22s^22p^5$				

6.82 Write the ions, formulas, and names for the ionic compounds using the electron configuration of the elements. (6.1, 6.2, 6.3)

Electron Configurations		Symbols of Ions			
Metal	**Nonmetal**	**Cation**	**Anion**	**Formula of Compound**	**Name of Compound**
$1s^22s^1$	$1s^22s^22p^63s^23p^4$				
$1s^22s^22p^63s^23p^64s^2$	$1s^22s^22p^63s^23p^3$				
$1s^22s^22p^63s^1$	$1s^22s^22p^63s^23p^5$				

6.83 Match the following physical and chemical properties with potassium chloride, KCl, used in salt substitutes, or butane, C_4H_{10}, used in lighters: (6.6)

a. melts at -138 °C
b. burns vigorously in air
c. melts at 770 °C
d. contains ionic bonds
e. is a gas at room temperature

6.84 Match the following physical and chemical properties with octane, C_8H_{18}, found in gasoline, or magnesium sulfate, $MgSO_4$, also called Epsom salts: (6.6)

a. contains only covalent bonds
b. melts at 1124 °C
c. is insoluble in water
d. is a liquid at room temperature
e. contains ions

6.85 Identify each of the following compounds as inorganic or organic and write the name: (6.3, 6.4, 6.5, 6.7)

a. C_7H_{16}
b. NO_2
c. K_3PO_4
d. C_2H_6

6.86 Identify each of the following compounds as inorganic or organic and write the name: (6.3, 6.4, 6.5, 6.7)

a. $Cr_2(SO_4)_3$
b. K_2S
c. PCl_5
d. $C_{10}H_{22}$

ADDITIONAL QUESTIONS AND PROBLEMS

6.87 Consider an ion with the symbol X^{2+} formed from a representative element. (6.1, 6.2, 6.3)
a. What is the group number of the element?
b. What is the electron-dot symbol of the element?
c. If X is in Period 2, what is the element?
d. What is the formula of the compound formed from X and the nitride ion?

6.88 Consider an ion with the symbol Y^{3-} formed from a representative element. (6.1, 6.2, 6.3)
a. What is the group number of the element?
b. What is the electron-dot symbol of the element?
c. If Y is in Period 3, what is the element?
d. What is the formula of the compound formed from the barium ion and Y?

6.89 One of the ions of tin is tin(IV). (6.1, 6.2, 6.4)
a. What is the symbol for this ion?
b. How many protons and electrons are in the ion?
c. What is the formula of tin(IV) oxide?
d. What is the formula of tin(IV) phosphate?

6.90 One of the ions of gold is gold(III). (6.1, 6.2, 6.4)
a. What is the symbol for this ion?
b. How many protons and electrons are in the ion?
c. What is the formula of gold(III) sulfate?
d. What is the formula of gold(III) chloride?

6.91 Identify the group number in the periodic table of X, a representative element, in each of the following ionic compounds: (6.2, 6.4)
a. XCl_3 **b.** Al_2X_3 **c.** XCO_3

6.92 Identify the group number in the periodic table of X, a representative element, in each of the following ionic compounds: (6.2, 6.4)
a. X_2O_3 **b.** X_2SO_3 **c.** Na_3X

6.93 Name each of the following ionic compounds: (6.3, 6.4, 6.5)
a. $FeBr_3$ **b.** $Ca_3(PO_4)_2$ **c.** $Al_2(CO_3)_3$
d. $PbCl_4$ **e.** $Mg(ClO_3)_2$ **f.** $SnSO_4$
g. CuS

6.94 Name each of the following ionic compounds: (6.3, 6.4, 6.5)
a. $CaSO_4$ **b.** $Ba(NO_3)_2$ **c.** MnS
d. $LiClO_4$ **e.** $CrPO_3$ **f.** Na_2HPO_4
g. $NiCl_2$

6.95 Write the formula for each of the following ionic compounds: (6.3, 6.4, 6.5)
a. copper(I) nitride
b. potassium hydrogen sulfite
c. lead(IV) sulfide
d. gold(III) carbonate
e. zinc perchlorate

6.96 Write the formula for each of the following ionic compounds: (6.3, 6.4, 6.5)
a. iron(III) nitrate
b. copper(II) hydrogen carbonate
c. tin(IV) sulfite
d. barium dihydrogen phosphate
e. cadmium hypochlorite

6.97 Write the formula for each of the following ionic compounds: (6.3, 6.4, 6.5)
a. nickel(III) chloride **b.** lead(IV) oxide
c. silver bromide **d.** calcium nitride
e. copper(I) phosphide **f.** chromium(II) sulfide

6.98 Write the formula for each of the following ionic compounds: (6.3, 6.4, 6.5)
a. tin(II) oxide **b.** bismuth(III) chloride
c. cobalt(II) sulfide **d.** chromium(III) iodide
e. lithium nitride **f.** gold(I) oxide

6.99 Write the name for each of the following ionic compounds: (6.3, 6.4, 6.5)
a. MgO **b.** $Cr(HCO_3)_3$ **c.** $Mn_2(CrO_4)_3$

6.100 Write the name for each of the following ionic compounds: (6.3, 6.4, 6.5)
a. Cu_2S **b.** $Fe_3(PO_4)_2$ **c.** $Ca(ClO)_2$

6.101 Name each of the following molecular compounds: (6.5)
a. NCl_3 **b.** N_2S_3 **c.** N_2O
d. IF **e.** PF_5 **f.** P_2O_5

6.102 Name each of the following molecular compounds: (6.5)
a. CBr_4 **b.** SF_6 **c.** BrCl
d. N_2O_4 **e.** SO_2 **f.** CS_2

6.103 Write the formula for each of the following molecular compounds: (6.5)
a. iodine heptafluoride
b. boron trifluoride
c. hydrogen iodide
d. sulfur dichloride

6.104 Write the formula for each of the following molecular compounds: (6.5)
a. diphosphorus pentasulfide
b. carbon tetraiodide
c. sulfur trioxide
d. dinitrogen difluoride

6.105 Classify each of the following as an ionic or molecular compound, and write its name: (6.3, 6.4, 6.5)
a. $CoCl_3$ **b.** Na_2SO_4 **c.** N_2O_3
d. LiBr **e.** ICl_3 **f.** CF_4

6.106 Classify each of the following as an ionic or molecular compound, and write its name: (6.3, 6.4, 6.5)
a. $Al_2(CO_3)_3$ **b.** ClF_5 **c.** S_2O
d. Mg_3N_2 **e.** ClO_2 **f.** $CrPO_4$

6.107 Write the formula for each of the following: (6.3, 6.4, 6.5)
a. tin(II) carbonate **b.** lithium phosphide
c. silicon tetrachloride **d.** chromium(II) sulfide
e. carbon dioxide **f.** calcium bromide
g. pentane

6.108 Write the formula for each of the following: (6.3, 6.4, 6.5)
a. sodium carbonate **b.** nitrogen dioxide
c. aluminum nitrate **d.** cobalt(II) nitride
e. potassium phosphate **f.** manganese(III) fluoride
g. nonane

CHALLENGE QUESTIONS

6.109 Indicate the type of compound (ionic or molecular) and complete the table: (6.3, 6.4, 6.5)

Formula of Compound	Type of Compound	Name of Compound
$FeSO_4$		
		Silicon dioxide
		Ammonium nitrate
$Al_2(SO_4)_3$		
		Cobalt(III) sulfide

6.110 Indicate the type of compound (ionic or molecular) and complete the table: (6.3, 6.4, 6.5)

Formula of Compound	Type of Compound	Name of Compound
$NaHSO_3$		
		Dinitrogen trioxide
		Magnesium hydrogen phosphate
Mn_2O_3		
		Lithium fluoride

6.111 Classify each of the following compounds as inorganic or organic, and name each: (6.3, 6.4, 6.5, 6.6, 6.7)
a. Li_2O **b.** $CH_3—CH_2—CH_3$ **c.** SiF_4
d. CH_4 **e.** MgF_2 **f.** C_4H_{10}

6.112 Classify each of the following compounds as inorganic or organic, and name each: (6.3, 6.4, 6.5, 6.6, 6.7)
a. $FeCl_2$ **b.** C_7H_{16} **c.** SF_4
d. $Ca_3(PO_4)_2$ **e.** PCl_3 **f.** $Al(NO_3)_3$

6.113 When sodium reacts with sulfur, an ionic compound forms. If a sample of this compound contains 4.8×10^{22} sodium ions, how many sulfide ions does it contain? (6.1)

6.114 When magnesium reacts with nitrogen, an ionic compound forms. If a sample of this compound contains 1.6×10^{23} magnesium ions, how many nitride ions does it contain? (6.1)

6.115 Draw the condensed structural and skeletal formula for each of the following: (6.7)
a. propane **b.** hexane

6.116 Draw the condensed structural and skeletal formula for each of the following: (6.7)
a. butane **b.** heptane

ANSWERS

Answers to Study Checks

6.1 a. metal
b. one valence electron
c. loses 1 e^-
d. K^+, potassium ion
e. $1s^22s^22p^63s^23p^6$

6.2 gallium sulfide

6.3 manganese(III) sulfide

6.4 Cr_2O_3

6.5 $(NH_4)_3PO_4$

6.6 calcium phosphate

6.7 iron(II) nitrate

6.8 a. silicon tetrabromide **b.** dibromine oxide

6.9 IF_7

6.10 octane

Answers to Selected Questions and Problems

6.1 a. 1 **b.** 2 **c.** 3 **d.** 1

6.3 a. $1s^2$ **b.** $1s^22s^22p^6$
c. $1s^22s^22p^63s^23p^63d^{10}$ **d.** $1s^22s^22p^63s^23p^6$

6.5 a. lose 2 e^- **b.** gain 3 e^-
c. gain 1 e^- **d.** lose 1 e^-

6.7 a. Li^+ **b.** I^-
c. Sr^{2+} **d.** Fe^{3+}

6.9 a. 8 protons, 10 electrons **b.** 19 protons, 18 electrons
c. 35 protons, 36 electrons **d.** 16 protons, 18 electrons

6.11 a. Cl^- **b.** Ba^{2+} **c.** Al^{3+} **d.** Se^{2-}

6.13 a and **c**

6.15 a. Na_2O **b.** $AlBr_3$ **c.** Ba_3N_2 **d.** MgF_2 **e.** Al_2S_3

6.17 a. K^+, S^{2-} K_2S **b.** Na^+, N^{3-} Na_3N
c. Al^{3+}, I^- AlI_3 **d.** Ga^{3+}, O^{2-} Ga_2O_3

6.19 a. aluminum oxide **b.** cesium sulfide
c. sodium oxide **d.** magnesium phosphide
e. potassium iodide **f.** barium fluoride

6.21 Most of the transition elements form more than one positive ion. The specific ion is indicated in a name by writing a Roman numeral that is the same as the ionic charge. For example, iron forms Fe^{2+} and Fe^{3+} ions, which are named iron(II) and iron(III).

6.23 a. iron(II) **b.** copper(II)
c. zinc **d.** lead(IV)
e. chromium(III) **f.** manganese(II)

6.25 a. tin(II) chloride **b.** iron(II) oxide
c. copper(I) sulfide **d.** copper(II) sulfide
e. cadmium bromide **f.** mercury(II) chloride

6.27 a. Au^{3+} **b.** Cr^{2+} **c.** Pb^{4+} **d.** Sn^{2+}

6.29 a. $MgCl_2$ **b.** Na_2S **c.** Cu_2O **d.** Zn_3P_2
e. AuN **f.** CoF_3

6.31 a. $CoCl_3$ **b.** PbO_2 **c.** AgI **d.** Ca_3N_2
e. Cu_3P **f.** $CrCl_2$

6.33 **a.** HCO_3^- **b.** NH_4^+ **c.** PO_4^{3-} **d.** HSO_4^- **e.** ClO^-

6.35 **a.** sulfate **b.** carbonate **c.** phosphate
d. nitrate **e.** perchlorate

6.37

	NO_2^-	CO_3^{2-}	HSO_4^-	PO_4^{3-}
Li^+	$LiNO_2$	Li_2CO_3	$LiHSO_4$	Li_3PO_4
	Lithium nitrite	Lithium carbonate	Lithium hydrogen sulfate	Lithium phosphate
Cu^{2+}	$Cu(NO_2)_2$	$CuCO_3$	$Cu(HSO_4)_2$	$Cu_3(PO_4)_2$
	Copper(II) nitrite	Copper(II) carbonate	Copper(II) hydrogen sulfate	Copper(II) phosphate
Ba^{2+}	$Ba(NO_2)_2$	$BaCO_3$	$Ba(HSO_4)_2$	$Ba_3(PO_4)_2$
	Barium nitrite	Barium carbonate	Barium hydrogen sulfate	Barium phosphate

6.39 **a.** CO_3^{2-}, sodium carbonate
b. NH_4^+, ammonium chloride
c. PO_3^{3-}, sodium phosphite
d. NO_2^-, manganese(II) nitrite
e. SO_3^{2-}, iron(II) sulfite
f. $C_2H_3O_2^-$, potassium acetate

6.41 **a.** $Ba(OH)_2$ **b.** $NaHSO_3$
c. $Fe(NO_3)_2$ **d.** $Zn_3(PO_4)_2$
e. $Fe_2(CO_3)_3$

6.43 **a.** aluminum sulfate **b.** magnesium phosphate
c. chromium(III) oxide **d.** sodium phosphate
e. ammonium sulfate **f.** bismuth(III) sulfide

6.45 The nonmetallic elements are most likely to form covalent bonds and therefore molecular compounds.

6.47 **a.** 2 valence electrons, 1 bonding pair and 0 lone pairs
b. 8 valence electrons, 1 bonding pair and 3 lone pairs
c. 14 valence electrons, 1 bonding pair and 6 lone pairs

6.49 **a.** phosphorus tribromide **b.** carbon tetrabromide
c. silicon dioxide **d.** hydrogen fluoride
e. nitrogen triiodide

6.51 **a.** dinitrogen trioxide **b.** nitrogen trichloride
c. silicon tetrabromide **d.** phosphorus pentachloride
e. dinitrogen trisulfide

6.53 **a.** CCl_4 **b.** CO **c.** PCl_3 **d.** N_2O_4

6.55 **a.** OF_2 **b.** BF_3 **c.** N_2O_3 **d.** SF_6

6.57 **a.** aluminum chloride **b.** diboron trioxide
c. dinitrogen tetroxide **d.** tin(II) nitrate
e. copper(II) chlorite

6.59 **a.** inorganic **b.** organic
c. organic **d.** inorganic
e. inorganic **f.** organic

6.61 **a.** inorganic **b.** organic
c. organic **d.** inorganic

6.63 **a.** ethane **b.** ethane
c. NaBr **d.** NaBr

6.65 **a.** pentane **b.** ethane
c. hexane

6.67 **a.** CH_4
b. $CH_3{-}CH_3$
c. $CH_3{-}CH_2{-}CH_2{-}CH_2{-}CH_3$

6.69 **a.** C_7H_{16}
b. $CH_3{-}CH_2{-}CH_2{-}CH_2{-}CH_2{-}CH_2{-}CH_3$ 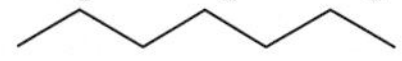
c. liquid
d. no
e. float

6.71 **a.** By losing two valence electrons from the fourth energy level, calcium achieves an octet in the third energy level.
b. $1s^22s^22p^63s^23p^6$
c. Group 1A (1) and 2A (2) elements acquire octets by losing electrons when they form compounds. Group 8A (18) elements are stable with octets (or two electrons for helium).

6.73 **a.** P^{3-} ion **b.** O atom
c. Zn^{2+} ion **d.** Fe^{3+} ion

6.75 **a.** Br^- **b.** Ag^+
c. Sn^{4+}

6.77 **a.** X = 1A(1); Y = 6A(16) **b.** ionic
c. X^+, Y^{2-} **d.** X_2Y
e. XCl **f.** Na_2Y
g. ionic

6.79

Period	Electron-Dot Symbols	Elements	Formula of Compound	Name of Compound
2	X· and ·Ÿ·	Li and N	Li_3N	Lithium nitride
4	Ẋ· and :Ÿ·	Ca and Br	$CaBr_2$	Calcium bromide
4	·Ẋ· and :Ÿ·	Ga and Se	Ga_2Se_3	Gallium selenide

6.81

Electron Configurations		Symbols of Ions			
Metal	Nonmetal	Cation	Anion	Formula of Compound	Name of Compound
$1s^22s^22p^63s^2$	$1s^22s^22p^3$	Mg^{2+}	N^{3-}	Mg_3N_2	Magnesium nitride
$1s^22s^22p^63s^23p^64s^1$	$1s^22s^22p^4$	K^+	O^{2-}	K_2O	Potassium oxide
$1s^22s^22p^63s^23p^1$	$1s^22s^22p^5$	Al^{3+}	F^-	AlF_3	Aluminum fluoride

6.83 **a.** butane **b.** butane
c. potassium chloride **d.** potassium chloride
e. butane

6.85 **a.** organic, heptane
b. inorganic, nitrogen dioxide
c. inorganic, potassium phosphate
d. organic, ethane

6.87 **a.** 2A (2) **b.** ·X·
c. Be **d.** X_3N_2

6.89 **a.** Sn^{4+}
b. 50 protons, 46 electrons
c. SnO_2
d. $Sn_3(PO_4)_4$

6.91 **a.** 3A (13) **b.** 6A (16)
c. 2A (2)

6.93 **a.** iron(III) bromide
b. calcium phosphate
c. aluminum carbonate
d. lead(IV) chloride
e. magnesium chlorate
f. tin(II) sulfate
g. copper(II) sulfide

6.95 **a.** Cu_3N **b.** $KHSO_3$
c. PbS_2 **d.** $Au_2(CO_3)_3$
e. $Zn(ClO_4)_2$

6.97 **a.** $NiCl_3$ **b.** PbO_2
c. AgBr **d.** Ca_3N_2
e. Cu_3P **f.** CrS

6.99 **a.** magnesium oxide
b. chromium(III) hydrogen carbonate or chromium(III) bicarbonate
c. manganese(III) chromate

6.101 **a.** nitrogen trichloride
b. dinitrogen trisulfide
c. dinitrogen oxide
d. iodine fluoride
e. phosphorus pentafluoride
f. diphosphorus pentoxide

6.103 **a.** IF_7 **b.** BF_3
c. HI **d.** SCl_2

6.105 **a.** ionic, cobalt(III) chloride
b. ionic, sodium sulfate
c. molecular, dinitrogen trioxide
d. ionic, lithium bromide
e. molecular, iodine trichloride
f. molecular, carbon tetrafluoride

6.107 **a.** $SnCO_3$ **b.** Li_3P
c. $SiCl_4$ **d.** CrS
e. CO_2 **f.** $CaBr_2$
g. $CH_3{-}CH_2{-}CH_2{-}CH_2{-}CH_3$, C_5H_{12}

6.109

Formula of Compound	Type of Compound	Name of Compound
$FeSO_4$	Ionic	Iron(II) sulfate
SiO_2	Molecular	Silicon dioxide
NH_4NO_3	Ionic	Ammonium nitrate
$Al_2(SO_4)_3$	Ionic	Aluminum sulfate
Co_2S_3	Ionic	Cobalt(III) sulfide

6.111 **a.** inorganic, lithium oxide
b. organic, propane
c. inorganic, silicon tetrafluoride
d. organic, methane
e. inorganic, magnesium fluoride
f. organic, butane

6.113 2.4×10^{22} S^{2-} ions

6.115 **a.** $CH_3{-}CH_2{-}CH_3$
b. $CH_3{-}CH_2{-}CH_2{-}CH_2{-}CH_2{-}CH_3$

Chemical Quantities 7

LOOKING AHEAD

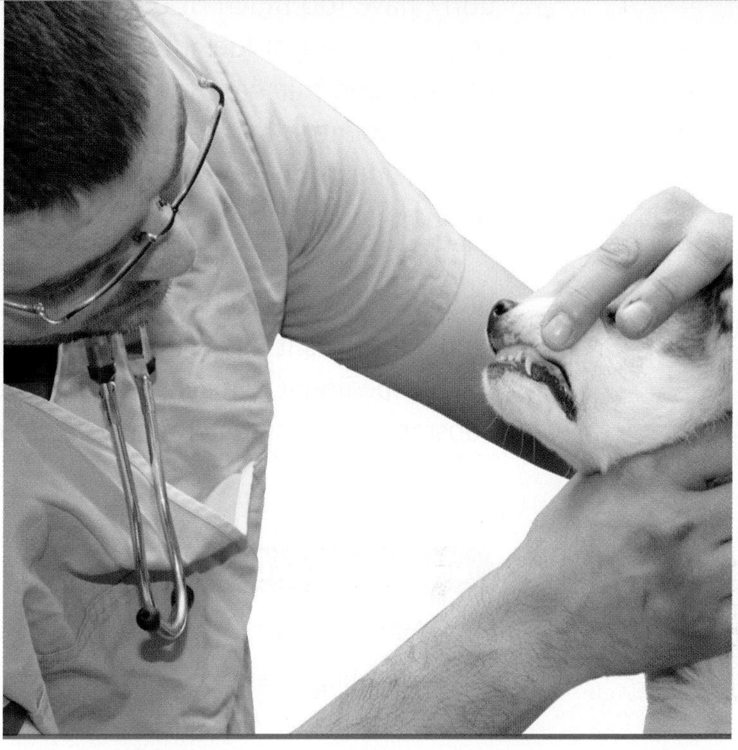

Max, a six-year-old dog, is listless, drinking large amounts of water, and not eating his food. His owner takes Max to his veterinarian, Sean, for an examination. Sean weighs Max and obtains a blood sample for a blood chemistry profile, which determines the overall health, detects any metabolic disorders, and measures the concentration of electrolytes.

The results of the lab tests for Max indicate that the white blood count is elevated, which may indicate an infection or inflammation. His electrolytes, which are also indicators of good health, were all in the normal ranges. The electrolyte chloride (Cl^-) was in the normal range of 0.106–0.118 mol/L, and the electrolyte sodium (Na^+) has a normal range of 0.144–0.160 mol/L. Potassium (K^+), another important electrolyte, has a normal range of 0.0035–0.0058 mol/L. To treat the possible infection, Sean ordered 375 mg tablets of Clavamox, which is a broad-spectrum antibiotic approved for veterinary use in dogs.

Career: Veterinarian

Veterinarians care for domesticated pets such as rats, birds, dogs, and cats. Some veterinarians specialize in the treatment of large animals, such as horses and cattle. Veterinarians interact with pet owners as they give advice about feeding, behavior, and breeding. In the assessment of an ill animal, they record the animal's symptoms and medical history including dietary intake, medications, eating habits, weight, and any signs of disease.

To diagnose health problems, veterinarians perform laboratory tests on animals including a complete blood count and urinalysis. They also obtain tissue and blood samples, as well as vaccinate against distemper, rabies, and other diseases. Veterinarians prescribe medication if an animal has an infection or illness. If an animal is injured, a veterinarian treats wounds, and sets fractures. A veterinarian also performs surgery such as neutering and spaying, provides dental cleanings, removes tumors, and euthanizes animals.

In chemistry, we calculate and measure the amounts of substances to use in the lab. Actually, measuring the amount of a substance is something you do every day. When you cook, you measure out the proper amounts of ingredients so that you don't have too much of one and too little of another. At the gas station, you pump a certain amount of fuel into your gas tank. If you paint the walls of a room, you measure the area and purchase the amount of paint that will cover the walls. If you take a pain reliever, you read the label to see how many tablets of aspirin or ibuprofen are needed. You read the nutrition label on food packaging to determine the quantities of carbohydrate, fat, sodium, iron, or zinc.

Each substance that we use in the chemistry lab is measured so that it functions properly in an experiment. The chemical formula of a substance tells us the number and kinds of atoms it has, which we then use to determine the mass of the substance to use in an experiment. Similarly, when we know the percentage and mass of the elements in a substance, we can determine its formula.

CHAPTER READINESS*

Key Math Skills

- Calculating a Percentage (1.4C)
- Solving Equations (1.4D)
- Using Scientific Notation (2.2)

Core Chemistry Skills

- Counting Significant Figures (2.3)
- Using Significant Figures in Calculations (2.4)
- Writing Conversion Factors from Equalities (2.6)
- Using Conversion Factors (2.7)

*These Key Math Skills and Core Chemistry Skills from previous chapters are listed here for your review as you proceed to the new material in this chapter.

LEARNING GOAL

Use Avogadro's number to determine the number of particles in a given number of moles.

7.1 The Mole

At the grocery store, you buy eggs by the dozen or soda by the case. In an office-supply store, pencils are ordered by the gross and paper by the ream. Common terms such as *dozen*, *case*, *gross*, and *ream* are used to count the number of items present. For example, when you buy a dozen eggs, you know you will get 12 eggs in the carton.

CORE CHEMISTRY SKILL

Converting Particles to Moles

Avogadro's Number

In chemistry, particles such as atoms, molecules, and ions are counted by the **mole** (abbreviated *mol* in calculations), a unit called **Avogadro's number** that contains 6.022×10^{23} items. Avogadro's number is a very big number because atoms are so small that it takes an extremely large number of atoms to provide a sufficient amount to weigh and use in chemical reactions. Avogadro's number is named for Amedeo Avogadro (1776–1856), an Italian physicist.

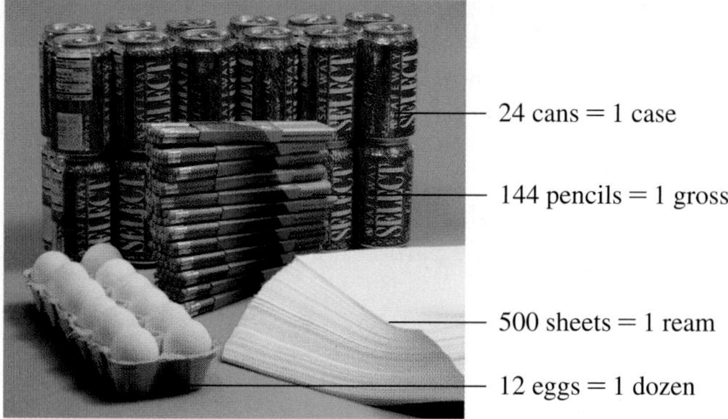

Collections of items include dozen, gross, and mole.

$$6.022 \times 10^{23} = 602\,200\,000\,000\,000\,000\,000\,000$$

One mole of any element always contains Avogadro's number of atoms. For example, 1 mol of carbon contains 6.022×10^{23} carbon atoms; 1 mol of aluminum contains 6.022×10^{23} aluminum atoms; 1 mol of sulfur contains 6.022×10^{23} sulfur atoms.

One mol of sulfur contains 6.022×10^{23} sulfur atoms.

1 mol of an element $= 6.022 \times 10^{23}$ atoms of that element

Avogadro's number tells us that 1 mol of a compound contains 6.022×10^{23} of the particular type of particles that make up that compound. One mol of a molecular compound contains Avogadro's number of molecules. For example, 1 mol of CO_2 contains 6.022×10^{23} molecules of CO_2. For an ionic compound, 1 mol contains Avogadro's number of **formula units**, which are the groups of ions represented by its formula. For the ionic formula, NaCl, 1 mol contains 6.022×10^{23} formula units of NaCl (Na^+, Cl^-). Table 7.1 gives examples of the number of particles in some 1-mol quantities.

TABLE 7.1 Number of Particles in 1-Mol Quantities

Substance	Number and Type of Particles
1 mol of Al	6.022×10^{23} atoms of Al
1 mol of Fe	6.022×10^{23} atoms of Fe
1 mol of water (H_2O)	6.022×10^{23} molecules of H_2O
1 mol of vitamin C ($C_6H_8O_6$)	6.022×10^{23} molecules of vitamin C
1 mol of NaCl	6.022×10^{23} formula units of NaCl

We can use Avogadro's number as a conversion factor to convert between the moles of a substance and the number of particles it contains.

$$\frac{6.022 \times 10^{23} \text{ particles}}{1 \text{ mol}} \quad \text{and} \quad \frac{1 \text{ mol}}{6.022 \times 10^{23} \text{ particles}}$$

For example, we use Avogadro's number to convert 4.00 mol of iron to atoms of iron.

$$4.00 \cancel{\text{mol Fe}} \times \frac{6.022 \times 10^{23} \text{ atoms Fe}}{1 \cancel{\text{mol Fe}}} = 2.41 \times 10^{24} \text{ atoms of Fe}$$

Avogadro's number as a conversion factor

We can also use Avogadro's number to convert 3.01×10^{24} molecules of CO_2 to moles of CO_2.

$$3.01 \times 10^{24} \cancel{\text{molecules } CO_2} \times \frac{1 \text{ mol } CO_2 \text{ molecules}}{6.022 \times 10^{23} \cancel{\text{molecules } CO_2}} = 5.00 \text{ mol of } CO_2 \text{ molecules}$$

Avogadro's number as a conversion factor

In calculations that convert between moles and particles, the number of moles will be small compared to the number of atoms or molecules, which will be large.

CONCEPT CHECK 7.1 Moles and Particles

Explain why 0.20 mol of aluminum is a small number, but the number of atoms in 0.20 mol is a large number: 1.2×10^{23} atoms of aluminum.

ANSWER

The term *mole*, abbreviated *mol*, is a unit that represents 6.022×10^{23} particles. Because atoms are submicroscopic particles, a large number of atoms are present in 1 mol of aluminum.

SAMPLE PROBLEM 7.1 Calculating the Number of Molecules

How many molecules are present in 1.75 mol of carbon dioxide?

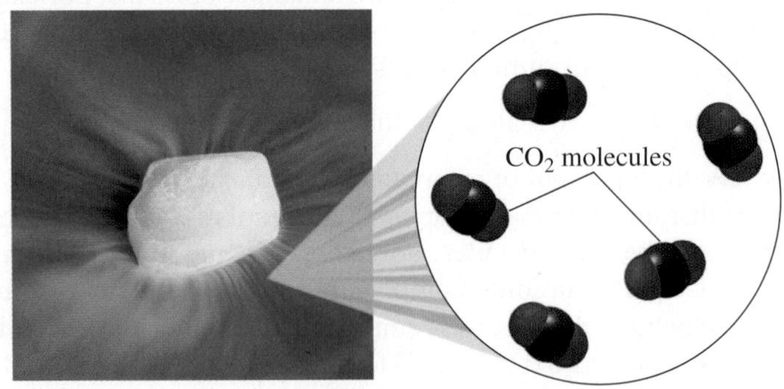

The solid form of carbon dioxide is known as "dry ice."

SOLUTION

Step 1 State the given and needed quantities.

Analyze the Problem	Given	Need
	1.75 mol of CO_2	molecules of CO_2

Step 2 Write a plan to convert moles to atoms or molecules.

moles of CO_2 → Avogadro's number → molecules of CO_2

Step 3 Use Avogadro's number to write conversion factors.

$$1 \text{ mol of } CO_2 = 6.022 \times 10^{23} \text{ molecules of } CO_2$$

$$\frac{6.022 \times 10^{23} \text{ molecules } CO_2}{1 \text{ mol } CO_2} \quad \text{and} \quad \frac{1 \text{ mol } CO_2}{6.022 \times 10^{23} \text{ molecules } CO_2}$$

Step 4 Set up the problem to calculate the number of particles.

$$1.75 \cancel{\text{mol } CO_2} \times \frac{6.022 \times 10^{23} \text{ molecules } CO_2}{1 \cancel{\text{mol } CO_2}} = 1.05 \times 10^{24} \text{ molecules of } CO_2$$

STUDY CHECK 7.1

How many moles of water, H_2O, contain 2.60×10^{23} molecules of water?

Guide to Calculating the Atoms or Molecules of a Substance

1. State the given and needed quantities.
2. Write a plan to convert moles to atoms or molecules.
3. Use Avogadro's number to write conversion factors.
4. Set up the problem to calculate the number of particles.

Moles of Elements in a Chemical Formula

We have seen that the subscripts in a chemical formula indicate the number of atoms of each type of element in a compound. For example, one molecule of NH_3 consists of 1 N atom and 3 H atoms. If we have 6.022×10^{23} molecules (1 mol) of NH_3, it would contain 6.022×10^{23} atoms (1 mol) of N and $3 \times 6.022 \times 10^{23}$ atoms (3 mol) of H. Thus, each subscript in a formula also refers to the moles of each kind of atom in 1 mol of a compound. For example, the subscripts in the NH_3 formula specify that 1 mol of NH_3 molecules contains 1 mol of N atoms and 3 mol of H atoms.

The chemical formula subscripts specify the

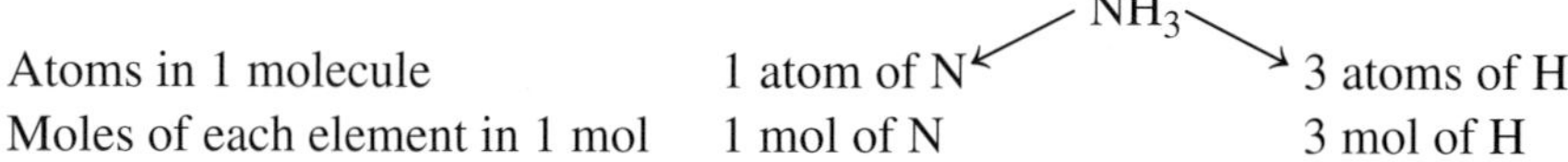

	NH_3	
Atoms in 1 molecule	1 atom of N	3 atoms of H
Moles of each element in 1 mol	1 mol of N	3 mol of H

Aspirin, $C_9H_8O_4$, is a drug used to reduce pain and inflammation in the body. Using the subscripts in the chemical formula of aspirin shows that there are 9 carbon atoms, 8 hydrogen atoms, and 4 oxygen atoms. The subscripts of the formula of aspirin, $C_9H_8O_4$, also tell us the number of moles of each element in 1 mol of aspirin: 9 mol of C atoms, 8 mol of H atoms, and 4 mol of O atoms.

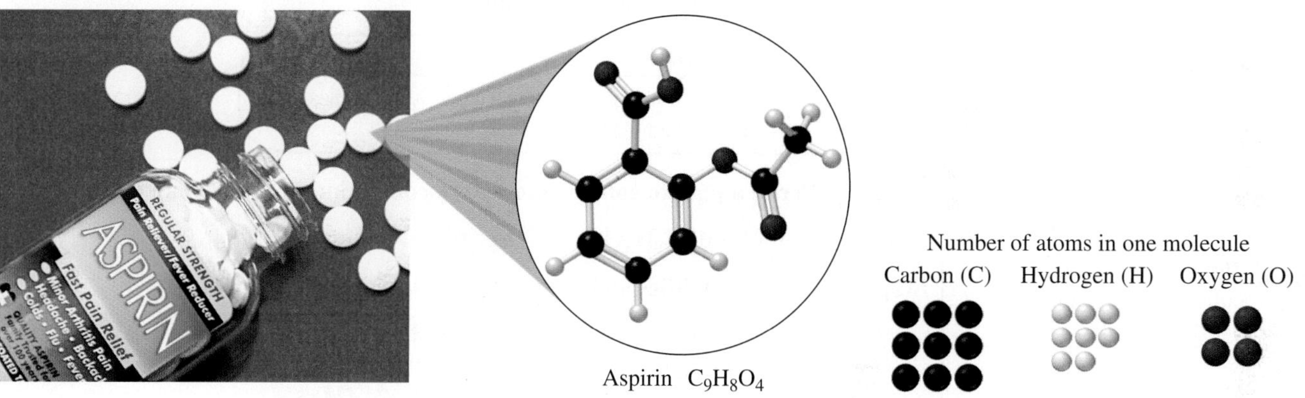

Aspirin $C_9H_8O_4$

The chemical formula subscripts specify the

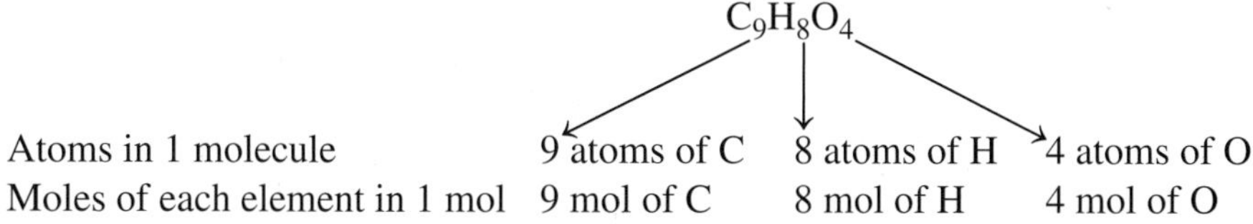

	$C_9H_8O_4$		
Atoms in 1 molecule	9 atoms of C	8 atoms of H	4 atoms of O
Moles of each element in 1 mol	9 mol of C	8 mol of H	4 mol of O

Using the subscripts from the formula, $C_9H_8O_4$, we can write the conversion factors for each of the elements in one mol of aspirin:

$$\frac{9 \text{ mol C}}{1 \text{ mol } C_9H_8O_4} \quad \frac{8 \text{ mol H}}{1 \text{ mol } C_9H_8O_4} \quad \frac{4 \text{ mol O}}{1 \text{ mol } C_9H_8O_4}$$

$$\frac{1 \text{ mol } C_9H_8O_4}{9 \text{ mol C}} \quad \frac{1 \text{ mol } C_9H_8O_4}{8 \text{ mol H}} \quad \frac{1 \text{ mol } C_9H_8O_4}{4 \text{ mol O}}$$

CONCEPT CHECK 7.2 Using Subscripts of a Formula

Indicate the moles of each element in 1 mol of each of the following:

a. $C_8H_9NO_2$, acetaminophen used in Tylenol
b. $Zn(C_2H_3O_2)_2$, zinc dietary supplement

ANSWER

a. The subscripts in the formula for acetaminophen, $C_8H_9NO_2$, indicate that 1 mol of acetaminophen contains 8 mol of C, 9 mol of H, 1 mol of N, and 2 mol of O.
b. In the formula, $Zn(C_2H_3O_2)_2$, the subscript 1 is understood for Zn as 1 mol of Zn. The subscript 2 outside the parentheses indicates that there are 2 mol of the ion $C_2H_3O_2^-$ in the chemical formula. Thus, there is 1 mol of Zn, 4 mol of C, 6 mol of H, and 4 mol of O in 1 mol of $Zn(C_2H_3O_2)_2$.

SAMPLE PROBLEM 7.2 Calculating the Moles of an Element in a Compound

How many moles of carbon are present in 1.50 mol of aspirin, $C_9H_8O_4$?

SOLUTION

Guide to Calculating Moles

1 State the given and needed quantities.
2 Write a plan to convert moles of a compound to moles of an element.
3 Write equalities and conversion factors using subscripts.
4 Set up the problem to calculate the moles of an element.

Step 1 State the given and needed quantities.

Analyze the Problem	Given	Need
	1.50 mol of aspirin, chemical formula $C_9H_8O_4$	moles of C

Step 2 Write a plan to convert moles of a compound to moles of an element.

moles of $C_9H_8O_4$ → Subscript → moles of C

Step 3 Write equalities and conversion factors using subscripts.

$$1 \text{ mol of } C_9H_8O_4 = 9 \text{ mol of C}$$

$$\frac{9 \text{ mol C}}{1 \text{ mol } C_9H_8O_4} \quad \text{and} \quad \frac{1 \text{ mol } C_9H_8O_4}{9 \text{ mol C}}$$

Step 4 Set up the problem to calculate the moles of an element.

$$1.50 \cancel{\text{mol } C_9H_8O_4} \times \frac{9 \text{ mol C}}{1 \cancel{\text{mol } C_9H_8O_4}} = 13.5 \text{ mol of C}$$

STUDY CHECK 7.2

How many moles of aspirin, $C_9H_8O_4$, contain 0.480 mol of O?

QUESTIONS AND PROBLEMS

7.1 The Mole

LEARNING GOAL: *Use Avogadro's number to determine the number of particles in a given number of moles.*

7.1 Calculate each of the following:
a. number of Ag atoms in 0.200 mol of Ag
b. number of C_3H_8O molecules in 0.750 mol of C_3H_8O
c. number of Cr atoms in 1.25 mol of Cr

7.2 Calculate each of the following:
a. number of Ni atoms in 3.4 mol of Ni
b. number of $Mg(OH)_2$ formula units in 1.20 mol of $Mg(OH)_2$
c. number of Li atoms in 4.5 mol of Li

7.3 Quinine, $C_{20}H_{24}N_2O_2$, is a component of tonic water and bitter lemon.
a. How many moles of hydrogen are in 1.0 mol of quinine?
b. How many moles of carbon are in 5.0 mol of quinine?
c. How many moles of nitrogen are in 0.020 mol of quinine?

7.4 Aluminum sulfate, $Al_2(SO_4)_3$, is used in some antiperspirants.
a. How many moles of sulfur are present in 3.0 mol of $Al_2(SO_4)_3$?
b. How many moles of aluminum ions are present in 0.40 mol of $Al_2(SO_4)_3$?
c. How many moles of sulfate ions (SO_4^{2-}) are present in 1.5 mol of $Al_2(SO_4)_3$?

7.5 Calculate each of the following:
a. number of C atoms in 0.500 mol of C
b. number of SO_2 molecules in 1.28 mol of SO_2
c. moles of Fe in 5.22×10^{22} atoms of Fe

7.6 Calculate each of the following:
a. number of Co atoms in 2.2 mol of Co
b. number of CO_2 molecules in 0.0180 mol of CO_2
c. moles of Cu in 7.8×10^{21} atoms of Cu

7.7 Calculate each of the following in 2.00 mol of H_3PO_4:
a. moles of H **b.** moles of O
c. atoms of P **d.** atoms of O

7.8 Calculate each of the following in 0.185 mol of $(C_3H_7)_2O$:
a. moles of C **b.** moles of O
c. atoms of H **d.** atoms of C

7.2 Molar Mass

LEARNING GOAL

Given the chemical formula of a substance, calculate its molar mass.

A single atom or molecule is much too small to weigh, even on the most accurate balance. In fact, it takes a huge number of atoms or molecules to make enough of a substance for you to see. An amount of water that contains Avogadro's number of water molecules is only a few sips. However, in the laboratory, we can use a balance to weigh out Avogadro's number of particles for 1 mol of substance.

For any element, the quantity called **molar mass** is the quantity in grams that equals the atomic mass of that element. We are counting 6.022×10^{23} atoms of an element when we weigh out the number of grams equal to its molar mass. For example, carbon has an atomic mass of 12.01 on the periodic table. This means 1 mol of carbon atoms has a mass of 12.01 g. Then to obtain 1 mol of carbon atoms, we would need to weigh out 12.01 g of carbon. Thus, the molar mass of carbon is found by looking at its atomic mass on the periodic table.

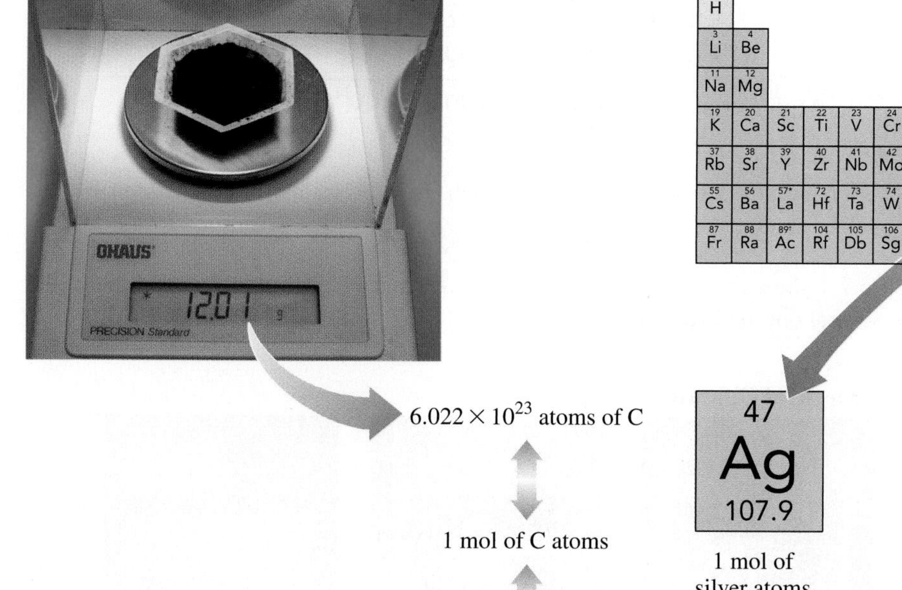

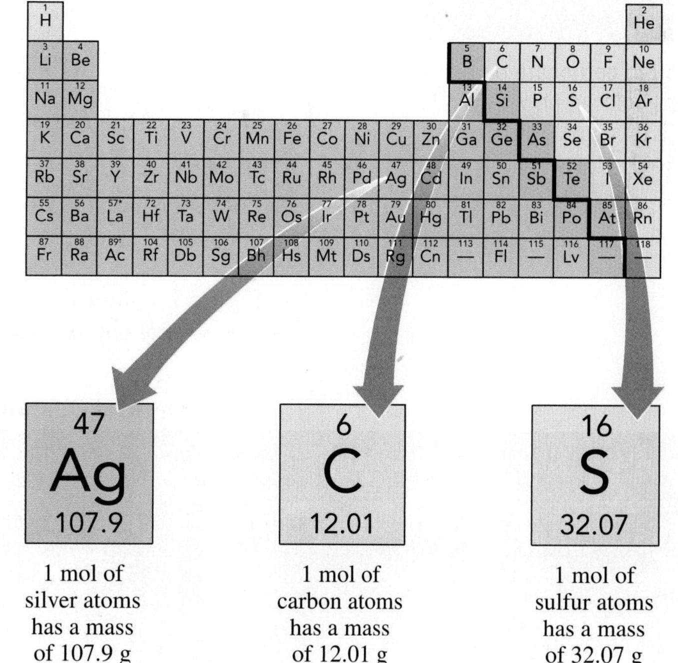

1 mol of silver atoms has a mass of 107.9 g

1 mol of carbon atoms has a mass of 12.01 g

1 mol of sulfur atoms has a mass of 32.07 g

Molar Mass of a Compound

CORE CHEMISTRY SKILL 

Calculating Molar Mass

To determine the molar mass of a compound, multiply the molar mass of each element by its subscript in the formula and add the results as shown in Sample Problem 7.3. ***In this text, we round the molar mass of an element to the hundredths place (0.01) place or use at least four significant figures for calculations.***

SAMPLE PROBLEM 7.3 Calculating the Molar Mass of a Compound

Calculate the molar mass for lithium carbonate, Li_2CO_3, used to produce red color in fireworks.

Guide to Calculating Molar Mass

1. Obtain the molar mass of each element.
2. Multiply each molar mass by the number of moles (subscript) in the formula.
3. Calculate the molar mass by adding the masses of the elements.

SOLUTION

Analyze the Problem	Given	Need
	formula Li_2CO_3	molar mass of Li_2CO_3

Step 1 **Obtain the molar mass of each element.**

$$\frac{6.941\text{ g Li}}{1\text{ mol Li}} \quad \frac{12.01\text{ g C}}{1\text{ mol C}} \quad \frac{16.00\text{ g O}}{1\text{ mol O}}$$

Step 2 **Multiply each molar mass by the number of moles (subscript) in the formula.**

Grams from 2 mol of Li

$$2\,\cancel{\text{mol Li}} \times \frac{6.941\text{ g Li}}{1\,\cancel{\text{mol Li}}} = 13.88\text{ g of Li}$$

Grams from 1 mol of C

$$1\,\cancel{\text{mol C}} \times \frac{12.01\text{ g C}}{1\,\cancel{\text{mol C}}} = 12.01\text{ g of C}$$

Grams from 3 mol of O

$$3\,\cancel{\text{mol O}} \times \frac{16.00\text{ g O}}{1\,\cancel{\text{mol O}}} = 48.00\text{ g of O}$$

Step 3 **Calculate the molar mass by adding the masses of the elements.**

$$\begin{aligned}
2\text{ mol of Li} &= 13.88\text{ g of Li}\\
1\text{ mol of C} &= 12.01\text{ g of C}\\
3\text{ mol of O} &= +48.00\text{ g of O}\\
\hline
\text{Molar mass of } Li_2CO_3 &= 73.89\text{ g of } Li_2CO_3
\end{aligned}$$

Lithium carbonate produces a red color in fireworks.

STUDY CHECK 7.3

Calculate the molar mass for salicylic acid, $C_7H_6O_3$, which is used to make aspirin.

Figure 7.1 shows some one mol quantities of substances. Table 7.2 lists the molar mass for several one-mol samples.

One–Mol Quantities

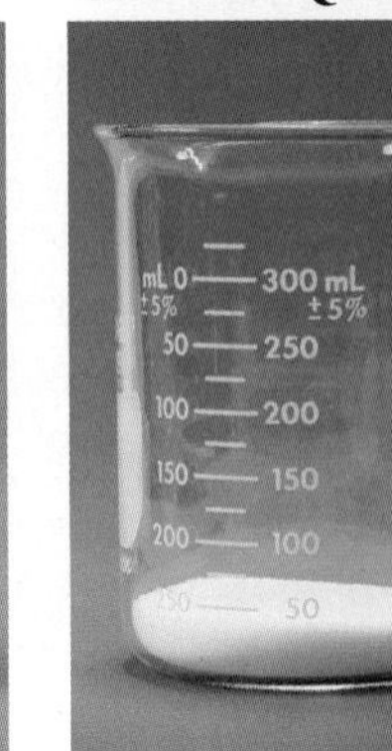

S Fe NaCl $K_2Cr_2O_7$ $C_{12}H_{22}O_{11}$

FIGURE 7.1 One-mol samples: sulfur, S (32.07 g); iron, Fe (55.85 g); salt, NaCl (58.44 g); potassium dichromate, $K_2Cr_2O_7$ (294.2 g); and sucrose, $C_{12}H_{22}O_{11}$ (342.3 g).

Q How is the molar mass for $K_2Cr_2O_7$ obtained?

TABLE 7.2 The Molar Mass of Selected Elements and Compounds

Substance	Molar Mass
1 mol of C	12.01 g
1 mol of Na	22.99 g
1 mol of Fe	55.85 g
1 mol of NaF	41.99 g
1 mol of $C_6H_{12}O_6$ (glucose)	180.16 g
1 mol of $C_8H_{10}N_4O_2$ (caffeine)	194.20 g

QUESTIONS AND PROBLEMS

7.2 Molar Mass

LEARNING GOAL: *Given the chemical formula of a substance, calculate its molar mass.*

7.9 Calculate the molar mass for each of the following:
- **a.** NaCl, table salt
- **b.** Fe_2O_3, rust
- **c.** $C_{19}H_{20}FNO_3$, Paxil, an antidepressant

7.10 Calculate the molar mass for each of the following:
- **a.** $FeSO_4$, iron supplement
- **b.** Al_2O_3, absorbent and abrasive
- **c.** $C_7H_5NO_3S$, saccharin, an artificial sweetener

7.11 Calculate the molar mass for each of the following:
- **a.** $Al_2(SO_4)_3$, antiperspirant
- **b.** $KC_4H_5O_6$, cream of tartar
- **c.** $C_{16}H_{19}N_3O_5S$, amoxicillin, an antibiotic

7.12 Calculate the molar mass for each of the following:
- **a.** C_3H_8O, rubbing alcohol
- **b.** $(NH_4)_2CO_3$, baking powder
- **c.** $Zn(C_2H_3O_2)_2$, zinc dietary supplement

7.13 Calculate the molar mass for each of the following:
- **a.** Cl_2
- **b.** $C_3H_6O_3$
- **c.** $Mg_3(PO_4)_2$

7.14 Calculate the molar mass for each of the following:
- **a.** O_2
- **b.** KH_2PO_4
- **c.** $Fe(ClO_4)_3$

7.15 Calculate the molar mass for each of the following:
- **a.** AlF_3
- **b.** $C_2H_4Cl_2$
- **c.** SnF_2

7.16 Calculate the molar mass for each of the following:
- **a.** $C_4H_8O_4$
- **b.** $Ga_2(CO_3)_3$
- **c.** $KBrO_4$

7.3 Calculations Using Molar Mass

LEARNING GOAL

Given the number of moles of a substance, calculate the mass in grams; given the mass, calculate the number of moles.

The molar mass of an element or a compound is one of the most useful conversion factors in chemistry because it converts moles of a substance to grams, or grams to moles. For example, 1 mol of magnesium has a mass of 24.31 g. To express molar mass as an equality, we can write

$$1 \text{ mol of Mg} = 24.31 \text{ g of Mg}$$

From this equality, two conversion factors can be written as

$$\frac{24.31 \text{ g Mg}}{1 \text{ mol Mg}} \quad \text{and} \quad \frac{1 \text{ mol Mg}}{24.31 \text{ g Mg}}$$

CORE CHEMISTRY SKILL 

Using Molar Mass as a Conversion Factor

SAMPLE PROBLEM 7.4 Converting Moles of an Element to Grams

Silver metal is used in the manufacture of tableware, mirrors, jewelry, and dental alloys. If the design for a piece of jewelry requires 0.750 mol of silver, how many grams of silver are needed?

SOLUTION

Step 1 **State the given and needed quantities.**

Analyze the Problem	Given	Need
	0.750 mol of Ag	grams of Ag

Silver metal is used to make jewelry.

Guide to Calculating the Moles (or Grams) of a Substance from Grams (or Moles)

1 State the given and needed quantities.

2 Write a plan to convert moles to grams (or grams to moles).

3 Determine the molar mass and write conversion factors.

4 Set up the problem to convert moles to grams (or grams to moles).

Step 2 **Write a plan to convert moles to grams.**

moles of Ag → Molar mass factor → grams of Ag

Step 3 **Determine the molar mass and write conversion factors.**

$$1 \text{ mol of Ag} = 107.9 \text{ g of Ag}$$

$$\frac{107.9 \text{ g Ag}}{1 \text{ mol Ag}} \quad \text{and} \quad \frac{1 \text{ mol Ag}}{107.9 \text{ g Ag}}$$

Step 4 **Set up the problem to convert moles to grams.**
Calculate the grams of silver using the molar mass factor that cancels mol Ag.

$$0.750 \cancel{\text{mol Ag}} \times \frac{107.9 \text{ g Ag}}{1 \cancel{\text{mol Ag}}} = 80.9 \text{ g of Ag}$$

STUDY CHECK 7.4

Calculate the number of grams of gold (Au) present in 0.124 mol of gold.

Conversion factors are written for compounds in the same way. For example, the molar mass of the compound H_2O is written

$$1 \text{ mol of } H_2O = 18.02 \text{ g of } H_2O$$

From this equality, conversion factors for the molar mass of H_2O are written as

$$\frac{18.02 \text{ g } H_2O}{1 \text{ mol } H_2O} \quad \text{and} \quad \frac{1 \text{ mol } H_2O}{18.02 \text{ g } H_2O}$$

We can now change from moles to grams, or grams to moles, using the conversion factors derived from the molar mass as shown in Sample Problem 7.4. (Remember, you must determine the molar mass first.)

Table salt is sodium chloride, NaCl.

SAMPLE PROBLEM 7.5 Converting Mass of a Compound to Moles

A box of salt contains 737 g of NaCl. How many moles of NaCl are present in the box?

SOLUTION

Step 1 **State the given and needed quantities.**

Analyze the Problem	Given	Need
	737 g of NaCl	moles of NaCl

Step 2 **Write a plan to convert grams to moles.**

grams of NaCl → Molar mass factor → moles of NaCl

Step 3 **Determine the molar mass and write conversion factors.**

$$(1 \times 22.99) + (1 \times 35.45) = 58.44 \text{ g/mol}$$

$$1 \text{ mol of NaCl} = 58.44 \text{ g of NaCl}$$

$$\frac{58.44 \text{ g NaCl}}{1 \text{ mol NaCl}} \quad \text{and} \quad \frac{1 \text{ mol NaCl}}{58.44 \text{ g NaCl}}$$

Step 4 **Set up the problem to convert grams to moles.**
Calculate the moles of NaCl using the molar mass factor that cancels g NaCl.

$$737 \text{ g NaCl} \times \frac{1 \text{ mol NaCl}}{58.44 \text{ g NaCl}} = 12.6 \text{ mol of NaCl}$$

STUDY CHECK 7.5

One gel cap of an antacid contains 311 mg of $CaCO_3$. In a recommended dosage of two gel caps, how many moles of $CaCO_3$ are present?

Figure 7.2 gives a summary of all the calculations in this section by showing the connections between the moles, mass in grams, and number of molecules or formula units, and the moles and atoms of each element in that compound.

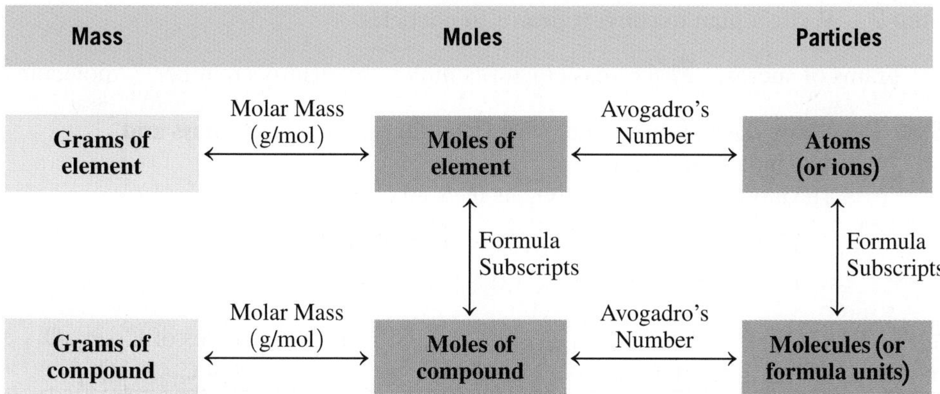

FIGURE 7.2 The moles of a compound are related to its mass in grams by molar mass, to the number of molecules (or formula units) by Avogadro's number, and to the moles of each element by the subscripts in the formula.

Q What steps are needed to calculate the number of atoms of H in 5.00 g of CH_4?

CONCEPT CHECK 7.3 Comparing Grams, Moles, and Atoms

Compounds called chlorofluorocarbons (CFCs) were used for many years in aerosol cans and in refrigerators. Eventually, it was determined that, in the stratosphere, CFCs interacted with sunlight, which has destroyed part of the ozone layer. The CFC Freon-13 has the formula of $CClF_3$.

a. Are there more moles of Cl or F in 1 mol of Freon-13?
b. Are there more grams of Cl or F in 1 mol of Freon-13?
c. Is the number of moles of carbon larger or smaller than the number of atoms of carbon?

ANSWER

a. From the formula $CClF_3$, there are 1 mol of Cl and 3 mol of F. Thus, there are more moles of F than Cl in 1 mol of Freon-13.
b. To determine the greater number of grams, we multiply the molar mass of each by the number of moles (subscripts). One mol of Cl $\times$ 35.45 g/mol $=$ 35.45 g of Cl, and 3 mol of F $\times$ 19.00 g/mol $=$ 57.00 g of F. Thus, there are more grams of fluorine than chlorine in the compound.
c. Because there is Avogadro's number of atoms in 1 mol, the number of moles of carbon is smaller than the number of atoms of carbon.

Table sugar is sucrose, $C_{12}H_{22}O_{11}$.

Guide to Calculating the Particles of a Substance from Grams

1 State the given and needed quantities.

2 Write a plan to convert grams to particles.

3 Write the equalities and conversion factors for molar mass and Avogadro's number.

4 Set up the problem to convert grams to particles.

We can now convert the mass in grams of a compound to the number of molecules. In these calculations as shown in Sample Problem 7.6, we see the central role of moles in the conversion of mass to particles.

SAMPLE PROBLEM 7.6 Converting Grams to Particles

A 10.00-lb bag of table sugar contains 4536 g of sucrose, $C_{12}H_{22}O_{11}$. How many molecules of sucrose are present?

SOLUTION

Step 1 State the given and needed quantities.

Analyze the Problem	Given	Need
	4536 g of sucrose, $C_{12}H_{22}O_{11}$	molecules of sucrose

Step 2 Write a plan to convert grams to particles.

grams of sucrose → Molar mass factor → moles → Avogadro's number → molecules

Step 3 Write the equalities and conversion factors for molar mass and Avogadro's number.
The molar mass of $C_{12}H_{22}O_{11}$ is the sum of the masses of

12 mol of C + 22 mol of H + 11 mol of O:

$$(12 \times 12.01) + (22 \times 1.008) + (11 \times 16.00) = 342.3\text{ g/mol}$$

$$1\text{ mol of } C_{12}H_{22}O_{11} = 342.3\text{ g of } C_{12}H_{22}O_{11}$$

$$\frac{342.3\text{ g } C_{12}H_{22}O_{11}}{1\text{ mol } C_{12}H_{22}O_{11}} \text{ and } \frac{1\text{ mol } C_{12}H_{22}O_{11}}{342.3\text{ g } C_{12}H_{22}O_{11}}$$

$$1\text{ mol of } C_{12}H_{22}O_{11} = 6.022 \times 10^{23}\text{ molecules of } C_{12}H_{22}O_{11}$$

$$\frac{6.022 \times 10^{23}\text{ molecules}}{1\text{ mol } C_{12}H_{22}O_{11}} \text{ and } \frac{1\text{ mol } C_{12}H_{22}O_{11}}{6.022 \times 10^{23}\text{ molecules}}$$

Step 4 Set up the problem to convert grams to particles. Use molar mass to convert the grams of sucrose to moles of sucrose, and then use Avogadro's number to convert moles of sucrose to molecules.

$$4536\ \cancel{\text{g } C_{12}H_{22}O_{11}} \times \frac{1\ \cancel{\text{mol } C_{12}H_{22}O_{11}}}{342.3\ \cancel{\text{g } C_{12}H_{22}O_{11}}} \times \frac{6.022 \times 10^{23}\text{ molecules}}{1\ \cancel{\text{mol } C_{12}H_{22}O_{11}}}$$

$$= 7.980 \times 10^{24}\text{ molecules of sucrose}$$

STUDY CHECK 7.6

In the body, caffeine, $C_8H_{10}N_4O_2$, acts as a stimulant and diuretic. How many moles of nitrogen are in 2.50 g of caffeine?

QUESTIONS AND PROBLEMS

7.3 Calculations Using Molar Mass

LEARNING GOAL: *Given the number of moles of a substance, calculate the mass in grams; given the mass, calculate the number of moles.*

7.17 Calculate the mass, in grams, for each of the following:
a. 1.50 mol of Na
b. 2.80 mol of Ca
c. 0.125 mol of CO_2
d. 0.0485 mol of Na_2CO_3
e. 7.14×10^2 mol of PCl_3

7.18 Calculate the mass, in grams, for each of the following:
a. 5.12 mol of Al **b.** 0.75 mol of Cu
c. 3.52 mol of $MgBr_2$ **d.** 0.145 mol of C_2H_6O
e. 2.08 mol of $(NH_4)_2SO_4$

7.19 Calculate the mass, in grams, in 0.150 mol of each of the following:
a. Ne **b.** I_2 **c.** Na_2O
d. $Ca(NO_3)_2$ **e.** C_6H_{14}

7.20 Calculate the mass, in grams, in 2.28 mol of each of the following:
a. N_2 **b.** SO_3 **c.** $C_3H_6O_3$
d. $Mg(HCO_3)_2$ **e.** SF_6

7.21 Calculate the number of moles in each of the following:
a. 82.0 g of Ag
b. 0.288 g of C
c. 15.0 g of ammonia, NH_3
d. 7.25 g of propane, C_3H_8
e. 245 g of Fe_2O_3

7.22 Calculate the number of moles in each of the following:
a. 85.2 g of Ni
b. 144 g of K
c. 6.4 g of H_2O
d. 308 g of $BaSO_4$
e. 252.8 g of fructose, $C_6H_{12}O_6$

7.23 Calculate the number of moles in 25.0 g of each of the following:
a. He **b.** O_2 **c.** $Al(OH)_3$
d. Ga_2S_3 **e.** C_4H_{10}, butane

7.24 Calculate the number of moles in 4.00 g of each of the following:
a. Au **b.** SnO_2 **c.** $Cr(OH)_3$
d. Ca_3N_2 **e.** $C_6H_8O_6$, vitamin C

7.25 Calculate the number of atoms of C in each of the following:
a. 25.0 g of C
b. 0.688 mol of CO_2
c. 275 g of C_3H_8
d. 1.84 mol of C_2H_6O
e. 7.5×10^{24} molecules of CH_4

7.26 Calculate the number of atoms of N in each of the following:
a. 0.755 mol of N_2
b. 0.82 g of $NaNO_3$
c. 40.0 g of N_2O
d. 6.24×10^{23} molecules of NH_3
e. 1.4×10^{22} molecules of N_2O_4

7.27 Propane gas, C_3H_8, is used as a fuel for many barbecues.
a. How many grams are in 1.50 mol of propane?
b. How many moles are in 34.0 g of propane?
c. How many grams of carbon are in 34.0 g of propane?
d. How many atoms of hydrogen are in 0.254 g of propane?

7.28 Allyl sulfide, $(C_3H_5)_2S$, gives garlic, onions, and leeks their characteristic odor.
a. How many moles of sulfur are in 23.2 g of $(C_3H_5)_2S$?
b. How many atoms of hydrogen are in 0.75 mol of $(C_3H_5)_2S$?
c. How many grams of carbon are in 4.20×10^{23} molecules of $(C_3H_5)_2S$?
d. How many atoms of carbon are in 15.0 g of $(C_3H_5)_2S$?

The characteristic odor of garlic is due to a sulfur-containing compound.

7.4 Mass Percent Composition and Empirical Formulas

LEARNING GOAL

Given the formula of a compound, calculate the mass percent composition; from the mass percent composition, determine the empirical formula of a compound.

Because the atoms of the elements in a compound are combined in a definite proportion, they are also combined in a definite proportion by mass. Thus, when we know the mass of an element in a sample of a compound, we can calculate its **mass percent composition** or **mass percent**, which is the mass of an element divided by the total mass of the compound and multiplied by 100%.

$$\text{Mass percent of an element} = \frac{\text{mass of an element}}{\text{total mass of the compound}} \times 100\%$$

CORE CHEMISTRY SKILL 

Calculating Mass Percent Composition

CONCEPT CHECK 7.4 Calculating Mass Percent from Experimental Data

What is the mass percent of N if 7.64 g of N are present in 12.0 g of N_2O, "laughing gas," which is used as an anaesthetic for surgery and in dentistry?

ANSWER

From the grams of N and the grams of N_2O, we calculate the mass percent of nitrogen as follows:

$$\text{Mass percent of an element} = \frac{\text{mass of an element}}{\text{total mass of the compound}} \times 100\%$$

$$\text{Mass percent of N} = \frac{7.64\ \cancel{\text{g N}}}{12.0\ \cancel{\text{g N}}} \times 100\% = 63.7\%\ \text{N}$$

Mass Percent Composition Using Molar Mass

We can also calculate mass percent composition of a compound by using its molar mass. Then the total mass of each element is divided by the molar mass of the compound and multiplied by 100%.

$$\text{Mass percent composition} = \frac{\text{mass of each element}}{\text{molar mass of the compound}} \times 100\%$$

The odor of pears is due to propyl acetate, $C_5H_{10}O_2$.

Guide to Calculating Mass Percent Composition

1 Determine the total mass of each element in the molar mass of a formula.

2 Divide the total mass of each element by the molar mass and multiply by 100%.

SAMPLE PROBLEM 7.7 Calculating Mass Percent Composition from Molar Mass

The odor of pears is due to the organic compound called propyl acetate, which has a formula of $C_5H_{10}O_2$. What is its mass percent composition?

SOLUTION

Step 1 Determine the total mass of each element in the molar mass of a formula.

Analyze the Problem	Given	Need
	$C_5H_{10}O_2$	mass percent composition: %C, %H, %O

$$5\ \cancel{\text{mol C}} \times \frac{12.01\ \text{g C}}{1\ \cancel{\text{mol C}}} = 60.05\ \text{g of C}$$

$$10\ \cancel{\text{mol H}} \times \frac{1.008\ \text{g H}}{1\ \cancel{\text{mol H}}} = 10.08\ \text{g of H}$$

$$2\ \cancel{\text{mol O}} \times \frac{16.00\ \text{g O}}{1\ \cancel{\text{mol O}}} = 32.00\ \text{g of O}$$

$$\text{Molar mass of } C_5H_{10}O_2 = 102.13\ \text{g of } C_5H_{10}O_2$$

Step 2 Divide the total mass of each element by the molar mass and multiply by 100%.

$$\text{Mass \% C} = \frac{60.05\ \text{g C}}{102.13\ \text{g } C_5H_{10}O_2} \times 100\% = 58.80\%\ \text{C}$$

$$\text{Mass \% H} = \frac{10.08\ \text{g H}}{102.13\ \text{g } C_5H_{10}O_2} \times 100\% = 9.870\%\ \text{H}$$

$$\text{Mass \% O} = \frac{32.00\ \text{g O}}{102.13\ \text{g } C_5H_{10}O_2} \times 100\% = 31.33\%\ \text{O}$$

The total mass percent for all the elements in the compound should equal 100%.

$$58.80\%\ C + 9.870\%\ H + 31.33\%\ O = 100.00\%$$

STUDY CHECK 7.7

The organic compound ethylene glycol, $C_2H_6O_2$, used as automobile antifreeze, is a sweet-tasting liquid, which is toxic to humans and animals. What is the mass percent composition of ethylene glycol?

Empirical Formulas

Calculating an Empirical Formula

Up to now, the formulas you have seen have been **molecular formulas**, which are the actual formulas of compounds. If we write a formula that represents the lowest whole-number ratio of the atoms in a compound, it is called the simplest or **empirical formula**. For example, the compound benzene, with molecular formula C_6H_6, has the

Chemistry Link to the Environment

FERTILIZERS

Every year in the spring, homeowners and farmers add fertilizers to the soil to produce greener lawns and larger crops. Plants require several nutrients, but the major ones are nitrogen, phosphorus, and potassium. Nitrogen promotes green growth, phosphorus promotes strong root development for strong plants and abundant flowers, and potassium helps plants defend against diseases and weather extremes. The numbers on a package of fertilizer give the percentages each of N, P, and K by mass. For example, the set of numbers 30−3−4 describes a fertilizer that contains 30% N, 3% P, and 4% K.

The major nutrient, nitrogen, is present in huge quantities as N_2 in the atmosphere, but plants cannot utilize nitrogen in this form. Bacteria in the soil convert atmospheric N_2 to usable forms by nitrogen fixation. To provide additional nitrogen to plants, several types of nitrogen-containing chemicals, including ammonia, nitrates, and ammonium compounds, are added to soil. The nitrates are absorbed directly, but ammonia and ammonium salts are first converted to nitrates by the soil bacteria.

The percent nitrogen depends on the type of nitrogen compound used in the fertilizer. The percent nitrogen by mass in each type is calculated using mass percent composition.

Type of Fertilizer	Percent Nitrogen by Mass
NH_3	$\dfrac{14.01\ g\ N}{17.03\ g\ NH_3} \times 100\% = 82.27\%\ N$
NH_4NO_3	$\dfrac{28.02\ g\ N}{80.05\ g\ NH_4NO_3} \times 100\% = 35.00\%\ N$
$(NH_4)_2SO_4$	$\dfrac{28.02\ g\ N}{132.15\ g\,(NH_4)_2SO_4} \times 100\% = 21.20\%\ N$
$(NH_4)_2HPO_4$	$\dfrac{28.02\ g\ N}{132.06\ g\,(NH_4)_2HPO_4} \times 100\% = 21.22\%\ N$

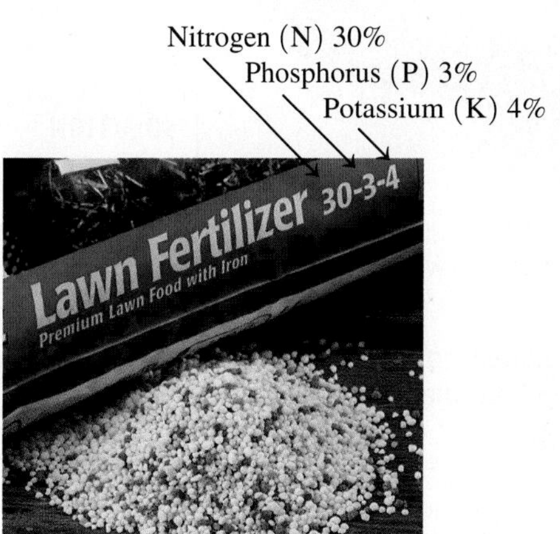

The label on a bag of fertilizer states the percentages of N, P, and K.

The choice of a fertilizer depends on its use and convenience. A fertilizer can be prepared as crystals or a powder, in a liquid solution, or as a gas such as ammonia. The ammonia and ammonium fertilizers are water soluble and quick-acting. Other forms may be made to slow-release by enclosing water-soluble ammonium salts in a thin plastic coating. The most commonly used fertilizer is NH_4NO_3 because it is easy to apply and has a high percent of N by mass.

empirical formula CH. Some molecular formulas and their empirical formulas are shown in Table 7.3.

TABLE 7.3 Examples of Molecular and Empirical Formulas

Name	Molecular (actual formula)	Empirical (simplest formula)
Acetylene	C_2H_2	CH
Benzene	C_6H_6	CH
Ammonia	NH_3	NH_3
Hydrazine	N_2H_4	NH_2
Ribose	$C_5H_{10}O_5$	CH_2O
Glucose	$C_6H_{12}O_6$	CH_2O

The empirical formula of a compound is determined by converting the number of grams of each element to moles and finding the lowest whole-number ratio to use as subscripts, as shown in Sample Problem 7.8.

Water-treatment plants use chemicals to purify sewage.

Guide to Calculating an Empirical Formula

1. Calculate the moles of each element.
2. Divide by the smallest number of moles.
3. Use the lowest whole-number ratio of moles as subscripts.

SAMPLE PROBLEM 7.8 Calculating an Empirical Formula

An iron compound is used to purify water in water-treatment plants. What is the empirical formula of the compound if experimental analysis shows that a sample of the compound contains 6.87 g of iron and 13.1 g of chlorine?

SOLUTION

Step 1 Calculate the moles of each element.

Analyze the Problem	Given	Need
	6.87 g of Fe, 13.1 g of Cl	empirical formula

$$6.87\ \cancel{g\ Fe} \times \frac{1\ \text{mol Fe}}{55.85\ \cancel{g\ Fe}} = 0.123\ \text{mol of Fe}$$

$$13.1\ \cancel{g\ Cl} \times \frac{1\ \text{mol Cl}}{35.45\ \cancel{g\ Cl}} = 0.370\ \text{mol of Cl}$$

Step 2 Divide by the smallest number of moles. In this problem, the 0.123 mol of Fe is the smaller number of moles.

$$\frac{0.123\ \text{mol Fe}}{0.123} = 1.00\ \text{mol of Fe}$$

$$\frac{0.370\ \text{mol Cl}}{0.123} = 3.01\ \text{mol of Cl}$$

Step 3 Use the lowest whole-number ratio of moles as subscripts. The relationship of moles of Fe to moles of Cl is 1 to 3, which we obtain by rounding off 3.01 to 3.

$$Fe_{1.00}Cl_{3.01} \longrightarrow Fe_1Cl_3\text{, written as } FeCl_3 \quad \text{Empirical formula}$$

STUDY CHECK 7.8

Phosphine is a highly toxic compound used for pest and rodent control. If a sample of phosphine contains 0.456 g of P and 0.0440 g of H, what is its empirical formula?

Often, the mass percent of each element in a compound is given. The mass percent composition is true for any quantity of the compound. For example, methane, CH_4, always has a mass percent composition of 74.9% C and 25.1% H. Thus, if we assume that we have a sample of exactly 100. g of the compound, we can determine the grams of each element in that 100. g sample as shown in Sample Problem 7.9.

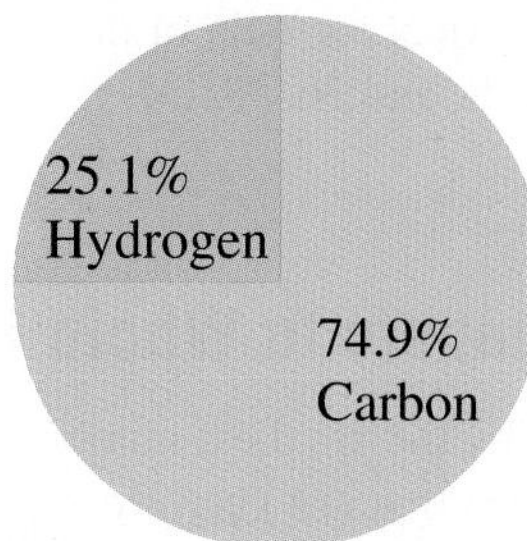

Mass percent composition of methane, CH_4

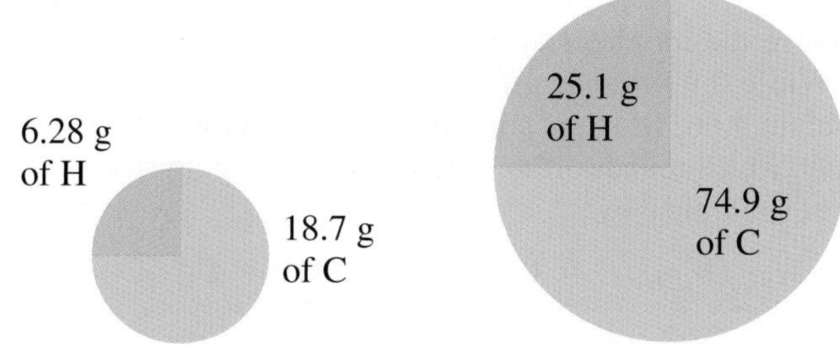

Composition, in grams, for 25.0 g of methane, CH_4

Composition, in grams, for 100. g of methane, CH_4

The mass percent composition for any amount of methane is always the same.

SAMPLE PROBLEM 7.9 Calculating an Empirical Formula from the Mass Percent Composition

Tetrachloroethene is a colorless liquid used for dry cleaning. What is the empirical formula of tetrachloroethene if its mass percent composition is 14.5% C and 85.5% Cl?

SOLUTION

	Given	Need
Analyze the Problem	14.5% C, 85.5% Cl	empirical formula

Step 1 **Calculate the moles of each element.** In a sample size of exactly 100. g of this compound, there are 14.5 g of C and 85.5 g of Cl.

$$14.5\ \cancel{g\ C} \times \frac{1\ \text{mol C}}{12.01\ \cancel{g\ C}} = 1.21\ \text{mol of C}$$

$$85.5\ \cancel{g\ Cl} \times \frac{1\ \text{mol Cl}}{35.45\ \cancel{g\ Cl}} = 2.41\ \text{mol of Cl}$$

Step 2 **Divide by the smallest number of moles.**

$$\frac{1.21\ \text{mol C}}{1.21} = 1.00\ \text{mol of C}$$

$$\frac{2.41\ \text{mol Cl}}{1.21} = 1.99\ \text{mol of Cl}$$

Sulfate of potash supplies sulfur and potassium.

Step 3 **Use the lowest whole-number ratio of moles as subscripts.**

$$C_{1.00}Cl_{1.99} \longrightarrow C_1Cl_2 = CCl_2$$

STUDY CHECK 7.9

Sulfate of potash is the common name of a compound used in fertilizers to supply potassium and sulfur. What is the empirical formula of this compound if it has a mass percent composition of 44.9% K, 18.4% S, and 36.7% O?

Converting Decimal Numbers to Whole Numbers

Sometimes the result of dividing by the smallest number of moles gives a decimal instead of a whole number. Decimal values that are very close to whole numbers can be rounded off. For example, 2.04 rounds off to 2 and 6.98 rounds off to 7. *However, a decimal that is greater than 0.1 or less than 0.9 should not be rounded off.* Instead, we multiply by a small integer until we obtain a whole number. Some multipliers that are typically used are listed in Table 7.4.

Let us suppose the numbers of moles we obtain give subscripts in the ratio of $C_{1.00}H_{2.33}O_{0.99}$. While 0.99 rounds off to 1, we cannot round off 2.33. If we multiply 2.33 × 2, we obtain 4.66, which is still not a whole number. If we multiply 2.33 by 3, the answer is 6.99, which rounds off to 7. To complete the empirical formula, all the other subscripts must be multiplied by 3.

$$C_{(1.00 \times 3)}H_{(2.33 \times 3)}O_{(0.99 \times 3)} = C_{3.00}H_{6.99}O_{2.97} \longrightarrow C_3H_7O_3$$

TABLE 7.4 Some Multipliers That Convert Decimals to Whole-Number Subscripts

Decimal	Multiplier	Example		Whole Number
0.20	5	1.20 × 5	=	6
0.25	4	2.25 × 4	=	9
0.33	3	1.33 × 3	=	4
0.50	2	2.50 × 2	=	5
0.67	3	1.67 × 3	=	5

SAMPLE PROBLEM 7.10 Calculating an Empirical Formula Using Multipliers

Citrus fruits are a good source of vitamin C.

Ascorbic acid (vitamin C), found in citrus fruits and vegetables, is important in metabolic reactions in the body, in the synthesis of collagen, and in the prevention of scurvy. If the mass percent composition of ascorbic acid is 40.9% C, 4.58% H, and 54.5% O, what is the empirical formula of ascorbic acid?

SOLUTION

	Given	Need
Analyze the Problem	40.9% C, 4.58% H, 54.5% O	empirical formula

Step 1 **Calculate the moles of each element.** In a sample size of exactly 100. g, there are 40.9 g of C, 4.58 g of H, and 54.5 g of O.

$$40.9 \text{ g C} \times \frac{1 \text{ mol C}}{12.01 \text{ g C}} = 3.41 \text{ mol of C}$$

$$4.58 \text{ g H} \times \frac{1 \text{ mol H}}{1.008 \text{ g H}} = 4.54 \text{ mol of H}$$

$$54.5 \text{ g O} \times \frac{1 \text{ mol O}}{16.00 \text{ g O}} = 3.41 \text{ mol of O}$$

Step 2 **Divide by the smallest number of moles.** For this problem, the smallest number of moles is 3.41.

$$\frac{3.41 \text{ mol C}}{3.41} = 1.00 \text{ mol of C}$$

$$\frac{4.54 \text{ mol H}}{3.41} = 1.33 \text{ mol of H}$$

$$\frac{3.41 \text{ mol O}}{3.41} = 1.00 \text{ mol of O}$$

Step 3 **Use the lowest whole-number ratio of moles as subscripts.** As calculated thus far, the ratio of moles gives the formula

$$C_{1.00}H_{1.33}O_{1.00}$$

Because the subscript for H has a decimal that is greater than 0.1 and less than 0.9, it should not be rounded off. Thus, we multiply each of the subscripts by 3 to obtain a whole number for H, which is 4. Thus, the empirical formula of ascorbic acid is $C_3H_4O_3$.

$$C_{(1.00\times3)}H_{(1.33\times3)}O_{(1.00\times3)} = C_{3.00}H_{3.99}O_{3.00} \longrightarrow C_3H_4O_3$$

STUDY CHECK 7.10

An organic compound called glyoxylic acid is used by plants and bacteria to convert fats into glucose. What is the empirical formula of glyoxylic acid if it has a mass percent composition of 32.5% C, 2.70% H, and 64.8% O?

QUESTIONS AND PROBLEMS

7.4 Mass Percent Composition and Empirical Formulas

LEARNING GOAL: *Given the formula of a compound, calculate the mass percent composition; from the mass percent composition, determine the empirical formula of a compound.*

7.29 Calculate the mass percent composition of each of the following:
- **a.** 4.68 g of Si and 5.32 g of O
- **b.** 5.72 g of C and 1.28 g of H
- **c.** 16.1 of Na, 22.5 g of S, and 11.3 g of O
- **d.** 6.22 g of C, 1.04 g of H, and 4.14 g of O

7.30 Calculate the mass percent composition of each of the following:
- **a.** 0.890 g of Ba and 1.04 g of Br
- **b.** 3.82 g of K and 1.18 g of I
- **c.** 3.29 of N, 0.946 g of H, and 3.76 g of S
- **d.** 4.14 g of C, 0.695 g of H, and 2.76 g of O

7.31 Calculate the mass percent composition of each of the following:
- **a.** MgF_2, magnesium fluoride
- **b.** $Ca(OH)_2$, calcium hydroxide
- **c.** $C_4H_8O_4$, erythrose, a carbohydrate
- **d.** $(NH_4)_3PO_4$, ammonium phosphate, fertilizer
- **e.** $C_{17}H_{19}NO_3$, morphine, a painkiller

7.32 Calculate the mass percent composition of each of the following:
a. $CaCl_2$, calcium chloride
b. $Na_2Cr_2O_7$, sodium dichromate
c. $C_2H_3Cl_3$, trichloroethane, a cleaning solvent
d. $Ca_3(PO_4)_2$, calcium phosphate, found in bone and teeth
e. $C_{18}H_{36}O_2$, stearic acid, a fatty acid

7.33 Calculate the mass percent of N in each of the following:
a. N_2O_5, dinitrogen pentoxide
b. NH_4Cl, expectorant in cough medicine
c. $C_2H_8N_2$, dimethylhydrazine, rocket fuel
d. $C_9H_{15}N_5O$, Rogaine, stimulates hair growth
e. $C_{14}H_{22}N_2O$, Lidocaine, local anesthetic

7.34 Calculate the mass percent of S in each of the following:
a. Na_2SO_4, sodium sulfate
b. Al_2S_3, aluminum sulfide
c. SO_3, sulfur trioxide
d. C_2H_6SO, dimethylsulfoxide, topical anti-inflammatory
e. $C_{10}H_{10}N_4O_2S$, sulfadiazine, antibacterial

7.35 Calculate the empirical formula for each of the following:
a. 3.57 g of N and 2.04 g of O
b. 7.00 g of C and 1.75 g of H
c. 0.175 g of H, 2.44 g of N, and 8.38 g of O
d. 2.06 g of Ca, 2.66 g of Cr, and 3.28 g of O

7.36 Calculate the empirical formula for each of the following:
a. 2.90 g of Ag and 0.430 g of S
b. 2.22 g of Na and 0.774 g of O
c. 2.11 g of Na, 0.0900 g of H, 2.94 g of S, and 5.86 g of O
d. 5.52 g of K, 1.45 g of P, and 3.00 g of O

7.37 Calculate the empirical formula for each of the following:
a. 70.9% K and 29.1% S
b. 55.0% Ga and 45.0% F
c. 31.0% B and 69.0% O
d. 18.8% Li, 16.3% C, and 64.9% O
e. 51.7% C, 6.95% H, and 41.3% O

7.38 Calculate the empirical formula for each of the following:
a. 55.5% Ca and 44.5% S
b. 78.3% Ba and 21.7% F
c. 76.0% Zn and 24.0% P
d. 29.1% Na, 40.6% S, and 30.3% O
e. 19.8% C, 2.20% H, and 78.0% Cl

LEARNING GOAL

Determine the molecular formula of a substance from the empirical formula and molar mass.

7.5 Molecular Formulas

An empirical formula represents the lowest whole-number ratio of atoms in a compound. However, empirical formulas do not necessarily represent the actual number of atoms in a molecule. A molecular formula is related to the empirical formula by a small integer such as 1, 2, or 3.

Molecular formula = small integer × empirical formula

For example, in Table 7.5, we see several different compounds that have the same empirical formula, CH_2O. The molecular formulas are related to the empirical formulas by small whole numbers (integers). The same relationship is true for the molar mass and empirical formula mass. The molar mass of each of the different compounds is related to the mass of the empirical formula (30.03 g) by the same small integer.

TABLE 7.5 Comparing the Molar Mass of Some Compounds with the Empirical Formula of CH_2O

Compound	Empirical Formula	Molecular Formula	Molar Mass (g)	Integer × Empirical Formula	Integer × Empirical Formula Mass
Acetaldehyde	CH_2O	CH_2O	30.03	$1(CH_2O)$	1 × 30.03
Acetic acid	CH_2O	$C_2H_4O_2$	60.06	$2(CH_2O)$	2 × 30.03
Lactic acid	CH_2O	$C_3H_6O_3$	90.09	$3(CH_2O)$	3 × 30.03
Erythrose	CH_2O	$C_4H_8O_4$	120.12	$4(CH_2O)$	4 × 30.03
Ribose	CH_2O	$C_5H_{10}O_5$	150.15	$5(CH_2O)$	5 × 30.03

CONCEPT CHECK 7.5 Empirical and Molecular Formulas

A compound has an empirical formula of CH_2O. Indicate if each of the following could be a possible molecular formula. Explain your answer.

a. CH_2O **b.** C_2H_4O **c.** $C_2H_4O_2$
d. $C_5H_{10}O_5$ **e.** $C_6H_{12}O$

ANSWER

a. The empirical formula and molecular formula have a ratio of 1:1, which gives an empirical formula that is the same as the molecular formula.
b. Because only the C and H are twice their moles in the empirical formula, this cannot be a corresponding molecular formula.
c. This can be a possible molecular formula because the C, H, and O are twice the moles of the empirical formula.
d. This can be a possible molecular formula because the C, H, and O are five times the moles of the empirical formula.
e. Because only the C and H are six times their moles in the empirical formula, this cannot be a corresponding molecular formula.

Relating Empirical and Molecular Formulas

Once we determine the empirical formula, we can calculate its mass in grams. If we are given the molar mass of the compound, we can calculate the value of the small integer.

$$\text{Small integer} = \frac{\text{molar mass of compound}}{\text{empirical formula mass}}$$

For example, when the molar mass of ribose is divided by the empirical formula mass, the integer is 5.

$$\text{Small integer} = \frac{\text{molar mass of ribose}}{\text{empirical formula mass of ribose}} = \frac{150.15\ \cancel{g}}{30.03\ \cancel{g}} = 5$$

Multiplying the subscripts in the empirical formula (CH_2O) by 5 gives the molecular formula of ribose, $C_5H_{10}O_5$.

$$5 \times \text{empirical formula } (CH_2O) = \text{molecular formula } (C_5H_{10}O_5)$$

Calculating a Molecular Formula

CORE CHEMISTRY SKILL

Calculating a Molecular Formula

Earlier, in Sample Problem 7.10, we determined that the empirical formula of ascorbic acid (vitamin C) was $C_3H_4O_3$. If the molar mass for ascorbic acid is 176.12 g, we can calculate its molecular formula as follows:

The mass of the empirical formula $C_3H_4O_3$ is obtained in the same way as molar mass.

$$\text{Empirical formula} = 3\text{ mol of C} + 4\text{ mol of H} + 3\text{ mol of O}$$

$$\text{Empirical formula mass} = (3 \times 12.01\text{ g}) + (4 \times 1.008\text{ g}) + (3 \times 16.00\text{ g}) = 88.06\text{ g}$$

$$\text{Small integer} = \frac{\text{molar mass of ascorbic acid}}{\text{empirical formula mass of } C_3H_4O_3} = \frac{176.12\ \cancel{g}}{88.06\ \cancel{g}} = 2$$

Multiplying all the subscripts in the empirical formula of ascorbic acid by 2 gives its molecular formula.

$$C_{(3\times2)}H_{(4\times2)}O_{(3\times2)} = C_6H_8O_6 \quad \text{Molecular formula}$$

Brightly colored dishes are made of melamine.

Guide to Calculating a Molecular Formula from an Empirical Formula

1 Obtain the empirical formula and calculate the empirical formula mass.

2 Divide the molar mass by the empirical formula mass to obtain a small integer.

3 Multiply the empirical formula by the small integer to obtain the molecular formula.

SAMPLE PROBLEM 7.11 Determination of a Molecular Formula

Melamine, which is used to make plastic items such as dishes and toys, contains 28.57% carbon, 4.80% hydrogen, and 66.64% nitrogen. If the experimental molar mass is 125 g, what is the molecular formula of melamine?

SOLUTION

	Given	Need
Analyze the Problem	28.57% C, 4.80% H, 66.64% N, molar mass 125 g	molecular formula

Step 1 **Obtain the empirical formula and calculate the empirical formula mass.** Write each percentage as the number of grams in exactly 100. g of melamine and determine the number of moles of each.

$$\text{C} = 28.57 \text{ g} \qquad \text{H} = 4.80 \text{ g} \qquad \text{N} = 66.64 \text{ g}$$

$$28.57 \text{ g C} \times \frac{1 \text{ mol C}}{12.01 \text{ g C}} = 2.38 \text{ mol of C}$$

$$4.80 \text{ g H} \times \frac{1 \text{ mol H}}{1.008 \text{ g H}} = 4.76 \text{ mol of H}$$

$$66.64 \text{ g N} \times \frac{1 \text{ mol N}}{14.01 \text{ g N}} = 4.76 \text{ mol of N}$$

Divide the moles of each element by the smallest number of moles, 2.38, to obtain the subscripts of each element in the formula.

$$\frac{2.38 \text{ mol C}}{2.38} = 1.00 \text{ mol of C}$$

$$\frac{4.76 \text{ mol H}}{2.38} = 2.00 \text{ mol of H}$$

$$\frac{4.76 \text{ mol N}}{2.38} = 2.00 \text{ mol of N}$$

Using these values as subscripts, $C_{1.00}H_{2.00}N_{2.00}$, we write the empirical formula for melamine as CH_2N_2.

$$C_{1.00}H_{2.00}N_{2.00} = CH_2N_2$$

Now we calculate the molar mass for this empirical formula as follows:

$$\text{Empirical formula} = 1 \text{ mol of C} + 2 \text{ mol of H} + 2 \text{ mol of N}$$

$$\text{Empirical formula mass} = (1 \times 12.01) + (2 \times 1.008) + (2 \times 14.01) = 42.05 \text{ g}$$

Step 2 **Divide the molar mass by the empirical formula mass to obtain a small integer.**

$$\text{Small integer} = \frac{\text{molar mass of melamine}}{\text{empirical formula mass of } CH_2N_2} = \frac{125 \text{ g}}{42.05 \text{ g}} = 2.97$$

Step 3 **Multiply the empirical formula by the small integer to obtain the molecular formula.** Because the experimental molar mass is close to 3 times the empirical formula mass, the subscripts in the empirical formula are multiplied by 3 to give the molecular formula.

$$C_{(1\times3)}H_{(2\times3)}N_{(2\times3)} = C_3H_6N_6 \quad \text{Molecular formula}$$

STUDY CHECK 7.11

The insecticide lindane has a mass percent composition of 24.78% C, 2.08% H, and 73.14% Cl. If its experimental molar mass is 290 g, what is the molecular formula?

QUESTIONS AND PROBLEMS

7.5 Molecular Formulas

LEARNING GOAL: *Determine the molecular formula of a substance from the empirical formula and molar mass.*

7.39 Write the empirical formula for each of the following substances:

a. H_2O_2, peroxide
b. $C_{18}H_{12}$, chrysene, used in the manufacture of dyes
c. $C_{10}H_{16}O_2$, chrysanthemic acid, in pyrethrum flowers
d. $C_9H_{18}N_6$, altretamine, an anticancer medication
e. $C_2H_4N_2O_2$, oxamide, a fertilizer

7.40 Write the empirical formula for each of the following substances:

a. $C_6H_6O_3$, pyrogallol, a developer in photography
b. $C_6H_{12}O_6$, galactose, a carbohydrate
c. $C_8H_6O_4$, terephthalic acid, used in the manufacture of plastic bottles
d. C_6Cl_6, hexachlorobenzene, a fungicide
e. $C_{24}H_{16}O_{12}$, laccaic acid, a crimson dye

7.41 The carbohydrate fructose found in honey and fruits has an empirical formula of CH_2O. If the experimental molar mass of fructose is 180 g, what is its molecular formula?

7.42 Caffeine has an empirical formula of $C_4H_5N_2O$. If it has an experimental molar mass of 194 g, what is the molecular formula of caffeine?

Coffee beans are a source of caffeine.

7.43 Benzene and acetylene have the same empirical formula, CH. However, benzene has an experimental molar mass of 78 g, and acetylene has an experimental molar mass of 26 g. What are the molecular formulas of benzene and acetylene?

7.44 Glyoxyl, used in textiles; maleic acid, used to retard oxidation of fats and oils; and acontic acid, a plasticizer, all have the same empirical formula, CHO. However, the experimental molar masses are glyoxyl 58 g, maleic acid 117 g, and acontic acid 174 g. What are the molecular formulas of glyoxyl, maleic acid, and acontic acid?

7.45 Mevalonic acid is involved in the biosynthesis of cholesterol. Mevalonic acid is 48.64% C, 8.16% H, and 43.20% O. If mevalonic acid has an experimental molar mass of 148 g, what is its molecular formula?

7.46 Chloral hydrate, a sedative, contains 14.52% C, 1.83% H, 64.30% Cl, and 19.35% O. If it has an experimental molar mass of 165 g, what is the molecular formula of chloral hydrate?

7.47 Vanillic acid contains 57.14% C, 4.80% H, and 38.06% O, and has an experimental molar mass of 168 g. What is the molecular formula of vanillic acid?

7.48 Lactic acid, the substance that builds up in muscles during exercise, has a mass percent composition of 40.0% C, 6.71% H, and 53.3% O, and an experimental molar mass of 90. g. What is the molecular formula of lactic acid?

7.49 A sample of nicotine, a poisonous compound found in tobacco leaves, is 74.0% C, 8.7% H, and 17.3% N. If the experimental molar mass of nicotine is 162 g, what is its molecular formula?

7.50 Adenine, a nitrogen-containing compound found in DNA and RNA, is 44.5% C, 3.70% H, and 51.8% N. If adenine has an experimental molar mass of 135 g, what is its molecular formula?

CHAPTER REVIEW

7.1 The Mole

LEARNING GOAL: *Use Avogadro's number to determine the number of particles in a given number of moles.*

- One mol of an element contains 6.022×10^{23} atoms.
- One mol of a compound contains 6.022×10^{23} molecules or formula units.

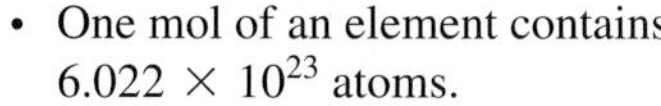

7.2 Molar Mass

LEARNING GOAL: *Given the chemical formula of a substance, calculate its molar mass.*

- The molar mass (g/mol) of a substance is the mass in grams equal numerically to its atomic mass, or the sum of the atomic masses, which have been multiplied by their subscripts in a formula.

7.3 Calculations Using Molar Mass

LEARNING GOAL: *Given the number of moles of a substance, calculate the mass in grams; given the mass, calculate the number of moles.*

- The molar mass is used as a conversion factor to change a quantity from grams to moles, or from moles to grams.

7.4 Mass Percent Composition and Empirical Formulas

LEARNING GOAL: *Given the formula of a compound, calculate the mass percent composition; from the mass percent composition, determine the empirical formula of a compound.*

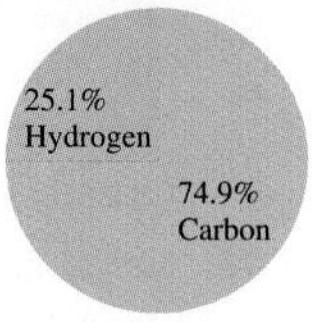

25.1% Hydrogen

74.9% Carbon

Mass percent of CH_4

- The mass percent composition is obtained by dividing the mass in grams of one or all elements in a compound by the mass of that compound.
- The empirical formula is calculated by determining the lowest whole-number mole ratio from the grams of the elements present in a sample.

7.5 Molecular Formulas

LEARNING GOAL: *Determine the molecular formula of a substance from the empirical formula and molar mass.*

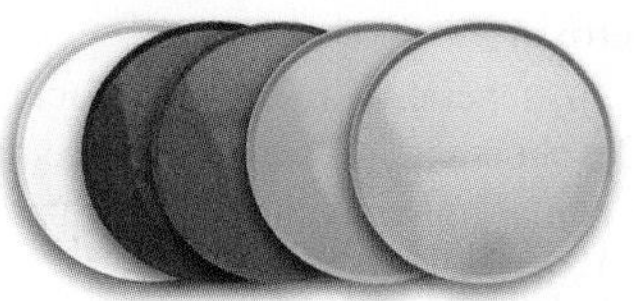

- A molecular formula is equal to, or a multiple of, the empirical formula.
- The experimental molar mass, which must be known, is divided by the mass of the empirical formula to obtain the small integer used to convert the empirical formula to the molecular formula.

CONCEPT MAP

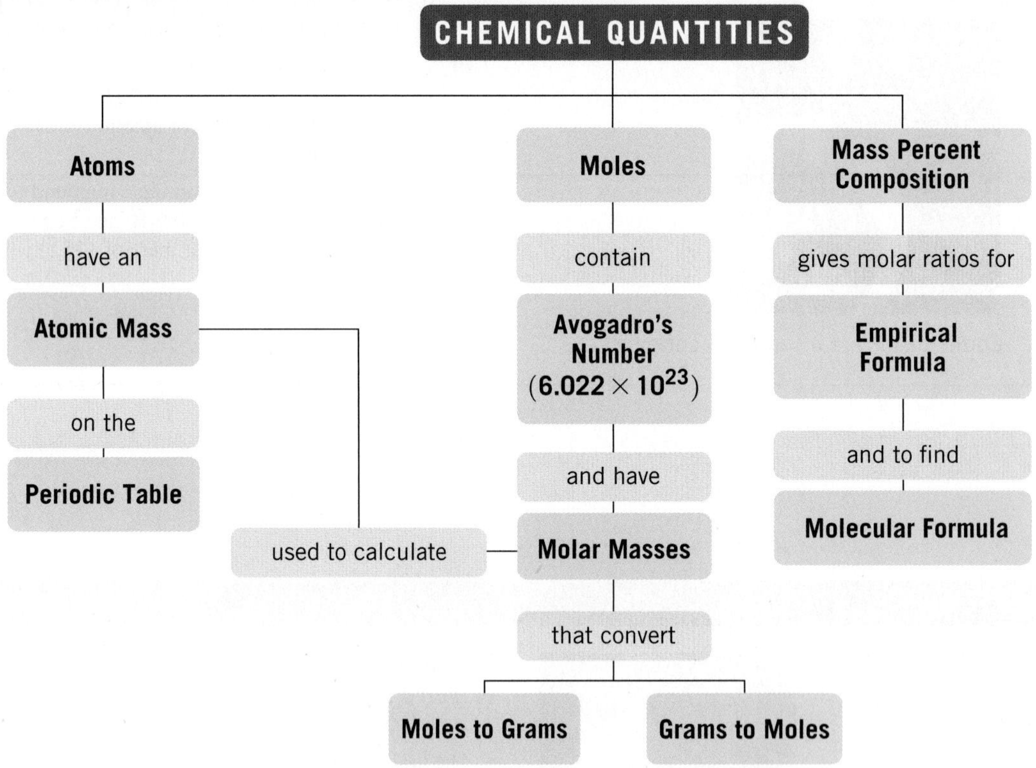

CHEMICAL QUANTITIES

- **Atoms**
  - have an
  - **Atomic Mass**
    - on the
    - **Periodic Table**
    - used to calculate → **Molar Masses**
- **Moles**
  - contain
  - **Avogadro's Number (6.022×10^{23})**
  - and have
  - **Molar Masses**
  - that convert
  - **Moles to Grams** / **Grams to Moles**
- **Mass Percent Composition**
  - gives molar ratios for
  - **Empirical Formula**
  - and to find
  - **Molecular Formula**

KEY TERMS

Avogadro's number The number of items in a mole, equal to 6.022×10^{23}.

empirical formula The simplest or smallest whole-number ratio of the atoms in a formula.

formula unit The group of ions represented by the formula of an ionic compound.

mass percent composition The percent by mass of the elements in a formula.

molar mass The mass in grams of 1 mol of an element is equal numerically to its atomic mass. The molar mass of a compound is equal to the sum of the masses of the elements in the formula.

mole A group of atoms, molecules, or formula units that contains 6.022×10^{23} of these items.

molecular formula The actual formula that gives the number of atoms of each type of element in the compound.

CORE CHEMISTRY SKILLS

The chapter section containing each Core Chemistry Skill is shown in parentheses at the end of each heading.

Converting Particles to Moles (7.1)

- In chemistry, atoms, molecules, and ions are counted by the mole (abbreviated *mol* in calculations), a unit that contains 6.022×10^{23} items, which is Avogadro's number.
- For example, 1 mol of carbon contains 6.022×10^{23} atoms of carbon and 1 mol of H_2O contains 6.022×10^{23} molecules of H_2O.
- Avogadro's number is used to convert between particles and moles.

Example: How many moles of nickel contain 2.45×10^{24} Ni atoms?

Answer:

$$2.45 \times 10^{24} \cancel{\text{Ni atoms}} \times \frac{1 \text{ mol Ni atoms}}{6.022 \times 10^{23} \cancel{\text{Ni atoms}}}$$

$$= 4.07 \text{ mol of Ni atoms}$$

Calculating Molar Mass (7.2)

- The molar mass of a compound is the sum of the molar mass of each element in its chemical formula multiplied by its subscript in the formula.

Example: Calculate the molar mass for pinene, $C_{10}H_{16}$, a component of pine tree sap.

Pinene is a component of pine sap.

Answer:

$$10 \cancel{\text{mol C}} \times \frac{12.01 \text{ g C}}{1 \cancel{\text{mol C}}} = 120.1 \text{ g of C}$$

$$16 \cancel{\text{mol H}} \times \frac{1.008 \text{ g H}}{1 \cancel{\text{mol H}}} = 16.13 \text{ g of H}$$

$$\text{Molar mass of } C_{10}H_{16} = 136.2 \text{ g of } C_{10}H_{16}$$

Using Molar Mass as a Conversion Factor (7.3)

- The molar mass of an element is its mass in grams equal numerically to its atomic mass.
- The molar mass of a compound is its mass in grams equal numerically to the sum of the masses of its elements.
- Molar mass is used as a conversion factor to convert between the moles and grams of a substance.

Equality: 1 mol of Al = 26.98 g of Al

Conversion Factors: $\frac{26.98 \text{ g Al}}{1 \text{ mol Al}}$ and $\frac{1 \text{ mol Al}}{26.98 \text{ g Al}}$

A bicycle with an aluminum frame.

Example: The frame of a bicycle contains 6500 g of aluminum. How many moles of aluminum are in the bicycle frame?

Answer: $6500 \cancel{\text{g Al}} \times \frac{1 \text{ mol Al}}{26.98 \cancel{\text{g Al}}} = 240 \text{ mol of Al}$

Calculating Mass Percent Composition (7.4)

- The mass of a compound contains a definite proportion by mass of its elements.
- The mass percent of an element in a compound is calculated by dividing the mass of that element by the mass of the compound.

$$\text{Mass percent of an element} = \frac{\text{mass of an element}}{\text{mass of the compound}} \times 100\%$$

Example: Dinitrogen tetroxide, N_2O_4, is used in liquid fuels for rockets. If it has a molar mass of 92.02 g/mol, what is the mass percent of nitrogen?

Answer: $\text{Mass \% N} = \frac{28.02 \text{ g N}}{92.02 \text{ g } N_2O_4} \times 100\% = 30.45\% \text{ N}$

Calculating an Empirical Formula (7.4)

- The empirical formula or simplest formula represents the lowest whole-number ratio of the atoms and therefore moles of elements in a compound.
- For example, dinitrogen tetroxide, N_2O_4, has the empirical formula NO_2.
- To calculate the empirical formula, the grams of each element are converted to moles and divided by the smallest number of moles to obtain the lowest whole-number ratio.

Example: Calculate the empirical formula for a compound that contains 3.28 g of Cr and 6.72 g of Cl.

Answer: Convert the grams of each element to moles.

$$3.28 \text{ g Cr} \times \frac{1 \text{ mol Cr}}{52.00 \text{ g Cr}} = 0.0631 \text{ mol of Cr}$$

$$6.72 \text{ g Cl} \times \frac{1 \text{ mol Cl}}{35.45 \text{ g Cl}} = 0.190 \text{ mol of Cl}$$

Divide by the smallest number of moles (0.0631 mol of Cr) to obtain the empirical formula.

$$\frac{0.0631 \text{ mol Cr}}{0.0631} = 1.00 \text{ mol of Cr}$$

$$\frac{0.190 \text{ mol Cl}}{0.0631} = 3.01 \text{ (round off to 3) mol of Cl}$$

Write the empirical formula using the whole-number ratios of moles.

Cr_1Cl_3 or $CrCl_3$

Calculating a Molecular Formula (7.5)

- A molecular formula is related to the empirical formula by a small whole number (integer) such as 1, 2, or 3.

$$\text{Molecular formula} = \text{small integer} \times \text{empirical formula}$$

- If the empirical formula mass and the molar mass are known for a compound, an integer can be calculated by dividing the molar mass by the empirical formula mass.

$$\text{Small integer} = \frac{\text{molar mass of compound}}{\text{empirical formula mass}}$$

Example: Cymene, a component in oil of thyme, has an empirical formula C_5H_7 and an experimental molar mass of 135 g. What is the molecular formula of cymene?

Answer: Empirical formula = 5 mol of C + 7 mol of H

$$\text{Empirical formula mass} = (5 \times 12.01 \text{ g}) + (7 \times 1.008 \text{ g}) = 67.11 \text{ g}$$

$$\frac{\text{Molar mass of cymene}}{\text{Empirical formula mass of cymene}} = \frac{135 \text{ g}}{67.11 \text{ g}} = 2.01 \text{ (round off to 2)}$$

The molecular formula of cymene is calculated by multiplying each of the subscripts in the empirical formula by 2.

$$C_{(5\times2)}H_{(7\times2)} = C_{10}H_{14}$$

UNDERSTANDING THE CONCEPTS

The chapter sections to review are shown in parentheses at the end of each question.

7.51 A dandruff shampoo contains dipyrithione, $C_{10}H_8N_2O_2S_2$, an antibacterial and antifungal agent. (7.1, 7.2, 7.3, 7.4)

Dandruff shampoo contains dipyrithione.

a. What is the empirical formula of dipyrithione?
b. What is the molar mass of dipyrithione?
c. What is the mass percent composition of dipyrithione?
d. How many atoms of C are in 25.0 g of dipyrithione?
e. How many moles of dipyrithione are in 25.0 g?

7.52 Ibuprofen, the anti-inflammatory ingredient in Advil, has the formula $C_{13}H_{18}O_2$. (7.1, 7.2, 7.3, 7.4)

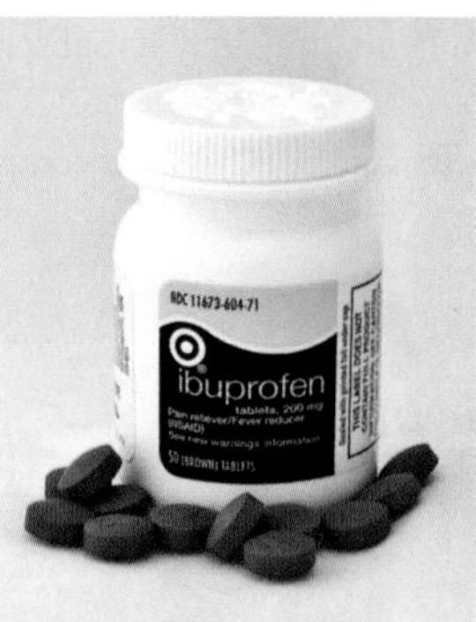

Ibuprofen is an anti-inflammatory drug.

a. What is the molar mass of ibuprofen?
b. How many atoms of H are in 0.100 mol of ibuprofen?
c. What is the mass percent of oxygen in ibuprofen?
d. How many atoms of carbon are in 0.425 g of ibuprofen?
e. How many grams of hydrogen are in 2.45 g of ibuprofen?

7.53 Using the models of the molecules (black = C, white = H, yellow = S, green = Cl), determine each of the following for models of compounds **1** and **2**: (7.2, 7.4, 7.5)

1.

2.

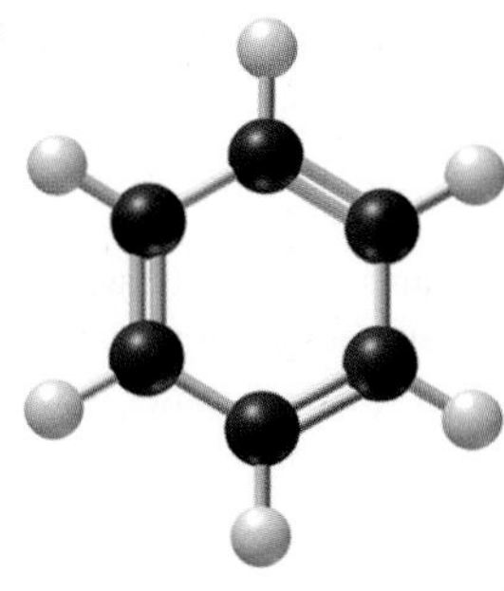

a. molecular formula **b.** empirical formula
c. molar mass **d.** mass percent composition

7.54 Using the models of the molecules (black = C, white = H, yellow = S, red = O), determine each of the following for models of compounds **1** and **2**: (7.2, 7.4, 7.5)

1.

2.

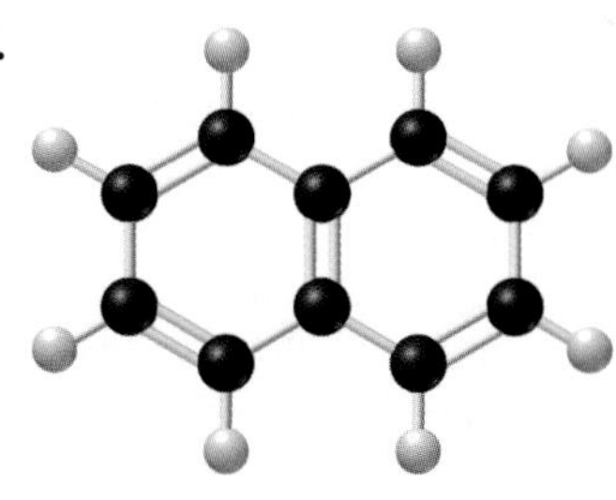

a. molecular formula **b.** empirical formula
c. molar mass **d.** mass percent composition

ADDITIONAL QUESTIONS AND PROBLEMS

7.55 Calculate the molar mass for each of the following: (7.2)
a. $ZnSO_4$, zinc sulfate, zinc supplement
b. $Ca(IO_3)_2$, calcium iodate, iodine source in table salt
c. $C_5H_8NNaO_4$, monosodium glutamate, flavor enhancer
d. $C_6H_{12}O_2$, isoamyl formate, used to make artificial fruit syrups

7.56 Calculate the molar mass for each of the following: (7.2)
a. $MgCO_3$, magnesium carbonate, an antacid
b. $Au(OH)_3$, gold(III) hydroxide, used in gold plating
c. $C_{18}H_{34}O_2$, oleic acid, from olive oil
d. $C_{21}H_{26}O_5$, prednisone, anti-inflammatory

7.57 Calculate the mass percent composition for each of the following compounds: (7.4)
a. 3.85 g of Ca and 3.65 g of F
b. 0.389 g of Na and 0.271 g of O
c. 12.4 of K, 17.4 g of Mn, and 20.3 g of O

7.58 Calculate the mass percent composition for each of the following compounds: (7.4)
a. 3.65 g of Na, 2.54 g of S, and 3.81 g of O
b. 0.457 g of C and 0.043 g of H
c. 0.907 g of Na, 1.40 g of Cl, and 1.89 g of O

7.59 Calculate the mass percent composition for each of the following compounds: (7.4)
a. K_2CrO_4
b. $Al(HCO_3)_3$
c. $C_6H_{12}O_6$

7.60 Calculate the mass percent composition for each of the following compounds: (7.4)
a. $CaCO_3$
b. $NaC_2H_3O_2$
c. $Ba(NO_3)_2$

7.61 Aspirin, $C_9H_8O_4$, is used to reduce inflammation and reduce fever. (7.1, 7.2, 7.3, 7.4)
a. What is the mass percent composition of aspirin?
b. How many moles of aspirin contain 5.0×10^{24} atoms of carbon?
c. How many atoms of oxygen are in 7.50 g of aspirin?
d. How many molecules of aspirin contain 2.50 g of hydrogen?

7.62 Ammonium sulfate, $(NH_4)_2SO_4$, is used in fertilizers. (7.1, 7.2, 7.3, 7.4)
a. What is the mass percent composition of $(NH_4)_2SO_4$?
b. How many atoms of hydrogen are in 0.75 mol of $(NH_4)_2SO_4$?
c. How many grams of oxygen are in 4.50×10^{23} formula units of $(NH_4)_2SO_4$?
d. What mass of $(NH_4)_2SO_4$ contains 2.50 g of sulfur?

7.63 A mixture contains 0.250 mol of Mn_2O_3 and 20.0 g of MnO_2. (7.1, 7.2, 7.3)
a. How many atoms of oxygen are present in the mixture?
b. How many grams of manganese are in the mixture?

7.64 A mixture contains 4.00×10^{23} molecules of PCl_3 and 0.250 mol of PCl_5. (7.1, 7.2, 7.3)
a. How many grams of chlorine are present in the mixture?
b. How many moles of phosphorus are in the mixture?

7.65 Write the empirical formula for each of the following: (7.4)
a. $C_5H_5N_5$, adenine, a nitrogen compound in RNA and DNA
b. FeC_2O_4, iron(II) oxalate, a photographic developer
c. $C_{16}H_{16}N_4$, stilbamidine, an antibiotic for animals
d. $C_6H_{14}N_2O_2$, lysine, an amino acid needed for growth

7.66 Write the empirical formula for each of the following: (7.4)
a. $C_{12}H_{24}N_2O_4$, carisoprodol, a skeletal muscle relaxant
b. $C_{10}H_{10}O_5$, opianic acid, used to synthesize a drug to treat tuberculosis
c. $CrCl_3$, chromium(III) chloride, used in chrome plating
d. $C_{16}H_{16}N_2O_2$, lysergic acid, a controlled substance from ergot

7.67 Calculate the empirical formula for each of the following compounds: (7.4)
a. 2.20 g of S and 7.81 g of F
b. 6.35 g of Ag, 0.825 g of N, and 2.83 g of O
c. 43.6% P and 56.4% O
d. 22.1% Al, 25.4% P, and 52.5% O

7.68 Calculate the empirical formula for each of the following compounds: (7.4)
a. 5.13 g of Cr and 2.37 g of O
b. 2.82 g of K, 0.870 g of C, and 2.31 g of O
c. 61.0% Sn and 39.0% F
d. 25.9% N and 74.1% O

7.69 Oleic acid, a component of olive oil, is 76.54% C, 12.13% H, and 11.33% O. The experimental value of the molar mass is 282 g. (7.1, 7.2, 7.3, 7.4, 7.5)

a. What is the molecular formula of oleic acid?

b. If oleic acid has a density of 0.895 g/mL, how many molecules of oleic acid are in 3.00 mL of oleic acid?

7.70 Iron pyrite, commonly known as "fool's gold," is 46.5% Fe and 53.5% S. (7.1, 7.2, 7.3, 7.4, 7.5)

a. If the empirical formula and the molecular formula are the same, what is the molecular formula of the compound?

b. If the crystal contains 4.85 g of iron, how many atoms of iron are in the crystal?

Iron pyrite is commonly known as "fool's gold."

7.71 Succinic acid is 40.7% C, 5.12% H, and 54.2% O. If it has an experimental molar mass of 118 g, what are the empirical and molecular formulas? (7.4, 7.5)

7.72 A compound is 70.6% Hg, 12.5% Cl, and 16.9% O. If it has an experimental molar mass of 568 g, what are the empirical and molecular formulas? (7.4, 7.5)

7.73 A sample of a compound contains 1.65×10^{23} atoms of C, 0.552 g of H, and 4.39 g of O. If 1 mol of the compound contains 4 mol of O, what is the molecular formula and molar mass of the compound? (7.4, 7.5)

7.74 What is the molecular formula of a compound if 0.500 mol of the compound contains 0.500 mol of Sr, 1.81×10^{24} atoms of O, and 35.5 g of Cl? (7.4, 7.5)

CHALLENGE QUESTIONS

7.75 A toothpaste contains 0.240% by mass sodium fluoride used to prevent tooth decay and 0.30% by mass triclosan, $C_{12}H_7Cl_3O_2$, a preservative and antigingivitis agent. One tube contains 119 g of toothpaste. (7.1, 7.2, 7.3, 7.4)

Components in toothpaste include triclosan and NaF.

a. How many moles of NaF are in the tube of toothpaste?

b. How many fluoride ions, F^-, are in the tube of toothpaste?

c. How many grams of sodium ion, Na^+, are in 1.50 g of toothpaste?

d. How many molecules of triclosan are in the tube of toothpaste?

e. What is the mass percent composition of triclosan?

7.76 Sorbic acid, an inhibitor of mold in cheese, has a mass percent composition of 64.27% C, 7.19% H, and 28.54% O. If sorbic acid has an experimental molar mass of 112 g, what is its molecular formula? (7.4, 7.5)

Cheese contains sorbic acid, which prevents the growth of mold.

7.77 Iron(III) chromate, a yellow powder used as a pigment in paints, contains 24.3% Fe, 33.9% Cr, and 41.8% O. If it has an experimental molar mass of 460 g, what are its empirical and molecular formulas? (7.4, 7.5)

Iron(III) chromate is a yellow pigment used in paints.

7.78 A gold bar is 5.50 cm long, 3.10 cm wide, and 0.300 cm thick. (7.1, 7.2, 7.3, 7.4, 7.5)

a. If gold has a density of 19.3 g/cm^3, what is the mass of the gold bar?

b. How many atoms of gold are in the bar?

c. When the same mass of gold combines with oxygen, the oxide product has a mass of 111 g. How many moles of O are combined with the gold?

d. What is the molecular formula of the oxide product if it is the same as the empirical formula?

A gold bar consists of gold atoms.

ANSWERS

Answers to Study Checks

7.1 0.432 mol of H_2O

7.2 0.120 mol of aspirin

7.3 138.12 g

7.4 24.4 g of Au

7.5 6.21×10^{-3} mol of $CaCO_3$

7.6 0.0515 mol of N

7.7 38.70% C; 9.744% H; 51.55% O

7.8 PH_3

7.9 K_2SO_4

7.10 $C_2H_2O_3$

7.11 $C_6H_6Cl_6$

Answers to Selected Questions and Problems

7.1 **a.** 1.20×10^{23} atoms of Ag
b. 4.52×10^{23} molecules of C_3H_8O
c. 7.53×10^{23} atoms of Cr

7.3 **a.** 24 mol of H
b. 1.0×10^2 mol of C
c. 0.040 mol of N

7.5 **a.** 3.01×10^{23} atoms of C
b. 7.71×10^{23} molecules of SO_2
c. 0.0867 mol of Fe

7.7 **a.** 6.00 mol of H
b. 8.00 mol of O
c. 1.20×10^{24} atoms of P
d. 4.82×10^{24} atoms of O

7.9 **a.** 58.44 g **b.** 159.7 g **c.** 329.4 g

7.11 **a.** 342.2 g **b.** 188.18 g **c.** 365.5 g

7.13 **a.** 70.90 g **b.** 90.08 g **c.** 262.9 g

7.15 **a.** 83.98 g **b.** 98.95 g **c.** 156.7 g

7.17 **a.** 34.5 g **b.** 112 g **c.** 5.50 g
d. 5.14 g **e.** 9.80×10^4 g

7.19 **a.** 3.03 g **b.** 38.1 g **c.** 9.30 g
d. 24.6 g **e.** 12.9 g

7.21 **a.** 0.760 mol of Ag **b.** 0.0240 mol of C
c. 0.881 mol of NH_3 **d.** 0.164 mol of C_3H_8
e. 1.53 mol of Fe_2O_3

7.23 **a.** 6.25 mol of He **b.** 0.781 mol of O_2
c. 0.321 mol of $Al(OH)_3$ **d.** 0.106 mol of Ga_2S_3
e. 0.430 mol of C_4H_{10}

7.25 **a.** 1.25×10^{24} atoms of C **b.** 4.14×10^{23} atoms of C
c. 1.13×10^{25} atoms of C **d.** 2.22×10^{24} atoms of C
e. 7.5×10^{24} atoms of C

7.27 **a.** 66.1 g of propane
b. 0.771 mol of propane
c. 27.8 g of C
d. 2.78×10^{22} atoms of H

7.29 **a.** 46.8% Si; 53.2% O
b. 81.7% C; 18.3% H
c. 32.3% Na; 45.1% S; 22.6% O
d. 54.6% C; 9.12% H; 36.3% O

7.31 **a.** 39.01% Mg; 60.99% F
b. 54.09% Ca; 43.18% O; 2.72% H
c. 40.00% C; 6.71% H; 53.29% O
d. 28.19% N; 8.12% H; 20.77% P; 42.92% O
e. 71.55% C; 6.71% H; 4.91% N; 16.82% O

7.33 **a.** 25.94% N **b.** 26.19% N
c. 46.62% N **d.** 33.47% N
e. 11.96% N

7.35 **a.** N_2O **b.** CH_3
c. HNO_3 **d.** $CaCrO_4$

7.37 **a.** K_2S **b.** GaF_3
c. B_2O_3 **d.** Li_2CO_3
e. $C_5H_8O_3$

7.39 **a.** HO **b.** C_3H_2
c. C_5H_8O **d.** $C_3H_6N_2$
e. CH_2NO

7.41 $C_6H_{12}O_6$

7.43 benzene C_6H_6; acetylene C_2H_2

7.45 $C_6H_{12}O_4$

7.47 $C_8H_8O_4$

7.49 $C_{10}H_{14}N_2$

7.51 **a.** C_5H_4NOS
b. 252.3 g
c. 47.60% C; 3.20% H; 11.11% N; 12.68% O; 25.42% S
d. 5.97×10^{23} atoms of C
e. 0.991 mol of dipyrithione

7.53 **1.** **a.** S_2Cl_2 **b.** SCl
c. 135.04 g **d.** 47.50% S; 52.50% Cl
2. **a.** C_6H_6 **b.** CH
c. 78.11 g **d.** 92.25% C; 7.74% H

7.55 **a.** 161.48 g **b.** 389.9 g
c. 169.11 g **d.** 116.16 g

7.57 **a.** 51.3% Ca; 48.7% F
b. 58.9% Na; 41.1% O
c. 24.8% K; 34.7% Mn; 40.5% O

7.59 **a.** 40.27% K; 26.78% Cr; 32.96% O
b. 12.85% Al; 1.44% H; 17.16% C; 68.57% O
c. 40.00% C; 6.72% H; 53.29% O

7.61 **a.** 59.99% C; 4.48% H; 35.52% O
b. 0.92 mol of aspirin

c. 1.00×10^{23} atoms of O
d. 1.87×10^{23} molecules of aspirin

7.63 **a.** 7.29×10^{23} atoms of O
b. 40.1 g of Mn

7.65 **a.** CHN **b.** FeC_2O_4
c. C_4H_4N **d.** C_3H_7NO

7.67 **a.** SF_6 **b.** $AgNO_3$
c. P_2O_5 **d.** $AlPO_4$

7.69 **a.** $C_{18}H_{34}O_2$
b. 5.72×10^{21} molecules of oleic acid

7.71 The empirical formula is $C_2H_3O_2$; the molecular formula is $C_4H_6O_4$.

7.73 The molecular formula is $C_4H_8O_4$; the molar mass is 120.10 g.

7.75 **a.** 0.00680 mol of NaF
b. 4.10×10^{21} F^- ions
c. 0.00197 g of Na^+ ions
d. 7.4×10^{20} molecules of triclosan
e. 49.76% C; 2.44% H; 36.74% Cl; 11.05% O

7.77 The empirical formula is $Fe_2Cr_3O_{12}$; the molecular formula is $Fe_2Cr_3O_{12}$.

Combining Ideas from Chapters 4 to 7

CI.7 For parts **a** to **f**, consider the loss of electrons by atoms of the element X, and a gain of electrons by atoms of the element Y. Element X is in Group 2A (2), Period 3, and Y is in Group 7A (17), Period 3. (4.2, 5.4, 5.5, 6.2, 6.3)

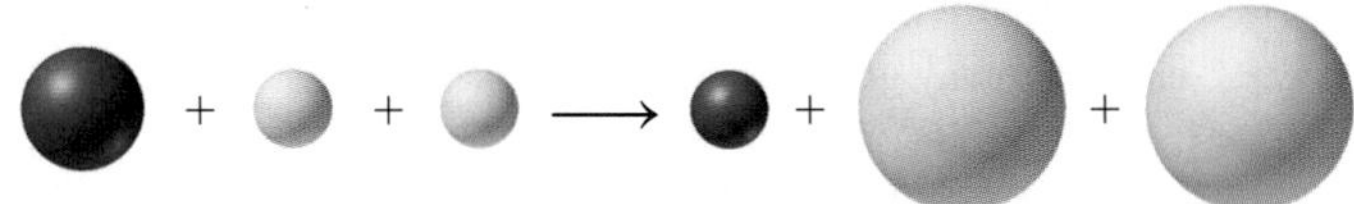

a. Which element is a metal, X or Y?
b. Which element is a nonmetal, X or Y?
c. What are the ionic charges of X and Y?
d. Write the electron configurations of the atoms X and Y.
e. Write the electron configurations of the ions of X and Y.
f. Write the actual formula and name of the ionic compound indicated by the ions.

CI.8 A bracelet of sterling silver marked 925 contains 92.5% silver by mass and 7.5% other metals. It has a volume of 25.6 cm^3 and a density of 10.2 g/cm^3. (2.6, 2.8, 4.4, 7.1)

a. What is the mass, in kilograms, of the sterling silver bracelet?
b. How many atoms of silver are in the bracelet?
c. Determine the number of protons and neutrons in each of the two stable isotopes of silver:

$$^{107}_{47}Ag \text{ and } ^{109}_{47}Ag$$

d. When silver combines with oxygen, a compound forms that contains 93.10% Ag by mass. What are the name and the molecular formula of the oxide product if the molecular formula is the same as the empirical formula?

CI.9 Oxalic acid, an organic compound found in plants and vegetables such as rhubarb, has a mass percent composition of 26.7% C, 2.24% H, and 71.1% O. Oxalic acid can interfere with respiration and cause kidney or bladder stones. If a large quantity of rhubarb leaves is ingested, the oxalic acid can be toxic. The lethal dose (LD_{50}) in rats for oxalic acid is 375 mg/kg. Rhubarb leaves contain about 0.5% by mass of oxalic acid. (2.7, 7.4, 7.5)

Rhubarb leaves are a source of oxalic acid.

a. What is the empirical formula of oxalic acid?
b. If oxalic acid has an experimental molar mass of 90. g, what is its molecular formula?
c. Using the LD_{50}, how many grams of oxalic acid would be toxic for a 160-lb person?
d. How many kilograms of rhubarb leaves would the person in part **c** need to eat to reach the toxic level of oxalic acid?

CI.10 The active ingredient in Tums has the following mass percent composition: 40.0% Ca, 12.0% C, and 48.0% O. (2.7, 6.3, 7.1, 7.4, 7.5)

a. If the empirical and molecular formulas are the same, what is its molecular formula?
b. What is the name of the ingredient?
c. If one Tums tablet contains 500. mg of this ingredient and a person takes two tablets a day, how many calcium ions does this person obtain from the Tums tablets?

CI.11 Tamiflu (Oseltamivir), $C_{16}H_{28}N_2O_4$, is a drug that is used to treat influenza. The preparation of Tamiflu begins with the extraction of shikimic acid from the seedpods of the Chinese spice, star anise. From 2.6 g of star anise, 0.13 g of shikimic acid can be obtained and used to produce one capsule containing 75 mg of Tamiflu. The usual adult dosage for treatment of influenza is 75 mg of Tamiflu twice daily for 5 days. (2.7, 6.5, 7.2, 7.3, 7.4, 7.5)

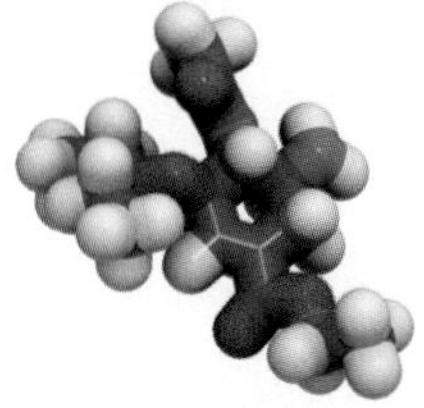

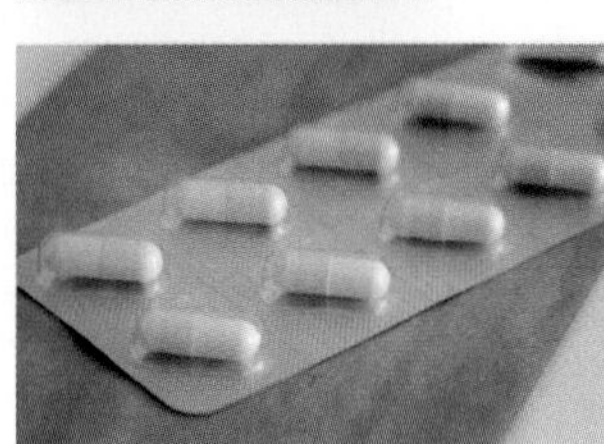

The spice called star anise is a plant source of shikimic acid.

a. What is the empirical formula of Tamiflu?
b. What is the mass percent composition of Tamiflu?
c. What is the molecular formula of shikimic acid? (Black spheres are carbon, white spheres are hydrogen, and red spheres are oxygen.)
d. How many moles of shikimic acid are contained in 1.3 g of shikimic acid?

e. How many capsules containing 75 mg of Tamiflu could be produced from 155 g of star anise?
f. How many grams of carbon are in one dose (75 mg) of Tamiflu?
g. How many kilograms of Tamiflu would be needed to treat all the people in a city with a population of 500 000 people?

CI.12 The compound butyric acid gives rancid butter its characteristic odor. (2.7, 2.8, 6.5, 7.1, 7.2, 7.3, 7.4, 7.5)

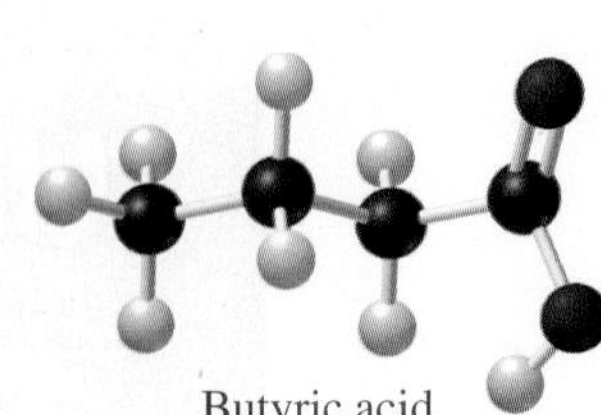

Butyric acid

a. If black spheres are carbon atoms, white spheres are hydrogen atoms, and red spheres are oxygen atoms, what is the molecular formula of butyric acid?
b. What is the empirical formula of butyric acid?
c. What is the mass percent composition of butyric acid?
d. How many grams of carbon are in 0.850 g of butyric acid?
e. How many grams of butyric acid contain 3.28×10^{23} oxygen atoms?
f. Butyric acid has a density of 0.959 g/mL at 20 °C. How many moles of butyric acid are contained in 0.565 mL of butyric acid?

ANSWERS

CI.7 **a.** X is a metal; elements in Group 2A (2) are metals.
b. Y is a nonmetal; elements in Group 7A (17) are nonmetals.
c. X^{2+}, Y^-
d. $X = 1s^22s^22p^63s^2$ $Y = 1s^22s^22p^63s^23p^5$
e. $X^{2+} = 1s^22s^22p^6$ $Y^- = 1s^22s^22p^63s^23p^6$
f. $MgCl_2$, magnesium chloride

CI.9 **a.** CHO_2
b. $C_2H_2O_4$
c. 27 g of oxalic acid
d. 5 kg of rhubarb

CI.11 **a.** $C_8H_{14}NO_2$
b. 61.52% C; 9.03% H; 8.97% N; 20.49% O
c. $C_7H_{10}O_5$
d. 7.5×10^{-3} mol of shikimic acid
e. 59 capsules
f. 0.046 g of C
g. 4×10^2 kg

Chemical Reactions 8

LOOKING AHEAD

Natalie was recently diagnosed with mild emphysema due to secondhand cigarette smoke. She has been referred to Angela, an exercise physiologist, who begins to assess Natalie's condition by connecting her to an EKG, a pulse oximeter, and a blood pressure cuff. The EKG tracks Natalie's heart rate and rhythm, the pulse oximeter tracks the oxygen levels in her blood, while the blood pressure cuff determines the pressure exerted by the heart in pumping her blood. Natalie then walks on a treadmill to determine her overall physical condition.

Based on Natalie's results, Angela creates a workout regime. They begin with low-intensity exercises that utilize smaller muscles instead of larger muscles, which require more O_2 and can deplete a significant amount of the O_2 in her blood. During the exercises, Angela continues to monitor Natalie's heart rate, blood O_2 level, and blood pressure to ensure that Natalie is exercising at a level that will enable her to become stronger without breaking down muscle due to a lack of oxygen.

Oxygen is necessary for metabolism and the production of ATP. In the mitochondria, O_2 is required for the final step in electron transport as it reacts with hydrogen ions to form water. These reactions associated with electron transport are coupled with oxidative phosphorylation to produce ATP.

Career: Exercise Physiologist

Exercise physiologists work with athletes as well as patients who have been diagnosed with diabetes, heart disease, pulmonary disease, or other chronic disability or disease. Patients who have been diagnosed with one of these diseases are often prescribed exercise as a form of treatment, and they are referred to an exercise physiologist. The exercise physiologist evaluates the patient's overall health and then creates a customized exercise program for that individual.

A program for an athlete might focus on reducing the number of injuries, while a program for a cardiac patient would focus on strengthening the heart muscles. The exercise physiologist also monitors the patient for improvement and notes if the exercise is reducing or reversing the progression of the disease.

The fuel in our cars burns with oxygen to provide energy to make the cars move and run the air conditioner. When we cook our food or bleach our hair, chemical reactions take place. In our bodies, chemical reactions convert food into molecules that build muscles and move them. In the leaves of trees and plants, carbon dioxide and water are converted into carbohydrates.

Some chemical reactions are simple, whereas others are quite complex. However, they can all be written with equations used to describe chemical reactions. In every chemical reaction, the atoms in the reacting substances, called *reactants*, are rearranged to give new substances called *products*.

In this chapter, we will see how equations are written and how we can determine the amount of reactant or product involved. We do the same thing at home when we use a recipe to make bread or cookies. At the automotive repair shop, a mechanic does essentially the same thing by adjusting the fuel system of an engine to allow for the correct amounts of fuel and oxygen. In the hospital, a respiratory therapist evaluates the levels of CO_2 and O_2 in the blood.

CHAPTER READINESS*

Key Math Skills

- Solving Equations (1.4D)

Core Chemistry Skills

- Writing Ionic Formulas (6.2, 6.4)
- Naming Ionic Compounds (6.3, 6.4)
- Writing the Names and Formulas for Molecular Compounds (6.5)

*These Key Math Skills and Core Chemistry Skills from previous chapters are listed here for your review as you proceed to the new material in this chapter.

LEARNING GOAL

Identify a balanced chemical equation and determine the number of atoms in the reactants and products.

8.1 Equations for Chemical Reactions

A *chemical change* occurs when a substance is converted into one or more new substances. For example, when silver tarnishes, the shiny silver metal (Ag) reacts with sulfur (S) to become the dull, black substance we call tarnish (Ag_2S) (see Figure 8.1).

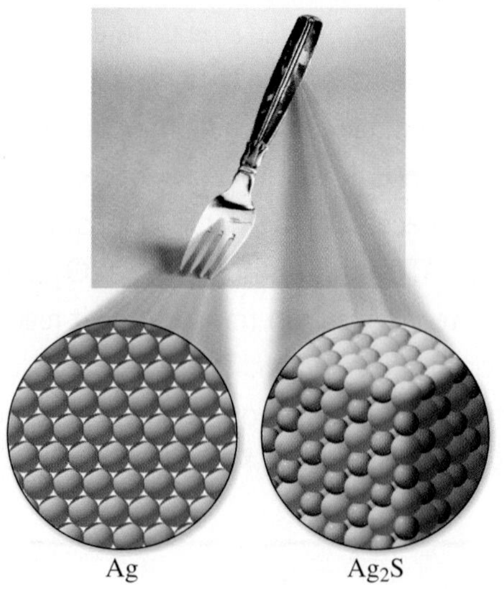

FIGURE 8.1 A chemical change produces new substances with new properties.

Q Why is the formation of tarnish a chemical change?

A **chemical reaction** always involves chemical change because atoms of the reacting substances form new combinations with new properties. During a chemical change, there is usually visual evidence that a chemical reaction has taken place (see Figure 8.2). For example, a chemical reaction occurs when an antacid tablet is dropped into a glass of water. The $NaHCO_3$ and citric acid ($C_6H_8O_7$) in the tablet react to form bubbles (gas) of carbon dioxide (CO_2). Other types of visible evidence of a chemical reaction are listed in Table 8.1.

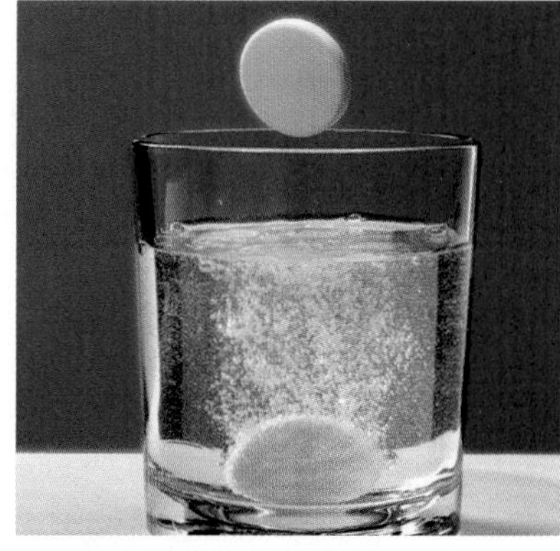

FIGURE 8.2 A chemical reaction forms new products with different properties. An antacid ($NaHCO_3$) tablet in water produces bubbles of carbon dioxide (CO_2).

Q What is the evidence for chemical change in this chemical reaction?

CONCEPT CHECK 8.1 Evidence of a Chemical Reaction

Indicate the visible evidence of a chemical reaction in each of the following:

a. burning propane fuel in a barbecue
b. using peroxide to change the color of hair

ANSWER

a. The production of heat during the burning of propane fuel is evidence of a chemical reaction.
b. The change in hair color is evidence of a chemical reaction.

When you build a model airplane, prepare a new recipe, or mix a medication formulation, you follow a set of directions. These directions tell you what materials to use and the products you will obtain. In chemistry, a **chemical equation** tells us the materials we need and the products that will form in a chemical reaction.

TABLE 8.1 Types of Visible Evidence of a Chemical Reaction

1. Formation of a gas (bubbles)
2. Change in color
3. Formation of a solid (precipitate)
4. Heat (or a flame) produced or heat absorbed

Writing a Chemical Equation

Suppose you work in a bicycle shop assembling wheels and frames into bicycles. You could represent this process by a simple equation:

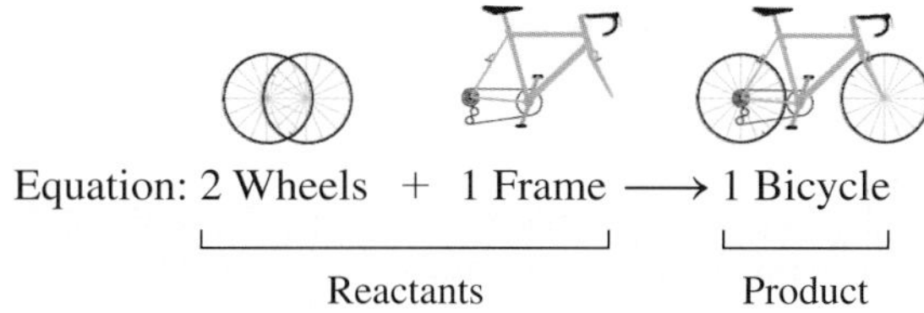

Equation: 2 Wheels + 1 Frame ⟶ 1 Bicycle

Reactants — Product

When you burn charcoal in a grill, the carbon in the charcoal combines with oxygen in the air to form carbon dioxide. We can represent this reaction by the following chemical equation:

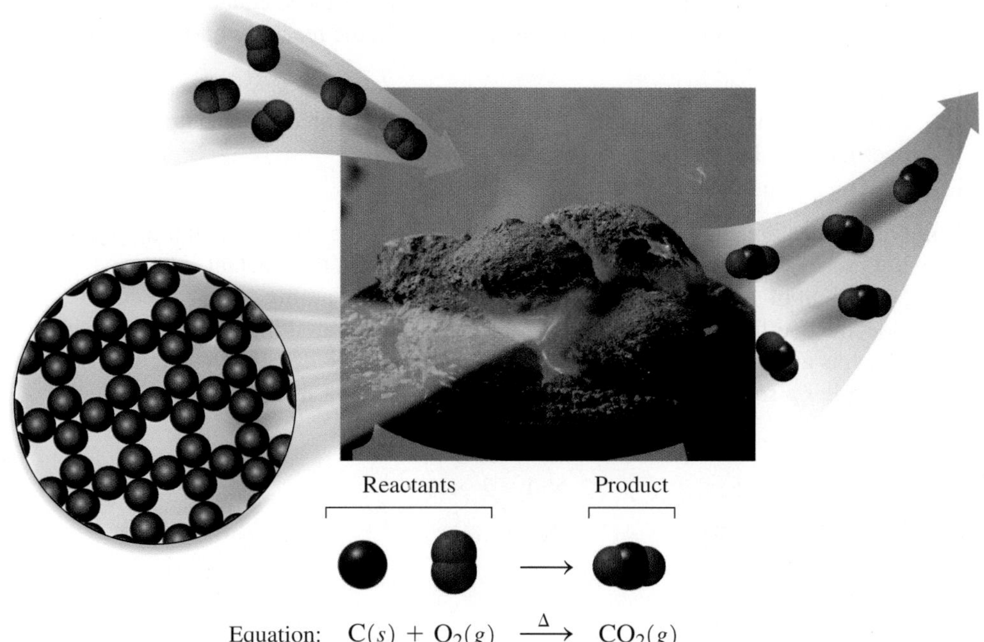

Equation: $C(s) + O_2(g) \xrightarrow{\Delta} CO_2(g)$

TABLE 8.2 Some Symbols Used in Writing Equations

Symbol	Meaning
+	Separates two or more formulas
$\longrightarrow$	Reacts to form products
$\xrightarrow{\Delta}$	Reactants are heated
(s)	Solid
(l)	Liquid
(g)	Gas or vapor
(aq)	Aqueous

In an equation, the formulas of the **reactants** are written on the left of the arrow and the formulas of the **products** on the right. When there are two or more formulas on the same side, they are separated by plus $(+)$ signs. The delta sign (Δ) indicates that heat was used to start the reaction.

Generally, each formula in an equation is followed by an abbreviation, in parentheses, that gives the physical state of the substance: solid (s), liquid (l), or gas (g). If a substance is dissolved in water, it is in an aqueous (aq) solution. Table 8.2 summarizes some of the symbols used in equations.

Identifying a Balanced Chemical Equation

When a chemical reaction takes place, the bonds between the atoms of the reactants are broken and new bonds are formed to give the products. All atoms are conserved, which means that atoms cannot be gained, lost, or changed into other types of atoms during a chemical reaction. Every chemical reaction is written as a **balanced equation**, in order to have the same number of atoms for each element in the reactants as in the products.

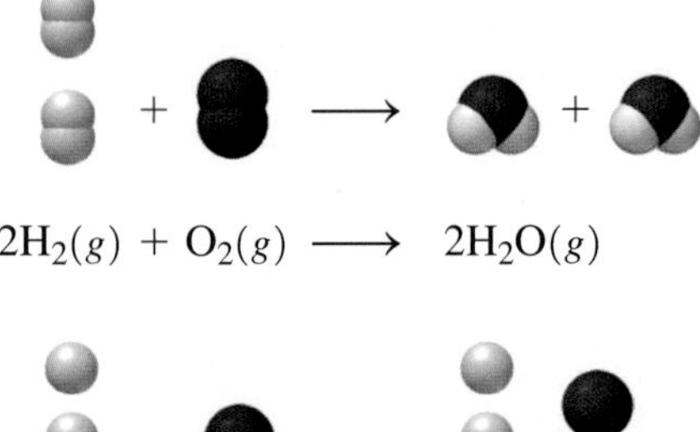

H O H O

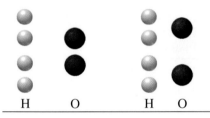

Reactant atoms = Product atoms

Now consider the balanced reaction in which hydrogen reacts with oxygen to form water written as follows:

$$2H_2(g) + O_2(g) \longrightarrow 2H_2O(g)$$

In the *balanced* equation, there are whole numbers called **coefficients** in front of the formulas. On the reactant side, the coefficient of 2 in front of the H_2 formula represents two molecules of hydrogen, which is 4 atoms of H. A coefficient of 1 is understood for O_2, which gives 2 atoms of O. On the product side, the coefficient of 2 in front of the H_2O formula represents 2 molecules of water. Because the coefficient of 2 multiplies all the atoms in H_2O, there are 4 hydrogen atoms and 2 oxygen atoms in the products. Because there are the same number of hydrogen atoms and oxygen atoms in the reactants as in the products, we know that the equation is *balanced.* This illustrates the *Law of Conservation of Matter*, which states that matter cannot be created or destroyed during a chemical reaction.

CONCEPT CHECK 8.2 Atoms in a Balanced Chemical Equation

Hydrogen and nitrogen react to form ammonia, NH_3. The balanced equation is written as

$$3H_2(g) + N_2(g) \longrightarrow \underset{\text{Ammonia}}{2NH_3(g)}$$

a. Identify the coefficient for H_2, N_2, and NH_3 in the balanced equation.
b. Calculate the number of atoms for each element in the reactants and products.

ANSWER

a. The coefficient of H_2 is 3; the coefficient of N_2 is 1, which is understood; the coefficient of NH_3 is 2.

$$3H_2(g) + 1N_2(g) \longrightarrow 2NH_3(g)$$

b. On the reactant side, the coefficient of 3 in front of the H_2 is used to multiply a subscript of 2, which gives $3 \times 2 = 6$ H atoms. On the reactant side, a coefficient of 1 is understood for N_2, which gives 2 N atoms. On the product side, the coefficient of 2 in front of the NH_3 is used to multiply a subscript of 1, which is understood, for the N, and gives 2 atoms of N. The coefficient of 2 also multiplies a subscript of 3 for H, which gives $2 \times 3 = 6$ H atoms.

$$3H_2(g) + 1N_2(g) \longrightarrow 2NH_3(g)$$

$3H_2(g)$	$1N_2(g)$		$2NH_3(g)$	
3×2	1×2		2×1	2×3
6 H	2 N	=	2 N	6 H

SAMPLE PROBLEM 8.1 Number of Atoms in Balanced Chemical Equations

Indicate the number of each type of atom in the following balanced equation:

$$Fe_2S_3(s) + 6HCl(aq) \longrightarrow 2FeCl_3(aq) + 3H_2S(g)$$

	Reactants	Products
Fe		
S		
H		
Cl		

SOLUTION

The total number of atoms in each formula is obtained by multiplying the coefficient by each subscript in a chemical formula.

	Reactants	Products
Fe	$2\ (1 \times 2)$	$2\ (2 \times 1)$
S	$3\ (1 \times 3)$	$3\ (3 \times 1)$
H	$6\ (6 \times 1)$	$6\ (3 \times 2)$
Cl	$6\ (6 \times 1)$	$6\ (2 \times 3)$

STUDY CHECK 8.1

When the alkane ethane, C_2H_6, burns in oxygen, the products are carbon dioxide and water. The balanced equation is written as

$$2C_2H_6(g) + 7O_2(g) \xrightarrow{\Delta} 4CO_2(g) + 6H_2O(g)$$

Calculate the number of each type of atom in the reactants and in the products.

QUESTIONS AND PROBLEMS

8.1 Equations for Chemical Reactions

LEARNING GOAL: *Identify a balanced chemical equation and determine the number of atoms in the reactants and products.*

8.1 State the number of atoms of oxygen in the reactants and in the products for each of the following equations:

a. $3NO_2(g) + H_2O(l) \longrightarrow NO(g) + 2HNO_3(aq)$
b. $5C(s) + 2SO_2(g) \longrightarrow CS_2(g) + 4CO(g)$
c. $2C_2H_2(g) + 5O_2(g) \xrightarrow{\Delta} 4CO_2(g) + 2H_2O(g)$
d. $N_2H_4(g) + 2H_2O_2(g) \longrightarrow N_2(g) + 4H_2O(g)$

8.2 State the number of atoms of oxygen in the reactants and in the products for each of the following equations:

a. $CH_4(g) + 2O_2(g) \xrightarrow{\Delta} CO_2(g) + 2H_2O(g)$
b. $4P(s) + 5O_2(g) \longrightarrow P_4O_{10}(s)$
c. $4NH_3(g) + 6NO(g) \longrightarrow 5N_2(g) + 6H_2O(g)$
d. $6CO_2(g) + 6H_2O(l) \longrightarrow C_6H_{12}O_6(aq) + 6O_2(g)$
Glucose

8.3 Determine whether each of the following equations is balanced or not balanced:

a. $S(s) + O_2(g) \longrightarrow SO_3(g)$
b. $2Al(s) + 3Cl_2(g) \longrightarrow 2AlCl_3(s)$
c. $2NaOH(aq) + H_2SO_4(aq) \longrightarrow Na_2SO_4(aq) + H_2O(l)$
d. $C_3H_8(g) + 5O_2(g) \xrightarrow{\Delta} 3CO_2(g) + 4H_2O(g)$

8.4 Determine whether each of the following equations is balanced or not balanced:

a. $PCl_3(l) + Cl_2(g) \longrightarrow PCl_5(s)$
b. $CO(g) + 2H_2(g) \longrightarrow CH_3OH(l)$
c. $2KClO_3(s) \longrightarrow 2KCl(s) + O_2(g)$
d. $Mg(s) + N_2(g) \longrightarrow Mg_3N_2(s)$

8.5 All of the following are balanced equations. State the number of atoms of each element in the reactants and in the products.

a. $2Na(s) + Cl_2(g) \longrightarrow 2NaCl(s)$
b. $PCl_3(l) + 3H_2(g) \longrightarrow PH_3(g) + 3HCl(g)$
c. $P_4O_{10}(s) + 6H_2O(l) \longrightarrow 4H_3PO_4(aq)$

8.6 All of the following are balanced equations. State the number of atoms of each element in the reactants and in the products.

a. $2N_2(g) + 3O_2(g) \longrightarrow 2N_2O_3(g)$
b. $Al_2O_3(s) + 6HCl(aq) \longrightarrow 2AlCl_3(aq) + 3H_2O(l)$
c. $C_5H_{12}(l) + 8O_2(g) \xrightarrow{\Delta} 5CO_2(g) + 6H_2O(g)$

LEARNING GOAL

Write a balanced chemical equation from the formulas of the reactants and products for a chemical reaction.

8.2 Balancing a Chemical Equation

We can now show the process of how to balance a chemical equation for the reaction of the alkane methane, CH_4, with oxygen, which produces carbon dioxide and water. This is the reaction that occurs in the flame of a laboratory burner or a gas cooktop as shown in Sample Problem 8.2.

CORE CHEMISTRY SKILL

Balancing a Chemical Equation

Guide to Balancing a Chemical Equation

1. Write an equation using the correct formulas of the reactants and products.
2. Count the atoms of each element in the reactants and products.
3. Use coefficients to balance each element.
4. Check the final equation to confirm it is balanced.

SAMPLE PROBLEM 8.2 Balancing a Chemical Equation

Write a balanced chemical equation for the combustion of methane, CH_4, using the following unbalanced equation:

$$CH_4(g) + O_2(g) \xrightarrow{\Delta} CO_2(g) + H_2O(g) \quad \text{Unbalanced}$$

SOLUTION

Step 1 **Write an equation using the correct formulas of the reactants and products.**

$$CH_4(g) + O_2(g) \xrightarrow{\Delta} CO_2(g) + H_2O(g)$$

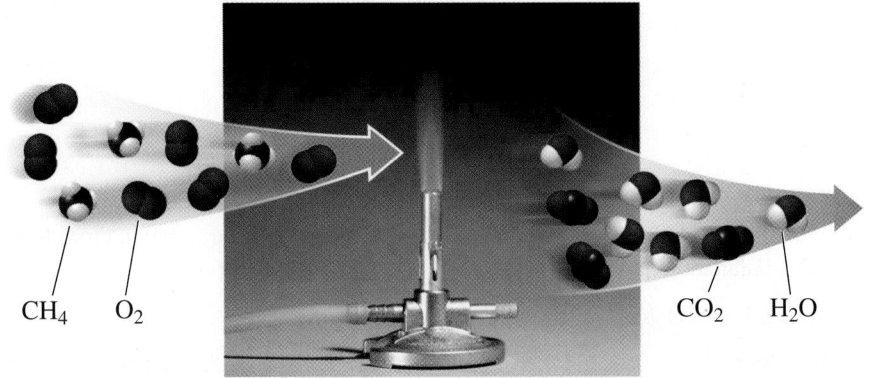

Step 2 **Count the atoms of each element in the reactants and products.** When we compare the atoms on the reactant side and the product side, we see that there are more H atoms in the reactants and more O atoms in the products.

$$CH_4(g) + O_2(g) \xrightarrow{\Delta} CO_2(g) + H_2O(g)$$

Reactants	Products	
1 C atom	1 C atom	Balanced
4 H atoms	2 H atoms	Not balanced
2 O atoms	3 O atoms	Not balanced

Step 3 **Use coefficients to balance each element.** We will start by balancing the H in CH_4 because it has the most atoms. By placing a coefficient of 2 in front of the formula for H_2O, a total of 4 H atoms in the products is obtained. *Only use coefficients to balance an equation. Do not change any of the subscripts: this would alter the chemical formula of a reactant or product.*

$$CH_4(g) + O_2(g) \xrightarrow{\Delta} CO_2(g) + 2H_2O(g)$$

Reactants	Products	
1 C atom	1 C atom	Balanced
4 H atoms	4 H atoms	Balanced
2 O atoms	4 O atoms	Not balanced

We can balance the O atoms on the reactant side by placing a coefficient of 2 in front of the formula O_2. There are now 4 O atoms and 4 H atoms in both the reactants and products.

$$CH_4(g) + 2O_2(g) \xrightarrow{\Delta} CO_2(g) + 2H_2O(g) \quad \text{Balanced}$$

Step 4 **Check the final equation to confirm it is balanced.** A check of the total number of atoms indicates that the equation is balanced.

$$CH_4(g) + 2O_2(g) \xrightarrow{\Delta} CO_2(g) + 2H_2O(g)$$

Reactants	Products	
1 C atom	1 C atom	Balanced
4 H atoms	4 H atoms	Balanced
4 O atoms	4 O atoms	Balanced

In a balanced equation, the coefficients must be the *lowest possible whole numbers*. Suppose you had obtained the following for the balanced equation:

$$2CH_4(g) + 4O_2(g) \xrightarrow{\Delta} 2CO_2(g) + 4H_2O(g) \quad \text{Incorrect}$$

Although there are equal numbers of atoms in the reactants and in the products, this is not balanced correctly. To obtain coefficients that are the lowest whole numbers, we divide all the coefficients by 2.

STUDY CHECK 8.2

Balance the following chemical equation:

$$Al(s) + Br_2(l) \longrightarrow AlBr_3(s)$$

SAMPLE PROBLEM 8.3 Balancing Chemical Equations with Polyatomic Ions

Balance the following chemical equation:

$$Na_3PO_4(aq) + MgCl_2(aq) \longrightarrow Mg_3(PO_4)_2(s) + NaCl(aq) \quad \text{Unbalanced}$$

SOLUTION

Step 1 **Write an equation using the correct formulas of the reactants and products.**

$$Na_3PO_4(aq) + MgCl_2(aq) \longrightarrow Mg_3(PO_4)_2(s) + NaCl(aq) \quad \text{Unbalanced}$$

Step 2 **Count the atoms (ions) of each element in the reactants and products.** When we compare the number of ions in the reactants and products, we find that the equation is not balanced. In this equation, we can balance the phosphate ion as a group of atoms because it appears on both sides of the equation.

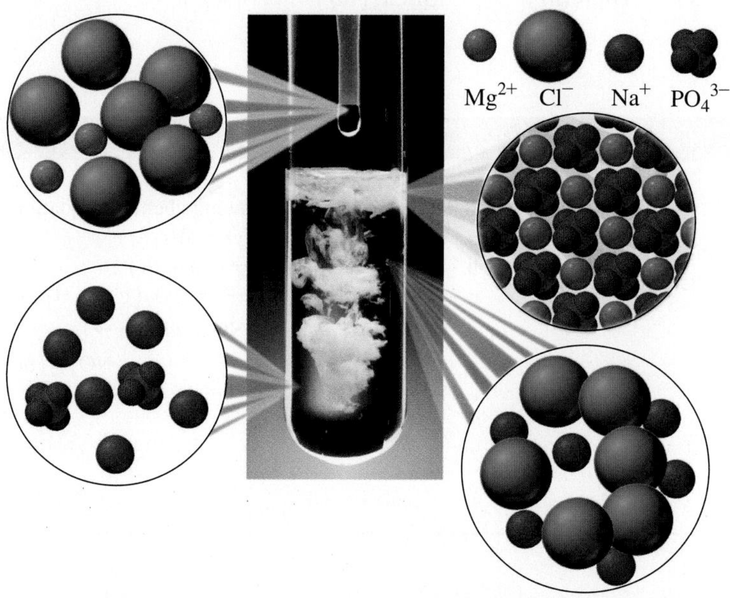

$$Na_3PO_4(aq) + MgCl_2(aq) \longrightarrow Mg_3(PO_4)_2(s) + NaCl(aq)$$

Reactants	Products	
3 Na^+	1 Na^+	Not balanced
1 PO_4^{3-}	2 PO_4^{3-}	Not balanced
1 Mg^{2+}	3 Mg^{2+}	Not balanced
2 Cl^-	1 Cl^-	Not balanced

Step 3 **Use coefficients to balance each element.** We begin with the formula that has the highest subscript values, which in this equation is $Mg_3(PO_4)_2$. The subscript 3 in $Mg_3(PO_4)_2$ is used as a coefficient for $MgCl_2$ to balance magnesium. The subscript 2 of the phosphate in $Mg_3(PO_4)_2$ is used as a coefficient for Na_3PO_4 to balance the phosphate ion.

$$2Na_3PO_4(aq) + 3MgCl_2(aq) \longrightarrow Mg_3(PO_4)_2(s) + NaCl(aq)$$

Reactants	Products	
6 Na^+	1 Na^+	Not balanced
2 PO_4^{3-}	2 PO_4^{3-}	Balanced
3 Mg^{2+}	3 Mg^{2+}	Balanced
6 Cl^-	1 Cl^-	Not balanced

Looking again at each of the ions in the reactants and products, we see that the sodium and chloride ions are not yet balanced. A coefficient of 6 is placed in front of the NaCl to balance the equation.

$$2Na_3PO_4(aq) + 3MgCl_2(aq) \longrightarrow Mg_3(PO_4)_2(s) + 6NaCl(aq)$$

Step 4 **Check the final equation to confirm it is balanced.** A check of the total number of ions confirms that the equation is balanced.

$$2Na_3PO_4(aq) + 3MgCl_2(aq) \longrightarrow Mg_3(PO_4)_2(s) + 6NaCl(aq) \quad \text{Balanced}$$

Reactants	Products	
6 Na^+	6 Na^+	Balanced
2 PO_4^{3-}	2 PO_4^{3-}	Balanced
3 Mg^{2+}	3 Mg^{2+}	Balanced
6 Cl^-	6 Cl^-	Balanced

STUDY CHECK 8.3

Balance the following chemical equation:

$$Sb_2S_3(s) + HCl(aq) \longrightarrow SbCl_3(aq) + H_2S(g)$$

QUESTIONS AND PROBLEMS

8.2 Balancing a Chemical Equation

LEARNING GOAL: *Write a balanced chemical equation from the formulas of the reactants and products for a chemical reaction.*

8.7 Balance each of the following chemical equations:

a. $N_2(g) + O_2(g) \longrightarrow NO(g)$

b. $HgO(s) \longrightarrow Hg(l) + O_2(g)$

c. $Fe(s) + O_2(g) \longrightarrow Fe_2O_3(s)$

d. $Na(s) + Cl_2(g) \longrightarrow NaCl(s)$

e. $Cu_2O(s) + O_2(g) \longrightarrow CuO(s)$

8.8 Balance each of the following chemical equations:

a. $Ca(s) + Br_2(l) \longrightarrow CaBr_2(s)$

b. $P_4(s) + O_2(g) \longrightarrow P_4O_{10}(s)$

c. $C_4H_8(g) + O_2(g) \xrightarrow{\Delta} CO_2(g) + H_2O(g)$

d. $Ca(OH)_2(aq) + HNO_3(aq) \longrightarrow Ca(NO_3)_2(aq) + H_2O(l)$

e. $Fe_2O_3(s) + C(s) \longrightarrow Fe(s) + CO(g)$

8.9 Balance each of the following chemical equations:
a. $Mg(s) + AgNO_3(aq) \longrightarrow Mg(NO_3)_2(aq) + Ag(s)$
b. $CuCO_3(s) \longrightarrow CuO(s) + CO_2(g)$
c. $Al(s) + CuSO_4(aq) \longrightarrow Cu(s) + Al_2(SO_4)_3(aq)$
d. $Pb(NO_3)_2(aq) + NaCl(aq) \longrightarrow PbCl_2(s) + NaNO_3(aq)$
e. $Al(s) + HCl(aq) \longrightarrow AlCl_3(aq) + H_2(g)$

8.10 Balance each of the following chemical equations:
a. $Zn(s) + HNO_3(aq) \longrightarrow Zn(NO_3)_2(aq) + H_2(g)$
b. $Al(s) + H_2SO_4(aq) \longrightarrow Al_2(SO_4)_3(aq) + H_2(g)$
c. $K_2SO_4(aq) + BaCl_2(aq) \longrightarrow BaSO_4(s) + KCl(aq)$
d. $CaCO_3(s) \longrightarrow CaO(s) + CO_2(g)$
e. $AlCl_3(aq) + KOH(aq) \longrightarrow Al(OH)_3(s) + KCl(aq)$

8.11 Balance each of the following chemical equations:
a. $Fe_2O_3(s) + CO(g) \longrightarrow Fe(s) + CO_2(g)$
b. $Li_3N(s) \longrightarrow Li(s) + N_2(g)$
c. $Al(s) + HBr(aq) \longrightarrow AlBr_3(aq) + H_2(g)$
d. $Ba(OH)_2(aq) + Na_3PO_4(aq) \longrightarrow Ba_3(PO_4)_2(s) + NaOH(aq)$
e. $As_4S_6(s) + O_2(g) \longrightarrow As_4O_6(s) + SO_2(g)$

8.12 Balance each of the following chemical equations:
a. $K(s) + H_2O(l) \longrightarrow KOH(aq) + H_2(g)$
b. $Cr(s) + S_8(s) \longrightarrow Cr_2S_3(s)$
c. $BCl_3(s) + H_2O(l) \longrightarrow H_3BO_3(aq) + HCl(aq)$
d. $Fe(OH)_3(s) + H_2SO_4(aq) \longrightarrow Fe_2(SO_4)_3(aq) + H_2O(l)$
e. $BaCl_2(aq) + Na_3PO_4(aq) \longrightarrow Ba_3(PO_4)_2(s) + NaCl(aq)$

8.13 Write a balanced equation using the correct formulas and include conditions (*s*, *l*, *g*, or *aq*) for each of the following chemical reactions:
a. Lithium metal reacts with liquid water to form hydrogen gas and aqueous lithium hydroxide.
b. Solid phosphorus reacts with chlorine gas to form solid phosphorus pentachloride.
c. Solid iron(II) oxide reacts with carbon monoxide gas to form solid iron and carbon dioxide gas.
d. Liquid pentene (C_5H_{10}) burns in oxygen gas to form carbon dioxide gas and water vapor.
e. Hydrogen sulfide gas and solid iron(III) chloride react to form solid iron(III) sulfide and hydrogen chloride gas.

8.14 Write a balanced equation using the correct formulas and include conditions (*s*, *l*, *g*, or *aq*) for each of the following chemical reactions:
a. Solid sodium carbonate decomposes to produce solid sodium oxide and carbon dioxide gas.
b. Nitrogen oxide gas reacts with carbon monoxide gas to produce nitrogen gas and carbon dioxide gas.
c. Iron metal reacts with solid sulfur to produce solid iron(III) sulfide.
d. Solid calcium reacts with nitrogen gas to produce solid calcium nitride.
e. In the *Apollo* lunar module, hydrazine gas, N_2H_4, reacts with dinitrogen tetroxide gas to produce gaseous nitrogen and water vapor.

8.3 Types of Reactions

LEARNING GOAL

Identify a reaction as a combination, decomposition, single replacement, double replacement, or combustion.

A great number of reactions occur in nature, in biological systems, and in the laboratory. However, there are some general patterns among all reactions that help us classify reactions. Some reactions may fit into more than one reaction type.

Combination Reactions

In a **combination reaction**, two or more elements or compounds bond to form one product. For example, sulfur and oxygen combine to form the product sulfur dioxide.

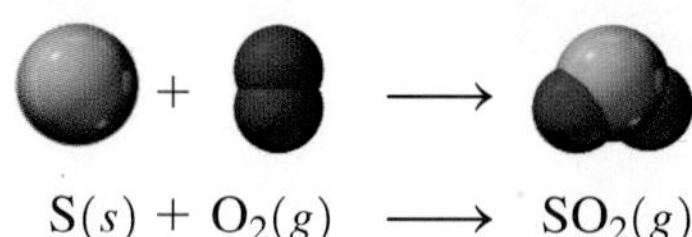

$$S(s) + O_2(g) \longrightarrow SO_2(g)$$

Combination

Two or more reactants combine to yield a single product

 +  $\longrightarrow$ 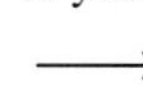 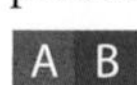

CORE CHEMISTRY SKILL 

Classifying Types of Chemical Reactions

In Figure 8.3, the elements magnesium and oxygen combine to form a single product, which is the ionic compound magnesium oxide formed from Mg^{2+} and O^{2-} ions.

$$2Mg(s) + O_2(g) \longrightarrow 2MgO(s)$$

In other examples of combination reactions, elements or compounds combine to form a single product.

$$N_2(g) + 3H_2(g) \longrightarrow \underset{\text{Ammonia}}{2NH_3(g)}$$

$$Cu(s) + S(s) \longrightarrow CuS(s)$$

$$MgO(s) + CO_2(g) \longrightarrow MgCO_3(s)$$

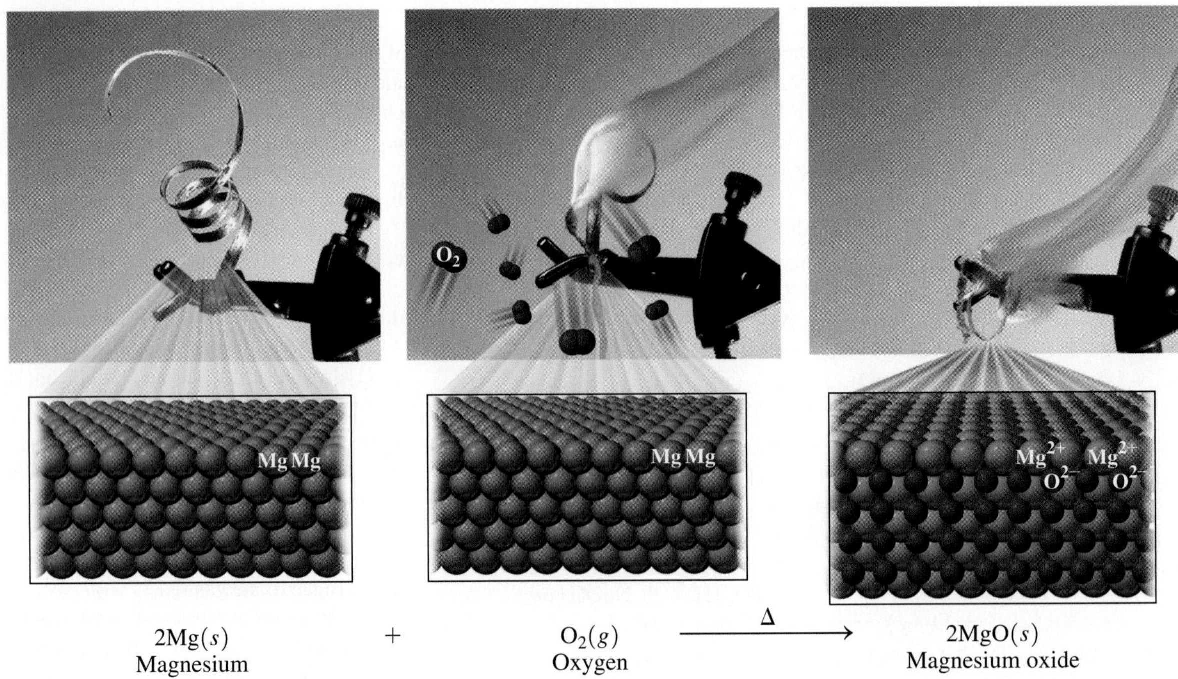

FIGURE 8.3 In a combination reaction, two or more substances combine to form one substance as the product.

Q What happens to the atoms of the reactants in a combination reaction?

Decomposition Reactions

Decomposition

A reactant splits into two or more products

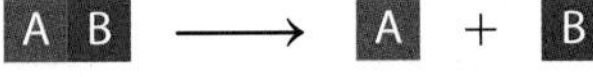

In a **decomposition reaction**, a single reactant splits into two or more products. For example, when mercury(II) oxide is heated, the products are the elements mercury and oxygen (see Figure 8.4).

$$2HgO(s) \xrightarrow{\Delta} 2Hg(l) + O_2(g)$$

FIGURE 8.4 In a decomposition reaction, one reactant breaks down into two or more products.

Q How do the differences in the reactant and products classify this as a decomposition reaction?

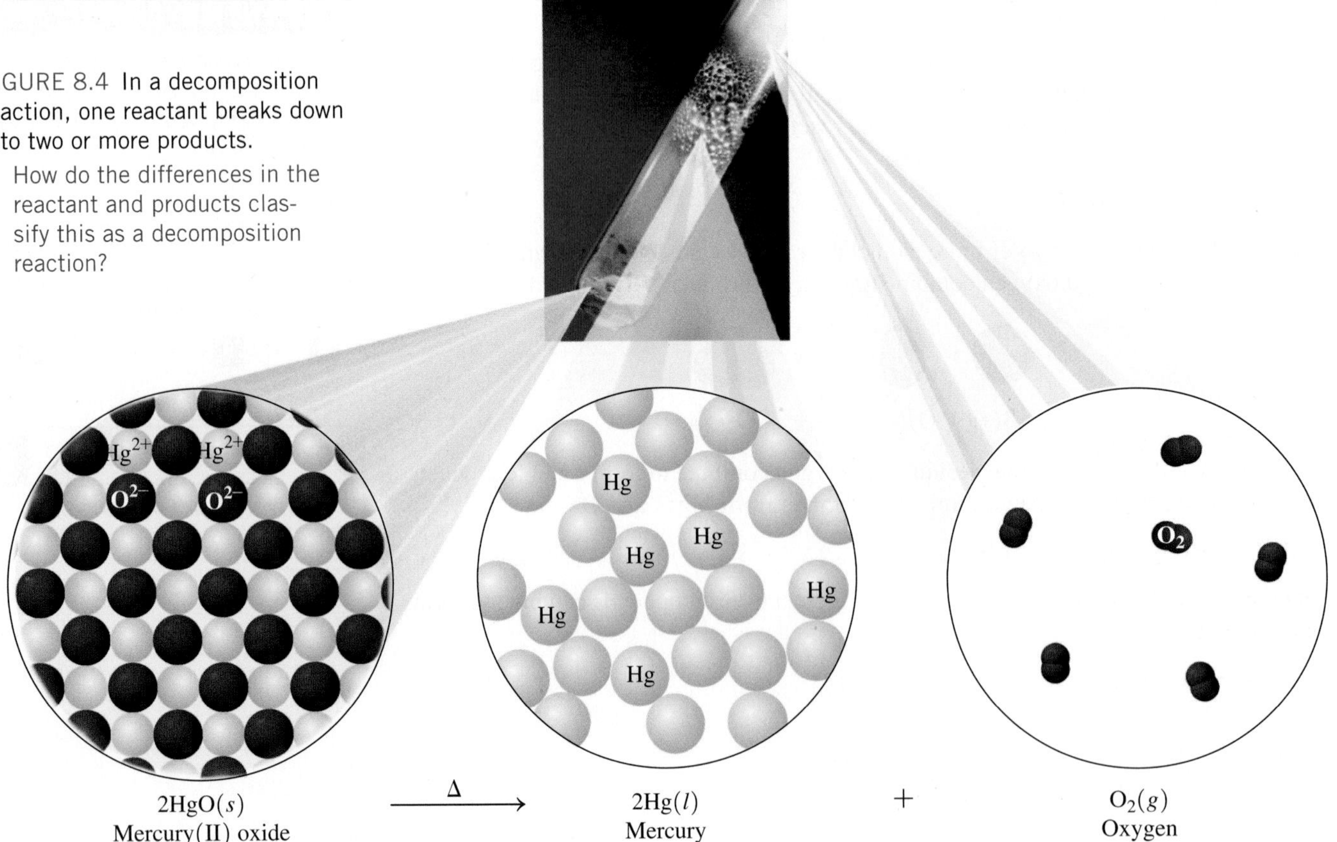

In another example of a decomposition reaction, calcium carbonate breaks apart into simpler compounds of calcium oxide and carbon dioxide.

$$CaCO_3(s) \xrightarrow{\Delta} CaO(s) + CO_2(g)$$

Chemistry Link to Health

SMOG AND HEALTH CONCERNS

There are two types of smog. One, photochemical smog, requires sunlight to initiate reactions that produce pollutants such as nitrogen oxides and ozone. The other type of smog, called industrial or London smog, occurs in areas where coal containing sulfur is burned and the unwanted product sulfur dioxide is emitted.

Photochemical smog is most prevalent in cities where people are dependent on cars for transportation. On a typical day in Los Angeles, for example, nitrogen oxide (NO) emissions from car exhausts increase as traffic increases on the roads. The nitrogen oxide is formed when N_2 and O_2 react at high temperatures in car and truck engines.

$$N_2(g) + O_2(g) \xrightarrow{\Delta} 2NO(g)$$

Then, NO reacts with oxygen in the air to produce NO_2, a reddish-brown gas that is irritating to the eyes and damaging to the respiratory tract.

$$2NO(g) + O_2(g) \xrightarrow{\Delta} 2NO_2(g)$$

When NO_2 molecules are exposed to sunlight, they are converted to NO molecules and oxygen atoms.

$$NO_2(g) \xrightarrow{\text{Sunlight}} NO(g) + \underset{\text{Oxygen atoms}}{O(g)}$$

The reddish-brown color of smog is due to nitrogen dioxide.

Single oxygen atoms are so reactive that they combine with oxygen molecules in the atmosphere, forming ozone.

$$O(g) + O_2(g) \longrightarrow \underset{\text{Ozone}}{O_3(g)}$$

In the upper atmosphere (the stratosphere), ozone is beneficial because it protects us from harmful ultraviolet radiation that comes from the Sun. However, in the lower atmosphere, ozone irritates the eyes and respiratory tract, which causes coughing and decreased lung function. In addition, ozone causes fabric to deteriorate and rubber to crack; it also damages trees and crops.

Industrial smog is produced when sulfur is converted to sulfur dioxide during the burning of coal or other sulfur-containing fuels.

$$S(s) + O_2(g) \longrightarrow SO_2(g)$$

The SO_2 is damaging to plants and is corrosive to metals such as steel. The SO_2 is also damaging to humans and can cause lung impairment and respiratory difficulties. In the air, SO_2 reacts with oxygen to form SO_3, which can combine with water to form sulfuric acid. When rain falls, it absorbs the sulfuric acid, which makes acid rain.

$$2SO_2(g) + O_2(g) \longrightarrow 2SO_3(g)$$
$$SO_3(g) + H_2O(l) \longrightarrow \underset{\text{Sulfuric acid}}{H_2SO_4(aq)}$$

The presence of sulfuric acid in rivers and lakes causes an increase in the acidity of the water, reducing the ability of animals and plants to survive.

Single Replacement Reactions

In a **single replacement reaction**, an uncombined element takes the place of an element in a compound.

In the single replacement reaction shown in Figure 8.5, zinc replaces hydrogen in hydrochloric acid, HCl(aq).

$$Zn(s) + 2HCl(aq) \longrightarrow ZnCl_2(aq) + H_2(g)$$

In another single replacement reaction, chlorine replaces bromine in the compound potassium bromide.

$$Cl_2(g) + 2KBr(s) \longrightarrow 2KCl(s) + Br_2(l)$$

Single replacement

One element replaces another element

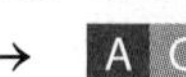

FIGURE 8.5 In a single replacement reaction, an atom or ion replaces an atom or ion in a compound.

Q What changes in the formulas of the reactants identify this equation as a single replacement reaction?

Double Replacement Reactions

Double replacement

Two elements replace each other

A B + C D ⟶ A D + C B

In a **double replacement reaction**, the positive ions in the reacting compounds switch places. In the reaction shown in Figure 8.6, barium ions change places with sodium ions in the reactants to form sodium chloride and a white solid precipitate of barium sulfate.

$$Na_2SO_4(aq) + BaCl_2(aq) \longrightarrow BaSO_4(s) + 2NaCl(aq)$$

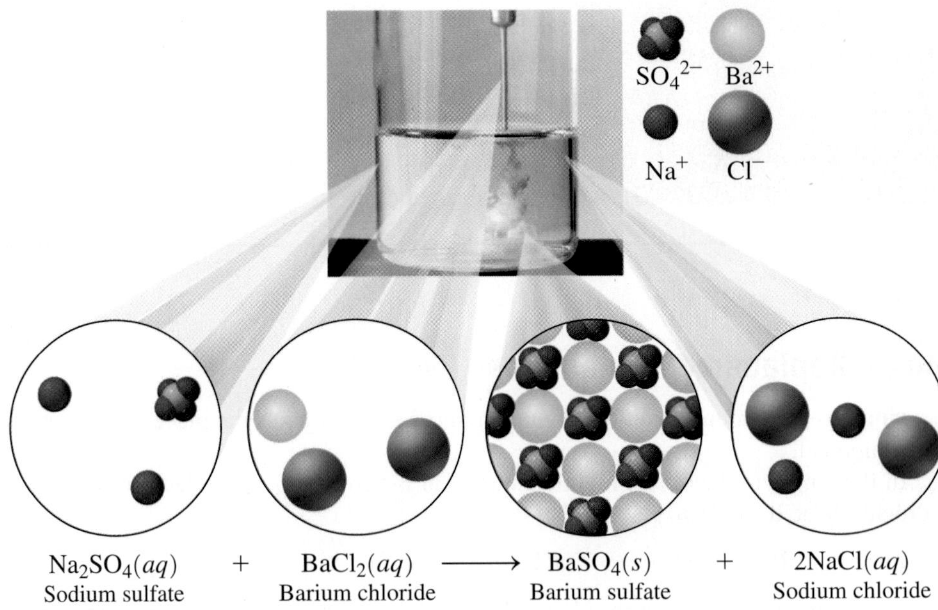

FIGURE 8.6 In a double replacement reaction, the positive ions in the reactants replace each other.

Q How do the changes in the formulas of the reactants identify this equation as a double replacement reaction?

When sodium hydroxide and hydrochloric acid (HCl) react, sodium and hydrogen ions switch places, forming sodium chloride and water.

$$NaOH(aq) + HCl(aq) \longrightarrow NaCl(aq) + HOH(l)$$

Combustion Reactions

In a combustion reaction, a candle burns using the oxygen in the air.

The burning of a candle and the burning of fuel in the engine of a car are examples of combustion reactions. In a **combustion reaction**, a carbon-containing compound that is the fuel burns in oxygen from the air to produce carbon dioxide, CO_2, water, H_2O, and energy in the form of heat or a flame. For example, methane gas, CH_4, undergoes combustion when used to cook our food on a gas cooktop and to heat our homes. In the equation for the combustion of methane, each element in the fuel, CH_4, forms a compound with oxygen.

$$\underset{\text{Methane}}{CH_4(g)} + 2O_2(g) \xrightarrow{\Delta} CO_2(g) + 2H_2O(g) + \text{energy}$$

SAMPLE PROBLEM 8.4 Writing an Equation for Combustion

A portable burner is fueled with butane, C_4H_{10}. Write the reactants and products for the complete combustion of butane, and balance the equation.

SOLUTION

Butane is an alkane with 4 C atoms and 10 H atoms. In a combustion reaction, butane reacts with oxygen to form carbon dioxide, water, and energy. We write the unbalanced equation as

$$C_4H_{10}(g) + O_2(g) \xrightarrow{\Delta} CO_2(g) + H_2O(g) + \text{energy}$$

We can begin by using the subscripts in C_4H_{10} to balance the C atoms in CO_2 and the H atoms in H_2O. However, we notice this gives a total of 13 O atoms in the products, which is an odd number.

$$C_4H_{10}(g) + O_2(g) \xrightarrow{\Delta} \underbrace{4CO_2(g) + 5H_2O(g)}_{\text{13 O atoms}} + \text{energy}$$

To obtain an even number of O atoms, we double the number of C_4H_{10}, CO_2, and H_2O molecules.

$$2C_4H_{10}(g) + O_2(g) \xrightarrow{\Delta} 8CO_2(g) + 10H_2O(g) + \text{energy}$$

Now the total number of O atoms in the products is 26, which can be balanced with a coefficient of 13 in front of O_2. The balanced equation for the complete combustion of butane is written

$$2C_4H_{10}(g) + 13O_2(g) \xrightarrow{\Delta} 8CO_2(g) + 10H_2O(g) + \text{energy}$$

STUDY CHECK 8.4

Ethene, used to ripen fruit, has the formula C_2H_4. Write a balanced equation for the complete combustion of ethene.

CORE CHEMISTRY SKILL 

Balancing Combustion Reactions

When camping, a butane cartridge provides fuel for a portable burner.

Chemistry Link to Health

INCOMPLETE COMBUSTION: TOXICITY OF CARBON MONOXIDE

When a propane heater, fireplace, or woodstove is used in a closed room, there must be adequate ventilation. If the supply of oxygen is limited, incomplete combustion from burning gas, oil, or wood produces carbon monoxide. The incomplete combustion of methane in natural gas is written

$$2CH_4(g) + \underset{\text{Limited oxygen supply}}{3O_2(g)} \xrightarrow{\Delta} \underset{\text{Carbon monoxide}}{2CO(g)} + 4H_2O(g) + \text{heat}$$

Carbon monoxide (CO) is a colorless, odorless, poisonous gas. When inhaled, CO passes into the bloodstream, where it attaches to hemoglobin, which reduces the amount of oxygen (O_2) reaching the cells. As a result, a person can experience a reduction in exercise capability, visual perception, and manual dexterity.

Hemoglobin is the protein that transports O_2 in the blood. When the amount of hemoglobin bound to CO (COHb) is about 10%, a person may experience shortness of breath, mild headache, and drowsiness. Heavy smokers can have levels of COHb in their blood as high as 9%. When as much as 30% of the hemoglobin is bound to CO, a person may experience more severe symptoms, including dizziness, mental confusion, severe headache, and nausea. If 50% or more of the hemoglobin is bound to CO, a person could become unconscious and die if not treated immediately with oxygen.

Table 8.3 summarizes the reaction types and gives examples.

TABLE 8.3 Summary of Reaction Types

Type of Reaction	Example
Combination	
$A + B \longrightarrow AB$	$Ca(s) + Cl_2(g) \longrightarrow CaCl_2(s)$
Decomposition	
$AB \longrightarrow A + B$	$Fe_2S_3(s) \longrightarrow 2Fe(s) + 3S(s)$
Single Replacement	
$A + BC \longrightarrow AC + B$	$Cu(s) + 2AgNO_3(aq) \longrightarrow Cu(NO_3)_2(aq) + 2Ag(s)$
Double Replacement	
$AB + CD \longrightarrow AD + CB$	$BaCl_2(aq) + K_2SO_4(aq) \longrightarrow BaSO_4(s) + 2KCl(aq)$
Combustion	
$C_XH_Y(g) + ZO_2(g) \xrightarrow{\Delta} XCO_2(g) + Y/2H_2O(g) + \text{energy}$	$CH_4(g) + 2O_2(g) \xrightarrow{\Delta} CO_2(g) + 2H_2O(g) + \text{energy}$

CONCEPT CHECK 8.3 Predicting Products

Predict the product(s) for each of the following and balance the equation:

a. Single replacement: $Al(s) + CuCl_2(aq) \longrightarrow$ ________ + ________
b. Combination: $K(s) + Cl_2(g) \longrightarrow$ ________

ANSWER

a. $2Al(s) + 3CuCl_2(aq) \longrightarrow 2AlCl_3(aq) + 3Cu(s)$
b. $K(s) + Cl_2(g) \longrightarrow 2KCl(s)$

SAMPLE PROBLEM 8.5 Classifying Types of Reactions

Classify each of the following as a combination, decomposition, single replacement, double replacement, or combustion reaction:

a. $2Fe_2O_3(s) + 3C(s) \longrightarrow 3CO_2(g) + 4Fe(s)$
b. $2KClO_3(s) \xrightarrow{\Delta} 2KCl(s) + 3O_2(g)$
c. $C_2H_4(g) + 3O_2(g) \xrightarrow{\Delta} 2CO_2(g) + 2H_2O(g) + \text{energy}$

SOLUTION

a. In this single replacement reaction, a C atom replaces Fe in Fe_2O_3 to form the compound CO_2 and Fe atoms.

b. When one reactant breaks down to produce two products, the reaction is decomposition.

c. The reaction of a carbon compound with oxygen to produce carbon dioxide, water, and energy makes this a combustion reaction.

STUDY CHECK 8.5

Nitrogen gas (N_2) and oxygen gas (O_2) react to form nitrogen dioxide gas. Write the balanced equation using the correct chemical formulas of the reactants and product, and identify the reaction type.

QUESTIONS AND PROBLEMS

8.3 Types of Reactions

LEARNING GOAL: *Identify a reaction as a combination, decomposition, single replacement, double replacement, or combustion.*

8.15 Classify each of the following as a combination, decomposition, single replacement, double replacement, or combustion reaction:

a. $2Al_2O_3(s) \xrightarrow{\Delta} 4Al(s) + 3O_2(g)$

b. $Br_2(g) + BaI_2(s) \longrightarrow BaBr_2(s) + I_2(g)$

c. $2C_2H_2(g) + 5O_2(g) \xrightarrow{\Delta} 4CO_2(g) + 2H_2O(g)$

d. $BaCl_2(aq) + K_2CO_3(aq) \longrightarrow BaCO_3(s) + 2KCl(aq)$

e. $Pb(s) + O_2(g) \longrightarrow PbO_2(s)$

8.16 Classify each of the following as a combination, decomposition, single replacement, double replacement, or combustion reaction:

a. $H_2(g) + Br_2(g) \longrightarrow 2HBr(g)$

b. $AgNO_3(aq) + NaCl(aq) \longrightarrow AgCl(s) + NaNO_3(aq)$

c. $2H_2O_2(aq) \longrightarrow 2H_2O(l) + O_2(g)$

d. $Zn(s) + CuCl_2(aq) \longrightarrow Cu(s) + ZnCl_2(aq)$

e. $C_5H_8(g) + 7O_2(g) \xrightarrow{\Delta} 5CO_2(g) + 4H_2O(g)$

8.17 Classify each of the following as a combination, decomposition, single replacement, double replacement, or combustion reaction:

a. $4Fe(s) + 3O_2(g) \longrightarrow 2Fe_2O_3(s)$

b. $Mg(s) + 2AgNO_3(aq) \longrightarrow Mg(NO_3)_2(aq) + 2Ag(s)$

c. $CuCO_3(s) \xrightarrow{\Delta} CuO(s) + CO_2(g)$

d. $2C_6H_6(l) + 15O_2(g) \xrightarrow{\Delta} 12CO_2(g) + 6H_2O(g)$

e. $Al_2(SO_4)_3(aq) + 6KOH(aq) \longrightarrow 2Al(OH)_3(s) + 3K_2SO_4(aq)$

8.18 Classify each of the following as a combination, decomposition, single replacement, double replacement, or combustion reaction:

a. $CuO(s) + 2HCl(aq) \longrightarrow CuCl_2(aq) + H_2O(l)$

b. $2Al(s) + 3Br_2(g) \longrightarrow 2AlBr_3(s)$

c. $Fe_2O_3(s) + 3C(s) \longrightarrow 2Fe(s) + 3CO(g)$

d. $C_6H_{12}(l) + 9O_2(g) \xrightarrow{\Delta} 6CO_2(g) + 6H_2O(g)$

e. $C_6H_{12}O_6(aq) \longrightarrow 2C_2H_6O(aq) + 2CO_2(g)$

8.19 Complete each of the following equations by writing the correct formulas of the products and balancing the equation:

a. combination: $Mg(s) + Cl_2(g) \longrightarrow$ ________

b. decomposition: $HBr(g) \longrightarrow$ ________ + ________

c. single replacement: $Mg(s) + Zn(NO_3)_2(aq) \longrightarrow$ ________ + ________

d. double replacement: $K_2S(aq) + Pb(NO_3)_2(aq) \longrightarrow$ ______ + ______

e. combustion: $C_5H_{10}(l) + O_2(g) \xrightarrow{\Delta}$ ________ + ________

8.20 Complete each of the following equations by writing the correct formulas of the products and balancing the equation:

a. combination: $Ca(s) + O_2(g) \longrightarrow$ ________

b. combustion: $C_3H_4(g) + O_2(g) \xrightarrow{\Delta}$ ________ + ________

c. decomposition: $PbO_2(s) \longrightarrow$ ________ + ________

d. single replacement: $KI(s) + Cl_2(g) \longrightarrow$ ________ + ________

e. double replacement: $CuCl_2(aq) + Na_2S(aq) \longrightarrow$ ________ + ________

8.4 Functional Groups and Reactions of Organic Compounds: Extended Topic

LEARNING GOAL

Classify organic molecules according to their functional groups; draw the condensed structural formulas for the products of reactions of organic compounds.

The most common type of reaction of organic compounds is the combustion reaction, which is typical of hydrocarbons used as fuels. Gasoline, a mixture of liquid hydrocarbons, is the fuel that powers our cars, lawn mowers, and snow blowers. Propane is the fuel

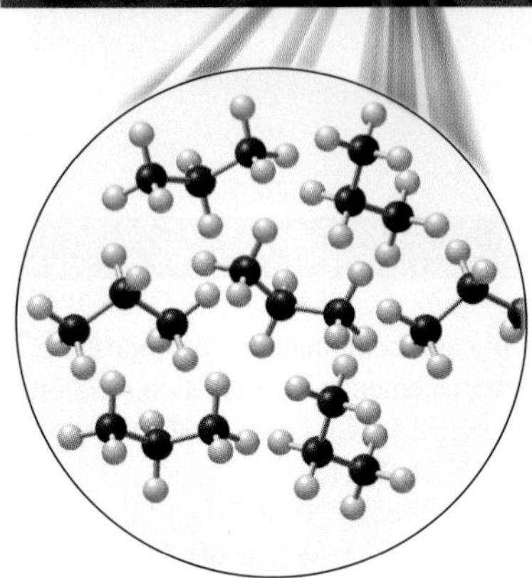

The propane from the torch undergoes combustion, which provides energy to solder metals.

used in portable heaters and gas barbecues. The balanced equation for the combustion of propane, C_3H_8, is

$$C_3H_8(g) + 5O_2(g) \xrightarrow{\Delta} 3CO_2(g) + 4H_2O(g) + \text{energy}$$

Now we can look at other organic compounds in which carbon atoms may also bond with the nonmetals oxygen and nitrogen. Table 8.4 lists the number of covalent bonds formed by elements found in organic compounds. In a typical organic compound, carbon forms four covalent bonds, hydrogen forms one covalent bond, nitrogen forms three covalent bonds, and oxygen forms two covalent bonds.

TABLE 8.4 Covalent Bonds for Elements in Organic Compounds

Element	Group	Covalent Bonds	Structure of Atoms	Representation of Atoms
H	1A (1)	1	—H	H atom
C	4A (14)	4	—C— (four bonds)	C atom
N	5A (15)	3	—N̈— (three bonds, one lone pair)	N atom
O	6A (16)	2	—Ö— (two bonds, two lone pairs)	O atom

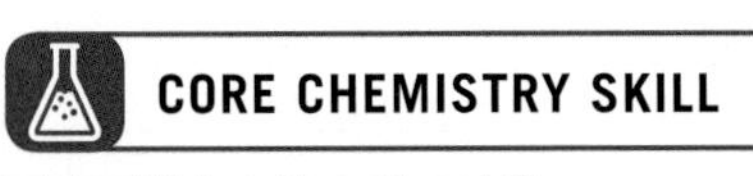

CORE CHEMISTRY SKILL
Identifying Functional Groups

Functional Groups

Organic compounds number in the millions, and more are synthesized every day. We organize many of the organic compounds according to their **functional groups**, which are specific groups of atoms that undergo characteristic chemical reactions. Organic compounds with the same functional group have similar properties and reactions. By identifying the functional group, we can classify organic compounds, predict their typical reactions, and draw the structures for their products.

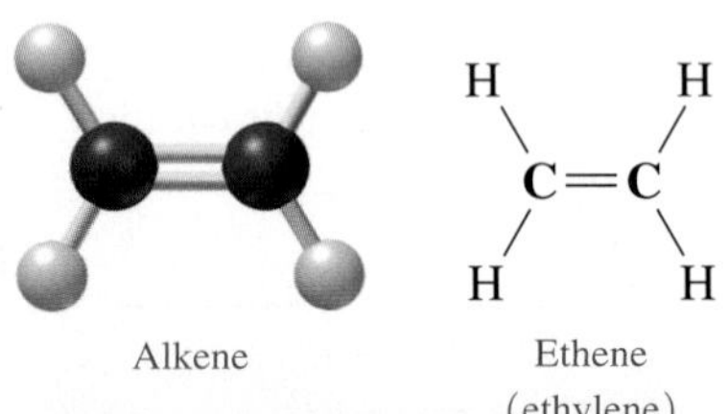

Alkene Ethene (ethylene)

Alkenes

In addition to the alkanes, the hydrocarbon family includes the classes of compounds known as *alkenes* and *aromatics*. An **alkene** contains at least one double bond, which forms when two adjacent carbon atoms share two pairs of valence electrons. The simplest alkene, ethene (or ethylene), is $H_2C{=}CH_2$. In the double bond of ethene, each carbon atom is attached to two hydrogen atoms, which gives four bonds. For an alkene, the ending of the name of the corresponding alkane is changed from *ane* to *ene*.

Ethene is an important plant hormone involved in promoting the ripening of fruit. Avocados, bananas, and tomatoes are often picked before they are ripe. Before the fruit is brought to market, it is exposed to ethene to accelerate the ripening process. Ethene also accelerates the breakdown of cellulose in plants, which causes flowers to wilt and leaves to fall from trees.

You may recognize the name ethylene in the word polyethylene, a synthetic polymer used for plastic bottles, film, and insulation material. Many of the small alkenes are used to make long-chain polymers such as polypropylene in clothing and carpets, and polystyrene used for plastic coffee cups.

Fruit that is picked early is ripened by exposure to ethene.

Chemistry Link to the Environment

PHEROMONES IN INSECT COMMUNICATION

Many insects emit minute quantities of chemicals called *pheromones* to send messages to other individuals of the same species. Some pheromones warn of danger, while others call for defense, mark a trail, or attract the opposite sex. During the past 40 years, the structures of many pheromones have been chemically determined. One of the most studied is bombykol, the sex pheromone produced by the female silkworm moth. Even a few nanograms of bombykol will attract male silkworm moths from distances of over 1 km. The bombykol molecule is a 16-carbon chain with two double bonds and an alcohol group. Scientists are interested in synthesizing pheromones to use as nontoxic alternatives to pesticides. When placed in a trap, bombykol can be used to isolate male silkworm moths. When a synthetic pheromone is released in a field, the males cannot locate the females, which disrupts the reproductive cycle. This technique has been successful in controlling the oriental fruit moth, the grapevine moth, and the pink bollworm.

Pheromones allow insects to attract mates from a great distance.

$$HO-CH_2-(CH_2)_7-CH_2-CH{=}CH-CH{=}CH-CH_2-CH_2-CH_3$$

Bombykol, sex attractant for the silkworm moth

Hydrogenation of Alkenes

The most characteristic reaction of alkenes is the *addition* of atoms to the double bond. Addition reactions occur because a double bond is easily broken, which provides electrons to form new single bonds. In *hydrogenation*, atoms of hydrogen from H_2 attach to the carbons in a double bond of an alkene to form an alkane. A catalyst such as platinum (Pt), nickel (Ni), or palladium (Pd) is added to speed up the reaction.

$$\underset{\text{2-Butene}}{CH_3-CH{=}CH-CH_3} + \mathbf{H-H} \xrightarrow{Pt} \underset{\text{Butane}}{CH_3-\overset{\mathbf{H}}{\overset{|}{C}}H-\overset{\mathbf{H}}{\overset{|}{C}}H-CH_3}$$

CONCEPT CHECK 8.4 Writing an Equation for Hydrogenation

Draw the condensed structural formula for the product of the following hydrogenation reaction:

$$CH_3-CH{=}CH_2 + H_2 \xrightarrow{Ni}$$

ANSWER

In a hydrogenation reaction, hydrogen adds to a double bond to give an alkane.

$$CH_3-CH_2-CH_3$$

Aromatic Compounds

In 1825, Michael Faraday isolated a hydrocarbon called *benzene*, which had the formula C_6H_6. Because compounds containing benzene often had fragrant odors, the class became known as **aromatic compounds**. A benzene molecule consists of a ring of six carbon atoms, with one hydrogen atom attached to each carbon. Later, scientists proposed that the carbon atoms be arranged in a ring with alternating single and double bonds. Today, the benzene structure is typically represented as a hexagon with a circle in the center.

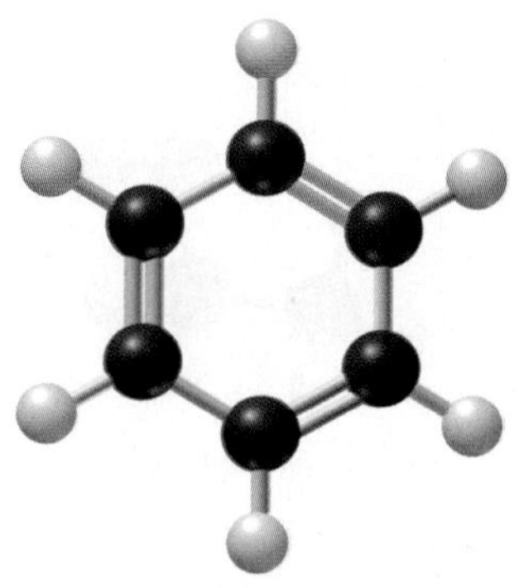

Aromatic

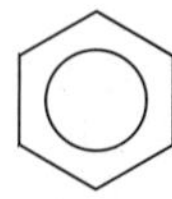

Benzene

An example of an aromatic compound that we use as a spice for flavor is thymol, which comes from the herb thyme.

Thymol

The aroma and flavor of the herb thyme is due to the aromatic compound thymol.

Chemistry Link to Health

POLYCYCLIC AROMATIC HYDROCARBONS (PAHs)

Large aromatic compounds known as *polycyclic aromatic hydrocarbons* are formed by fusing together two or more benzene rings edge to edge. In a fused-ring compound, neighboring benzene rings share two or more carbon atoms. Naphthalene, with two benzene rings, is known for its use in mothballs. Anthracene, with three rings, is used in the manufacture of dyes.

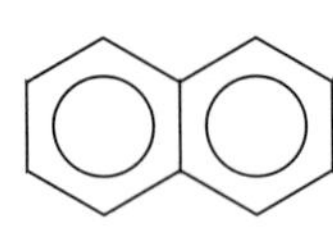

Naphthalene

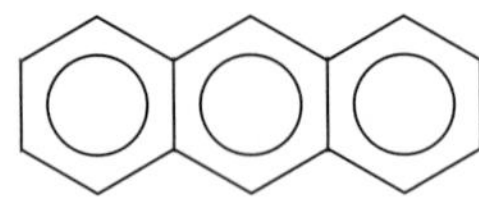

Anthracene

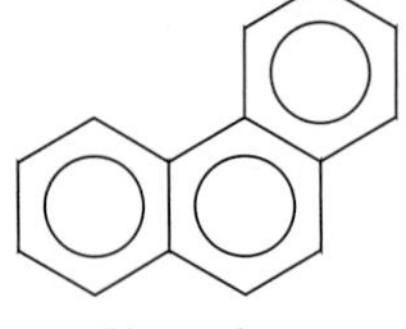

Phenanthrene

When a polycyclic compound contains the three fused rings of phenanthrene, it may act as a carcinogen, a substance known to cause cancer.

Compounds containing five or more fused benzene rings such as benzo[*a*]pyrene are potent carcinogens. The molecules interact with the DNA in the cells, causing abnormal cell growth and cancer. Increased exposure to carcinogens increases the chance of DNA alterations in the cells. Benzo[*a*]pyrene, a product of combustion, has been identified in coal tar, tobacco smoke, barbecued meats, and automobile exhaust.

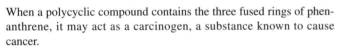

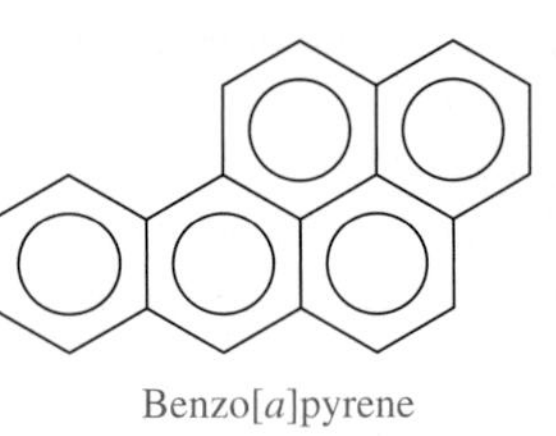

Benzo[*a*]pyrene

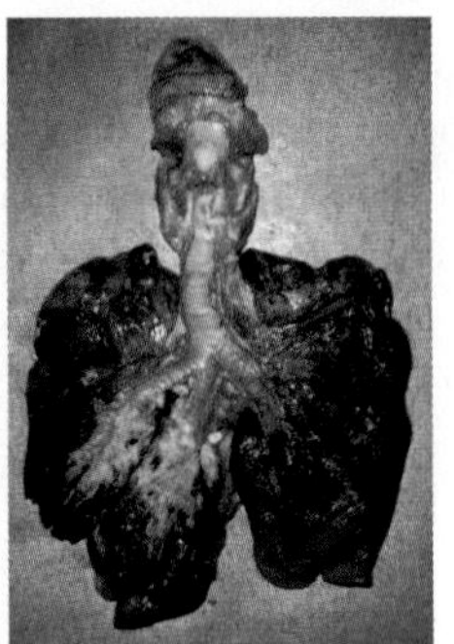

Aromatic compounds such as benzo[*a*]pyrene are strongly associated with lung cancers.

Alcohols

Alcohol

In an **alcohol**, a *hydroxyl* (—OH) *group* replaces a hydrogen atom in a hydrocarbon.

$$CH_3-CH_2-\mathbf{OH}$$

Ethanol

Ethanol (ethyl alcohol), CH_3-CH_2-OH, has been known since prehistoric times as an intoxicating product formed by the fermentation of grains, sugars, and starches.

$$C_6H_{12}O_6 \xrightarrow{\text{Fermentation}} 2CH_3-CH_2-OH + 2CO_2$$

Today, ethanol for commercial use is produced by reacting ethene and water at high temperatures and pressures. Ethanol is also used as a solvent for perfumes, varnishes, and some medicines, such as tincture of iodine. Recent interest in alternative fuels has led to increased production of ethanol by the fermentation of sugars from grains such as corn, wheat, and rice. "Gasohol" is a fuel comprised of ethanol and gasoline.

A flaming dessert is prepared using a liquor containing ethanol that undergoes combustion.

Combustion of Alcohols

We have seen that hydrocarbons undergo combustion in the presence of oxygen. Alcohols burn with oxygen, too. For example, in a restaurant, a dessert may be prepared by pouring a liquor on fruit or ice cream and lighting it. The balanced equation for the combustion of the ethanol in the liquor proceeds as follows:

$$CH_3{-}CH_2{-}OH(g) + 3O_2(g) \xrightarrow{\Delta} 2CO_2(g) + 3H_2O(g) + \text{energy}$$

Chemistry Link to Health

HAND SANITIZERS AND ETHANOL

Hand sanitizers are used as an alternative to washing hands to kill most bacteria and viruses that spread colds and flu. Many hand sanitizers use ethanol as their active ingredient. While safe for most adults, supervision is recommended when used by children because there is some concern about their risk to the health of children. After using an alcohol-based hand sanitizer, children might ingest enough alcohol to make them sick. In an alcohol-containing sanitizer, the amount of ethanol is typically 60% but can be as high as 85%. This amount of ethanol can make hand sanitizers a fire hazard in the home because ethanol is highly flammable. When ethanol undergoes combustion, it produces a transparent blue flame. When using an ethanol-containing sanitizer, it is important to rub hands until they are completely dry. It is also recommended that sanitizers containing ethanol be placed in storage areas that are away from heat sources in the home.

Hand sanitizers that contain ethanol are used to kill bacteria on the hands.

CONCEPT CHECK 8.5 Identifying Alkanes, Alkenes, and Alcohols

Classify each of the following condensed structural formulas as an alkane, alkene, or alcohol:

a. $CH_3{-}CH_2{-}CH_2{-}OH$
b. $CH_3{-}CH_2{-}CH_3$
c. $CH_3{-}CH_2{-}CH_2{-}CH{=}CH_2$

ANSWER

a. This is an alcohol because it has a hydroxyl ($-OH$) group attached to a carbon chain.
b. This is an alkane because it has only single bonds between the carbon atoms.
c. This is an alkene because it has a double bond between two carbon atoms.

Aldehydes and Ketones

Aldehydes and ketones contain a *carbonyl* ($C{=}O$) *group*, which is a carbon atom attached to an oxygen atom with a double bond. In an **aldehyde**, the carbon atom of the carbonyl group is also bonded to a hydrogen atom. In a **ketone**, the carbonyl group is bonded to two other carbon atoms.

Ketones and aldehydes are in many items we use or eat each day. For example, they are used in the food industry to produce flavorings such as vanilla, cinnamon, and spearmint. When we buy a small bottle of liquid flavoring, the aldehyde or ketone is dissolved in alcohol because the compounds are not very soluble in water.

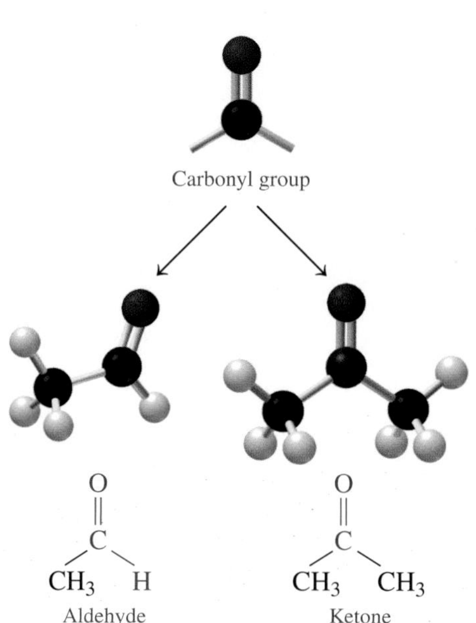

Formaldehyde, the simplest aldehyde, is a colorless gas with a pungent odor. An aqueous solution called formalin, which contains 40% formaldehyde, is used as a germicide and to preserve biological specimens. Industrially, it is a reactant in the synthesis of polymers used to make fabrics, insulation materials, carpeting, pressed wood products such as plywood, and plastics for kitchen counters. Exposure to formaldehyde fumes can irritate the eyes, nose, and upper respiratory tract and cause skin rashes, headaches, dizziness, and general fatigue.

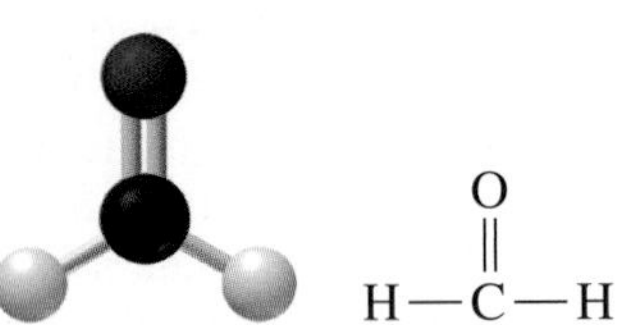

The ball-and-stick model and condensed structural formula are shown for formaldehyde, which is used to preserve biological specimens.

The simplest ketone, known as *acetone* or propanone (dimethyl ketone), is a colorless liquid with a mild odor that has wide use as a solvent in cleaning fluids, paint and nail polish removers, and rubber cement. Acetone is extremely flammable, and care must be taken when using it. In the body, acetone may be produced in uncontrolled diabetes, fasting, and high-protein diets when large amounts of fats are metabolized for energy.

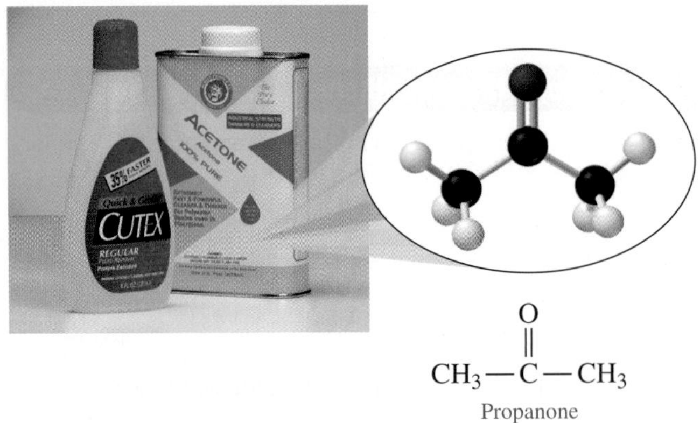

The ball-and-stick model and condensed structural formula are shown for propanone, also known as acetone, which is used as a solvent for paint and nail polish.

Carboxylic Acids

In a **carboxylic acid**, the functional group is the *carboxyl group*, which is a combination of the *carb*onyl and hydr*oxyl* groups.

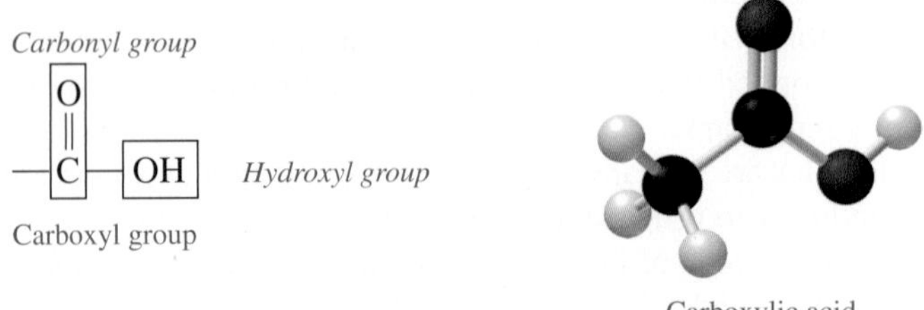

Carboxylic acid

The functional group in the formula of a carboxylic acid can be drawn as follows:

$$\mathbf{CH_3{-}\overset{\overset{\displaystyle O}{\|}}{C}{-}O{-}H} \qquad \text{or} \qquad CH_3{-}\mathbf{COOH}$$

Carboxylic acid

Carboxylic acids are common in nature. For example, formic acid, HCOOH, is injected under the skin from red ant and bee stings.

Acetic acid, $CH_3{-}COOH$, is formed when the ethanol in wine and apple cider reacts with oxygen in the air. A solution of acetic acid and water is the vinegar used in food preparation and salad dressings.

The sour taste of vinegar is due to ethanoic acid (acetic acid).

Esters

An **ester** is similar to a carboxylic acid, except the oxygen is attached to a carbon and not to hydrogen.

The functional group in the formula of an ester can be drawn as follows:

$$\mathrm{CH_3{-}}\overset{\overset{\displaystyle \mathbf{O}}{\|}}{\mathbf{C}}{-}\mathbf{O}{-}\mathrm{CH_3} \qquad \text{or} \qquad CH_3{-}\mathbf{COO}{-}CH_3$$

Ester

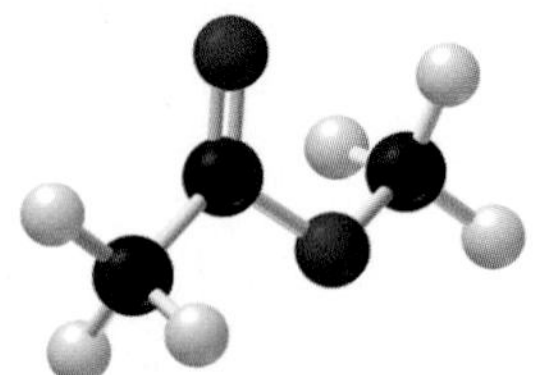
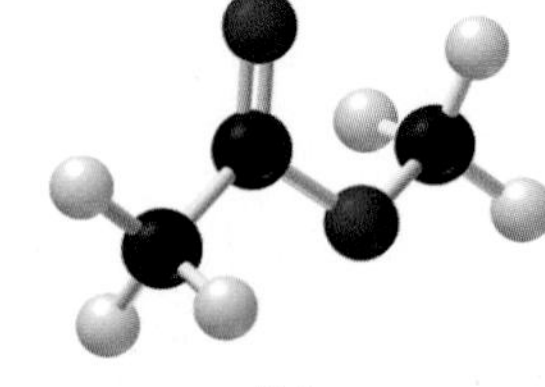
Ester

Many of the fragrances of perfumes and flowers and the flavors of fruits are due to esters. Small esters are volatile, so we can smell them, and soluble in water, so we can taste them. Esters are responsible for the odor and flavor of oranges, bananas, pears, pineapples, and strawberries. For example, the ester named ethyl butanoate produces the smell and flavor of pineapples.

$$CH_3{-}CH_2{-}CH_2{-}\overset{\overset{\displaystyle O}{\|}}{C}{-}O{-}CH_2{-}CH_3$$

Ethyl butanoate
(ethyl butyrate)

Esters such as ethyl butanoate provide the odor and flavor of many fruits such as pineapples.

Chemistry Link to Health

SALICYLIC ACID FROM THE WILLOW TREE

For many centuries, relief from pain and fever was obtained by chewing on the leaves or a piece of bark from the willow tree. By the 1800s, chemists discovered that salicin was the agent in the bark responsible for the relief of pain. However, the body converts salicin to salicylic acid, which has a carboxyl group and a hydroxyl group that irritates the stomach lining.

Salicylic acid: benzene ring with $\overset{\overset{\displaystyle O}{\|}}{C}{-}OH$ and OH (ortho)

Acetylsalicylic acid (aspirin): benzene ring with $\overset{\overset{\displaystyle O}{\|}}{C}{-}OH$ and $O{-}\overset{\overset{\displaystyle O}{\|}}{C}{-}CH_3$ (ortho)

In 1899, the Bayer chemical company in Germany produced an ester of salicylic acid and acetic acid, called acetylsalicylic acid (aspirin), which is less irritating. Today, aspirin is used as an analgesic (pain reliever), antipyretic (fever reducer), and anti-inflammatory agent. Many people take a daily low-dose aspirin, which has been found to lower the risk of heart attack and stroke.

The discovery of salicin in the leaves and bark of the willow tree led to the development of aspirin.

CONCEPT CHECK 8.6 Identifying Functional Groups

Classify each of the following organic compounds:

a. $CH_3—CH_2—CH_2—CH_2—OH$

b. $CH_3—CH=CH—CH_3$

c. $CH_3—CH_2—\overset{\overset{\displaystyle O}{\|}}{C}—CH_2—CH_3$

ANSWER

a. $CH_3—CH_2—CH_2—CH_2—\text{(OH)}$

This compound contains the —OH group, which makes it an alcohol.

b. $CH_3—\text{(CH=CH)}—CH_3$

This compound contains a double bond between two carbon atoms, which makes it an alkene.

c. $CH_3—CH_2—\overset{\overset{\displaystyle O}{\|}}{C}—CH_2—CH_3$

This compound contains the carbonyl (C=O) group attached to two carbon groups, which makes it a ketone.

Amines

Amines are derivatives of ammonia, NH_3, in which a nitrogen atom is attached to one, two, or three carbon groups. From Table 8.4, we know that a nitrogen atom forms three bonds.

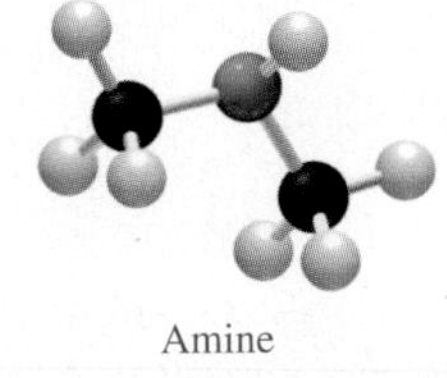

Amine

NH_3 (Ammonia)

Examples of amines: $CH_3—NH_2$; $CH_3—NH—CH_3$; $CH_3—N(CH_3)—CH_3$

One characteristic of fish is their odor, which is due to amines. Amines such as putrescine and cadaverine have a particularly pungent and offensive odor, which is produced when proteins decay.

$$H_2N—CH_2—CH_2—CH_2—CH_2—NH_2$$

Putrescine

$$H_2N—CH_2—CH_2—CH_2—CH_2—CH_2—NH_2$$

Cadaverine

Chemistry Link to Health

AMINES IN HEALTH AND MEDICINE

In response to allergic reactions or injury to cells, the body increases the production of an amine known as histamine, which causes blood vessels to dilate and redness and swelling to occur. Administering an antihistamine helps block the effects of histamine.

In the body, hormones called *biogenic amines* carry messages between the central nervous system and nerve cells. Epinephrine (adrenaline) and norepinephrine (noradrenaline) are released by the adrenal medulla in "fight-or-flight" situations to raise the blood glucose level and move the blood to the muscles. Used in remedies for colds, hay fever, and asthma, Benzedrine, Neo-Synephrine (phenylephrine), and norepinephrine contract the capillaries in the mucous membranes of the respiratory passages. Sometimes Benzedrine is taken internally to combat the desire to sleep, but it has side effects. Parkinson's disease is a result of a deficiency in another biogenic amine called dopamine.

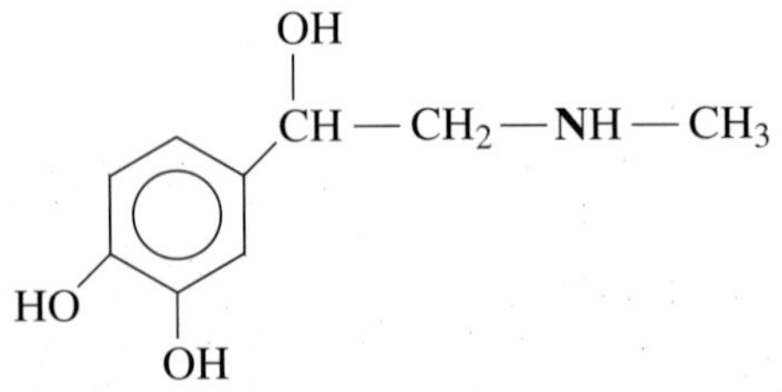

[Structure: benzene ring with two OH groups (HO, OH) bearing $CH(OH)—CH_2—NH—CH_3$]

Epinephrine (adrenaline)

Produced synthetically, amphetamines (known as "uppers") are stimulants of the central nervous system much like epinephrine, but they also increase cardiovascular activity and depress the appetite. They are sometimes used to bring about weight loss, but they can cause chemical dependency. Methedrine is used to treat depression and in the illegal form is known as "crank" or "crystal meth." The prefix meth means that there is one more CH_3- group on the nitrogen atom.

$$C_6H_5-CH_2-\underset{}{\overset{CH_3}{\overset{|}{CH}}}-NH_2$$

Benzedrine (amphetamine)

$$C_6H_5-CH_2-\overset{CH_3}{\overset{|}{CH}}-\overset{H}{\overset{|}{N}}-CH_3$$

Methamphetamine (methedrine)

Amides

In an **amide**, the hydroxyl group of a carboxylic acid is replaced by a nitrogen atom.

$$CH_3-\overset{O}{\overset{\|}{C}}-NH_2$$

Amide

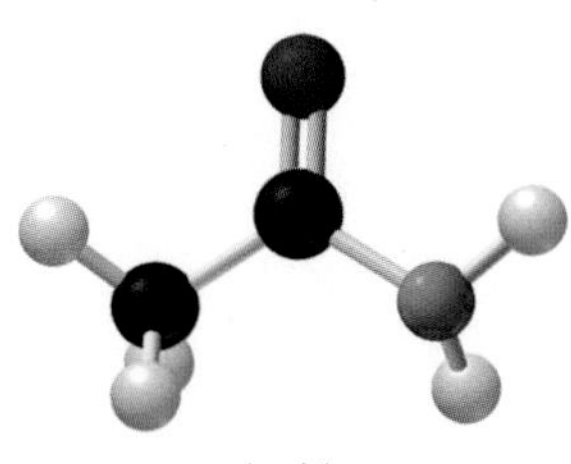

Amide

Many compounds that are amides are used to reduce fever and relieve pain. For example, the amide called acetaminophen is found in Tylenol.

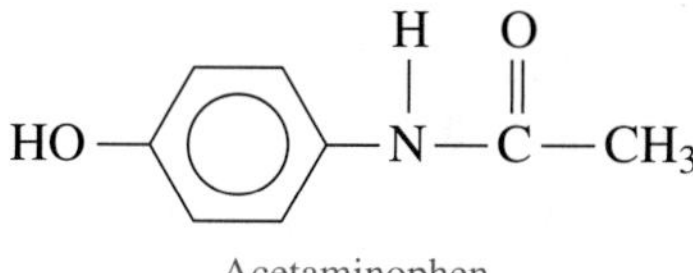

Acetaminophen

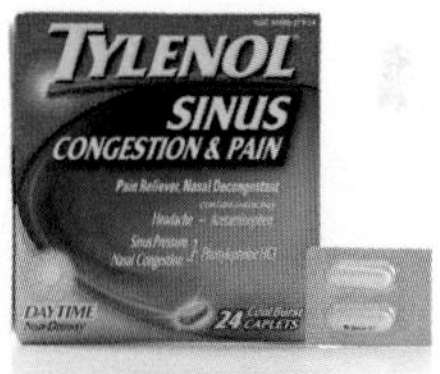

Amides such as acetaminophen are found in pain relievers.

A list of the common functional groups in organic compounds is shown in Table 8.5.

TABLE 8.5 Classes of Organic Compounds

Class	Functional Group	Example/Name	Uses
Alkene	$>C=C<$	$H_2C=CH_2$ Ethene (ethylene)	Ripening of fruit, used to make polyethylene
Alcohol	$-OH$	$CH_3-CH_2-\mathbf{OH}$ Ethanol (ethyl alcohol)	Solvent
Aldehyde	$-\overset{O}{\overset{\|}{C}}-H$	$CH_3-\overset{\mathbf{O}}{\overset{\|}{\mathbf{C}}}-\mathbf{H}$ Ethanal (acetaldehyde)	Preparation of acetic acid
Ketone	$-\overset{O}{\overset{\|}{C}}-$	$CH_3-\overset{\mathbf{O}}{\overset{\|}{\mathbf{C}}}-CH_3$ Propanone (acetone)	Solvent, paint and fingernail polish remover
Carboxylic acid	$-\overset{O}{\overset{\|}{C}}-O-H$	$CH_3-\overset{\mathbf{O}}{\overset{\|}{\mathbf{C}}}-\mathbf{O}-\mathbf{H}$ Ethanoic acid (acetic acid)	Component of vinegar
Ester	$-\overset{O}{\overset{\|}{C}}-O-$	$CH_3-\overset{\mathbf{O}}{\overset{\|}{\mathbf{C}}}-\mathbf{O}-CH_3$ Methyl ethanoate (methyl acetate)	Rum flavoring

TABLE 8.5 Classes of Organic Compounds (*continued*)

Class	Functional Group	Example/Name	Uses
Amine	$-\overset{\vert}{N}-$	CH_3-NH_2 Methylamine	Odor of fish
Amide	$-\overset{O}{\overset{\Vert}{C}}-\overset{\vert}{N}-$	$CH_3-\overset{O}{\overset{\Vert}{C}}-NH_2$ Ethanamide (acetamide)	Odor of mice

SAMPLE PROBLEM 8.6 Identifying Functional Groups

Classify the following organic compounds according to their functional groups:

a. $CH_3-CH_2-NH-CH_3$

b. $CH_3-CH_2-\overset{O}{\overset{\Vert}{C}}-NH_2$

c. CH_3-CH_2-COOH

d. $CH_3-\overset{CH_3}{\overset{\vert}{CH}}-\overset{O}{\overset{\Vert}{C}}-H$

SOLUTION

a. amine **b.** amide
c. carboxylic acid **d.** aldehyde

STUDY CHECK 8.6

How does a carboxylic acid differ from an ester?

QUESTIONS AND PROBLEMS

8.4 Functional Groups and Reactions of Organic Compounds: Extended Topic

LEARNING GOAL: *Classify organic molecules according to their functional groups; draw the condensed structural formulas for the products of reactions of organic compounds.*

8.21 Classify the organic compound that contains the following functional groups (**a–c**):
a. a hydroxyl group attached to a carbon chain
b. a carbon–carbon double bond
c. a carbonyl group attached to a hydrogen atom

8.22 Classify the organic compound that contains the following functional groups (**a–c**):
a. a nitrogen atom attached to one or more carbon atoms
b. a carbonyl group between two carbon atoms
c. a carboxyl group attached to two carbon atoms

8.23 Classify each of the molecules (**a–d**) according to its functional group.
a. $CH_3-\overset{OH}{\overset{\vert}{CH}}-CH_3$
b. $CH_3-\overset{O}{\overset{\Vert}{C}}-O-CH_2-CH_3$
c. $CH_3-CH_2-CH_2-CH_2-CH_2-COOH$
d. $CH_3-CH_2-NH_2$

8.24 Classify each of the molecules (**a–d**) according to its functional group.
a. $CH_3-\overset{O}{\overset{\Vert}{C}}-CH_2-CH_3$
b. $CH_3-\overset{CH_3}{\overset{\vert}{N}}-CH_3$
c. $CH_3-CH_2-CH_2-\overset{O}{\overset{\Vert}{C}}-H$
d. CH_3-CH_2-COOH

8.25 Write a balanced equation for the complete combustion of each of the following:
a. propane
b. octane
c. $CH_3-CH_2-CH_2-OH$
d. C_6H_{12}

8.26 Write a balanced equation for the complete combustion of each of the following:
a. ethane
b. heptane
c. $CH_3-CH_2-CH_2-CH_2-OH$
d. C_3H_6O

8.27 Draw the condensed structural formula for the product in each of the following:

a. $CH_3{-}CH_2{-}CH_2{-}CH{=}CH_2 + H_2 \xrightarrow{Pt}$

b. $CH_3{-}CH{=}CH{-}CH_3 + H_2 \xrightarrow{Ni}$

8.28 Draw the condensed structural formula for the product in each of the following:

a. $CH_3{-}CH_2{-}CH{=}CH_2 + H_2 \xrightarrow{Pt}$

b. $CH_3{-}\underset{}{\overset{CH_3}{\overset{|}{C}}}{=}CH{-}CH_2{-}CH_3 + H_2 \xrightarrow{Pt}$

8.5 Biochemical Compounds: Extended Topic

LEARNING GOAL

Identify the type of a biochemical compound from its structure and name its functional groups.

Biochemical compounds are organic compounds that are found in living things. Biochemical processes and reactions are part of every cell from which we derive energy and cellular components. Our diets are rich with biochemical compounds including carbohydrates, lipids, and proteins. All of the biochemical compounds are very large molecules, but each contains the same functional groups that are present in organic compounds.

Carbohydrates

The **carbohydrates** are a group of biochemical compounds consisting of monosaccharides, which contain many alcohol groups and an aldehyde or ketone group, disaccharides, and polysaccharides. Carbohydrates are the most abundant of all the organic compounds in nature. In plants, energy from the Sun converts carbon dioxide and water into the carbohydrate glucose. Many of the glucose molecules are made into long-chain polymers of starch that store energy or into cellulose to build the structural framework of the plant. About 65% of the foods in our diet consist of carbohydrates.

Carbohydrates contained in foods such as pasta and bread provide energy for the body.

Monosaccharides

The simplest carbohydrates are *monosaccharides*, which consist of a chain of carbon atoms. They all contain several hydroxyl (—OH) groups as well as an aldehyde (—CHO) group as the first carbon, or a ketone (C=O) group as the second carbon. The most common monosaccharide—glucose, also known as blood sugar—is an aldehyde. Fructose, the sweetest carbohydrate, is a ketone. Both glucose and fructose are found in honey.

CONCEPT CHECK 8.7 Functional Groups in Monosaccharides

Galactose, a monosaccharide found in milk and milk products, has the structure shown at right:

a. What is the molecular formula of galactose?

b. What functional groups are present in galactose?

```
  H     O
   \\  //
     C
    1|
  H—C—OH
    2|
 HO—C—H
    3|
 HO—C—H
    4|
  H—C—OH
    5|
    CH2OH
    6
```

Galactose

ANSWER

a. The total number of C atoms is 6, of H atoms is 12, and of O atoms is 6. The molecular formula is $C_6H_{12}O_6$.

b. The functional groups are an aldehyde group on carbon 1, and five alcohol (hydroxyl) groups on the other carbon atoms.

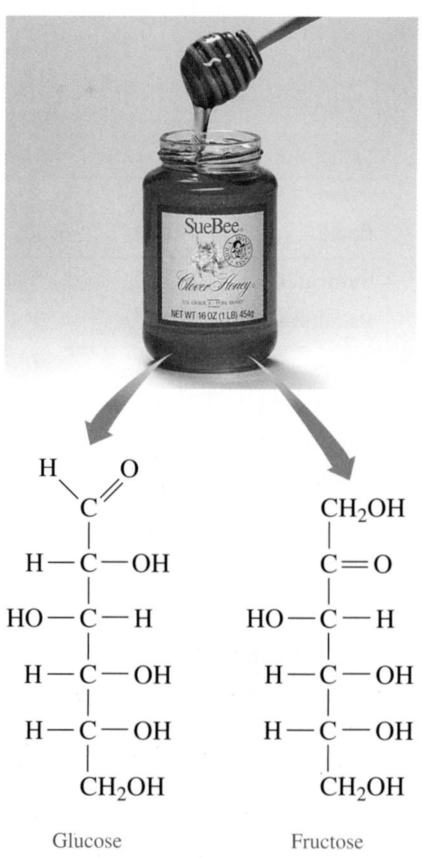

Honey is a mixture of fructose and glucose.

Disaccharides and Polysaccharides

A *disaccharide* consists of two monosaccharide units joined together. For example, ordinary table sugar, sucrose, is a disaccharide that contains one molecule of glucose and one molecule of fructose. *Polysaccharides* are carbohydrates that are naturally occurring polymers such as amylose and cellulose, which contain many monosaccharide units of glucose. Although we have represented monosaccharides in an open chain, the most stable form is a six-atom ring formed when the aldehyde or ketone group reacts with the hydroxyl group of a carbon at the other end of the chain. The cyclic representations of the saccharides are shown below:

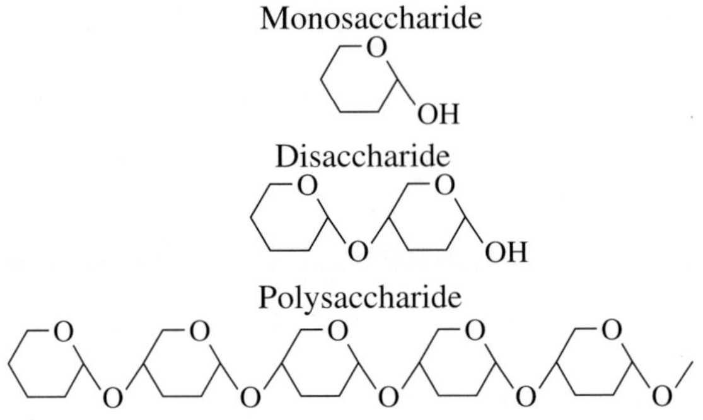

Monosaccharide

Disaccharide

Polysaccharide

Lipids

Lipids are a family of biochemical molecules that have the common property of being soluble in organic solvents but not in water. Lipids are important in cell membranes, fats, cholesterol, and steroid hormones.

Fatty Acids

The fats and oils in our diets contain fatty acids, which are long chains of carbon atoms with a carboxylic acid group at one end. An example is lauric acid, a 12-carbon acid found in coconut oil that can be written as

$$CH_3—(CH_2)_{10}—COOH$$

$$CH_3—CH_2—CH_2—CH_2—CH_2—CH_2—CH_2—CH_2—CH_2—CH_2—CH_2—C(=O)—OH$$

Condensed structural formula

Saturated fatty acids, which are generally solids at room temperature, contain only single bonds between carbons. Unsaturated fatty acids have one or more double bonds in the carbon chain and are usually liquids at room temperature. Table 8.6 lists some common fatty acids.

TABLE 8.6 Structures and Sources of Some Common Fatty Acids

Name	Carbon Atoms	Double Bonds	Condensed Structural Formula	Sources
Saturated				
Palmitic acid	16	0	$CH_3—(CH_2)_{14}—COOH$	Palm
Stearic acid	18	0	$CH_3—(CH_2)_{16}—COOH$	Animal fat
Unsaturated				
Oleic acid	18	1	$CH_3—(CH_2)_7—CH=CH—(CH_2)_7—COOH$	Olives, corn
Linoleic acid	18	2	$CH_3—(CH_2)_4—CH=CH—CH_2—CH=CH—(CH_2)_7—COOH$	Soybean, safflower, sunflower

Chemistry Link to Health

OMEGA-3 FATTY ACIDS IN FISH OILS

Because unsaturated fatty acids are now recognized as beneficial to health, American diets have changed to include more unsaturated fatty acids and less saturated fatty acids. This change is a response to research that indicates that atherosclerosis and heart disease are associated with diets that contain high levels of fats. However, the Inuit peoples of Alaska have a diet with high levels of unsaturated fats as well as high levels of blood cholesterol, but they have a very low occurrence of heart disease. The fats in the Inuit diet are primarily unsaturated fats from fish rather than from land animals.

The fatty acids in vegetable oils are omega-6, in which the first double bond occurs at the sixth carbon, counting from the $CH_3—$ end. However, the fatty acids in fish oils are mostly the omega-3 type, in which the first double bond occurs at the third carbon from the $CH_3—$ end.

In atherosclerosis and heart disease, cholesterol forms plaques that adhere to the walls of the blood vessels. As more plaque forms, there is also a possibility of blood clots blocking the blood vessels and causing a heart attack. Omega-3 fatty acids lower the tendency of blood clots blocking the blood vessels. It appears that a diet that includes fish such as salmon, tuna, and herring can provide higher amounts of the omega-3 fatty acids, which lessen the possibility of developing heart disease.

Cold-water fish are a source of omega-3 fatty acids.

Omega-6 Fatty Acid

Linoleic acid

$$\underset{1}{CH_3}—(CH_2)_4—\underset{6}{CH}{=}CH—CH_2—CH{=}CH—(CH_2)_7—COOH$$

Omega-3 Fatty Acid

Linolenic acid

$$\underset{1}{CH_3}—CH_2—(\underset{3}{CH}{=}CH—CH_2)_3—(CH_2)_6—COOH$$

Triacylglycerols (Fats)

In a *triacylglycerol*, also known as a *fat* or *oil*, the hydroxyl groups on the trialcohol glycerol form ester bonds with the carboxyl groups of three fatty acids. For example, glycerol and three molecules of stearic acid form a triacylglycerol.

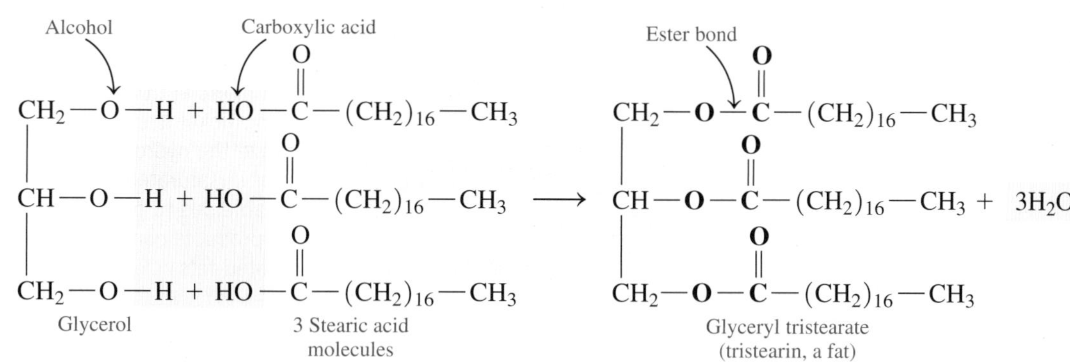

Prior to hibernation, a polar bear eats food with a high content of fats and oils.

Triacylglycerols are the major form of energy storage for animals. Animals that hibernate eat large quantities of plants, seeds, and nuts that contain high levels of fats and oils. Prior to hibernation, animals, such as polar bears, gain as much as 14 kg every week. As the external temperature drops, the animal goes into hibernation. Its body temperature drops to nearly freezing, and cellular activity, respiration, and heart rate are drastically reduced. Animals that live in extremely cold climates will hibernate for 4 to 7 months. During this time, stored fat is their only source of energy.

Chemistry Link to Industry

HYDROGENATION OF UNSATURATED FATS

Vegetable oils such as corn oil or safflower oil contain a high proportion of unsaturated fatty acids with double bonds. Commercially, the process of hydrogenation is used to convert many, but not all, of the double bonds to single bonds, which produces more saturated solid fats, such as margarine. In commercial hydrogenation, the addition of hydrogen is stopped before all the double bonds in a vegetable oil become completely saturated. As the fat becomes more saturated, the substances become more solid at room temperature. By controlling the amount of hydrogen, manufacturers can produce the various types of products on the market today, such as soft margarines, solid stick margarines, and solid shortenings. Although these products now contain more saturated fatty acids than the original oils, they contain no cholesterol, unlike similar products from animal sources, such as butter and lard. For example, when oleic acid, a typical unsaturated fatty acid in olive oil, is hydrogenated, it is converted to stearic acid, a saturated fatty acid.

$$\underset{\substack{\text{Oleic acid}\\\text{(unsaturated)}}}{CH_3-(CH_2)_7-CH{=}CH-(CH_2)_7-COOH} + H_2 \xrightarrow{Pt} \underset{\substack{\text{Stearic acid}\\\text{(saturated)}}}{CH_3-(CH_2)_{16}-COOH}$$

In nature, the more prevalent structure of the double bonds in unsaturated fatty acids is the *cis* structure, which means that the hydrogen atoms are on one side of the double bond and the carbon chains attached to the double bond are on the other side. During the process of hydrogenation of vegetable oils, some of the cis double bonds are changed to *trans* double bonds, which have the hydrogen atoms and carbon chains on opposite sides. If the label on a product states that the oils have been "partially" or "fully hydrogenated," that product will also contain trans fatty acids.

Cis double bond

Trans double bond

The concern about trans fatty acids is that they behave like saturated fatty acids in the body. Several studies reported that trans fatty acids raise the levels of LDL-cholesterol, low-density lipoproteins containing cholesterol that can accumulate in the arteries. More research is still needed to determine the overall impact of trans fatty acids present in fats in our diets. Since 2006, food labels have given the grams of trans fat per serving.

In commercial hydrogenation, nickel is used to catalyze the hydrogenation of unsaturated fats in vegetable oils to produce solid products containing saturated fats.

Proteins are found in foods such as eggs, milk, meat, and fish as well as plants such as grains, beans, and nuts.

Proteins

Proteins are biologically active polymers consisting of just 20 different amino acid building blocks, which are repeated numerous times with different sequences. There are many kinds of proteins in the body. Some proteins form cartilage, muscles, hair, and nails. Proteins also function as enzymes, which regulate biological reactions such as digestion and cellular metabolism. Other proteins, such as hemoglobin and myoglobin, transport oxygen in the blood and muscle.

Amino Acids

Amino acids, which are the molecular building blocks of proteins, contain an amino ($-NH_2$) group and a carboxylic acid ($-COOH$) group bonded to the central, alpha carbon atom. The unique characteristics of amino acids are due to different side chains (R). In biological systems, the amino and carboxylic acids groups are present in ionic forms.

General Structure of an α-Amino Acid

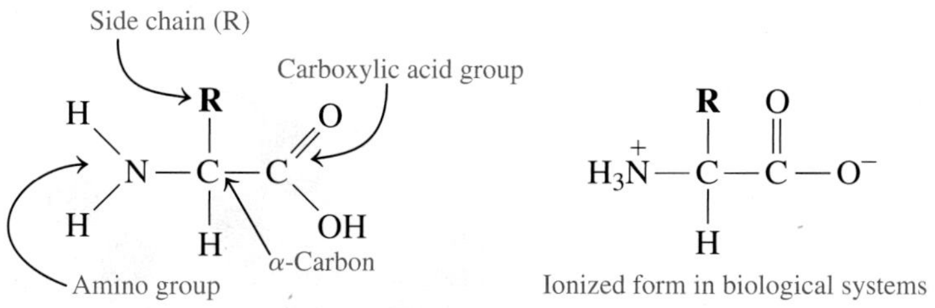

Side chain (R)
Carboxylic acid group
Amino group
α-Carbon

$$H_2N-CH(R)-COOH$$

$$H_3\overset{+}{N}-CH(R)-C(=O)-O^-$$

Ionized form in biological systems

The structures, names, and three-letter abbreviations of some common amino acids found in proteins are listed in Table 8.7.

TABLE 8.7 Some Typical Amino Acids in Proteins

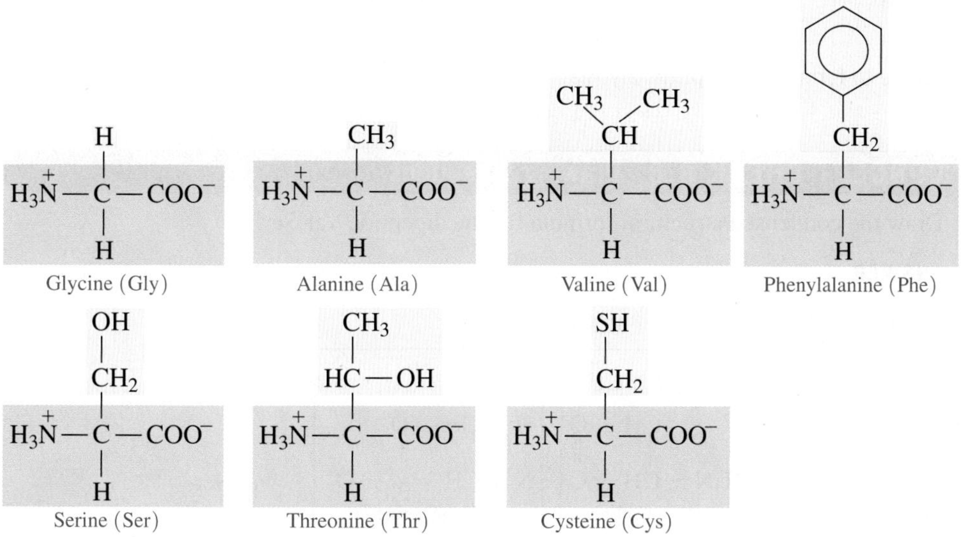

Structure	Name
$H_3\overset{+}{N}-CH(H)-COO^-$	Glycine (Gly)
$H_3\overset{+}{N}-CH(CH_3)-COO^-$	Alanine (Ala)
$H_3\overset{+}{N}-CH(CH(CH_3)_2)-COO^-$	Valine (Val)
$H_3\overset{+}{N}-CH(CH_2C_6H_5)-COO^-$	Phenylalanine (Phe)
$H_3\overset{+}{N}-CH(CH_2OH)-COO^-$	Serine (Ser)
$H_3\overset{+}{N}-CH(CH(OH)CH_3)-COO^-$	Threonine (Thr)
$H_3\overset{+}{N}-CH(CH_2SH)-COO^-$	Cysteine (Cys)

Peptides

The linking of two or more amino acids forms a *peptide*. A *peptide bond* is an amide bond that forms when the $-COO^-$ group of one amino acid reacts with the $H_3\overset{+}{N}-$ group of the next amino acid. For example, the combination of the amino acids glycine and alanine produces an amide bond in the dipeptide Gly-Ala. The order of amino acids in the peptide is written as the sequence of three-letter abbreviations going from left to right.

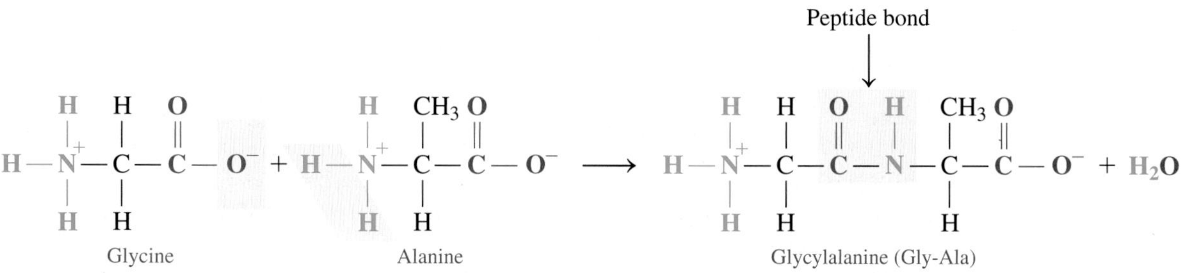

$$\underset{\text{Glycine}}{H_3\overset{+}{N}-CH_2-C(=O)-O^-} + \underset{\text{Alanine}}{H_3\overset{+}{N}-CH(CH_3)-C(=O)-O^-} \longrightarrow \underset{\text{Glycylalanine (Gly-Ala)}}{H_3\overset{+}{N}-CH_2-C(=O)-NH-CH(CH_3)-C(=O)-O^-} + H_2O$$

Peptide bond

The ball-and-stick model of the formation of this peptide bond is shown as follows:

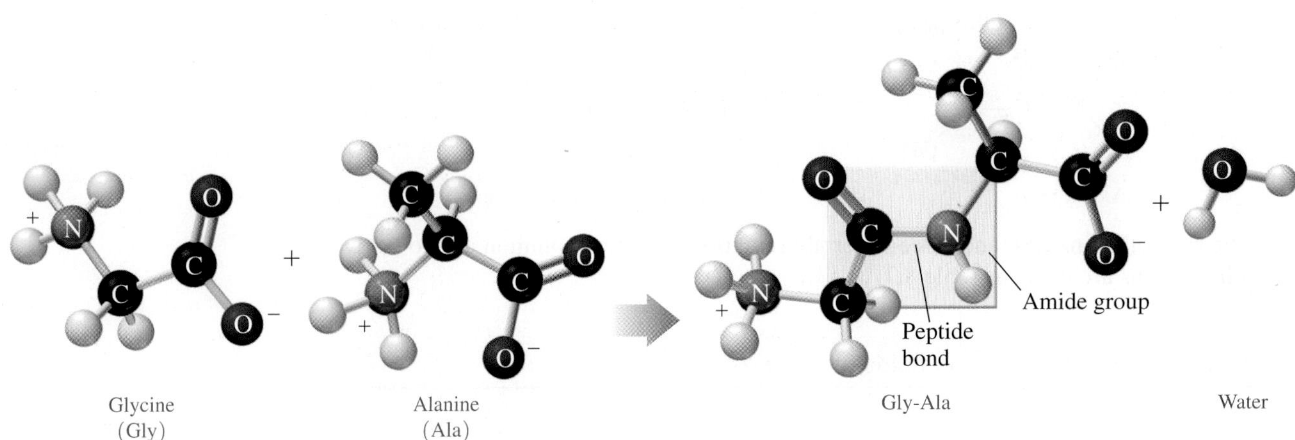

A peptide bond links glycine and alanine to form the dipeptide Gly-Ala.

CONCEPT CHECK 8.8 Drawing Dipeptides

Draw the condensed structural formula for the dipeptide Val-Ser.

ANSWER

Valine is joined to serine by a peptide bond.

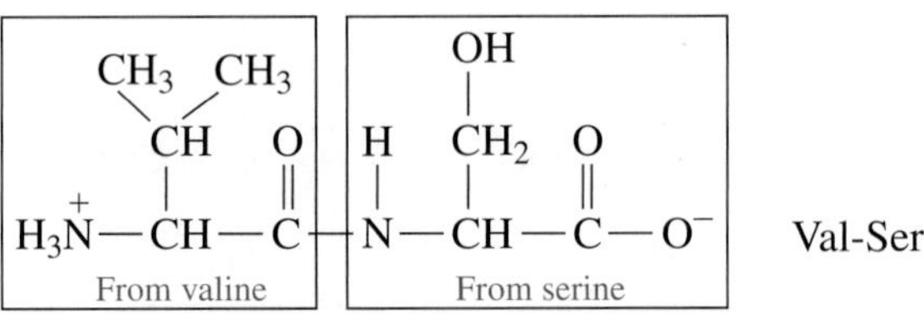

Some artificial sweeteners contain amino acids.

Amino acids are used to make the sugar substitute Aspartame, marketed as NutraSweet and Equal, which is 180 times sweeter than sucrose (table sugar). It is a noncarbohydrate sweetener made of aspartic acid and a methyl ester of phenylalanine. However, one breakdown product, phenylalanine, poses a danger to anyone who cannot metabolize it properly, a condition called *phenylketonuria* (PKU).

$$\overset{+}{H_3N}-\underset{\underset{COO^-}{|}}{\overset{CH_2-COO^-}{CH}}$$

$$H_3\overset{+}{N}-CH(CH_2COO^-)-C(=O)-NH-CH(CH_2C_6H_5)-C(=O)-O-CH_3$$

Aspartic acid — Phenylalanine — Methyl ester

Aspartame (NutraSweet)

QUESTIONS AND PROBLEMS

8.5 Biochemical Compounds: Extended Topic

LEARNING GOAL: *Identify the type of a biochemical compound from its structure and name its functional groups.*

8.29 Identify the functional groups in each of the following monosaccharides:

a.

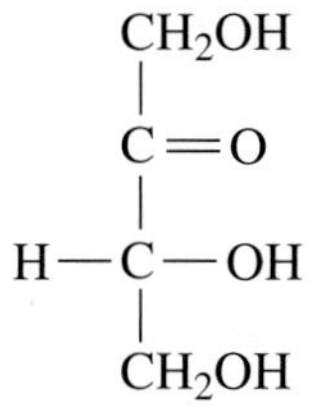

```
      CH2OH
        |
       C=O
        |
   H—C—OH
        |
      CH2OH
```

Erythrulose

b.

```
  H     O
    \  //
     C
     |
  H—C—OH
     |
  H—C—OH
     |
  H—C—OH
     |
    CH2OH
```

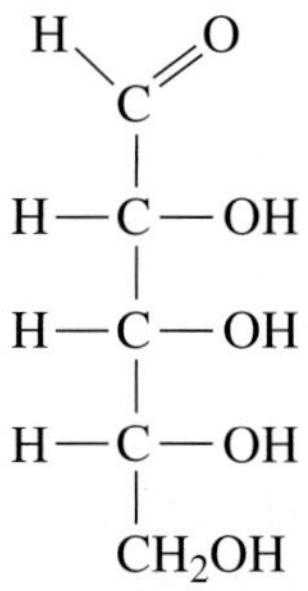

Ribose

8.30 Identify the functional groups in each of the following monosaccharides:

a.

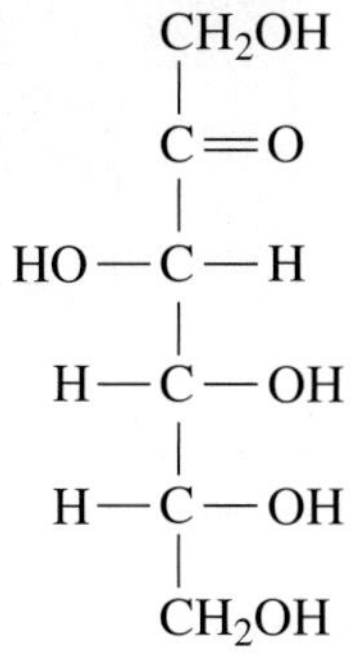

```
       CH2OH
         |
        C=O
         |
   HO—C—H
         |
    H—C—OH
         |
    H—C—OH
         |
       CH2OH
```

Fructose

b.

```
   H     O
     \  //
      C
      |
  HO—C—H
      |
   H—C—OH
      |
     CH2OH
```

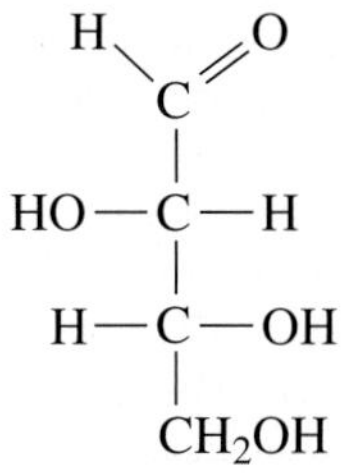

Threose

8.31 Match each of the following biochemical molecules (**1–3**) with the definitions (**a–e**) below:

1. carbohydrate **2.** lipid **3.** protein

a. a polymer of amino acids
b. a biochemical compound that is not soluble in water
c. contains many alcohol groups and an aldehyde or ketone group
d. fats
e. a polysaccharide

8.32 Match each of the following biochemical molecules (**1–3**) with the definitions (**a–e**) below:

1. carbohydrate **2.** lipid **3.** protein

a. a long-chain fatty acid
b. a biochemical compound that is the main source of energy in the body
c. contains 20 different amino acids
d. a disaccharide
e. glucose, which is also known as blood sugar

CHAPTER REVIEW

8.1 Equations for Chemical Reactions

LEARNING GOAL: *Identify a balanced chemical equation and determine the number of atoms in the reactants and products.*

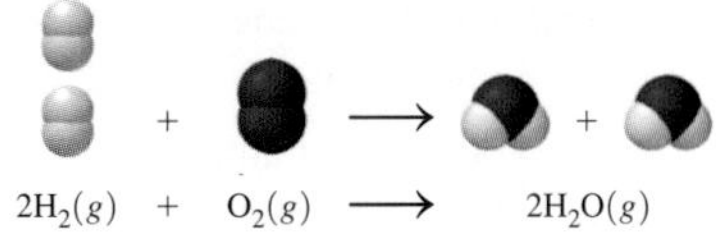

- A chemical change occurs when the atoms of the initial substances rearrange to form new substances.
- A chemical equation shows the formulas of the substances that react on the left side of the reaction arrow and the products that form on the right side of the reaction arrow.

8.2 Balancing a Chemical Equation

LEARNING GOAL: *Write a balanced chemical equation from the formulas of the reactants and products for a chemical reaction.*

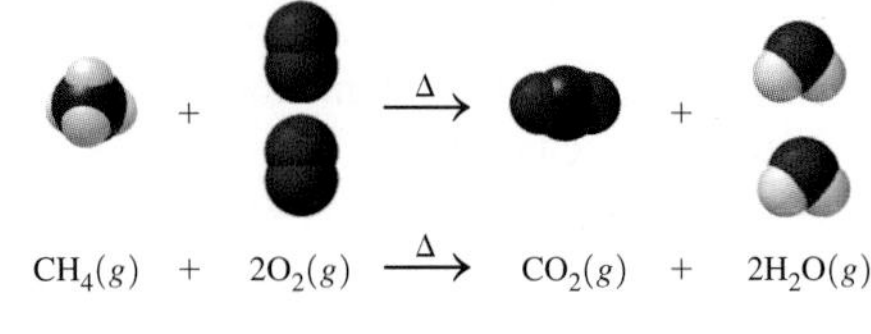

- An equation is balanced by writing coefficients, which are small whole numbers, in front of formulas to balance the atoms or ions of each element in the reactants and in the products.

8.3 Types of Reactions

LEARNING GOAL: *Identify a reaction as a combination, decomposition, single replacement, double replacement, or combustion.*

Single replacement

One element replaces another element

A + BC ⟶ AC + B

- Many chemical reactions are organized by reaction type: combination, decomposition, single replacement, double replacement, or combustion.

8.4 Functional Groups and Reactions of Organic Compounds: Extended Topic

LEARNING GOAL: *Classify organic molecules according to their functional groups; draw the condensed structural formulas for the products of reactions of organic compounds.*

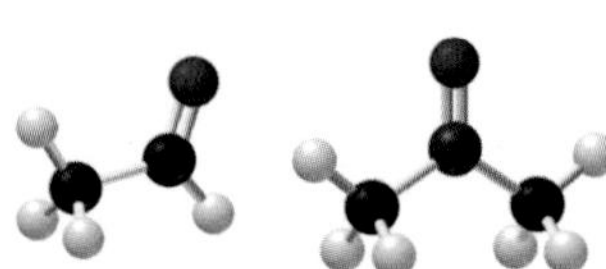

- An organic molecule contains a characteristic group of atoms called a functional group that determines the molecule's family and chemical reactivity.
- Functional groups are used to classify organic compounds, act as reactive sites in the molecule, and provide a system of naming for organic compounds.
- Some common functional groups include the hydroxyl group in alcohols, the carbonyl group in aldehydes and ketones, and a nitrogen atom in amines.
- Combustion is a characteristic reaction of alkanes and other organic compounds.
- In hydrogenation, hydrogen atoms are attached to the carbon atoms in a double bond, which converts an alkene to an alkane.

8.5 Biochemical Compounds: Extended Topic

LEARNING GOAL: *Identify the type of a biochemical compound from its structure and name its functional groups.*

- Carbohydrates are classified as monosaccharides (simple sugars), disaccharides (two monosaccharide units), or polysaccharides (many monosaccharide units).
- Carbohydrates consist of carbon chains that contain an aldehyde or ketone group, and hydroxyl groups on all the other carbons.
- Lipids are biochemical compounds that are not soluble in water.
- Fatty acids consist of long chains of carbon atoms with a carboxylic acid group on one end.
- Fatty acids may be saturated with single bonds between carbon atoms, or unsaturated with one or more double bonds.
- A fat or oil (triacylglycerol) is a biochemical compound consisting of glycerol (three alcohol groups) with ester bonds to three fatty acids.
- An amino acid consists of an amino group, a carboxylic acid group, and a unique side group attached to the central alpha carbon atom.
- Peptides form when an amide bond forms between the carboxylic acid group of one amino acid and the amino group of the second amino acid.
- Proteins are biologically active polymers of amino acids connected by peptide bonds.

CONCEPT MAP

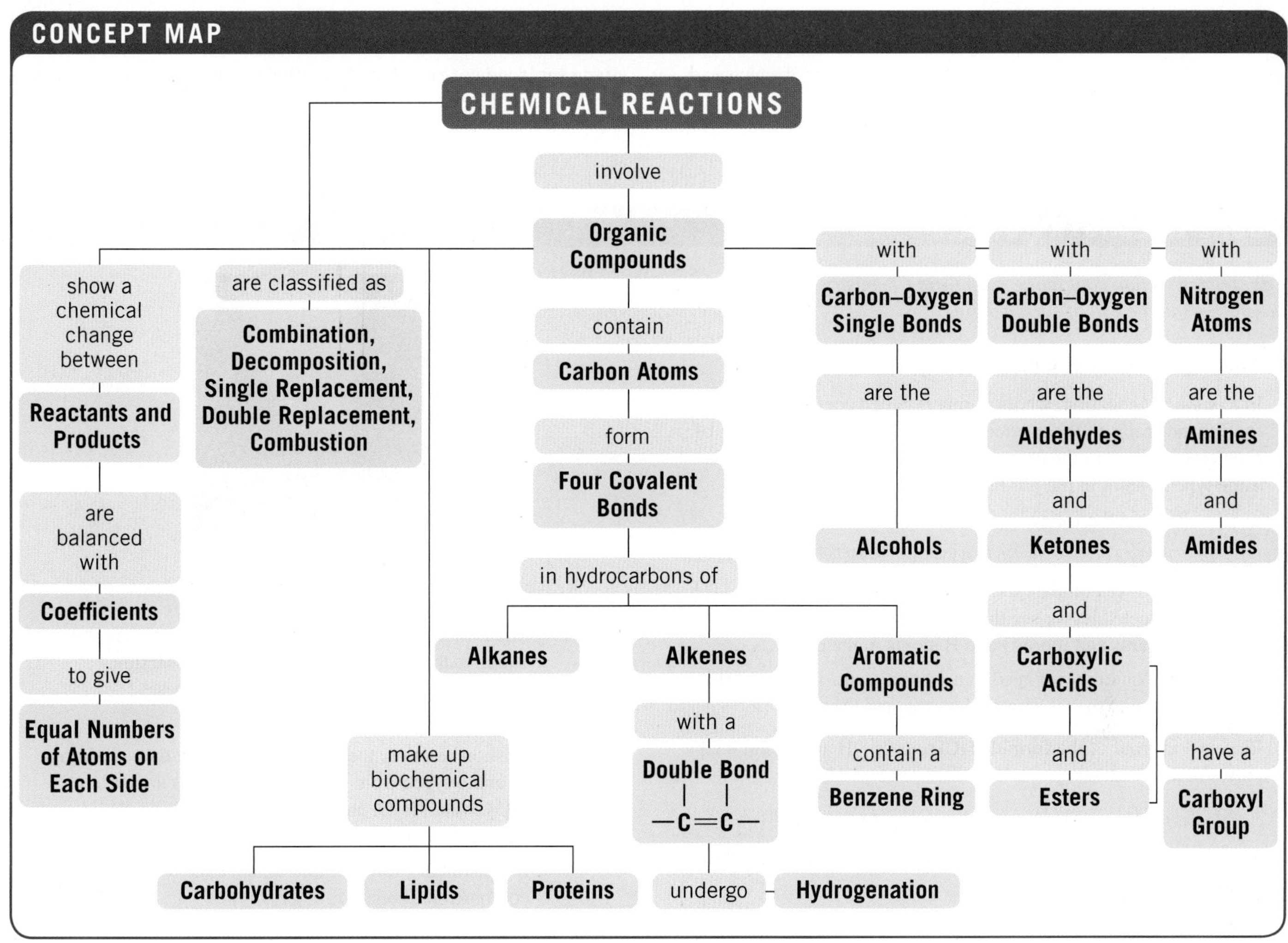

KEY TERMS

alcohol An organic compound that contains the hydroxyl (—OH) group bonded to a carbon atom.

aldehyde A class of organic compounds that contains a carbonyl (C=O) group bonded to at least one hydrogen atom.

alkene A type of hydrocarbon that contains carbon–carbon double bonds (C=C).

amide An organic compound in which a carbon containing the carbonyl group is attached to a nitrogen atom.

amine An organic compound that contains a nitrogen atom bonded to one or more carbon atoms.

amino acid The building block of proteins, consisting of an amino group, a carboxylic acid group, and a unique side group attached to the alpha carbon.

aromatic compound A compound that contains the ring structure of benzene.

balanced equation The final form of a chemical reaction that shows the same number of atoms of each element in the reactants and products.

carbohydrate A group of biochemical compounds that are monosaccharides containing many alcohol groups and an aldehyde or ketone group, disaccharides, and polysaccharides.

carboxylic acid An organic compound that contains the carboxyl (—COOH) group.

chemical equation A shorthand way to represent a chemical reaction using chemical formulas to indicate the reactants and products.

chemical reaction The process by which a chemical change takes place.

coefficient Whole numbers placed in front of the formulas in an equation to balance the number of atoms of each element.

combination reaction A reaction in which reactants combine to form a single product.

combustion reaction A chemical reaction in which an organic compound reacts with oxygen to produce CO_2, H_2O, and energy.

decomposition reaction A reaction in which a single reactant splits into two or more simpler substances.

double replacement reaction A reaction in which the positive ions of two different reactants exchange places.

ester An organic compound that contains a carboxyl (—COO—) group with an oxygen atom bonded to carbon.

functional group A group of atoms that determines the physical and chemical properties and naming of a class of organic compounds.

ketone An organic compound in which a carbonyl (C=O) group is bonded to two carbon atoms.

lipid A type of biochemical compound that is not soluble in water.
products The substances formed as a result of a chemical reaction.
protein A biologically active compound that is a polymer of amino acids.
reactants The initial substances that undergo change in a chemical reaction.
single replacement reaction A reaction in which an element replaces a different element in a compound.

CORE CHEMISTRY SKILLS

The chapter section containing each Core Chemistry Skill is shown in parentheses at the end of each heading.

Balancing a Chemical Equation (8.2)

- In a *balanced* equation, whole numbers called coefficients multiply each of the atoms in the chemical formulas so that the number of each type of atom in the reactants is equal to the number of the same type of atom in the products.

Example: Balance the following equation:

$SnCl_4(aq) + H_2O(l) \longrightarrow Sn(OH)_4(s) + HCl(aq)$ Unbalanced

Answer: When we compare the atoms on the reactant side and the product side, we see that there are more Cl atoms in the reactants and more O and H atoms in the products.

To balance the equation, we need to use coefficients in front of the formulas containing the Cl atoms, H atoms, and O atoms.

- Place a 4 in front of the formula HCl to give 8 H atoms and 4 Cl atoms in the products.

$$SnCl_4(aq) + H_2O(l) \longrightarrow Sn(OH)_4(s) + 4HCl(aq)$$

- Place a 4 in front of the formula H_2O to give 8 H atoms and 4 O atoms in the reactants.

$$SnCl_4(aq) + 4H_2O(l) \longrightarrow Sn(OH)_4(s) + 4HCl(aq)$$

- The total number of Sn (1), Cl (4), H (8), and O (4) atoms is now equal on both sides of the equation.

$SnCl_4(aq) + 4H_2O(l) \longrightarrow Sn(OH)_4(s) + 4HCl(aq)$ Balanced

Classifying Types of Chemical Reactions (8.3)

- Chemical reactions are classified by identifying general patterns in their equations.
- In a combination reaction, two or more elements or compounds bond to form one product.
- In a decomposition reaction, a single reactant splits into two or more products.
- In a single replacement reaction, an uncombined element takes the place of an element in a compound.
- In a double replacement reaction, the positive ions in the reacting compounds switch places.
- In combustion reaction, a carbon-containing compound that is the fuel burns in oxygen from the air to produce carbon dioxide, CO_2, water, H_2O, and energy.

Example: Classify the thermite reaction used to cut or weld railroad tracks.

$$2Al(s) + Fe_2O_3(s) \xrightarrow{\Delta} Al_2O_3(s) + 2Fe(l)$$

The thermite reaction produces molten iron.

Answer: The iron in iron(III) oxide is replaced by aluminum, which makes this a single replacement reaction.

Balancing Combustion Reactions (8.3)

- In a combustion reaction, the reactants are a carbon-containing compound and oxygen from the air; the products are carbon dioxide, CO_2, water, H_2O, and energy.

Example: Butanol, an alcohol, has been proposed as a replacement for gasoline. Complete and balance the reaction of the combustion of butanol, $C_4H_{10}O(l)$.

Answer: The formulas for the reactants and products in the reaction are written as

$$C_4H_{10}O(l) + O_2(g) \xrightarrow{\Delta} CO_2(g) + H_2O(g) + \text{energy}$$

Using the subscripts in $C_4H_{10}O$, we place a coefficient of 4 in front of CO_2 and a coefficient of 5 in front of H_2O.

$$C_4H_{10}O(l) + O_2(g) \xrightarrow{\Delta} 4CO_2(g) + 5H_2O(g) + \text{energy}$$

There are now 13 O atoms in the products. With one O atom in butanol, a coefficient of 6 is placed in front of O_2 to give 12 more O atoms, or a total of 13 O atoms in the reactants.

$$C_4H_{10}O(l) + 6O_2(g) \xrightarrow{\Delta} 4CO_2(g) + 5H_2O(g) + \text{energy}$$

- The total number of C (4), H (10), and O (13) atoms is now equal on both sides of the equation.

Identifying Functional Groups (8.4)

- Functional groups are specific groups of atoms in organic compounds, which undergo characteristic chemical reactions.
- Organic compounds with the same functional group have similar properties and reactions.

Example: Identify the functional groups in the following molecule, which is a component of skincare products.

$$HO-CH_2-\overset{\overset{\displaystyle O}{\|}}{C}-OH$$

Answer: The hydroxyl ($-OH$) group makes it an alcohol. It also contains the carboxyl $-COOH$ group, which means it is also a carboxylic acid.

SUMMARY OF REACTIONS

Combination

$S(s) + O_2(g) \longrightarrow SO_2(g)$

Decomposition

$2HgO(s) \longrightarrow 2Hg(l) + O_2(g)$

Single Replacement

$Zn(s) + 2HCl(aq) \longrightarrow ZnCl_2(aq) + H_2(g)$

Double Replacement

$AgNO_3(aq) + HCl(aq) \longrightarrow AgCl(s) + HNO_3(aq)$

Combustion

$C_3H_8(g) + 5O_2(g) \xrightarrow{\Delta} 3CO_2(g) + 4H_2O(g) + \text{energy}$

Hydrogenation

$CH_3{-}CH{=}CH_2(g) + H_2(g) \xrightarrow{Pt} CH_3{-}CH_2{-}CH_3(g)$

UNDERSTANDING THE CONCEPTS

The chapter sections to review are shown in parentheses at the end of each question.

8.33 If red spheres represent oxygen atoms, blue spheres represent nitrogen atoms, and all the molecules are gases, (8.1, 8.2, 8.3)

Reactants Products

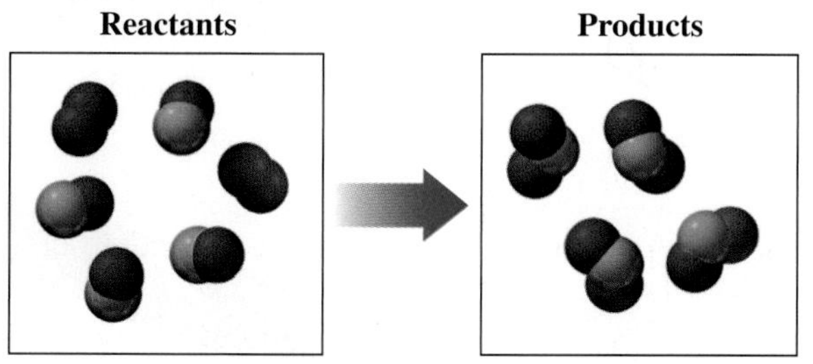

a. write the formula for each of the reactants and products
b. write a balanced equation for the reaction
c. indicate the type of reaction as combination, decomposition, single replacement, double replacement, or combustion

8.34 If purple spheres represent iodine atoms, white spheres represent hydrogen atoms, and all the molecules are gases, (8.1, 8.2, 8.3)

Reactants Products

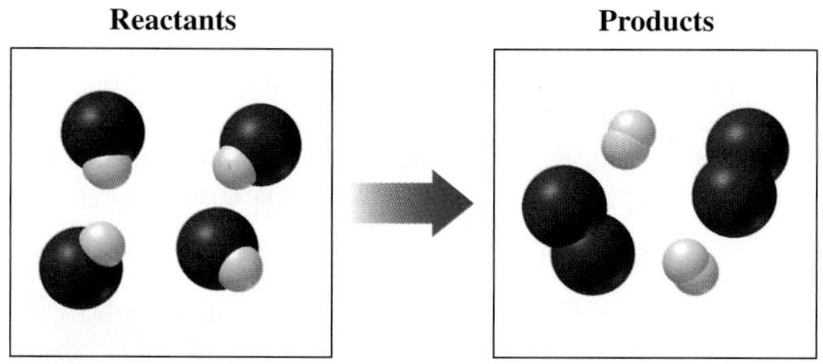

a. write the formula for each of the reactants and products
b. write a balanced equation for the reaction
c. indicate the type of reaction as combination, decomposition, single replacement, double replacement, or combustion

8.35 If blue spheres represent nitrogen atoms, purple spheres represent iodine atoms, the reacting molecules are solid, and the products are gases, (8.1, 8.2, 8.3)

Reactants Products

a. write the formula for each of the reactants and products
b. write a balanced equation for the reaction
c. indicate the type of reaction as combination, decomposition, single replacement, double replacement, or combustion

8.36 If green spheres represent chlorine atoms, yellow-green spheres represent fluorine atoms, white spheres represent hydrogen atoms, and all the molecules are gases, (8.1, 8.2, 8.3)

Reactants Products

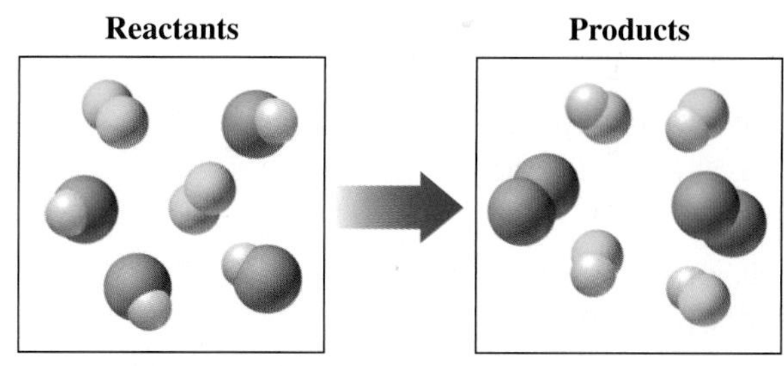

a. write the formula for each of the reactants and products
b. write a balanced equation for the reaction
c. indicate the type of reaction as combination, decomposition, single replacement, double replacement, or combustion

8.37 If green spheres represent chlorine atoms, red spheres represent oxygen atoms, and all the molecules are gases, (8.1, 8.2, 8.3)

Reactants Products

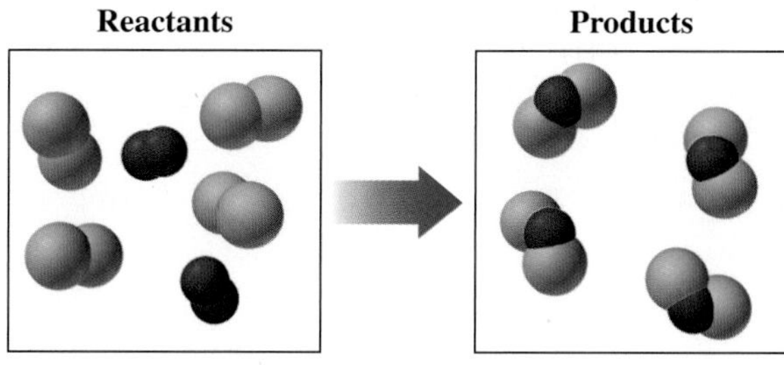

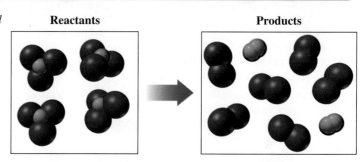

a. write the formula for each of the reactants and products
b. write a balanced equation for the reaction
c. indicate the type of reaction as combination, decomposition, single replacement, double replacement, or combustion

8.38 If blue spheres represent nitrogen atoms, purple spheres represent iodine atoms, the reacting molecules are gases, and the products are solid, (8.1, 8.2, 8.3)

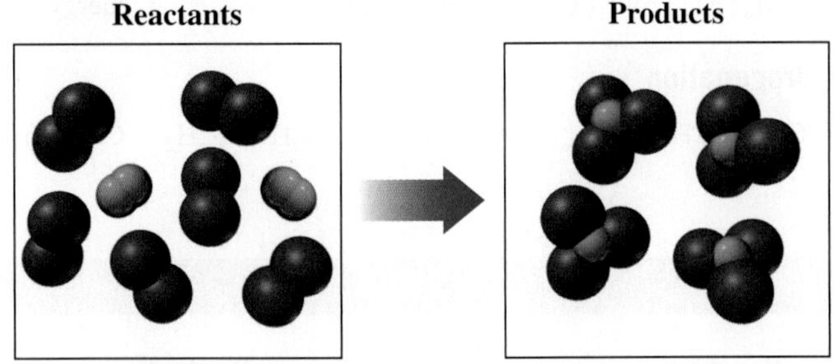

a. write the formula for each of the reactants and products
b. write a balanced equation for the reaction
c. indicate the type of reaction as combination, decomposition, single replacement, double replacement, or combustion

8.39 Balance each of the following by adding coefficients; identify the type of reaction for each: (8.1, 8.2, 8.3)

a. ___ + ___ $\longrightarrow$ ___

b. ___ $\longrightarrow$ ___ + ___

8.40 Balance each of the following by adding coefficients; identify the type of reaction for each: (8.1, 8.2, 8.3)

a. ___ + ___ $\longrightarrow$ ___ + ___

b. ___ + ___ $\longrightarrow$ ___

8.41 Classify each of the following according to its functional group: (8.4)

a. $CH_3-CH_2-CH_2-\overset{O}{\overset{\|}{C}}-CH_3$

b. $CH_3-CH{=}CH_2$

c. $CH_3-\overset{O}{\overset{\|}{C}}-O-CH_3$

d. $CH_3-CH_2-CH_2-NH_2$

8.42 Classify each of the following according to its functional group: (8.4)

a. CH_3-NH_2

b. $CH_3-\overset{O}{\overset{\|}{C}}-CH_3$

c. $CH_3-\overset{CH_3}{\overset{|}{CH}}-CH_2-OH$

d. $CH_3-\overset{CH_3}{\overset{|}{CH}}-\overset{O}{\overset{\|}{C}}-H$

8.43 Select the class of organic compound that matches each of the following definitions (**a–d**): alkane, alkene, alcohol, aldehyde, ketone, carboxylic acid, ester, amine, or amide. (8.4)

a. contains a hydroxyl group
b. contains one or more carbon–carbon double bonds
c. contains a carbonyl group bonded to a hydrogen
d. contains only carbon–carbon single bonds

8.44 Select the class of organic compound that matches each of the following definitions (**a–d**): alkane, alkene, alcohol, aldehyde, ketone, carboxylic acid, ester, amine, or amide. (8.4)

a. contains a carboxyl group in which the hydrogen atom is replaced by a carbon atom
b. contains a carbonyl group bonded to a hydroxyl group
c. contains a nitrogen atom bonded to one or more carbon atoms
d. contains a carbonyl group bonded to two carbon atoms

8.45 Classify each of the following according to its functional group(s): (8.4)

a. $C_6H_5-\overset{O}{\overset{\|}{C}}-H$ (benzene ring bonded to C)

b. $C_6H_5-CH{=}CH-\overset{O}{\overset{\|}{C}}-H$ (benzene ring bonded to CH)

c. $CH_3-\overset{O}{\overset{\|}{C}}-\overset{O}{\overset{\|}{C}}-CH_3$

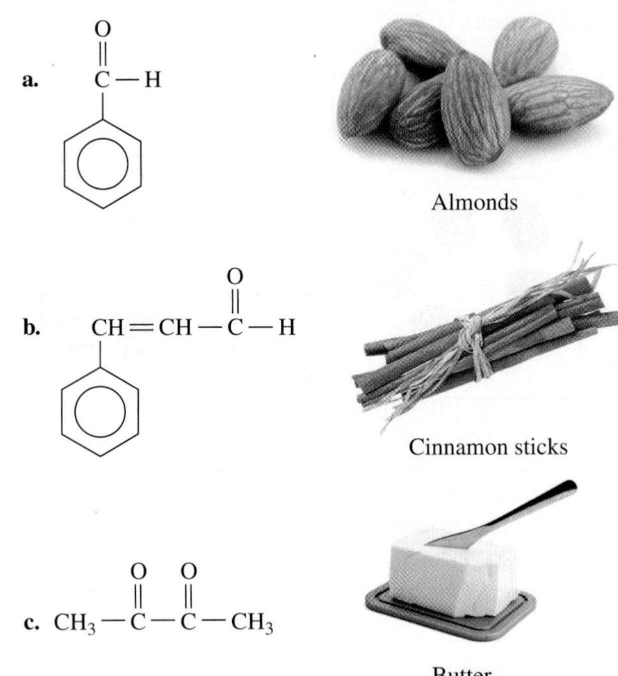

Almonds

Cinnamon sticks

Butter

8.46 Classify each of the following according to its functional group(s): (8.4)

a. BHA is an antioxidant used as a preservative in foods such as baked goods, butter, meats, and snack foods.

Benzene ring with OH; $-\overset{CH_3}{\underset{CH_3}{\overset{|}{\underset{|}{C}}}}-CH_3$; and $O-CH_3$

Baked goods contain BHA as a preservative.

b. Vanillin is a flavoring obtained from the seeds of the vanilla bean.

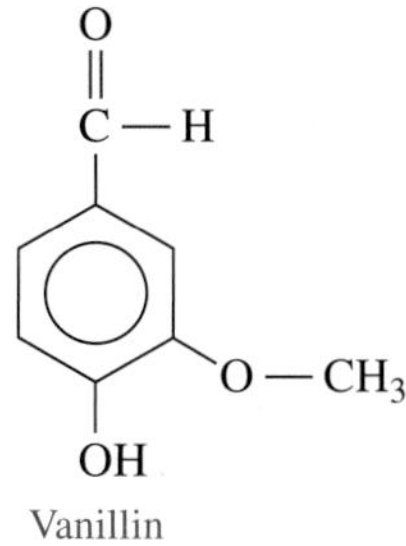

Vanillin

Vanilla extract is a solution containing the compound vanillin.

8.47 The sweetener aspartame is made from two amino acids: aspartic acid and phenylalanine. Classify aspartame according to its functional group(s). (8.4)

The sweetener in Equal is aspartame.

8.48 Phenacetin was previously used to reduce fever but is now banned. Classify phenacetin according to its functional group(s). (8.4)

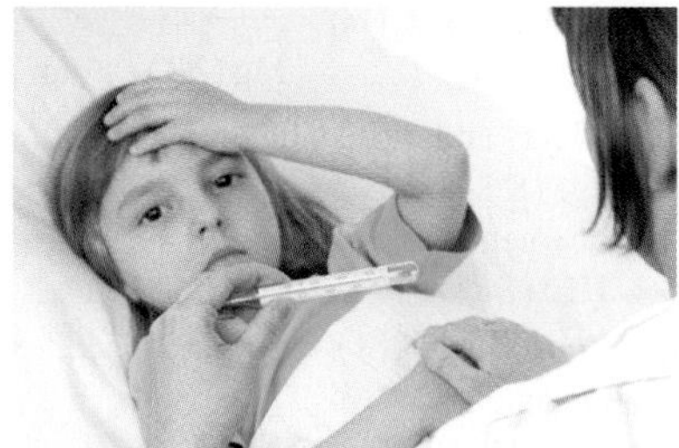

Phenacetin

Phenacetin is no longer used because it is a carcinogen.

8.49 State whether each of the following statements is *true* or *false*: (8.5)

a. An amino acid contains an amino group and a carboxylic acid group.
b. Lipids are water soluble.
c. Polysaccharides are a type of protein.
d. A protein is a polymer of amino acids.

8.50 State whether each of the following statements is *true* or *false*: (8.5)

a. In a fat, fatty acids are bonded to glycerol molecules by peptide bonds.
b. Lipids are not water soluble.
c. Disaccharides are a type of carbohydrate.
d. Proteins are polymers of monosaccharides.

ADDITIONAL QUESTIONS AND PROBLEMS

8.51 Identify the type of reaction for each of the following as combination, decomposition, single replacement, double replacement, or combustion: (8.1, 8.2, 8.3)

a. A metal and a nonmetal element form an ionic compound.
b. A hydrocarbon reacts with oxygen to produce carbon dioxide and water.
c. Two compounds react to produce two new compounds.
d. Heating calcium carbonate produces calcium oxide and carbon dioxide.
e. Zinc replaces copper in $Cu(NO_3)_2$.

8.52 Identify the type of reaction for each of the following as combination, decomposition, single replacement, double replacement, or combustion: (8.1, 8.2, 8.3)

a. A compound breaks apart into its elements.
b. An element replaces the ion in a compound.
c. Copper and bromine form copper(II) bromide.
d. Iron(II) sulfite breaks down to iron(II) oxide and sulfur dioxide.
e. Silver ion from $AgNO_3(aq)$ forms a solid with bromide ion from $KBr(aq)$.

8.53 Balance each of the following unbalanced equations and identify the type of reaction: (8.1, 8.2, 8.3)

a. $NH_3(g) + HCl(g) \longrightarrow NH_4Cl(s)$
b. $C_4H_8(g) + O_2(g) \xrightarrow{\Delta} CO_2(g) + H_2O(g)$
c. $Sb(s) + Cl_2(g) \longrightarrow SbCl_3(s)$
d. $NI_3(s) \longrightarrow N_2(g) + I_2(g)$
e. $KBr(aq) + Cl_2(g) \longrightarrow KCl(aq) + Br_2(l)$
f. $Fe(s) + H_2SO_4(aq) \longrightarrow Fe_2(SO_4)_3(aq) + H_2(g)$
g. $Al_2(SO_4)_3(aq) + NaOH(aq) \longrightarrow Na_2SO_4(aq) + Al(OH)_3(s)$

8.54 Balance each of the following unbalanced equations and identify the type of reaction: (8.1, 8.2, 8.3)

a. $Si_3N_4(s) \longrightarrow Si(s) + N_2(g)$

b. $Mg(s) + N_2(g) \longrightarrow Mg_3N_2(s)$

c. $C_3H_4(g) + O_2(g) \xrightarrow{\Delta} CO_2(g) + H_2O(g)$

d. $Mg(s) + H_3PO_4(aq) \longrightarrow Mg_3(PO_4)_2(s) + H_2(g)$

e. $Cr_2O_3(s) + H_2(g) \longrightarrow Cr(s) + H_2O(g)$

f. $Al(s) + Cl_2(g) \longrightarrow AlCl_3(s)$

g. $MgCl_2(aq) + AgNO_3(aq) \longrightarrow Mg(NO_3)_2(aq) + AgCl(s)$

8.55 Predict the products and write a balanced equation for each of the following: (8.1, 8.2, 8.3)

a. single replacement:
$Zn(s) + HCl(aq) \longrightarrow$ ______ + ______

b. decomposition: $BaCO_3(s) \xrightarrow{\Delta}$ ______ + ______

c. double replacement:
$NaOH(aq) + HCl(aq) \longrightarrow$ ______ + ______

d. combination: $Al(s) + F_2(g) \longrightarrow$ ______

8.56 Predict the products and write a balanced equation for each of the following:

a. decomposition: $NaCl(s) \xrightarrow{\text{Electricity}}$ ______ + ______

b. combination: $Ca(s) + Br_2(g) \longrightarrow$ ______

c. combustion:
$C_2H_4(g) + O_2(g) \xrightarrow{\Delta}$ ______ + ______

d. double replacement:
$NiCl_2(aq) + NaOH(aq) \longrightarrow$ ______ + ______

8.57 Write a balanced equation for each of the following reactions and identify the type of reaction: (8.1, 8.2, 8.3)

a. Sodium metal reacts with oxygen gas to form solid sodium oxide.

b. Aqueous sodium chloride and aqueous silver nitrate react to form solid silver chloride and aqueous sodium nitrate.

c. Gasohol is a fuel that contains ethanol (C_2H_6O), which burns in oxygen (O_2) to give two gases, carbon dioxide and water.

8.58 Write a balanced equation for each of the following reactions and identify the type of reaction: (8.1, 8.2, 8.3)

a. Solid potassium chlorate is heated to form solid potassium chloride and oxygen gas.

b. Carbon monoxide gas and oxygen gas combine to form carbon dioxide gas.

c. Ethene gas, C_2H_4, reacts with chlorine gas, Cl_2, to form dichloroethane, $C_2H_4Cl_2$.

8.59 Classify vitamin B_5 according to its functional group(s). (8.4)

$$HO-CH_2-\underset{\large CH_3}{\overset{\large CH_3}{C}}-\overset{\large OH}{CH}-\overset{\large O}{\overset{\|}{C}}-\overset{\large H}{N}-CH_2-CH_2-\overset{\large O}{\overset{\|}{C}}-OH$$

8.60 Classify epinephrine (adrenaline) according to its functional group(s). (8.4)

[Structure: benzene ring bearing HO and OH substituents, attached to $\overset{OH}{CH}-CH_2-\overset{H}{N}-CH_3$]

8.61 Classify novocaine (procaine), which is used as a local anesthetic, according to its functional group(s). (8.4)

[Structure: H_2N–benzene ring–$\overset{O}{\overset{\|}{C}}-O-CH_2-CH_2-N(CH_2-CH_3)_2$]

8.62 Classify lidocaine (xylocaine), which is used as a local anesthetic, according to its functional group(s). (8.4)

[Structure: benzene ring with two CH_3 groups, attached to $\overset{H}{N}-\overset{O}{\overset{\|}{C}}-CH_2-N(CH_2-CH_3)_2$]

CHALLENGE QUESTIONS

8.63 Write the correct formulas for the reactants and products, balanced equation for each of the following reaction descriptions, and identify each type of reaction: (8.1, 8.2, 8.3)

a. An aqueous solution of lead(II) nitrate is mixed with aqueous sodium phosphate to produce solid lead(II) phosphate and aqueous sodium nitrate.

b. Gallium metal heated in oxygen gas forms solid gallium(III) oxide.

c. When solid sodium nitrate is heated, solid sodium nitrite and oxygen gas are produced.

8.64 Write the correct formulas for the reactants and products, balanced equation for each of the following reaction descriptions, and identify each type of reaction: (8.1, 8.2, 8.3)

a. Solid bismuth(III) oxide and solid carbon react to form bismuth metal and carbon monoxide gas.

b. Solid sodium bicarbonate is heated and forms solid sodium carbonate, gaseous carbon dioxide, and water.

c. Butane gas (C_4H_{10}) reacts with oxygen gas to form two gaseous products: carbon dioxide and water.

8.65 In the following diagram, if blue spheres are the element X and yellow spheres are the element Y, (8.1, 8.2, 8.3)

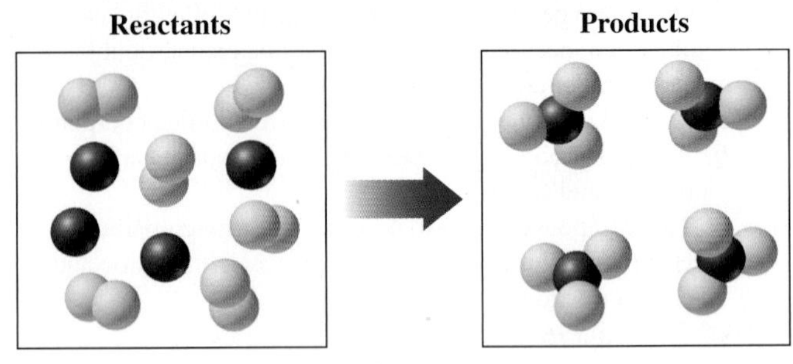

a. write the formula for each of the reactants and products

b. write a balanced equation for the reaction

c. indicate the type of reaction as combination, decomposition, single replacement, double replacement, or combustion

8.66 In the following diagram, if red spheres are the element A, white spheres are the element B, and green spheres are the element C, (8.1, 8.2, 8.3)

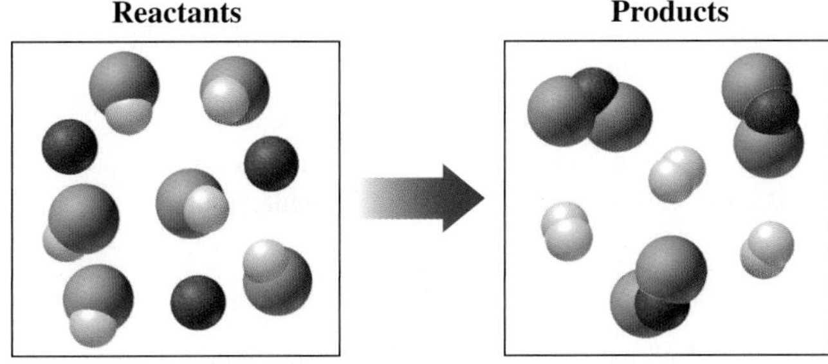

a. write the formula for each of the reactants and products
b. write a balanced equation for the reaction
c. indicate the type of reaction as combination, decomposition, single replacement, double replacement, or combustion

8.67 Toradol is used in dentistry to relieve pain. Classify toradol according to its functional group(s). (8.4)

(structure: benzene ring–C(=O)–pyrrolizine ring (N)–C(=O)–OH)

8.68 Voltaren is indicated for acute and chronic treatment of the symptoms of rheumatoid arthritis. Classify voltaren according to its functional group(s). (8.4)

(structure: benzene ring bearing $CH_2-\overset{O}{\overset{\|}{C}}-OH$ and NH; NH attached to a benzene ring bearing Cl and Cl)

8.69 Classify each of the following according to its functional group(s): (8.4)
a. $CH_3-CH_2-CH_2-OH$
b. $CH_3-CH_2-CH_2-NH-CH_3$
c. $CH_3-\underset{}{\overset{CH_3}{\overset{|}{CH}}}-\overset{O}{\overset{\|}{C}}-CH_3$

8.70 Classify each of the following according to its functional group(s): (8.4)
a. $CH_3-\overset{CH_3}{\overset{|}{CH}}-CH=CH-CH_3$
b. $CH_3-CH_2-\overset{O}{\overset{\|}{C}}-OH$
c. $CH_3-CH_2-\overset{O}{\overset{\|}{C}}-H$

8.71 Complete and balance each of the following reactions: (8.1, 8.2, 8.3)
a. $C_5H_{12} + O_2 \xrightarrow{\Delta}$
b. $CH_3-CH_2-CH=CH-CH_2-CH_3 + H_2 \xrightarrow{Pt}$

8.72 Complete and balance each of the following reactions: (8.1, 8.2, 8.3)
a. $H_2C=CH_2 + H_2 \xrightarrow{Pt}$
b. $CH_3-CH_2-CH_2-CH_2-CH=CH_2 + O_2 \xrightarrow{\Delta}$

ANSWERS

Answers to Study Checks

8.1 reactants/products: 4 C atoms, 12 H atoms, 14 O atoms

8.2 $2Al(s) + 3Br_2(l) \longrightarrow 2AlBr_3(s)$

8.3 $Sb_2S_3(s) + 6HCl(aq) \longrightarrow 2SbCl_3(aq) + 3H_2S(g)$

8.4 $C_2H_4(g) + 3O_2(g) \xrightarrow{\Delta} 2CO_2(g) + 2H_2O(g)$ + energy

8.5 $N_2(g) + 2O_2(g) \longrightarrow 2NO_2(g)$ combination reaction

8.6 A carboxylic acid contains a carboxyl group attached to H, while an ester contains a carboxyl group attached to C.

Answers to Selected Questions and Problems

8.1 **a.** reactants/products: 7 O atoms
b. reactants/products: 4 O atoms
c. reactants/products: 10 O atoms
d. reactants/products: 4 O atoms

8.3 **a.** not balanced **b.** balanced
c. not balanced **d.** balanced

8.5 **a.** 2 Na atoms, 2 Cl atoms
b. 1 P atom, 3 Cl atoms, 6 H atoms
c. 4 P atoms, 16 O atoms, 12 H atoms

8.7 **a.** $N_2(g) + O_2(g) \longrightarrow 2NO(g)$
b. $2HgO(s) \longrightarrow 2Hg(l) + O_2(g)$
c. $4Fe(s) + 3O_2(g) \longrightarrow 2Fe_2O_3(s)$
d. $2Na(s) + Cl_2(g) \longrightarrow 2NaCl(s)$
e. $2Cu_2O(s) + O_2(g) \longrightarrow 4CuO(s)$

8.9 **a.** $Mg(s) + 2AgNO_3(aq) \longrightarrow Mg(NO_3)_2(aq) + 2Ag(s)$
b. $CuCO_3(s) \longrightarrow CuO(s) + CO_2(g)$
c. $2Al(s) + 3CuSO_4(aq) \longrightarrow 3Cu(s) + Al_2(SO_4)_3(aq)$
d. $Pb(NO_3)_2(aq) + 2NaCl(aq) \longrightarrow PbCl_2(s) + 2NaNO_3(aq)$
e. $2Al(s) + 6HCl(aq) \longrightarrow 2AlCl_3(aq) + 3H_2(g)$

8.11 **a.** $Fe_2O_3(s) + 3CO(g) \longrightarrow 2Fe(s) + 3CO_2(g)$
b. $2Li_3N(s) \longrightarrow 6Li(s) + N_2(g)$
c. $2Al(s) + 6HBr(aq) \longrightarrow 2AlBr_3(aq) + 3H_2(g)$
d. $3Ba(OH)_2(aq) + 2Na_3PO_4(aq) \longrightarrow Ba_3(PO_4)_2(s) + 6NaOH(aq)$
e. $As_4S_6(s) + 9O_2(g) \longrightarrow As_4O_6(s) + 6SO_2(g)$

8.13 **a.** $2Li(s) + 2H_2O(l) \longrightarrow H_2(g) + 2LiOH(aq)$
b. $2P(s) + 5Cl_2(g) \longrightarrow 2PCl_5(s)$
c. $FeO(s) + CO(g) \longrightarrow Fe(s) + CO_2(g)$
d. $2C_5H_{10}(l) + 15O_2(g) \xrightarrow{\Delta} 10CO_2(g) + 10H_2O(g)$
e. $3H_2S(g) + 2FeCl_3(s) \longrightarrow Fe_2S_3(s) + 6HCl(g)$

8.15 **a.** decomposition **b.** single replacement
c. combustion **d.** double replacement
e. combination

8.17 **a.** combination **b.** single replacement
c. decomposition **d.** combustion
e. double replacement

8.19 **a.** $Mg(s) + Cl_2(g) \longrightarrow MgCl_2(s)$
b. $2HBr(g) \longrightarrow H_2(g) + Br_2(g)$
c. $Mg(s) + Zn(NO_3)_2(aq) \longrightarrow Mg(NO_3)_2(aq) + Zn(s)$
d. $K_2S(aq) + Pb(NO_3)_2(aq) \longrightarrow PbS(s) + 2KNO_3(aq)$
e. $2C_5H_{10}(l) + 15O_2(g) \xrightarrow{\Delta} 10CO_2(g) + 10H_2O(g)$

8.21 **a.** alcohol **b.** alkene **c.** aldehyde

8.23 **a.** alcohol **b.** ester
c. carboxylic acid **d.** amine

8.25 **a.** $C_3H_8(g) + 5O_2(g) \xrightarrow{\Delta} 3CO_2(g) + 4H_2O(g) + \text{energy}$
b. $2C_8H_{18}(l) + 25O_2(g) \xrightarrow{\Delta} 16CO_2(g) + 18H_2O(g) + \text{energy}$
c. $2C_3H_8O(l) + 9O_2(g) \xrightarrow{\Delta} 6CO_2(g) + 8H_2O(g) + \text{energy}$
d. $C_6H_{12}(l) + 9O_2(g) \xrightarrow{\Delta} 6CO_2(g) + 6H_2O(g) + \text{energy}$

8.27 **a.** $CH_3—CH_2—CH_2—CH_2—CH_3$
b. $CH_3—CH_2—CH_2—CH_3$

8.29 **a.** hydroxyl, carbonyl (ketone)
b. hydroxyl, carbonyl (aldehyde)

8.31 **a.** **3.** protein **b.** **2.** lipid **c.** **1.** carbohydrate
d. **2.** lipid **e.** **1.** carbohydrate

8.33 **a.** reactants NO and O_2; product NO_2
b. $2NO(g) + O_2(g) \longrightarrow 2NO_2(g)$
c. combination

8.35 **a.** reactant NI_3; products N_2 and I_2
b. $2NI_3(s) \longrightarrow N_2(g) + 3I_2(g)$
c. decomposition

8.37 **a.** reactants Cl_2 and O_2; products OCl_2
b. $2Cl_2(g) + O_2(g) \longrightarrow 2OCl_2(g)$
c. combination

8.39 **a.** 1,1,2 combination reaction
b. 2,2,1 decomposition reaction

8.41 **a.** ketone **b.** alkene
c. ester **d.** amine

8.43 **a.** alcohol **b.** alkene
c. aldehyde **d.** alkane

8.45 **a.** aromatic, aldehyde
b. aromatic, aldehyde, alkene
c. ketone

8.47 carboxylic acid, aromatic, amine, amide, ester

8.49 **a.** true **b.** false
c. false **d.** true

8.51 **a.** combination **b.** combustion
c. double replacement **d.** decomposition
e. single replacement

8.53 **a.** $NH_3(g) + HCl(g) \longrightarrow NH_4Cl(s)$ combination
b. $C_4H_8(g) + 6O_2(g) \xrightarrow{\Delta} 4CO_2(g) + 4H_2O(g)$ combustion
c. $2Sb(s) + 3Cl_2(g) \longrightarrow 2SbCl_3(s)$ combination
d. $2NI_3(s) \longrightarrow N_2(g) + 3I_2(g)$ decomposition
e. $2KBr(aq) + Cl_2(g) \longrightarrow 2KCl(aq) + Br_2(l)$ single replacement
f. $2Fe(s) + 3H_2SO_4(aq) \longrightarrow Fe_2(SO_4)_3(aq) + 3H_2(g)$ single replacement
g. $Al_2(SO_4)_3(aq) + 6NaOH(aq) \longrightarrow 3Na_2SO_4(aq) + 2Al(OH)_3(s)$ double replacement

8.55 **a.** $Zn(s) + 2HCl(aq) \longrightarrow ZnCl_2(aq) + H_2(g)$
b. $BaCO_3(s) \xrightarrow{\Delta} BaO(s) + CO_2(g)$
c. $NaOH(aq) + HCl(aq) \longrightarrow NaCl(aq) + H_2O(l)$
d. $2Al(s) + 3F_2(g) \longrightarrow 2AlF_3(s)$

8.57 **a.** $4Na(s) + O_2(g) \longrightarrow 2Na_2O(s)$ combination
b. $NaCl(aq) + AgNO_3(aq) \longrightarrow AgCl(s) + NaNO_3(aq)$ double replacement
c. $C_2H_6O(g) + 3O_2(g) \xrightarrow{\Delta} 2CO_2(g) + 3H_2O(g)$ combustion

8.59 carboxylic acid, alcohol, amide

8.61 aromatic, amine, ester

8.63 **a.** $3Pb(NO_3)_2(aq) + 2Na_3PO_4(aq) \longrightarrow Pb_3(PO_4)_2(s) + 6NaNO_3(aq)$ double replacement
b. $4Ga(s) + 3O_2(g) \xrightarrow{\Delta} 2Ga_2O_3(s)$ combination
c. $2NaNO_3(s) \xrightarrow{\Delta} 2NaNO_2(s) + O_2(g)$ decomposition

8.65 **a.** reactants: X and Y_2; products: XY_3
b. $2X + 3Y_2 \longrightarrow 2XY_3$
c. combination

8.67 aromatic, alkene, ketone, amine, carboxylic acid

8.69 **a.** alcohol **b.** amine **c.** ketone

8.71 **a.** $C_5H_{12} + 8O_2 \xrightarrow{\Delta} 5CO_2 + 6H_2O$
b. $CH_3—CH_2—CH{=}CH—CH_2—CH_3 + H_2 \xrightarrow{Pt} CH_3—CH_2—CH_2—CH_2—CH_2—CH_3$

Chemical Quantities in Reactions 9

LOOKING AHEAD

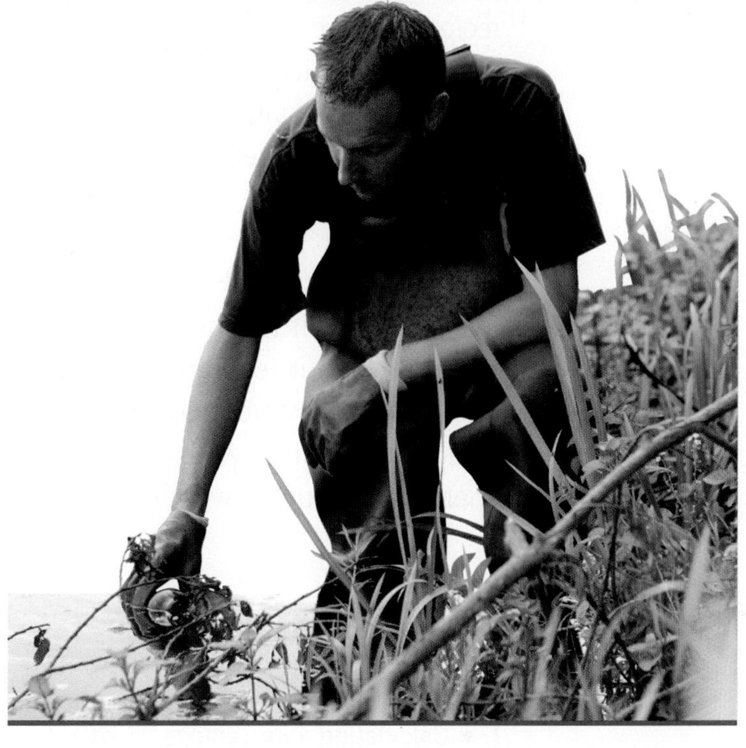

Lance, an environmental scientist, is collecting soil and water samples at a nearby farm to test for the presence and concentration of any pesticides and pharmaceuticals. Farmers use pesticides to increase food production and pharmaceuticals to treat and prevent animal-related diseases. Due to the common use of these chemicals, they may pass into the soil and water supply, potentially contaminating the environment and causing health problems.

Recently, a farmer's sheep were treated with a dewormer, fenbendazole, to destroy gastrointestinal worms. Lance detects small amounts of fenbendazole in the soil. He advises the farmer to decrease the dosage he administers to his sheep in order to reduce the amounts of the dewormer currently in the soil. Lance then indicates he will be back in a month to retest the soil and water.

Career: Environmental Scientist

Environmental scientists monitor environmental pollution to protect the health of the public. By using specialized equipment, environmental scientists measure pollution levels in soil, air, and water, as well as noise and radiation levels. They can specialize in a specific area, such as air quality or hazardous and solid waste. For instance, air-quality experts monitor indoor air for allergens, mold, and toxins; they measure outdoor air pollutants created by businesses, vehicles, and agriculture. Since environmental scientists obtain and measure samples containing potentially hazardous materials, they must be knowledgeable about safety protocols and wear personal protective equipment. They may also recommend methods to diminish various pollutants, and they may assist in cleanup and remediation efforts.

When we know the balanced chemical equation for a reaction, we can determine the mole and mass relationships between the reactants and products. Then we use molar masses to calculate the quantities of substances used or produced in a particular reaction. We do much the same thing at home when we use a recipe to make a cake or add the right quantity of water to make soup. In the manufacturing of chemical compounds, side reactions decrease the percent of product obtained. From the actual amount of product, we can determine the percent yield for a reaction. Knowing how to determine the quantitative results of a chemical reaction is essential to chemists, engineers, pharmacists, respiratory therapists, and other scientists and health professionals.

We will also look at energy changes in a balanced chemical equation. A reaction is exothermic if it produces heat along with the other products. A reaction is endothermic when it requires heat for the reaction. In the body, chemical reactions require energy when we need to produce large molecules such as protein and glycogen from smaller molecules. When chemical reactions in the body break down large molecules, energy is produced, which is stored in high-energy compounds.

CHAPTER READINESS*

Key Math Skills

- Calculating a Percentage (1.4C)

Core Chemistry Skills

- Counting Significant Figures (2.3)
- Using Significant Figures in Calculations (2.4)
- Writing Conversion Factors from Equalities (2.6)
- Using Conversion Factors (2.7)
- Using Energy Units (3.4)
- Calculating Molar Mass (7.2)
- Using Molar Mass as a Conversion Factor (7.3)
- Balancing a Chemical Equation (8.2)
- Balancing Combustion Reactions (8.3)

*These Key Math Skills and Core Chemistry Skills from previous chapters are listed here for your review as you proceed to the new material in this chapter.

LEARNING GOAL

Given a quantity in moles of reactant or product, use a mole–mole factor from the balanced equation to calculate the number of moles of another substance in the reaction.

9.1 Mole Relationships in Chemical Equations

In any chemical reaction, the total amount of matter in the reactants is equal to the total amount of matter in the products. Thus, the total mass of all the reactants must be equal to the total mass of all the products. This is known as the **law of conservation of mass**, which states that there is no change in the total mass of the substances reacting in a balanced chemical reaction. Thus, no material is lost or gained as original substances are changed to new substances.

In the chemical reaction of Ag and S, the mass of the reactants is the same as the mass of the product, Ag_2S.

For example, tarnish (Ag_2S) forms when silver reacts with sulfur to form silver sulfide.

$$2Ag(s) + S(s) \longrightarrow Ag_2S(s)$$

In this reaction, the number of silver atoms that reacts is twice the number of sulfur atoms. When 200 silver atoms react, 100 sulfur atoms are required. However, in the actual chemical reaction, many more atoms of both silver and sulfur would react. If we are dealing with molar amounts, then the coefficients in the equation can be interpreted in terms of moles. Thus, 2 mol of silver reacts with 1 mol of sulfur to produce 1 mol of Ag_2S. Because the molar mass of each can be determined, the moles of Ag, S, and Ag_2S can also be stated in terms of mass in grams of each. Thus, 215.8 g of Ag and 32.1 g of S react to form 247.9 g of Ag_2S. The total mass of the reactants (247.9 g) is equal to the mass of product (247.9 g). The various ways in which a chemical equation can be interpreted are seen in Table 9.1.

TABLE 9.1 Information Available from a Balanced Equation

	Reactants		Products
Equation	$2Ag(s)$	$+ S(s)$	$\longrightarrow Ag_2S(s)$
Atoms	2 Ag atoms	+ 1 S atom	$\longrightarrow$ 1 Ag_2S formula unit
	200 Ag atoms	+ 100 S atoms	$\longrightarrow$ 100 Ag_2S formula units
Avogadro's Number of Atoms	$2(6.022 \times 10^{23})$ Ag atoms	$+ 1(6.022 \times 10^{23})$ S atoms	$\longrightarrow 1(6.022 \times 10^{23})$ Ag_2S formula units
Moles	2 mol of Ag	+ 1 mol of S	$\longrightarrow$ 1 mol of Ag_2S
Mass (g)	2(107.9 g) of Ag	+ 1(32.1 g) of S	$\longrightarrow$ 1(247.9 g) of Ag_2S
Total Mass (g)	247.9 g		$\longrightarrow$ 247.9 g

CONCEPT CHECK 9.1 Conservation of Mass

The combustion of the alkane CH_4 with oxygen produces carbon dioxide and water. Calculate the total mass of reactants and products for the following equation when 1 mol of CH_4 reacts:

$$CH_4(g) + 2O_2(g) \xrightarrow{\Delta} CO_2(g) + 2H_2O(g)$$

ANSWER

Interpreting the coefficients in the equation as the number of moles of each substance and multiplying by the respective molar masses gives the total mass of reactants and products. The quantities of moles are exact because the coefficients in the balanced equation are exact.

	Reactants		Products
Equation	$CH_4(g) + 2O_2(g)$	$\xrightarrow{\Delta}$	$CO_2(g) + 2H_2O(g)$
Moles	1 mol of CH_4 + 2 mol of O_2	$\longrightarrow$	1 mol of CO_2 + 2 mol of H_2O
Mass	16.04 g of CH_4 + 64.00 g of O_2	$\longrightarrow$	44.01 g of CO_2 + 36.03 g of H_2O
Total Mass	80.04 g of reactants	=	80.04 g of products

Mole–Mole Factors from a Balanced Equation

When iron reacts with sulfur, the product is iron(III) sulfide.

$$2Fe(s) + 3S(s) \longrightarrow Fe_2S_3(s)$$

Iron (Fe) $2Fe(s)$ + Sulfur (S) $3S(s)$ $\longrightarrow$ Iron(III) sulfide (Fe_2S_3) $Fe_2S_3(s)$

From the balanced equation, we see that 2 mol of iron reacts with 3 mol of sulfur to form 1 mol of iron(III) sulfide. Actually, any amount of iron or sulfur may be used, but the *ratio* of iron reacting with sulfur will always be the same. From the coefficients, we can write **mole–mole factors** between reactants and between reactants and products. The coefficients used in the mole–mole factors are exact numbers; they do not limit the number of significant figures.

Fe and S: $\dfrac{2\text{ mol Fe}}{3\text{ mol S}}$ and $\dfrac{3\text{ mol S}}{2\text{ mol Fe}}$

Fe and Fe_2S_3: $\dfrac{2\text{ mol Fe}}{1\text{ mol }Fe_2S_3}$ and $\dfrac{1\text{ mol }Fe_2S_3}{2\text{ mol Fe}}$

S and Fe_2S_3: $\dfrac{3\text{ mol S}}{1\text{ mol }Fe_2S_3}$ and $\dfrac{1\text{ mol }Fe_2S_3}{3\text{ mol S}}$

CORE CHEMISTRY SKILL

Using Mole–Mole Factors

Using Mole–Mole Factors in Calculations

Whenever you prepare a recipe, adjust an engine for the proper mixture of fuel and air, or prepare medicines in a pharmaceutical laboratory, you need to know the proper amounts of reactants to use and how much of the product will form. Now that we have written all the possible conversion factors for the balanced equation $2Fe(s) + 3S(s) \longrightarrow Fe_2S_3(s)$, we will use those mole–mole factors in a chemical calculation in Sample Problem 9.1.

SAMPLE PROBLEM 9.1 Calculating Moles of a Reactant

In the chemical reaction of iron and sulfur, how many moles of sulfur are needed to react with 1.42 mol of iron?

$$2Fe(s) + 3S(s) \longrightarrow Fe_2S_3(s)$$

SOLUTION

Step 1 **State the given and needed quantities (moles).**

Analyze the Problem	Given	Need
	1.42 mol of Fe	moles of S
	Equation	
	$2Fe(s) + 3S(s) \longrightarrow Fe_2S_3(s)$	

Step 2 **Write a plan to convert the given to the needed quantity (moles).**

moles of Fe → Mole–mole factor → moles of S

Step 3 **Use coefficients to write mole–mole factors.**

2 mol of Fe = 3 mol of S

$$\frac{2 \text{ mol Fe}}{3 \text{ mol S}} \quad \text{and} \quad \frac{3 \text{ mol S}}{2 \text{ mol Fe}}$$

Step 4 **Set up the problem to give the needed quantity (moles).**

$$1.42 \text{ }\cancel{\text{mol Fe}} \times \frac{3 \text{ mol S}}{2 \text{ }\cancel{\text{mol Fe}}} = 2.13 \text{ mol of S}$$

Three SFs — Exact — Three SFs

STUDY CHECK 9.1

Using the equation in Sample Problem 9.1, calculate the number of moles of iron needed to react with 2.75 mol of sulfur.

Guide to Calculating the Quantities of Reactants and Products in a Chemical Reaction

1. State the given and needed quantities (moles or grams).
2. Write a plan to convert the given to the needed quantity (moles or grams).
3. Use coefficients to write mole–mole factors; write molar mass factors if needed.
4. Set up the problem to give the needed quantity (moles or grams).

SAMPLE PROBLEM 9.2 Calculating Moles of a Product

Propane gas (C_3H_8), a fuel used in camp stoves, soldering torches, and specially equipped automobiles, reacts with oxygen to produce carbon dioxide, water, and energy. How many moles of CO_2 can be produced when 2.25 mol of C_3H_8 reacts?

$$\underset{\text{Propane}}{C_3H_8(g)} + 5O_2(g) \xrightarrow{\Delta} 3CO_2(g) + 4H_2O(g)$$

SOLUTION

Step 1 **State the given and needed quantities (moles).**

Analyze the Problem	Given	Need
	2.25 mol of C_3H_8	moles of CO_2
	Equation	
	$C_3H_8(g) + 5O_2(g) \xrightarrow{\Delta} 3CO_2(g) + 4H_2O(g)$ Propane	

Step 2 **Write a plan to convert the given to the needed quantity (moles).**

moles of C_3H_8 → Mole–mole factor → moles of CO_2

Propane fuel reacts with O_2 in the air to produce CO_2, H_2O, and energy.

Step 3 **Use coefficients to write mole–mole factors.**

$$1 \text{ mol of } C_3H_8 = 3 \text{ mol of } CO_2$$

$$\frac{1 \text{ mol } C_3H_8}{3 \text{ mol } CO_2} \text{ and } \frac{3 \text{ mol } CO_2}{1 \text{ mol } C_3H_8}$$

Step 4 **Set up the problem to give the needed quantity (moles).**

$$\underset{\text{Three SFs}}{2.25 \cancel{\text{mol } C_3H_8}} \times \overset{\text{Exact}}{\underset{\text{Exact}}{\frac{3 \text{ mol } CO_2}{1 \cancel{\text{mol } C_3H_8}}}} = \underset{\text{Three SFs}}{6.75 \text{ mol of } CO_2}$$

STUDY CHECK 9.2

Using the equation in Sample Problem 9.2, calculate the moles of oxygen that must react to produce 0.756 mol of water.

QUESTIONS AND PROBLEMS

9.1 Mole Relationships in Chemical Equations

LEARNING GOAL: *Given a quantity in moles of reactant or product, use a mole–mole factor from the balanced equation to calculate the number of moles of another substance in the reaction.*

9.1 Calculate the total masses of the reactants and the products for each of the following equations:
a. $2SO_2(g) + O_2(g) \longrightarrow 2SO_3(g)$
b. $4P(s) + 5O_2(g) \longrightarrow 2P_2O_5(s)$

9.2 Calculate the total masses of the reactants and the products for each of the following equations:
a. $2Al(s) + 3Cl_2(g) \longrightarrow 2AlCl_3(s)$
b. $4HCl(g) + O_2(g) \longrightarrow 2Cl_2(g) + 2H_2O(g)$

9.3 Write all of the mole–mole factors for each of the equations in Problem 9.1.

9.4 Write all of the mole–mole factors for each of the equations in Problem 9.2.

9.5 For the equations in Problem 9.1, write the setup with the correct mole–mole factor:
a. moles of SO_3 from the moles of SO_2
b. moles of O_2 needed to react with moles of P

9.6 For the equations in Problem 9.2, write the setup with the correct mole–mole factor:
a. moles of $AlCl_3$ from the moles of Cl_2
b. moles of O_2 needed to react with moles of HCl

9.7 The reaction of hydrogen with oxygen produces water.

$$2H_2(g) + O_2(g) \longrightarrow 2H_2O(g)$$

a. How many moles of O_2 are required to react with 2.0 mol of H_2?
b. How many moles of H_2 are needed to react with 5.0 mol of O_2?
c. How many moles of H_2O form when 2.5 mol of O_2 reacts?

9.8 Ammonia is produced by the reaction of nitrogen and hydrogen.

$$N_2(g) + 3H_2(g) \longrightarrow \underset{\text{Ammonia}}{2NH_3(g)}$$

a. How many moles of H_2 are needed to react with 1.0 mol of N_2?
b. How many moles of N_2 reacted if 0.60 mol of NH_3 is produced?
c. How many moles of NH_3 are produced when 1.4 mol of H_2 reacts?

9.9 Carbon disulfide and carbon monoxide are produced when carbon is heated with sulfur dioxide.

$$5C(s) + 2SO_2(g) \longrightarrow CS_2(l) + 4CO(g)$$

a. How many moles of C are needed to react with 0.500 mol of SO_2?
b. How many moles of CO are produced when 1.2 mol of C reacts?
c. How many moles of SO_2 are required to produce 0.50 mol of CS_2?
d. How many moles of CS_2 are produced when 2.5 mol of C reacts?

9.10 In the acetylene torch, acetylene gas (C_2H_2) burns in oxygen to produce carbon dioxide and water.

$$2C_2H_2(g) + 5O_2(g) \xrightarrow{\Delta} 4CO_2(g) + 2H_2O(g)$$

a. How many moles of O_2 are needed to react with 2.00 mol of C_2H_2?
b. How many moles of CO_2 are produced when 3.5 mol of C_2H_2 reacts?
c. How many moles of C_2H_2 are required to produce 0.50 mol of H_2O?
d. How many moles of CO_2 are produced from 0.100 mol of O_2?

9.2 Mass Calculations for Reactions

LEARNING GOAL

Given the mass in grams of a substance in a reaction, calculate the mass in grams of another substance in the reaction.

When we have the balanced chemical equation for a reaction, we can use the mass of one of the substances (A) in the reaction to calculate the mass of another substance (B) in the reaction. However, the calculations require us to convert the mass of A to moles of A using the molar mass factor for A. Then we use the mole–mole factor that links substance A to substance B, which we obtain from the coefficients in the balanced equation. This mole–mole factor (B/A) will convert the moles of A to moles of B. Then the molar mass factor of B is used to calculate the grams of substance B.

Substance A → Substance B

grams of A → [Molar mass factor A] → moles of A → [Mole–mole factor B/A] → moles of B → [Molar mass factor B] → grams of B

CONCEPT CHECK 9.2 Mass of Product from Mass of Reactant

In the engines of cars and trucks, nitrogen and oxygen from the air react at high temperature to produce nitrogen oxide, a component of smog. Complete the following to help answer the question: How many grams of NO can be produced when 12.5 g of O_2 reacts?

$$N_2(g) + O_2(g) \longrightarrow 2NO(g)$$

a. What molar mass factor is needed to convert grams of O_2 to moles of O_2?
b. What mole–mole factor is needed to convert moles of O_2 to moles of NO?
c. What molar mass factor is needed to convert moles of NO to grams of NO?

ANSWER

a. The molar mass factor that gives the moles of O_2 is

$$\frac{1 \text{ mol } O_2}{32.00 \text{ g } O_2}$$

b. The mole–mole factor that gives the moles of NO is

$$\frac{2 \text{ mol NO}}{1 \text{ mol } O_2}$$

c. The molar mass factor that gives the grams of NO is

$$\frac{30.01 \text{ g NO}}{1 \text{ mol NO}}$$

CORE CHEMISTRY SKILL 

Converting Grams to Grams

SAMPLE PROBLEM 9.3 Mass of Product

When acetylene, C_2H_2, burns in oxygen, high temperatures are produced that are used for welding metals.

$$2C_2H_2(g) + 5O_2(g) \xrightarrow{\Delta} 4CO_2(g) + 2H_2O(g)$$

How many grams of CO_2 are produced when 54.6 g of C_2H_2 is burned?

SOLUTION

Step 1 State the given and needed quantities (grams).

	Given	Need
Analyze the Problem	54.6 g of C_2H_2	grams of CO_2
	Equation	
	$2C_2H_2(g) + 5O_2(g) \xrightarrow{\Delta} 4CO_2(g) + 2H_2O(g) + \text{energy}$ Acetylene	

A mixture of acetylene and oxygen undergoes combustion during the welding of metals.

Step 2 **Write a plan to convert the given to the needed quantity (grams).**

grams of C_2H_2 → Molar mass → moles of C_2H_2 → Mole–mole factor → moles of CO_2 → Molar mass → grams of CO_2

Step 3 **Use coefficients to write mole–mole factors; write molar mass factors if needed.**

$$1 \text{ mol of } C_2H_2 = 26.04 \text{ g of } C_2H_2$$
$$\frac{26.04 \text{ g } C_2H_2}{1 \text{ mol } C_2H_2} \text{ and } \frac{1 \text{ mol } C_2H_2}{26.04 \text{ g } C_2H_2}$$

$$2 \text{ mol of } C_2H_2 = 4 \text{ mol of } CO_2$$
$$\frac{2 \text{ mol } C_2H_2}{4 \text{ mol } CO_2} \text{ and } \frac{4 \text{ mol } CO_2}{2 \text{ mol } C_2H_2}$$

$$1 \text{ mol of } CO_2 = 44.01 \text{ g of } CO_2$$
$$\frac{44.01 \text{ g } CO_2}{1 \text{ mol } CO_2} \text{ and } \frac{1 \text{ mol } CO_2}{44.01 \text{ g } CO_2}$$

Step 4 **Set up the problem to give the needed quantity (grams).**

$$\underset{\text{Three SFs}}{54.6 \text{ g } \cancel{C_2H_2}} \times \overset{\text{Exact}}{\underset{\text{Four SFs}}{\frac{1 \cancel{\text{mol } C_2H_2}}{26.04 \text{ g } \cancel{C_2H_2}}}} \times \overset{\text{Exact}}{\underset{\text{Exact}}{\frac{4 \cancel{\text{mol } CO_2}}{2 \cancel{\text{mol } C_2H_2}}}} \times \overset{\text{Four SFs}}{\underset{\text{Exact}}{\frac{44.01 \text{ g } CO_2}{1 \cancel{\text{mol } CO_2}}}} = \underset{\text{Three SFs}}{185 \text{ g of } CO_2}$$

STUDY CHECK 9.3

Using the equation in Sample Problem 9.3, calculate the grams of CO_2 that can be produced when 25.0 g of O_2 reacts.

SAMPLE PROBLEM 9.4 Mass of Reactant

The alkane heptane, C_7H_{16}, is designated as the zero point in the octane rating of gasoline. Heptane is an undesirable compound in gasoline because it burns rapidly and causes engine knocking. How many grams of O_2 are required to react with 22.50 g of C_7H_{16}?

$$C_7H_{16}(g) + 11O_2(g) \xrightarrow{\Delta} 7CO_2(g) + 8H_2O(g)$$

SOLUTION

Step 1 **State the given and needed quantities (grams).**

	Given	Need
Analyze the Problem	22.50 g of C_7H_{16}	grams of O_2
	Equation	
	$C_7H_{16}(g) + 11O_2(g) \xrightarrow{\Delta} 7CO_2(g) + 8H_2O(g)$ Heptane	

Step 2 **Write a plan to convert the given to the needed quantity (grams).**

grams of C_7H_{16} → Molar mass → moles of C_7H_{16} → Mole–mole factor → moles of O_2 → Molar mass → grams of O_2

Step 3 **Use coefficients to write mole–mole factors; write molar mass factors if needed.**

$$1 \text{ mol of } C_7H_{16} = 100.2 \text{ g of } C_7H_{16}$$
$$\frac{100.2 \text{ g } C_7H_{16}}{1 \text{ mol } C_7H_{16}} \text{ and } \frac{1 \text{ mol } C_7H_{16}}{100.2 \text{ g } C_7H_{16}}$$

$1 \text{ mol of } C_7H_{16} = 11 \text{ mol of } O_2$	$1 \text{ mol of } O_2 = 32.00 \text{ g of } O_2$
$\dfrac{1 \text{ mol } C_7H_{16}}{11 \text{ mol } O_2}$ and $\dfrac{11 \text{ mol } O_2}{1 \text{ mol } C_7H_{16}}$	$\dfrac{32.00 \text{ g } O_2}{1 \text{ mol } O_2}$ and $\dfrac{1 \text{ mol } O_2}{32.00 \text{ g } O_2}$

Step 4 **Set up the problem to give the needed quantity (grams).**

$$\underset{\text{Four SFs}}{22.50 \text{ g } C_7H_{16}} \times \overset{\text{Exact}}{\dfrac{1 \text{ mol } C_7H_{16}}{100.2 \text{ g } C_7H_{16}}} \times \overset{\text{Exact}}{\dfrac{11 \text{ mol } O_2}{1 \text{ mol } C_7H_{16}}} \times \overset{\text{Four SFs}}{\dfrac{32.00 \text{ g } O_2}{1 \text{ mol } O_2}} = \underset{\text{Four SFs}}{79.07 \text{ g of } O_2}$$

(Denominators: 100.2 g C_7H_{16} — Four SFs; 1 mol C_7H_{16} — Exact; 1 mol O_2 — Exact)

STUDY CHECK 9.4

Using the equation in Sample Problem 9.4, calculate the grams of C_7H_{16} that are needed to produce 15.0 g of H_2O.

QUESTIONS AND PROBLEMS

9.2 Mass Calculations for Reactions

LEARNING GOAL: *Given the mass in grams of a substance in a reaction, calculate the mass in grams of another substance in the reaction.*

9.11 Sodium reacts with oxygen to produce sodium oxide.

$$4Na(s) + O_2(g) \longrightarrow 2Na_2O(s)$$

a. How many grams of Na_2O are produced when 57.5 g of Na reacts?
b. If you have 18.0 g of Na, how many grams of O_2 are required for reaction?
c. How many grams of O_2 are needed in a reaction that produces 75.0 g of Na_2O?

9.12 Nitrogen gas reacts with hydrogen gas to produce ammonia.

$$N_2(g) + 3H_2(g) \longrightarrow 2NH_3(g)$$

a. If you have 3.64 g of H_2, how many grams of NH_3 can be produced?
b. How many grams of H_2 are needed to react with 2.80 g of N_2?
c. How many grams of NH_3 can be produced from 12.0 g of H_2?

9.13 Ammonia and oxygen react to form nitrogen and water.

$$4NH_3(g) + 3O_2(g) \longrightarrow 2N_2(g) + 6H_2O(g)$$

a. How many grams of O_2 are needed to react with 13.6 g of NH_3?
b. How many grams of N_2 can be produced when 6.50 g of O_2 reacts?
c. How many grams of H_2O are formed from the reaction of 34.0 g of NH_3?

9.14 Iron(III) oxide reacts with carbon to give iron and carbon monoxide.

$$Fe_2O_3(s) + 3C(s) \longrightarrow 2Fe(s) + 3CO(g)$$

a. How many grams of C are required to react with 16.5 g of Fe_2O_3?
b. How many grams of CO are produced when 36.0 g of C reacts?
c. How many grams of Fe can be produced when 6.00 g of Fe_2O_3 reacts?

9.15 Nitrogen dioxide and water react to produce nitric acid, HNO_3, and nitrogen oxide.

$$3NO_2(g) + H_2O(l) \longrightarrow 2HNO_3(aq) + NO(g)$$

a. How many grams of H_2O are required to react with 28.0 g of NO_2?
b. How many grams of NO are produced from 15.8 g of H_2O?
c. How many grams of HNO_3 are produced from 8.25 g of NO_2?

9.16 Calcium cyanamide, $CaCN_2$, reacts with water to form calcium carbonate and ammonia.

$$CaCN_2(s) + 3H_2O(l) \longrightarrow CaCO_3(s) + 2NH_3(g)$$

a. How many grams of H_2O are needed to react with 75.0 g of $CaCN_2$?
b. How many grams of NH_3 are produced from 5.24 g of $CaCN_2$?
c. How many grams of $CaCO_3$ form if 155 g of H_2O reacts?

9.17 When lead(II) sulfide reacts with oxygen (O_2) gas, the products are lead(II) oxide and sulfur dioxide gas.
a. Write the balanced equation for the reaction.
b. How many grams of oxygen are required to react with 29.9 g of lead(II) sulfide?
c. How many grams of sulfur dioxide can be produced when 65.0 g of lead(II) sulfide reacts?
d. How many grams of lead(II) sulfide are used to produce 128 g of lead(II) oxide?

9.18 When the gases dihydrogen sulfide and oxygen (O_2) react, they form the gases sulfur dioxide and water.
a. Write the balanced equation for the reaction.
b. How many grams of oxygen are required to react with 2.50 g of dihydrogen sulfide?
c. How many grams of sulfur dioxide can be produced when 38.5 g of oxygen reacts?
d. How many grams of oxygen are required to produce 55.8 g of water?

LEARNING GOAL

Identify a limiting reactant when given the quantities of two reactants; calculate the amount of product formed from the limiting reactant.

9.3 Limiting Reactants

When you make peanut butter sandwiches for lunch, you need 2 slices of bread and 1 tablespoon of peanut butter for each sandwich. As an equation, we could write:

2 slices of bread + 1 tablespoon of peanut butter $\longrightarrow$ 1 peanut butter sandwich

If you have 8 slices of bread and a full jar of peanut butter, you will run out of bread after you make 4 peanut butter sandwiches. You cannot make any more sandwiches once the bread is used up, even though there is a lot of peanut butter left in the jar. The number of slices of bread has limited the number of sandwiches you can make.

On a different day, you might have 8 slices of bread but only a tablespoon of peanut butter left in the peanut butter jar. You will run out of peanut butter after you make just 1 peanut butter sandwich and have 6 slices of bread left over. The small amount of peanut butter available has limited the number of sandwiches you can make.

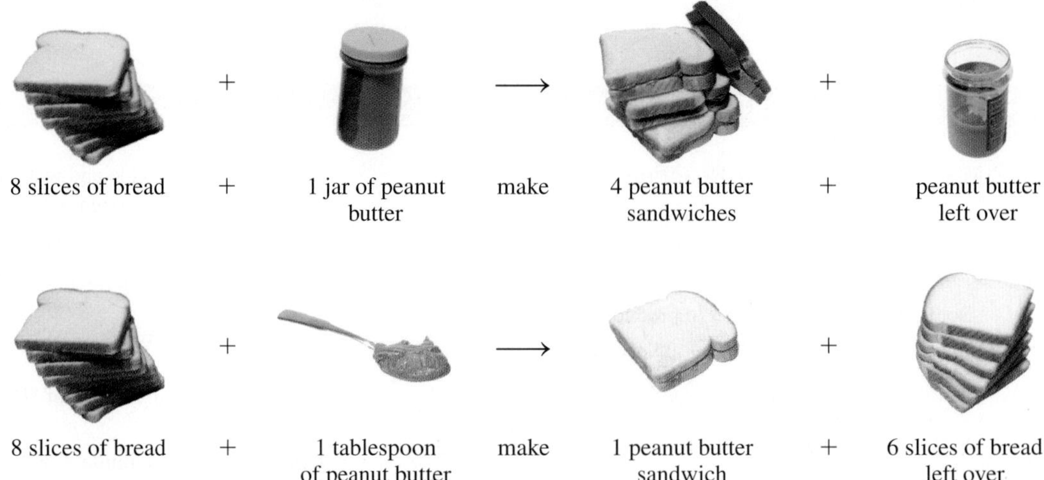
8 slices of bread + 1 jar of peanut butter make 4 peanut butter sandwiches + peanut butter left over
8 slices of bread + 1 tablespoon of peanut butter make 1 peanut butter sandwich + 6 slices of bread left over

The reactant that is completely used up is the **limiting reactant**. The reactant that does not completely react and is left over is called the *excess reactant.*

Bread	Peanut Butter	Sandwiches	Limiting Reactant	Excess Reactant
1 loaf (20 slices)	1 tablespoon	1	Peanut butter	Bread
4 slices	1 full jar	2	Bread	Peanut butter
8 slices	1 full jar	4	Bread	Peanut butter

CONCEPT CHECK 9.3 Limiting Reactants

For a picnic that you are planning, you have 10 spoons, 8 forks, and 6 knives. If each person requires 1 spoon, 1 fork, and 1 knife, how many people can be served at your picnic?

ANSWER

The relationship of utensils required by each person can be written:

1 person = 1 spoon, 1 fork, and 1 knife

The maximum number of people for each utensil can be determined as follows:

$$10\ \cancel{\text{spoons}} \times \frac{1\ \text{person}}{1\ \cancel{\text{spoon}}} = 10\ \text{people}$$

$$8\ \cancel{\text{forks}} \times \frac{1\ \text{person}}{1\ \cancel{\text{fork}}} = 8\ \text{people}$$

$$6\ \cancel{\text{knives}} \times \frac{1\ \text{person}}{1\ \cancel{\text{knife}}} = 6\ \text{people}$$ Smallest number of people

The limiting utensil is six knives, which means that six people can be served at your picnic.

Calculating Moles of Product from a Limiting Reactant

In a similar way, the reactants in a chemical reaction do not always combine in quantities that allow each to be used up at exactly the same time. In many reactions, there is a limiting reactant that determines the amount of product that can be formed. When we know the quantities of the reactants of a chemical reaction, we calculate the amount of product that is possible from each reactant if it were completely consumed. We are looking for the *limiting reactant*, which is the one that runs out first, producing the smaller amount of product.

CORE CHEMISTRY SKILL 

Calculating Quantity of Product from a Limiting Reactant

SAMPLE PROBLEM 9.5 Moles of Product from Limiting Reactant

The chemical reaction of carbon monoxide and hydrogen is used to produce methanol (CH_3OH).

$$CO(g) + 2H_2(g) \longrightarrow CH_3OH(g)$$

If 3.00 mol of CO and 5.00 mol of H_2 are the initial reactants, how many moles of methanol can be produced and what is the limiting reactant?

SOLUTION

Step 1 State the given and needed moles.

Analyze the Problem	Given	Need
	3.00 mol of CO, 5.00 mol of H_2	moles of CH_3OH produced, limiting reactant
	Equation	
	$CO(g) + 2H_2(g) \longrightarrow CH_3OH(g)$	

Step 2 Write a plan to convert the moles of each reactant to moles of product.

moles of CO → Mole–mole factor → moles of CH_3OH

moles of H_2 → Mole–mole factor → moles of CH_3OH

Step 3 Write the mole–mole factors from the equation.

1 mol of CO = 1 mol of CH_3OH

$$\frac{1 \text{ mol CO}}{1 \text{ mol } CH_3OH} \text{ and } \frac{1 \text{ mol } CH_3OH}{1 \text{ mol CO}}$$

2 mol of H_2 = 1 mol of CH_3OH

$$\frac{2 \text{ mol } H_2}{1 \text{ mol } CH_3OH} \text{ and } \frac{1 \text{ mol } CH_3OH}{2 \text{ mol } H_2}$$

Step 4 Calculate the number of moles of product from each reactant and select the smaller number of moles as the amount of product from the limiting reactant.

Moles of CH_3OH (product) from CO:

$$3.00 \cancel{\text{mol CO}} \times \frac{1 \text{ mol } CH_3OH}{1 \cancel{\text{mol CO}}} = 3.00 \text{ mol of } CH_3OH$$

Guide to Calculating the Moles of Product from a Limiting Reactant

1. State the given and needed moles.
2. Write a plan to convert the moles of each reactant to moles of product.
3. Write the mole–mole factors from the equation.
4. Calculate the number of moles of product from each reactant and select the smaller number of moles as the amount of product from the limiting reactant.

Moles of CH_3OH (product) from H_2:

$$5.00 \cancel{\text{mol } H_2} \times \frac{1 \text{ mol } CH_3OH}{2 \cancel{\text{mol } H_2}} = 2.50 \text{ mol of } CH_3OH$$

Limiting reactant — Smaller amount of product

The smaller amount, 2.50 mol of CH_3OH, is the maximum amount of methanol that can be produced from the limiting reactant, H_2, when it is completely consumed.

STUDY CHECK 9.5

If the initial mixture of reactants for Sample Problem 9.5 contains 4.00 mol of CO and 4.00 mol of H_2, what is the limiting reactant and how many moles of methanol can be produced?

A ceramic brake disc in a sports car withstands temperatures of 1400 °C.

Calculating Mass of Product from a Limiting Reactant

The quantities of the reactants can also be given in grams. The calculations to identify the limiting reactant are the same as before, but the grams of each reactant must first be converted to moles, then to moles of product, and finally to grams of product. Then select the smaller mass of product, which is from complete use of the limiting reactant. This calculation is shown in Sample Problem 9.6.

Guide to Calculating the Grams of Product from a Limiting Reactant

1. State the given and needed grams.
2. Write a plan to convert the grams of each reactant to grams of product.
3. Write the molar mass factors and the mole–mole factors from the equation.
4. Calculate the number of grams of product from each reactant and select the smaller number of grams as the amount of product from the limiting reactant.

SAMPLE PROBLEM 9.6 Mass of Product from a Limiting Reactant

When silicon dioxide (sand) and carbon are heated, the products are silicon carbide, SiC, and carbon monoxide. Silicon carbide is a ceramic material that tolerates extreme temperatures and is used as an abrasive and in the brake discs of sports cars. How many grams of CO are formed from 70.0 g of SiO_2 and 50.0 g of C?

$$SiO_2(s) + 3C(s) \xrightarrow{\text{Heat}} SiC(s) + 2CO(g)$$

SOLUTION

Step 1 State the given and needed grams.

	Given	Need
Analyze the Problem	70.0 g of SiO_2, 50.0 g of C	grams of CO from limiting reactant
	Equation	
	$SiO_2(s) + 3C(s) \xrightarrow{\text{Heat}} SiC(s) + 2CO(g)$	

Step 2 Write a plan to convert the grams of each reactant to grams of product.

grams of SiO_2 → Molar mass → moles of SiO_2 → Mole–mole factor → moles of CO → Molar mass → grams of CO

grams of C → Molar mass → moles of C → Mole–mole factor → moles of CO → Molar mass → grams of CO

Step 3 **Write the molar mass factors and mole–mole factors from the equation.**

Molar mass factors

$$1 \text{ mol of } SiO_2 = 60.09 \text{ g of } SiO_2 \qquad \frac{1 \text{ mol } SiO_2}{60.09 \text{ g } SiO_2} \text{ and } \frac{60.09 \text{ g } SiO_2}{1 \text{ mol } SiO_2}$$

$$1 \text{ mol of C} = 12.01 \text{ g of C} \qquad \frac{1 \text{ mol C}}{12.01 \text{ g C}} \text{ and } \frac{12.01 \text{ g C}}{1 \text{ mol C}}$$

$$1 \text{ mol of CO} = 28.01 \text{ g of CO} \qquad \frac{1 \text{ mol CO}}{28.01 \text{ g CO}} \text{ and } \frac{28.01 \text{ g CO}}{1 \text{ mol CO}}$$

Mole–mole factors

$$2 \text{ mol of CO} = 1 \text{ mol of } SiO_2 \qquad \frac{2 \text{ mol CO}}{1 \text{ mol } SiO_2} \text{ and } \frac{1 \text{ mol } SiO_2}{2 \text{ mol CO}}$$

$$2 \text{ mol of CO} = 3 \text{ mol of C} \qquad \frac{2 \text{ mol CO}}{3 \text{ mol C}} \text{ and } \frac{3 \text{ mol C}}{2 \text{ mol CO}}$$

Step 4 **Calculate the number of grams of product from each reactant and select the smaller number of grams as the amount of product from the limiting reactant.**

Grams of CO (product) from SiO_2:

$$70.0 \text{ g } \cancel{SiO_2} \times \frac{1 \text{ } \cancel{\text{mol } SiO_2}}{60.09 \text{ g } \cancel{SiO_2}} \times \frac{2 \text{ } \cancel{\text{mol CO}}}{1 \text{ } \cancel{\text{mol } SiO_2}} \times \frac{28.01 \text{ g CO}}{1 \text{ } \cancel{\text{mol CO}}} = 65.3 \text{ g of CO}$$

Limiting reactant — Smaller amount of product

Grams of CO (product) from C:

$$50.0 \text{ g } \cancel{C} \times \frac{1 \text{ } \cancel{\text{mol C}}}{12.01 \text{ g } \cancel{C}} \times \frac{2 \text{ } \cancel{\text{mol CO}}}{3 \text{ } \cancel{\text{mol C}}} \times \frac{28.01 \text{ g CO}}{1 \text{ } \cancel{\text{mol CO}}} = 77.7 \text{ g of CO}$$

The smaller amount, 65.3 g of CO, is the most CO that can be produced.

STUDY CHECK 9.6

Hydrogen sulfide burns with oxygen to give sulfur dioxide and water. How many grams of sulfur dioxide are formed from the reaction of 8.52 g of H_2S and 9.60 g of O_2?

$$2H_2S(g) + 3O_2(g) \xrightarrow{\Delta} 2SO_2(g) + 2H_2O(g)$$

QUESTIONS AND PROBLEMS

9.3 Limiting Reactants

LEARNING GOAL: *Identify a limiting reactant when given the quantities of two reactants; calculate the amount of product formed from the limiting reactant.*

9.19 A taxi company has 10 taxis.

a. On a certain day, only eight taxi drivers show up for work. How many taxis can be used to pick up passengers?

b. On another day, 10 taxi drivers show up for work but three taxis are in the repair shop. How many taxis can be driven?

9.20 A clock maker has 15 clock faces. Each clock requires one face and two hands.

a. If the clock maker has 42 hands, how many clocks can be produced?

b. If the clock maker has only eight hands, how many clocks can be produced?

9.21 Nitrogen and hydrogen react to form ammonia.

$$N_2(g) + 3H_2(g) \longrightarrow 2NH_3(g)$$

Determine the limiting reactant in each of the following mixtures of reactants:

a. 3.0 mol of N_2 and 5.0 mol of H_2

b. 8.0 mol of N_2 and 4.0 mol of H_2

c. 3.0 mol of N_2 and 12.0 mol of H_2

9.22 Iron and oxygen react to form iron(III) oxide.

$$4Fe(s) + 3O_2(g) \longrightarrow 2Fe_2O_3(s)$$

Determine the limiting reactant in each of the following mixtures of reactants:

a. 2.0 mol of Fe and 6.0 mol of O_2
b. 5.0 mol of Fe and 4.0 mol of O_2
c. 16.0 mol of Fe and 20.0 mol of O_2

9.23 For each of the following reactions, 20.0 g of each reactant is present initially. Determine the limiting reactant, and calculate the grams of product in parentheses that would be produced.

a. $2Al(s) + 3Cl_2(g) \longrightarrow 2AlCl_3(s)$ $(AlCl_3)$
b. $4NH_3(g) + 5O_2(g) \longrightarrow 4NO(g) + 6H_2O(g)$ (H_2O)
c. $CS_2(g) + 3O_2(g) \xrightarrow{\Delta} CO_2(g) + 2SO_2(g)$ (SO_2)

9.24 For each of the following reactions, 20.0 g of each reactant is present initially. Determine the limiting reactant, and calculate the grams of product in parentheses that would be produced.

a. $4Al(s) + 3O_2(g) \longrightarrow 2Al_2O_3(s)$ (Al_2O_3)
b. $3NO_2(g) + H_2O(l) \longrightarrow 2HNO_3(aq) + NO(g)$ (HNO_3)
c. $C_2H_5OH(l) + 3O_2(g) \xrightarrow{\Delta} 2CO_2(g) + 3H_2O(g)$ (H_2O)

9.25 For each of the following reactions, calculate the grams of indicated product when 25.0 g of the first reactant and 40.0 g of the second reactant is used:

a. $2SO_2(g) + O_2(g) \longrightarrow 2SO_3(g)$ (SO_3)
b. $3Fe(s) + 4H_2O(l) \longrightarrow Fe_3O_4(s) + 4H_2(g)$ (Fe_3O_4)
c. $C_7H_{16}(g) + 11O_2(g) \xrightarrow{\Delta} 7CO_2(g) + 8H_2O(g)$ (CO_2)

9.26 For each of the following reactions, calculate the grams of indicated product when 15.0 g of the first reactant and 10.0 g of the second reactant is used:

a. $4Li(s) + O_2(g) \longrightarrow 2Li_2O(s)$ (Li_2O)
b. $Fe_2O_3(s) + 3H_2(g) \longrightarrow 2Fe(s) + 3H_2O(l)$ (Fe)
c. $Al_2S_3(s) + 6H_2O(l) \longrightarrow 2Al(OH)_3(aq) + 3H_2S(g)$ (H_2S)

LEARNING GOAL

Given the actual quantity of product, determine the percent yield for a reaction.

9.4 Percent Yield

In our problems up to now, we assumed that all of the reactants changed completely to product. Thus, we have calculated the amount of product as the maximum quantity possible, or 100%. While this would be an ideal situation, it does not usually happen. As we carry out a reaction and transfer products from one container to another, some product is usually lost. In the lab as well as commercially, the starting materials may not be completely pure, and side reactions may use some of the reactants to give unwanted products. Thus, 100% of the desired product is not actually obtained.

When we do a chemical reaction in the laboratory, we measure out specific quantities of the reactants. We calculate the **theoretical yield** for the reaction, which is the amount of product (100%) we would expect if all the reactants were converted to the desired product. When the reaction ends, we collect and measure the mass of the product, which is the **actual yield** for the product. Because some product is usually lost, the actual yield is less than the theoretical yield. Using the actual yield and the theoretical yield for a product, we can calculate the **percent yield**.

Calculating Percent Yield

$$\text{Percent yield } (\%) = \frac{\text{actual yield}}{\text{theoretical yield}} \times 100\%$$

CONCEPT CHECK 9.4 Calculating Percent Yield

For your chemistry class party, you have prepared cookie dough from a recipe that makes 5 dozen cookies. You place dough for 12 cookies on a baking sheet and place it in the oven. But then the phone rings and you run to answer it. While you are talking, the cookies on the baking sheet burn and you have to throw them out. You proceed to prepare four more baking sheets with 12 cookies each. If the rest of the cookies are edible, what is the percent yield of cookies you provide for the chemistry party?

ANSWER

The theoretical yield of cookies is 5 dozen or 60 cookies, which is the maximum or 100% of the possible number of cookies. The actual yield is 48 edible cookies, which is

60 cookies minus the 12 cookies that burned. The percent yield is the ratio of 48 edible cookies divided by the theoretical yield of 60 cookies that were possible multiplied by 100%.

Theoretical yield: 60 cookies possible

Actual yield: 48 cookies to eat

Percent yield: $\frac{48 \text{ cookies (actual)}}{60 \text{ cookies (theoretical)}} \times 100\% = 80\%$

SAMPLE PROBLEM 9.7 Calculating Percent Yield

On a space shuttle, LiOH is used to absorb exhaled CO_2 from breathing air to form $LiHCO_3$.

$$LiOH(s) + CO_2(g) \longrightarrow LiHCO_3(s)$$

What is the percent yield of $LiHCO_3$ for the reaction if 50.0 g of LiOH gives 72.8 g of $LiHCO_3$?

SOLUTION

Step 1 State the given and needed quantities.

Analyze the Problem	Given	Need
	50.0 g of LiOH (reactant), 72.8 g of $LiHCO_3$ (actual product)	theoretical yield of $LiHCO_3$, percent yield of $LiHCO_3$
	Equation	
	$LiOH(s) + CO_2(g) \longrightarrow LiHCO_3(s)$	

Step 2 Write a plan to calculate the theoretical yield and the percent yield.

Calculation of theoretical yield:

grams of LiOH → Molar mass → moles of LiOH → Mole–mole factor → moles of $LiHCO_3$ → Molar mass → grams of $LiHCO_3$

Theoretical yield

Calculation of percent yield:

$$\text{Percent yield }(\%) = \frac{\text{actual yield of } LiHCO_3}{\text{theoretical yield of } LiHCO_3} \times 100\%$$

Step 3 Write the molar mass factors and the mole–mole factor from the balanced equation.

Molar mass factors

$$1 \text{ mol of LiOH} = 23.95 \text{ g of LiOH}$$

$$\frac{1 \text{ mol LiOH}}{23.95 \text{ g LiOH}} \text{ and } \frac{23.95 \text{ g LiOH}}{1 \text{ mol LiOH}}$$

$$1 \text{ mol of } LiHCO_3 = 67.96 \text{ g of } LiHCO_3$$

$$\frac{1 \text{ mol } LiHCO_3}{67.96 \text{ g } LiHCO_3} \text{ and } \frac{67.96 \text{ g } LiHCO_3}{1 \text{ mol } LiHCO_3}$$

Mole–mole factor

$$1 \text{ mol of } LiHCO_3 = 1 \text{ mol of LiOH}$$

$$\frac{1 \text{ mol } LiHCO_3}{1 \text{ mol LiOH}} \text{ and } \frac{1 \text{ mol LiOH}}{1 \text{ mol } LiHCO_3}$$

Guide to Calculations for Percent Yield

1 State the given and needed quantities.

2 Write a plan to calculate the theoretical yield and the percent yield.

3 Write the molar mass factors and the mole–mole factor from the balanced equation.

4 Calculate the percent yield by dividing the actual yield (given) by the theoretical yield and multiplying the result by 100%.

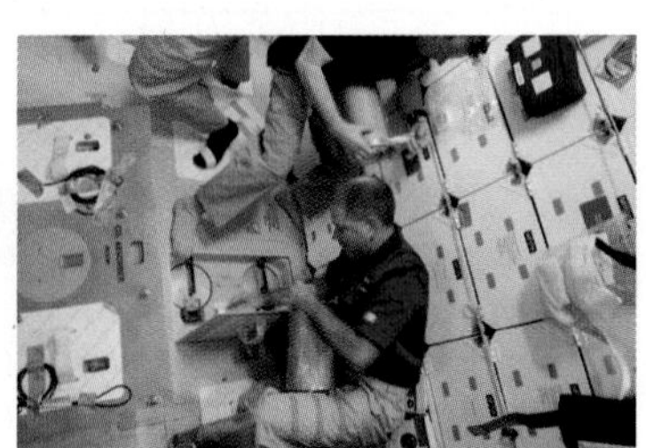

On a space shuttle, the LiOH in the canisters removes CO_2 from the air.

Step 4 **Calculate the percent yield by dividing the actual yield (given) by the theoretical yield and multiplying the result by 100%.**

Calculation of theoretical yield:

$$50.0\ \text{g}\ \cancel{\text{LiOH}} \times \frac{1\ \cancel{\text{mol LiOH}}}{23.95\ \text{g}\ \cancel{\text{LiOH}}} \times \frac{1\ \cancel{\text{mol LiHCO}_3}}{1\ \cancel{\text{mol LiOH}}} \times \frac{67.96\ \text{g LiHCO}_3}{1\ \cancel{\text{mol LiHCO}_3}}$$

$= 142$ g of $LiHCO_3$

Calculation of percent yield:

$$\frac{\text{actual yield (given)}}{\text{theoretical yield (calculated)}} \times 100\% = \frac{72.8\ \text{g}\ \cancel{\text{LiHCO}_3}}{142\ \text{g}\ \cancel{\text{LiHCO}_3}} \times 100\% = 51.3\%$$

A percent yield of 51.3% means that 72.8 g of the theoretical amount of 142 g of $LiHCO_3$ was actually produced by the reaction.

STUDY CHECK 9.7

For the reaction in Sample Problem 9.7, what is the percent yield of $LiHCO_3$ if 8.00 g of CO_2 produces 10.5 g of $LiHCO_3$?

QUESTIONS AND PROBLEMS

9.4 Percent Yield

LEARNING GOAL: *Given the actual quantity of product, determine the percent yield for a reaction.*

9.27 Carbon disulfide is produced by the reaction of carbon and sulfur dioxide.

$$5\text{C}(s) + 2\text{SO}_2(g) \longrightarrow \text{CS}_2(g) + 4\text{CO}(g)$$

a. What is the percent yield of carbon disulfide if the reaction of 40.0 g of carbon produces 36.0 g of carbon disulfide?

b. What is the percent yield of carbon disulfide if the reaction of 32.0 g of sulfur dioxide produces 12.0 g of carbon disulfide?

9.28 Iron(III) oxide reacts with carbon monoxide to produce iron and carbon dioxide.

$$\text{Fe}_2\text{O}_3(s) + 3\text{CO}(g) \longrightarrow 2\text{Fe}(s) + 3\text{CO}_2(g)$$

a. What is the percent yield of iron if the reaction of 65.0 g of iron(III) oxide produces 15.0 g of iron?

b. What is the percent yield of carbon dioxide if the reaction of 75.0 g of carbon monoxide produces 85.0 g of carbon dioxide?

9.29 Aluminum reacts with oxygen to produce aluminum oxide.

$$4\text{Al}(s) + 3\text{O}_2(g) \longrightarrow 2\text{Al}_2\text{O}_3(s)$$

Calculate the mass of Al_2O_3 that can be produced if the reaction of 50.0 g of aluminum and sufficient oxygen has a 75.0% yield.

9.30 Propane (C_3H_8) burns in oxygen to produce carbon dioxide and water.

$$\text{C}_3\text{H}_8(g) + 5\text{O}_2(g) \xrightarrow{\Delta} 3\text{CO}_2(g) + 4\text{H}_2\text{O}(g)$$

Calculate the mass of CO_2 that can be produced if the reaction of 45.0 g of propane and sufficient oxygen has a 60.0% yield.

9.31 When 30.0 g of carbon is heated with silicon dioxide, 28.2 g of carbon monoxide is produced. What is the percent yield of carbon monoxide for this reaction?

$$\text{SiO}_2(s) + 3\text{C}(s) \longrightarrow \text{SiC}(s) + 2\text{CO}(g)$$

9.32 When 56.6 g of calcium is reacted with nitrogen gas, 32.4 g of calcium nitride is produced. What is the percent yield of calcium nitride for this reaction?

$$3\text{Ca}(s) + \text{N}_2(g) \longrightarrow \text{Ca}_3\text{N}_2(s)$$

LEARNING GOAL

Given the heat of reaction (enthalpy change), calculate the loss or gain of heat for an exothermic or endothermic reaction.

9.5 Energy in Chemical Reactions

Almost every chemical reaction involves a loss or gain of energy. To discuss energy change for a reaction, we look at the energy of the reactants before the reaction and the energy of the products after the reaction.

Energy Units for Chemical Reactions

The SI unit for energy is the *joule* (J). Often, the unit of *kilojoules* (kJ) is used to show the energy change in a reaction.

1 kilojoule (kJ) = 1000 joules (J)

Heat of Reaction (Enthalpy Change)

The **heat of reaction** is the amount of heat absorbed or released during a reaction that takes place at constant pressure. A change of energy occurs as reactants interact, bonds break apart, and products form. We determine a heat of reaction or *enthalpy change*, symbol ΔH, as the difference in the energy of the products and the reactants.

$$\Delta H = H_{\text{products}} - H_{\text{reactants}}$$

Exothermic Reactions

In an **exothermic reaction** (*exo* means "out"), the energy of the products is lower than that of the reactants. This means that heat is released along with the products that form. Let us look at the equation for the exothermic reaction in which 185 kJ of heat is released when 1 mol of hydrogen and 1 mol of chlorine react to form 2 mol of hydrogen chloride. For an exothermic reaction, the heat of reaction can be written as one of the products. It can also be written as a ΔH value with a negative sign $(-)$.

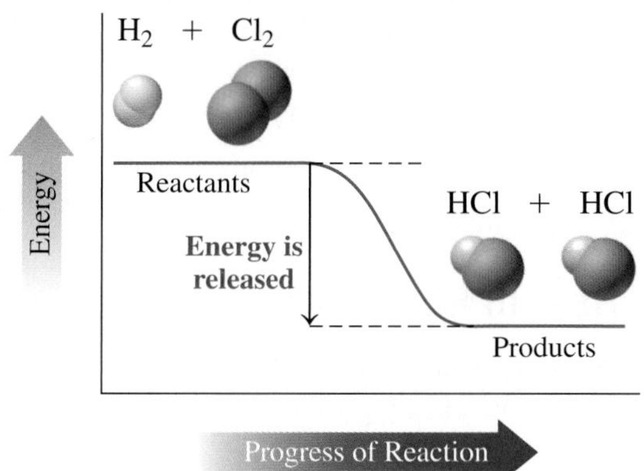

Exothermic, Heat Released	Heat Is a Product
$H_2(g) + Cl_2(g) \longrightarrow 2HCl(g) + 185\text{ kJ}$	$\Delta H = -185\text{ kJ}$ Negative sign

Endothermic Reactions

In an **endothermic reaction** (*endo* means "within"), the energy of the products is higher than that of the reactants. Heat is required to convert the reactants to products. Let us look at the equation for the endothermic reaction in which 180 kJ of heat is needed to convert 1 mol of nitrogen and 1 mol of oxygen to 2 mol of nitrogen oxide. For an endothermic reaction, the heat of reaction can be written as one of the reactants. It can also be written as a ΔH value with a positive sign $(+)$.

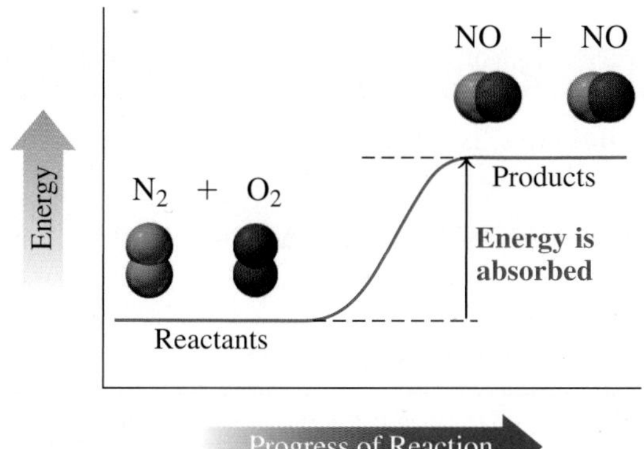

Endothermic, Heat Absorbed	Heat Is a Reactant
$N_2(g) + O_2(g) + 180\text{ kJ} \longrightarrow 2NO(g)$	$\Delta H = +180\text{ kJ}$ Positive sign

Reaction	Energy Change	Heat in the Equation	Sign of ΔH
Endothermic	Heat absorbed	Reactant side	Positive sign $(+)$
Exothermic	Heat released	Product side	Negative sign $(-)$

CONCEPT CHECK 9.5 Exothermic and Endothermic Reactions

In the reaction of 1 mol of carbon with oxygen gas, the energy of the carbon dioxide produced is 393 kJ less than that of the reactants.

a. Is the reaction exothermic or endothermic?
b. Write the balanced chemical equation including the heat of the reaction.
c. What is the value (in kJ) for the heat of reaction?

ANSWER

a. When the energy of the products is lower than that of the reactants, the reaction gives off heat, which means that it is exothermic.
b. In an exothermic reaction, the heat is written as a product.

$$C(s) + O_2(g) \longrightarrow CO_2(g) + 393\text{ kJ}$$

c. The heat of reaction for an exothermic reaction has a negative sign: $\Delta H = -393$ kJ

Calculations of Heat in Reactions

The value of ΔH refers to the heat change in kilojoules for the each substance in the balanced equation for the reaction. Consider the following decomposition reaction:

$$2H_2O(l) \longrightarrow 2H_2(g) + O_2(g) \quad \Delta H = +572\text{ kJ}$$
$$2H_2O(l) + 572\text{ kJ} \longrightarrow 2H_2(g) + O_2(g)$$

For this reaction, 572 kJ are absorbed by 2 mol of H_2O to produce 2 mol of H_2 and 1 mol of O_2. We can write heat conversion factors for each substance in this reaction as follows:

$$\frac{+572\text{ kJ}}{2\text{ mol }H_2O} \quad \frac{+572\text{ kJ}}{2\text{ mol }H_2} \quad \frac{+572\text{ kJ}}{1\text{ mol }O_2}$$

Suppose in this reaction that 9.00 g of H_2O undergoes reaction. We can calculate the heat as

$$9.00\text{ g }\cancel{H_2O} \times \frac{1\text{ }\cancel{\text{mol }H_2O}}{18.02\text{ }\cancel{\text{g }H_2O}} \times \frac{572\text{ kJ}}{2\text{ }\cancel{\text{mol }H_2O}} = +143\text{ kJ}$$

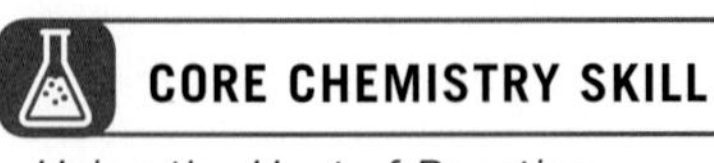

Using the Heat of Reaction

SAMPLE PROBLEM 9.8 Calculating Heat in a Reaction

How much heat, in kilojoules, is released when nitrogen and hydrogen react to form 50.0 g of ammonia?

$$N_2(g) + 3H_2(g) \longrightarrow 2NH_3(g) \qquad \Delta H = -92.2\text{ kJ}$$

SOLUTION

Step 1 State the given and needed quantities.

Analyze the Problem	Given	Need
	50.0 g of NH_3, $\Delta H = -92.2$ kJ	heat released, in kilojoules
	Equation	
	$N_2(g) + 3H_2(g) \longrightarrow 2NH_3(g)$	

Step 2 **Write a plan using the heat of reaction and any molar mass needed.**

grams of NH_3 → Molar mass → moles of NH_3 → Heat of reaction → kilojoules

Step 3 **Write the conversion factors including heat of reaction.**

$$1 \text{ mol of } NH_3 = 17.03 \text{ g of } NH_3 \qquad 2 \text{ mol of } NH_3 = -92.2 \text{ kJ}$$

$$\frac{17.03 \text{ g } NH_3}{1 \text{ mol } NH_3} \text{ and } \frac{1 \text{ mol } NH_3}{17.03 \text{ g } NH_3} \qquad \frac{-92.2 \text{ kJ}}{2 \text{ mol } NH_3} \text{ and } \frac{2 \text{ mol } NH_3}{-92.2 \text{ kJ}}$$

Step 4 **Set up the problem to calculate the heat.**

$$50.0 \text{ g } \cancel{NH_3} \times \frac{1 \text{ } \cancel{\text{mol } NH_3}}{17.03 \text{ } \cancel{\text{g } NH_3}} \times \frac{-92.2 \text{ kJ}}{2 \text{ } \cancel{\text{mol } NH_3}} = -135 \text{ kJ}$$

STUDY CHECK 9.8

Mercury(II) oxide decomposes to mercury and oxygen.

$$2HgO(s) \longrightarrow 2Hg(l) + O_2(g) \quad \Delta H = +182 \text{ kJ}$$

a. Is the reaction exothermic or endothermic?
b. How many kilojoules are needed to react 25.0 g of mercury(II) oxide?

Guide to Calculations Using the Heat of Reaction (ΔH)

1. State the given and needed quantities.
2. Write a plan using the heat of reaction and any molar mass needed.
3. Write the conversion factors including heat of reaction.
4. Set up the problem to calculate the heat.

Chemistry Link to Health

COLD PACKS AND HOT PACKS

In a hospital, at a first-aid station, or at an athletic event, an instant *cold pack* may be used to reduce swelling from an injury, remove heat from inflammation, or decrease capillary size to lessen the effect of hemorrhaging. Inside the plastic container of a cold pack, there is a compartment containing solid ammonium nitrate (NH_4NO_3) that is separated from a compartment containing water. The pack is activated when it is hit or squeezed hard enough to break the walls between the compartments and cause the ammonium nitrate to mix with the water (shown as H_2O over the reaction arrow). In an endothermic process, 1 mol of NH_4NO_3 that dissolves absorbs 26 kJ of heat. The temperature drops to about 4–5 °C to give a cold pack that is ready to use.

Endothermic Reaction in a Cold Pack

$$NH_4NO_3(s) + 26 \text{ kJ} \xrightarrow{H_2O} NH_4NO_3(aq)$$

Hot packs are used to relax muscles, lessen aches and cramps, and increase circulation by expanding capillary size. Constructed in the same way as cold packs, a hot pack contains a salt such as $CaCl_2$. When 1 mol of $CaCl_2$ dissolves in water, 82 kJ are released as heat. The temperature increases as much as 66 °C to give a hot pack that is ready to use.

Exothermic Reaction in a Hot Pack

$$CaCl_2(s) \xrightarrow{H_2O} CaCl_2(aq) + 82 \text{ kJ}$$

Cold packs use an endothermic reaction.

QUESTIONS AND PROBLEMS

9.5 Energy in Chemical Reactions

LEARNING GOAL: *Given the heat of reaction (enthalpy change), calculate the loss or gain of heat for an exothermic or endothermic reaction.*

9.33 In an exothermic reaction, is the energy of the products higher or lower than that of the reactants?

9.34 In an endothermic reaction, is the energy of the products higher or lower than that of the reactants?

9.35 Classify each of the following as exothermic or endothermic:
a. A reaction releases 550 kJ.
b. The energy level of the products is higher than that of the reactants.
c. The metabolism of glucose in the body provides energy.

9.36 Classify each of the following as exothermic or endothermic:
a. The energy level of the products is lower than that of the reactants.
b. In the body, the synthesis of proteins requires energy.
c. A reaction absorbs 125 kJ.

9.37 Classify each of the following as exothermic or endothermic and give the ΔH for each:
a. $CH_4(g) + 2O_2(g) \xrightarrow{\Delta} CO_2(g) + 2H_2O(g) + 802\text{ kJ}$
b. $Ca(OH)_2(s) + 65.3\text{ kJ} \longrightarrow CaO(s) + H_2O(l)$
c. $2Al(s) + Fe_2O_3(s) \longrightarrow Al_2O_3(s) + 2Fe(l) + 850\text{ kJ}$

The thermite reaction of aluminum and iron(III) oxide produces very high temperatures used to cut or weld railroad tracks.

9.38 Classify each of the following as exothermic or endothermic and give the ΔH for each:
a. $C_3H_8(g) + 5O_2(g) \xrightarrow{\Delta} 3CO_2(g) + 4H_2O(g) + 2220\text{ kJ}$
b. $2Na(s) + Cl_2(g) \longrightarrow 2NaCl(s) + 819\text{ kJ}$
c. $PCl_5(g) + 67\text{ kJ} \longrightarrow PCl_3(g) + Cl_2(g)$

9.39 **a.** How many kilojoules are released when 125 g of Cl_2 reacts with silicon?

$$Si(s) + 2Cl_2(g) \longrightarrow SiCl_4(g) \quad \Delta H = -657\text{ kJ}$$

b. How many kilojoules are absorbed when 278 g of PCl_5 reacts?

$$PCl_5(g) \longrightarrow PCl_3(g) + Cl_2(g) \quad \Delta H = +67\text{ kJ}$$

9.40 **a.** How many kilojoules are released when 75.0 g of methanol reacts?

$$2CH_3OH(l) + 3O_2(g) \xrightarrow{\Delta} 2CO_2(g) + 4H_2O(l) \quad \Delta H = -726\text{ kJ}$$

b. How many kilojoules are absorbed when 315 g of $Ca(OH)_2$ reacts?

$$Ca(OH)_2(s) \longrightarrow CaO(s) + H_2O(l) \quad \Delta H = +65.3\text{ kJ}$$

CHAPTER REVIEW

9.1 Mole Relationships in Chemical Equations

LEARNING GOAL: *Given a quantity in moles of reactant or product, use a mole–mole factor from the balanced equation to calculate the number of moles of another substance in the reaction.*

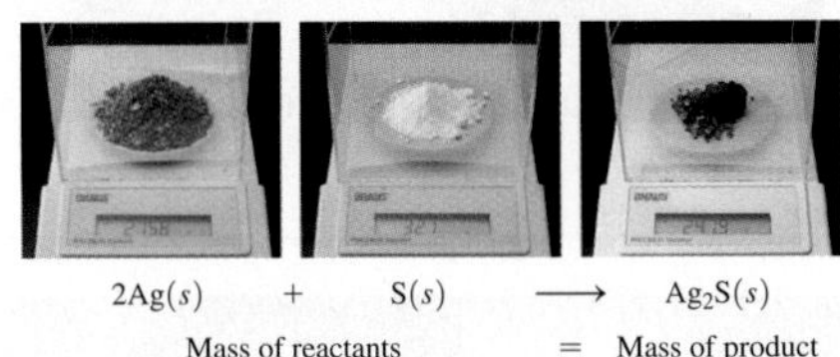

$2Ag(s) + S(s) \longrightarrow Ag_2S(s)$

Mass of reactants = Mass of product

- In a balanced equation, the total mass of the reactants is equal to the total mass of the products.
- The coefficients in an equation describing the relationship between the moles of any two components are used to write mole–mole factors.
- When the number of moles for one substance is known, a mole–mole factor is used to find the moles of a different substance in the reaction.

9.2 Mass Calculations for Reactions

LEARNING GOAL: *Given the mass in grams of a substance in a reaction, calculate the mass in grams of another substance in the reaction.*

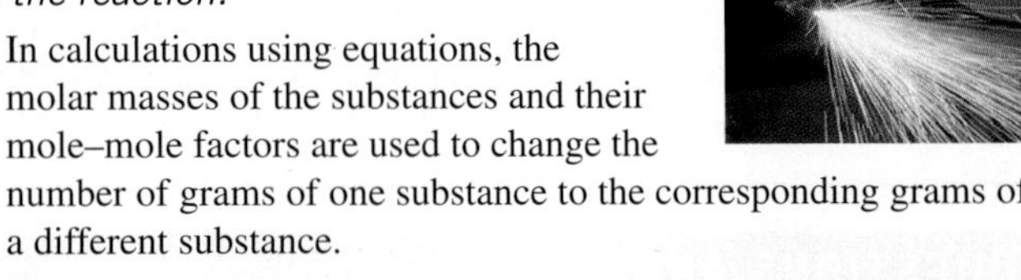

- In calculations using equations, the molar masses of the substances and their mole–mole factors are used to change the number of grams of one substance to the corresponding grams of a different substance.

9.3 Limiting Reactants

LEARNING GOAL: *Identify a limiting reactant when given the quantities of two reactants; calculate the amount of product formed from the limiting reactant.*

- A limiting reactant is the reactant that produces the smaller amount of product while the other reactant is left over.
- When the masses of two reactants are given, the mass of a product is calculated from the limiting reactant.

9.4 Percent Yield

LEARNING GOAL: *Given the actual quantity of product, determine the percent yield for a reaction.*

- The percent yield for a reaction indicates the percent of product actually produced during a reaction.
- The percent yield is calculated by dividing the actual yield in grams of a product by the theoretical yield in grams and multiplying by 100%.

9.5 Energy in Chemical Reactions

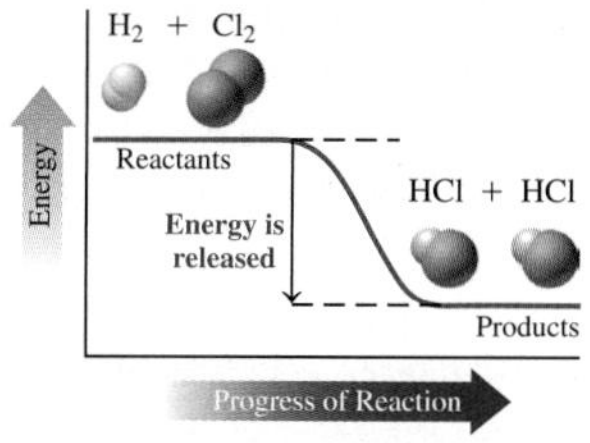

LEARNING GOAL: *Given the heat of reaction (enthalpy change), calculate the loss or gain of heat for an exothermic or endothermic reaction.*

- In chemical reactions, the heat of reaction (ΔH) is the energy difference between the products and the reactants.
- In an exothermic reaction, the energy of the products is lower than that of the reactants. Heat is released, and ΔH is negative.
- In an endothermic reaction, the energy of the products is higher than that of the reactants; heat is absorbed, and ΔH is positive.

CONCEPT MAP

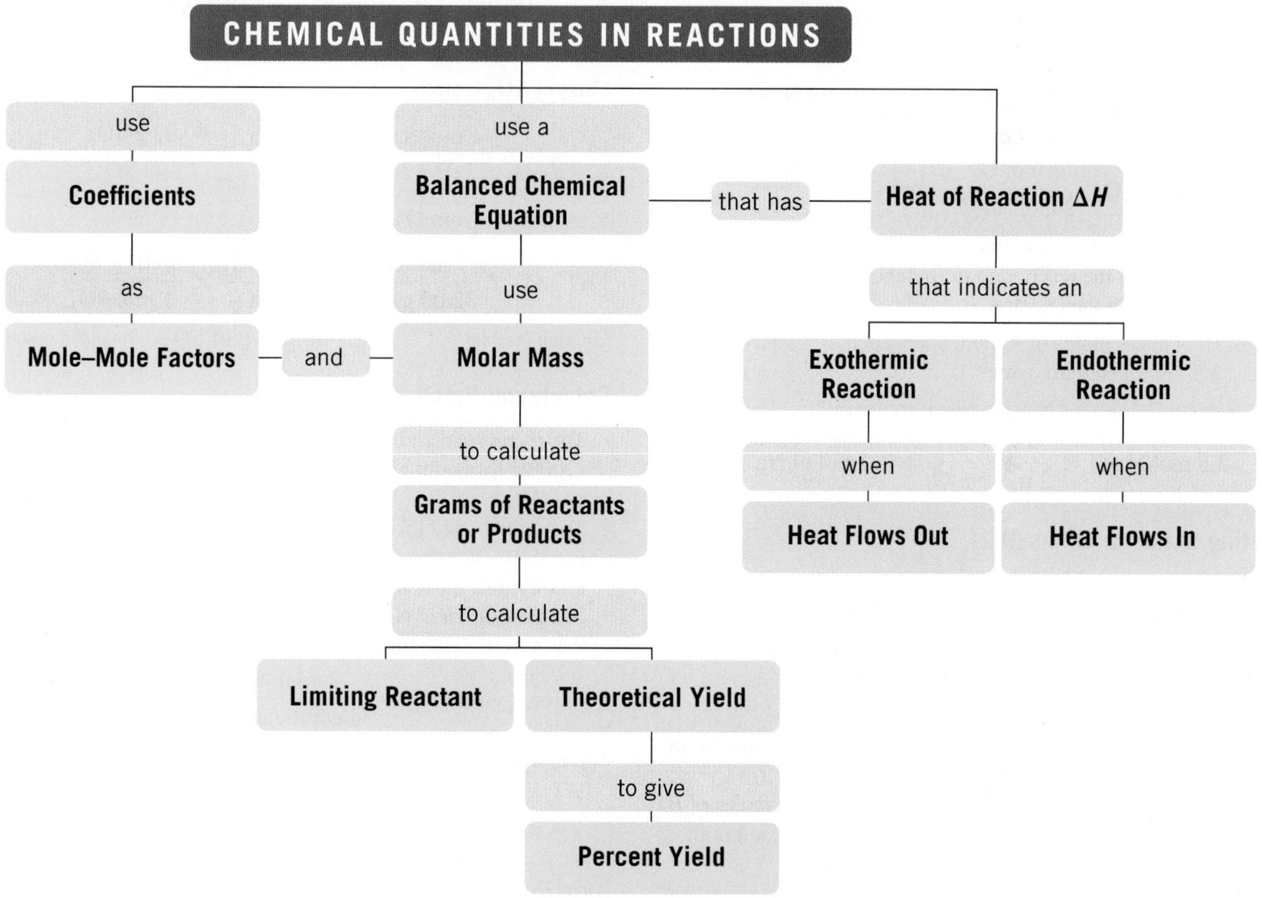

CHEMICAL QUANTITIES IN REACTIONS

use
Coefficients
as
Mole–Mole Factors — and —

use a
Balanced Chemical Equation — that has — **Heat of Reaction ΔH**
use
Molar Mass
to calculate
Grams of Reactants or Products
to calculate
Limiting Reactant | **Theoretical Yield**
to give
Percent Yield

Heat of Reaction ΔH
that indicates an
Exothermic Reaction | **Endothermic Reaction**
when | when
Heat Flows Out | **Heat Flows In**

KEY TERMS

actual yield The actual amount of product produced by a reaction.

endothermic reaction A reaction wherein the energy of the products is higher than that of the reactants.

exothermic reaction A reaction wherein the energy of the products is lower than that of the reactants.

heat of reaction The heat (symbol ΔH) absorbed or released when a reaction takes place at constant pressure.

law of conservation of mass In a chemical reaction, the total mass of the reactants is equal to the total mass of the products; matter is neither lost nor gained.

limiting reactant The reactant used up during a chemical reaction, which limits the amount of product that can form.

mole–mole factor A conversion factor that relates the number of moles of two compounds in an equation derived from their coefficients.

percent yield The ratio of the actual yield for a reaction to the theoretical yield possible for the reaction.

theoretical yield The maximum amount of product that a reaction can produce from a given amount of reactant.

CORE CHEMISTRY SKILLS

The chapter section containing each Core Chemistry Skill is shown in parentheses at the end of each heading.

Using Mole–Mole Factors (9.1)

Consider the balanced equation

$$4Na(s) + O_2(g) \longrightarrow 2Na_2O(s)$$

- The coefficients in a balanced chemical equation represent the moles of reactants and the moles of products. Thus, 4 mol of Na react with 1 mol of O_2 to form 2 mol of Na_2O.
- From the coefficients, mole–mole factors can be written for any two substances as follows:

Na and O_2 $\quad \dfrac{4 \text{ mol Na}}{1 \text{ mol } O_2}$ and $\dfrac{1 \text{ mol } O_2}{4 \text{ mol Na}}$

Na and Na_2O $\quad \dfrac{4 \text{ mol Na}}{2 \text{ mol } Na_2O}$ and $\dfrac{2 \text{ mol } Na_2O}{4 \text{ mol Na}}$

O_2 and Na_2O $\quad \dfrac{1 \text{ mol } O_2}{2 \text{ mol } Na_2O}$ and $\dfrac{2 \text{ mol } Na_2O}{1 \text{ mol } O_2}$

- A mole–mole factor is used to convert the number of moles of one substance in the reaction to the number of moles of another substance in the reaction.

Example: How many moles of sodium are needed to produce 3.5 mol of sodium oxide?

Answer: **Given:** 3.5 mol of Na_2O **Need:** moles of Na

$$3.5 \cancel{\text{mol } Na_2O} \times \frac{4 \text{ mol Na}}{2 \cancel{\text{mol } Na_2O}} = 7.0 \text{ mol of Na}$$

Converting Grams to Grams (9.2)

- When we have the balanced chemical equation for a reaction, we can use the mass of substance A and then calculate the mass of substance B.

$$A \longrightarrow B$$

- The process is as follows:

(1) Use the molar mass factor to convert the mass, in grams, of A to moles of A.
(2) Use the mole–mole factor that converts moles of A to moles of B.
(3) Use the molar mass factor of B to calculate the mass, in grams, of B.

$$\text{grams of A} \xrightarrow{\textit{molar mass A}} \text{moles of A} \xrightarrow{\textit{mole–mole factor}} \text{moles of B} \xrightarrow{\textit{molar mass B}} \text{grams of B}$$

Example: How many grams of O_2 are needed to completely react with 14.6 g of Na?

$$4Na(s) + O_2(g) \longrightarrow 2Na_2O(s)$$

Answer:

	Molar mass of Na	Mole–mole factor	Molar mass of O_2	
	Exact	Exact	Four SFs	

$$14.6 \cancel{\text{g Na}} \times \frac{1 \cancel{\text{mol Na}}}{22.99 \cancel{\text{g Na}}} \times \frac{1 \cancel{\text{mol } O_2}}{4 \cancel{\text{mol Na}}} \times \frac{32.00 \text{ g } O_2}{1 \cancel{\text{mol } O_2}} = 5.08 \text{ g of } O_2$$

Three SFs — Four SFs — Exact — Exact — Three SFs

Calculating Quantity of Product from a Limiting Reactant (9.3)

Often in reactions, the reactants are not consumed at exactly the same time. Then one of the reactants, called the *limiting reactant*, determines the maximum amount of product that can form.

- To determine the limiting reactant, we calculate the amount of product that is possible from each reactant.
- The limiting reactant is the one that produces the smaller amount of product.

Example: If 12.5 g of S reacts with 17.2 g of O_2, what is the limiting reactant and the mass, in grams, of SO_3 produced?

$$2S(s) + 3O_2(g) \longrightarrow 2SO_3(g)$$

Answer:

Mass of SO_3 from S:

$$12.5 \cancel{\text{g S}} \times \frac{1 \cancel{\text{mol S}}}{32.07 \cancel{\text{g S}}} \times \frac{2 \cancel{\text{mol } SO_3}}{2 \cancel{\text{mol S}}} \times \frac{80.07 \text{ g } SO_3}{1 \cancel{\text{mol } SO_3}} = 31.2 \text{ g of } SO_3$$

Mass of SO_3 from O_2:

$$17.2 \cancel{\text{g } O_2} \times \frac{1 \cancel{\text{mol } O_2}}{32.00 \cancel{\text{g } O_2}} \times \frac{2 \cancel{\text{mol } SO_3}}{3 \cancel{\text{mol } O_2}} \times \frac{80.07 \text{ g } SO_3}{1 \cancel{\text{mol } SO_3}}$$

Limiting reactant $= 28.7 \text{ g of } SO_3$ Smaller amount of SO_3

Calculating Percent Yield (9.4)

- The *theoretical yield* for a reaction is the amount of product (100%) formed if all the reactants were converted to desired product.
- The *actual yield* for the reaction is the mass, in grams, of the product obtained at the end of the experiment. Because some product is usually lost, the actual yield is less than the theoretical yield.
- The *percent yield* is calculated from the actual yield divided by the theoretical yield and multiplied by 100%.

$$\text{Percent yield}(\%) = \frac{\text{actual yield}}{\text{theoretical yield}} \times 100\%$$

Example: If 22.6 g of Al reacts completely with O_2, and 37.8 g of Al_2O_3 is obtained, what is the percent yield of Al_2O_3 for the reaction?

$$4Al(s) + 3O_2(g) \longrightarrow 2Al_2O_3(s)$$

Answer:

Calculation of theoretical yield:

$$22.6 \cancel{\text{g Al}} \times \frac{1 \cancel{\text{mol Al}}}{26.98 \cancel{\text{g Al}}} \times \frac{2 \cancel{\text{mol } Al_2O_3}}{4 \cancel{\text{mol Al}}} \times \frac{101.96 \text{ g } Al_2O_3}{1 \cancel{\text{mol } Al_2O_3}}$$

$= 42.7 \text{ g of } Al_2O_3$
Theoretical yield

Calculation of percent yield:

$$\frac{\text{actual yield (given)}}{\text{theoretical yield (calculated)}} \times 100\% = \frac{37.8 \cancel{\text{g } Al_2O_3}}{42.7 \cancel{\text{g } Al_2O_3}} \times 100\%$$

$= 88.5\%$

Using the Heat of Reaction (9.5)

- The heat of reaction is the amount of heat, usually in kJ, that is absorbed or released during a reaction.
- The heat of reaction or *enthalpy change*, symbol ΔH, is the difference in the energy of the products and the reactants.

$$\Delta H = H_{\text{products}} - H_{\text{reactants}}$$

- In an exothermic reaction (*exo* means "out"), the energy of the products is lower than that of the reactants. This means that heat is released along with the products that form. Then the sign for the heat of reaction, ΔH, is negative.
- In an endothermic reaction (*endo* means "within"), the energy of the products is higher than that of the reactants. The heat is required to convert the reactants to products. Then the sign for the heat of reaction, ΔH, is positive.

Example: How many kilojoules are released when 3.50 g of CH_4 undergoes combustion?

$$CH_4(g) + 2O_2(g) \xrightarrow{\Delta} CO_2(g) + 2H_2O(g) \quad \Delta H = -802 \text{ kJ}$$

Answer: $3.50 \text{ g } \cancel{CH_4} \times \frac{1 \text{ } \cancel{\text{mol } CH_4}}{16.04 \text{ } \cancel{\text{g } CH_4}} \times \frac{-802 \text{ kJ}}{1 \text{ } \cancel{\text{mol } CH_4}} = -175 \text{ kJ}$

UNDERSTANDING THE CONCEPTS

The chapter sections to review are shown in parentheses at the end of each question.

9.41 If red spheres represent oxygen atoms and blue spheres represent nitrogen atoms, (9.1, 9.2, 9.3)

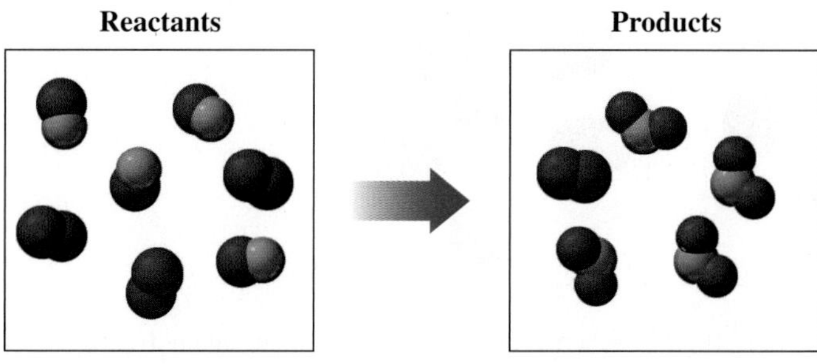

a. write a balanced equation for the reaction
b. identify the limiting reactant

9.42 If green spheres represent chlorine atoms, yellow-green spheres represent fluorine atoms, and white spheres represent hydrogen atoms, (9.1, 9.2, 9.3)

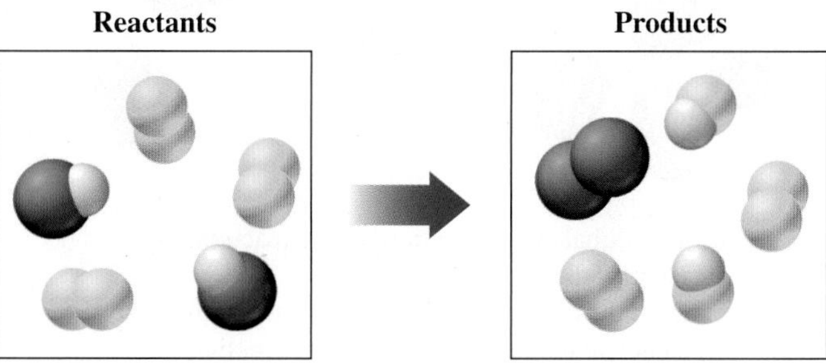

a. write a balanced equation for the reaction
b. identify the limiting reactant

9.43 If blue spheres represent nitrogen atoms and white spheres represent hydrogen atoms, (9.1, 9.2, 9.3)

Reactants

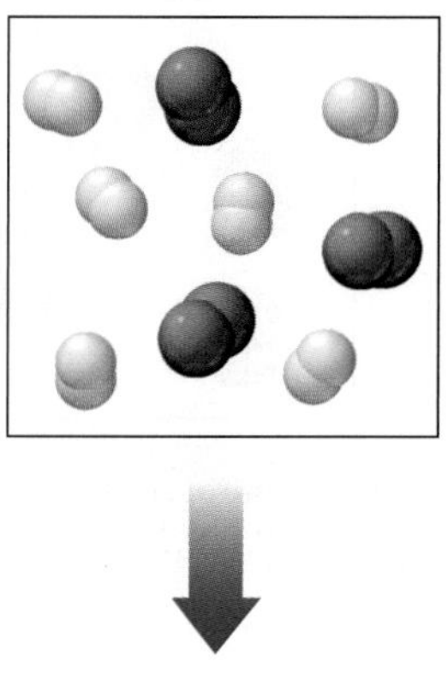

Products

A

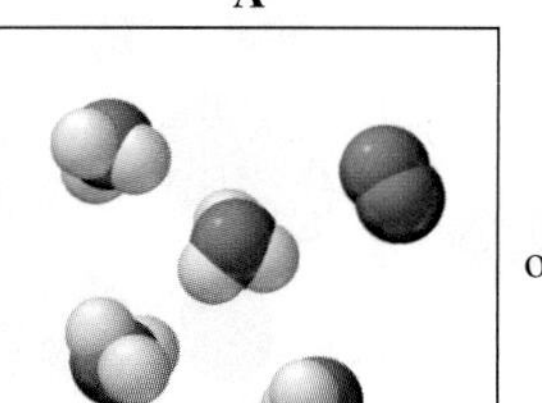

or

B

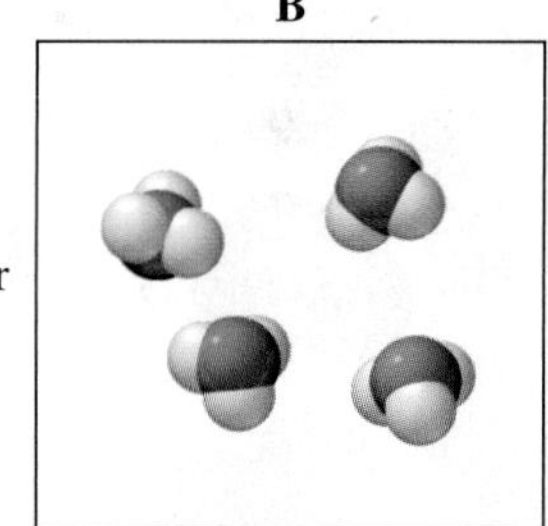

a. write a balanced equation for the reaction
b. identify the diagram that shows the products

9.44 If purple spheres represent iodine atoms and white spheres represent hydrogen atoms, (9.1, 9.2, 9.3)

a. write a balanced equation for the reaction

b. identify the diagram that shows the products

Reactants

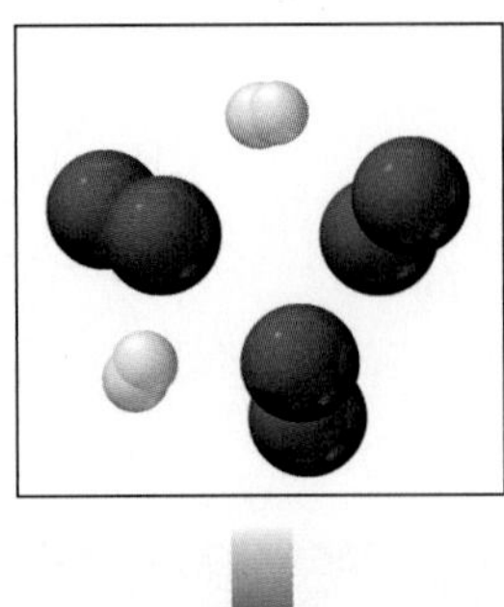

Products

A or **B** or **C**

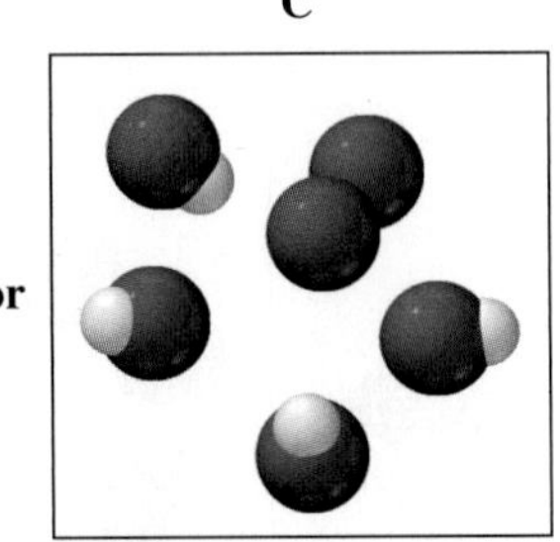

9.45 If blue spheres represent nitrogen atoms and purple spheres represent iodine atoms, (9.1, 9.2, 9.3, 9.4)

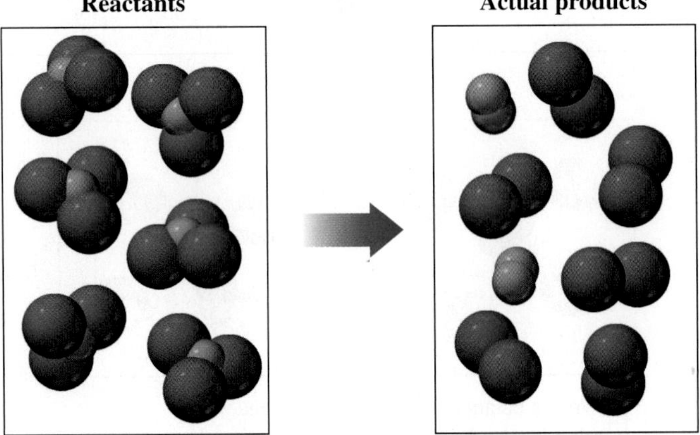

a. write a balanced equation for the reaction

b. from the diagram of the actual products that result, calculate the percent yield for the reaction

9.46 If green spheres represent chlorine atoms and red spheres represent oxygen atoms, (9.1, 9.2, 9.3, 9.4)

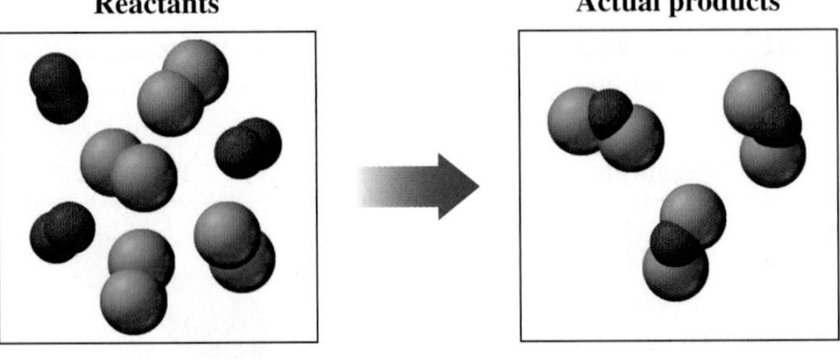

a. write a balanced equation for the reaction.

b. identify the limiting reactant

c. from the diagram of the actual products that result, calculate the percent yield for the reaction

ADDITIONAL QUESTIONS AND PROBLEMS

9.47 When ammonia (NH_3) reacts with fluorine (F_2), the products are dinitrogen tetrafluoride and hydrogen fluoride. (9.1, 9.2)

$$2NH_3(g) + 5F_2(g) \longrightarrow N_2F_4(g) + 6HF(g)$$

a. How many moles of each reactant are needed to produce 4.00 mol of HF?

b. How many grams of F_2 are required to react with 25.5 g of NH_3?

c. How many grams of N_2F_4 can be produced when 3.40 g of NH_3 reacts?

9.48 Gasohol is a fuel that contains ethanol (C_2H_6O) that burns in oxygen (O_2) to give carbon dioxide and water. (9.1, 9.2)

$$C_2H_6O(g) + 3O_2(g) \xrightarrow{\Delta} 2CO_2(g) + 3H_2O(g)$$

a. How many moles of O_2 are needed to completely react with 4.0 mol of C_2H_6O?

b. If a car produces 88 g of CO_2, how many grams of O_2 are used up in the reaction?

c. If you add 125 g of C_2H_6O to your fuel, how many grams of CO_2 can be produced from the ethanol?

9.49 When hydrogen peroxide (H_2O_2) is used in rocket fuels, it produces water and oxygen (O_2). (9.1, 9.2)

$$2H_2O_2(l) \longrightarrow 2H_2O(l) + O_2(g)$$

a. How many moles of H_2O_2 are needed to produce 3.00 mol of H_2O?
b. How many grams of H_2O_2 are required to produce 36.5 g of O_2?
c. How many grams of H_2O can be produced when 12.2 g of H_2O_2 reacts?

9.50 Propane gas, C_3H_8, reacts with oxygen to produce water and carbon dioxide. (9.1, 9.2)

$$C_3H_8(g) + 5O_2(g) \xrightarrow{\Delta} 3CO_2(g) + 4H_2O(l)$$

a. How many moles of H_2O form when 5.00 mol of C_3H_8 completely reacts?
b. How many grams of CO_2 are produced from 18.5 g of oxygen gas?
c. How many grams of H_2O can be produced when 46.3 g of C_3H_8 reacts?

9.51 When 12.8 g of Na and 10.2 g of Cl_2 react, what is the mass, in grams, of NaCl that is produced? (9.1, 9.2, 9.3)

$$2Na(s) + Cl_2(g) \longrightarrow 2NaCl(s)$$

9.52 If 35.8 g of CH_4 and 75.5 g of S react, how many grams of H_2S are produced? (9.1, 9.2, 9.3)

$$CH_4(g) + 4S(g) \longrightarrow CS_2(g) + 2H_2S(g)$$

9.53 Pentane gas, C_5H_{12}, reacts with oxygen to produce carbon dioxide and water. (9.1, 9.2, 9.3)

$$C_5H_{12}(g) + 8O_2(g) \xrightarrow{\Delta} 5CO_2(g) + 6H_2O(g)$$

a. How many moles of C_5H_{12} must react to produce 4.00 mol of water?
b. How many grams of CO_2 are produced from 32.0 g of O_2?
c. How many grams of CO_2 are formed if 44.5 g of C_5H_{12} is mixed with 108 g of O_2?

9.54 When nitrogen dioxide (NO_2) from car exhaust combines with water in the air, it forms nitrogen oxide and nitric acid (HNO_3), which causes acid rain. (9.1, 9.2, 9.3)

$$3NO_2(g) + H_2O(l) \longrightarrow NO(g) + 2HNO_3(aq)$$

a. How many moles of NO_2 are needed to react with 0.250 mol of H_2O?
b. How many grams of HNO_3 are produced when 60.0 g of NO_2 completely reacts?
c. How many grams of HNO_3 can be produced if 225 g of NO_2 is mixed with 55.2 g of H_2O?

9.55 The gaseous hydrocarbon acetylene, C_2H_2, used in welders' torches, burns according to the following equation: (9.1, 9.2, 9.3, 9.4)

$$2C_2H_2(g) + 5O_2(g) \xrightarrow{\Delta} 4CO_2(g) + 2H_2O(g)$$

a. What is the theoretical yield, in grams, of CO_2, if 22.0 g of C_2H_2 completely reacts?
b. If the actual yield in part **a** is 64.0 g of CO_2, what is the percent yield of CO_2 for the reaction?

9.56 The equation for the decomposition of potassium chlorate is written as (9.1, 9.2, 9.3, 9.4)

$$2KClO_3(s) \xrightarrow{\Delta} 2KCl(s) + 3O_2(g)$$

a. When 46.0 g of $KClO_3$ is completely decomposed, what is the theoretical yield, in grams, of O_2?
b. If 12.1 g of O_2 is produced, what is the percent yield of O_2?

9.57 When 28.0 g of acetylene reacts with hydrogen, 24.5 g of ethane is produced. What is the percent yield of C_2H_6 for the reaction? (9.1, 9.2, 9.3, 9.4)

$$C_2H_2(g) + 2H_2(g) \xrightarrow{Pt} C_2H_6(g)$$

9.58 When 50.0 g of iron(III) oxide reacts with carbon monoxide, 32.8 g of iron is produced. What is the percent yield of Fe for the reaction? (9.1, 9.2, 9.3, 9.4)

$$Fe_2O_3(s) + 3CO(g) \longrightarrow 2Fe(s) + 3CO_2(g)$$

9.59 Nitrogen and hydrogen combine to form ammonia. (9.1, 9.2, 9.3, 9.4)

$$N_2(g) + 3H_2(g) \longrightarrow 2NH_3(g)$$

a. If 50.0 g of N_2 is mixed with 20.0 g of H_2, what is the theoretical yield, in grams, of NH_3?
b. If the reaction in part **a** has a percent yield of 62.0%, what is the actual yield, in grams, of ammonia?

9.60 Sodium and nitrogen combine to form sodium nitride. (9.1, 9.2, 9.3, 9.4)

$$6Na(s) + N_2(g) \longrightarrow 2Na_3N(s)$$

a. If 80.0 g of Na is mixed with 20.0 g of nitrogen gas, what is the theoretical yield, in grams, of Na_3N?
b. If the reaction in part a has a percent yield of 75.0%, what is the actual yield, in grams, of Na_3N?

9.61 The equation for the reaction of nitrogen and oxygen to form nitrogen oxide is written as (9.1, 9.2, 9.3, 9.4)

$$N_2(g) + O_2(g) \longrightarrow 2NO(g) \qquad \Delta H = +90.2\ kJ$$

a. How many kilojoules are required to form 3.00 g of NO?
b. What is the complete equation (including heat) for the decomposition of NO?
c. How many kilojoules are released when 5.00 g of NO decomposes to N_2 and O_2?

9.62 The equation for the reaction of iron and oxygen gas to form rust (Fe_2O_3) is written as (9.1, 9.2, 9.5)

$$4Fe(s) + 3O_2(g) \longrightarrow 2Fe_2O_3(s) \quad \Delta H = -1.7 \times 10^3\ kJ$$

a. How many kilojoules are released when 2.00 g of Fe reacts?
b. How many grams of rust form when 150 kJ are released?

9.63 Each of the following is a reaction that occurs in the cells of the body. Identify which is exothermic and endothermic. (9.1, 9.2, 9.5)

a. Succinyl-CoA + H_2O $\longrightarrow$ succinate + CoA + 8.9 kcal
b. GDP + P_i + 34 kJ $\longrightarrow$ GTP + H_2O

9.64 Each of the following is a reaction that is needed by the cells of the body. Identify which is exothermic and endothermic. (9.1, 9.2, 9.5)

a. Phosphocreatine + H_2O $\longrightarrow$ creatine + P_i + 10.2 kcal
b. Fructose-6-phosphate + P_i + 16 kJ $\longrightarrow$ fructose-1,6-bisphosphate

CHALLENGE QUESTIONS

9.65 Chromium and oxygen combine to form chromium(III) oxide. (9.1, 9.2, 9.3, 9.4)

$$4Cr(s) + 3O_2(g) \longrightarrow 2Cr_2O_3(s)$$

a. How many moles of O_2 react with 4.50 mol of Cr?
b. How many grams of Cr_2O_3 are produced when 24.8 g of Cr reacts?
c. When 26.0 g of Cr reacts with 8.00 g of O_2, how many grams of Cr_2O_3 can form?
d. If 74.0 g of Cr and 62.0 g of O_2 are mixed, and 87.3 g of Cr_2O_3 is actually obtained, what is the percent yield of Cr_2O_3 for the reaction?

9.66 Aluminum and chlorine combine to form aluminum chloride. (9.1, 9.2, 9.3, 9.4)

$$2Al(s) + 3Cl_2(g) \longrightarrow 2AlCl_3(s)$$

a. How many moles of Cl_2 are needed to react with 4.50 mol of Al?
b. How many grams of $AlCl_3$ are produced when 50.2 g of Al reacts?
c. When 13.5 g of Al reacts with 8.00 g of Cl_2, how many grams of $AlCl_3$ can form?
d. If 45.0 g of Al and 62.0 g of Cl_2 are mixed, and 66.5 g of $AlCl_3$ is actually obtained, what is the percent yield of $AlCl_3$ for the reaction?

9.67 The combustion of propyne, $CH_3—C≡CH$, releases heat when it burns according to the following equation: (9.1, 9.2, 9.3, 9.4)

$$C_3H_4(g) + 4O_2(g) \xrightarrow{\Delta} 3CO_2(g) + 2H_2O(g)$$

a. How many moles of O_2 are needed to react completely with 0.225 mol of C_3H_4?
b. How many grams of water are produced from the complete reaction of 64.0 g of O_2?
c. How many grams of CO_2 are produced from the complete reaction of 78.0 g of C_3H_4?
d. If the reaction in part **c** produces 186 g of CO_2, what is the percent yield of CO_2 for the reaction?

9.68 The gaseous hydrocarbon butane, C_4H_{10}, burns according to the following equation: (9.1, 9.2, 9.3, 9.4)

$$2C_4H_{10}(g) + 13O_2(g) \xrightarrow{\Delta} 8CO_2(g) + 10H_2O(g)$$

a. How many moles of H_2O are produced from the complete reaction of 2.50 mol of C_4H_{10}?
b. How many grams of O_2 are needed to react completely with 22.5 g of C_4H_{10}?
c. How many grams of CO_2 are produced from the complete reaction of 55.0 g of C_4H_{10}?
d. If the reaction in part **c** produces 145 g of CO_2, what is the percent yield of CO_2 for the reaction?

9.69 Sulfur trioxide decomposes to sulfur and oxygen. (9.1, 9.2, 9.5)

$$2SO_3(g) \longrightarrow 2S(s) + 3O_2(g) \quad \Delta H = +790 \text{ kJ}$$

a. Is the reaction endothermic or exothermic?
b. How many kilojoules are required when 1.5 mol of SO_3 reacts?
c. How many kilojoules are required when 150 g of O_2 is formed?

9.70 When hydrogen peroxide (H_2O_2) is used in rocket fuels, it produces water, oxygen, and heat. (9.1, 9.2, 9.5)

$$2H_2O_2(l) \longrightarrow 2H_2O(l) + O_2(g) \quad \Delta H = -196 \text{ kJ}$$

a. Is the reaction endothermic or exothermic?
b. How many kilojoules are released when 2.50 mol of H_2O_2 reacts?
c. How many kilojoules are released when 275 g of O_2 is produced?

ANSWERS

Answers to Study Checks

9.1 1.83 mol of Fe

9.2 0.945 mol of O_2

9.3 27.5 g of CO_2

9.4 10.4 g of C_7H_{16}

9.5 4.00 mol of CH_3OH from CO, 2.00 mol of CH_3OH from H_2; H_2 is the limiting reactant; 2.00 mol of CH_3OH can be produced.

9.6 12.8 g of SO_2

9.7 84.7%

9.8 a. endothermic **b.** 10.5 kJ

Answers to Selected Questions and Problems

9.1 a. 160.14 g of reactants = 160.14 g of products
b. 283.88 g of reactants = 283.88 g of products

9.3 a. $\frac{2 \text{ mol } SO_2}{1 \text{ mol } O_2}$ and $\frac{1 \text{ mol } O_2}{2 \text{ mol } SO_2}$

$\frac{2 \text{ mol } SO_2}{2 \text{ mol } SO_3}$ and $\frac{2 \text{ mol } SO_3}{2 \text{ mol } SO_2}$

$\frac{2 \text{ mol } SO_3}{1 \text{ mol } O_2}$ and $\frac{1 \text{ mol } O_2}{2 \text{ mol } SO_3}$

b. $\frac{4 \text{ mol P}}{5 \text{ mol } O_2}$ and $\frac{5 \text{ mol } O_2}{4 \text{ mol P}}$

$\frac{4 \text{ mol P}}{2 \text{ mol } P_2O_5}$ and $\frac{2 \text{ mol } P_2O_5}{4 \text{ mol P}}$

$\frac{5 \text{ mol } O_2}{2 \text{ mol } P_2O_5}$ and $\frac{2 \text{ mol } P_2O_5}{5 \text{ mol } O_2}$

9.5 a. $\cancel{\text{mol } SO_2} \times \frac{2 \text{ mol } SO_3}{2 \cancel{\text{mol } SO_2}} = \text{mol of } SO_3$

b. $\cancel{\text{mol P}} \times \frac{5 \text{ mol } O_2}{4 \cancel{\text{mol P}}} = \text{mol of } O_2$

9.7 a. 1.0 mol of O_2 **b.** 10. mol of H_2
c. 5.0 mol of H_2O

9.9 a. 1.25 mol of C **b.** 0.96 mol of CO
c. 1.0 mol of SO_2 **d.** 0.50 mol of CS_2

9.11 a. 77.5 g of Na_2O **b.** 6.26 g of O_2
c. 19.4 g of O_2

9.13 a. 19.2 g of O_2 **b.** 3.79 g of N_2
c. 54.0 g of H_2O

9.15 a. 3.66 g of H_2O **b.** 26.3 g of NO
c. 7.53 g of HNO_3

9.17 a. $2PbS(s) + 3O_2(g) \longrightarrow 2PbO(s) + 2SO_2(g)$
b. 6.00 g of O_2 **c.** 17.4 g of SO_2
d. 137 g of PbS

9.19 a. Eight taxis can be used to pick up passengers.
b. Seven taxis can be driven.

9.21 a. 5.0 mol of H_2 **b.** 4.0 mol of H_2
c. 3.0 mol of N_2

9.23 a. 25.1 g of $AlCl_3$ **b.** 13.5 g of H_2O
c. 26.7 g of SO_2

9.25 a. 31.2 g of SO_3 **b.** 34.6 g of Fe_3O_4
c. 35.0 g of CO_2

9.27 a. 71.0% **b.** 63.2%

9.29 70.9 g of Al_2O_3

9.31 60.5%

9.33 a. In exothermic reactions, the energy of the products is lower than that of the reactants.

9.35 a. exothermic **b.** endothermic
c. exothermic

9.37 a. Heat is released, exothermic, $\Delta H = -802$ kJ
b. Heat is absorbed, endothermic, $\Delta H = +65.3$ kJ
c. Heat is released, exothermic, $\Delta H = -850$ kJ

9.39 a. 579 kJ **b.** 89 kJ

9.41 a. $2NO + O_2 \longrightarrow 2NO_2$
b. NO is the limiting reactant.

9.43 a. $N_2 + 3H_2 \longrightarrow 2NH_3$ **b.** A

9.45 a. $2NI_3 \longrightarrow N_2 + 3I_2$ **b.** 67%

9.47 a. 1.33 mol of NH_3 and 3.33 mol of F_2
b. 142 g of F_2
c. 10.4 g of N_2F_4

9.49 a. 3.00 mol of H_2O_2 **b.** 77.6 g of H_2O_2
c. 6.46 g of H_2O

9.51 16.8 g of NaCl

9.53 a. 0.667 mol of C_5H_{12} **b.** 27.5 g of CO_2
c. 92.8 g of CO_2

9.55 a. 74.4 g of CO_2 **b.** 86.0%

9.57 75.9%

9.59 a. 60.8 g of NH_3 **b.** 37.7 g of NH_3

9.61 a. 4.51 kJ
b. $2NO(g) \longrightarrow N_2(g) + O_2(g) + 90.2$ kJ
c. 7.51 kJ

9.63 a. exothermic **b.** endothermic

9.65 a. 3.38 mol of oxygen
b. 36.2 g of chromium(III) oxide
c. 25.3 g of chromium(III) oxide
d. 80.8 %

9.67 a. 0.900 mol of oxygen **b.** 18.0 g of water
c. 257 g of carbon dioxide **d.** 72.4%

9.69 a. endothermic **b.** 590 kJ
c. 1200 kJ

10 Properties of Solids and Liquids

LOOKING AHEAD

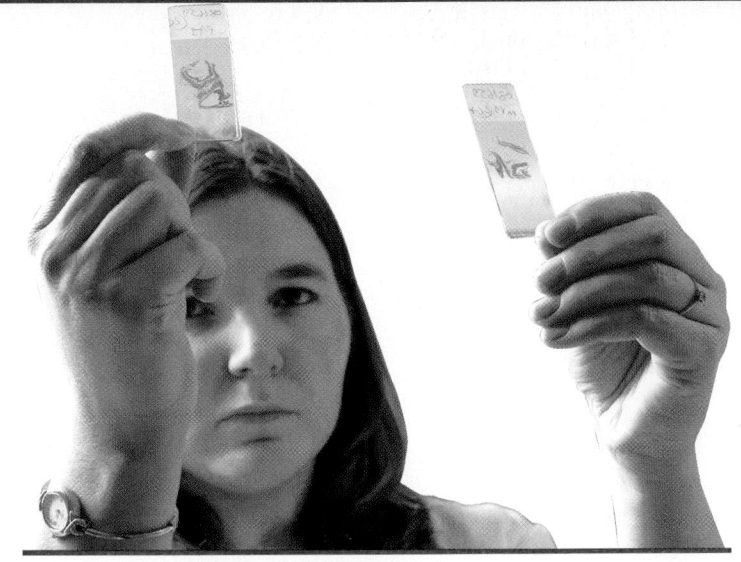

Bill has been diagnosed with basal cell carcinoma, the most common form of skin cancer. He has an appointment to undergo Mohs surgery, a specialized procedure to remove the cancerous growth found on his shoulder. The surgeon begins the process by removing the abnormal growth, in addition to a thin layer of surrounding (margin) tissue, which he sends to Lisa, a histologist. Lisa prepares the tissue sample to be viewed by a pathologist. Tissue preparation requires Lisa to cut the tissue into a very thin section (normally about 0.001 cm), which is then mounted onto a microscope slide.

Lisa then treats the tissue with a dye to stain the cells, as this enables the pathologist to view any abnormal cells more easily. The pathologist examines the tissue sample and reports back to the surgeon that no abnormal cells were present in the margin tissue and that Bill's tumor has been completely removed. No further tissue removal is necessary.

DNA, or deoxyribonucleic acid, contains all of a person's genetic information such as skin and eye color. This information is copied every time a cell divides. However, changes can occur in the DNA sequence during cell division, resulting in a mutation, which can lead to cancer.

Career: Histologist

Histologists study the microscopic make-up of tissues, cells, and bodily fluids in order to detect and identify the presence of a specific disease. They determine blood types and the concentrations of drugs and other substances in the blood. Histologists also help establish a rationale as to why a patient may not be responding to his or her treatment. Sample preparation is a critical component of a histologist's job, as they prepare tissue samples from humans, animals, and plants. The tissue samples are cut into extremely thin sections, which are then mounted and stained using various chemical dyes. The dyes provide contrast for the cells to be viewed and help highlight any abnormalities that may exist. Utilization of various dyes requires the histologist to be familiar with solution preparation and the handling of potentially hazardous chemicals.

Now we can investigate more complex chemical bonds and how they contribute to the structure of a molecule or a polyatomic ion. Once we have this basis of understanding, we can look at the differences in properties and reactivity of compounds.

Electron-dot formulas can be used to diagram the sharing of valence electrons in molecules and polyatomic ions. The presence of multiple bonds can be identified, and possible resonance structures can be drawn. From the electron-dot formulas, we can predict the three-dimensional shapes and polarities of molecules. Then we examine how the different attractive forces between the particles of ions and molecules influence their physical properties, such as melting and boiling point. Finally, we discuss the physical states of solids, liquids, and gases and describe the energy involved in changes of state.

CHAPTER READINESS*

Core Chemistry Skills

- Using Significant Figures in Calculations (2.4)
- Using Conversion Factors (2.7)
- Classifying Matter (3.1)
- Identifying Physical and Chemical Changes (3.2)
- Using Energy Units (3.4)
- Using the Heat Equation (3.5)
- Drawing Electron-Dot Symbols (5.6)

*These Key Math Skills and Core Chemistry Skills from previous chapters are listed here for your review as you proceed to the new material in this chapter.

10.1 Electron-Dot Formulas

LEARNING GOAL

Draw the electron-dot formulas for molecular compounds or polyatomic ions with multiple bonds and show resonance structures.

Electron-dot formulas for molecular compounds or polyatomic ions use the electron-dot symbols as shown in Table 10.1. For elements with one to four valence electrons, the dots are placed one at a time on the sides, top, and bottom of the atomic symbol. For elements with more than four valence electrons, each added dot is paired with one of the first four dots.

TABLE 10.1 Valence Electrons of Some Representative Elements and Their Electron-Dot Symbols

	Group Number							
	1A (1)	2A (1)	3A (13)	4A (14)	5A (15)	6A (16)	7A (17)	8A (18)
Number of Valence Electrons	1	2	3	4	5	6	7	8*
Electron-Dot Symbol	H·							He:
	Li·	Be·	·B·	·C·	·N·	·O:	·F:	:Ne:
	Na·	Mg·	·Al·	·Si·	·P·	·S:	·Cl:	:Ar:
	K·	Ca·	·Ga·	·Ge·	·As·	·Se:	·Br:	:Kr:

* Helium (He) is stable with 2 valence electrons.

CORE CHEMISTRY SKILL

Drawing Electron-Dot Formulas

Drawing Electron-Dot Formulas

When we draw an electron-dot formula for a molecule or polyatomic ion, we show the sequence of atoms, the bonding pairs of electrons shared between atoms, and the nonbonding or *lone pairs* of electrons. From the formula, we identify the central atom, which is the element that has the fewer atoms. Then, the central atom is bonded to the other atoms, as shown in Concept Check 10.1.

CONCEPT CHECK 10.1 Lone Pairs and Bonding Pairs

State the number of valence electrons, bonding pairs, and nonbonding (lone) electron pairs in each of the following electron-dot formulas:

a. H:Ö: with H above O (electron-dot formula of H_2O) **b.** :Br:Ö: with :Br: above O (electron-dot formula of Br_2O)

ANSWER

a. The atom of O is the central atom because there are fewer atoms of O than of H. The H atoms are then placed around the O atom. There are eight valence electrons: each H has one valence electron, and the O atom has six valence electrons. There are two bonding pairs: one between each H atom and the central O atom. The O atom has two lone pairs.

b. The atom of O is the central atom because there are fewer atoms of O than of Br. The Br atoms are then placed around the O atom. There are 20 valence electrons: each Br has seven valence electrons, and the O atom has six valence electrons. There are two bonding pairs: one between each Br atom and the central O atom. The O atom has two lone pairs; each Br atom has three lone pairs.

SAMPLE PROBLEM 10.1 Drawing Electron-Dot Formulas

Draw the electron-dot formula for PCl_3, phosphorus trichloride, used commercially to prepare insecticides and flame retardants.

SOLUTION

Guide to Drawing Electron-Dot Formulas

1. Determine the arrangement of atoms.
2. Determine the total number of valence electrons.
3. Attach each bonded atom to the central atom with a pair of electrons.
4. Place the remaining electrons using single or multiple bonds to complete the octets.

Step 1 **Determine the arrangement of atoms.** In PCl_3, the central atom is P because there is only one P atom.

Cl P Cl
  Cl

Step 2 **Determine the total number of valence electrons.** We use the group number to determine the number of valence electrons for each of the atoms in the molecule.

Element	Group	Atoms	Valence Electrons	=	Total
P	5A (15)	1 P	$\times 5\,e^-$	=	$5\,e^-$
Cl	7A (17)	3 Cl	$\times 7\,e^-$	=	$21\,e^-$
	Total valence electrons for PCl_3			=	$26\,e^-$

Step 3 **Attach each bonded atom to the central atom with a pair of electrons.** Each bonding pair can also be represented by a bond line.

Cl:P:Cl with :Cl below P or Cl—P—Cl with Cl bonded below P

Step 4 **Place the remaining electrons using single or multiple bonds to complete the octets.** Six electrons $(3 \times 2\,e^-)$ are used to bond the central P atom to three Cl atoms. Twenty valence electrons are left.

$$26 \text{ valence } e^- - 6 \text{ bonding } e^- = 20\,e^- \text{ remaining}$$

The ball-and-stick model of PCl_3 consists of P and Cl atoms connected by single bonds.

We use the remaining 20 electrons as lone pairs, which are placed around the outer Cl atoms and on the P atom, such that all the atoms have octets.

$$:\ddot{\underset{..}{Cl}}:\ddot{\underset{..}{P}}:\ddot{\underset{..}{Cl}}: \quad \text{or} \quad :\ddot{\underset{..}{Cl}}-\ddot{P}-\ddot{\underset{..}{Cl}}:$$
$$:\underset{..}{Cl}: \qquad\qquad\qquad :\underset{..}{Cl}:$$

STUDY CHECK 10.1

Draw the electron-dot formula for Cl_2O.

SAMPLE PROBLEM 10.2 Drawing Electron-Dot Formulas for Polyatomic Ions

Sodium chlorite, $NaClO_2$, is an ionic compound that contains the chlorite ion ClO_2^-. It is used to bleach textiles, pulp, and paper. Draw the electron-dot formula for the chlorite ion.

SOLUTION

Step 1 **Determine the arrangement of atoms.** For the polyatomic ion ClO_2^-, the central atom is Cl because there is only one Cl atom. For a polyatomic ion, the atoms and electrons are placed in brackets, and the charge is written outside to the upper right.

$$[\text{O Cl O}]^-$$

Step 2 **Determine the total number of valence electrons.** We use the group numbers to determine the number of valence electrons for each of the atoms in the ion. Because the ion has a negative charge, one more electron is added to the valence electrons.

Element	Group	Atoms	Valence Electrons	=	Total
O	6A (16)	2 O	$\times 6\ e^-$	=	$12\ e^-$
Cl	7A (17)	1 Cl	$\times 7\ e^-$	=	$7\ e^-$
Ionic charge (negative) add			$1\ e^-$	=	$1\ e^-$
	Total valence electrons for ClO_2^-			=	$20\ e^-$

Step 3 **Attach each bonded atom to the central atom with a pair of electrons.** Each bonding pair can also be represented by a line, which indicates a single bond.

$$[\text{O:Cl:O}]^- \quad \text{or} \quad [\text{O—Cl—O}]^-$$

Step 4 **Place the remaining electrons using single or multiple bonds to complete the octets.** Four electrons are used to bond the O atoms to the central Cl atom, which leaves 16 valence electrons. Of these, 12 electrons are drawn as lone pairs to complete the octets of the O atoms.

$$\left[:\ddot{\underset{..}{O}}:Cl:\ddot{\underset{..}{O}}:\right]^- \quad \text{or} \quad \left[:\ddot{\underset{..}{O}}-Cl-\ddot{\underset{..}{O}}:\right]^-$$

The remaining four electrons are placed as two lone pairs on the central Cl atom.

$$\left[:\ddot{\underset{..}{O}}:\ddot{\underset{..}{Cl}}:\ddot{\underset{..}{O}}:\right]^- \quad \text{or} \quad \left[:\ddot{\underset{..}{O}}-\ddot{\underset{..}{Cl}}-\ddot{\underset{..}{O}}:\right]^-$$

In ClO_2^-, the central Cl atom is bonded to two O atoms.

When we check the electron-dot formula, we see that all 20 available valence electrons—two bonding pairs and eight lone pairs—have been used to draw complete octets for all the atoms.

STUDY CHECK 10.2

Draw the electron-dot formula for the polyatomic ion, amide or amino ion, NH_2^-.

Multiple Covalent Bonds and Resonance

Up to now, we have looked at covalent bonding in molecules or polyatomic ions that have only single bonds. However, in some molecular compounds, atoms share two or three pairs of electrons to complete their octets. A **double bond** occurs when two pairs of electrons are shared; in a **triple bond**, three pairs of electrons are shared. Atoms of carbon, oxygen, nitrogen, and sulfur are most likely to form multiple bonds. Atoms of hydrogen and the halogens do not form double or triple bonds.

Double and triple bonds form when there are not enough valence electrons to complete the octets for some of the atoms in the molecule or polyatomic ion. Then one or more lone pairs from the atoms attached to the central atom are shared with the central atom.

For example, there are double bonds in CO_2 because two pairs of electrons are shared between the carbon atom and each oxygen atom to give octets. The process of drawing an electron-dot formula for CO_2 is shown in Sample Problem 10.3.

SAMPLE PROBLEM 10.3 Drawing Electron-Dot Formulas with Multiple Bonds

Draw the electron-dot formula for carbon dioxide, CO_2.

SOLUTION

Step 1 **Determine the arrangement of atoms.** The central atom is C because there is only one C atom.

O C O

Step 2 **Determine the total number of valence electrons.** Using the group numbers to determine valence electrons, the carbon atom has four valence electrons, while each oxygen atom has six valence electrons, which gives a total of 16 valence electrons for the molecule.

Element	Group	Atoms	Valence Electrons	=	Total
C	4A (14)	1 C	$\times 4\,e^-$	=	$4\,e^-$
O	6A (16)	2 O	$\times 6\,e^-$	=	$12\,e^-$
	Total valence electrons for CO_2			=	$16\,e^-$

Step 3 **Attach each bonded atom to the central atom with a pair of electrons.**

O:C:O or O—C—O

Step 4 **Place the remaining electrons using single or multiple bonds to complete the octets.** Because we used four valence electrons to attach the C atom to two O atoms, there are 12 valence electrons remaining.

16 valence $e^- - 4$ bonding $e^- = 12\,e^-$ remaining

The remaining 12 electrons are placed as six lone pairs of electrons on the O atoms. However, this does not complete the octet for the C atom.

:Ö:C:Ö: or :Ö—C—Ö:

To complete the octet for the C atom, it shares a lone pair of electrons from each of the O atoms. When two bonding pairs occur between atoms, it is a double bond.

Lone pairs converted to bonding pairs

$:\ddot{O}:C:\ddot{O}:$ or $:\ddot{O}-C-\ddot{O}:$

Double bonds — Double bonds — Molecule of carbon dioxide

$:\ddot{O}::C::\ddot{O}:$ or $:\ddot{O}=C=\ddot{O}:$

STUDY CHECK 10.3

Draw the electron-dot formula for H_2CCH_2 (atoms arranged as H C C H, with an H above each C).

CONCEPT CHECK 10.2 Multiple Bonds in Molecular Compounds

The covalent molecule N_2 contains a triple bond. Show how the N atoms achieve octets by forming a triple bond.

ANSWER

Because nitrogen is in Group 5A (15), each N atom has five valence electrons. One pair of electrons is used to bond the two N atoms; each N atom now has six electrons. Each N atom achieves an octet by sharing two more bonding pairs of electrons, which is called a triple bond.

Octets

$\cdot\ddot{N}:\ddot{N}\cdot \longrightarrow :N:::N: \quad :N\equiv N:$

Three shared pairs — Triple bond — Nitrogen molecule

Resonance Structures

CORE CHEMISTRY SKILL

Drawing Resonance Structures

When a molecule or polyatomic ion contains multiple bonds, it may be possible to draw more than one electron-dot formula. We can see how this happens when we draw the electron-dot formula for ozone, O_3, a component in the stratosphere that protects us from the ultraviolet rays of the Sun.

To draw the electron-dot formula for O_3, we need to determine the number of valence electrons for an O atom, and then the total number of valence electrons for O_3. Because O is in Group 6A (16), it has six valence electrons. Therefore, the compound O_3 would have a total of 18 valence electrons.

Element	Group	Atoms	Valence Electrons	=	Total
O	6A (16)	3 O	$\times 6\,e^-$	=	$18\,e^-$

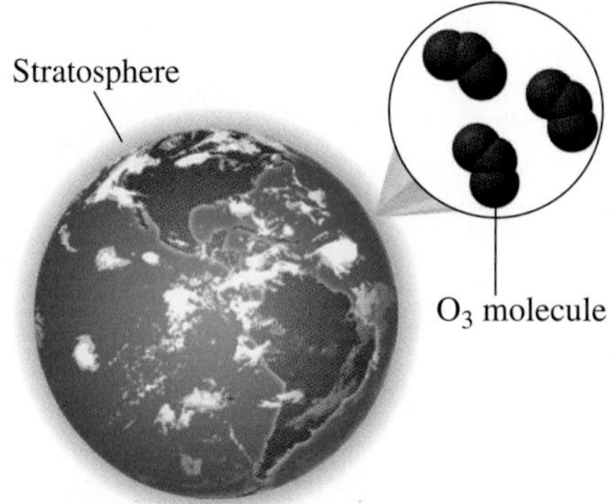

Ozone, O_3, is a component in the stratosphere that protects us from the ultraviolet rays of the Sun.

For the electron-dot formula for O_3, we place three O atoms in a row and identify the O atom in the middle as the central atom. Using four of the available valence electrons, we draw a bonding pair between the O atoms on the end and the central O atom. Two bonding pairs use four valence electrons.

O—O—O

The remaining valence electrons (14) are placed as lone pairs of electrons around the O atoms on both ends of the electron-dot formula, and one lone pair goes on the central O atom.

$$:\ddot{\underset{\cdot\cdot}{O}}-\ddot{O}-\ddot{\underset{\cdot\cdot}{O}}:$$

To complete an octet for the central O atom, one lone pair of electrons from an end O atom needs to be shared. But which lone pair should be used? One possibility is to form a double bond between the central O atom and the O on the left, and the other possibility is to form a double bond between the central O atom and the O on the right.

$$:\ddot{\underset{\cdot\cdot}{O}}-\ddot{O}-\ddot{\underset{\cdot\cdot}{O}}: \quad \text{or} \quad :\ddot{\underset{\cdot\cdot}{O}}-\ddot{O}-\ddot{\underset{\cdot\cdot}{O}}:$$

Thus it is possible to draw two or more electron-dot formulas for a molecule such as O_3 or for a polyatomic ion. When this happens, all the possible electron-dot formulas are called **resonance structures**, and their relationship is shown by drawing a double-headed arrow between them.

$$:\ddot{O}=\ddot{O}-\ddot{\underset{\cdot\cdot}{O}}: \longleftrightarrow :\ddot{\underset{\cdot\cdot}{O}}-\ddot{O}=\ddot{O}:$$

Resonance structures

Experiments show that the actual bond lengths in ozone are equivalent to a molecule with a "one-and-a-half" bond between the central O atom and each outside O atom. In an actual ozone molecule, the electrons are spread equally over all the O atoms. When we draw resonance structures of molecules or polyatomic ions, the true structure is really an average of those structures.

SAMPLE PROBLEM 10.4 Drawing Resonance Structures

Sulfur dioxide is produced by volcanic activity and the burning of sulfur-containing coal. Once in the atmosphere, the SO_2 is converted to SO_3, which combines with water forming sulfuric acid, H_2SO_4, a component of acid rain. Draw two resonance structures for sulfur dioxide.

SOLUTION

Step 1 **Determine the arrangement of atoms.** In SO_2, the S atom is the central atom because there is only one S atom.

O S O

Step 2 **Determine the total number of valence electrons.** We can use the group numbers to determine the number of valence electrons.

Element	Group	Atoms	Valence Electrons	=	Total
S	6A (16)	1 S	$\times 6\ e^-$	=	$6\ e^-$
O	6A (16)	2 O	$\times 6\ e^-$	=	$12\ e^-$
	Total valence electrons for SO_2			=	$18\ e^-$

Step 3 **Attach each bonded atom to the central atom with a pair of electrons.**

O—S—O

Step 4 **Place the remaining electrons using single or multiple bonds to complete the octets.** After four electrons are used to form single bonds between the S atom and the O atoms, the remaining 14 electrons are drawn as lone pairs, which complete the octets for the O atoms but not the S atom.

$$:\ddot{\underset{\cdot\cdot}{O}}-\ddot{S}-\ddot{\underset{\cdot\cdot}{O}}:$$

To complete the octet for S, one lone pair of electrons from one of the O atoms is shared to form a double bond. One possibility is to form a double bond between the central S atom and the O on the left, and the other possibility is to form a double bond between the central S atom and the O on the right.

$$:\ddot{O}=\ddot{S}-\ddot{O}: \longleftrightarrow :\ddot{O}-\ddot{S}=\ddot{O}:$$

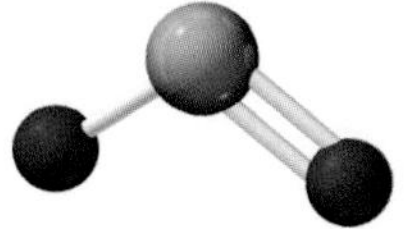

The ball-and-stick model of SO_2 consists of S (yellow) and O (red) atoms.

STUDY CHECK 10.4

Draw three resonance structures for SO_3.

CONCEPT CHECK 10.3 Resonance Structures

Explain why SO_2 has resonance structures but SCl_2 does not.

ANSWER

In the electron-dot formula of SCl_2, the sharing of the valence electrons of each chlorine atom completes the octet of the sulfur atom. However, in SO_2, the central sulfur atom must form a double bond with one of the oxygen atoms. Thus, when two or more electron-dot formulas can be drawn, the molecule has two or more resonance structures.

Table 10.2 summarizes this method of drawing electron-dot formulas for several molecules and ions.

Exceptions to the Octet Rule

While the octet rule is useful for bonding in many compounds, there are exceptions. We have already seen that a hydrogen (H_2) molecule requires just two electrons or a single bond. Usually the nonmetals form octets. However, in BCl_3, the B atom has only three valence electrons to share. Boron compounds typically have six valence electrons on the central B atoms and form just three bonds. While we will generally see compounds of P, S, Cl, Br, and I with octets, they can form molecules in which they share more of their valence electrons. This expands their valence electrons to 10, 12, or even 14 electrons.

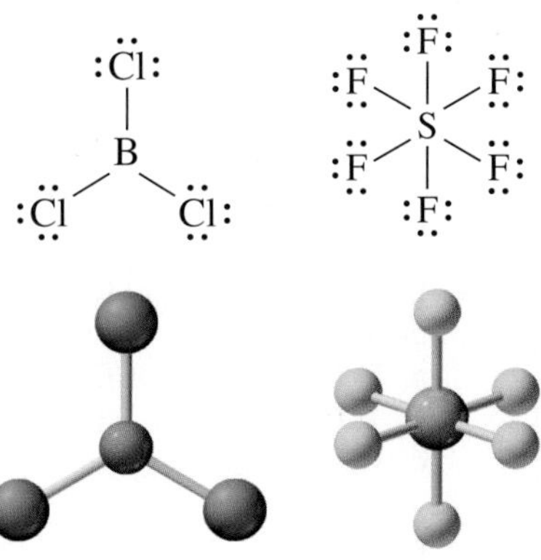

In BCl_3, the central B atom is bonded to three Cl atoms.

In SF_6, the central S atom is bonded to six F atoms.

TABLE 10.2 Using Valence Electrons to Draw Electron-Dot Formulas

Molecule or Polyatomic Ion	Total Valence Electrons	Form Single Bonds to Attach Atoms (electrons used)	Electrons Remaining	Completed Octets (or H:)
Cl_2	$2(7) = 14$	Cl—Cl ($2e^-$)	$14 - 2 = 12$	:C̤̈l—C̤̈l:
HCl	$1 + 7 = 8$	H—Cl ($2e^-$)	$8 - 2 = 6$	H—C̤̈l:
H_2O	$2(1) + 6 = 8$	H—O—H ($4e^-$)	$8 - 4 = 4$	H—Ö̤—H
PCl_3	$5 + 3(7) = 26$	Cl—P(—Cl)—Cl ($6e^-$)	$26 - 6 = 20$	:C̤̈l—P̤(—C̤̈l:)—C̤̈l:
ClO_3^-	$7 + 3(6) + 1 = 26$	[O—Cl(—O)—O]$^-$ ($6e^-$)	$26 - 6 = 20$	[:Ö̤—C̤l(—Ö̤:)—Ö̤:]$^-$
NO_2^-	$5 + 2(6) + 1 = 18$	[O—N—O]$^-$ ($4e^-$)	$18 - 4 = 14$	[:Ö̤—N̈=Ö:]$^-$ ↕ [:Ö=N̈—Ö̤:]$^-$

For example, we have seen that the P atom in PCl_3 has an octet, but in PCl_5, the P atom has five bonds with 10 valence electrons. In H_2S, the S atom has an octet, but in SF_6, there are six bonds to sulfur with 12 valence electrons.

QUESTIONS AND PROBLEMS

10.1 Electron-Dot Formulas

LEARNING GOAL: *Draw the electron-dot formulas for molecular compounds or polyatomic ions with multiple bonds and show resonance structures.*

10.1 Determine the total number of valence electrons for each of the following:
a. H_2S **b.** I_2 **c.** CCl_4 **d.** OH^-

10.2 Determine the total number of valence electrons for each of the following:
a. SBr_2 **b.** NBr_3 **c.** CH_3OH **d.** NH_4^+

10.3 Draw the electron-dot formula for each of the following molecules or ions:
a. HF **b.** SF_2 **c.** NBr_3 **d.** BH_4^-

```
                              H
e. CH3OH (methyl alcohol)   H C O H
                              H

                          H H
f. N2H4 (hydrazine)     H N N H
```

10.4 Draw the electron-dot formula for each of the following molecules or ions:
a. H_2O **b.** CCl_4
c. H_3O^+ **d.** SiF_4
e. CF_2Cl_2

```
             H H
f. C2H6    H C C H
             H H
```

10.5 When is it necessary to draw a multiple bond in an electron-dot formula?

10.6 If the available number of valence electrons for a molecule or polyatomic ion does not complete all of the octets in an electron-dot formula, what should you do?

10.7 What is resonance?

10.8 When does a molecular compound have resonance?

10.9 Draw the electron-dot formula for each of the following molecules or ions:
a. CO
b. HCN
c. H_2CO (C is the central atom)

10.10 Draw the electron-dot formula for each of the following molecules or ions:
a. HCCH (ethyne)
b. CS_2
c. NO^+

10.11 Draw resonance structures for each of the following molecules or ions:
a. $ClNO_2$ (N is the central atom)
b. OCN^- (C is the central atom)

10.12 Draw resonance structures for each of the following molecules or ions:
a. HCO_2^- (C is the central atom)
b. N_2O (N N O)

LEARNING GOAL

Predict the three-dimensional structure of a molecule or polyatomic ion and classify it as polar or nonpolar.

10.2 Shapes of Molecules and Ions (VSEPR Theory)

The three-dimensional shape of a molecule or polyatomic ion is determined by drawing an electron-dot formula and identifying the number of electron groups (one or more electron pairs) around the central atom. We count lone pairs of electrons, single, double, or triple bonds as *one* electron group. In the **valence shell electron-pair repulsion (VSEPR) theory**, the electron groups are arranged as far apart as possible around a central atom to minimize the repulsion between their negative charges.

Once we have counted the number of electron groups surrounding the central atom, we can determine its specific shape from the number of atoms bonded to the central atom.

CORE CHEMISTRY SKILL

Predicting Shape

Central Atoms with Two Electron Groups

In the electron-dot formula of CO_2, there are two electron groups (two double bonds) attached to the central atom. According to VSEPR theory, minimal repulsion occurs when two electron groups are on opposite sides of the central C atom. This gives the CO_2 molecule a linear electron-group geometry and a **linear** shape with a bond angle of 180°.

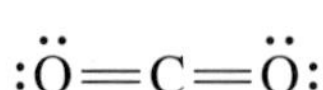

Linear electron-group geometry

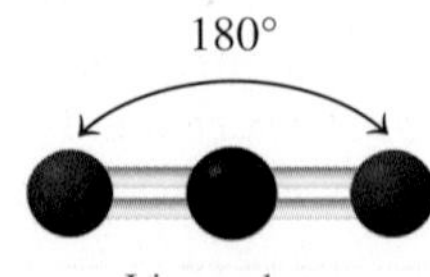

Linear shape

Central Atoms with Three Electron Groups

In the electron-dot formula of formaldehyde, H_2CO, the central atom C is attached to two H atoms by single bonds and to the O atom by a double bond. Minimal repulsion occurs when three electron groups are as far apart as possible around the central C atom, which gives 120° bond angles. This type of electron-group geometry is *trigonal planar* and gives a shape for H_2CO called **trigonal planar**.

Electron-dot formula

Trigonal planar electron-group geometry (120°)

Trigonal planar shape

In the electron-dot formula for SO_2, there are also three electron groups around the central S atom: a single bond to an O atom, a double bond to another O atom, and a lone pair of electrons. As in H_2CO, three electron groups have minimal repulsion when they form trigonal-planar electron-group geometry. However, in SO_2 one of the electron groups is a lone pair of electrons. Therefore, the shape of the SO_2 molecule is determined by the two O atoms bonded to the central S atom, which gives the SO_2 molecule a **bent** shape with a bond angle of 120°. When there are one or more lone pairs on the central atom, the shape has a different name than that of the electron-group geometry.

Electron-dot formula

Trigonal planar electron-group geometry

120°
Bent shape

Central Atoms with Four Electron Groups

In a molecule of methane, CH_4, the central C atom is bonded to four H atoms. From the electron-dot formula, you may think that CH_4 is planar with 90° bond angles. However, the best geometry for minimum repulsion is *tetrahedral*, which places the four electron groups at the corners of a tetrahedron, giving bond angles of 109°. When there are four atoms attached to four electron groups, the shape of the molecule or polyatomic ion is **tetrahedral**.

A way to represent the three-dimensional structure of methane is to use the wedge–dash notation. In this representation, the two bonds connecting carbon to hydrogen by solid lines are in the plane of the paper. The wedge represents a carbon-to-hydrogen bond coming out of the page toward us, whereas the dash represents a carbon-to-hydrogen bond going into the page away from us.

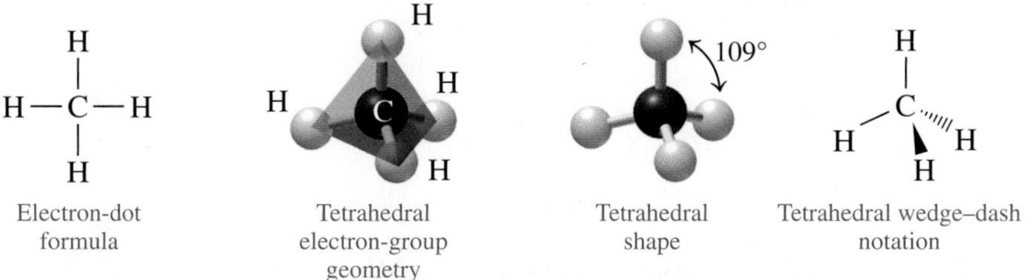

Electron-dot formula

Tetrahedral electron-group geometry

Tetrahedral shape

Tetrahedral wedge–dash notation

Now we can look at molecules that also have four electron groups, of which one or more are lone pairs of electrons. Then the central atom is attached to only two or three atoms. For example, in the electron-dot formula of ammonia, NH_3, four electron groups have a tetrahedral electron-group geometry. However, in NH_3 one of the electron groups is a lone pair of electrons. Therefore, the shape of NH_3 is determined by the three hydrogen atoms bonded to the central N atom. The shape of the NH_3 molecule is **trigonal pyramidal**, with a bond angle of 109°. The wedge–dash notation can also represent this three-dimensional structure of ammonia with one N—H bond in the plane, one N—H bond coming toward us, and one N—H bond going away from us.

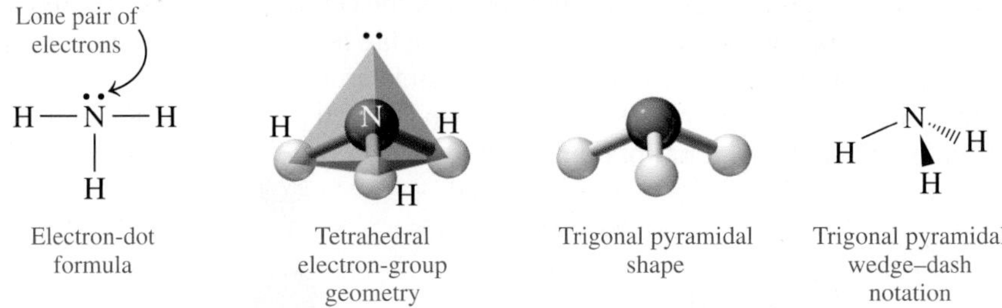

In the electron-dot formula of water, H_2O, there are also four electron groups, which have minimal repulsion when the electron-group geometry is tetrahedral. However, in H_2O, two of the electron groups are lone pairs of electrons. Because the shape of H_2O is determined by the two H atoms bonded to the central O atom, the H_2O molecule has a **bent** shape with a bond angle of 109°. Table 10.3 gives the molecular shapes for molecules with two, three, and four bonded atoms.

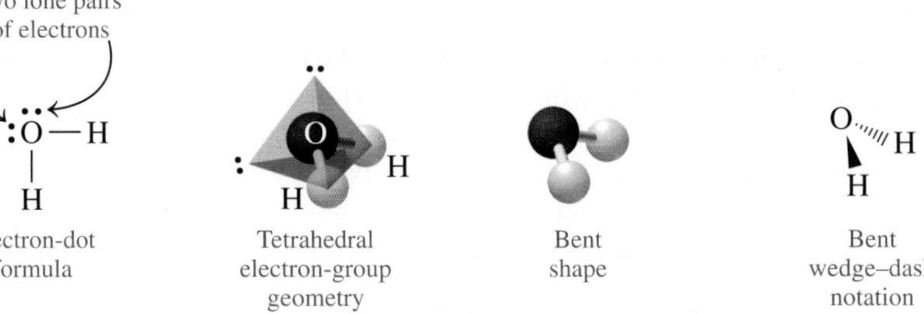

TABLE 10.3 Molecular Shapes for a Central Atom with Two, Three, and Four Bonded Atoms

Electron Groups	Electron-Group Geometry	Bonded Atoms	Lone Pairs	Bond Angle*	Shape	Example
2	Linear	2	0	180°	Linear	CO_2
3	Trigonal planar	3	0	120°	Trigonal planar	H_2CO
3	Trigonal planar	2	1	120°	Bent	SO_2
4	Tetrahedral	4	0	109°	Tetrahedral	CH_4
4	Tetrahedral	3	1	109°	Trigonal pyramidal	NH_3
4	Tetrahedral	2	2	109°	Bent	H_2O

*The bond angles in actual molecular compounds or polyatomic ions may vary slightly.

CONCEPT CHECK 10.4 Shapes of Molecules

If the four electron groups in a PH_3 molecule form a tetrahedron, why does a PH_3 molecule have a trigonal pyramidal shape?

ANSWER

Four electron groups achieve minimal repulsion when the electron-group geometry is tetrahedral. However, in PH_3, one of the electron groups is a lone pair of electrons. Because the shape of the PH_3 molecule is determined by the three H atoms bonded to the central P atom, the shape of PH_3 is trigonal pyramidal.

SAMPLE PROBLEM 10.5 Predicting Shapes

Use VSEPR theory to predict the shape of the following molecules or polyatomic ions:

a. H_2Se **b.** NO_3^-

SOLUTION

a. Step 1 **Draw the electron-dot formula.** In the electron-dot formula for H_2Se, there are four electron groups, including two lone pairs of electrons.

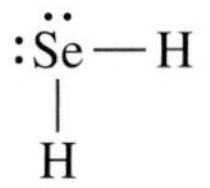

```
 ..
:Se—H
  |
  H
```

Step 2 **Arrange the electron groups around the central atom to minimize repulsion.** To minimize repulsion, the electron-group geometry would be tetrahedral.

Step 3 **Use the atoms bonded to the central atom to determine the shape.** Because the central atom Se is bonded to two H atoms, it has a *bent* shape with a bond angle of 109°.

b. Step 1 **Draw the electron-dot formula.** The polyatomic ion, NO_3^-, contains three electron groups (two single bonds between the central N atom and O atoms, and one double bond between N and O). Note that the double bond can be drawn to all of the O atoms in turn, which results in three possible resonance structures. However, we have represented just one of the structures here.

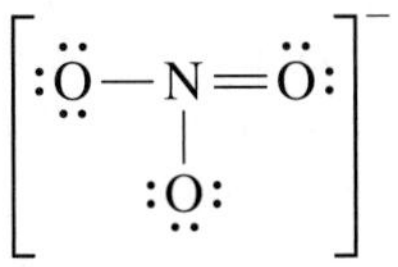

```
[ ..      .. ]-
[:O—N=O:]
[ ''  |      ]
[    :O:     ]
[     ''     ]
```

Step 2 **Arrange the electron groups around the central atom to minimize repulsion.** To minimize repulsion, three electron groups would have a trigonal planar geometry.

Step 3 **Use the atoms bonded to the central atom to determine the shape.** Because NO_3^- has three bonded atoms, it has a *trigonal planar* shape.

STUDY CHECK 10.5

Use VSEPR theory to predict the shape of ClO_2^-.

Guide to Predicting Molecular Shape (VSEPR Theory)

1. Draw the electron-dot formula.
2. Arrange the electron groups around the central atom to minimize repulsion.
3. Use the atoms bonded to the central atom to determine the shape.

QUESTIONS AND PROBLEMS

10.2 Shapes of Molecules and Ions (VSEPR Theory)

LEARNING GOAL: *Predict the three-dimensional structure of a molecule or polyatomic ion and classify it as polar or nonpolar.*

10.13 Choose the shape (**1–6**) that matches each of the following descriptions (**a–c**):

1. linear **2.** bent (109°) **3.** trigonal planar
4. bent (120°) **5.** trigonal pyramidal **6.** tetrahedral

a. a molecule with a central atom that has four electron groups and four bonded atoms
b. a molecule with a central atom that has four electron groups and three bonded atoms
c. a molecule with a central atom that has three electron groups and three bonded atoms

10.14 Choose the shape (**1–6**) that matches each of the following descriptions (**a–c**):

1. linear **2.** bent (109°) **3.** trigonal planar
4. bent (120°) **5.** trigonal pyramidal **6.** tetrahedral

a. a molecule with a central atom that has four electron groups and two bonded atoms
b. a molecule with a central atom that has two electron groups and two bonded atoms
c. a molecule with a central atom that has three electron groups and two bonded atoms

10.15 Complete each of the following statements for a molecule of SeO_3:

a. There are ______ electron groups around the central Se atom.
b. The electron-group geometry is ______.
c. The number of atoms attached to the central Se atom is ______.
d. The shape of the molecule is ______.

10.16 Complete each of the following statements for a molecule of H_2S:

a. There are ______ electron groups around the central S atom.
b. The electron-group geometry is ______.
c. The number of atoms attached to the central S atom is ______.
d. The shape of the molecule is ______.

10.17 Compare the electron-dot formulas of CF_4 and NF_3. Why do these molecules have different shapes?

10.18 Compare the electron-dot formulas of CH_4 and H_2O. Why do these molecules have similar bond angles but different names for their shapes?

10.19 Use VSEPR theory to predict the shape of each of the following:

a. GaH_3 **b.** OF_2 **c.** HCN **d.** CCl_4

10.20 Use VSEPR theory to predict the shape of each of the following:

a. CF_4 **b.** NCl_3 **c.** SCl_2 **d.** CS_2

10.21 Draw the electron-dot formula and predict the shape for each of the following:

a. CO_3^{2-} **b.** SO_4^{2-} **c.** NH_4^+ **d.** NO_2^+

10.22 Draw the electron-dot formula and predict the shape for each of the following:

a. NO_2^- **b.** PO_4^{3-} **c.** ClO_4^- **d.** SF_3^+

LEARNING GOAL

Use electronegativity to determine the polarity of a bond or a molecule.

10.3 Electronegativity and Polarity

We can learn more about the chemistry of compounds by looking at how electrons are shared between atoms. The bonding electrons are shared equally in a bond between identical nonmetal atoms. However, when a bond is between atoms of different elements, the electron pairs are usually shared unequally. Then the shared pairs of electrons are attracted to one atom in the bond more than the other.

CORE CHEMISTRY SKILL

Using Electronegativity

Electronegativity

The **electronegativity** of an atom is its ability to attract the shared electrons in a chemical bond. Nonmetals have higher electronegativities than do metals because nonmetals have a greater attraction for electrons than metals. On the electronegativity scale, fluorine was assigned a value of 4.0, and the electronegativities for all other elements were determined relative to the attraction of fluorine for shared electrons. The nonmetal fluorine, which has the highest electronegativity (4.0), is located in the upper right corner of the periodic table. The metal cesium, which has the lowest electronegativity (0.7), is located in the lower left corner of the periodic table. The electronegativity values for the representative elements are shown in Figure 10.1.

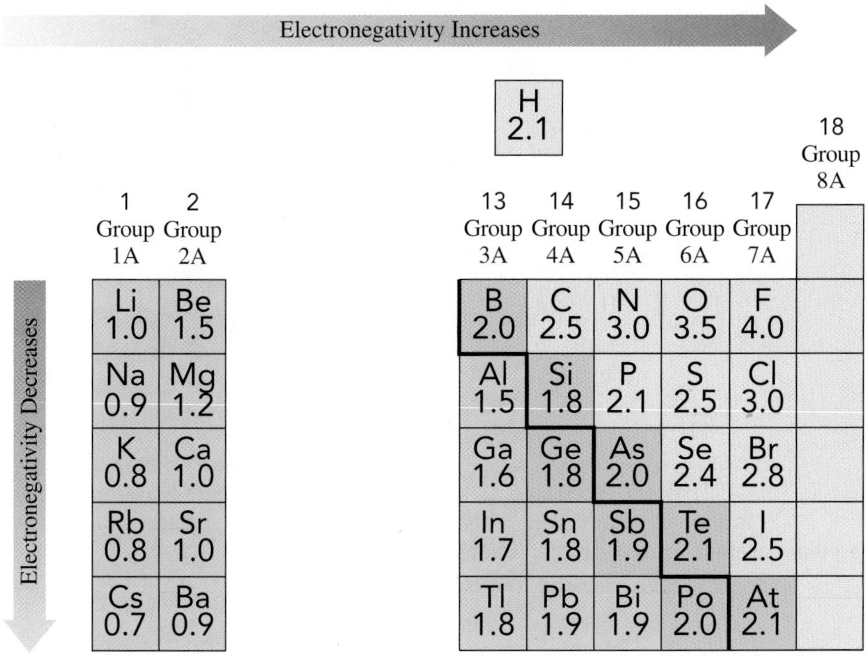

Electronegativity Increases →

Electronegativity Decreases ↓

1 Group 1A	2 Group 2A	13 Group 3A	14 Group 4A	15 Group 5A	16 Group 6A	17 Group 7A	18 Group 8A
						H 2.1	
Li 1.0	Be 1.5	B 2.0	C 2.5	N 3.0	O 3.5	F 4.0	
Na 0.9	Mg 1.2	Al 1.5	Si 1.8	P 2.1	S 2.5	Cl 3.0	
K 0.8	Ca 1.0	Ga 1.6	Ge 1.8	As 2.0	Se 2.4	Br 2.8	
Rb 0.8	Sr 1.0	In 1.7	Sn 1.8	Sb 1.9	Te 2.1	I 2.5	
Cs 0.7	Ba 0.9	Tl 1.8	Pb 1.9	Bi 1.9	Po 2.0	At 2.1	

FIGURE 10.1 The electronegativity values of the representative elements in Group 1A (1) to Group 7A (17), which indicate the ability of atoms to attract shared electrons, increase going across a period from left to right and decrease going down a group.

Q What element on the periodic table has the strongest attraction for shared electrons?

Going across each period from left to right, there is an increase in the positive charge of the nuclei, which causes a greater attraction for the electrons. This results in an increase in the electronegativity values going across each period from left to right.

Within each group, the attraction for electrons decreases going down the group as the size of the atoms increases. Thus the highest electronegativities are at the top and decrease going down within a group. The electronegativities for the transition elements are low, but we will not include them in our discussion. There are no electronegativities assigned to the noble gases because they do not typically form bonds.

CONCEPT CHECK 10.5 Electronegativity

Using the periodic table, predict the element with the higher electronegativity in each of the following pairs:

a. Mg and Cl **b.** N and As

ANSWER

a. Because electronegativity values increase going across a period from left to right, Cl would have a higher electronegativity than Mg.

b. Because electronegativity values decrease going down a group, N would have a higher electronegativity than As.

Types of Bonds

The difference in the electronegativity values of two atoms can be used to predict the type of chemical bond, ionic or covalent, that forms. For the H—H bond, the electronegativity difference is zero $(2.1 - 2.1 = 0.0)$, which means the bonding electrons are shared equally. Thus, we see a symmetrical electron cloud around the H atoms. A covalent bond between atoms with identical or very similar electronegativity values is a **nonpolar covalent bond**. However, in covalent bonds between atoms with different electronegativity values, the electrons are shared unequally; the bond is a **polar covalent bond**. The electron cloud for a polar covalent bond is unsymmetrical. For the H—Cl bond, there is an electronegativity difference of 0.9 $(3.0 - 2.1 = 0.9)$, which means that the H—Cl bond is polar covalent (see Figure 10.2). When finding the electronegativity difference, the smaller electronegativity is always subtracted from the larger; thus the difference is always a positive number.

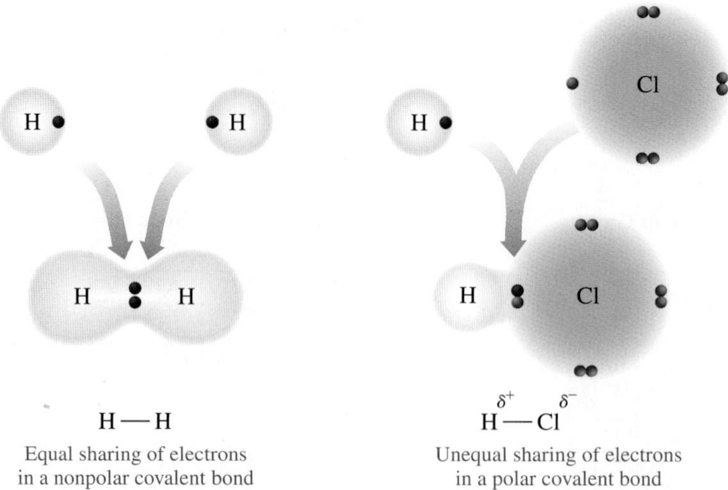

FIGURE 10.2 In the nonpolar covalent bond of H_2, electrons are shared equally. In the polar covalent bond of HCl, electrons are shared unequally.

Q H_2 has a nonpolar covalent bond, but HCl has a polar covalent bond. Explain.

Dipoles and Bond Polarity

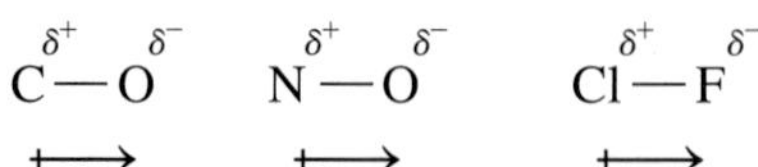

The **polarity** of a bond depends on the difference in the electronegativity values of its atoms. In a polar covalent bond, the shared electrons are attracted to the more electronegative atom, which makes it partially negative, due to the negatively charged electrons around that atom. At the other end of the bond, the atom with the lower electronegativity becomes partially positive due to a lack of electrons around that atom.

A bond becomes more *polar* as the electronegativity difference increases. A polar covalent bond that has a separation of charges is called a **dipole**. The positive and negative ends are indicated by the lowercase Greek letter delta with a positive or negative sign, δ^+ and δ^-. Sometimes we use an arrow that points from the positive charge to the negative charge $\mapsto$ to indicate the dipole.

Variations in Bonding

The variations in bonding are continuous; there is no definite point at which one type of bond stops and the next one starts. When the electronegativity difference is from 0.0 to 0.4, the electrons are considered to be shared equally in a *nonpolar covalent bond*. For example, the H—H bond with an electronegativity difference of 0.0 $(2.1 - 2.1 = 0.0)$ and the C—H bond with an electronegativity difference of 0.4 $(2.5 - 2.1 = 0.4)$ are classified as nonpolar covalent bonds.

As the electronegativity difference increases, the shared electrons are attracted more closely to the more electronegative atom, which increases the polarity of the bond. When the electronegativity difference is from 0.5 to 1.8, the bond is classified as a *polar covalent bond*. For example, the O—H bond with an electronegativity difference of 1.4 $(3.5 - 2.1 = 1.4)$ is a polar covalent bond.

When the difference in electronegativity is greater than 1.8, electrons are transferred from one atom to another, which results in an *ionic bond*. For example, the electronegativity difference for the ionic compound NaCl is 2.1 $(3.0 - 0.9 = 2.1)$. Thus, for large differences in electronegativity, we would predict an ionic bond (see Table 10.4). Table 10.5 gives examples of predicting bond type from the electronegativity difference.

TABLE 10.4 Electronegativity Difference and Types of Bonds

Electronegativity Difference	0	0.4	1.8	3.3
Bond Type	Covalent nonpolar	Covalent polar	Ionic	
Electron Bonding	Electrons shared equally	Electrons shared unequally	Electron transfer	
		δ^+ δ^-	+ −	

TABLE 10.5 Predicting Bond Type from Electronegativity Differences

Molecule	Bond	Type of Electron Sharing	Electronegativity Difference*	Type of Bond	Reason
H_2	H—H	Shared equally	2.1 − 2.1 = 0.0	Nonpolar covalent	Between 0.0 and 0.4
BrCl	Br—Cl	Shared about equally	3.0 − 2.8 = 0.2	Nonpolar covalent	Between 0.0 and 0.4
HBr	$\overset{\delta^+}{H}—\overset{\delta^-}{Br}$	Shared unequally	2.8 − 2.1 = 0.7	Polar covalent	Greater than 0.4, but less than 1.8
HCl	$\overset{\delta^+}{H}—\overset{\delta^-}{Cl}$	Shared unequally	3.0 − 2.1 = 0.9	Polar covalent	Greater than 0.4, but less than 1.8
NaCl	Na^+Cl^-	Electron transfer	3.0 − 0.9 = 2.1	Ionic	Greater than 1.8
MgO	$Mg^{2+}O^{2-}$	Electron transfer	3.5 − 1.2 = 2.3	Ionic	Greater than 1.8

*Values are taken from Figure 10.1.

CONCEPT CHECK 10.6 Using Electronegativity to Determine the Polarity of Bonds

Complete the following table for each of the bonds indicated:

Bond	Electronegativity Difference	Type of Bond	Reason
Si—S			
Cs—Cl			
Si—P			

ANSWER

Bond	Electronegativity Difference	Type of Bond	Reason
Si—S	2.5 − 1.8 = 0.7	Polar covalent	Greater than 0.4, but less than 1.8
Cs—Cl	3.0 − 0.7 = 2.3	Ionic	Greater than 1.8
Si—P	2.1 − 1.8 = 0.3	Nonpolar covalent	Between 0.0 and 0.4

SAMPLE PROBLEM 10.6 Bond Polarity

Using electronegativity values, classify each bond as nonpolar covalent, polar covalent, or ionic:

O—K, Cl—As, N—N, O—H

SOLUTION

For each bond, we obtain the electronegativity values and calculate the difference.

Bond	Electronegativity Difference	Type of Bond
O—K	3.5 − 0.8 = 2.7	Ionic
Cl—As	3.0 − 2.0 = 1.0	Polar covalent
N—N	3.0 − 3.0 = 0.0	Nonpolar covalent
O—H	3.5 − 2.1 = 1.4	Polar covalent

STUDY CHECK 10.6

Using electronegativity values, classify each bond as nonpolar covalent, polar covalent, or ionic:

a. P—Cl **b.** Br—Br **c.** Na—O

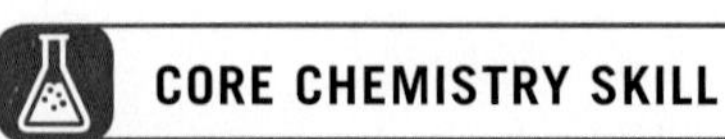

Identifying Polarity of Molecules

Polarity of Molecules

We have seen that covalent bonds in molecules can be polar or nonpolar. Now we will look at how the bonds in a molecule and its shape determine whether that molecule is classified as polar or nonpolar.

Nonpolar Molecules

In a **nonpolar molecule**, all the bonds are nonpolar or the polar bonds cancel each other out. Molecules such as H_2, Cl_2, and CH_4 are nonpolar because they contain only nonpolar covalent bonds.

H—H Cl—Cl H—C(—H)(—H)—H

Nonpolar molecules

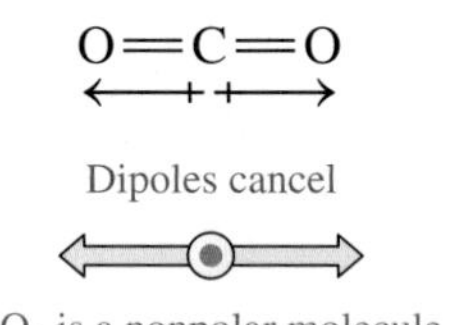

CO_2 is a nonpolar molecule.

A *nonpolar molecule* also occurs when polar bonds (dipoles) cancel each other because they are in a symmetrical arrangement. For example, CO_2, a linear molecule, contains two equal polar covalent bonds whose dipoles point in opposite directions. As a result, the dipoles cancel out, which makes a CO_2 molecule nonpolar.

Another example of a nonpolar molecule is the CCl_4 molecule, which has four polar bonds symmetrically arranged around the central C atom. Each of the C—Cl bonds has the same polarity, but because they have a tetrahedral arrangement, their opposing dipoles cancel out. As a result, a molecule of CCl_4 is nonpolar.

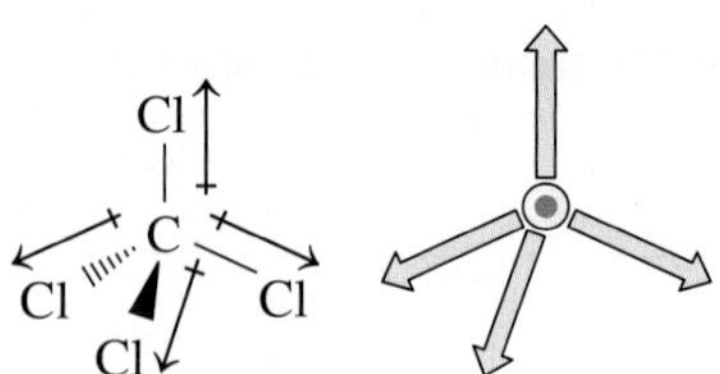

The four C—Cl dipoles cancel out.

H—Cl

A single dipole does not cancel.

Polar Molecules

In a **polar molecule**, one end of the molecule is more negatively charged than the other end. Polarity in a molecule occurs when the dipoles from the individual polar bonds do not cancel each other. For example, HCl is a polar molecule because it has one covalent bond that is polar.

In molecules with two or more electron groups, the shape, such as bent or trigonal pyramidal, determines whether or not the dipoles cancel. For example, we have seen that H_2O has a bent shape. Thus, a water molecule is polar because the individual dipoles do not cancel.

More negative end of molecule

More positive end of molecule

H_2O is a polar molecule because its dipoles do not cancel.

The NH_3 molecule has a tetrahedral electron geometry with three bonded atoms, which gives it a trigonal pyramidal shape. Thus, a NH_3 molecule is polar because the individual N—H dipoles do not cancel.

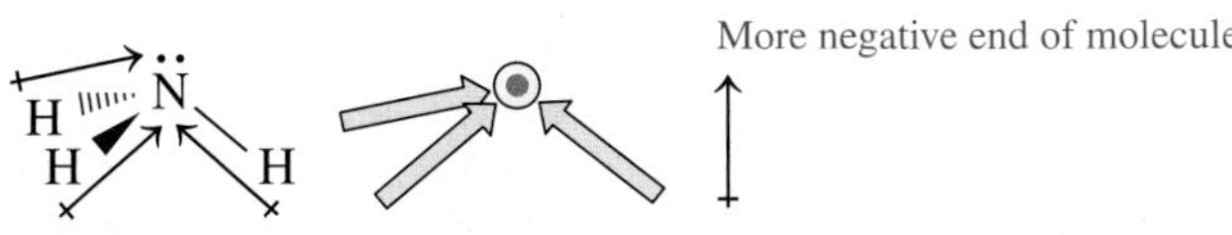

NH_3 is a polar molecule because its dipoles do not cancel.

In the molecule CH_3F, the C—F bond is polar covalent, but the three C—H bonds are nonpolar covalent. Because there is only one dipole in CH_3F, which does not cancel, CH_3F is a polar molecule.

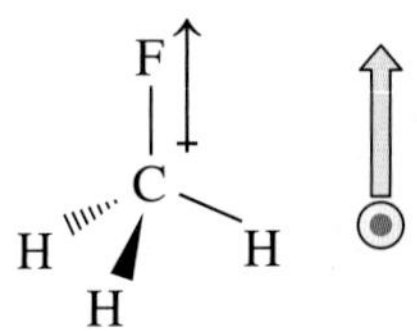

CH_3F is a polar molecule.

SAMPLE PROBLEM 10.7 Polarity of Molecules

Determine whether each of the following molecules is polar or nonpolar:

a. $SiCl_4$ **b.** OF_2

SOLUTION

a. Step 1 **Determine if the bonds are polar covalent or nonpolar covalent.** From Figure 10.1, Cl 3.0 and Si 1.8 give an electronegativity difference of 1.2, which makes the Si—Cl bonds polar covalent.

Step 2 **If the bonds are polar covalent, draw the electron-dot formula and determine if the dipoles cancel.** The electron-dot formula for $SiCl_4$ has four electron groups and four bonded atoms. The molecule has a tetrahedral shape. The dipoles of the Si—Cl bonds point away from each other and cancel out, which makes $SiCl_4$ a nonpolar molecule.

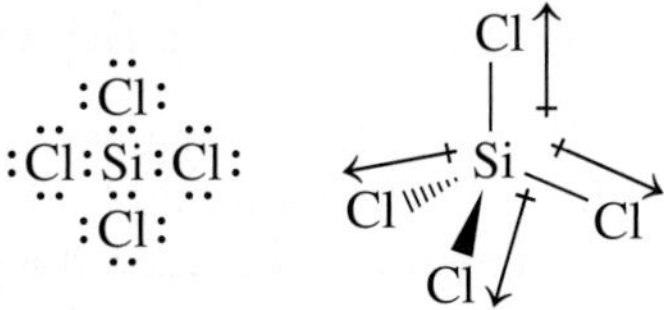

$SiCl_4$ is a nonpolar molecule.

b. Step 1 **Determine if the bonds are polar or nonpolar.** From Figure 10.1, F 4.0 and O 3.5 give an electronegativity difference of 0.5, which makes the O—F bonds polar covalent.

Step 2 **If the bonds are polar covalent, draw the electron-dot formula and determine if the dipoles cancel.** The electron-dot formula for OF_2 has four electron groups and two bonded atoms. The molecule has a bent shape in which the dipoles of the O—F bonds do not cancel. This makes one end of the molecule positive and the other end negative. The OF_2 molecule would be a polar molecule.

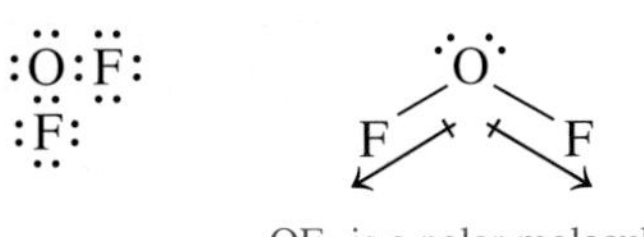

OF_2 is a polar molecule.

STUDY CHECK 10.7

Would PCl_3 be a polar or nonpolar molecule?

Guide to Determination of Polarity of a Molecule

1 Determine if the bonds are polar covalent or nonpolar covalent.

2 If the bonds are polar covalent, draw the electron-dot formula and determine if the dipoles cancel.

QUESTIONS AND PROBLEMS

10.3 Electronegativity and Polarity

LEARNING GOAL: *Use electronegativity to determine the polarity of a bond or a molecule.*

10.23 Describe the trend in electronegativity as *increases* or *decreases* for each of the following:
a. from B to F **b.** from Mg to Ba **c.** from F to I

10.24 Describe the trend in electronegativity as *increases* or *decreases* for each of the following:
a. from Al to Cl **b.** from Br to K **c.** from Li to Cs

10.25 What electronegativity difference (**a–c**) would you expect for a nonpolar covalent bond?
a. between 0.0 and 0.4
b. from 0.5 to 1.8
c. 1.9 or greater

10.26 What electronegativity difference (**a–c**) would you expect for a polar covalent bond?
a. between 0.0 and 0.4
b. from 0.5 to 1.8
c. 1.9 or greater

10.27 Using the periodic table, arrange the atoms in each of the following sets in order of increasing electronegativity:
a. Li, Na, K **b.** Na, Cl, P **c.** Se, Ca, O

10.28 Using the periodic table, arrange the atoms in each of the following sets in order of increasing electronegativity:
a. Cl, F, Br **b.** B, O, N **c.** Mg, F, S

10.29 For each of the following bonds, indicate the positive δ^+ end and the negative δ^- end. Draw an arrow to show the dipole for each.
a. N—F **b.** Si—Br **c.** C—O
d. P—Br **e.** N—P

10.30 For each of the following bonds, indicate the positive δ^+ end and the negative δ^- end. Draw an arrow to show the dipole for each.
a. P—Cl **b.** Se—F **c.** Br—F
d. N—H **e.** B—Cl

10.31 Predict whether each of the following bonds is nonpolar covalent, polar covalent, or ionic:
a. Si—Br **b.** Li—F **c.** Br—F
d. I—I **e.** N—P **f.** C—P

10.32 Predict whether each of the following bonds is nonpolar covalent, polar covalent, or ionic:
a. Si—O **b.** K—Cl **c.** S—F
d. P—Br **e.** Li—O **f.** N—S

10.33 Why is F_2 a nonpolar molecule, but HF is a polar molecule?

10.34 Why is CCl_4 a nonpolar molecule, but PCl_3 is a polar molecule?

10.35 Identify each of the following molecules as polar or nonpolar:
a. CS_2 **b.** NF_3
c. CHF_3 **d.** SO_3

10.36 Identify each of the following molecules as polar or nonpolar:
a. SeF_2 **b.** PBr_3
c. SiF_4 **d.** SO_2

10.37 The molecule CO_2 is nonpolar, but CO is a polar molecule. Explain.

10.38 The molecules CH_4 and CH_3Cl both have tetrahedral shapes. Why is CH_4 nonpolar whereas CH_3Cl is polar?

LEARNING GOAL

Describe the attractive forces between ions, polar covalent molecules, and nonpolar covalent molecules.

CORE CHEMISTRY SKILL

Identifying Attractive Forces

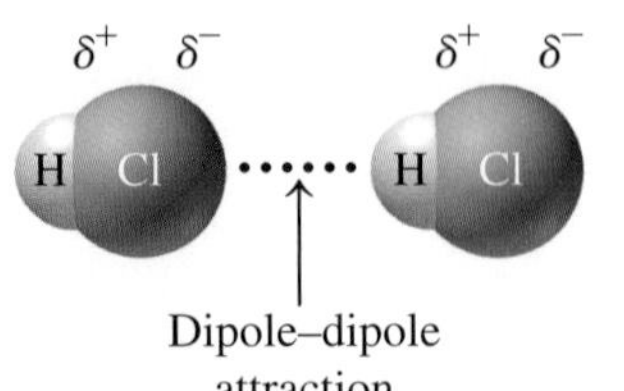

Dipole–dipole attraction

10.4 Attractive Forces in Compounds

Now we will look at the attractive forces that hold molecules and ions close together in liquids and solids. A solid melts and a liquid boils when the quantity of heat added is enough to disrupt the attractive forces between the particles. When the attractive forces in a substance are weak, it has relatively low melting and boiling points. When the attractive forces are strong, the substance has relatively high melting and boiling points. Such differences in properties are explained by looking at the various kinds of attractive forces between particles including *dipole–dipole attractions*, *hydrogen bonding*, and *dispersion forces*.

Dipole–Dipole Attractions

All polar molecules are attracted to each other by **dipole–dipole attractions**. Because polar molecules have dipoles, the positively charged end of the dipole in one molecule is attracted to the negatively charged end of the dipole in another molecule. For example, the polar molecules of HCl form an attraction between the partially positive H atom of one HCl molecule and the partially negative Cl atom in another HCl molecule.

Hydrogen Bonds

Polar molecules containing hydrogen atoms bonded to the highly electronegative atoms fluorine, oxygen, or nitrogen form especially strong dipole–dipole attractions. These attractions, called **hydrogen bonds**, occur between the partially positive hydrogen atom in one molecule and the partially negative nitrogen, oxygen, or fluorine atom in another. Hydrogen bonds are the strongest type of attractive forces between polar covalent molecules, but they are weaker than covalent or ionic bonds. They are a major factor in the formation and structure of biological molecules such as proteins and DNA.

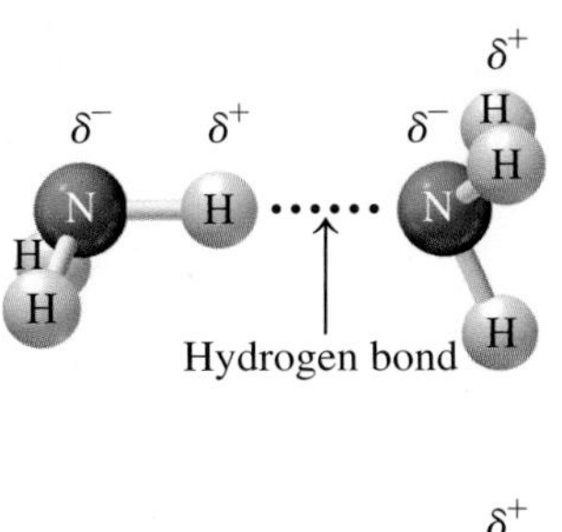

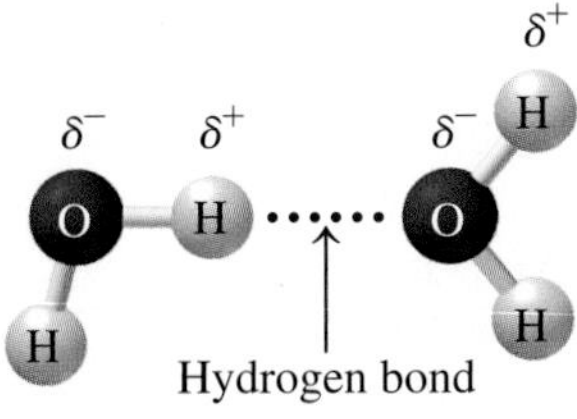

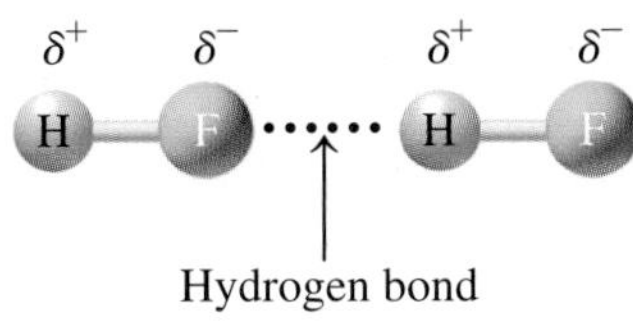

Dispersion Forces

Very weak attractive forces called **dispersion forces** are the only attractions that occur between nonpolar molecules. Usually, the electrons in a nonpolar covalent molecule are distributed symmetrically. However, the movement of the electrons may place more electrons on one end of the molecule than the other, forming a *temporary dipole*. These momentary dipoles in what is normally a nonpolar substance align the molecules so that the positive end of one molecule is attracted to the negative end of another molecule. Although dispersion forces are very weak, they make it possible for nonpolar molecules to form liquids and solids.

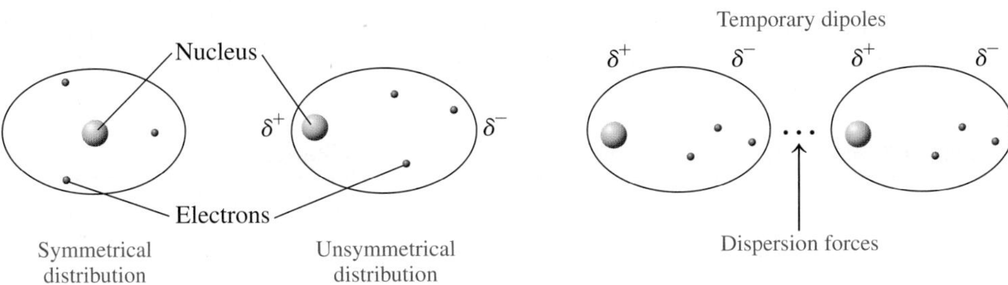

Nonpolar molecules have weak attractions when they form temporary dipoles.

The various types of attractions within ionic and molecular compounds and between the particles in solids and liquids are summarized in Table 10.6.

TABLE 10.6 Comparison of Bonding and Attractive Forces

Type of Force	Particle Arrangement	Example	Strength
Between Atoms or Ions		$Na^{+}Cl^{-}$	Strong
Ionic bond	+ − + / − + −		↑
Covalent bond (X = nonmetal)	X:X	Cl—Cl	
Between Molecules			
Hydrogen bond (X = F, O, or N)	$\overset{\delta^+}{H}\overset{\delta^-}{X}\cdots\overset{\delta^+}{H}\overset{\delta^-}{X}$	$\overset{\delta^+}{H}—\overset{\delta^-}{F}\cdots\overset{\delta^+}{H}—\overset{\delta^-}{F}$	
Dipole–dipole attractions (X and Y = nonmetals)	$\overset{\delta^+}{Y}\overset{\delta^-}{X}\cdots\overset{\delta^+}{Y}\overset{\delta^-}{X}$	$\overset{\delta^+}{H}—\overset{\delta^-}{Cl}\cdots\overset{\delta^+}{H}—\overset{\delta^-}{Cl}$	
Dispersion forces (temporary shift of electrons in nonpolar bonds)	$\overset{\delta^+}{X}\!:\!\overset{\delta^-}{X}\cdots\overset{\delta^+}{X}\!:\!\overset{\delta^-}{X}$ (temporary dipoles)	$\overset{\delta^+}{F}—\overset{\delta^-}{F}\cdots\overset{\delta^+}{F}—\overset{\delta^-}{F}$	Weak

CONCEPT CHECK 10.7 Attractive Forces Between Particles

Indicate the major type of molecular interaction—dipole–dipole attractions, hydrogen bonding, or dispersion forces—expected of each of the following:

a. HF **b.** F_2 **c.** PCl_3

ANSWER

a. An HF molecule interacts with other HF molecules by hydrogen bonding.
b. Because F_2 is nonpolar, the only molecular interactions are dispersion forces.
c. The polarity of the PCl_3 molecules provides dipole–dipole attractions.

Size, Mass, and Boiling Points

As the size and mass of similar types of molecular compounds increase, there are more electrons that produce stronger temporary dipoles. In general, larger nonpolar molecules with increased molar masses also have higher boiling points. As the molar mass of similar compounds increases, the dispersion forces also increase due to the increase in the number of electrons. We see this trend in the boiling points of the first four alkanes shown in Table 10.7.

TABLE 10.7 Mass and Boiling Points of the First Four Alkanes

Alkane	Formula		Molar Mass	Boiling Point (°C)
Methane	CH_4	CH_4	16.04 g/mol	−162
Ethane	C_2H_6	$CH_3{-}CH_3$	30.07 g/mol	−89
Propane	C_3H_8	$CH_3{-}CH_2{-}CH_3$	44.09 g/mol	−42
Butane	C_4H_{10}	$CH_3{-}CH_2{-}CH_2{-}CH_3$	58.12 g/mol	−1

CONCEPT CHECK 10.8 Boiling Points with Increasing Molar Masses

Which compound would have the higher boiling point: CH_4 or GeH_4?

ANSWER

The compound with the greater molar mass will have the higher boiling point. As molar mass increases, there are more electrons and stronger dispersion forces.

CH_4 16.04 g/mol GeH_4 76.67 g/mol

Therefore, GeH_4, which has the larger molar mass, would have the higher boiling point.

TABLE 10.8 Melting Points of Selected Substances

Substance	Melting Point (°C)
Ionic Bonds	
MgF_2	1248
NaCl	801
Hydrogen Bonds	
H_2O	0
NH_3	−78
Dipole–Dipole Attractions	
HI	−51
HBr	−89
HCl	−115
Dispersion Forces	
Br_2	−7
Cl_2	−101
F_2	−220
CH_4	−182

Attractive Forces and Melting Points

The melting point of a substance is related to the strength of the attractive forces between its particles. A compound with weak attractive forces such as dispersion forces has a low melting point because only a small amount of energy is needed to separate the molecules of the solid and form a liquid. A compound with dipole–dipole attractions requires more energy to break the attractive forces that hold particles together. A compound that can form hydrogen bonds requires even more energy to overcome the attractive forces that exist between its molecules. The highest melting points are seen with ionic compounds that have very strong attractions between positive and negative ions. Large amounts of energy are needed to overcome the strong attractive forces between positive and negative ions and to melt an ionic solid. For example, the ionic solid NaCl melts at 801 °C. Table 10.8 compares the melting points of some substances that have various kinds of attractive forces.

Chemistry Link to Health

ATTRACTIVE FORCES IN BIOLOGICAL COMPOUNDS

The proteins in our bodies are biological molecules that have many different functions. They are needed for structural components such as cartilage, muscles, hair, and nails, and for the formation of enzymes that regulate biological reactions. Other proteins, such as hemoglobin and myoglobin, transport oxygen in the blood and muscle.

Proteins are composed of building blocks called *amino acids*. Every amino acid has a central carbon atom bonded to $-NH_3^+$ from an amine, a $-COO^-$ from a carboxylic acid, an H atom, and a side chain called an R group, which is unique for each amino acid. For example, the R group for the amino acid alanine is a methyl group ($-CH_3$).

Methyl group

Carboxylate group

Amino group

Alanine, an amino acid

(a)

(b)

(a) The ionized form of alanine contains $-NH_3^+$, $-COO^-$, H, and a $-CH_3$ group. **(b)** The structure of alanine represented as a ball-and-stick model.

Several of the amino acids have side chains that contain functional groups such as: hydroxyl $-OH$, amide $-CONH_2$, amine $-NH_2$, which is ionized as ammonium $-NH_3^+$, and carboxyl $-COOH$, which is ionized as carboxylate $-COO^-$.

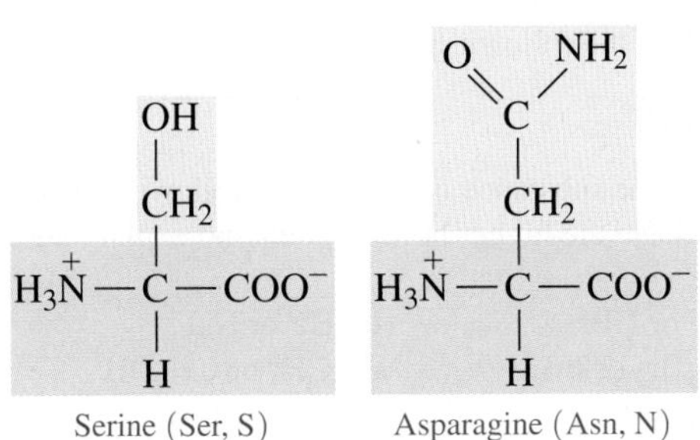

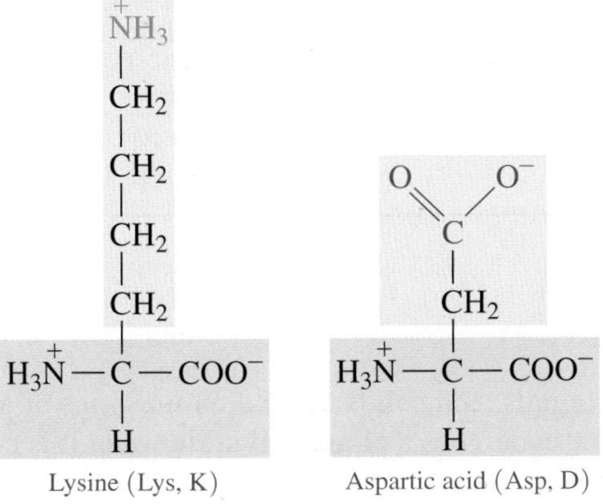

In the primary structure of proteins, amino acids are linked together by peptide bonds, which are amide bonds that form between the $-COO^-$ group of one amino acid and the $-NH_3^+$ group of the next amino acid. When there are more than 50 amino acids in a chain, it is called a protein. Every protein in our bodies has a unique sequence of amino acids in a primary structure that determines its biological function. In addition, proteins have higher levels of structure. In an *alpha helix*, hydrogen bonds form between the hydrogen atom of the N—H groups and the oxygen atom of a C=O group in the next turn. Because many hydrogen bonds form, the backbone of a protein takes a helical shape similar to a corkscrew or a spiral staircase.

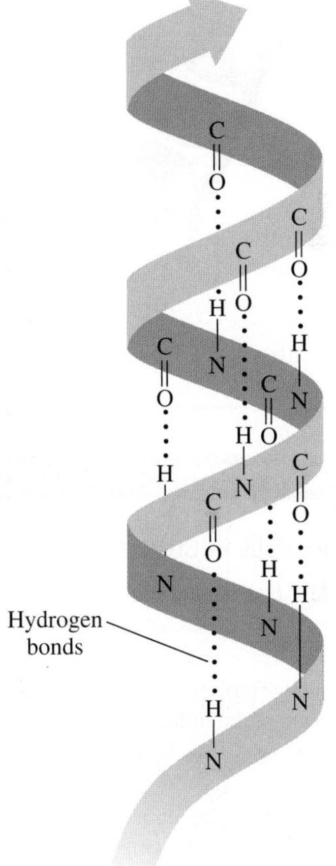

The shape of an alpha helix is stabilized by hydrogen bonds.

Shapes of Biologically Active Proteins

Many proteins have compact, spherical shapes because sections of the chain fold over on top of other sections of the chain. This shape is stabilized by attractive forces between functional groups of side chains (R groups), causing the protein to twist and bend into a specific three-dimensional shape.

Hydrogen bonds form between the side chains within the protein. For example, a hydrogen bond can occur between the $-OH$ groups on two serines or between the $-OH$ of a serine and the $-NH_2$

of asparagine. Hydrogen bonding also occurs between the polar side chains of the amino acids on the outer surface of the protein and —OH or —H of polar water molecules in the external aqueous environment.

Ionic bonds can form between the positively and negatively charged R groups of acidic and basic amino acids. For example, an ionic bond can form between the $—NH_3^+$ in the R group of lysine and the $—COO^-$ of aspartic acid.

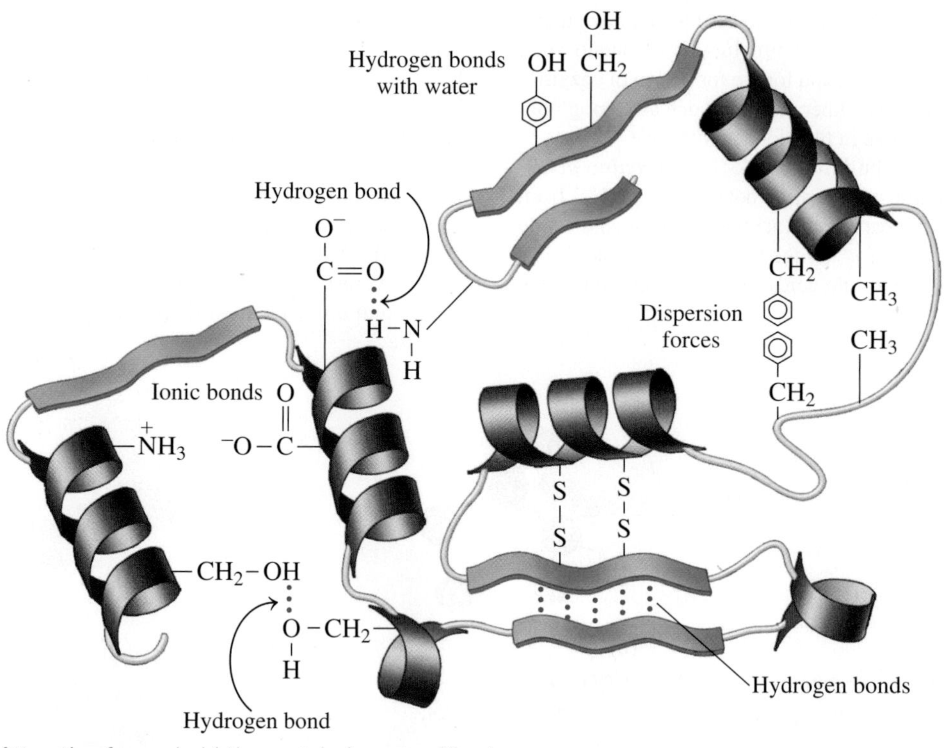

Attractive forces hold the protein in a specific shape.

QUESTIONS AND PROBLEMS

10.4 Attractive Forces in Compounds

LEARNING GOAL: *Describe the attractive forces between ions, polar covalent molecules, and nonpolar covalent molecules.*

10.39 Identify the major type of attractive force between the particles of each of the following:
a. BrF **b.** KCl
c. NF_3 **d.** Cl_2

10.40 Identify the major type of attractive force between the particles of each of the following:
a. HCl **b.** MgF_2
c. PBr_3 **d.** NH_3

10.41 Identify the strongest attractive forces between the particles of each of the following:
a. CH_3OH **b.** CO
c. CF_4 **d.** $CH_3—CH_3$

10.42 Identify the strongest attractive forces between the particles of each of the following:
a. O_2 **b.** SiH_4
c. CH_3Cl **d.** H_2O_2

10.43 Identify the substance in each of the following pairs that would have the higher boiling point and explain your choice:
a. HF or HBr **b.** HF or NaF
c. $MgBr_2$ or PBr_3 **d.** CH_4 or CH_3OH

10.44 Identify the substance in each of the following pairs that would have the higher boiling point and explain your choice:
a. NaCl or HCl **b.** H_2O or H_2Se
c. NH_3 or PH_3 **d.** F_2 or HF

LEARNING GOAL

Describe the changes of state between solids, liquids, and gases; calculate the energy involved.

10.5 Changes of State

The states and properties of gases, liquids, and solids depend on the types of attractive forces between their particles. Matter undergoes a **change of state** when it is converted from one state to another state (see Figure 10.3).

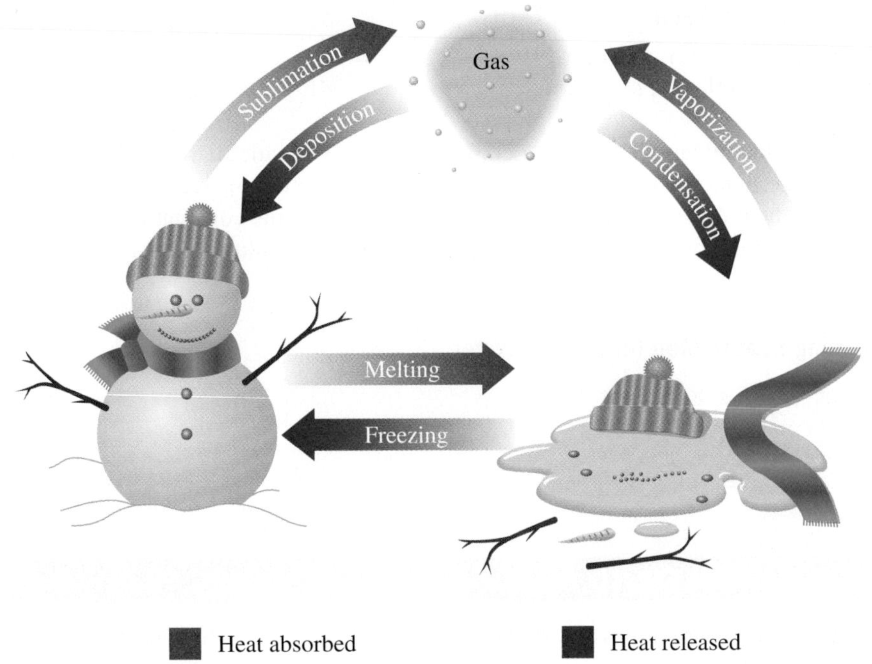

FIGURE 10.3 Changes of state include melting and freezing, boiling and condensation, sublimation and deposition.

Q Is heat added or released when liquid water freezes?

Melting and Freezing

When heat is added to a solid, the particles move faster. At a temperature called the **melting point (mp)**, enough energy is absorbed to overcome the attractive forces such as ionic or dipole–dipole forces that hold the particles together in the solid; the rigid solid structure changes to a random association of particles in the liquid. The substance is **melting**, changing from a solid to a liquid. During a change of state, the temperature of a substance remains constant.

If the temperature of a liquid is lowered, the reverse process takes place. Heat is removed from the liquid, which causes its particles to move slower. Eventually, the attractive forces between the particles are sufficient to form a solid. The substance is in the process of **freezing**, changing from a liquid to a solid at the **freezing point (fp)**, which is the same temperature as the melting point.

Every substance has its own freezing (melting) point: Solid water (ice) melts at 0 °C when heat is added, and freezes at 0 °C when heat is removed. Gold melts at 1064 °C when heat is added, and freezes at 1064 °C when heat is removed.

During a change of state, the temperature of a substance remains constant. Suppose we have a glass containing ice and water. The ice melts when heat is added at 0 °C, forming more liquid. When heat is removed at 0 °C, the liquid water freezes, forming more solid. The process of melting requires heat; it is endothermic. The process of freezing releases heat; it is exothermic. Melting and freezing are reversible at 0 °C.

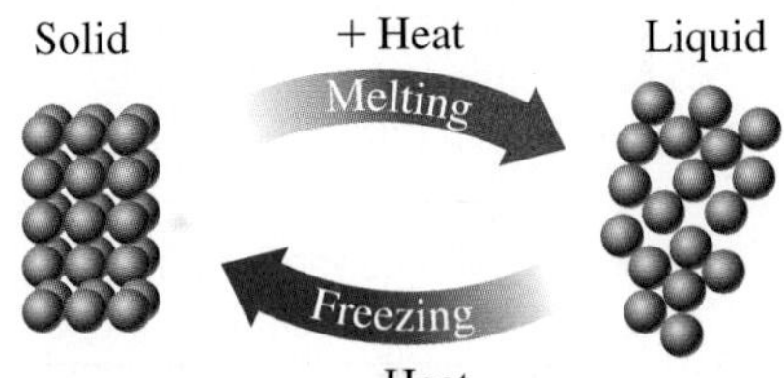

Melting and freezing are reversible processes.

Heat of Fusion

During melting, the **heat of fusion** is the energy that must be added to convert exactly 1 g of solid to liquid at the melting point. For example, 334 J of heat is needed to melt exactly 1 g of ice at its melting point (0 °C).

$$H_2O(s) + 334\ \text{J/g} \longrightarrow H_2O(l) \quad \text{Endothermic}$$

The heat of fusion (334 J/g) is also the quantity of heat that must be removed to freeze 1 g of water at its freezing point (0 °C).

$$H_2O(l) \longrightarrow H_2O(s) + 334\ \text{J/g} \quad \text{Exothermic}$$

Water is sometimes sprayed in fruit orchards during subfreezing weather. If the air temperature drops to 0 °C, the water begins to freeze. Because heat is released as the water molecules form solid ice, the air warms above 0 °C and protects the fruit.

Heat of Fusion for Water

$$\frac{334\ \text{J}}{1\ \text{g}\ H_2O} \quad \text{and} \quad \frac{1\ \text{g}\ H_2O}{334\ \text{J}}$$

The heat of fusion can be used as a conversion factor in calculations. For example, to determine the heat needed to melt a sample of ice, the mass of ice, in grams, is multiplied by the heat of fusion. Because the temperature remains constant as long as the ice is melting, there is no temperature change given in the calculation, as shown in Sample Problem 10.8.

CORE CHEMISTRY SKILL

Calculating Heat for Change of State

Calculating Heat to Melt (or Freeze) Water

Heat = mass × heat of fusion

$$\text{J} = \cancel{\text{g}} \times \frac{334\ \text{J}}{\cancel{\text{g}}}$$

Guide to Calculations Using Heat of Fusion

1. State the given and needed quantities.
2. Write a plan to convert the given quantity to the needed quantity.
3. Write the heat of fusion factor and any metric factor needed.
4. Set up the problem and calculate the needed quantity.

SAMPLE PROBLEM 10.8 Heat of Fusion

Ice cubes at 0 °C with a mass of 26.0 g are added to your soft drink (heat of fusion for water = 334 J/g).

a. How much heat (joules) will be absorbed to melt all the ice?
b. What happens to the temperature of your soft drink? Why?

SOLUTION

a. The heat in joules required to melt the ice is calculated as follows:

Step 1 **State the given and needed quantities.**

Analyze the Problem	Given	Need
	26.0 g of ice at 0 °C, heat of fusion = 334 J/g	joules to melt ice at 0 °C

Step 2 **Write a plan to convert the given quantity to the needed quantity.**

grams of ice → Heat of fusion → joules

Step 3 **Write the heat of fusion factor and any metric factor needed.**

$$1\ \text{g of}\ H_2O\ (s \rightarrow l) = 334\ \text{J}$$

$$\frac{334\ \text{J}}{1\ \text{g}\ H_2O} \quad \text{and} \quad \frac{1\ \text{g}\ H_2O}{334\ \text{J}}$$

Step 4 **Set up the problem and calculate the needed quantity.**

$$\underset{\text{Three SFs}}{26.0\ \cancel{\text{g}\ H_2O}} \times \underset{\text{Exact}}{\overset{\text{Three SFs}}{\frac{334\ \text{J}}{1\ \cancel{\text{g}\ H_2O}}}} = \underset{\text{Three SFs}}{8680\ \text{J}}$$

b. The temperature of the soft drink will decrease as heat is removed from the soft drink to melt the ice.

STUDY CHECK 10.8

In a freezer, 125 g of water at 0 °C is placed in an ice cube tray. How much heat, in kilojoules, must be removed to form ice cubes at 0 °C?

Evaporation, Boiling, and Condensation

Water in a mud puddle disappears, unwrapped food dries out, and clothes hung on a clothesline dry. **Evaporation** is taking place as molecules of liquid water with sufficient energy escape from the liquid surface and enter the gas phase (see Figure 10.4a). The loss of the "hot" molecules removes heat, which cools the remaining liquid water. At higher temperatures, more and more water molecules gain sufficient energy to evaporate. At the **boiling point (bp)**, all the molecules within a liquid have enough energy to overcome their attractive forces and become a gas. We observe the **boiling** of a liquid such as water as gas bubbles form throughout the liquid, rise to the surface, and escape (see Figure 10.4b).

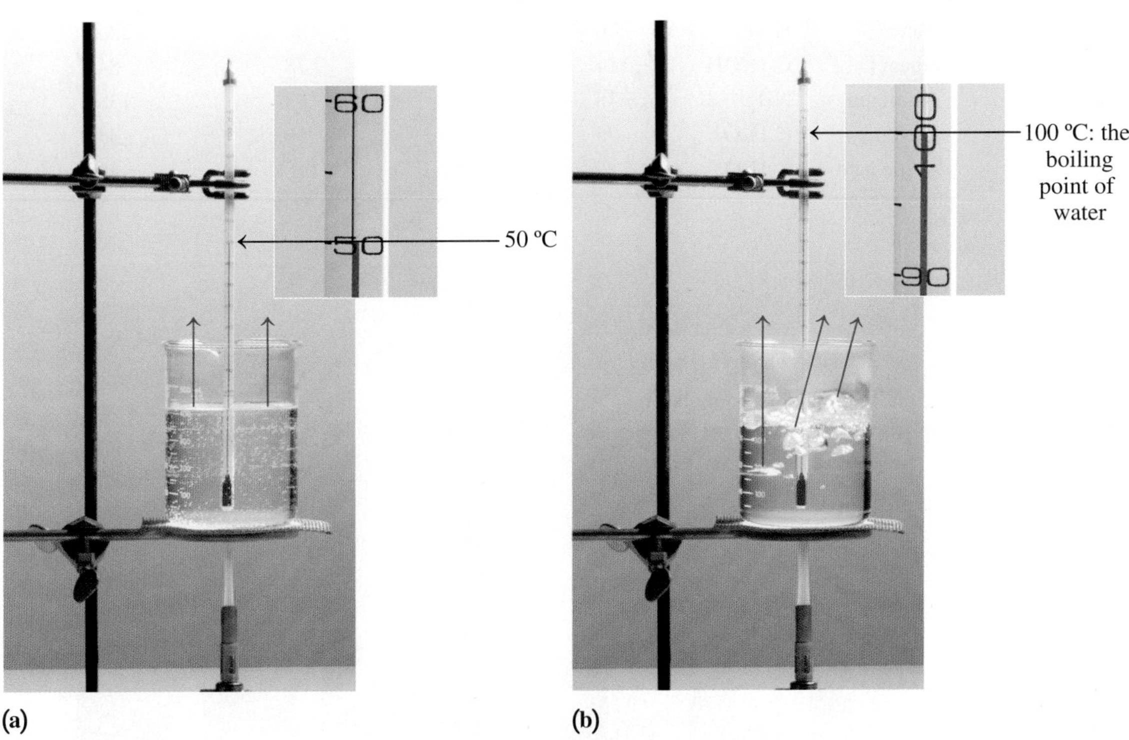

FIGURE 10.4 **(a)** Evaporation occurs at the surface of a liquid. **(b)** Boiling occurs as bubbles of gas form throughout the liquid.

Q Why does water evaporate faster at 80 °C than at 20 °C?

When heat is removed from a gas, a reverse process takes place. In **condensation**, water vapor is converted back to liquid as the water molecules lose kinetic energy and slow down. Condensation occurs at the same temperature as boiling but differs because heat is removed. You may have noticed that condensation occurs when you take a hot shower and the water vapor forms water droplets on a mirror. Because a substance loses heat as it condenses, its surroundings become warmer. That is why, when a rainstorm is approaching, we may notice a warming of the air as gaseous water molecules condense to rain.

Liquid + Heat Gas

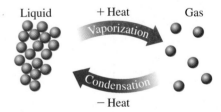

Vaporization

Condensation

− Heat

Vaporization and condensation are reversible processes.

Heat of Vaporization

The **heat of vaporization** is the energy that must be added to convert exactly 1 g of liquid to gas at its boiling point. For water, 2260 J is needed to convert 1 g of water to vapor at 100 °C.

$$H_2O(l) + 2260\ J/g \longrightarrow H_2O(g) \quad \text{Endothermic}$$

This is also the amount of heat released when 1 g of water vapor (gas) changes to liquid at 100 °C. Therefore, 2260 J/g is also the *heat of condensation* of water.

$$H_2O(g) \longrightarrow H_2O(l) + 2260\ J/g \quad \text{Exothermic}$$

Just as substances have different melting and boiling points, they also have different heats of fusion and vaporization (see Table 10.9). As seen in Figure 10.5, the heats of vaporization are larger than the heats of fusion.

TABLE 10.9 Heats of Fusion and Heats of Vaporization for Selected Substances

Liquid	Formula	Melting Point (°C)	Heat of Fusion (J/g)	Boiling Point (°C)	Heat of Vaporization (J/g)
Water	H_2O	0	334	100	2260
Ethanol	C_2H_5OH	−114	109	78	841
Ammonia	NH_3	−78	351	−33	1380
Acetone	C_3H_6O	−95	99.3	56	335
Acetic acid	$C_2H_4O_2$	17	192	118	390

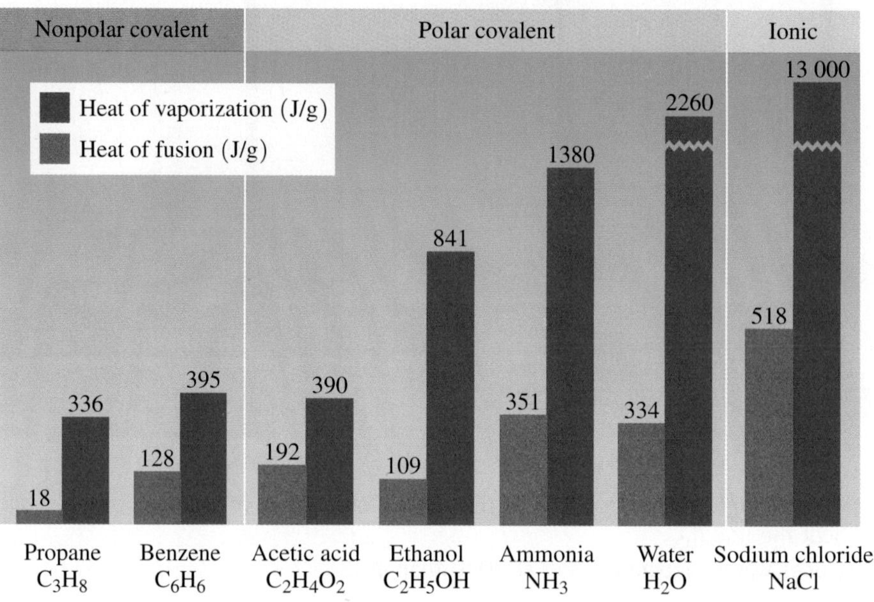

FIGURE 10.5 For any substance, the heat of vaporization is greater than the heat of fusion.

Q Why does the formation of a gas require more energy than the formation of a liquid of the same compound?

The heat of vaporization can be used as a conversion factor in calculations.

Heat of Vaporization for Water

$$\frac{2260\ J}{1\ g\ H_2O} \quad \text{and} \quad \frac{1\ g\ H_2O}{2260\ J}$$

To determine the heat needed to boil a sample of water, the mass, in grams, is multiplied by the heat of vaporization. Because the temperature remains constant as long as the water is boiling, there is no temperature change given in the calculation, as shown in Sample Problem 10.9.

Calculating Heat to Vaporize (or Condense) Water

$$\text{Heat} = \text{mass} \times \text{heat of vaporization}$$

$$J = \cancel{g} \times \frac{2260\ J}{\cancel{g}}$$

SAMPLE PROBLEM 10.9 Using Heat of Vaporization

In a sauna, 122 g of water is converted to steam at 100 °C. How many kilojoules of heat are needed?

SOLUTION

Step 1 **State the given and needed quantities.**

Analyze the Problem	Given	Need
	122 g of $H_2O(l)$ at 100 °C, heat of vaporization = 2260 J/g	kilojoules to convert to $H_2O(g)$ at 100 °C

Step 2 **Write a plan to convert the given quantity to the needed quantity.**

grams of water → (Heat of vaporization) → joules → (Metric factor) → kilojoules

Step 3 **Write the heat of vaporization factor and any metric factor needed.**

$$1 \text{ g of } H_2O\ (l \rightarrow g) = 2260 \text{ J}$$
$$\frac{2260 \text{ J}}{1 \text{ g } H_2O} \text{ and } \frac{1 \text{ g } H_2O}{2260 \text{ J}}$$

$$1 \text{ kJ} = 1000 \text{ J}$$
$$\frac{1000 \text{ J}}{1 \text{ kJ}} \text{ and } \frac{1 \text{ kJ}}{1000 \text{ J}}$$

Step 4 **Set up the problem and calculate the needed quantity.**

$$122 \text{ g } H_2O \times \frac{2260 \text{ J}}{1 \text{ g } H_2O} \times \frac{1 \text{ kJ}}{1000 \text{ J}} = 276 \text{ kJ}$$

3 SFs, Exact, Exact → 3 SFs

STUDY CHECK 10.9

When steam from a pan of boiling water reaches a cool window, it condenses. How much heat, in kilojoules, is released when 25.0 g of steam condenses at 100 °C?

Guide to Calculations Using Heat of Vaporization

1. State the given and needed quantities.
2. Write a plan to convert the given quantity to the needed quantity.
3. Write the heat of vaporization factor and any metric factor needed.
4. Set up the problem and calculate the needed quantity.

Heating and Cooling Curves

All the changes of state during the heating of a solid can be illustrated visually. On a **heating curve**, the temperature is shown on the vertical axis, and the addition of heat is shown on the horizontal axis (see Figure 10.6).

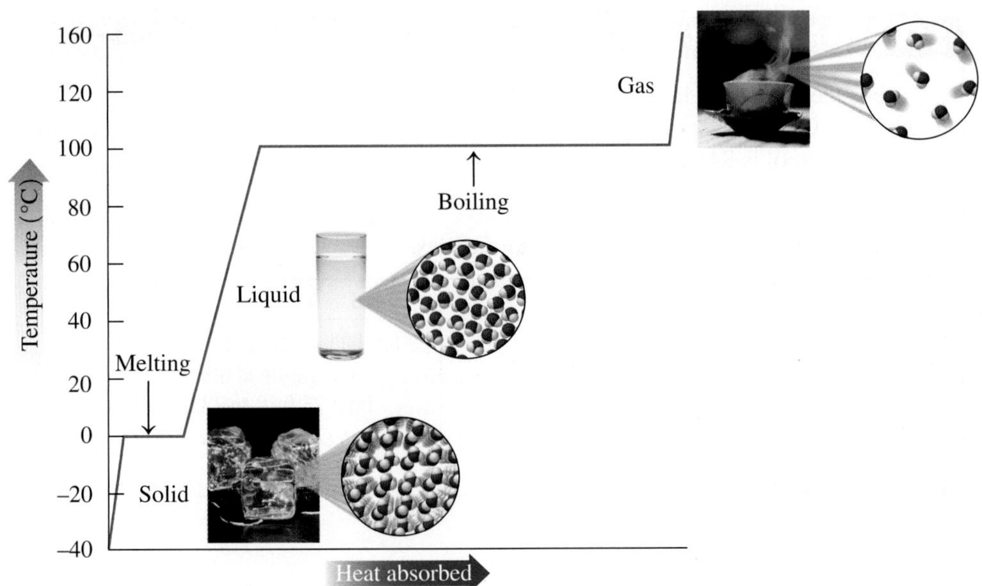

FIGURE 10.6 A heating curve diagrams the temperature increases and changes of state as heat is added.

Q What does the plateau at 100 °C represent on the heating curve for water?

Steps on a Heating Curve

The first diagonal line indicates a warming of a solid as heat is added. When the melting temperature is reached, a horizontal line, or plateau, indicates that solid is melting. As melting takes place, the solid is changing to a liquid without any change in temperature (see Figure 10.6).

Once all of the particles are in the liquid state, heat that is added will increase the temperature of the liquid. This increase is drawn as a diagonal line from the melting point to the boiling point temperature. Once the liquid reaches its boiling point, a horizontal line indicates that the temperature remains constant as liquid changes to gas. Because the heat of vaporization is greater than the heat of fusion, the horizontal line at the boiling point is longer than the line at the melting point. Once all the liquid becomes gas, adding more heat increases the temperature of the gas.

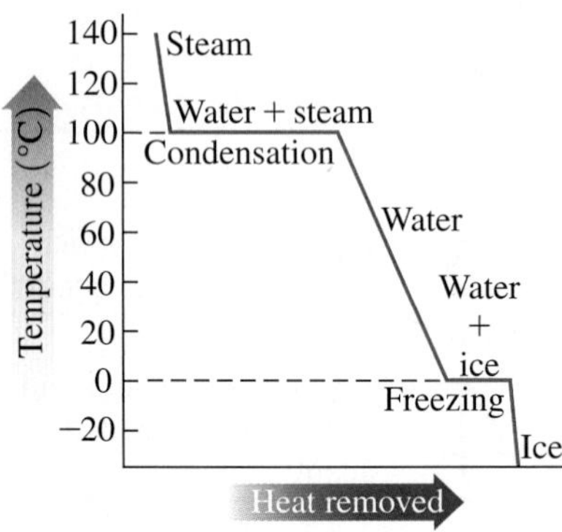

A cooling curve for water illustrates the change in temperature and changes of state as heat is removed.

Steps on a Cooling Curve

A **cooling curve** is a diagram of the cooling process, which is the reverse of a heating curve. In the diagram, the temperature is plotted on the vertical axis, and the removal of heat is plotted on the horizontal axis. Initially, a diagonal line to the boiling (condensation) point is drawn to show that heat is removed from a substance, cooling the gas until it begins to condense. A horizontal line (plateau) is drawn at the condensation point (same as the boiling point) to indicate the change of state as the gas condenses to form a liquid. After all of the gas has changed into liquid, further cooling lowers the temperature. The decrease in temperature is shown as a diagonal line from the condensation point temperature to the freezing point temperature. At the freezing point, another horizontal line indicates that liquid is changing to solid at the freezing point temperature. Once all of the substance is frozen, a loss of more heat decreases the temperature of the solid below its freezing point, which is shown as a diagonal line below its freezing point.

Combining Energy Calculations

Up to now, we have calculated one step in a heating or cooling curve. However, a problem may require a combination of steps in which a substance may change state and then the new state undergoes a temperature change followed by another change of state. When the temperature of a substance is changing and not its state, we need to use the heat equation, which includes the ΔT.

$$\text{Heat (J)} = \text{mass (g)} \times \text{temperature change } (\Delta T) \times \text{specific heat (J/g °C)}$$

The heat is calculated for each step separately, and the results are added together to give the total energy, as seen in Sample Problem 10.10.

SAMPLE PROBLEM 10.10 Combining Heat Calculations

Calculate the total heat, in joules, needed to convert 15.0 g of liquid ethanol at 25.0 °C to gas at 78.0 °C. The specific heat of ethanol is 2.46 J/g °C. The heat of vaporization for liquid ethanol is 841 J/g (see Table 10.9).

SOLUTION

Step 1 **State the given and needed quantities.**

	Given	Need
Analyze the Problem	15.0 g of ethanol at 25.0 °C, specific heat of ethanol = 2.46 J/g °C, heat of vaporization of ethanol = 841 J/g	total joules to raise temperature of ethanol from 25.0 °C to 78.0 °C, and convert to gas (78.0 °C)

Step 2 **Write a plan to convert the given quantity to the needed quantity.** When several changes occur, draw a diagram of heating and changes of state.

Total joules =

(1) joules to heat ethanol from 25.0 °C → 78.0 °C

$$\text{Joules} = \text{mass (g)} \times \text{temperature change } (\Delta T) \times \text{specific heat} \left(\frac{\text{J}}{\text{g °C}}\right)$$

(2) joules to change liquid ethanol to gas at 78.0 °C

$$\text{Joules} = \text{mass (g)} \times \text{heat of vaporization} \left(\frac{\text{J}}{\text{g}}\right)$$

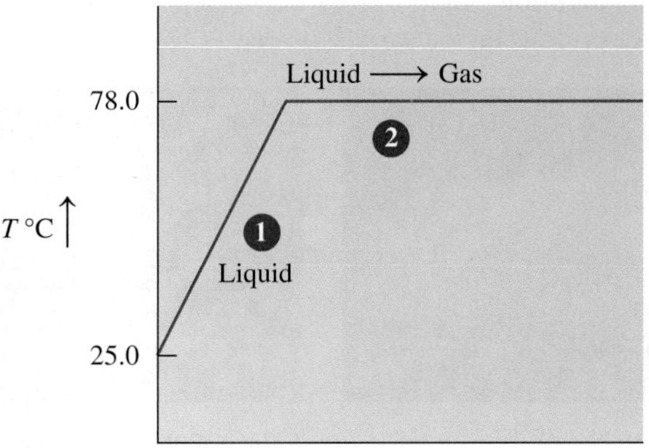

Step 3 **Write the heat conversion factors needed.**

$$SH_{\text{Ethanol}} = \frac{2.46 \text{ J}}{\text{g °C}}$$

$$\frac{2.46 \text{ J}}{\text{g °C}} \text{ and } \frac{\text{g °C}}{2.46 \text{ J}}$$

$$1 \text{ g of ethanol } (l \rightarrow g) = 841 \text{ J}$$

$$\frac{841 \text{ J}}{1 \text{ g ethanol}} \text{ and } \frac{1 \text{ g ethanol}}{841 \text{ J}}$$

Step 4 **Set up the problem and calculate the needed quantity.**

$$\Delta T = 78.0 \text{ °C} - 25.0 \text{ °C} = 53.0 \text{ °C}$$

Temperature change: Heat needed to warm ethanol (liquid) from 25.0 °C to 78.0 °C.

$$15.0 \cancel{\text{g}} \times 53.0 \cancel{\text{°C}} \times \frac{2.46 \text{ J}}{\cancel{\text{g}} \cancel{\text{°C}}} = 1960 \text{ J}$$

Change of state at constant temperature: Heat needed to convert ethanol (liquid) to ethanol (gas) at 78.0 °C.

$$15.0 \cancel{\text{g ethanol}} \times \frac{841 \text{ J}}{1 \cancel{\text{g ethanol}}} = 12\,600 \text{ J}$$

Calculate the total heat:

Heating ethanol (25.0 °C to 78.0 °C)	1 960 J
Changing liquid to gas (78.0 °C)	12 600 J
Total heat needed	14 600 J (rounded off)

STUDY CHECK 10.10

How many kilojoules are released when 75.0 g of steam at 100 °C condenses, cools to 0 °C, and freezes? (*Hint:* The solution will require three energy calculations.)

Sublimation

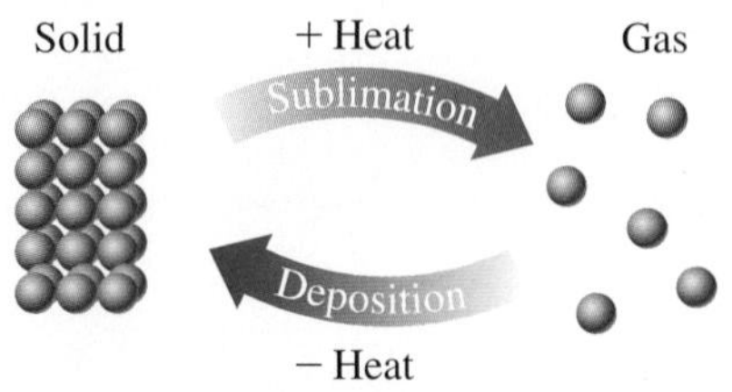

Sublimation and deposition are reversible processes.

In a process called **sublimation**, the particles on the surface of a solid change directly to a gas with no temperature change and without going through the liquid state. In the reverse process of sublimation, called **deposition**, gas particles change directly to solid.

For example, dry ice, which is solid carbon dioxide, undergoes sublimation at −78 °C. It is called "dry" because it does not form a liquid as it warms. In extremely cold areas, snow does not melt, but sublimes directly to water vapor. In a frost-free refrigerator, the water in the ice on the walls of the freezer and in frozen foods sublimes when warm air is circulated though the compartment during the defrost cycle. When frozen foods are left in the freezer for a long time, so much water sublimes that foods, especially meats, become dry and shrunken, a condition called *freezer burn*. Deposition occurs in a freezer when water vapor forms ice crystals on the surface of freezer bags and frozen food.

Dry ice sublimes at −78 °C.

Water vapor will change to solid on contact with a cold surface.

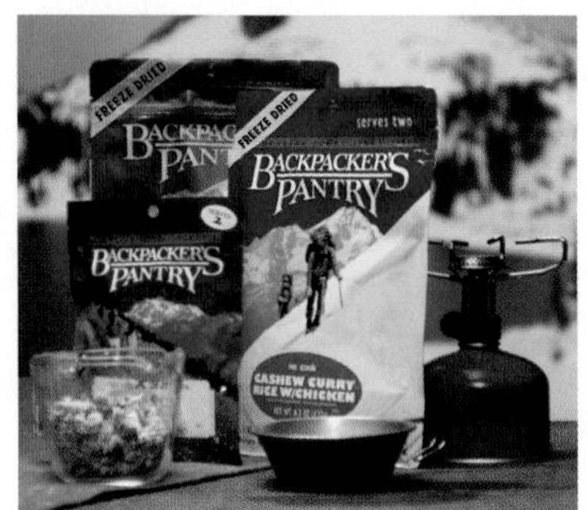

Freeze-dried food is prepared by sublimation.

Freeze-dried foods prepared by sublimation are convenient for long-term storage and for camping and hiking. A food that has been frozen is placed in a vacuum chamber where it dries as the ice sublimes. The dried food retains all of its nutritional value and needs only water to be edible. A food that is freeze-dried does not need refrigeration because bacteria cannot grow without water.

Chemistry Link to Health

STEAM BURNS

Hot water at 100 °C can cause burns and damage to the skin. If 25 g of hot water at 100 °C falls on a person's skin, the temperature of the water will drop to body temperature, 37 °C. The heat released during cooling can cause severe burns. Using the heat equation, the amount of heat to cool the water is calculated from the temperature change, 63 °C (100 °C − 37 °C), and the specific heat of water, 4.184 J/g °C.

$$25\ \cancel{g} \times 63\ \cancel{^\circ C} \times \frac{4.184\ J}{\cancel{g}\ \cancel{^\circ C}} = 6600\ J \text{ released when water cools from 100 °C to 37 °C}$$

However, getting steam on the skin is even more damaging. The condensation of the same quantity of steam to liquid at 100 °C releases much more heat—almost ten times as much. This amount of heat can be calculated using the heat of vaporization, which is 2260 J/g for water at 100 °C.

$$25\ \cancel{g} \times \frac{2260\ J}{1\ \cancel{g}} = 57\,000\ J \text{ released when water (gas) condenses to water (liquid) at 100 °C}$$

The total heat released is calculated by combining the heat from the condensation at 100 °C and the heat from cooling of the steam from 100 °C to 37 °C (body temperature). We can see that most of the heat is from the condensation of steam. This large amount of heat released on the skin is what causes damage from steam burns.

Condensation (100 °C)	=	57 000 J
Cooling (100 °C to 37 °C)	=	6 600 J
Heat released	=	64 000 J (rounded off)

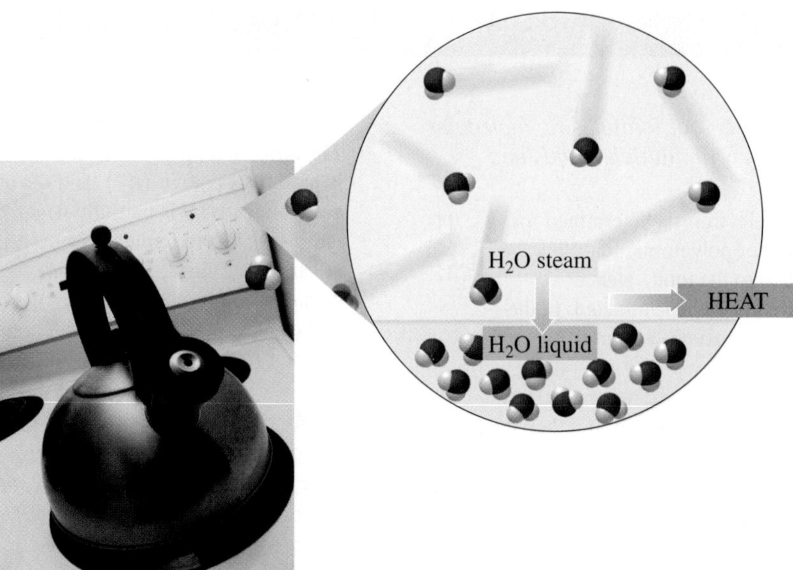

When steam condenses, a large quantity of heat is released.

QUESTIONS AND PROBLEMS

10.5 Changes of State

LEARNING GOAL: *Describe the changes of state between solids, liquids, and gases; calculate the energy involved.*

10.45 Using Table 10.9, calculate the heat change needed for each of the following at the melting/freezing point:
- **a.** joules to melt 65.0 g of ice
- **b.** joules to melt 17.0 g of ethanol
- **c.** kilojoules to freeze 225 g of acetone
- **d.** kilojoules to freeze 0.0500 kg of water

10.46 Using Table 10.9, calculate the heat change needed for each of the following at the melting/freezing point:
- **a.** joules to freeze 35.2 g of acetic acid
- **b.** joules to freeze 275 g of water
- **c.** kilojoules to melt 145 g of ammonia
- **d.** kilojoules to melt 5.00 kg of ice

10.47 Using Table 10.9, calculate the heat change needed for each of the following at the boiling/condensation point:
- **a.** joules to vaporize 10.0 g of water
- **b.** kilojoules to vaporize 50.0 g of ethanol
- **c.** joules to condense 8.00 g of acetic acid
- **d.** kilojoules to condense 0.175 kg of ammonia

10.48 Using Table 10.9, calculate the heat change needed for each of the following at the boiling/condensation point:
- **a.** joules to condense 10.0 g of steam
- **b.** kilojoules to condense 76.0 g of acetic acid
- **c.** joules to vaporize 44.0 g of ammonia
- **d.** kilojoules to vaporize 5.0 kg of water

10.49 Using Table 10.9 and the specific heat of water, 4.184 J/g °C, calculate the total amount of heat for each of the following:
- **a.** joules needed to warm 20.0 g of water at 15 °C to 72 °C
- **b.** joules needed to melt 50.0 g of ice at 0.0 °C and to warm the liquid to 65.0 °C
- **c.** kilojoules released when 15.0 g of steam condenses at 100 °C and the liquid cools to 0 °C
- **d.** kilojoules needed to melt 24.0 g of ice at 0 °C, warm the liquid to 100 °C, and change it to steam at 100 °C

10.50 Using Table 10.9 and the specific heat of water, 4.184 J/g °C, calculate the total amount of heat for each of the following:
- **a.** joules to condense 125 g of steam at 100 °C and to cool the liquid to 15.0 °C
- **b.** joules needed to melt a 525-g ice sculpture at 0 °C and to warm the liquid to 15.0 °C
- **c.** kilojoules released when 85.0 g of steam condenses at 100 °C, the liquid cools to 0 °C, and freezes
- **d.** joules to warm 55.0 mL of water (density = 1.00 g/mL) from 10.0 °C to 100 °C and vaporize it at 100 °C

10.51 An ice bag containing 275 g of ice at 0 °C was used to treat sore muscles. When the bag was removed, the ice had melted and the liquid water had a temperature of 24.0 °C. How many kilojoules of heat were absorbed?

10.52 A 115-g sample of steam at 100 °C is emitted from a volcano. It condenses, cools, and falls as snow at 0 °C. How many kilojoules of heat were released?

CHAPTER REVIEW

10.1 Electron-Dot Formulas

LEARNING GOAL: *Draw the electron-dot formulas for molecular compounds or polyatomic ions with multiple bonds and show resonance structures.*

H
H:Ö:

- The total number of valence electrons is determined for all the atoms in the molecule or polyatomic ion.
- Any negative charge is added to the total valence electrons, while any positive charge is subtracted. In the electron-dot formulas, a bonding pair is placed between the central atom and attached atoms.
- The remaining valence electrons are used as lone pairs to complete the octets of the surrounding atoms and then the central atom.
- When octets are not completed, lone pairs of electrons are converted to bonding pairs forming double or triple bonds.
- Resonance structures can be drawn when two or more electron-dot formulas can be drawn for a molecule or ion with a multiple bond.

10.2 Shapes of Molecules and Ions (VSEPR Theory)

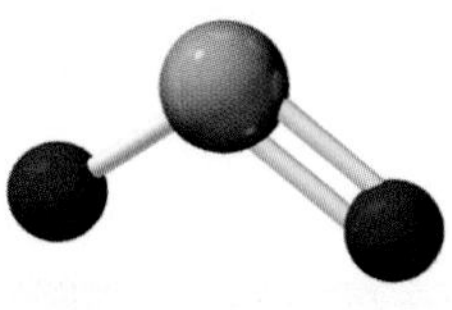

LEARNING GOAL: *Predict the three-dimensional structure of a molecule or polyatomic ion and classify it as polar or nonpolar.*

- The shape of a molecule is determined from the electron-dot formula, the electron-group geometry, and the number of bonded atoms.
- The electron-group geometry around a central atom with two electron groups is linear; with three electron groups, the geometry is trigonal planar; and with four electron groups, the geometry is tetrahedral.
- When all the electron groups are bonded to atoms, the shape has the same name as the electron arrangement.
- A central atom with three electron groups and two bonded atoms has a bent shape, 120°.
- A central atom with four electron groups and three bonded atoms has a trigonal pyramidal shape.
- A central atom with four electron groups and two bonded atoms has a bent shape, 109°.

10.3 Electronegativity and Polarity

LEARNING GOAL: *Use electronegativity to determine the polarity of a bond or a molecule.*

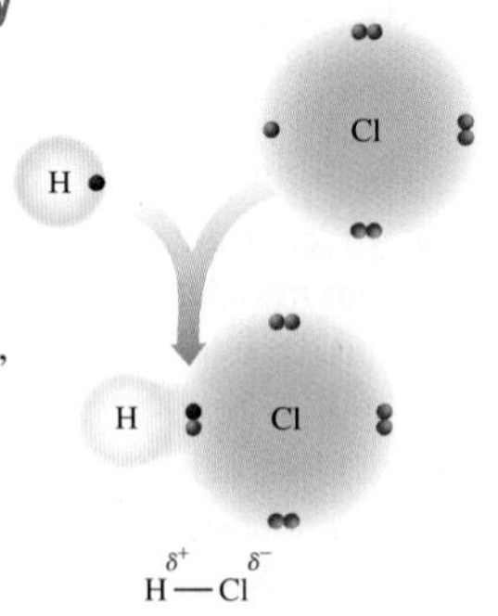

- Electronegativity is the ability of an atom to attract the electrons it shares with another atom. In general, the electronegativities of metals are low, while nonmetals have high electronegativities.
- In a nonpolar covalent bond, atoms share electrons equally.
- In a polar covalent bond, the electrons are unequally shared because they are attracted to the more electronegative atom.
- The atom in a polar bond with the lower electronegativity is partially positive (δ^+), and the atom with the higher electronegativity is partially negative (δ^-).
- Atoms that form ionic bonds have large differences in electronegativities. Nonpolar molecules contain nonpolar covalent bonds or have an arrangement of bonded atoms that causes the dipoles to cancel out.
- In polar molecules, the dipoles do not cancel.

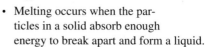

10.4 Attractive Forces in Compounds

LEARNING GOAL: *Describe the attractive forces between ions, polar covalent molecules, and nonpolar covalent molecules.*

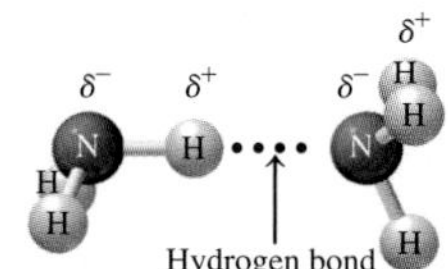

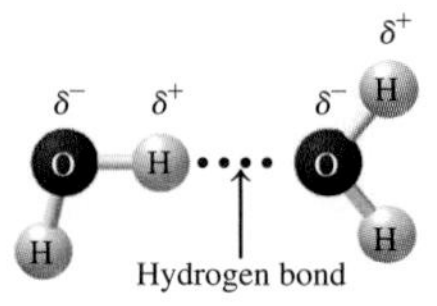

- In ionic solids, oppositely charged ions are held in a rigid structure by ionic bonds.
- Attractive forces called dipole–dipole attractions and hydrogen bonds hold the solid and liquid states of molecular compounds together.
- Nonpolar compounds form solids and liquids by weak attractions between temporary dipoles called dispersion forces.

10.5 Changes of State

LEARNING GOAL: *Describe the changes of state between solids, liquids, and gases; calculate the energy involved.*

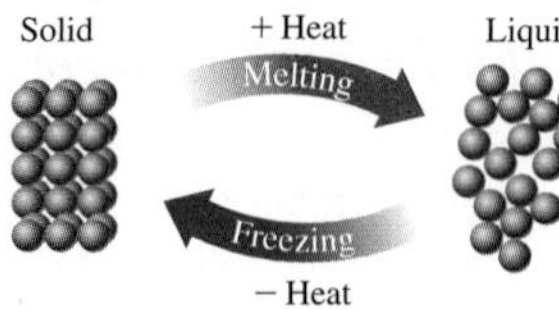

- Melting occurs when the particles in a solid absorb enough energy to break apart and form a liquid.
- The amount of energy required to convert exactly 1 g of solid to liquid is called the heat of fusion.
- For water, 334 J is needed to melt 1 g of ice or must be removed to freeze 1 g of water.
- Evaporation occurs when particles in a liquid state absorb enough energy to break apart and form gaseous particles.
- Boiling is the vaporization of liquid at its boiling point. The heat of vaporization is the amount of heat needed to convert exactly 1 g of liquid to vapor.
- For water, 2260 J is needed to vaporize 1 g of water or must be removed to condense 1 g of steam.
- A heating or cooling curve illustrates the changes in temperature and state as heat is added to or removed from a substance. Plateaus on the graph indicate changes of state.
- The total heat absorbed or removed from a substance undergoing temperature changes and changes of state is the sum of energy calculations for change(s) of state and change(s) in temperature.
- Sublimation is a process whereby a solid changes directly to a gas.

CONCEPT MAP

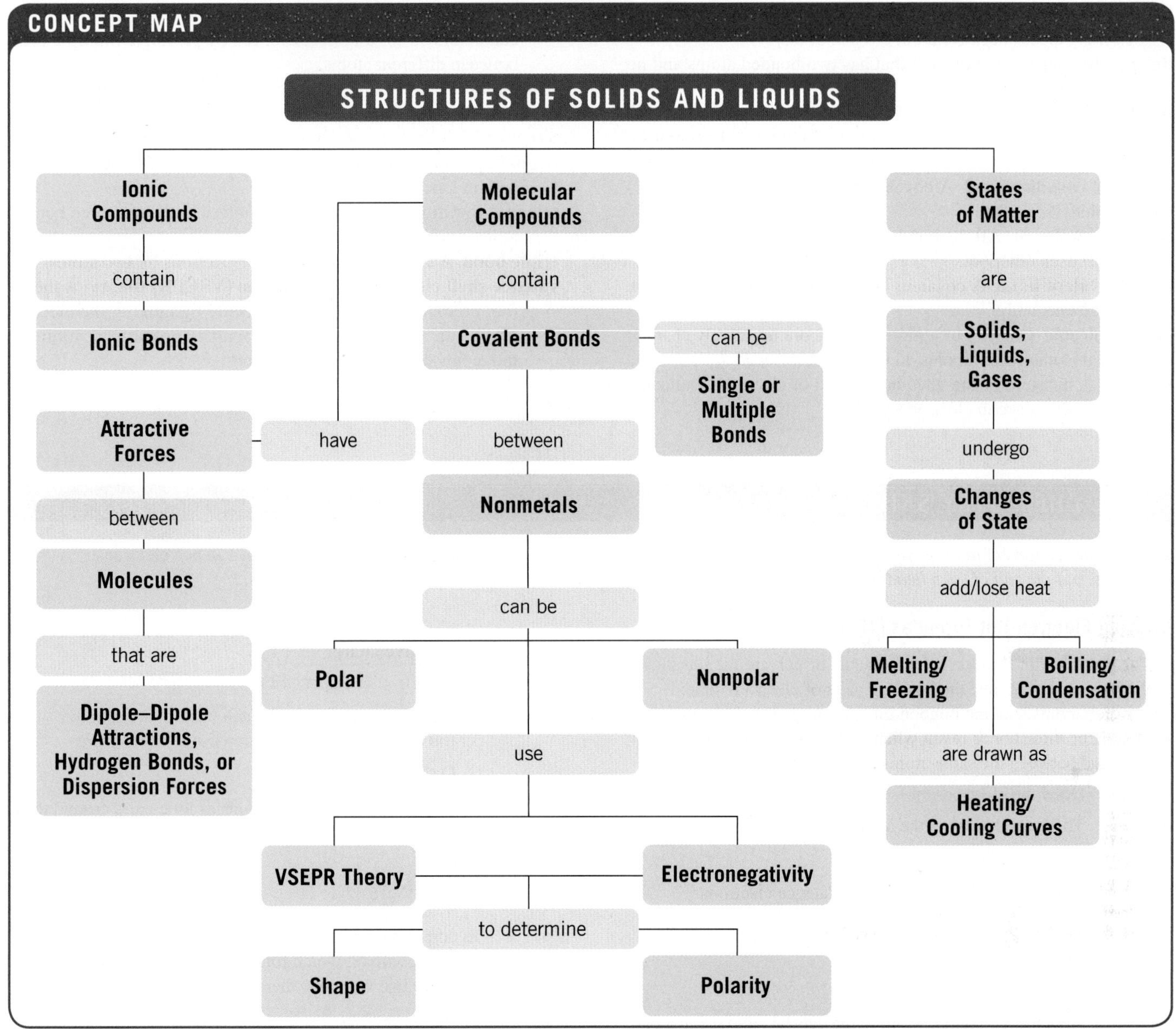

KEY TERMS

bent The shape of a molecule with two bonded atoms and one lone pair or two lone pairs.

boiling The formation of bubbles of gas throughout a liquid.

boiling point (bp) The temperature at which a substance exists as a liquid and gas; liquid changes to gas (boils), and gas changes to liquid (condenses).

change of state The transformation of one state of matter to another, for example, solid to liquid, liquid to solid, liquid to gas.

condensation The change of state of a gas to a liquid.

cooling curve A diagram that illustrates temperature changes and changes of state for a substance as heat is removed.

deposition The change of a gas directly to a solid; the reverse of sublimation.

dipole The separation of positive and negative charge in a polar bond indicated by an arrow that is drawn from the more positive atom to the more negative atom.

dipole–dipole attractions Attractive forces between oppositely charged ends of polar molecules.

dispersion forces Weak dipole bonding that results from a momentary polarization of nonpolar molecules in a substance.

double bond A sharing of two pairs of electrons by two atoms.

electronegativity The relative ability of an element to attract electrons in a bond.

evaporation The formation of a gas (vapor) by the escape of high-energy molecules from the surface of a liquid.

freezing A change of state from liquid to solid.

freezing point (fp) The temperature at which a liquid changes to a solid (freezes) and a solid changes to a liquid (melts).

heat of fusion The energy required to melt exactly 1 g of a substance. For water, 334 J is needed to melt 1 g of ice; 334 J is released when 1 g of water freezes.

heat of vaporization The energy required to vaporize 1 g of a substance. For water, 2260 J is needed to vaporize exactly 1 g of water; 1 g of steam gives off 2260 J when it condenses.

heating curve A diagram that shows the temperature changes and changes of state of a substance as it is heated.

hydrogen bond The attraction between a partially positive H and a strongly electronegative atom of F, O, or N.
linear The shape of a molecule that has two bonded atoms and no lone pairs.
melting The conversion of a solid to a liquid.
melting point (mp) The temperature at which a solid becomes a liquid (melts). It is the same temperature as the freezing point.
nonpolar covalent bond A covalent bond in which the electrons are shared equally.
nonpolar molecule All the bonds are nonpolar or the polar bonds cancel each other out.
polar covalent bond A covalent bond in which the electrons are shared unequally.
polar molecule One end of a molecule is more negatively charged than the other end; dipoles do not cancel.
polarity A measure of the unequal sharing of electrons, indicated by the difference in electronegativities.
resonance structures Two or more electron-dot formulas that can be drawn for a molecule or ion by placing a multiple bond between different atoms.
sublimation The change of state in which a solid is transformed directly to a gas without forming a liquid.
tetrahedral The shape of a molecule with four bonded atoms.
trigonal planar The shape of a molecule with three bonded atoms and no lone pairs.
trigonal pyramidal The shape of a molecule that has three bonded atoms and one lone pair.
triple bond A sharing of three pairs of electrons by two atoms.
valence shell electron-pair repulsion (VSEPR) theory A theory that predicts the shape of a molecule by moving the electron groups on a central atom as far apart as possible to minimize the repulsion of the negative regions.

CORE CHEMISTRY SKILLS

The chapter section containing each Core Chemistry Skill is shown in parentheses at the end of each heading.

Drawing Electron-Dot Formulas (10.1)

- The electron-dot formula for a molecule or polyatomic ion shows the sequence of atoms, the bonding pairs of electrons shared between atoms, and the nonbonding or *lone pairs* of electrons.
- Double or triple bonds result when a second or third electron pair is shared between the same atoms to complete octets.

Example: Draw the electron-dot formula for CS_2.

Answer: The central atom in the atom arrangement is C.

S C S

Determine the total number of valence electrons.

$2\,S \times 6\,e^- = 12\,e^-$
$1\,C \times 4\,e^- = 4\,e^-$
Total $= 16\,e^-$

Attach each bonded atom to the central atom using a pair of electrons. Two bonding pairs use four electrons.

S:C:S

Place the 12 remaining electrons as lone pairs around the S atoms.

:S̤̈:C:S̤̈:

To complete the octet for C, a lone pair of electrons from each of the S atoms is shared with C, which forms two double bonds.

:S̤̈::C::S̤̈: ⟶ :S̈=C=S̈:

Electron pairs moved to form double bonds

Drawing Resonance Structures (10.1)

- When a molecule or polyatomic ion contains multiple bonds, it may be possible to draw more than one electron-dot formula called resonance structures.

Example: Draw the electron-dot formula for NO_2^-.

Answer: The central atom in the atom arrangement is N.

O N O

Determine the total number of valence electrons.

$1\,N \times 5\,e^- = 5\,e^-$
$2\,O \times 6\,e^- = 12\,e^-$
negative charge $= 1\,e^-$
Total $= 18\,e^-$

Use electron pairs to attach each bonded atom to the central atom. Two bonding pairs use four electrons.

O:N:O

Place the 14 remaining electrons as lone pairs around the O and N atoms.

[:Ö̤:N̈:Ö̤:]⁻

To complete the octet for N, a lone pair from one O atom is shared with N, which forms one double bond. Because there are two O atoms, there are two resonance structures.

[:O̤=N̈—Ö̤:]⁻ ⟷ [:Ö̤—N̈=O̤:]⁻

Electron pair moved to form double bonds

Predicting Shape (10.2)

- The three-dimensional shape of a molecule or polyatomic ion is determined by drawing an electron-dot formula and identifying the number of electron groups (one or more electron pairs) around the central atom and the number of bonded atoms.
- In the valence shell electron-pair repulsion (VSEPR) theory, the electron groups are arranged as far apart as possible around a central atom to minimize the repulsion.
- A central atom with two electron groups bonded to two atoms is linear. A central atom with three electron groups bonded to three atoms is trigonal planar, and to two atoms is bent (120°). A central atom with four electron groups bonded to four atoms is tetrahedral, to three atoms is trigonal pyramidal, and to two atoms is bent (109°).

Example: Predict the shape for NO_2^-.

Answer: Using the electron-dot formula we drew for NO_2^-, we count three electron groups around the central N atom: one double bond, one single bond, and a lone pair of electrons.

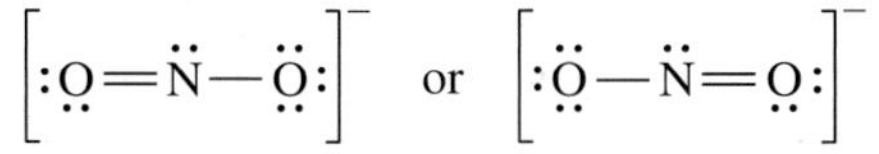

$$\left[:\ddot{O}=\ddot{N}-\ddot{O}:\right]^- \quad \text{or} \quad \left[:\ddot{O}-\ddot{N}=\ddot{O}:\right]^-$$

The electron-group geometry is trigonal planar, but with the central N atom bonded to two O atoms, the shape is bent, 120°.

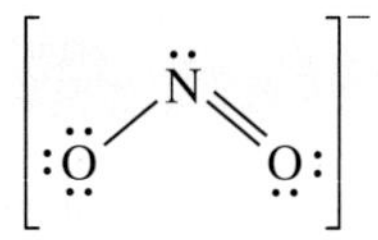

$$\left[:\ddot{O} \diagup \ddot{N} \diagdown \ddot{O}:\right]^-$$

Using Electronegativity (10.3)

- The electronegativity values indicate the ability of atoms to attract shared electrons.
- Electronegativity values increase going across a period from left to right, and decrease going down a group.
- A nonpolar covalent bond occurs between atoms with identical or very similar electronegativity values such that the electronegativity difference is 0.0 to 0.4.
- A polar covalent bond typically occurs when electrons are shared unequally between atoms with electronegativity differences from 0.5 to 1.8.
- An ionic bond typically occurs when the difference in electronegativity for two atoms is greater than 1.8.

Example: Use electronegativity values to classify each of the following bonds as nonpolar covalent, polar covalent, or ionic:

a. Sr—Cl **b.** C—S **c.** O—Br

Answer: **a.** An electronegativity difference of 2.0 (Cl 3.0 − Sr 1.0) makes this an ionic bond.
b. An electronegativity difference of 0.0 (C 2.5 − S 2.5) makes this a nonpolar covalent bond.
c. An electronegativity difference of 0.7 (O 3.5 − Br 2.8) makes this a polar covalent bond.

Identifying Polarity of Molecules (10.3)

- A molecule is nonpolar if all of its bonds are nonpolar or it has polar bonds that cancel out. CCl_4 is a nonpolar molecule that consists of four polar bonds that cancel out.

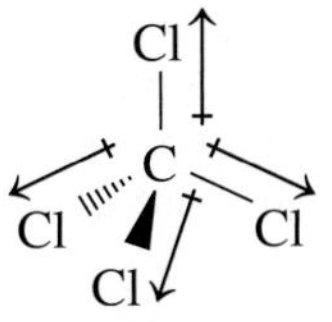

- A molecule is polar if it contains polar bonds that do not cancel out. H_2O is a polar molecule that consists of polar bonds that do not cancel out.

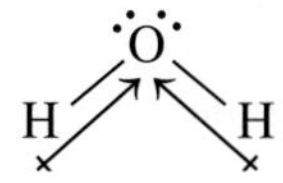

Example: Predict whether $AsCl_3$ is polar or nonpolar.

Answer: From its electron-dot formula, we see that $AsCl_3$ has four electron groups with three bonded atoms.

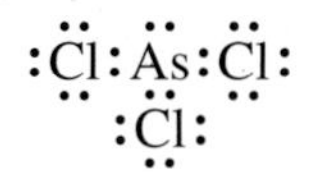

$$:\ddot{Cl}:\ddot{As}:\ddot{Cl}:$$
$$:\ddot{Cl}:$$

The shape of a molecule of $AsCl_3$ would be trigonal pyramidal with three polar bonds (As—Cl = 3.0 − 2.0 = 1.0) that do not cancel. Thus it is a polar molecule.

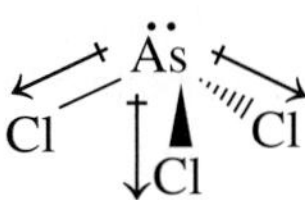

Identifying Attractive Forces (10.4)

- Dipole–dipole attractions occur between the dipoles in polar compounds because the positively charged end of one molecule is attracted to the negatively charged end of another molecule.

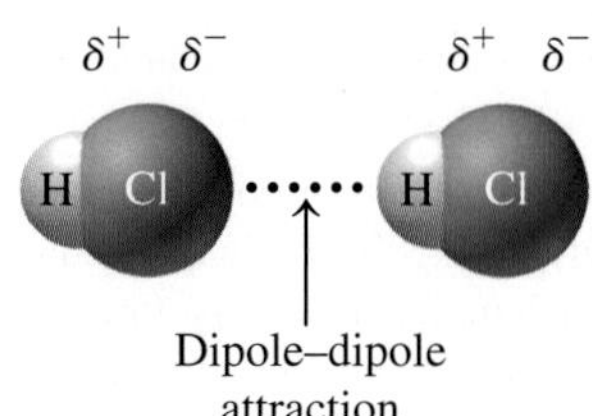

- Strong dipole–dipole attractions called hydrogen bonds occur in compounds in which H is bonded to F, O, or N. The partially positive H atom in one molecule has a strong attraction to the partially negative F, O, or N in another molecule.
- Dispersion forces are very weak attractive forces between nonpolar molecules that occur when *temporary dipoles* form as electrons are unequally distributed.

Example: Identify the strongest type of attractive forces in each of the following:

a. HF **b.** F_2 **c.** NF_3

Answer: **a.** HF molecules, which are polar with H bonded to F, have hydrogen bonding.
b. Nonpolar F_2 molecules have only dispersion forces.
c. NF_3 molecules, which are polar, have dipole–dipole attractions.

- Substances with ionic bonds have the highest melting and boiling points. Substances with hydrogen bonds have higher melting and boiling points than compounds with only dipole–dipole attractions. Substances with only dispersion forces would typically have the lowest melting and boiling points, which increase as molar mass increases.

Example: Identify the compound with the highest boiling point in each of the following:

a. HI, HBr, HF **b.** F_2, Cl_2, I_2

Answer: **a.** HBr and HI have dipole–dipole attractions, but HF has hydrogen bonding, which gives HF the highest boiling point.
b. Because F_2, Cl_2, and I_2 have only dispersion forces, I_2 with the greatest molar mass would have the highest boiling point.

Calculating Heat for Change of State (10.5)

- At the melting/freezing point, the heat of fusion is absorbed/released to convert 1 g of a solid to a liquid or 1 g of liquid to a solid.
- For example, 334 J of heat is needed to melt (freeze) exactly 1 g of ice at its melting (freezing) point (0 °C).

- At the boiling/condensation point, the heat of vaporization is absorbed/released to convert exactly 1 g of liquid to gas or 1 g of gas to liquid.
- For example, 2260 J of heat is needed to boil (condense) exactly 1 g of water/steam at its boiling (condensation) point, 100 °C.

Example: What is the quantity of heat, in kilojoules, released when 45.8 g of steam (water) condenses at its boiling (condensation) point?

Answer:

$$\underset{\text{3 SFs}}{45.8\ \cancel{\text{g steam}}} \times \frac{\overset{\text{3 SFs}}{2260\ \cancel{\text{J}}}}{\underset{\text{Exact}}{1\ \cancel{\text{g steam}}}} \times \frac{\overset{\text{Exact}}{1\ \text{kJ}}}{\underset{\text{Exact}}{1000\ \cancel{\text{J}}}} = \underset{\text{3 SFs}}{104\ \text{kJ}}$$

UNDERSTANDING THE CONCEPTS

The chapter sections to review are shown in parentheses at the end of each question.

10.53 Match each of the electron-dot formulas (**a–c**) with the correct diagram (**1–3**) of its shape, and name the shape; indicate if each molecule is polar or nonpolar. Assume X and Y are nonmetals and all bonds are polar covalent. (10.1, 10.2, 10.3)

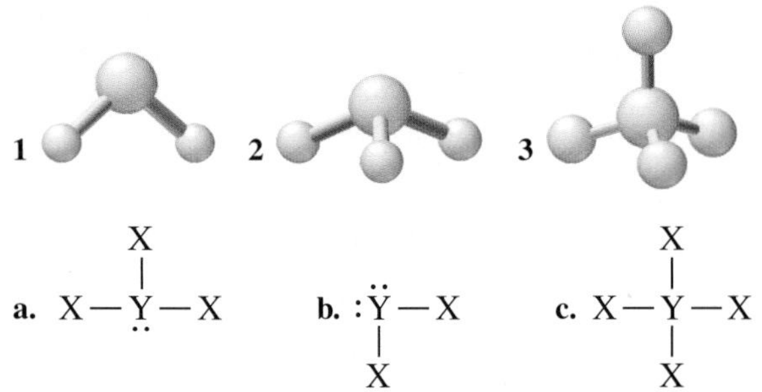

10.54 Match each of the formulas (**a–c**) with the correct diagram (**1–3**) of its shape, and name the shape; indicate if each molecule is polar or nonpolar. (10.1, 10.2, 10.3)

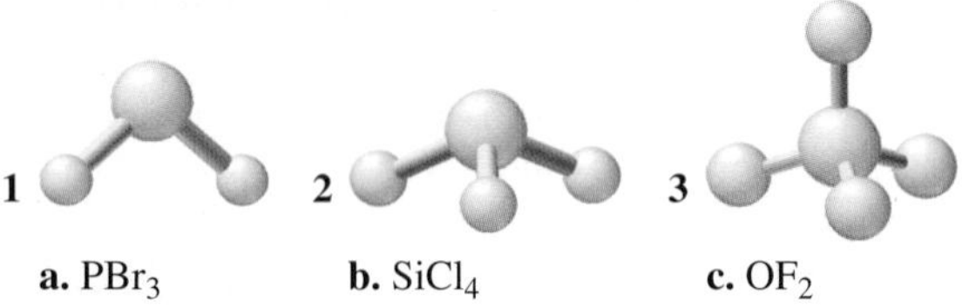

a. PBr_3 **b.** $SiCl_4$ **c.** OF_2

10.55 Consider the following bonds: Ca—O, C—O, K—O, O—O, and N—O. (10.3)
a. Which bonds are polar covalent?
b. Which bonds are nonpolar covalent?
c. Which bonds are ionic?
d. Arrange the covalent bonds in order of decreasing polarity.

10.56 Consider the following bonds: F—Cl, Cl—Cl, Cs—Cl, O—Cl, and Ca—Cl. (10.3)
a. Which bonds are polar covalent?
b. Which bonds are nonpolar covalent?
c. Which bonds are ionic?
d. Arrange the covalent bonds in order of decreasing polarity.

10.57 Identify the major attractive force between each of the following atoms or molecules: (10.4)
a. PH_3 **b.** NO_2
c. $CH_3—NH_2$ **d.** Ar

10.58 Identify the major attractive force between each of the following atoms or molecules: (10.4)
a. He **b.** HBr
c. SnH_4 **d.** $CH_3—CH_2—CH_2—OH$

10.59 Use your knowledge of changes of state to explain the following: (10.5)
a. How does perspiration during heavy exercise cool the body?
b. Why do towels dry more quickly on a hot summer day than on a cold winter day?
c. Why do wet clothes stay wet in a plastic bag?

Perspiration forms on the skin during heavy exercise.

10.60 Use your knowledge of changes of state to explain the following: (10.5)

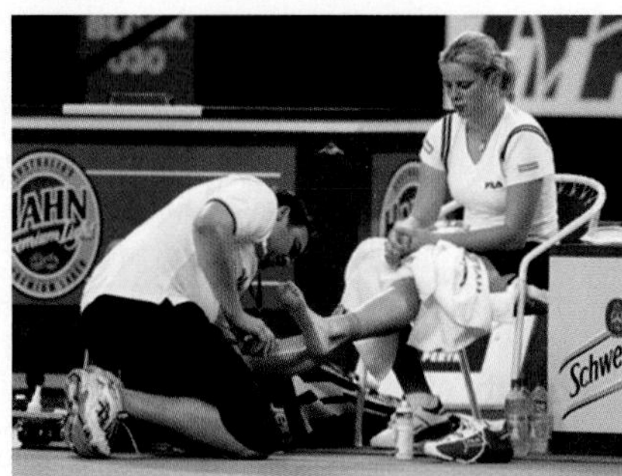

A spray is used to numb a sports injury.

a. Why is a spray that evaporates quickly, such as ethyl chloride, used to numb a sports injury during a game?
b. Why does water in a wide, flat, shallow dish evaporate more quickly than the same amount of water in a tall, narrow vase?
c. Why does a sandwich on a plate dry out faster than a sandwich in plastic wrap?

10.61 Draw a heating curve for a sample of ice that is heated from −20 °C to 150 °C. Indicate the segment of the graph that corresponds to each of the following: (10.5)
a. solid **b.** melting **c.** liquid
d. boiling **e.** gas

10.62 Draw a cooling curve for a sample of steam that cools from 110 °C to −10 °C. Indicate the segment of the graph that corresponds to each of the following: (10.5)

a. solid **b.** freezing **c.** liquid
d. condensing **e.** gas

10.63 The following is a heating curve for chloroform, a solvent for fats, oils, and waxes: (10.5)

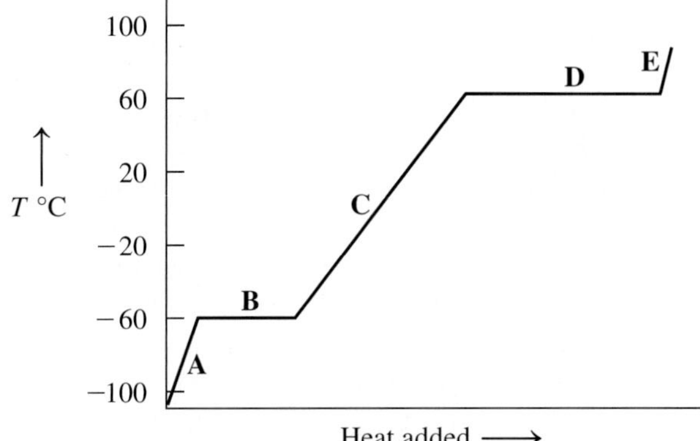

a. What is the melting point of chloroform?
b. What is the boiling point of chloroform?
c. On the heating curve, identify the segments **A**, **B**, **C**, **D**, and **E** as solid, liquid, gas, melting, or boiling.
d. At the following temperatures, is chloroform a solid, liquid, or gas: −80 °C; −40 °C; 25 °C; 80 °C?

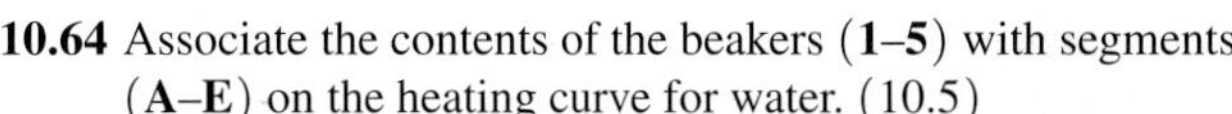

10.64 Associate the contents of the beakers (**1–5**) with segments (**A–E**) on the heating curve for water. (10.5)

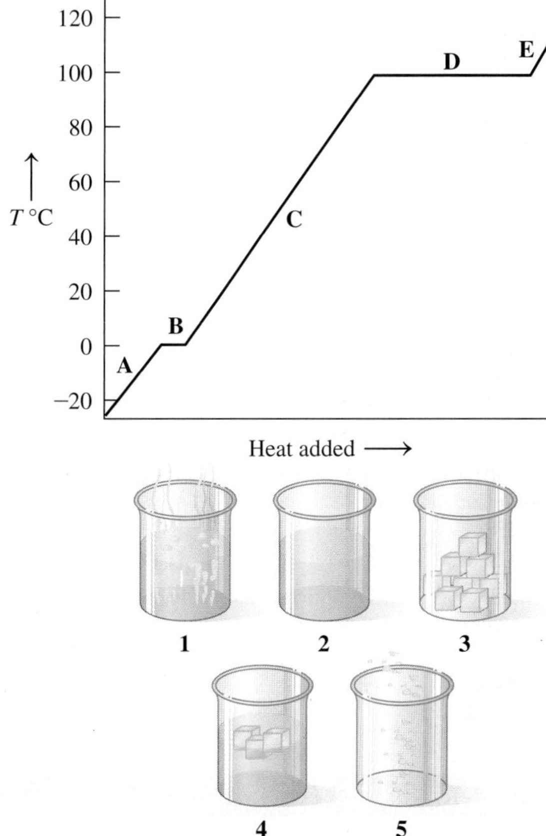

ADDITIONAL QUESTIONS AND PROBLEMS

10.65 Determine the total number of valence electrons in each of the following: (10.1)

a. HNO_2 **b.** CH_3CHO
c. PH_4^+ **d.** SO_3^{2-}

10.66 Determine the total number of valence electrons in each of the following: (10.1)

a. $COCl_2$ **b.** N_2O
c. ClO_2^- **d.** $SeCl_2$

10.67 Draw the electron-dot formula for each of the following: (10.1)

a. BF_4^- **b.** Cl_2O
c. H_2NOH (N is the central atom)
d. H_2CCl_2

10.68 Draw the electron-dot formula for each of the following: (10.1)

a. H_3COCH_3 (the atoms are in the order C O C)
b. HNO_2 (the atoms are in the order HONO)
c. ClO_2^- **d.** BrO^-

10.69 Draw resonance structures for each of the following: (10.1)

a. N_3^- **b.** NO_2^+ **c.** CNS^-

10.70 Draw resonance structures for each of the following: (10.1)

a. NO_3^- **b.** CO_3^{2-} **c.** SCN^-

10.71 Use the periodic table to arrange the following atoms in order of increasing electronegativity: (10.3)

a. I, F, Cl **b.** Li, K, S, Cl
c. Mg, Sr, Ba, Be

10.72 Use the periodic table to arrange the following atoms in order of increasing electronegativity: (10.3)

a. Cl, Br, Se **b.** Na, Cs, O, S
c. O, F, B, Li

10.73 Select the more polar bond in each of the following pairs: (10.3)

a. C—N or C—O **b.** N—F or N—Br
c. Br—Cl or S—Cl **d.** Br—Cl or Br—I
e. N—F or N—O

10.74 Select the more polar bond in each of the following pairs: (10.3)

a. C—C or C—O **b.** P—Cl or P—Br
c. Si—S or Si—Cl **d.** F—Cl or F—Br
e. P—O or P—S

10.75 Show the dipole arrow for each of the following bonds: (10.3)

a. Si—Cl **b.** C—N **c.** F—Cl
d. C—F **e.** N—O

10.76 Show the dipole arrow for each of the following bonds: (10.3)

a. P—O **b.** N—F **c.** O—Cl
d. S—Cl **e.** P—F

10.77 Classify each of the following bonds as nonpolar covalent, polar covalent, or ionic: (10.3)

a. Si—Cl **b.** C—C **c.** Na—Cl
d. C—H **e.** F—F

10.78 Classify each of the following bonds as nonpolar covalent, polar covalent, or ionic: (10.3)

a. C—N **b.** Cl—Cl **c.** K—Br
d. H—H **e.** N—F

10.79 For each of the following, draw the electron-dot formula and determine the shape: (10.1, 10.2)

a. NF_3 **b.** $SiBr_4$
c. CSe_2 **d.** SO_2

10.80 For each of the following, draw the electron-dot formula and determine the shape: (10.1, 10.2)

a. PCl_4^+ **b.** O_2^{2-}
c. $COCl_2$ (C is the central atom)
d. HCCH

10.81 Use the electron-dot formula to determine the shape for each of the following molecules and ions: (10.1, 10.2)

a. BrO_2^- **b.** H_2O
c. CBr_4 **d.** PO_3^{3-}

10.82 Use the electron-dot formula to determine the shape for each of the following molecules and ions: (10.1, 10.2)

a. PH_3 **b.** NO_3^-
c. HCN **d.** SO_3^{2-}

10.83 Classify each of the following molecules as polar or nonpolar: (10.2, 10.3)

a. HBr **b.** SiO_2 **c.** NCl_3
d. CH_3Cl **e.** NI_3 **f.** H_2O

10.84 Classify each of the following molecules as polar or nonpolar: (10.2, 10.3)

a. GeH_4 **b.** I_2 **c.** CF_3Cl
d. PCl_3 **e.** BCl_3 **f.** SCl_2

10.85 Indicate the major type of attractive force—(1) ionic bonds, (2) dipole–dipole attractions, (3) hydrogen bonds, (4) dispersion forces—that occurs between particles of the following: (10.4)

a. NF_3 **b.** ClF **c.** Br_2
d. Cs_2O **e.** C_4H_{10} **f.** CH_3OH

10.86 Indicate the major type of attractive force—(1) ionic bonds, (2) dipole–dipole attractions, (3) hydrogen bonds, (4) dispersion forces—that occurs between particles of the following: (10.4)

a. $CHCl_3$ **b.** H_2O **c.** LiCl
d. OBr_2 **e.** HBr **f.** IBr

10.87 When it rains or snows, the air temperature seems warmer. Explain. (10.5)

10.88 Water is sprayed on the ground of an orchard when temperatures are near freezing to keep the fruit from freezing. Explain. (10.5)

10.89 Using Table 10.9, calculate the grams of ice that will melt at 0 °C if 1540 J is absorbed. (10.5)

10.90 Using Table 10.9, calculate the grams of ethanol that will vaporize at 78 °C if 4620 J is absorbed. (10.5)

10.91 Using Table 10.9, calculate the grams of acetic acid that will freeze at 17 °C if 5.25 kJ is removed. (10.5)

10.92 Using Table 10.9, calculate the grams of acetone that will condense at 56 °C if 8.46 kJ is removed. (10.5)

CHALLENGE QUESTIONS

10.93 Complete the electron-dot formula for each of the following: (10.1)

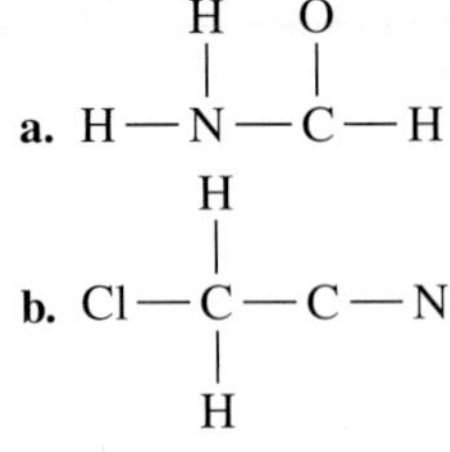

c. H—N—N—H

d. Cl—C—O—C—H (O on the first C; H above and below the second C)

10.94 Identify the errors in each of the following electron-dot formulas and draw the correct formula: (10.1)

a. $:\ddot{Cl}{=}O{=}\ddot{Cl}:$

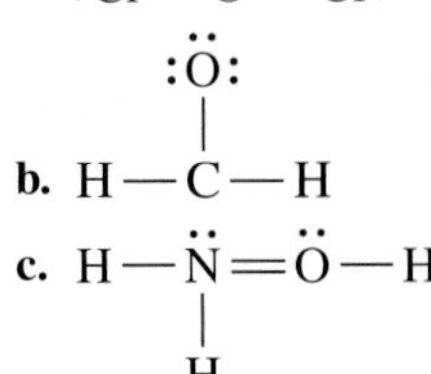

10.95 Predict the shape of each of the following molecules or ions: (10.2)

a. NH_2Cl (N is the central atom)
b. PH_4^+
c. SCN^-

10.96 Classify each of the following molecules as polar or nonpolar: (10.2, 10.3)

a. N_2 **b.** TeO_2 **c.** NH_2Cl

10.97 The melting point of carbon tetrachloride is −23 °C and its boiling point is 77 °C. Draw a heating curve for carbon tetrachloride from −100 °C to 100 °C. (10.5)

a. What is the state of carbon tetrachloride at −50 °C?
b. What happens on the curve at −23 °C?
c. What is the state of carbon tetrachloride at 20 °C?
d. What is the state of carbon tetrachloride at 90 °C?
e. At what temperature will both solid and liquid be present?

10.98 The melting point of benzene is 5.5 °C and its boiling point is 80.1 °C. Draw a heating curve for benzene from 0 °C to 100 °C. (10.5)

a. What is the state of benzene at 15 °C?
b. What happens on the curve at 5.5 °C?
c. What is the state of benzene at 63 °C?
d. What is the state of benzene at 98 °C?
e. At what temperature will both liquid and gas be present?

10.99 A 45.0-g piece of ice at 0.0 °C is added to a sample of water at 8.0 °C. All of the ice melts, and the temperature of the water decreases to 0.0 °C. How many grams of water were in the sample? (10.5)

10.100 An ice cube at 0 °C with a mass of 115 g is added to H_2O in a beaker that has a temperature of 64.0 °C. If the final temperature of the mixture is 24.0 °C, what was the initial mass of the warm water? (10.5)

10.101 An ice cube tray holds 325 g of water. If the water initially has a temperature of 25 °C, how many kilojoules of heat must be removed to cool and freeze the water at 0 °C? (10.5)

10.102 A 3.0-kg block of lead is taken from a furnace at 300 °C and placed on a large block of ice at 0 °C. The specific heat of lead is 0.13 J/g °C. If all the heat given up by the lead is used to melt ice, how much ice is melted when the temperature of the lead drops to 0 °C? (10.5)

ANSWERS

Answers to Study Checks

10.1 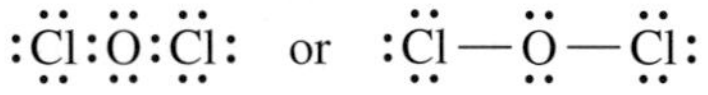

10.2 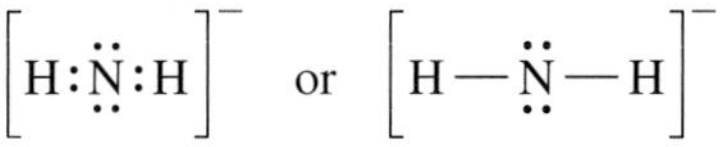

10.3 H_2CCH_2 $(12\ e^-)$ 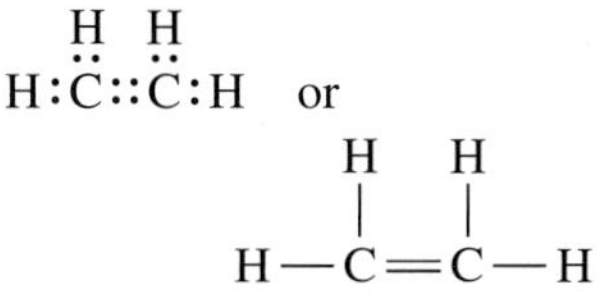

10.4 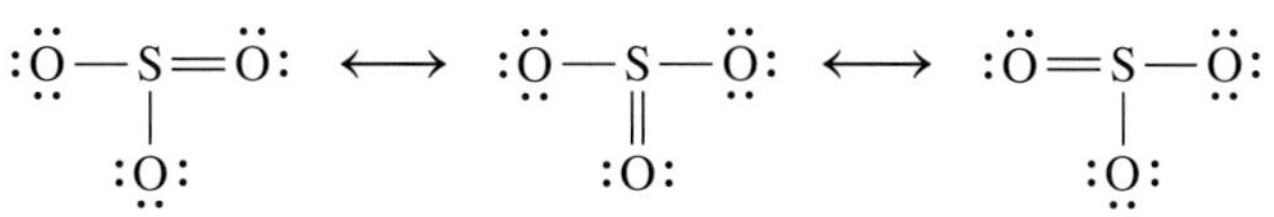

10.5 With two bonded atoms and two lone pairs of electrons, the shape of ClO_2^- is bent with a bond angle of 109°.

10.6 **a.** polar covalent (0.9)
b. nonpolar covalent (0.0)
c. ionic (2.6)

10.7 The PCl_3 molecule is trigonal pyramidal with polar P—Cl bonds, which makes it a polar molecule.

10.8 41.8 kJ removed

10.9 56.5 kJ released

10.10 226 kJ released

Answers to Selected Questions and Problems

10.1 **a.** 8 valence electrons **b.** 14 valence electrons
c. 32 valence electrons **d.** 8 valence electrons

10.3 **a.** HF $(8\ e^-)$ 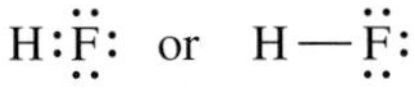

b. SF_2 $(20\ e^-)$ 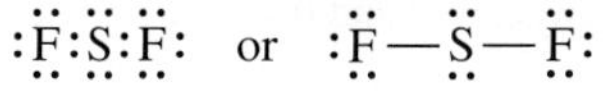

c. NBr_3 $(26\ e^-)$ 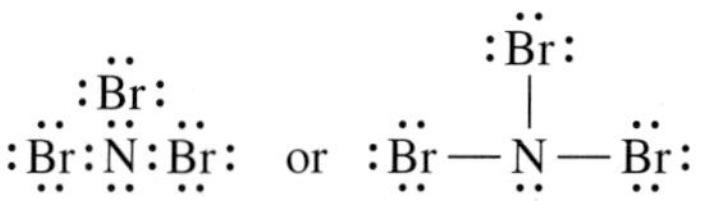

d. BH_4^- $(8\ e^-)$ 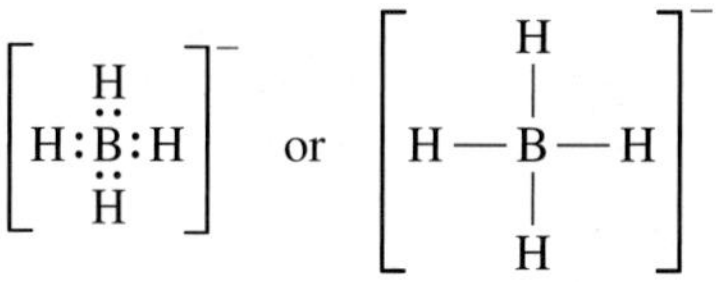

e. CH_3OH $(14\ e^-)$ 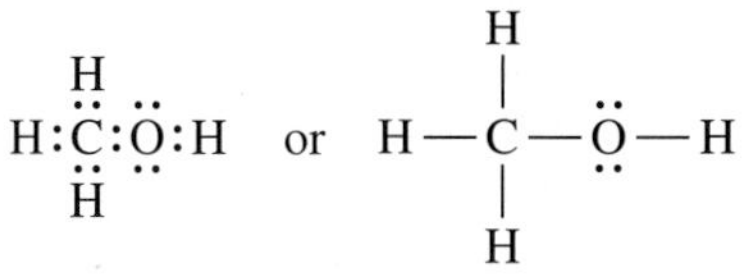

f. N_2H_4 $(14\ e^-)$ 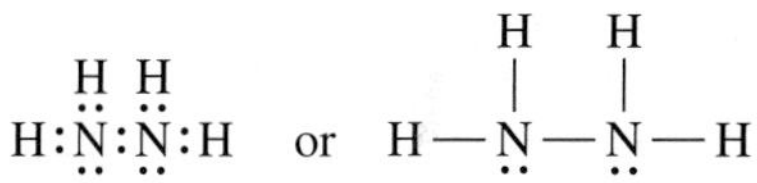

10.5 If complete octets cannot be formed by using all the valence electrons, it is necessary to draw multiple bonds.

10.7 Resonance occurs when we can draw two or more electron-dot formulas for the same molecule or ion.

10.9 **a.** CO $(10\ e^-)$ 
b. 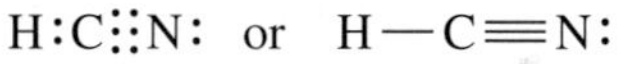 In HCN, there is a triple bond between C and N atoms.
c. H_2CO $(12\ e^-)$ 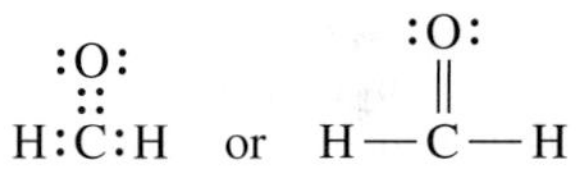

10.11 **a.** $ClNO_2$ $(24\ e^-)$ 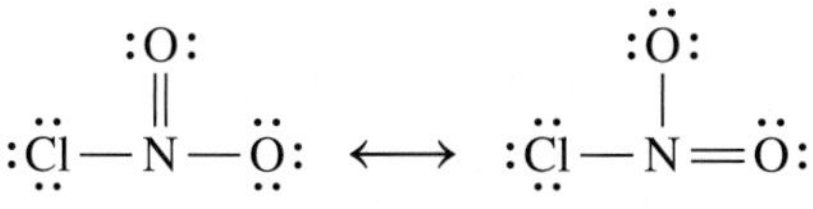

b. OCN^- $(16\ e^-)$ 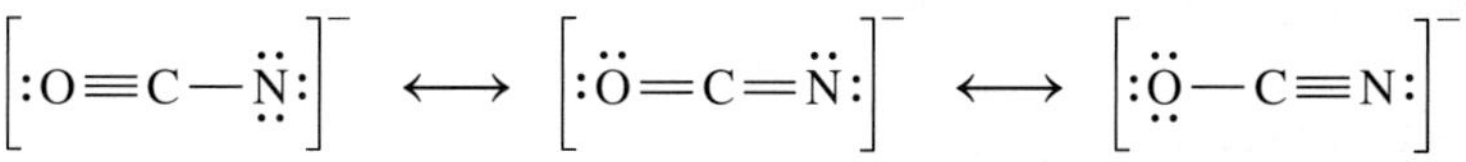

10.13 **a.** **6** tetrahedral
b. **5** trigonal pyramidal
c. **3** trigonal planar

10.15 **a.** three **b.** trigonal planar
c. three **d.** trigonal planar

10.17 In CF_4, the central atom C has four bonded atoms and no lone pairs of electrons, which gives it a tetrahedral shape. In NF_3, the central atom N has three bonded atoms and one lone pair of electrons, which gives NF_3 a trigonal pyramidal shape.

10.19 **a.** trigonal planar **b.** bent (109°)
c. linear **d.** tetrahedral

10.21 **a.** CO_3^{2-} $(24\ e^-)$ 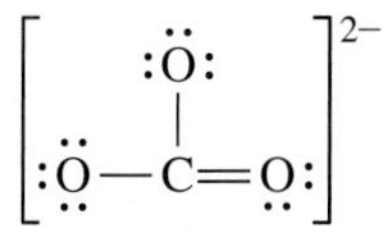 trigonal planar

b. SO_4^{2-} $(32\ e^-)$ 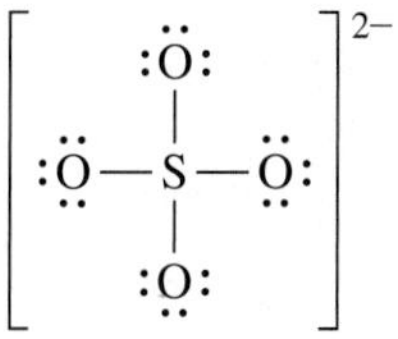 tetrahedral

c. NH_4^+ ($8\,e^-$) $\left[\begin{array}{c} \text{H} \\ | \\ \text{H—N—H} \\ | \\ \text{H} \end{array}\right]^+$ tetrahedral

d. NO_2^+ ($16\,e^-$) $[:\ddot{\text{O}}{=}\text{N}{=}\ddot{\text{O}}:]^+$ linear

10.23 **a.** increases **b.** decreases **c.** decreases

10.25 **a.** between 0.0 and 0.4

10.27 **a.** K, Na, Li **b.** Na, P, Cl **c.** Ca, Se, O

10.29 **a.** $\overset{\delta^+}{\text{N}}—\overset{\delta^-}{\text{F}}$ **b.** $\overset{\delta^+}{\text{Si}}—\overset{\delta^-}{\text{Br}}$

c. $\overset{\delta^+}{\text{C}}—\overset{\delta^-}{\text{O}}$ **d.** $\overset{\delta^+}{\text{P}}—\overset{\delta^-}{\text{Br}}$

e. $\overset{\delta^-}{\text{N}}—\overset{\delta^+}{\text{P}}$

10.31 **a.** polar covalent **b.** ionic
c. polar covalent **d.** nonpolar covalent
e. polar covalent **f.** nonpolar covalent

10.33 Electrons are shared equally between two identical atoms and unequally between nonidentical atoms.

10.35 **a.** nonpolar **b.** polar
c. polar **d.** nonpolar

10.37 In the molecule CO_2, the two C—O dipoles cancel; in CO, there is only one dipole.

10.39 **a.** dipole–dipole attractions **b.** ionic bonds
c. dipole–dipole attractions **d.** dispersion forces

10.41 **a.** hydrogen bonds **b.** dipole–dipole attractions
c. dispersion forces **d.** dispersion forces

10.43 **a.** HF; hydrogen bonds are stronger than the dipole–dipole attractions in HBr.
b. NaF; ionic bonds are stronger than the hydrogen bonds in HF.
c. $MgBr_2$; ionic bonds are stronger than the dipole–dipole attractions in PBr_3.
d. CH_3OH; hydrogen bonds are stronger than the dispersion forces in CH_4.

10.45 **a.** 21 700 J **b.** 1850 J
c. 22.3 kJ **d.** 16.7 kJ

10.47 **a.** 22 600 J **b.** 42.1 kJ
c. 3100 J **d.** 242 kJ

10.49 **a.** 4800 J **b.** 30 300 J
c. 40.2 kJ **d.** 72.2 kJ

10.51 119.5 kJ

10.53 **a.** 2, trigonal pyramidal, polar
b. 1, bent (109°), polar
c. 3, tetrahedral, nonpolar

10.55 **a.** C—O and N—O
b. O—O
c. Ca—O and K—O
d. C—O, N—O, O—O

10.57 **a.** dispersion forces **b.** dipole–dipole attractions
c. hydrogen bonds **d.** dispersion forces

10.59 **a.** The heat from the skin is used to evaporate the water (perspiration). Therefore, the skin is cooled.
b. On a hot day, there are more molecules with sufficient energy to become water vapor.
c. In a closed bag, some molecules evaporate, but they cannot escape and will condense back to liquid; the clothes will not dry.

10.61

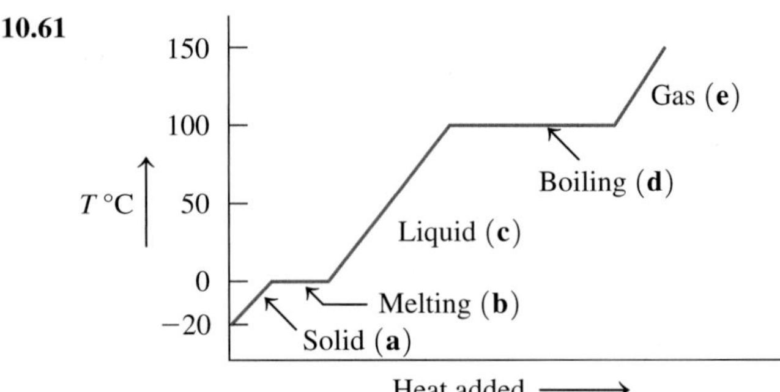

10.63 **a.** about −60 °C **b.** about 60 °C
c. A represents the solid state. B represents the change from solid to liquid or melting of the substance. C represents the liquid state as temperature increases. D represents the change from liquid to gas or boiling of the liquid. E represents the gas state.
d. At −80 °C, solid; at −40 °C, liquid; at 25 °C, liquid; 80 °C, gas

10.65 **a.** $1 + 5 + 2(6) = 18$ valence electrons
b. $2(4) + 4(1) + 6 = 18$ valence electrons
c. $5 + 4(1) - 1 = 8$ valence electrons
d. $6 + 3(6) + 2 = 26$ valence electrons

10.67 **a.** BF_4^- ($32\,e^-$) $\left[\begin{array}{c} :\ddot{\text{F}}: \\ :\ddot{\text{F}}:\text{B}:\ddot{\text{F}}: \\ :\ddot{\text{F}}: \end{array}\right]^-$ or $\left[\begin{array}{c} :\ddot{\text{F}}: \\ | \\ :\ddot{\text{F}}—\text{B}—\ddot{\text{F}}: \\ | \\ :\ddot{\text{F}}: \end{array}\right]^-$

b. Cl_2O ($20\,e^-$) $:\ddot{\text{Cl}}:\ddot{\text{O}}:\ddot{\text{Cl}}:$ or $:\ddot{\text{Cl}}—\ddot{\text{O}}—\ddot{\text{Cl}}:$

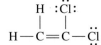

c. H_2NOH ($14\,e^-$) $\begin{array}{c} \text{H} \\ \text{H}:\ddot{\text{N}}:\ddot{\text{O}}:\text{H} \end{array}$ or $\begin{array}{c} \text{H} \\ | \\ \text{H—}\ddot{\text{N}}\text{—}\ddot{\text{O}}\text{—H} \end{array}$

d. H_2CCCl_2 ($24\,e^-$) $\begin{array}{c} \text{H}\;:\ddot{\text{Cl}}: \\ \text{H}:\text{C}::\text{C}:\ddot{\text{Cl}}: \end{array}$ or $\begin{array}{c} \text{H}\;\;:\ddot{\text{Cl}}: \\ |\quad\;\; | \\ \text{H—C=C—}\ddot{\text{Cl}}: \end{array}$

10.69 a. 16 valence electrons $[:N::N::N:]^-$ or

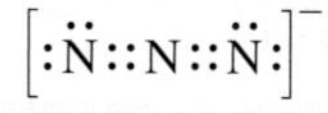

$[:N-N\equiv N:]^- \longleftrightarrow [:N=N=N:]^- \longleftrightarrow [:N\equiv N-N:]^-$

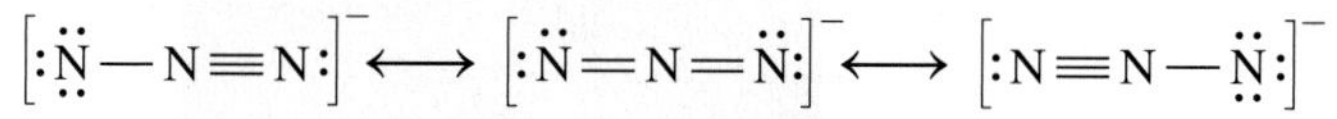

b. 16 valence electrons $[:O::N::O:]^+$ or

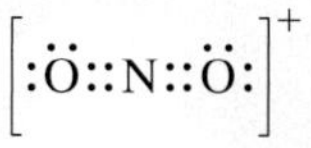

$[:O-N\equiv O:]^+ \longleftrightarrow [:O=N=O:]^+ \longleftrightarrow [:O\equiv N-O:]^+$

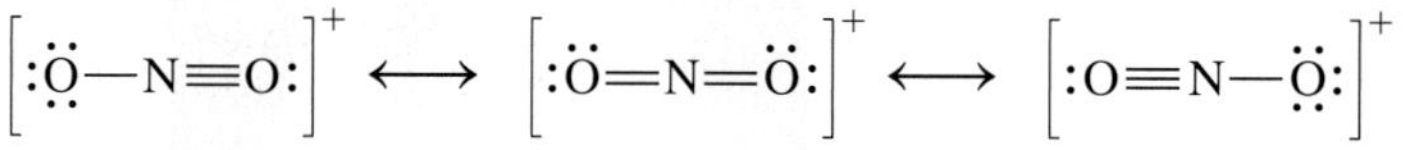

c. 16 valence electrons $[:C::N:S:]^-$ or

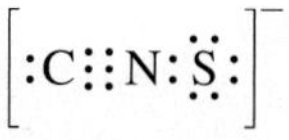

$[:C-N\equiv S:]^- \longleftrightarrow [:C=N=S:]^- \longleftrightarrow [:C\equiv N-S:]^-$

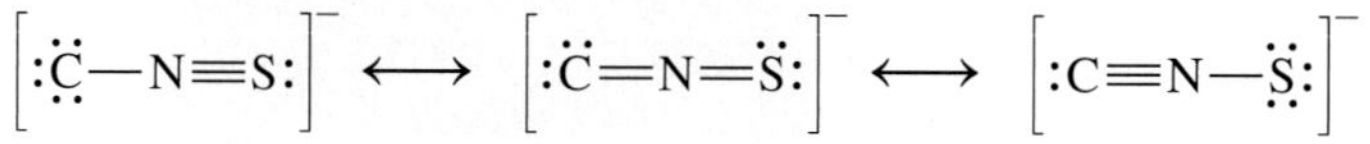

10.71 a. I, Cl, F **b.** K, Li, S, Cl **c.** Ba, Sr, Mg, Be

10.73 a. C—O **b.** N—F
c. S—Cl **d.** Br—I
e. N—F

10.75 a. Si—Cl (arrow toward Cl) **b.** C—N (arrow toward N)
c. F—Cl (arrow toward F) **d.** C—F (arrow toward F)
e. N—O (arrow toward O)

10.77 a. polar covalent **b.** nonpolar covalent
c. ionic **d.** nonpolar covalent
e. nonpolar covalent

10.79 a. NF_3 ($26\ e^-$) :F—N—F: with :F: bonded below N; trigonal pyramidal

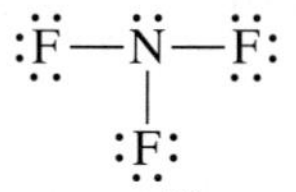

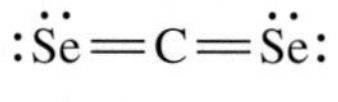

b. $SiBr_4$ ($32\ e^-$) :Br—Si—Br: with :Br: above and :Br: below Si; tetrahedral

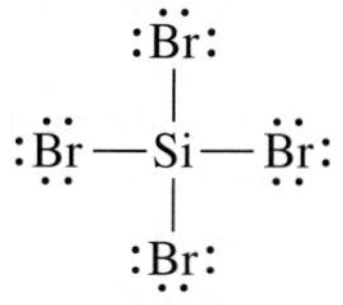

c. CSe_2 ($16\ e^-$) :Se=C=Se: linear

d. SO_2 ($18\ e^-$) :O=S—O: ⟷ :O—S=O: bent (120°)

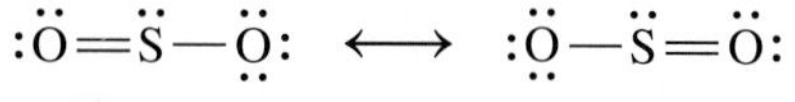

10.81 a. bent (109°) **b.** bent (109°)
c. tetrahedral **d.** trigonal pyramidal

10.83 a. polar **b.** nonpolar
c. nonpolar **d.** polar
e. polar **f.** polar

10.85 a. (2) dipole–dipole attractions
b. (2) dipole–dipole attractions
c. (4) dispersion forces
d. (1) ionic bonds
e. (4) dispersion forces
f. (3) hydrogen bonds

10.87 When water vapor condenses or liquid water freezes, heat is released, which warms the air.

10.89 4.61 g of water

10.91 27.3 g of acetic acid

10.93 a. ($18\ e^-$) H—N(—H)—C(=O:)—H

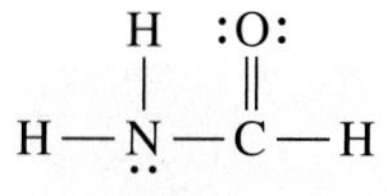

b. ($22\ e^-$) :Cl—C(H)(H)—C≡N:

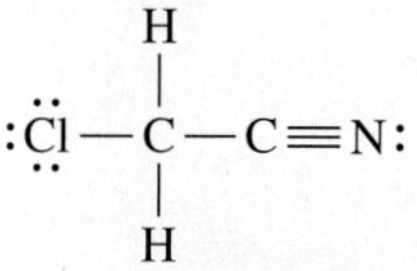

c. ($12\ e^-$) H—N=N—H

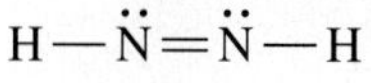

d. ($30\ e^-$) :Cl—C(=O:)—O—C(H)(H)—H

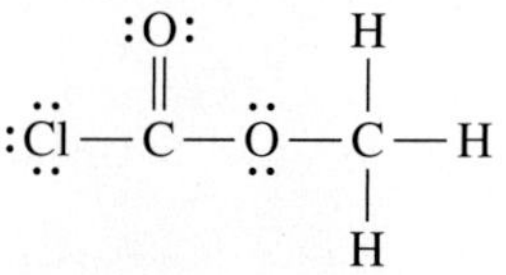

10.95 a. trigonal pyramidal **b.** tetrahedral **c.** linear

10.97 a. solid **b.** solid carbon tetrachloride melts
c. liquid **d.** gas **e.** −23 °C

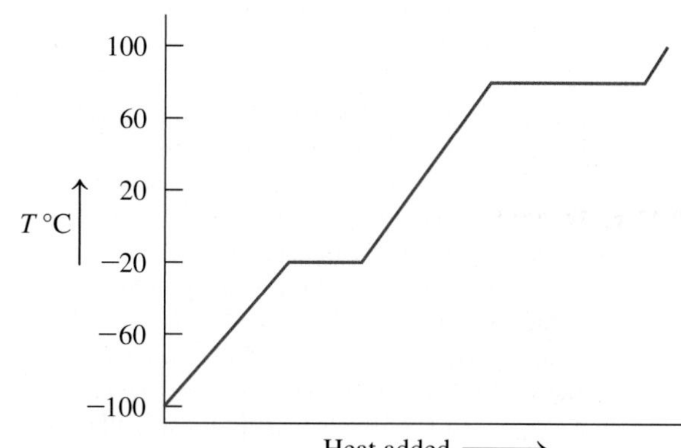

10.99 450 g of water

10.101 143 kJ of heat is removed.

Combining Ideas from Chapters 8 to 10

CI.13 In an experiment, the mass of a piece of copper is determined to be 8.56 g. Then the copper is reacted with sufficient oxygen gas to produce solid copper(II) oxide. (7.1, 8.1, 8.2, 8.3, 9.1, 9.2, 9.3, 9.4)

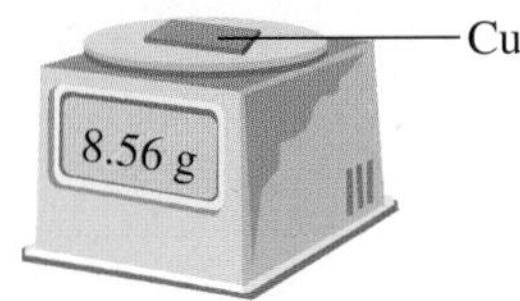

a. How many copper atoms are in the sample?
b. Write the balanced chemical equation for the reaction.
c. Classify the type of reaction.
d. How many grams of O_2 are required to completely react with the Cu?
e. How many grams of CuO will result from the reaction of 8.56 g of Cu and 3.72 g of oxygen?
f. How many grams of CuO will result in part **e**, if the yield for the reaction is 85.0%?

CI.14 One of the alkanes in gasoline is octane, C_8H_{18}, which has a density of 0.803 g/cm^3 and $\Delta H = -510$ kJ/mol. Suppose a hybrid car has a fuel tank with a capacity of 11.9 gal and has a gas mileage of 45 mi/gal. (1.10, 6.7, 8.3, 8.5, 9.5)

Octane is one of the components of motor fuel.

a. Draw the condensed structural formula for octane.
b. Write a balanced chemical equation for the complete combustion of octane including the heat of reaction.
c. What is the energy, in kilojoules, produced from one tank of fuel assuming it is all octane?
d. How many molecules of C_8H_{18} are present in one tank of fuel assuming it is all octane?
e. If this hybrid car is driven 24 500 miles in one year, how many kilograms of carbon dioxide will be produced from the combustion of the fuel assuming it is all octane?

CI.15 When clothes have stains, bleach may be added to the wash to react with the soil and make the stains colorless. The bleach solution is prepared by bubbling chlorine gas into a solution of sodium hydroxide to produce a solution of sodium hypochlorite, sodium chloride, and water. One brand of bleach contains 5.25% sodium hypochlorite by mass (active ingredient) with a density of 1.08 g/mL. (6.4, 7.1, 7.2, 8.2, 9.2, 9.3, 9.4, 10.1)

Bleach is a solution of sodium hypochlorite.

a. What is the formula and molar mass of sodium hypochlorite?
b. Draw the electron-dot formula for the hypochlorite ion.
c. How many hypochlorite ions are present in 1.00 gallon of bleach solution?
d. Write the balanced chemical equation for the preparation of bleach.
e. How many grams of NaOH are required to produce the sodium hypochlorite for 1.00 gallon of bleach?
f. If 165 g of Cl_2 is passed through a solution containing 275 g of NaOH and 162 g of sodium hypochlorite is produced, what is the percent yield of sodium hypochlorite for the reaction?

CI.16 Ethanol, $CH_3—CH_2—OH$, is obtained from renewable crops such as corn, which use the Sun as their source of energy. In the United States, automobiles can now use a fuel known as E85 that contains 85.0% ethanol and 15.0% gasoline by volume. Ethanol has a melting point of −115 °C, a boiling point of 78 °C, a heat of fusion of 109 J/g, and a heat of vaporization of 841 J/g. Liquid ethanol has a density of 0.796 g/mL and a specific heat of 2.46 J/g °C. (8.3, 8.5, 9.1, 9.2, 10.4, 10.5)

E85 fuel contains 85% ethanol.

a. Draw a heating curve for ethanol from $-150\ °C$ to $100\ °C$.

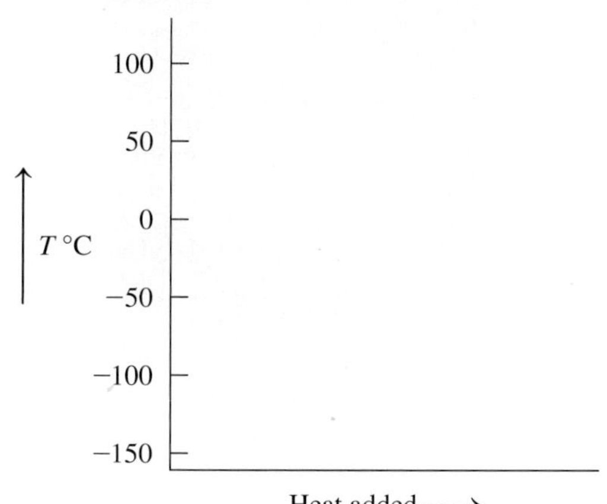

b. When 20.0 g of ethanol at $-62\ °C$ is heated and completely vaporized at $78\ °C$, how much energy, in kilojoules, is required?
c. If a 15.0-gal gas tank is filled with E85, how many liters of ethanol are in the gas tank?
d. Write the balanced chemical equation for the complete combustion of ethanol.
e. How many kilograms of CO_2 are produced by the complete combustion of the ethanol in a full 15.0-gal gas tank?
f. What is the strongest attractive force between liquid ethanol molecules?

CI.17 Chloral hydrate, a sedative and hypnotic, was the first drug used to treat insomnia. Chloral hydrate has a melting point of $57\ °C$. At its boiling point of $98\ °C$, it breaks down to chloral and water. (7.4, 7.5, 8.4, 10.1)

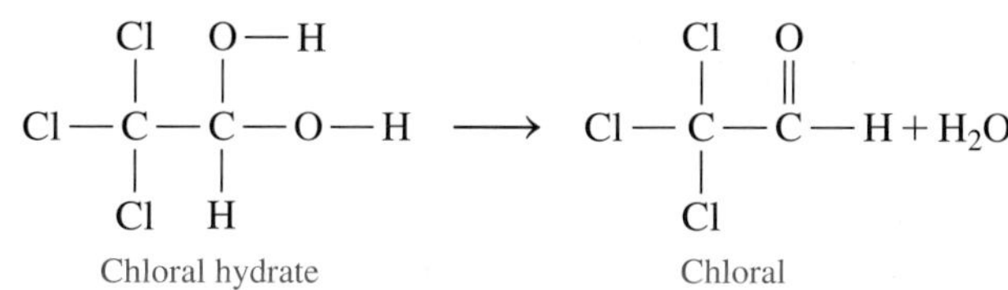

a. Draw the electron-dot formulas for chloral hydrate and chloral.
b. What functional groups are in chloral hydrate and chloral?
c. What are the empirical formulas of chloral hydrate and chloral?
d. What is the mass percent of Cl in chloral hydrate?

CI.18 Ethylene glycol, $C_2H_6O_2$, used as a coolant and antifreeze, has a density of 1.11 g/mL. As a sweet-tasting liquid, it can be appealing to pets and small children, but it can be toxic, with an LD_{50} of 4700 mg/kg. Its accidental ingestion can cause kidney damage and difficulty with breathing. In the body, ethylene glycol is converted to another toxic substance, oxalic acid, $H_2C_2O_4$. (2.8, 7.4, 7.5, 8.2, 8.4, 10.1, 10.3, 10.4)

a. What are the empirical formulas of ethylene glycol and oxalic acid?
b. If ethylene glycol has a C—C single bond with two H atoms attached to each C atom, what is its electron-dot formula?
c. Which bonds in ethylene glycol are polar and which are nonpolar?
d. How many milliliters of ethylene glycol could be toxic for an 11.0-lb cat?
e. What would be the strongest attractive force in ethylene glycol?

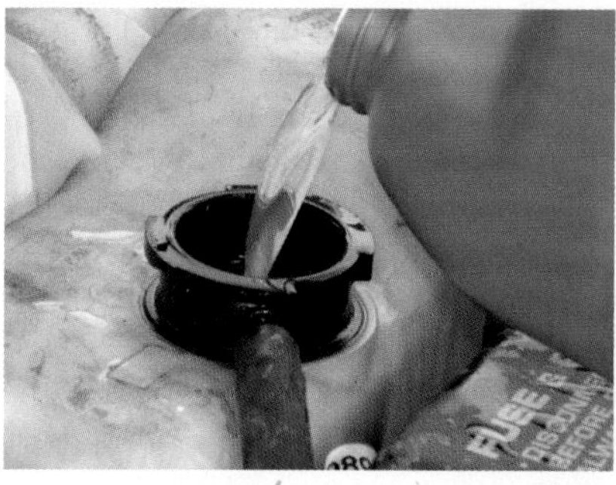

Antifreeze often contains ethylene glycol.

f. If oxalic acid has two carboxylic acid groups attached by a C—C single bond, what is its electron-dot formula?
g. Write the balanced chemical equation for the reaction of ethylene glycol and oxygen (O_2) to give oxalic acid and water.

CI.19 Acetone (propanone), a clear liquid solvent with an acrid odor, is used to remove nail polish, paints, and resins. It has a low boiling point and is highly flammable. Acetone has a density of 0.786 g/mL and a heat of combustion of -1790 kJ/mol. (2.8, 7.2, 8.3, 8.4, 9.2, 9.5)

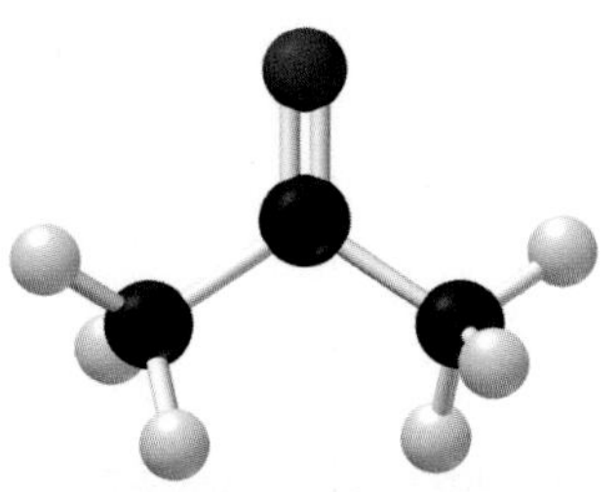

Acetone has carbon atoms (black), hydrogen atoms (white), and an oxygen atom (red).

a. Draw the condensed structural formula for acetone.
b. What are the molecular formula and molar mass of acetone?
c. Write a balanced chemical equation for the complete combustion of acetone, including the heat of reaction.
d. Is the combustion of acetone an endothermic or exothermic reaction?
e. How much heat, in kilojoules, is released if 2.58 g of acetone reacts completely with oxygen?
f. How many grams of oxygen gas are needed to react with 15.0 mL of acetone?

CI.20 The compound dihydroxyacetone (DHA) is used in "sunless" tanning lotions, which darken the skin by reacting with the amino acids in the outer surface of the skin. A typical drugstore lotion contains 4.0% (mass/volume) DHA. (2.8, 7.2, 8.4)

a. Draw the condensed structural formula for DHA.
b. Identify the functional groups in DHA.
c. What are the molecular formula and molar mass of DHA?
d. A bottle of sunless tanning lotion contains 177 mL of lotion. How many milligrams of DHA are in a bottle?

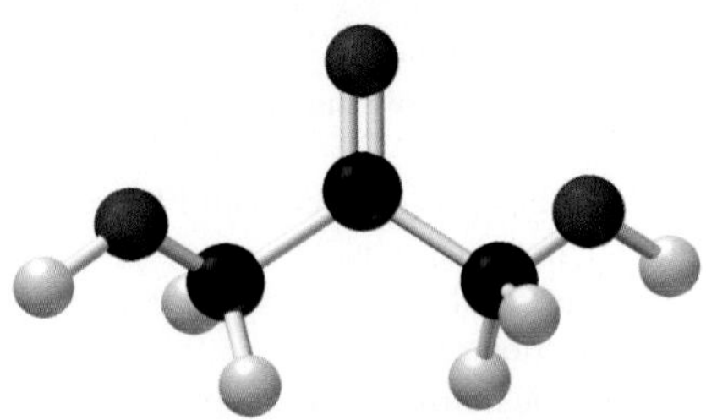

The model of dihydroxyacetone has carbon atoms (black), hydrogen atoms (white), and oxygen atoms (red).

ANSWERS

CI.13 a. 8.11×10^{22} atoms of copper
b. $2Cu(s) + O_2(g) \longrightarrow 2CuO(s)$
c. combination reaction
d. 2.16 g of O_2
e. 10.7 g of CuO
f. 9.10 g of CuO

CI.15 a. NaOCl, 74.44 g/mol
b. ($14\ e^-$) $\left[:\ddot{\underset{..}{Cl}}-\ddot{\underset{..}{O}}:\right]^-$
c. 1.74×10^{24} OCl^- ions
d. $2NaOH(aq) + Cl_2(g) \longrightarrow NaOCl(aq) + NaCl(aq) + H_2O(l)$
e. 231 g of NaOH
f. 93.6%

CI.17 a. ($44\ e^-$)

$$\begin{array}{ccccccc} & & :\ddot{Cl}: & & :\ddot{O}-H & & \\ & & | & & | & & \\ :\ddot{\underset{..}{Cl}} & - & C & - & C & - & \ddot{\underset{..}{O}}-H \\ & & | & & | & & \\ & & :\underset{..}{Cl}: & & H & & \end{array}$$

($36\ e^-$)

$$\begin{array}{ccccccc} & & :\ddot{Cl}: & & :O: & & \\ & & | & & \| & & \\ :\ddot{\underset{..}{Cl}} & - & C & - & C & - & H \\ & & | & & & & \\ & & :\underset{..}{Cl}: & & & & \end{array}$$

b. chloral hydrate: alcohol (two); chloral: aldehyde
c. chloral hydrate: $C_2H_3O_2Cl_3$
chloral: C_2HOCl_3
d. 64.33% Cl (by mass)

CI.19 a.

$$\begin{array}{ccccc} & & O & & \\ & & \| & & \\ CH_3 & - & C & - & CH_3 \end{array}$$

b. C_3H_6O; 58.08 g/mol
c. $C_3H_6O(g) + 4O_2(g) \xrightarrow{\Delta} 3CO_2(g) + 3H_2O(g) + 1790\ kJ$
d. exothermic
e. 79.5 kJ
f. 26.0 g of O_2

Gases 11

LOOKING AHEAD

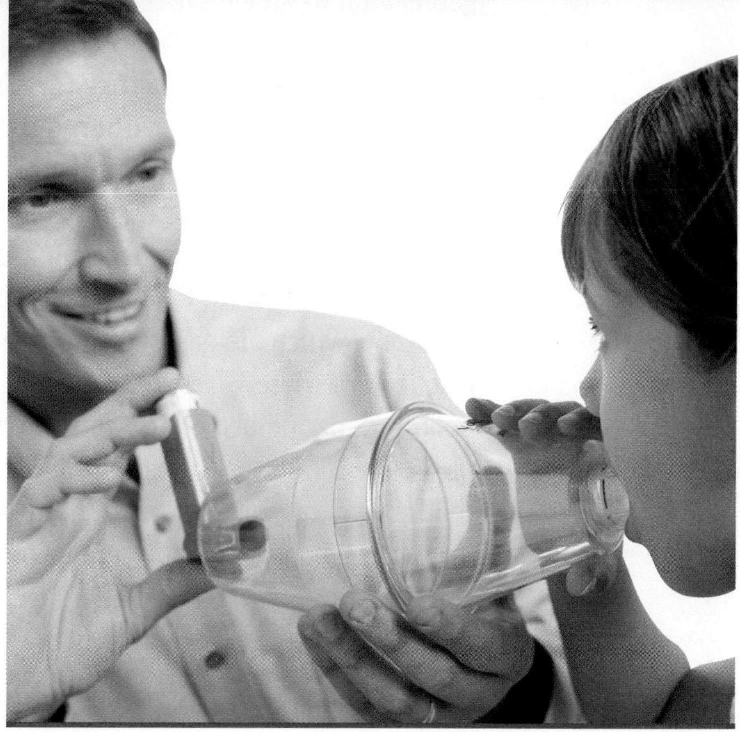

After soccer practice, Whitney complained that she was having difficulty breathing. Her father quickly took her to the emergency room where she was seen by a respiratory therapist. The respiratory therapist listened to Whitney's chest and then tested her breathing capacity using a spirometer. Based on her limited breathing capacity and the wheezing noise in her chest, Whitney was diagnosed as having asthma.

The therapist gave Whitney a nebulizer containing a bronchodilator that opens the airways and allows more air to go into the lungs. During the breathing treatment, the respiratory therapist measured the amount of oxygen (O_2) in her blood and explained to Whitney and her father that air is a mixture of gases containing 78% nitrogen (N_2) gas and 21% O_2 gas. Because Whitney had difficulty obtaining sufficient oxygen breathing air, the respiratory therapist gave her supplemental oxygen through an oxygen mask. Within a short period of time, Whitney's breathing returned to normal. The therapist then explained that the lungs work according to Boyle's law: the volume of the lungs increases upon inhalation, and the pressure decreases to make air flow in. However, during an asthma attack, the airways become restricted, and it becomes more difficult to expand the volume of the lungs.

Career: Respiratory Therapist

Respiratory therapists assess and treat a range of patients, including premature infants whose lungs have not developed and asthmatics or patients with emphysema or cystic fibrosis. In assessing patients, they perform a variety of diagnostic tests including breathing capacity, concentrations of oxygen and carbon dioxide in a patient's blood, as well as blood pH. In order to treat patients, therapists provide oxygen or aerosol medications to the patient, as well as chest physiotherapy to remove mucus from their lungs. Respiratory therapists also educate patients on how to correctly use their inhalers.

We all live at the bottom of a sea of gases called the atmosphere. The most important of these gases is oxygen, which constitutes about 21% of the atmosphere. Without oxygen, life on this planet would be impossible: Oxygen is vital to all life processes of plants and animals. Ozone (O_3), formed in the upper atmosphere by the interaction of oxygen with ultraviolet light, absorbs some of the harmful radiation before it can strike Earth's surface. The other gases in the atmosphere include nitrogen (78%), argon, carbon dioxide (CO_2), and water vapor. Carbon dioxide gas, a product of combustion and metabolism, is used by plants in photosynthesis, which produces the oxygen that is essential for humans and animals.

The atmosphere has become a dumping ground for other gases, such as methane, chlorofluorocarbons (CFCs), and nitrogen oxides, as well as volatile organic compounds (VOCs), which are gases from paints, paint thinners, and cleaning supplies. The chemical reactions of these gases with sunlight and oxygen in the atmosphere are contributing to air pollution, ozone depletion, climate change, and acid rain. Such chemical changes can seriously affect our health and our lifestyle. An understanding of gases and some of the laws that govern gas behavior can help us understand the nature of matter and allow us to make decisions concerning important environmental and health issues.

CHAPTER READINESS*

Key Math Skills

- Solving Equations (1.4D)

Core Chemistry Skills

- Using Significant Figures in Calculations (2.4)
- Writing Conversion Factors from Equalities (2.6)
- Using Conversion Factors (2.7)
- Using Molar Mass as a Conversion Factor (7.3)
- Converting Moles to Moles (9.1)

*These Key Math Skills and Core Chemistry Skills from previous chapters are listed here for your review as you proceed to the new material in this chapter.

LEARNING GOAL

Describe the kinetic molecular theory of gases and the properties of gases.

11.1 Properties of Gases

We are surrounded by gases but are not often aware of their presence. Of the elements on the periodic table, only a few exist as gases at room temperature: H_2, N_2, O_2, F_2, Cl_2, and the noble gases. Another group of gases includes the oxides of the nonmetals on the upper corner of the periodic table, such as CO, CO_2, NO, NO_2, SO_2, and SO_3. Organic compounds such as methane, ethane, propane, and butane that have small molar masses are also gases at room temperatures. Generally, molecules that are gases at room temperature have fewer than five atoms from the first or second period.

The behavior of gases is quite different from that of liquids and solids. Gas particles are far apart, whereas particles of both liquids and solids are held close together. A gas has no definite shape or volume and will completely fill any container. Because there are great distances between gas particles, a gas is less dense than a solid or liquid, and easy to compress. A model for the behavior of a gas, called the **kinetic molecular theory of gases**, helps us understand gas behavior.

Kinetic Molecular Theory of Gases

1. **A gas consists of small particles (atoms or molecules) that move randomly with high velocities.** Gas molecules moving in random directions at high speeds cause a gas to fill the entire volume of a container.
2. **The attractive forces between the particles of a gas are usually very small.** Gas particles are far apart and fill a container of any size and shape.
3. **The actual volume occupied by gas molecules is extremely small compared to the volume that the gas occupies.** The volume of the gas is considered equal to the volume of the container. Most of the volume of a gas is empty space, which allows gases to be easily compressed.
4. **Gas particles are in constant motion, moving rapidly in straight paths.** When gas particles collide, they rebound and travel in new directions. Every time they hit the walls of the container, they exert pressure. An increase in the number or force of collisions against the walls of the container causes an increase in the pressure of the gas.
5. **The average kinetic energy of gas molecules is proportional to the Kelvin temperature.** Gas particles move faster as the temperature increases. At higher temperatures, gas particles hit the walls of the container more often and with more force, producing higher pressures.

The kinetic molecular theory helps explain some of the characteristics of gases. For example, we can smell perfume when a bottle is opened on the other side of a room because its particles move rapidly in all directions. At room temperatures, the molecules of air are moving at about 450 m/s, which is 1000 mi/h. They move faster at higher temperatures and more slowly at lower temperatures. Sometimes tires and gas-filled containers explode when temperatures are too high. From the kinetic molecular theory, we know that gas particles move faster when heated, hit the walls of a container with more force, and cause a buildup of pressure inside a container.

CONCEPT CHECK 11.1 Properties of Gases

Use the kinetic molecular theory to explain why a gas completely fills a container of any size and shape.

ANSWER

Gas particles move at high speeds in random directions, moving as far apart as possible until they hit the walls of a container. Thus gas particles completely fill a container of any size and shape.

When we talk about a gas, we describe it in terms of four properties: pressure, volume, temperature, and the amount of gas.

Pressure (*P*)

Gas particles are extremely small and move rapidly. When they hit the walls of a container, they exert a *pressure* (see Figure 11.1). If we heat the container, the molecules move faster and smash into the walls of the container more often and with increased force, thus increasing the pressure. The gas particles in the air, mostly oxygen and nitrogen, exert a pressure on us called **atmospheric pressure** (see Figure 11.2). As you go to higher altitudes, the atmospheric pressure is less because there are fewer particles in the air. The most common units used for gas measurement are the *atmosphere* (atm) and *millimeters of mercury* (mmHg). On the TV weather report, you may hear or see the atmospheric pressure given in inches of mercury, or in kilopascals in countries other than the United States.

FIGURE 11.1 Gas particles move in straight lines within a container. The gas particles exert pressure when they collide with the walls of the container.

Q Why does heating the container increase the pressure of the gas within it?

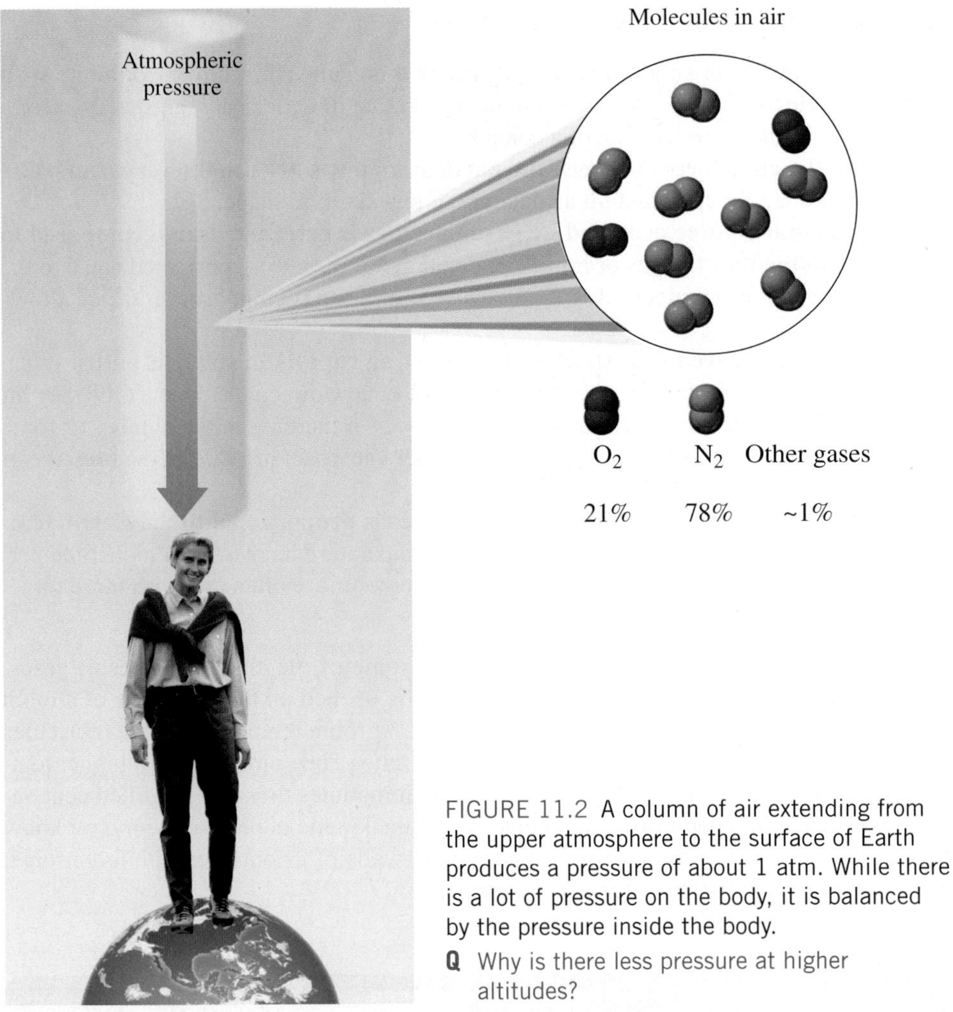

FIGURE 11.2 A column of air extending from the upper atmosphere to the surface of Earth produces a pressure of about 1 atm. While there is a lot of pressure on the body, it is balanced by the pressure inside the body.

Q Why is there less pressure at higher altitudes?

Volume (*V*)

The volume of gas equals the size of the container in which the gas is placed. When you inflate a tire or a basketball, you are adding more gas particles. The increase in the number of particles hitting the walls of the tire or basketball increases the volume. Sometimes, on a cold morning, a tire looks flat. The volume of the tire has decreased because a lower temperature decreases the speed of the molecules, which in turn reduces the force of their impacts on the walls of the tire. The most common units for volume measurement are liters (L) and milliliters (mL).

Temperature (*T*)

The temperature of a gas is related to the kinetic energy of its particles. For example, if we have a gas at 200 K in a rigid container and heat it to a temperature of 400 K, the gas particles will have twice the kinetic energy that they did at 200 K. This also means that the gas at 400 K exerts twice the pressure of the gas at 200 K. Although you measure gas temperature using a Celsius thermometer, all comparisons of gas behavior and all calculations related to temperature must use the Kelvin temperature scale. No one has yet achieved the conditions for absolute zero (0 K), but we predict that the particles will have zero kinetic energy and exert zero pressure at absolute zero.

Amount of Gas (*n*)

When you add air to a bicycle tire, you increase the amount of gas, which results in a higher pressure in the tire. Usually, we measure the amount of gas by its mass (grams). In gas law calculations, we need to change the grams of gas to moles.

A summary of the four properties of a gas is given in Table 11.1.

TABLE 11.1 Properties That Describe a Gas

Property	Description	Unit(s) of Measurement
Pressure (P)	The force exerted by a gas against the walls of the container	atmosphere (atm); millimeters of mercury (mmHg); torr; pascal (Pa)
Volume (V)	The space occupied by a gas	liter (L); milliliter (mL); cubic meter (m^3)
Temperature (T)	The determining factor of the kinetic energy and rate of motion of gas particles	degree Celsius (°C); kelvin (K) *is required in calculations*
Amount (n)	The quantity of gas present in a container	grams (g); moles (n) *is required in calculations*

SAMPLE PROBLEM 11.1 Properties of Gases

Identify the property of a gas that is described by each of the following:

a. increases the kinetic energy of gas particles
b. the force of the gas particles hitting the walls of the container
c. the space that is occupied by a gas

SOLUTION

a. temperature **b.** pressure **c.** volume

STUDY CHECK 11.1

When helium is added to a balloon, the mass of the gas, in grams, increases. What property of a gas is described?

Chemistry Link to Health

MEASURING BLOOD PRESSURE

Your blood pressure is one of the vital signs a doctor or nurse checks during a physical examination. It actually consists of two separate measurements. Acting as a pump, the heart contracts to create the pressure that pushes blood through the circulatory system. During contraction, the blood pressure is at its highest; this is your *systolic* pressure. When the heart muscles relax, the blood pressure falls; this is your *diastolic* pressure. The normal range for systolic pressure is 100–120 mmHg. For diastolic pressure, it is 60–80 mmHg. These two measurements are usually expressed as a ratio such as 100/80. These values are somewhat higher in older people. When blood pressures are elevated, such as 140/90, there is a greater risk of stroke, heart attack, or kidney damage. Low blood pressure prevents the brain from receiving adequate oxygen, causing dizziness and fainting.

The blood pressures are measured by a sphygmomanometer, an instrument consisting of a stethoscope and an inflatable cuff connected to a tube of mercury called a manometer. After the cuff is wrapped around the upper arm, it is pumped up with air until it cuts off the flow of blood. With the stethoscope over the artery, the air is slowly released from the cuff, decreasing the pressure on the artery. When the blood flow first starts again in the artery, a noise can be heard through the stethoscope signifying the systolic blood pressure as the pressure shown on the manometer. As air continues to be released, the cuff deflates until no sound is heard in the artery. A second pressure reading is taken at the moment of silence and denotes the diastolic pressure, the pressure when the heart is not contracting.

The use of digital blood pressure monitors is becoming more common. However, they have not been validated for use in all situations and can sometimes give inaccurate readings.

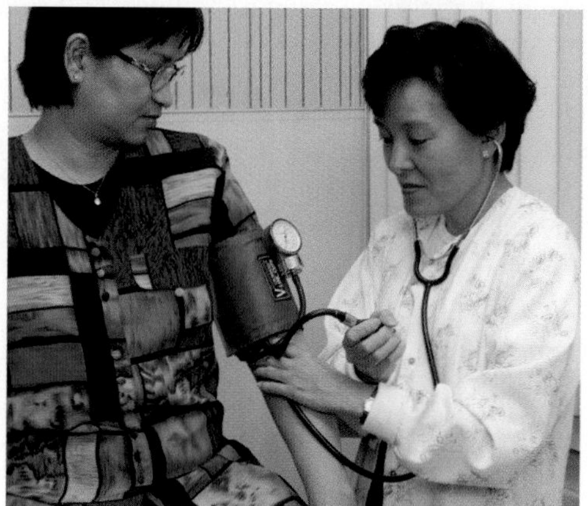

The measurement of blood pressure is part of a routine health checkup.

QUESTIONS AND PROBLEMS

11.1 Properties of Gases

LEARNING GOAL: *Describe the kinetic molecular theory of gases and the properties of gases.*

11.1 Use the kinetic molecular theory of gases to explain each of the following:
a. Gases move faster at higher temperatures.
b. Gases can be compressed much more easily than liquids or solids.
c. Gases have low densities.

11.2 Use the kinetic molecular theory of gases to explain each of the following:
a. A container of nonstick cooking spray explodes when thrown into a fire.
b. The air in a hot-air balloon is heated to make the balloon rise.
c. You can smell the odor of cooking onions from far away.

11.3 Identify the property of a gas that is measured in each of the following:
a. 350 K **b.** 125 mL
c. 2.00 g of O_2 **d.** 755 mmHg

11.4 Identify the property of a gas that is measured in each of the following:
a. 425 K **b.** 1.0 atm
c. 10.0 L **d.** 0.50 mol of He

LEARNING GOAL

Describe the units of measurement used for pressure, and change from one unit to another.

11.2 Gas Pressure

When billions and billions of gas particles hit against the walls of a container, they exert **pressure**, which is defined as a force acting on a certain area.

$$\text{Pressure } (P) = \frac{\text{force}}{\text{area}}$$

The atmospheric pressure can be measured using a barometer (see Figure 11.3). At a pressure of exactly 1 atmosphere (atm), a mercury column in an inverted tube would be *exactly* 760 mm high. One **atmosphere (atm)** is defined as *exactly* 760 mmHg (millimeters of mercury). One atmosphere is also 760 **torr**, a pressure unit named to honor Evangelista Torricelli, the inventor of the barometer. Because the units of torr and mmHg are equal, they are used interchangeably.

$$1 \text{ atm} = 760 \text{ mmHg} = 760 \text{ torr (exact)}$$
$$1 \text{ mmHg} = 1 \text{ torr (exact)}$$

In SI units, pressure is measured in pascals (Pa); 1 atm is equal to 101 325 Pa. Because a pascal is a very small unit, pressures are usually reported in kilopascals.

$$1 \text{ atm} = 1.01325 \times 10^5 \text{ Pa} = 101.325 \text{ kPa}$$

The U.S. equivalent of 1 atm is 14.7 lb/in.^{2} (psi). When you use a pressure gauge to check the air pressure in the tires of a car, it may read 30–35 psi. This measurement is actually 30–35 psi above the pressure that the atmosphere exerts on the outside of the tire. Table 11.2 summarizes the various units used in the measurement of pressure.

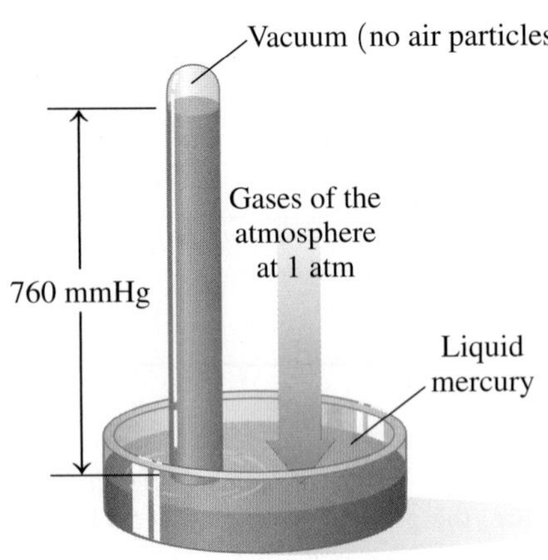

FIGURE 11.3 A barometer: the pressure exerted by the gases in the atmosphere is equal to the downward pressure of a mercury column in a closed glass tube. The height of the mercury column measured in mmHg is called atmospheric pressure.

Q Why does the height of the mercury column change from day to day?

TABLE 11.2 Units for Measuring Pressure

Unit	Abbreviation	Unit Equivalent to 1 atm
Atmosphere	atm	1 atm (exact)
Millimeters of Hg	mmHg	760 mmHg (exact)
Torr	torr	760 torr
Inches of Hg	in. Hg	29.9 in. Hg
Pounds per square inch	lb/in.^{2} (psi)	14.7 lb/in.^{2}
Pascal	Pa	101 325 Pa
Kilopascal	kPa	101.325 kPa

If you have a barometer in your home, it probably gives pressure in inches of mercury. One atmosphere is equal to the pressure of a column of mercury that is 29.9 in. high. Atmospheric pressure changes with variations in weather and altitude. On a hot, sunny day, a column of air has more particles, which increases the pressure on the mercury surface. The mercury column rises, which indicates a higher atmospheric pressure. On a rainy day, the atmosphere exerts less pressure, which causes the mercury column to fall. In the weather report, this type of weather is called a *low-pressure system*. Above sea level, the density of the gases in the air decreases, which causes lower atmospheric pressures; the atmospheric pressure is greater than 760 mmHg at the Dead Sea because it is below sea level and the column of air above it is taller (see Table 11.3).

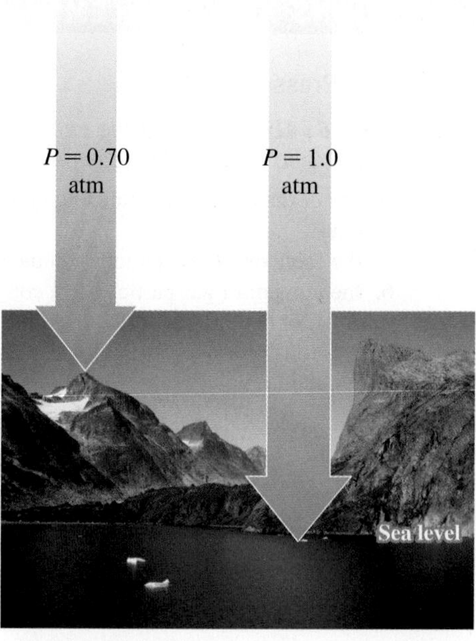

The atmospheric pressure decreases as the altitude increases.

TABLE 11.3 Altitude and Atmospheric Pressure

Location	Altitude (km)	Atmospheric Pressure (mmHg)
Dead Sea	−0.40	800
Sea level	0.00	760
Los Angeles	0.09	752
Las Vegas	0.70	700
Denver	1.60	630
Mount Whitney	4.50	440
Mount Everest	8.90	253

Divers must be concerned about increasing pressures on their ears and lungs when they dive below the surface of the ocean. Because water is more dense than air, the pressure on a diver increases rapidly as the diver descends. At a depth of 33 ft below the surface of the ocean, an additional 1 atm of pressure is exerted by the water on a diver, which gives a total pressure of 2 atm. At 100 ft, there is a total pressure of 4 atm on a diver. The regulator that a diver uses continuously adjusts the pressure of the breathing mixture to match the increase in pressure.

CONCEPT CHECK 11.2 Units of Pressure

A sample of neon gas has a pressure of 0.50 atm. Calculate the pressure, in mmHg, of the neon.

ANSWER

The equality 1 atm = 760 mmHg can be written as two conversion factors:

$$\frac{760\ \text{mmHg}}{1\ \text{atm}} \quad \text{and} \quad \frac{1\ \text{atm}}{760\ \text{mmHg}}$$

Using the conversion factor that cancels atm and gives mmHg, we can set up the problem as

$$0.50\ \cancel{\text{atm}} \times \frac{760\ \text{mmHg}}{1\ \cancel{\text{atm}}} = 380\ \text{mmHg}$$

QUESTIONS AND PROBLEMS

11.2 Gas Pressure

LEARNING GOAL: *Describe the units of measurement used for pressure, and change from one unit to another.*

11.5 Which of the following statement(s) describes the pressure of a gas?
- **a.** the force of the gas particles on the walls of the container
- **b.** the number of gas particles in a container
- **c.** 4.5 L of helium gas
- **d.** 750 torr
- **e.** 28.8 lb/in.^{2}

11.6 Which of the following statement(s) describes the pressure of a gas?
- **a.** the temperature of the gas
- **b.** the volume of the container
- **c.** 3.00 atm
- **d.** 0.25 mol of O_2
- **e.** 101 kPa

11.7 An oxygen tank contains oxygen (O_2) at a pressure of 2.00 atm. What is the pressure in the tank in terms of the following units?
- **a.** torr
- **b.** lb/in.^{2}
- **c.** mmHg
- **d.** kPa

11.8 On a climb up Mount Whitney, the atmospheric pressure drops to 467 mmHg. What is the pressure in terms of the following units?
- **a.** atm
- **b.** torr
- **c.** in. Hg
- **d.** Pa

LEARNING GOAL

Use the pressure–volume relationship (Boyle's law) to determine the final pressure or volume when the temperature and amount of gas are constant.

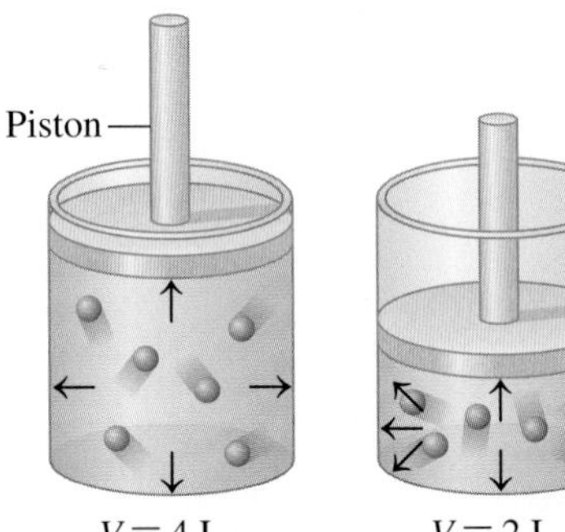

FIGURE 11.4 **Boyle's law:** As volume decreases, gas molecules become more crowded, which causes the pressure to increase. Pressure and volume are inversely related.

Q If the volume of a gas increases, what will happen to its pressure?

11.3 Pressure and Volume (Boyle's Law)

Imagine that you can see air particles hitting the walls inside a bicycle tire pump. What happens to the pressure inside the pump as we push down on the handle? As the volume decreases, there is a decrease in the surface area of the container. The air particles are crowded together, more collisions occur, and the pressure increases within the container.

When a change in one property (in this case, volume) causes a change in another property (in this case, pressure), the properties are related. If the change occurs in opposite directions, the properties have an **inverse relationship**. The inverse relationship between the pressure and volume of a gas is known as **Boyle's law**. The law states that the volume (V) of a sample of gas changes inversely with the pressure (P) of the gas as long as there is no change in the temperature (T) or amount of gas (n), as illustrated in Figure 11.4.

If the volume or pressure of a gas changes without any change occurring in the temperature or in the amount of the gas, then the final pressure and volume will give the same PV product as the initial pressure and volume. Then we can set the initial and final PV products equal to each other.

Boyle's Law

$P_1V_1 = P_2V_2$ No change in number of moles and temperature

CONCEPT CHECK 11.3 Boyle's Law

State and explain the reason for the change (*increases, decreases*) in the pressure of a gas that occurs in each of the following when n and T do not change:

	Pressure (P)	Volume (V)	Amount (n)	Temperature (T)
a.		decreases	constant	constant
b.		increases	constant	constant

ANSWER

a. When the volume of a gas decreases at constant n and T, the gas particles are closer together, which increases the number of collisions with the container walls. Therefore, the *pressure increases* when volume decreases with no change in n and T.

b. When the volume of a gas increases with no change in n and T, the gas particles move farther apart, which decreases the number of collisions with the container walls. Therefore the *pressure decreases* when the volume increases with no change in n and T.

	Pressure (P)	Volume (V)	Amount (n)	Temperature (T)
a.	increases	decreases	constant	constant
b.	decreases	increases	constant	constant

SAMPLE PROBLEM 11.2 Calculating Pressure When Volume Changes

CORE CHEMISTRY SKILL 

Using the Gas Laws

A sample of hydrogen gas (H_2) has a volume of 5.0 L and a pressure of 1.0 atm. What is the final pressure, in atmospheres, if the volume is decreased to 2.0 L with no change in temperature and amount of gas?

SOLUTION

Step 1 **Organize the data in a table of initial and final conditions.** In this problem, we want to know the final pressure (P_2) for the change in volume. We place the properties that change, which are the volume and pressure, in a table. The properties that do not change, which are temperature (T) and amount of gas (n), are shown below the table. Because we are given the initial and final volumes of the gas, we know that the volume decreases. We can predict that the pressure will increase.

Analyze the Problem	Conditions 1	Conditions 2	Know	Predict
	$V_1 = 5.0$ L	$V_2 = 2.0$ L	V decreases	
	$P_1 = 1.0$ atm	$P_2 = ?$ atm		P increases

Factors that remain constant: T and n

Step 2 **Rearrange the gas law equation to solve for the unknown quantity.** For a PV relationship, we use Boyle's law and solve for P_2 by dividing both sides by V_2.

$$P_1V_1 = P_2V_2$$

$$\frac{P_1V_1}{V_2} = \frac{P_2\cancel{V_2}}{\cancel{V_2}}$$

$$P_2 = P_1 \times \frac{V_1}{V_2}$$

Step 3 **Substitute values into the gas law equation and calculate.** When we substitute in the values, we see that the ratio of the volumes (volume factor) is greater than 1, which increases the pressure as we predicted in Step 1. Note that the units of volume (L) cancel to give the final pressure in atmospheres.

$$P_2 = 1.0 \text{ atm} \times \underbrace{\frac{5.0 \cancel{\text{L}}}{2.0 \cancel{\text{L}}}}_{\substack{\text{Volume factor} \\ \text{increases pressure}}} = 2.5 \text{ atm}$$

STUDY CHECK 11.2

A sample of helium gas has a volume of 312 mL at 648 torr. If the volume expands to 825 mL at constant temperature, what is the final pressure, in torr?

Guide to Using the Gas Laws

1. Organize the data in a table of initial and final conditions.
2. Rearrange the gas law equation to solve for the unknown quantity.
3. Substitute values into the gas law equation and calculate.

SAMPLE PROBLEM 11.3 Calculating Volume When Pressure Changes

A gauge indicates the pressure of a gas in a tank.

The gauge on a 12-L tank of compressed oxygen reads 3800 mmHg. How many liters would this same gas occupy at a pressure of 0.75 atm at constant temperature and amount of gas?

SOLUTION

Step 1 **Organize the data in a table of initial and final conditions.** To match the units for initial and final pressure, we can either convert atm to mmHg or mmHg to atm.

$$0.75 \cancel{\text{atm}} \times \frac{760 \text{ mmHg}}{1 \cancel{\text{atm}}} = 570 \text{ mmHg}$$

$$3800 \cancel{\text{mmHg}} \times \frac{1 \text{ atm}}{760 \cancel{\text{mmHg}}} = 5.0 \text{ atm}$$

We place the gas data using units of mmHg for pressure and liters for volume in a table. (We could have both pressures in units of atm as well.) The properties that do not change, which are temperature and amount of gas, are shown below the table. We know that pressure decreases. We can predict that the volume increases.

	Conditions 1	Conditions 2	Know	Predict
Analyze the Problem	$P_1 = 3800$ mmHg (5.0 atm)	$P_2 = 570$ mmHg (0.75 atm)	P decreases	
	$V_1 = 12$ L	$V_2 = ?$ L		V increases

Factors that remain constant: T and n

Step 2 **Rearrange the gas law equation to solve for the unknown quantity.** For a PV relationship, we use Boyle's law and solve for V_2 by dividing both sides by P_2. According to Boyle's law, a decrease in the pressure will cause an increase in the volume when T and n remain constant.

$$P_1V_1 = P_2V_2$$

$$\frac{P_1V_1}{P_2} = \frac{\cancel{P_2}V_2}{\cancel{P_2}}$$

$$V_2 = V_1 \times \frac{P_1}{P_2}$$

Step 3 **Substitute values into the gas law equation and calculate.** When we substitute in the values with pressures in units of mmHg or atm, the ratio of pressures (pressure factor) is greater than 1, which increases the volume as predicted in Step 1.

$$V_2 = 12 \text{ L} \times \frac{3800 \cancel{\text{mmHg}}}{570 \cancel{\text{mmHg}}} = 80. \text{ L}$$

Pressure factor increases volume

or

$$V_2 = 12 \text{ L} \times \frac{5.0 \cancel{\text{atm}}}{0.75 \cancel{\text{atm}}} = 80. \text{ L}$$

Pressure factor increases volume

STUDY CHECK 11.3

In an underground gas reserve, a bubble of methane gas (CH_4) has a volume of 45.0 mL at 1.60 atm pressure and 25 °C. What volume, in milliliters, will it occupy when it reaches the surface where the atmospheric pressure is 745 mmHg, if there is no change in the temperature and amount of gas?

Chemistry Link to Health

PRESSURE–VOLUME RELATIONSHIP IN BREATHING

The importance of Boyle's law becomes more apparent when you consider the mechanics of breathing. Our lungs are elastic, balloon-like structures contained within an airtight chamber called the thoracic cavity. The diaphragm, a muscle, forms the flexible floor of the cavity.

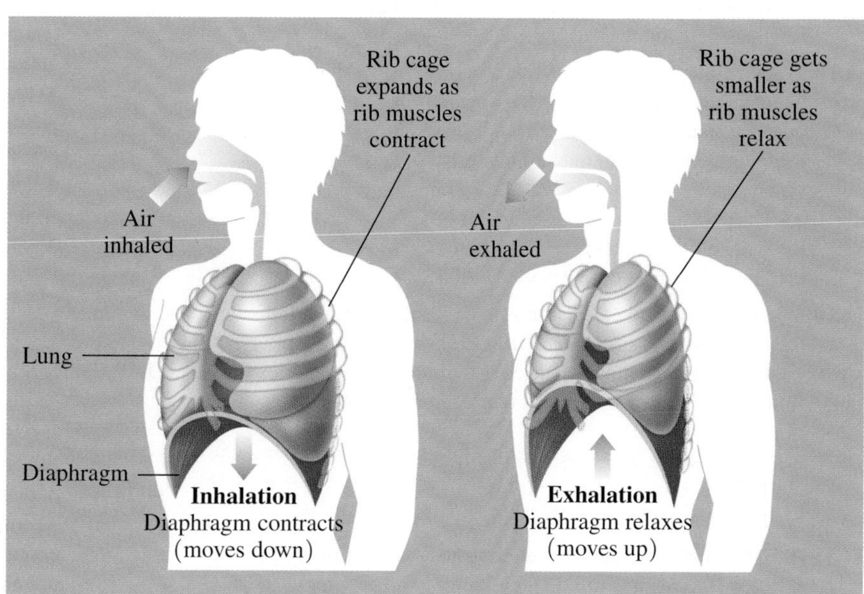

Inspiration

The process of taking a breath of air begins when the diaphragm flattens and the rib cage expands, causing an increase in the volume of the thoracic cavity. The elasticity of the lungs allows them to expand when the thoracic cavity expands. According to Boyle's law, the pressure inside the lungs decreases when their volume increases, causing the pressure inside the lungs to fall below the pressure of the atmosphere. This difference in pressures produces a *pressure gradient* between the lungs and the atmosphere. In a pressure gradient, molecules flow from an area of greater pressure to an area of lower pressure. Thus, we inhale as air flows into the lungs (*inspiration*), until the pressure within the lungs becomes equal to the pressure of the atmosphere.

Expiration

Expiration, or the exhalation phase of breathing, occurs when the diaphragm relaxes and moves back up into the thoracic cavity to its resting position. The volume of the thoracic cavity decreases, which squeezes the lungs and decreases their volume. Now the pressure in the lungs is greater than the pressure of the atmosphere, so air flows out of the lungs. Thus, breathing is a process in which pressure gradients are continuously created between the lungs and the environment because of the changes in the volume and pressure.

QUESTIONS AND PROBLEMS

11.3 Pressure and Volume (Boyle's Law)

LEARNING GOAL: *Use the pressure–volume relationship (Boyle's law) to determine the final pressure or volume when the temperature and amount of gas are constant.*

11.9 Why do scuba divers need to exhale air when they ascend to the surface of the water?

11.10 Why does a sealed bag of chips expand when you take it to a higher altitude?

11.11 The air in a cylinder with a piston has a volume of 220 mL and a pressure of 650 mmHg.

a. To obtain a higher pressure inside the cylinder at constant temperature and amount of gas, should the cylinder change as shown in **A** or **B**? Explain your choice.

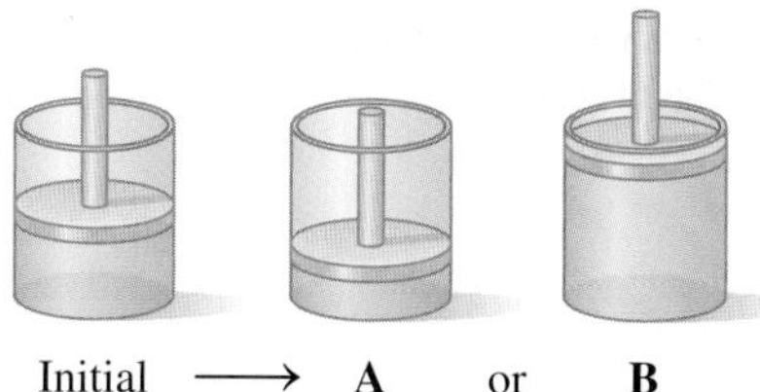

b. If the pressure inside the cylinder increases to 1.2 atm, what is the final volume, in milliliters, of the cylinder? Complete the following table:

Property	Conditions 1	Conditions 2	Know	Predict
Pressure (P)				
Volume (V)				

11.12 A balloon is filled with helium gas. When each of the following changes are made at constant temperature, which of these diagrams (**A**, **B**, or **C**) shows the final volume of the balloon?

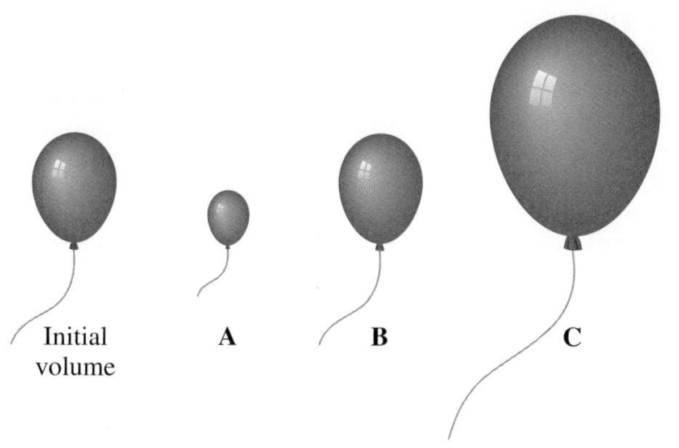

a. The balloon floats to a higher altitude where the outside pressure is lower.
b. The balloon is taken inside the house, but the atmospheric pressure remains the same.
c. The balloon is put in a hyperbaric chamber in which the pressure is increased.

11.13 A gas with a volume of 4.0 L is in a closed container. Indicate the changes (*increases*, *decreases*, *does not change*) in its pressure that must have occurred if the volume undergoes the following changes at constant temperature and amount of gas:
a. The volume is compressed to 2.0 L.
b. The volume expands to 12 L.
c. The volume is compressed to 0.40 L.

11.14 A gas at a pressure of 2.0 atm is in a closed container. Indicate the changes (*increases*, *decreases*, *does not change*) in its volume that must have occurred if the pressure undergoes the following changes at constant temperature and amount of gas:
a. The pressure increases to 6.0 atm.
b. The pressure remains at 2.0 atm.
c. The pressure drops to 0.40 atm.

11.15 A 10.0-L balloon contains helium gas at a pressure of 655 mmHg. What is the final pressure, in millimeters of mercury, of the helium gas at each of the following volumes, if there is no change in temperature and amount of gas?
a. 20.0 L
b. 2.50 L
c. 13 800 mL
d. 1250 mL

11.16 The air in a 5.00-L tank has a pressure of 1.20 atm. What is the final pressure, in atmospheres, of the air when the air is placed in tanks that have the following volumes, if there is no change in temperature and amount of gas?
a. 1.00 L
b. 2500. mL
c. 750. mL
d. 8.00 L

11.17 A sample of nitrogen (N_2) has a volume of 50.0 L at a pressure of 760. mmHg. What is the volume, in liters, of the gas at each of the following pressures, if there is no change in temperature and amount of gas?
a. 725 mmHg
b. 2.0 atm
c. 0.500 atm
d. 850 torr

11.18 A sample of methane (CH_4) has a volume of 25 mL at a pressure of 0.80 atm. What is the volume, in milliliters, of the gas at each of the following pressures, if there is no change in temperature and amount of gas?
a. 0.40 atm
b. 2.00 atm
c. 2500 mmHg
d. 80.0 torr

11.19 Cyclopropane, C_3H_6, is a general anesthetic. A 5.0-L sample has a pressure of 5.0 atm. What is the volume, in liters, of this gas given to a patient at a pressure of 1.0 atm with no change in temperature and amount of gas?

11.20 A tank of oxygen holds 20.0 L of oxygen (O_2) at a pressure of 15.0 atm. What is the volume, in liters, of this gas when it is released at a pressure of 1.00 atm with no change in temperature and amount of gas?

11.21 Use the words *inspiration* and *expiration* to describe the part of the breathing cycle that occurs because of each of the following:
a. The diaphragm contracts (flattens out).
b. The volume of the lungs decreases.
c. The pressure within the lungs is less than that of the atmosphere.

11.22 Use the words *inspiration* and *expiration* to describe the part of the breathing cycle that occurs because of each of the following:
a. The diaphragm relaxes, moving up into the thoracic cavity.
b. The volume of the lungs expands.
c. The pressure within the lungs is greater than that of the atmosphere.

LEARNING GOAL

Use the temperature–volume relationship (Charles's law) to determine the final temperature or volume when the pressure and amount of gas are constant.

11.4 Temperature and Volume (Charles's Law)

Suppose that you are going to take a ride in a hot-air balloon. The captain turns on a propane burner to heat the air inside the balloon. As the air is heated, it expands and becomes less dense than the air outside, causing the balloon and its passengers to lift off. In 1787, Jacques Charles, a balloonist as well as a physicist, proposed that the volume of a gas is related to the temperature. This proposal became **Charles's law**, which states that the volume (V) of a gas is directly related to the temperature (K) when there is no change in the pressure (P) or amount (n) of gas. A **direct relationship** is one in which the related properties increase or decrease together. For two conditions, initial and final, we can write Charles's law as follows:

Charles's Law

$$\frac{V_1}{T_1} = \frac{V_2}{T_2}$$ No change in number of moles and pressure

All temperatures used in gas law calculations must be converted to their corresponding Kelvin (K) temperatures.

To determine the effect of changing temperature on the volume of a gas, the pressure and the amount of gas are kept constant. If we increase the temperature of a gas sample, we know from the kinetic molecular theory that the motion (kinetic energy) of the gas particles will also increase. To keep the pressure constant, the volume of the container must increase (see Figure 11.5). If the temperature of the gas is decreased, the volume of the container must also decrease to maintain the same pressure.

As a gas in a hot-air balloon is heated, it expands.

CONCEPT CHECK 11.4 Charles's Law

State and explain the reason for the change (*increases*, *decreases*) in a gas that occurs in each of the following when n and P do not change:

	Temperature (T)	Volume (V)	Amount (n)	Pressure (P)
a.	increases		constant	constant
b.	decreases		constant	constant

ANSWER

a. When the temperature of a gas increases at constant n and P, the gas particles move faster. To keep the pressure constant, the volume of the container must increase when temperature increases with no change in n and P.

b. When the temperature of a gas decreases at constant n and P, the gas particles move more slowly. To keep the pressure constant, the volume of the container must decrease when the temperature decreases with no change in n and P.

	Temperature (T)	Volume (V)	Amount (n)	Pressure (P)
a.	increases	increases	constant	constant
b.	decreases	decreases	constant	constant

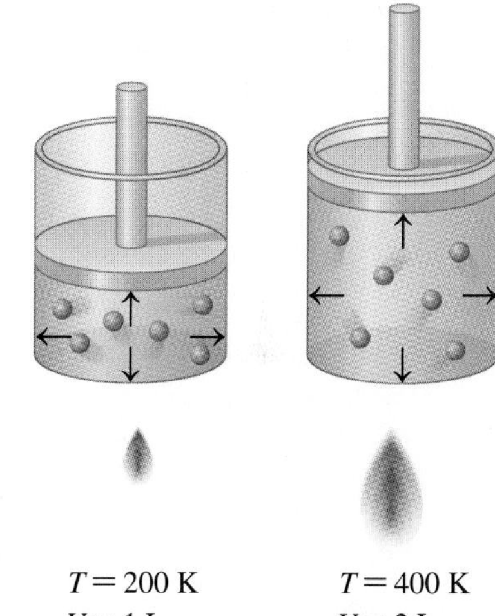

FIGURE 11.5 **Charles's law:** The Kelvin temperature of a gas is directly related to the volume of the gas when there is no change in the pressure and amount of gas. When the temperature increases, making the molecules move faster, the volume must increase to maintain constant pressure.

Q If the temperature of a gas decreases at a constant pressure, how will the volume change?

SAMPLE PROBLEM 11.4 Calculating Volume When Temperature Changes

A sample of argon gas has a volume of 5.40 L and a temperature of 15 °C. What is the final volume, in liters, of the gas after the temperature has been increased to 42 °C at constant pressure and amount of gas?

SOLUTION

Step 1 Organize the data in a table of initial and final conditions. The properties that change, which are the temperature and volume, are listed in the following table. The properties that do not change, which are pressure and amount of gas, are shown below the table. When the temperature is given in degrees Celsius, it must be changed to kelvins. Because we know the initial and final temperatures of the gas, we know that the temperature increases. Thus, we can predict that the volume increases.

$$T_1 = 15\ °C + 273 = 288\ K$$
$$T_2 = 42\ °C + 273 = 315\ K$$

	Conditions 1	Conditions 2	Know	Predict
Analyze the Problem	$T_1 = 288$ K	$T_2 = 315$ K	T increases	
	$V_1 = 5.40$ L	$V_2 = ?$ L		V increases

Factors that remain constant: P and n

Step 2 **Rearrange the gas law equation to solve for the unknown quantity.** In this problem, we want to know the final volume (V_2) when the temperature increases. Using Charles's law, we solve for V_2 by multiplying both sides by T_2.

$$\frac{V_1}{T_1} = \frac{V_2}{T_2}$$

$$T_2 \times \frac{V_1}{T_1} = \cancel{T_2} \times \frac{V_2}{\cancel{T_2}}$$

$$V_2 = V_1 \times \frac{T_2}{T_1}$$

Step 3 **Substitute values into the gas law equation and calculate.** From the table, we see that the temperature has increased. Because temperature is directly related to volume, the volume must increase. When we substitute in the values, we see that the ratio of the temperatures (temperature factor) is greater than 1, which increases the volume, as predicted in Step 1.

$$V_2 = 5.40\text{ L} \times \frac{315\ \cancel{\text{K}}}{288\ \cancel{\text{K}}} = 5.91\text{ L}$$

Temperature factor increases volume

STUDY CHECK 11.4

A mountain climber with a body temperature of 37 °C inhales 486 mL of air at a temperature of −8 °C. What volume, in milliliters, will the air occupy in the lungs, if the pressure and amount of gas do not change?

Chemistry Link to the Environment

GREENHOUSE GASES

The term *greenhouse gases* was first used during the early 1800s for the gases in the atmosphere that trap heat. Among the greenhouse gases are carbon dioxide (CO_2), methane (CH_4), dinitrogen oxide (N_2O), and chlorofluorocarbons (CFCs). The molecules of greenhouse gases consist of more than two atoms that vibrate when heat is absorbed. By contrast, oxygen and nitrogen do not trap heat and are not greenhouse gases. Because the two atoms in their molecules are tightly bonded, they do not absorb heat.

Greenhouse gases are beneficial in keeping the average surface temperature for Earth at 15 °C. Without greenhouse gases, it is estimated that the average surface temperature of Earth would be −18 °C. Most scientists say that the concentration of greenhouse gases in the atmosphere and the surface temperature of Earth are increasing because of human activities. The increase in atmospheric carbon dioxide is mostly a result of the burning of fossil fuels and wood.

Methane (CH_4) is a colorless, odorless gas that is released by livestock, rice farming, the decomposition of organic plant material in landfills, and the mining, drilling, and transport of coal and oil. The contribution from livestock comes from the breakdown of organic material in the digestive tracts of cows, sheep, and camels. The level of methane in the atmosphere has increased about 150% since industrialization. In one year, as much as 5×10^{11} kg of methane are added to the atmosphere. Livestock produce about 20% of the greenhouse gases. In one day, one cow emits about 200 g of methane. For a global population of 1.5 billion livestock, a total of 3×10^8 kg of methane is produced every day. In the past few years, methane levels have stabilized due to improvements in the recovery of methane. Methane remains in the atmosphere for about ten years, but its molecular structure causes it to trap 20 times more heat than does carbon dioxide.

Dinitrogen oxide (N_2O), commonly called nitrous oxide, is a colorless greenhouse gas that has a sweet odor. Most people recognize it as an anesthetic used in dentistry called "laughing gas." Although some dinitrogen oxide is released naturally from soil bacteria, its major sources are from agricultural and industrial processes. Atmospheric dinitrogen oxide has increased by about 15% since industrialization, caused by the extensive use of fertilizers, sewage treatment plants, and car exhaust. Each year, 1×10^{10} kg of dinitrogen oxide is added to the atmosphere. Dinitrogen oxide released today will remain in the atmosphere for about 150–180 years where it has a greenhouse effect that is 300 times greater than that of carbon dioxide.

Chlorofluorinated gases (CFCs) are synthetic compounds containing chlorine, fluorine, and carbon. Chlorofluorocarbons were used as propellants in aerosol cans and refrigerants in refrigerators and air conditioners. During the 1970s, scientists determined that CFCs in the atmosphere were destroying the protective ozone layer. Since then, many countries banned the production and use of CFCs, and their levels in the atmosphere have declined slightly. Hydrofluorocarbons (HFCs), in which hydrogen atoms replace chlorine atoms, are now used as refrigerants. Although HFCs do not destroy the ozone layer, they are greenhouse gases because they trap heat in the atmosphere.

Based on current trends and climate models, scientists estimate that levels of atmospheric carbon dioxide will increase by about 2% each year up to 2025. As long as the greenhouse gases trap more heat than is reflected back into space, average surface temperatures on Earth will continue to rise. Efforts are taking place around the world to slow or decrease the emissions of greenhouse gases into the atmosphere. It is anticipated that temperature will stabilize only when the amount of energy that reaches the surface of Earth is equal to the heat that is reflected back into space.

In 2007, former U.S. Vice President Al Gore and the United Nations Panel on Climate Change were awarded the Nobel Prize for increasing global awareness of the relationship between human activities and global warming.

Percentages of Greenhouse Gases in the Atmosphere

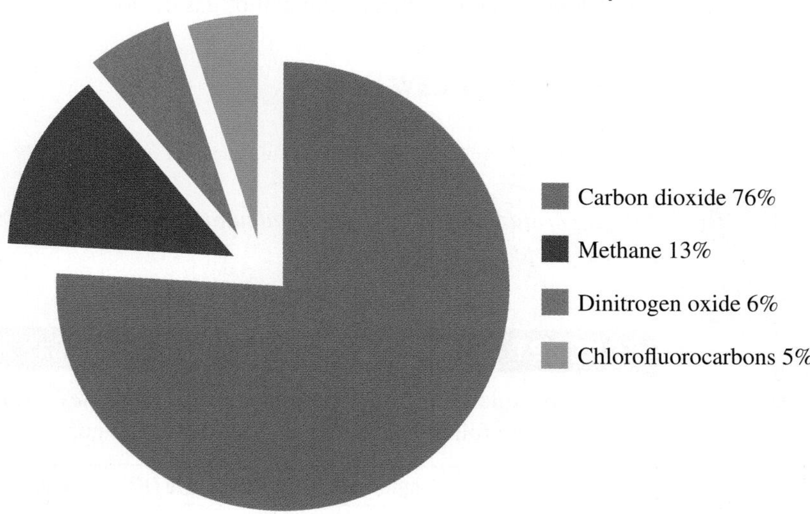

QUESTIONS AND PROBLEMS

11.4 Temperature and Volume (Charles's Law)

LEARNING GOAL: *Use the temperature–volume relationship (Charles's law) to determine the final temperature or volume when the pressure and amount of gas are constant.*

11.23 Select the diagram that shows the final volume of a balloon when the following changes are made at constant pressure:

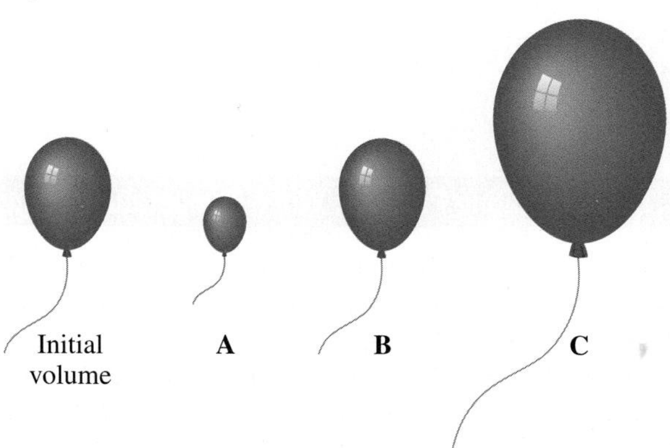

a. The temperature is changed from 100 K to 300 K.
b. The balloon is placed in a freezer.
c. The balloon is first warmed and then returned to its starting temperature.

11.24 Indicate whether the final volume of gas in each of the following is the *same*, *larger*, or *smaller* than the initial volume, if pressure and amount of gas do not change:
a. A volume of 505 mL of air on a cold winter day at −15 °C is breathed into the lungs, when body temperature is 37 °C.
b. The heater used to heat the air in a hot-air balloon is turned off.
c. A balloon filled with helium at the amusement park is left in a car on a hot day.

11.25 A sample of neon initially has a volume of 2.50 L at 15 °C. What final temperature, in degrees Celsius, is needed to change the volume of the gas to each of the following, if n and P do not change?
a. 5.00 L **b.** 1250 mL **c.** 7.50 L **d.** 3550 mL

11.26 A gas has a volume of 4.00 L at 0 °C. What final temperature, in degrees Celsius, is needed to change the volume of the gas to each of the following, if n and P do not change?
a. 1.50 L **b.** 1200 mL **c.** 10.0 L **d.** 50.0 mL

11.27 A balloon contains 2500 mL of helium gas at 75 °C. What is the final volume, in milliliters, of the gas when the temperature changes to each of the following, if n and P do not change?
a. 55 °C **b.** 680. K **c.** −25 °C **d.** 240. K

11.28 An air bubble has a volume of 0.500 L at 18 °C. What is the final volume, in liters, of the gas when the temperature changes to each of the following, if n and P do not change?
a. 0 °C **b.** 425 K **c.** −12 °C **d.** 575 K

LEARNING GOAL

Use the temperature–pressure relationship (Gay-Lussac's law) to determine the final temperature or pressure when the volume and amount of gas are constant.

11.5 Temperature and Pressure (Gay-Lussac's Law)

If we could observe the molecules of a gas as the temperature rises, we would notice that they move faster and hit the sides of the container more often and with greater force. If we maintain a constant volume and amount of gas, the pressure would increase. In the temperature–pressure relationship known as **Gay-Lussac's law**, the pressure of a gas is directly related to its Kelvin temperature. This means that an increase in temperature increases the pressure of a gas, and a decrease in temperature decreases the pressure of the gas as long as the volume and amount of gas do not change (see Figure 11.6).

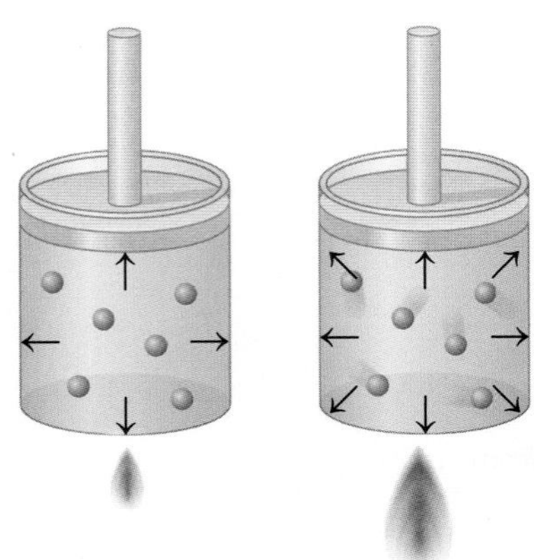

$T = 200$ K $\quad$ $T = 400$ K

$P = 1$ atm $\quad$ $P = 2$ atm

FIGURE 11.6 **Gay-Lussac's law:** When the Kelvin temperature of a gas is doubled at constant volume and amount of gas, the pressure also doubles.

Q How does a decrease in the temperature of a gas affect its pressure at constant volume?

Gay-Lussac's Law

$$\frac{P_1}{T_1} = \frac{P_2}{T_2} \quad \text{No change in number of moles and volume}$$

All temperatures used in gas law calculations must be converted to their corresponding Kelvin (K) temperatures.

CONCEPT CHECK 11.5 Gay-Lussac's Law

State and explain the reason for the change (*increases*, *decreases*) in a gas that occurs in each of the following when n and V do not change:

	Temperature (T)	Pressure (P)	Amount (n)	Volume (V)
a.	increases		constant	constant
b.	decreases		constant	constant

ANSWER

a. When the temperature of a gas increases with no change in n and V, the particles of gas move faster. At constant volume, the gas particles collide more often with the container walls and with more force, increasing the pressure.

b. When the temperature of a gas decreases with no change in n and V, the particles of gas move more slowly. At constant volume, the gas particles collide less often with the container walls and with less force, decreasing the pressure.

	Temperature (T)	Pressure (P)	Amount (n)	Volume (V)
a.	increases	increases	constant	constant
b.	decreases	decreases	constant	constant

SAMPLE PROBLEM 11.5 Calculating Pressure When Temperature Changes

Aerosol containers can be dangerous if they are heated, because they can explode. Suppose a container of hair spray with a pressure of 4.0 atm at a room temperature of 25 °C is thrown into a fire. If the temperature of the gas inside the aerosol can reaches 402 °C, what will be its pressure, in atmospheres, if the volume and amount of gas do not change? The aerosol container may explode if the pressure inside exceeds 8.0 atm. Would you expect it to explode?

SOLUTION

Step 1 **Organize the data in a table of initial and final conditions.** We list the properties that change, which are the pressure and temperature, in a table. The properties that do not change, which are volume and amount of gas, are shown below the table. The temperatures given in degrees Celsius must be changed to kelvins. Because we know the initial and final temperatures of the gas, we know that the temperature increases. Thus, we can predict that the pressure increases.

$$T_1 = 25\ °C + 273 = 298\ K$$
$$T_2 = 402\ °C + 273 = 675\ K$$

Analyze the Problem	Conditions 1	Conditions 2	Know	Predict
	$P_1 = 4.0$ atm	$P_2 = ?$ atm		P increases
	$T_1 = 298$ K	$T_2 = 675$ K	T increases	

Factors that remain constant: V and n

Step 2 **Rearrange the gas law equation to solve for the unknown quantity.** Using Gay-Lussac's law, we solve for P_2 by multiplying both sides by T_2.

$$\frac{P_1}{T_1} = \frac{P_2}{T_2}$$

$$T_2 \times \frac{P_1}{T_1} = \cancel{T_2} \times \frac{P_2}{\cancel{T_2}}$$

$$P_2 = P_1 \times \frac{T_2}{T_1}$$

Step 3 **Substitute values into the gas law equation and calculate.** When we substitute in the values, we see that the ratio of the temperatures (temperature factor) is greater than 1, which increases pressure as predicted in Step 1.

$$P_2 = 4.0\ \text{atm} \times \underbrace{\frac{675\ \cancel{K}}{298\ \cancel{K}}}_{\text{Temperature factor increases pressure}} = 9.1\ \text{atm}$$

Because the calculated pressure of 9.1 atm exceeds the limit of 8.0 atm, we would expect the aerosol can to explode.

STUDY CHECK 11.5

In a storage area where the temperature has reached 55 °C, the pressure of oxygen gas in a 15.0-L steel cylinder is 965 torr. To what temperature, in degrees Celsius, would the gas have to be cooled to reduce the pressure to 850 torr, when the volume and the amount of the gas do not change?

Vapor Pressure and Boiling Point

When liquid molecules with sufficient kinetic energy break away from the surface, they become gas particles or vapor. In an open container, all the liquid will eventually evaporate. In a closed container, the vapor accumulates and creates pressure called **vapor pressure**. Each liquid exerts its own vapor pressure at a given temperature. As temperature increases, more vapor forms, and vapor pressure increases. Table 11.4 lists the vapor pressure of water at various temperatures.

A liquid reaches its boiling point when its vapor pressure becomes equal to the external pressure. As boiling occurs, bubbles of the gas form within the liquid and quickly rise to the surface. For example, at an atmospheric pressure of 760 mmHg, water will boil at 100 °C, the temperature at which its vapor pressure reaches 760 mmHg (see Table 11.4).

At high altitudes, where atmospheric pressures are lower than 760 mmHg, the boiling point of water is lower than 100 °C. For example, a typical atmospheric pressure in Denver is 630 mmHg. This means that water in Denver boils when the vapor pressure is 630 mmHg. From Table 11.5, we see that water has a vapor pressure of 630 mmHg at 95 °C, which means that water boils at 95 °C in Denver.

TABLE 11.4 Vapor Pressure of Water

Temperature (°C)	Vapor Pressure (mmHg)
0	5
10	9
20	18
30	32
37*	47
40	55
50	93
60	149
70	234
80	355
90	528
100	760

*At body temperature.

In a closed container such as a pressure cooker, a pressure greater than 1 atm can be obtained, which means that water boils at a temperature higher than 100 °C. Laboratories and hospitals use closed containers called *autoclaves* to sterilize laboratory and surgical equipment. Table 11.5 shows how the boiling point of water increases as pressure increases.

TABLE 11.5 Pressure and the Boiling Point of Water

Pressure (mmHg)	Boiling Point (°C)
270	70
467	87
630	95
752	99
760	100
800	100.4
1075	110
1520 (2 atm)	120
3800 (5 atm)	160
7600 (10 atm)	180

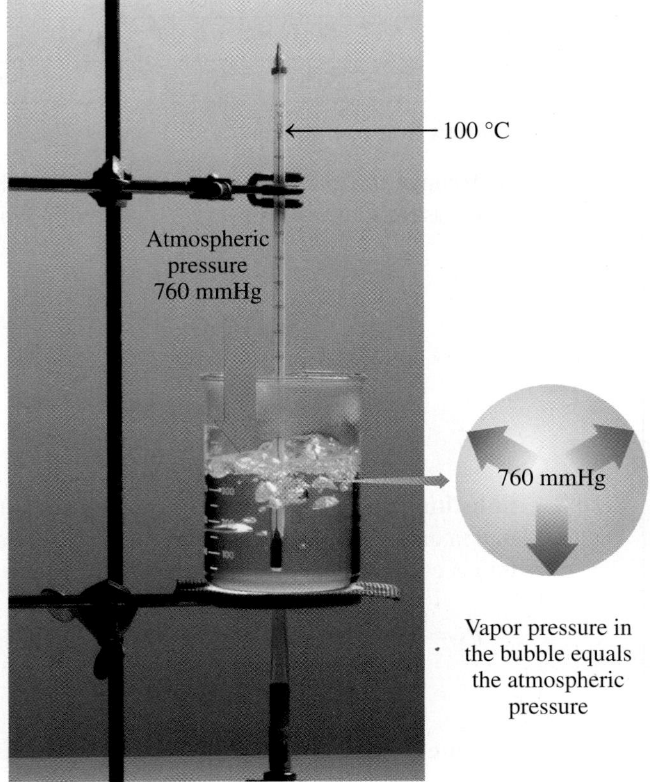

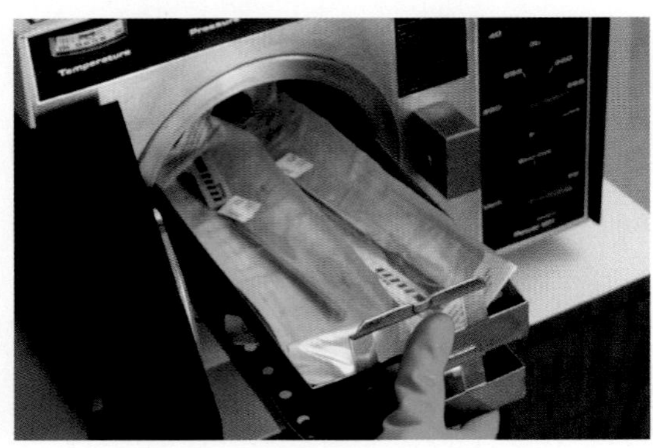

An autoclave used to sterilize equipment attains a temperature higher than 100 °C.

QUESTIONS AND PROBLEMS

11.5 Temperature and Pressure (Gay-Lussac's Law)

LEARNING GOAL: *Use the temperature–pressure relationship (Gay-Lussac's law) to determine the final temperature or pressure when the volume and amount of gas are constant.*

11.29 Calculate the final pressure, in millimeters of mercury, for each of the following, with n and V constant:
- **a.** A gas with an initial pressure of 1200 torr at 155 °C is cooled to 0 °C.
- **b.** A gas in an aerosol can at an initial pressure of 1.40 atm at 12 °C is heated to 35 °C.

11.30 Calculate the final pressure, in atmospheres, for each of the following, with n and V constant:
- **a.** A gas with an initial pressure of 1.20 atm at 75 °C is cooled to −22 °C.
- **b.** A sample of N_2 with an initial pressure of 780. mmHg at −75 °C is heated to 28 °C.

11.31 Calculate the final temperature, in degrees Celsius, °C, for each of the following, with n and V constant:
- **a.** A sample of xenon at 25 °C and 740. mmHg is cooled to give a pressure of 620. mmHg.
- **b.** A tank of argon gas with a pressure of 0.950 atm at −18 °C is heated to give a pressure of 1250 torr.

11.32 Calculate the final temperature, in degrees Celsius, °C, for each of the following, with n and V constant:
- **a.** A sample of helium gas with a pressure of 250 torr at 0 °C is heated to give a pressure of 1500 torr.
- **b.** A sample of air at 40 °C and 740. mmHg is cooled to give a pressure of 680. mmHg.

11.33 Match the terms *vapor pressure*, *atmospheric pressure*, and *boiling point* to the following descriptions:
- **a.** the temperature at which bubbles of vapor appear within the liquid
- **b.** the pressure exerted by a gas above the surface of its liquid

11.34 Match the terms *vapor pressure*, *atmospheric pressure*, and *boiling point* to the following descriptions:

a. the pressure exerted on Earth by the particles in the air
b. the temperature at which the vapor pressure of a liquid becomes equal to the external pressure

11.35 Explain each of the following observations:

a. Water boils at 87 °C on the top of Mount Whitney.
b. Food cooks more quickly in a pressure cooker than in an open pan.

11.36 Explain each of the following observations:

a. Boiling water at sea level is hotter than boiling water in the mountains.
b. Water used to sterilize surgical equipment is heated to 120 °C at 2.0 atm in an autoclave.

11.6 The Combined Gas Law

LEARNING GOAL

Use the combined gas law to find the final pressure, volume, or temperature of a gas when changes in two of these properties are given and the amount of gas is constant.

All of the pressure–volume–temperature relationships for gases that we have studied may be combined into a single relationship called the **combined gas law**. This expression is useful for studying the effect of changes in two of these variables on the third as long as the amount of gas (number of moles) remains constant.

Combined Gas Law

$$\frac{P_1V_1}{T_1} = \frac{P_2V_2}{T_2}$$ No change in number of moles of gas

By using the combined gas law, we can derive any of the gas laws by omitting those properties that do not change, as seen in Table 11.6.

TABLE 11.6 Summary of Gas Laws

Combined Gas Law	Properties Held Constant	Relationship	Name of Gas Law
$\frac{P_1V_1}{\cancel{T_1}} = \frac{P_2V_2}{\cancel{T_2}}$	T, n	$P_1V_1 = P_2V_2$	Boyle's law
$\frac{\cancel{P_1}V_1}{T_1} = \frac{\cancel{P_2}V_2}{T_2}$	P, n	$\frac{V_1}{T_1} = \frac{V_2}{T_2}$	Charles's law
$\frac{P_1\cancel{V_1}}{T_1} = \frac{P_2\cancel{V_2}}{T_2}$	V, n	$\frac{P_1}{T_1} = \frac{P_2}{T_2}$	Gay-Lussac's law

CONCEPT CHECK 11.6 The Combined Gas Law

State and explain the reason for the change (*increases, decreases, no change*) in a gas that occurs for the following when n does not change:

	Pressure (P)	Volume (V)	Temperature (K)	Amount (n)
a.		twice as large	half the Kelvin temperature	constant
b.	twice as large		twice as large	constant

ANSWER

a. Pressure decreases by one-half when the volume (at constant n) doubles. If the temperature in Kelvin is halved, the pressure is also halved. The changes in both V and T decrease the pressure to one-fourth its initial value.

b. No change. When the Kelvin temperature of a gas (at constant n) is doubled, the volume is doubled. But when the pressure is twice as much, the volume must decrease to one-half. The changes offset each other, and no change occurs in the volume.

	Pressure (P)	Volume (V)	Temperature (K)	Amount (n)
a.	one-fourth as large	twice as large	half the Kelvin temperature	constant
b.	twice as large	no change	twice as large	constant

Under water, the pressure on a diver is greater than the atmospheric pressure.

SAMPLE PROBLEM 11.6 Using the Combined Gas Law

A 25.0-mL bubble is released from a diver's air tank at a pressure of 4.00 atm and a temperature of 11 °C. What is the volume, in milliliters, of the bubble when it reaches the ocean surface where the pressure is 1.00 atm and the temperature is 18 °C, when the amount of gas does not change?

SOLUTION

Step 1 **Organize the data in a table of initial and final conditions.** We list the properties that change, which are the pressure, volume, and temperature, in a table. The property that remains constant, which is the amount of gas, is shown below the table. The temperatures in degrees Celsius must be changed to kelvins.

$$T_1 = 11\ °\text{C} + 273 = 284\ \text{K}$$
$$T_2 = 18\ °\text{C} + 273 = 291\ \text{K}$$

	Conditions 1	Conditions 2
Analyze the Problem	$P_1 = 4.00$ atm	$P_2 = 1.00$ atm
	$V_1 = 25.0$ mL	$V_2 = ?$ mL
	$T_1 = 284$ K	$T_2 = 291$ K

Factor that remains constant: *n*

Step 2 **Rearrange the gas law equation to solve for the unknown quantity.** For changes in two conditions, pressure and temperature, we rearrange the combined gas law equation to solve for V_2.

$$\frac{P_1V_1}{T_1} = \frac{P_2V_2}{T_2}$$

$$\frac{P_1V_1}{T_1} \times \frac{T_2}{P_2} = \frac{\cancel{P_2}V_2}{\cancel{T_2}} \times \frac{\cancel{T_2}}{\cancel{P_2}}$$

$$V_2 = V_1 \times \frac{P_1}{P_2} \times \frac{T_2}{T_1}$$

Step 3 **Substitute values into the gas law equation and calculate.** From the data table, we determine that both the pressure decrease and the temperature increase will increase the volume. However, when one change decreases the unknown, but the second change increases the unknown, it is difficult to predict the overall change for the unknown.

$$V_2 = 25.0\ \text{mL} \times \frac{4.00\ \cancel{\text{atm}}}{1.00\ \cancel{\text{atm}}} \times \frac{291\ \cancel{\text{K}}}{284\ \cancel{\text{K}}} = 102\ \text{mL}$$

Pressure factor increases volume; Temperature factor increases volume

STUDY CHECK 11.6

A weather balloon is filled with 15.0 L of helium at a temperature of 25 °C and a pressure of 685 mmHg. What is the pressure, in millimeters of mercury, of the helium in the balloon in the upper atmosphere when the final temperature is −35 °C and the final volume becomes 34.0 L, if the amount of He does not change?

QUESTIONS AND PROBLEMS

11.6 The Combined Gas Law

LEARNING GOAL: *Use the combined gas law to find the final pressure, volume, or temperature of a gas when changes in two of these properties are given and the amount of gas is constant.*

11.37 Rearrange the variables in the combined gas law to solve for T_2.

11.38 Rearrange the variables in the combined gas law to solve for P_2.

11.39 A sample of helium gas has a volume of 6.50 L at a pressure of 845 mmHg and a temperature of 25 °C. What is the final pressure of the gas, in atmospheres, when the volume and temperature of the gas sample are changed to the following, if the amount of gas does not change?
a. 1850 mL and 325 K
b. 2.25 L and 12 °C
c. 12.8 L and 47 °C

11.40 A sample of argon gas has a volume of 735 mL at a pressure of 1.20 atm and a temperature of 112 °C. What is the final volume of the gas, in milliliters, when the pressure and temperature of the gas sample are changed to the following, if the amount of gas does not change?
a. 658 mmHg and 281 K
b. 0.55 atm and 75 °C
c. 15.4 atm and −15 °C

11.41 A 124-mL bubble of hot gas initially at 212 °C and 1.80 atm is emitted from an active volcano. What is the final temperature, in degrees Celsius, of the gas in the bubble outside the volcano if the final volume of the bubble is 138 mL and the pressure is 0.800 atm, if the amount of gas remains constant?

11.42 A scuba diver 60 ft below the ocean surface inhales 50.0 mL of compressed air from a scuba tank at a pressure of 3.00 atm and a temperature of 8 °C. What is the final pressure of air, in atmospheres, in the lungs when the gas expands to 150.0 mL at a body temperature of 37 °C, and the amount of gas remains constant?

11.7 Volume and Moles (Avogadro's Law)

LEARNING GOAL

Use Avogadro's law to determine the amount or volume of a gas when the pressure and temperature are constant.

In our study of the gas laws, we have looked at changes in properties for a specified amount (n) of gas. Now we will consider how the properties of a gas change when there is a change in the number of moles or grams of the gas.

When you blow up a balloon, its volume increases because you add more air molecules. If the balloon has a small hole in it, air leaks out, causing its volume to decrease. In 1811, Amedeo Avogadro formulated **Avogadro's law**, which states that the volume of a gas is directly related to the number of moles of a gas when temperature and pressure do not change. For example, if the number of moles of a gas is doubled, then the volume will double as long as we do not change the pressure or the temperature (see Figure 11.7). At constant pressure and temperature, we can write Avogadro's law as follows:

Avogadro's Law

$$\frac{V_1}{n_1} = \frac{V_2}{n_2} \quad \text{No change in pressure or temperature}$$

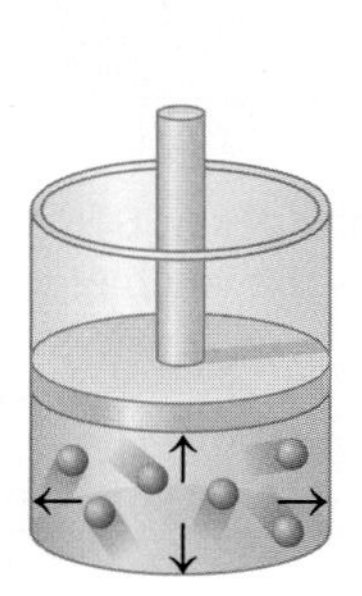

$n = 1$ mol
$V = 1$ L

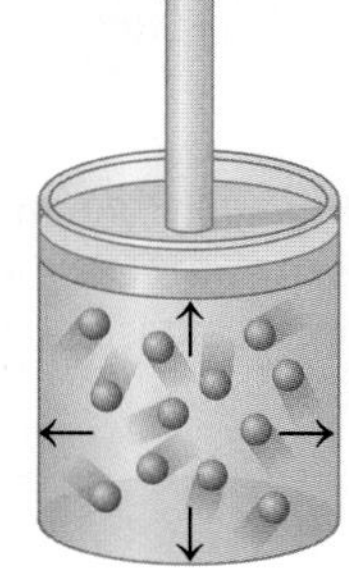

$n = 2$ mol
$V = 2$ L

FIGURE 11.7 **Avogadro's law:** The volume of a gas is directly related to the number of moles of the gas. If the number of moles is doubled, the volume must double at constant temperature and pressure.

Q If a balloon has a leak, what happens to its volume?

SAMPLE PROBLEM 11.7 Calculating Volume for a Change in Moles

A weather balloon with a volume of 44 L is filled with 2.0 mol of helium. What is the final volume, in liters, if 3.0 mol of helium are added, to give a total of 5.0 mol of helium, if the pressure and temperature do not change?

SOLUTION

Step 1 **Organize the data in a table of initial and final conditions.** We list those properties that change, which are volume and amount (moles) of gas, in a table. The properties that do not change, which are pressure and temperature, are shown below the table. Because there is an increase in the number of moles of gas, we can predict that the volume increases.

	Conditions 1	Conditions 2	Know	Predict
Analyze the Problem	$V_1 = 44$ L	$V_2 = ?$ L		V increases
	$n_1 = 2.0$ mol	$n_2 = 5.0$ mol	n increases	

Factors that remain constant: P and T

Step 2 **Rearrange the gas law equation to solve for the unknown quantity.** Using Avogadro's law, we can solve for V_2 by multiplying both sides of the equation by n_2.

$$\frac{V_1}{n_1} = \frac{V_2}{n_2}$$

$$n_2 \times \frac{V_1}{n_1} = \frac{V_2}{\cancel{n_2}} \times \cancel{n_2}$$

$$V_2 = V_1 \times \frac{n_2}{n_1}$$

Step 3 **Substitute values into the gas law equation and calculate.** When we substitute in the values, we see that the mole factor is greater than 1, which increases volume as predicted in Step 1.

$$V_2 = 44\text{ L} \times \underbrace{\frac{5.0\ \cancel{\text{mol}}}{2.0\ \cancel{\text{mol}}}}_{\text{Mole factor increases volume}} = 110\text{ L}$$

STUDY CHECK 11.7

A sample containing 8.00 g of oxygen has a volume of 5.00 L. What is the volume, in liters, after 4.00 g of oxygen is added to the 8.00 g of oxygen in the balloon, if the temperature and pressure do not change?

The molar volume of a gas at STP is about the same as the volume of three basketballs.

STP and Molar Volume

Using Avogadro's law, we can say that any two gases will have equal volumes if they contain the same number of moles of gas at the same temperature and pressure. To help us make comparisons between different gases, arbitrary conditions called *standard temperature* (273 K) and *standard pressure* (1 atm), together abbreviated **STP**, were selected by scientists:

STP Conditions

Standard temperature is *exactly* 0 °C (273 K).

Standard pressure is *exactly* 1 atm (760 mmHg).

At STP, 1 mol of any gas occupies a volume of 22.4 L, which is about the same as the volume of three basketballs. This volume, 22.4 L, of any gas is called the **molar volume** (see Figure 11.8).

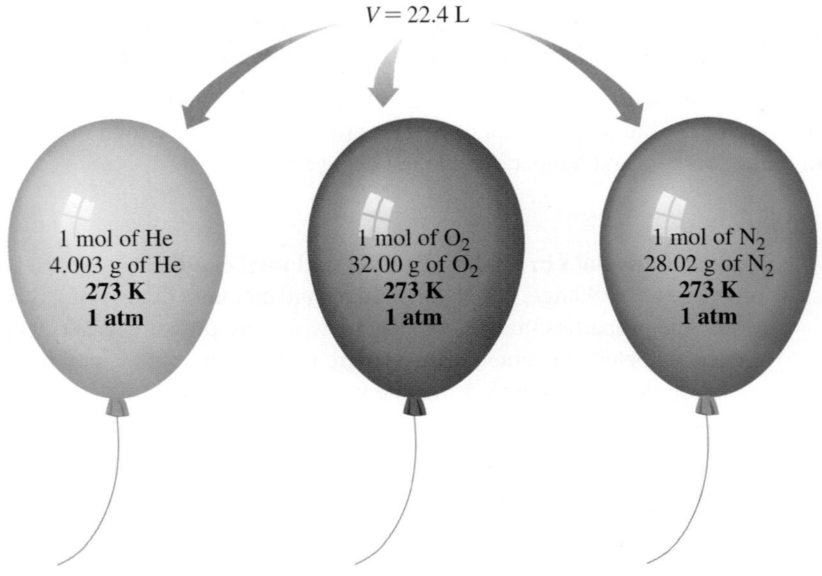

FIGURE 11.8 Avogadro's law indicates that 1 mol of any gas at STP has a volume of 22.4 L.

Q What volume of gas is occupied by 16.0 g of methane gas, CH_4, at STP?

When a gas is at STP conditions (0 °C and 1 atm), its molar volume can be written as a conversion factor and used to convert between the number of moles of gas and its volume, in liters.

1 mol of gas = 22.4 L (STP)

Molar Volume Conversion Factors

$$\frac{1 \text{ mol gas}}{22.4 \text{ L (STP)}} \quad \text{and} \quad \frac{22.4 \text{ L (STP)}}{1 \text{ mol gas}}$$

SAMPLE PROBLEM 11.8 Using Molar Volume to Find Volume at STP

What is the volume, in liters, of 64.0 g of O_2 gas at STP?

SOLUTION

Once we convert the mass of O_2 to moles of O_2, the molar volume of a gas at STP can be used to calculate the volume (L) of O_2.

Step 1 State the given and needed quantities.

Analyze the Problem	Given	Need
	64.0 g of $O_2(g)$ at STP	liters of O_2 gas at STP

Step 2 Write a plan to calculate the needed quantity.

grams of O_2 → Molar mass → moles of O_2 → Molar volume → liters of O_2

Step 3 Write the equalities and conversion factors including 22.4 L/mol at STP.

1 mol of O_2 = 32.00 g of O_2

$$\frac{32.00 \text{ g } O_2}{1 \text{ mol } O_2} \quad \text{and} \quad \frac{1 \text{ mol } O_2}{32.00 \text{ g } O_2}$$

1 mol of O_2 = 22.4 L of O_2 (STP)

$$\frac{22.4 \text{ L } O_2 \text{ (STP)}}{1 \text{ mol } O_2} \quad \text{and} \quad \frac{1 \text{ mol } O_2}{22.4 \text{ L } O_2 \text{ (STP)}}$$

Step 4 Set up the problem with factors to cancel units.

$$64.0 \cancel{\text{g } O_2} \times \frac{1 \cancel{\text{mol } O_2}}{32.00 \cancel{\text{g } O_2}} \times \frac{22.4 \text{ L } O_2 \text{ (STP)}}{1 \cancel{\text{mol } O_2}} = 44.8 \text{ L of } O_2 \text{ (STP)}$$

STUDY CHECK 11.8

How many grams of $Cl_2(g)$ are in 5.00 L of $Cl_2(g)$ at STP?

Guide to Using Molar Volume

1. State the given and needed quantities.
2. Write a plan to calculate the needed quantity.
3. Write the equalities and conversion factors including 22.4 L/mol at STP.
4. Set up the problem with factors to cancel units.

Density of a Gas at STP

We have seen that at the same temperature and pressure, 1 mol of any gas occupies the same volume. Thus, the density (D = g/L) of any gas depends on its molar mass. For example, at STP, oxygen, O_2, has a density of 1.43 g/L while the carbon dioxide, CO_2, that we exhale has a density of 1.96 g/L. A bubble or balloon filled with carbon dioxide would settle to the ground because the density of CO_2 is greater than the density of air, which is 1.29 g/L. On the other hand, balloons filled with helium rise in the air because helium has a density of 0.179 g/L, which is less dense than air. For any gas at STP, we can calculate density (g/L) using the molar mass and the molar volume, as shown in Sample Problem 11.9.

Balloons rise in the air because helium is less dense than air.

SAMPLE PROBLEM 11.9 Density of a Gas at STP

What is the density, in grams per liter, of nitrogen gas (N_2) at STP?

SOLUTION

Step 1 **State the given and needed quantities.**

Analyze the Problem	Given	Need
	$N_2(g)$ at STP	density (g/L) of N_2 gas at STP

Step 2 **Write a plan to calculate the needed quantity.** At STP, the density (g/L) of any gas can be calculated by dividing its molar mass by the molar volume.

$$\text{Density} = \frac{\text{molar mass}}{\text{molar volume}} = \frac{\text{g/}\cancel{\text{mol}}}{\text{L/}\cancel{\text{mol}}} = \frac{\text{g}}{\text{L}}$$

Step 3 **Write the equalities and conversion factors including 22.4 L/mol at STP.**

$$1 \text{ mol of } N_2 = 28.02 \text{ g of } N_2$$
$$\frac{28.02 \text{ g } N_2}{1 \text{ mol } N_2} \text{ and } \frac{1 \text{ mol } N_2}{28.02 \text{ g } N_2}$$

$$1 \text{ mol of } N_2 = 22.4 \text{ L of } N_2 \text{ (STP)}$$
$$\frac{22.4 \text{ L } N_2 \text{ (STP)}}{1 \text{ mol } N_2} \text{ and } \frac{1 \text{ mol } N_2}{22.4 \text{ L } N_2 \text{ (STP)}}$$

Step 4 **Set up the problem with factors to cancel units.**

$$\text{Density (g/L) of } N_2 = \frac{\text{mass}}{\text{volume}} = \frac{\dfrac{28.02 \text{ g } N_2}{1 \cancel{\text{mol } N_2}}}{\dfrac{22.4 \text{ L } N_2 \text{ (STP)}}{1 \cancel{\text{mol } N_2}}} = 1.25 \text{ g/L (STP)}$$

STUDY CHECK 11.9

What is the density, in grams per liter, of hydrogen gas (H_2) at STP?

QUESTIONS AND PROBLEMS

11.7 Volume and Moles (Avogadro's Law)

LEARNING GOAL: *Use Avogadro's law to determine the amount or volume of a gas when the pressure and temperature are constant.*

11.43 What happens to the volume of a bicycle tire or a basketball when you use an air pump to add air?

11.44 Sometimes when you blow up a balloon and release it, it flies around the room. What is happening to the air that was in the balloon and its volume?

11.45 A sample containing 1.50 mol of Ne gas has an initial volume of 8.00 L. What is the final volume, in liters, when the following changes occur in the quantity of the gas at constant pressure and temperature?
- **a.** A leak allows one-half of Ne atoms to escape.
- **b.** A sample of 3.50 mol of Ne is added to the 1.50 mol of Ne gas in the container.
- **c.** A sample of 25.0 g of Ne is added to the 1.50 mol of Ne gas in the container.

11.46 A sample containing 4.80 g of O_2 gas has an initial volume of 15.0 L. What is the final volume, in liters, when the following changes occur in the quantity of the gas at constant pressure and temperature?
- **a.** A sample of 0.500 mol of O_2 is added to the 4.80 g of O_2 in the container.
- **b.** A sample of 2.00 g of O_2 is removed.
- **c.** A sample of 4.00 g of O_2 is added to the 4.80 g of O_2 gas in the container.

11.47 Use the molar volume to calculate each of the following at STP:
- **a.** the number of moles of O_2 in 44.8 L of O_2 gas
- **b.** the number of moles of CO_2 in 4.00 L of CO_2 gas
- **c.** the volume (L) occupied by 6.40 g of O_2 gas
- **d.** the volume (mL) occupied by 50.0 g of Ne gas

11.48 Use the molar volume to calculate each of the following at STP:
- **a.** the volume (L) occupied by 2.50 mol of N_2 gas
- **b.** the volume (mL) occupied by 0.420 mol of He gas
- **c.** the number of grams of neon contained in 11.2 L of Ne gas
- **d.** the number of moles of H_2 in 1620 mL of H_2 gas

11.49 Calculate the density of each of the following gases, in grams per liter, at STP:
a. F_2 **b.** CH_4 **c.** Ne **d.** SO_2

11.50 Calculate the density of each of the following gases, in grams per liter, at STP:
a. C_3H_8 **b.** NH_3 **c.** Cl_2 **d.** Ar

11.8 The Ideal Gas Law

LEARNING GOAL

Use the ideal gas law equation to solve for P, V, T, or n of a gas when given three of the four values in the ideal gas law equation. Calculate density, molar mass, or volume of a gas in a chemical reaction.

The **ideal gas law** is the combination of the four properties used in the measurement of a gas—pressure (P), volume (V), temperature (T), and amount of a gas (n)—to give a single expression, which is written as

Ideal Gas Law

$$PV = nRT$$

Rearranging the ideal gas law equation shows that the four gas properties equal the gas law constant, R.

$$\frac{PV}{nT} = R$$

To calculate the value of R, we substitute the STP conditions for molar volume into the expression: 1 mol of any gas occupies 22.4 L at STP (273 K and 1 atm).

$$R = \frac{(1.00\ \text{atm})(22.4\ \text{L})}{(1.00\ \text{mol})(273\ \text{K})} = \frac{0.0821\ \text{L} \cdot \text{atm}}{\text{mol} \cdot \text{K}}$$

The value for the **ideal gas constant, *R***, is 0.0821 L · atm per mol · K. If we use 760 mmHg for the pressure, we obtain another useful value for R of 62.4 L · mmHg per mol · K.

$$R = \frac{(760\ \text{mmHg})(22.4\ \text{L})}{(1.00\ \text{mol})(273\ \text{K})} = \frac{62.4\ \text{L} \cdot \text{mmHg}}{\text{mol} \cdot \text{K}}$$

The ideal gas law is a useful expression when you are given the quantities for any three of the four properties of a gas. Although real gases show some deviations in behavior, the ideal gas law closely approximates the behavior of real gases at typical conditions. In working problems using the ideal gas law, the units of each variable must match the units in the R you select.

Ideal Gas Constant (*R*)	$\frac{0.0821\ \text{L} \cdot \text{atm}}{\text{mol} \cdot \text{K}}$	$\frac{62.4\ \text{L} \cdot \text{mmHg}}{\text{mol} \cdot \text{K}}$
Pressure (*P*)	atm	mmHg
Volume (*V*)	L	L
Amount (*n*)	mol	mol
Temperature (*T*)	K	K

CORE CHEMISTRY SKILL 

Using the Ideal Gas Law

SAMPLE PROBLEM 11.10 Using the Ideal Gas Law

Dinitrogen oxide, N_2O, which is used in dentistry, is an anesthetic also called laughing gas. What is the pressure, in atmospheres, of 0.350 mol of N_2O at 22 °C in a 5.00-L container?

SOLUTION

Step 1 **State the given and needed quantities.** When three of the four quantities (P, V, n, and T) are known, we use the ideal gas law equation to solve for the unknown quantity. It is helpful to organize the data in a table. The temperature is converted from degrees Celsius to kelvins so that the units of V, n, and T match the unit of the gas constant R.

Analyze the Problem		*P*	*V*	*n*	*R*	*T*
	Given		5.00 L	0.350 mol	$\frac{0.0821\ \text{L} \cdot \text{atm}}{\text{mol} \cdot \text{K}}$	22 °C + 273 = 295 K
	Need	? atm				

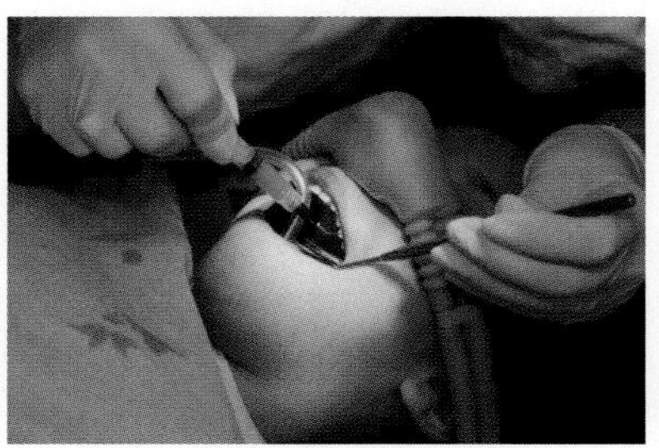

Dinitrogen oxide is used as an anesthetic in dentistry.

Guide to Using the Ideal Gas Law

1. State the given and needed quantities.
2. Rearrange the ideal gas law equation to solve for the needed quantity.
3. Substitute the gas data into the equation and calculate the needed quantity.

Step 2 **Rearrange the ideal gas law equation to solve for the needed quantity.** By dividing both sides of the ideal gas law by V, we solve for pressure, P.

$$PV = nRT \quad \text{Ideal gas law equation}$$

$$\frac{P\cancel{V}}{\cancel{V}} = \frac{nRT}{V}$$

$$P = \frac{nRT}{V}$$

Step 3 **Substitute the gas data into the equation and calculate the needed quantity.**

$$P = \frac{0.350\ \cancel{\text{mol}} \times \dfrac{0.0821\ \cancel{\text{L}} \cdot \text{atm}}{\cancel{\text{mol}} \cdot \cancel{\text{K}}} \times 295\ \cancel{\text{K}}}{5.00\ \cancel{\text{L}}} = 1.70\ \text{atm}$$

STUDY CHECK 11.10

Chlorine gas, Cl_2, is used to purify the water. How many moles of chlorine gas are in a 7.00-L tank if the gas has a pressure of 865 mmHg and a temperature of 24 °C?

Many times we need to know the amount of gas, in grams, involved in a reaction. Then the ideal gas law equation can be rearranged to solve for the amount (n) of gas, which is converted to mass in grams using its molar mass as shown in Sample Problem 11.11.

SAMPLE PROBLEM 11.11 Calculating Mass Using the Ideal Gas Law

Butane, C_4H_{10}, is used as a fuel for barbecues and as an aerosol propellant. If you have 108 mL of butane at 715 mmHg and 25 °C, what is the mass, in grams, of butane?

SOLUTION

Step 1 **State the given and needed quantities.** When three of the quantities (P, V, and T) are known, we use the ideal gas law equation to solve for the unknown quantity, moles (n). Because the pressure is given in mmHg, we will use R in mmHg. The volume given in milliliters (mL) is converted to a volume in liters (L). The temperature is converted from degrees Celsius to kelvins.

Analyze the Problem		P	V	n	R	T
	Given	715 mmHg	108 mL (0.108 L)		$\frac{62.4\ \text{L} \cdot \text{mmHg}}{\text{mol} \cdot \text{K}}$	25 °C + 273 = 298 K
	Need			? g of C_4H_{10} (? mol of C_4H_{10})		

Step 2 **Rearrange the ideal gas law equation to solve for the needed quantity.** By dividing both sides of the ideal gas law equation by RT, we solve for moles, n.

$$PV = n\,RT \quad \text{Ideal gas law equation}$$

$$\frac{PV}{RT} = \frac{n\,\cancel{RT}}{\cancel{RT}}$$

$$n = \frac{PV}{RT}$$

Step 3 **Substitute the gas data into the equation and calculate the needed quantity.**

$$n = \frac{715 \cancel{\text{mmHg}} \times 0.108 \cancel{\text{L}}}{\dfrac{62.4 \cancel{\text{L}} \cdot \cancel{\text{mmHg}}}{\text{mol} \cdot \cancel{\text{K}}} \times 298 \cancel{\text{K}}} = 0.00415 \text{ mol } (4.15 \times 10^{-3} \text{ mol})$$

Now we can convert the moles of butane to grams using its molar mass of 58.12 g/mol:

$$0.00415 \cancel{\text{mol } C_4H_{10}} \times \frac{58.12 \text{ g } C_4H_{10}}{1 \cancel{\text{mol } C_4H_{10}}} = 0.241 \text{ g of } C_4H_{10}$$

STUDY CHECK 11.11

What is the volume, in liters, of 1.20 g of carbon monoxide at 8 °C if it has a pressure of 724 mmHg?

Molar Mass of a Gas

Another use of the ideal gas law is to determine the molar mass of a gas. If the mass, in grams, of the gas is known, we calculate the number of moles of the gas using the ideal gas law equation. Then the molar mass (g/mol) can be determined.

SAMPLE PROBLEM 11.12 Molar Mass of a Gas Using the Ideal Gas Law

What is the molar mass, in grams per mole, of a gas if a 3.16-g sample of gas at 0.750 atm and 45 °C occupies a volume of 2.05 L?

SOLUTION

Step 1 **State the given and needed quantities.** When the mass of a gas is given, it is combined with the moles of gas using the ideal gas law equation, to determine its molar mass.

		P	*V*	*n*	*R*	*T*
Analyze the Problem	**Given**	0.750 atm	2.05 L	mass = 3.16 g	$\frac{0.0821 \text{ L} \cdot \text{atm}}{\text{mol} \cdot \text{K}}$	45 °C + 273 = 318 K
	Need			? mol of C_4H_{10}		

Guide to Calculating the Molar Mass of a Gas

1. State the given and needed quantities.
2. Rearrange the ideal gas law equation to solve for the number of moles.
3. Obtain the molar mass by dividing the given number of grams by the number of moles.

Step 2 **Rearrange the ideal gas law equation to solve for the number of moles.** To solve for moles, n, divide both sides of the ideal gas law equation by RT.

$$PV = n\,RT \quad \text{Ideal gas law equation}$$

$$\frac{PV}{RT} = \frac{n\,\cancel{RT}}{\cancel{RT}}$$

$$n = \frac{PV}{RT}$$

$$n = \frac{0.750 \cancel{\text{atm}} \times 2.05 \cancel{\text{L}}}{\dfrac{0.0821 \cancel{\text{L}} \cdot \cancel{\text{atm}}}{\text{mol} \cdot \cancel{\text{K}}} \times 318 \cancel{\text{K}}} = 0.0589 \text{ mol}$$

Step 3 **Obtain the molar mass by dividing the given number of grams by the number of moles.**

$$\text{Molar mass} = \frac{\text{mass}}{\text{moles}} = \frac{3.16 \text{ g}}{0.0589 \text{ mol}} = 53.7 \text{ g/mol}$$

STUDY CHECK 11.12

What is the molar mass, in grams per mole, of an unknown gas in a 1.50-L container if 0.488 g of the gas has a pressure of 0.0750 atm at 19.0 °C?

QUESTIONS AND PROBLEMS

11.8 The Ideal Gas Law

LEARNING GOAL: *Use the ideal gas law equation to solve for P, V, T, or n of a gas when given three of the four values in the ideal gas law equation. Calculate density, molar mass, or volume of a gas in a chemical reaction.*

11.51 Calculate the pressure, in atmospheres, of 2.00 mol of helium gas in a 10.0-L container at 27 °C.

11.52 What is the volume, in liters, of 4.00 mol of methane gas, CH_4, at 18 °C and 1.40 atm?

11.53 An oxygen gas container has a volume of 20.0 L. How many grams of oxygen are in the container if the gas has a pressure of 845 mmHg at 22 °C?

11.54 A 10.0-g sample of krypton has a temperature of 25 °C at 575 mmHg. What is the volume, in milliliters, of the krypton gas?

11.55 A 25.0-g sample of nitrogen, N_2, has a volume of 50.0 L and a pressure of 630. mmHg. What is the temperature, in kelvins and degrees Celsius, of the gas?

11.56 A 0.226-g sample of carbon dioxide, CO_2, has a volume of 525 mL and a pressure of 455 mmHg. What is the temperature, in kelvins and degrees Celsius, of the gas?

11.57 Determine the molar mass of each of the following gases:

a. 0.84 g of a gas that occupies 450 mL at 0 °C and 1.00 atm (STP)

b. 1.28 g of a gas that occupies 1.00 L at 0 °C and 760 mmHg (STP)

c. 1.48 g of a gas that occupies 1.00 L at 685 mmHg and 22 °C

d. 2.96 g of a gas that occupies 2.30 L at 0.95 atm and 24 °C

11.58 Determine the molar mass of each of the following gases:

a. 2.90 g of a gas that occupies 0.500 L at 0 °C and 1.00 atm (STP)

b. 1.43 g of a gas that occupies 2.00 L at 0 °C and 760 mmHg (STP)

c. 0.726 g of a gas that occupies 855 mL at 1.20 atm and 18 °C

d. 2.32 g of a gas that occupies 1.23 L at 685 mmHg and 25 °C

LEARNING GOAL

Determine the mass or volume of a gas that reacts or forms in a chemical reaction.

CORE CHEMISTRY SKILL

Calculating Mass or Volume of a Gas in a Chemical Reaction

11.9 Gas Laws and Chemical Reactions

Gases are involved as reactants and products in many chemical reactions. For example, we have seen that the combustion of organic fuels with oxygen gas produces carbon dioxide gas and water vapor. In combination reactions, we have seen that hydrogen gas and nitrogen gas react to form ammonia gas, and hydrogen gas and oxygen gas produce water. Typically, the information given for a gas in a reaction is its pressure (P), volume (V), and temperature (T). Then we can use the ideal gas law equation to determine the moles of a gas in a reaction. If we are given the number of moles for one of the gases in a reaction, we can use a mole–mole factor to determine the moles of any other substance.

SAMPLE PROBLEM 11.13 Gases in Chemical Reactions

Limestone ($CaCO_3$) reacts with HCl to produce aqueous calcium chloride, carbon dioxide gas, and water.

$$CaCO_3(s) + 2HCl(aq) \longrightarrow CaCl_2(aq) + CO_2(g) + H_2O(l)$$

How many liters of CO_2 are produced at 752 mmHg and 24 °C from a 25.0-g sample of limestone?

SOLUTION

Step 1 State the given and needed quantities.

	Given	Need
Analyze the Problem	Reactant: 25.0 g of $CaCO_3$	liters of $CO_2(g)$
	Product: $CO_2(g)$ at 752 mmHg, 24 °C (24 °C + 273 = 297 K)	
	Equation	
	$CaCO_3(s) + 2HCl(aq) \longrightarrow CaCl_2(aq) + CO_2(g) + H_2O(l)$	

Step 2 **Write a plan to convert the given quantity to the needed moles.**

grams of CaO_3 → Molar mass → moles of CaO_3 → Mole-mole factor → moles of CO_2

Step 3 **Write the equalities and conversion factors for molar mass and mole–mole factors.**

$$1 \text{ mol of } CaCO_3 = 100.09 \text{ g of } CaCO_3$$
$$\frac{100.09 \text{ g } CaCO_3}{1 \text{ mol } CaCO_3} \text{ and } \frac{1 \text{ mol } CaCO_3}{100.09 \text{ g } CaCO_3}$$

$$1 \text{ mol of } CaCO_3 = 1 \text{ mol of } CO_2$$
$$\frac{1 \text{ mol } CaCO_3}{1 \text{ mol } CO_2} \text{ and } \frac{1 \text{ mol } CO_2}{1 \text{ mol } CaCO_3}$$

Step 4 **Set up the problem to calculate moles of needed quantity.**

$$25.0 \cancel{\text{g } CaCO_3} \times \frac{1 \cancel{\text{mol } CaCO_3}}{100.09 \cancel{\text{g } CaCO_3}} \times \frac{1 \text{ mol } CO_2}{1 \cancel{\text{mol } CaCO_3}} = 0.250 \text{ mol of } CO_2$$

Step 5 **Convert the moles of needed quantity to mass or volume using the molar mass or the ideal gas law equation.**

$$V = \frac{nRT}{P}$$

$$V = \frac{0.250 \cancel{\text{mol}} \times \dfrac{62.4 \text{ L} \cdot \cancel{\text{mmHg}}}{\cancel{\text{K}} \cdot \cancel{\text{mol}}} \times 297 \cancel{\text{K}}}{752 \cancel{\text{mmHg}}} = 6.16 \text{ L of } CO_2$$

STUDY CHECK 11.13

If 12.8 g of aluminum reacts with HCl, how many liters of H_2 would be formed at 715 mmHg and 19 °C?

$$2Al(s) + 6HCl(aq) \longrightarrow 3H_2(g) + 2AlCl_3(aq)$$

Guide to Reactions Involving the Ideal Gas Law

1 State the given and needed quantities.

2 Write a plan to convert the given quantity to the needed moles.

3 Write the equalities and conversion factors for molar mass and mole–mole factors.

4 Set up the problem to calculate moles of needed quantity.

5 Convert the moles of needed quantity to mass or volume using the molar mass or the ideal gas law equation.

When aluminum reacts with HCl, bubbles of H_2 gas form.

QUESTIONS AND PROBLEMS

11.9 Gas Laws and Chemical Reactions

LEARNING GOAL: *Determine the mass or volume of a gas that reacts or forms in a chemical reaction.*

11.59 Mg metal reacts with HCl to produce hydrogen gas.

$$Mg(s) + 2HCl(aq) \longrightarrow H_2(g) + MgCl_2(aq)$$

a. What volume, in liters, of hydrogen at 0 °C and 1.00 atm (STP) is released when 8.25 g of Mg reacts?

b. How many grams of magnesium are needed to prepare 5.00 L of H_2 at 735 mmHg and 18 °C?

11.60 When heated to 350 °C at 0.950 atm, ammonium nitrate decomposes to produce nitrogen, water, and oxygen gases.

$$2NH_4NO_3(s) \xrightarrow{\Delta} 2N_2(g) + 4H_2O(g) + O_2(g)$$

a. How many liters of water vapor are produced when 25.8 g of NH_4NO_3 decomposes?

b. How many grams of NH_4NO_3 are needed to produce 10.0 L of oxygen?

11.61 Butane undergoes combustion when it reacts with oxygen to produce carbon dioxide and water. What volume, in liters, of oxygen is needed to react with 55.2 g of butane at 0.850 atm and 25 °C?

$$2C_4H_{10}(g) + 13O_2(g) \xrightarrow{\Delta} 8CO_2(g) + 10H_2O(g)$$

11.62 Potassium nitrate decomposes to potassium nitrite and oxygen. What volume, in liters, of O_2 can be produced from the decomposition of 50.0 g of KNO_3 at 35 °C and 1.19 atm?

$$2KNO_3(s) \longrightarrow 2KNO_2(s) + O_2(g)$$

11.63 Aluminum and oxygen react to form aluminum oxide. How many liters of oxygen at 0 °C and 760 mmHg (STP) are required to completely react with 5.4 g of aluminum?

$$4Al(s) + 3O_2(g) \longrightarrow 2Al_2O_3(s)$$

11.64 Nitrogen dioxide reacts with water to produce oxygen and ammonia. How many grams of NH_3 can be produced when 4.00 L of NO_2 reacts at 415 °C and 725 mmHg?

$$4NO_2(g) + 6H_2O(g) \longrightarrow 7O_2(g) + 4NH_3(g)$$

LEARNING GOAL

Use Dalton's law of partial pressures to calculate the total pressure of a mixture of gases.

11.10 Partial Pressures (Dalton's Law)

Many gas samples are a mixture of gases. For example, the air you breathe is a mixture of mostly oxygen and nitrogen gases. In ideal gas mixtures, scientists observed that all gas particles behave in the same way. Therefore, the total pressure of the gases in a mixture is a result of the collisions of the gas particles regardless of what type of gas they are.

In a gas mixture, each gas exerts its **partial pressure**, which is the pressure it would exert if it were the only gas in the container. **Dalton's law** states that the total pressure of a gas mixture is the sum of the partial pressures of the gases in the mixture.

CORE CHEMISTRY SKILL

Calculating Partial Pressure

Dalton's Law

$$P_{\text{total}} = P_1 + P_2 + P_3 + \cdots$$

Total pressure of a gas mixture = Sum of the partial pressures of the gases in the mixture

Suppose we have two separate tanks, one filled with helium at a pressure of 2.0 atm and the other filled with argon at a pressure of 4.0 atm. When the gases are combined in a single tank with the same volume and temperature, the number of gas molecules, not the type of gas, determines the pressure in a container. There the pressure of the gas mixture would be 6.0 atm, which is the sum of their individual or partial pressures.

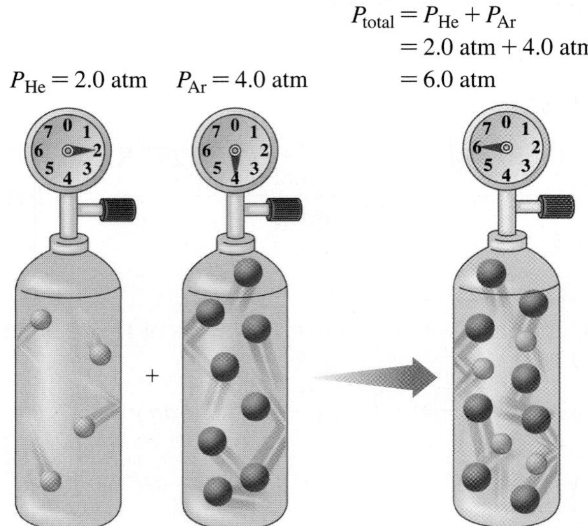

$P_{\text{total}} = P_{\text{He}} + P_{\text{Ar}}$
$= 2.0 \text{ atm} + 4.0 \text{ atm}$
$= 6.0 \text{ atm}$
$P_{\text{He}} = 2.0 \text{ atm}$
$P_{\text{Ar}} = 4.0 \text{ atm}$
+

The total pressure of two gases is the sum of their partial pressures.

CONCEPT CHECK 11.7 Pressure of a Gas Mixture

A scuba tank is filled with Trimix, a breathing gas mixture for deep scuba diving. The tank contains oxygen with a partial pressure of 20. atm, nitrogen with a partial pressure of 40. atm, and helium with a partial pressure of 140. atm. What is the total pressure of the breathing mixture, in atmospheres?

ANSWER

Using Dalton's law of partial pressures, we add together the partial pressures of oxygen, nitrogen, and helium present in the mixture.

$$P_{\text{total}} = P_{\text{oxygen}} + P_{\text{nitrogen}} + P_{\text{helium}}$$
$$P_{\text{total}} = 20. \text{ atm} + 40. \text{ atm} + 140. \text{ atm}$$
$$= 200. \text{ atm}$$

Therefore, when oxygen, nitrogen, and helium are placed in the same container, the sum of their partial pressures is the total pressure of the mixture, which is 200. atm.

Air Is a Gas Mixture

The air you breathe is a mixture of gases. What we call the *atmospheric pressure* is actually the sum of the partial pressures of the gases in the air. Table 11.7 lists partial pressures for the gases in air on a typical day.

TABLE 11.7 Typical Composition of Air

Gas	Partial Pressure (mmHg)	Percentage (%)
Nitrogen, N_2	594	78.2
Oxygen, O_2	160.	21.0
Carbon dioxide, CO_2; Argon, Ar; Water vapor, H_2O	6	0.8
Total air	760.	100

SAMPLE PROBLEM 11.14 Partial Pressure of a Gas in a Mixture

A Heliox breathing mixture of oxygen and helium is prepared for a scuba diver who is going to descend 200 ft below the ocean surface. At that depth, the diver breathes a gas mixture that has a total pressure of 7.00 atm. If the partial pressure of the oxygen in the tank at that depth is 1140 mmHg, what is the partial pressure, in atmospheres, of the helium in the breathing mixture?

SOLUTION

Step 1 Write the equation for the sum of the partial pressures.

$$P_{\text{total}} = P_{O_2} + P_{\text{He}}$$

Step 2 Rearrange the equation to solve for the unknown pressure. To solve for the partial pressure of helium (P_{He}), we rearrange the equation to give the following:

$$P_{\text{He}} = P_{\text{total}} - P_{O_2}$$

Convert units to match.

$$P_{O_2} = 1140\ \cancel{\text{mmHg}} \times \frac{1\ \text{atm}}{760\ \cancel{\text{mmHg}}} = 1.50\ \text{atm}$$

Step 3 Substitute known pressures into the equation and calculate the unknown partial pressure.

$$P_{\text{He}} = P_{\text{total}} - P_{O_2}$$

$$P_{\text{He}} = 7.00\ \text{atm} - 1.50\ \text{atm} = 5.50\ \text{atm}$$

STUDY CHECK 11.14

An anesthetic consists of a mixture of cyclopropane gas, C_3H_6, and oxygen gas, O_2. If the mixture has a total pressure of 1.09 atm, and the partial pressure of the cyclopropane is 73 mmHg, what is the partial pressure, in millimeters of mercury, of the oxygen in the anesthetic?

Guide to Calculating Partial Pressure

1. Write the equation for the sum of the partial pressures.
2. Rearrange the equation to solve for the unknown pressure.
3. Substitute known pressures into the equation and calculate the unknown partial pressure.

Gases Collected Over Water

In the laboratory, gases are often collected by bubbling them through water into a container (see Figure 11.9). In a reaction, magnesium (Mg) reacts with HCl to form H_2 gas and $MgCl_2$.

$$Mg(s) + 2HCl(aq) \longrightarrow H_2(g) + MgCl_2(aq)$$

As hydrogen is produced during the reaction, it displaces some of the water in the container. Because of the vapor pressure of water, the gas that is collected is a mixture of hydrogen and water vapor. For our calculation, we need the pressure of the dry hydrogen gas. We use the vapor pressure of water (Table 11.4) at the experimental temperature, and subtract it from the total gas pressure. Then we can use the ideal gas law to determine the moles or grams of the hydrogen gas that were collected.

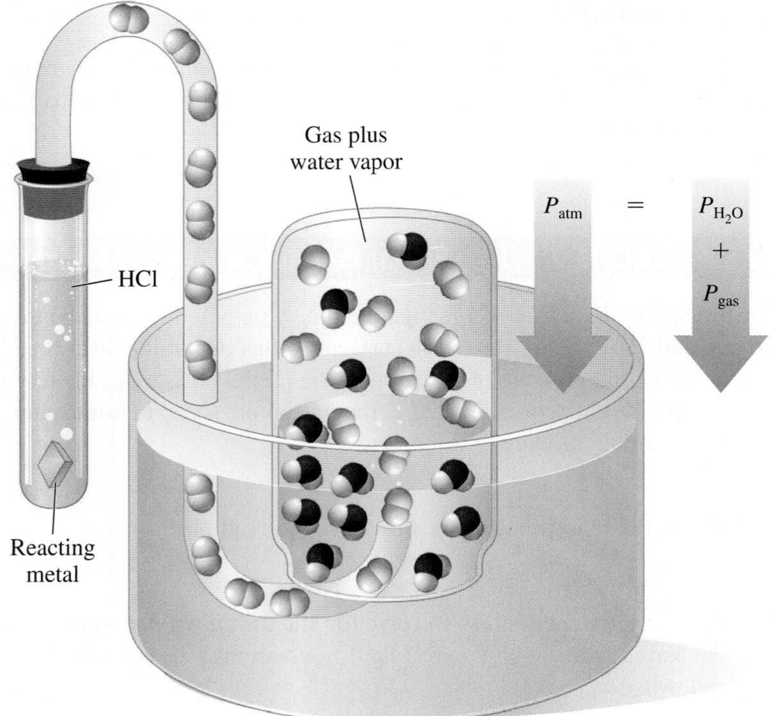

FIGURE 11.9 A gas from a reaction is collected by bubbling through water. Due to evaporation of water, the total pressure is equal to the partial pressure of the gas and the vapor pressure of water.

Q How is the pressure of the dry gas determined?

SAMPLE PROBLEM 11.15 Moles of Gas Collected Over Water

When magnesium reacts with HCl, a volume of 0.355 L of hydrogen gas is collected over water at 26 °C. The vapor pressure of water at 26 °C is 25 mmHg.

$$Mg(s) + 2HCl(aq) \longrightarrow H_2(g) + MgCl_2(aq)$$

If the total pressure is 752 mmHg, how many moles of $H_2(g)$ were collected?

SOLUTION

Guide to Gases Collected over Water

1. Obtain the vapor pressure of water.
2. Subtract the vapor pressure from the total P of gas mixture to give the partial pressure of needed gas.
3. Use the ideal gas law to convert P_{gas} to moles or grams of gas collected.

Step 1 **Obtain the vapor pressure of water.** The vapor pressure of water at 26 °C is 25 mmHg.

Step 2 **Subtract the vapor pressure from the total *P* of gas mixture to give the partial pressure of needed gas.** Using Dalton's law of partial pressures, determine the partial pressure of H_2.

$$P_{total} = P_{H_2} + P_{H_2O}$$

Solving for the partial pressure of H_2 gives

$$P_{H_2} = P_{total} - P_{H_2O}$$
$$P_{H_2} = 752\ \text{mmHg} - 25\ \text{mmHg}$$
$$= 727\ \text{mmHg}$$

Step 3 **Use the ideal gas law to convert P_{gas} to moles or grams of gas collected.** By dividing both sides of the ideal gas law equation by RT, we solve for moles, n, of gas.

$$PV = nRT \quad \text{Ideal gas law equation}$$

$$\frac{PV}{RT} = \frac{n\cancel{RT}}{\cancel{RT}}$$

$$n = \frac{PV}{RT}$$

Solve for the moles of H_2 gas by placing the partial pressure of H_2 (727 mmHg), volume of gas container (0.355 L), temperature (26 °C + 273 = 299 K), and R, using mmHg, into the ideal gas law equation.

$$n = \frac{727 \cancel{\text{mmHg}} \times 0.355 \cancel{\text{L}}}{\frac{62.4 \cancel{\text{L}} \cdot \cancel{\text{mmHg}}}{\text{mol} \cdot \cancel{\text{K}}} \times 299 \cancel{\text{K}}} = 0.0138 \text{ mol of } H_2 \, (1.38 \times 10^{-2} \text{ mol of } H_2)$$

STUDY CHECK 11.15

A 456-mL sample of oxygen gas (O_2) is collected over water at a pressure of 744 mmHg and a temperature of 20. °C. How many grams of dry O_2 are collected?

Chemistry Link to Health

BLOOD GASES

Our cells continuously use oxygen and produce carbon dioxide. Both gases move in and out of the lungs through the membranes of the alveoli, the tiny air sacs at the ends of the airways in the lungs. An exchange of gases occurs in which oxygen from the air diffuses into the lungs and into the blood, while carbon dioxide produced in the cells is carried to the lungs to be exhaled. In Table 11.8, partial pressures are given for the gases in air that we inhale (inspired air), air in the alveoli, and air that we exhale (expired air). The partial pressure of water vapor increases within the lungs because the vapor pressure of water is 47 mmHg at body temperature.

At sea level, oxygen normally has a partial pressure of 100 mmHg in the alveoli of the lungs. Because the partial pressure of oxygen in venous blood is 40 mmHg, oxygen diffuses from the alveoli into the bloodstream. The oxygen combines with hemoglobin, which carries it to the tissues of the body where the partial pressure of oxygen can be very low, less than 30 mmHg. Oxygen diffuses from the blood, where the partial pressure of O_2 is high, into the tissues, where O_2 pressure is low.

As oxygen is used in the cells of the body during metabolic processes, carbon dioxide is produced, so the partial pressure of CO_2 may be as high as 50 mmHg or more. Carbon dioxide diffuses from the tissues into the bloodstream and is carried to the lungs. There it diffuses out of the blood, where CO_2 has a partial pressure of 46 mmHg, into the alveoli, where CO_2 is at 40 mmHg and is exhaled. Table 11.9 summarizes the partial pressures of blood gases in the tissues and in oxygenated and deoxygenated blood.

TABLE 11.8 Partial Pressures of Gases during Breathing

	Partial Pressure (mmHg)		
Gas	**Inspired Air**	**Alveolar Air**	**Expired Air**
Nitrogen, N_2	594	573	569
Oxygen, O_2	160	100	116
Carbon dioxide, CO_2	0.3	40	28
Water vapor, H_2O	5.7	47	47
Total	760.	760.	760.

TABLE 11.9 Partial Pressures of Oxygen and Carbon Dioxide in Blood and Tissues

	Partial Pressure (mmHg)		
Gas	**Oxygenated Blood**	**Deoxygenated Blood**	**Tissues**
O_2	100	40	30 or less
CO_2	40	46	50 or greater

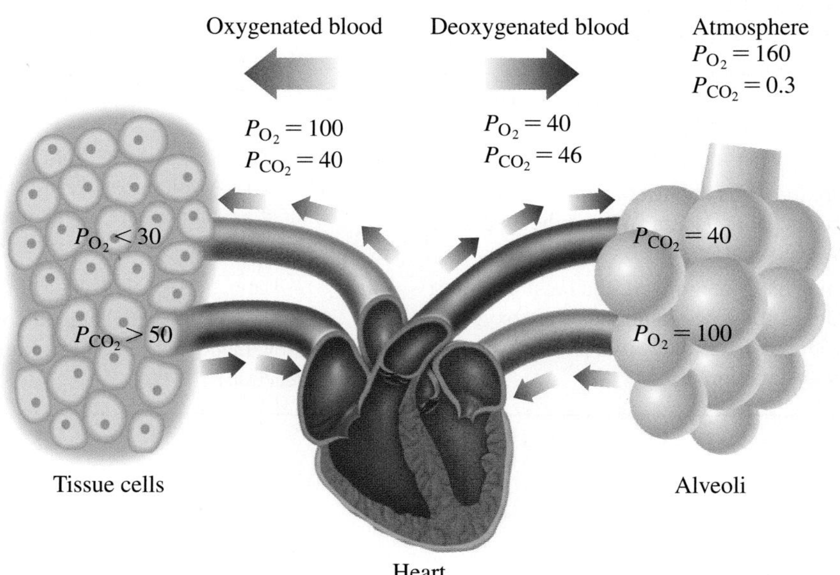

Chemistry Link to Health

HYPERBARIC CHAMBERS

A burn patient may undergo treatment for burns and infections in a hyperbaric chamber, a device in which pressures can be obtained that are two to three times greater than atmospheric pressure. A greater oxygen pressure increases the level of dissolved oxygen in the blood and tissues, where it fights bacterial infections. High levels of oxygen are toxic to many strains of bacteria. The hyperbaric chamber may also be used during surgery, to help counteract carbon monoxide (CO) poisoning, and to treat some cancers.

The blood is normally capable of dissolving up to 95 percent of the oxygen. Thus, if the partial pressure of the oxygen in the hyperbaric chamber is 2280 mmHg (3 atm), about 2170 mmHg of oxygen can dissolve in the blood, saturating the tissues. In the treatment for carbon monoxide poisoning, oxygen at high pressure is used to displace the CO from the hemoglobin faster than breathing pure oxygen at 1 atm.

A patient undergoing treatment in a hyperbaric chamber must also undergo decompression (reduction of pressure) at a rate that slowly reduces the concentration of dissolved oxygen in the blood. If decompression is too rapid, the oxygen dissolved in the blood may form gas bubbles in the circulatory system.

Similarly, if a scuba diver does not decompress slowly, a condition called the "bends" may occur. While below the surface of the ocean, a diver uses a breathing mixture with higher pressures. If there is nitrogen in the mixture, higher quantities of nitrogen gas will dissolve in the blood. If the diver ascends to the surface too quickly, the dissolved nitrogen forms gas bubbles that can block a blood vessel and cut off the flow of blood in the joints and tissues of the body and be quite painful. A diver suffering from the bends is placed immediately into a hyperbaric chamber where pressure is first increased and then slowly decreased. The dissolved nitrogen can then diffuse through the lungs until atmospheric pressure is reached.

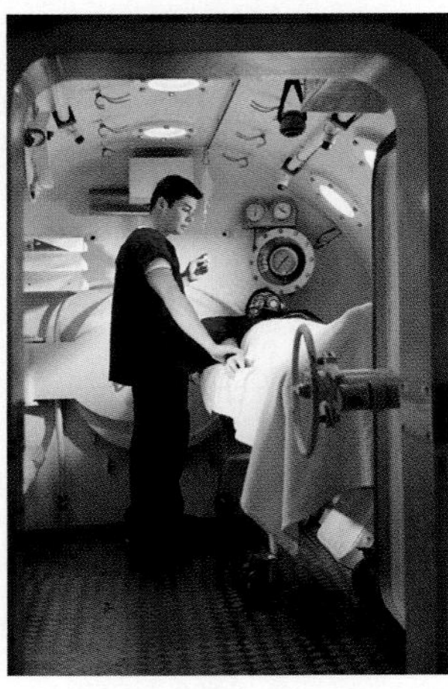

A hyperbaric chamber is used in the treatment of certain diseases.

QUESTIONS AND PROBLEMS

11.10 Partial Pressures (Dalton's Law)

LEARNING GOAL: *Use Dalton's law of partial pressures to calculate the total pressure of a mixture of gases.*

11.65 In a gas mixture, the partial pressures are nitrogen 425 torr, oxygen 115 torr, and helium 225 torr. What is the total pressure, in torr, exerted by the gas mixture?

11.66 In a gas mixture, the partial pressures are argon 415 mmHg, neon 75 mmHg, and nitrogen 125 mmHg. What is the total pressure, in millimeters of mercury, exerted by the gas mixture?

11.67 An air sample in the lungs contains oxygen at 93 mmHg, nitrogen at 565 mmHg, carbon dioxide at 38 mmHg, and water vapor at 47 mmHg. What is the total pressure, in atmospheres, exerted by the gas mixture?

11.68 A Nitrox II gas mixture for scuba diving contains oxygen gas at 53 atm and nitrogen gas at 94 atm. What is the total pressure, in torr, of the scuba gas mixture?

11.69 A gas mixture containing oxygen, nitrogen, and helium exerts a total pressure of 925 torr. If the partial pressures are oxygen 425 torr and helium 75 torr, what is the partial pressure, in torr, of the nitrogen in the mixture?

11.70 A gas mixture containing oxygen, nitrogen, and neon exerts a total pressure of 1.20 atm. If helium added to the mixture increases the pressure to 1.50 atm, what is the partial pressure, in atmospheres, of the helium?

11.71 When solid $KClO_3$ is heated, it decomposes to give solid KCl and O_2 gas. A volume of 256 mL of gas is collected over water at a total pressure of 765 mmHg and 24 °C. The vapor pressure of water at 24 °C is 22 mmHg.

$$2KClO_3(s) \xrightarrow{\Delta} 2KCl(s) + 3O_2(g)$$

a. What was the partial pressure of the O_2 gas?
b. How many moles of O_2 gas were produced in the reaction?

11.72 When Zn reacts with HCl solution, the products are H_2 gas and $ZnCl_2$. A volume of 425 mL of H_2 gas is collected over water at a total pressure of 758 mmHg and 16 °C. The vapor pressure of water at 16 °C is 14 mmHg.

$$Zn(s) + HCl(aq) \longrightarrow H_2(g) + ZnCl_2(aq)$$

a. What was the partial pressure of the H_2 gas?
b. How many moles of H_2 gas were produced in the reaction?

CHAPTER REVIEW

11.1 Properties of Gases

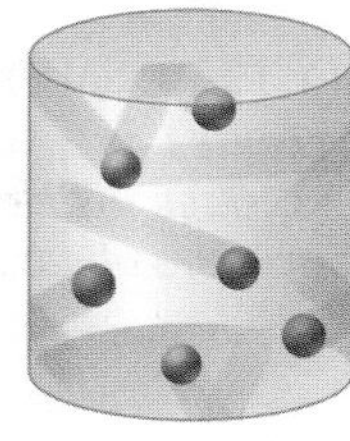

LEARNING GOAL: *Describe the kinetic molecular theory of gases and the properties of gases.*

- In a gas, particles are so far apart and moving so fast that their attractions are negligible.
- A gas is described by the physical properties of pressure (P), volume (V), temperature (T), and amount in moles (n).

11.2 Gas Pressure

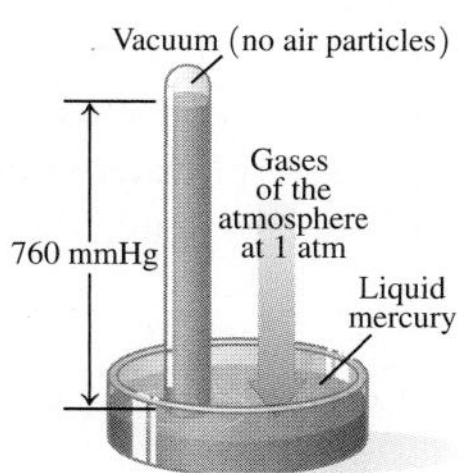

LEARNING GOAL: *Describe the units of measurement used for pressure, and change from one unit to another.*

- A gas exerts pressure, the force of the gas particles striking the surface of a container.
- Gas pressure is measured in units such as torr, mmHg, atm, and Pa.

11.3 Pressure and Volume (Boyle's Law)

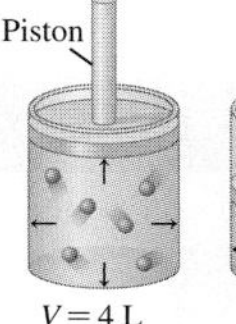

LEARNING GOAL: *Use the pressure–volume relationship (Boyle's law) to determine the final pressure or volume when the temperature and amount of gas are constant.*

- The volume (V) of a gas changes inversely with the pressure (P) of the gas if there is no change in the amount and temperature.

$$P_1V_1 = P_2V_2$$

- The pressure of a gas increases if its volume decreases; its pressure decreases if the volume increases.

11.4 Temperature and Volume (Charles's Law)

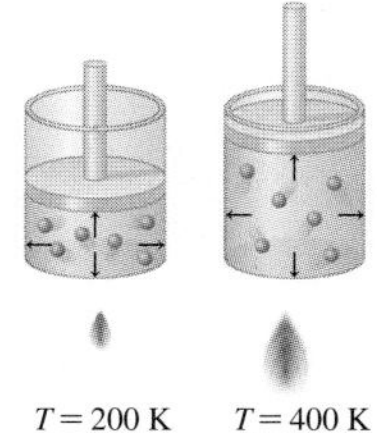

LEARNING GOAL: *Use the temperature–volume relationship (Charles's law) to determine the final temperature or volume when the pressure and amount of gas are constant.*

- The volume (V) of a gas is directly related to its Kelvin temperature (T) when there is no change in the pressure and amount of the gas.

$$\frac{V_1}{T_1} = \frac{V_2}{T_2}$$

- If the temperature of a gas increases, its volume increases; if its temperature decreases, the volume decreases.

11.5 Temperature and Pressure (Gay-Lussac's Law)

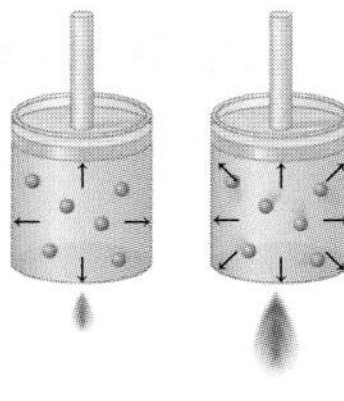

LEARNING GOAL: *Use the temperature–pressure relationship (Gay-Lussac's law) to determine the final temperature or pressure when the volume and amount of gas are constant.*

- The pressure (P) of a gas is directly related to its Kelvin temperature (T).

$$\frac{P_1}{T_1} = \frac{P_2}{T_2}$$

- An increase in temperature increases the pressure of a gas, and a decrease in temperature decreases the pressure, as long as the volume and amount stay constant.
- Vapor pressure is the pressure of the gas that forms when a liquid evaporates.
- At the boiling point of a liquid, the vapor pressure equals the external pressure.

11.6 The Combined Gas Law

LEARNING GOAL: *Use the combined gas law to find the final pressure, volume, or temperature of a gas when changes in two of these properties are given and the amount of gas is constant.*

- The combined gas law is the relationship of pressure (P), volume (V), and temperature (T) for a constant amount of gas.
- The combined gas law is used to determine the effect of changes in two of the variables on the third.

$$\frac{P_1V_1}{T_1} = \frac{P_2V_2}{T_2}$$

11.7 Volume and Moles (Avogadro's Law)

LEARNING GOAL: *Use Avogadro's law to determine the amount or volume of a gas when the pressure and temperature are constant.*

- The volume (V) of a gas is directly related to the number of moles (n) of the gas when the pressure and temperature of the gas do not change.

$$\frac{V_1}{n_1} = \frac{V_2}{n_2}$$

- If the moles of gas increase, the volume must increase; if the moles of gas decrease, the volume must decrease.
- At standard temperature (273 K) and standard pressure (1 atm), abbreviated STP, 1 mol of any gas has a volume of 22.4 L.
- The density of a gas at STP is the ratio of the molar mass to the molar volume.

11.8 The Ideal Gas Law

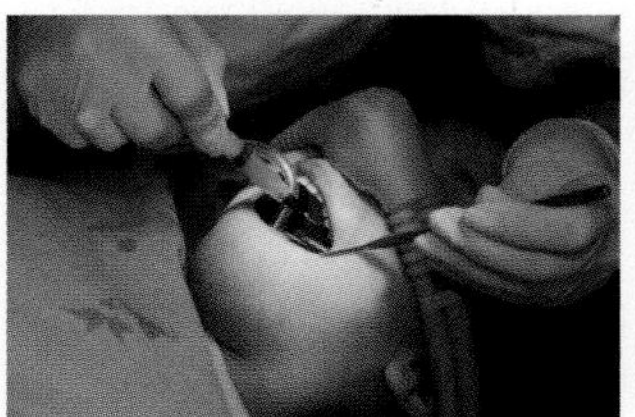

LEARNING GOAL: *Use the ideal gas law equation to solve for P, V, T, or n of a gas when given three of the four values in the ideal gas law equation. Calculate density, molar mass, or volume of a gas in a chemical reaction.*

- The ideal gas law gives the relationship of the quantities P, V, n, and T that describe and measure a gas.

$$PV = nRT$$

- Any of the four variables can be calculated if the values of the other three are known.
- The molar mass of a gas can be calculated using molar volume at STP or the ideal gas law.

11.9 Gas Laws and Chemical Reactions

LEARNING GOAL: *Determine the mass or volume of a gas that reacts or forms in a chemical reaction.*

- The ideal gas law equation is used to convert the quantities (P, V, and T) of gases to moles in a chemical reaction.
- The moles of gases can be used to determine the number of moles or grams of other substances in the reaction.
- The pressure and volume of other gases in the reaction can be calculated using the ideal gas law equation.

11.10 Partial Pressures (Dalton's Law)

LEARNING GOAL: *Use Dalton's law of partial pressures to calculate the total pressure of a mixture of gases.*

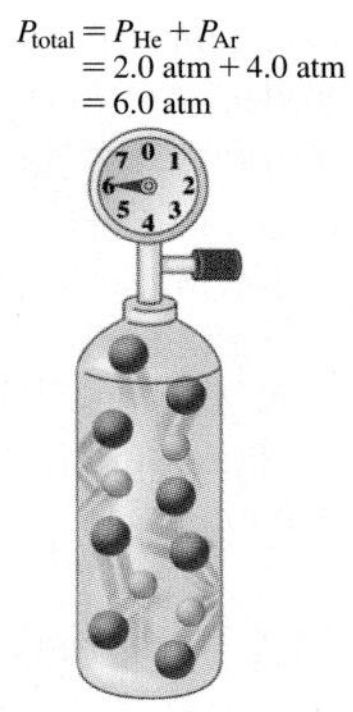

- In a mixture of two or more gases, the total pressure is the sum of the partial pressures of the individual gases.

$$P_{total} = P_1 + P_2 + P_3 + \cdots$$

- The partial pressure of a gas in a mixture is the pressure it would exert if it were the only gas in the container.
- For gases collected over water, the vapor pressure of water is subtracted from the total pressure of the gas mixture to obtain the partial pressure of the dry gas.

CONCEPT MAP

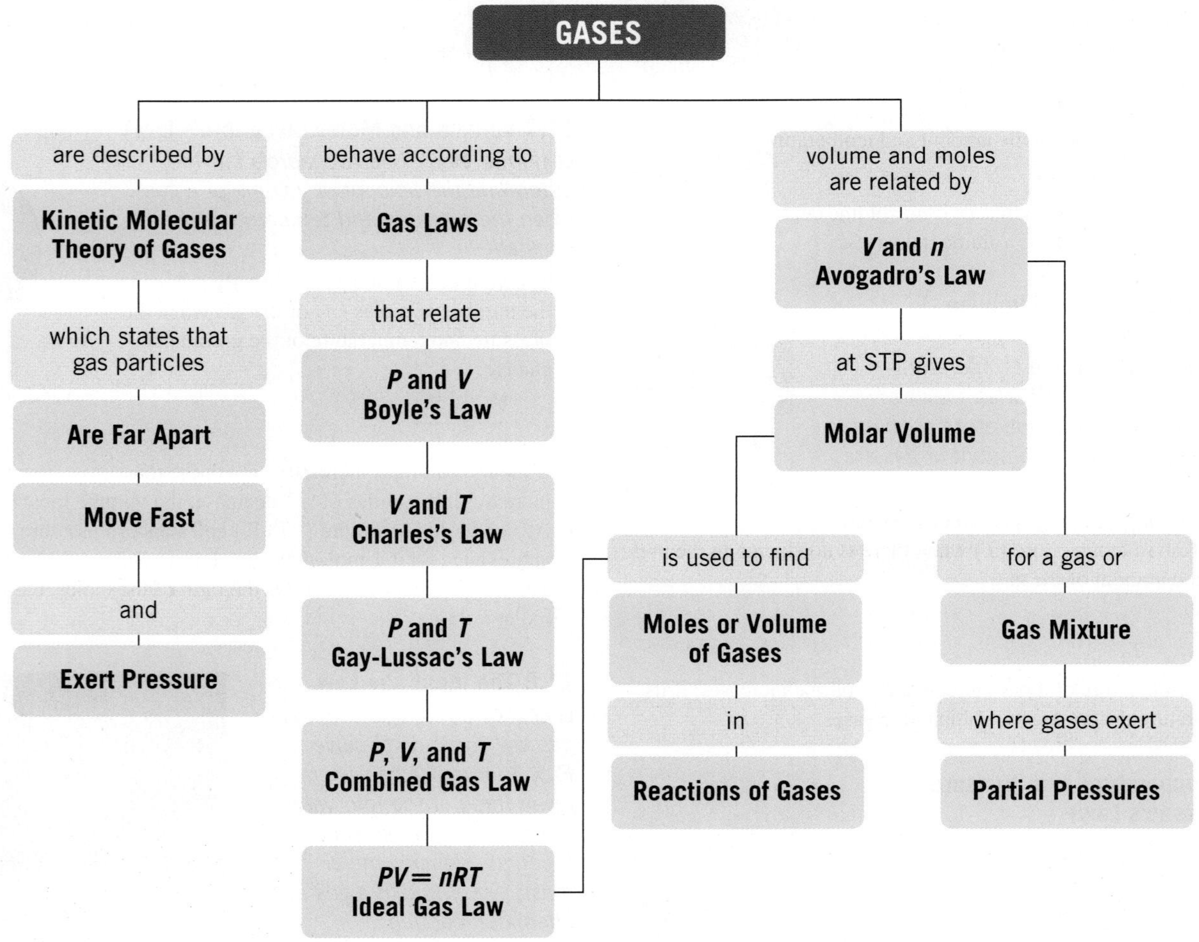

GASES

- are described by **Kinetic Molecular Theory of Gases**
  - which states that gas particles **Are Far Apart**, **Move Fast**
  - and **Exert Pressure**
- behave according to **Gas Laws**
  - that relate
    - ***P* and *V* Boyle's Law**
    - ***V* and *T* Charles's Law**
    - ***P* and *T* Gay-Lussac's Law**
    - ***P*, *V*, and *T* Combined Gas Law**
    - ***PV* = *nRT* Ideal Gas Law**
- volume and moles are related by **_V_ and _n_ Avogadro's Law**
  - at STP gives **Molar Volume**
    - (with Ideal Gas Law) is used to find **Moles or Volume of Gases** in **Reactions of Gases**
  - for a gas or **Gas Mixture** where gases exert **Partial Pressures**

KEY TERMS

atmosphere (atm) A unit equal to the pressure exerted by a column of mercury 760 mm high.

atmospheric pressure The pressure exerted by the atmosphere.

Avogadro's law A gas law stating that the volume of a gas changes directly with the number of moles of gas when pressure and temperature do not change.

Boyle's law A gas law stating that the pressure of a gas is inversely related to the volume when temperature and moles of the gas do not change; that is, if volume decreases, pressure increases.

Charles's law A gas law stating that the volume of a gas changes directly with a change in Kelvin temperature when pressure and moles of the gas do not change.

combined gas law A relationship that combines several gas laws relating pressure, volume, and temperature.

$$\frac{P_1V_1}{T_1} = \frac{P_2V_2}{T_2}$$

Dalton's law A gas law stating that the total pressure exerted by a mixture of gases in a container is the sum of the partial pressures that each gas would exert alone.

direct relationship A relationship in which two properties increase or decrease together.

Gay-Lussac's law A gas law stating that the pressure of a gas changes directly with a change in Kelvin temperature when the number of moles of a gas and its volume do not change.

ideal gas constant, *R* A numerical value that relates the quantities P, V, n, and T in the ideal gas law, $PV = nRT$.

ideal gas law A law that combines the four measured properties of a gas: $PV = nRT$.

inverse relationship A relationship in which two properties change in opposite directions.

kinetic molecular theory of gases A model used to explain the behavior of gases.

molar volume A volume of 22.4 L occupied by 1 mol of a gas at STP conditions of 0 °C (273 K) and 1 atm.

partial pressure The pressure exerted by a single gas in a gas mixture.

pressure The force exerted by gas particles that hit the walls of a container.

STP Standard conditions of exactly 0 °C (273 K) temperature and 1 atm pressure used for the comparison of gases.

torr A unit of pressure equal to 1 mmHg; 760 torr = 1 atm.

vapor pressure The pressure exerted by the particles of vapor above a liquid.

CORE CHEMISTRY SKILLS

The chapter section containing each Core Chemistry Skill is shown in parentheses at the end of each heading.

Using the Gas Laws (11.3)

- Boyle's, Charles's, Gay-Lussac's, and Avogadro's law show the relationships between two properties of a gas.

$P_1V_1 = P_2V_2$ Boyle's law

$\frac{V_1}{T_1} = \frac{V_2}{T_2}$ Charles's law

$\frac{P_1}{T_1} = \frac{P_2}{T_2}$ Gay-Lussac's law

$\frac{V_1}{n_1} = \frac{V_2}{n_2}$ Avogadro's law

- The combined gas law shows the relationship between P, V, and T for a gas.

$$\frac{P_1V_1}{T_1} = \frac{P_2V_2}{T_2}$$

- When two properties of a gas vary and the other two are constant, we list the initial and final conditions of each property in a table.

Example: A sample of helium gas (He) has a volume of 6.8 L and a pressure of 2.5 atm. What is the final volume, in liters, if it has a final pressure of 1.2 atm with no change in temperature and amount of gas?

Answer:

Analyze the Problem	Conditions 1	Conditions 2	Know	Predict
	$V_1 = 6.8$ L	$V_2 = ?$ L		V increases
	$P_1 = 2.5$ atm	$P_2 = 1.2$ atm	P decreases	

Factors that remain constant: T and n

Using Boyle's law, we can write the relationship for V_2, which we predict will increase.

$$V_2 = V_1 \times \frac{P_1}{P_2}$$

$$V_2 = 6.8\text{ L} \times \frac{2.5\text{ atm}}{1.2\text{ atm}} = 14\text{ L}$$

Using the Ideal Gas Law (11.8)

- The ideal gas law equation combines the relationships of the four properties of a gas into one equation.

$PV = nRT$

- When three of the four properties are given, we rearrange the ideal gas law equation for the needed quantity.

Example: What is the volume, in liters, of 0.750 mol of CO_2 at a pressure of 1340 mmHg and a temperature of 295 K?

Answer:

$$V = \frac{nRT}{P}$$

$$= \frac{0.750\text{ mol} \times \frac{62.4\text{ L}\cdot\text{mmHg}}{\text{mol}\cdot\text{K}} \times 295\text{ K}}{1340\text{ mmHg}} = 10.3\text{ L}$$

Calculating Mass or Volume of a Gas in a Chemical Reaction (11.9)

- The ideal gas law equation is used to calculate the pressure, volume, moles (or grams) of a gas in a chemical reaction.

Example: What is the volume, in liters, of N_2 required to react with 18.5 g of magnesium at a pressure of 1.20 atm and a temperature of 303 K?

$$3Mg(s) + N_2(g) \longrightarrow Mg_3N_2(s)$$

Answer: Initially, we convert the grams of Mg to moles and use mole–mole conversion factors from the balanced equation to calculate the moles of N_2 gas.

$$18.5\ \text{g Mg} \times \frac{1\ \text{mol Mg}}{24.31\ \text{g Mg}} \times \frac{1\ \text{mol } N_2}{3\ \text{mol Mg}} = 0.254\ \text{mol of } N_2$$

Now, we use the moles of N_2 in the ideal gas law equation and solve for liters, the needed quantity.

$$V = \frac{nRT}{P} = \frac{0.254\ \text{mol } N_2 \times \dfrac{0.0821\ \text{L} \cdot \text{atm}}{\text{mol} \cdot \text{K}} \times 303\ \text{K}}{1.20\ \text{atm}} = 5.27\ \text{L}$$

Calculating Partial Pressure (11.10)

- In a gas mixture, each gas exerts its partial pressure, which is the pressure it would exert if it were the only gas in the container.
- Dalton's law states that the total pressure of a gas mixture is the sum of the partial pressures of the gases in the mixture.

$$P_{\text{total}} = P_1 + P_2 + P_3 + \cdots$$

Example: A gas mixture with a total pressure of 1.18 atm contains helium gas at a partial pressure of 465 mmHg and nitrogen gas. What is the partial pressure, in atmospheres, of the nitrogen gas?

Answer: Initially, we convert the partial pressure of helium gas from mmHg to atm.

$$465\ \text{mmHg} \times \frac{1\ \text{atm}}{760\ \text{mmHg}} = 0.612\ \text{atm of He gas}$$

Using Dalton's law, we solve for the needed quantity, P_{N_2} in atm.

$$P_{\text{total}} = P_{N_2} + P_{\text{He}}$$
$$P_{N_2} = P_{\text{total}} - P_{\text{He}}$$
$$P_{N_2} = 1.18\ \text{atm} - 0.612\ \text{atm} = 0.568\ \text{atm}$$

UNDERSTANDING THE CONCEPTS

The chapter sections to review are shown in parentheses at the end of each question.

11.73 Two flasks of equal volume and at the same temperature contain different gases. One flask contains 10.0 g of Ne, and the other flask contains 10.0 g of He. Is each of the following statements *true* or *false*? Explain. (11.1)

a. The flask that contains He has a higher pressure than the flask that contains Ne.
b. The densities of the gases are the same.

11.74 Two flasks of equal volume and at the same temperature contain different gases. One flask contains 5.0 g of O_2, and the other flask contains 5.0 g of H_2. Is each of the following statements *true* or *false*? Explain. (11.1)

a. Both flasks contain the same number of molecules.
b. The pressures in the flasks are the same.

11.75 At 100 °C, which of the following diagrams (**1**, **2**, or **3**) represents a gas sample that exerts the: (11.7)

a. lowest pressure? **b.** highest pressure?

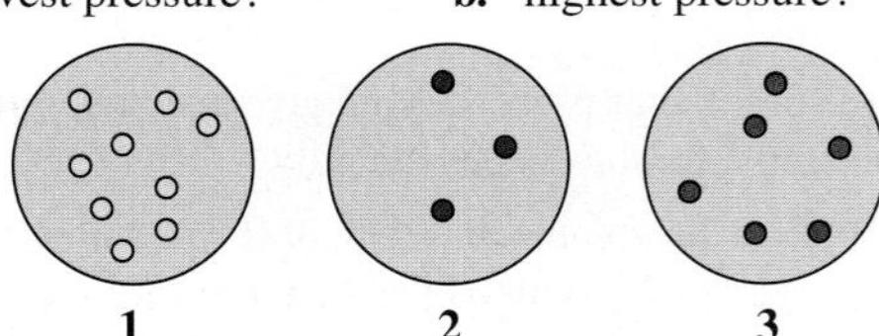

11.76 Indicate which diagram (**1**, **2**, or **3**) represents the volume of the gas sample in a flexible container when each of the following changes takes place: (11.3, 11.4)

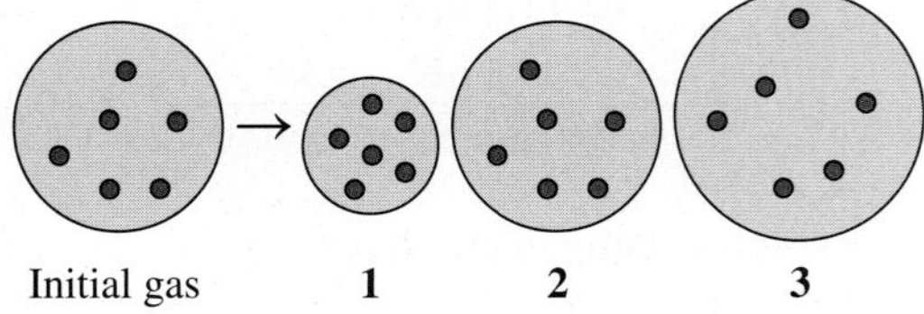

a. Temperature increases at constant pressure.
b. Temperature decreases at constant pressure.
c. Pressure decreases at constant temperature.
d. Doubling the pressure and doubling the Kelvin temperature.

11.77 A balloon is filled with helium gas with a pressure of 1.00 atm and neon gas with a pressure of 0.50 atm. For each of the following changes of the initial balloon, select the diagram (**A**, **B**, or **C**) that shows the final volume of the balloon: (11.3, 11.4, 11.7)

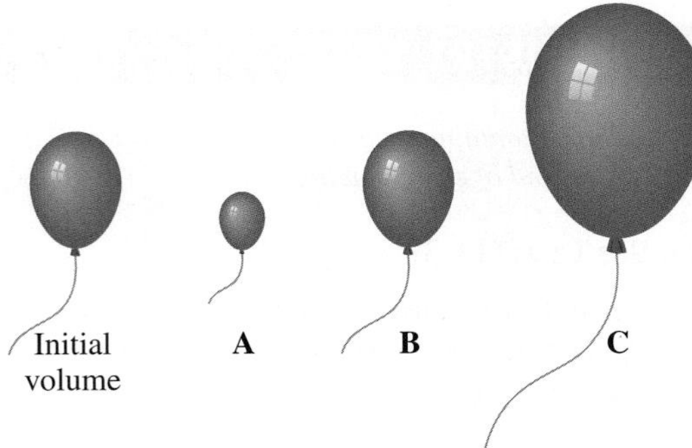

a. The balloon is put in a cold storage unit (P and n constant).
b. The balloon floats to a higher altitude where the pressure is less (n and T constant).
c. All of the helium gas is removed (T and P constant).
d. The Kelvin temperature doubles, and half of the gas atoms leak out (P constant).
e. 2.0 mol of O_2 gas is added at constant T and P.

11.78 Indicate if pressure *increases*, *decreases*, or *stays the same* in each of the following: (11.3, 11.5, 11.7)

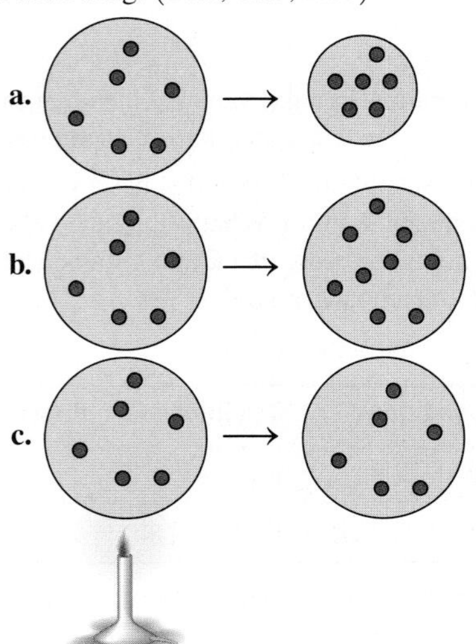

11.79 An airplane is pressurized to 650. mmHg. (11.10)

a. If air is 21% oxygen, what is the partial pressure of oxygen on the plane?

b. If the partial pressure of oxygen drops below 100. mmHg, passengers become drowsy. If this happens, oxygen masks are released. What is the total cabin pressure at which oxygen masks are dropped?

11.80 At a restaurant, a customer chokes on a piece of food. You put your arms around the person's waist and use your fists to push up on the person's abdomen, an action called the Heimlich maneuver. (11.3)

a. How would this action change the volume of the chest and lungs?

b. Why does it cause the person to expel the food item from the airway?

ADDITIONAL QUESTIONS AND PROBLEMS

11.81 In 1783, Jacques Charles launched his first balloon filled with hydrogen gas, which he chose because it was lighter than air. The balloon had a volume of 31 000 L when it reached an altitude of 1000 m, where the pressure was 658 mmHg and the temperature was −8 °C. How many kilograms of hydrogen were used to fill the balloon at STP? (11.6, 11.7)

Jacques Charles used hydrogen to launch his balloon in 1783.

11.82 Your spaceship has docked at a space station above Mars. The temperature inside the space station is a carefully controlled 24 °C at a pressure of 745 mmHg. A balloon with a volume of 425 mL drifts into the airlock where the temperature is −95 °C and the pressure is 0.115 atm. What is the final volume, in milliliters, of the balloon if *n* remains constant and the balloon is very elastic? (11.6)

11.83 A gas sample has a volume of 4250 mL at 15 °C and 745 mmHg. What is the final temperature, in degrees Celsius, after the sample is transferred to a different container with a volume of 2.50 L and a pressure of 1.20 atm, when *n* remains constant? (11.6)

11.84 A weather balloon has a volume of 750 L when filled with helium at 8 °C at a pressure of 380 torr. What is the final volume, in liters, of the balloon when the pressure is 0.20 atm, the temperature is −45 °C, and *n* remains constant? (11.6)

11.85 A 2.00-L container is filled with methane gas, CH_4, at a pressure of 2500. mmHg and a temperature of 18 °C. How many grams of methane are in the container? (11.8)

11.86 A steel cylinder with a volume of 15.0 L is filled with 50.0 g of nitrogen gas at 25 °C. What is the pressure, in atmospheres, of the N_2 gas in the cylinder? (11.8)

11.87 A sample of gas with a mass of 1.62 g occupies a volume of 941 mL at a pressure of 748 torr and a temperature of 20.0 °C. What is the molar mass of the gas? (11.8)

11.88 What is the molar mass of a gas if 1.15 g of the gas has a volume of 225 mL at 0 °C and 1.00 atm (STP)? (11.8)

11.89 How many grams of CO_2 are in 35.0 L of $CO_2(g)$ at 1.20 atm and 5 °C? (11.8)

11.90 A container is filled with 0.644 g of O_2 at 5 °C and 845 mmHg. What is the volume, in milliliters, of the container? (11.8)

11.91 How many liters of H_2 gas can be produced at 0 °C and 1.00 atm (STP) from 25.0 g of Zn? (11.8, 11.9)

$$Zn(s) + 2HCl(aq) \longrightarrow H_2(g) + ZnCl_2(aq)$$

11.92 In the formation of smog, nitrogen and oxygen gas react to form nitrogen dioxide. How many grams of NO_2 will be produced when 2.0 L of nitrogen at 840 mmHg and 24 °C are completely reacted? (11.8, 11.9)

$$N_2(g) + 2O_2(g) \longrightarrow 2NO_2(g)$$

11.93 Nitrogen dioxide reacts with water to produce oxygen and ammonia. A 5.00-L sample of $H_2O(g)$ reacts at a temperature of 375 °C and a pressure of 725 mmHg. How many grams of NH_3 can be produced? (11.8, 11.9)

$$4NO_2(g) + 6H_2O(g) \longrightarrow 7O_2(g) + 4NH_3(g)$$

11.94 Hydrogen gas can be produced in the laboratory through the reaction of magnesium metal with hydrochloric acid. When 12.0 g of Mg reacts, what volume, in liters, of H_2 gas is produced at 24 °C and 835 mmHg? (11.8, 11.9)

$$Mg(s) + 2HCl(aq) \longrightarrow H_2(g) + MgCl_2(aq)$$

11.95 A gas mixture with a total pressure of 2400 torr is used by a scuba diver. If the mixture contains 2.0 mol of helium and 6.0 mol of oxygen, what is the partial pressure, in torr, of each gas in the sample? (11.10)

11.96 What is the total pressure, in millimeters of mercury, of a gas mixture containing argon gas at 0.25 atm, helium gas at 350 mmHg, and nitrogen gas at 360 torr? (11.10)

11.97 A gas mixture contains oxygen and argon at partial pressures of 0.60 atm and 425 mmHg. If nitrogen gas added to the sample increases the total pressure to 1250 torr, what is the partial pressure, in torr, of the nitrogen added? (11.10)

11.98 A gas mixture contains helium and oxygen at partial pressures of 255 torr and 0.450 atm. What is the total pressure, in millimeters of mercury, of the mixture after it is placed in a container one-half the volume of the original container? (11.10)

CHALLENGE QUESTIONS

11.99 Solid aluminum reacts with aqueous H_2SO_4 to form H_2 gas and aluminum sulfate. When a sample of Al is allowed to react, 415 mL of gas is collected over water at 23 °C, at a pressure of 755 mmHg. At 23 °C, the vapor pressure of water is 21 mmHg. (11.8, 11.9, 11.10)

$$2Al(s) + 3H_2SO_4(aq) \longrightarrow 3H_2(g) + Al_2(SO_4)_3(aq)$$

a. What is the pressure, in millimeters of mercury, of the dry H_2 gas?
b. How many moles of H_2 were produced?
c. How many grams of Al were reacted?

11.100 When heated, $KClO_3$ forms KCl and O_2. When a sample of $KClO_3$ is heated, 226 mL of gas with a pressure of 744 mmHg is collected over water at 26 °C. At 26 °C, the vapor pressure of water is 25 mmHg. (11.8, 11.9, 11.10)

$$2KClO_3(s) \xrightarrow{\Delta} 2KCl(s) + 3O_2(g)$$

a. What is the pressure, in millimeters of mercury, of the dry O_2 gas?
b. How many moles of O_2 were produced?
c. How many grams of $KClO_3$ were reacted?

11.101 A sample of gas with a mass of 1.020 g occupies a volume of 762 mL at a pressure of 760. mmHg and a temperature of 0.0 °C. (7.4, 7.5, 11.7, 11.8)
a. What is the molar mass of the gas?
b. If the unknown gas is composed of 0.815 g of carbon and the rest is hydrogen, what is its molecular formula?

11.102 A sample of an unknown gas with a mass of 3.24 g occupies a volume of 1.88 L at a pressure of 748 mmHg and a temperature of 20.0 °C. (7.4, 7.5, 11.7, 11.8)
a. What is the molar mass of the gas?
b. If the unknown gas is composed of 2.78 g of carbon and the rest is hydrogen, what is its molecular formula?

11.103 The propane, C_3H_8, in a fuel cylinder, undergoes combustion with oxygen in the air. How many liters of CO_2 are produced at STP if the cylinder contains 881 g of propane? (11.7, 11.9)

$$C_3H_8(g) + 5O_2(g) \xrightarrow{\Delta} 3CO_2(g) + 4H_2O(g)$$

11.104 When sensors in a car detect a collision, they cause the reaction of sodium azide, NaN_3, which generates nitrogen gas to fill the airbags within 0.03 s. How many liters of N_2 are produced at STP if the airbag contains 132 g of NaN_3? (11.7, 11.9)

$$2NaN_3(s) \longrightarrow 2Na(s) + 3N_2(g)$$

11.105 Glucose, $C_6H_{12}O_6$, is metabolized in living systems. How many grams of water can be produced from the reaction of 18.0 g of glucose and 7.50 L of O_2 at 1.00 atm and 37 °C? (9.2, 9.3, 11.8, 11.9)

$$C_6H_{12}O_6(s) + 6O_2(g) \longrightarrow 6CO_2(g) + 6H_2O(l)$$

11.106 2.00 L of N_2, at 25 °C and 1.08 atm, is mixed with 4.00 L of O_2, at 25 °C and 0.118 atm, and the mixture is allowed to react. How much NO, in grams, is produced? (9.2, 9.3, 11.8, 11.9)

$$N_2(g) + O_2(g) \longrightarrow 2NO(g)$$

ANSWERS

Answers to Study Checks

11.1 The mass in grams gives the amount of gas.

11.2 245 torr

11.3 73.5 mL

11.4 569 mL

11.5 16 °C

11.6 241 mmHg

11.7 7.50 L

11.8 15.8 g of Cl_2

11.9 0.0900 g/L

11.10 0.327 mol of Cl_2

11.11 1.04 L

11.12 104 g/mol

11.13 18.1 L of H_2

11.14 755 mmHg

11.15 0.579 g of O_2

Answers to Selected Questions and Problems

11.1 **a.** At a higher temperature, gas particles have greater kinetic energy, which makes them move faster.
b. Because there are great distances between the particles of a gas, they can be pushed closer together and still remain a gas.
c. Gas particles are very far apart, which means that the mass of a gas in a certain volume is very small, resulting in a low density.

11.3 **a.** temperature **b.** volume
c. amount **d.** pressure

11.5 Statements **a**, **d**, and **e** describe the pressure of a gas.

11.7 **a.** 1520 torr **b.** 29.4 lb/in.^{2}
c. 1520 mmHg **d.** 203 kPa

11.9 As a diver ascends to the surface, external pressure decreases. If the air in the lungs were not exhaled, its volume would expand and severely damage the lungs. The pressure in the lungs must adjust to changes in the external pressure.

11.11 **a.** The pressure is greater in cylinder A. According to Boyle's law, a decrease in volume pushes the gas particles closer together, which will cause an increase in the pressure.
b.

Property	Conditions 1	Conditions 2	Know	Predict
Pressure (P)	650 mmHg	1.2 atm (910 mmHg)	P increases	
Volume (V)	220 mL	160 mL		V decreases

11.13 a. increases **b.** decreases
c. increases

11.15 a. 328 mmHg **b.** 2620 mmHg
c. 475 mmHg **d.** 5240 mmHg

11.17 a. 52.4 L **b.** 25 L
c. 100. L **d.** 45 L

11.19 25 L of cyclopropane

11.21 a. inspiration **b.** expiration
c. inspiration

11.23 a. C **b.** A
c. B

11.25 a. 303 °C **b.** −129 °C
c. 591 °C **d.** 136 °C

11.27 a. 2400 mL **b.** 4900 mL
c. 1800 mL **d.** 1700 mL

11.29 a. 770 mmHg **b.** 1150 mmHg

11.31 a. −23 °C **b.** 168 °C

11.33 a. boiling point **b.** vapor pressure

11.35 a. On top of a mountain, water boils below 100 °C because the atmospheric (external) pressure is less than 1 atm.
b. Because the pressure inside a pressure cooker is greater than 1 atm, water boils above 100 °C. At a higher temperature, food cooks faster.

11.37 $T_2 = T_1 \times \frac{P_2}{P_1} \times \frac{V_2}{V_1}$

11.39 a. 4.26 atm **b.** 3.07 atm
c. 0.606 atm

11.41 −33 °C

11.43 The volume increases because the number of gas particles is increased.

11.45 a. 4.00 L **b.** 26.7 L
c. 14.6 L

11.47 a. 2.00 mol of O_2 **b.** 0.179 mol of CO_2
c. 4.48 L **d.** 55 500 mL

11.49 a. 1.70 g/L **b.** 0.716 g/L
c. 0.901 g/L **d.** 2.86 g/L

11.51 4.93 atm

11.53 29.4 g of O_2

11.55 566 K (293 °C)

11.57 a. 42 g/mol **b.** 28.7 g/mol
c. 39.8 g/mol **d.** 33 g/mol

11.59 a. 7.60 L of H_2 **b.** 4.92 g of Mg

11.61 178 L of O_2

11.63 3.4 L of O_2

11.65 765 torr

11.67 0.978 atm

11.69 425 torr

11.71 a. 743 mmHg **b.** 0.0103 mol of O_2

11.73 a. True. The flask containing helium has more moles of helium and thus more helium atoms.
b. True. The mass and volume of each are the same, which means the mass/volume ratio or density is the same in both flasks.

11.75 a. 2 Fewest number of gas particles exerts the lowest pressure.
b. 1 Greatest number of gas particles exerts the highest pressure.

11.77 a. A: Volume decreases when temperature decreases.
b. C: Volume increases when pressure decreases.
c. A: Volume decreases when the moles of gas decrease.
d. B: Doubling the temperature, in kelvins, would double the volume, but when half of the gas escapes, the volume would decrease by half. These two opposing effects cancel each other, and there is no change in the volume.
e. C: Increasing the moles increases the volume to keep *T* and *P* constant.

11.79 a. 140 mmHg **b.** 480 mmHg

11.81 2.5 kg of H_2

11.83 −66 °C

11.85 4.41 g of CH_4

11.87 42.1 g/mol

11.89 81.0 g of CO_2

11.91 8.56 L of H_2

11.93 1.02 g of NH_3

11.95 He 600 torr, O_2 1800 torr

11.97 370 torr

11.99 a. 734 mmHg **b.** 0.0165 mol of H_2
c. 0.297 g of Al

11.101 a. 30.0 g/mol
b. C_2H_6

11.103 1340 L of CO_2

11.105 5.31 g of water

12 Solutions

LOOKING AHEAD

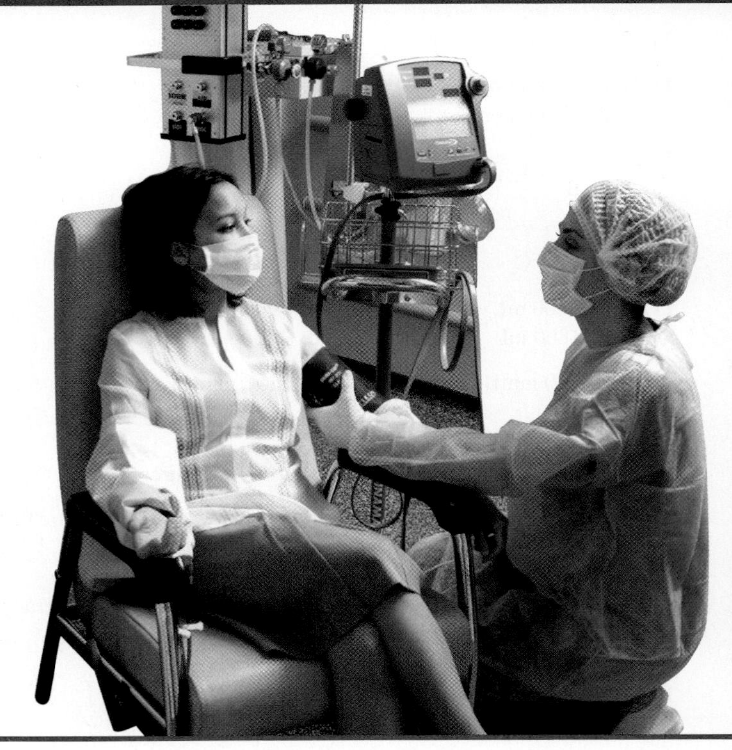

When Michelle's kidneys stopped functioning, she was placed on dialysis three times a week. As she enters the dialysis unit, her dialysis nurse, Amanda, asks Michelle how she is feeling. Michelle indicates that she feels tired today and has considerable swelling around her ankles.

The dialysis nurse informs Michelle that her side effects are due to her body's inability to regulate the amount of water in her cells. She explains that the amount of water is regulated by the concentration of electrolytes in her body fluids and the rate at which waste products are removed from her body. Amanda explains that although water is essential for the many chemical reactions that occur in the body, the amount of water can become too high or too low, due to various diseases and conditions.

Because Michelle's kidneys no longer perform dialysis, she cannot regulate the amount of electrolytes or waste in her body fluids. As a result, she has an electrolyte imbalance and a buildup of waste products, so her body is retaining water. Amanda then explains that the dialysis machine does the work of her kidneys to reduce the high levels of electrolytes and waste products.

Career: Dialysis Nurse

A dialysis nurse specializes in assisting patients with kidney disease undergoing dialysis. This requires monitoring the patient before, during, and after dialysis for any complications such as a drop in blood pressure or cramping. The dialysis nurse connects the patient to the dialysis unit via a dialysis catheter that is inserted into the neck or chest, which must be kept clean to prevent infection. A dialysis nurse must have considerable knowledge about how the dialysis machine functions to ensure that it is operating correctly at all times.

Solutions are everywhere around us. Most of the gases, liquids, and solids we see are mixtures of at least one substance dissolved in another. There are different types of solution. The air we breathe is a solution that is primarily oxygen and nitrogen gases. Carbon dioxide gas dissolved in water makes our carbonated drinks. When we make solutions of coffee or tea, we use hot water to dissolve substances from coffee beans or tea leaves. The ocean is also a solution, consisting of many salts, such as sodium chloride, dissolved in water. In your medicine cabinet, the antiseptic tincture of iodine is a solution of iodine dissolved in ethanol.

Because the individual components in any mixture are not bonded to each other, the composition of those components can vary. Also, some of the physical properties of the individual components are still noticeable. For example, in ocean water, we detect the dissolved sodium chloride by the salty taste. The flavor we associate with coffee is due to the dissolved components. In a solution, the components cannot be distinguished one from the other. Syrup is a solution of sugar and water: the sugar cannot be distinguished from the water.

Solutions can be described by their concentration, which is the amount of solute in a specific amount of that solution. These relationships, which include mass % (m/m), volume % (v/v), mass/volume % (m/v), and molarity (M), are used to convert between the amount of a solute and the quantity of its solution. Solutions are also diluted by adding a specific amount of solvent to a solution. Solutions have different properties that depend on the concentration of particles. The particles in a solution lower the freezing point of the solvent and elevate its boiling point. In osmosis, water flows through a semipermeable membrane from a solution with a lower concentration of particles into a solution with a higher concentration of particles.

CHAPTER READINESS*

Key Math Skills

- Calculating a Percentage (1.4C)
- Interpreting a Line Graph (1.4E)

Core Chemistry Skills

- Writing Conversion Factors from Equalities (2.6)
- Using Conversion Factors (2.7)
- Using Mole–Mole Factors (9.1)
- Identifying Attractive Forces (10.4)
- Using the Ideal Gas Law (11.8)

*These Key Math Skills and Core Chemistry Skills from previous chapters are listed here for your review as you proceed to the new material in this chapter.

12.1 Solutions

LEARNING GOAL

Identify the solute and solvent in a solution; describe the formation of a solution.

A **solution** is a homogeneous mixture in which one substance, called the **solute**, is uniformly dispersed in another substance called the **solvent**. When a small amount of salt is dissolved in water, the salt-water solution tastes slightly salty. When more salt is added, the salt-water solution tastes very salty. Usually, the solute (in this case, salt) is the substance present in the smaller amount, whereas the solvent (in this case, water) is present in the larger amount. For example, in a solution composed of 5.0 g of salt and 50. g of water, salt is the solute and water is the solvent. In a solution, the particles of the solute are evenly dispersed among the molecules within the solvent (see Figure 12.1).

A solution consists of at least one solute dispersed in a solvent.

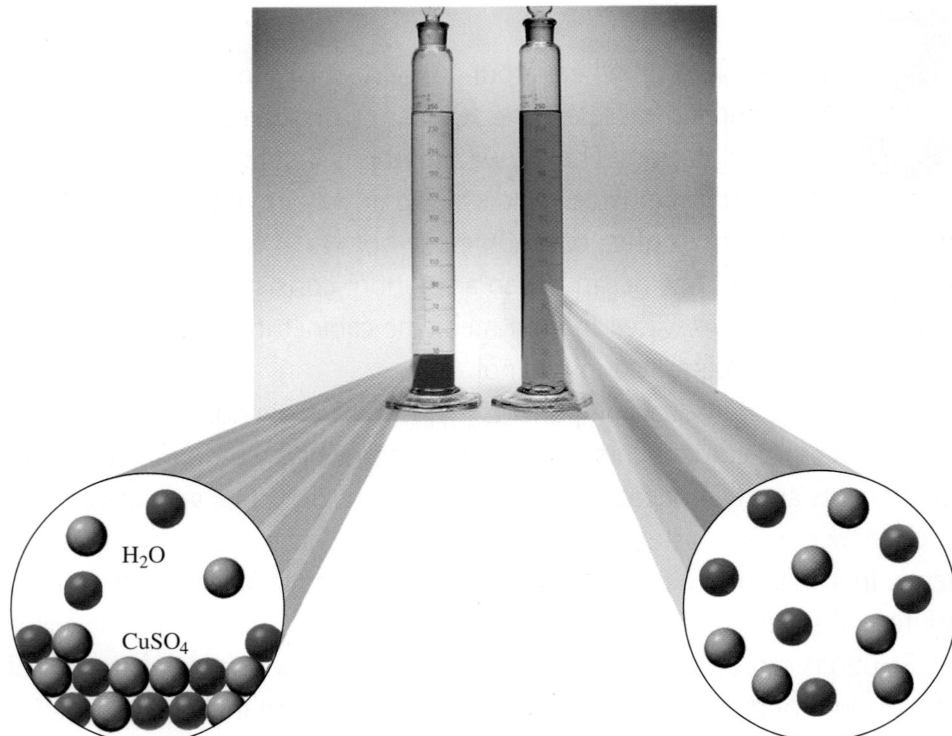

FIGURE 12.1 A solution of copper(II) sulfate ($CuSO_4$) forms as particles of solute dissolve, move away from the crystals, and become evenly dispersed among the solvent (water) molecules.

Q What does the uniform blue color indicate about the $CuSO_4$ solution?

Types of Solutes and Solvents

Solutes and solvents may be solids, liquids, or gases. The solution that forms has the same physical state as the solvent. When sugar crystals are dissolved in water, the resulting sugar solution is liquid. Sugar is the solute, and water is the solvent. Soda water and soft drinks are prepared by dissolving carbon dioxide gas in water. The carbon dioxide gas is the solute, and water is the solvent. Table 12.1 lists some solutes and solvents and their solutions.

TABLE 12.1 Some Examples of Solutions

Type	Example	Primary Solute	Solvent
Gas Solutions			
Gas in a gas	Air	Oxygen (gas)	Nitrogen (gas)
Liquid Solutions			
Gas in a liquid	Soda water	Carbon dioxide (gas)	Water (liquid)
	Household ammonia	Ammonia (gas)	Water (liquid)
Liquid in a liquid	Vinegar	Acetic acid (liquid)	Water (liquid)
Solid in a liquid	Seawater	Sodium chloride (solid)	Water (liquid)
	Tincture of iodine	Iodine (solid)	Ethanol (liquid)
Solid Solutions			
Solid in a solid	Brass	Zinc (solid)	Copper (solid)
	Steel	Carbon (solid)	Iron (solid)

Water as a Solvent

Water is one of the most common substances in nature. In the H_2O molecule, an oxygen atom shares electrons with two hydrogen atoms. Because oxygen is much more electronegative than hydrogen, the O—H bonds are polar. In each polar bond, the oxygen atom has a partial negative (δ^-) charge and the hydrogen atom has a partial positive (δ^+) charge. Because the water molecule has a bent shape, water is a *polar solvent.*

Attractive forces known as *hydrogen bonds* occur between molecules where partially positive hydrogen atoms are attracted to the partially negative atoms of N, O, or F. In the diagram, the hydrogen bonds are shown as dots between the water molecules. Although hydrogen bonds are much weaker than covalent or ionic bonds, there are many of them linking water molecules together. Hydrogen bonds also are important in the properties of biological compounds such as proteins, carbohydrates, and DNA.

Partial negative charge
Partial positive charge
Hydrogen bonds

In water, hydrogen bonds form between the lone pairs of an oxygen in one water molecule and the hydrogen in another.

Chemistry Link to Health

WATER IN THE BODY

The average adult contains about 60% water by mass, and the average infant about 75%. About 60% of the body's water is contained within the cells as intracellular fluids; the other 40% makes up extracellular fluids, which include the interstitial fluid in tissue and the plasma in the blood. These external fluids carry nutrients and waste materials between the cells and the circulatory system.

Every day, you lose between 1500 and 3000 mL of water from the kidneys as urine, from the skin as perspiration, from the lungs as you exhale, and from the gastrointestinal tract. Serious dehydration can occur in an adult who experiences a 10% net loss in total body fluid; a 20% loss of fluid can be fatal. An infant suffers severe dehydration with just a 5–10% loss in body fluid.

24 Hours

Water gain	
Liquid	1000 mL
Food	1200 mL
Metabolism	300 mL
Total	2500 mL

Water loss	
Urine	1500 mL
Perspiration	300 mL
Breath	600 mL
Feces	100 mL
Total	2500 mL

Water loss is continually replaced by the liquids and foods in the diet and from metabolic processes that produce water in the cells of the body. Table 12.2 lists the percentage of water by mass contained in some foods.

The water lost from the body is replaced by the intake of fluids.

TABLE 12.2 Percentage of Water in Some Foods

Food	Water (% by mass)	Food	Water (% by mass)
Vegetables		**Meats/Fish**	
Carrot	88	Chicken, cooked	71
Celery	94	Hamburger, broiled	60
Cucumber	96	Salmon	71
Tomato	94		
Fruits		**Milk Products**	
Apple	85	Cottage cheese	78
Cantaloupe	91	Milk, whole	87
Orange	86	Yogurt	88
Strawberry	90		
Watermelon	93		

Formation of Solutions

The interactions between solute and solvent will determine whether or not a solution will form. Initially, energy is needed to separate both the particles in the solute and the solvent particles. Then energy is released as solute particles move between the solvent particles to form a solution. However, there must be attractions between the solute and the solvent particles to provide the energy for the initial separation. These attractions occur when the solute and the solvent have similar polarities. The expression "like dissolves like" is a way of saying that the polarities of a solute and a solvent must be similar in order to form a solution (see Figure 12.2). In the absence of attractions between a solute and a solvent, there is insufficient energy to form a solution (see Table 12.3).

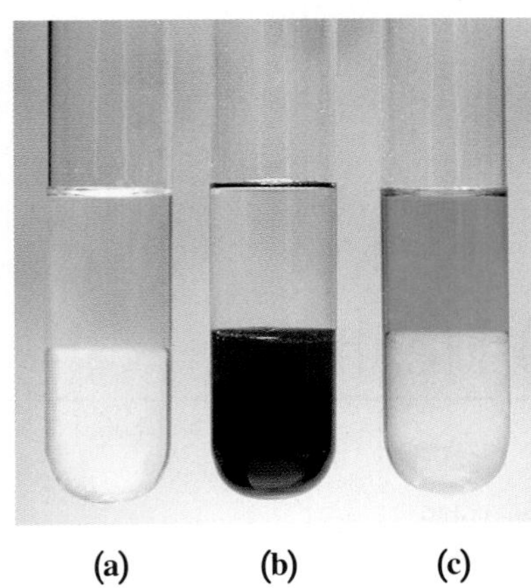

FIGURE 12.2 Like dissolves like. In each test tube, the lower layer is CH_2Cl_2 (more dense), and the upper layer is water (less dense). **(a)** CH_2Cl_2 is nonpolar and water is polar; the two layers do not mix. **(b)** The nonpolar solute I_2 (purple) is soluble in the nonpolar solvent CH_2Cl_2. **(c)** The ionic solute $Ni(NO_3)_2$ (green) is soluble in the polar solvent water.

Q In which layer would polar molecules of sucrose ($C_{12}H_{22}O_{11}$) be soluble?

TABLE 12.3 Possible Combinations of Solutes and Solvents

Solutions Will Form		Solutions Will Not Form	
Solute	**Solvent**	**Solute**	**Solvent**
Polar	Polar	Polar	Nonpolar
Nonpolar	Nonpolar	Nonpolar	Polar

Solutions with Ionic and Polar Solutes

In ionic solutes such as sodium chloride, NaCl, strong solute–solute attractions take place between positively charged Na^+ ions and negatively charged Cl^- ions. In water, a polar solvent, the hydrogen bonds provide strong solvent–solvent attractions. When NaCl crystals are placed in water, partially negative oxygen atoms in water molecules attract positive Na^+ ions, and the partially positive hydrogen atoms in other water molecules attract negative Cl^- ions (see Figure 12.3). As soon as the Na^+ ions and the Cl^- ions form a solution, they undergo **hydration** as water molecules surround each ion. Hydration of the ions diminishes their attraction to other ions and keeps them in solution. The strong solute–solvent attractions between Na^+ and Cl^- ions and the polar water molecules provide energy needed to form the solution.

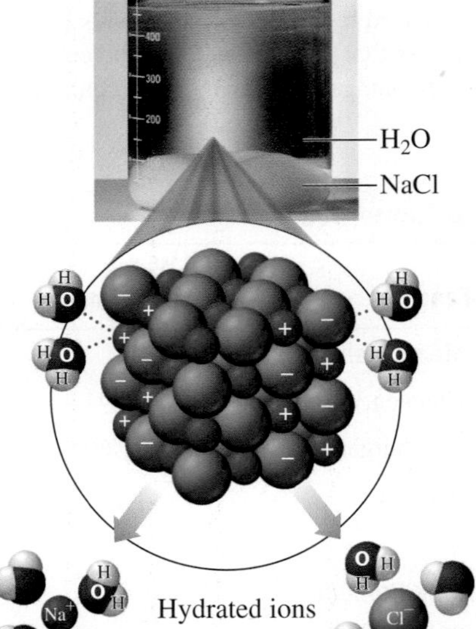

FIGURE 12.3 Ions on the surface of a crystal of NaCl dissolve in water as they are attracted to the polar water molecules that pull the ions into solution and surround them.

Q What helps keep Na^+ and Cl^- ions in solution?

In the equation for the formation of the NaCl solution, the solid and aqueous NaCl are shown with the formula H_2O over the arrow, which indicates that water is needed for the dissociation process but is not a reactant.

$$NaCl(s) \xrightarrow{H_2O} Na^+(aq) + Cl^-(aq)$$

In another example, we find that a polar molecular compound such as methanol, $CH_3—OH$, is soluble in water because methanol has a polar —OH group that forms hydrogen bonds with water (see Figure 12.4). Polar solutes require polar solvents for a solution to form.

Solutions with Nonpolar Solutes

Compounds containing nonpolar molecules, such as iodine (I_2), oil, or grease, do not dissolve in water because there are little or no attractions between the particles of a nonpolar solute and the polar solvent. The expression "like dissolves like" is a way of saying that the polarities of a solute and a solvent must be similar in order to form a solution (see Figure 12.4).

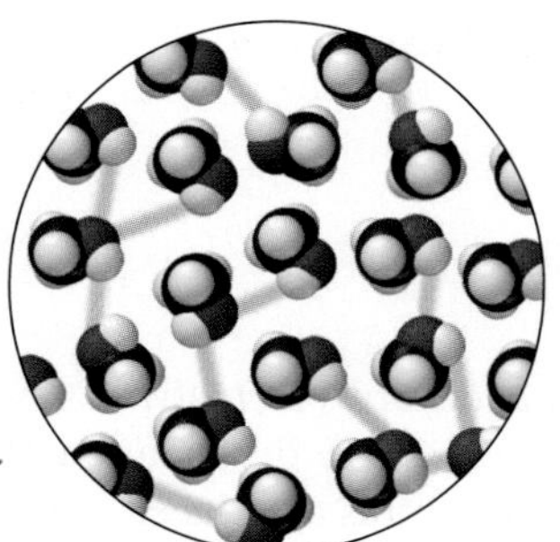

Methanol ($CH_3—OH$) solute

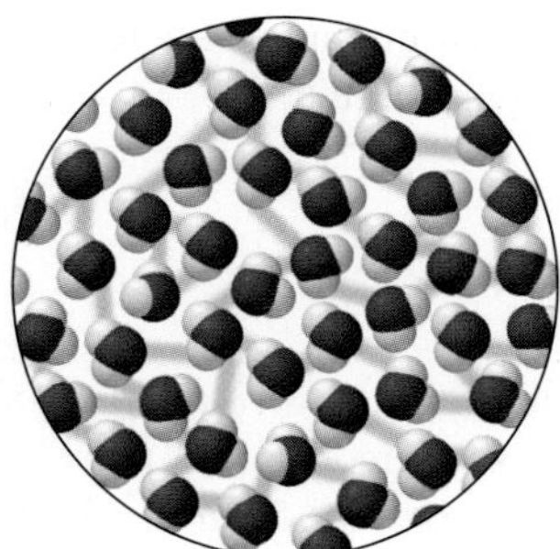

Water solvent

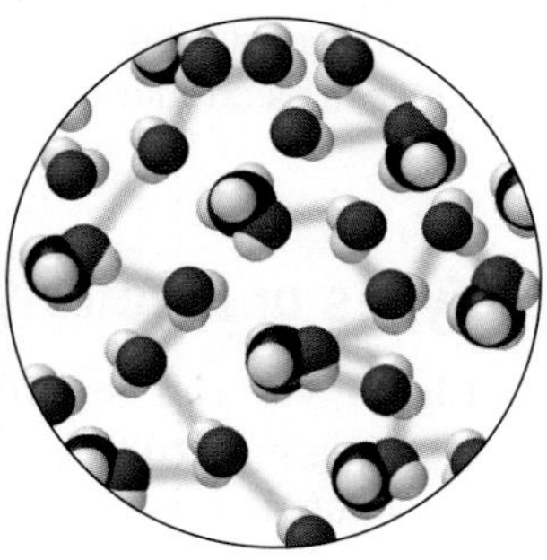

Methanol–water solution with hydrogen bonding

FIGURE 12.4 Molecules of the polar molecular compound methanol, $CH_3—OH$, form hydrogen bonds with polar water molecules to form a methanol–water solution.

Q Why is the methanol–water solution an example of "like dissolves like"?

CONCEPT CHECK 12.1 Polar and Nonpolar Solutes

Indicate whether each of the following substances will form a solution with water. Explain.

a. $KCl(s)$
b. hexane, $CH_3—CH_2—CH_2—CH_2—CH_2—CH_3$
c. ethanol, $CH_3—CH_2—OH$

ANSWER

a. Yes. KCl is an ionic compound. The solute–solvent attractions between the ions K^+ and Cl^- and polar water molecules provide the energy to break solute–solute and solvent–solvent bonds. Thus, a KCl solution will form.

b. No. Hexane is a nonpolar compound, which means it does not form a solution with the polar water molecules. There are no attractions between a nonpolar solute and a polar solvent. Thus, no solution forms.

c. Ethanol with its —OH group is a polar solute. Because attractions between a polar solute and the polar solvent water provide energy to break solute–solute and solvent–solvent bonds, ethanol will form a solution with water.

QUESTIONS AND PROBLEMS

12.1 Solutions

LEARNING GOAL: *Identify the solute and solvent in a solution; describe the formation of a solution.*

12.1 Identify the solute and the solvent in each solution composed of the following:
a. 10.0 g of NaCl and 100.0 g of H_2O
b. 50.0 mL of ethanol, $CH_3—CH_2—OH(l)$, and 10.0 mL of H_2O
c. 0.20 L of O_2 and 0.80 L of N_2

12.2 Identify the solute and the solvent in each solution composed of the following:
a. 10 mL of acetic acid and 200 mL of water
b. 100.0 mL of water and 5.0 g of sugar
c. 1.0 g of Br_2 and 50.0 mL of methylene chloride(l)

12.3 Water is a polar solvent; CCl_4 is a nonpolar solvent. In which solvent is each of the following more likely to be soluble?
a. $NaNO_3$, ionic
b. I_2, nonpolar
c. sucrose (table sugar), polar
d. octane, nonpolar

12.4 Water is a polar solvent; hexane is a nonpolar solvent. In which solvent is each of the following more likely to be soluble?
a. vegetable oil, nonpolar
b. benzene, nonpolar
c. LiCl, ionic
d. Na_2SO_4, ionic

12.5 Describe the formation of an aqueous KI solution when KI dissolves in water.

12.6 Describe the formation of an aqueous LiBr solution when LiBr dissolves in water.

LEARNING GOAL

Identify solutes as electrolytes or nonelectrolytes.

12.2 Electrolytes and Nonelectrolytes

Solutes can be classified by their ability to conduct an electrical current. When **electrolytes** dissolve in water, the process of *dissociation* separates them into ions forming solutions that conduct electricity. When **nonelectrolytes** dissolve in water, they do not separate into ions and their solutions do not conduct electricity.

To test solutions for the presence of ions, we can use an apparatus that consists of a battery and a pair of electrodes connected by wires to a light bulb. The light bulb glows when electricity flows, which can only happen when electrolytes provide ions that move between electrodes to complete the circuit.

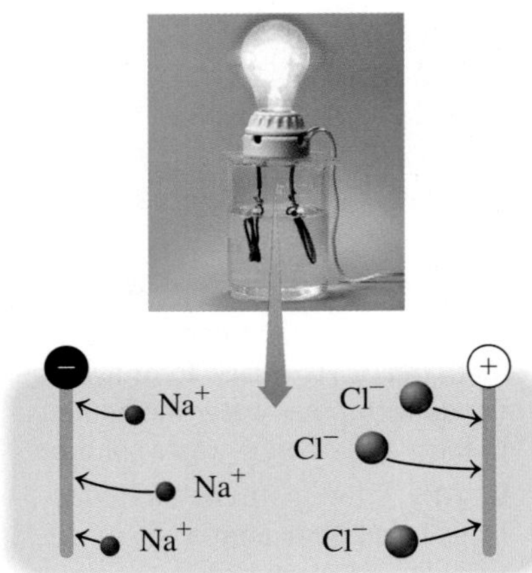

A strong electrolyte in an aqueous solution completely dissociates into ions.

Types of Electrolytes

Electrolytes can be further classified as *strong electrolytes* and *weak electrolytes*. For a **strong electrolyte**, such as sodium chloride (NaCl), there is 100% dissociation of the solute into ions. When the electrodes from the light bulb apparatus are placed in the NaCl solution, the light bulb is very bright.

In an equation for dissociation, the charges must balance. For example, magnesium nitrate dissociates to give one magnesium ion for every two nitrate ions. However, only the ionic bonds between Mg^{2+} and NO_3^- are broken; the covalent bonds within the polyatomic ion are retained. The dissociation for $Mg(NO_3)_2$ is written as follows:

$$Mg(NO_3)_2(s) \xrightarrow{H_2O} Mg^{2+}(aq) + 2NO_3^-(aq)$$

A **weak electrolyte** is a compound that dissolves in water mostly as undissociated molecules. Only a few of the dissolved solute molecules separate, producing a small number of ions in solution. Thus, solutions of weak electrolytes do not conduct electrical current as well as solutions of strong electrolytes. When the electrodes are placed in a solution of a weak electrolyte, the glow of the light bulb is very dim. For example, an aqueous solution of the weak electrolyte HF contains mostly HF molecules and only a few H^+ and F^- ions. As more H^+ and F^- ions form, some recombine to give HF molecules. These forward and reverse reactions of molecules to ions and back again are indicated by two arrows between the reactants and products that point in opposite directions:

$$HF(aq) \overset{H_2O}{\rightleftarrows} H^+(aq) + F^-(aq)$$

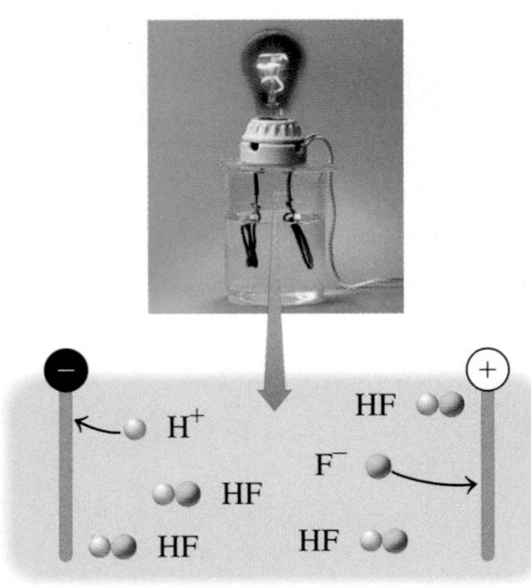

A weak electrolyte forms mostly molecules and a few ions in an aqueous solution.

A nonelectrolyte such as sucrose (sugar) dissolves in water as molecules, which do not dissociate into ions. When electrodes of the light bulb apparatus are placed in a solution of a nonelectrolyte, the light bulb does not glow, because the solution does not contain ions and cannot conduct electricity.

$$C_{12}H_{22}O_{11}(s) \xrightarrow{H_2O} C_{12}H_{22}O_{11}(aq)$$

Table 12.4 summarizes the classification of solutes in aqueous solutions.

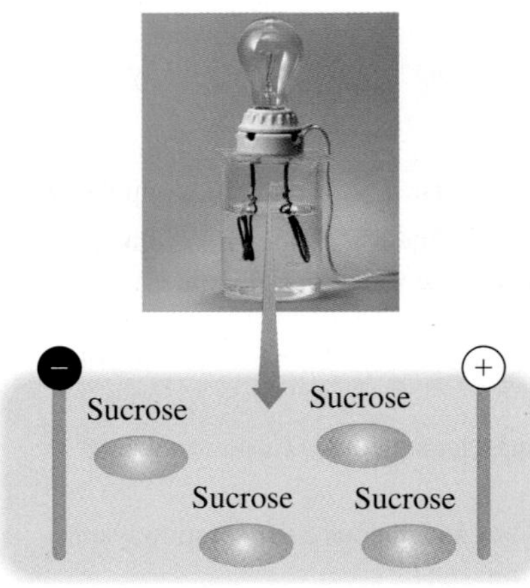

A nonelectrolyte dissolves as molecules in an aqueous solution.

TABLE 12.4 Classification of Solutes in Aqueous Solutions

Types of Solute	Dissociation	Types of Particles in Solution	Conducts Electricity?	Examples
Strong electrolyte	Completely	Ions only	Yes	Ionic compounds such as $NaCl$, KBr, $MgCl_2$, $NaNO_3$, $NaOH$, KOH, HCl, HBr, HI, HNO_3, $HClO_4$, H_2SO_4
Weak electrolyte	Partially	Mostly molecules and a few ions	Weakly	HF, H_2O, NH_3, $HC_2H_3O_2$ (acetic acid)
Nonelectrolyte	None	Molecules only	No	Organic compounds such as $CH_3—OH$ (methanol), $CH_3—CH_2—OH$ (ethanol), $C_{12}H_{22}O_{11}$ (sucrose), CH_4N_2O (urea)

CONCEPT CHECK 12.2 Electrolytes and Nonelectrolytes

Indicate whether solutions of each of the following contain only ions, only molecules, or mostly molecules and a few ions. Write the equation for the formation of a solution for each of the following:

a. Na_2SO_4, a strong electrolyte **b.** urea, CH_4N_2O, a nonelectrolyte
c. hypobromous acid, HBrO, a weak electrolyte

ANSWER

a. An aqueous solution of Na_2SO_4 contains only the ions Na^+ and SO_4^{2-}.

$$Na_2SO_4(s) \xrightarrow{H_2O} 2Na^+(aq) + SO_4^{2-}(aq)$$

b. An aqueous solution of the nonelectrolyte CH_4N_2O contains only molecules of urea, CH_4N_2O.

$$CH_4N_2O(s) \xrightarrow{H_2O} CH_4N_2O(aq)$$

c. An aqueous solution of the weak electrolyte HBrO contains mostly HBrO molecules and only a few H^+ and BrO^- ions. The equation for the formation of a solution with a weak electrolyte is shown with two arrows between the reactant and the products in opposite directions.

$$HBrO(aq) \underset{}{\overset{H_2O}{\rightleftarrows}} H^+(aq) + BrO^-(aq)$$

QUESTIONS AND PROBLEMS

12.2 Electrolytes and Nonelectrolytes

LEARNING GOAL: *Identify solutes as electrolytes or nonelectrolytes.*

12.7 KF is a strong electrolyte, and HF is a weak electrolyte. How is the solution of KF different from that of HF?

12.8 NaOH is a strong electrolyte, and $CH_3—OH$ is a nonelectrolyte. How is the solution of NaOH different from that of $CH_3—OH$?

12.9 Write a balanced equation for the dissociation of each of the following strong electrolytes in water:
a. KCl **b.** $CaCl_2$
c. K_3PO_4 **d.** $Fe(NO_3)_3$

12.10 Write a balanced equation for the dissociation of each of the following strong electrolytes in water:
a. LiBr **b.** $NaNO_3$
c. $CuCl_2$ **d.** K_2CO_3

12.11 Indicate whether aqueous solutions of each of the following solutes contain only ions, only molecules, or mostly molecules and a few ions:
a. acetic acid, $CH_3—COOH$, a weak electrolyte
b. NaBr, a strong electrolyte
c. fructose, $C_6H_{12}O_6$, a nonelectrolyte

12.12 Indicate whether aqueous solutions of each of the following solutes contain only ions, only molecules, or mostly molecules and a few ions:
a. NH_4Cl, a strong electrolyte
b. ethanol, $CH_3—CH_2—OH$, a nonelectrolyte
c. HCN, hydrocyanic acid, a weak electrolyte

12.13 Classify each solute represented in the following equations as a strong, weak, or nonelectrolyte:

a. $K_2SO_4(s) \xrightarrow{H_2O} 2K^+(aq) + SO_4^{2-}(aq)$

b. $NH_3(g) + H_2O(l) \rightleftarrows NH_4^+(aq) + OH^-(aq)$

c. $C_6H_{12}O_6(s) \xrightarrow{H_2O} C_6H_{12}O_6(aq)$

12.14 Classify each solute represented in the following equations as a strong, weak, or nonelectrolyte:

a. $CH_3—OH(l) \xrightarrow{H_2O} CH_3—OH(aq)$

b. $MgCl_2(s) \xrightarrow{H_2O} Mg^{2+}(aq) + 2Cl^-(aq)$

c. $HClO(aq) \overset{H_2O}{\rightleftarrows} H^+(aq) + ClO^-(aq)$

LEARNING GOAL

Define solubility; distinguish between an unsaturated and a saturated solution. Identify a salt as soluble or insoluble.

12.3 Solubility

The term *solubility* describes the amount of a solute that can dissolve in a given amount of solvent. Many factors, such as type of solute, type of solvent, and temperature, affect the solubility of a solute. **Solubility**, usually expressed in grams of solute in 100 g of solvent, is the maximum amount of solute that dissolves at a certain temperature. If a solute readily dissolves when added to the solvent, the solution does not contain the maximum amount of solute. We call this solution an **unsaturated solution**.

A solution that contains all the solute that can dissolve is a **saturated solution**. When a solution is saturated, the rate at which the solute dissolves becomes equal to the rate at which solid forms, a process known as recrystallization. Then there is no further change in the amount of dissolved solute in the solution.

$$\text{Solute} + \text{solvent} \underset{\text{Solute recrystallizes}}{\overset{\text{Solute dissolves}}{\rightleftarrows}} \text{Saturated solution}$$

We can prepare a saturated solution by adding an amount of solute greater than that needed for solubility (saturation). Stirring the solution will dissolve the maximum amount of solute and leave the excess on the bottom of the container. Once we have a saturated solution, the addition of more solute will only increase the amount of undissolved solute.

More solute can dissolve in an unsaturated solution but not in a saturated solution.

SAMPLE PROBLEM 12.1 Saturated Solutions

At 20 °C, the solubility of KCl is 34 g/100 g of water. In the laboratory, a student mixes 75 g of KCl with 200. g of water at a temperature of 20 °C.

a. How much of the KCl can dissolve?
b. Is the solution saturated or unsaturated?
c. What is the mass, in grams, of any solid KCl left undissolved?

SOLUTION

a. KCl has a solubility of 34 g of KCl in 100 g of water. Using its solubility as a conversion factor, we can calculate the maximum amount of KCl that can dissolve in 200. g of water as follows:

$$200.\ \text{g}\ \cancel{H_2O} \times \frac{34\ \text{g KCl}}{100\ \text{g}\ \cancel{H_2O}} = 68\ \text{g of KCl}$$

b. Because 75 g of KCl exceeds the maximum amount of 68 g for KCl that can dissolve in 200. g of water, the KCl solution is saturated.
c. If we add 75 g of KCl to 200. g of water and only 68 g of KCl can dissolve, there is 7 g (75 g − 68 g) of solid (undissolved) KCl on the bottom of the container.

STUDY CHECK 12.1

At 40 °C, the solubility of KNO_3 is 65 g/100 g of water. How many grams of KNO_3 will dissolve in 120 g of water at 40 °C?

Rock candy can be made from a saturated solution of sugar (sucrose).

Effect of Temperature on Solubility

The solubility of most solids becomes greater as temperature increases, which means that solutions usually contain more dissolved solute at higher temperatures. A few substances show little change in solubility at higher temperatures, and a few are less soluble (see Figure 12.5). For example, when you add sugar to iced tea, some undissolved sugar may form on the bottom of the glass. But if you add sugar to hot tea, many teaspoons of sugar are needed before solid sugar appears. Hot tea dissolves more sugar than does cold tea because the solubility of sugar is much greater at a higher temperature.

When a saturated solution is carefully cooled, it might become a *supersaturated solution* because it contains more solute than the solubility allows. Such a solution is unstable, and if the solution is agitated or if a solute crystal is added, the excess solute will crystallize to give a saturated solution again.

Conversely, the solubility of a gas in water decreases as the temperature increases. At higher temperatures, more gas molecules have the energy to escape from the solution. Perhaps you have observed the bubbles escaping from a carbonated drink as it warms. At high temperatures, bottles containing carbonated solutions may burst as more gas molecules leave the solution and increase the gas pressure inside the bottle.

Biologists have found that increased temperatures in rivers and lakes cause the amount of dissolved oxygen to decrease until the warm water can no longer support a biological community. In the early morning, the surface of a lake or pond contains cooler water, which has more dissolved oxygen and therefore more fish. Electricity-generating plants are required to have their own ponds to use with their cooling towers to lessen the threat of thermal pollution to surrounding waterways.

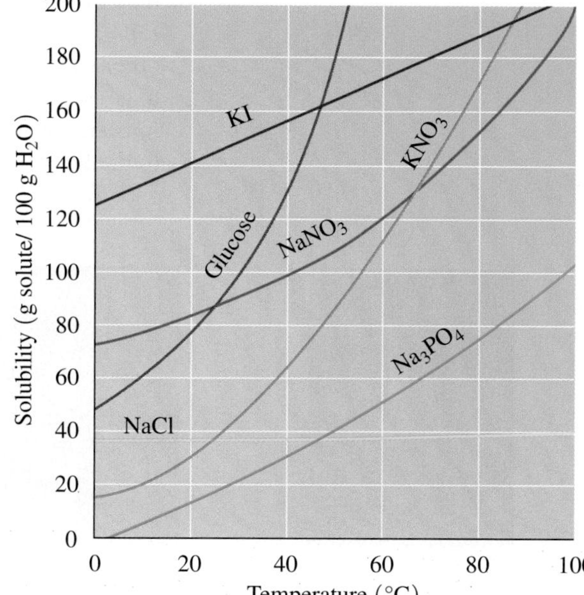

FIGURE 12.5 In water, most common solids are more soluble as the temperature increases.

Q Compare the solubility of $NaNO_3$ at 20 °C and 60 °C.

Henry's Law

Henry's law states that the solubility of gas in a liquid is directly related to the pressure of that gas above the liquid. At higher pressures, more gas molecules are available to enter and dissolve in the liquid. A can of soda is carbonated by using CO_2 gas at high pressure to increase the solubility of the CO_2 in the beverage. When you open the soda can at atmospheric pressure, the pressure of the CO_2 drops, which decreases the solubility of CO_2. As a result, bubbles of CO_2 rapidly escape from the solution. The burst of bubbles is even more noticeable when you open a warm can of soda.

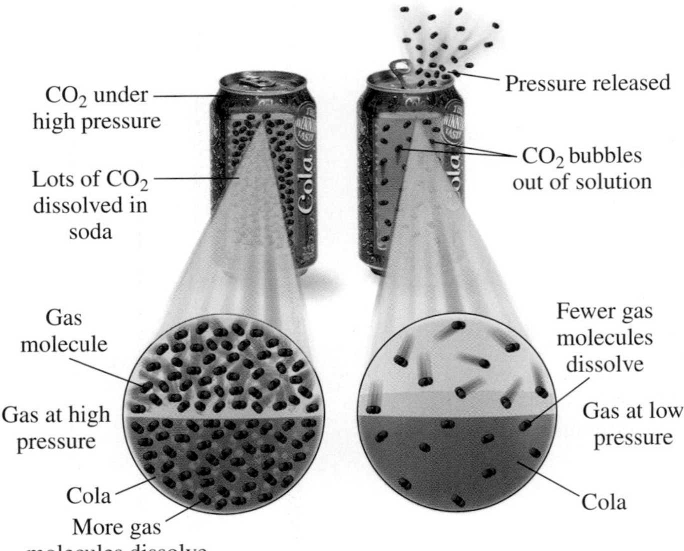

When the pressure of a gas above a solution decreases, the solubility of that gas in the solution also decreases.

SAMPLE PROBLEM 12.2 Factors Affecting Solubility

Indicate whether there is an increase or decrease in each of the following:

a. the solubility of sugar in water when the temperature increases from 25 °C to 45 °C

b. the solubility of O_2 in a lake as the water warms

SOLUTION

a. An increase in the temperature from 25 °C to 45 °C increases the solubility of sugar in water.

b. An increase in the temperature decreases the solubility of O_2 gas in water.

STUDY CHECK 12.2

At 40 °C, the solubility of KNO_3 is 65 g of KNO_3/100 g of H_2O. Would you expect the solubility of KNO_3 to be higher or lower at 80 °C? Explain.

TABLE 12.5 Solubility Rules for Ionic Solids in Water

An Ionic Solid Is:	
Soluble If It Contains:	**Insoluble If It Contains:**
Li^+, Na^+, K^+	None
NH_4^+	None
NO_3^-, $C_2H_3O_2^-$	None
Cl^-, Br^-, I^-	Ag^+, Pb^{2+}, or Hg_2^{2+}
SO_4^{2-}	Ba^{2+}, Pb^{2+}, Ca^{2+}, Sr^{2+}, CO_3^{2-}, S^{2-}, PO_4^{3-}, OH^-

Soluble and Insoluble Salts

In our discussion up to now, we have used ionic compounds that dissolve in water, which are known as **soluble salts**. However, some ionic compounds do not separate into ions in water. They are **insoluble salts** that remain as solids even in contact with water.

Salts that are soluble in water typically contain at least one of the following ions: Li^+, Na^+, K^+, NH_4^+, NO_3^- or $C_2H_3O_2^-$ (acetate). *Only a salt containing a soluble cation or anion will dissolve in water.* Salts containing Cl^-, Br^-, or I^- are soluble unless they are combined with Ag^+, Pb^{2+}, or Hg_2^{2+}; then they are insoluble. Similarly, most salts containing SO_4^{2-} are soluble, but a few are insoluble, as shown in Table 12.5. Most other salts including those containing the anions CO_3^{2-}, S^{2-}, PO_4^{3-}, or OH^- are insoluble (see Figure 12.6). In an insoluble salt, attractions between its positive and negative ions are too strong for the polar water molecules to break. We can use the solubility rules to predict whether a salt (a solid ionic compound) would be expected to dissolve in water (see Table 12.6).

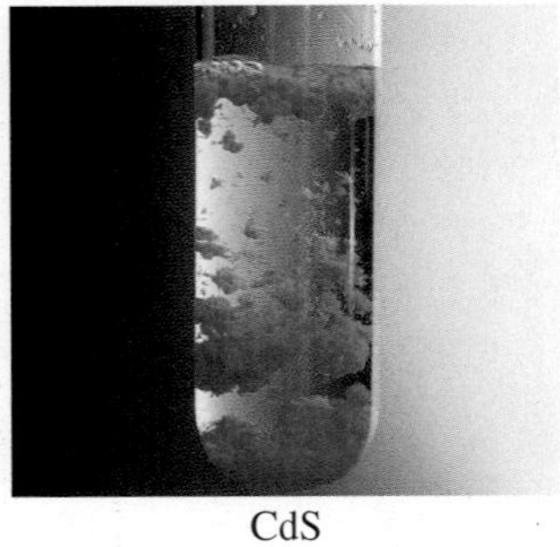
CdS

FeS

PbI_2

$Ni(OH)_2$

FIGURE 12.6 If a salt contains a combination of a cation and an anion that are not soluble, that salt is insoluble. For example, combinations of cadmium and sulfide, iron and sulfide, lead and iodide, and nickel and hydroxide do not contain any soluble ions. Thus, they form insoluble salts.

Q What ions make each of these salts insoluble in water?

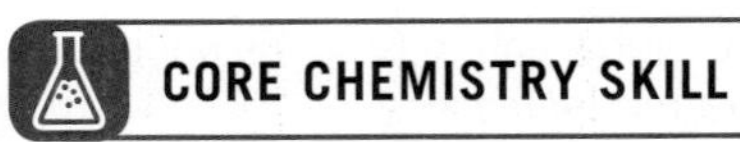

Using Solubility Rules

TABLE 12.6 Using Solubility Rules

Ionic Compound	Solubility in Water	Reasoning
K_2S	Soluble	Contains K^+
$Ca(NO_3)_2$	Soluble	Contains NO_3^-
$PbCl_2$	Insoluble	Forms an insoluble chloride
NaOH	Soluble	Contains Na^+
$AlPO_4$	Insoluble	Contains no soluble ions

In medicine, the insoluble salt $BaSO_4$ is used as an opaque substance to enhance X-rays of the gastrointestinal tract. $BaSO_4$ is so insoluble that it does not dissolve in gastric fluids (see Figure 12.7). Other barium salts cannot be used because they would dissolve in water, releasing Ba^{2+}, which is poisonous.

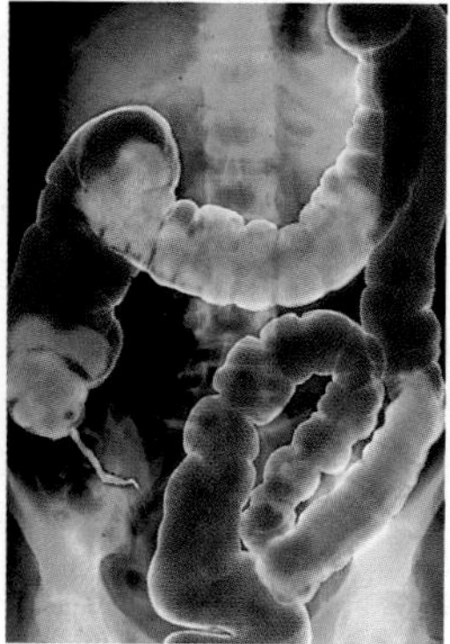

FIGURE 12.7 A barium sulfate-enhanced X-ray of the abdomen shows the large intestine.

Q Is $BaSO_4$ a soluble or an insoluble substance?

CONCEPT CHECK 12.3 Soluble and Insoluble Salts

Predict whether each of the following salts is soluble in water and explain why:

a. Na_3PO_4 **b.** $CaCO_3$

ANSWER

a. The salt Na_3PO_4 is soluble in water because any compound that contains Na^+ is soluble.
b. The salt $CaCO_3$ is not soluble in water because it does not contain a soluble positive ion or a soluble negative ion.

Chemistry Link to Health

GOUT AND KIDNEY STONES: A PROBLEM OF SATURATION IN BODY FLUIDS

The conditions of gout and kidney stones involve compounds in the body that exceed their solubility levels and form solid products. Gout affects adults, primarily men, over the age of 40. Attacks of gout may occur when the concentration of uric acid in blood plasma exceeds its solubility, which is 7 mg/100 mL of plasma at 37 °C. Insoluble deposits of needlelike crystals of uric acid can form in the cartilage, tendons, and soft tissues, where they cause painful gout attacks. They may also form in the tissues of the kidneys, where they can cause renal damage. High levels of uric acid in the body can be caused by an increase in uric acid production, failure of the kidneys to remove uric acid, or a diet with an overabundance of foods containing purines, which are metabolized to uric acid in the body. Foods in the diet that contribute to high levels of uric acid include certain meats, sardines, mushrooms, asparagus, and beans. Drinking alcoholic beverages may also significantly increase uric acid levels and bring about gout attacks.

Treatment for gout involves diet changes and drugs. Depending on the levels of uric acid, a medication such as probenecid is used, which helps the kidneys eliminate uric acid, or allopurinol can be administered to block the production of uric acid by the body.

Kidney stones are solid materials that form in the urinary tract. Most kidney stones are composed of calcium phosphate and calcium oxalate, although they can be solid uric acid. The excessive ingestion of minerals and insufficient water intake can cause the concentration of mineral salts to exceed their solubility and lead to the formation of kidney stones. When a kidney stone passes through the urinary tract, it causes considerable pain and discomfort, necessitating the use of painkillers and surgery. Sometimes ultrasound is used to break up kidney stones. Persons prone to kidney stones are advised to drink six to eight glasses of water every day to prevent saturation levels of minerals in the urine.

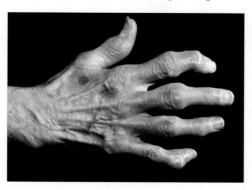

Gout occurs when uric acid exceeds its solubility.

Kidney stones form when calcium phosphate exceeds its solubility.

SAMPLE PROBLEM 12.3 Writing Equations for the Formation of an Insoluble Salt

Guide to Writing an Equation for the Formation of an Insoluble Salt

1. Write the ions of the reactants.
2. Write the combinations of ions and determine if any are insoluble.
3. Write the ionic equation including any solid.
4. Write the net ionic equation.

When solutions of $AgNO_3$ and NaCl are mixed, a white solid forms. Write the ionic and net ionic equations for the reaction.

SOLUTION

Step 1 **Write the ions of the reactants.**

$$Ag^+(aq) + NO_3^-(aq) + Na^+(aq) + Cl^-(aq)$$

Step 2 **Write the combinations of ions and determine if any are insoluble.** When we look at the ions of each solution, we see that the combination of Ag^+ and Cl^- forms an insoluble salt.

Analyze the Problem	Mixture (new combinations)	Product	Soluble?
	$Ag^+(aq) + Cl^-(aq)$	$AgCl(s)$	no
	$Na^+(aq) + NO_3^-(aq)$	$NaNO_3(aq)$	yes

Step 3 **Write the ionic equation including any solid.** In the **ionic equation**, we show all the ions of the reactants and products. The products include the solid AgCl that forms along with the remaining ions Na^+ and NO_3^-.

$$Ag^+(aq) + NO_3^-(aq) + Na^+(aq) + Cl^-(aq) \longrightarrow AgCl(s) + Na^+(aq) + NO_3^-(aq)$$

Step 4 **Write the net ionic equation.** Now we remove the Na^+ and NO_3^- ions, known as *spectator ions*, because they are unchanged during the reaction.

$$Ag^+(aq) + \underbrace{\cancel{NO_3^-(aq)} + \cancel{Na^+(aq)}}_{\text{Spectator ions}} + Cl^-(aq) \longrightarrow AgCl(s) + \underbrace{\cancel{Na^+(aq)} + \cancel{NO_3^-(aq)}}_{\text{Spectator ions}}$$

Finally, a **net ionic equation** is written for the chemical reaction that occurred.

$$Ag^+(aq) + Cl^-(aq) \longrightarrow AgCl(s) \quad \text{Net ionic equation}$$

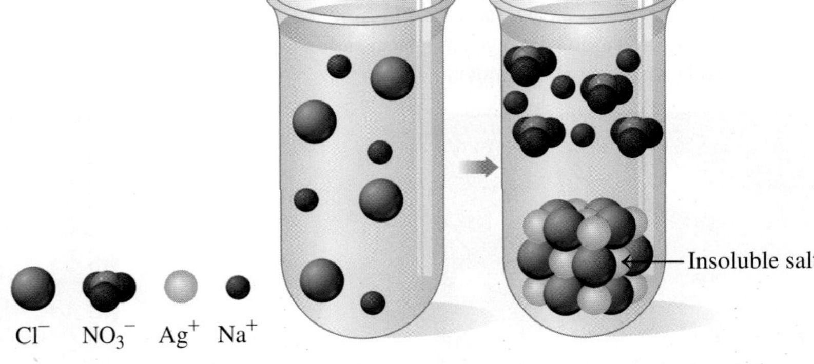

Type of Equation			
Chemical	$AgNO_3(aq)$	$+ NaCl(aq) \longrightarrow$	$AgCl(s) + NaNO_3(aq)$
Ionic	$Ag^+(aq) + NO_3^-(aq)$	$+ Na^+(aq) + Cl^-(aq) \longrightarrow$	$AgCl(s) + Na^+(aq) + NO_3^-(aq)$
Net Ionic	$Ag^+(aq)$	$+ Cl^-(aq) \longrightarrow$	$AgCl(s)$

STUDY CHECK 12.3

Predict whether a solid might form in each of the following mixtures of solutions. If so, write the net ionic equation for the reaction.

a. $NH_4Cl(aq)$ and $Ca(NO_3)_2(aq)$ **b.** $BaCl_2(aq)$ and $Na_2SO_4(aq)$

QUESTIONS AND PROBLEMS

12.3 Solubility

LEARNING GOAL: *Define solubility; distinguish between an unsaturated and a saturated solution. Identify a salt as soluble or insoluble.*

12.15 State whether each of the following refers to a saturated or an unsaturated solution:

a. A crystal added to a solution does not change in size.

b. A sugar cube completely dissolves when added to a cup of coffee.

12.16 State whether each of the following refers to a saturated or an unsaturated solution:

a. A spoonful of salt added to boiling water dissolves.

b. A layer of sugar forms on the bottom of a glass of tea as ice is added.

Use the following table for Problems 12.17–12.20:

	Solubility (g/100 g H_2O)	
Substance	**20 °C**	**50 °C**
KCl	34	43
$NaNO_3$	88	110
$C_{12}H_{22}O_{11}$ (sugar)	204	260

12.17 Using the previous table, determine whether each of the following solutions will be saturated or unsaturated at 20 °C:

a. adding 25 g of KCl to 100. g of H_2O

b. adding 11 g of $NaNO_3$ to 25 g of H_2O

c. adding 400. g of sugar to 125 g of H_2O

12.18 Using the previous table, determine whether each of the following solutions will be saturated or unsaturated at 50 °C:

a. adding 25 g of KCl to 50. g of H_2O

b. adding 150. g of $NaNO_3$ to 75 g of H_2O

c. adding 80. g of sugar to 25 g of H_2O

12.19 A solution containing 80. g of KCl in 200. g of H_2O at 50 °C is cooled to 20 °C.

a. How many grams of KCl remain in solution at 20 °C?

b. How many grams of solid KCl crystallized after cooling?

12.20 A solution containing 80. g of $NaNO_3$ in 75 g of H_2O at 50 °C is cooled to 20 °C.

a. How many grams of $NaNO_3$ remain in solution at 20 °C?

b. How many grams of solid $NaNO_3$ crystallized after cooling?

12.21 Explain the following observations:

a. More sugar dissolves in hot tea than in iced tea.

b. Champagne in a warm room goes flat.

c. A warm can of soda has more spray when opened than a cold one.

12.22 Explain the following observations:

a. An open can of soda loses its "fizz" more quickly at room temperature than in the refrigerator.

b. Chlorine gas in tap water escapes as the sample warms to room temperature.

c. Less sugar dissolves in iced coffee than in hot coffee.

12.23 Predict whether each of the following ionic compounds is soluble in water:

a. LiCl **b.** AgCl

c. $BaCO_3$ **d.** K_2O

e. $Fe(NO_3)_3$

12.24 Predict whether each of the following ionic compounds is soluble in water:

a. PbS **b.** KI

c. Na_2S **d.** Ag_2O

e. $CaSO_4$

12.25 Determine whether a solid forms when solutions containing the following salts are mixed. If so, write the net ionic equation for the reaction.

a. $KCl(aq)$ and $Na_2S(aq)$

b. $AgNO_3(aq)$ and $K_2S(aq)$

c. $CaCl_2(aq)$ and $Na_2SO_4(aq)$

d. $CuCl_2(aq)$ and $Li_3PO_4(aq)$

12.26 Determine whether a solid forms when solutions containing the following salts are mixed. If so, write the net ionic equation for the reaction.

a. $Na_3PO_4(aq)$ and $AgNO_3(aq)$

b. $K_2SO_4(aq)$ and $Na_2CO_3(aq)$

c. $Pb(NO_3)_2(aq)$ and $Na_2CO_3(aq)$

d. $BaCl_2(aq)$ and $KOH(aq)$

12.4 Concentration of Solutions

LEARNING GOAL

Calculate the concentration of a solute in a solution; use concentration units to calculate the amount of solute or solution.

The amount of solute dissolved in a certain amount of solution is called the **concentration** of the solution. We will look at the concentrations that are a ratio of a certain amount of solute in a given amount of solution.

$$\text{Concentration of a solution} = \frac{\text{amount of solute}}{\text{amount of solution}}$$

Mass Percent (m/m) Concentration

Mass percent (m/m) describes the mass of the solute in grams for exactly 100 g of solution. In the calculation of mass percent (m/m), the units of mass of the solute and solution must be the same. If the mass of the solute is given as grams, then the mass of the solution must also be grams. The mass of the solution is the sum of the mass of the solute and the mass of the solvent.

$$\text{Mass percent (m/m)} = \frac{\text{mass of solute (g)}}{\text{mass of solute (g)} + \text{mass of solvent (g)}} \times 100\%$$
$$= \frac{\text{mass of solute (g)}}{\text{mass of solution (g)}} \times 100\%$$

Suppose we prepared a solution by mixing 8.00 g of KCl (solute) with 42.00 g of water (solvent). Together, the mass of the solute and the mass of the solvent give the mass of the solution (8.00 g + 42.00 g = 50.00 g). Mass percent is calculated by substituting the values into the mass percent expression.

$$\frac{8.00 \text{ g KCl}}{\underbrace{50.00 \text{ g solution}}_{\substack{8.00 \text{ g KCl} + 42.00 \text{ g } H_2O \\ \text{(Solute + Solvent)}}}} \times 100\% = 16.0\% \text{ (m/m) KCl solution}$$

Add 8.00 g of KCl

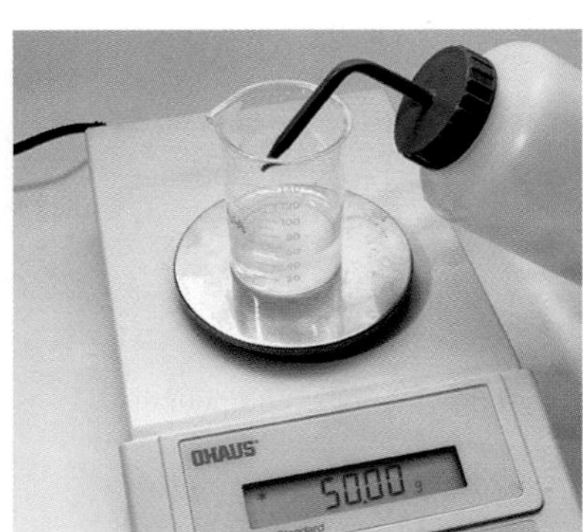

Add water until the solution has a mass of 50.00 g

When water is added to 8.00 g of KCl to form 50.00 g of KCl solution, the mass percent concentration is 16.0% (m/m).

CONCEPT CHECK 12.4 Mass Percent (m/m) Concentration

A NaBr solution is prepared by adding 4.0 g of NaBr to 50.0 g of H_2O.

a. What is the mass of the solution?
b. Is the final concentration of the NaBr solution equal to 7.4% (m/m), 8.0% (m/m), or 80.% (m/m)?

ANSWER

a. The mass of the NaBr solution is the sum of 4.0 g of NaBr solute and 50.0 g of H_2O solvent, which is 54.0 g (4.0 g NaBr + 50.0 g H_2O).
b. The mass percent of the NaBr solution is 7.4% (m/m).

$$\frac{4.0 \text{ g NaBr}}{54.0 \text{ g solution}} \times 100\% = 7.4\% \text{ (m/m) NaBr solution}$$

CORE CHEMISTRY SKILL

Calculating Concentration

Guide to Calculating Solution Concentration

1 State the given and needed quantities.

2 Write the concentration expression.

3 Substitute solute and solution quantities into the expression and calculate.

SAMPLE PROBLEM 12.4 Calculating Mass Percent (m/m) Concentration

What is the mass percent (m/m) of a solution prepared by dissolving 30.0 g of NaOH in 120.0 g of H_2O?

SOLUTION

Step 1 State the given and needed quantities.

	Given	Need
Analyze the Problem	30.0 g of NaOH solute	mass percent (m/m)
	30.0 g NaOH + 120.0 g H_2O = 150.0 g of NaOH solution	

Step 2 Write the concentration expression.

$$\text{Mass percent (m/m)} = \frac{\text{grams of solute}}{\text{grams of solution}} \times 100\%$$

Step 3 **Substitute solute and solution quantities into the expression and calculate.**

$$\text{Mass percent (m/m)} = \frac{30.0 \text{ g NaOH}}{150.0 \text{ g solution}} \times 100\%$$
$$= 20.0\% \text{ (m/m) NaOH solution}$$

STUDY CHECK 12.4

What is the mass percent (m/m) of NaCl in a solution made by dissolving 2.0 g of NaCl in 56.0 g of H_2O?

Volume Percent (v/v) Concentration

Because the volumes of liquids or gases are easily measured, the concentrations of their solutions are often expressed as **volume percent (v/v)**. The units of volume used in the ratio must be the same—for example, both in milliliters or both in liters.

$$\text{Volume percent (v/v)} = \frac{\text{volume of solute}}{\text{volume of solution}} \times 100\%$$

We interpret a volume/volume percent as the volume of solute in exactly 100 mL of solution. On a bottle of extract of vanilla, a label that reads alcohol 35% (v/v) means 35 mL of ethanol solute in exactly 100 mL of vanilla solution.

The label indicates that vanilla extract contains 35% (v/v) alcohol.

SAMPLE PROBLEM 12.5 Calculating Volume Percent (v/v) Concentration

A bottle contains 59 mL of lemon extract solution. If the extract contains 49 mL of alcohol, what is the volume percent (v/v) of the alcohol in the extract solution?

SOLUTION

Step 1 **State the given and needed quantities.**

	Given	Need
Analyze the Problem	49 mL of alcohol solute	volume percent (v/v)
	59 mL of extract solution	

Step 2 **Write the concentration expression.**

$$\text{Volume percent (v/v)} = \frac{\text{volume of solute}}{\text{volume of solution}} \times 100\%$$

Step 3 **Substitute solute and solution quantities into the expression and calculate.**

$$\text{Volume percent (v/v)} = \frac{49 \text{ mL alcohol}}{59 \text{ mL solution}} \times 100\%$$
$$= 83\% \text{ (v/v) alcohol solution}$$

Lemon extract is a mixture of lemon flavor and alcohol.

STUDY CHECK 12.5

What is the volume percent (v/v) of Br_2 in a solution prepared by dissolving 12 mL of bromine (Br_2) in enough carbon tetrachloride to prepare 250. mL of solution?

Mass/Volume Percent (m/v) Concentration

Mass/volume percent (m/v) describes the mass of the solute in grams for exactly 100 mL of solution. In the calculation of mass/volume percent, the unit of mass of the solute is grams and the unit of volume is milliliters.

$$\text{Mass/volume percent (m/v)} = \frac{\text{grams of solute}}{\text{milliliters of solution}} \times 100\%$$

The mass/volume percent is widely used in hospitals and pharmacies for the preparation of intravenous solutions and medicines. For example, a 5% (m/v) glucose solution contains 5 g of glucose in exactly 100 mL of solution. The volume of solution represents the combined volumes of the glucose and H_2O.

Molarity (M) Concentration

When chemists work with solutions, they often use **molarity (M)**, a concentration that states the number of moles of solute in exactly 1 liter of solution.

The molarity of a solution can be calculated knowing the moles of solute and the volume of solution in liters.

$$\text{Molarity (M)} = \frac{\text{moles of solute}}{\text{liters of solution}} = \frac{\text{mol of solute}}{\text{L of soln}}$$

For example, if 1.0 mol of NaCl were dissolved in enough water to prepare 1.0 L of solution, the resulting NaCl solution would have a molarity of 1.0 M. The abbreviation M indicates the units of moles per liter (mol/L).

$$\text{M} = \frac{\text{moles of solute}}{\text{liters of solution}} = \frac{1.0 \text{ mol NaCl}}{1.0 \text{ L solution}} = 1.0 \text{ M NaCl solution}$$

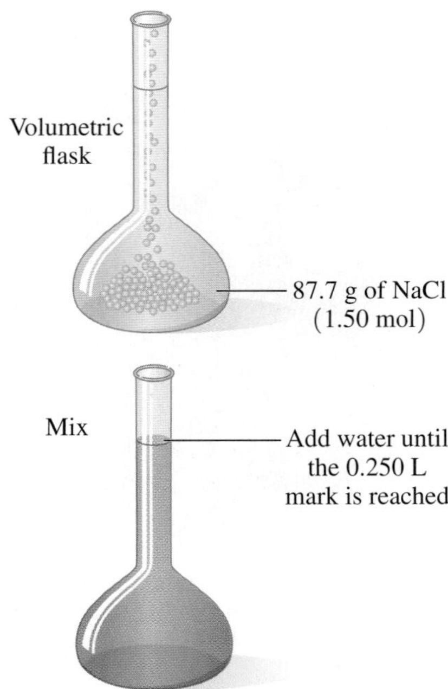

A solution of 1.50 mol of NaCl and water added to the 0.250-L mark is a 6.00 M NaCl solution.

SAMPLE PROBLEM 12.6 Calculating Molarity

What is the molarity (M) of 87.7 g of NaCl in 0.250 L of NaCl solution?

SOLUTION

Step 1 State the given and needed quantities.

	Given	Need
Analyze the Problem	87.7 g of NaCl	molarity (mol/L)
	0.250 L of NaCl solution	

To calculate the moles of NaCl, we need to write the equality and conversion factors for the molar mass of NaCl. Then the moles in 87.7 g of NaCl can be determined.

$$1 \text{ mol of NaCl} = 58.44 \text{ g of NaCl}$$
$$\frac{1 \text{ mol NaCl}}{58.44 \text{ g NaCl}} \quad \text{and} \quad \frac{58.44 \text{ g NaCl}}{1 \text{ mol NaCl}}$$

$$\text{moles of NaCl} = 87.7 \text{ g } \cancel{\text{NaCl}} \times \frac{1 \text{ mol NaCl}}{58.44 \text{ g } \cancel{\text{NaCl}}} = 1.50 \text{ mol of NaCl}$$

Step 2 Write the concentration expression.

$$\text{Molarity (M)} = \frac{\text{moles of solute}}{\text{liters of solution}}$$

Step 3 Substitute solute and solution quantities into the expression and calculate.

$$\text{M} = \frac{1.50 \text{ mol NaCl}}{0.250 \text{ L solution}} = \frac{6.00 \text{ mol NaCl}}{1 \text{ L solution}} = 6.00 \text{ M NaCl solution}$$

STUDY CHECK 12.6

What is the molarity of a solution that contains 75.0 g of KNO_3 dissolved in 0.350 L of solution?

Table 12.7 summarizes the types of units used in the various types of concentration expressions for solutions.

TABLE 12.7 Summary of Types of Concentration Expressions and Their Units

Concentration Units	Mass Percent (m/m)	Volume Percent (v/v)	Mass/Volume Percent (m/v)	Molarity (M)
Solute	g	mL	g	mol
Solution	g	mL	mL	L

Using Concentration as a Conversion Factor

CORE CHEMISTRY SKILL 

Using Concentration as a Conversion Factor

In the preparation of solutions, we often need to calculate the amount of solute or solution. Then the concentration is useful as a conversion factor. Some examples of concentrations, their meanings, and possible conversion factors are given in Table 12.8. The value of 100 in the denominator of a percent expression is an *exact* number. Some examples of using percent concentration or molarity as conversion factors are given in Sample Problems 12.7 and 12.8.

TABLE 12.8 Conversion Factors from Percent Concentrations

Percent Concentration	Meaning	Conversion Factors		
15% (m/m) KCl solution	15 g of KCl in 100 g of KCl solution	$\frac{15 \text{ g KCl}}{100 \text{ g solution}}$	and	$\frac{100 \text{ g solution}}{15 \text{ g KCl}}$
12% (v/v) ethanol solution	12 mL of ethanol in 100 mL of ethanol solution	$\frac{12 \text{ mL ethanol}}{100 \text{ mL solution}}$	and	$\frac{100 \text{ mL solution}}{12 \text{ mL ethanol}}$
5% (m/v) glucose solution	5 g of glucose in 100 mL of glucose solution	$\frac{5 \text{ g glucose}}{100 \text{ mL solution}}$	and	$\frac{100 \text{ mL solution}}{5 \text{ g glucose}}$
Molarity				
6.0 M HCl solution	6.0 mol of HCl in 1 liter of HCl solution	$\frac{6.0 \text{ mol HCl}}{1 \text{ L solution}}$	and	$\frac{1 \text{ L solution}}{6.0 \text{ mol HCl}}$

SAMPLE PROBLEM 12.7 Using Mass Percent to Find Mass of Solute

The topical antibiotic ointment Neosporin is 3.5% (m/m) neomycin solution. How many grams of neomycin are in a tube containing 64 g of ointment?

SOLUTION

Step 1 State the given and needed quantities.

Analyze the Problem	Given	Need
	64 g of 3.5% (m/m) neomycin solution	grams of neomycin

Step 2 Write a plan to calculate the mass or volume.

grams of ointment → % (m/m) factor → grams of neomycin

Step 3 Write equalities and conversion factors. The mass percent (m/m) indicates the grams of a solute in every 100 g of a solution. The mass percent (3.5% m/m) can be written as two conversion factors.

$$100 \text{ g of ointment} = 3.5 \text{ g of neomycin}$$

$$\frac{3.5 \text{ g neomycin}}{100 \text{ g ointment}} \quad \text{and} \quad \frac{100 \text{ g ointment}}{3.5 \text{ g neomycin}}$$

Guide to Using Concentration to Calculate Mass or Volume

1. State the given and needed quantities.
2. Write a plan to calculate the mass or volume.
3. Write equalities and conversion factors.
4. Set up the problem to calculate the mass or volume.

Step 4 **Set up the problem to calculate the mass or volume.**

$$64 \cancel{\text{g ointment}} \times \frac{3.5 \text{ g neomycin}}{100 \cancel{\text{g ointment}}} = 2.2 \text{ g of neomycin}$$

STUDY CHECK 12.7

Calculate the grams of KCl in 225 g of an 8.00% (m/m) KCl solution.

SAMPLE PROBLEM 12.8 Using Molarity to Calculate Volume

How many liters of a 2.00 M NaCl solution are needed to provide 67.3 g of NaCl?

SOLUTION

Step 1 **State the given and needed quantities.**

Analyze the Problem	Given	Need
	67.3 g of NaCl	liters of NaCl solution
	2.00 M NaCl solution	

Step 2 **Write a plan to calculate mass or volume.**

grams of NaCl → Molar mass → moles of NaCl → Molarity → liters of NaCl solution

Step 3 **Write equalities and conversion factors.**

1 mol of NaCl = 58.44 g of NaCl

$$\frac{1 \text{ mol NaCl}}{58.44 \text{ g NaCl}} \text{ and } \frac{58.44 \text{ g NaCl}}{1 \text{ mol NaCl}}$$

1 L of solution = 2.00 mol of NaCl

$$\frac{1 \text{ L solution}}{2.00 \text{ mol NaCl}} \text{ and } \frac{2.00 \text{ mol NaCl}}{1 \text{ L solution}}$$

Step 4 **Set up the problem to calculate the mass or volume.**

$$\text{liters of NaCl solution} = 67.3 \cancel{\text{g NaCl}} \times \frac{1 \cancel{\text{mol NaCl}}}{58.44 \cancel{\text{g NaCl}}} \times \frac{1 \text{ L solution}}{2.00 \cancel{\text{mol NaCl}}}$$

$$= 0.576 \text{ L of solution}$$

STUDY CHECK 12.8

How many milliliters of a 2.25 M HCl solution will provide 4.12 g of HCl?

QUESTIONS AND PROBLEMS

12.4 Concentration of Solutions

LEARNING GOAL: *Calculate the concentration of a solute in a solution; use concentration units to calculate the amount of solute or solution.*

12.27 What is the difference between a 5.00% (m/m) glucose solution and a 5.00% (m/v) glucose solution?

12.28 What is the difference between a 10.0% (v/v) methanol (CH_3OH) solution and a 10.0% (m/m) methanol solution?

12.29 Calculate the mass percent (m/m) for the solute in each of the following solutions:

a. 25 g of KCl and 125 g of H_2O

b. 8.0 g of $CaCl_2$ in 80.0 g of $CaCl_2$ solution

c. 12 g of sucrose in 225 g of sucrose solution

12.30 Calculate the mass percent (m/m) for the solute in each of the following solutions:

a. 75 g of NaOH in 325 g of NaOH solution

b. 2.0 g of KOH and 20.0 g of H_2O

c. 48.5 g of Na_2CO_3 in 250.0 g of Na_2CO_3 solution

12.31 Calculate the mass/volume percent (m/v) for the solute in each of the following solutions:

a. 75 g of Na_2SO_4 in 250 mL of Na_2SO_4 solution

b. 39 g of sucrose in 355 mL of a carbonated drink

12.32 Calculate the mass/volume percent (m/v) for the solute in each of the following solutions:

a. 2.50 g of KCl in 50.0 mL of KCl solution

b. 7.5 g of casein in 120 mL of low-fat milk

12.33 Calculate the molarity (M) of each of the following solutions:
a. 2.00 mol of glucose in 4.00 L of a glucose solution
b. 5.85 g of NaCl in 40.0 mL of a NaCl solution
c. 4.00 g of KOH in 2.00 L of a KOH solution

12.34 Calculate the molarity (M) of each of the following solutions:
a. 0.500 mol of sucrose in 0.200 L of a sucrose solution
b. 30.4 g of LiBr in 350. mL of a LiBr solution
c. 73.0 g of HCl in 2.00 L of a HCl solution

12.35 Calculate the amount of solute, in grams or milliliters, needed to prepare the following solutions:
a. 50.0 g of a 5.0% (m/m) KCl solution
b. 1250 g of a 4.0% (m/m) NH_4Cl solution
c. 250 mL of a 10.0% (v/v) acetic acid solution

12.36 Calculate the amount of solute, in grams or milliliters, needed to prepare the following solutions:
a. 150. g of a 40.0% (m/m) LiBr solution
b. 450 g of a 2.0% (m/m) KCl solution
c. 225 mL of a 15% (v/v) isopropyl alcohol solution

12.37 A mouthwash contains 22.5% (v/v) alcohol. If the bottle of mouthwash contains 355 mL, how many milliliters of alcohol are present?

12.38 A bottle of champagne is 11% (v/v) alcohol. If there are 750 mL of champagne in the bottle, how many milliliters of alcohol are present?

12.39 Calculate the amount of solution, in grams or milliliters, that contains each of the following amounts of solute:
a. 5.0 g of $LiNO_3$ from a 25% (m/m) $LiNO_3$ solution
b. 40.0 g of KOH from a 10.0% (m/v) KOH solution
c. 2.0 mL of formic acid from a 10.0% (v/v) formic acid solution

12.40 Calculate the amount of solution, in grams or milliliters, that contains each of the following amounts of solute:
a. 7.50 g of NaCl from a 2.0% (m/m) NaCl solution
b. 4.0 g of NaOH from a 25% (m/v) NaOH solution
c. 20.0 mL of ethanol from an 8.0% (v/v) ethanol solution

12.41 Calculate the grams of solute needed to prepare each of the following:
a. 2.00 L of a 1.50 M NaOH solution
b. 125 mL of a 0.200 M KCl solution
c. 25.0 mL of a 3.50 M HCl solution

12.42 Calculate the grams of solute needed to prepare each of the following:
a. 2.00 L of a 5.00 M NaOH solution
b. 325 mL of a 0.100 M $CaCl_2$ solution
c. 15.0 mL of a 0.500 M $LiNO_3$ solution

12.43 Calculate the volume indicated for each of the following:
a. liters of a 2.00 M NaOH solution to obtain 3.00 mol of NaOH
b. liters of a 1.50 M NaCl solution to obtain 15.0 mol of NaCl
c. milliliters of a 0.800 M $Ca(NO_3)_2$ solution to obtain 0.0500 mol of $Ca(NO_3)_2$

12.44 Calculate the volume indicated for each of the following:
a. liters of 4.00 M KCl solution to obtain 0.100 mol of KCl
b. liters of a 6.00 M HCl solution to obtain 5.00 mol of HCl
c. milliliters of a 2.50 M K_2SO_4 solution to obtain 1.20 mol of K_2SO_4

12.45 Calculate the volume, in milliliters, for each of the following that provides the given amount of solute:
a. 12.5 g of Na_2CO_3 from a 0.120 M Na_2CO_3 solution
b. 0.850 mol of $NaNO_3$ from a 0.500 M $NaNO_3$ solution
c. 30.0 g of LiOH from a 2.70 M LiOH solution

12.46 Calculate the volume, in liters, for each of the following that provides the given amount of solute:
a. 5.00 mol of NaOH from a 12.0 M NaOH solution
b. 15.0 g of Na_2SO_4 from a 4.00 M Na_2SO_4 solution
c. 28.0 g of $NaHCO_3$ from a 1.50 M $NaHCO_3$ solution

12.5 Dilution and Chemical Reactions in Solution

LEARNING GOAL

Calculate the new concentration or volume of a diluted solution. Given the volume and concentration of a solution, calculate the amount of another reactant or product in a reaction.

In chemistry and biology, we often prepare diluted solutions from more concentrated solutions. In a process called **dilution**, a solvent, usually water, is added to a solution, which increases the volume. As a result, the concentration of the solution decreases. In an everyday example, you are making a dilution when you add three cans of water to a can of concentrated orange juice.

1 can of orange juice concentrate + 3 cans of water = 4 cans of orange juice

Although the addition of solvent increases the volume, the amount of solute does not change; it is the same in the concentration solution and the diluted solution (see Figure 12.8).

Grams or moles of solute = grams or moles of solute
Concentrated solution — Diluted solution

We can write this equality in terms of the concentration, C, and the volume, *V*. The concentration, C, may be percent concentration or molarity.

$$\underset{\text{Concentrated solution}}{C_1V_1} = \underset{\text{Diluted solution}}{C_2V_2}$$

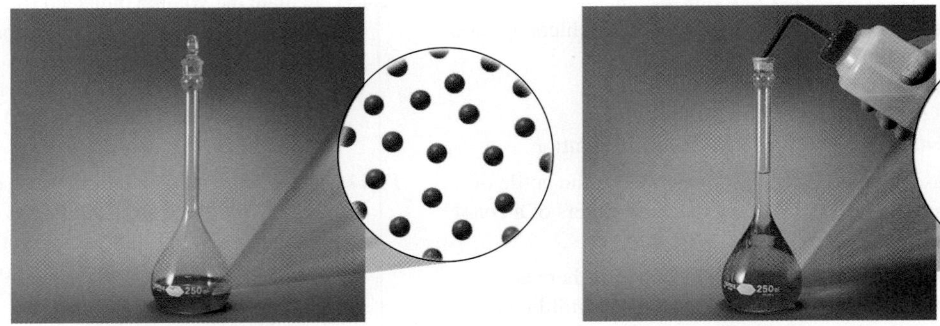

FIGURE 12.8 When water is added to a concentrated solution, there is no change in the number of particles. The solute particles spread out as the volume of the diluted solution increases.

Q What is the concentration of the diluted solution after an equal volume of water is added to a sample of a 6 M HCl solution?

If we are given any three of the four variables (C_1, C_2, V_1, or V_2), we can rearrange the expression to solve for the unknown quantity.

CONCEPT CHECK 12.5 Volume of a Diluted Solution

A 50.0-mL sample of a 20.0% (m/v) $SrCl_2$ solution is diluted with water to give a 5.00% (m/v) $SrCl_2$ solution. Use this data to complete the following table with the given concentrations and volumes of the solutions. Indicate what we know as *increases* or *decreases*, and predict the change in the unknown as *increases* or *decreases*.

Concentrated Solution	Diluted Solution	Know	Predict
$C_1 =$	$C_2 =$		
$V_1 =$	$V_2 =$		

ANSWER

Concentrated Solution	Diluted Solution	Know	Predict
$C_1 = 20.0\%$ (m/v)	$C_2 = 5.00\%$ (m/v)	C decreases	
$V_1 = 50.0$ mL	$V_2 = ?$ mL		*V* increases

SAMPLE PROBLEM 12.9 Volume of a Diluted Solution

What volume, in milliliters, of a 2.5% (m/v) KOH solution can be prepared by diluting 50.0 mL of a 12% (m/v) KOH solution?

SOLUTION

Step 1 **Prepare a table of the concentrations and volumes of the solutions.** For our problem analysis, we organize the solution data in a table, making sure that the units of concentration and volume are the same.

	Concentrated Solution	Diluted Solution	Know	Predict
Analyze the Problem	$C_1 = 12\%$ (m/v) KOH	$C_2 = 2.5\%$ (m/v) KOH	C decreases	
	$V_1 = 50.0$ mL	$V_2 = ?$ mL		V increases

Step 2 **Rearrange the dilution expression to solve for the unknown quantity.**

$$C_1V_1 = C_2V_2$$

$$\frac{C_1V_1}{C_2} = \frac{\cancel{C_2}V_2}{\cancel{C_2}} \quad \text{Divide both sides by } C_2$$

$$V_2 = V_1 \times \frac{C_1}{C_2}$$

Step 3 **Substitute the known quantities into the dilution expression and calculate.**

$$V_2 = 50.0 \text{ mL} \times \frac{12\%}{2.5\%} = 240 \text{ mL (diluted KOH solution)}$$

Concentration factor increases volume

When the initial volume (V_1) is multiplied by a ratio of the percent concentrations (concentration factor) that is greater than 1, the volume of the solution increases as predicted in Step 1.

STUDY CHECK 12.9

What is the final volume, in milliliters, when 25.0 mL of a 15% (m/v) KCl solution is diluted to a 3.0% (m/v) KCl solution?

Guide to Calculating Dilution Quantities

1. Prepare a table of the concentrations and volumes of the solutions.
2. Rearrange the dilution expression to solve for the unknown quantity.
3. Substitute the known quantities into the dilution expression and calculate.

SAMPLE PROBLEM 12.10 Molarity of a Diluted Solution

What is the molarity of a solution prepared when 75.0 mL of a 4.00 M KCl solution is diluted to a volume of 500. mL?

SOLUTION

Step 1 **Prepare a table of the concentrations and volumes of the solutions.** For our problem analysis, we organize the solution data in a table, making sure that the units of concentration and volume are the same.

	Concentrated Solution	Diluted Solution	Know	Predict
Analyze the Problem	$C_1 = 4.00$ M KCl	$C_2 = ?$ M KCl		C (molarity) decreases
	$V_1 = 75.0$ mL $= 0.0750$ L	$V_2 = 500.$ mL $= 0.500$ L	V increases	

Step 2 **Rearrange the dilution expression to solve for the unknown quantity.**

$$C_1V_1 = C_2V_2$$

$$\frac{C_1V_1}{V_2} = \frac{C_2\cancel{V_2}}{\cancel{V_2}} \quad \text{Divide both sides by } V_2$$

$$C_2 = C_1 \times \frac{V_1}{V_2}$$

Step 3 **Substitute the known quantities into the dilution expression and calculate.**

$$C_2 = 4.00 \text{ M} \times \frac{75.0 \cancel{\text{mL}}}{500. \cancel{\text{mL}}} = 0.600 \text{ M (diluted KCl solution)}$$

Volume factor decreases concentration

The final concentration has decreased as predicted in Step 1.

STUDY CHECK 12.10

You need to prepare 450. mL of a 2.00 M NaOH solution from a 10.0 M NaOH solution. What volume of the 10.0 M NaOH solution do you need?

CORE CHEMISTRY SKILL

Calculating the Quantity of a Reactant or Product for a Chemical Reaction in Solution

Guide to Calculations Involving Solutions in Chemical Reactions

1 State the given and needed quantities.

2 Write a plan to calculate the needed quantity or concentration.

3 Write equalities and conversion factors including mole–mole and concentration factors.

4 Set up the problem to calculate the needed quantity or concentration.

Chemical Reactions in Solution

When chemical reactions involve aqueous solutions, we use the balanced chemical equation, the molarity, and the volume to determine the moles or grams of the reactants or products. For example, we can determine the volume of a solution from the molarity and the grams of reactant as seen in Sample Problem 12.11.

SAMPLE PROBLEM 12.11 Volume of a Solution in a Reaction

Zinc reacts with HCl to produce hydrogen gas, H_2, and $ZnCl_2$.

$$Zn(s) + 2HCl(aq) \longrightarrow H_2(g) + ZnCl_2(aq)$$

How many liters of a 1.50 M HCl solution completely react with 5.32 g of zinc?

SOLUTION

Step 1 **State the given and needed quantities.**

	Given	Need
Analyze the Problem	5.32 g of Zn	
	1.50 M HCl solution	liters of HCl solution
	Equation	
	$Zn(s) + 2HCl(aq) \longrightarrow H_2(g) + ZnCl_2(aq)$	

Step 2 **Write a plan to calculate the needed quantity or concentration.**

grams of Zn → Molar mass → moles of Zn → Mole–mole factor → moles of HCl → Molarity → liters of HCl solution

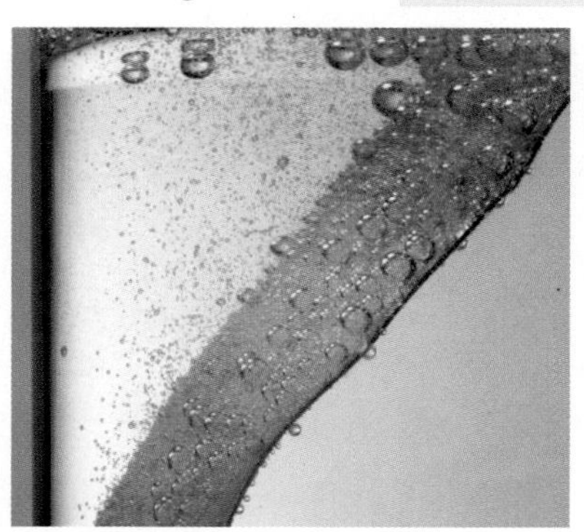

Zinc reacts when placed in a HCl solution.

Step 3 **Write equalities and conversion factors including mole–mole and concentration factors.**

1 mol of Zn = 65.41 g of Zn

$$\frac{1 \text{ mol Zn}}{65.41 \text{ g Zn}} \text{ and } \frac{65.41 \text{ g Zn}}{1 \text{ mol Zn}}$$

1 mol of Zn = 2 mol of HCl

$$\frac{1 \text{ mol Zn}}{2 \text{ mol HCl}} \text{ and } \frac{2 \text{ mol HCl}}{1 \text{ mol Zn}}$$

1 L of solution = 1.50 mol of HCl

$$\frac{1 \text{ L solution}}{1.50 \text{ mol HCl}} \text{ and } \frac{1.50 \text{ mol HCl}}{1 \text{ L solution}}$$

Step 4 **Set up the problem to calculate the needed quantity or concentration.**

$$5.32\ \cancel{g\ Zn} \times \frac{1\ \cancel{mol\ Zn}}{65.41\ \cancel{g\ Zn}} \times \frac{2\ \cancel{mol\ HCl}}{1\ \cancel{mol\ Zn}} \times \frac{1\ L\ solution}{1.50\ \cancel{mol\ HCl}} = 0.108\ L\ of\ HCl\ solution$$

STUDY CHECK 12.11

Using the reaction in Sample Problem 12.11, how many grams of zinc can react with 225 mL of a 0.200 M HCl solution?

SAMPLE PROBLEM 12.12 Volume of a Reactant in a Solution

When a $BaCl_2$ solution is added to a Na_2SO_4 solution, $BaSO_4$, a white solid, forms.

How many milliliters of a 0.250 M $BaCl_2$ solution are needed to react with 0.0325 L of a 0.160 M Na_2SO_4 solution?

$$Na_2SO_4(aq) + BaCl_2(aq) \longrightarrow BaSO_4(s) + 2NaCl(aq)$$

SOLUTION

Step 1 **State the given and needed quantities.**

Analyze the Problem	Given	Need
	0.0325 L of 0.160 M Na_2SO_4 solution	
	0.250 M $BaCl_2$ solution	milliliters of $BaCl_2$ solution
	Equation	
	$Na_2SO_4(aq) + BaCl_2(aq) \longrightarrow BaSO_4(s) + 2NaCl(aq)$	

Step 2 **Write a plan to calculate the needed quantity or concentration.**

liters of Na_2SO_4 solution → Molarity → moles of Na_2SO_4 → Mole–mole factor → moles of $BaCl_2$

→ Molarity → liters of $BaCl_2$ solution → Metric factor → milliliters of $BaCl_2$ solution

Step 3 **Write equalities and conversion factors including mole–mole and concentration factors.**

1 L of solution = 0.160 mol of Na_2SO_4

$$\frac{1\ L\ solution}{0.160\ mol\ Na_2SO_4} \text{ and } \frac{0.160\ mol\ Na_2SO_4}{1\ L\ solution}$$

1 mol of Na_2SO_4 = 1 mol of $BaCl_2$

$$\frac{1\ mol\ Na_2SO_4}{1\ mol\ BaCl_2} \text{ and } \frac{1\ mol\ BaCl_2}{1\ mol\ Na_2SO_4}$$

1 L of solution = 0.250 mol of $BaCl_2$

$$\frac{1\ L\ solution}{0.250\ mol\ BaCl_2} \text{ and } \frac{0.250\ mol\ BaCl_2}{1\ L\ solution}$$

1 L = 1000 mL

$$\frac{1\ L}{1000\ mL} \text{ and } \frac{1000\ mL}{1\ L}$$

Step 4 **Set up the problem to calculate the needed quantity or concentration.**

$$0.0325\ \cancel{L\ solution} \times \frac{0.160\ \cancel{mol\ Na_2SO_4}}{1\ \cancel{L\ solution}} \times \frac{1\ \cancel{mol\ BaCl_2}}{1\ \cancel{mol\ Na_2SO_4}} \times \frac{1\ \cancel{L\ solution}}{0.250\ \cancel{mol\ BaCl_2}} \times \frac{1000\ mL\ BaCl_2\ solution}{1\ \cancel{L\ solution}}$$

$$= 20.8\ mL\ of\ BaCl_2\ solution$$

STUDY CHECK 12.12

For the reaction in Sample Problem 12.12, how many milliliters of a 0.330 M Na_2SO_4 solution are needed to react with 26.8 mL of a 0.216 M $BaCl_2$ solution?

SAMPLE PROBLEM 12.13 Volume of a Gas from a Solution

Acid rain results from the reaction of nitrogen dioxide with water in the air.

$$3NO_2(g) + H_2O(l) \longrightarrow 2HNO_3(aq) + NO(g)$$

At STP, how many liters of NO_2 gas are required to produce 0.275 L of a 0.400 M HNO_3 solution?

SOLUTION

Step 1 **State the given and needed quantities.**

	Given	Need
Analyze the Problem	0.275 L of HNO_3 solution	
	0.400 M HNO_3 solution	liters of $NO_2(g)$ at STP
	Equation	
	$3NO_2(g) + H_2O(l) \longrightarrow 2HNO_3(aq) + NO(g)$	

Step 2 **Write a plan to calculate the needed quantity or concentration.** We start the problem with the volume and molarity of the HNO_3 solution to calculate moles. Then we can use the mole–mole factor and the molar volume to calculate the liters of NO_2 gas.

liters of solution → Molarity → moles of HNO_3 → Mole–mole factor → moles of NO_2 → Molar volume → liters of NO_2 (at STP)

Step 3 **Write equalities and conversion factors including mole–mole and concentration factors.**

1 L of solution = 0.400 mol of HNO_3

$$\frac{1 \text{ L solution}}{0.400 \text{ mol HNO}_3} \quad \text{and} \quad \frac{0.400 \text{ mol HNO}_3}{1 \text{ L solution}}$$

3 mol of NO_2 = 2 mol of HNO_3

$$\frac{2 \text{ mol HNO}_3}{3 \text{ mol NO}_2} \quad \text{and} \quad \frac{3 \text{ mol NO}_2}{2 \text{ mol HNO}_3}$$

1 mol of NO_2 (STP) = 22.4 L of NO_2 (STP)

$$\frac{22.4 \text{ L NO}_2 \text{ (STP)}}{1 \text{ mol NO}_2} \quad \text{and} \quad \frac{1 \text{ mol NO}_2}{22.4 \text{ L NO}_2 \text{ (STP)}}$$

Step 4 **Set up the problem to calculate needed quantity or concentration.**

$$0.275 \cancel{\text{L solution}} \times \frac{0.400 \cancel{\text{mol HNO}_3}}{1 \cancel{\text{L solution}}} \times \frac{3 \cancel{\text{mol NO}_2}}{2 \cancel{\text{mol HNO}_3}} \times \frac{22.4 \text{ L NO}_2 \text{ (STP)}}{1 \cancel{\text{mol NO}_2}} = 3.70 \text{ L of NO}_2 \text{ (STP)}$$

STUDY CHECK 12.13

Using the equation in Sample Problem 12.13, determine the volume of NO produced at 100 °C and 1.20 atm, when 2.20 L of a 1.50 M HNO_3 solution is produced.

Figure 12.9 gives a summary of the pathways and conversion factors needed for substances including solutions involved in chemical reactions.

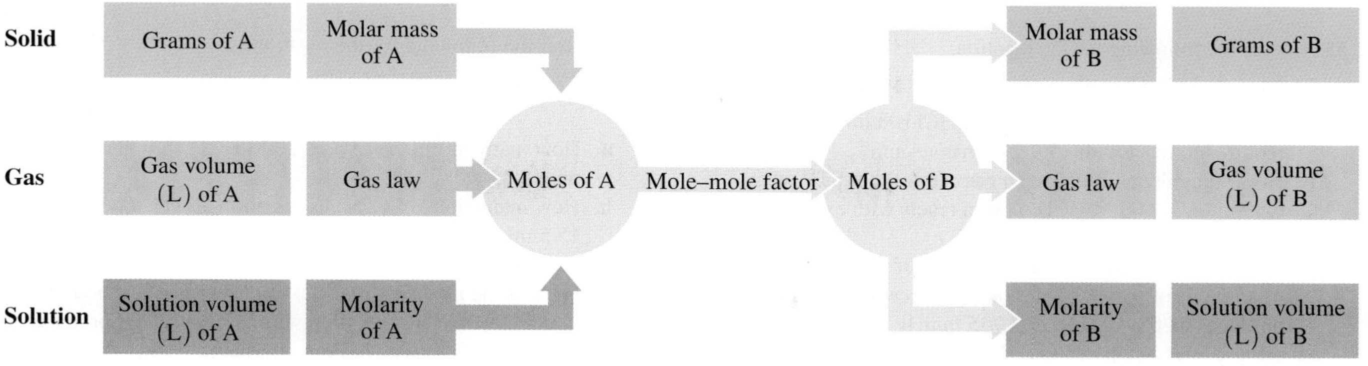

FIGURE 12.9 In calculations involving chemical reactions, substance A is converted to moles of A using molar mass (if solid), gas laws (if gas), or molarity (if solution). Then moles of A are converted to moles of substance B, which are converted to grams of solid, liters of gas, or liters of solution, as needed.

Q What sequence of conversion factors would you use to calculate the number of grams of $CaCO_3$ needed to react with 1.50 L of a 2.00 M HCl solution in the reaction $CaCO_3(s) + 2HCl(aq) \longrightarrow CO_2(g) + H_2O(l) + CaCl_2(aq)$?

QUESTIONS AND PROBLEMS

12.5 Dilution and Chemical Reactions in Solutions

LEARNING GOAL: *Calculate the new concentration or volume of a diluted solution. Given the volume and concentration of a solution, calculate the amount of another reactant or product in a reaction.*

12.47 Calculate the final concentration of each of the following:

a. 0.150 L of a 6.00 M HCl solution is added to water to give a final volume of 0.500 L.

b. Water is added to 0.50 L of a 12 M NaOH solution to make 3.0 L of a diluted NaOH solution.

c. A 10.0-mL sample of a 25% (m/v) KOH solution is diluted with water so that the final volume is 100.0 mL.

d. A 50.0-mL sample of a 15% (m/v) H_2SO_4 solution is added to water to give a final volume of 250 mL.

12.48 Calculate the final concentration of each of the following:

a. 1.0 L of a 4.0 M HNO_3 solution is added to water so that the final volume is 8.0 L.

b. Water is added to 0.25 L of a 6.0 M NaF solution to make 2.0 L of a diluted NaF solution.

c. A 50.0-mL sample of an 8.0% (m/v) KBr solution is diluted with water so that the final volume is 200.0 mL.

d. A 5.0-mL sample of a 50.0% (m/v) acetic acid $HC_2H_3O_2$ solution is added to water to give a final volume of 25 mL.

12.49 Determine the volume, in milliliters, for each of the following:

a. a 1.50 M HCl solution prepared from 20.0 mL of a 6.00 M HCl solution

b. a 2.0% (m/v) LiCl solution prepared from 50.0 mL of a 10.0% (m/v) LiCl solution

c. a 0.500 M H_3PO_4 solution prepared from 50.0 mL of a 6.00 M H_3PO_4 solution

d. a 5.0% (m/v) glucose solution prepared from 75 mL of a 12% (m/v) glucose solution

12.50 Determine the volume, in milliliters, for each of the following:

a. a 1.00% (m/v) H_2SO_4 solution prepared from 10.0 mL of a 20.0% H_2SO_4 solution

b. a 0.10 M HCl solution prepared from 25 mL of a 6.0 M HCl solution

c. a 1.0 M NaOH solution prepared from 50.0 mL of a 12 M NaOH solution

d. a 1.0% (m/v) $CaCl_2$ solution prepared from 18 mL of a 4.0% (m/v) $CaCl_2$ solution

12.51 Determine the volume, in milliliters, required to prepare each of the following:

a. 255 mL of a 0.200 M HNO_3 solution using a 4.00 M HNO_3 solution

b. 715 mL of a 0.100 M $MgCl_2$ solution using a 6.00 M $MgCl_2$ solution

c. 0.100 L of a 0.150 M KCl solution using an 8.00 M KCl solution

12.52 Determine the volume, in milliliters, required to prepare each of the following:

a. 20.0 mL of a 0.250 M KNO_3 solution using a 6.00 M KNO_3 solution

b. 25.0 mL of a 2.50 M H_2SO_4 solution using a 12.0 M H_2SO_4 solution

c. 0.500 L of a 1.50 M NH_4Cl solution using a 10.0 M NH_4Cl solution

12.53 Answer the following for the reaction:

$$Pb(NO_3)_2(aq) + 2KCl(aq) \longrightarrow PbCl_2(s) + 2KNO_3(aq)$$

a. How many grams of $PbCl_2$ will be formed from 50.0 mL of a 1.50 M KCl solution?

b. How many milliliters of a 2.00 M $Pb(NO_3)_2$ solution will react with 50.0 mL of a 1.50 M KCl solution?

c. What is the molarity of 20.0 mL of a KCl solution that reacts completely with 30.0 mL of a 0.400 M $Pb(NO_3)_2$ solution?

12.54 Answer the following for the reaction:

$$NiCl_2(aq) + 2NaOH(aq) \longrightarrow Ni(OH)_2(s) + 2NaCl(aq)$$

a. How many milliliters of a 0.200 M NaOH solution are needed to react with 18.0 mL of a 0.500 M $NiCl_2$ solution?

b. How many grams of $Ni(OH)_2$ are produced from the reaction of 35.0 mL of a 1.75 M NaOH solution and excess $NiCl_2$?

c. What is the molarity of 30.0 mL of a $NiCl_2$ solution that reacts completely with 10.0 mL of a 0.250 M NaOH solution?

12.55 Answer the following for the reaction:

$$Mg(s) + 2HCl(aq) \longrightarrow H_2(g) + MgCl_2(aq)$$

a. How many milliliters of a 6.00 M HCl solution are required to react with 15.0 g of magnesium?
b. How many liters of hydrogen gas can form at STP when 0.500 L of a 2.00 M HCl solution reacts with excess magnesium?
c. What is the molarity of a HCl solution if the reaction of 45.2 mL of the HCl solution with excess magnesium produces 5.20 L of H_2 gas at 735 mmHg and 25 °C?

12.56 Answer the following for the reaction:

$$CaCO_3(s) + 2HCl(aq) \longrightarrow CO_2(g) + H_2O(l) + CaCl_2(aq)$$

a. How many milliliters of a 0.200 M HCl solution can react with 8.25 g of $CaCO_3$?
b. How many liters of CO_2 gas can form at STP when 15.5 mL of a 3.00 M HCl solution reacts with excess $CaCO_3$?
c. What is the molarity of a HCl solution if the reaction of 200. mL of the HCl solution with excess $CaCO_3$ produces 12.0 L of CO_2 gas at 725 mmHg and 18 °C?

LEARNING GOAL

Identify a mixture as a solution, a colloid, or a suspension. Describe how the number of particles in a solution affects the freezing point, boiling point, and osmotic pressure.

12.6 Properties of Solutions

The solute particles in a solution play an important role in determining the properties of that solution. In most of the solutions discussed so far, the solute is dissolved as small particles that are uniformly dispersed throughout the solvent to give a homogeneous solution. When you observe a solution, such as salt water, you cannot visually distinguish the solute from the solvent. The solution appears transparent, although it may have a color. The particles are so small that they go through filters and through semipermeable membranes. A *semipermeable membrane* allows solvent molecules such as water and very small solute particles to pass through, but does not allow the passage of large solute molecules.

Colloids

The particles in a colloidal dispersion, or *colloid*, are much larger than solute particles in a solution. Colloidal particles are large molecules, such as proteins, or groups of molecules or ions. Colloids are homogeneous mixtures that do not separate or settle out. Colloidal particles are small enough to pass through filters but too large to pass through semipermeable membranes. Table 12.9 lists several examples of colloids.

TABLE 12.9 Examples of Colloids

	Substance Dispersed	Dispersing Medium
Fog, clouds, sprays	Liquid	Gas
Dust, smoke	Solid	Gas
Shaving cream, whipped cream, soapsuds	Gas	Liquid
Styrofoam, marshmallows	Gas	Solid
Mayonnaise, homogenized milk, hand lotions	Liquid	Liquid
Cheese, butter	Liquid	Solid
Blood plasma, paints (latex), gelatin	Solid	Liquid

Suspensions

Suspensions are heterogeneous, nonuniform mixtures containing very large particles that are trapped by filters and do not pass through semipermeable membranes. If you stir muddy water, it mixes but then quickly separates as the suspension particles settle to the bottom. Before you use suspensions such as Kaopectate, calamine lotion, antacid mixtures, and liquid penicillin, it is important that you "shake well before using" to suspend all the particles they contain.

Water-treatment plants make use of the properties of suspensions to purify water. When chemicals such as aluminum sulfate or iron(III) sulfate are added to untreated water, they react with small particles to form large suspension particles called *floc*. In the water-treatment plant, a system of filters traps the suspension particles, but clean water passes through.

Table 12.10 compares the different types of mixtures, and Figure 12.10 illustrates some properties of solutions, colloids, and suspensions.

TABLE 12.10 Comparison of Solutions, Colloids, and Suspensions

Type of Mixture	Type of Particle	Settling	Separation
Solution	Small particles such as atoms, ions, or small molecules	Particles do not settle	Particles cannot be separated by filters or semipermeable membranes
Colloid	Larger molecules or groups of molecules or ions	Particles do not settle	Particles can be separated by semipermeable membranes but not by filters
Suspension	Very large particles that may be visible	Particles settle rapidly	Particles can be separated by filters

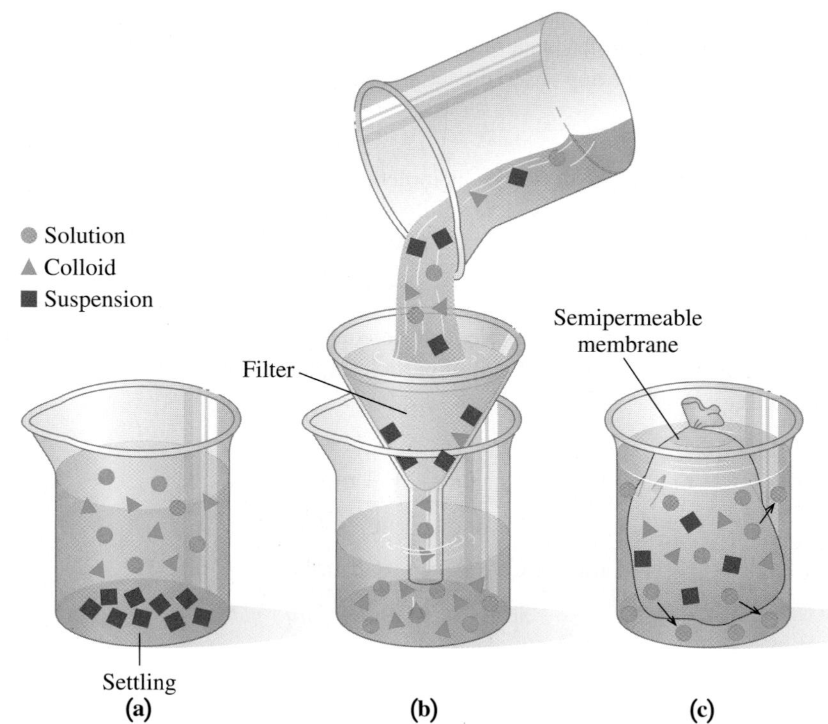

FIGURE 12.10 Properties of different types of mixtures: **(a)** suspensions settle out; **(b)** suspensions are separated by a filter; **(c)** solution particles pass through a semipermeable membrane, but colloids and suspensions do not.

Q Why is a filter paper used to separate suspension particles from a solution, but a semipermeable membrane is needed to separate colloids from a solution?

CONCEPT CHECK 12.6 Classifying Types of Mixtures

Classify each of the following as a solution, colloid, or suspension:

a. a mixture that has particles that settle out upon standing
b. a mixture whose solute particles pass through both filters and membranes
c. an enzyme, which is a large protein molecule that cannot pass through cellular membranes but does pass through a filter

ANSWER

a. A suspension has very large particles that settle out upon standing.
b. A solution contains particles small enough to pass through both filters and membranes.
c. A colloid contains particles that are small enough to pass through a filter but too large to pass through a membrane.

Freezing Point Lowering and Boiling Point Elevation

When a solute is added to water, the physical properties such as freezing point and boiling point change. Therefore, an aqueous solution will have a lower freezing point and a higher boiling point than pure water. These types of changes in physical properties, known as **colligative properties**, depend on the number of solute particles in the solution.

Ethylene glycol is added to a radiator to form an aqueous solution that has a lower freezing point than water.

Probably one familiar example is the process of spreading salt on icy sidewalks and roads when temperatures drop below freezing. The particles from the salt combine with water to lower the freezing point, which causes the ice to melt. Another example is the addition of antifreeze, such as ethylene glycol $HO—CH_2—CH_2—OH$, to the water in a car radiator. Ethylene glycol is an organic compound with two alcohol functional groups, which form hydrogen bonds to make it very soluble in water. If the ethylene glycol and water mixture is about 50–50% by mass, it does not freeze until the temperature drops to about −30 °F, and does not boil unless the temperature reaches about 225 °F. The solution in the radiator prevents the water in the radiator from forming ice in cold weather and boiling over on a hot desert highway.

Insects and fish in climates with subfreezing temperatures control ice formation by producing biological antifreezes made of glycerol, proteins, and sugars, such as glucose, within their bodies. Some insects can survive temperatures below −60 °C. These forms of biological antifreezes may one day be applied to the long-term preservation of human organs.

The Alaska Upis beetle produces biological antifreeze to survive subfreezing temperatures.

Particles in Solution

A solute that is a nonelectrolyte dissolves as molecules, whereas a solute that is a strong electrolyte dissolves entirely as ions. The solute in antifreeze, which is ethylene glycol, $C_2H_6O_2$—a nonelectrolyte—dissolves as molecules.

$$\text{Nonelectrolyte: } 1 \text{ mol of } C_2H_6O_2(l) = 1 \text{ mol of } C_2H_6O_2(aq)$$

However, when 1 mol of a strong electrolyte, such as NaCl or $CaCl_2$, dissolves in water, the NaCl solution will contain 2 mol of particles and the $CaCl_2$ solution will contain 3 mol of particles.

Strong electrolytes:

$$1 \text{ mol of NaCl}(s) = \underbrace{1 \text{ mol of Na}^+(aq) + 1 \text{ mol of Cl}^-(aq)}_{2 \text{ mol of particles } (aq)}$$

$$1 \text{ mol of CaCl}_2(s) = \underbrace{1 \text{ mol of Ca}^{2+}(aq) + 2 \text{ mol of Cl}^-(aq)}_{3 \text{ mol of particles } (aq)}$$

Molality (*m*)

The calculation for freezing point lowering or boiling point elevation uses a concentration unit of *molality*. The **molality**, abbreviation ***m***, of a solution is the number of moles of solute particles per kilogram of solvent. This may seem similar to molarity, but the denominator for molality refers to the mass of the solvent, not the volume of the solution.

$$\text{Molality}(m) = \frac{\text{moles of solute}}{\text{kilograms of solvent}}$$

Guide to Calculating Molality

1. State the given and needed quantities.
2. Write the molality expression.
3. Substitute solute and solvent quantities into the expression and calculate.

SAMPLE PROBLEM 12.14 Calculating Molality

Calculate the molality of a solution containing 35.5 g of the nonelectrolyte glucose ($C_6H_{12}O_6$) in 0.400 kg of water.

SOLUTION

Step 1 State the given and needed quantities.

	Given	Need
Analyze the Problem	35.5 g of glucose ($C_6H_{12}O_6$)	
	0.400 kg of water	molality (m)

Step 2 Write the molality expression.

$$\text{Molality}(m) \text{ of glucose solution} = \frac{\text{moles of glucose}}{\text{kilograms of water}}$$

Step 3 **Substitute solute and solvent quantities into the expression and calculate.** To match the unit of moles in the molality expression, we convert the grams of glucose to moles of glucose, using its molar mass.

$$1 \text{ mol of glucose} = 180.2 \text{ g of glucose}$$
$$\frac{1 \text{ mol glucose}}{180.2 \text{ g glucose}} \quad \text{and} \quad \frac{180.2 \text{ g glucose}}{1 \text{ mol glucose}}$$

$$\text{moles of glucose} = 35.5 \cancel{\text{g glucose}} \times \frac{1 \text{ mol glucose}}{180.2 \cancel{\text{g glucose}}} = 0.197 \text{ mol of glucose}$$

$$\text{Molality } (m) = \frac{0.197 \text{ mol glucose}}{0.400 \text{ kg water}} = 0.493\ m$$

STUDY CHECK 12.14

Calculate the molality of a solution containing 15.8 g of urea, CH_4N_2O, a nonelectrolyte, in 250. g of water.

Using Molality to Calculate Freezing Point Lowering and Boiling Point Elevation

CORE CHEMISTRY SKILL
Calculating Temperature Change

One mol of particles in 1000 g of water lowers the freezing point from 0 °C to −1.86 °C. A similar change occurs with the boiling point of water. One mol of particles in 1000 g of water raises the boiling point from 100. °C to 100.52 °C.

The freezing point lowering (ΔT_f) is determined from the molality (m) of the particles in the solution and the freezing point constant, K_f.

$$\Delta T_f = mK_f$$

Then we can calculate the new, lower freezing point as

$$T_{\text{solution}} = T_{\text{solvent}} - \Delta T_f$$

The freezing point constant (K_f) for water is 1.86 °C/m.

$$\Delta T_f = mK_f = 1\ \cancel{m} \times \frac{1.86\ °\text{C}}{\cancel{m}} = 1.86\ °\text{C}$$

$$\begin{aligned} T_{\text{solution}} &= T_{\text{water}} - \Delta T_f \\ &= 0\ °\text{C} - 1.86\ °\text{C} \\ &= -1.86\ °\text{C} \end{aligned}$$

If there are 2 mol of particles dissolved in 1 kg of water, the freezing point decreases twice that much to −3.72 °C. For example, a solution of 1 mol of NaCl in 1 kg of water produces 2 mol of particles, 1 mol of Na^+, and 1 mol of Cl^-. Thus, 1 mol of NaCl in 1 kg of water produces a 2 m solution of particles.

$$\Delta T_f = mK_f = 2\ \cancel{m} \times \frac{1.86\ °\text{C}}{\cancel{m}} = 3.72\ °\text{C}$$

$$\begin{aligned} T_{\text{solution}} &= T_{\text{water}} - \Delta T_f \\ &= 0\ °\text{C} - 3.72\ °\text{C} \\ &= -3.72\ °\text{C} \end{aligned}$$

A similar change occurs with the boiling point of water. The boiling point elevation (ΔT_b) is determined from the molality (m) of the particles in the solution and the boiling point constant, K_b.

$$\Delta T_b = mK_b$$

Then we can calculate the new, higher boiling point as

$$T_{solution} = T_{water} + \Delta T_b$$

The boiling point constant (K_b) for water is 0.52 °C/m.

$$\Delta T_b = mK_b = 1\, \cancel{m} \times \frac{0.52\ ^\circ\text{C}}{\cancel{m}} = 0.52\ ^\circ\text{C}$$

$$\begin{aligned} T_{solution} &= T_{water} + \Delta T_b \\ &= 100.\ ^\circ\text{C} + 0.52\ ^\circ\text{C} \\ &= 100.52\ ^\circ\text{C} \end{aligned}$$

The effect of some solutes on freezing and boiling point is summarized in Table 12.11.

TABLE 12.11 Effect of Solute Concentration on Freezing and Boiling Points of 1 kg of Water

Substance/kg water	Type of Solute	Molality of Particles	Freezing Point	Boiling Point
Pure water	None	0	0 °C	100 °C
1 mol of $C_2H_6O_2$	Nonelectrolyte	1 m	−1.86 °C	100.52 °C
1 mol of NaCl	Strong electrolyte	2 m	−3.72 °C	101.04 °C
1 mol of $CaCl_2$	Strong electrolyte	3 m	−5.58 °C	101.56 °C

CONCEPT CHECK 12.7 Freezing Point Changes

In each pair, identify the solution that will have a lower freezing point. Explain.

a. 1.0 mol of NaOH (strong electrolyte) and 1.0 mol of ethylene glycol (nonelectrolyte) each in 1.0 kg of water

b. 0.20 mol of KNO_3 (strong electrolyte) and 0.20 mol of $Ca(NO_3)_2$ (strong electrolyte) each in 1.0 kg of water

ANSWER

a. When 1.0 mol of NaOH dissolves in water, it will produce 2.0 mol of particles because each NaOH dissociates to give two particles, Na^+ and OH^-. However, 1.0 mol of ethylene glycol dissolves as molecules to produce only 1.0 mol of particles. Thus, 1.0 mol of NaOH in 1.0 kg of water will have the lower freezing point.

b. When 0.20 mol of KNO_3 dissolves in water, it will produce 0.40 mol of particles because each KNO_3 dissociates to give two particles, K^+ and NO_3^-. When 0.20 mol of $Ca(NO_3)_2$ dissolves in water, it will produce 0.60 mol of particles because each $Ca(NO_3)_2$ dissociates to give three particles, Ca^{2+} and $2NO_3^-$. Thus, 0.20 mol of $Ca(NO_3)_2$ in 1.0 kg of water will have the lower freezing point.

SAMPLE PROBLEM 12.15 Calculating Freezing Point Lowering

In the northeastern United States during freezing temperatures, $CaCl_2$ is spread on icy highways to melt the ice. Calculate the freezing point lowering and freezing point of a solution containing 225 g of $CaCl_2$ in 500. g of water.

Guide to Using Molality

1. State the given and needed quantities.
2. Write the expression for the change in freezing or boiling point.
3. Substitute molality into the expression and calculate.

SOLUTION

Step 1 State the given and needed quantities.

Analyze the Problem	Given	Need
	225 g of $CaCl_2$	
	500. g of water = 0.500 kg of water	ΔT_f, fp

Step 2 Write the expression for the change in freezing or boiling point.

$$\Delta T_f = mK_f$$

Step 3 **Substitute molality into the expression and calculate.** We use molar mass to calculate the moles of $CaCl_2$. Then we multiply by three to obtain the number of moles of ions (particles) produced by 1 mol of $CaCl_2$ in solution.

The molality (m) of the particles in solution is obtained by dividing the moles of particles by the number of kilograms of water in the solution.

$$m = \frac{\text{moles of particles}}{\text{kilograms of water}}$$

Calculating the molality of the $CaCl_2$ solution:

$$\text{moles of particles} = 225\ \cancel{\text{g CaCl}_2} \times \frac{1\ \cancel{\text{mol CaCl}_2}}{110.98\ \cancel{\text{g CaCl}_2}} \times \frac{3\ \text{mol particles}}{1\ \cancel{\text{mol CaCl}_2}}$$

$$= 6.08\ \text{mol of particles}$$

$$\text{Molality } (m) = \frac{6.08\ \text{mol particles}}{0.500\ \text{kg water}} = 12.2\ m$$

The freezing point lowering is calculated using the molality and the freezing point constant. Finally, the freezing point lowering is subtracted from 0 °C to obtain the new freezing point of the $CaCl_2$ solution.

$$\Delta T_f = 12.2\ \cancel{m} \times \frac{1.86\ °\text{C}}{\cancel{m}} = 22.7\ °\text{C}$$

$$T_{\text{solution}} = T_{\text{water}} - \Delta T_f$$

$$= 0\ °\text{C} - 22.7\ °\text{C} = -22.7\ °\text{C}$$

A truck spreads calcium chloride on the road to melt ice and snow.

STUDY CHECK 12.15

Ethylene glycol, $C_2H_6O_2$, a nonelectrolyte, is added to the water in a radiator to give a solution containing 515 g of ethylene glycol in 565 g of water (solvent). What are the boiling point elevation and the boiling point of the solution?

Osmotic Pressure

The movement of water into and out of the cells of plants as well as our own bodies is an important biological process that also depends on the solute concentration. In **osmosis**, a semipermeable membrane allows molecules of the solvent, water, to move through but retains the solute molecules. In this process of diffusion, water moves from the compartment where its concentration is higher to the side where it has a lower concentration. In terms of solute concentration, water flows through the membrane in the direction that will equalize or attempt to equalize the concentrations of solute on both sides. Although water can flow in both directions through the semipermeable membrane, the net flow of water is from the side with the lower solute concentration into the side with the higher solute concentration.

If an osmosis apparatus contains water on one side and a sucrose solution on the other side, the net flow of water will be from the pure water into the sucrose solution, which increases its volume and lowers its sucrose concentration. In the case where two sucrose solutions with different concentrations are placed on each side of the semipermeable membrane, water will flow from the side containing the lower sucrose concentration into the side containing the higher sucrose concentration.

Eventually the height of the sucrose solution creates sufficient pressure to equalize the flow of water between the two compartments. This pressure, called **osmotic pressure**, prevents the flow of additional water into the more concentrated solution. Then there is no further change in the volumes of the two solutions. The osmotic pressure depends on the concentration of solute particles in the solution. The greater the number of particles dissolved, the higher its osmotic pressure. In this example, the sucrose solution has a higher osmotic pressure than pure water, which has an osmotic pressure of zero.

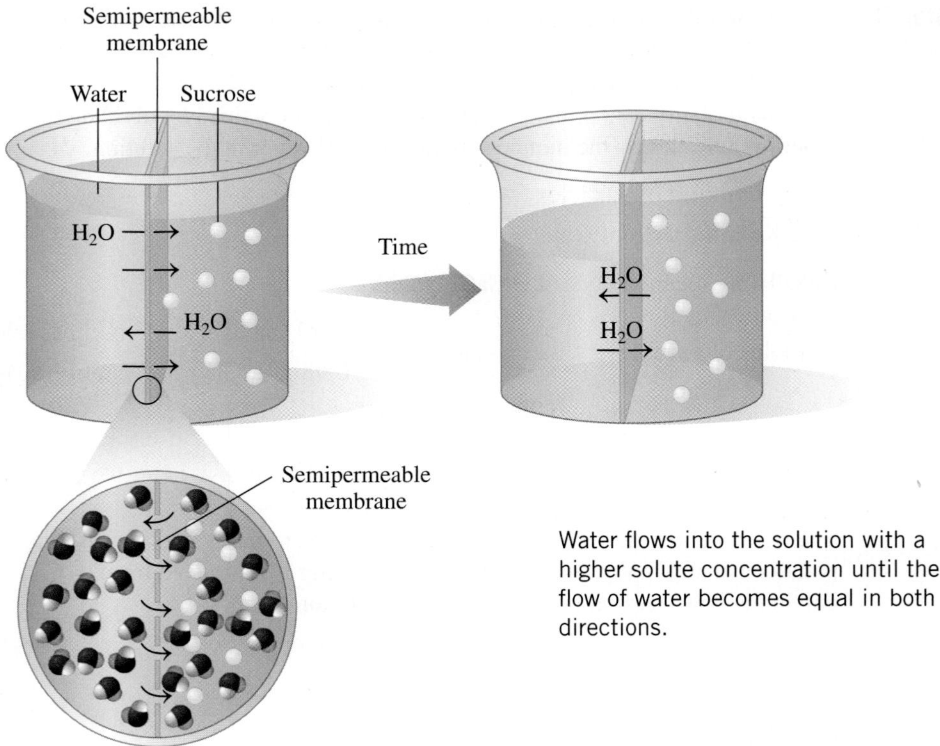

Water flows into the solution with a higher solute concentration until the flow of water becomes equal in both directions.

In a process called *reverse osmosis*, a pressure greater than the osmotic pressure is applied to a solution so that it is forced through a purification membrane. The flow of water is reversed because water flows from an area of lower water concentration to an area of higher water concentration. The molecules and ions in solution stay behind, trapped by the membrane, while water passes through the membrane. This process of reverse osmosis is used in a few desalination plants to obtain pure water from sea (salt) water. However, the pressure that must be applied requires so much energy that reverse osmosis is not yet an economical method for obtaining pure water in most parts of the world.

CONCEPT CHECK 12.8 Osmotic Pressure

A 2% (m/m) sucrose solution and an 8% (m/m) sucrose solution are separated by a semipermeable membrane.

a. Which sucrose solution exerts the greater osmotic pressure?
b. In what direction does water flow initially?
c. Which solution will have the higher level of liquid at equilibrium?

ANSWER

a. The 8% (m/m) sucrose solution has the higher solute concentration, more solute particles, and the greater osmotic pressure.
b. Initially, water will flow out of the 2% (m/m) solution into the more concentrated 8% (m/m) solution.
c. The level of the 8% (m/m) solution will be higher.

Isotonic Solutions

Because the cell membranes in biological systems are semipermeable, osmosis is an ongoing process. The solutes in body solutions such as blood, tissue fluids, lymph, and plasma all exert osmotic pressure. Most intravenous (IV) solutions used in a hospital are *isotonic* solutions, which exert the same osmotic pressure as body fluids such as blood. The percent concentration typically used in IV solutions is similar to the types of percent concentrations we have already discussed, except that the concentration of IV solutions is *mass/volume percent* (*m/v*). The most typical isotonic solutions are 0.9% (m/v)

NaCl solution, or 0.9 g NaCl/100 mL of solution, and 5% (m/v) glucose solution, or 5 g glucose/100 mL of solution. Although they do not contain the same kinds of particles, a 0.9% (m/v) NaCl solution as well as a 5% (m/v) glucose solution are both 0.3 M (Na^+ and Cl^- ions or glucose molecules). A red blood cell placed in an isotonic solution retains its volume because there is an equal flow of water into and out of the cell (see Figure 12.11a).

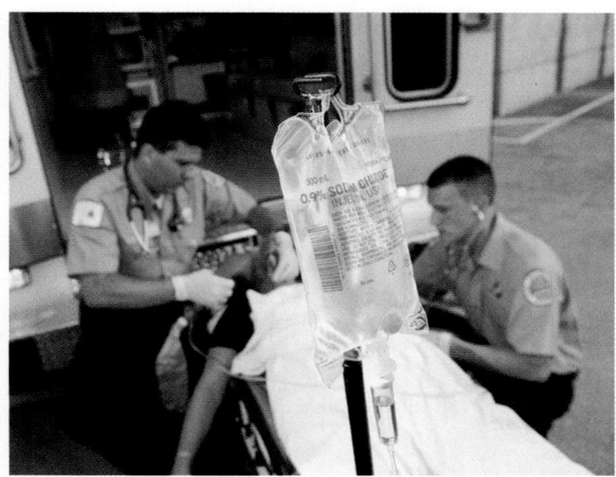

A 0.9% NaCl solution is isotonic with the solute concentration of the blood cells of the body.

Hypotonic and Hypertonic Solutions

If a red blood cell is placed in a solution that is not isotonic, the differences in osmotic pressure inside and outside the cell can drastically alter the volume of the cell. When a red blood cell is placed in a *hypotonic* solution, which has a lower solute concentration (*hypo* means "lower than"), water flows into the cell by osmosis. The increase in fluid causes the cell to swell and possibly burst—a process called *hemolysis* (see Figure 12.11b). A similar process occurs when you place dehydrated food, such as raisins or dried fruit, in water. The water enters the cells, and the food becomes plump and smooth.

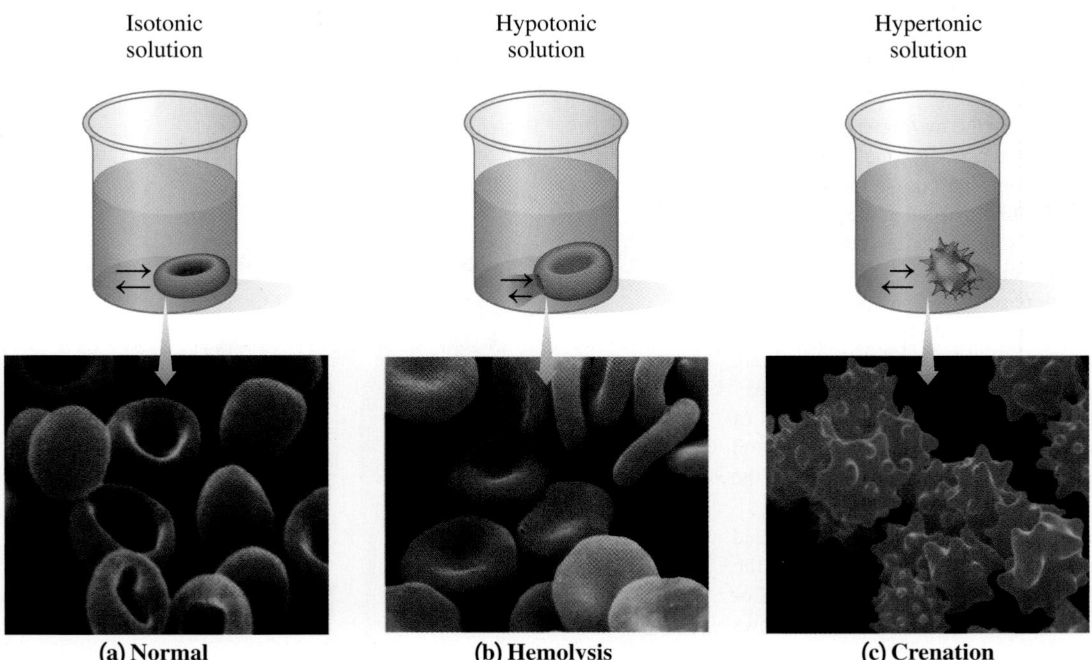

FIGURE 12.11 **(a)** In an isotonic solution, a red blood cell retains its normal volume. **(b)** Hemolysis: In a hypotonic solution, water flows into a red blood cell, causing it to swell and burst. **(c)** Crenation: In a hypertonic solution, water leaves the red blood cell, causing it to shrink.

Q What happens to a red blood cell placed in a 4% NaCl solution?

If a red blood cell is placed in a *hypertonic* solution, which has a higher solute concentration (*hyper* means "greater than"), water flows out of the cell into the hypertonic solution by osmosis. Suppose a red blood cell is placed in a 10% (m/v) NaCl solution. Because the osmotic pressure in the cell is equal to that of a 0.9% (m/v) NaCl solution, the cell shrinks, a process called *crenation* (see Figure 12.11c). A similar process occurs when making pickles, which uses a hypertonic salt solution that causes the cucumbers to shrivel as they lose water.

SAMPLE PROBLEM 12.16 Isotonic, Hypotonic, and Hypertonic Solutions

Describe each of the following solutions as isotonic, hypotonic, or hypertonic. Indicate whether a red blood cell placed in each solution will undergo hemolysis, crenation, or no change.

a. a 5.0% (m/v) glucose solution **b.** a 0.2% (m/v) NaCl solution

SOLUTION

a. A 5.0% (m/v) glucose solution is isotonic. A red blood cell will not undergo any change.
b. A 0.2% (m/v) NaCl solution is hypotonic. A red blood cell will undergo hemolysis.

STUDY CHECK 12.16

What is the effect of a 10% (m/v) glucose solution on a red blood cell?

Dialysis

Dialysis is a process that is similar to osmosis. In dialysis, a semipermeable membrane called a dialyzing membrane permits small solute molecules and ions as well as solvent water molecules to pass through, but it retains large particles, such as colloids. Dialysis is a way to separate solution particles from colloids.

Chemistry Link to Health

DIALYSIS BY THE KIDNEYS AND THE ARTIFICIAL KIDNEY

The fluids of the body undergo dialysis by the membranes of the kidneys, which remove waste materials, excess salts, and water. In an adult, each kidney contains about 2 million nephrons. At the top of each nephron, there is a network of arterial capillaries called the glomerulus.

As blood flows into the glomerulus, small particles, such as amino acids, glucose, urea, water, and certain ions, will move through the capillary membranes into the nephron. As this solution moves through the nephron, substances still of value to the body (such as amino acids, glucose, certain ions, and 99% of the water) are reabsorbed. The major waste product, urea, is excreted in the urine.

If the kidneys fail to dialyze waste products, increased levels of urea can become life-threatening in a relatively short time. A person with kidney failure must use an artificial kidney, which cleanses the blood by *hemodialysis*.

A typical artificial-kidney machine contains a large tank filled with about 100 L of water containing selected electrolytes. In the center of this dialyzing bath (dialysate), there is a dialyzing coil or membrane made of cellulose tubing. As the patient's blood flows through the dialyzing coil, the highly concentrated waste products dialyze out of the blood. No blood is lost because the membrane is not permeable to large particles such as red blood cells.

Dialysis patients do not produce much urine. As a result, they retain large amounts of water between dialysis treatments, which produces a strain on the heart. The intake of fluids for a dialysis patient

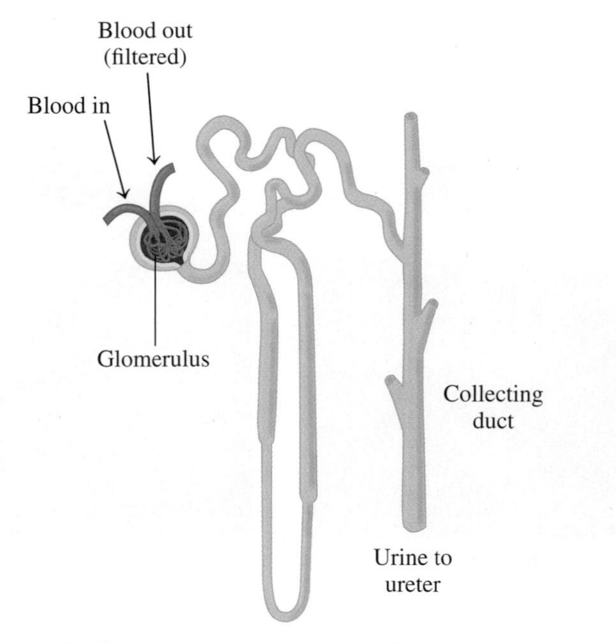

In the kidneys, each nephron contains a glomerulus where urea and waste products are removed to form urine.

may be restricted to as little as a few teaspoons of water a day. In the dialysis procedure, the pressure of the blood is increased as it circulates through the dialyzing coil so that water can be squeezed out of the blood. For some dialysis patients, 2–10 L of water may be removed during one treatment. Dialysis patients typically have two to three treatments a week, each treatment lasting about 5 to 7 h. Some of the newer treatments require less time. For many patients, dialysis is done at home with a home dialysis unit.

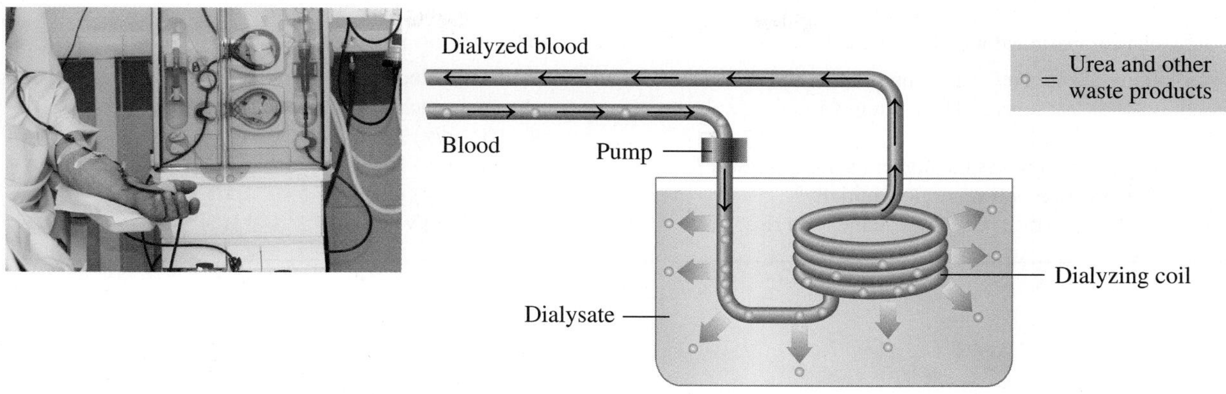

During dialysis, waste products and excess water are removed from the blood.

QUESTIONS AND PROBLEMS

12.6 Properties of Solutions

LEARNING GOAL: *Identify a mixture as a solution, a colloid, or a suspension. Describe how the number of particles in a solution affects the freezing point, boiling point, and osmotic pressure.*

12.57 Identify the following as characteristic of a solution, colloid, or suspension:

a. a mixture that cannot be separated by a semipermeable membrane

b. a mixture that settles out upon standing

12.58 Identify the following as characteristic of a solution, colloid, or suspension:

a. Particles of this mixture remain inside a semipermeable membrane but pass through filters.

b. The particles of solute in this mixture are very large and visible.

12.59 In each pair, identify the solution that will have a lower freezing point. Explain.

a. 1.0 mol of glycerol (nonelectrolyte) and 2.0 mol of ethylene glycol (nonelectrolyte) each in 1.0 kg of water

b. 0.50 mol of KCl (strong electrolyte) and 0.50 mol of $MgCl_2$ (strong electrolyte) each in 2.0 kg of water

12.60 In each pair, identify the solution that will have a higher boiling point. Explain.

a. 1.50 mol of LiOH (strong electrolyte) and 3.00 mol of KOH (strong electrolyte) each in 0.50 kg of water

b. 0.40 mol of $Al(NO_3)_3$ (strong electrolyte) and 0.40 mol of CsCl (strong electrolyte) each in 0.50 kg of water

12.61 Calculate the molality (m) of the following solutions:

a. 325 g of methanol, $CH_3—OH$, a nonelectrolyte, added to 455 g of water

b. 640. g of the antifreeze propylene glycol, $C_3H_8O_2$, a nonelectrolyte, dissolved in 1.22 kg of water

12.62 Calculate the molality (m) of the following solutions:

a. 65.0 g of glucose, $C_6H_{12}O_6$, a nonelectrolyte, added to 112 g of water

b. 110. g of sucrose, $C_{12}H_{22}O_{11}$, a nonelectrolyte, dissolved in 1.50 kg of water

12.63 Calculate the freezing point and boiling point of each solution in Problem 12.61.

12.64 Calculate the freezing point and boiling point of each solution in Problem 12.62.

12.65 Indicate the compartment (**A** or **B**) that will increase in volume for each of the following pairs of solutions separated by a semipermeable membrane:

A	B
a. 5.0% (m/v) starch	10% (m/v) starch
b. 4% (m/v) albumin	8% (m/v) albumin
c. 10% (m/v) sucrose	0.1% (m/v) sucrose

12.66 Indicate the compartment (**A** or **B**) that will increase in volume for each of the following pairs of solutions separated by a semipermeable membrane:

A	B
a. 20% (m/v) starch	10% (m/v) starch
b. 10% (m/v) albumin	2% (m/v) albumin
c. 0.5% (m/v) sucrose	5% (m/v) sucrose

12.67 Two solutions, a 10% (m/v) starch solution and a 1% (m/v) starch solution, are separated by a semipermeable membrane. (Starch is a colloid.)
a. Which compartment has the higher osmotic pressure?
b. In which direction will water flow initially?
c. In which compartment will the volume level rise?

12.68 Two solutions, a 0.1% (m/v) albumin solution and a 2% (m/v) albumin solution, are separated by a semipermeable membrane. (Albumin is a colloid.)
a. Which compartment has the higher osmotic pressure?
b. In which direction will water flow initially?
c. In which compartment will the volume level rise?

12.69 Are the following solutions isotonic, hypotonic, or hypertonic compared with a red blood cell?
a. distilled H_2O
b. 1% (m/v) glucose
c. 0.9% (m/v) NaCl
d. 15% (m/v) glucose

12.70 Will a red blood cell undergo crenation, hemolysis, or no change in each of the following solutions?
a. 1% (m/v) glucose
b. 2% (m/v) NaCl
c. 5% (m/v) glucose
d. 0.1% (m/v) NaCl

CHAPTER REVIEW

12.1 Solutions

LEARNING GOAL: *Identify the solute and solvent in a solution; describe the formation of a solution.*

- A solution forms when a solute, usually the smaller quantity, dissolves in a solvent.
- In a solution, the particles of solute are evenly dispersed in the solvent.
- The solute and the solvent may be solid, liquid, or gas.
- The polar O—H groups form hydrogen bonds between water molecules.
- An ionic solute dissolves in water—a polar solvent—because the polar water molecules attract and pull the ions into solution, where they become hydrated.
- The expression "like dissolves like" means that a polar or an ionic solute dissolves in a polar solvent and a nonpolar solute requires a nonpolar solvent.

12.2 Electrolytes and Nonelectrolytes

LEARNING GOAL: *Identify solutes as electrolytes or nonelectrolytes.*

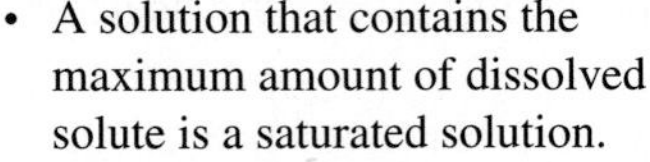

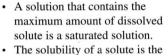

Strong electrolyte

- Substances that produce ions in water are called electrolytes because their solution will conduct an electrical current.
- Strong electrolytes are completely ionized, whereas weak electrolytes are only partially ionized.
- Nonelectrolytes are substances that dissolve in water to produce molecules and cannot conduct electrical currents.

12.3 Solubility

LEARNING GOAL: *Define solubility; distinguish between between an unsaturated and a saturated solution. Identify a salt as soluble or insoluble.*

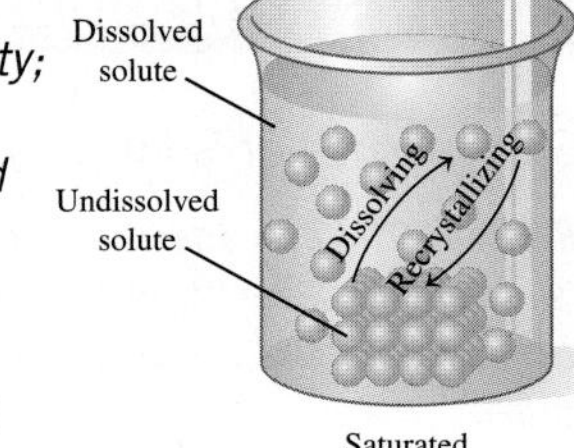

Saturated solution

- A solution that contains the maximum amount of dissolved solute is a saturated solution.
- The solubility of a solute is the maximum amount of a solute that can dissolve in 100 g of solvent.
- A solution containing less than the maximum amount of dissolved solute is unsaturated.
- An increase in temperature increases the solubility of most solids in water but decreases the solubility of gases in water.
- Salts that are soluble in water usually contain Li^+, Na^+, K^+, NH_4^+, NO_3^-, or acetate, $CH_3—COO^-$.
- An ionic equation consists of writing all the dissolved substances in an equation for the formation of an insoluble salt as individual ions.
- A net ionic equation is written by removing all the ions not involved in the chemical change (spectator ions) from the ionic equation.

12.4 Concentration of Solutions

LEARNING GOAL: *Calculate the concentration of a solute in a solution; use concentration units to calculate the amount of solute or solution.*

- Mass percent (m/m) expresses the ratio of the mass of solute to the mass of solution multiplied by 100%.
- Percent concentration can also be expressed as a volume/volume (v/v) ratio or mass/volume (m/v) ratio.
- Molarity is the moles of solute per liter of solution.
- In calculations of grams or milliliters of solute or solution, the concentration is used as a conversion factor.

12.5 Dilution and Chemical Reactions in Solution

LEARNING GOAL: *Calculate the new concentration or volume of a diluted solution. Given the volume and concentration of a solution, calculate the amount of another reactant or product in a reaction.*

- In dilution, a solvent such as water is added to a solution, which increases the volume and decreases the concentration.
- When solutions are involved in chemical reactions, the moles of a substance in solution can be determined from the volume and molarity of the solution.
- When mass, volume, and molarities of substances in a reaction are given, the balanced equation is used to determine the quantities or concentrations of other substances in the reaction.

12.6 Properties of Solutions

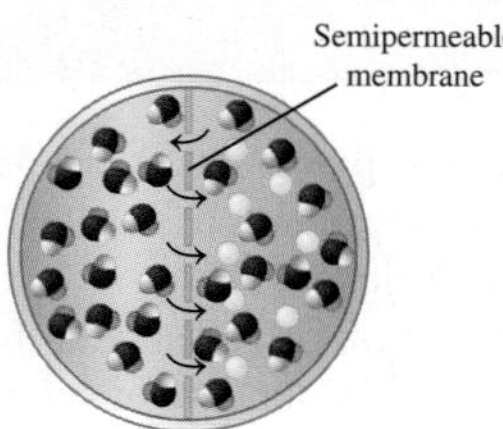

LEARNING GOAL: *Identify a mixture as a solution, a colloid, or a suspension. Describe how the number of particles in a solution affects the freezing point, boiling point, and osmotic pressure.*

- Colloids contain particles that pass through most filters but do not settle out or pass through semipermeable membranes.
- Suspensions have very large particles that settle out of solution.
- The particles in a solution lower the freezing point, raise the boiling point, and increase the osmotic pressure. In osmosis, solvent (water) passes through a semipermeable membrane from a solution with a lower osmotic pressure (lower solute concentration) to a solution with a higher osmotic pressure (higher solute concentration). Isotonic solutions have osmotic pressures equal to that of body fluids.
- A red blood cell maintains its volume in an isotonic solution but swells in a hypotonic solution and shrinks in a hypertonic solution.

CONCEPT MAP

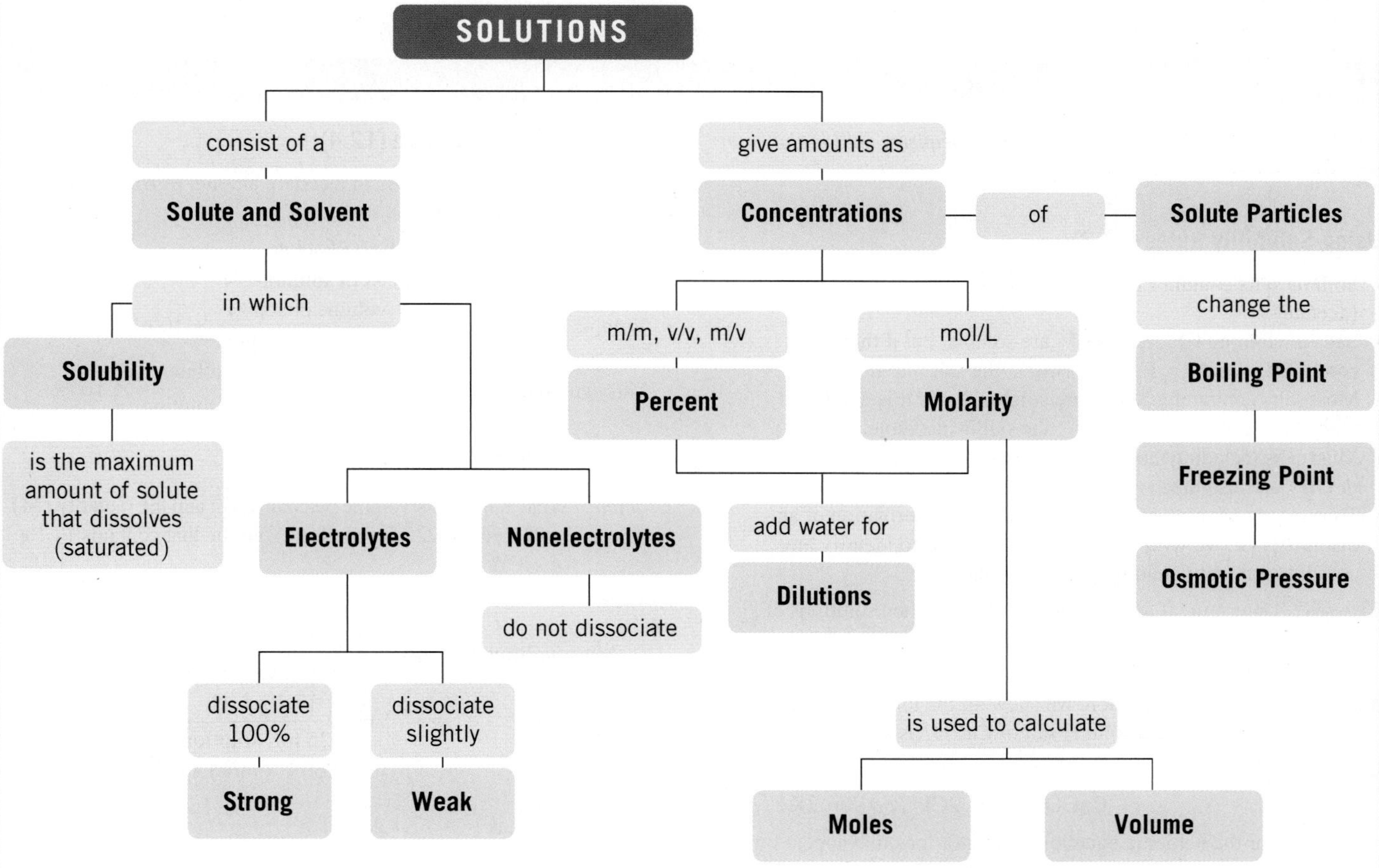

SOLUTIONS

- consist of a **Solute and Solvent**
  - in which
    - **Solubility** — is the maximum amount of solute that dissolves (saturated)
    - **Electrolytes**
      - dissociate 100% — **Strong**
      - dissociate slightly — **Weak**
    - **Nonelectrolytes** — do not dissociate
- give amounts as **Concentrations** — of — **Solute Particles**
  - m/m, v/v, m/v — **Percent**
  - mol/L — **Molarity**
    - is used to calculate **Moles**, **Volume**
  - (Percent, Molarity) add water for **Dilutions**
  - Solute Particles change the **Boiling Point**, **Freezing Point**, **Osmotic Pressure**

KEY TERMS

colligative property A property of solution that depends on the number of solute particles in solution but not the specific type of particle.
concentration A measure of the amount of solute that is dissolved in a specified amount of solution.
dilution A process by which water (solvent) is added to a solution to increase the volume and decrease (dilute) the solute concentration.
electrolyte A substance that produces ions when dissolved in water; its solution conducts electricity.
Henry's law The solubility of a gas in a liquid is directly related to the pressure of that gas above the liquid.
hydration The process of surrounding dissolved ions by water molecules.
insoluble salt An ionic compound that does not dissolve in water.
ionic equation An equation for a reaction in solution that gives all the individual ions, both reacting ions and spectator ions.
mass percent (m/m) The grams of solute in exactly 100 g of solution.
mass/volume percent (m/v) The grams of solute in exactly 100 mL of solution.
molality (*m*) The number of moles of solute in exactly 1 kg of solvent.
molarity (M) The number of moles of solute in exactly 1 L of solution.
net ionic equation An equation for a reaction that gives only the reactants undergoing chemical change and leaves out spectator ions.
nonelectrolyte A substance that dissolves in water as molecules; its solution will not conduct an electrical current.
osmosis The flow of a solvent, usually water, through a semipermeable membrane into a solution of higher solute concentration.
osmotic pressure The pressure that prevents the flow of water into the more concentrated solution.
saturated solution A solution containing the maximum amount of solute that can dissolve at a given temperature. Any additional solute will remain undissolved in the container.
solubility The maximum amount of solute that can dissolve in exactly 100 g of solvent, usually water, at a given temperature.
soluble salt An ionic compound that dissolves in water.
solute A substance that is the smaller amount uniformly dispersed in another substance called the solvent.
solution A homogeneous mixture in which the solute is made up of small particles (ions or molecules).
solvent The substance in which the solute dissolves; usually the component present in greater amount.
strong electrolyte A compound that ionizes completely when it dissolves in water; its solution is a good conductor of electricity.
unsaturated solution A solution that contains less solute than can be dissolved.
volume percent (v/v) A percent concentration that relates the volume of the solute to the volume of the solution.
weak electrolyte A substance that produces only a few ions along with many molecules when it dissolves in water; its solution is a weak conductor of electricity.

CORE CHEMISTRY SKILLS

The chapter section containing each Core Chemistry Skill is shown in parentheses at the end of each heading.

Using Solubility Rules (12.3)

- Soluble salts contain Li^+, Na^+, K^+, NH_4^+, NO_3^-, or $C_2H_3O_2^-$ (acetate).
- Salts containing Cl^-, Br^-, or I^- are soluble, but if they are combined with Ag^+, Pb^{2+}, or Hg_2^{2+}, the salts are insoluble.
- Most salts containing SO_4^{2-} are soluble, but if it is combined with Ba^{2+}, Pb^{2+}, Ca^{2+}, or Sr^{2+}, the salt is insoluble.
- Most salts including those containing the anions CO_3^{2-}, S^{2-}, PO_4^{3-}, or OH^- are insoluble.
- To write an equation or ionic equation for the formation of an insoluble salt, we write the cations and anions to identify any combination that would form an insoluble salt.

Example: Determine if an insoluble salt forms when solutions of $CaCl_2$ and K_2CO_3 are mixed. If so, write the net ionic equation for the reaction.

Answer: In the ionic equation, we show all the ions of the reactants and show the insoluble salt of $CaCO_3$ as a solid.

$$Ca^{2+}(aq) + 2Cl^-(aq) + 2K^+(aq) + CO_3^{2-}(aq) \longrightarrow CaCO_3(s) + 2Cl^-(aq) + 2K^+(aq)$$

For the net ionic equation, spectator ions that appear on both sides of the equation are removed.

$$Ca^{2+}(aq) + CO_3^{2-}(aq) \longrightarrow CaCO_3(s)$$

Net ionic equation

Calculating Concentration (12.4)

The amount of solute dissolved in a certain amount of solution is called the concentration of the solution.

- Mass percent (m/m) $= \dfrac{\text{mass of solute}}{\text{mass of solution}} \times 100\%$
- Volume percent (v/v) $= \dfrac{\text{volume of solute}}{\text{volume of solution}} \times 100\%$
- Mass/volume percent (m/v) $= \dfrac{\text{grams of solute}}{\text{milliliters of solution}} \times 100\%$
- Molarity (M) $= \dfrac{\text{moles of solute}}{\text{liters of solution}}$

Example: What is the mass/volume percent (m/v) and the molarity (M) of 225 mL (0.225 L) of a LiCl solution that contains 17.1 g of LiCl?

Answer:

$$\text{Mass/volume \% (m/v)} = \frac{\text{grams of solute}}{\text{milliliters of solution}} \times 100\% = \frac{17.1\text{ g LiCl}}{225\text{ mL solution}} \times 100\% = 7.60\%\text{ (m/v) LiCl solution}$$

$$\text{moles of LiCl} = 17.1\text{ g LiCl} \times \frac{1\text{ mol LiCl}}{42.39\text{ g LiCl}} = 0.403\text{ mol of LiCl}$$

$$\text{Molarity (M)} = \frac{\text{moles of solute}}{\text{liters of solution}} = \frac{0.403\text{ mol LiCl}}{0.225\text{ L solution}} = 1.79\text{ M LiCl solution}$$

Using Concentration as a Conversion Factor (12.4)

- When we need to calculate the amount of solute or solution, we use the concentration as a conversion factor.
- For example, the concentration of a 4.50 M HCl solution means there are 4.50 mol of HCl in 1 L of HCl solution, which gives two conversion factors written as

$$\frac{4.50\text{ mol HCl}}{1\text{ L solution}} \quad \text{and} \quad \frac{1\text{ L solution}}{4.50\text{ mol HCl}}$$

Example: How many milliliters of a 4.50 M HCl solution will provide 41.2 g of HCl?

Answer:

$$41.2\ \cancel{\text{g HCl}} \times \frac{1\ \cancel{\text{mol HCl}}}{36.46\ \cancel{\text{g HCl}}} \times \frac{1\ \cancel{\text{L solution}}}{4.50\ \cancel{\text{mol HCl}}} \times \frac{1000\text{ mL solution}}{1\ \cancel{\text{L solution}}}$$

$= 251$ mL of HCl solution

Calculating the Quantity of a Reactant or Product for a Chemical Reaction in Solution (12.5)

- When chemical reactions involve aqueous solutions of reactants or products, we use the balanced chemical equation, the molarity, and the volume to determine the moles or grams of the reactants or products.

Example: How many grams of zinc metal will react with 0.315 L of a 1.20 M HCl solution?

$$Zn(s) + 2HCl(aq) \longrightarrow H_2(g) + ZnCl_2(aq)$$

Answer:

$$0.315\ \cancel{\text{L solution}} \times \frac{1.20\ \cancel{\text{mol HCl}}}{1\ \cancel{\text{L solution}}} \times \frac{1\ \cancel{\text{mol Zn}}}{2\ \cancel{\text{mol HCl}}} \times \frac{65.41\text{ g Zn}}{1\ \cancel{\text{mol Zn}}}$$

$= 12.4$ g of Zn

Calculating Temperature Change (12.6)

- The particles in a solution lower the freezing point, raise the boiling point, and increase the osmotic pressure.
- The freezing point lowering (ΔT_f) is determined from the molality (m) of the particles in the solution and the freezing point constant, K_f.

$$\Delta T_f = mK_f$$

- The boiling point elevation (ΔT_b) is determined from the molality (m) of the particles in the solution and the boiling point constant, K_b.

$$\Delta T_b = mK_b$$

Example: What is the boiling point of a solution that contains 1.5 mol of the strong electrolyte KCl in 1 kg of water?

Answer: A solution of 1.5 mol of KCl in 1 kg of water, which contains 3.0 mol of particles, 1.5 mol of K^+, and 1.5 mol of Cl^-, is a 3.0 m solution.

$$\Delta T_b = mK_b = 3.0\ \cancel{m} \times \frac{0.52\ ^\circ\text{C}}{\cancel{m}} = 1.6\ ^\circ\text{C}$$

$$T_{\text{solution}} = T_{\text{solvent}} + \Delta T_b$$

$$= 100.\ ^\circ\text{C} + 1.6\ ^\circ\text{C}$$

$$= 101.6\ ^\circ\text{C}$$

UNDERSTANDING THE CONCEPTS

The chapter sections to review are shown in parentheses at the end of each question.

12.71 Select the diagram that represents the solution formed by a solute ●● that is a (12.1)

a. nonelectrolyte **b.** weak electrolyte
c. strong electrolyte

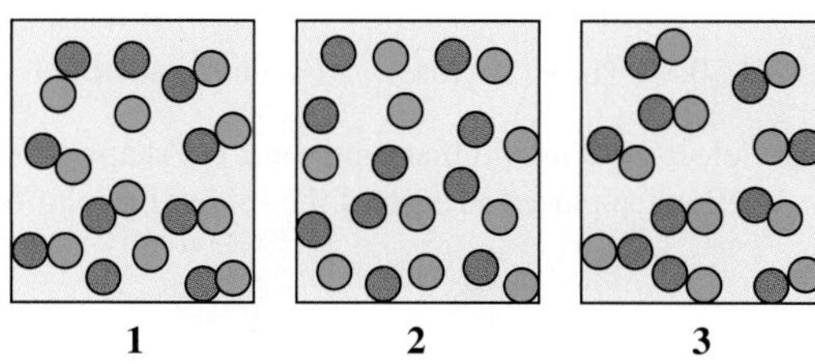

12.72 Match the diagrams with the following: (12.1)

a. a polar solute and a polar solvent
b. a nonpolar solute and a polar solvent
c. a nonpolar solute and a nonpolar solvent

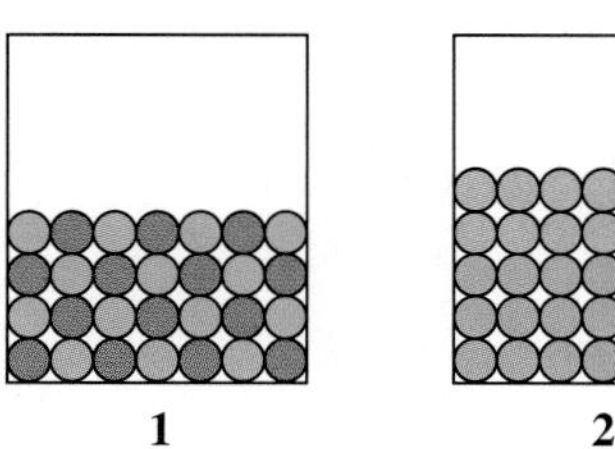

12.73 Select the container that represents the dilution of a 4% (m/m) KCl solution to each of the following: (12.5)

a. 2% (m/m) KCl solution
b. 1% (m/m) KCl solution

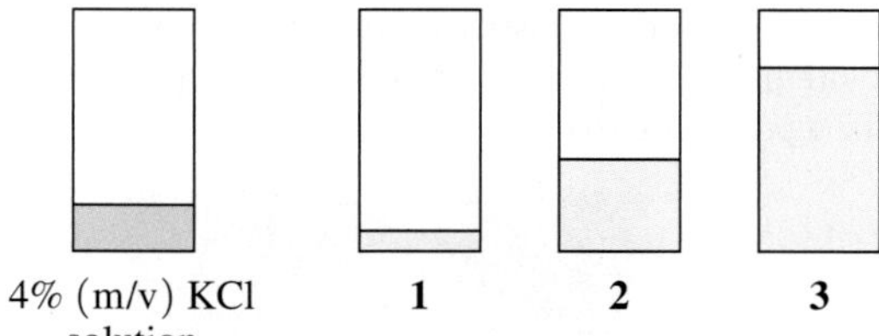

12.74 If all the solute is dissolved in diagram **1**, how would heating or cooling the solution cause each of the following changes? (12.5)

a. **2** to **3**
b. **2** to **1**

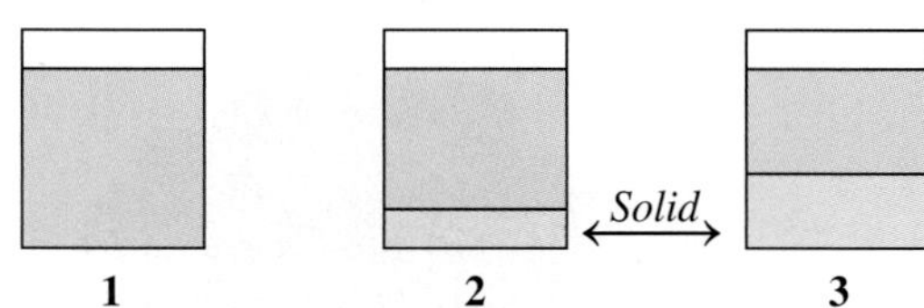

Use the following illustration of beakers and solutions for Problems 12.75 and 12.76:

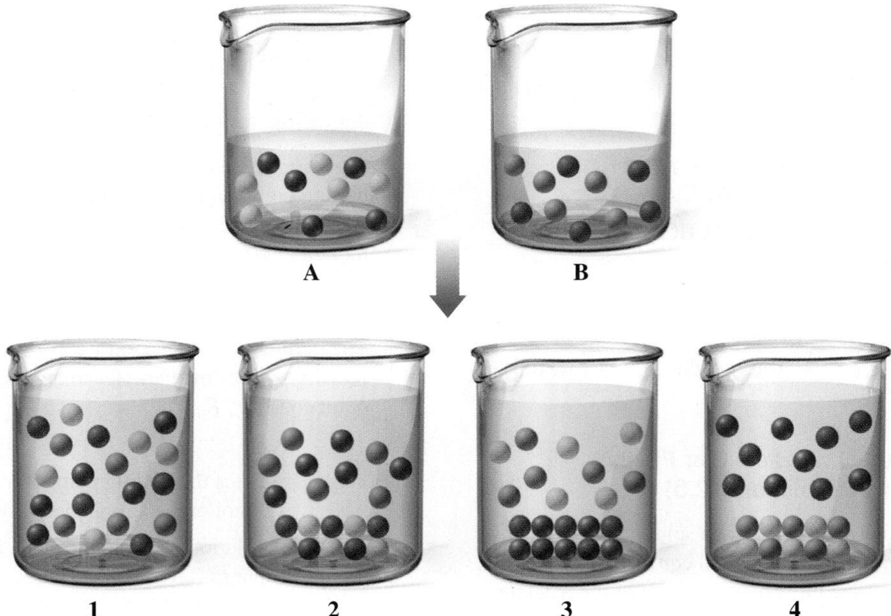

12.75 Use the following types of ions: (12.3)

Na^+ Cl^- Ag^+ NO_3^-

a. Select the beaker (**1**, **2**, **3**, or **4**) that contains the products after the solutions in beakers **A** and **B** are mixed.
b. If an insoluble salt forms, write the ionic equation.
c. If a reaction occurs, write the net ionic equation.

12.76 Use the following types of ions: (12.3)

K^+ NO_3^- NH_4^+ Br^-

a. Select the beaker (**1**, **2**, **3**, or **4**) that contains the products after the solutions in beakers **A** and **B** are mixed.
b. If an insoluble salt forms, write the ionic equation.
c. If a reaction occurs, write the net ionic equation.

12.77 A pickle is made by soaking a cucumber in brine, a salt-water solution. What makes the smooth cucumber become wrinkled like a prune? (12.6)

12.78 Why do lettuce leaves in a salad wilt after a vinaigrette dressing containing salt is added? (12.6)

12.79 A semipermeable membrane separates two compartments, **A** and **B**. If the levels of solutions in **A** and **B** are equal initially, select the diagram that illustrates the final levels for each of the following: (12.6)

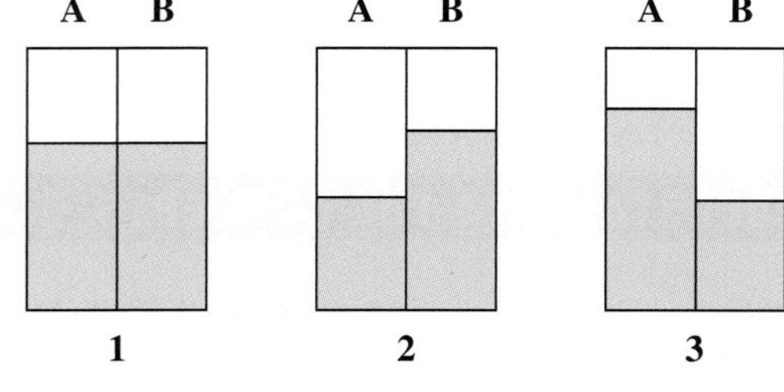

Solution in A	Solution in B
a. 2% (m/v) starch	8% (m/v) starch
b. 1% (m/v) starch	1% (m/v) starch
c. 5% (m/v) sucrose	1% (m/v) sucrose
d. 0.1% (m/v) sucrose	1% (m/v) sucrose

12.80 Select the diagram that represents the shape of a red blood cell when placed in each of the following solutions: (12.6)

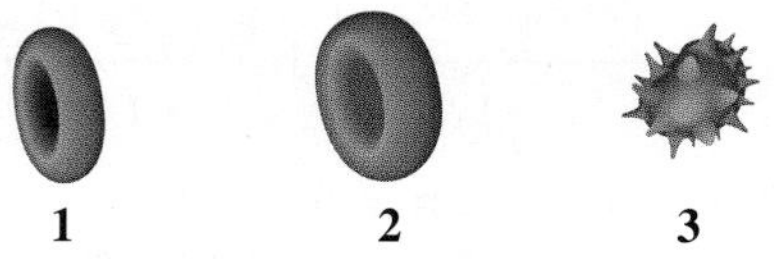

Normal red blood cell

a. 0.9% (m/v) NaCl solution
b. 10% (m/v) glucose solution
c. 0.01% (m/v) NaCl solution
d. 5% (m/v) glucose solution
e. 1% (m/v) glucose solution

ADDITIONAL QUESTIONS AND PROBLEMS

12.81 Why does iodine dissolve in hexane but not in water? (12.1)

12.82 How do temperature and pressure affect the solubility of solids and gases in water? (12.3)

12.83 If NaCl has a solubility of 36.0 g in 100 g of H_2O at 20 °C, how many grams of water are needed to prepare a saturated solution containing 80.0 g of NaCl? (12.3)

12.84 If the solid NaCl in a saturated solution of NaCl continues to dissolve, why is there no change in the concentration of the NaCl solution? (12.3)

12.85 Potassium nitrate has a solubility of 32 g of KNO_3 in 100 g of H_2O at 20 °C. State if each of the following forms an unsaturated or saturated solution at 20 °C: (12.3)

a. 32 g of KNO_3 and 200. g of H_2O
b. 19 g of KNO_3 and 50. g of H_2O
c. 68 g of KNO_3 and 150. g of H_2O

12.86 Potassium fluoride has a solubility of 92 g of KF in 100 g of H_2O at 18 °C. State if each of the following forms an unsaturated or saturated solution at 18 °C: (12.3)

a. 46 g of KF and 100. g of H_2O
b. 46 g of KF and 50. g of H_2O
c. 184 g of KF and 150. g of H_2O

12.87 Indicate whether each of the following ionic compounds is soluble or insoluble in water: (12.3)

a. $CuCO_3$ **b.** $NaHCO_3$
c. $Mg_3(PO_4)_2$ **d.** $(NH_4)_2SO_4$
e. FeO **f.** $Ca(OH)_2$

12.88 Indicate whether each of the following ionic compounds is soluble in water: (12.3)

a. KCl **b.** $PbBr_2$
c. CuS **d.** $AgNO_3$
e. $MgCO_3$ **f.** $FePO_4$

12.89 Write the net ionic equation to show the formation of a precipitate (insoluble salt) when the following solutions are mixed. Write *none* if there is not a precipitate. (12.3)

a. $AgNO_3(aq)$ and $LiCl(aq)$
b. $NaCl(aq)$ and $KNO_3(aq)$
c. $Na_2SO_4(aq)$ and $BaCl_2(aq)$

12.90 Write the net ionic equation to show the formation of a precipitate (insoluble salt) when the following solutions are mixed. Write *none* if there is not a precipitate. (12.3)

a. $Ca(NO_3)_2(aq)$ and $Na_2S(aq)$
b. $Na_3PO_4(aq)$ and $Pb(NO_3)_2(aq)$
c. $FeCl_3(aq)$ and $NH_4NO_3(aq)$

12.91 Calculate the mass percent (m/m) of a solution containing 15.5 g of Na_2SO_4 and 75.5 g of H_2O. (12.4)

12.92 Calculate the mass percent (m/m) of a solution containing 26 g of K_2CO_3 and 724 g of H_2O. (12.4)

12.93 What is the molarity of a solution containing 8.0 g of NaOH in 400. mL of NaOH solution? (12.4)

12.94 What is the molarity of a solution containing 15.6 g of KCl in 274 mL of KCl solution? (12.4)

12.95 How many milliliters of a 12% (v/v) propyl alcohol solution would you need to obtain 4.5 mL of propyl alcohol? (12.4)

12.96 An 80-proof brandy is a 40.0% (v/v) ethanol solution. The "proof" is twice the percent concentration of alcohol in the beverage. How many milliliters of alcohol are present in 750. mL of brandy? (12.4)

12.97 How many grams of solute are in each of the following solutions? (12.4)

a. 2.52 L of a 3.00 M KNO_3 solution
b. 75.0 mL of a 0.506 M Na_2SO_4 solution
c. 45.2 mL of a 1.80 M HCl solution

12.98 How many grams of solute are in each of the following solutions? (12.4)

a. 0.428 L of a 0.450 M K_2CO_3 solution
b. 10.5 mL of a 2.50 M $AgNO_3$ solution
c. 28.4 mL of a 6.00 M H_3PO_4 solution

12.99 How many milliliters of a 1.75 M LiCl solution contain 15.2 g of LiCl? (12.4)

12.100 How many milliliters of a 1.50 M NaBr solution contain 75.0 g of NaBr? (12.4)

12.101 How many liters of a 2.50 M KNO_3 solution can be prepared from 60.0 g of KNO_3? (12.4)

12.102 How many liters of a 4.00 M NaCl solution will provide 25.0 g of NaCl? (12.4)

12.103 The antacid Amphogel contains aluminum hydroxide $Al(OH)_3$. How many milliliters of a 6.00 M HCl solution are required to react with 60.0 mL of a 2.00 M $Al(OH)_3$ solution? (12.5)

$$Al(OH)_3(s) + 3HCl(aq) \longrightarrow 3H_2O(l) + AlCl_3(aq)$$

12.104 Cadmium reacts with HCl to produce hydrogen gas and cadmium chloride. What is the molarity (M) of the HCl solution if 250. mL of the HCl solution reacts with excess cadmium to produce 4.20 L of H_2 gas measured at STP? (12.5)

$$Cd(s) + 2HCl(aq) \longrightarrow H_2(g) + CdCl_2(aq)$$

12.105 Calcium carbonate, $CaCO_3$, reacts with stomach acid (HCl, hydrochloric acid) according to the following equation: (12.5)

$$CaCO_3(s) + 2HCl(aq) \longrightarrow CO_2(g) + H_2O(l) + CaCl_2(aq)$$

One tablet of Tums, an antacid, contains 500.0 mg of $CaCO_3$. If one tablet of Tums is added to 20.0 mL of a 0.100 M HCl solution, how many liters of CO_2 gas are produced at STP?

12.106 How many liters of NO gas can be produced at STP from 80.0 mL of a 4.00 M HNO_3 solution and 10.0 g of Cu? (12.5)

$$3Cu(s) + 8HNO_3(aq) \longrightarrow 3Cu(NO_3)_2(aq) + 4H_2O(l) + 2NO(g)$$

12.107 Calculate the concentration, percent or molarity, of the solution when water is added to prepare each of the following solutions: (12.5)

a. 25.0 mL of a 0.200 M NaBr solution diluted to 50.0 mL
b. 15.0 mL of a 12.0% (m/v) K_2SO_4 solution diluted to 40.0 mL
c. 75.0 mL of a 6.00 M NaOH solution diluted to 255 mL

12.108 Calculate the concentration, percent or molarity, of the solution when water is added to prepare each of the following solutions: (12.5)

a. 25.0 mL of an 18.0 M HCl solution diluted to 500. mL
b. 50.0 mL of a 15.0% (m/v) NH_4Cl solution diluted to 125 mL
c. 4.50 mL of an 8.50 M KOH solution diluted to 75.0 mL

12.109 What is the final volume, in milliliters, when 25.0 mL of each of the following solutions is diluted to provide the given concentration? (12.5)
a. 10.0% (m/v) HCl solution to give a 2.50% (m/v) HCl solution
b. 5.00 M HCl solution to give a 1.00 M HCl solution
c. 6.00 M HCl solution to give a 0.500 M HCl solution

12.110 What is the final volume, in milliliters, when 5.00 mL of each of the following solutions is diluted to provide the given concentration? (12.5)
a. 20.0% (m/v) NaOH solution to give a 4.00% (m/v) NaOH solution
b. 0.600 M NaOH solution to give a 0.100 M NaOH solution
c. 16.0% (m/v) NaOH solution to give a 2.00% (m/v) NaOH solution

CHALLENGE QUESTIONS

12.111 Write the net ionic equation to show the formation of a precipitate (insoluble salt) when the following solutions are mixed. Write *none* if no insoluble salt forms. (12.3)
a. $AgNO_3(aq) + Na_2SO_4(aq)$
b. $KCl(aq) + Pb(NO_3)_2(aq)$
c. $CaCl_2(aq) + (NH_4)_3PO_4(aq)$
d. $K_2SO_4(aq) + BaCl_2(aq)$

12.112 Write the net ionic equation to show the formation of a precipitate (insoluble salt) when the following solutions are mixed. Write *none* if no insoluble salt forms. (12.3)
a. $Pb(NO_3)_2(aq) + NaBr(aq)$
b. $AgNO_3(aq) + (NH_4)_2CO_3(aq)$
c. $Na_3PO_4(aq) + Al(NO_3)_3(aq)$
d. $NaOH(aq) + CuCl_2(aq)$

12.113 A solution is prepared with 70.0 g of HNO_3 and 130.0 g of H_2O. The HNO_3 solution has a density of 1.21 g/mL. (12.4)
a. What is the mass percent (m/m) of the HNO_3 solution?
b. What is the total volume, in milliliters, of the solution?
c. What is the mass/volume percent (m/v)?
d. What is the molarity (M) of the solution?

12.114 A solution is prepared by dissolving 22.0 g of NaOH in 118.0 g of water. The NaOH solution has a density of 1.15 g/mL. (12.4)
a. What is the mass percent (m/m) of the NaOH solution?
b. What is the total volume, in milliliters, of the solution?
c. What is the mass/volume percent (m/v)?
d. What is the molarity (M) of the solution?

12.115 In a laboratory experiment, a 10.0-mL sample of NaCl solution is poured into an evaporating dish with a mass of 24.10 g. The combined mass of the evaporating dish and the NaCl solution is 36.15 g. After heating, the evaporating dish and dry NaCl have a combined mass of 25.50 g. (12.4)
a. What is the mass percent (m/m) of the NaCl solution?
b. What is the molarity (M) of the NaCl solution?
c. If water is added to 10.0 mL of the initial NaCl solution to give a final volume of 60.0 mL, what is the molarity of the diluted NaCl solution?

12.116 In a laboratory experiment, a 15.0-mL sample of KCl solution is poured into an evaporating dish with a mass of 24.10 g. The combined mass of the evaporating dish and KCl solution is 41.50 g. After heating, the evaporating dish and dry KCl have a combined mass of 28.28 g. (12.4)
a. What is the mass percent (m/m) of the KCl solution?
b. What is the molarity (M) of the KCl solution?
c. If water is added to 10.0 mL of the initial KCl solution to give a final volume of 60.0 mL, what is the molarity of the diluted KCl solution?

12.117 A 355-mL sample of a HCl solution reacts with excess Mg to produce 4.20 L of H_2 gas measured at 745 mmHg and 35 °C. What is the molarity (M) of the HCl solution? (12.5)

$$Mg(s) + 2HCl(aq) \longrightarrow H_2(g) + MgCl_2(aq)$$

12.118 A 255-mL sample of a HCl solution reacts with excess Ca to produce 14.0 L of H_2 gas measured at 732 mmHg and 22 °C. What is the molarity (M) of the HCl solution? (12.5)

$$Ca(s) + 2HCl(aq) \longrightarrow H_2(g) + CaCl_2(aq)$$

12.119 How many moles of each of the following strong electrolytes are needed to give the same freezing point lowering as 1.2 mol of the nonelectrolyte ethylene glycol in 1 kg of water? (12.6)
a. NaCl **b.** K_3PO_4

12.120 How many moles of each of the following are needed to give the same freezing point lowering as 3.0 mol of the nonelectrolyte ethylene glycol in 1 kg of water? (12.6)
a. $CH_3—OH$, a nonelectrolyte
b. KNO_3, a strong electrolyte

12.121 The boiling point of a NaCl solution is 101.04 °C. (12.6)
a. What is the molality (*m*) of the NaCl solution?
b. What is the freezing point of the NaCl solution?

12.122 The freezing point of a $CaCl_2$ solution is −25 °C. (12.6)
a. What is the molality (*m*) of the $CaCl_2$ solution?
b. What is the boiling point of the $CaCl_2$ solution?

ANSWERS

Answers to Study Checks

12.1 78 g of KNO_3

12.2 The solubility of KNO_3 is expected to be higher because the solubility of most solids increases when the temperature increases.

12.3 a. No solid forms.
b. $Ba^{2+}(aq) + SO_4^{2-}(aq) \longrightarrow BaSO_4(s)$

12.4 3.4% (m/m) NaCl solution

12.5 4.8% (v/v) Br_2 in CCl_4

12.6 2.12 M KNO_3 solution

12.7 18.0 g of KCl

12.8 50.2 mL of HCl solution

12.9 125 mL

12.10 90.0 mL of 10.0 M NaOH solution

12.11 1.47 g of Zn

12.12 17.5 mL of a Na_2SO_4 solution

12.13 42.1 L of NO

12.14 1.05 *m*

12.15 $\Delta T_b = 7.6$ °C; boiling point is 107.6 °C

12.16 The red blood cell will undergo crenation.

Answers to Selected Questions and Problems

12.1 **a.** NaCl, solute; water, solvent
b. water, solute; ethanol, solvent
c. oxygen, solute; nitrogen, solvent

12.3 **a.** water **b.** CCl_4 **c.** water **d.** CCl_4

12.5 The polar water molecules pull the K^+ and I^- ions away from the solid and into solution, where they are hydrated.

12.7 In a solution of KF, only the ions of K^+ and F^- are present in the solvent. In an HF solution, there are a few ions of H^+ and F^- present but mostly dissolved HF molecules.

12.9 **a.** $KCl(s) \xrightarrow{H_2O} K^+(aq) + Cl^-(aq)$
b. $CaCl_2(s) \xrightarrow{H_2O} Ca^{2+}(aq) + 2Cl^-(aq)$
c. $K_3PO_4(s) \xrightarrow{H_2O} 3K^+(aq) + PO_4^{3-}(aq)$
d. $Fe(NO_3)_3(s) \xrightarrow{H_2O} Fe^{3+}(aq) + 3NO_3^-(aq)$

12.11 **a.** mostly molecules and a few ions
b. ions only **c.** molecules only

12.13 **a.** strong electrolyte
b. weak electrolyte
c. nonelectrolyte

12.15 **a.** saturated **b.** unsaturated

12.17 **a.** unsaturated **b.** unsaturated
c. saturated

12.19 **a.** 68 g of KCl **b.** 12 g of KCl

12.21 **a.** The solubility of solid solutes typically increases as temperature increases.
b. The solubility of a gas is less at a higher temperature.
c. Gas solubility is less at a higher temperature, and the CO_2 pressure in the can is increased.

12.23 **a.** soluble **b.** insoluble **c.** insoluble
d. soluble **e.** soluble

12.25 **a.** no solid forms
b. $2Ag^+(aq) + S^{2-}(aq) \longrightarrow Ag_2S(s)$
c. $Ca^{2+}(aq) + SO_4^{2-}(aq) \longrightarrow CaSO_4(s)$
d. $3Cu^{2+}(aq) + 2PO_4^{3-}(aq) \longrightarrow Cu_3(PO_4)_2(s)$

12.27 A 5.00% (m/m) glucose solution can be made by adding 5.00 g of glucose to 95.00 g of water, while a 5.00% (m/v) glucose solution can be made by adding 5.00 g of glucose to enough water to make 100.0 mL of solution.

12.29 **a.** 17% (m/m) KCl solution
b. 10.% (m/m) $CaCl_2$ solution
c. 5.3% (m/m) sucrose solution

12.31 **a.** 30.% (m/v) Na_2SO_4 solution
b. 11% (m/v) sucrose solution

12.33 **a.** 0.500 M glucose solution
b. 2.50 M NaCl solution
c. 0.0356 M KOH solution

12.35 **a.** 2.5 g of KCl **b.** 50. g of NH_4Cl
c. 25 mL of acetic acid

12.37 79.9 mL of alcohol

12.39 **a.** 20. g of $LiNO_3$ solution
b. 400. mL of KOH solution
c. 20. mL of formic acid solution

12.41 **a.** 120. g of NaOH **b.** 1.86 g of KCl
c. 3.19 g of HCl

12.43 **a.** 1.50 L of NaOH solution
b. 10.0 L of NaCl solution
c. 62.5. mL of $Ca(NO_3)_2$ solution

12.45 **a.** 983 mL **b.** 1700 mL (1.70×10^3 mL)
c. 464 mL

12.47 **a.** 1.80 M HCl solution **b.** 2.0 M NaOH solution
c. 2.5% (m/v) KOH solution
d. 3.0% (m/v) H_2SO_4 solution

12.49 **a.** 80.0 mL of HCl solution **b.** 250 mL of LiCl solution
c. 600. mL of H_3PO_4 solution
d. 180 mL of glucose solution

12.51 **a.** 12.8 mL of the HNO_3 solution
b. 11.9 mL of the $MgCl_2$ solution
c. 1.88 mL of the KCl solution

12.53 **a.** 10.4 g of $PbCl_2$
b. 18.8 mL of $Pb(NO_3)_2$ solution
c. 1.20 M KCl solution

12.55 **a.** 206 mL of HCl solution **b.** 11.2 L of H_2 gas
c. 9.09 M HCl solution

12.57 **a.** solution
b. suspension

12.59 **a.** 2.0 mol of ethylene glycol in 1.0 kg of water will have a lower freezing point because it has more particles in solution.
b. 0.50 mol of $MgCl_2$ in 2.0 kg of water has a lower freezing point because each formula unit of $MgCl_2$ dissociates in water to give three particles, whereas each formula unit of KCl dissociates to give only two particles.

12.61 **a.** 22.3 *m*
b. 6.89 *m*

12.63 **a.** freezing point: −41.5 °C; boiling point: 111.6 °C
b. freezing point: −12.8 °C; boiling point: 103.6 °C

12.65 **a.** **B**; 10% (m/v) starch solution
b. **B**; 8% (m/v) albumin solution
c. **A**; 10% (m/v) sucrose solution

12.67 **a.** 10% (m/v) starch solution
b. from the 1% (m/v) starch solution into the 10% (m/v) starch solution
c. 10% (m/v) starch solution

12.69 **a.** hypotonic
b. hypotonic
c. isotonic
d. hypertonic

12.71 **a.** **3** (no dissociation)
b. **1** (some dissociation, a few ions)
c. **2** (all ionized)

12.73 **a.** **2**; to halve the % concentration, the volume would double.
b. **3**; to go to one-fourth the % concentration, the volume would be four times the initial volume.

12.75 **a.** beaker **3**
b. $Na^+(aq) + Cl^-(aq) + Ag^+(aq) + NO_3^-(aq) \longrightarrow AgCl(s) + Na^+(aq) + NO_3^-(aq)$
c. $Ag^+(aq) + Cl^-(aq) \longrightarrow AgCl(s)$

12.77 The skin of the cucumber acts like a semipermeable membrane, and water from the more dilute solution inside flows into the more concentrated brine solution.

12.79 **a.** **2** **b.** **1** **c.** **3** **d.** **2**

12.81 Because iodine is a nonpolar molecule, it will dissolve in hexane, a nonpolar solvent. Iodine does not dissolve in water because water is a polar solvent.

12.83 222 g of water

12.85 **a.** unsaturated solution **b.** saturated solution
c. saturated solution

12.87 **a.** insoluble **b.** soluble **c.** insoluble
d. soluble **e.** insoluble **f.** insoluble

12.89 **a.** $Ag^+(aq) + Cl^-(aq) \longrightarrow AgCl(s)$
b. none
c. $Ba^{2+}(aq) + SO_4^{2-}(aq) \longrightarrow BaSO_4(s)$

12.91 17.0% (m/m) Na_2SO_4 solution

12.93 0.50 M NaOH solution

12.95 38 mL of propyl alcohol solution

12.97 **a.** 764 g of KNO_3 **b.** 5.39 g of Na_2SO_4
c. 2.97 g of HCl

12.99 205 mL of LiCl solution

12.101 0.237 L of KNO_3 solution

12.103 60.0 mL of HCl solution

12.105 0.0224 L of CO_2

12.107 **a.** 0.100 M NaBr solution
b. 4.50% (m/v) K_2SO_4 solution
c. 1.76 M NaOH solution

12.109 **a.** 100. mL **b.** 125 mL **c.** 300. mL

12.111 **a.** $2Ag^+(aq) + SO_4^{2-}(aq) \longrightarrow Ag_2SO_4(s)$
b. $Pb^{2+}(aq) + 2Cl^-(aq) \longrightarrow PbCl_2(s)$
c. $3Ca^{2+}(aq) + 2PO_4^{3-}(aq) \longrightarrow Ca_3(PO_4)_2(s)$
d. $Ba^{2+}(aq) + SO_4^{2-}(aq) \longrightarrow BaSO_4(s)$

12.113 **a.** 35.0% (m/m) HNO_3 solution
b. 165 mL
c. 42.4% (m/v) HNO_3 solution
d. 6.73 M HNO_3 solution

12.115 **a.** 11.6% (m/m) NaCl solution
b. 2.40 M NaCl solution
c. 0.400 M NaCl solution

12.117 0.917 M HCl solution

12.119 **a.** 0.60 mol of NaCl
b. 0.30 mol of K_3PO_4

12.121 **a.** 2.0 *m* **b.** −3.7 °C

Reaction Rates and Chemical Equilibrium 13

LOOKING AHEAD

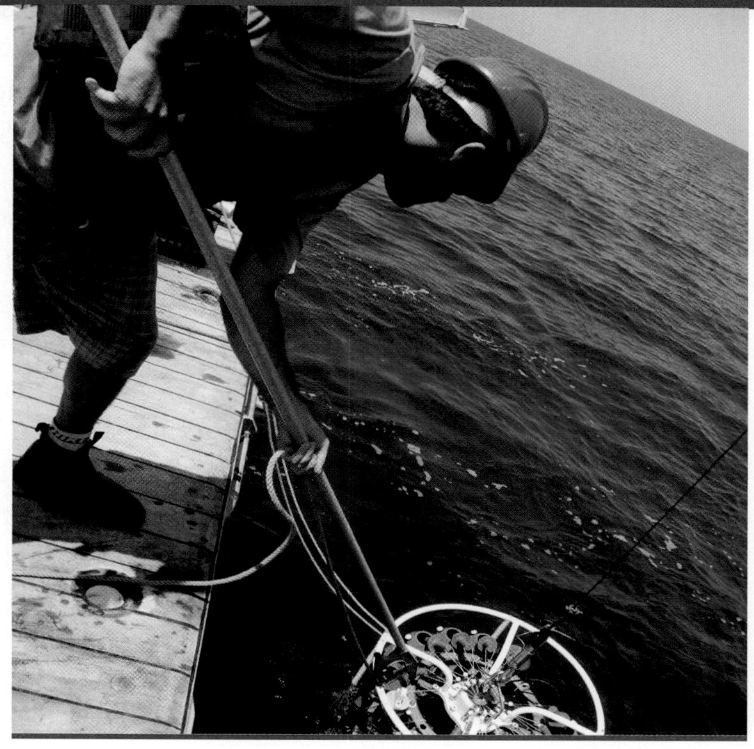

Peter, a chemical oceanographer, is collecting data concerning the amount of dissolved gases, specifically carbon dioxide (CO_2) in the Atlantic Ocean. Studies indicate that CO_2 in the atmosphere has increased as much as 25% since the eighteenth century, which has resulted in a scientific debate regarding its effects. The exact role of the oceans in this debate is currently unknown. Peter's research involves measuring the amount of dissolved CO_2 in the oceans and determining its impact on global conditions such as temperature. The oceans are a complex mixture of many different chemicals including gases, elements and minerals, and organic and particulate matter. As a result, the oceans have been called a "chemical soup," which can complicate a study like Peter's. Peter understands that CO_2 is absorbed in the ocean through a series of equilibrium reactions. An equilibrium reaction is a reversible reaction in which both the products and the reactants are present. If the equilibrium reactions shift according to Le Châtelier's principle, an increase in the CO_2 concentration could eventually increase the amount of dissolved calcium carbonate, $CaCO_3$, which makes up coral reefs and shells. However, Peter must first determine the rate at which CO_2 is absorbed into the seawater and how it affects the amount of $CaCO_3$ in the water to determine if this is occurring.

Career: Chemical Oceanographer

A chemical oceanographer, also called a marine chemist, studies the chemistry of the ocean. One area of study includes how chemicals or pollutants enter into and affect the ocean. These include sewage, oil or fuels, chemical fertilizers, and storm drain overflows. Oceanographers analyze how these chemicals interact with seawater, marine life, and sediments, as they can behave differently due to the ocean's varied environmental conditions. Chemical oceanographers also study how the various elements are cycled within the ocean. For instance, oceanographers quantify the amount and rate at which carbon dioxide is absorbed at the ocean's surface and eventually transferred to deep waters. Chemical oceanographers also aid ocean engineers in the development of instruments and vessels that enable researchers to collect data and discover previously unknown marine life.

Earlier we looked at chemical reactions and determined the amounts of substances that react and the products that form. Now we are interested in how fast a reaction goes. If we know how fast a medication acts on the body, we can adjust the time over which the medication is taken. In construction, substances are added to cement to make it dry faster so that work can continue. Some reactions such as explosions or the formation of precipitates in a solution are very fast. When we roast a turkey or bake a cake, the reaction is slower. Some reactions such as the tarnishing of silver and the aging of the body are much slower (see Figure 13.1). We will see that some reactions need energy while other reactions produce energy. We burn gasoline in our automobile engines to produce energy to make our cars move. In this chapter, we will also look at the effect of changing the concentrations of reactants or products on the rate of reaction.

Up to now, we have considered a reaction as proceeding in a forward direction from reactants to products. However, in many reactions a reverse reaction also takes place as products collide to re-form reactants. When the forward and reverse reactions occur at the same rate, the amounts of reactants and products stay the same. When this balance in the rates of the forward and reverse reactions is reached, we say that the reaction has reached *equilibrium*. At equilibrium, both reactants and products are present. Some reaction mixtures contain mostly reactants and form only a few products, whereas others contain mostly products and a few reactants.

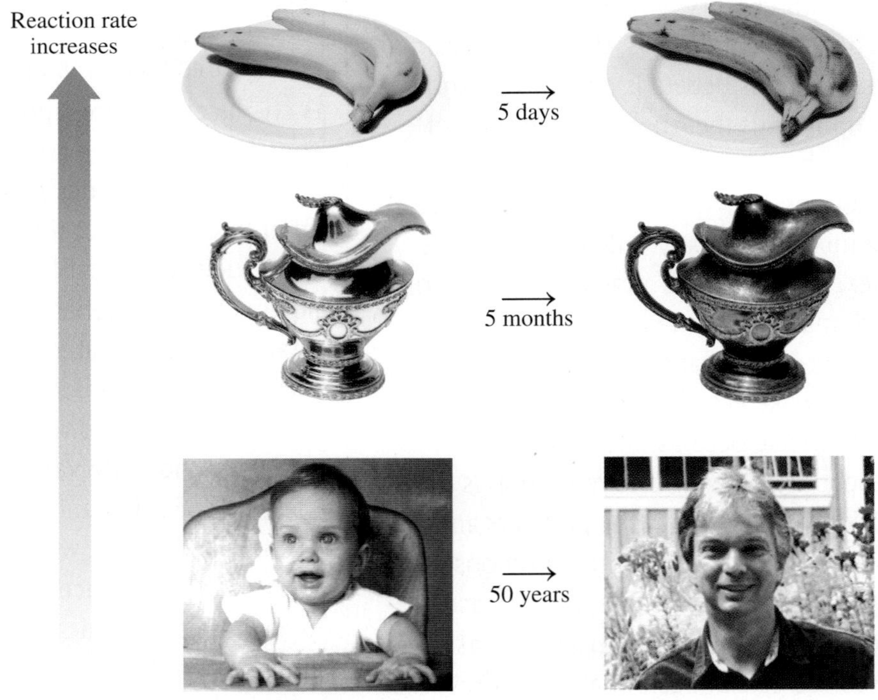

FIGURE 13.1 Reaction rates vary greatly for everyday processes. A banana ripens in a few days, silver tarnishes in a few months, while the aging process of humans takes many years.

Q How would you compare the rates of the reaction that forms sugars in plants by photosynthesis with the reactions that digest sugars in the body?

CHAPTER READINESS*

Key Math Skills

- Solving Equations (1.4D)
- Using Scientific Notation (2.2)

Core Chemistry Skills

- Using Significant Figures in Calculations (2.4)
- Balancing a Chemical Equation (8.2)
- Using Solubility Rules (12.3)
- Calculating Concentration (12.4)

*These Key Math Skills and Core Chemistry Skills from previous chapters are listed here for your review as you proceed to the new material in this chapter.

13.1 Rates of Reactions

LEARNING GOAL

Describe how temperature, concentration, and catalysts affect the rate of a reaction.

For a chemical reaction to take place, the molecules of the reactants must come in contact with each other. The **collision theory** indicates that a reaction takes place only when molecules collide with the proper orientation and sufficient energy. Many collisions can occur, but only a few actually lead to the formation of product. For example, consider the reaction of nitrogen and oxygen molecules (see Figure 13.2). To form nitrogen oxide (NO) product, the collisions between N_2 and O_2 molecules must place the atoms in the proper alignment. If the molecules are not aligned properly, no reaction takes place.

Collision that forms products

Collisions that do not form products

Insufficient energy

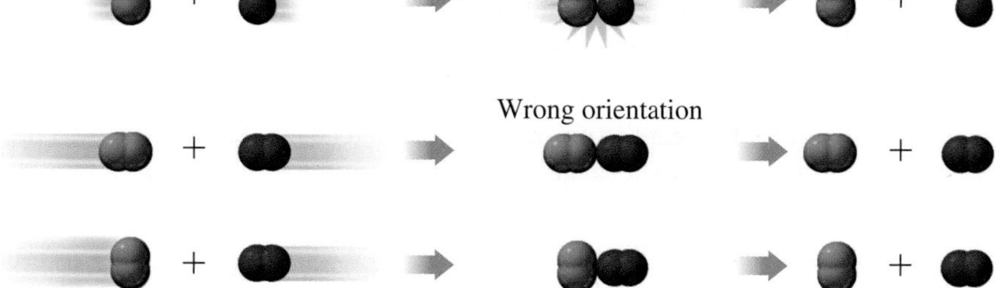

FIGURE 13.2 Reacting molecules must collide, have a minimum amount of energy, and have the proper orientation to form products.

Q What happens when reacting molecules collide with the minimum energy but don't have the proper orientation?

Activation Energy

Even when a collision has the proper orientation, there still must be sufficient energy to break the bonds between the atoms of the reactants. The **activation energy** is the minimum amount of energy required to break the bonds between atoms of the reactants. In Figure 13.3, activation energy appears as an energy hill. The concept of activation energy is analogous to climbing a hill. To reach a destination on the other side, we must have the energy needed to climb to the top of the hill. Once we are at the top, we can run down the other side. The energy needed to get us from our starting point to the top of the hill would be our activation energy.

Energy

N_2 O_2

Reactants

Activation energy

NO NO

Products

Progress of Reaction

FIGURE 13.3 The activation energy is the minimum energy needed to convert the colliding molecules into product.

Q What happens in a collision of reacting molecules that have the proper orientation, but not the energy of activation?

In the same way, a collision must provide enough energy to push the reactants to the top of the energy hill. Then the reactants may be converted to products. If the energy provided by the collision is less than the activation energy, the molecules simply bounce apart and no reaction occurs. The features that lead to a successful reaction are summarized next.

Three Conditions Required for a Reaction to Occur

1. **Collision** The reactants must collide.
2. **Orientation** The reactants must align properly to break and form bonds.
3. **Energy** The collision must provide the energy of activation.

Reaction Rates

The **rate** (or speed) **of reaction** is determined by measuring the amount of a reactant used up, or the amount of a product formed, in a certain period of time.

$$\text{Rate of reaction} = \frac{\text{change in concentration of reactant or product}}{\text{change in time}}$$

Perhaps we can describe the rate of reaction with the analogy of eating a pizza. When we start to eat, we have a whole pizza. As time goes by, there are fewer slices of pizza left. If we know how long it took to eat the pizza, we could determine the rate at which the pizza was consumed. Let's assume 4 slices are eaten every 8 minutes. That gives a rate of $\frac{1}{2}$ slice per minute. After 16 min, all 8 slices are gone.

Rate at Which Pizza Slices Are Eaten

Slices Eaten	0	4 slices	6 slices	8 slices
Time (min)	0	8 min	12 min	16 min

$$\text{Rate} = \frac{4\text{ slices}}{8\text{ min}} = \frac{1\text{ slice}}{2\text{ min}} = \frac{\frac{1}{2}\text{ slice}}{1\text{ min}}$$

Factors That Affect the Rate of a Reaction

Some reactions go very fast, while others are very slow. For any reaction, the rate is affected by changes in temperature and in the concentration of the reactants, and by the addition of catalysts.

Temperature

At higher temperatures, the increase in kinetic energy makes the reacting molecules move faster. As a result, more collisions occur and more colliding molecules have sufficient energy to react and form products. If we want food to cook faster, we use more heat to raise the temperature. When body temperature rises, the pulse rate, rate of breathing, and metabolic rate all increase. On the other hand, we slow down reactions by lowering the temperature. We refrigerate perishable foods to retard spoilage and make them last longer. For some injuries, we apply ice to lessen the bruising process.

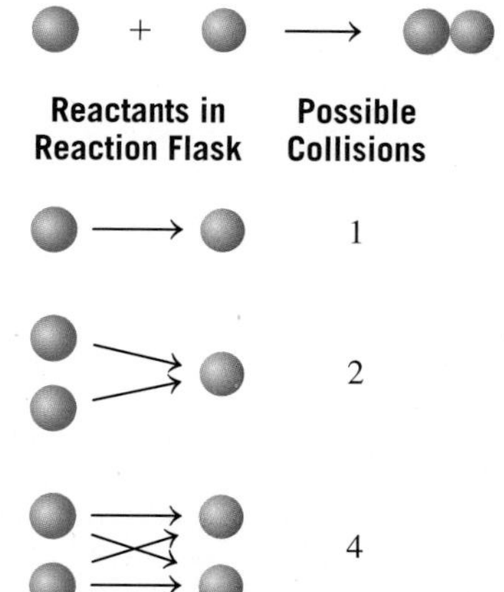

FIGURE 13.4 Increasing the concentration of a reactant increases the number of collisions that are possible.

Q Why does doubling the reactants increase the rate of reaction?

Concentrations of Reactants

For virtually all reactions, the rate of a reaction increases when the concentration of the reactants increases. When there are more reacting molecules, more collisions that form products can occur, and the reaction goes faster (see Figure 13.4). For example, a person having difficulty breathing may be given oxygen. The increase in the number of oxygen molecules in the lungs increases the rate at which oxygen combines with hemoglobin and helps the person breathe more easily.

Catalysts

Another way to speed up a reaction is to lower the energy of activation. The energy of activation is the minimum energy needed to break apart the bonds of the reacting molecules. If a collision provides less than the activation energy, the bonds do not break and the reactant molecules bounce apart. A **catalyst** speeds up a reaction by providing an alternative pathway that has a lower energy of activation. When activation energy is lowered, more collisions provide sufficient energy for reactants to form product. During a reaction, a catalyst is not changed or consumed.

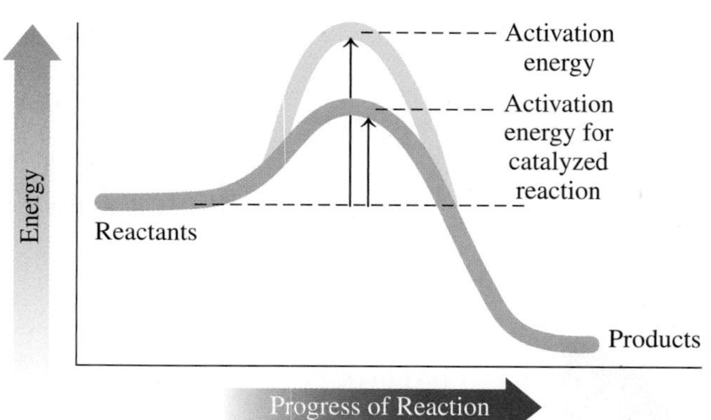

When a catalyst lowers the activation energy, the reaction occurs at a faster rate.

Catalysts have many uses in industry. In the manufacturing of margarine, hydrogen (H_2) is added to vegetable oils. Normally, the reaction is very slow because it has a high activation energy. However, when platinum (Pt) is used as a catalyst, the reaction occurs rapidly. In the body, biocatalysts called enzymes make most metabolic reactions proceed at rates necessary for proper cellular activity. Enzymes are added to laundry detergents to break down proteins (proteases), starches (amylases), or greases (lipases) that have stained clothes. Such enzymes function at the low temperatures that are used in home washing machines, and they are biodegradable as well.

The factors affecting reaction rates are summarized in Table 13.1.

TABLE 13.1 Factors That Increase Reaction Rate

Factor	Reason
Increasing reactant concentration	More collisions
Increasing temperature	More collisions, more collisions with energy of activation
Adding a catalyst	Lowers energy of activation

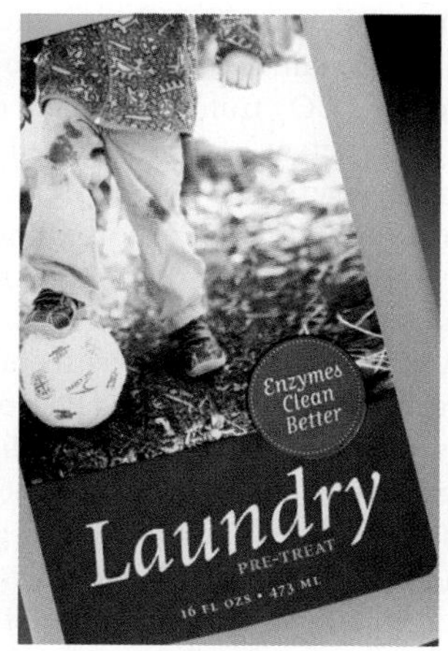

Enzymes in laundry detergent catalyze the removal of stains at low temperatures.

CONCEPT CHECK 13.1 Rate of Reactions

Will a decrease in the concentration of a reactant cause an increase or a decrease in the rate of a reaction? Explain.

ANSWER

When the concentration of a reactant is decreased, there are fewer collisions between the reactant molecules, which decreases the rate of reaction.

SAMPLE PROBLEM 13.1 Factors That Affect the Rate of Reaction

Indicate whether the following changes will increase, decrease, or have no effect on the rate of reaction:

a. increasing the temperature
b. increasing the number of reacting molecules
c. adding a catalyst

SOLUTION

a. A higher temperature increases the kinetic energy of the particles, which increases the number of collisions and makes more collisions effective, causing an increase in the rate of reaction.
b. Increasing the number of reacting molecules increases the number of collisions and the rate of the reaction.
c. Adding a catalyst increases the rate of reaction by lowering the activation energy, which increases the number of collisions that form product.

STUDY CHECK 13.1

How does the lowering of temperature affect the rate of reaction?

Chemistry Link to the Environment

CATALYTIC CONVERTERS

For over 30 years, manufacturers have been required to include catalytic converters in the exhaust systems of gasoline automobile engines. When gasoline burns, the products found in the exhaust of a car contain high levels of pollutants. These include carbon monoxide (CO) from incomplete combustion, hydrocarbons such as C_8H_{18} (octane) from unburned fuel, and nitrogen oxide (NO) from the reaction of N_2 and O_2 at the high temperatures reached within the engine. Carbon monoxide is toxic, and unburned hydrocarbons and nitrogen oxide are involved in the formation of smog and acid rain.

A catalytic converter consists of solid-particle catalysts, such as platinum (Pt) and palladium (Pd), on a ceramic honeycomb that provides a large surface area and facilitates contact with pollutants. As the pollutants pass through the converter, they react with the catalysts. Today, we all use unleaded gasoline because lead interferes with the ability of the Pt and Pd catalysts in the converter to react with the pollutants. The purpose of a catalytic converter is to lower the activation energy for reactions that convert each of these pollutants into substances such as CO_2, N_2, O_2, and H_2O, which are already present in the atmosphere.

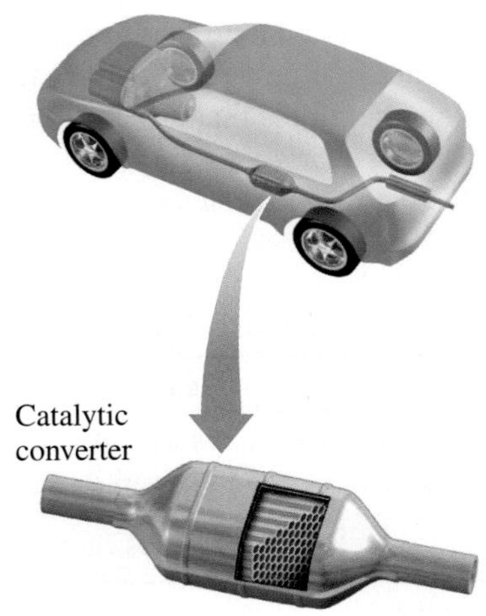

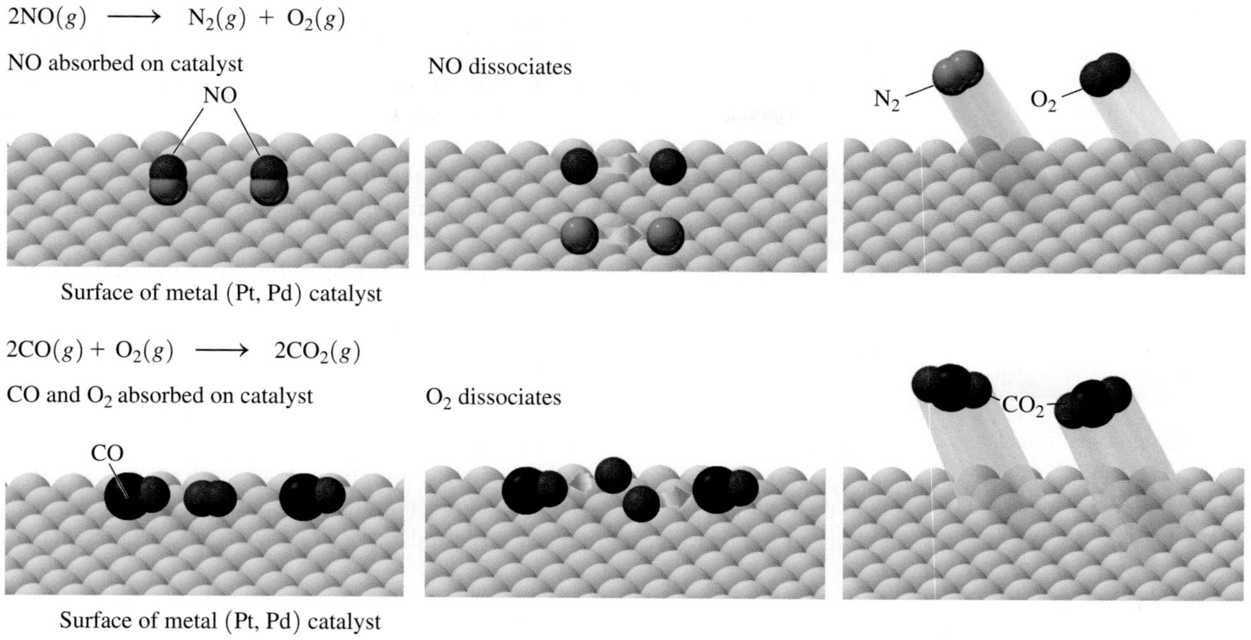

$2NO(g) \longrightarrow N_2(g) + O_2(g)$

NO absorbed on catalyst

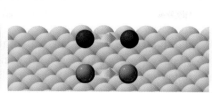

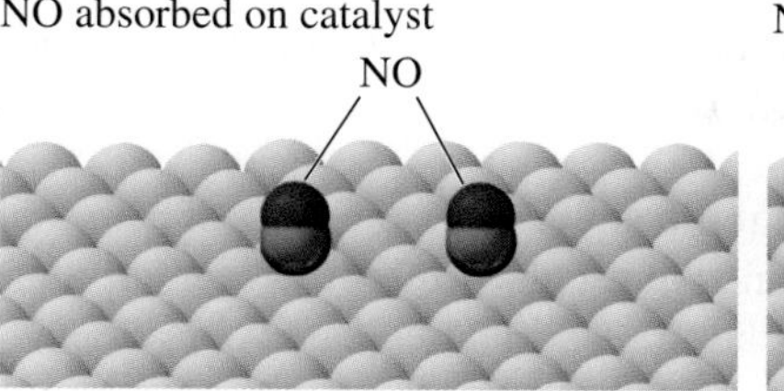

NO dissociates

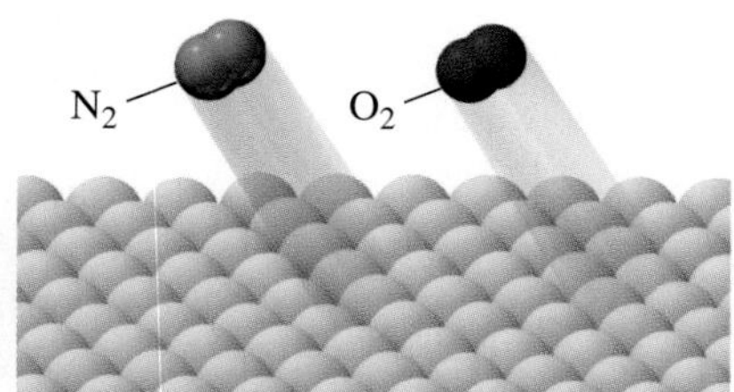

Surface of metal (Pt, Pd) catalyst

$2CO(g) + O_2(g) \longrightarrow 2CO_2(g)$

CO and O_2 absorbed on catalyst

O_2 dissociates

Surface of metal (Pt, Pd) catalyst

QUESTIONS AND PROBLEMS

13.1 Rates of Reactions

LEARNING GOAL: *Describe how temperature, concentration, and catalysts affect the rate of a reaction.*

13.1 **a.** What is meant by the rate of a reaction?
b. Why does bread grow mold more quickly at room temperature than in the refrigerator?

13.2 **a.** How does a catalyst affect the activation energy?
b. Why is pure oxygen used in respiratory distress?

13.3 In the following reaction, what happens to the number of collisions when more $Br_2(g)$ molecules are added?

$$H_2(g) + Br_2(g) \longrightarrow 2HBr(g)$$

13.4 In the following reaction, what happens to the number of collisions when the temperature of the reaction is decreased?

$$2H_2(g) + CO(g) \longrightarrow CH_3OH(g)$$

13.5 How would each of the following changes affect the rate of the reaction shown here?

$$2SO_2(g) + O_2(g) \longrightarrow 2SO_3(g)$$

a. add some $SO_2(g)$
b. raise the temperature
c. add a catalyst
d. remove some $O_2(g)$

13.6 How would each of the following changes affect the rate of the reaction shown here?

$$2NO(g) + 2H_2(g) \longrightarrow N_2(g) + 2H_2O(g)$$

a. add some $NO(g)$
b. lower the temperature
c. remove some $H_2(g)$
d. add a catalyst

13.2 Chemical Equilibrium

LEARNING GOAL

Use the concept of reversible reactions to explain chemical equilibrium.

In earlier chapters, we considered the *forward reaction* in an equation and assumed that all of the reactants were converted to products. However, most of the time reactants are not completely converted to products because a *reverse reaction* takes place in which products collide to form the reactants. When a reaction proceeds in both a forward and reverse direction, it is said to be reversible. We have looked at other reversible processes. For example, the melting of solids to form liquids and the freezing of liquids to solids is a reversible physical change. Even in our daily life we have reversible events. We go from home to school and we return from school to home. We go up an escalator and we come back down. We put money in our bank account and we take money out.

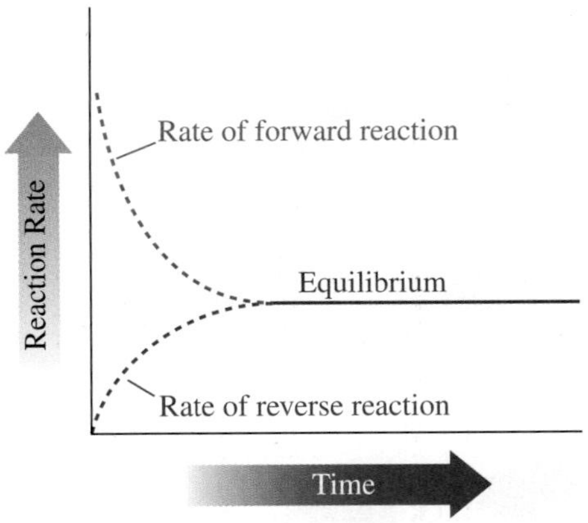

As a reaction progresses, the rate of the forward reaction decreases and that of the reverse reaction increases until they become equal.

An analogy for a forward and reverse reaction can be found in the phrase "We are going to the grocery store." Although we mention our trip in one direction, we know that we will also return home from the store. Because our trip has both a forward and reverse direction, we can say the trip is reversible. It is not very likely that we would stay at the store forever.

A trip to the grocery store can be used to illustrate another aspect of reversible reactions. Perhaps the grocery store is nearby and we usually walk. However, we can change our rate. Suppose that one day we drive to the store, which increases our rate and gets us to the store faster. Correspondingly, a car also increases the rate at which we return home.

Reversible Chemical Reactions

A **reversible reaction** proceeds in both the forward and reverse direction. That means there are two reaction rates: one is the rate of the forward reaction, and the other is the rate of the reverse reaction. When molecules begin to react, the rate of the forward reaction is faster than the rate of the reverse reaction. As reactants are consumed and products accumulate, the rate of the forward reaction decreases and the rate of the reverse reaction increases.

SAMPLE PROBLEM 13.2 Reversible Reactions

Write the forward and reverse reactions for each of the following:

a. $N_2(g) + 3H_2(g) \rightleftarrows 2NH_3(g)$
b. $2CO(g) + O_2(g) \rightleftarrows 2CO_2(g)$

SOLUTION

The equations are separated into forward and reverse reactions.

a. Forward reaction: $N_2(g) + 3H_2(g) \longrightarrow 2NH_3(g)$
Reverse reaction: $2NH_3(g) \longrightarrow N_2(g) + 3H_2(g)$

b. Forward reaction: $2CO(g) + O_2(g) \longrightarrow 2CO_2(g)$
Reverse reaction: $2CO_2(g) \longrightarrow 2CO(g) + O_2(g)$

STUDY CHECK 13.2

Write the equilibrium equation for the reaction that contains the following reverse reaction:

$2HBr(g) \longrightarrow H_2(g) + Br_2(g)$

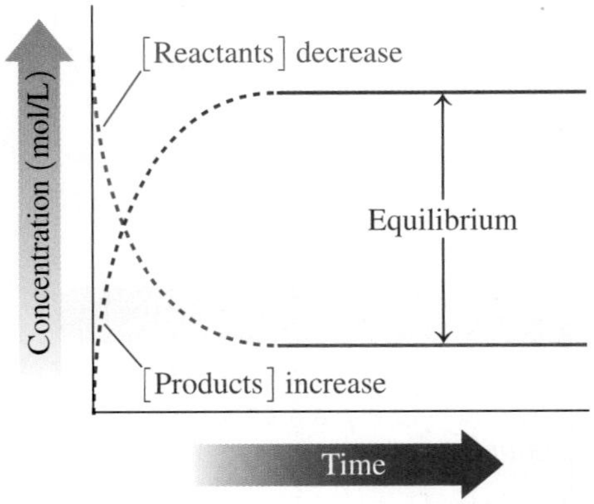

Equilibrium is reached when there are no further changes in the concentrations of reactants and products.

Equilibrium

Eventually, the rates of the forward and reverse reactions become equal; the reactants form products at the same rate that the products form reactants. A reaction reaches **chemical equilibrium** when no further change takes place in the concentrations of the reactants and products, even though the two reactions continue at equal but opposite rates.

At Equilibrium:

The rate of the forward reaction is equal to the rate of the reverse reaction.

No further changes occur in the concentrations of reactants and products, even though the two reactions continue at equal but opposite rates.

Let us look at the process as the reaction of H_2 and I_2 proceeds to equilibrium. Initially, only the reactants H_2 and I_2 are present. Soon, a few molecules of HI are produced by the forward reaction. With more time, additional HI molecules are produced. As the concentration of HI increases, more HI molecules collide and react in the reverse direction (see Figure 13.5).

$$\text{Forward reaction: } H_2(g) + I_2(g) \longrightarrow 2HI(g)$$
$$\text{Reverse reaction: } 2HI(g) \longrightarrow H_2(g) + I_2(g)$$

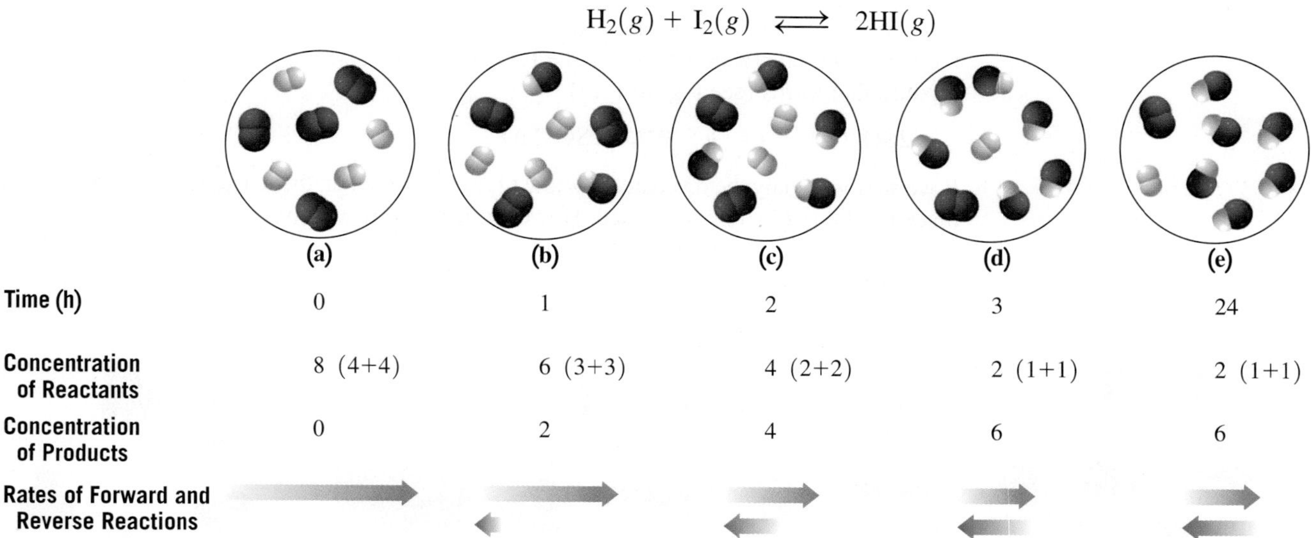

FIGURE 13.5 **(a)** Initially, the reaction flask contains only the reactants H_2 (white) and I_2 (purple). **(b)** The forward reaction between H_2 and I_2 begins to produce HI. **(c)** As the reaction proceeds, there are fewer molecules of H_2 and I_2 and more molecules of HI, which increases the rate of the reverse reaction. **(d)** At equilibrium, the concentrations of reactants H_2 and I_2 and product HI are constant. **(e)** The reaction continues with the rate of the forward reaction equal to the rate of the reverse reaction.

Q How do the rates of the forward and reverse reactions compare once a chemical reaction reaches equilibrium?

As HI product builds up, the rate of the reverse reaction increases, while the rate of the forward reaction decreases. Eventually, the rates become equal, which means the reaction has reached equilibrium. Even though the concentrations remain constant at equilibrium, the forward and reverse reactions continue to occur. The forward and reverse reactions are usually shown together in a single equation by using a double arrow. A reversible reaction is two opposing reactions that occur at the same time.

$$H_2(g) + I_2(g) \underset{\text{Reverse reaction}}{\overset{\text{Forward reaction}}{\rightleftarrows}} 2HI(g)$$

CONCEPT CHECK 13.2 Reaction Rates and Equilibrium

Complete each of the following with *equal* or *not equal*, *faster* or *slower*, *change* or *do not change*:

a. Before equilibrium is reached, the concentrations of the reactants and products ________.

b. Initially, reactants placed in a container have a ________ rate of reaction than the rate of reaction of the products.

c. At equilibrium, the rate of the forward reaction is ________ to the rate of the reverse reaction.

d. At equilibrium, the concentrations of the reactants and products ________.

ANSWER

a. Before equilibrium is reached, the concentrations of the reactants and products *change*.
b. Initially, reactants placed in a container have a *faster* rate of reaction than the rate of reaction of the products.
c. At equilibrium, the rate of the forward reaction is *equal* to the rate of the reverse reaction.
d. At equilibrium, the concentrations of the reactants and products *do not change*.

We can also set up a reaction starting with only reactants or with only products. Let's look at the initial reactions in each, the forward and reverse reactions, and the equilibrium mixture that forms (see Figure 13.6).

$$2SO_2(g) + O_2(g) \rightleftharpoons 2SO_3(g)$$

If we start with only the reactants SO_2 and O_2 in the container, the reaction to form SO_3 takes place until equilibrium is reached. However, if we start with only the product SO_3 in the container, the reaction to form SO_2 and O_2 takes place until equilibrium is reached. In both containers, the equilibrium mixture contains the same concentrations of SO_2, O_2, and SO_3.

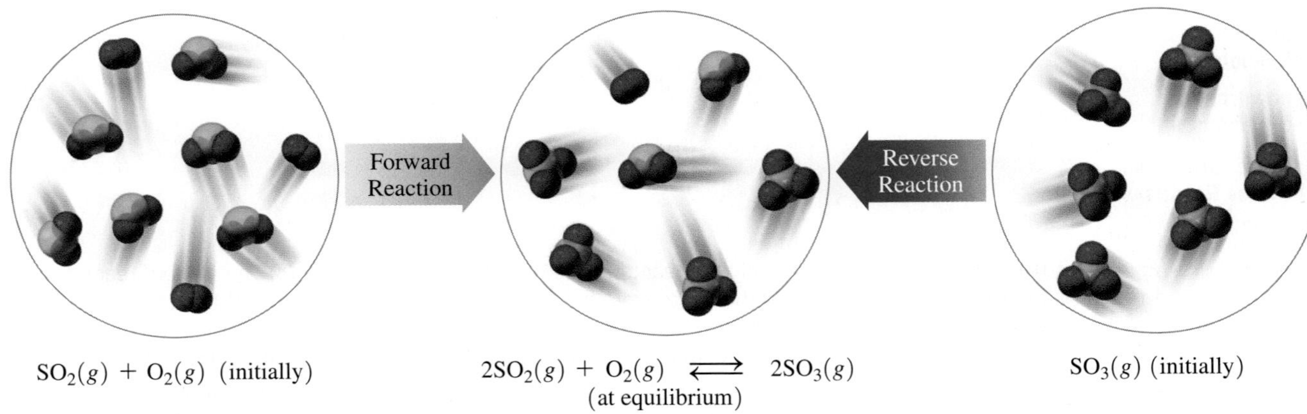

$SO_2(g) + O_2(g)$ (initially) $2SO_2(g) + O_2(g) \rightleftharpoons 2SO_3(g)$ (at equilibrium) $SO_3(g)$ (initially)

FIGURE 13.6 One sample initially contains $SO_2(g)$ and $O_2(g)$, while another sample contains only $SO_3(g)$. At equilibrium, mostly $SO_3(g)$ and only small amounts of $SO_2(g)$ and $O_2(g)$, are present in the equilibrium mixture.

Q Why is the same equilibrium mixture obtained from $SO_2(g)$ and $O_2(g)$ as from $SO_3(g)$?

QUESTIONS AND PROBLEMS

13.2 Chemical Equilibrium

LEARNING GOAL: *Use the concept of reversible reactions to explain chemical equilibrium.*

13.7 What is meant by the term *reversible reaction*?

13.8 When does a reversible reaction reach equilibrium?

13.9 Which of the following are at equilibrium?
a. The rate of the forward reaction is twice as fast as the rate of the reverse reaction.
b. The concentrations of the reactants and the products do not change.
c. The rate of the reverse reaction does not change.

13.10 Which of the following are not at equilibrium?
a. The rates of the forward and reverse reactions are equal.
b. The rate of the forward reaction does not change.
c. The concentrations of reactants and the products are not constant.

LEARNING GOAL

Calculate the equilibrium constant for a reversible reaction given the concentrations of reactants and products at equilibrium.

13.3 Equilibrium Constants

At equilibrium, the concentrations of the reactants and products are constant. We can use a ski lift as an analogy. Early in the morning, skiers at the bottom of the mountain begin to ride the ski lift up to the slopes. After the skiers reach the top of the mountain, they ski down. Eventually, the number of people riding up the ski lift becomes equal to the number of people skiing down the mountain. There is no further change in the number of skiers on the slopes; the system is at equilibrium.

At equilibrium, the number of people riding the lift and the number of people skiing on the slope are constant.

Equilibrium Constant Expression

At equilibrium, the concentrations can be used to set up a relationship between the products and the reactants. Suppose we write a general equation for reactants A and B that form products C and D. The small italic letters are the coefficients in the balanced equation.

$$aA + bB \rightleftarrows cC + dD$$

An **equilibrium constant expression** for a reversible chemical reaction multiplies the concentrations of the products together and divides by the concentrations of the reactants. Each concentration is raised to a power that is equal to its coefficient in the balanced chemical equation. The square bracket around each substance indicates that the concentration is expressed in moles per liter (M). For our general reaction, this is written as:

CORE CHEMISTRY SKILL 

Writing the Equilibrium Constant Expression

$$K_c = \frac{[\text{Products}]}{[\text{Reactants}]} = \frac{[C]^c[D]^d}{[A]^a[B]^b}$$

Coefficients

Equilibrium constant expression

We can now describe how to write the equilibrium constant expression for the reaction of H_2 and I_2 that forms HI. First, we need to write the balanced chemical equation with a double arrow between the reactants and the products.

$$H_2(g) + I_2(g) \rightleftarrows 2HI(g)$$

Second, we show the concentration of the products using brackets in the numerator and the concentrations of the reactants in brackets in the denominator.

$$\frac{\text{Products}}{\text{Reactants}} \longrightarrow \frac{[HI]}{[H_2][I_2]}$$

Finally, we write any coefficient in the balanced chemical equation as an exponent of its concentration (the coefficient 1 is understood) and set it equal to K_c.

$$K_c = \frac{[HI]^2}{[H_2][I_2]}$$

CONCEPT CHECK 13.3 The Equilibrium Constant Expression

Select the correctly written equilibrium constant expression for the following reaction, and explain your choice:

$$CH_4(g) + H_2O(g) \rightleftarrows CO(g) + 3H_2(g)$$

a. $K_c = \frac{[CO][3H_2]}{[CH_4][H_2O]}$ **b.** $K_c = \frac{[CO][H_2]^3}{[CH_4][H_2O]}$

c. $K_c = \frac{[CH_4][H_2O]}{[CO][H_2]^3}$ **d.** $K_c = \frac{[CO][H_2]}{[CH_4][H_2O]}$

ANSWER

The correct equilibrium constant expression is **b**. The products are written in the numerator and the reactants are written in the denominator. Because H_2 has a coefficient of 3 in the balanced equation, an exponent of 3 is used with the concentration of H_2.

Guide to Writing the Equilibrium Constant Expression

1. Write the balanced chemical equation.
2. Write the concentrations of the products as the numerator and the reactants as the denominator.
3. Write any coefficient in the equation as an exponent.

SAMPLE PROBLEM 13.3 Writing Equilibrium Constant Expressions

Write the equilibrium constant expression for the following reaction:

$$2SO_2(g) + O_2(g) \rightleftarrows 2SO_3(g)$$

SOLUTION

Step 1 **Write the balanced chemical equation.**

$$2SO_2(g) + O_2(g) \rightleftarrows 2SO_3(g)$$

Step 2 **Write the concentrations of the products as the numerator and the reactants as the denominator.**

$$\frac{[\text{Products}]}{[\text{Reactants}]} \longrightarrow \frac{[SO_3]}{[SO_2][O_2]}$$

Step 3 **Write any coefficient in the equation as an exponent.**

$$K_c = \frac{[SO_3]^2}{[SO_2]^2[O_2]}$$

STUDY CHECK 13.3

Write the balanced chemical equation that would give the following equilibrium constant expression:

$$K_c = \frac{[NO_2]^2}{[NO]^2[O_2]}$$

$$CaCO_3(s) \rightleftarrows CaO(s) + CO_2(g)$$

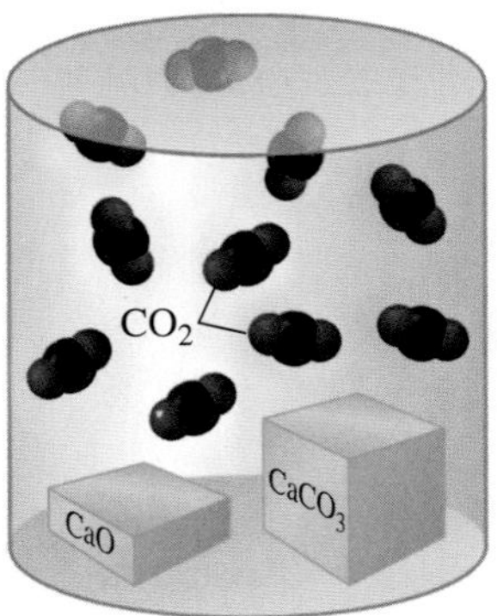

$T = 800\ ^\circ C$

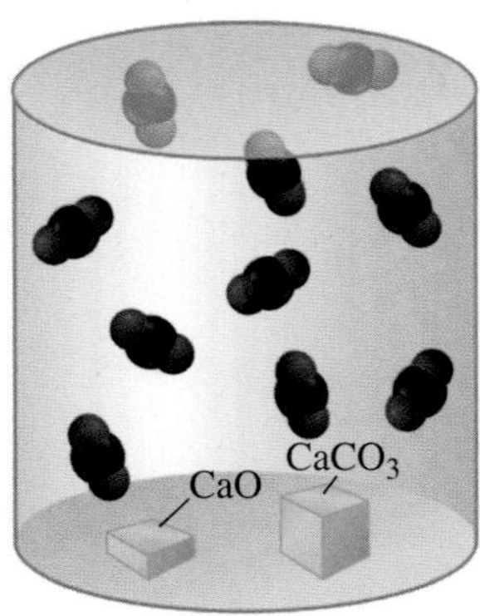

$T = 800\ ^\circ C$

FIGURE 13.7 At equilibrium at constant temperature, the concentration of CO_2 is the same regardless of the amounts of $CaCO_3(s)$ and $CaO(s)$ in the container.

Q Why are the concentrations of $CaO(s)$ and $CaCO_3(s)$ not included in K_c for the decomposition of $CaCO_3(s)$?

Heterogeneous Equilibrium

Up to now, our examples have been reactions that involve only gases. A reaction in which all the reactants and products are in the same state reaches **homogeneous equilibrium**. When the reactants and products are in two or more states, the equilibrium is termed a **heterogeneous equilibrium**. In the following reaction, solid calcium carbonate reaches heterogeneous equilibrium with solid calcium oxide and carbon dioxide gas (see Figure 13.7).

$$CaCO_3(s) \rightleftarrows CaO(s) + CO_2(g)$$

In contrast to gases, the concentrations of pure solids and pure liquids are constant; they do not change. Therefore, pure solids and liquids are not included in the equilibrium constant expression. For this heterogeneous equilibrium, the K_c expression does not include the concentration of $CaCO_3(s)$ or $CaO(s)$. It is written as $K_c = [CO_2]$.

CONCEPT CHECK 13.4 Equilibrium Constant Expression for a Heterogeneous Equilibrium

Select the correctly written equilibrium constant expression for the following reaction:

$$CO(g) + 2H_2(g) \rightleftarrows CH_3OH(l)$$

a. $\frac{[CH_3OH]}{[CO][H_2]^2}$ **b.** $[CO][H_2]^2$ **c.** $\frac{1}{[CO][H_2]^2}$

ANSWER

In a heterogeneous equilibrium, only the gases are included in the equilibrium constant expression. The concentration of the liquid CH_3OH remains constant; it is not included in the equilibrium constant expression. Therefore, the correct answer **c** gives the concentrations of the gases, CO and H_2, in the denominator.

SAMPLE PROBLEM 13.4 Heterogeneous Equilibrium Constant Expression

Write the equilibrium constant expression for the following reaction at equilibrium:

$$4HCl(g) + O_2(g) \rightleftharpoons 2H_2O(l) + 2Cl_2(g)$$

SOLUTION

Step 1 **Write the balanced chemical equation.**

$$4HCl(g) + O_2(g) \rightleftharpoons 2H_2O(l) + 2Cl_2(g)$$

Step 2 **Write the concentrations of the products as the numerator and the reactants as the denominator.** In this heterogeneous reaction, the concentration of the liquid H_2O is not included in the equilibrium constant expression.

$$\frac{\text{Products}}{\text{Reactants}} \begin{matrix} \longrightarrow \\ \longrightarrow \end{matrix} \frac{[Cl_2]}{[HCl][O_2]}$$

Step 3 **Write any coefficient in the equation as an exponent.**

$$K_c = \frac{[Cl_2]^2}{[HCl]^4[O_2]}$$

STUDY CHECK 13.4

Solid iron(II) oxide and carbon monoxide gas react to produce solid iron and carbon dioxide gas. Write the balanced chemical equation and the equilibrium constant expression for this reaction at equilibrium.

Calculating Equilibrium Constants

CORE CHEMISTRY SKILL 

Calculating an Equilibrium Constant

The **equilibrium constant, K_c,** is the numerical value obtained by substituting experimentally measured molar concentrations at equilibrium into the equilibrium constant expression. For example, the equilibrium constant expression for the reaction of H_2 and I_2 is written

$$H_2(g) + I_2(g) \rightleftharpoons 2HI(g) \qquad K_c = \frac{[HI]^2}{[H_2][I_2]}$$

In the first experiment, the molar concentrations for the reactants and products at equilibrium are found to be $[H_2] = 0.10$ M, $[I_2] = 0.20$ M, and $[HI] = 1.04$ M. When we substitute these values into the equilibrium constant expression, we obtain its numerical value.

In additional experiments 2 and 3, the mixtures have different equilibrium concentrations for the system at equilibrium at the same temperature. However, when these concentrations are used to calculate the equilibrium constant, we obtain the same value of K_c for each (see Table 13.2). *Thus, a reaction at a specific temperature can have only one value for the equilibrium constant.*

TABLE 13.2 Equilibrium Constant for $H_2(g) + I_2(g) \rightleftharpoons 2HI(g)$ at 427 °C

Experiment	Concentrations at Equilibrium			Equilibrium Constant
	$[H_2]$	$[I_2]$	$[HI]$	$K_c = \frac{[HI]^2}{[H_2][I_2]}$
1	0.10 M	0.20 M	1.04 M	$K_c = \frac{[1.04]^2}{[0.10][0.20]} = 54$
2	0.20 M	0.20 M	1.47 M	$K_c = \frac{[1.47]^2}{[0.20][0.20]} = 54$
3	0.30 M	0.17 M	1.66 M	$K_c = \frac{[1.66]^2}{[0.30][0.17]} = 54$

The units of K_c depend on the specific equation. In this example, the units of $[M]^2/[M]^2$ cancel out to give a value of 54. In other equations, the concentration units do not cancel. However, in this text, the numerical value will be given without any units as shown in Sample Problem 13.5.

Guide to Calculating the K_c Value

1. State the given and needed quantities.
2. Write the K_c expression for the equilibrium.
3. Substitute equilibrium (molar) concentrations and calculate K_c.

SAMPLE PROBLEM 13.5 Calculating an Equilibrium Constant

The decomposition of dinitrogen tetroxide forms nitrogen dioxide.

$$N_2O_4(g) \rightleftharpoons 2NO_2(g)$$

What is the numerical value of K_c at 100 °C if a reaction mixture at equilibrium contains 0.45 M N_2O_4 and 0.31 M NO_2?

SOLUTION

Step 1 State the given and needed quantities.

Analyze the Problem	Given		Need
	Reactant	Product	
	0.45 M N_2O_4	0.31 M NO_2	K_c
	Equation		
	$N_2O_4(g) \rightleftharpoons 2NO_2(g)$		

Step 2 Write the K_c expression for the equilibrium.

$$K_c = \frac{[NO_2]^2}{[N_2O_4]}$$

Step 3 Substitute equilibrium (molar) concentrations and calculate K_c.

$$K_c = \frac{[0.31]^2}{[0.45]} = 0.21$$

STUDY CHECK 13.5

Calculate the numerical value of K_c if an equilibrium mixture contains 0.040 M NH_3, 0.60 M H_2, and 0.20 M N_2.

$$2NH_3(g) \rightleftharpoons 3H_2(g) + N_2(g)$$

QUESTIONS AND PROBLEMS

13.3 Equilibrium Constants

LEARNING GOAL: *Calculate the equilibrium constant for a reversible reaction given the concentrations of reactants and products at equilibrium.*

13.11 Write the equilibrium constant expression for each of the following reactions:

a. $CH_4(g) + 2H_2S(g) \rightleftharpoons CS_2(g) + 4H_2(g)$
b. $2NO(g) \rightleftharpoons N_2(g) + O_2(g)$
c. $2SO_3(g) + CO_2(g) \rightleftharpoons CS_2(g) + 4O_2(g)$

13.12 Write the equilibrium constant expression for each of the following reactions:

a. $2HBr(g) \rightleftharpoons H_2(g) + Br_2(g)$
b. $2BrNO(g) \rightleftharpoons Br_2(g) + 2NO(g)$
c. $CH_4(g) + Cl_2(g) \rightleftharpoons CH_3Cl(g) + HCl(g)$

13.13 Identify each of the following as a homogeneous or heterogeneous equilibrium:

a. $2O_3(g) \rightleftharpoons 3O_2(g)$
b. $2NaHCO_3(s) \rightleftharpoons Na_2CO_3(s) + CO_2(g) + H_2O(g)$
c. $CH_4(g) + H_2O(g) \rightleftharpoons 3H_2(g) + CO(g)$
d. $4HCl(g) + Si(s) \rightleftharpoons SiCl_4(l) + 2H_2(g)$

13.14 Identify each of the following as a homogeneous or heterogeneous equilibrium:

a. $CO(g) + H_2(g) \rightleftharpoons C(s) + H_2O(g)$
b. $NH_4Cl(s) \rightleftharpoons NH_3(g) + HCl(g)$
c. $CS_2(g) + 4H_2(g) \rightleftharpoons CH_4(g) + 2H_2S(g)$
d. $Br_2(g) + Cl_2(g) \rightleftharpoons 2BrCl(g)$

13.15 Write the equilibrium constant expression for each of the reactions in Problem 13.13.

13.16 Write the equilibrium constant expression for each of the reactions in Problem 13.14.

13.17 What is the numerical value of K_c for the following reaction if the equilibrium mixture contains 0.030 M N_2O_4 and 0.21 M NO_2?

$$N_2O_4(g) \rightleftarrows 2NO_2(g)$$

13.18 What is the numerical value of K_c for the following reaction if the equilibrium mixture contains 0.30 M CO_2, 0.033 M H_2, 0.20 M CO, and 0.30 M H_2O?

$$CO_2(g) + H_2(g) \rightleftarrows CO(g) + H_2O(g)$$

13.19 What is the numerical value of K_c for the following reaction if the equilibrium mixture contains 0.51 M CO, 0.30 M H_2, 1.8 M CH_4, and 2.0 M H_2O?

$$CO(g) + 3H_2(g) \rightleftarrows CH_4(g) + H_2O(g)$$

13.20 What is the numerical value of K_c for the following reaction if the equilibrium mixture contains 0.44 M N_2, 0.40 M H_2, and 2.2 M NH_3?

$$N_2(g) + 3H_2(g) \rightleftarrows 2NH_3(g)$$

13.21 What is the numerical value of K_c for the following reaction if the equilibrium mixture at 750 °C contains 0.20 M CO and 0.052 M CO_2?

$$FeO(s) + CO(g) \rightleftarrows Fe(s) + CO_2(g)$$

13.22 What is the numerical value of K_c for the following reaction if the equilibrium mixture at 800 °C contains 0.030 M CO_2?

$$CaCO_3(s) \rightleftarrows CaO(s) + CO_2(g)$$

13.4 Using Equilibrium Constants

LEARNING GOAL

Use an equilibrium constant to predict the extent of reaction and to calculate equilibrium concentrations.

The values of K_c can be large or small. The size of the equilibrium constant depends on whether equilibrium is reached with more products than reactants, or more reactants than products. However, the size of an equilibrium constant does not affect how fast equilibrium is reached.

Equilibrium with a Large K_c

When a reaction has a large equilibrium constant, it means that the forward reaction produced a large amount of products when equilibrium was reached. Then the equilibrium mixture contains mostly products, which makes the concentrations of the products in the numerator higher than the concentrations of the reactants in the denominator. Thus at equilibrium, this reaction has a large K_c. Consider the reaction of SO_2 and O_2, which has a large K_c. At equilibrium, the reaction mixture contains mostly product and few reactants (see Figure 13.8).

$$2SO_2(g) + O_2(g) \rightleftarrows 2SO_3(g)$$

$$K_c = \frac{[SO_3]^2}{[SO_2]^2[O_2]} \quad \frac{\text{Mostly product}}{\text{Few reactants}} = 3.4 \times 10^2$$

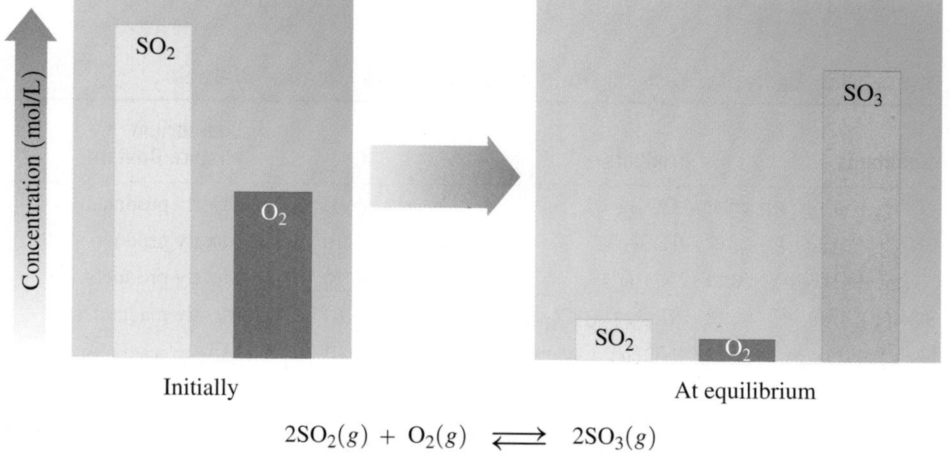

FIGURE 13.8 In the reaction of $SO_2(g)$ and $O_2(g)$, the equilibrium mixture contains mostly product $SO_3(g)$, which results in a large K_c.

Q Why does an equilibrium mixture containing mostly product have a large K_c?

Equilibrium with a Small K_c

When a reaction has a small equilibrium constant, the equilibrium mixture contains a high concentration of reactants and a low concentration of products. Then the equilibrium expression has a small number in the numerator and a large number in the denominator.

Thus at equilibrium, this reaction has a small K_c. Consider the reaction for the formation of $NO(g)$ from $N_2(g)$ and $O_2(g)$, which has a small K_c (see Figure 13.9).

$$N_2(g) + O_2(g) \rightleftarrows 2NO(g)$$

$$K_c = \frac{[NO]^2}{[N_2][O_2]} \quad \frac{\text{Few products}}{\text{Mostly reactants}} = 2 \times 10^{-9}$$

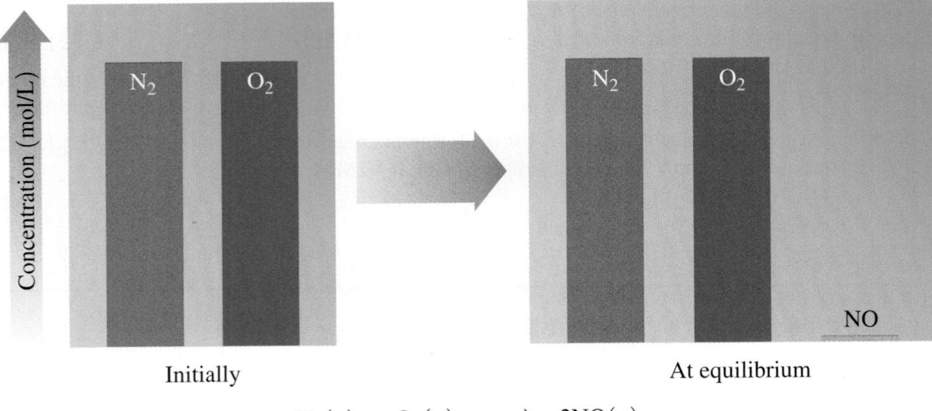

FIGURE 13.9 The equilibrium mixture contains a very small amount of the product NO and a large amount of the reactants N_2 and O_2, which results in a small K_c.

Q Does a reaction with a $K_c = 3.2 \times 10^{-5}$ contain mostly reactants or products at equilibrium?

A few reactions have equilibrium constants close to 1, which means they have about equal concentrations of reactants and products. Moderate amounts of reactants have been converted to products upon reaching equilibrium (see Figure 13.10).

Small K_c	$K_c \approx 1$	Large K_c
Mostly reactants		Mostly products
Products << Reactants Little reaction takes place	Reactants ≈ Products Moderate reaction	Products >> Reactants Reaction essentially complete

FIGURE 13.10 At equilibrium, a reaction with a large K_c contains mostly products, whereas a reaction with a small K_c contains mostly reactants.

Q Does a reaction with a $K_c = 1.2$ contain mostly reactants, mostly products, or about equal amounts of both reactants and products at equilibrium?

Table 13.3 lists some equilibrium constants and the extent of their reaction.

TABLE 13.3 Examples of Reactions with Large and Small K_c Values

Reactants		Products	K_c	Equilibrium Mixture Contains
$2CO(g) + O_2(g)$	$\rightleftarrows$	$2CO_2(g)$	2×10^{11}	Mostly products
$2H_2(g) + S_2(g)$	$\rightleftarrows$	$2H_2S(g)$	1.1×10^{7}	Mostly products
$N_2(g) + 3H_2(g)$	$\rightleftarrows$	$2NH_3(g)$	1.6×10^{2}	Mostly products
$PCl_5(g)$	$\rightleftarrows$	$PCl_3(g) + Cl_2(g)$	1.2×10^{-2}	Mostly reactants
$N_2(g) + O_2(g)$	$\rightleftarrows$	$2NO(g)$	2×10^{-9}	Mostly reactants

CONCEPT CHECK 13.5 Extent of Reaction

Predict whether the equilibrium mixture contains mostly reactants or mostly products for each of the following:

a. $2H_2(g) + O_2(g) \rightleftarrows 2H_2O(g) \quad K_c = 2.9 \times 10^{82}$
b. $N_2O_4(g) \rightleftarrows 2NO_2(g) \quad K_c = 5.9 \times 10^{-3}$

ANSWER

a. When K_c has a large value, it indicates that there are high concentrations of products in the numerator and low concentrations of reactants in the denominator. Thus, this equilibrium mixture contains mostly product.

b. When K_c has a small value, it indicates that there are low concentrations of products in the numerator and high concentrations of reactants in the denominator. Thus, this equilibrium mixture contains mostly reactants.

Calculating Concentrations at Equilibrium

CORE CHEMISTRY SKILL 

Calculating Equilibrium Concentrations

When we know the numerical value of the equilibrium constant and all the equilibrium concentrations except one, we can calculate the unknown concentration as shown in Sample Problem 13.6.

SAMPLE PROBLEM 13.6 Calculating Concentration Using an Equilibrium Constant

For the reaction of carbon dioxide and hydrogen, the equilibrium concentrations are 0.25 M CO_2, 0.80 M H_2, and 0.50 M H_2O. What is the equilibrium concentration of $CO(g)$?

$$CO_2(g) + H_2(g) \rightleftarrows CO(g) + H_2O(g) \qquad K_c = 0.11$$

SOLUTION

Step 1 State the given and needed quantities.

	Given		Need
	Reactants	Product	
Analyze the Problem	$[CO_2] = 0.25$ M $[H_2] = 0.80$ M	$[H_2O] = 0.50$ M	$[CO]$
	Equation		
	$CO_2(g) + H_2(g) \rightleftarrows CO(g) + H_2O(g)$		$K_c = 0.11$

Step 2 Write the K_c expression for the equilibrium and solve for the needed concentration.

$$K_c = \frac{[CO][H_2O]}{[CO_2][H_2]}$$

We can rearrange K_c to solve for the unknown $[CO]$ by multiplying both sides by $[CO_2][H_2]$ and then dividing both sides by $[H_2O]$.

$$K_c \times [CO_2][H_2] = \frac{[CO][H_2O]}{\cancel{[CO_2]}\cancel{[H_2]}} \times \cancel{[CO_2]}\cancel{[H_2]}$$

$$K_c[CO_2][H_2] = [CO][H_2O]$$

$$K_c\frac{[CO_2][H_2]}{[H_2O]} = \frac{[CO]\cancel{[H_2O]}}{\cancel{[H_2O]}}$$

$$[CO] = K_c\frac{[CO_2][H_2]}{[H_2O]}$$

Step 3 Substitute the equilibrium (molar) concentrations and calculate the needed concentration.

$$[CO] = K_c\frac{[CO_2][H_2]}{[H_2O]} = 0.11\frac{[0.25][0.80]}{[0.50]}$$

$$[CO] = 0.044 \text{ M}$$

Guide to Using the Equilibrium Constant

1. State the given and needed quantities.
2. Write the K_c expression for the equilibrium and solve for the needed concentration.
3. Substitute the equilibrium (molar) concentrations and calculate the needed concentration.

STUDY CHECK 13.6

When the alkene ethene (C_2H_4) reacts with water vapor, ethanol, an alcohol, is produced. If an equilibrium mixture contains 0.020 M C_2H_4 and 0.015 M H_2O, what is the equilibrium concentration of C_2H_5OH? At 327 °C, the K_c is 9.0×10^3.

$$C_2H_4(g) + H_2O(g) \rightleftharpoons C_2H_5OH(g)$$

QUESTIONS AND PROBLEMS

13.4 Using Equilibrium Constants

LEARNING GOAL: *Use an equilibrium constant to predict the extent of reaction and to calculate equilibrium concentrations.*

13.23 Indicate whether each of the following equilibrium mixtures contains mostly products or mostly reactants:

a. $Cl_2(g) + NO(g) \rightleftharpoons 2NOCl(g) \quad K_c = 3.7 \times 10^8$

b. $2H_2(g) + S_2(g) \rightleftharpoons 2H_2S(g) \quad K_c = 1.1 \times 10^7$

c. $3O_2(g) \rightleftharpoons 2O_3(g) \quad K_c = 1.7 \times 10^{-56}$

13.24 Indicate whether each of the following equilibrium mixtures contains mostly products or mostly reactants:

a. $CO(g) + Cl_2(g) \rightleftharpoons COCl_2(g) \quad K_c = 5.0 \times 10^{-9}$

b. $2HF(g) \rightleftharpoons H_2(g) + F_2(g) \quad K_c = 1.0 \times 10^{-95}$

c. $2NO(g) + O_2(g) \rightleftharpoons 2NO_2(g) \quad K_c = 6.0 \times 10^{13}$

13.25 The equilibrium constant, K_c, for this reaction is 54.

$$H_2(g) + I_2(g) \rightleftharpoons 2HI(g)$$

If the equilibrium mixture contains 0.015 M I_2 and 0.030 M HI, what is the molar concentration of H_2?

13.26 The equilibrium constant, K_c, for the following reaction is 4.6×10^{-3}. If the equilibrium mixture contains 0.050 M NO_2, what is the molar concentration of N_2O_4?

$$N_2O_4(g) \rightleftharpoons 2NO_2(g)$$

13.27 The K_c for the following reaction at 100 °C is 2.0. If the equilibrium mixture contains 2.0 M NO and 1.0 M Br_2, what is the molar concentration of NOBr?

$$2NOBr(g) \rightleftharpoons 2NO(g) + Br_2(g)$$

13.28 The K_c for the following reaction at 225 °C is 1.7×10^2. If the equilibrium mixture contains 0.18 M H_2 and 0.020 M N_2, what is the molar concentration of NH_3?

$$3H_2(g) + N_2(g) \rightleftharpoons 2NH_3(g)$$

LEARNING GOAL

Use Le Châtelier's principle to describe the changes made in equilibrium concentrations when reaction conditions change.

13.5 Changing Equilibrium Conditions: Le Châtelier's Principle

We have seen that when a reaction reaches equilibrium, the rates of the forward and reverse reactions are equal and the concentrations remain constant. Now we will look at what happens to a system at equilibrium when changes occur in reaction conditions, such as changes in concentration, volume, and temperature.

Le Châtelier's Principle

When we alter any of the conditions of a system at equilibrium, the rates of the forward and reverse reactions will no longer be equal. We say that a *stress* is placed on the equilibrium. Then the system responds by changing the rate of the forward or reverse reaction in the direction that relieves that stress to reestablish equilibrium. We can use **Le Châtelier's principle**, which states that when a system at equilibrium is disturbed, the system will shift in the direction that will reduce that stress.

Le Châtelier's Principle

When a stress (change in conditions) is placed on a reaction at equilibrium, the equilibrium will shift in the direction that relieves the stress.

Suppose we have two water tanks connected by a pipe. When the water levels in the tanks are equal, water flows in the forward direction from Tank A to Tank B at the same rate as it flows in the reverse direction from Tank B to Tank A. Suppose we add more water to Tank A. With a higher level of water in Tank A, more water flows in the forward direction from Tank A to Tank B than in the reverse direction from Tank B to Tank A, which is shown with a longer arrow. Eventually, equilibrium is reached as the levels in both tanks become equal, but higher than before. Then the rate of water flows equally between Tank A and Tank B.

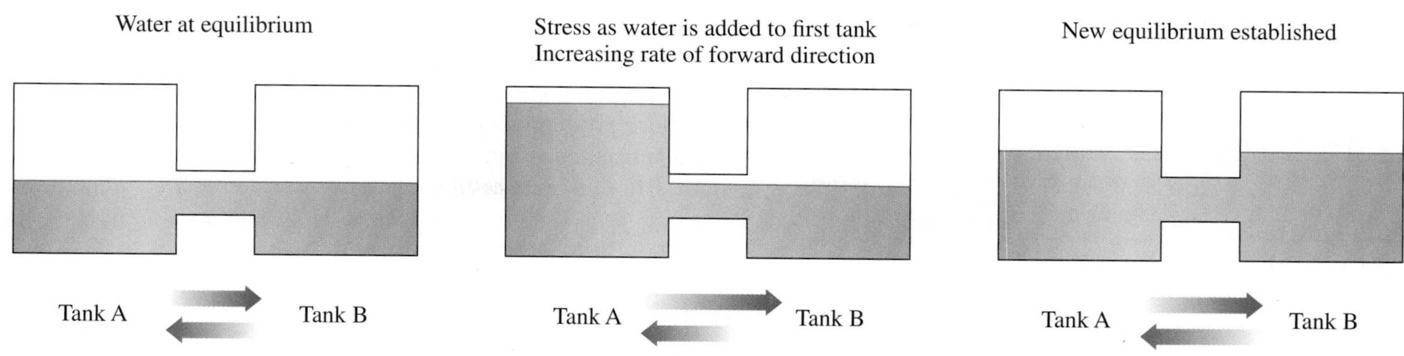

When water is added to one tank, the levels readjust to equalize.

Effect of Concentration Changes on Equilibrium

CORE CHEMISTRY SKILL

Using Le Châtelier's Principle

We will now use the reaction of H_2 and I_2 to illustrate how a change in concentration disturbs the equilibrium and how the system responds to that stress.

$$H_2(g) + I_2(g) \rightleftharpoons 2HI(g)$$

Suppose that more of the reactant H_2 is added to the equilibrium mixture, which increases the concentration of H_2. Because a K_c cannot change for a reaction at a given temperature, adding more H_2 places a stress on the system (see Figure 13.11). Then the system relieves this stress by increasing the rate of the forward reaction. Thus, more products are formed until the system is again at equilibrium. According to Le Châtelier's principle, adding more reactant causes the system to *shift* in the direction of the products until equilibrium is reestablished.

Add H_2

$$H_2(g) + I_2(g) \rightleftharpoons 2HI(g)$$

Suppose now that some H_2 is removed from the reaction mixture at equilibrium, which lowers the concentration of H_2 and slows the rate of the forward reaction. From using Le Châtelier's principle, we know that when some of the reactants are removed, the system will *shift* in the direction of the reactants until equilibrium is reestablished.

Remove H_2

$$H_2(g) + I_2(g) \rightleftharpoons 2HI(g)$$

The concentrations of the products of an equilibrium mixture can also increase or decrease. For example, if more HI is added, there is an increase in the rate of the reaction in the reverse direction, which converts some of the products to reactants. The concentration of the products decreases and the concentration of the reactants increases until equilibrium is reestablished. Using Le Châtelier's principle, we see that the addition of a product causes the system to *shift* in the direction of the reactants.

Add HI

$$H_2(g) + I_2(g) \rightleftharpoons 2HI(g)$$

In another example, some HI is removed from an equilibrium mixture, which decreases the concentration of the products. Then there is a *shift* in the direction of the products to reestablish equilibrium.

Remove HI

$$H_2(g) + I_2(g) \rightleftharpoons 2HI(g)$$

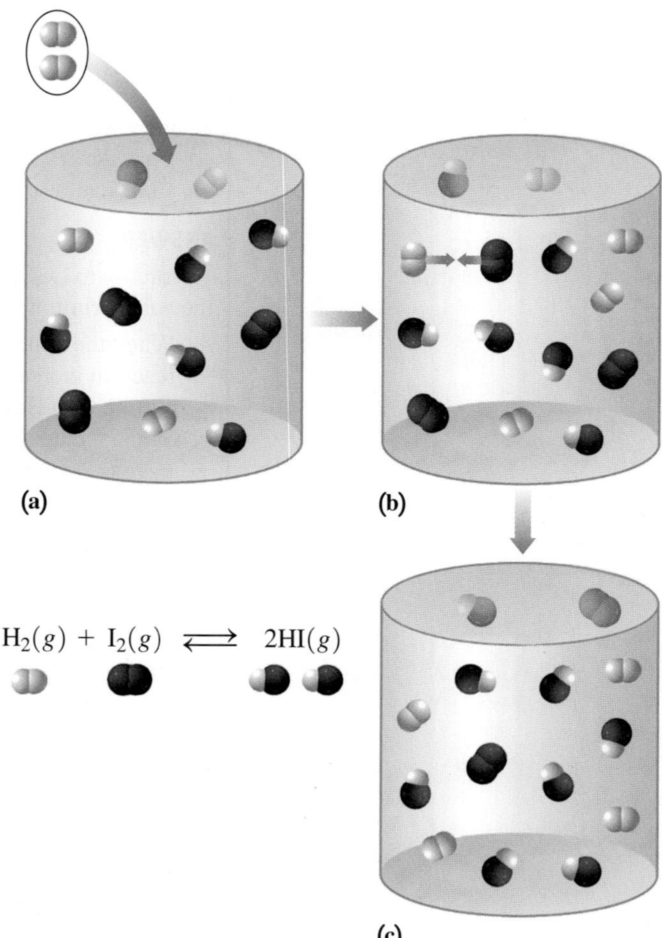

FIGURE 13.11 **(a)** The addition of H_2 places stress on the equilibrium system of $H_2(g) + I_2(g) \rightleftharpoons 2HI(g)$. **(b)** To relieve the stress, the forward reaction converts some reactants H_2 and I_2 to product HI. **(c)** A new equilibrium is established when the rates of the forward reaction and the reverse reaction become equal.

Q If more product HI is added, will the equilibrium shift in the direction of the products or reactants? Why?

TABLE 13.4 Effect of Concentration Changes on Equilibrium $H_2(g) + I_2(g) \rightleftarrows 2HI(g)$

Stress	Shift in the Direction of
Increase $[H_2]$	Products
Decrease $[H_2]$	Reactants
Increase $[I_2]$	Products
Decrease $[I_2]$	Reactants
Increase $[HI]$	Reactants
Decrease $[HI]$	Products

In summary, Le Châtelier's principle indicates that a stress caused by adding a substance at equilibrium is relieved when the equilibrium system shifts the reaction away from that substance. Adding more reactant causes an increase in the forward reaction to products. Adding more products causes an increase in the reverse reaction to reactants. When some of a substance is removed, the equilibrium system shifts in the direction of that substance. These features of Le Châtelier's principle are summarized in Table 13.4.

Effect of a Catalyst on Equilibrium

Sometimes a catalyst is added to a reaction to speed up a reaction by lowering the activation energy. As a result, the rates of both the forward and reverse reactions increase. The time required to reach equilibrium is shorter, but the same ratios of products and reactants are attained. Therefore, a catalyst speeds up the forward and reverse reactions, but it has no effect on the equilibrium mixture.

CONCEPT CHECK 13.6 Effect of Changes in Concentrations on Equilibrium

Describe the effect of each of the following changes on the equilibrium mixture for the following reaction:

$$CO(g) + H_2O(g) \rightleftarrows CO_2(g) + H_2(g)$$

a. increase $[CO]$
b. increase $[H_2]$
c. decrease $[H_2O]$
d. decrease $[CO_2]$
e. add a catalyst

ANSWER

According to Le Châtelier's principle, when stress is applied to a reaction at equilibrium, the equilibrium will shift to relieve that stress.

a. When the concentration of the reactant CO increases, the rate of the forward reaction increases to shift the equilibrium in the direction of the products until equilibrium is reestablished.

b. When the concentration of the product H_2 increases, the rate of the reverse reaction increases to shift the equilibrium in the direction of the reactants until equilibrium is reestablished.

c. When the concentration of the reactant H_2O decreases, the rate of the forward reaction decreases to shift the equilibrium in the direction of the reactants until equilibrium is reestablished.

d. When the concentration of the product CO_2 decreases, the rate of the reverse reaction decreases to shift the equilibrium in the direction of the products until equilibrium is reestablished.

e. When a catalyst is added, the rates of the forward and reverse reactions increase equally without a change in the equilibrium mixture.

Effect of Volume Change on Equilibrium

If there is a change in the volume of a gas mixture at equilibrium, there will also be a change in the concentrations of those gases. Decreasing the volume will increase the concentration of gases, whereas increasing the volume will decrease their concentration. Then the system responds to reestablish equilibrium.

Let's look at the effect of decreasing the volume of the equilibrium mixture of the following reaction:

$$2CO(g) + O_2(g) \rightleftarrows 2CO_2(g)$$

If we decrease the volume, all the concentrations increase. According to Le Châtelier's principle, the increase in concentration is relieved when the system shifts in the direction of the smaller number of moles.

Decrease V

$$2CO(g) + O_2(g) \rightleftharpoons 2CO_2(g)$$

3 mol of gas — 2 mol of gas

On the other hand, when the volume of the equilibrium gas mixture increases, the concentrations of all the gases decrease. Then the system shifts in the direction of the greater number of moles to reestablish equilibrium (see Figure 13.12).

Increase V

$$2CO(g) + O_2(g) \rightleftharpoons 2CO_2(g)$$

3 mol of gas — 2 mol of gas

When a reaction has the same number of moles of reactants as products, a volume change does not affect the equilibrium mixture because the concentrations of the reactants and products change in the same way.

$$H_2(g) + I_2(g) \rightleftharpoons 2HI(g)$$

2 mol of gas — 2 mol of gas

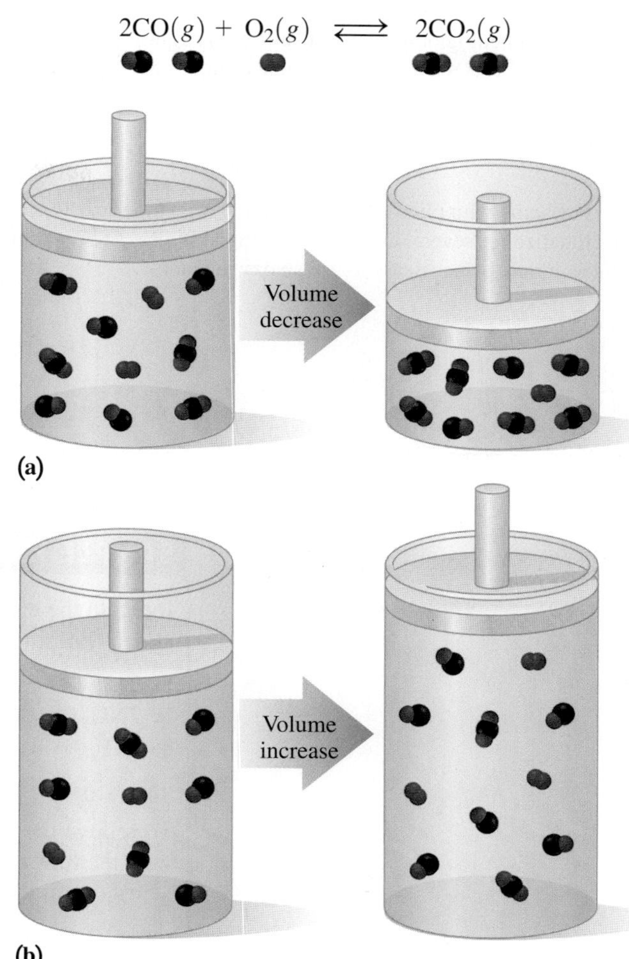

FIGURE 13.12 **(a)** A decrease in the volume of the container causes the system to shift in the direction of fewer moles of gas. **(b)** An increase in the volume of the container causes the system to shift in the direction of more moles of gas.

Q If you want to increase the products, should you increase or decrease the volume of the container?

Chemistry Link to Health

OXYGEN–HEMOGLOBIN EQUILIBRIUM AND HYPOXIA

The transport of oxygen involves an equilibrium between hemoglobin (Hb), oxygen, and oxyhemoglobin (HbO_2).

$$Hb(aq) + O_2(g) \rightleftharpoons HbO_2(aq)$$

When the O_2 level is high in the alveoli of the lung, the reaction shifts in the direction of the product HbO_2. In the tissues where O_2 concentration is low, the reverse reaction releases the oxygen from the hemoglobin. The equilibrium expression is written

$$K_c = \frac{[HbO_2]}{[Hb][O_2]}$$

At normal atmospheric pressure, oxygen diffuses into the blood because the partial pressure of oxygen in the alveoli is higher than that in the blood. At an altitude above 8000 ft, a decrease in the atmospheric pressure results in a significant reduction in the partial pressure of oxygen, which means that less oxygen is available for the blood and body tissues. The fall in atmospheric pressure at higher altitudes decreases the partial pressure of inhaled oxygen, and there is less driving pressure for gas exchange in the lungs. At an altitude of 18 000 ft, a person will obtain 29% less oxygen. When oxygen levels are lowered, a person may experience *hypoxia*, characterized by increased respiratory rate, headache, decreased mental acuteness, fatigue, decreased physical coordination, nausea, vomiting, and cyanosis. A similar problem occurs in persons with a history of lung disease that impairs gas diffusion in the alveoli or in persons with a reduced number of red blood cells, such as smokers.

According to Le Châtelier's principle, we see that a decrease in oxygen will shift the equilibrium in the direction of the reactants. Such a shift depletes the concentration of HbO_2 and causes the hypoxia.

$$Hb(aq) + O_2(g) \longleftarrow HbO_2(aq)$$

Immediate treatment of altitude sickness includes hydration, rest, and if necessary, descending to a lower altitude. The adaptation to lowered oxygen levels requires about 10 days. During this time the bone marrow increases red blood cell production, providing more red blood cells and more hemoglobin. A person living at a high altitude can have 50% more red blood cells than someone at sea level. This increase in hemoglobin causes a shift in the equilibrium back in the direction of HbO_2 product. Eventually, the higher concentration of HbO_2 will provide more oxygen to the tissues and the symptoms of hypoxia will lessen.

$$Hb(aq) + O_2(g) \longrightarrow HbO_2(aq)$$

For some who climb high mountains, it is important to stop and acclimatize for several days at increasing altitudes. At very high altitudes, it may be necessary to use an oxygen tank.

Hypoxia may occur at high altitudes where the oxygen concentration is lower.

SAMPLE PROBLEM 13.7 Effect of Changes in Volume

Indicate the effect of decreasing the volume of the container for each of the following at equilibrium:

a. $C_2H_2(g) + 2H_2(g) \rightleftarrows C_2H_6(g)$
b. $2NO_2(g) \rightleftarrows 2NO(g) + O_2(g)$
c. $CO(g) + H_2O(g) \rightleftarrows CO_2(g) + H_2(g)$

SOLUTION

To relieve the stress of decreasing the volume, the equilibrium shifts in the direction with the fewer moles of gas.

a. The equilibrium shifts in the direction of the product, which has fewer moles of gas.

$$\underset{\text{3 mol of gas}}{C_2H_2(g) + 2H_2(g)} \longrightarrow \underset{\text{1 mol of gas}}{C_2H_6(g)}$$

b. The equilibrium system shifts in the direction of the reactant, which has fewer moles of gas.

$$\underset{\text{2 mol of gas}}{2NO_2(g)} \longleftarrow \underset{\text{3 mol of gas}}{2NO(g) + O_2(g)}$$

c. There is no shift in equilibrium because the moles of reactant are equal to the moles of product.

$$\underset{\text{2 mol of gas}}{CO(g) + H_2O(g)} \rightleftarrows \underset{\text{2 mol of gas}}{CO_2(g) + H_2(g)}$$

STUDY CHECK 13.7

Suppose you want to increase the yield of product in the following reaction. Would you increase or decrease the volume of the reaction container?

$$CO(g) + 2H_2(g) \rightleftarrows CH_3OH(g)$$

Effect of a Change in Temperature on Equilibrium

We can think of heat as a reactant or a product in a reaction. For example, in the equation for an endothermic reaction, heat is written on the reactant side. When the temperature of an endothermic reaction increases, the system responds by shifting in the direction of the products to remove heat.

Increase T

$$N_2(g) + O_2(g) + \text{heat} \rightleftarrows 2NO(g)$$

If the temperature is lowered for an endothermic reaction, there is a decrease in heat. Then the system shifts in the direction of the reactants to add heat.

Decrease *T*

$$N_2(g) + O_2(g) + \text{heat} \rightleftarrows 2NO(g)$$

In the equation for an exothermic reaction, heat is written on the product side. When the temperature of an exothermic reaction increases, the system responds by shifting in the direction of the reactants to remove heat.

Increase *T*

$$2SO_2(g) + O_2(g) \rightleftarrows 2SO_3(g) + \text{heat}$$

If the temperature is lowered for an exothermic reaction, there is a decrease in heat. Then the system shifts in the direction of the products to add heat.

Decrease *T*

$$2SO_2(g) + O_2(g) \rightleftarrows 2SO_3(g) + \text{heat}$$

SAMPLE PROBLEM 13.8 Effect of Temperature Change on Equilibrium

Indicate the change in equilibrium that takes place when the temperature is increased for each of the following at equilibrium:

a. $N_2(g) + 3H_2(g) \rightleftarrows 2NH_3(g) + 92\text{ kJ}$
b. $2HF(g) + Cl_2(g) + 357\text{ kJ} \rightleftarrows 2HCl(g) + F_2(g)$

SOLUTION

a. When the temperature is increased for an exothermic reaction, the equilibrium shifts in the direction of the reactants to remove heat.
b. When the temperature is increased for an endothermic reaction, the equilibrium shifts in the direction of the products to remove heat.

STUDY CHECK 13.8

Indicate the change in equilibrium that takes place when the temperature is decreased for each of the reactions in Sample Problem 13.8.

Table 13.5 summarizes the ways we can use Le Châtelier's principle to determine the shift in equilibrium that relieves a stress caused by the change in a condition.

TABLE 13.5 Effects of Condition Changes on Equilibrium

Condition	Change (Stress)	Remove Stress in the Direction of
Concentration	Add a reactant	Products (forward reaction)
	Remove a reactant	Reactants (reverse reaction)
	Add a product	Reactants (reverse reaction)
	Remove a product	Products (forward reaction)
Volume (container)	Decrease volume	Fewer moles of gas
	Increase volume	More moles of gas
Temperature	**Endothermic reaction**	
	Raise *T*	Products (forward reaction to remove heat)
	Lower *T*	Reactants (reverse reaction to add heat)
	Exothermic reaction	
	Raise *T*	Reactants (reverse reaction to remove heat)
	Lower *T*	Products (forward reaction to add heat)
Catalyst	Increases rates equally	No effect

Chemistry Link to Health

HOMEOSTASIS: REGULATION OF BODY TEMPERATURE

In a physiological system of equilibrium called *homeostasis*, changes in our environment are balanced by changes in our bodies. It is crucial to our survival that we balance heat gain with heat loss. If we do not lose enough heat, our body temperature rises. At high temperatures, the body can no longer regulate our metabolic reactions. If we lose too much heat, body temperature drops. At low temperatures, essential functions proceed too slowly.

The skin plays an important role in the maintenance of body temperature. When the outside temperature rises, receptors in the skin send signals to the brain. The temperature-regulating part of the brain stimulates the sweat glands to produce perspiration. As perspiration evaporates from the skin, heat is removed and the body temperature is lowered.

In cold temperatures, epinephrine is released, causing an increase in metabolic rate, which increases the production of heat. Receptors on the skin signal the brain to constrict the blood vessels. Less blood flows through the skin, and heat is conserved. The production of perspiration stops, thereby lessening the heat lost by evaporation.

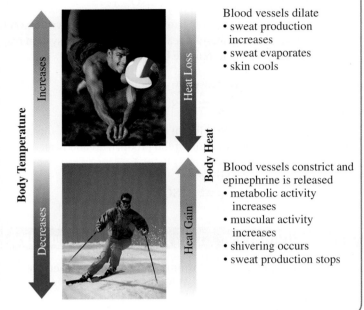

Blood vessels dilate
- sweat production increases
- sweat evaporates
- skin cools

Blood vessels constrict and epinephrine is released
- metabolic activity increases
- muscular activity increases
- shivering occurs
- sweat production stops

QUESTIONS AND PROBLEMS

13.5 Changing Equilibrium Conditions: Le Châtelier's Principle

LEARNING GOAL: *Use Le Châtelier's principle to describe the changes made in equilibrium concentrations when reaction conditions change.*

13.29 In the lower atmosphere, oxygen is converted to ozone (O_3) by the energy provided from lightning.

$$3O_2(g) + \text{heat} \rightleftarrows 2O_3(g)$$

For each of the following changes at equilibrium, indicate whether the equilibrium shifts in the direction of products, reactants, or does not change:

a. add more $O_2(g)$
b. add more $O_3(g)$
c. increase the temperature
d. increase the volume of the container
e. add a catalyst

13.30 Ammonia is produced by reacting nitrogen gas and hydrogen gas.

$$N_2(g) + 3H_2(g) \rightleftarrows 2NH_3(g) + 92\text{ kJ}$$

For each of the following changes at equilibrium, indicate whether the equilibrium shifts in the direction of products, reactants, or does not change:

a. remove some $N_2(g)$
b. decrease the temperature
c. add more $NH_3(g)$
d. add more $H_2(g)$
e. increase the volume of the container

13.31 Hydrogen chloride can be made by reacting hydrogen gas and chlorine gas.

$$H_2(g) + Cl_2(g) + \text{heat} \rightleftarrows 2HCl(g)$$

For each of the following changes at equilibrium, indicate whether the equilibrium shifts in the direction of products, reactants, or does not change:

a. add more $H_2(g)$
b. increase the temperature
c. remove some $HCl(g)$
d. add a catalyst
e. remove some $Cl_2(g)$

13.32 When heated, carbon reacts with water to produce carbon monoxide and hydrogen.

$$C(s) + H_2O(g) + \text{heat} \rightleftarrows CO(g) + H_2(g)$$

For each of the following changes at equilibrium, indicate whether the equilibrium shifts in the direction of products, reactants, or does not change:

a. decrease the temperature
b. add more $C(s)$
c. remove $CO(g)$ as its forms
d. add more $H_2O(g)$
e. decrease the volume of the container

13.6 Equilibrium in Saturated Solutions

LEARNING GOAL

Write the solubility product expression for a slightly soluble salt and calculate the K_{sp}; use K_{sp} to determine the solubility.

Until now, we have looked primarily at equilibrium systems that involve gases. However, there are also equilibrium systems that involve aqueous saturated solutions between solid solutes of slightly soluble salts and their ions. Everyday examples of solubility equilibrium in solution are found in the slightly soluble salts that are found in bone and kidney stones. Bone is composed of calcium phosphate, $Ca_3(PO_4)_2$, which produces ions during bone loss. Kidney stones are composed of calcium salts such as calcium oxalate, CaC_2O_4.

CORE CHEMISTRY SKILL 

Writing the Solubility Product Expression

Solubility Product Constant Expression

In a saturated solution, a solid slightly soluble salt is in equilibrium with its ions. As long as the temperature remains constant, the concentration of the ions in the saturated solution is constant. Let us look at the solubility equilibrium equation for CaC_2O_4, which is written with the solid solute on the left and the ions in solution on the right.

$$CaC_2O_4(s) \rightleftarrows Ca^{2+}(aq) + C_2O_4^{2-}(aq)$$

Calcium oxalate, a slightly soluble salt, produces small amounts of Ca^{2+} and $C_2O_4^{2-}$ in aqueous solution.

The *solubility* of a substance is the quantity that dissolves to form a saturated solution. We represent the solubility in a saturated aqueous solution of solid CaC_2O_4 by the **solubility product expression, K_{sp},** which is the product of the ion concentrations. As in other heterogeneous equilibria, the concentration of the solid CaC_2O_4 is constant and is not included in the solubility product expression.

$$K_{sp} = [Ca^{2+}][C_2O_4^{2-}]$$

In another example, we look at the equilibrium of solid calcium phosphate and its ions Ca^{2+} and PO_4^{3-}.

$$Ca_3(PO_4)_2(s) \rightleftarrows 3Ca^{2+}(aq) + 2PO_4^{3-}(aq)$$

As with other equilibrium expressions, the molar concentration of each product ion is raised to a power that is equal to its coefficient in the balanced equilibrium equation. For this equilibrium equation, the solubility product expression consists of $[Ca^{2+}]$ raised to the power of 3 and $[PO_4^{3-}]$ raised to the power of 2.

$$K_{sp} = [Ca^{2+}]^3[PO_4^{3-}]^2$$

CONCEPT CHECK 13.7 Writing the Solubility Product Expression

For each of the following slightly soluble salts, write the solubility equilibrium equation and the solubility product expression:

a. AgBr **b.** Cu_2CO_3

ANSWER

a. In the solubility equilibrium equation, the solid salt is written on the left with the ions Ag^+ and Br^- in aqueous solution on the right. The solubility product expression is written as the product of the molar concentrations of the ions. At equilibrium, the solubility product expression is equal to K_{sp}, the solubility product constant.

$$AgBr(s) \rightleftarrows Ag^+(aq) + Br^-(aq) \qquad K_{sp} = [Ag^+][Br^-]$$

b. In the solubility equilibrium equation, the solid salt is written on the left with the ions $2Cu^+$ and CO_3^{2-} in aqueous solution on the right. The solubility product expression, K_{sp}, is written as the product of the molar concentrations of the ions with $[Cu^+]$ raised to a power of 2, which is its coefficient in the balanced equation.

$$Cu_2CO_3(s) \rightleftarrows 2Cu^+(aq) + CO_3^{2-}(aq) \qquad K_{sp} = [Cu^+]^2[CO_3^{2-}]$$

CORE CHEMISTRY SKILL

Calculating a Solubility Product Constant

Solubility Product Constant

The numerical value of the solubility product expression is the **solubility product constant, K_{sp}**. In this text, solubility will be expressed as the molar solubility, which is the moles of solute that dissolve in 1 liter of saturated solution. The calculation of a solubility product constant is shown in Sample Problem 13.9.

Terraces in Pamukkale, Turkey, are composed of calcium carbonate, which is a slightly soluble salt.

Guide to Calculating K_{sp}

1. State the given and needed quantities.
2. Write the equilibrium equation for the dissociation of the slightly soluble salt.
3. Write the solubility product expression (K_{sp}).
4. Substitute the molar concentration of each ion into the K_{sp} expression and calculate.

SAMPLE PROBLEM 13.9 Calculating the Solubility Product Constant

We can make a saturated solution of $CaCO_3$ by adding solid $CaCO_3$ to water and stirring until equilibrium is reached. What is the numerical value of K_{sp} for $CaCO_3$ if the equilibrium mixture contains 7.1×10^{-5} M Ca^{2+} and 7.1×10^{-5} M CO_3^{2-}?

Step 1 State the given and needed quantities.

	Given	Need
Analyze the Problem	$[Ca^{2+}] = 7.1 \times 10^{-5}$ M $[CO_3^{2-}] = 7.1 \times 10^{-5}$ M	numerical value of K_{sp}

Step 2 Write the equilibrium equation for the dissociation of the slightly soluble salt.

$$CaCO_3(s) \rightleftarrows Ca^{2+}(aq) + CO_3^{2-}(aq)$$

Step 3 Write the solubility product expression (K_{sp}).

$$K_{sp} = [Ca^{2+}][CO_3^{2-}]$$

Step 4 Substitute the molar concentration of each ion into the K_{sp} expression and calculate.

$$K_{sp} = [7.1 \times 10^{-5}][7.1 \times 10^{-5}] = 5.0 \times 10^{-9}$$

STUDY CHECK 13.9

A saturated solution of AgBr contains 7.3×10^{-7} M Ag^+ and 7.3×10^{-7} M Br^-. What is the numerical value of K_{sp} for AgBr?

Table 13.6 gives values of K_{sp} for a selected group of slightly soluble salts at 25 °C.

TABLE 13.6 Examples of Solubility Product Constants (K_{sp})

Formula	K_{sp}
AgCl	1.8×10^{-10}
Ag_2SO_4	1.2×10^{-5}
$BaCO_3$	2.0×10^{-9}
$BaSO_4$	1.1×10^{-10}
CaF_2	3.2×10^{-11}
$Ca(OH)_2$	6.5×10^{-6}
$CaSO_4$	2.4×10^{-5}
$PbCl_2$	1.5×10^{-6}
$PbCO_3$	7.4×10^{-14}

SAMPLE PROBLEM 13.10 Calculating the Solubility Product Constant Using Coefficients

A saturated solution of strontium fluoride, SrF_2, contains 8.7×10^{-4} M Sr^{2+} and 1.7×10^{-3} M F^-. What is the numerical value of K_{sp} for SrF_2?

SOLUTION

Step 1 State the given and needed quantities.

	Given	Need
Analyze the Problem	$[Sr^{2+}] = 8.7 \times 10^{-4}$ M $[F^-] = 1.7 \times 10^{-3}$ M	numerical value of K_{sp}

Step 2 Write the equilibrium equation for the dissociation of the slightly soluble salt.

$$SrF_2(s) \rightleftarrows Sr^{2+}(aq) + 2F^-(aq)$$

Step 3 Write the solubility product expression (K_{sp}).

$$K_{sp} = [Sr^{2+}][F^-]^2$$

Step 4 **Substitute the molar concentration of each ion into the K_{sp} expression and calculate.**

$$K_{sp} = [8.7 \times 10^{-4}][1.7 \times 10^{-3}]^2 = 2.5 \times 10^{-9}$$

STUDY CHECK 13.10

What is the numerical value of K_{sp} for silver oxalate, $Ag_2C_2O_4$, if a saturated solution contains 2.2×10^{-4} M Ag^+ and 1.1×10^{-4} M $C_2O_4^{2-}$?

CORE CHEMISTRY SKILL 

Calculating the Molar Solubility

Molar Solubility, *S*

The molar solubility, *S*, of a slightly soluble salt is the number of moles of solute that dissolves in 1 liter of solution. For example, the molar solubility of CdS is found experimentally to be 1×10^{-12} M.

$$CdS(s) \rightleftarrows Cd^{2+}(aq) + S^{2-}(aq)$$

Because CdS dissociates into Cd^{2+} and S^{2-} ions, they each have a concentration equal to the solubility *S*.

$$S = [Cd^{2+}] = [S^{2-}] = 1 \times 10^{-12}\ M$$

If we know the K_{sp} of a slightly soluble salt, we can determine its molar solubility, as shown in Sample Problem 13.11.

Cadmium sulfide is a slightly soluble salt.

SAMPLE PROBLEM 13.11 Calculating the Molar Solubility from K_{sp}

Calculate the molar solubility, *S*, of $PbSO_4$ if it has a $K_{sp} = 1.6 \times 10^{-8}$.

SOLUTION

Step 1 **State the given and needed quantities.**

Analyze the Problem	Given	Need
	$K_{sp} = 1.6 \times 10^{-8}$	molar solubility (S) of $PbSO_4(s)$

Step 2 **Write the equilibrium equation for the dissociation of the slightly soluble salt.**

$$PbSO_4(s) \rightleftarrows Pb^{2+}(aq) + SO_4^{2-}(aq)$$

Step 3 **Write the solubility product expression, K_{sp}, using *S*.**

$$K_{sp} = [Pb^{2+}][SO_4^{2-}] = S \times S = S^2 = 1.6 \times 10^{-8}$$

Step 4 **Calculate the molar solubility *S*.**

$$S^2 = 1.6 \times 10^{-8}$$
$$S = \sqrt{1.6 \times 10^{-8}} = 1.3 \times 10^{-4}\ M$$

Thus, 1.3×10^{-4} mol of $PbSO_4$ will dissolve in 1 L of solution.

STUDY CHECK 13.11

Calculate the molar solubility, *S*, of MnS if it has a $K_{sp} = 2.5 \times 10^{-10}$.

Guide to Calculating Molar Solubility from K_{sp}

1. State the given and needed quantities.
2. Write the equilibrium equation for the dissociation of the slightly soluble salt.
3. Write the solubility product expression, K_{sp}, using *S*.
4. Calculate the molar solubility *S*.

Effect on Solubility of Adding a Common Ion

We have seen that when a slightly soluble salt such as $MgCO_3$ dissolves in water, small amounts of Mg^{2+} and CO_3^{2-} ions are produced in equal quantities.

$$MgCO_3(s) \rightleftarrows Mg^{2+}(aq) + CO_3^{2-}(aq) \quad K_{sp} = 3.5 \times 10^{-8}$$

When we calculate the molar solubility of $MgCO_3$ from its K_{sp}, it is 1.9×10^{-4} M and the concentrations of both Mg^{2+} and CO_3^{2-} are the same (1.9×10^{-4} M).

$$S = [Mg^{2+}] = [CO_3^{2-}] = 1.9 \times 10^{-4}\text{ M}$$

We know from Le Châtelier's principle that adding one of the products to a system at equilibrium causes the equilibrium to shift in the direction of the reactants. The same principle applies to the solubility of a slightly soluble salt. For example, we can decrease the solubility of the slightly soluble salt $MgCO_3$ by adding a salt that dissolves completely to give one of the ions Mg^{2+} or CO_3^{2-}. When $MgCl_2$ is added to the above solution, it increases the concentration of Mg^{2+}, the common ion. Because the K_{sp} for $MgCO_3$ must stay the same, some Mg^{2+} combines with CO_3^{2-} to form solid $MgCO_3$. This reverse reaction decreases $[CO_3^{2-}]$ and decreases the solubility of $MgCO_3$.

Mg^{2+} added

$$MgCO_3(s) \rightleftharpoons Mg^{2+}(aq) + CO_3^{2-}(aq)$$

Concentration increases Concentration decreases

Suppose $MgCl_2$ is added to the equilibrium mixture to give $[Mg^{2+}]$ equal to 1.0×10^{-2} M. Using the K_{sp}, we can calculate the new solubility S, of $MgCO_3$, which is equal to the $[CO_3^{2-}]$.

$$K_{sp} = [Mg^{2+}][CO_3^{2-}] = 3.5 \times 10^{-8}$$
$$K_{sp} = [Mg^{2+}]\,S = 3.5 \times 10^{-8}$$

We substitute the known concentration of Mg^{2+} and solve for $[CO_3^{2-}]$, which is equal to the new S.

$$[1.0 \times 10^{-2}]\,S = 3.5 \times 10^{-8}$$

We rearrange the equation for S and solve for the molar solubility S, which is the amount of $MgCO_3(s)$ that can dissolve when a common ion has increased $[Mg^{2+}]$.

$$S = \frac{3.5 \times 10^{-8}}{1.0 \times 10^{-2}} = 3.5 \times 10^{-6}\text{ M}$$

Thus, the new solubility S is reduced to 3.5×10^{-6} M for $MgCO_3$ compared to 1.9×10^{-4} M when there is no common ion added.

The solubility of $MgCO_3$ can also be decreased by adding Na_2CO_3, which increases the common ion $[CO_3^{2-}]$. According to Le Châtelier's principle, the addition of the product CO_3^{2-} causes the equilibrium to shift in the direction of the reactants, which means it decreases the solubility of $MgCO_3$. In the reverse reaction, the common ion CO_3^{2-} combines with some of the Mg^{2+} in solution to form solid $MgCO_3$, which reduces both the concentration of Mg^{2+} and the molar solubility S of $MgCO_3$.

CO_3^{2-} added

$$MgCO_3(s) \rightleftharpoons Mg^{2+}(aq) + CO_3^{2-}(aq)$$

Concentration decreases Concentration increases

SAMPLE PROBLEM 13.12 Calculating Molar Solubility with a Common Ion

CaC_2O_4 has a K_{sp} of 2.7×10^{-9}. If $Na_2C_2O_4$ is added to the solution to give $[C_2O_4^{2-}] = 3.5 \times 10^{-2}$ M, what is the molar solubility, S, of CaC_2O_4?

SOLUTION

Step 1 State the given and needed quantities.

	Given	Need
Analyze the Problem	$K_{sp} = 2.7 \times 10^{-9}$ $[C_2O_4^{2-}] = 3.5 \times 10^{-2}$ M	molar solubility (S) of $CaC_2O_4(s)$

Step 2 Write the equilibrium equation for the dissociation of the slightly soluble salt.

$$CaC_2O_4(s) \rightleftharpoons Ca^{2+}(aq) + C_2O_4^{2-}(aq)$$

Step 3 Write the solubility product expression, K_{sp}, using S.

$$K_{sp} = [Ca^{2+}][C_2O_4^{2-}] = S[C_2O_4^{2-}]$$

Step 4 Calculate the molar solubility S.

$$K_{sp} = S[3.5 \times 10^{-2}] = 2.7 \times 10^{-9}$$

$$S = \frac{2.7 \times 10^{-9}}{[3.5 \times 10^{-2}]} = 7.7 \times 10^{-8}\ \text{M}$$

Thus, 7.7×10^{-8} mol of CaC_2O_4 will dissolve in 1 L of solution.

STUDY CHECK 13.12

Nickel(II) carbonate, $NiCO_3$, has a K_{sp} of 1.3×10^{-7}. What is the molar solubility of $NiCO_3$ in a solution if Na_2CO_3 is added to the solution to give $[CO_3^{2-}] = 4.2 \times 10^{-2}$ M?

QUESTIONS AND PROBLEMS

13.6 Equilibrium in Saturated Solutions

LEARNING GOAL: *Write the solubility product expression for a slightly soluble salt and calculate K_{sp}; use K_{sp} to determine the solubility.*

13.33 For each of the following slightly soluble salts, write the equilibrium equation for dissociation and the solubility product expression:
a. $BaCO_3$ **b.** CaF_2 **c.** Ag_3PO_4

13.34 For each of the following slightly soluble salts, write the equilibrium equation for dissociation and the solubility product expression:
a. Ag_2S **b.** $Al(OH)_3$ **c.** BaF_2

13.35 A saturated solution of barium sulfate, $BaSO_4$, has $[Ba^{2+}]$ 1×10^{-5} M and $[SO_4^{2-}]$ 1×10^{-5} M. What is the numerical value of K_{sp} for $BaSO_4$?

13.36 A saturated solution of copper(II) sulfide, CuS, has $[Cu^{2+}] = 1.1 \times 10^{-18}$ M and $[S^{2-}] = 1.1 \times 10^{-18}$ M. What is the numerical value of K_{sp} for CuS?

13.37 A saturated solution of silver carbonate, Ag_2CO_3, has $[Ag^+] = 2.6 \times 10^{-4}$ M and $[CO_3^{2-}] = 1.3 \times 10^{-4}$ M. What is the numerical value of K_{sp} for Ag_2CO_3?

13.38 A saturated solution of barium fluoride, BaF_2, has $[Ba^{2+}] = 3.6 \times 10^{-3}$ M and $[F^-] = 7.2 \times 10^{-3}$ M. What is the numerical value of K_{sp} for BaF_2?

13.39 What are the molar concentrations of Cu^+ and I^- in a saturated CuI solution if K_{sp} of CuI is 1×10^{-12}?

13.40 What are the molar concentrations of Sn^{2+} and S^{2-} in a saturated SnS solution if K_{sp} of SnS is 1×10^{-26}?

13.41 What is the molar solubility, S, of AgCl in a solution that has $[Ag^+] = 2.0 \times 10^{-3}$ M (see Table 13.6 for K_{sp})?

13.42 What is the molar solubility, S, of $PbCO_3$ in a solution that has $[CO_3^{2-}] = 3.0 \times 10^{-4}$ M (see Table 13.6 for K_{sp})?

CHAPTER REVIEW

13.1 Rates of Reactions

LEARNING GOAL: *Describe how temperature, concentration, and catalysts affect the rate of a reaction.*

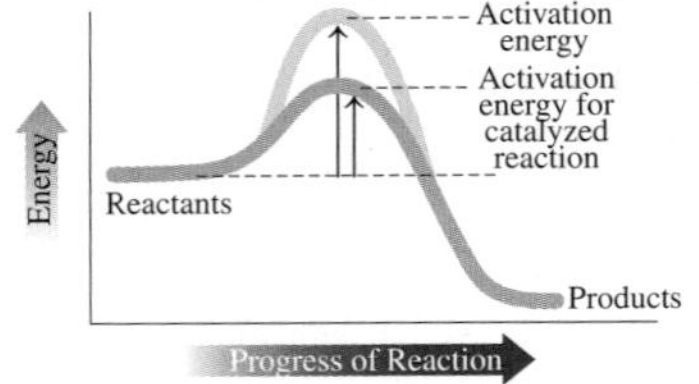

- The rate of a reaction is the speed at which the reactants are converted to products.
- Increasing the concentrations of reactants, raising the temperature, or adding a catalyst can increase the rate of a reaction.

13.2 Chemical Equilibrium

LEARNING GOAL: *Use the concept of reversible reactions to explain chemical equilibrium.*

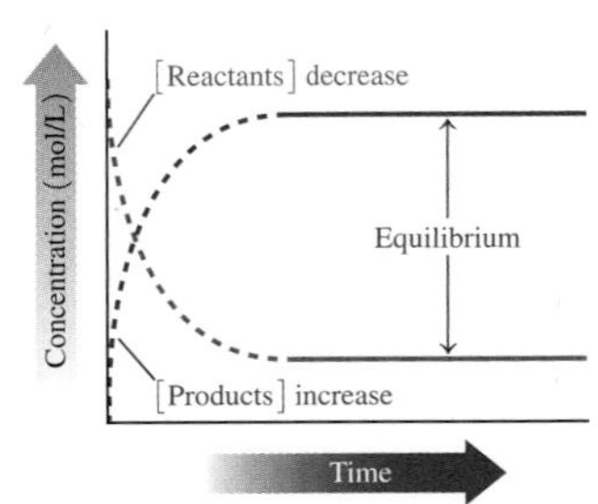

- Chemical equilibrium occurs in a reversible reaction when the rate of the forward reaction becomes equal to the rate of the reverse reaction.
- At equilibrium, no further change occurs in the concentrations of the reactants and products as the forward and reverse reactions continue.

13.3 Equilibrium Constants

LEARNING GOAL: *Calculate the equilibrium constant for a reversible reaction given the concentrations of reactants and products at equilibrium.*

- An equilibrium constant, K_c, is the ratio of the concentrations of the products to the concentrations of the reactants, with each concentration raised to a power equal to its coefficient in the balanced chemical equation.
- For heterogeneous reactions, only the molar concentrations of gases are placed in the equilibrium expression.

13.4 Using Equilibrium Constants

LEARNING GOAL: *Use an equilibrium constant to predict the extent of reaction and to calculate equilibrium concentrations.*

$$2SO_2(g) + O_2(g) \rightleftharpoons 2SO_3(g)$$

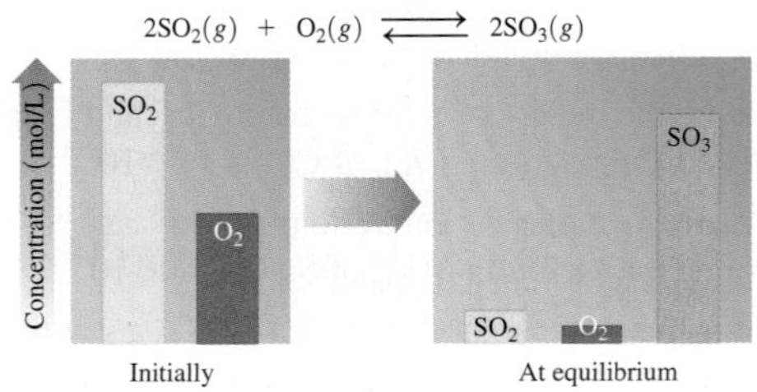

- A large value of K_c indicates that an equilibrium mixture contains mostly products and few reactants, whereas a small value of K_c indicates that the equilibrium mixture contains mostly reactants.
- Equilibrium constants can be used to calculate the concentration of a component in the equilibrium mixture.

13.5 Changing Equilibrium Conditions: Le Châtelier's Principle

LEARNING GOAL: *Use Le Châtelier's principle to describe the changes made in equilibrium concentrations when reaction conditions change.*

- When reactants are removed or products are added to an equilibrium mixture, the system shifts in the direction of the reactants.
- When reactants are added or products are removed from an equilibrium mixture, the system shifts in the direction of the products.
- A decrease in the volume of a reaction container causes a shift in the direction of the smaller number of moles of gas.
- An increase in the volume of a reaction container causes a shift in the direction of the greater number of moles of gas.
- Raising the temperature of an endothermic reaction or lowering the temperature of an exothermic reaction will cause the system to shift in the direction of products.
- Lowering the temperature of an endothermic reaction or raising the temperature of an exothermic reaction will cause the system to shift in the direction of reactants.

13.6 Equilibrium in Saturated Solutions

LEARNING GOAL: *Write the solubility product expression for a slightly soluble salt and calculate K_{sp}; use K_{sp} to determine the solubility.*

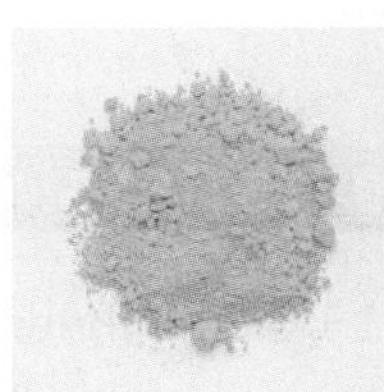

- In a saturated solution, a slightly soluble salt is in equilibrium with its ions.
- In a saturated solution, the concentrations of the ions from the slightly soluble salt are constant and can be used to calculate the solubility product constant, K_{sp}, for the salt.
- If K_{sp} for a slightly soluble salt is known, its solubility can be calculated.

CONCEPT MAP

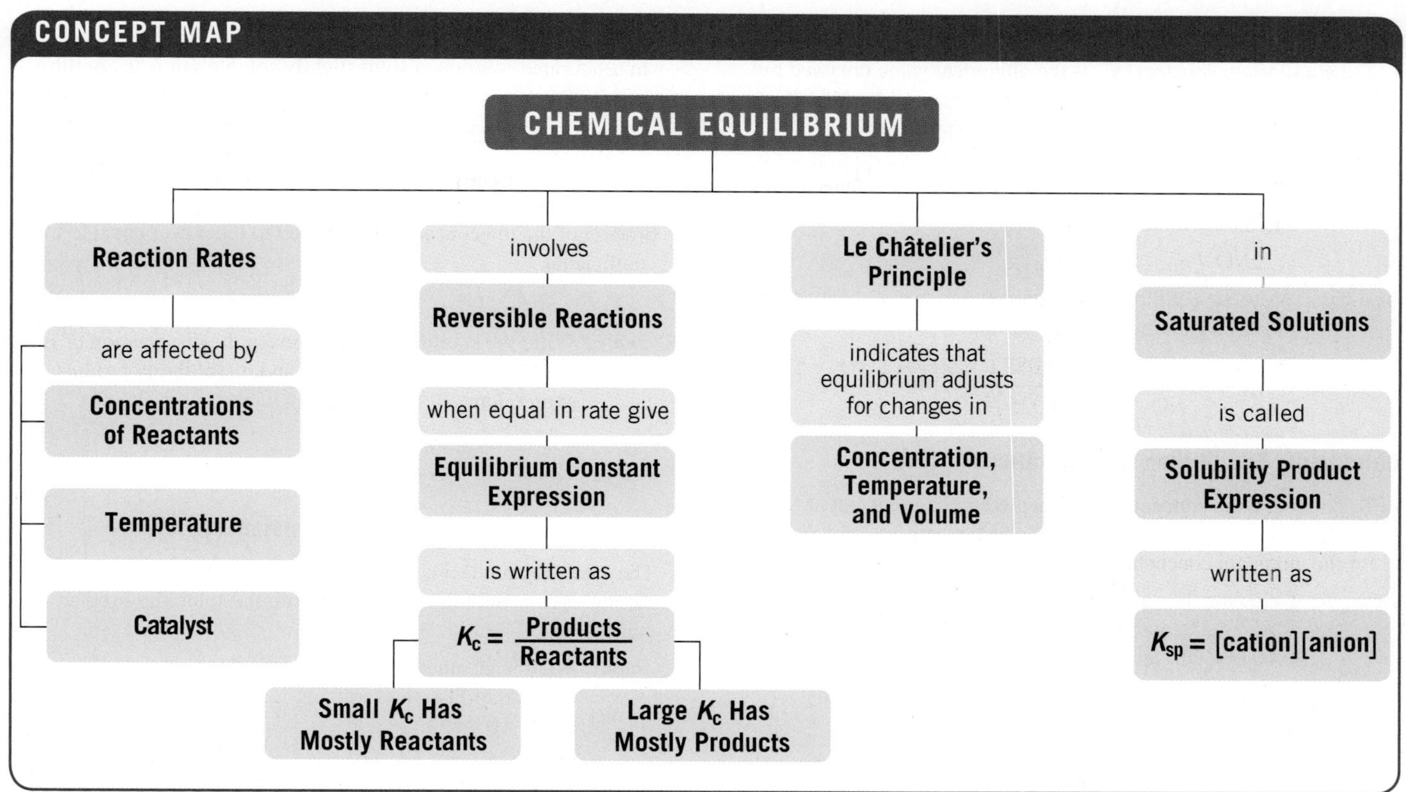

KEY TERMS

activation energy The energy that must be provided by a collision to break apart the bonds of the reacting molecules.

catalyst A substance that increases the rate of reaction by lowering the activation energy.

chemical equilibrium The point at which the rate of forward and reverse reactions are equal so that no further change in concentrations of reactants and products takes place.

collision theory A model for a chemical reaction stating that molecules must collide with sufficient energy and proper orientation in order to form products.

equilibrium constant, K_c The numerical value obtained by substituting the equilibrium concentrations of the components into the equilibrium constant expression.

equilibrium constant expression The ratio of the concentrations of products to the concentrations of reactants, with each component raised to an exponent equal to the coefficient of that compound in the balanced chemical equation.

heterogeneous equilibrium An equilibrium system in which the components are in different states.

homogeneous equilibrium An equilibrium system in which all components are in the same state.

Le Châtelier's principle When a stress is placed on a system at equilibrium, the equilibrium shifts to relieve that stress.

rate of reaction The speed at which reactants are used to form product(s).

reversible reaction A reaction in which a forward reaction occurs from reactants to products, and a reverse reaction occurs from products back to reactants.

solubility product constant, K_{sp} The product of the concentrations of the ions in a saturated solution of a slightly soluble salt, with each concentration raised to a power equal to its coefficient in the balanced equilibrium equation.

solubility product expression, K_{sp} The product of the ion concentration, with each concentration raised to an exponent equal to the coefficient in the balanced chemical equation.

CORE CHEMISTRY SKILLS

The chapter section containing each Core Chemistry Skill is shown in parentheses at the end of each heading.

Writing the Equilibrium Constant Expression (13.3)

- An equilibrium constant expression for a reversible reaction is written by multiplying the concentrations of the products in the numerator and dividing by the product of the concentrations of the reactants in the denominator.
- Each concentration is raised to a power equal to its coefficient in the balanced chemical equation:

$$K_c = \frac{[\text{Products}]}{[\text{Reactants}]} = \frac{[C]^c[D]^d}{[A]^a[B]^b} \quad \text{Coefficients}$$

Example: Write the equilibrium constant expression for the following chemical reaction:

$$2NO_2(g) \rightleftarrows N_2O_4(g)$$

Answer: $K_c = \frac{[N_2O_4]}{[NO_2]^2}$

Calculating an Equilibrium Constant (13.3)

- The equilibrium constant, K_c, is the numerical value obtained by substituting experimentally measured molar concentrations at equilibrium into the equilibrium constant expression.

Example: Calculate the numerical value of K_c for the following reaction when the equilibrium mixture contains 0.025 M NO_2 and 0.087 M N_2O_4:

$$2NO_2(g) \rightleftarrows N_2O_4(g)$$

Answer: Write the equilibrium constant expression, substitute the molar concentrations, and calculate.

$$K_c = \frac{[N_2O_4]}{[NO_2]^2} = \frac{[0.087]}{[0.025]^2} = 140$$

Calculating Equilibrium Concentrations (13.4)

- To determine the concentration of a product or a reactant at equilibrium, we use the equilibrium constant expression to solve for the unknown concentration.

Example: Calculate the equilibrium concentration for CF_4 if $K_c = 2.0$, and the equilibrium mixture contains 0.10 M COF_2 and 0.050 M CO_2.

$$2COF_2(g) \rightleftarrows CO_2(g) + CF_4(g)$$

Answer: Write the equilibrium constant expression.

$$K_c = \frac{[CO_2][CF_4]}{[COF_2]^2}$$

Rearrange the equation, substitute the molar concentrations, and calculate $[CF_4]$.

$$[CF_4] = \frac{K_c[COF_2]^2}{[CO_2]} = \frac{2.0[0.10]^2}{[0.050]} = 0.40 \text{ M}$$

Using Le Châtelier's Principle (13.5)

- Le Châtelier's principle states that when a system at equilibrium is disturbed by changes in concentration, volume, or temperature, the system will shift in the direction that will reduce that stress.

Example: Nitrogen and oxygen form dinitrogen pentoxide in an exothermic, combination reaction.

$$2N_2(g) + 5O_2(g) \rightleftarrows 2N_2O_5(g) + \text{heat}$$

For each of the following changes at equilibrium, indicate whether the equilibrium shifts in the direction of products, or reactants, or does not change:

a. remove some $N_2(g)$
b. decrease the temperature
c. increase the volume of the container

Answer:

a. Removing a reactant shifts the equilibrium in the direction of the reactants.
b. Decreasing the temperature shifts the equilibrium of an exothermic reaction in the direction of products, which produces heat.
c. Increasing the volume of the container shifts the equilibrium in the direction of the greater number of moles of gas, which is in the direction of the reactants.

Writing the Solubility Product Expression (13.6)

- In a saturated solution, a solid slightly soluble salt is in equilibrium with its ions.

$$FeF_2(s) \rightleftarrows Fe^{2+}(aq) + 2F^-(aq)$$

- We represent the solubility of solid FeF_2 in a saturated aqueous solution by the solubility product expression, K_{sp}, which is the product of the ion concentrations raised to the power equal to the coefficients.

$$K_{sp} = [Fe^{2+}][F^-]^2$$

Example: Write the equilibrium equation for the dissociation of the slightly soluble salt PbI_2, and its solubility product expression.

Answer:

$$PbI_2(s) \rightleftarrows Pb^{2+}(aq) + 2I^-(aq) \quad K_{sp} = [Pb^{2+}][I^-]^2$$

Calculating a Solubility Product Constant (13.6)

- The solubility product constant, K_{sp}, is calculated by substituting the molar concentrations of the ions into the solubility product expression.

Example: What is the numerical value of K_{sp} for a saturated solution of PbI_2 that contains 1.3×10^{-3} M Pb^{2+} and 2.6×10^{-3} M I^-?

Answer: The K_{sp} is calculated by substituting the molar concentrations into the solubility product expression.

$$K_{sp} = [Pb^{2+}][I^-]^2 = [1.3 \times 10^{-3}][2.6 \times 10^{-3}]^2 = 8.8 \times 10^{-9}$$

Calculating the Molar Solubility (13.6)

- The molar solubility, S, of a slightly soluble salt is the number of moles of solute that dissolves in 1 liter of solution.
- If we know the K_{sp} of a slightly soluble salt, we can calculate the molar solubility, S, of the slightly soluble salt.

Example A: What is the solubility product expression and the molar solubility, S, of $NiS(s)$, which has a K_{sp} of 4.0×10^{-20}?

Answer A: $K_{sp} = [Ni^{2+}][S^{2-}] = S \times S = S^2 = 4.0 \times 10^{-20}$

$$S = \sqrt{4.0 \times 10^{-20}} = 2.0 \times 10^{-10} \text{ M}$$

Therefore, 2.0×10^{-10} mol of NiS will dissolve in 1 L of saturated solution.

Example B: For the above example, calculate the molar solubility of NiS when the soluble salt $NiCl_2$ is added to the saturated solution of NiS to give 1.0×10^{-2} M Ni^{2+}.

Answer B: We substitute the $[Ni^{2+}]$ into the K_{sp} for NiS, and rearrange the equation to solve for the new molar solubility, S, of NiS.

$$K_{sp} = [Ni^{2+}][S^{2-}] = [1.0 \times 10^{-2}]S = 4.0 \times 10^{-20}$$

$$S = \frac{4.0 \times 10^{-20}}{[1.0 \times 10^{-2}]} = 4.0 \times 10^{-18} \text{ M}$$

Therefore, only 4.0×10^{-18} mol of NiS will dissolve in 1 L of saturated solution with the common ion Ni^{2+}.

UNDERSTANDING THE CONCEPTS

The chapter sections to review are shown in parentheses at the end of each question.

13.43 Write the equilibrium constant expression for each of the following reactions: (13.3)

a. $CH_4(g) + 2O_2(g) \rightleftharpoons CO_2(g) + 2H_2O(g)$

b. $4NH_3(g) + 3O_2(g) \rightleftharpoons 2N_2(g) + 6H_2O(g)$

c. $C(s) + 2H_2(g) \rightleftharpoons CH_4(g)$

13.44 Write the equilibrium constant expression for each of the following reactions: (13.3)

a. $2C_2H_6(g) + 7O_2(g) \rightleftharpoons 4CO_2(g) + 6H_2O(g)$

b. $2KHCO_3(s) \rightleftharpoons K_2CO_3(s) + CO_2(g) + H_2O(g)$

c. $4NH_3(g) + 5O_2(g) \rightleftharpoons 4NO(g) + 6H_2O(g)$

13.45 Would the equilibrium constant, K_c, for the reaction in the diagrams have a large or small value? (13.4)

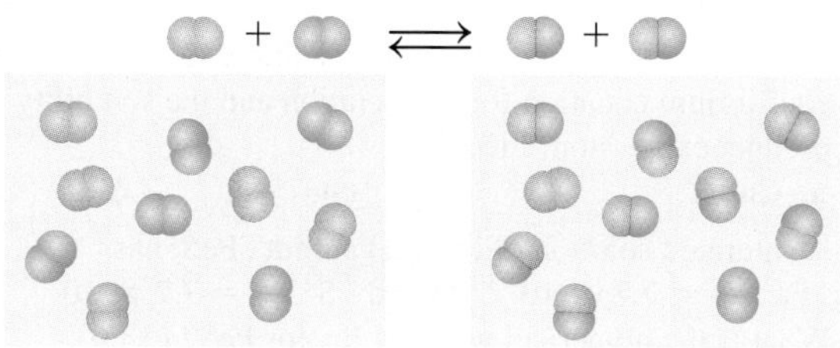

Initially — At equilibrium

13.46 Would the equilibrium constant, K_c, for the reaction in the diagrams have a large or small value? (13.4)

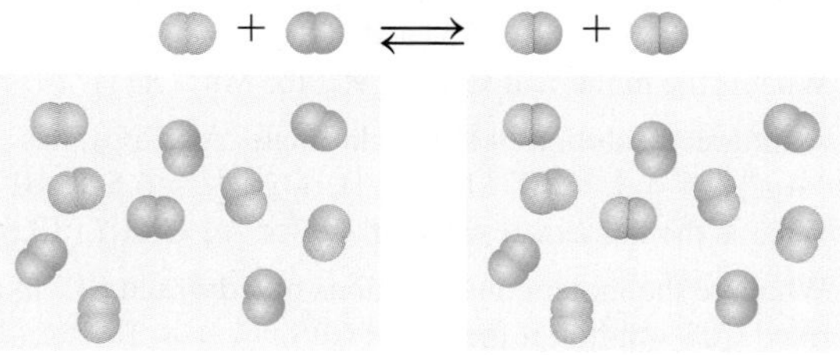

Initially — At equilibrium

13.47 Would T_2 be higher or lower than T_1 for the reaction shown in the diagrams? (13.5)

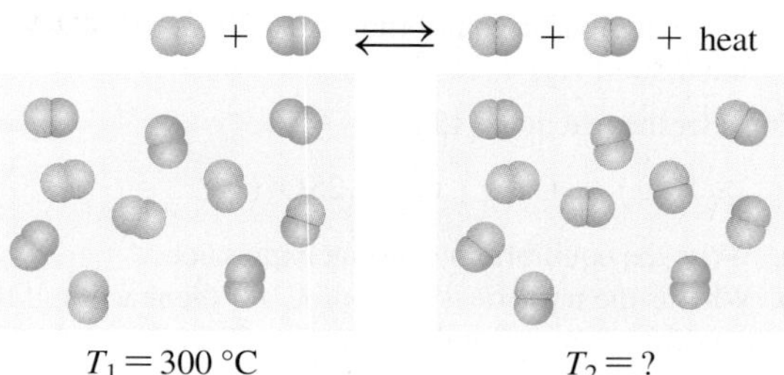

$T_1 = 300\ °C$ — $T_2 = ?$

13.48 Would the reaction shown in the diagrams be exothermic or endothermic? (13.5)

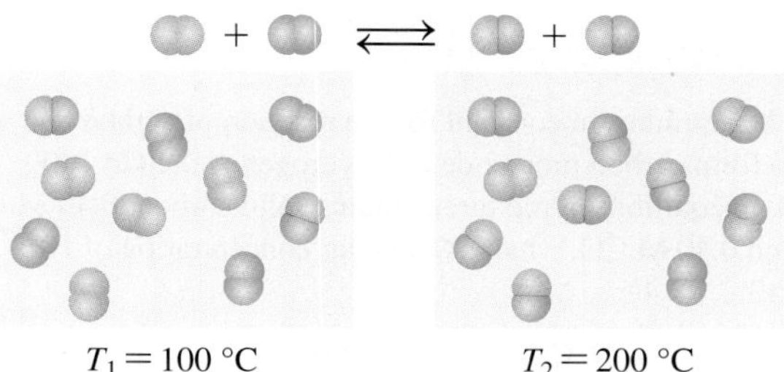

$T_1 = 100\ °C$ — $T_2 = 200\ °C$

ADDITIONAL QUESTIONS AND PROBLEMS

13.49 For each of the following changes at equilibrium, indicate whether the equilibrium shifts in the direction of products, reactants, or does not change: (13.5)

$$C_2H_4(g) + Cl_2(g) \rightleftharpoons C_2H_4Cl_2(g) + \text{heat}$$

a. raise the temperature of the reaction

b. decrease the volume of the reaction container

c. add a catalyst

d. add more $Cl_2(g)$

13.50 For each of the following changes at equilibrium, indicate whether the equilibrium shifts in the direction of products, reactants, or does not change: (13.5)

$$N_2(g) + O_2(g) + \text{heat} \rightleftharpoons 2NO(g)$$

a. raise the temperature of the reaction

b. decrease the volume of the reaction container

c. add a catalyst

d. add some $N_2(g)$

13.51 For each of the following reactions, indicate if the equilibrium mixture contains mostly products, mostly reactants, or both reactants and products: (13.4)

a. $H_2(g) + Cl_2(g) \rightleftharpoons 2HCl(g)$ $K_c = 1.3 \times 10^{34}$

b. $2NOBr(g) \rightleftharpoons 2NO(g) + Br_2(g)$ $K_c = 2.0$

c. $2NOCl(g) \rightleftharpoons Cl_2(g) + 2NO(g)$ $K_c = 2.7 \times 10^{-9}$

d. $C(s) + H_2O(g) \rightleftharpoons CO(g) + H_2(g)$ $K_c = 6.3 \times 10^{-1}$

13.52 For each of the following reactions, indicate if the equilibrium mixture contains mostly products, mostly reactants, or both reactants and products: (13.4)

a. $2H_2O(g) \rightleftharpoons 2H_2(g) + O_2(g)$ $K_c = 4 \times 10^{-48}$

b. $N_2(g) + 3H_2(g) \rightleftharpoons 2NH_3(g)$ $K_c = 0.30$

c. $2SO_2(g) + O_2(g) \rightleftharpoons 2SO_3(g)$ $K_c = 1.2 \times 10^9$

d. $H_2(g) + S(s) \rightleftharpoons 2H_2S(g)$ $K_c = 7.8 \times 10^5$

13.53 Consider the reaction: (13.3)

$$2NH_3(g) \rightleftharpoons N_2(g) + 3H_2(g)$$

a. Write the equilibrium constant expression.
b. What is the numerical value of K_c for the reaction if the concentrations at equilibrium are 0.20 M NH_3, 3.0 M N_2, and 0.50 M H_2?

13.54 Consider the reaction: (13.3)

$$2SO_2(g) + O_2(g) \rightleftharpoons 2SO_3(g)$$

a. Write the equilibrium constant expression.
b. What is the numerical value of K_c for the reaction if the concentrations at equilibrium are 0.10 M SO_2, 0.12 M O_2, and 0.60 M SO_3?

13.55 The equilibrium constant for the following reaction is 5.0 at 100 °C. If an equilibrium mixture contains 0.50 M NO_2, what is the molar concentration of N_2O_4? (13.3, 13.4)

$$2NO_2(g) \rightleftharpoons N_2O_4(g)$$

13.56 The equilibrium constant for the reaction of carbon and water to form carbon monoxide and hydrogen is 0.20 at 1000 °C. If an equilibrium mixture contains solid carbon, 0.40 M H_2O, and 0.40 M CO, what is the molar concentration of H_2? (13.3, 13.4)

$$C(s) + H_2O(g) \rightleftharpoons CO(g) + H_2(g)$$

13.57 According to Le Châtelier's principle, does the equilibrium shift in the direction of products or reactants when O_2 is added to the equilibrium mixture of each of the following reactions? (13.5)
a. $3O_2(g) \rightleftharpoons 2O_3(g)$
b. $2CO_2(g) \rightleftharpoons 2CO(g) + O_2(g)$
c. $P_4(g) + 5O_2(g) \rightleftharpoons P_4O_{10}(s)$
d. $2SO_2(g) + 2H_2O(g) \rightleftharpoons H_2S(g) + 3O_2(g)$

13.58 According to Le Châtelier's principle, does the equilibrium shift in the direction of products or reactants when N_2 is added to the equilibrium mixture of each of the following reactions? (13.5)
a. $2NH_3(g) \rightleftharpoons 3H_2(g) + N_2(g)$
b. $N_2(g) + O_2(g) \rightleftharpoons 2NO(g)$
c. $2NO_2(g) \rightleftharpoons N_2(g) + 2O_2(g)$
d. $4NH_3(g) + 3O_2(g) \rightleftharpoons 2N_2(g) + 6H_2O(g)$

13.59 Would decreasing the volume of the container for each of the following reactions cause the equilibrium to shift in the direction of products or reactants, or not change? (13.5)
a. $3O_2(g) \rightleftharpoons 2O_3(g)$
b. $2CO_2(g) \rightleftharpoons 2CO(g) + O_2(g)$
c. $P_4(g) + 5O_2(g) \rightleftharpoons P_4O_{10}(s)$
d. $2SO_2(g) + 2H_2O(g) \rightleftharpoons 2H_2S(g) + 3O_2(g)$

13.60 Would increasing the volume of the container for each of the following reactions cause the equilibrium to shift in the direction of products or reactants, or not change? (13.5)
a. $2NH_3(g) \rightleftharpoons 3H_2(g) + N_2(g)$
b. $N_2(g) + O_2(g) \rightleftharpoons 2NO(g)$
c. $N_2(g) + 2O_2(g) \rightleftharpoons 2NO_2(g)$
d. $4NH_3(g) + 3O_2(g) \rightleftharpoons 2N_2(g) + 6H_2O(g)$

13.61 For each of the following slightly soluble salts, write the equilibrium equation for dissociation and the solubility product expression: (13.6)
a. $CuCO_3$ **b.** PbF_2 **c.** $Fe(OH)_3$

13.62 For each of the following slightly soluble salts, write the equilibrium equation for dissociation and the solubility product expression: (13.6)
a. CuS **b.** Ag_2SO_4 **c.** $Zn(OH)_2$

13.63 A saturated solution of iron(II) sulfide, FeS, has $[Fe^{2+}] = 7.7 \times 10^{-10}$ M and $[S^{2-}] = 7.7 \times 10^{-10}$ M. What is the numerical value of K_{sp} for FeS? (13.6)

13.64 A saturated solution of copper(I) chloride, CuCl, has $[Cu^+] = 1.1 \times 10^{-3}$ M and $[Cl^-] = 1.1 \times 10^{-3}$ M. What is the numerical value of K_{sp} for CuCl? (13.6)

13.65 A saturated solution of manganese(II) hydroxide, $Mn(OH)_2$, has $[Mn^{2+}] = 3.7 \times 10^{-5}$ M and $[OH^-] = 7.4 \times 10^{-5}$ M. What is the numerical value of K_{sp} for $Mn(OH)_2$? (13.6)

13.66 A saturated solution of silver chromate, Ag_2CrO_4, has $[Ag^+] = 1.3 \times 10^{-4}$ M and $[CrO_4^{2-}] = 6.5 \times 10^{-5}$ M. What is the numerical value of K_{sp} for Ag_2CrO_4? (13.6)

13.67 What are the molar concentrations of Cd^{2+} and S^{2-} in a saturated CdS solution if the K_{sp} of CdS is 1.0×10^{-24}? (13.6)

13.68 What are the molar concentrations of Cu^{2+} and CO_3^{2-} in a saturated $CuCO_3$ solution if the K_{sp} of $CuCO_3$ is 1×10^{-26}? (13.6)

13.69 What is the molar solubility, *S*, of $BaSO_4$ in a solution that has $[Ba^{2+}] = 1.0 \times 10^{-3}$ M (see Table 13.6 for the K_{sp})? (13.6)

13.70 What is the molar solubility, *S*, of AgCl in a solution that has $[Cl^-] = 2.0 \times 10^{-2}$ M (see Table 13.6 for the K_{sp})? (13.6)

CHALLENGE QUESTIONS

13.71 For each of the following K_c values, indicate whether the equilibrium mixture contains mostly reactants, mostly products, or similar amounts of reactants and products: (13.4)
a. $N_2(g) + O_2(g) \rightleftharpoons 2NO(g)$ $K_c = 1 \times 10^{-30}$
b. $H_2(g) + Br_2(g) \rightleftharpoons 2HBr(g)$ $K_c = 2.0 \times 10^{19}$

13.72 For each of the following K_c values, indicate whether the equilibrium mixture contains mostly reactants, mostly products, or similar amounts of reactants and products: (13.4)
a. $Cl_2(g) + 2NO(g) \rightleftharpoons 2NOCl(g)$ $K_c = 3.7 \times 10^8$
b. $N_2(g) + 2H_2(g) \rightleftharpoons 2N_2H_4(g)$ $K_c = 7.4 \times 10^{-26}$

13.73 The K_c at 100 °C is 2.0 for the decomposition reaction of NOBr. (13.3, 13.4, 13.5)

$$2NOBr(g) \rightleftharpoons 2NO(g) + Br_2(g)$$

In an experiment, 1.0 mol of NOBr, 1.0 mol of NO, and 1.0 mol of Br_2 were placed in a 1.0 L container.
a. Write the equilibrium constant expression for the reaction.
b. Is the system at equilibrium?
c. If not, will the rate of the forward or reverse reaction initially speed up?
d. At equilibrium, which concentration(s) will be greater than 1.0 mol/L, and which will be less than 1.0 mol/L?

13.74 Consider the following reaction: (13.3, 13.4, 13.5)

$$PCl_5(g) \rightleftharpoons PCl_3(g) + Cl_2(g)$$

a. Write the equilibrium constant expression for the reaction.
b. Initially, 0.60 mol of PCl_5 is placed in a 1.0 L flask. At equilibrium, there is 0.16 mol of PCl_3 in the flask. What are the equilibrium concentrations of PCl_5 and Cl_2?

c. What is the numerical value of the equilibrium constant, K_c, for the reaction?
d. If 0.20 mol of Cl_2 is added to the equilibrium mixture, will the concentration of PCl_5 increase or decrease?

13.75 Indicate how each of the following will affect the equilibrium concentration of CO in the following reaction: (13.3, 13.5)

$$C(s) + H_2O(g) + 31\text{ kcal} \rightleftharpoons CO(g) + H_2(g)$$

a. add more $H_2(g)$
b. increase the temperature of the reaction
c. increase the volume of the container
d. decrease the volume of the container
e. add a catalyst

13.76 Indicate how each of the following will affect the equilibrium concentration of NH_3 in the following reaction: (13.3, 13.5)

$$4NH_3(g) + 5O_2(g) \rightleftharpoons 4NO(g) + 6H_2O(g) + 906\text{ kJ}$$

a. add more $O_2(g)$
b. increase the temperature of the reaction
c. increase the volume of the container
d. add more $NO(g)$
e. remove some $H_2O(g)$

13.77 Indicate if you would increase or decrease the volume of the container to *increase* the yield of the products in each of the following: (13.5)
a. $2C(s) + O_2(g) \rightleftharpoons 2CO(g)$
b. $2CH_4(g) \rightleftharpoons C_2H_2(g) + 3H_2(g)$
c. $2H_2(g) + O_2(g) \rightleftharpoons 2H_2O(g)$

13.78 Indicate if you would increase or decrease the volume of the container to *increase* the yield of the products in each of the following: (13.5)
a. $Cl_2(g) + 2NO(g) \rightleftharpoons 2NOCl(g)$
b. $N_2(g) + 2H_2(g) \rightleftharpoons N_2H_4(g)$
c. $N_2O_4(g) \rightleftharpoons 2NO_2(g)$

13.79 The antacid milk of magnesia, which contains $Mg(OH)_2$, is used to neutralize excess stomach acid. If the solubility of $Mg(OH)_2$ in water is 9.7×10^{-3} g/L, what is the numerical value of K_{sp}? (13.6)

13.80 The slightly soluble salt PbF_2 has a solubility in water of 0.74 g/L. What is the numerical value of K_{sp} of PbF_2? (13.6)

ANSWERS

Answers to Study Checks

13.1 Lowering the temperature will decrease the rate of reaction.

13.2 $H_2(g) + Br_2(g) \rightleftharpoons 2HBr(g)$

13.3 $2NO(g) + O_2(g) \rightleftharpoons 2NO_2(g)$

13.4 $FeO(s) + CO(g) \rightleftharpoons Fe(s) + CO_2(g) \quad K_c = \dfrac{[CO_2]}{[CO]}$

13.5 $K_c = 27$

13.6 $[C_2H_5OH] = 2.7\text{ M}$

13.7 Decreasing the volume of the reaction container will shift the equilibrium in the direction of the product side, which has fewer moles of gas.

13.8 a. A decrease in temperature for an exothermic reaction will cause a shift in the direction of products to add heat.
b. A decrease in temperature for an endothermic reaction will cause a shift in the direction of reactants to add heat.

13.9 $K_{sp} = 5.3 \times 10^{-13}$

13.10 $K_{sp} = 5.3 \times 10^{-12}$

13.11 $S = 1.6 \times 10^{-5}\text{ M}$

13.12 $S = 3.1 \times 10^{-6}\text{ M}$

Answers to Selected Questions and Problems

13.1 a. The rate of the reaction indicates how fast the products form or how fast the reactants are used up.
b. At room temperature, the reactions involved in the growth of bread mold will proceed at a faster rate than at the lower temperature of the refrigerator.

13.3 The number of collisions will increase when the number of Br_2 molecules is increased.

13.5 a. increase b. increase
c. increase d. decrease

13.7 A reversible reaction is one in which a forward reaction converts reactants to products, whereas a reverse reaction converts products to reactants.

13.9 a. not at equilibrium b. at equilibrium
c. at equilibrium

13.11 a. $K_c = \dfrac{[CS_2][H_2]^4}{[CH_4][H_2S]^2}$ b. $K_c = \dfrac{[N_2][O_2]}{[NO]^2}$
c. $K_c = \dfrac{[CS_2][O_2]^4}{[SO_3]^2[CO_2]}$

13.13 a. homogeneous equilibrium
b. heterogeneous equilibrium
c. homogeneous equilibrium
d. heterogeneous equilibrium

13.15 a. $K_c = \dfrac{[O_2]^3}{[O_3]^2}$ b. $K_c = [CO_2][H_2O]$
c. $K_c = \dfrac{[H_2]^3[CO]}{[CH_4][H_2O]}$ d. $K_c = \dfrac{[H_2]^2}{[HCl]^4}$

13.17 $K_c = 1.5$

13.19 $K_c = 260$

13.21 $K_c = 0.26$

13.23 a. mostly products b. mostly products
c. mostly reactants

13.25 $[H_2] = 1.1 \times 10^{-3}\text{ M}$

13.27 $[NOBr] = 1.4\text{ M}$

13.29 a. Equilibrium shifts in the direction of the product.
b. Equilibrium shifts in the direction of the reactants.
c. Equilibrium shifts in the direction of the product.
d. Equilibrium shifts in the direction of the reactants.
e. No shift in equilibrium occurs.

13.31 **a.** Equilibrium shifts in the direction of the product.
b. Equilibrium shifts in the direction of the product.
c. Equilibrium shifts in the direction of the product.
d. No shift in equilibrium occurs.
e. Equilibrium shifts in the direction of the reactants.

13.33 **a.** $BaCO_3(s) \rightleftharpoons Ba^{2+}(aq) + CO_3^{2+}(aq)$; $K_{sp} = [Ba^{2+}][CO_3^{2-}]$
b. $CaF_2(s) \rightleftharpoons Ca^{2+}(aq) + 2F^-(aq)$; $K_{sp} = [Ca^{2+}][F^-]^2$
c. $Ag_3PO_4(s) \rightleftharpoons 3Ag^+(aq) + PO_4^{3-}(aq)$; $K_{sp} = [Ag^+]^3[PO_4^{3-}]$

13.35 $K_{sp} = 1 \times 10^{-10}$

13.37 $K_{sp} = 8.8 \times 10^{-12}$

13.39 $[Cu^+] = 1 \times 10^{-6}\,M$; $[I^-] = 1 \times 10^{-6}\,M$

13.41 $S = 9.0 \times 10^{-8}\,M$

13.43 **a.** $K_c = \dfrac{[CO_2][H_2O]^2}{[CH_4][O_2]^2}$ **b.** $K_c = \dfrac{[N_2]^2[H_2O]^6}{[NH_3]^4[O_2]^3}$
c. $K_c = \dfrac{[CH_4]}{[H_2]^2}$

13.45 The equilibrium constant for the reaction would have a large value.

13.47 T_2 is lower than T_1.

13.49 **a.** Equilibrium shifts in the direction of the reactants.
b. Equilibrium shifts in the direction of the products.
c. There is no change in equilibrium.
d. Equilibrium shifts in the direction of the products.

13.51 **a.** mostly products **b.** both reactants and products
c. mostly reactants **d.** both reactants and products

13.53 **a.** $K_c = \dfrac{[N_2][H_2]^3}{[NH_3]^2}$ **b.** $K_c = 9.4$

13.55 $[N_2O_4] = 1.3\,M$

13.57 **a.** Equilibrium shifts in the direction of the products.
b. Equilibrium shifts in the direction of the reactants.
c. Equilibrium shifts in the direction of the products.
d. Equilibrium shifts in the direction of the reactants.

13.59 **a.** Equilibrium shifts in the direction of the products.
b. Equilibrium shifts in the direction of the reactants.
c. Equilibrium shifts in the direction of the products.
d. Equilibrium shifts in the direction of the reactants.

13.61 **a.** $CuCO_3(s) \rightleftharpoons Cu^{2+}(aq) + CO_3^{2-}(aq)$; $K_{sp} = [Cu^{2+}][CO_3^{2-}]$
b. $PbF_2(s) \rightleftharpoons Pb^{2+}(aq) + 2F^-(aq)$; $K_{sp} = [Pb^{2+}][F^-]^2$
c. $Fe(OH)_3(s) \rightleftharpoons Fe^{3+}(aq) + 3OH^-(aq)$; $K_{sp} = [Fe^{3+}][OH^-]^3$

13.63 $K_{sp} = 5.9 \times 10^{-19}$

13.65 $K_{sp} = 2.0 \times 10^{-13}$

13.67 $[Cd^{2+}] = 1.0 \times 10^{-12}\,M$; $[S^{2-}] = 1.0 \times 10^{-12}\,M$

13.69 $S = 1.1 \times 10^{-7}\,M$

13.71 **a.** A small K_c value indicates that the equilibrium mixture contains mostly reactants.
b. A large K_c value indicates that the equilibrium mixture contains mostly products.

13.73 **a.** $K_c = \dfrac{[NO]^2[Br_2]}{[NOBr]^2}$
b. When the concentrations are placed in the expression, the result is 1.0, which is not equal to K_c. The system is not at equilibrium.
c. The rate of the forward reaction will increase.
d. The $[Br_2]$ and $[NO]$ will increase and $[NOBr]$ will decrease.

13.75 **a.** decrease **b.** increase
c. increase **d.** decrease
e. no change

13.77 **a.** increase **b.** increase
c. decrease

13.79 $K_{sp} = 2.0 \times 10^{-11}$

14 Acids and Bases

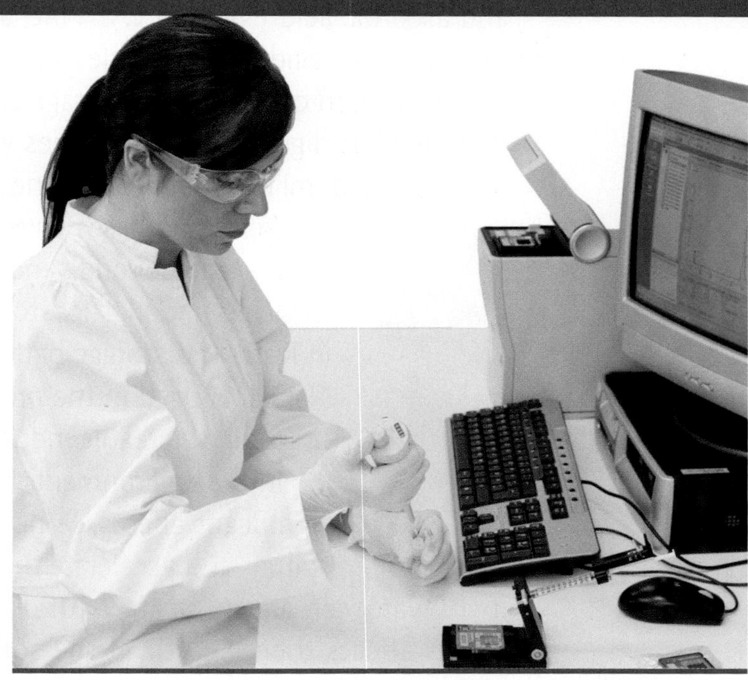

LOOKING AHEAD

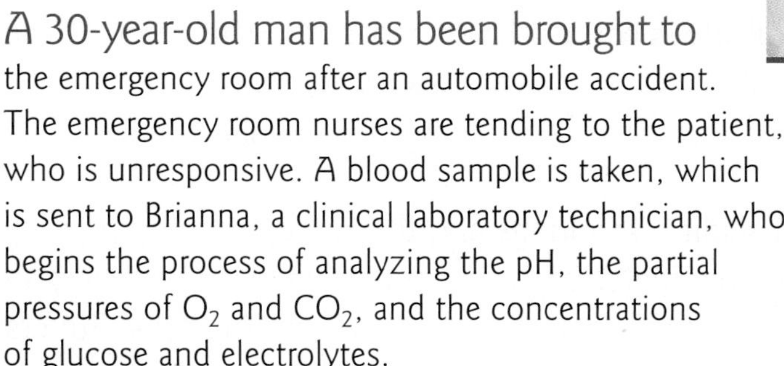

A 30-year-old man has been brought to the emergency room after an automobile accident. The emergency room nurses are tending to the patient, who is unresponsive. A blood sample is taken, which is sent to Brianna, a clinical laboratory technician, who begins the process of analyzing the pH, the partial pressures of O_2 and CO_2, and the concentrations of glucose and electrolytes.

Within minutes, Brianna determines that the patient's blood pH is 7.30 and the partial pressure of CO_2 gas is above the desired level. Blood pH is typically in the range of 7.35–7.45, and a value less than 7.35 indicates a state of acidosis. Respiratory acidosis occurs due to an increase in the partial pressure of CO_2 gas in the bloodstream which prevents the biochemical buffers in blood from making a change in the pH.

Brianna recognizes these signs and immediately contacts the emergency room to inform them that the patient's airway may be blocked. In the emergency room, they provide the patient with an IV containing bicarbonate to increase the blood pH and begin the process of unblocking the patient's airway. Shortly afterward, the patient's airway is cleared, and his blood pH and partial pressure of CO_2 gas return to normal.

Career: Clinical Laboratory Technician

Clinical laboratory technicians, also known as medical laboratory technicians, perform a wide variety of tests on body fluids and cells that help in the diagnosis and treatment of patients. These tests range from determining blood concentrations of glucose and cholesterol to determining drug levels in the blood for transplant patients or a patient undergoing treatment. Clinical laboratory technicians also prepare specimens in the detection of cancerous tumors, and type blood samples for transfusions. Clinical laboratory technicians must also interpret and analyze the test results, which are then passed on to the physician.

Acids and bases are important substances in health, industry, and the environment. One of the most common characteristics of acids is their sour taste. Lemons and grapefruits are sour because they contain organic acids such as citric and ascorbic acid (vitamin C). Vinegar tastes sour because it contains acetic acid. We produce lactic acid in our muscles when we exercise. Acid from bacteria turns milk sour in the production of yogurt and cottage cheese. We have hydrochloric acid in our stomachs that helps us digest food. Sometimes we take antacids, which are bases such as sodium bicarbonate or milk of magnesia, to neutralize the effects of too much stomach acid.

Citrus fruits are sour because of the presence of acids.

Acids and bases have many uses in the chemical industry. Sulfuric acid, H_2SO_4, is the world's most widely produced chemical. It is used to produce fertilizers and plastics, to manufacture detergents, and to conduct electricity in lead–acid storage batteries for automobiles. The base sodium hydroxide, NaOH, is used in the production of pulp and paper, in the manufacture of soaps, in the textile industries, and in the manufacture of glass.

In the environment, the acidity, or pH, of rain, water, and soil can have significant effects. When rain becomes too acidic, it can dissolve marble statues and accelerate the corrosion of metals. In lakes and ponds, the acidity of water can affect the ability of plants and fish to survive. The acidity of soil around plants affects their growth. If the soil pH is too acidic or too basic, the roots of the plant cannot take up some nutrients. Most plants thrive in soil with a nearly neutral pH, although certain plants, such as orchids, camellias, and blueberries, require a more acidic soil.

The pH of a solution describes its acidity. The lungs and the kidneys are the primary organs that regulate the pH of body fluids, including blood and urine. Major changes in the pH of the body fluids can severely affect biological activities within the cells. Buffers are present to prevent large fluctuations in pH.

CHAPTER READINESS*

Key Math Skills

- Solving Equations (1.4D)
- Using Scientific Notation (2.2)

Core Chemistry Skills

- Writing Ionic Formulas (6.2, 6.4)
- Balancing a Chemical Equation (8.2)
- Identifying Functional Groups (8.4)
- Using Concentration as a Conversion Factor (12.4)
- Writing the Equilibrium Constant Expression (13.3)
- Calculating Equilibrium Concentrations (13.4)
- Using Le Châtelier's Principle (13.5)

*These Key Math Skills and Core Chemistry Skills from previous chapters are listed here for your review as you proceed to the materials in this chapter.

14.1 Acids and Bases

LEARNING GOAL

Describe and name Arrhenius acids and bases, and organic acids.

The term *acid* comes from the Latin word *acidus*, which means "sour." We are familiar with the sour tastes of vinegar and lemons and other common acids in foods.

In 1887, the Swedish chemist Svante Arrhenius was the first to describe **acids** as substances that produce hydrogen ions (H^+) when they dissolve in water. For example, hydrogen chloride ionizes in water to give hydrogen ions, H^+, and chloride ions, Cl^-. It is the hydrogen ions that give acids a sour taste, change the blue litmus indicator to red, and corrode some metals.

$$\underset{\text{Polar molecular compound}}{HCl(g)} \xrightarrow[\text{Ionization}]{H_2O} \underset{\text{Hydrogen ion}}{H^+(aq)} + Cl^-(aq)$$

Naming Acids

Acids dissolve in water to produce hydrogen ions, along with a negative ion that may be a simple nonmetal anion or a polyatomic ion.

When an acid dissolves in water to produce a hydrogen ion and a simple nonmetal anion, the prefix *hydro* is used before the name of the nonmetal, and its *ide* ending is changed to *ic acid*. For example, hydrogen chloride (HCl) dissolves in water to form $HCl(aq)$, which is named hydrochloric acid. An exception is hydrogen cyanide (HCN), which as an acid is named hydrocyanic acid, $HCN(aq)$. When the anion is an oxygen-containing polyatomic ion, the *ate* in the name of the polyatomic anion is replaced by *ic acid*. If the acid contains a polyatomic ion with an *ite* ending, its name ends in *ous acid*.

The halogens in Group 7A (17) can form more than two oxygen-containing acids. For chlorine, the common form is chloric acid, $HClO_3$, which contains the chlorate polyatomic ion (ClO_3^-). For the acid that contains one more oxygen atom than the common form, the prefix *per* is used; $HClO_4$ is named *perchloric acid*. When the polyatomic ion in the acid has one oxygen atom less than the common form, the suffix *ous* is used. Thus, $HClO_2$ is named *chlorous acid*; it contains the chlorite ion, ClO_2^-. The prefix *hypo* is used for the acid that has two oxygen atoms less than the common form; $HClO$ is named *hypochlorous acid*. The names of some common acids and their anions are listed in Table 14.1.

TABLE 14.1 Naming Common Acids

Acid	Name of Acid	Anion	Name of Anion
HCl	Hydrochloric acid	Cl^-	Chloride
HBr	Hydrobromic acid	Br^-	Bromide
HCN	Hydrocyanic acid	CN^-	Cyanide
HNO_3	Nitric acid	NO_3^-	Nitrate
HNO_2	Nitrous acid	NO_2^-	Nitrite
H_2SO_4	Sulfuric acid	SO_4^{2-}	Sulfate
H_2SO_3	Sulfurous acid	SO_3^{2-}	Sulfite
H_2CO_3	Carbonic acid	CO_3^{2-}	Carbonate
H_3PO_4	Phosphoric acid	PO_4^{3-}	Phosphate
$HClO_4$	Perchloric acid	ClO_4^-	Perchlorate
$HClO_3$	Chloric acid	ClO_3^-	Chlorate
$HClO_2$	Chlorous acid	ClO_2^-	Chlorite
$HClO$	Hypochlorous acid	ClO^-	Hypochlorite
$HC_2H_3O_2$	Acetic acid	$C_2H_3O_2^-$	Acetate

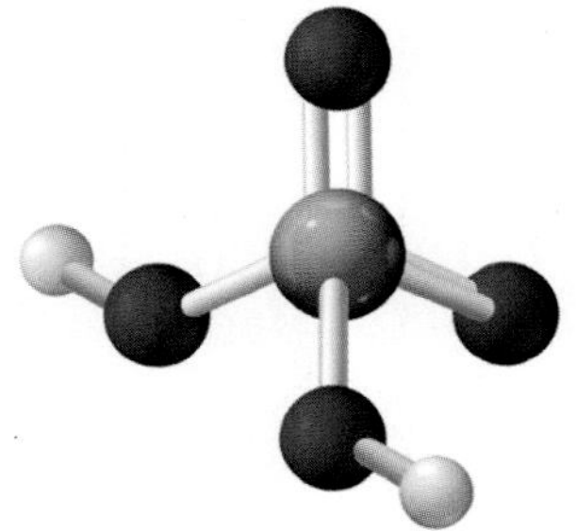

Sulfuric acid contains two H atoms that can dissociate in aqueous solutions.

CONCEPT CHECK 14.1 Naming Acids

a. If H_2SO_4 is named sulfuric acid, what is the name of H_2SO_3? Why?
b. In part **a**, why is the prefix *hydro* not used at the beginning of either name?

ANSWER

a. H_2SO_3 is named sulfurous acid. The acid of the polyatomic anion that ends in *ite* replaces the *ite* ending with *ous acid.*
b. The prefix *hydro* is used only when the anion is a simple nonmetal anion, and not with an acid that includes a polyatomic ion.

Red ants inject formic acid under the skin, which causes burning and irritation.

Naming Carboxylic Acids

A *carboxylic acid* contains a *carboxyl group*, which is a hydroxyl group attached to a carbonyl group. Many carboxylic acids have common names, which are derived from their natural sources. Formic acid is injected under the skin from bee or red ant stings and other insect bites. Acetic acid is produced when ethanol in wines and apple cider reacts with the oxygen in the air. Propionic acid is obtained from the fats in dairy products. Butyric acid gives the foul odor to rancid butter (see Table 14.2).

TABLE 14.2 Names and Natural Sources of Carboxylic Acids

Condensed Structural Formula	IUPAC Name	Common Name	Occurs In
$H-\overset{O}{\overset{\|}{C}}-OH$	Methanoic acid	Formic acid	Ant and bee stings (Latin *formica*, "ant")
$CH_3-\overset{O}{\overset{\|}{C}}-OH$	Ethanoic acid	Acetic acid	Vinegar (Latin *acetum*, "vinegar")
$CH_3-CH_2-\overset{O}{\overset{\|}{C}}-OH$	Propanoic acid	Propionic acid	Dairy products (Greek *pro*, "first," *pion*, "fat")
$CH_3-CH_2-CH_2-\overset{O}{\overset{\|}{C}}-OH$	Butanoic acid	Butyric acid	Rancid butter (Latin *butyrum*, "butter")

The IUPAC names of carboxylic acids are based on the alkane names of the corresponding carbon chains. We identify the longest carbon chain containing the carboxyl group and replace the final *e* with *oic acid* (see Figure 14.1).

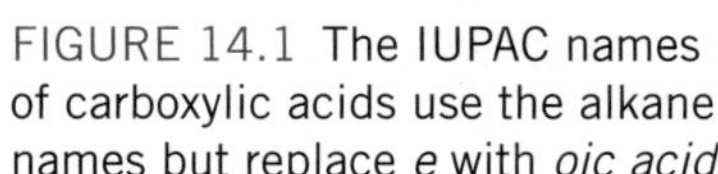

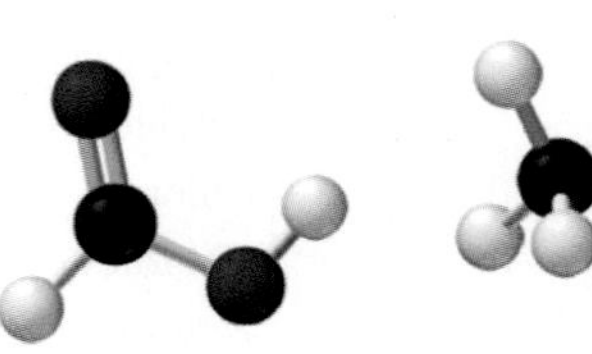

Methanoic acid (formic acid)

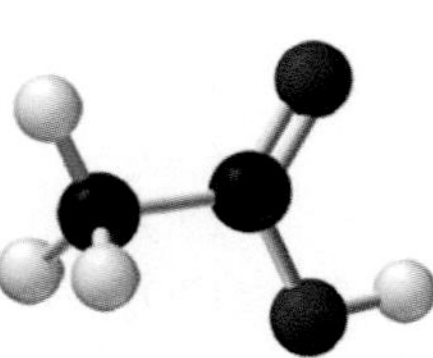

Ethanoic acid (acetic acid)

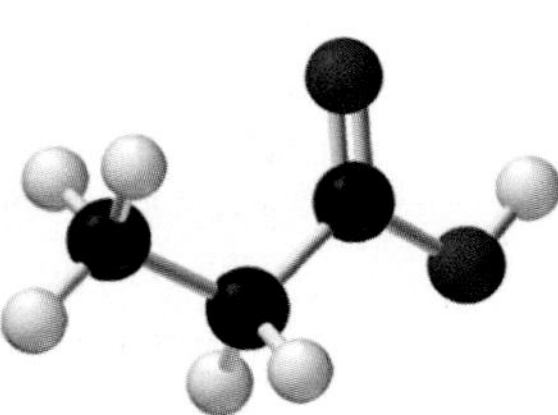

Propanoic acid (propionic acid)

FIGURE 14.1 The IUPAC names of carboxylic acids use the alkane names but replace *e* with *oic acid.*

Q What is the IUPAC and common name of a carboxylic acid with a chain of four carbons?

Bases

You may be familiar with some household bases such as antacids, drain openers, and oven cleaners. According to the Arrhenius theory, **bases** are ionic compounds that dissociate into cations and hydroxide ions (OH^-) when they dissolve in water. They are another example of strong electrolytes. For example, sodium hydroxide is an Arrhenius base that dissociates completely in water to give sodium ions, Na^+, and hydroxide ions, OH^-.

Most Arrhenius bases are metals from Groups 1A (1) and 2A (2), such as NaOH, KOH, LiOH, and $Ca(OH)_2$. The hydroxide ions (OH^-) give Arrhenius bases common characteristics, such as a bitter taste and a slippery feel. A base turns litmus indicator blue and phenolphthalein indicator pink. Table 14.3 compares some characteristics of acids and bases.

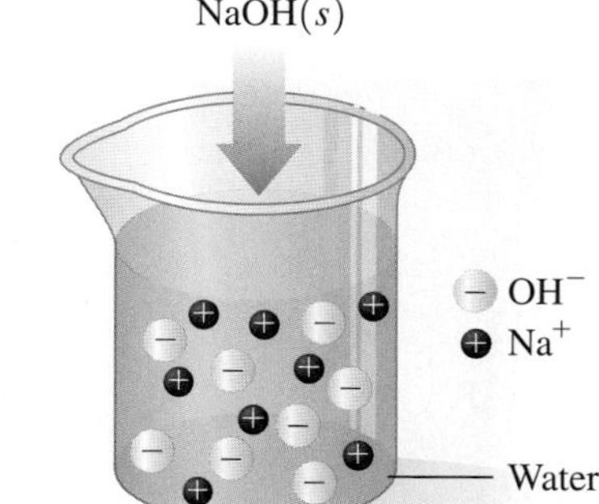

$$NaOH(s) \xrightarrow{H_2O} Na^+(aq) + OH^-(aq)$$

Ionic compound | Ionization | Hydroxide ion

An Arrhenius base produces a cation and an OH^- anion in an aqueous solution.

TABLE 14.3 Some Characteristics of Acids and Bases

Characteristic	Acids	Bases
Arrhenius	Produce H^+	Produce OH^-
Electrolytes	Yes	Yes
Taste	Sour	Bitter, chalky
Feel	May sting	Soapy, slippery
Litmus	Red	Blue
Phenolphthalein	Colorless	Pink
Neutralization	Neutralize bases	Neutralize acids

Naming Bases

Typical Arrhenius bases are named as *hydroxides*.

Base	Name
NaOH	Sodium **hydroxide**
KOH	Potassium **hydroxide**
$Ca(OH)_2$	Calcium **hydroxide**
$Al(OH)_3$	Aluminum **hydroxide**

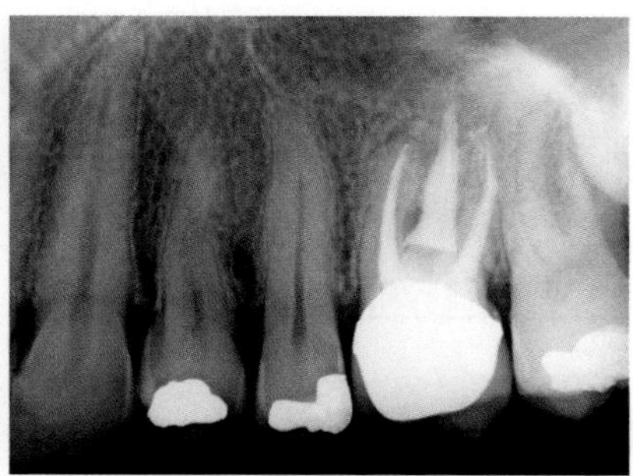

Calcium hydroxide, $Ca(OH)_2$, also called slaked lime, is used in the food industry to produce beverages, in tanning to neutralize acids, and in dentistry as a filler for root canals.

CONCEPT CHECK 14.2 Ionization of an Arrhenius Base

When dried corn kernels are soaked in limewater (calcium hydroxide solution), the product is hominy, which is used to make grits. Write an equation for the ionization of calcium hydroxide in water.

ANSWER

When calcium hydroxide, which has the formula $Ca(OH)_2$, dissolves in water, the solution contains calcium ions (Ca^{2+}) and twice as many hydroxide ions (OH^-). The equation is written as

$$Ca(OH)_2(s) \xrightarrow{H_2O} Ca^{2+}(aq) + 2OH^-(aq)$$

Hominy for grits is prepared by soaking corn kernels in a calcium hydroxide solution.

A soft drink contains H_3PO_4 and H_2CO_3.

SAMPLE PROBLEM 14.1 Names and Formulas of Acids and Bases

a. Identify each of the following as an acid or a base and give its name:
   1. H_3PO_4, ingredient in soft drinks
   2. NaOH, ingredient in oven cleaner
b. Write the formula for each of the following:
   1. magnesium hydroxide, ingredient in antacids
   2. hydrobromic acid, used industrially to prepare bromide compounds

SOLUTION

a. 1. acid; phosphoric acid **2.** base; sodium hydroxide
b. 1. $Mg(OH)_2$ **2.** HBr

STUDY CHECK 14.1

a. Identify as an acid or base and give the name for $HClO_3$.
b. Write the formula for iron(III) hydroxide.

QUESTIONS AND PROBLEMS

14.1 Acids and Bases

LEARNING GOAL: *Describe and name Arrhenius acids and bases, and organic acids.*

14.1 Indicate whether each of the following statements indicates an acid, a base, or both:
a. has a sour taste
b. neutralizes bases
c. produces H^+ ions in water
d. is named barium hydroxide
e. is an electrolyte

14.2 Indicate whether each of the following statements indicates an acid, a base, or both:
a. makes a red ant sting burn
b. produces OH^- in water
c. has a slippery feel
d. conducts an electrical current
e. turns litmus red

14.3 Name each of the following as an acid or a base:
a. HCl **b.** $Ca(OH)_2$ **c.** H_2CO_3
d. HNO_3 **e.** H_2SO_3 **f.** $HBrO_2$
g. $CH_3—\overset{\overset{\displaystyle O}{\|}}{C}—OH$

14.4 Name each of the following as an acid or a base:
a. $Al(OH)_3$ **b.** HBr **c.** H_2SO_4
d. KOH **e.** HNO_2 **f.** $HClO_2$
g. $CH_3—CH_2—\overset{\overset{\displaystyle O}{\|}}{C}—OH$

14.5 Write formulas for each of the following acids and bases:
a. rubidium hydroxide **b.** hydrofluoric acid
c. formic acid **d.** lithium hydroxide
e. ammonium hydroxide **f.** periodic acid

14.6 Write formulas for each of the following acids and bases:
a. barium hydroxide **b.** hydroiodic acid
c. nitric acid **d.** strontium hydroxide
e. acetic acid **f.** hypochlorous acid

LEARNING GOAL

Identify conjugate acid–base pairs for Brønsted–Lowry acids and bases.

14.2 Brønsted–Lowry Acids and Bases

In 1923, J. N. Brønsted in Denmark and T. M. Lowry in Great Britain expanded the definition of acids and bases to include bases that do not contain OH^- ions. A **Brønsted–Lowry acid** can donate a hydrogen ion, H^+, to another substance, and a **Brønsted–Lowry base** can accept a hydrogen ion.

A Brønsted–Lowry acid is a substance that donates H^+.

A Brønsted–Lowry base is a substance that accepts H^+.

A free hydrogen ion, H^+, does not actually exist in water. Its attraction to polar water molecules is so strong that the H^+ bonds to a water molecule and forms a **hydronium ion, H_3O^+**.

$$H—\ddot{O}\!:\!(—H) + H^+ \longrightarrow \left[H—\ddot{O}(—H)—H\right]^+$$

Water Hydrogen ion Hydronium ion

We can write the formation of a hydrochloric acid solution as a transfer of H^+ from hydrogen chloride to water. By accepting an H^+ in the reaction, water is acting as a base according to the Brønsted–Lowry concept.

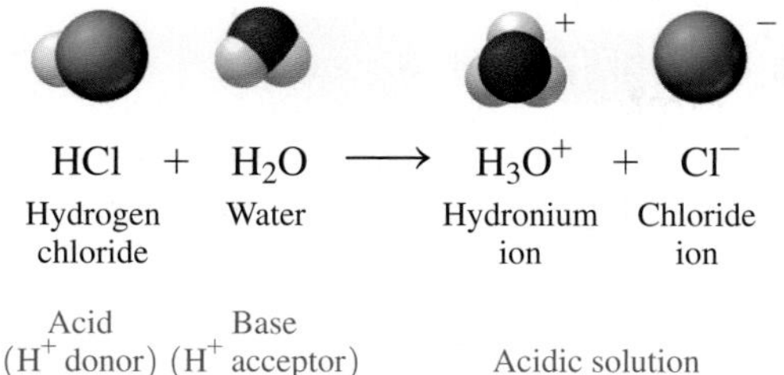

In another reaction, ammonia (NH_3) reacts with water. Because the nitrogen atom of NH_3 has a stronger attraction for H^+, water acts as an acid by donating H^+.

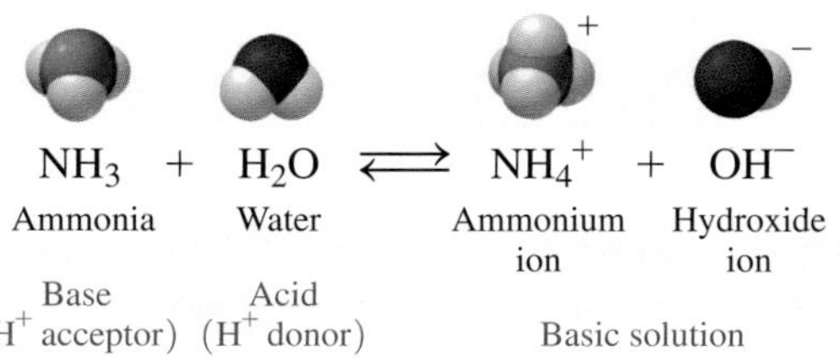

SAMPLE PROBLEM 14.2 Acids and Bases

In each of the following equations, identify the reactant that is a Brønsted–Lowry acid and the reactant that is a Brønsted–Lowry base:

a. $HBr(aq) + H_2O(l) \longrightarrow H_3O^+(aq) + Br^-(aq)$
b. $H_2O(l) + HS^-(aq) \longrightarrow H_2S(aq) + OH^-(aq)$

SOLUTION

a. HBr, Brønsted–Lowry acid; H_2O, Brønsted–Lowry base
b. H_2O, Brønsted–Lowry acid; HS^-, Brønsted–Lowry base

STUDY CHECK 14.2

When HNO_3 reacts with water, water acts as a Brønsted–Lowry base. Write the equation for the reaction.

Conjugate Acid–Base Pairs

CORE CHEMISTRY SKILL 

Identifying Conjugate Acid–Base Pairs

According to the Brønsted–Lowry theory, a **conjugate acid–base pair** consists of molecules or ions related by the loss of one H^+ by an acid, and the gain of one H^+ by a base. Every acid–base reaction contains two conjugate acid–base pairs because an H^+ is transferred in both the forward and reverse directions. When an acid such as HF loses one H^+, the conjugate base F^- is formed. When the base H_2O gains an H^+, its conjugate acid, H_3O^+, is formed.

Because the overall reaction of HF is reversible, the conjugate acid H_3O^+ can donate H^+ to the conjugate base F^- and re-form the acid HF and the base H_2O. Using the relationship of loss and gain of one H^+, we can now identify the conjugate acid–base pairs as HF/F^- along with H_3O^+/H_2O.

Conjugate acid–base pair

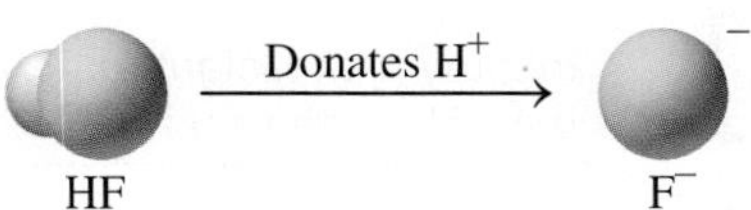

Conjugate acid–base pair

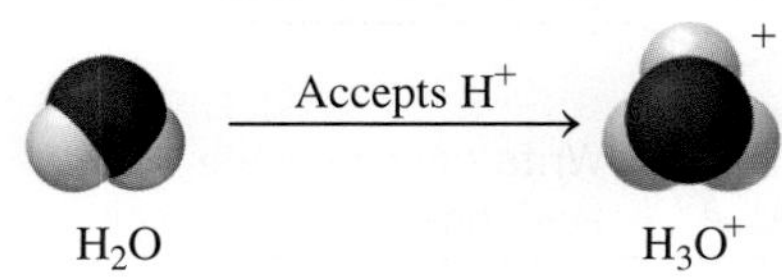

H$^+$ gain

H$^+$ loss

Acid — Conjugate base

$HF(aq) + H_2O(l) \rightleftarrows F^-(aq) + H_3O^+(aq)$

Base — Conjugate acid

H$^+$ gain

H$^+$ loss

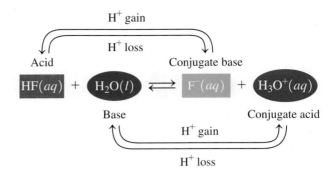

Table 14.4 gives some more examples of conjugate acid–base pairs.

In another reaction, ammonia, NH_3, accepts H^+ from H_2O to form the conjugate acid NH_4^+ and conjugate base OH^-. Each of these conjugate acid–base pairs, NH_4^+/NH_3 and H_2O/OH^-, is related by the loss and gain of one H^+.

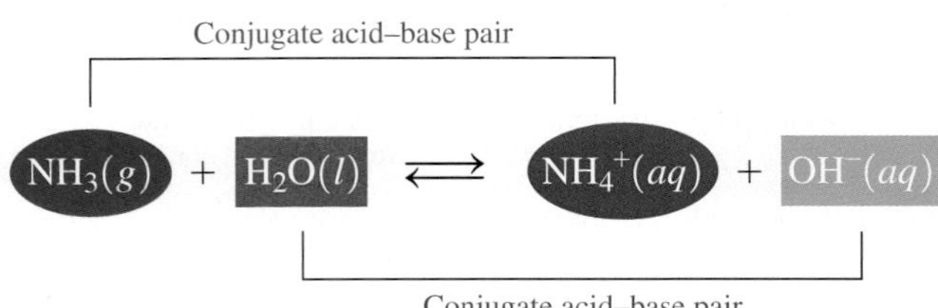

Ammonia, NH_3, acts as a base when it gains one H^+ to form its conjugate acid NH_4^+. Water acts as an acid by losing one H^+ to form its conjugate base OH^-.

In these two examples, we see that water can act as an acid when it donates H^+ or as a base when it accepts H^+. Substances that can act as both acids and bases are **amphoteric** or *amphiprotic*. For water, the most common amphoteric substance, the acidic or basic behavior depends on the other reactant. Water donates H^+ when it reacts with a stronger base, and it accepts H^+ when it reacts with a stronger acid. Another example of an amphoteric substance is bicarbonate, HCO_3^-. With a base, HCO_3^- acts as an acid and donates one H^+ to give CO_3^{2-}. However, when HCO_3^- reacts with an acid, it acts as a base and accepts one H^+ to form H_2CO_3.

Amphoteric substances act as both acids and bases.

H_3O^+ / H_2CO_3 ← Acts as a base — H_2O / HCO_3^- — Acts as an acid → OH^- / CO_3^{2-}

CONCEPT CHECK 14.3 Conjugate Acid–Base Pairs

a. Write the formula for the conjugate base of $HClO_3$.
b. Write the conjugate acid of HS^-.

ANSWER

a. A conjugate base forms when a Brønsted–Lowry acid loses H^+. When $HClO_3$ loses H^+, it forms its conjugate base ClO_3^-.
b. A conjugate acid forms when a Brønsted–Lowry base gains H^+. When HS^- gains H^+, it forms its conjugate acid H_2S.

Guide to Writing Conjugate Acid–Base Pairs

1 Identify the reactant that loses H$^+$ as the acid.

2 Identify the reactant that gains H$^+$ as the base.

3 Write the conjugate acid–base pairs for each.

SAMPLE PROBLEM 14.3 Identifying Conjugate Acid–Base Pairs

Identify the conjugate acid–base pairs in the following reaction:

$$HBr(aq) + NH_3(aq) \rightleftarrows Br^-(aq) + NH_4^+(aq)$$

SOLUTION

Step 1 Identify the reactant that loses H$^+$ as the acid.
In the reaction, HBr loses H^+ to form the product Br^-. Thus HBr is the conjugate acid and Br^- is its base.

Step 2 **Identify the reactant that gains H^+ as the base.**
In the reaction, NH_3 gains H^+ to form NH_4^+. Thus, NH_3 is a conjugate base and NH_4^+ is its acid.

Step 3 **Write the conjugate acid–base pairs for each.**

$$HBr/Br^-, NH_4^+/NH_3$$

STUDY CHECK 14.3

Identify the conjugate acid–base pairs in the following reaction:

$$HCN(aq) + SO_4^{2-}(aq) \rightleftharpoons CN^-(aq) + HSO_4^-(aq)$$

QUESTIONS AND PROBLEMS

14.2 Brønsted–Lowry Acids and Bases

LEARNING GOAL: *Identify conjugate acid–base pairs for Brønsted–Lowry acids and bases.*

14.7 Identify the reactant that is a Brønsted–Lowry acid and the reactant that is a Brønsted–Lowry base in each of the following:

a. $HI(aq) + H_2O(l) \longrightarrow I^-(aq) + H_3O^+(aq)$
b. $F^-(aq) + H_2O(l) \rightleftharpoons HF(aq) + OH^-(aq)$
c. $H_2S(aq) + CH_3{-}CH_2{-}NH_2(aq) \rightleftharpoons HS^-(aq) + CH_3{-}CH_2{-}NH_3^+(aq)$

14.8 Identify the reactant that is a Brønsted–Lowry acid and the reactant that is a Brønsted–Lowry base in each of the following:

a. $CO_3^{2-}(aq) + H_2O(l) \rightleftharpoons HCO_3^-(aq) + OH^-(aq)$
b. $H_2SO_4(aq) + H_2O(l) \longrightarrow HSO_4^-(aq) + H_3O^+(aq)$
c. $C_2H_3O_2^-(aq) + H_3O^+(aq) \rightleftharpoons HC_2H_3O_2(aq) + H_2O(l)$

14.9 Write the formula for the conjugate base for each of the following acids:

a. HF **b.** H_2O **c.** $H_2PO_3^-$
d. HSO_4^- **e.** $HClO_2$

14.10 Write the formula for the conjugate base for each of the following acids:

a. HCO_3^- **b.** $CH_3{-}NH_3^+$ **c.** HPO_4^{2-}
d. HNO_2 **e.** $HBrO$

14.11 Write the formula for the conjugate acid for each of the following bases:

a. CO_3^{2-} **b.** H_2O **c.** $H_2PO_4^-$
d. Br^- **e.** ClO_4^-

14.12 Write the formula for the conjugate acid for each of the following bases:

a. SO_4^{2-} **b.** CN^- **c.** NH_3
d. ClO_2^- **e.** HS^-

14.13 Identify the Brønsted–Lowry acid–base pairs in each of the following equations:

a. $H_2CO_3(aq) + H_2O(l) \rightleftharpoons HCO_3^-(aq) + H_3O^+(aq)$
b. $NH_4^+(aq) + H_2O(l) \rightleftharpoons NH_3(aq) + H_3O^+(aq)$
c. $HCN(aq) + NO_2^-(aq) \rightleftharpoons CN^-(aq) + HNO_2(aq)$
d. $CHO_2^-(aq) + HF(aq) \rightleftharpoons HCHO_2(aq) + F^-(aq)$

14.14 Identify the Brønsted–Lowry acid–base pairs in each of the following equations:

a. $H_3PO_4(aq) + H_2O(l) \rightleftharpoons H_2PO_4^-(aq) + H_3O^+(aq)$
b. $CO_3^{2-}(aq) + H_2O(l) \rightleftharpoons HCO_3^-(aq) + OH^-(aq)$
c. $H_3PO_4(aq) + NH_3(aq) \rightleftharpoons H_2PO_4^-(aq) + NH_4^+(aq)$
d. $HNO_2(aq) + CH_3{-}CH_2{-}NH_2(aq) \rightleftharpoons CH_3{-}CH_2{-}NH_3^+(aq) + NO_2^-(aq)$

14.15 When ammonium chloride dissolves in water, the ammonium ion NH_4^+ donates an H^+ to water. Write a balanced equation for the reaction of the ammonium ion with water.

14.16 When sodium carbonate dissolves in water, the carbonate ion CO_3^{2-} acts as a base. Write a balanced equation for the reaction of the carbonate ion with water.

14.3 Strengths of Acids and Bases

LEARNING GOAL

Write equations for the dissociation of strong and weak acids; identify the direction of reaction.

In the process called **dissociation**, an acid or a base separates into ions in water. The *strength* of an acid is determined by the moles of H_3O^+ that are produced for each mole of acid that dissociates. The *strength* of a base is determined by the moles of OH^- that are produced for each mole of base that dissolves. Strong acids and strong bases dissociate completely in water, whereas weak acids and weak bases dissociate only slightly, leaving most of the initial acid or base undissociated.

Strong and Weak Acids

Strong acids are examples of strong electrolytes because they donate hydrogen ions so easily that their dissociation in water is nearly complete. For example, when HCl, a strong acid, dissociates in water, H^+ is transferred to H_2O; the resulting solution contains essentially only the

Acids produce hydrogen ions in aqueous solution.

ions H_3O^+ and Cl^-. We consider the reaction of HCl in H_2O to go 100% to products. Thus, the equation for a strong acid such as HCl is written with a single arrow to the products.

$$HCl(g) + H_2O(l) \longrightarrow H_3O^+(aq) + Cl^-(aq)$$

There are only six common strong acids. All other acids are weak. Table 14.4 lists the relative strengths of acids and bases.

Weak acids are weak electrolytes because they dissociate slightly in water, which means that only a small percentage of H^+ is transferred from a weak acid to H_2O, forming only a small amount of H_3O^+ ions. A weak acid has a strong conjugate base, which is why the reverse reaction is more prevalent. Even at high concentrations, weak acids produce low concentrations of H_3O^+ ions (see Figure 14.2).

Many of the products we use at home contain weak acids. Organic acids such as citric acid and acetic acid are weak acids. Citric acid is a weak acid found in fruits and fruit juices such as lemons, oranges, and grapefruit. In the vinegar used in salad dressings, acetic acid ($HC_2H_3O_2$) is present typically as a 5% acetic acid solution. In water, a few $HC_2H_3O_2$ molecules donate H^+ to H_2O to form H_3O^+ ions and acetate ions $C_2H_3O_2^-$. The formation of hydronium ions from vinegar is the reason we notice the sour taste of vinegar. In a weak acid, a reverse reaction also takes place, which converts the H_3O^+ ions and acetate ions $C_2H_3O_2^-$ back to reactants. This means that a weak acid such as acetic acid reaches equilibrium between the mostly undissociated acid and its ions. We write the equation for a weak acid in an aqueous solution with a double arrow to indicate that the forward and reverse reactions are at equilibrium.

$$\underset{\text{Acetic acid}}{HC_2H_3O_2(aq)} + H_2O(l) \rightleftarrows \underset{\text{Acetate ion}}{C_2H_3O_2^-(aq)} + H_3O^+(aq)$$

Diprotic Acids

Some weak acids, such as carbonic acid, are *diprotic acids* that have two H^+, which dissociate one at a time. For example, carbonated soft drinks are prepared by dissolving

TABLE 14.4 Relative Strengths of Acids and Bases

Increasing Acid Strength ↑

Acid		Base	
Strong Acids			
Hydroiodic acid	HI	I^-	Iodide ion
Hydrobromic acid	HBr	Br^-	Bromide ion
Perchloric acid	$HClO_4$	ClO_4^-	Perchlorate ion
Hydrochloric acid	HCl	Cl^-	Chloride ion
Sulfuric acid	H_2SO_4	HSO_4^-	Hydrogen sulfate ion
Nitric acid	HNO_3	NO_3^-	Nitrate ion
Weak Acids			
Hydronium ion	H_3O^+	H_2O	Water
Hydrogen sulfate ion	HSO_4^-	SO_4^{2-}	Sulfate ion
Phosphoric acid	H_3PO_4	$H_2PO_4^-$	Dihydrogen phosphate ion
Hydrofluoric acid	HF	F^-	Fluoride ion
Nitrous acid	HNO_2	NO_2^-	Nitrite ion
Acetic acid	$HC_2H_3O_2$	$C_2H_3O_2^-$	Acetate ion
Carbonic acid	H_2CO_3	HCO_3^-	Bicarbonate ion
Hydrosulfuric acid	H_2S	HS^-	Hydrogen sulfide ion
Dihydrogen phosphate ion	$H_2PO_4^-$	HPO_4^{2-}	Hydrogen phosphate ion
Ammonium ion	NH_4^+	NH_3	Ammonia
Hydrocyanic acid	HCN	CN^-	Cyanide ion
Bicarbonate ion	HCO_3^-	CO_3^{2-}	Carbonate ion
Methylammonium ion	$CH_3{-}NH_3^+$	$CH_3{-}NH_2$	Methylamine
Hydrogen sulfide ion	HS^-	S^{2-}	Sulfide ion
Water	H_2O	OH^-	Hydroxide ion

Increasing Base Strength ↓

FIGURE 14.2 A strong acid such as HCl is completely dissociated ($\approx$100%), whereas a weak acid such as $HC_2H_3O_2$ is only slightly ionized to form a weak acid solution that contains mostly molecules and a few ions.

Q What is the difference between a strong acid and a weak acid?

CO_2 in water to form carbonic acid, H_2CO_3. A weak acid such as H_2CO_3 reaches equilibrium between the mostly undissociated H_2CO_3 molecules and the ions H_3O^+ and HCO_3^-.

$$H_2CO_3(aq) + H_2O(l) \rightleftarrows H_3O^+(aq) + HCO_3^-(aq)$$

Carbonic acid — Bicarbonate ion (hydrogen carbonate)

Because HCO_3^- is also a weak acid, a second dissociation can take place to produce another hydronium ion and the carbonate ion, CO_3^{2-}.

$$HCO_3^-(aq) + H_2O(l) \rightleftarrows H_3O^+(aq) + CO_3^{2-}(aq)$$

Bicarbonate ion (hydrogen carbonate) — Carbonate ion

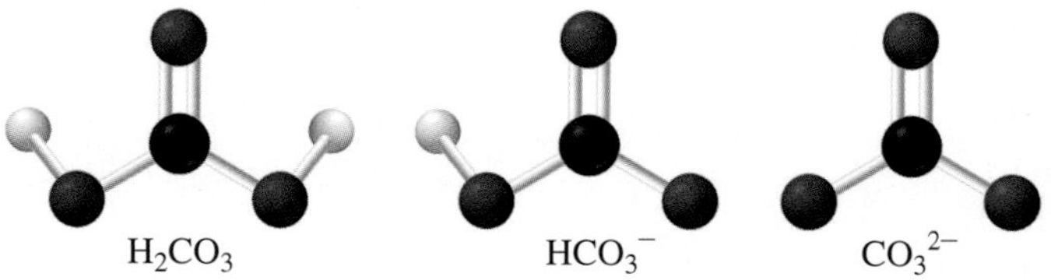

Carbonic acid, a weak acid, loses one H^+ to form hydrogen carbonate ion, which loses a second H^+ to form carbonate ion.

Sulfuric acid, H_2SO_4, is also a diprotic acid. However, its first dissociation is complete (100%), which means H_2SO_4 is a strong acid. The product, hydrogen sulfate HSO_4^-, can dissociate again but only slightly, which means that the hydrogen sulfate ion is a weak acid.

$$H_2SO_4(aq) + H_2O(l) \longrightarrow H_3O^+(aq) + HSO_4^-(aq)$$

Sulfuric acid — Bisulfate ion (hydrogen sulfate)

$$HSO_4^-(aq) + H_2O(l) \rightleftarrows H_3O^+(aq) + SO_4^{2-}(aq)$$

Bisulfate ion (hydrogen sulfate) — Sulfate ion

In summary, a strong acid such as HI in water dissociates completely to form an aqueous solution of the ions H_3O^+ and I^-. A weak acid such as HF dissociates only slightly in water to form an aqueous solution that consists mostly of undissociated HF molecules and only a few H_3O^+ and F^- ions (see Figure 14.3).

Strong acid: $HI(aq) + H_2O(l) \longrightarrow H_3O^+(aq) + I^-(aq)$ Completely dissociated

Weak acid: $HF(aq) + H_2O(l) \rightleftarrows H_3O^+(aq) + F^-(aq)$ Slightly dissociated

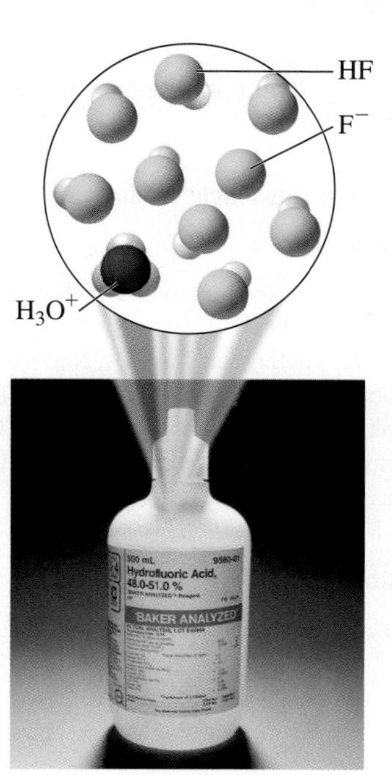

Hydrofluoric acid is the only halogen acid that is a weak acid.

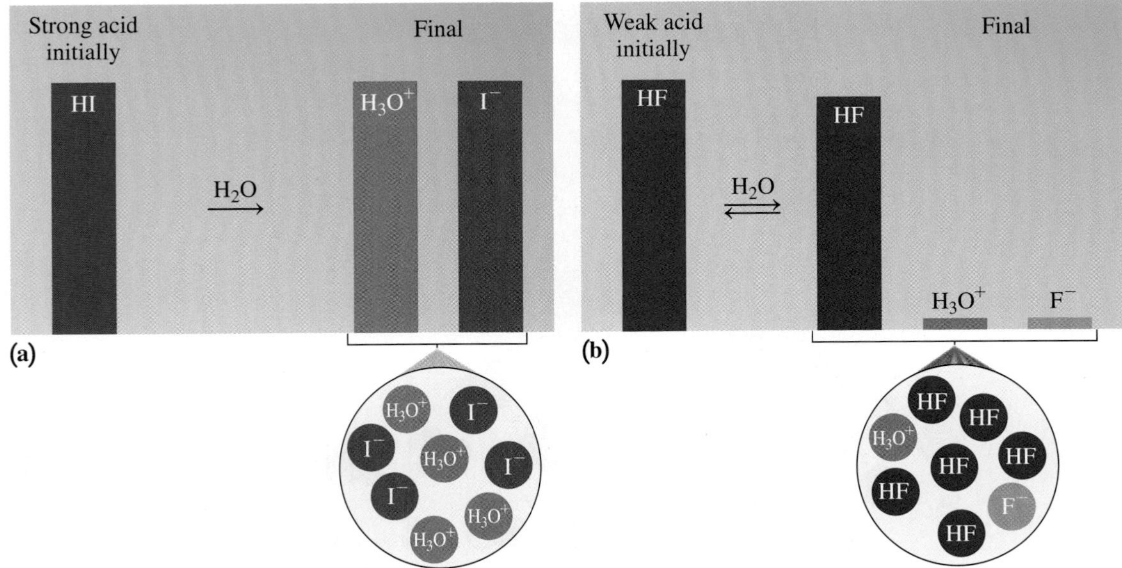

FIGURE 14.3 After dissociation in water, **(a)** a strong acid (HA) has a high concentration of H_3O^+ and A^-, and **(b)** a weak acid (HA) has a high concentration of HA and low concentrations of H_3O^+ and A^-.

Q How does the height of H_3O^+ and A^- in the bar diagram change for a weak acid?

Bases in household products are used to remove grease and to open drains.

Bases in Household Products

Weak Bases

Window cleaner, ammonia, NH_3
Bleach, NaOCl
Laundry detergent, Na_2CO_3, Na_3PO_4
Toothpaste and baking soda, $NaHCO_3$
Baking powder, scouring powder, Na_2CO_3
Lime for lawns and agriculture, $CaCO_3$
Laxatives, antacids, $Mg(OH)_2$, $Al(OH)_3$

Strong Bases

Drain cleaner, oven cleaner, NaOH

Strong and Weak Bases

As strong electrolytes, **strong bases** dissociate completely in water. Because these strong bases are ionic compounds, they dissociate in water to give an aqueous solution of metal ions and hydroxide ions. The Group 1A (1) hydroxides are very soluble in water, which can give high concentrations of OH^- ions. A few strong bases are less soluble in water, but what does dissolve dissociates completely as ions. For example, when KOH forms a KOH solution, it contains only the ions K^+ and OH^-.

$$KOH(s) \xrightarrow{H_2O} K^+(aq) + OH^-(aq)$$

Strong Bases

Lithium hydroxide LiOH
Sodium hydroxide NaOH
Potassium hydroxide KOH
Strontium hydroxide $Sr(OH)_2$*
Calcium hydroxide $Ca(OH)_2$*
Barium hydroxide $Ba(OH)_2$*

*Low solubility, but they dissociate completely

Sodium hydroxide, NaOH (also known as lye), is used in household products to remove grease from ovens and to clean drains. Because high concentrations of hydroxide ions cause severe damage to the skin and eyes, directions must be followed carefully when such products are used in the home and in the chemistry laboratory. If you spill an acid or a base on your skin or get some in your eyes, be sure to flood the area immediately with water for at least 10 minutes and seek medical attention.

Weak bases are weak electrolytes that are poor acceptors of hydrogen ions and produce very few ions in solution. A typical weak base, ammonia, NH_3, is found in window cleaners. In an aqueous solution, only a few ammonia molecules accept hydrogen ions to form NH_4^+ and OH^-.

$$\underset{\text{Ammonia}}{NH_3(g)} + H_2O(l) \rightleftharpoons \underset{\text{Ammonium hydroxide}}{NH_4^+(aq) + OH^-(aq)}$$

Direction of Reaction

There is a relationship between the components in each conjugate acid–base pair. Strong acids have weak conjugate bases that do not readily accept H^+. As the strength of the acid decreases, the strength of its conjugate base increases.

In any acid–base reaction, there are two acids and two bases. However, one acid is stronger than the other acid, and one base is stronger than the other base. By comparing their relative strengths, we can determine the direction of the reaction. For example, the strong acid H_2SO_4 readily gives up H^+ to water. The hydronium ion H_3O^+ produced is a weaker acid than H_2SO_4, and the conjugate base HSO_4^- is a weaker base than water.

$$\underset{\text{Stronger acid}}{H_2SO_4(aq)} + \underset{\text{Stronger base}}{H_2O(l)} \longrightarrow \underset{\text{Weaker acid}}{H_3O^+(aq)} + \underset{\text{Weaker base}}{HSO_4^-(aq)} \quad \text{Mostly products}$$

Let's look at another reaction in which water donates one H^+ to carbonate, CO_3^{2-}, to form HCO_3^- and OH^-. From Table 14.4, we see that HCO_3^- is a stronger acid than H_2O. We also see that OH^- is a stronger base than CO_3^{2-}. To reach equilibrium, the strong acid and strong base react in the direction of the weaker acid and weaker base.

$$\underset{\text{Weaker base}}{CO_3^{2-}(aq)} + \underset{\text{Weaker acid}}{H_2O(l)} \rightleftarrows \underset{\text{Stronger acid}}{HCO_3^-(aq)} + \underset{\text{Stronger base}}{OH^-(aq)} \quad \text{Mostly reactants}$$

CONCEPT CHECK 14.4 Strengths of Acids and Bases

For each of the following questions, select from HCO_3^-, HSO_4^-, or HNO_2:

a. Which is the strongest acid?
b. Which acid has the strongest conjugate base?

ANSWER

a. The strongest acid in this group is the acid listed closest to the top of Table 14.4, which is HSO_4^-.
b. The weakest acid, the acid listed nearest the bottom of Table 14.4, HCO_3^-, has the strongest conjugate base CO_3^{2-}.

SAMPLE PROBLEM 14.4 Direction of Reaction

Does the equilibrium mixture of the following reaction contain mostly reactants or products?

$$HF(aq) + H_2O(l) \rightleftarrows H_3O^+(aq) + F^-(aq)$$

SOLUTION

From Table 14.4, we see that HF is a weaker acid than H_3O^+ and that H_2O is a weaker base than F^-. Thus, the equilibrium mixture contains mostly reactants.

$$\underset{\text{Weaker acid}}{HF(aq)} + \underset{\text{Weaker base}}{H_2O(l)} \rightleftarrows \underset{\text{Stronger acid}}{H_3O^+(aq)} + \underset{\text{Stronger base}}{F^-(aq)}$$

STUDY CHECK 14.4

Does the equilibrium mixture for reaction of nitric acid and water contain mostly reactants or products?

QUESTIONS AND PROBLEMS

14.3 Strengths of Acids and Bases

LEARNING GOAL: *Write equations for the dissociation of strong and weak acids; identify the direction of reaction.*

14.17 What is meant by the phrase "A strong acid has a weak conjugate base"?

14.18 What is meant by the phrase "A weak acid has a strong conjugate base"?

14.19 Identify the stronger acid in each of the following pairs:
- **a.** HBr or HNO_2
- **b.** H_3PO_4 or HSO_4^-
- **c.** HCN or H_2CO_3

14.20 Identify the stronger acid in each of the following pairs:
- **a.** NH_4^+ or H_3O^+
- **b.** H_2SO_4 or HCl
- **c.** H_2O or H_2CO_3

14.21 Identify the weaker acid in each of the following pairs:
- **a.** HCl or HSO_4^-
- **b.** HNO_2 or HF
- **c.** HCO_3^- or NH_4^+

14.22 Identify the weaker acid in each of the following pairs:
- **a.** HNO_3 or HCO_3^-
- **b.** HSO_4^- or H_2O
- **c.** H_2SO_4 or H_2CO_3

14.23 Predict whether each of the following reactions contains mostly reactants or products at equilibrium:
- **a.** $H_2CO_3(aq) + H_2O(l) \rightleftarrows HCO_3^-(aq) + H_3O^+(aq)$
- **b.** $NH_4^+(aq) + H_2O(l) \rightleftarrows NH_3(aq) + H_3O^+(aq)$
- **c.** $HNO_2(aq) + NH_3(aq) \rightleftarrows NO_2^-(aq) + NH_4^+(aq)$

14.24 Predict whether each of the following reactions contains mostly reactants or products at equilibrium:
- **a.** $H_3PO_4(aq) + H_2O(l) \rightleftarrows H_3O^+(aq) + H_2PO_4^-(aq)$
- **b.** $CO_3^{2-}(aq) + H_2O(l) \rightleftarrows OH^-(aq) + HCO_3^-(aq)$
- **c.** $HS^-(aq) + F^-(aq) \rightleftarrows HF(aq) + S^{2-}(aq)$

14.25 Write an equation for the acid–base reaction between ammonium ion and sulfate ion. Why does the equilibrium mixture contain mostly reactants?

14.26 Write an equation for the acid–base reaction between nitrous acid and hydroxide ion. Why does the equilibrium mixture contain mostly products?

LEARNING GOAL

Write the expression for the dissociation constant of a weak acid or weak base.

14.4 Dissociation Constants for Acids and Bases

As we have seen, acids have different strengths depending on how much they dissociate in water. Because the dissociation of strong acids in water is essentially complete, the reaction is not considered to be an equilibrium situation. However, because weak acids in water dissociate only slightly, the ion products reach equilibrium with the undissociated weak acid molecules. For example, formic acid $HCHO_2$, the acid found in bee and ant stings, is a weak acid. Formic acid is an organic acid or a *carboxylic acid* in which the H^+ written on the left of the formula dissociates to form formate ion.

$$HCHO_2(aq) + H_2O(l) \rightleftarrows H_3O^+(aq) + CHO_2^-(aq)$$

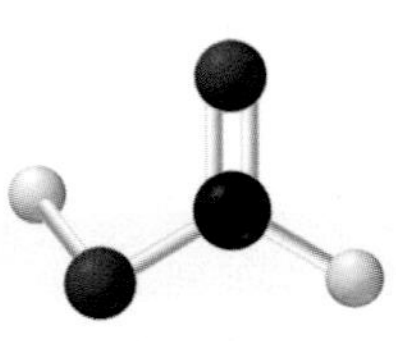

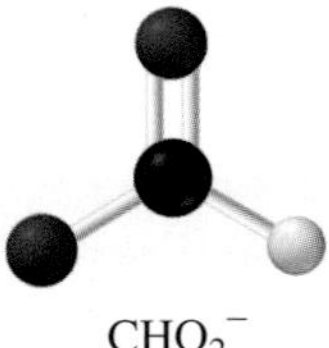

Formic acid, a weak acid, loses one H^+ to form formate ion.

Dissociation Constants for Weak Acids and Weak Bases

An equilibrium expression can be written for weak acids or weak bases that gives the ratio of the concentrations of products to the weak acid or base reactants. As with other equilibrium expressions, the molar concentration of the products is divided by the molar concentration of the reactants. Because water is a pure liquid with a constant concentration, it is omitted from the equilibrium expression. The numerical value of the acid equilibrium expression is the **acid dissociation constant, K_a** (or acid ionization constant). For example, the value of the K_a for formic acid at 25 °C is determined by experiment to be 1.8×10^{-4}. Thus, for the weak acid $HCHO_2$, the K_a is written

$$\frac{[H_3O^+][CHO_2^-]}{[HCHO_2]} = 1.8 \times 10^{-4} \quad \text{Acid dissociation constant}$$

The K_a for formic acid is small, which confirms that the equilibrium mixture of formic acid in water contains mostly reactants and only small amounts of the products. (Recall that the concentration units are omitted in the values given for equilibrium constants).

Weak acids have small K_a values. However, strong acids, which are essentially 100% dissociated, have very large K_a values, but these values are not usually given. Table 14.5 gives K_a values for selected weak acids.

TABLE 14.5 K_a and K_b Values for Selected Weak Acids and Bases

Acids (K_a)		
Phosphoric acid	H_3PO_4	7.5×10^{-3}
Hydrofluoric acid	HF	7.2×10^{-4}
Nitrous acid	HNO_2	4.5×10^{-4}
Formic acid	$HCHO_2$	1.8×10^{-4}
Acetic acid	$HC_2H_3O_2$	1.8×10^{-5}
Carbonic acid	H_2CO_3	4.3×10^{-7}
Hydrosulfuric acid	H_2S	9.1×10^{-8}
Dihydrogen phosphate	$H_2PO_4^-$	6.2×10^{-8}
Hydrocyanic acid	HCN	4.9×10^{-10}
Hydrogen phosphate	HPO_4^{2-}	2.2×10^{-13}
Bases (K_b)		
Methylamine	$CH_3{-}NH_2$	4.4×10^{-4}
Carbonate	CO_3^{2-}	2.2×10^{-4}
Ammonia	NH_3	1.8×10^{-5}

Let us now consider the equilibrium expression for the weak base methylamine:

$$CH_3{-}NH_2(aq) + H_2O(l) \rightleftharpoons CH_3{-}NH_3^+(aq) + OH^-(aq)$$

As we did with the acid dissociation expression, the concentration of water is omitted from the equilibrium expression, which gives the **base dissociation constant, K_b** (or base ionization constant). Thus, for a weak base such as methylamine, the K_b is written

$$K_b = \frac{[CH_3{-}NH_3^+][OH^-]}{[CH_3{-}NH_2]} = 4.4 \times 10^{-4}$$

Table 14.6 summarizes the characteristics of acids and bases in terms of strength and equilibrium position.

TABLE 14.6 Characteristics of Acids and Bases

Characteristic	**Strong Acids**	**Weak Acids**
Equilibrium Position	Toward products (ionized)	Toward reactants (not ionized)
K_a	Large	Small
$[H_3O^+]$ and $[A^-]$	100% of [HA] reacts	Small percent of [HA] reacts
Conjugate Base	Weak	Strong
Characteristic	**Strong Bases**	**Weak Bases**
Equilibrium Position	Toward products (ionized)	Toward reactants (not ionized)
K_b	Large	Small
$[BH^+]$ and $[OH^-]$	100% of [B] reacts	Small percent of [B] reacts
Conjugate Acid	Weak	Strong

CONCEPT CHECK 14.5 Acid Dissociation Constants

Nitrous acid, HNO_2, has a K_a of 4.5×10^{-4} and hypochlorous acid, HOCl, has a K_a of 3.5×10^{-4}. If each acid has a 0.10 M concentration, which solution has the higher concentration of H_3O^+?

ANSWER

Nitrous acid has a larger K_a value than does hypochlorous acid. When nitrous acid dissolves in water, there is more dissociation of HNO_2, which gives a higher concentration of H_3O^+ in solution.

SAMPLE PROBLEM 14.5 Writing an Acid Dissociation Constant Expression

Write the acid dissociation constant expression for nitrous acid.

SOLUTION

The equation for the dissociation of nitrous acid is written

$$HNO_2(aq) + H_2O(l) \rightleftarrows H_3O^+(aq) + NO_2^-(aq)$$

The acid dissociation constant expression is written as the concentration of the products divided by the concentration of the undissociated weak acid.

$$K_a = \frac{[H_3O^+][NO_2^-]}{[HNO_2]}$$

STUDY CHECK 14.5

Write the acid dissociation constant expression for hydrogen phosphate.

QUESTIONS AND PROBLEMS

14.4 Dissociation Constants for Acids and Bases

LEARNING GOAL: *Write the expression for the dissociation constant of a weak acid or weak base.*

14.27 Answer *true* or *false* for each of the following: A strong acid

- **a.** is completely ionized in aqueous solution
- **b.** has a small value of K_a
- **c.** has a strong conjugate base
- **d.** has a weak conjugate base
- **e.** is slightly ionized in aqueous solution

14.28 Answer *true* or *false* for each of the following: A weak acid

- **a.** is completely ionized in aqueous solution
- **b.** has a small value of K_a
- **c.** has a strong conjugate base
- **d.** has a weak conjugate base
- **e.** is slightly ionized in aqueous solution

14.29 Consider the following acids and their dissociation constants:

$$H_2SO_3(aq) + H_2O(l) \rightleftarrows H_3O^+(aq) + HSO_3^-(aq) \quad K_a = 1.2 \times 10^{-2}$$

$$HS^-(aq) + H_2O(l) \rightleftarrows H_3O^+(aq) + S^{2-}(aq) \quad K_a = 1.3 \times 10^{-19}$$

- **a.** Which is the stronger acid, H_2SO_3 or HS^-?
- **b.** What is the conjugate base of H_2SO_3?
- **c.** Which acid has the weaker conjugate base?
- **d.** Which acid has the stronger conjugate base?
- **e.** Which acid produces more ions?

14.30 Consider the following acids and their dissociation constants:

$$HPO_4^{2-}(aq) + H_2O(l) \rightleftarrows H_3O^+(aq) + PO_4^{3-}(aq) \quad K_a = 2.2 \times 10^{-13}$$

$$HCHO_2(aq) + H_2O(l) \rightleftarrows H_3O^+(aq) + CHO_2^-(aq) \quad K_a = 1.8 \times 10^{-4}$$

- **a.** Which is the weaker acid, HPO_4^{2-} or $HCHO_2$?
- **b.** What is the conjugate base of HPO_4^{2-}?
- **c.** Which acid has the weaker conjugate base?
- **d.** Which acid has the stronger conjugate base?
- **e.** Which acid produces more ions?

14.31 Phosphoric acid dissociates to form dihydrogen phosphate and hydronium ion. Phosphoric acid has a K_a of 7.5×10^{-3}. Write the equation for the reaction and the acid dissociation constant expression for phosphoric acid.

14.32 Aniline, $C_6H_5{-}NH_2$, a weak base with a K_b of 4.0×10^{-10}, reacts with water to form its conjugate acid, $C_6H_5{-}NH_3^+$. Write the equation for the reaction and the base dissociation constant expression for aniline.

LEARNING GOAL

Use the ion product of water to calculate the $[H_3O^+]$ *and* $[OH^-]$ *in an aqueous solution.*

14.5 Ionization of Water

We have seen that in some acid–base reactions, water is amphoteric, which means that it can act either as an acid or as a base. In pure water, there is a forward reaction between two water molecules that transfers H^+ from one water molecule to the other. One molecule acts as an acid by losing H^+, and the water molecule that gains H^+ acts as a base. Every time H^+ is transferred between two water molecules, the products are one H_3O^+ and one OH^-, which react in the reverse direction to re-form two water molecules. Thus, equilibrium is reached between the conjugate acid–base pairs of water.

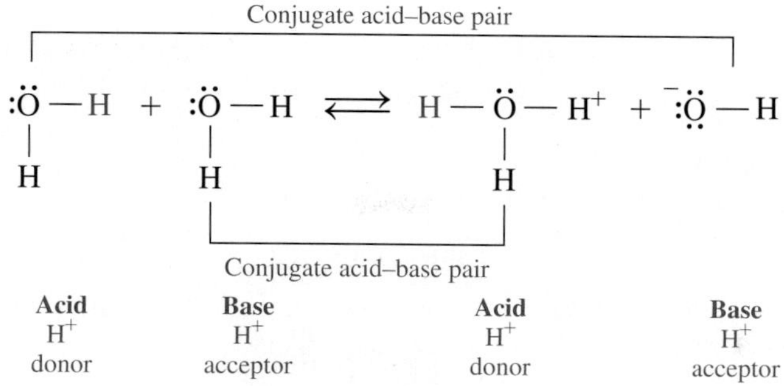

Writing the Ion Product Constant for Water, K_w

Using the equation for the reaction in water at equilibrium, we can write its equilibrium constant expression that shows the concentrations of the products divided by the concentrations of the reactants. Recall that square brackets around the symbols indicate their concentrations in moles per liter (M).

$$H_2O(l) + H_2O(l) \rightleftharpoons H_3O^+(aq) + OH^-(aq)$$

$$K_a = \frac{[H_3O^+][OH^-]}{[H_2O][H_2O]}$$

As we did for the acid and base dissociation constant expressions, we omit the constant concentration of pure liquid water to give the **ion product constant for water, K_w.**

$$K_w = [H_3O^+][OH^-]$$

Experiments have determined that in pure water, the concentration of H_3O^+ at 25 °C is 1.0×10^{-7} M.

Pure water $[H_3O^+] = 1.0 \times 10^{-7}\,M$

Because pure water contains an equal number of OH^- ions and H_3O^+ ions, the concentration of hydroxide ion must also be 1.0×10^{-7} M.

Pure water $[OH^-] = 1.0 \times 10^{-7}\,M$

When we place the $[H_3O^+]$ and $[OH^-]$ into the ion product expression, we obtain the numerical value of K_w, which is 1.0×10^{-14} at 25 °C. As before, the concentration units are omitted in the K_w value.

$$\begin{aligned} K_w &= [H_3O^+][OH^-] \\ &= [1.0 \times 10^{-7}][1.0 \times 10^{-7}] = 1.0 \times 10^{-14} \end{aligned}$$

Neutral, Acidic, and Basic Solution

When the $[H_3O^+]$ and $[OH^-]$ in a solution are equal, the solution is **neutral**. However, most solutions are not neutral and have different concentrations of $[H_3O^+]$ and $[OH^-]$. If acid is added to water, there is an increase in $[H_3O^+]$ and a decrease in $[OH^-]$, which makes an acidic solution. If base is added, $[OH^-]$ increases and $[H_3O^+]$ decreases, which gives a basic solution (see Figure 14.4). However, for any aqueous solution, whether it is neutral, acidic, or basic, the product $[H_3O^+][OH^-]$ is equal to K_w (1.0×10^{-14}) at 25 °C (see Table 14.7).

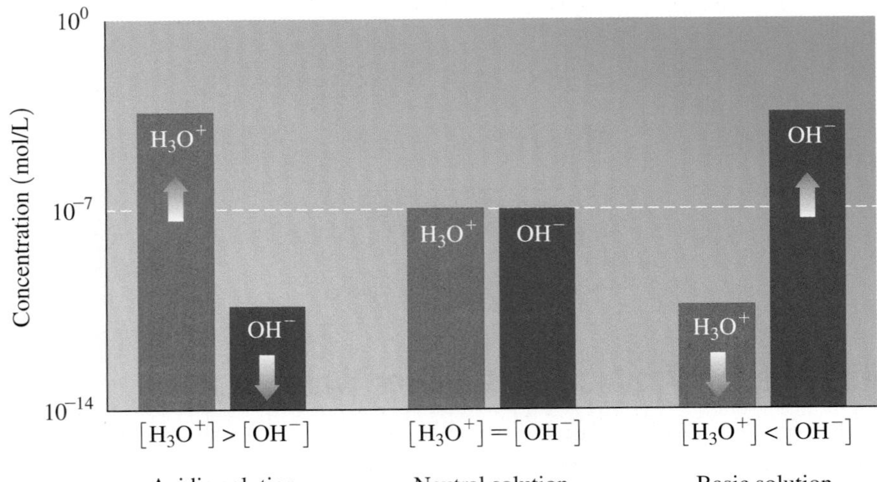

FIGURE 14.4 In a neutral solution, $[H_3O^+]$ and $[OH^-]$ are equal. In acidic solutions, the $[H_3O^+]$ is greater than the $[OH^-]$. In basic solutions, the $[OH^-]$ is greater than the $[H_3O^+]$.

Q If the $[H_3O^+] = 1.0 \times 10^{-3}$ M, is the solution acidic, basic, or neutral?

TABLE 14.7 Examples of $[H_3O^+]$ and $[OH^-]$ in Neutral, Acidic, and Basic Solutions

Type of Solution	$[H_3O^+]$	$[OH^-]$	K_w
Neutral	1.0×10^{-7} M	1.0×10^{-7} M	1.0×10^{-14}
Acidic	1.0×10^{-2} M	1.0×10^{-12} M	1.0×10^{-14}
Acidic	2.5×10^{-5} M	4.0×10^{-10} M	1.0×10^{-14}
Basic	1.0×10^{-8} M	1.0×10^{-6} M	1.0×10^{-14}
Basic	5.0×10^{-11} M	2.0×10^{-4} M	1.0×10^{-14}

CORE CHEMISTRY SKILL

Calculating $[H_3O^+]$ and $[OH^-]$ in Solutions

Using the K_w to Calculate $[H_3O^+]$ and $[OH^-]$ in a Solution

If we know the $[H_3O^+]$ of a solution, we can use the K_w to calculate the $[OH^-]$. If we know the $[OH^-]$ of a solution, we can calculate $[H_3O^+]$ from their relationship in the K_w, as shown in Sample Problem 14.6.

$$K_w = [H_3O^+][OH^-]$$

$$[OH^-] = \frac{K_w}{[H_3O^+]} \qquad [H_3O^+] = \frac{K_w}{[OH^-]}$$

Guide to Calculating $[H_3O^+]$ and $[OH^-]$ in Aqueous Solutions

1. State the given and needed quantities.
2. Write the K_w for water and solve for the unknown $[H_3O^+]$ or $[OH^-]$.
3. Substitute the known $[H_3O^+]$ or $[OH^-]$ into the equation and calculate.

SAMPLE PROBLEM 14.6 Calculating $[H_3O^+]$ and $[OH^-]$ in Solution

A vinegar solution has a $[H_3O^+] = 2.0 \times 10^{-3}$ M at 25 °C. What is the $[OH^-]$ of the vinegar solution? Is the solution acidic, basic, or neutral?

SOLUTION

Step 1 State the given and needed quantities.

Analyze the Problem	Given	Need	Know
	$[H_3O^+] = 2.0 \times 10^{-3}$ M	$[OH^-]$	$K_w = [H_3O^+][OH^-] = 1.0 \times 10^{-14}$

Step 2 Write the K_w for water and solve for the unknown $[H_3O^+]$ or $[OH^-]$.

$$K_w = [H_3O^+][OH^-] = 1.0 \times 10^{-14}$$

Solve for $[OH^-]$ by dividing both sides by $[H_3O^+]$.

$$\frac{K_w}{[H_3O^+]} = \frac{\cancel{[H_3O^+]}[OH^-]}{\cancel{[H_3O^+]}} = \frac{1.0 \times 10^{-14}}{[H_3O^+]}$$

$$[OH^-] = \frac{1.0 \times 10^{-14}}{[H_3O^+]}$$

Step 3 **Substitute the known $[H_3O^+]$ or $[OH^-]$ into the equation and calculate.**

$$[OH^-] = \frac{1.0 \times 10^{-14}}{[2.0 \times 10^{-3}]} = 5.0 \times 10^{-12}\text{ M}$$

Because the $[H_3O^+]$ of 2.0×10^{-3} M is much larger than the $[OH^-]$ of 5.0×10^{-12} M, the solution is acidic.

STUDY CHECK 14.6

What is the $[H_3O^+]$ of an ammonia cleaning solution with $[OH^-] = 4.0 \times 10^{-4}$ M? Is the solution acidic, basic, or neutral?

QUESTIONS AND PROBLEMS

14.5 Ionization of Water

LEARNING GOAL: *Use the ion product of water to calculate the $[H_3O^+]$ and $[OH^-]$ in an aqueous solution.*

14.33 Why are the concentrations of H_3O^+ and OH^- equal in pure water?

14.34 What is the meaning and value of K_w at 25 °C?

14.35 In an acidic solution, how does the concentration of H_3O^+ compare to the concentration of OH^-?

14.36 If a base is added to pure water, why does the $[H_3O^+]$ decrease?

14.37 Indicate whether each of the following solutions is an acidic, basic, or neutral:

a. $[H_3O^+] = 2.0 \times 10^{-5}$ M
b. $[H_3O^+] = 1.4 \times 10^{-9}$ M
c. $[OH^-] = 8.0 \times 10^{-3}$ M
d. $[OH^-] = 3.5 \times 10^{-10}$ M

14.38 Indicate whether each of the following solutions is an acidic, basic, or neutral solution:

a. $[H_3O^+] = 6.0 \times 10^{-12}$ M
b. $[H_3O^+] = 1.4 \times 10^{-4}$ M
c. $[OH^-] = 5.0 \times 10^{-12}$ M
d. $[OH^-] = 4.5 \times 10^{-2}$ M

14.39 Calculate the $[H_3O^+]$ of each aqueous solution with the following $[OH^-]$:

a. coffee, 1.0×10^{-9} M
b. soap, 1.0×10^{-6} M
c. cleanser, 2.0×10^{-5} M
d. lemon juice, 4.0×10^{-13} M

14.40 Calculate the $[H_3O^+]$ of each aqueous solution with the following $[OH^-]$:

a. NaOH, 1.0×10^{-2} M
b. milk of magnesia, 1.0×10^{-5} M
c. aspirin, 1.8×10^{-11} M
d. seawater, 2.5×10^{-6} M

14.41 Calculate the $[OH^-]$ of each aqueous solution with the following $[H_3O^+]$:

a. vinegar, 1.0×10^{-3} M
b. urine, 5.0×10^{-6} M
c. ammonia solution, 1.8×10^{-12} M
d. KOH solution, 4.0×10^{-13} M

14.42 Calculate the $[OH^-]$ of each aqueous solution with the following $[H_3O^+]$:

a. baking soda, 1.0×10^{-8} M
b. orange juice, 2.0×10^{-4} M
c. milk, 5.0×10^{-7} M
d. bleach, 4.8×10^{-12} M

14.6 The pH Scale

LEARNING GOAL

Calculate pH from $[H_3O^+]$; given the pH, calculate the $[H_3O^+]$ and $[OH^-]$ of a solution.

Personnel working in food processing, medicine, agriculture, spa and pool maintenance, soap manufacturing, and wine making measure the $[H_3O^+]$ and $[OH^-]$ of solutions. Although we have expressed H_3O^+ and OH^- as molar concentrations, it is more convenient to describe the acidity of solutions using the *pH scale*. On this scale, a number between 0 and 14 represents the H_3O^+ concentration for common solutions. A neutral solution has a pH of 7.0 at 25 °C. An acidic solution has a pH less than 7.0; a basic solution has a pH greater than 7.0 (see Figure 14.5).

Acidic solution	pH $<$ 7.0	$[H_3O^+] > 1.0 \times 10^{-7}$ M
Neutral solution	pH $=$ 7.0	$[H_3O^+] = 1.0 \times 10^{-7}$ M
Basic solution	pH $>$ 7.0	$[H_3O^+] < 1.0 \times 10^{-7}$ M

When we relate acidity and pH, we are using an inverse relationship, which is when one component increases while the other component decreases. When an acid is added to pure water, the $[H_3O^+]$ (acidity) of the solution increases but its pH decreases. When a base is added to pure water, it becomes more basic, which means its acidity decreases and the pH increases.

In the laboratory, a pH meter is commonly used to determine the pH of a solution. There are also various indicators and pH papers that turn specific colors when placed in solutions of different pH values. The pH is found by comparing the color on the test paper or the color of the solution to a color chart (see Figure 14.6).

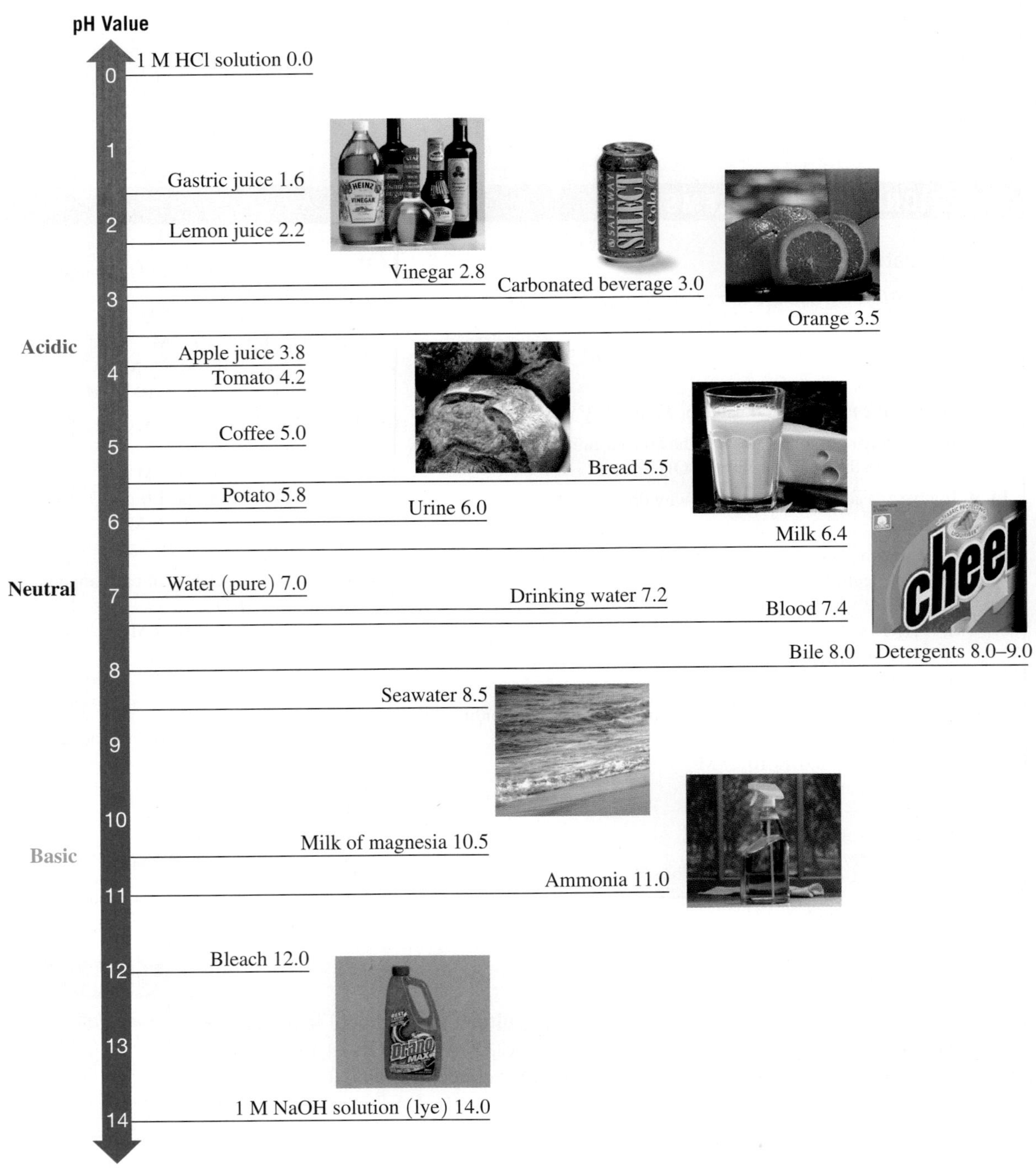

FIGURE 14.5 On the pH scale, values below 7.0 are acidic, a value of 7.0 is neutral, and values above 7.0 are basic.

Q Is apple juice an acidic, a basic, or a neutral solution?

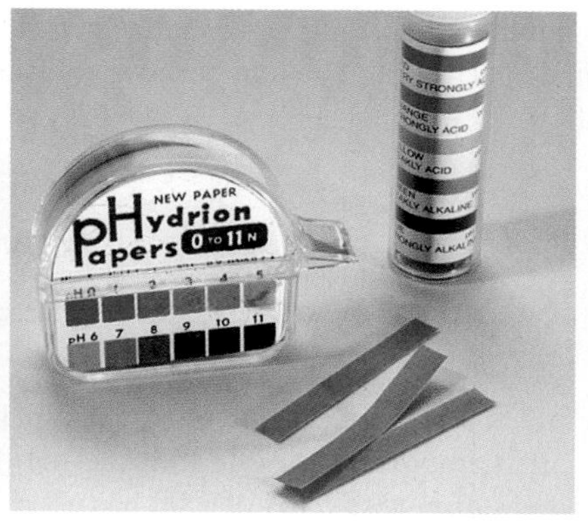

(a) (b) (c)

FIGURE 14.6 The pH of a solution can be determined using **(a)** a pH meter, **(b)** pH paper, and **(c)** indicators that turn different colors corresponding to different pH values.

Q If a pH meter reads 4.00, is the solution acidic, basic, or neutral?

CONCEPT CHECK 14.6 pH of Solutions

Consider the pH of the following items:

Item	pH
Root beer	5.8
Kitchen cleaner	10.9
Pickles	3.5
Glass cleaner	7.6
Cranberry juice	2.9

a. Place the pH values of the items on the list in order of most acidic to most basic.
b. Which item has the highest $[H_3O^+]$?
c. Which item has the highest $[OH^-]$?

ANSWER

a. The most acidic item is the one with the lowest pH, and the most basic is the item with the highest pH: cranberry juice (2.9), pickles (3.5), root beer (5.8), glass cleaner (7.6), kitchen cleaner (10.9).
b. The item with the highest $[H_3O^+]$ would have the lowest pH value, which is cranberry juice.
c. The item with the highest $[OH^-]$ would have the highest pH value, which is kitchen cleaner.

Cranberry juice has a pH of 2.9, which makes it acidic.

Calculating the pH of Solutions

KEY MATH SKILL
Calculating pH from $[H_3O^+]$

The pH scale is a logarithmic scale that corresponds to the hydrogen ion concentrations of aqueous solutions. Mathematically, **pH** is the negative logarithm (base 10) of the $[H_3O^+]$.

$$pH = -\log[H_3O^+]$$

Essentially, the negative powers of 10 in the molar concentrations are converted to positive numbers. For example, a lemon juice solution with $[H_3O^+] = 1.0 \times 10^{-2}$ M has a pH of 2.00. This can be calculated using the pH equation:

$$pH = -\log[1.0 \times 10^{-2}]$$
$$pH = -(-2.00)$$
$$= 2.00$$

If soil is too acidic, nutrients are not absorbed by crops. Then lime ($CaCO_3$), which acts as a base, may be added to increase the soil pH.

The number of *decimal places* in the pH value is the same as the number of significant figures in the $[H_3O^+]$. The number to the left of the decimal point in the pH value is the power of 10.

$$[H_3O^+] = \mathbf{1.0} \times 10^{-2} \qquad \text{pH} = 2.\mathbf{00}$$

Two SFs — Two SFs

Because pH is a log scale, a change of one pH unit corresponds to a tenfold change in $[H_3O^+]$. It is important to note that the pH decreases as the $[H_3O^+]$ increases. For example, a solution with a pH of 2.00 has a $[H_3O^+]$ that is ten times greater than a solution with a pH of 3.00 and 100 times greater than a solution with a pH of 4.00.

CONCEPT CHECK 14.7 Calculating pH

Indicate if the pH values given for each of the following are correct or incorrect and why:

a. $[H_3O^+] = 1 \times 10^{-6}$ pH = −6.0
b. $[OH^-] = 1.0 \times 10^{-10}$ pH = 10.00
c. $[H_3O^+] = 1.0 \times 10^{-6}$ pH = 6.00

ANSWER

a. Incorrect. The pH of this solution is 6.0, which has a positive value, not negative.
b. Incorrect. The pH is calculated from the $[H_3O^+]$, not $[OH^-]$. This solution has a $[H_3O^+]$ of 1.0×10^{-4} M, which has a pH of 4.00. There are two zeros after the decimal point to match the two significant figures in the coefficient of the molarity.
c. The pH is correctly calculated from the $[H_3O^+]$ because there are two zeros after the decimal point to match the two significant figures in the coefficient of the molarity.

pH Calculation

The pH of a solution is calculated from the $[H_3O^+]$ by using the *log* key and changing the sign as shown in Sample Problem 14.7.

SAMPLE PROBLEM 14.7 Calculating pH from $[H_3O^+]$

Aspirin, which is acetylsalicylic acid, was the first nonsteroidal anti-inflammatory drug used to alleviate pain and fever. If a solution of aspirin has a $[H_3O^+] = 1.7 \times 10^{-3}$ M, what is the pH of the solution?

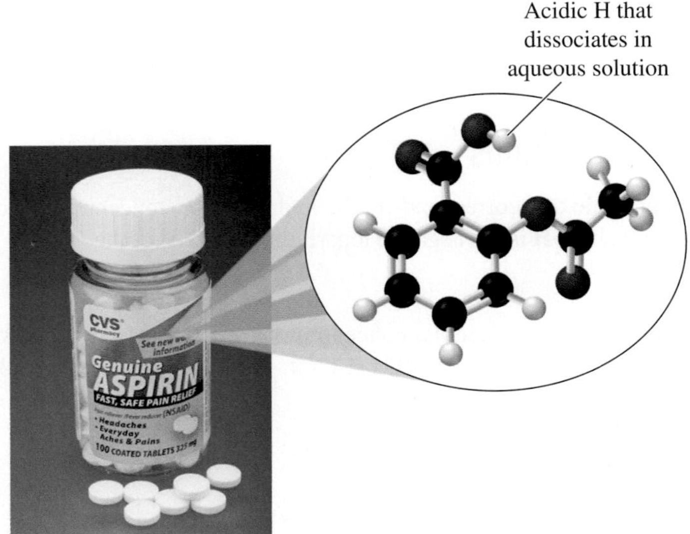

Aspirin, which is acetylsalicylic acid, has a K_a of 3.0×10^{-4}.

SOLUTION

Step 1 State the given and needed quantities.

Analyze the Problem	Given	Need	Know
	$[H_3O^+] = 1.7 \times 10^{-3}$ M	pH	$pH = -\log[H_3O^+]$

Step 2 Enter the $[H_3O^+]$ into the pH equation.

$$pH = -\log[H_3O^+] = -\log[1.7 \times 10^{-3}]$$

Procedure	Calculator Display
Enter 1.7 and press [EE or EXP]	1.7⁰⁰ or 1.7 00 or 1.7E00
Enter 3 and press [+/−] to change the sign.	1.7⁻⁰³ or 1.7−03 or 1.7E−03

Step 3 Press the *log* key and change the sign. Adjust the number of SFs on the *right* of the decimal point.

Procedure	Calculator Display
[log] [+/−]	2.769551079

The steps can be combined to give the calculator sequence as follows:

$$pH = -\log[1.7 \times 10^{-3}] = 1.7 \text{ [EE or EXP] } 3 \text{ [+/−] [log] [+/−]}$$
$$= 2.769551079$$

Be sure to check the instructions for your calculator. On some calculators, the log key is used first, followed by the concentration.

In a pH value, the number to the *left* of the decimal point is an *exact* number derived from the power of 10. Thus, the two SFs in the coefficient determine that there are two SFs after the decimal point in the pH value.

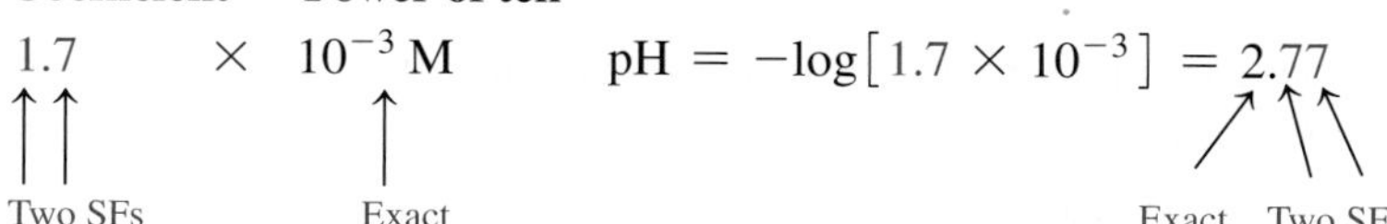

STUDY CHECK 14.7

What is the pH of bleach with $[H_3O^+] = 4.2 \times 10^{-12}$ M?

When we need to calculate the pH from $[OH^-]$, we use the K_w to calculate $[H_3O^+]$, place it in the pH equation, and calculate the pH of the solution as shown in Sample Problem 14.8.

SAMPLE PROBLEM 14.8 Calculating pH from $[OH^-]$

What is the pH of an ammonia solution with $[OH^-] = 3.7 \times 10^{-3}$ M?

SOLUTION

Step 1 State the given and needed quantities.

Analyze the Problem	Given	Need	Know
	$[OH^-] = 3.7 \times 10^{-3}$ M	$[H_3O^+]$ pH	$K_w = [H_3O^+][OH^-] = 1.0 \times 10^{-14}$ $pH = -\log[H_3O^+]$

Guide to Calculating pH of an Aqueous Solution

1. State the given and needed quantities.
2. Enter the $[H_3O^+]$ into the pH equation.
3. Press the *log* key and change the sign. Adjust the number of SFs on the *right* of the decimal point.

Step 2 **Enter the $[H_3O^+]$ into the pH equation.** Because $[OH^-]$ is given for the ammonia solution, we have to calculate $[H_3O^+]$. Using the ion product constant for water, K_w, we divide both sides by $[OH^-]$ to obtain $[H_3O^+]$.

$$K_w = [H_3O^+][OH^-] = 1.0 \times 10^{-14}$$

$$\frac{K_w}{[OH^-]} = \frac{[H_3O^+]\,[\cancel{OH^-}]}{[\cancel{OH^-}]}$$

$$[H_3O^+] = \frac{1.0 \times 10^{-14}}{[3.7 \times 10^{-3}]} = 2.7 \times 10^{-12}\ \text{M}$$

Now, we enter the $[H_3O^+]$ into the pH equation.

$$pH = -\log[H_3O^+]$$

	Procedure	Calculator Display
$pH = -\log[2.7 \times 10^{-12}]$ =	2.7 (EE or EXP) 12 (+/−) (=)	2.7^{-12} or 2.7−12 or 2.7E−12

Step 3 **Press the *log* key and change the sign. Adjust the number of SFs on the *right* of the decimal point.**

Procedure		Calculator Display
(log) (+/−)		11.56863624
2.7×10^{-12} M	pH = 11.57	
Two SFs	Two SFs to the *right* of the decimal point	

STUDY CHECK 14.8

Calculate the pH of a sample of acid rain that has $[OH^-] = 2 \times 10^{-10}$ M.

pOH

The **pOH** scale is similar to the pH scale except that pOH is associated with the $[OH^-]$ of an aqueous solution.

$$pOH = -\log[OH^-]$$

Solutions with high $[OH^-]$ have low pOH values; solutions with low $[OH^-]$ have high pOH values. In any aqueous solution, the sum of the pH and pOH is equal to 14.00, which is the negative logarithm of the K_w.

$$pH + pOH = 14.00$$

For example, if the pH of a solution is 3.50, the pOH can be calculated as follows:

$$pH + pOH = 14.00$$
$$pOH = 14.00 - pH = 14.00 - 3.50 = 10.50$$

A comparison of $[H_3O^+]$, $[OH^-]$, and their corresponding pH and pOH values is given in Table 14.8.

TABLE 14.8 A Comparison of $[H_3O^+]$, $[OH^-]$, and Corresponding pH Values at 25 °C

$[H_3O^+]$	pH	$[OH^-]$	pOH	
10^0	0	10^{-14}	14	Acidic
10^{-1}	1	10^{-13}	13	
10^{-2}	2	10^{-12}	12	
10^{-3}	3	10^{-11}	11	
10^{-4}	4	10^{-10}	10	
10^{-5}	5	10^{-9}	9	
10^{-6}	6	10^{-8}	8	
10^{-7}	7	10^{-7}	7	Neutral
10^{-8}	8	10^{-6}	6	
10^{-9}	9	10^{-5}	5	
10^{-10}	10	10^{-4}	4	Basic
10^{-11}	11	10^{-3}	3	
10^{-12}	12	10^{-2}	2	
10^{-13}	13	10^{-1}	1	
10^{-14}	14	10^0	0	

Calculating $[H_3O^+]$ from pH

If we are given the pH of the solution and asked to determine the $[H_3O^+]$, we need to reverse the calculation of pH.

$$[H_3O^+] = 10^{-pH}$$

For example, if the pH of a solution is 3.0, we can substitute it into this equation. The number of significant figures in $[H_3O^+]$ is equal to the number of decimal places in the pH value.

$$[H_3O^+] = 10^{-pH} = 10^{-3.0} = 1 \times 10^{-3}\,M$$

For pH values that are not whole numbers, the calculation requires the use of the *10^x* key, which is usually a *2nd function* key. On some calculators, this operation is done using the *inverse* key and the *log* key as shown in Sample Problem 14.9.

KEY MATH SKILL

Calculating $[H_3O^+]$ from pH

SAMPLE PROBLEM 14.9 Calculating $[H_3O^+]$ from pH

Calculate $[H_3O^+]$ for a solution of baking soda with a pH of 8.25.

SOLUTION

Step 1 **State the given and needed quantities.**

Analyze the Problem	Given	Need	Know
	pH = 8.25	$[H_3O^+]$	$[H_3O^+] = 10^{-pH}$

Step 2 **Enter the pH value into the inverse log equation and change the sign.** Press the *2nd function* key and then the *10^x* key.

Calculator Display

8.25 +/−   −8.25

2nd 10^x 5.623413252^{-09} or 5.623413252−09 or 5.623413252E−09

Or press the *inverse* key and then the *log* key.

inv log

Step 3 **Adjust the SFs in the coefficient.** Because the pH value of 8.25 has two digits to the *right* of the decimal point, the coefficient for $[H_3O^+]$ is written with two SFs.

$$[H_3O^+] = 5.6 \times 10^{-9}\,M$$

Two SFs

STUDY CHECK 14.9

What are the $[H_3O^+]$ and $[OH^-]$ of beer that has a pH of 4.50?

Guide to Calculating $[H_3O^+]$ from pH

1. State the given and needed quantities.
2. Enter the pH value into the inverse log equation and change the sign.
3. Adjust the SFs in the coefficient.

Chemistry Link to Health

STOMACH ACID, HCl

Gastric acid, which contains HCl, is produced by parietal cells that line the stomach. When the stomach expands with the intake of food, the gastric glands begin to secrete a strongly acidic solution of HCl. In a single day, a person may secrete 2000 mL of gastric juice, which contains hydrochloric acid, mucins, and the enzymes pepsin and lipase.

The HCl in the gastric juice activates a digestive enzyme from the chief cells called *pepsinogen* to form *pepsin*, which breaks down proteins in food entering the stomach. The secretion of HCl continues until the stomach has a pH of about 2, which is the optimum for activating the digestive enzymes without ulcerating the stomach lining. In addition, the low pH is beneficial by destroying bacteria that reach the stomach. Normally, large quantities of viscous mucus are secreted within the stomach to protect its lining from acid and enzyme damage. Gastric acid may also form under conditions of stress when the nervous system activates the production of HCl. As the contents of the stomach move into the small intestine, cells produce bicarbonate that neutralizes the gastric acid until the pH is about 5.

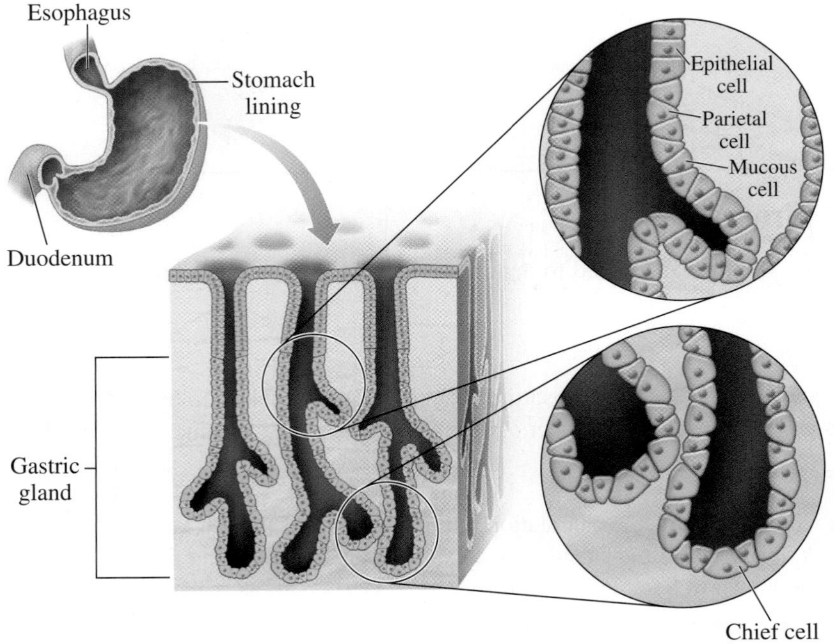

Parietal cells in the lining of the stomach secrete gastric acid HCl.

QUESTIONS AND PROBLEMS

14.6 The pH Scale

LEARNING GOAL: *Calculate pH from* $[H_3O^+]$; *given the pH, calculate the* $[H_3O^+]$ *and* $[OH^-]$ *of a solution.*

14.43 Why does a neutral solution have a pH of 7.00?

14.44 If you know the $[OH^-]$, how can you determine the pH of a solution?

14.45 State whether each of the following solutions is acidic, basic, or neutral:
- **a.** blood, pH 7.38
- **b.** vinegar, pH 2.8
- **c.** drain cleaner, pOH 2.8
- **d.** coffee, pH 5.52
- **e.** tomatoes, pH 4.2
- **f.** chocolate cake, pH 7.6

14.46 State whether each of the following solutions is acidic, basic, or neutral:
- **a.** soda, pH 3.22
- **b.** shampoo, pOH 8.3
- **c.** laundry detergent, pOH 4.56
- **d.** rain, pH 5.8
- **e.** honey, pH 3.9
- **f.** cheese, pH 7.4

14.47 A solution with a pH of 3 is 10 times more acidic than a solution with pH 4. Explain.

14.48 A solution with a pH of 10 is 100 times more basic than a solution with pH 8. Explain.

14.49 Calculate the pH of each solution given the following:
- **a.** $[H_3O^+] = 1.0 \times 10^{-4}$ M
- **b.** $[H_3O^+] = 3.0 \times 10^{-9}$ M
- **c.** $[OH^-] = 1.0 \times 10^{-5}$ M
- **d.** $[OH^-] = 2.5 \times 10^{-11}$ M
- **e.** $[H_3O^+] = 6.7 \times 10^{-8}$ M
- **f.** $[OH^-] = 8.2 \times 10^{-4}$ M

14.50 Calculate the pH of each solution given the following:

a. $[H_3O^+] = 1.0 \times 10^{-8}$ M
b. $[H_3O^+] = 5.0 \times 10^{-6}$ M
c. $[OH^-] = 4.0 \times 10^{-2}$ M
d. $[OH^-] = 8.0 \times 10^{-3}$ M
e. $[H_3O^+] = 4.7 \times 10^{-2}$ M
f. $[OH^-] = 3.9 \times 10^{-6}$ M

14.51 Complete the following table:

$[H_3O^+]$	$[OH^-]$	pH	pOH	Acidic, Basic, or Neutral?
	1.0×10^{-6} M			
		3.49		
2.8×10^{-5} M				
			2.00	

14.52 Complete the following table:

$[H_3O^+]$	$[OH^-]$	pH	pOH	Acidic, Basic, or Neutral?
		10.00		
				Neutral
			5.66	
6.4×10^{-12} M				

14.7 Reactions of Acids and Bases

LEARNING GOAL

Write balanced equations for reactions of acids with metals, carbonates, and bases.

Typical reactions of acids and bases include the reactions of acids with metals, bases, and carbonate or bicarbonate ions. For example, when you drop an antacid tablet in water, the bicarbonate ion and citric acid in the tablet react to produce carbon dioxide bubbles, water, and a salt. A **salt** is an ionic compound that does not have H^+ as the cation or OH^- as the anion.

Acids and Metals

Acids react with certain metals to produce hydrogen gas (H_2) and a salt. Active metals include potassium, sodium, calcium, magnesium, aluminum, zinc, iron, and tin. In these single replacement reactions, the metal ion replaces the hydrogen in the acid.

$$\underset{\text{Metal}}{Mg(s)} + \underset{\text{Acid}}{2HCl(aq)} \longrightarrow \underset{\text{Hydrogen}}{H_2(g)} + \underset{\text{Salt}}{MgCl_2(aq)}$$

$$\underset{\text{Metal}}{Zn(s)} + \underset{\text{Acid}}{2HNO_3(aq)} \longrightarrow \underset{\text{Hydrogen}}{H_2(g)} + \underset{\text{Salt}}{Zn(NO_3)_2(aq)}$$

Magnesium reacts rapidly with acid and forms H_2 gas and a salt of magnesium.

CONCEPT CHECK 14.8 Equations for Metals and Acids

Write the balanced equation for the reaction of $Al(s)$ with $HCl(aq)$.

ANSWER

When the metal $Al(s)$ reacts with HCl, it forms $H_2(g)$ and Al^{3+}, which is balanced by $3Cl^-$ from HCl to give the salt $AlCl_3(aq)$. Using the formula of the salt gives the unbalanced equation.

$$Al(s) + HCl(aq) \longrightarrow H_2(g) + AlCl_3(aq)$$

Now the equation can be balanced with the proper coefficients.

$$2Al(s) + 6HCl(aq) \longrightarrow 3H_2(g) + 2AlCl_3(aq)$$

CORE CHEMISTRY SKILL

Writing Equations for Reactions of Acids and Bases

Acids React with Carbonates and Bicarbonates

When an acid is added to a carbonate or bicarbonate, the products are carbon dioxide gas, water, and a salt. The acid reacts with CO_3^{2-} or HCO_3^- to produce carbonic acid, H_2CO_3, which breaks down rapidly to CO_2 and H_2O.

$$\underset{\text{Acid}}{2HCl(aq)} + \underset{\text{Carbonate}}{Na_2CO_3(aq)} \longrightarrow \underset{\text{Carbon dioxide}}{CO_2(g)} + \underset{\text{Water}}{H_2O(l)} + \underset{\text{Salt}}{2NaCl(aq)}$$

$$\underset{\text{Acid}}{HBr(aq)} + \underset{\text{Bicarbonate}}{NaHCO_3(aq)} \longrightarrow \underset{\text{Carbon dioxide}}{CO_2(g)} + \underset{\text{Water}}{H_2O(l)} + \underset{\text{Salt}}{NaBr(aq)}$$

When sodium bicarbonate (baking soda) reacts with an acid (vinegar), the products are carbon dioxide gas, water, and a salt.

Acids and Hydroxides: Neutralization

Neutralization is a reaction between a strong or weak acid with a strong base to produce a salt and water. The H^+ of an acid and the OH^- of the base combine to form water. The salt is the combination of the cation from the base and the anion from the acid. We can write the following equation for the neutralization reaction between HCl and NaOH:

$$\underset{\text{Acid}}{HCl(aq)} + \underset{\text{Base}}{NaOH(aq)} \longrightarrow \underset{\text{Water}}{H_2O(l)} + \underset{\text{Salt}}{NaCl(aq)}$$

If we write the strong acid HCl and the strong base NaOH as ions, we see that H^+ combines with OH^- to form water, leaving the ions Na^+ and Cl^- in solution.

$$H^+(aq) + Cl^-(aq) + Na^+(aq) + OH^-(aq) \longrightarrow H_2O(l) + Na^+(aq) + Cl^-(aq)$$

When we omit the ions that do not change during the reaction (*spectator ions*), we obtain the net ionic equation.

$$H^+(aq) + \cancel{Cl^-(aq)} + \cancel{Na^+(aq)} + OH^-(aq) \longrightarrow H_2O(l) + \cancel{Na^+(aq)} + \cancel{Cl^-(aq)}$$

The net ionic equation for the neutralization of H^+ and OH^- to form H_2O is

$$H^+(aq) + OH^-(aq) \longrightarrow H_2O(l) \quad \text{Net ionic equation}$$

Chemistry Link to the Environment

ACID RAIN

Natural rain is slightly acidic, with a pH of 5.6. In the atmosphere, carbon dioxide combines with water to form carbonic acid, a weak acid, which dissociates to give hydronium ions and bicarbonate.

$$CO_2(g) + H_2O(l) \rightleftarrows H_2CO_3(aq)$$
$$H_2CO_3(aq) + H_2O(l) \rightleftarrows H_3O^+(aq) + HCO_3^-(aq)$$

However, in many parts of the world, rain has become considerably more acidic. *Acid rain* is a term given to precipitation such as rain, snow, hail, or fog, in which the water has a pH that is less than 5.6. In the United States, pH values of rain have decreased to about 4–4.5. In some parts of the world, pH values have been reported as low as 2.6, which is about as acidic as lemon juice or vinegar. Because the calculation of pH involves powers of 10, a pH value of 2.6 would be 1000 times more acidic than natural rain.

Although natural sources such as volcanoes and forest fires release SO_2, the primary sources of acid rain today are from the burning of fossil fuels in automobiles and coal in industrial plants. When coal and oil are burned, sulfur impurities combine with oxygen in the air to produce SO_2 and SO_3. The reaction of SO_3 with water forms sulfuric acid, H_2SO_4, which is a strong acid.

$$S(s) + O_2(g) \longrightarrow O_2(g)$$
$$2SO_2(g) + O_2(g) \longrightarrow 2SO_3(g)$$
$$SO_3(g) + H_2O(l) \longrightarrow H_2SO_4(aq)$$

In an effort to decrease the formation of acid rain, legislation has required a reduction in SO_2 emissions. Coal-burning plants have installed equipment called "scrubbers" that absorb SO_2 before it is emitted. In a smokestack, "scrubbing" removes 95% of the SO_2 as the flue gases containing SO_2 pass through limestone ($CaCO_3$) and water. The end product, $CaSO_4$, also called "gypsum," is used in agriculture and to prepare cement products.

Nitrogen oxide forms at high temperatures in the engines of automobiles as air containing nitrogen and oxygen gases is burned. As nitrogen oxide is emitted into the air, it combines with more oxygen to form nitrogen dioxide, which is responsible for the brown color of smog. When nitrogen dioxide dissolves in water in the atmosphere, nitric acid forms.

$$N_2(g) + O_2(g) \longrightarrow 2NO(g)$$
$$2NO(g) + O_2(g) \longrightarrow 2NO_2(g)$$
$$3NO_2(g) + H_2O(g) \longrightarrow 2HNO_3(aq) + NO(g)$$

Air currents in the atmosphere carry the sulfuric acid and nitric acid many thousands of kilometers before they precipitate in areas far away from the site of the initial contamination. The acids in acid rain have detrimental effects on marble and limestone structures, lakes, and forests. Throughout the world, monuments made of marble (a form of $CaCO_3$) are deteriorating as acid rain dissolves the marble.

$$CaCO_3(s) + H_2SO_4(aq) \longrightarrow CO_2(g) + H_2O(l) + CaSO_4(aq)$$

Acid rain is changing the pH of many lakes and streams in parts of the United States and Europe. When the pH of a lake falls below 4.5–5, most fish and plant life cannot survive. As the soil near a lake becomes more acidic, aluminum becomes more soluble. Increased levels of aluminum ion in lakes are toxic to fish and other water animals.

Trees and forests are susceptible to acid rain, too. Acid rain breaks down the protective waxy coating on leaves and interferes with photosynthesis. Tree growth is impaired as nutrients and minerals in the soil dissolve and wash away. In eastern Europe, acid rain is causing an environmental disaster. Nearly 70% of the forests in the Czech Republic have been severely damaged, and some parts of the land are so acidic that crops will not grow.

A marble statue in Washington Square Park that has been eroded by acid rain.

Acid rain has severely damaged forests in eastern Europe.

Balancing Neutralization Equations

In a neutralization reaction, one H^+ always reacts with one OH^-. Therefore, a neutralization equation may need coefficients to balance the H^+ from the acid with the OH^- from the base as shown in Sample Problem 14.10.

SAMPLE PROBLEM 14.10 Balancing a Neutralization Equation

Write the balanced equation for the neutralization of $HCl(aq)$ and $Ba(OH)_2(s)$.

SOLUTION

Step 1 **Write the reactants and products.**

$$HCl(aq) + Ba(OH)_2(s) \longrightarrow H_2O(l) + \text{salt}$$

Step 2 **Balance the H^+ in the acid with the OH^- in the base.** Placing a coefficient of 2 in front of the HCl provides $2H^+$ for the $2OH^-$ from $Ba(OH)_2$.

$$2HCl(aq) + Ba(OH)_2(s) \longrightarrow H_2O(l) + \text{salt}$$

Step 3 **Balance the H_2O with the H^+ and the OH^-.** Use a coefficient of 2 in front of H_2O to balance $2H^+$ and $2OH^-$.

$$2HCl(aq) + Ba(OH)_2(s) \longrightarrow 2H_2O(l) + \text{salt}$$

Step 4 **Write the salt from the remaining ions.** Use the ions Ba^{2+} and $2Cl^-$ and write the formula for the salt as $BaCl_2$.

$$2HCl(aq) + Ba(OH)_2(s) \longrightarrow 2H_2O(l) + BaCl_2(aq)$$

STUDY CHECK 14.10

Write the balanced equation for the neutralization of $H_2SO_4(aq)$ and $LiOH(s)$.

Guide to Balancing an Equation for Neutralization

1. Write the reactants and products.
2. Balance the H^+ in the acid with the OH^- in the base.
3. Balance the H_2O with the H^+ and the OH^-.
4. Write the salt from the remaining ions.

CONCEPT CHECK 14.9 Reactions of Acids

Write a balanced equation for the reaction of $H_2SO_4(aq)$ with each of the following:

a. $Al(s)$ **b.** $K_2CO_3(s)$

ANSWER

a. $Al(s)$

When an active metal reacts with an acid, the products are $H_2(g)$ and a salt.

$$Al(s) + H_2SO_4(aq) \longrightarrow H_2(g) + \text{salt}$$

The metal ion Al^{3+} and the anion SO_4^{2-} combine to form a salt $Al_2(SO_4)_3(aq)$.

$$Al(s) + H_2SO_4(aq) \longrightarrow H_2(g) + Al_2(SO_4)_3(aq)$$

Now coefficients are added to balance the equation.

$$2Al(s) + 3H_2SO_4(aq) \longrightarrow 3H_2(g) + Al_2(SO_4)_3(aq)$$

b. $K_2CO_3(s)$

When a carbonate reacts with an acid, the products are $CO_2(g)$, $H_2O(l)$, and a salt.

$$K_2CO_3(s) + H_2SO_4(aq) \longrightarrow CO_2(g) + H_2O(l) + \text{salt}$$

The metal ion K^+ and the anion SO_4^{2-} combine to form a salt K_2SO_4. The equation is balanced.

$$K_2CO_3(s) + H_2SO_4(aq) \longrightarrow CO_2(g) + H_2O(l) + K_2SO_4(aq)$$

QUESTIONS AND PROBLEMS

14.7 Reactions of Acids and Bases

LEARNING GOAL: *Write balanced equations for reactions of acids with metals, carbonates, and bases.*

14.53 Complete and balance the equation for each of the following reactions:

a. $ZnCO_3(s) + HBr(aq) \longrightarrow$

b. $Zn(s) + HCl(aq) \longrightarrow$

c. $HCl(aq) + NaHCO_3(s) \longrightarrow$

d. $H_2SO_4(aq) + Mg(OH)_2(s) \longrightarrow$

14.54 Complete and balance the equation for each of the following reactions:

a. $KHCO_3(s) + HBr(aq) \longrightarrow$

b. $Ca(s) + H_2SO_4(aq) \longrightarrow$

c. $H_2SO_4(aq) + Ca(OH)_2(s) \longrightarrow$

d. $Na_2CO_3(s) + H_2SO_4(aq) \longrightarrow$

14.55 Balance each of the following neutralization reactions:

a. $HCl(aq) + Mg(OH)_2(s) \longrightarrow H_2O(l) + MgCl_2(aq)$

b. $H_3PO_4(aq) + LiOH(aq) \longrightarrow H_2O(l) + Li_3PO_4(aq)$

14.56 Balance each of the following neutralization reactions:

a. $HNO_3(aq) + Ba(OH)_2(s) \longrightarrow H_2O(l) + Ba(NO_3)_2(aq)$

b. $H_2SO_4(aq) + Al(OH)_3(s) \longrightarrow H_2O(l) + Al_2(SO_4)_3(aq)$

14.57 Write a balanced equation for the neutralization of each of the following:

a. $H_2SO_4(aq)$ and $NaOH(aq)$

b. $HCl(aq)$ and $Fe(OH)_3(s)$

c. $H_2CO_3(aq)$ and $Mg(OH)_2(s)$

14.58 Write a balanced equation for the neutralization of each of the following:

a. $H_3PO_4(aq)$ and $NaOH(aq)$

b. $HI(aq)$ and $LiOH(aq)$

c. $HNO_3(aq)$ and $Ca(OH)_2(s)$

Chemistry Link to Health

ANTACIDS

Antacids are substances used to neutralize excess stomach acid (HCl). Some antacids are mixtures of aluminum hydroxide and magnesium hydroxide. These hydroxides are not very soluble in water, so the levels of available OH^- are not damaging to the intestinal tract. However, aluminum hydroxide has the side effects of producing constipation and binding phosphate in the intestinal tract, which may cause weakness and loss of appetite. Magnesium hydroxide has a laxative effect. These side effects are less likely when a combination of the antacids is used.

$$Al(OH)_3(s) + 3HCl(aq) \longrightarrow 3H_2O(l) + AlCl_3(aq)$$
$$Mg(OH)_2(s) + 2HCl(aq) \longrightarrow 2H_2O(l) + MgCl_2(aq)$$

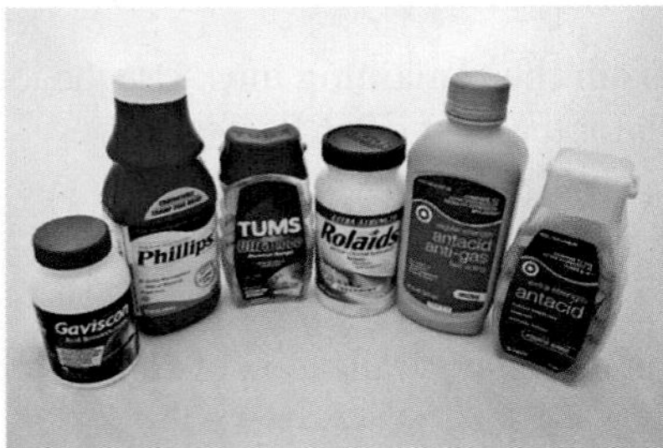

Antacids neutralize excess stomach acid.

Some antacids use calcium carbonate to neutralize excess stomach acid. About 10% of the calcium is absorbed into the bloodstream, where it elevates the level of serum calcium. Calcium carbonate is not recommended for patients who have peptic ulcers or a tendency to form kidney stones, which typically consist of an insoluble calcium salt.

$$CaCO_3(s) + 2HCl(aq) \longrightarrow CO_2(g) + H_2O(l) + CaCl_2(aq)$$

Still other antacids contain sodium bicarbonate. This type of antacid neutralizes excess gastric acid, increases blood pH, but also elevates sodium levels in the body fluids. It also is not recommended in the treatment of peptic ulcers.

$$NaHCO_3(s) + HCl(aq) \longrightarrow CO_2(g) + H_2O(l) + NaCl(aq)$$

The neutralizing substances in some antacid preparations are given in Table 14.9.

TABLE 14.9 Basic Compounds in Some Antacids

Antacid	Base(s)
Amphojel	$Al(OH)_3$
Milk of magnesia	$Mg(OH)_2$
Mylanta, Maalox, Di-Gel, Gelusil, Riopan	$Mg(OH)_2$, $Al(OH)_3$
Bisodol, Rolaids	$CaCO_3$, $Mg(OH)_2$
Titralac, Tums, Pepto-Bismol	$CaCO_3$
Alka-Seltzer	$NaHCO_3$, $KHCO_3$

14.8 Acid–Base Titration

LEARNING GOAL

Calculate the molarity or volume of an acid or base from titration information.

Suppose we need to find the molarity of a solution of HCl, which has an unknown concentration. We can do this by a laboratory procedure called **titration** in which we neutralize an acid sample with a known amount of base. In a titration, we place a measured volume of the acid in a flask and add a few drops of an **indicator**, such as phenolphthalein. An indicator is a compound that dramatically changes color when pH of the solution changes. In an acidic solution, phenolphthalein is colorless. Then we fill a buret with a NaOH solution of known molarity and carefully add NaOH solution to neutralize the acid in the flask (see Figure 14.7). We know that neutralization has taken place when the phenolphthalein in the solution changes from colorless to pink. This is called the neutralization **endpoint**. From the measured volume of the NaOH solution and its molarity, we calculate the number of moles of NaOH, the moles of acid, and the concentration of the acid.

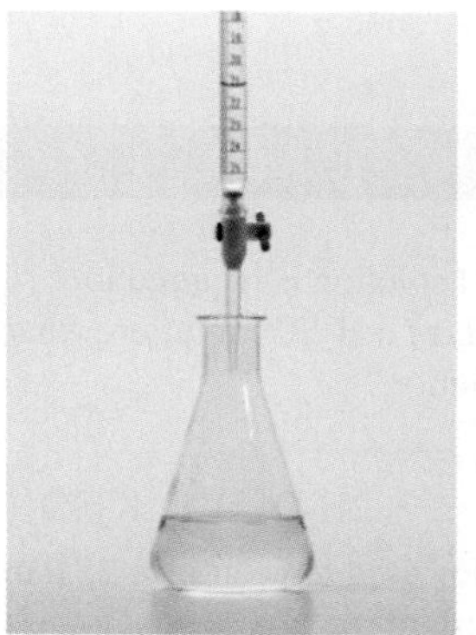

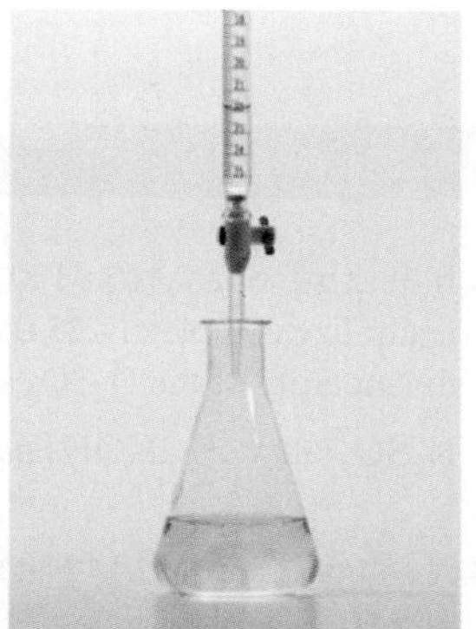

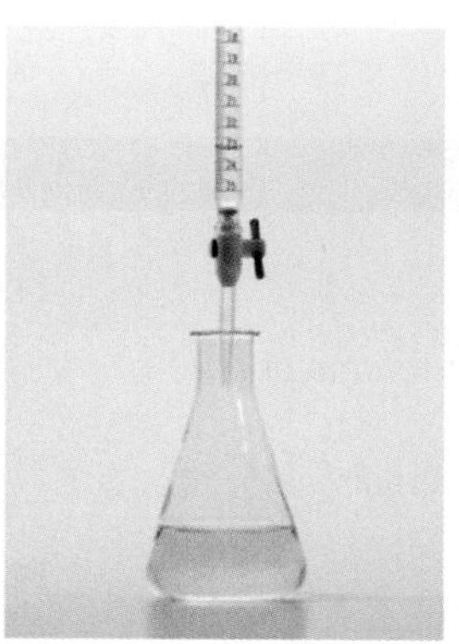

FIGURE 14.7 The titration of an acid. A known volume of an acid is placed in a flask with an indicator and titrated with a measured volume of a base solution, such as NaOH, to the neutralization endpoint.

Q What data is needed to determine the molarity of the acid in the flask?

SAMPLE PROBLEM 14.11 Titration of An Acid

CORE CHEMISTRY SKILL

Calculating Molarity or Volume of an Acid or Base in a Titration

A 25.0-mL sample of an HCl solution is placed in a flask with a few drops of phenolphthalein (indicator). If 32.6 mL of a 0.185 M NaOH solution is needed to reach the endpoint, what is the concentration (M) of the HCl solution?

$$NaOH(aq) + HCl(aq) \longrightarrow H_2O(l) + NaCl(aq)$$

SOLUTION

Step 1 State the given and needed quantities and concentrations.

	Given	Need
Analyze the Problem	25.0 mL (0.0250 L) of HCl solution	molarity of the HCl solution
	32.6 mL of 0.185 M NaOH solution	
	Neutralization Equation	
	$NaOH(aq) + HCl(aq) \longrightarrow H_2O(l) + NaCl(aq)$	

Step 2 **Write a plan to calculate the molarity or volume.**

mL of NaOH solution → (Metric factor) → L of NaOH solution → (Molarity) → moles of NaOH → (Mole–mole factor) → moles of HCl → (Divide by liters) → molarity of HCl solution

Step 3 **State equalities and conversion factors, including concentrations.**

1 L of NaOH solution = 1000 mL of NaOH solution

$$\frac{1 \text{ L NaOH solution}}{1000 \text{ mL NaOH solution}} \text{ and } \frac{1000 \text{ mL NaOH solution}}{1 \text{ L NaOH solution}}$$

1 L of NaOH solution = 0.185 mol of NaOH

$$\frac{1 \text{ L NaOH solution}}{0.185 \text{ mol NaOH}} \text{ and } \frac{0.185 \text{ mol NaOH}}{1 \text{ L NaOH solution}}$$

1 mol of HCl = 1 mol of NaOH

$$\frac{1 \text{ mol HCl}}{1 \text{ mol NaOH}} \text{ and } \frac{1 \text{ mol NaOH}}{1 \text{ mol HCl}}$$

Guide to Calculations for an Acid–Base Titration

1. State the given and needed quantities and concentrations.
2. Write a plan to calculate the molarity or volume.
3. State equalities and conversion factors, including concentrations.
4. Set up the problem to calculate the needed quantity.

Step 4 **Set up the problem to calculate the needed quantity.**

$$32.6 \cancel{\text{mL NaOH solution}} \times \frac{1 \cancel{\text{L NaOH solution}}}{1000 \cancel{\text{mL NaOH solution}}} \times \frac{0.185 \cancel{\text{mol NaOH}}}{1 \cancel{\text{L solution}}} \times \frac{1 \text{ mol HCl}}{1 \cancel{\text{mol NaOH}}}$$

$$= 0.00603 \text{ mol of HCl}$$

$$\text{molarity of HCl solution} = \frac{0.00603 \text{ mol HCl}}{0.0250 \text{ L HCl}} = 0.241 \text{ M HCl solution}$$

STUDY CHECK 14.11

What is the molarity of an HCl solution if 28.6 mL of a 0.175 M NaOH solution is needed to neutralize a 25.0-mL sample of the HCl solution?

QUESTIONS AND PROBLEMS

14.8 Acid–Base Titration

LEARNING GOAL: *Calculate the molarity or volume of an acid or base from titration information.*

14.59 If you need to determine the molarity of a formic acid solution, $HCHO_2$, how would you proceed?

$$HCHO_2(aq) + H_2O(l) \rightleftharpoons H_3O^+(aq) + CHO_2^-(aq)$$

14.60 If you need to determine the molarity of an acetic acid solution, $HC_2H_3O_2$, how would you proceed?

$$HC_2H_3O_2(aq) + H_2O(l) \rightleftharpoons H_3O^+(aq) + C_2H_3O_2^-(aq)$$

14.61 What is the molarity of a solution of HCl if 5.00 mL of the HCl solution is titrated with 28.6 mL of 0.145 M NaOH solution?

$$HCl(aq) + NaOH(aq) \longrightarrow H_2O(l) + NaCl(aq)$$

14.62 If 29.7 mL of a 0.205 M KOH solution is required to neutralize completely 25.0 mL of a solution of $HC_2H_3O_2$, what is the molarity of the acetic acid solution?

$$HC_2H_3O_2(aq) + KOH(aq) \longrightarrow H_2O(l) + KC_2H_3O_2(aq)$$

14.63 If 38.2 mL of a 0.163 M KOH solution is required to neutralize completely 25.0 mL of a H_2SO_4 solution, what is the molarity of the H_2SO_4 solution?

$$H_2SO_4(aq) + 2KOH(aq) \longrightarrow 2H_2O(l) + K_2SO_4(aq)$$

14.64 A solution of 0.162 M NaOH is used to neutralize 25.0 mL of a H_2SO_4 solution. If 32.8 mL of the NaOH solution is required to reach the endpoint, what is the molarity of the H_2SO_4 solution?

$$H_2SO_4(aq) + 2NaOH(aq) \longrightarrow 2H_2O(l) + Na_2SO_4(aq)$$

14.65 A solution of 0.204 M NaOH is used to neutralize 50.0 mL of a 0.0224 M H_3PO_4 solution. What volume, in milliliters, of the NaOH solution is required to reach the endpoint?

$$H_3PO_4(aq) + 3NaOH(aq) \longrightarrow 3H_2O(l) + Na_3PO_4(aq)$$

14.66 A solution of 0.312 M KOH is used to neutralize 15.0 mL of a 0.186 M H_3PO_4 solution. What volume, in milliliters, of the KOH solution is required to reach the endpoint?

$$H_3PO_4(aq) + 3KOH(aq) \longrightarrow 3H_2O(l) + K_3PO_4(aq)$$

14.9 Buffers

LEARNING GOAL

Describe the role of buffers in maintaining the pH of a solution; calculate the pH of a buffer.

The pH of water and most solutions changes drastically when a small amount of acid or base is added. However, when acids or bases are added to a *buffer* solution, there is little change in pH. A **buffer solution** is a solution that maintains the pH of a solution by neutralizing small amounts of added acid or base. For example, blood contains buffers that maintain a consistent pH of about 7.4. If the pH of the blood goes slightly above or below 7.4, changes in our oxygen levels and our metabolic processes can be drastic enough to cause death. Even though we obtain acids and bases from foods and cellular reactions, the buffers in the body absorb those compounds so effectively that the pH of our blood remains essentially unchanged (see Figure 14.8).

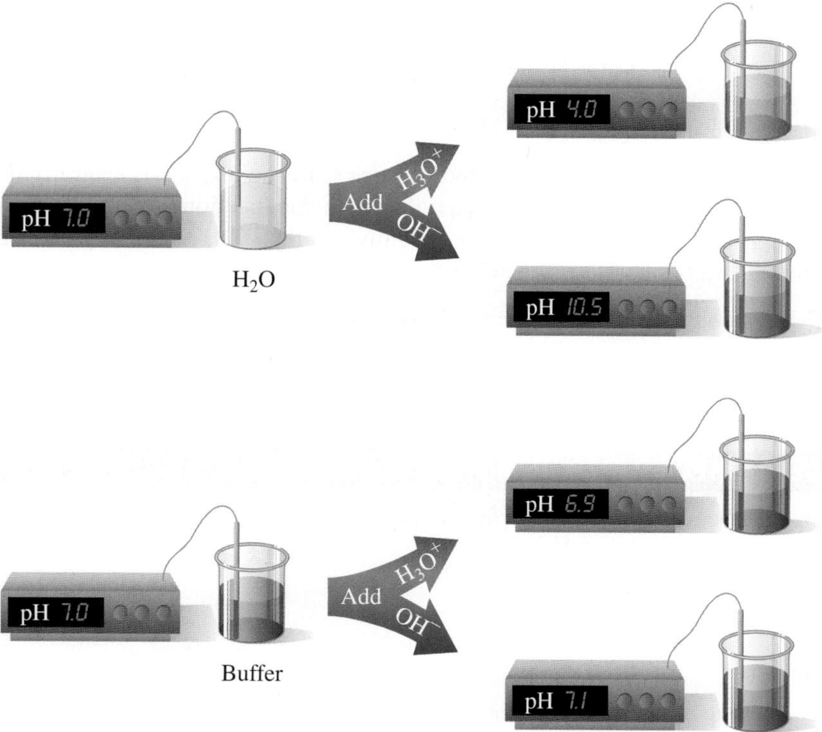

FIGURE 14.8 Adding an acid or a base to water changes the pH drastically, but a buffer resists pH change when small amounts of acid or base are added.

Q Why does the pH change several pH units when acid is added to water, but not when acid is added to a buffer?

In a buffer, an acid must be present to react with any OH^- that is added, and a base must be available to react with any added H_3O^+. However, that acid and base must not neutralize each other. Therefore, a combination of an acid–base conjugate pair is used in buffers. Most buffer solutions consist of nearly equal concentrations of a weak acid and a salt containing its conjugate base (see Figure 14.9). Buffers may also contain a weak base and the salt of the weak base, which contains its conjugate acid.

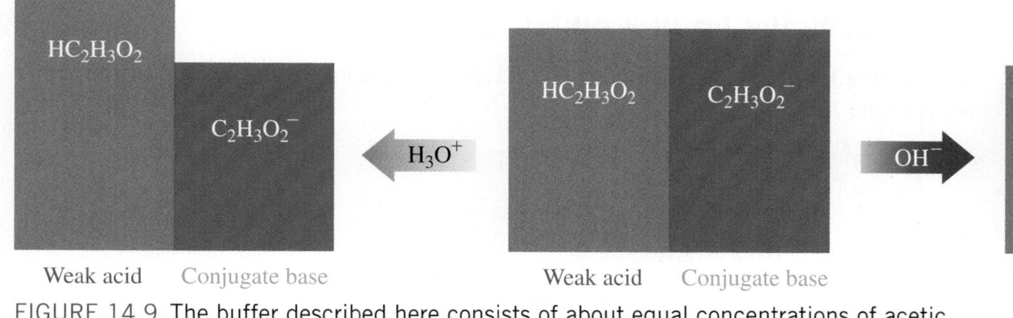

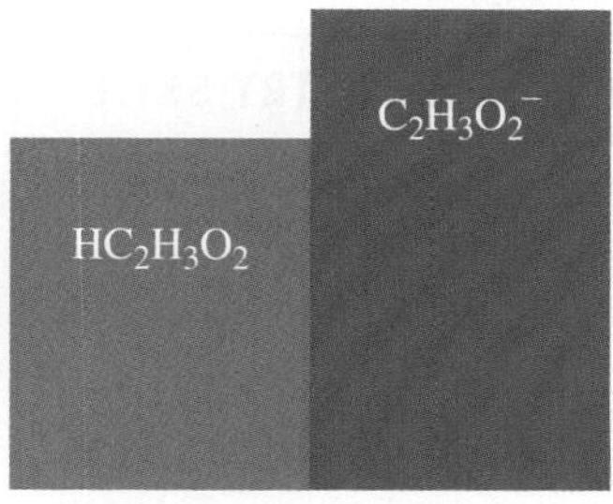

FIGURE 14.9 The buffer described here consists of about equal concentrations of acetic acid ($HC_2H_3O_2$) and its conjugate base acetate ion ($C_2H_3O_2^-$). Adding H_3O^+ to the buffer uses up some $C_2H_3O_2^-$, whereas adding OH^- neutralizes some $HC_2H_3O_2$. The pH of the solution is maintained as long as the added amounts of acid or base are small compared to the concentrations of the buffer components.

Q How does this acetic acid/acetate ion buffer maintain pH?

For example, a typical buffer can be made from the weak acid acetic acid $(HC_2H_3O_2)$ and its salt, sodium acetate $(NaC_2H_3O_2)$. As a weak acid, acetic acid dissociates slightly in water to form H_3O^+ and a very small amount of $C_2H_3O_2^-$. The addition of its salt, sodium acetate, provides a much larger concentration of acetate ion $(C_2H_3O_2^-)$, which is necessary for its buffering capability.

$$\underset{\text{Large amount}}{HC_2H_3O_2(aq)} + H_2O(l) \rightleftharpoons H_3O^+(aq) + \underset{\text{Large amount}}{C_2H_3O_2^-(aq)}$$

We can now describe how this buffer solution maintains the $[H_3O^+]$. When a small amount of acid is added, the additional H_3O^+ combines with the acetate ion, $C_2H_3O_2^-$, causing the equilibrium to shift in the direction of the reactants, acetic acid and water. There will be a slight decrease in the $[C_2H_3O_2^-]$ and a slight increase in the $[HC_2H_3O_2]$, but both the $[H_3O^+]$ and pH are maintained.

$$HC_2H_3O_2(aq) + H_2O(l) \longleftarrow H_3O^+(aq) + C_2H_3O_2^-(aq)$$

Equilibrium shifts in the direction of the reactants

If a small amount of base is added to this same buffer solution, it is neutralized by the acetic acid, $HC_2H_3O_2$, which shifts the equilibrium in the direction of the products acetate ion and water. The $[HC_2H_3O_2]$ decreases slightly and the $[C_2H_3O_2^-]$ increases slightly, but again the $[H_3O^+]$ and thus the pH of the solution are maintained.

$$HC_2H_3O_2(aq) + OH^-(aq) \longrightarrow H_2O(l) + C_2H_3O_2^-(aq)$$

Equilibrium shifts in the direction of the products

CONCEPT CHECK 14.10 Identifying Buffer Solutions

Indicate whether each of the following could be used as a buffer solution:

a. HCl (a strong acid) and NaCl
b. H_3PO_4 (a weak acid)
c. HF (a weak acid) and NaF

ANSWER

a. No. A strong acid will change the pH of a solution. A buffer requires a weak acid and a salt containing its conjugate base.
b. No. A weak acid is part of a buffer, but the salt containing the conjugate base of the weak acid is also needed.
c. Yes. This mixture would be a buffer because it contains a weak acid and a salt with its conjugate base.

CORE CHEMISTRY SKILL

Calculating the pH of a Buffer

Calculating the pH of a Buffer

By rearranging the K_a expression to give $[H_3O^+]$, we can obtain the ratio of the acetic acid/acetate buffer.

$$K_a = \frac{[H_3O^+][C_2H_3O_2^-]}{[HC_2H_3O_2]}$$

Solving for $[H_3O^+]$ gives:

$$[H_3O^+] = K_a \times \frac{[HC_2H_3O_2]}{[C_2H_3O_2^-]} \begin{array}{l} \longleftarrow \text{Weak acid} \\ \longleftarrow \text{Conjugate base} \end{array}$$

In this rearrangement of K_a, the weak acid is in the numerator and the conjugate base in the denominator. We can now calculate the $[H_3O^+]$ and pH for an acetic acid buffer as shown in Sample Problem 14.12.

SAMPLE PROBLEM 14.12 Calculating the pH of a Buffer

The K_a for acetic acid, $HC_2H_3O_2$, is 1.8×10^{-5}. What is the pH of a buffer prepared with 1.0 M $HC_2H_3O_2$ and 1.0 M $C_2H_3O_2^-$?

$$HC_2H_3O_2(aq) + H_2O(l) \rightleftarrows H_3O^+(aq) + C_2H_3O_2^-(aq)$$

SOLUTION

Step 1 State the given and needed quantities.

	Given	Need	Know
Analyze the Problem	1.0 M $HC_2H_3O_2$		$K_a = \frac{[H_3O^+][C_2H_3O_2^-]}{[HC_2H_3O_2]}$
	1.0 M $C_2H_3O_2^-$	pH	$pH = -\log[H_3O^+]$
	Equation $HC_2H_3O_2(aq) + H_2O(l) \rightleftarrows H_3O^+(aq) + C_2H_3O_2^-(aq)$		

Step 2 Write the K_a expression and rearrange for $[H_3O^+]$.

$$K_a = \frac{[H_3O^+][C_2H_3O_2^-]}{[HC_2H_3O_2]}$$

$$[H_3O^+] = K_a \times \frac{[HC_2H_3O_2]}{[C_2H_3O_2^-]}$$

Step 3 Substitute [HA] and [A⁻] into the K_a expression.

$$[H_3O^+] = 1.8 \times 10^{-5} \times \frac{[1.0]}{[1.0]}$$

$$[H_3O^+] = 1.8 \times 10^{-5}\,M$$

Step 4 Use $[H_3O^+]$ to calculate pH. Placing the $[H_3O^+]$ into the pH equation gives the pH of the buffer.

$$pH = -\log[1.8 \times 10^{-5}] = 4.74$$

STUDY CHECK 14.12

One of the conjugate acid–base pairs that buffers the blood is $H_2PO_4^-/HPO_4^{2-}$, which has a K_a of 6.2×10^{-8}. What is the pH of a buffer that is prepared from 0.10 M $H_2PO_4^-$ and 0.50 M HPO_4^{2-}?

Guide to Calculating pH of a Buffer

1. State the given and needed quantities.
2. Write the K_a expression and rearrange for $[H_3O^+]$.
3. Substitute [HA] and [A⁻] into the K_a expression.
4. Use $[H_3O^+]$ to calculate pH.

Because K_a is a constant at a given temperature, the $[H_3O^+]$ is determined by the $[HC_2H_3O_2]/[C_2H_3O_2^-]$ ratio. As long as the addition of small amounts of either acid or base changes the ratio of $[HC_2H_3O_2]/[C_2H_3O_2^-]$ only slightly, the changes in $[H_3O^+]$ will be small and the pH will be maintained. If a large amount of acid or base is added, the *buffering capacity* of the system may be exceeded. Buffers can be prepared from conjugate acid–base pairs such as $H_2PO_4^-/HPO_4^{2-}$, HPO_4^{2-}/PO_4^{3-}, HCO_3^-/CO_3^{2-}, or NH_4^+/NH_3. The pH of the buffer solution will depend on the conjugate acid–base pair chosen.

Using a common phosphate buffer for biological specimens, we can look at the effect of using different ratios of $[H_2PO_4^-]/[HPO_4^{2-}]$ on the $[H_3O^+]$ and pH. The K_a of $H_2PO_4^-$ is 6.2×10^{-8}. The equation and the $[H_3O^+]$ are written as follows:

$$H_2PO_4^-(aq) + H_2O(l) \rightleftarrows H_3O^+(aq) + HPO_4^{2-}(aq)$$

$$[H_3O^+] = K_a \times \frac{[H_2PO_4^-]}{[HPO_4^{2-}]}$$

K_a	$\frac{[H_2PO_4^-]}{[HPO_4^{2-}]}$	Ratio	$[H_3O^+]$	pH
6.2×10^{-8}	$\frac{1.0\,M}{0.10\,M}$	$\frac{10}{1}$	6.2×10^{-7}	6.21
6.2×10^{-8}	$\frac{1.0\,M}{1.0\,M}$	$\frac{1}{1}$	6.2×10^{-8}	7.21
6.2×10^{-8}	$\frac{0.10\,M}{1.0\,M}$	$\frac{1}{10}$	6.2×10^{-9}	8.21

To prepare a phosphate buffer with a pH close to the pH of a biological sample, 7.4, we would choose concentrations that are about equal, such as 1.0 M $H_2PO_4^-$ and 1.0 M HPO_4^{2-}.

CONCEPT CHECK 14.11 Preparation of Buffers

A buffer solution is needed to maintain a pH of 3.5 to 3.8 in a urine sample. Which of the following buffers would you use if 0.1 M solutions of the weak acid and conjugate base are available?

Formic acid/formate $K_a = 1.8 \times 10^{-4}$

Carbonic acid/bicarbonate $K_a = 4.3 \times 10^{-7}$

Ammonium/ammonia $K_a = 5.6 \times 10^{-10}$

ANSWER

Because formic acid has a K_a of 1.8×10^{-4}, the pH of a formic acid/formate buffer would be around 4, whereas the carbonic acid/bicarbonate buffer would be around pH 7 and the ammonium/ammonia buffer around 10. Thus, we can calculate the $[H_3O^+]$ and pH of a formic acid/formate buffer that uses 0.1 M solutions of the weak acid and the conjugate base.

$$[H_3O^+] = K_a \times \frac{[HCHO_2]}{[CHO_2^-]}$$

$$[H_3O^+] = 1.8 \times 10^{-4} \times \frac{[0.1]}{[0.1]} = 1.8 \times 10^{-4}\,M$$

$$pH = -\log[1.8 \times 10^{-4}] = 3.74$$

Chemistry Link to Health

BUFFERS IN THE BLOOD

The arterial blood has a normal pH of 7.35–7.45. If changes in H_3O^+ lower the pH below 6.8 or raise it above 8.0, cells cannot function properly and death may result. In our cells, CO_2 is continually produced as an end product of cellular metabolism. Some CO_2 is carried to the lungs for elimination, and the rest dissolves in body fluids such as plasma and saliva, forming carbonic acid, H_2CO_3. As a weak acid, carbonic acid dissociates to give bicarbonate, HCO_3^-, and H_3O^+. More of the anion HCO_3^- is supplied by the kidneys to give an important buffer system in the body fluid—the H_2CO_3/HCO_3^- buffer.

$$CO_2(g) + H_2O(l) \rightleftarrows H_2CO_3(aq) \rightleftarrows H_3O^+(aq) + HCO_3^-(aq)$$

Excess H_3O^+ entering the body fluids reacts with the HCO_3^-, and excess OH^- reacts with the carbonic acid.

$$H_2CO_3(aq) + H_2O(l) \longleftarrow H_3O^+(aq) + HCO_3^-(aq)$$

Equilibrium shifts in the direction of the reactants

$$H_2CO_3(aq) + OH^-(aq) \longrightarrow H_2O(l) + HCO_3^-(aq)$$

Equilibrium shifts in the direction of the products

For carbonic acid, we can write the equilibrium expression as

$$K_a = \frac{[H_3O^+][HCO_3^-]}{[H_2CO_3]}$$

To maintain the normal blood pH (7.35–7.45), the ratio of $[H_2CO_3]/[HCO_3^-]$ needs to be about 1 to 10, which is obtained by the concentrations in the blood of 0.0024 M H_2CO_3 and 0.024 M HCO_3^-.

$$[H_3O^+] = K_a \times \frac{[H_2CO_3]}{[HCO_3^-]}$$

$$= 4.3 \times 10^{-7} \times \frac{[0.0024]}{[0.024]}$$

$$= 4.3 \times 10^{-7} \times 0.10 = 4.3 \times 10^{-8}\text{ M}$$

$$\text{pH} = -\log[4.3 \times 10^{-8}] = 7.37$$

In the body, the concentration of carbonic acid is closely associated with the partial pressure of CO_2, P_{CO_2}. Table 14.10 lists the normal values for arterial blood. If the CO_2 level rises, increasing $[H_2CO_3]$, the equilibrium shifts to produce more H_3O^+, which lowers the pH. This condition is called *acidosis*. Difficulty with ventilation or gas diffusion can lead to respiratory acidosis, which can happen in emphysema or when an accident or depressive drugs affect the medulla of the brain.

A lowering of the CO_2 level leads to a high blood pH, a condition called *alkalosis*. Excitement, trauma, or a high temperature may cause a person to hyperventilate, which expels large amounts of CO_2. As the partial pressure of CO_2 in the blood falls below normal, the equilibrium shifts from H_2CO_3 to CO_2 and H_2O. This shift decreases the $[H_3O^+]$ and raises the pH. The kidneys also regulate H_3O^+ and HCO_3^-, but they do so more slowly than the adjustment made by the lungs during ventilation.

TABLE 14.10 Normal Values for Blood Buffer in Arterial Blood

P_{CO_2}	40 mmHg
H_2CO_3	2.4 mmol/L of plasma
HCO_3^-	24 mmol/L of plasma
pH	7.35–7.45

QUESTIONS AND PROBLEMS

14.9 Buffers

LEARNING GOAL: *Describe the role of buffers in maintaining the pH of a solution; calculate the pH of a buffer.*

14.67 Which of the following represents a buffer system? Explain.
a. NaOH and NaCl
b. H_2CO_3 and $NaHCO_3$
c. HF and KF
d. KCl and NaCl

14.68 Which of the following represents a buffer system? Explain.
a. $HClO_2$
b. $NaNO_3$
c. $HC_2H_3O_2$ and $NaC_2H_3O_2$
d. HCl and NaOH

14.69 Consider the buffer system of hydrofluoric acid, HF, and its salt, NaF.

$$HF(aq) + H_2O(l) \rightleftharpoons H_3O^+(aq) + F^-(aq)$$

a. The purpose of this buffer system is to:
1. maintain [HF]
2. maintain $[F^-]$
3. maintain pH

b. The salt of the weak acid is needed to:
1. provide the conjugate base
2. neutralize added H_3O^+
3. provide the conjugate acid

c. The addition of OH^- is neutralized by:
1. the salt
2. H_2O
3. H_3O^+

d. When H_3O^+ is added, the equilibrium shifts in the direction of the:
1. reactants
2. products
3. does not change

14.70 Consider the buffer system of nitrous acid, HNO_2, and its salt, $NaNO_2$.

$$HNO_2(aq) + H_2O(l) \rightleftharpoons H_3O^+(aq) + NO_2^-(aq)$$

a. The purpose of this buffer system is to:
1. maintain $[HNO_2]$
2. maintain $[NO_2^-]$
3. maintain pH

b. The weak acid is needed to:
1. provide the conjugate base
2. neutralize added OH^-
3. provide the conjugate acid

c. The addition of H_3O^+ is neutralized by:
1. the salt
2. H_2O
3. OH^-

d. When OH^- is added, the equilibrium shifts in the direction of the:
1. reactants
2. products
3. does not change

14.71 Nitrous acid has a K_a of 4.5×10^{-4}. What is the pH of a buffer solution containing 0.10 M HNO_2 and 0.10 M NO_2^-?

14.72 Acetic acid has a K_a of 1.8×10^{-5}. What is the pH of a buffer solution containing 0.15 M $HC_2H_3O_2$ and 0.15 M $C_2H_3O_2^-$?

14.73 Using Table 14.5 for K_a values, compare the pH of a HF buffer that contains 0.10 M HF and 0.10 M NaF with another HF buffer that contains 0.060 M HF and 0.120 M NaF.

14.74 Using Table 14.5 for K_a values, compare the pH of a H_2CO_3 buffer that contains 0.10 M H_2CO_3 and 0.10 M $NaHCO_3$ with another H_2CO_3 buffer that contains 0.15 M H_2CO_3 and 0.050 M $NaHCO_3$.

CHAPTER REVIEW

14.1 Acids and Bases

LEARNING GOAL: *Describe and name Arrhenius acids and bases, and organic acids.*

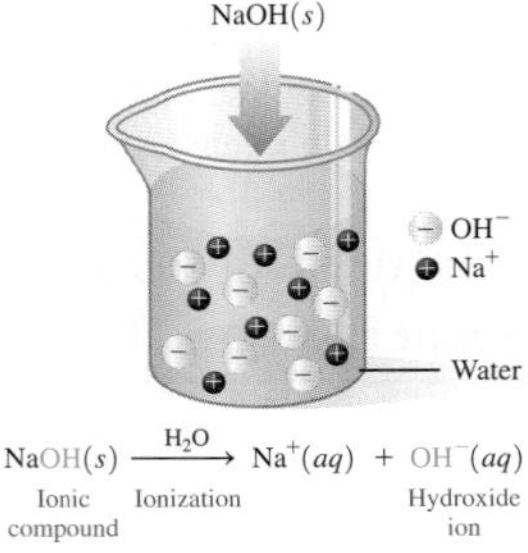

- An Arrhenius acid produces H^+ and an Arrhenius base produces OH^- in aqueous solutions.
- Acids taste sour, may sting, and neutralize bases.
- Bases taste bitter, feel slippery, and neutralize acids.
- Acids containing a simple anion use a *hydro* prefix, whereas acids with oxygen-containing polyatomic anions are named as *ic* or *ous acids*.
- Organic acids use common names such as formic acid and acetic acid. Their IUPAC names are derived from their alkane names by replacing the *e* with *oic acid*.

14.2 Brønsted–Lowry Acids and Bases

LEARNING GOAL: *Identify conjugate acid–base pairs for Brønsted–Lowry acids and bases.*

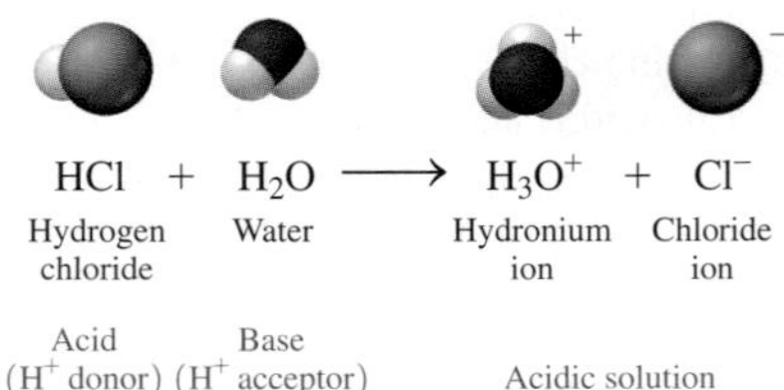

- According to the Brønsted–Lowry theory, acids are H^+ donors and bases are H^+ acceptors.
- A conjugate acid–base pair is related by the loss or gain of one H^+.
- For example, when the acid HF donates H^+, the F^- is its conjugate base. The other acid–base pair would be H_3O^+/H_2O.

$$HF(aq) + H_2O(l) \rightleftarrows H_3O^+(aq) + F^-(aq)$$

14.3 Strengths of Acids and Bases

LEARNING GOAL: *Write equations for the dissociation of strong and weak acids; identify the direction of reaction.*

- Strong acids dissociate completely in water, and the H^+ is accepted by H_2O acting as a base.
- A weak acid dissociates slightly in water, producing only a small percentage of H_3O^+.

- Strong bases are hydroxides of Groups 1A (1) and 2A (2) that dissociate completely in water.
- An important weak base is ammonia, NH_3.

14.4 Dissociation Constants for Acids and Bases

LEARNING GOAL: *Write the expression for the dissociation constant of a weak acid or weak base.*

- In water, weak acids and weak bases produce only a few ions when equilibrium is reached.
- Weak acids have small K_a values whereas strong acids, which are essentially 100% dissociated, have very large K_a values.
- The reaction for a weak acid can be written as $HA + H_2O \rightleftarrows H_3O^+ + A^-$. The acid dissociation constant expression is written as

$$K_a = \frac{[H_3O^+][A^-]}{[HA]}.$$

- For a weak base, $B + H_2O \rightleftarrows BH^+ + OH^-$, the base dissociation constant expression is written as

$$K_b = \frac{[BH^+][OH^-]}{[B]}.$$

14.5 Ionization of Water

LEARNING GOAL: *Use the ion product of water to calculate the $[H_3O^+]$ and $[OH^-]$ in an aqueous solution.*

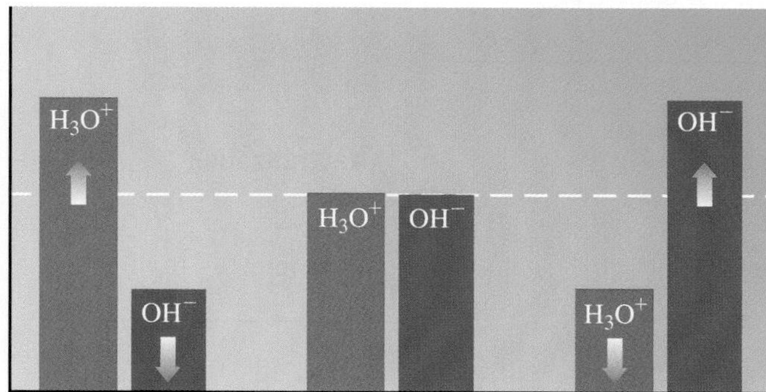

- In pure water, a few water molecules transfer H^+ to other water molecules, producing small, but equal, amounts of $[H_3O^+]$ and $[OH^-]$.
- In pure water, the molar concentrations of H_3O^+ and OH^- are each 1.0×10^{-7} mol/L.
- The ion product constant for water, K_w, $[H_3O^+][OH^-] = 1.0 \times 10^{-14}$ at 25 °C.
- In acidic solutions, the $[H_3O^+]$ is greater than the $[OH^-]$.
- In basic solutions, the $[OH^-]$ is greater than the $[H_3O^+]$.

14.6 The pH Scale

LEARNING GOAL: *Calculate pH from $[H_3O^+]$; given the pH, calculate the $[H_3O^+]$ and $[OH^-]$ of a solution.*

- The pH scale is a range of numbers typically from 0 to 14, which represents the $[H_3O^+]$ of the solution.
- A neutral solution has a pH of 7.0. In acidic solutions, the pH is below 7.0; in basic solutions, the pH is above 7.0.
- Mathematically, pH is the negative logarithm of the hydronium ion concentration $pH = -\log[H_3O^+]$.
- The pOH is the negative log of the hydroxide ion concentration $pOH = -\log[OH^-]$.
- The sum of the pH + pOH is 14.00.

14.7 Reactions of Acids and Bases

LEARNING GOAL: *Write balanced equations for reactions of acids with metals, carbonates, and bases.*

- An acid reacts with a metal to produce hydrogen gas and a salt.
- The reaction of an acid with a carbonate or bicarbonate produces carbon dioxide, water, and a salt.
- In neutralization, an acid reacts with a base to produce water and a salt.

14.8 Acid–Base Titration

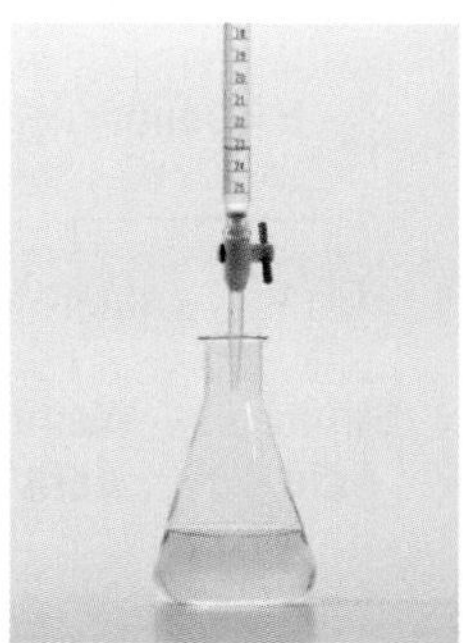

LEARNING GOAL: *Calculate the molarity or volume of an acid or base from titration information.*

- In a titration, an acid sample is neutralized with a known amount of a base.
- From the volume and molarity of the base, the concentration of the acid is calculated.

14.9 Buffers

LEARNING GOAL: *Describe the role of buffers in maintaining the pH of a solution; calculate the pH of a buffer.*

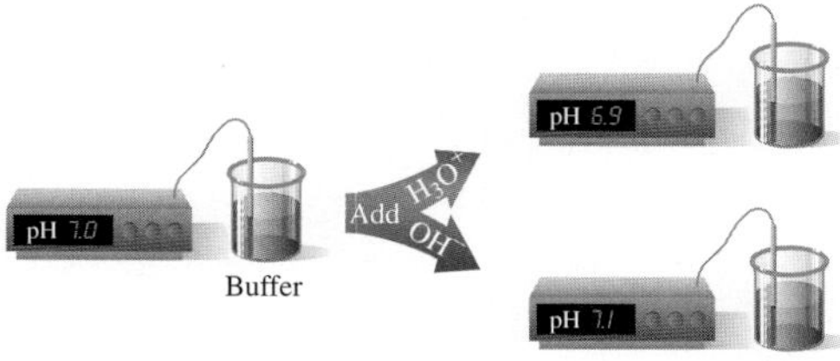

- A buffer solution resists changes in pH when small amounts of an acid or a base are added.
- A buffer contains either a weak acid and its salt or a weak base and its salt.
- In a buffer, the weak acid reacts with added OH^-, and the anion of the salt reacts with added H_3O^+.

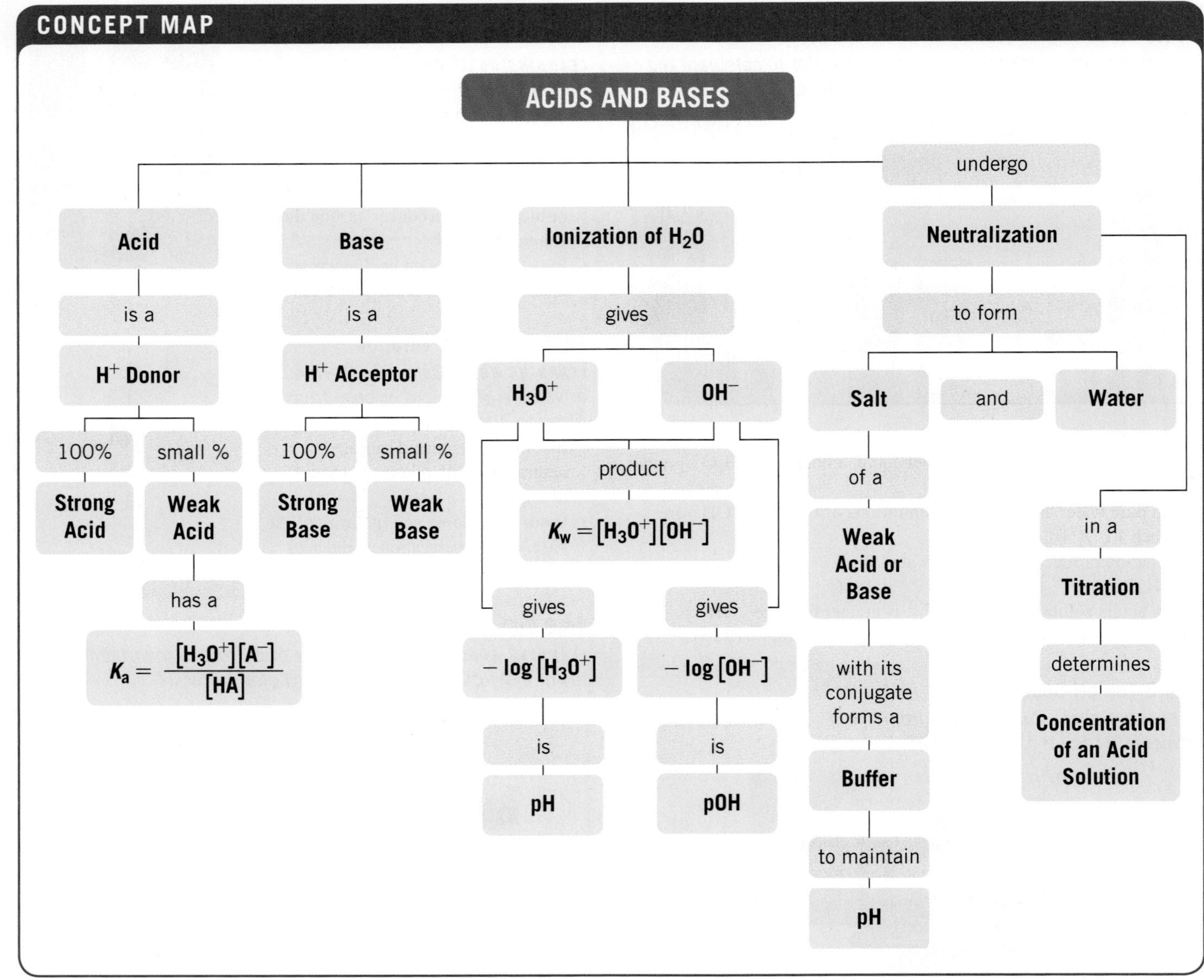

KEY TERMS

acid A substance that dissolves in water and produces hydrogen ions (H^+), according to the Arrhenius theory. All acids are hydrogen ion donors, according to the Brønsted–Lowry theory.

acid dissociation constant, K_a The product of the ions from the dissociation of a weak acid divided by the concentration of the weak acid.

amphoteric Substances that can act as either an acid or a base in water.

base A substance that dissolves in water and produces hydroxide ions (OH^-) according to the Arrhenius theory. All bases are hydrogen ion acceptors, according to the Brønsted–Lowry theory.

base dissociation constant, K_b The product of the ions from the dissociation of a weak base divided by the concentration of the weak base.

Brønsted–Lowry acids and bases An acid is a hydrogen ion donor; a base is a hydrogen ion acceptor.

buffer solution A solution of a weak acid and its conjugate base or a weak base and its conjugate acid that maintains the pH by neutralizing added acid or base.

conjugate acid–base pair An acid and a base that differ by one H^+. When an acid donates a hydrogen ion, the product is its conjugate base, which is capable of accepting a hydrogen ion in the reverse reaction.

dissociation The separation of an acid or a base into ions in water.

endpoint The point at which an indicator changes color. For the indicator phenolphthalein, the color change occurs when the number of moles of OH^- is equal to the number of moles of H_3O^+ in the sample.

hydronium ion, H_3O^+ The ion formed by the attraction of a hydrogen ion, H^+, to a water molecule.

indicator A substance added to a titration sample that changes color when the pH of the solution changes.

ion product constant for water, K_w The product of $[H_3O^+]$ and $[OH^-]$ in solution; $K_w = [H_3O^+][OH^-]$.

neutral The term that describes a solution with equal concentrations of $[H_3O^+]$ and $[OH^-]$.

neutralization A reaction between an acid and a base to form water and a salt.

pH A measure of the $[H_3O^+]$ in a solution; $pH = -\log[H_3O^+]$.

pOH A measure of the $[OH^-]$ in a solution; $pOH = -\log[OH^-]$.

salt An ionic compound that contains a metal ion or NH_4^+ and a nonmetal or polyatomic ion other than OH^-.

strong acid An acid that completely ionizes in water.

strong base A base that completely ionizes in water.

titration The addition of base to an acid sample to determine the concentration of the acid.

weak acid An acid that is a poor donor of H^+ and dissociates only slightly in water.

weak base A base that is a poor acceptor of H^+ and produces only a small number of ions in water.

KEY MATH SKILLS

The chapter section containing each Key Math Skill is shown in parentheses at the end of each heading.

Calculating pH from $[H_3O^+]$ (14.6)

- The pH of a solution is calculated from the negative log of the $[H_3O^+]$.

$pH = -\log[H_3O^+]$

Example: What is the pH of a solution that has $[H_3O^+] = 2.4 \times 10^{-11}$ M?

Answer: We substitute the given $[H_3O^+]$ into the pH equation and calculate the pH.

$$pH = -\log[H_3O^+]$$
$$pH = -\log[2.4 \times 10^{-11}]$$
$$pH = -(-10.62)$$
$$pH = 10.62$$ (Two decimal places equal the 2 SFs in the $[H_3O^+]$ coefficient.)

Calculating $[H_3O^+]$ from pH (14.6)

- The calculation of $[H_3O^+]$ from the pH is done by reversing the pH calculation using the negative pH or the inverse log (*2nd* 10^x).

$[H_3O^+] = 10^{-pH}$

Example: What is the $[H_3O^+]$ of a solution with a pH of 4.80?

Answer: $[H_3O^+] = 10^{-pH}$

$= 10^{-4.80}$

= INV log (−pH)

= 2nd 10^x (−4.80)

$= 1.6 \times 10^{-5}$ M

CORE CHEMISTRY SKILLS

The chapter section containing each Core Chemistry Skill is shown in parentheses at the end of each heading.

Identifying Conjugate Acid–Base Pairs (14.2)

- According to the Brønsted–Lowry theory, a conjugate acid–base pair consists of molecules or ions related by the loss of one H^+ by an acid, and the gain of one H^+ by a base.
- Every acid–base reaction contains two conjugate acid–base pairs because an H^+ is transferred in both the forward and reverse directions.
- When an acid such as HF loses one H^+, the conjugate base F^- is formed. When H_2O acts as a base, it gains an H^+, which forms its conjugate acid, H_3O^+.

Example: Identify the conjugate acid–base pairs in the following reaction:

$$H_2SO_4(aq) + H_2O(l) \rightleftharpoons HSO_4^-(aq) + H_3O^+(aq)$$

Answer:

$$\underbrace{\underset{\text{Acid}}{H_2SO_4(aq)} + \underset{\text{Base}}{H_2O(l)}} \rightleftharpoons \underbrace{\underset{\text{Conjugate base}}{HSO_4^-(aq)} + \underset{\text{Conjugate acid}}{H_3O^+(aq)}}$$

Conjugate acid–base pairs: H_2SO_4/HSO_4^- H_3O^+/H_2O

Calculating $[H_3O^+]$ and $[OH^-]$ in Solutions (14.5)

- For all aqueous solutions, the product of $[H_3O^+]$ and $[OH^-]$ is equal to the ion product constant for water, K_w.

$$K_w = [H_3O^+][OH^-]$$

- Because pure water contains equal numbers of OH^- ions and H_3O^+ ions each with molar concentrations of 1.0×10^{-7} M, the numerical value of K_w is 1.0×10^{-14} at 25 °C.

$$K_w = [H_3O^+][OH^-] = [1.0 \times 10^{-7}][1.0 \times 10^{-7}] = 1.0 \times 10^{-14}$$

- If we know the $[H_3O^+]$ of a solution, we can use the K_w to calculate the $[OH^-]$. If we know the $[OH^-]$ of a solution, we can calculate $[H_3O^+]$ using the K_w.

$$[OH^-] = \frac{K_w}{[H_3O^+]} \qquad [H_3O^+] = \frac{K_w}{[OH^-]}$$

Example: What is the $[OH^-]$ in a solution that has $[H_3O^+] = 2.4 \times 10^{-11}$ M? Is the solution acidic or basic?

Answer: We solve the K_w expression for $[OH^-]$ and substitute in the known values of K_w and $[H_3O^+]$.

$$[OH^-] = \frac{K_w}{[H_3O^+]} \qquad [OH^-] = \frac{1.0 \times 10^{-14}}{[2.4 \times 10^{-11}]} = 4.2 \times 10^{-4}\ M$$

Because the $[OH^-]$ is greater than the $[H_3O^+]$, this is a basic solution.

Writing Equations for Reactions of Acids and Bases (14.7)

- Acids react with certain metals to produce hydrogen gas (H_2) and a salt.

$$\underset{\text{Metal}}{Mg(s)} + \underset{\text{Acid}}{2HCl(aq)} \longrightarrow \underset{\text{Hydrogen}}{H_2(g)} + \underset{\text{Salt}}{MgCl_2(aq)}$$

- When an acid is added to a carbonate or bicarbonate, the products are carbon dioxide gas, water, and a salt.

$$\underset{\text{Acid}}{2HCl(aq)} + \underset{\text{Carbonate}}{Na_2CO_3(aq)} \longrightarrow \underset{\text{Carbon dioxide}}{CO_2(g)} + \underset{\text{Water}}{H_2O(l)} + \underset{\text{Salt}}{2NaCl(aq)}$$

- Neutralization is a reaction between a strong or weak acid with a strong base to produce water and a salt.

$$\underset{\text{Acid}}{HCl(aq)} + \underset{\text{Base}}{NaOH(aq)} \longrightarrow \underset{\text{Water}}{H_2O(l)} + \underset{\text{Salt}}{NaCl(aq)}$$

Example: Write the balanced chemical equation for the reaction of $ZnCO_3(s)$ and hydrobromic acid $HBr(aq)$.

Answer:

$$ZnCO_3(s) + 2HBr(aq) \longrightarrow CO_2(g) + H_2O(l) + ZnBr_2(aq)$$

Calculating Molarity or Volume of an Acid or Base in a Titration (14.8)

- In a titration, a measured volume of acid is neutralized by an NaOH solution of known molarity.
- From the measured volume of the NaOH solution required for titration and its molarity, the number of moles of NaOH, the moles of acid, and the concentration of the acid are calculated.

Example: A 15.0-mL sample of a H_2SO_4 solution is titrated with 24.0 mL of a 0.245 M NaOH solution. What is the molarity of the H_2SO_4 solution?

$$H_2SO_4(aq) + 2NaOH(aq) \longrightarrow 2H_2O(l) + Na_2SO_4(aq)$$

Answer:

$$24.0\ \text{mL NaOH solution} \times \frac{1\ \text{L NaOH solution}}{1000\ \text{mL NaOH solution}}$$

$$\times \frac{0.245\ \text{mol NaOH}}{1\ \text{L NaOH solution}} \times \frac{1\ \text{mol } H_2SO_4}{2\ \text{mol NaOH}} = 0.00294\ \text{mol of } H_2SO_4$$

$$\frac{0.00294\ \text{mol } H_2SO_4}{0.0150\ \text{L } H_2SO_4\ \text{solution}} = 0.196\ \text{M } H_2SO_4\ \text{solution}$$

Calculating the pH of a Buffer (14.9)

- A buffer solution maintains pH by neutralizing small amounts of added acid or base.
- Most buffer solutions consist of nearly equal concentrations of a weak acid and a salt containing its conjugate base such as acetic acid, $HC_2H_3O_2$, and its salt $NaC_2H_3O_2$.
- The $[H_3O^+]$ is calculated by solving the K_a expression for $[H_3O^+]$, which gives the ratio of the acetic acid/acetate buffer.

$$K_a = \frac{[H_3O^+][C_2H_3O_2^-]}{[HC_2H_3O_2]}$$

Solving for $[H_3O^+]$ gives:

$$[H_3O^+] = K_a \times \frac{[HC_2H_3O_2]}{[C_2H_3O_2^-]} \begin{array}{l} \longleftarrow \text{Weak acid} \\ \longleftarrow \text{Conjugate base} \end{array}$$

- The pH of the buffer is calculated from the $[H_3O^+]$.

$$pH = -\log[H_3O^+]$$

Example: What is the pH of a buffer prepared with 0.40 M $HC_2H_3O_2$ and 0.20 M $C_2H_3O_2^-$, if the K_a of acetic acid is 1.8×10^{-5}?

Answer:

$$[H_3O^+] = K_a \times \frac{[HC_2H_3O_2]}{[C_2H_3O_2^-]} = 1.8 \times 10^{-5} \times \frac{[0.40]}{[0.20]}$$

$$= 3.6 \times 10^{-5}\ \text{M}$$

$$pH = -\log[3.6 \times 10^{-5}] = 4.44$$

UNDERSTANDING THE CONCEPTS

The chapter sections to review are shown in parentheses at the end of each question.

14.75 Determine if each of the following diagrams represents a strong acid or a weak acid. The acid has the formula HX. (14.3)

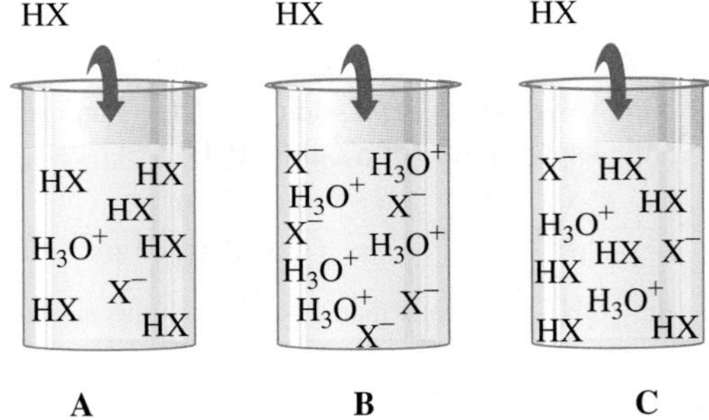

14.76 Adding a few drops of a strong acid to water will lower the pH appreciably. However, adding the same number of drops to a buffer does not appreciably alter the pH. Why? (14.4, 14.9)

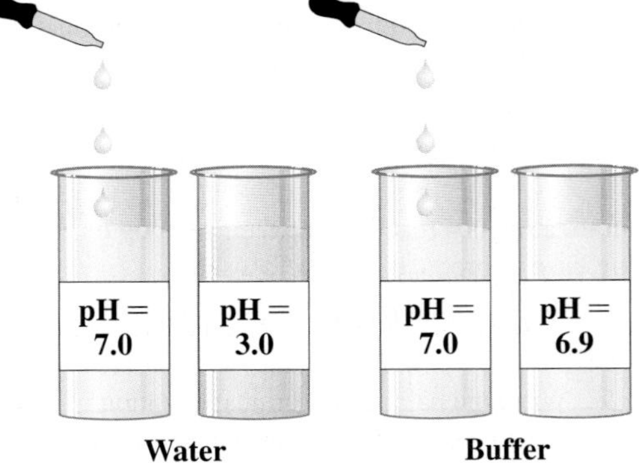

14.77 Sometimes, during stress or trauma, a person can start to hyperventilate. Then the person might breathe into a paper bag to avoid fainting. (14.9)

a. What changes occur in the blood pH during hyperventilation?

b. How does breathing into a paper bag help return blood pH to normal?

Breathing into a paper bag provides carbon dioxide.

14.78 In the blood plasma, pH is maintained by the carbonic acid–bicarbonate buffer system. (14.9)

a. How is pH maintained when acid is added to the buffer system?

b. How is pH maintained when base is added to the buffer system?

ADDITIONAL QUESTIONS AND PROBLEMS

14.79 Identify each of the following as an acid, base, or salt, and give its name: (14.1)

a. $HBrO_2$ **b.** RbOH
c. $Mg(NO_3)_2$ **d.** $CH_3—CH_2—CH_2—COOH$
e. $HClO_4$

14.80 Identify each of the following as an acid, base, or salt, and give its name: (14.1)

a. HI **b.** $MgBr_2$
c. NH_3 **d.** Li_2SO_3
e. $CH_3—CH_2—COOH$

14.81 Complete the following table: (14.2)

Acid	Conjugate Base
HI	
	Cl^-
NH_4^+	
	HS^-

14.82 Complete the following table: (14.2)

Base	Conjugate Acid
	HS^-
	$HC_2H_3O_2$
NH_3	
ClO^-	

14.83 Using Table 14.4, identify the stronger acid in each of the following pairs: (14.3)

a. HF or HCN **b.** H_3O^+ or H_2S
c. HNO_2 or $HC_2H_3O_2$ **d.** H_2O or HCO_3^-

14.84 Using Table 14.4, identify the stronger base in each of the following pairs: (14.3)

a. H_2O or Cl^- **b.** OH^- or NH_3
c. SO_4^{2-} or NO_2^- **d.** CO_3^{2-} or H_2O

14.85 Are each of the following solutions acidic, basic, or neutral? (14.6)

a. rain, pH 5.2 **b.** tears, pH 7.5
c. tea, pH 3.8 **d.** cola, pH 2.5
e. photo developer, pH 12.0

14.86 Are each of the following solutions acidic, basic, or neutral? (14.6)

a. saliva, pH 6.8 **b.** urine, pH 5.9
c. pancreatic juice, pH 8.0 **d.** bile, pH 8.4
e. blood, pH 7.45

14.87 Determine the pH and pOH for each of the following solutions: (14.6)

a. $[H_3O^+] = 2.0 \times 10^{-8}$ M
b. $[H_3O^+] = 5.0 \times 10^{-2}$ M
c. $[OH^-] = 3.5 \times 10^{-4}$ M
d. $[OH^-] = 0.0054$ M

14.88 Determine the pH and pOH for each of the following solutions: (14.6)

a. $[OH^-] = 1.0 \times 10^{-7}$ M
b. $[H_3O^+] = 4.2 \times 10^{-3}$ M
c. $[H_3O^+] = 0.0001$ M
d. $[OH^-] = 8.5 \times 10^{-9}$ M

14.89 Are the solutions in Problem 14.87 acidic, basic, or neutral? (14.6)

14.90 Are the solutions in Problem 14.88 acidic, basic, or neutral? (14.6)

14.91 Calculate the $[H_3O^+]$ and $[OH^-]$ for a solution with each of the following pH values: (14.6)

a. 3.00 **b.** 6.48
c. 8.85 **d.** 11.00

14.92 Calculate the $[H_3O^+]$ and $[OH^-]$ for a solution with each of the following pH values: (14.6)

a. 10.0 **b.** 5.0
c. 6.5 **d.** 1.82

14.93 Solution A has a pH of 4.5, and solution B has a pH of 6.7. (14.6)

a. Which solution is more acidic?
b. What is the $[H_3O^+]$ in each?
c. What is the $[OH^-]$ in each?

14.94 Solution X has a pH of 9.5, and solution Y has a pH of 7.5. (14.6)

a. Which solution is more acidic?
b. What is the $[H_3O^+]$ in each?
c. What is the $[OH^-]$ in each?

14.95 What is the $[OH^-]$ in a solution that contains 0.225 g of NaOH in 0.250 L of solution? (14.7)

14.96 What is the $[H_3O^+]$ in a solution that contains 1.54 g of HNO_3 in 0.500 L of solution? (14.7)

14.97 What is the pH and pOH of a solution prepared by dissolving 2.5 g of HCl in water to make 425 mL of solution? (14.6)

14.98 What is the pH and pOH of a solution prepared by dissolving 1.00 g of $Ca(OH)_2$ in water to make 875 mL of solution? (14.6)

CHALLENGE QUESTIONS

14.99 For each of the following: (14.2, 14.3)

1. H_2S **2.** H_3PO_4
a. Write the formula for the conjugate base.
b. Write the K_a expression.
c. Which is the weaker acid?

14.100 For each of the following: (14.2, 14.3)

1. HCO_3^- **2.** $HC_2H_3O_2$
a. Write the formula for the conjugate base.
b. Write the K_a expression.
c. Which is the stronger acid?

14.101 Using Table 14.4, identify the conjugate acid–base pairs in each of the following equations and whether the equilibrium mixture contains mostly products or mostly reactants: (14.2, 14.3)

a. $NH_3(aq) + HNO_3(aq) \rightleftarrows NH_4^+(aq) + NO_3^-(aq)$
b. $H_2O(l) + HBr(aq) \rightleftarrows H_3O^+(aq) + Br^-(aq)$

14.102 Using Table 14.4, identify the conjugate acid–base pairs in each of the following equations and whether the equilibrium mixture contains mostly products or mostly reactants: (14.2, 14.3)

a. $HNO_2(aq) + HS^-(aq) \rightleftarrows H_2S(g) + NO_2^-(aq)$
b. $Cl^-(aq) + H_2O(l) \rightleftarrows OH^-(aq) + HCl(aq)$

14.103 Complete and balance each of the following: (14.7)

a. $ZnCO_3(s) + H_2SO_4(aq) \longrightarrow$

b. $Al(s) + HNO_3(aq) \longrightarrow$

14.104 Complete and balance each of the following: (14.7)

a. $H_3PO_4(aq) + Ca(OH)_2(s) \longrightarrow$

b. $KHCO_3(s) + HNO_3(aq) \longrightarrow$

14.105 Determine each of the following for a 0.050 M KOH solution: (14.6, 14.7, 14.8)

a. $[H_3O^+]$

b. pH

c. pOH

d. the balanced equation for the reaction with H_2SO_4

e. milliliters of KOH solution required to neutralize 40.0 mL of a 0.035 M H_2SO_4 solution

14.106 Determine each of the following for a 0.100 M HBr solution: (14.6, 14.7, 14.8)

a. $[H_3O^+]$

b. pH

c. pOH

d. the balanced equation for the reaction with LiOH

e. milliliters of HBr solution required to neutralize 36.0 mL of a 0.250 M LiOH solution

14.107 One of the most acidic lakes in the United States is Little Echo Pond in the Adirondacks in New York. Recently, this lake had a pH of 4.2, well below the recommended pH of 6.5. (14.6, 14.8)

A helicopter drops calcium carbonate on an acidic lake to increase its pH.

a. What are the $[H_3O^+]$ and $[OH^-]$ of the lake?

b. What are the $[H_3O^+]$ and $[OH^-]$ of a lake that has a pH of 6.5?

c. One way to raise the pH of an acidic lake (and restore aquatic life) is to add limestone ($CaCO_3$). How many grams of $CaCO_3$ are needed to neutralize 1.0 kL of the acidic water from the lake if the acid is sulfuric acid?

$$H_2SO_4(aq) + CaCO_3(s) \longrightarrow CO_2(g) + H_2O(l) + CaSO_4(aq)$$

14.108 The daily output of stomach acid (gastric juice) is 1000 mL to 2000 mL. Prior to a meal, stomach acid (HCl) typically has a pH of 1.42. (14.6, 14.7, 14.8)

a. What is the $[H_3O^+]$ of stomach acid?

b. One chewable tablet of the antacid Maalox contains 600. mg of $CaCO_3$. Write the neutralization equation and calculate the milliliters of stomach acid neutralized by two tablets of Maalox.

c. The antacid milk of magnesia contains 400. mg of $Mg(OH)_2$ per teaspoon. Write the balanced equation for the neutralization and calculate the number of milliliters of stomach acid that are neutralized by 1 tablespoon of milk of magnesia (1 tablespoon = 3 teaspoons).

14.109 Calculate the volume, in milliliters, of a 0.150 M NaOH solution that will completely neutralize each of the following: (14.8)

a. 25.0 mL of a 0.288 M HCl solution

b. 10.0 mL of a 0.560 M H_2SO_4 solution

14.110 Calculate the volume, in milliliters, of a 0.215 M NaOH solution that will completely neutralize each of the following: (14.8)

a. 3.80 mL of a 1.25 M HNO_3 solution

b. 8.50 mL of a 0.825 M H_3PO_4 solution

14.111 A solution of 0.205 M NaOH is used to neutralize 20.0 mL of a H_2SO_4 solution. If 45.6 mL of the NaOH solution is required to reach the endpoint, what is the molarity of the H_2SO_4 solution? (14.8)

$$H_2SO_4(aq) + 2NaOH(aq) \longrightarrow 2H_2O(l) + Na_2SO_4(aq)$$

14.112 A 10.0-mL sample of vinegar, which is an aqueous solution of acetic acid, $HC_2H_3O_2$, requires 16.5 mL of a 0.500 M NaOH solution to reach the endpoint in a titration. What is the molarity of the acetic acid solution? (14.8)

$$HC_2H_3O_2(aq) + NaOH(aq) \longrightarrow H_2O(l) + NaC_2H_3O_2(aq)$$

14.113 A buffer solution is made by dissolving H_3PO_4 and NaH_2PO_4 in water. (14.9)

a. Write an equation that shows how this buffer neutralizes added acid.

b. Write an equation that shows how this buffer neutralizes added base.

c. Calculate the pH of this buffer if it contains 0.50 M H_3PO_4 and 0.20 M $H_2PO_4^-$. The K_a for H_3PO_4 is 7.5×10^{-3}.

14.114 A buffer solution is made by dissolving $HC_2H_3O_2$ and $NaC_2H_3O_2$ in water. (14.9)

a. Write an equation that shows how this buffer neutralizes added acid.

b. Write an equation that shows how this buffer neutralizes added base.

c. Calculate the pH of this buffer if it contains 0.20 M $HC_2H_3O_2$ and 0.40 M $C_2H_3O_2^-$. The K_a for $HC_2H_3O_2$ is 1.8×10^{-5}.

ANSWERS

Answers to Study Checks

14.1 **a.** chloric acid **b.** $Fe(OH)_3$

14.2 $HNO_3(aq) + H_2O(l) \longrightarrow H_3O^+(aq) + NO_3^-(aq)$

14.3 The conjugate acid–base pairs are HCN/CN^- and HSO_4^-/SO_4^{2-}.

14.4 $HNO_3(aq) + H_2O(l) \longrightarrow H_3O^+(aq) + NO_3^-(aq)$

The equilibrium mixture contains mostly products because HNO_3 is a stronger acid than H_3O^+, and H_2O is a stronger base than NO_3^-.

14.5 $K_a = 2.2 \times 10^{-13}$

14.6 $[H_3O^+] = 2.5 \times 10^{-11}$ M; basic

14.7 11.38

14.8 pH = 4.3

14.9 $[H_3O^+] = 3.2 \times 10^{-5}$ M; $[OH^-] = 3.1 \times 10^{-10}$ M

14.10 $H_2SO_4(aq) + 2LiOH(s) \longrightarrow 2H_2O(l) + Li_2SO_4(aq)$

14.11 0.200 M HCl solution

14.12 pH = 7.91

Answers to Selected Questions and Problems

14.1 **a.** acid **b.** acid **c.** acid **d.** base **e.** both

14.3 **a.** hydrochloric acid **b.** calcium hydroxide **c.** carbonic acid **d.** nitric acid **e.** sulfurous acid **f.** bromous acid **g.** ethanoic acid (IUPAC); acetic acid (common)

14.5 **a.** RbOH **b.** HF **c.** HCH_2O **d.** LiOH **e.** NH_4OH **f.** HIO_4

14.7 **a.** HI is the acid (hydrogen ion donor), and H_2O is the base (hydrogen ion acceptor).
b. H_2O is the acid (hydrogen ion donor), and F^- is the base (hydrogen ion acceptor).
c. H_2S is the acid (hydrogen ion donor), and $CH_3—CH_2—NH_2$ is the base (hydrogen ion acceptor).

14.9 **a.** F^- **b.** OH^- **c.** HPO_3^{2-} **d.** SO_4^{2-} **e.** ClO_2^-

14.11 **a.** HCO_3^- **b.** H_3O^+ **c.** H_3PO_4 **d.** HBr **e.** $HClO_4$

14.13 **a.** The conjugate acid–base pairs are H_2CO_3/HCO_3^-, and H_3O^+/H_2O.
b. The conjugate acid–base pairs are NH_4^+/NH_3, and H_3O^+/H_2O.
c. The conjugate acid–base pairs are HCN/CN^-, and HNO_2/NO_2^-.
d. The conjugate acid–base pairs are HF/F^-, and $HCHO_2/CHO_2^-$.

14.15 $NH_4^+(aq) + H_2O(l) \rightleftharpoons NH_3(aq) + H_3O^+(aq)$

14.17 A strong acid is a good hydrogen ion donor, whereas its conjugate base is a poor hydrogen ion acceptor.

14.19 **a.** HBr **b.** HSO_4^- **c.** H_2CO_3

14.21 **a.** HSO_4^- **b.** HNO_2 **c.** HCO_3^-

14.23 **a.** reactants **b.** reactants **c.** products

14.25 $NH_4^+(aq) + SO_4^{2-}(aq) \rightleftharpoons NH_3(aq) + HSO_4^-(aq)$

The equilibrium mixture contains mostly reactants because NH_4^+ is a weaker acid than HSO_4^-, and SO_4^{2-} is a weaker base than NH_3.

14.27 **a.** true **b.** false **c.** false **d.** true **e.** false

14.29 **a.** H_2SO_3 **b.** HSO_3^- **c.** H_2SO_3 **d.** HS^- **e.** H_2SO_3

14.31 $H_3PO_4(aq) + H_2O(l) \rightleftharpoons H_2PO_4^-(aq) + H_3O^+(aq)$

$$K_a = \frac{[H_3O^+][H_2PO_4^-]}{[H_3PO_4]}$$

14.33 In pure water, $[H_3O^+] = [OH^-]$ because one of each is produced every time a hydrogen ion is transferred from one water molecule to another.

14.35 In an acidic solution, the $[H_3O^+]$ is greater than the $[OH^-]$.

14.37 **a.** acidic **b.** basic **c.** basic **d.** acidic

14.39 **a.** 1.0×10^{-5} M **b.** 1.0×10^{-8} M **c.** 5.0×10^{-10} M **d.** 2.5×10^{-2} M

14.41 **a.** 1.0×10^{-11} M **b.** 2.0×10^{-9} M **c.** 5.6×10^{-3} M **d.** 2.5×10^{-2} M

14.43 In a neutral solution, the $[H_3O^+]$ is 1.0×10^{-7} M and the pH is 7.00, which is the negative value of the power of 10.

14.45 **a.** basic **b.** acidic **c.** basic **d.** acidic **e.** acidic **f.** basic

14.47 An increase or decrease of one pH unit changes the $[H_3O^+]$ by a factor of 10. Thus a pH of 3 is 10 times more acidic than a pH of 4.

14.49 **a.** 4.00 **b.** 8.52 **c.** 9.00 **d.** 3.40 **e.** 7.17 **f.** 10.92

14.51

$[H_3O^+]$	$[OH^-]$	pH	pOH	Acidic, Basic, or Neutral?
1.0×10^{-8} M	1.0×10^{-6} M	8.00	6.00	Basic
3.2×10^{-4} M	3.1×10^{-11} M	3.49	10.51	Acidic
2.8×10^{-5} M	3.6×10^{-10} M	4.55	9.45	Acidic
1.0×10^{-12} M	1.0×10^{-2} M	12.00	2.00	Basic

14.53 a. $ZnCO_3(s) + 2HBr(aq) \longrightarrow CO_2(g) + H_2O(l) + ZnBr_2(aq)$
b. $Zn(s) + 2HCl(aq) \longrightarrow H_2(g) + ZnCl_2(aq)$
c. $HCl(aq) + NaHCO_3(s) \longrightarrow CO_2(g) + H_2O(l) + NaCl(aq)$
d. $H_2SO_4(aq) + Mg(OH)_2(s) \longrightarrow 2H_2O(l) + MgSO_4(aq)$

14.55 a. $2HCl(aq) + Mg(OH)_2(s) \longrightarrow 2H_2O(l) + MgCl_2(aq)$
b. $H_3PO_4(aq) + 3LiOH(aq) \longrightarrow 3H_2O(l) + Li_3PO_4(aq)$

14.57 a. $H_2SO_4(aq) + 2NaOH(aq) \longrightarrow 2H_2O(l) + Na_2SO_4(aq)$
b. $3HCl(aq) + Fe(OH)_3(s) \longrightarrow 3H_2O(l) + FeCl_3(aq)$
c. $H_2CO_3(aq) + Mg(OH)_2(s) \longrightarrow 2H_2O(l) + MgCO_3(s)$

14.59 To a known volume of formic acid, add a few drops of indicator. Place a solution of NaOH of known molarity in a buret. Add base to acid until one drop changes the color of the solution. Use the volume and molarity of NaOH and the volume of formic acid to calculate the concentration of the formic acid in the sample.

14.61 0.830 M HCl solution

14.63 0.124 M H_2SO_4 solution

14.65 16.5 mL

14.67 **b** and **c** are buffer systems. **b** contains the weak acid H_2CO_3 and its salt $NaHCO_3$. **c** contains HF, a weak acid, and its salt KF.

14.69 a. 3 **b.** 1 and 2
c. 3 **d.** 1

14.71 pH = 3.35

14.73 The pH of the 0.10 M HF/0.10 M NaF buffer is 3.14.
The pH of the 0.060 M HF/0.120 M NaF buffer is 3.44.

14.75 a. This diagram represents a weak acid; only a few HX molecules separate into H_3O^+ and X^- ions.
b. This diagram represents a strong acid; all the HX molecules separate into H_3O^+ and X^- ions.
c. This diagram represents a weak acid; only a few HX molecules separate into H_3O^+ and X^- ions.

14.77 a. During hyperventilation, a person will lose CO_2 and the blood pH will rise.
b. Breathing into a paper bag will increase the CO_2 concentration and lower the blood pH.

14.79 a. acid, bromous acid
b. base, rubidium hydroxide
c. salt, magnesium nitrate
d. acid, butanoic acid (butyric acid)
e. acid, perchloric acid

14.81

Acid	Conjugate Base
HI	I^-
HCl	Cl^-
NH_4^+	NH_3
H_2S	HS^-

14.83 a. HF **b.** H_3O^+
c. HNO_2 **d.** HCO_3^-

14.85 a. acidic **b.** basic
c. acidic **d.** acidic
e. basic

14.87 a. pH = 7.70; pOH = 6.30
b. pH = 1.30; pOH = 12.70
c. pH = 10.54; pOH = 3.46
d. pH = 11.73; pOH = 2.27

14.89 a. basic **b.** acidic
c. basic **d.** basic

14.91 a. $[H_3O^+] = 1.0 \times 10^{-3}$ M; $[OH^-] = 1.0 \times 10^{-11}$ M
b. $[H_3O^+] = 3.3 \times 10^{-7}$ M; $[OH^-] = 3.0 \times 10^{-8}$ M
c. $[H_3O^+] = 1.4 \times 10^{-9}$ M; $[OH^-] = 7.1 \times 10^{-6}$ M
d. $[H_3O^+] = 1.0 \times 10^{-11}$ M; $[OH^-] = 1.0 \times 10^{-3}$ M

14.93 a. Solution A
b. Solution A $[H_3O^+] = 3 \times 10^{-5}$ M;
Solution B $[H_3O^+] = 2 \times 10^{-7}$ M
c. Solution A $[OH^-] = 3 \times 10^{-10}$ M;
Solution B $[OH^-] = 5 \times 10^{-8}$ M

14.95 $[OH^-] = 0.0225$ M

14.97 pH = 0.80; pOH = 13.20

14.99 a. 1. HS^-
2. $H_2PO_4^-$
b. 1. $\frac{[H_3O^+][HS^-]}{[H_2S]}$
2. $\frac{[H_3O^+][H_2PO_4^-]}{[H_3PO_4]}$
c. H_2S

14.101 a. HNO_3/NO_3^- and NH_4^+/NH_3; equilibrium mixture contains mostly products
b. HBr/Br^- and H_3O^+/H_2O; equilibrium mixture contains mostly products

14.103 a. $ZnCO_3(s) + H_2SO_4(aq) \longrightarrow CO_2(g) + H_2O(l) + ZnSO_4(aq)$
b. $2Al(s) + 6HNO_3(aq) \longrightarrow 3H_2(g) + 2Al(NO_3)_3(aq)$

14.105 a. $[H_3O^+] = 2.0 \times 10^{-13}$ M
b. pH = 12.70
c. pOH = 1.30
d. $2KOH(aq) + H_2SO_4(aq) \longrightarrow 2H_2O(l) + K_2SO_4(aq)$
e. 56 mL of the KOH solution

14.107 a. $[H_3O^+] = 6 \times 10^{-5}$ M; $[OH^-] = 2 \times 10^{-10}$ M
b. $[H_3O^+] = 3 \times 10^{-7}$ M; $[OH^-] = 3 \times 10^{-8}$ M
c. 3 g of $CaCO_3$

14.109 a. 48.0 mL of NaOH solution
b. 74.7 mL of NaOH solution

14.111 0.234 M H_2SO_4 solution

14.113 a. acid:
$H_2PO_4^-(aq) + H_3O^+(aq) \longrightarrow H_3PO_4(aq) + H_2O(l)$
b. base:
$H_3PO_4(aq) + OH^-(aq) \longrightarrow H_2PO_4^-(aq) + H_2O(l)$
c. pH = 1.72

Combining Ideas from Chapters 11 to 14

CI.21 Methane is a major component of purified natural gas used for heating and cooking. When 1.0 mol of methane gas burns with oxygen to produce carbon dioxide and water vapor, 883 kJ of heat is produced. At STP, methane gas has a density of 0.715 g/L. For transport, the natural gas is cooled to −163 °C to form liquefied natural gas (LNG) with a density of 0.45 g/mL. A tank on a ship can hold 7.0 million gallons of LNG. (2.8, 6.6, 7.1, 7.3, 8.2, 9.5, 11.7, 11.9)

An LNG carrier transports liquefied natural gas.

a. Draw the electron-dot formula for methane, which has the formula CH_4.

b. What is the mass, in kilograms, of LNG (assume that LNG is all methane) transported in one tank on a ship?

c. What is the volume, in liters, of LNG (methane) from one tank when the LNG (methane) from one tank is converted to methane gas at STP?

d. Write the balanced equation for the combustion of methane and oxygen in a gas burner, including the heat of reaction.

Methane is the fuel burned in a gas cooktop.

e. How many kilograms of oxygen are needed to react with all of the methane in one tank of LNG?

f. How much heat, in kilojoules, is released after burning all of the methane from one tank of LNG?

CI.22 Automobile exhaust is a major cause of air pollution. One pollutant is nitrogen oxide, which forms from nitrogen and oxygen gases in the air at the high temperatures in an automobile engine. Once emitted into the air, nitrogen oxide reacts with oxygen to produce nitrogen dioxide, a reddish brown gas with a sharp, pungent odor that makes up smog. One component of gasoline is octane, C_8H_{18}, which has a density of 0.803 g/mL. In one year, a typical automobile uses 550 gal of gasoline and produces 41 lb of nitrogen oxide. (2.8, 7.2, 7.3, 8.3, 9.2, 11.7, 11.9)

Two gases found in automobile exhaust are carbon dioxide and nitrogen oxide.

a. Write balanced equations for the production of nitrogen oxide and nitrogen dioxide.

b. If all the nitrogen oxide emitted by one automobile is converted to nitrogen dioxide in the atmosphere, how many kilograms of nitrogen dioxide are produced in one year by a single automobile?

c. Write a balanced equation for the combustion of octane.

d. How many moles of C_8H_{18} are present in 15.2 gal of octane?

e. How many liters of CO_2 at STP are produced in one year from the gasoline used by the typical automobile?

CI.23 A mixture of 25.0 g of CS_2 gas and 30.0 g of O_2 gas is placed in 10.0-L container and heated to 125 °C. The products of the reaction are carbon dioxide gas and sulfur dioxide gas. (7.2, 7.3, 8.2, 9.2, 11.8, 11.10)

a. Write a balanced equation for the reaction.

b. How many grams of CO_2 are produced?

c. What is the partial pressure, in millimeters of mercury, of the remaining reactant?

d. What is the final pressure, in millimeters of mercury, in the container?

CI.24 In wine-making, glucose ($C_6H_{12}O_6$) from grapes undergoes fermentation in the absence of oxygen to produce ethanol and carbon dioxide. A bottle of vintage port wine has a volume of 750 mL and contains 135 mL of ethanol (C_2H_6O). Ethanol has a density of 0.789 g/mL. In 1.5 lb of grapes, there are 26 g of glucose. (2.8, 7.2, 7.3, 8.2, 9.2, 12.4)

Port is a type of fortified wine that is produced in Portugal.

When the glucose in grapes is fermented, ethanol is produced.

a. Calculate the volume percent (v/v) of ethanol in the port wine.

b. What is the molarity (M) of ethanol in the port wine?

c. Write the balanced equation for the fermentation reaction of sugar in grapes.

d. How many grams of sugar from grapes are required to produce one bottle of port wine?

e. How many bottles of port wine can be produced from 1.0 ton of grapes (1 ton = 2000 lb)?

CI.25 Consider the following reaction at equilibrium:

$$2H_2(g) + S_2(g) \rightleftharpoons 2H_2S(g) + \text{heat}$$

In a 10.0-L container, an equilibrium mixture contains 2.02 g of H_2, 10.3 g of S_2, and 68.2 g of H_2S. (7.1, 7.2, 13.2, 13.3, 13.4, 13.5)

a. What is the numerical value of K_c for this equilibrium mixture?

b. If more H_2 is added to the equilibrium mixture, how will the equilibrium shift?

c. How will the equilibrium shift if the mixture is placed in a 5.00-L container with no change in temperature?

d. If a 5.00-L container has an equilibrium mixture of 0.300 mol of H_2 and 2.50 mol of H_2S, what is the $[S_2]$ if temperature remains constant?

CI.26 A saturated solution of cobalt(II) hydroxide has a pH of 9.36. (7.1, 7.2, 13.2, 13.6)

a. Write the solubility product expression for cobalt(II) hydroxide.
b. Calculate the numerical value of K_{sp} for cobalt(II) hydroxide.
c. How many grams of cobalt(II) hydroxide will dissolve in 2.0 L of water?
d. How many grams of cobalt(II) hydroxide will dissolve in 50.0 mL of a 0.0100 M NaOH solution?

Cobalt(II) hydroxide is a gelatinous blue solid.

CI.27 A metal M with a mass of 0.420 g completely reacts with 34.8 mL of a 0.520 M HCl solution to form H_2 gas and aqueous MCl_3. (7.1, 7.2, 8.2, 9.2, 11.8)

When a metal reacts with a strong acid, bubbles of hydrogen gas form.

a. Write a balanced equation for the reaction of the metal $M(s)$ and $HCl(aq)$.
b. What volume, in milliliters, of H_2 at 720. mmHg and 24 °C is produced?
c. How many moles of metal M reacted?
d. Using your results from part **c**, determine the molar mass and name of metal M.
e. Write the balanced equation for the reaction.

CI.28 In a teaspoon (5.0 mL) of a liquid antacid, there are 400. mg of $Mg(OH)_2$ and 400. mg of $Al(OH)_3$. A 0.080 M HCl solution, which is similar to stomach acid, is used to neutralize 5.0 mL of the liquid antacid. (12.6, 14.6, 14.7)

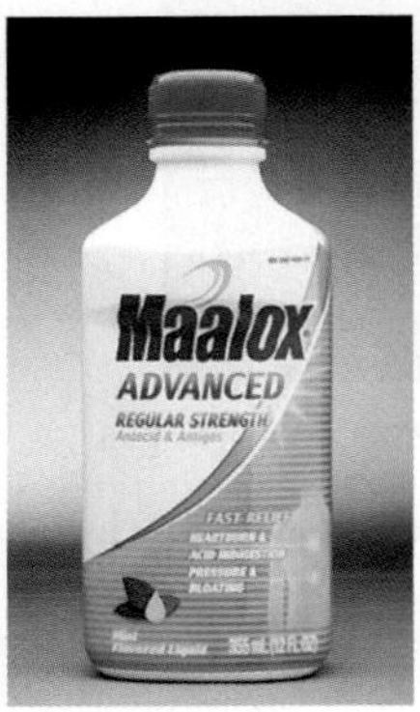

An antacid neutralizes stomach acid and raises the pH.

a. Write the equation for the neutralization of HCl and $Mg(OH)_2$.
b. Write the equation for the neutralization of HCl and $Al(OH)_3$.
c. What is the pH of the HCl solution?
d. How many milliliters of the HCl solution are needed to neutralize the $Mg(OH)_2$?
e. How many milliliters of the HCl solution are needed to neutralize the $Al(OH)_3$?

ANSWERS

CI.21 a. H:C̈:H (with H above and below, Lewis structure) or

$$\begin{array}{c} \text{H} \\ | \\ \text{H}-\text{C}-\text{H} \\ | \\ \text{H} \end{array}$$

b. 1.2×10^7 kg of LNG (methane)
c. 1.7×10^{10} L of LNG (methane)
d. $CH_4(g) + 2O_2(g) \xrightarrow{\Delta} CO_2(g) + 2H_2O(g) + 883\text{ kJ}$
e. 4.8×10^7 kg of O_2
f. 6.6×10^{11} kJ

CI.23 a. $CS_2(g) + 3O_2(g) \xrightarrow{\Delta} CO_2(g) + 2SO_2(g)$
b. 13.8 g of CO_2
c. 37 mmHg
d. 2370 mmHg

CI.25 a. $K_c = 248$
b. If H_2 is added, the equilibrium will shift in the direction of the products.
c. If the volume decreases, the equilibrium will shift in the direction of the products.
d. $[S_2] = 0.280M$

CI.27 a. $2M(s) + 6HCl(aq) \longrightarrow 3H_2(g) + 2MCl_3(aq)$
b. 233 mL of H_2
c. 6.03×10^{-3} mol of M
d. 69.7 g/mol; gallium
e. $2Ga(s) + 6HCl(aq) \longrightarrow 3H_2(g) + 2GaCl_3(aq)$

Oxidation and Reduction 15

LOOKING AHEAD

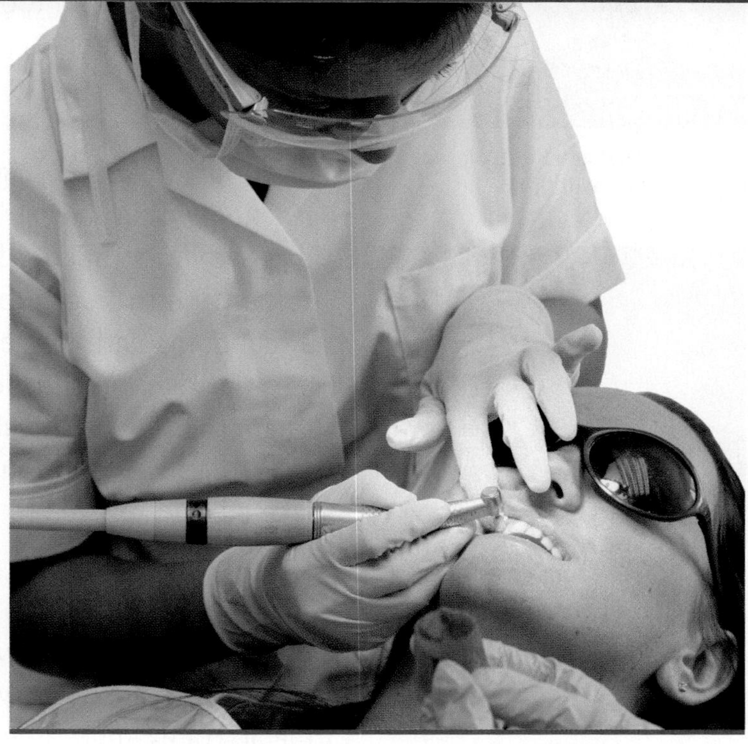

Kimberly's teeth have become badly stained due to drinking excessive amounts of coffee. She makes an appointment with her dentist to have her teeth whitened. Kimberly's teeth are cleaned and examined for any cavities. After that, the dentist begins the process of whitening Kimberly's teeth. She explains to Kimberly that she uses a gel of 15% hydrogen peroxide that penetrates into the enamel of the tooth, where it causes a chemical reaction that whitens the teeth. The chemical reaction is referred to as an oxidation–reduction reaction where one chemical (hydrogen peroxide) is reduced and the other chemical (the coffee stain) is oxidized. During the oxidation, the coffee stains on the teeth become lighter or colorless, and therefore, the teeth are whiter.

Career: Dentist

Dentists are involved in assessing and maintaining the health of the teeth, gums, mouth, and bones of the jaw. They also examine X-rays to determine if there is disease or decay of the teeth and gums. Dentists remove decay and fill cavities, or they may extract teeth if necessary. Local anesthetics are often used for dental procedures. Dentists also educate patients on proper care of teeth and gums. Many dentists operate their own businesses with a staff that includes dental hygienists and a dental technician. A dentist may specialize in certain areas of dentistry. An orthodontist fits a patient's teeth with wires to straighten teeth or correct a bite. A periodontist treats problems with soft tissues of the gums. Pediatric dentists treat the teeth of children.

Rust forms on a set of tools when oxygen reacts with iron.

Pure iron is obtained from reducing iron ores.

Perhaps you have never heard of an oxidation and reduction reaction. However, this type of reaction has many important applications in your everyday life. When you see tarnish on a silver spoon, rust on iron tools, or the green patina on a copper roof, you are observing oxidation.

$$4Fe(s) + 3O_2(g) \longrightarrow \underset{\text{Rust}}{2Fe_2O_3(s)}$$

When we turn the lights on in our automobiles, an oxidation–reduction reaction within the car battery provides the electricity. On a cold, wintry day, we might build a fire. As the wood burns, oxygen combines with carbon and hydrogen to produce carbon dioxide, water, and heat. When a fuel burns with oxygen, it is combustion, which we can now describe as an oxidation–reduction reaction. When we eat foods with starches in them, the starches break down to give glucose, which is oxidized in our cells to give energy along with carbon dioxide and water. Every breath we take provides oxygen to carry out oxidation in our cells.

$$\underset{\text{Glucose}}{C_6H_{12}O_6(aq)} + 6O_2(g) \xrightarrow{\Delta} 6CO_2(g) + 6H_2O(l) + \text{energy}$$

The term *reduction* was originally used for reactions that removed oxygen from compounds. Metal oxides in ores are reduced to obtain the pure metal. For example, iron metal is obtained by reducing the iron in iron ore with carbon.

$$2Fe_2O_3(l) + 3C(s) \longrightarrow 3CO_2(g) + 4Fe(l)$$

As more was learned about oxidation and reduction reactions, scientists found that oxidation and reduction do not always involve oxygen. Today an oxidation–reduction reaction is any reaction that involves the transfer of electrons from one substance to another.

CHAPTER READINESS*

Key Math Skills

- Using Positive and Negative Numbers in Calculations (1.4B)
- Solving Equations (1.4D)

Core Chemistry Skills

- Writing Positive and Negative Ions (6.1)
- Writing Ionic Formulas (6.2, 6.4)
- Balancing a Chemical Equation (8.2)
- Identifying Functional Groups (8.4)

*These Key Math Skills and the Core Chemistry Skills from previous chapters are listed here for your review as you proceed to the new material in this chapter.

15.1 Oxidation–Reduction Reactions

LEARNING GOAL

Identify what is oxidized and what is reduced in an oxidation–reduction reaction.

In an **oxidation–reduction reaction** (abbreviated *redox*), electrons are transferred from one substance to another. If one substance loses electrons, another substance must gain electrons. **Oxidation** is defined as the *loss* of electrons; **reduction** is defined as the *gain* of electrons.

CORE CHEMISTRY SKILL 

Identifying Oxidized and Reduced Substances

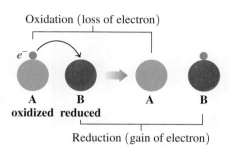

One way to remember these definitions is to use the following acronym:

OIL RIG

Oxidation **I**s **L**oss of electrons.

Reduction **I**s **G**ain of electrons.

In the formation of ionic compounds, we have seen that metals lose electrons to become positive ions and nonmetals gain electrons to become negative ions. We can now look at the oxidation and reduction reactions that take place when calcium metal reacts with sulfur to produce the ionic compound calcium sulfide.

$$Ca(s) + S(s) \longrightarrow CaS(s)$$

The element Ca in the reactants has a charge of 0, but in the CaS product, it is present as a Ca^{2+} ion. Because the charge is more positive, we know that the calcium atom lost two electrons, which means that calcium metal was oxidized in the reaction.

$$Ca^0 \longrightarrow Ca^{2+} + 2\,e^- \quad \text{Oxidation; loss of electrons by Ca}$$

At the same time, the element S in the reactants has a charge of 0, but in the CaS product, it is present as a S^{2-} ion. Because the charge is more negative, we know that the sulfur atom gained two electrons, which means that a reduction reaction took place.

$$S^0 + 2\,e^- \longrightarrow S^{2-} \quad \text{Reduction; gain of electrons by S}$$

Thus, the overall equation for the formation of CaS involves an oxidation and a reduction reaction that occur simultaneously. In every oxidation and reduction, the number of electrons lost must be equal to the number of electrons gained. Because each shows a loss or gain of two electrons, we can add them and write the overall equation for the formation of CaS.

$$\begin{array}{lll} Ca^0(s) & \longrightarrow & Ca^{2+}(s) + 2\,e^- \\ S^0(s) + 2\,e^- & \longrightarrow & S^{2-}(s) \\ \hline Ca^0(s) + S^0(s) & \longrightarrow & Ca^{2+} + S^{2-} = CaS(s) \end{array}$$

The overall equation without the charges is written as

$$Ca(s) + S(s) \longrightarrow CaS(s)$$

As we see in the next reaction between zinc and copper(II) sulfate, there is always an oxidation with every reduction (see Figure 15.1).

$$Zn(s) + CuSO_4(aq) \longrightarrow ZnSO_4(aq) + Cu(s)$$

We can rewrite the equation to show the atoms and ions:

$$Zn(s) + Cu^{2+}(aq) + SO_4^{2-}(aq) \longrightarrow Zn^{2+}(aq) + SO_4^{2-}(aq) + Cu(s)$$

Solution of Cu^{2+} and SO_4^{2-}

Zn strip

$Cu(s)$

Cu^{2+} ion

Zn^0

$Zn^0 \longrightarrow Zn^{2+}$

$2e^-$

$Cu^{2+} \longrightarrow Cu^0$

Zn^{2+} ion

Cu^0

FIGURE 15.1 In this single replacement reaction, $Zn(s)$ is oxidized to $Zn^{2+}(aq)$ when it provides two electrons to reduce $Cu^{2+}(aq)$ to $Cu(s)$:
$Zn(s) + Cu^{2+}(aq) \longrightarrow Zn^{2+}(aq) + Cu(s)$.
Q In this reaction, is $Zn(s)$ oxidized or reduced?

In this reaction, Zn atoms lose two electrons to form Zn^{2+}. The increase in positive charge indicates that Zn is oxidized. At the same time, Cu^{2+} gains two electrons to form Cu. The decrease in charge indicates that Cu^{2+} is reduced. The SO_4^{2-} ions are *spectator ions*, which means they are present in both the reactants and products and do not change.

$$Zn(s) \longrightarrow Zn^{2+}(aq) + 2e^- \quad \text{Oxidation of Zn}$$
$$Cu^{2+}(aq) + 2e^- \longrightarrow Cu(s) \quad \text{Reduction of } Cu^{2+}$$

CONCEPT CHECK 15.1 Identifying Oxidation and Reduction

Identify each of the following as an oxidation or a reduction:

a. $Be^0(s) \longrightarrow Be^{2+}(aq)$
b. $Mg^{2+}(aq) \longrightarrow Mg^0(s)$
c. $2Cl^-(aq) \longrightarrow Cl_2^0(g)$

ANSWER

a. When an atom of Be loses two electrons to form a 2+ ion, it is an oxidation.

$$Be^0(aq) \longrightarrow Be^{2+}(s) + 2e^-$$

b. When a magnesium ion with a 2+ charge gains two electrons to form a neutral magnesium atom, it is a reduction.

$$Mg^{2+}(aq) + 2e^- \longrightarrow Mg^0(s)$$

c. When two chloride ions each with a 1− charge lose two electrons to form neutral Cl atoms in a Cl_2 molecule, it is an oxidation.

$$2Cl^-(aq) \longrightarrow Cl_2^0(g) + 2e^-$$

QUESTIONS AND PROBLEMS

15.1 Oxidation–Reduction Reactions

LEARNING GOAL: *Identify what is oxidized and what is reduced in an oxidation–reduction reaction.*

15.1 Identify each of the following as an oxidation or a reduction reaction:

a. $Na^+(aq) + e^- \longrightarrow Na(s)$
b. $Ni(s) \longrightarrow Ni^{2+}(aq) + 2e^-$
c. $Cr^{3+}(aq) + 3e^- \longrightarrow Cr(s)$
d. $2H^+(aq) + 2e^- \longrightarrow H_2(g)$

15.2 Identify each of the following as an oxidation or a reduction reaction:

a. $O_2(g) + 4e^- \longrightarrow 2O^{2-}(aq)$

b. $Al(s) \longrightarrow Al^{3+}(aq) + 3e^-$

c. $Fe^{3+}(aq) + e^- \longrightarrow Fe^{2+}(aq)$

d. $2Br^-(aq) \longrightarrow Br_2(l) + 2e^-$

15.3 In each of the following reactions, identify the reactant that is oxidized and the reactant that is reduced:

a. $Zn(s) + Cl_2(g) \longrightarrow ZnCl_2(s)$

b. $Cl_2(g) + 2NaBr(aq) \longrightarrow 2NaCl(aq) + Br_2(l)$

c. $2Pb(s) + O_2(g) \longrightarrow 2PbO(s)$

d. $2Fe^{3+}(aq) + Sn^{2+}(aq) \longrightarrow 2Fe^{2+}(aq) + Sn^{4+}(aq)$

15.4 In each of the following reactions, identify the reactant that is oxidized and the reactant that is reduced:

a. $2Li(s) + F_2(g) \longrightarrow 2LiF(s)$

b. $Cl_2(g) + 2KI(aq) \longrightarrow 2KCl(aq) + I_2(s)$

c. $Sn(s) + Cu^{2+}(aq) \longrightarrow Sn^{2+}(aq) + Cu(s)$

d. $Fe(s) + CuSO_4(aq) \longrightarrow FeSO_4(aq) + Cu(s)$

15.2 Oxidation Numbers

LEARNING GOAL

Assign and use oxidation numbers to identify elements that are oxidized or reduced.

In more complex oxidation–reduction reactions, the identification of the substances oxidized and reduced is not as obvious as in the reactions in the previous section. To help identify the atoms or ions that are oxidized or reduced, we assign values called **oxidation numbers** (or sometimes oxidation states) to the elements of the reactants and products. It is important to recognize that oxidation numbers do not always represent actual charges, but they help us identify loss or gain of electrons.

Rules for Assigning Oxidation Numbers

CORE CHEMISTRY SKILL 

Assigning Oxidation Numbers

The rules for assigning oxidation numbers to the atoms or ions in the reactants and products are given in Table 15.1.

TABLE 15.1 Rules for Assigning Oxidation Numbers

1. The sum of the oxidation numbers in a molecule is zero (0), or for a polyatomic ion is equal to its charge.
2. The oxidation number of an element (monatomic or diatomic) is zero (0).
3. The oxidation number of a monatomic ion is equal to its charge.
4. In compounds, the oxidation number of Group 1A (1) metals is +1, and that of Group 2A (2) metals is +2.
5. In compounds, the oxidation number of fluorine is −1. Other nonmetals in Group 7A (17) are −1 except when combined with oxygen or fluorine.
6. In compounds, the oxidation number of oxygen is −2 except in OF_2.
7. In compounds with nonmetals, the oxidation number of hydrogen is +1; in compounds with metals, the oxidation number of hydrogen is −1.

We can now look at how these rules are used to assign oxidation numbers. For each formula, the oxidation numbers are written *below* the symbols of the elements (see Table 15.2).

TABLE 15.2 Examples of Using Rules to Assign Oxidation Numbers

Formula	Oxidation Numbers	Explanation
Br_2	Br_2 0	Each Br atom in diatomic bromine has an oxidation number of 0 (Rule 2).
Ba^{2+}	Ba^{2+} +2	The oxidation number of a monatomic ion is equal to its charge. (Rule 3).

TABLE 15.2 Examples of Using Rules to Assign Oxidation Numbers

Formula	Oxidation Numbers	Explanation
CO_2	CO_2 +4−2	In compounds, O has an oxidation number of −2 (Rule 6). Because CO_2 is neutral, the oxidation number of C is calculated as +4 (Rule 1). $1C + 2O = 0$ $C + 2(-2) = 0$ $C = +4$
Al_2O_3	Al_2O_3 +3−2	In compounds, the oxidation number of O is −2 (Rule 6). For Al_2O_3 (neutral), the oxidation number of Al is calculated as +3 (Rule 1). $2Al + 3O = 0$ $2Al + 3(-2) = 0$ $2Al = +6$ $Al = +3$
$HClO_3$	$HClO_3$ +1+5−2	The oxidation number of H is +1 (Rule 7), and O is −2 (Rule 6). For $HClO_3$ (neutral), the oxidation number of Cl is calculated as +5 (Rule 1). $H + Cl + 3O = 0$ $(+1) + Cl + 3(-2) = 0$ $Cl - 5 = 0$ $Cl = +5$
SO_4^{2-}	SO_4^{2-} +6−2	The oxidation number of O is −2 (Rule 6). For SO_4^{2-} (−2 charge), the oxidation number of S is calculated as +6 (Rule 1). $S + 4O = -2$ $S + 4(-2) = -2$ $S = +6$
CH_2O	CH_2O 0 +1−2	The oxidation number of H is +1 (Rule 7), and O is −2 (Rule 6). For CH_2O (neutral), the oxidation number of C is calculated as 0 (Rule 1). $C + 2H + O = 0$ $C + 2(+1) + (-2) = 0$ $C = 0$

SAMPLE PROBLEM 15.1 Assigning Oxidation Numbers

Assign oxidation numbers to the elements in each of the following:

a. NCl_3 **b.** CO_3^{2-}

SOLUTION

a. NCl_3: The oxidation number of Cl is −1 (Rule 5). For NCl_3 (neutral), the sum of the oxidation numbers of N and 3Cl must be equal to zero (Rule 1). Thus, the oxidation number of N is calculated as +3.

$$N + 3Cl = 0$$
$$N + 3(-1) = 0$$
$$N = +3$$

The oxidation numbers are written as

NCl_3
+3−1

b. CO_3^{2-}: The oxidation number of O is −2 (Rule 6). For CO_3^{2-}, the sum of oxidation numbers is equal to −2 (Rule 1). The oxidation number of C is calculated as +4.

$$C + 3O = -2$$
$$C + 3(-2) = -2$$
$$C = +4$$

The oxidation numbers are written as

$\underset{+4-2}{CO_3^{2-}}$

STUDY CHECK 15.1

Assign oxidation numbers to the elements in each of the following:

a. H_3PO_4 **b.** MnO_4^-

Using Oxidation Numbers to Identify Oxidation–Reduction

CORE CHEMISTRY SKILL 

Using Oxidation Numbers

Oxidation numbers can be used to identify the elements that are oxidized and the elements that are reduced in a reaction. In oxidation, the loss of electrons increases the oxidation number so that it is higher (more positive) in the product than in the reactant. In reduction, the gain of electrons decreases the oxidation number so that it is lower (more negative) in the product than in the reactant.

Reduction: oxidation number decreases

−7 −6 −5 −4 −3 −2 −1 0 +1 +2 +3 +4 +5 +6 +7

Oxidation: oxidation number increases

An oxidation reaction occurs when the charge becomes more positive. A reduction reaction occurs when the charge becomes more negative.

SAMPLE PROBLEM 15.2 Using Oxidation Numbers to Determine Oxidation and Reduction

Identify the element that is oxidized and the element that is reduced in the following equation:

$$CO_2(g) + H_2(g) \longrightarrow CO(g) + H_2O(g)$$

SOLUTION

Guide to Using Oxidation Numbers

1. Assign oxidation numbers to each element.
2. Identify the increase in oxidation number as oxidation; the decrease as reduction.

Step 1 **Assign oxidation numbers to each element.** In H_2, the oxidation number of H is 0. In H_2O, the oxidation number of H is +1. In CO_2, CO, and H_2O, the oxidation number of O is −2. Using the oxidation number −2 for O, the oxidation number of C would be +4 in CO_2, and +2 in CO.

$$\underset{+4\,-2}{CO_2(g)} + \underset{0}{H_2(g)} \longrightarrow \underset{+2\,-2}{CO(g)} + \underset{+1\,-2}{H_2O(g)} \quad \text{Oxidation numbers}$$

Step 2 **Identify the increase in oxidation number as oxidation; the decrease as reduction.** H is oxidized because its oxidation number increases from 0 to +1. C is reduced because its oxidation number decreases from +4 to +2.

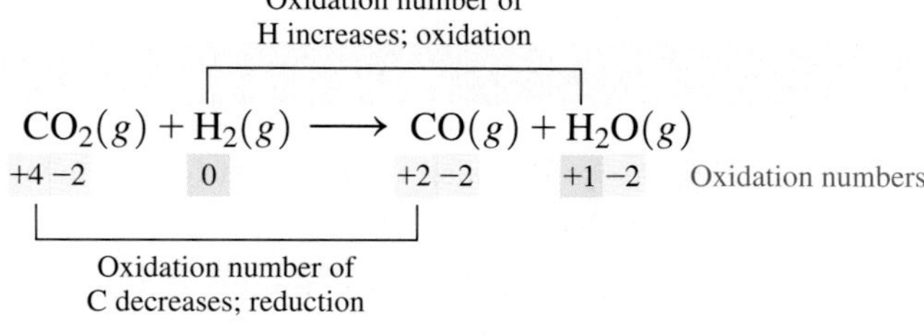

STUDY CHECK 15.2

In the following equation, which reactant is oxidized and which is reduced?

$$2Al(s) + 3Sn^{2+}(aq) \longrightarrow 2Al^{3+}(aq) + 3Sn(s)$$

CORE CHEMISTRY SKILL

Identifying Oxidizing and Reducing Agents

Oxidizing and Reducing Agents

We have seen that an oxidation reaction must always be accompanied by a reduction reaction. The substance that loses electrons is oxidized, and the substance that gains electrons is reduced. For example, Zn is oxidized to Zn^{2+} by losing 2 electrons and Cl_2 reduced to $2Cl^-$ by gaining 2 electrons.

$$Zn(s) + Cl_2(g) \longrightarrow ZnCl_2(s)$$

In an oxidation–reduction reaction, the substance that is oxidized is called the **reducing agent** because it provides electrons. The substance that is reduced is called the **oxidizing agent** because it accepts electrons. Because Zn is oxidized in this reaction, it is the *reducing agent*. In the same reaction Cl_2 is reduced, which makes it the *oxidizing agent*.

$$Zn \longrightarrow Zn^{2+} + 2e^- \quad \text{Zn is oxidized; Zn is the } \textit{reducing agent.}$$

$$Cl_2 + 2e^- \longrightarrow 2Cl^- \quad \text{Cl (in Cl}_2\text{) is reduced; Cl}_2 \text{ is the } \textit{oxidizing agent.}$$

The terms we have used to describe oxidation and reduction are listed in the margin on the left.

Oxidation–Reduction Terminology

Loss of electrons	Gain of electrons
Oxidized	Reduced
Reducing agent	Oxidizing agent
Oxidation number increases	Oxidation number decreases

Lead oxides, once used in paint, are now banned due to the toxicity of lead.

CONCEPT CHECK 15.2 Identifying Oxidizing and Reducing Agents

Identify the substance that is oxidized, the substance that is reduced, the oxidizing agent, and the reducing agent for the reaction of lead(II) oxide and carbon monoxide.

$$PbO(s) + CO(g) \longrightarrow Pb(s) + CO_2(g)$$

ANSWER

Using the oxidation number −2 for O, the oxidation number of Pb in PbO would be +2 and the oxidation number of C in CO would be +2. The element Pb has an oxidation number of 0. The C in CO_2 would have an oxidation number of +4.

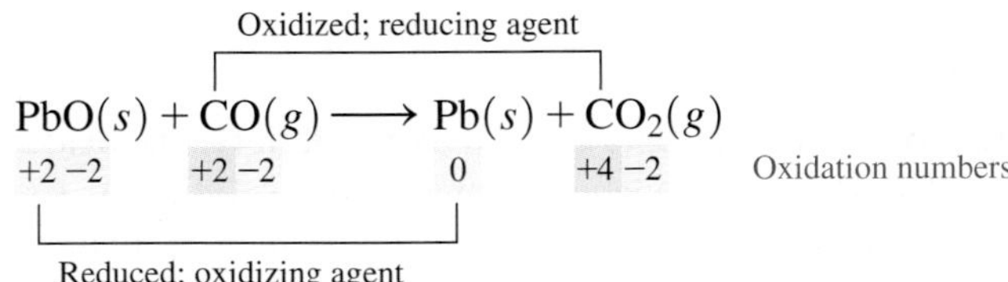

The Pb in PbO is reduced because the oxidation number of Pb decreases from +2 to 0. Thus, the compound PbO is the oxidizing agent. The C in CO is oxidized because the oxidation number of C increases from +2 to +4. Thus, the compound CO is the reducing agent.

QUESTIONS AND PROBLEMS

15.2 Oxidation Numbers

LEARNING GOAL: *Assign and use oxidation numbers to identify elements that are oxidized or reduced.*

15.5 Assign oxidation numbers to each of the following:
a. Cu **b.** F_2 **c.** Fe^{2+} **d.** Cl^-

15.6 Assign oxidation numbers to each of the following:
a. Al **b.** Al^{3+} **c.** F^- **d.** N_2

15.7 Assign oxidation numbers to all the elements in each of the following:
a. KCl **b.** MnO_2 **c.** NO **d.** Mn_2O_3

15.8 Assign oxidation numbers to all the elements in each of the following:
a. H_2S **b.** NO_2 **c.** CCl_4 **d.** PCl_3

15.9 Assign oxidation numbers to all the elements in each of the following:
a. Li_3PO_4 **b.** SO_3^{2-} **c.** Cr_2S_3 **d.** NO_3^-

15.10 Assign oxidation numbers to all the elements in each of the following:
a. $C_2H_3O_2^-$ **b.** $AlCl_3$ **c.** NH_4^+ **d.** $HBrO_4$

15.11 Assign oxidation numbers to all the elements in each of the following:
a. HSO_4^- **b.** H_3PO_3 **c.** $Cr_2O_7^{2-}$ **d.** Na_2CO_3

15.12 Assign oxidation numbers to all the elements in each of the following:
a. N_2O **b.** $LiOH$ **c.** SbO_2^- **d.** IO_4^-

15.13 What is the oxidation number of the specified element in each of the following?
a. N in HNO_3 **b.** C in C_3H_6
c. P in K_3PO_4 **d.** Cr in CrO_4^{2-}

15.14 What is the oxidation number of the specified element in each of the following?
a. C in $BaCO_3$ **b.** Fe in $FeBr_3$
c. Cl in ClF_4^- **d.** S in $S_2O_3^{2-}$

15.15 Indicate whether each of the following describes the oxidizing agent or the reducing agent in an oxidation–reduction reaction:
a. the substance that is oxidized
b. the substance that gains electrons

15.16 Indicate whether each of the following describes the oxidizing agent or the reducing agent in an oxidation–reduction reaction:
a. the substance that is reduced
b. the substance that loses electrons

15.17 For each of the following reactions, identify the substance that is oxidized, the substance that is reduced, the oxidizing agent, and the reducing agent:
a. $2Li(s) + Cl_2(g) \longrightarrow 2LiCl(s)$
b. $Cl_2(g) + 2NaBr(aq) \longrightarrow 2NaCl(aq) + Br_2(l)$
c. $2Pb(s) + O_2(g) \longrightarrow 2PbO(s)$
d. $Al(s) + 3Ag^+(aq) \longrightarrow Al^{3+}(aq) + 3Ag(s)$

15.18 For each of the following reactions, identify the substance that is oxidized, the substance that is reduced, the oxidizing agent, and the reducing agent:
a. $2Li(s) + F_2(g) \longrightarrow 2LiF(s)$
b. $Cl_2(g) + 2KI(aq) \longrightarrow 2KCl(aq) + I_2(s)$
c. $Zn(s) + Ni^{2+}(aq) \longrightarrow Zn^{2+}(aq) + Ni(s)$
d. $Fe(s) + CuSO_4(aq) \longrightarrow FeSO_4(aq) + Cu(s)$

15.19 For each of the following reactions, identify the substance that is oxidized, the substance that is reduced, the oxidizing agent, and the reducing agent:
a. $2NiS(s) + 3O_2(g) \longrightarrow 2NiO(s) + 2SO_2(g)$
b. $Sn^{2+}(aq) + 2Fe^{3+}(aq) \longrightarrow Sn^{4+}(aq) + 2Fe^{2+}(aq)$
c. $CH_4(g) + 2O_2(g) \longrightarrow CO_2(g) + 2H_2O(g)$
d. $2Cr_2O_3(s) + 3Si(s) \longrightarrow 4Cr(s) + 3SiO_2(s)$

15.20 For each of the following reactions, identify the substance that is oxidized, the substance that is reduced, the oxidizing agent, and the reducing agent:
a. $2HgO(s) \longrightarrow 2Hg(l) + O_2(g)$
b. $Zn(s) + 2HCl(aq) \longrightarrow ZnCl_2(aq) + H_2(g)$
c. $2Na(s) + 2H_2O(l) \longrightarrow 2Na^+(aq) + 2OH^-(aq) + H_2(g)$
d. $14H^+(aq) + 6Fe^{2+}(aq) + Cr_2O_7^{2-}(aq) \longrightarrow 6Fe^{3+}(aq) + 2Cr^{3+}(aq) + 7H_2O(l)$

15.3 Balancing Oxidation–Reduction Equations Using Half-Reactions

LEARNING GOAL

Balance oxidation–reduction equations using the half-reaction method.

In the **half-reaction method** for balancing equations, an oxidation–reduction reaction is written as two *half-reactions*. As each half-reaction is balanced for atoms and charge, it becomes apparent which one is oxidation and which one is reduction. Once the loss and gain of electrons are equalized for the half-reactions, they are combined to obtain the overall balanced equation. The half-reaction method is typically used to balance equations that are written as ionic equations. Let us consider the reaction between aluminum metal and a solution of Cu^{2+} as shown in Sample Problem 15.3.

CORE CHEMISTRY SKILL 

Using Half-Reactions to Balance Redox Equations

SAMPLE PROBLEM 15.3 Using Half-Reactions to Balance Equations

Use half-reactions to balance the following equation:

$$Al(s) + Cu^{2+}(aq) \longrightarrow Al^{3+}(aq) + Cu(s)$$

SOLUTION

	Reaction	Electrons	Equalize Electrons	Total Electron Loss and Gain
Analyze the Problem	**Oxidation** $Al(s) \longrightarrow Al^{3+}(aq)$	loss of 3 e^-	$\times$ 2	6 e^-
	Reduction $Cu^{2+}(aq) \longrightarrow Cu(s)$	gain of 2 e^-	$\times$ 3	6 e^-

Guide to Balancing Redox Equations Using Half-Reactions

1 Write two half-reactions for the equation.

2 For each half-reaction, balance the elements other than H and O. If necessary, balance O by adding H_2O, and H by adding H^+.

3 Balance each half-reaction for charge by adding electrons.

4 Multiply each half-reaction by factors that equalize the loss and gain of electrons.

5 Add half-reactions and cancel electrons, and any identical ions or molecules. Check balance of atoms and charge.

Step 1 **Write two half-reactions for the equation.**

$$Al(s) \longrightarrow Al^{3+}(aq)$$
$$Cu^{2+}(aq) \longrightarrow Cu(s)$$

Step 2 **For each half-reaction, balance the elements other than H and O. If necessary, balance O by adding H_2O, and H by adding H^+.** In these half-reactions, the Al and Cu are already balanced.

$$Al(s) \longrightarrow Al^{3+}(aq)$$
$$Cu^{2+}(aq) \longrightarrow Cu(s)$$

Step 3 **Balance each half-reaction for charge by adding electrons.** For the aluminum half-reaction, we need to add three electrons on the product side to balance the charge. With a loss of electrons, this is an oxidation.

$$Al(s) \longrightarrow Al^{3+}(aq) + \mathbf{3\,e^-} \quad \text{Oxidation}$$

0 charge = 0 charge

For the Cu^{2+} half-reaction, we need to add two electrons on the reactant side to balance the charge. With a gain of electrons, this is a reduction.

$$Cu^{2+}(aq) + \mathbf{2\,e^-} \longrightarrow Cu(s) \quad \text{Reduction}$$

0 charge = 0 charge

Step 4 **Multiply each half-reaction by factors that equalize the loss and gain of electrons.** To obtain the same number of electrons in each half-reaction, we need to multiply the oxidation half-reaction by 2 and the reduction half-reaction by 3.

$$\mathbf{2} \times [Al(s) \longrightarrow Al^{3+}(aq) + \mathbf{3\,e^-}]$$
$$2Al(s) \longrightarrow 2Al^{3+}(aq) + \mathbf{6\,e^-} \quad 6\,e^- \text{ lost}$$

$$\mathbf{3} \times [Cu^{2+}(aq) + \mathbf{2\,e^-} \longrightarrow Cu(s)]$$
$$3Cu^{2+}(aq) + \mathbf{6\,e^-} \longrightarrow 3Cu(s) \quad 6\,e^- \text{ gained}$$

Step 5 **Add half-reactions and cancel electrons, and any identical ions or molecules. Check balance of atoms and charge.**

$$2Al(s) \longrightarrow 2Al^{3+}(aq) + \mathbf{6\,e^-}$$
$$3Cu^{2+}(aq) + \mathbf{6\,e^-} \longrightarrow 3Cu(s)$$
$$2Al(s) + 3Cu^{2+}(aq) + \cancel{6e^-} \longrightarrow 2Al^{3+}(aq) + \cancel{6e^-} + 3Cu(s)$$

Final balanced equation:

$$2Al(s) + 3Cu^{2+}(aq) \longrightarrow 2Al^{3+}(aq) + 3Cu(s)$$

Check balance of atoms and charge.

	Reactants		Products
	2Al	=	**2Al**
	3Cu	=	**3Cu**
Charge:	**6+**	=	**6+**

STUDY CHECK 15.3

Use the half-reaction method to balance the following equation:

$$Zn(s) + Fe^{3+}(aq) \longrightarrow Zn^{2+}(aq) + Fe^{2+}(aq)$$

Balancing Oxidation–Reduction Equations in Acidic Solution

When we use the half-reaction method for balancing equations for reactions in acidic solution, we balance O by adding H_2O, and balance H by adding H^+ as shown in Sample Problem 15.4.

SAMPLE PROBLEM 15.4 Using Half-Reactions to Balance Equations in Acidic Solution

Use half-reactions to balance the following equation for a reaction that takes place in acidic solution:

$$I^-(aq) + Cr_2O_7^{2-}(aq) \longrightarrow I_2(s) + Cr^{3+}(aq)$$

A dichromate solution (yellow) and an iodide solution (colorless) form a brown solution of Cr^{3+} and iodine (I_2).

SOLUTION

Step 1 **Write two half-reactions for the equation.**

$$I^-(aq) \longrightarrow I_2(s)$$
$$Cr_2O_7^{2-}(aq) \longrightarrow Cr^{3+}(aq)$$

Step 2 **For each half-reaction, balance the elements other than H and O. If necessary, balance O by adding H_2O, and H by adding H^+.**

The two I atoms in I_2 are balanced with a coefficient of 2 for I^-.

$$2I^-(aq) \longrightarrow I_2(s)$$

The two Cr atoms are balanced with a coefficient of 2 for Cr^{3+}.

$$Cr_2O_7^{2-}(aq) \longrightarrow 2Cr^{3+}(aq)$$

Now balance O by adding H_2O to the product side.

$$Cr_2O_7^{2-}(aq) \longrightarrow 2Cr^{3+}(aq) + \mathbf{7H_2O}(l) \quad \text{H}_2\text{O balances O}$$

Balance H by adding H^+ to the reactant side.

$$\mathbf{14H^+}(aq) + Cr_2O_7^{2-}(aq) \longrightarrow 2Cr^{3+}(aq) + 7H_2O(l) \quad \text{H}^+ \text{ balances H}$$

Step 3 **Balance each half-reaction for charge by adding electrons.** A charge of −2 is balanced with two electrons on the product side.

$$\underset{-2}{2I^-(aq)} \longrightarrow \underbrace{I_2(s) + \mathbf{2}\,e^-}_{-2} \quad \text{Oxidation}$$

A charge of +6 is obtained on the reactant side by adding six electrons.

$$\underbrace{\mathbf{6}\,e^- + 14H^+(aq) + Cr_2O_7^{2-}(aq)}_{+6} \longrightarrow \underset{+6}{2Cr^{3+}(aq) + 7H_2O(l)} \quad \text{Reduction}$$

Step 4 **Multiply each half-reaction by factors that equalize the loss and gain of electrons.** The half-reaction with I is multiplied by 3 to equal the gain of 6 e^- by the Cr half-reaction.

$$3 \times [2I^-(aq) \longrightarrow I_2(s) + \mathbf{2}\,e^-]$$
$$6I^-(aq) \longrightarrow 3I_2(s) + \mathbf{6}\,e^- \quad 6\,e^- \text{ lost}$$
$$\mathbf{6}\,e^- + 14H^+(aq) + Cr_2O_7^{2-}(aq) \longrightarrow 2Cr^{3+}(aq) + 7H_2O(l) \quad 6\,e^- \text{ gained}$$

Step 5 **Add half-reactions and cancel electrons, and any identical ions or molecules. Check balance of atoms and charge.**

$$6I^-(aq) \longrightarrow 3I_2(s) + \mathbf{6}\,e^-$$
$$\mathbf{6}\,e^- + 14H^+(aq) + Cr_2O_7^{2-}(aq) \longrightarrow 2Cr^{3+}(aq) + 7H_2O(l)$$

$$\cancel{6e^-} + 14H^+(aq) + Cr_2O_7^{2-}(aq) + 6I^-(aq) \longrightarrow 2Cr^{3+}(aq) + 3I_2(s) + 7H_2O(l) + \cancel{6e^-}$$

Final balanced equation:

$$14H^+(aq) + Cr_2O_7^{2-}(aq) + 6I^-(aq) \longrightarrow 2Cr^{3+}(aq) + 3I_2(s) + 7H_2O(l)$$

Check balance of atoms and charge.

	Reactants		Products
	6I	=	**6I**
	2Cr	=	**2Cr**
	14H	=	**14H**
	7O	=	**7O**
Charge:	**6+**	=	**6+**

STUDY CHECK 15.4

Use half-reactions to balance the following equation in acidic solution:

$$Fe^{2+}(aq) + IO_3^-(aq) \longrightarrow Fe^{3+}(aq) + I_2(s)$$

Balancing Oxidation–Reduction Equations in Basic Solution

An oxidation–reduction reaction can also take place in basic solution. In that case, we use the same half-reaction method, but once we have the balanced equation, we will neutralize the H^+ with OH^- to form water. The H^+ is neutralized by adding OH^- to both sides of the equation to form H_2O as shown in Sample Problem 15.5.

SAMPLE PROBLEM 15.5 Using Half-Reactions to Balance Equations in Basic Solution

Use half-reactions to balance the following equation that takes place in basic solution:

$$Fe^{2+}(aq) + MnO_4^-(aq) \longrightarrow Fe^{3+}(aq) + MnO_2(s)$$

SOLUTION

Step 1 **Write two half-reactions for the equation.** We separate the equation into two half-reactions by writing one half-reaction for Fe and one for Mn.

$$Fe^{2+}(aq) \longrightarrow Fe^{3+}(aq)$$
$$MnO_4^-(aq) \longrightarrow MnO_2(s)$$

Step 2 **For each half-reaction, balance the elements other than H and O. If necessary, balance O by adding H_2O, and H by adding H^+.**

$$Fe^{2+}(aq) \longrightarrow Fe^{3+}(aq)$$
$$MnO_4^-(aq) \longrightarrow MnO_2(s) + \mathbf{2H_2O}(l)$$ H_2O balances O
$$\mathbf{4H^+}(aq) + MnO_4^-(aq) \longrightarrow MnO_2(s) + \mathbf{2H_2O}(l)$$ H^+ balances H

Step 3 **Balance each half-reaction for charge by adding electrons.**

$$Fe^{2+}(aq) \longrightarrow Fe^{3+}(aq) + \mathbf{1\,e^-}$$ Oxidation

+2 = +2

$$\mathbf{3\,e^-} + 4H^+(aq) + MnO_4^-(aq) \longrightarrow MnO_2(s) + 2H_2O(l)$$ Reduction

0 charge = 0 charge

Step 4 **Multiply each half-reaction by factors that equalize the loss and gain of electrons.** The half-reaction with Fe is multiplied by 3 to equal the gain of 3 e^- by Mn.

$$\mathbf{3} \times [Fe^{2+}(aq) \longrightarrow Fe^{3+}(aq) + \mathbf{1\,e^-}]$$
$$3Fe^{2+}(aq) \longrightarrow 3Fe^{3+}(aq) + \mathbf{3\,e^-}$$ 3 e^- lost
$$\mathbf{3\,e^-} + \mathbf{4H^+}(aq) + MnO_4^-(aq) \longrightarrow MnO_2(s) + \mathbf{2H_2O}(l)$$ 3 e^- gained

Step 5 **Add half-reactions and cancel electrons, and any identical ions or molecules. Check balance of atoms and charge.**

$$3Fe^{2+}(aq) \longrightarrow 3Fe^{3+}(aq) + 3\,e^-$$
$$4H^+(aq) + MnO_4^-(aq) + 3\,e^- \longrightarrow MnO_2(s) + 2H_2O(l)$$
$$\cancel{3e^-} + 4H^+(aq) + 3Fe^{2+}(aq) + MnO_4^-(aq) \longrightarrow 3Fe^{3+}(aq) + \cancel{3e^-} + MnO_2(s) + 2H_2O(l)$$

Final balanced equation:

$$3Fe^{2+}(aq) + 4H^+(aq) + MnO_4^-(aq) \longrightarrow 3Fe^{3+}(aq) + MnO_2(s) + 2H_2O(l)$$

To convert the equation to an oxidation–reduction reaction in basic solution, we neutralize H^+ with OH^- to form H_2O. For this equation, we add $4OH^-(aq)$ to both sides of the equation.

$$4H^+(aq) + \mathbf{4OH^-}(aq) + 3Fe^{2+}(aq) + MnO_4^-(aq) \longrightarrow 3Fe^{3+}(aq) + MnO_2(s) + 2H_2O(l) + \mathbf{4OH^-}(aq)$$

Combining $4H^+$ and $4OH^-$ gives $4H_2O$ on the reactant side.

$$4H_2O(l) + 3Fe^{2+}(aq) + MnO_4^-(aq) \longrightarrow 3Fe^{3+}(aq) + MnO_2(s) + 2H_2O(l) + 4OH^-(aq)$$

Canceling $2H_2O$ on both the reactant and the product side gives the balanced equation in basic solution:

Final balanced equation in basic solution:

$$2H_2O(l) + 3Fe^{2+}(aq) + MnO_4^-(aq) \longrightarrow 3Fe^{3+}(aq) + MnO_2(s) + 4OH^-(aq)$$

Check balance of atoms and charge.

	Reactants		Products
	3Fe	=	**3Fe**
	1Mn	=	**1Mn**
	4H	=	**4H**
	6O	=	**6O**
Charge:	**5+**	=	**5+**

STUDY CHECK 15.5

Use half-reactions to balance the following equation in basic solution:

$$N_2O(g) + ClO^-(aq) \longrightarrow NO_2^-(aq) + Cl^-(aq)$$

QUESTIONS AND PROBLEMS

15.3 Balancing Oxidation–Reduction Equations Using Half-Reactions

LEARNING GOAL: *Balance oxidation–reduction equations using the half-reaction method.*

15.21 Balance each of the following half-reactions in acidic solution:

a. $Sn^{2+}(aq) \longrightarrow Sn^{4+}(aq)$
b. $Mn^{2+}(aq) \longrightarrow MnO_4^{2-}(aq)$
c. $NO_2^-(aq) \longrightarrow NO_3^-(aq)$
d. $ClO_3^-(aq) \longrightarrow ClO_2(aq)$

15.22 Balance each of the following half-reactions in acidic solution:

a. $Cu(s) \longrightarrow Cu^{2+}(aq)$
b. $SO_4^{2-}(aq) \longrightarrow SO_3^{2-}(aq)$
c. $BrO_3^-(aq) \longrightarrow Br^-(aq)$
d. $IO_3^-(aq) \longrightarrow I_2(s)$

15.23 Use the half-reaction method to balance each of the following in acidic solution:

a. $Ag(s) + NO_3^-(aq) \longrightarrow Ag^+(aq) + NO_2(g)$
b. $NO_3^-(aq) + S(s) \longrightarrow NO(g) + SO_2(g)$
c. $S_2O_3^{2-}(aq) + Cu^{2+}(aq) \longrightarrow S_4O_6^{2-}(aq) + Cu(s)$

15.24 Use the half-reaction method to balance each of the following in acidic solution:

a. $Mn(s) + NO_3^-(aq) \longrightarrow Mn^{2+}(aq) + NO_2(g)$
b. $C_2O_4^{2-}(aq) + MnO_4^-(aq) \longrightarrow CO_2(g) + Mn^{2+}(aq)$
c. $ClO_3^-(aq) + SO_3^{2-}(aq) \longrightarrow Cl^-(aq) + SO_4^{2-}(aq)$

15.25 Use the half-reaction method to balance each of the following in basic solution:

a. $Fe(s) + CrO_4^{2-}(aq) \longrightarrow Fe_2O_3(s) + Cr_2O_3(s)$
b. $CN^-(aq) + MnO_4^-(aq) \longrightarrow CNO^-(aq) + MnO_2(s)$

15.26 Use the half-reaction method to balance each of the following in basic solution:

a. $Al(s) + ClO^-(aq) \longrightarrow AlO_2^-(aq) + Cl^-(aq)$
b. $Sn^{2+}(aq) + IO_4^-(aq) \longrightarrow Sn^{4+}(aq) + I^-(aq)$

LEARNING GOAL

Use the activity series to determine if an oxidation–reduction reaction is spontaneous. Write the half-reactions that occur in a voltaic cell and the cell notation.

CORE CHEMISTRY SKILL

Identifying Spontaneous Reactions

Because Cu is below Zn on the activity series, no oxidation–reduction reaction occurs.

15.4 Electrical Energy from Oxidation–Reduction Reactions

When we placed a zinc metal strip in a solution of Cu^{2+}, reddish-brown Cu metal accumulated on the Zn strip according to the following spontaneous reaction (see Figure 15.1).

$$Zn(s) + Cu^{2+}(aq) \longrightarrow Zn^{2+}(aq) + Cu(s) \quad \text{Spontaneous}$$

However, if we place a Cu metal strip in a Zn^{2+} solution, nothing will happen. The reaction does not run spontaneously in the reverse direction because Cu does not lose electrons as easily as Zn.

We can determine the direction of a spontaneous reaction from the *activity series*, which ranks the metals and H_2 in terms of how easily they lose electrons.

In the **activity series**, the metals that lose electrons most easily are placed at the top, and the metals that do not lose electrons easily are at the bottom. Thus the metals that are more easily oxidized are above the metals whose ions are more easily reduced (see Table 15.3). Active metals include K, Na, Ca, Mg, Al, Zn, Fe, and Sn. In single replacement reactions, the metal ion replaces the H in the acid. Metals listed below $H_2(g)$ will not react with H^+ from acids.

TABLE 15.3 Activity Series for Some Metals

	Metal		Ion
Most active oxidize easily	$Li(s)$	$\longrightarrow$	$Li^+(aq) + e^-$
	$K(s)$	$\longrightarrow$	$K^+(aq) + e^-$
	$Ca(s)$	$\longrightarrow$	$Ca^{2+}(aq) + 2e^-$
	$Na(s)$	$\longrightarrow$	$Na^+(aq) + e^-$
	$Mg(s)$	$\longrightarrow$	$Mg^{2+}(aq) + 2e^-$
	$Al(s)$	$\longrightarrow$	$Al^{3+}(aq) + 3e^-$
	$Zn(s)$	$\longrightarrow$	$Zn^{2+}(aq) + 2e^-$
	$Cr(s)$	$\longrightarrow$	$Cr^{3+}(aq) + 3e^-$
	$Fe(s)$	$\longrightarrow$	$Fe^{2+}(aq) + 2e^-$
	$Ni(s)$	$\longrightarrow$	$Ni^{2+}(aq) + 2e^-$
	$Sn(s)$	$\longrightarrow$	$Sn^{2+}(aq) + 2e^-$
	$Pb(s)$	$\longrightarrow$	$Pb^{2+}(aq) + 2e^-$
	$H_2(g)$	$\longrightarrow$	$2H^+(aq) + 2e^-$
	$Cu(s)$	$\longrightarrow$	$Cu^{2+}(aq) + 2e^-$
	$Ag(s)$	$\longrightarrow$	$Ag^+(aq) + e^-$
Least active oxidize with difficulty	$Au(s)$	$\longrightarrow$	$Au^{3+}(aq) + 3e^-$

According to the activity series, a metal will oxidize spontaneously when it is combined with the reverse of the half-reaction for any metal below it on the list. We use the activity series to predict the direction of the spontaneous reaction. Suppose we have two beakers. In one, we place a Mg strip in a solution containing Ni^{2+} ions. In the other, we place a Ni strip in a solution containing Mg^{2+} ions. Looking at the activity series we see that the half-reaction for the oxidation of Mg is listed above that for Ni, which means that Mg is the more active metal and loses electrons more easily than Ni. Using the activity series table, we write these two half-reactions as follows:

$$Mg(s) \longrightarrow Mg^{2+}(aq) + 2e^-$$
$$Ni(s) \longrightarrow Ni^{2+}(aq) + 2e^-$$

The reaction that will be spontaneous is the oxidation of Mg combined with the reverse (reduction) of Ni^{2+}.

$$\begin{array}{ll} Mg(s) & \longrightarrow Mg^{2+}(aq) + 2\,e^- \\ Ni^{2+}(aq) + 2\,e^- & \longrightarrow Ni(s) \end{array}$$

Therefore, we combine the half-reactions, which gives the following overall reaction that occurs spontaneously:

$$Mg(s) + Ni^{2+}(aq) + \cancel{2e^-} \longrightarrow Mg^{2+}(aq) + Ni(s) + \cancel{2e^-}$$

$$Mg(s) + Ni^{2+}(aq) \longrightarrow Mg^{2+}(aq) + Ni(s) \qquad \text{Spontaneous}$$

However, a reaction between a Mg strip and a solution containing K^+ ions will not occur spontaneously. We determine this by looking at the two half-reactions needed.

$$\begin{array}{ll} Mg(s) & \longrightarrow Mg^{2+}(aq) + 2\,e^- \\ K^+(aq) + e^- & \longrightarrow K(s) \end{array}$$

Because the half-reaction for the oxidation of K is above that for Mg, there will not be a spontaneous reaction between Mg and K^+.

$$Mg(s) + 2K^+(aq) \not\rightleftharpoons Mg^{2+}(aq) + 2K(s) \qquad \text{No reaction takes place}$$

CONCEPT CHECK 15.3 Predicting Spontaneous Reactions

Determine if the reaction for each of the following metals with an HCl (H^+) solution is spontaneous:

a. $Zn(s) + 2H^+(aq) \longrightarrow Zn^{2+}(aq) + H_2(g)$
b. $Cu(s) + 2H^+(aq) \longrightarrow Cu^{2+}(aq) + H_2(g)$

ANSWER

a. Using the activity series (see Table 15.3), we see that Zn oxidizes more easily than H_2. Thus the oxidation half-reaction for Zn is combined with the reverse half-reaction for H_2.

$$\begin{array}{ll} Zn(s) & \longrightarrow Zn^{2+}(aq) + 2\,e^- \\ 2H^+(aq) + 2\,e^- & \longrightarrow H_2(g) \\ Zn(s) + 2H^+(aq) & \longrightarrow Zn^{2+}(aq) + H_2(g) \end{array}$$

Thus, this reaction is spontaneous.

b. Using the activity series (see Table 15.3), we see that H_2 oxidizes more easily than Cu. In this reaction, we would be combining an oxidation half-reaction with one that is above it in the activity series.

$$\begin{array}{ll} 2H^+(aq) + 2\,e^- & \longrightarrow H_2(g) \\ Cu(s) & \longrightarrow Cu^{2+}(aq) + 2\,e^- \\ Cu(s) + 2H^+(aq) & \not\rightleftharpoons Cu^{2+}(aq) + H_2(g) \end{array}$$

Thus, this reaction is not spontaneous.

Voltaic Cells

We can generate electrical energy from a spontaneous oxidation–reduction reaction by using an apparatus called a **voltaic cell**. The two half-reactions still take place, but in a cell the electrons must flow through an external circuit. For example, a piece of zinc metal in a Cu^{2+} solution becomes coated with a rusty-brown coating of Cu, while the blue color (Cu^{2+}) of the solution fades. The oxidation of the zinc metal provides electrons for the reduction of the Cu^{2+} ions. We can write the two half-reactions as

$$\begin{array}{lll} Zn(s) & \longrightarrow Zn^{2+}(aq) + 2\,e^- & \text{Oxidation} \\ Cu^{2+}(aq) + 2\,e^- & \longrightarrow Cu(s) & \text{Reduction} \end{array}$$

The overall reaction is

$$Zn(s) + Cu^{2+}(aq) \longrightarrow Zn^{2+}(aq) + Cu(s)$$

As long as the Zn metal and Cu^{2+} ions are in the same container, the electrons are transferred directly from Zn to Cu^{2+}. However, when the components of the two half-reactions are placed in separate containers, called *half-cells*, the electrons flow from one half-cell to the other, producing an electrical current. In each half-cell, there is a strip of metal, called an *electrode*, in contact with the ionic solution. The electrode where oxidation takes place is called the **anode**; the **cathode** is the electrode where reduction takes place. In this example, the anode is a zinc metal strip placed in a $Zn^{2+}(ZnSO_4)$ solution. The cathode is a copper metal strip placed in a $Cu^{2+}(CuSO_4)$ solution. In this voltaic cell, the Zn anode and Cu cathode are connected by a wire that allows electrons to move from the oxidation half-cell to the reduction half-cell.

Anode is where
oxidation takes place
electrons are produced } $Zn(s) \longrightarrow Zn^{2+}(aq) + 2\,e^-$

Cathode is where
reduction takes place
electrons are used up } $Cu^{2+}(aq) + 2\,e^- \longrightarrow Cu(s)$

The circuit is completed by a *salt bridge* containing positive and negative ions that are placed in the half-cell solutions. The purpose of the salt bridge is to provide ions, such as Na^+ and SO_4^{2-} ions, to maintain an electrical balance in each half-cell solution. As oxidation occurs, there is an increase in Zn^{2+} ions, which is balanced by SO_4^{2-} anions from the salt bridge. At the cathode, there is a loss of Cu^{2+}, which is balanced by SO_4^{2-} moving into the salt bridge. The complete circuit involves the flow of electrons from the anode to the cathode and the flow of anions from the cathode solution to the anode solution (see Figure 15.2).

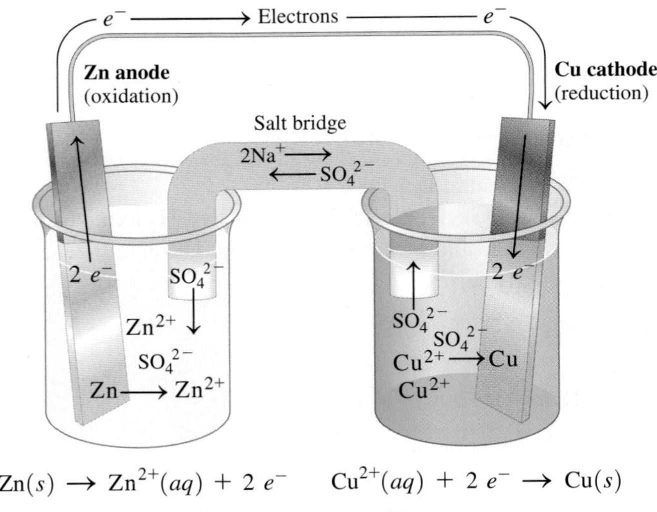

FIGURE 15.2 In this voltaic cell, the Zn anode is in a Zn^{2+} solution, and the Cu cathode is in a Cu^{2+} solution. Electrons produced by the oxidation of Zn flow from the anode through the wire to the cathode where they reduce Cu^{2+} to Cu. The circuit is completed by the flow of SO_4^{2-} through the salt bridge.

Q Which electrode will be heavier when the reaction ends?

We can diagram the oxidation and reduction reactions that take place in the cell using a *shorthand notation* as follows:

$$Zn(s)\,|\,Zn^{2+}(aq)\,\|\,Cu^{2+}(aq)\,|\,Cu(s)$$

The components of the oxidation half-cell (anode) are written on the left side, and the components of the reduction half-cell (cathode) are written on the right. A single vertical line separates the solid Zn anode from the Zn^{2+} solution, and another vertical line separates the Cu^{2+} solution from the Cu cathode. A double vertical line separates the two half-cells.

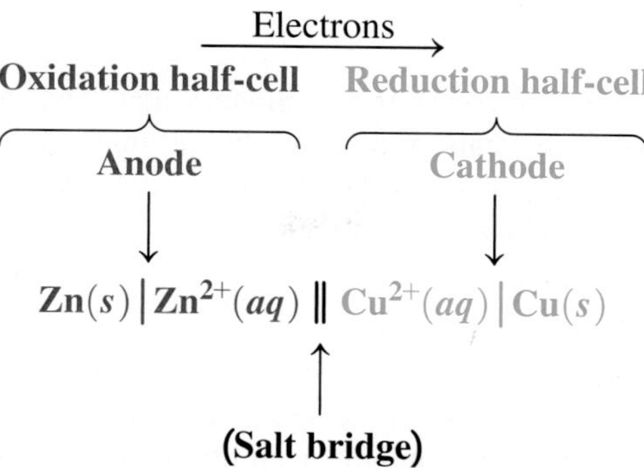

In some voltaic cells, there is no component in the half-reactions that can be used as an electrode. When this is the case, inert electrodes made of graphite or platinum are used for the transfer of electrons. If there are two ionic components in a cell, their symbols are separated by a comma. For example, suppose a voltaic cell consists of a platinum anode placed in a Sn^{2+} solution, and a silver cathode placed in a Ag^+ solution. The notation for the cell would be written as

$$Pt(s)\,|\,Sn^{2+}(aq),\,Sn^{4+}(aq)\,\|\,Ag^+(aq)\,|\,Ag(s)$$

The oxidation reaction at the anode is

$$Sn^{2+}(aq) \longrightarrow Sn^{4+}(aq) + 2\,e^-$$

The reduction reaction at the cathode is

$$Ag^+(aq) + e^- \longrightarrow Ag(s)$$

To balance the overall cell reaction, we multiply the cathode reduction by 2 and combine the two half-reactions.

$$\begin{array}{lll} 2Ag^+(aq) + \mathbf{2\,e^-} & \longrightarrow & 2Ag(s) \\ Sn^{2+}(aq) & \longrightarrow & Sn^{4+}(aq) + \mathbf{2\,e^-} \\ \hline Sn^{2+}(aq) + 2Ag^+(aq) & \longrightarrow & Sn^{4+}(aq) + 2Ag(s) \end{array}$$

SAMPLE PROBLEM 15.6 Diagramming a Voltaic Cell

A voltaic cell consists of an iron (Fe) anode in a Fe^{2+} solution and a tin (Sn) cathode placed in a Sn^{2+} solution. Write the cell notation, the oxidation and reduction half-reactions, and the overall cell reaction.

SOLUTION

The notation for the cell would be written as

$$Fe(s)\,|\,Fe^{2+}(aq)\,\|\,Sn^{2+}(aq)\,|\,Sn(s)$$

The oxidation reaction at the anode is

$$Fe(s) \longrightarrow Fe^{2+}(aq) + 2\,e^-$$

The reduction reaction at the cathode is

$$Sn^{2+}(aq) + 2\,e^- \longrightarrow Sn(s)$$

To write the overall cell reaction, we combine the two half-reactions.

$$\begin{array}{lll} Fe(s) & \longrightarrow & Fe^{2+}(aq) + 2\,e^- \\ Sn^{2+}(aq) + 2\,e^- & \longrightarrow & Sn(s) \\ \hline Fe(s) + Sn^{2+}(aq) & \longrightarrow & Fe^{2+}(aq) + Sn(s) \end{array}$$

STUDY CHECK 15.6

Write the half-reactions and the overall cell reaction for the following notation of a voltaic cell:

$$Co(s)\,|\,Co^{2+}(aq)\,\|\,Cu^{2+}(aq)\,|\,Cu(s)$$

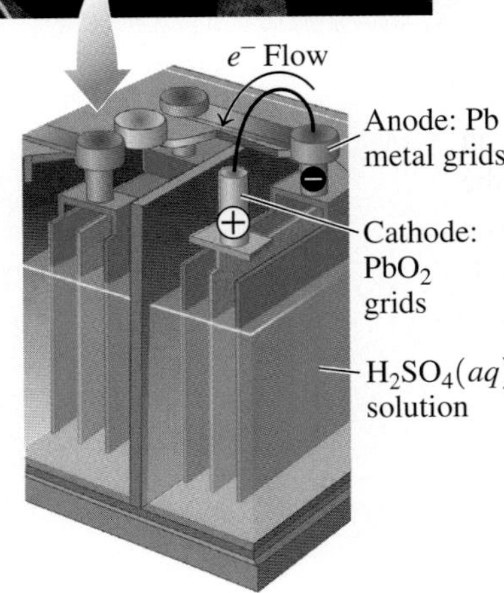

A 12-volt car battery is also known as a lead storage battery.

Batteries

Batteries are needed to power your cell phone, watch, and calculator. Batteries also are needed to make cars start, and flashlights produce light. Within each of these batteries are voltaic cells that produce electrical energy. Let's look at some examples of commonly used batteries.

Lead Storage Battery

A lead storage battery is used to operate the electrical system in a car. We need a car battery to start the engine, turn on the lights, or operate the radio. If the battery runs down, the car won't start and the lights won't turn on. A car battery or a lead storage battery is a type of voltaic cell. In a typical 12-V battery, there are six voltaic cells linked together. Each of the cells consists of a lead (Pb) plate that acts as the anode and a lead(IV) oxide (PbO_2) plate that acts as the cathode. Both half-cells contain a sulfuric acid (H_2SO_4) solution. When the car battery is producing electrical energy (discharging), the following half-reactions take place:

Anode (oxidation):

$$Pb(s) + SO_4^{2-}(aq) \longrightarrow PbSO_4(s) + \mathbf{2\,e^-}$$

Cathode (reduction):

$$\mathbf{2\,e^-} + 4H^+(aq) + PbO_2(s) + SO_4^{2-}(aq) \longrightarrow PbSO_4(s) + 2H_2O(l)$$

Overall cell reaction:

$$4H^+(aq) + Pb(s) + PbO_2(s) + 2SO_4^{2-}(aq) \longrightarrow 2PbSO_4(s) + 2H_2O(l)$$

In both half-reactions, Pb^{2+} is produced, which combines with SO_4^{2-} to form an insoluble salt $PbSO_4$. As a car battery is used, there is a buildup of $PbSO_4$ on the electrodes. At the same time, there is a decrease in the concentrations of the sulfuric acid components, H^+ and SO_4^{2-}. As a car runs, the battery is continuously recharged by an alternator, which is powered by the engine. The recharging reactions restore the Pb and PbO_2 electrodes as well as H_2SO_4. Without recharging, the car battery cannot continue to produce electrical energy.

Dry-Cell Batteries

Dry-cell batteries are used in calculators, watches, flashlights, and battery-operated toys. The term *dry cell* describes a battery that uses a paste rather than an aqueous solution. Dry cells can be acidic or alkaline. In an acidic dry cell, the anode is a zinc metal case that contains a paste of MnO_2, NH_4Cl, $ZnCl_2$, H_2O, and starch. Within this MnO_2 electrolyte mixture is a graphite cathode.

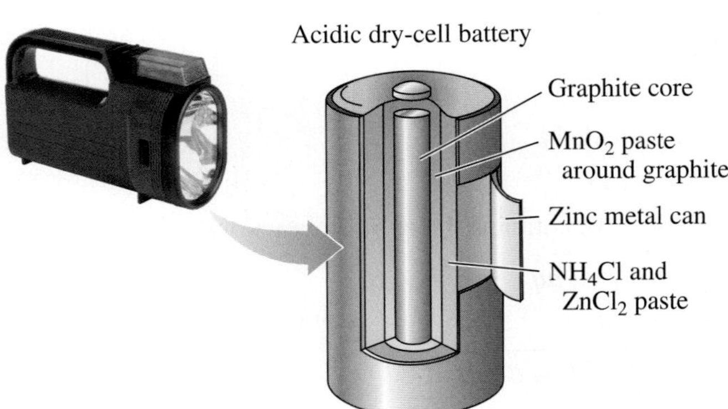

In an acidic dry-cell battery, the cathode is graphite, and the anode is a zinc case.

Anode (oxidation): $Zn(s) \longrightarrow Zn^{2+}(aq) + 2e^-$

Cathode (reduction): $2e^- + 2MnO_2(s) + 2NH_4^+(aq) \longrightarrow Mn_2O_3(s) + 2NH_3(aq) + H_2O(l)$

Overall cell reaction: $Zn(s) + 2MnO_2(s) + 2NH_4^+(aq) \longrightarrow Zn^{2+}(aq) + Mn_2O_3(s) + 2NH_3(aq) + H_2O(l)$

An alkaline battery has similar components except that NaOH or KOH replaces the NH_4Cl electrolyte. Under basic conditions, the product of oxidation is zinc oxide (ZnO). Alkaline batteries tend to be more expensive, but they last longer and produce more power than acidic dry-cell batteries.

Anode (oxidation): $Zn(s) + 2OH^-(aq) \longrightarrow ZnO(s) + H_2O(l) + 2e^-$

Cathode (reduction): $2e^- + 2MnO_2(s) + H_2O(l) \longrightarrow Mn_2O_3(s) + 2OH^-(aq)$

Overall cell reaction: $Zn(s) + 2MnO_2(s) \longrightarrow ZnO(s) + Mn_2O_3(s)$

Mercury and Lithium Batteries

Mercury and lithium batteries are similar to alkaline dry-cell batteries. For example, a mercury battery has a zinc anode, but the cathode is steel in a mixture of HgO, KOH, and $Zn(OH)_2$. The reduced product Hg is toxic and an environmental hazard. Mercury batteries come with warnings on the label and should be disposed of properly.

Anode (oxidation): $Zn(s) + 2OH^-(aq) \longrightarrow ZnO(s) + H_2O(l) + 2e^-$

Cathode (reduction): $2e^- + HgO(s) + H_2O(l) \longrightarrow Hg(l) + 2OH^-(aq)$

Overall cell reaction: $Zn(s) + HgO(s) \longrightarrow ZnO(s) + Hg(l)$

In a lithium battery, the anode is lithium, not zinc. Lithium is much less dense than zinc, and a lithium battery can be made very small.

Anode (oxidation): $2Li(s) \longrightarrow 2Li^+ + 2e^-$

Cathode (reduction): $2e^- + I_2(s) \longrightarrow 2I^-(aq)$

Overall cell reaction: $2Li(s) + I_2(s) \longrightarrow 2Li^+(aq) + 2I^-(aq)$

Nickel–Cadmium (NiCad) Batteries

Nickel–cadmium (NiCad) batteries can be recharged. They use a cadmium anode and a cathode of solid nickel oxide $NiO(OH)(s)$.

Anode (oxidation): $Cd(s) + 2OH^-(aq) \longrightarrow Cd(OH)_2(s) + 2e^-$

Cathode (reduction): $2e^- + 2NiO(OH)(s) + 2H_2O(l) \longrightarrow 2Ni(OH)_2(s) + 2OH^-(aq)$

Overall cell reaction: $Cd(s) + 2NiO(OH)(s) + 2H_2O(l) \longrightarrow Cd(OH)_2(s) + 2Ni(OH)_2(s)$

A NiCad battery in a cell phone can be recharged many times.

NiCad batteries are expensive, but they can be recharged many times. A charger provides an electrical current that converts the solid $Cd(OH)_2$ and $Ni(OH)_2$ products in the NiCad battery back to the reactants.

CONCEPT CHECK 15.4 Batteries

The following half-reaction takes place in a dry-cell battery used in portable radios and flashlights:

$$Zn(s) \longrightarrow Zn^{2+}(aq) + 2e^-$$

a. Why is this half-reaction an oxidation?
b. At which electrode does this half-reaction occur?

ANSWER

a. This half-reaction is an oxidation because $Zn(s)$ loses electrons.
b. The oxidation of Zn would take place at the anode.

Batteries come in many shapes and sizes.

Chemistry Link to the Environment

CORROSION: OXIDATION OF METALS

Metals used in building materials, such as iron, eventually oxidize, which causes deterioration of the metal. This oxidation process, known as *corrosion*, produces rust on cars, bridges, ships, and underground pipes.

$$4Fe(s) + 3O_2(g) \longrightarrow \underset{\text{Rust}}{2Fe_2O_3(s)}$$

The formation of rust requires both oxygen and water. The process of rusting requires an anode and cathode in different places on the surface of a piece of iron. In one area of the iron surface, called the *anode region*, the oxidation half-reaction takes place (see Figure 15.3).

$$\text{Anode (oxidation): } Fe(s) \longrightarrow Fe^{2+}(aq) + 2\,e^-$$

or

$$2Fe(s) \longrightarrow 2Fe^{2+}(aq) + 4\,e^-$$

The electrons move through the iron metal from the anode to an area called the *cathode region* where oxygen dissolved in water is reduced to water.

$$\text{Cathode (reduction): } 4\,e^- + 4H^+(aq) + O_2(g) \longrightarrow 2H_2O(l)$$

By combining the half-reactions that occur in the anode and cathode regions, we can write the overall oxidation–reduction equation.

$$4H^+(aq) + 2Fe(s) + O_2(g) \longrightarrow 2Fe^{2+}(aq) + 2H_2O(l)$$

The formation of rust occurs as Fe^{2+} ions move out of the anode region and come in contact with dissolved oxygen (O_2). The Fe^{2+} oxidizes to Fe^{3+}, which reacts with oxygen to form rust.

$$4H_2O(l) + 4Fe^{2+}(aq) + O_2(g) \longrightarrow \underset{\text{Rust}}{2Fe_2O_3(s)} + 8H^+(aq)$$

We can write the formation of rust starting with solid Fe reacting with O_2 as follows. There is no H^+ in the overall equation because H^+ is used and produced in equal quantities.

Corrosion of iron

$$4Fe(s) + 3O_2(g) \longrightarrow \underset{\text{Rust}}{2Fe_2O_3(s)}$$

Other metals such as aluminum, copper, and silver also undergo corrosion, but at a slower rate than iron. The oxidation of Al on the surface of an aluminum object produces Al^{3+}, which reacts with oxygen in the air to form a protective coating of Al_2O_3. This Al_2O_3 coating prevents further oxidation of the aluminum underneath it.

$$Al(s) \longrightarrow Al^{3+}(aq) + 3\,e^-$$

When copper is used on a roof, dome, or a steeple, it oxidizes to Cu^{2+}, which is converted to a green patina of $Cu_2(OH)_2CO_3$.

$$Cu(s) \longrightarrow Cu^{2+}(aq) + 2\,e^-$$

When we use silver dishes and utensils, the Ag^+ ion from oxidation reacts with sulfides in food to form Ag_2S, which we call "tarnish."

$$Ag(s) \longrightarrow Ag^+(aq) + e^-$$

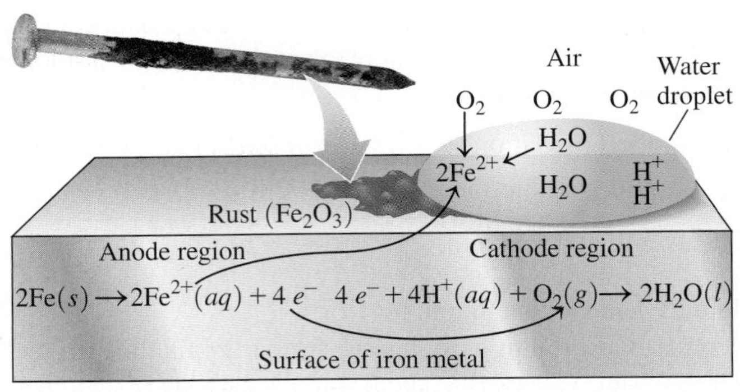

FIGURE 15.3 Rust forms when electrons from the oxidation of Fe flow from the anode region to the cathode region where oxygen is reduced. As Fe^{2+} ions come in contact with O_2 and H_2O, rust forms.

Q Why must both O_2 and H_2O be present for the corrosion of iron?

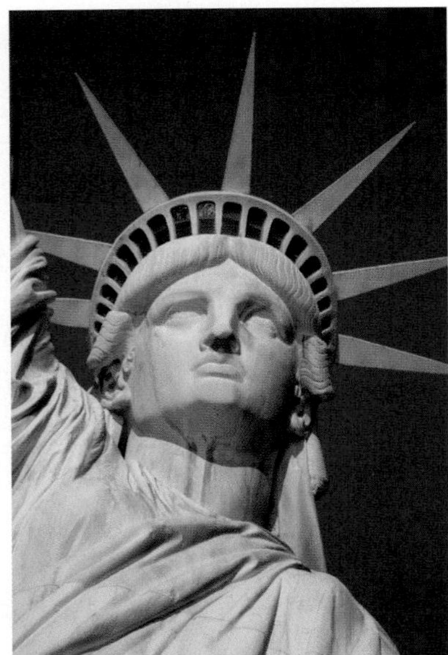

The green patina on copper is due to oxidation.

Prevention of Corrosion

Billions of dollars are spent each year to prevent corrosion and repair building materials made of iron. One way to prevent corrosion is to paint the bridges, cars, and ships with paints containing materials that seal the iron surface from H_2O and O_2. But it is necessary to repaint often; a scratch in the paint exposes the iron, which then begins to rust.

A more effective way to prevent corrosion is to place the iron in contact with a metal that substitutes for the anode region of iron. Metals such as Zn, Mg, or Al lose electrons more easily than iron. When one of these metals is in contact with iron, the metal acts as the anode instead of iron. For example, in a process called *galvanization*, an iron object is coated with zinc. The zinc becomes the anode because zinc is more easily oxidized than Fe. As long as Fe does not act as an anode, rust cannot form.

In a method called *cathodic protection*, structures such as iron pipes and underground storage containers are placed in contact with a piece of metal such as Mg, Al, or Zn, which is called the *sacrificial anode*. Again, because these metals lose electrons more easily than Fe, they become the anode, thereby preventing the rusting of the iron. A magnesium plate that is welded or bolted to a ship's hull loses electrons more easily than iron or steel and protects the hull from rusting. Occasionally, a new magnesium plate is added to replace the magnesium as it is used up. Magnesium stakes placed in the ground are connected to underground pipelines and storage containers to prevent corrosion damage.

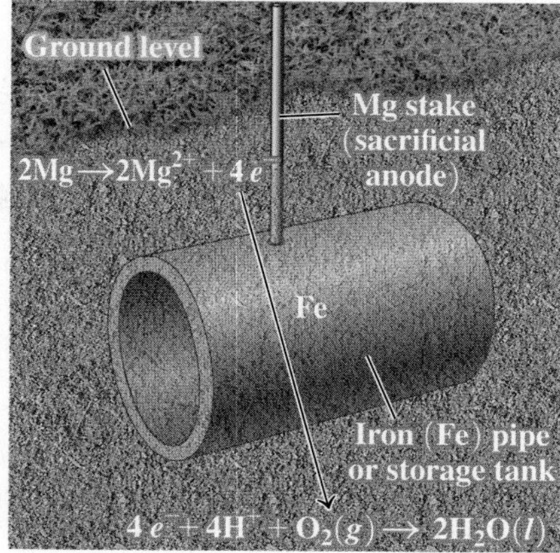

Rusting of an iron pipe is prevented by attaching a piece of magnesium, which oxidizes more easily than iron.

QUESTIONS AND PROBLEMS

15.4 Electrical Energy from Oxidation–Reduction Reactions

LEARNING GOAL: *Use the activity series to determine if an oxidation–reduction reaction is spontaneous. Write the half-reactions that occur in a voltaic cell and the cell notation.*

15.27 Use the activity series in Table 15.3 to predict whether each of the following reactions will occur spontaneously:

a. $2Au(s) + 6H^+(aq) \longrightarrow 2Au^{3+}(aq) + 3H_2(g)$
b. $Ni^{2+}(aq) + Fe(s) \longrightarrow Ni(s) + Fe^{2+}(aq)$
c. $2Ag(s) + Cu^{2+}(aq) \longrightarrow 2Ag^+(aq) + Cu(s)$

15.28 Use the activity series in Table 15.3 to predict whether each of the following reactions will occur spontaneously:

a. $2Ag(s) + 2H^+(aq) \longrightarrow 2Ag^+(aq) + H_2(g)$
b. $Mg(s) + Cu^{2+}(aq) \longrightarrow Mg^{2+}(aq) + Cu(s)$
c. $2Al(s) + 3Cu^{2+}(aq) \longrightarrow 2Al^{3+}(aq) + 3Cu(s)$

15.29 Write the half-reactions and the overall cell reaction for each of the following voltaic cells:

a. $Pb(s)\,|\,Pb^{2+}(aq)\,\|\,Cu^{2+}(aq)\,|\,Cu(s)$
b. $Cr(s)\,|\,Cr^{2+}(aq)\,\|\,Ag^+(aq)\,|\,Ag(s)$

15.30 Write the half-reactions and the overall cell reaction for each of the following voltaic cells:

a. $Al(s)\,|\,Al^{3+}(aq)\,\|\,Cd^{2+}(aq)\,|\,Cd(s)$
b. $Sn(s)\,|\,Sn^{2+}(aq)\,\|\,Fe^{3+}(aq), Fe^{2+}(aq)\,|\,C\ (graphite)$

15.31 Describe the voltaic cell and half-cell components and write the shorthand notation for the following oxidation–reduction reactions:

a. $Cd(s) + Sn^{2+}(aq) \longrightarrow Cd^{2+}(aq) + Sn(s)$
b. $Zn(s) + Cl_2(g) \longrightarrow Zn^{2+}(aq) + 2Cl^-(aq)$ (C graphite cathode)

15.32 Describe the voltaic cell and half-cell components and write the shorthand notation for the following oxidation–reduction reactions:

a. $Mn(s) + Sn^{2+}(aq) \longrightarrow Mn^{2+}(aq) + Sn(s)$
b. $Ni(s) + 2Ag^+(aq) \longrightarrow Ni^{2+}(aq) + 2Ag(s)$

15.33 The following half-reaction takes place in a nickel–cadmium battery used in a cordless drill:

$$Cd(s) + 2OH^-(aq) \longrightarrow Cd(OH)_2(s) + 2e^-$$

a. Is the half-reaction an oxidation or a reduction?
b. What substance is oxidized or reduced?
c. At which electrode would this half-reaction occur?

15.34 The following half-reaction takes place in a mercury battery used in hearing aids:

$$HgO(s) + H_2O(l) + 2e^- \longrightarrow Hg(l) + 2OH^-(aq)$$

a. Is the half-reaction an oxidation or a reduction?
b. What substance is oxidized or reduced?
c. At which electrode would this half-reaction occur?

15.35 The following half-reaction takes place in a mercury battery used in pacemakers and watches:

$$Zn(s) + 2OH^-(aq) \longrightarrow ZnO(s) + H_2O(l) + 2e^-$$

a. Is the half-reaction an oxidation or a reduction?
b. What substance is oxidized or reduced?
c. At which electrode would this half-reaction occur?

15.36 The following half-reaction takes place in a lead storage battery used in automobiles:

$$Pb(s) + SO_4^{2-}(aq) \longrightarrow PbSO_4(s) + 2e^-$$

a. Is the half-reaction an oxidation or a reduction?
b. What substance is oxidized or reduced?
c. At which electrode would this half-reaction occur?

Chemistry Link to the Environment

FUEL CELLS: CLEAN ENERGY FOR THE FUTURE

Fuel cells are of interest to scientists because they provide an alternative source of electrical energy that is more efficient, does not use up oil reserves, and generates products that do not pollute the atmosphere. Fuel cells are considered to be a clean way to produce energy.

Like other electrochemical cells, a fuel cell consists of an anode and a cathode connected by a wire. But unlike other cells, the reactants must continuously enter the fuel cell to produce energy; electrical current is generated only as long as the fuels are supplied. One type of hydrogen–oxygen fuel cell has been used in automobile prototypes. In this hydrogen cell, gas enters the fuel cell and comes in contact with a platinum catalyst embedded in a plastic membrane. The catalyst assists in the oxidation of hydrogen atoms to hydrogen ions and electrons (see Figure 15.4).

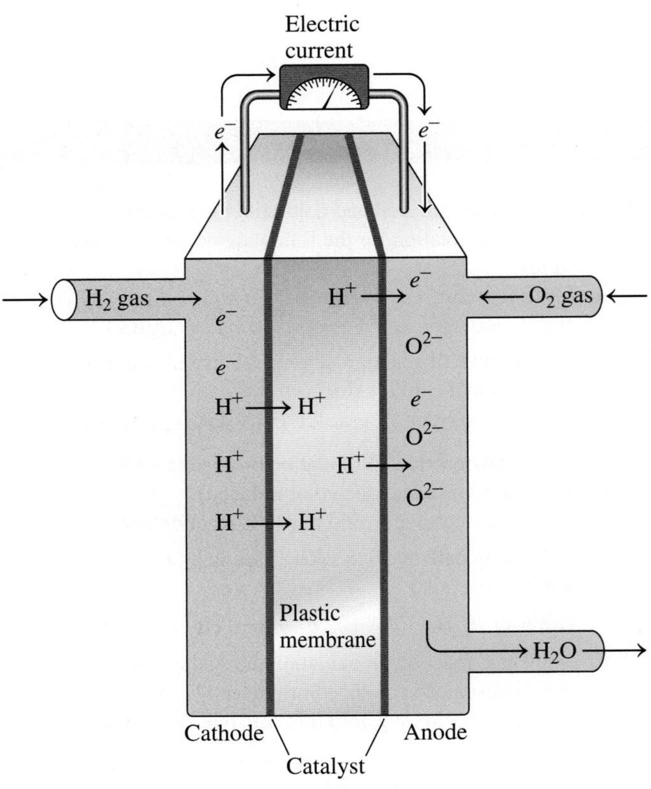

Oxidation
$H_2(g) \longrightarrow 4\,e^- + 4H^+(aq)$

Reduction
$4\,e^- + 4H^+(aq) + O_2(g) \longrightarrow 2H_2O(l)$

FIGURE 15.4 With a supply of hydrogen and oxygen, a fuel cell can generate electricity continuously.

Q In most electrochemical cells, the electrodes are eventually used up. Is this true for a fuel cell? Why or why not?

The electrons produce an electric current as they travel through the wire from the anode to the cathode. The hydrogen ions flow through the plastic membrane to the cathode. At the cathode, oxygen molecules are reduced to oxide ions that combine with the hydrogen ions to form water. The overall hydrogen–oxygen fuel cell reaction can be written as

$$2H_2(g) + O_2(g) \longrightarrow 2H_2O(l)$$

Fuel cells have already been used for power on the space shuttle and may soon be available to produce energy for cars and buses. A major drawback to the practical use of fuel cells is the economic impact of converting cars to fuel cell operation. The storage and cost of producing hydrogen are also problems. Some manufacturers are experimenting with systems that convert gasoline or methanol to hydrogen for immediate use in fuel cells.

In homes, fuel cells may one day replace the batteries currently used to provide electrical power for cell phones, DVD players, and laptop computers. Fuel cell design is still in the prototype phase, although there is much interest in their development. We already know they can work, but modifications must still be made before they become reasonably priced and part of our everyday lives.

Fuel cells are used to supply power on the space shuttle orbiter.

15.5 Oxidation–Reduction Reactions That Require Electrical Energy

LEARNING GOAL

Describe the half-cell reactions and the overall reactions that occur in electrolysis.

When we look at the activity series in Table 15.3, we see that the oxidation of Cu is below Zn. This means that the following oxidation–reduction reaction is not spontaneous:

$$\underset{\text{Less active}}{Cu(s)} + Zn^{2+}(aq) \longrightarrow Cu^{2+}(aq) + \underset{\text{More active}}{Zn(s)} \quad \text{Not spontaneous}$$

To make this reaction take place, we need an **electrolytic cell** that uses an electrical current to drive a nonspontaneous oxidation–reduction reaction. This process is called **electrolysis** (see Figure 15.5).

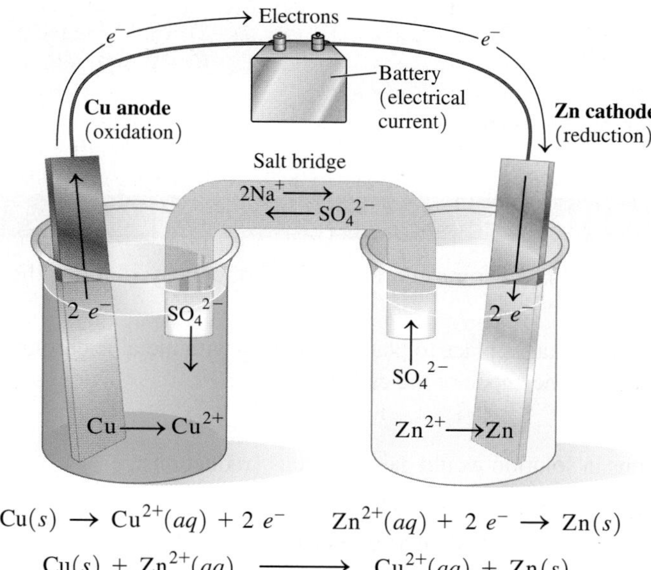

$$Cu(s) \rightarrow Cu^{2+}(aq) + 2\,e^- \qquad Zn^{2+}(aq) + 2\,e^- \rightarrow Zn(s)$$

$$Cu(s) + Zn^{2+}(aq) \longrightarrow Cu^{2+}(aq) + Zn(s)$$

FIGURE 15.5 In this electrolytic cell, the Cu anode is in a Cu^{2+} solution, and the Zn cathode is in a Zn^{2+} solution. Electrons provided by a battery reduce Zn^{2+} to Zn and drive the oxidation of Cu to Cu^{2+} at the Cu anode.

Q Why is an electrical current needed to make the reaction of $Cu(s)$ and $Zn^{2+}(aq)$ happen?

Electrolysis of Sodium Chloride

When molten sodium chloride is electrolyzed, the products are sodium metal and chlorine gas. In this electrolytic cell, electrodes are placed in the mixture of Na^+ and Cl^- and connected to a battery. The products are separated to prevent them from reacting spontaneously with each other. As electrons flow to the cathode, Na^+ is reduced to sodium metal. At the same time, electrons leave the anode as Cl^- is oxidized to Cl_2. The half-reactions and the overall reactions are

$$\begin{array}{lll} \text{Anode (oxidation):} & 2Cl^-(l) & \longrightarrow Cl_2(g) + 2\,e^- \\ \text{Cathode (reduction):} & 2Na^+(l) + 2\,e^- & \longrightarrow 2Na(l) \\ \hline & 2Na^+(l) + 2Cl^-(l) & \longrightarrow 2Na(l) + Cl_2(g) \quad \text{Not spontaneous} \end{array}$$

Electrical energy

Electroplating

In industry, the process of electroplating uses electrolysis to coat an object with a thin layer of a metal such as silver, platinum, or gold. Car bumpers are electroplated with chromium to prevent rusting. Silver-plated utensils, bowls, and platters are made by electroplating objects with a layer of silver.

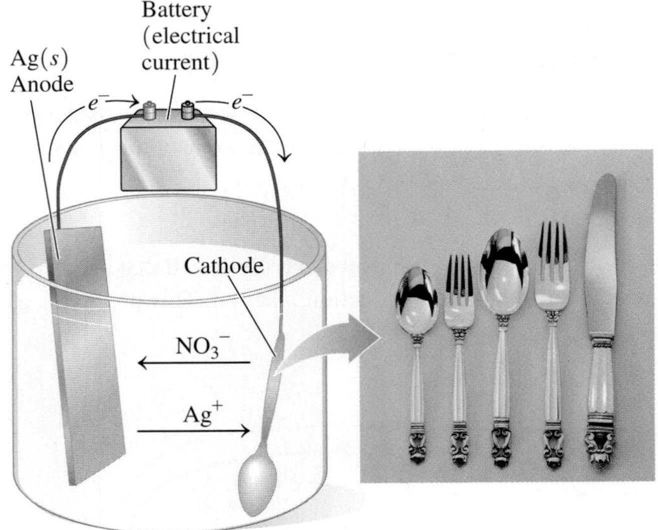

SAMPLE PROBLEM 15.7 Electrolysis

Electrolysis is used to chrome plate an iron hubcap by placing the hubcap in a Cr^{3+} solution.

a. What half-reaction takes place to plate the hubcap with metallic chromium?
b. Is the iron hubcap the anode or the cathode?

SOLUTION

a. The Cr^{3+} ions in solution would gain electrons (reduction).

$$Cr^{3+}(aq) + 3\,e^- \longrightarrow Cr(s)$$

b. The iron hubcap is the cathode where reduction takes place.

STUDY CHECK 15.7

Why is energy needed to chrome plate the iron in Sample Problem 15.7?

Using electrolysis, a thin layer of chromium is plated onto a hubcap.

QUESTIONS AND PROBLEMS

15.5 Oxidation–Reduction Reactions That Require Electrical Energy

LEARNING GOAL: *Describe the half-cell reactions and the overall reactions that occur in electrolysis.*

15.37 What we call "tin cans" are really iron cans coated with a thin layer of tin. The anode is a bar of tin and the cathode is the iron can. An electrical current is used to oxidize the Sn to Sn^{2+} in solution, which is reduced to produce a thin coating of Sn on the can.
a. What half-reaction takes place to tin plate an iron can?
b. Why is the iron can the cathode?
c. Why is the tin bar the anode?

15.38 Electrolysis is used to gold plate jewelry made of stainless steel.
a. What half-reaction takes place when a Au^{3+} solution is used to gold plate a stainless steel earring?
b. Is the earring the anode or the cathode?
c. Why is energy needed to gold plate the earring?

15.39 When the tin coating on an iron can is scratched, rust will form. Use the activity series in Table 15.3 to explain why this happens.

15.40 When the zinc coating on an iron can is scratched, rust does not form. Use the activity series in Table 15.3 to explain why this happens.

15.6 Oxidation of Alcohols: Extended Topic

LEARNING GOAL

Classify alcohols as primary, secondary, or tertiary; write equations for the oxidation of alcohols.

We have seen that oxidation involves the loss of electrons and that reduction involves the gain of electrons. For organic and biochemical compounds, oxidation typically involves the addition of oxygen or the loss of hydrogen, and reduction involves the loss of oxygen or the gain of hydrogen. In organic chemistry, oxidation occurs when there is an increase in the number of carbon–oxygen bonds. In a reduction reaction, the product has fewer bonds between carbon and oxygen.

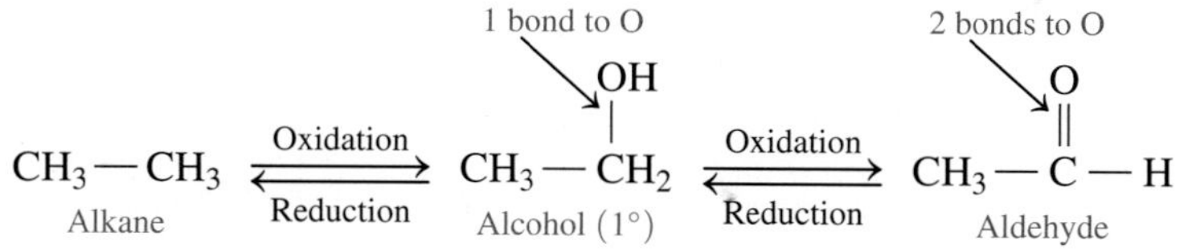

$$\underset{\text{Alkane}}{CH_3-CH_3} \underset{\text{Reduction}}{\overset{\text{Oxidation}}{\rightleftarrows}} \underset{\text{Alcohol }(1^\circ)}{CH_3-\overset{\overset{OH}{|}}{CH_2}} \underset{\text{Reduction}}{\overset{\text{Oxidation}}{\rightleftarrows}} \underset{\text{Aldehyde}}{CH_3-\overset{\overset{O}{\|}}{C}-H}$$

1 bond to O; 2 bonds to O

Classification of Alcohols

Alcohols are classified by the number of carbon groups attached to the carbon atom bonded to the hydroxyl ($-OH$) group. A **primary (1°) alcohol** has one carbon group attached to the carbon atom bonded to the $-OH$ group, a **secondary (2°) alcohol** has two carbon groups, and a **tertiary (3°) alcohol** has three carbon groups. The simplest alcohol, methanol, which has a carbon atom attached to three H atoms is considered a primary alcohol.

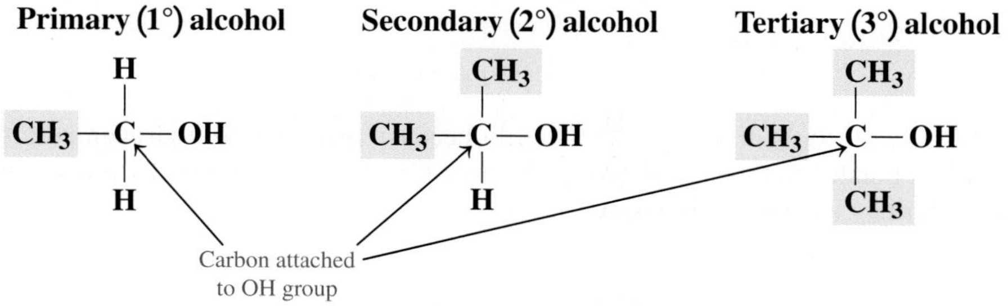

Primary (1°) alcohol

$$CH_3-\underset{\underset{H}{|}}{\overset{\overset{H}{|}}{C}}-OH$$

Secondary (2°) alcohol

$$CH_3-\underset{\underset{H}{|}}{\overset{\overset{CH_3}{|}}{C}}-OH$$

Tertiary (3°) alcohol

$$CH_3-\underset{\underset{CH_3}{|}}{\overset{\overset{CH_3}{|}}{C}}-OH$$

Carbon attached to OH group

CONCEPT CHECK 15.5 Classifying Alcohols

Classify each of the following alcohols as primary, secondary, or tertiary:

a. $CH_3-CH_2-CH_2-OH$

b. 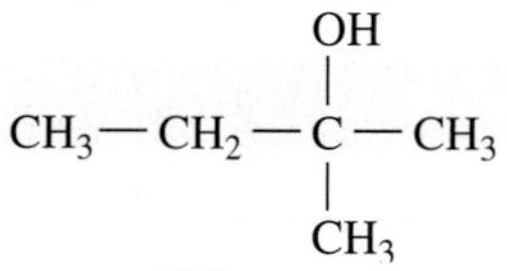 $CH_3-CH_2-\underset{\underset{CH_3}{|}}{\overset{\overset{OH}{|}}{C}}-CH_3$

c. $CH_3-\overset{\overset{OH}{|}}{CH}-CH_3$

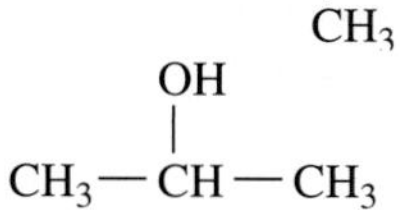

ANSWER

a. One carbon group attached to the carbon atom bonded to the $-OH$ group makes this a primary alcohol.

b. Three carbon groups attached to the carbon atom bonded to the $-OH$ group makes this a tertiary alcohol.

c. Two carbon groups attached to the carbon atom bonded to the $-OH$ group makes this a secondary alcohol.

Oxidation of Primary and Secondary Alcohols

When a primary alcohol is oxidized, it produces an aldehyde. The oxidation occurs by removing two hydrogen atoms, one from the —OH group and another from the carbon that is bonded to the —OH. To indicate the presence of an oxidizing agent such as $KMnO_4$ and $K_2Cr_2O_7$, reactions are written with the symbol [O] over the reaction arrow.

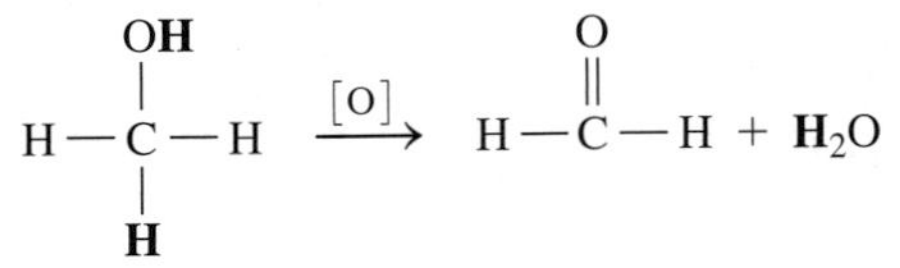

$$\underset{\text{Methanol}}{\mathrm{H{-}\overset{\displaystyle OH}{\overset{|}{\underset{\underset{\displaystyle H}{|}}{C}}}{-}H}} \xrightarrow{[O]} \underset{\text{Methanal}}{\mathrm{H{-}\overset{\displaystyle O}{\overset{\|}{C}}{-}H}} + H_2O$$

$$\underset{\text{Ethanol}}{\mathrm{CH_3{-}\overset{\displaystyle OH}{\overset{|}{CH_2}}}} \xrightarrow{[O]} \underset{\text{Ethanal}}{\mathrm{CH_3{-}\overset{\displaystyle O}{\overset{\|}{C}}{-}H}} + H_2O$$

The other product of the oxidation is H_2O, formed when two H atoms from the alcohol combine with an O atom from the oxidizing agent. In the oxidation of secondary alcohols, the products are ketones. One H is removed from the —OH, and another H is removed from the carbon bonded to the —OH group.

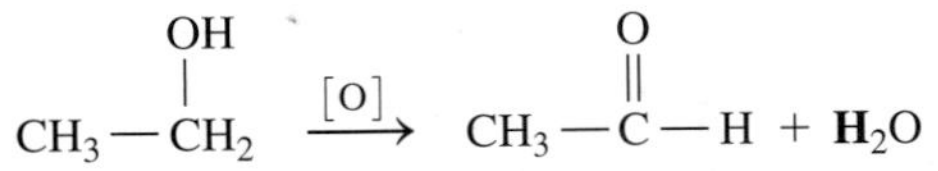

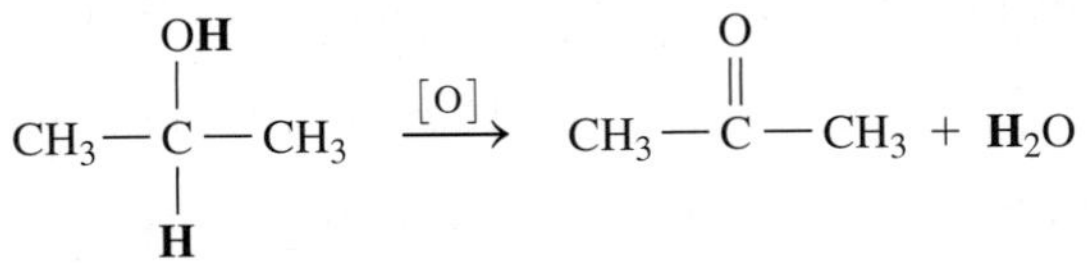

$$\underset{\text{2-Propanol}}{\mathrm{CH_3{-}\overset{\displaystyle OH}{\overset{|}{\underset{\underset{\displaystyle H}{|}}{C}}}{-}CH_3}} \xrightarrow{[O]} \underset{\text{Propanone, acetone}}{\mathrm{CH_3{-}\overset{\displaystyle O}{\overset{\|}{C}}{-}CH_3}} + H_2O$$

Tertiary alcohols do not oxidize readily because there are no hydrogen atoms on the carbon bonded to the —OH group. Because C—C bonds are usually too strong to oxidize, tertiary alcohols resist oxidation.

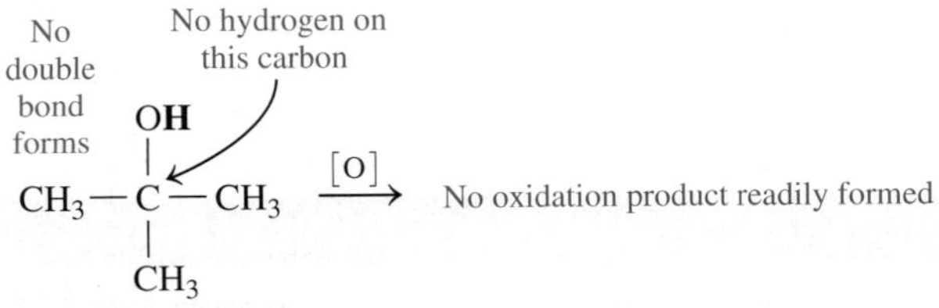

No double bond forms

No hydrogen on this carbon

$$\underset{3^\circ\ \text{Alcohol}}{\mathrm{CH_3{-}\overset{\displaystyle OH}{\overset{|}{\underset{\underset{\displaystyle CH_3}{|}}{C}}}{-}CH_3}} \xrightarrow{[O]} \text{No oxidation product readily formed}$$

SAMPLE PROBLEM 15.8 Oxidation of Alcohols

Draw the condensed structural formula for the aldehyde or ketone formed by the oxidation of each of the following:

a. 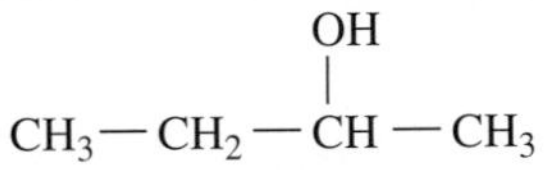 $\mathrm{CH_3{-}CH_2{-}\overset{\displaystyle OH}{\overset{|}{CH}}{-}CH_3}$

b. $CH_3—CH_2—CH_2—OH$

SOLUTION

a. The oxidation of a secondary alcohol produces a ketone.

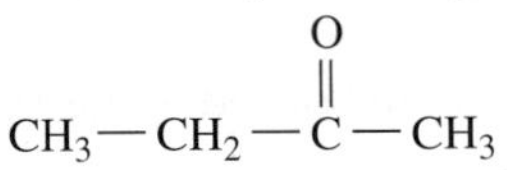

$$\mathrm{CH_3{-}CH_2{-}\overset{\displaystyle O}{\overset{\|}{C}}{-}CH_3}$$

b. The oxidation of a primary alcohol produces an aldehyde.

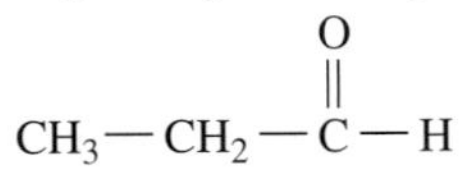

$$\mathrm{CH_3{-}CH_2{-}\overset{\displaystyle O}{\overset{\|}{C}}{-}H}$$

STUDY CHECK 15.8

Draw the condensed structural formula for the aldehyde or ketone formed by the oxidation of the following alcohol:

$$CH_3-\overset{CH_3}{\overset{|}{CH}}-\overset{CH_3}{\overset{|}{CH}}-CH_2-CH_2-OH$$

QUESTIONS AND PROBLEMS

15.6 Oxidation of Alcohols: Extended Topic

LEARNING GOAL: *Classify alcohols as primary, secondary, or tertiary; write equations for the oxidation of alcohols.*

15.41 Classify each of the following as a primary, secondary, or tertiary alcohol:

a. $CH_3-\overset{CH_3}{\overset{|}{CH}}-CH_2-CH_2-OH$

b. $CH_3-CH_2-CH_2-CH_2-OH$

c. $CH_3-\underset{\underset{CH_3}{|}}{\overset{OH}{\overset{|}{C}}}-CH_2-CH_3$

15.42 Classify each of the following as a primary, secondary, or tertiary alcohol:

a. $CH_3-\overset{CH_3}{\overset{|}{CH}}-CH_2-OH$

b. $CH_3-CH_2-\overset{OH}{\overset{|}{CH}}-CH_2-CH_3$

c. $CH_3-CH_2-CH_2-\underset{\underset{CH_3}{|}}{\overset{CH_3}{\overset{|}{C}}}-OH$

15.43 Draw the condensed structural formula for the aldehyde or ketone produced when each of the following alcohols is oxidized [O] (if no reaction, write *none*):

a. $CH_3-CH_2-CH_2-CH_2-CH_2-OH$

b. $CH_3-\underset{\underset{CH_3}{|}}{\overset{OH}{\overset{|}{C}}}-CH_2-CH_3$

c. $CH_3-\overset{OH}{\overset{|}{CH}}-CH_2-\overset{CH_3}{\overset{|}{CH}}-CH_3$

15.44 Draw the condensed structural formula for the aldehyde or ketone produced when each of the following alcohols is oxidized [O] (if no reaction, write *none*):

a. $CH_3-\overset{CH_3}{\overset{|}{CH}}-CH_2-CH_2-OH$

b. $CH_3-CH_2-\underset{\underset{CH_3}{|}}{\overset{OH}{\overset{|}{C}}}-CH_2-CH_2-CH_3$

c. $CH_3-CH_2-\overset{OH}{\overset{|}{CH}}-CH_2-CH_3$

Chemistry Link to Health

OXIDATION OF ETHANOL IN THE BODY

Ethanol is the most commonly abused drug in the United States. When ingested in small amounts, ethanol may produce a feeling of euphoria in the body despite the fact that it is a depressant. In the liver, enzymes such as alcohol dehydrogenase oxidize ethanol to acetaldehyde, a substance that impairs mental and physical coordination. If the blood alcohol concentration exceeds 0.4%, coma or death may occur. Table 15.4 gives some of the typical behaviors exhibited at various levels of blood alcohol.

$$\underset{\text{Ethanol (ethyl alcohol)}}{CH_3-CH_2-OH} \xrightarrow{[O]} \underset{\text{Ethanal (acetaldehyde)}}{CH_3-\overset{O}{\overset{\|}{C}}-H} \xrightarrow{[O]} \underset{\text{Ethanoic acid (acetic acid)}}{CH_3-\overset{O}{\overset{\|}{C}}-OH} \xrightarrow{[O]} 2CO_2 + H_2O$$

The acetaldehyde produced from ethanol in the liver is further oxidized to acetic acid, which is eventually converted to carbon dioxide and water in the citric acid cycle. However, the intermediate products can cause considerable damage while they are present within the cells of the liver.

A person weighing 150 lb requires about one hour to metabolize the alcohol in a 12 oz glass of beer. However, the rate of metabolism of ethanol varies between nondrinkers and drinkers. Typically, nondrinkers and social drinkers can metabolize 12–15 mg of ethanol/dL of blood in one hour, but an alcoholic can metabolize as much as

TABLE 15.4 Typical Behaviors Exhibited by a 150-lb Person Consuming Alcohol

Number of Beers (12 oz) or Glasses of Wine (5 oz) in 1 h	Percent Blood Alcohol Concentration (% m/v)	Typical Behavior
1	0.025	Slightly dizzy, talkative
2	0.05	Euphoria, loud talking, and laughing
4	0.10	Loss of inhibition, loss of coordination, drowsiness, legally drunk in most states
8	0.20	Intoxicated, quick to anger, exaggerated emotions
12	0.30	Unconscious
16–20	0.40–0.50	Coma and death

30 mg of ethanol/dL in one hour. Some effects of alcohol metabolism include an increase in liver lipids (fatty liver), gastritis, pancreatitis, ketoacidosis, alcoholic hepatitis, and psychological disturbances.

When alcohol is present in the blood, it evaporates through the lungs. Thus, the percentage of alcohol in the lungs can be used to calculate the blood alcohol concentration (BAC). Several devices are used to measure the BAC. When a Breathalyzer is used, a suspected drunk driver exhales through a mouthpiece into a solution containing

A breathalyzer test is used to determine blood level of ethanol.

the orange Cr^{6+} ion. Any alcohol present in the exhaled air is oxidized, which reduces the orange Cr^{6+} to green Cr^{3+}.

$$\underset{\text{Ethanol}}{CH_3-CH_2-OH} + \underset{\text{Orange}}{Cr^{6+}} \xrightarrow{[O]} \underset{\text{Acetic acid}}{CH_3-\overset{\overset{\displaystyle O}{\|}}{C}-OH} + \underset{\text{Green}}{Cr^{3+}}$$

The Alcosensor uses the oxidation of alcohol in a fuel cell to generate an electric current that is measured. The Intoxilyzer measures the amount of light absorbed by the alcohol molecules.

Sometimes alcoholics are treated with a drug called Antabuse (disulfiram), which prevents the oxidation of acetaldehyde to acetic acid. As a result, acetaldehyde accumulates in the blood, which causes nausea, profuse sweating, headache, dizziness, vomiting, and respiratory difficulties. Because of these unpleasant side effects, the patient is less likely to use alcohol.

CHAPTER REVIEW

15.1 Oxidation–Reduction Reactions

LEARNING GOAL: *Identify what is oxidized and what is reduced in an oxidation–reduction reaction.*

- In oxidation–reduction reactions, electrons are transferred from one reactant to another.
- The reactant that loses electrons is oxidized, and the reactant that gains electrons is reduced.
- Oxidation must always occur with reduction.

15.2 Oxidation Numbers

LEARNING GOAL: *Assign and use oxidation numbers to identify elements that are oxidized or reduced.*

- Oxidation numbers assigned to elements keep track of the changes in the loss and gain of electrons.

- Oxidation is an increase in oxidation number; reduction is a decrease in oxidation number.
- The reducing agent is the substance that provides electrons for reduction.
- The oxidizing agent is the substance that accepts the electrons from oxidation.
- In molecular compounds and polyatomic ions, oxidation numbers are assigned using a set of rules.
- The oxidation number of an element is zero, and the oxidation number of a monatomic ion is the same as the ionic charge of the ion.
- The sum of the oxidation numbers for a compound is equal to zero and for a polyatomic ion is equal to the overall charge.
- Balancing oxidation–reduction equations using oxidation numbers involves the following:

(1) assigning oxidation numbers
(2) determining the loss and gain of electrons
(3) equalizing the loss and gain of electrons
(4) balancing the remaining substances by inspection

15.3 Balancing Oxidation–Reduction Equations Using Half-Reactions

LEARNING GOAL: *Balance oxidation–reduction equations using the half-reaction method.*

- Balancing oxidation–reduction equations using half-reactions involves the following:
  (1) separating the equation into half-reactions
  (2) balancing elements other than H and O
  (3) balancing O with H_2O and H with H^+
  (4) balancing charge with electrons
  (5) equalizing the loss and gain of electrons
  (6) combining half-reactions, canceling electrons, and combining H_2O and H^+
  (7) using OH^- to neutralize H^+ to H_2O for an oxidation–reduction reaction in basic solution

15.4 Electrical Energy from Oxidation–Reduction Reactions

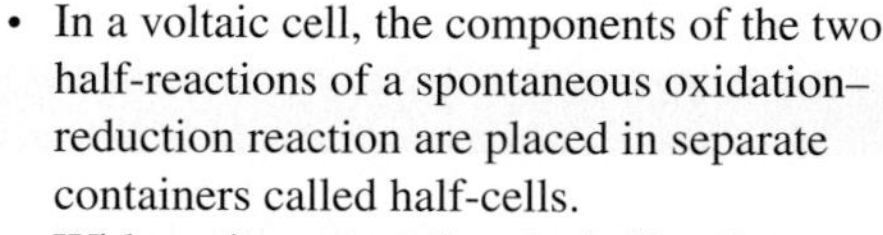

LEARNING GOAL: *Use the activity series to determine if an oxidation–reduction reaction is spontaneous. Write the half-reactions that occur in a voltaic cell and the cell notation.*

- In a voltaic cell, the components of the two half-reactions of a spontaneous oxidation–reduction reaction are placed in separate containers called half-cells.
- With a wire connecting the half-cells, an electrical current is generated as electrons move from the anode where oxidation takes place to the cathode where reduction takes place.

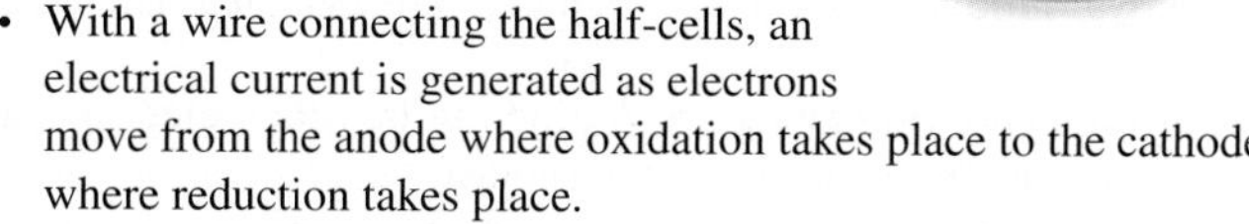

15.5 Oxidation–Reduction Reactions That Require Electrical Energy

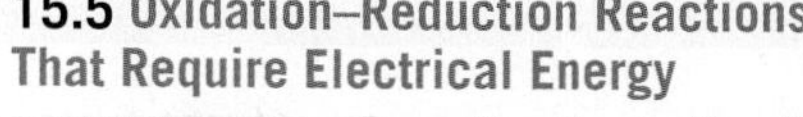

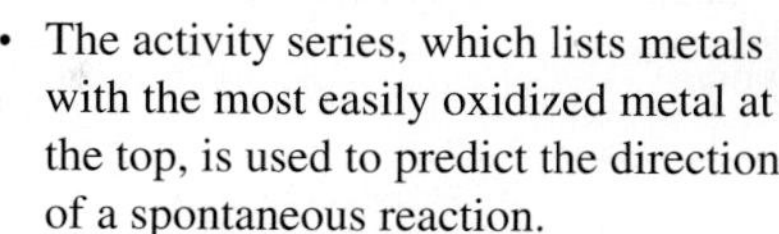

LEARNING GOAL: *Describe the half-cell reactions and the overall reactions that occur in electrolysis.*

- The activity series, which lists metals with the most easily oxidized metal at the top, is used to predict the direction of a spontaneous reaction.
- In an electrolytic cell, electrical energy from an external source is used to make reactions take place that are not spontaneous.
- A method called electrolysis is used to plate chrome on hubcaps, zinc on iron, or gold on stainless steel jewelry.

15.6 Oxidation of Alcohols: Extended Topic

LEARNING GOAL: *Classify alcohols as primary, secondary, or tertiary; write equations for the oxidation of alcohols.*

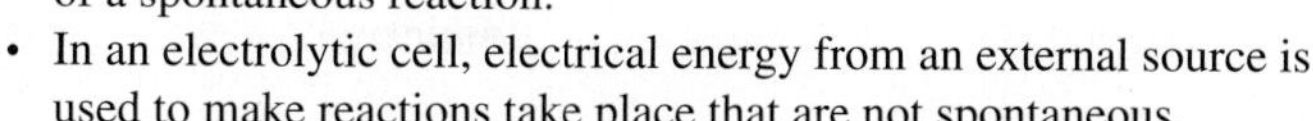

$$CH_3-CH_3 \underset{\text{Reduction}}{\overset{\text{Oxidation}}{\rightleftharpoons}} CH_3-CH_2(OH) \underset{\text{Reduction}}{\overset{\text{Oxidation}}{\rightleftharpoons}} CH_3-C(=O)-H$$

Alkane; Alcohol (1°) (1 bond to O); Aldehyde (2 bonds to O)

- Alcohols are classified according to the number of carbon groups bonded to the carbon that holds the —OH group.
- In a primary (1°) alcohol, one carbon group is attached to the carbon atom with the —OH group.
- In a secondary (2°) alcohol, two carbon groups are attached, and in a tertiary (3°) alcohol, there are three carbon groups.
- Primary alcohols are oxidized to aldehydes. Secondary alcohols are oxidized to ketones. Tertiary alcohols do not oxidize.

SUMMARY OF REACTIONS

Oxidation of Primary Alcohols to Form Aldehydes

$$\underset{\text{Ethanol}}{CH_3-CH_2-OH} \xrightarrow{[O]} \underset{\text{Ethanal}}{CH_3-C(=O)-H} + H_2O$$

Oxidation of Secondary Alcohols to Form Ketones

$$\underset{\text{2-Propanol}}{CH_3-CH(OH)-CH_3} \xrightarrow{[O]} \underset{\text{Propanone}}{CH_3-C(=O)-CH_3} + H_2O$$

CONCEPT MAP

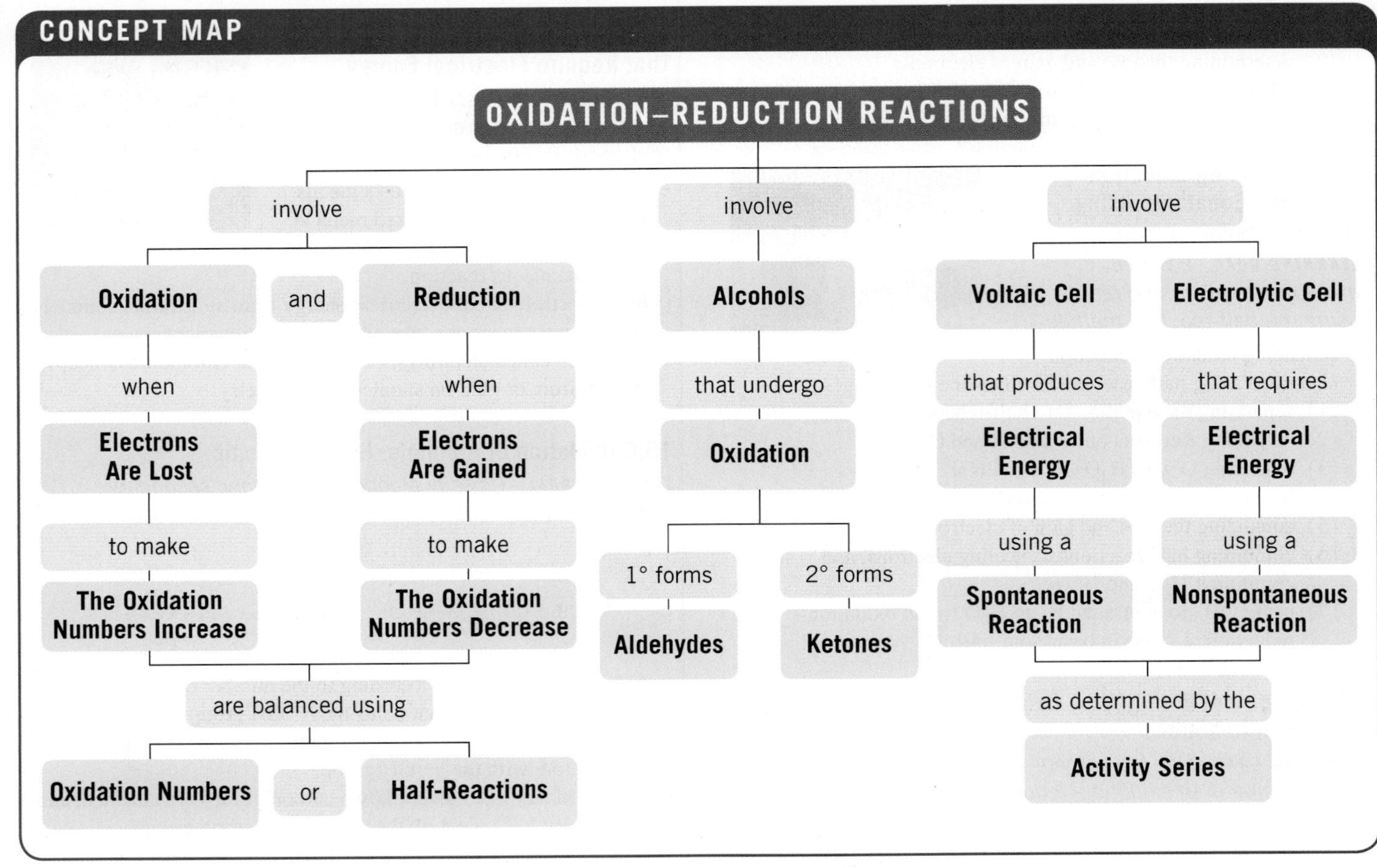

KEY TERMS

activity series A table of half-reactions with the metals that oxidize most easily at the top, and the metals that do not oxidize easily at the bottom.

anode The electrode where oxidation takes place.

cathode The electrode where reduction takes place.

electrolysis The use of electrical energy to run a nonspontaneous oxidation–reduction reaction in an electrolytic cell.

electrolytic cell A cell in which electrical energy is used to make a nonspontaneous oxidation–reduction reaction happen.

half-reaction method A method of balancing oxidation–reduction reactions in which the half-reactions are balanced separately and then combined to give the complete reaction.

oxidation The loss of electrons by a substance.

oxidation number A number equal to zero in an element or the charge of a monatomic ion; in molecular compounds and polyatomic ions, oxidation numbers are assigned using a set of rules.

oxidation–reduction reaction A reaction in which electrons are transferred from one reactant to another.

oxidizing agent The reactant that gains electrons and is reduced.

primary (1°) alcohol An alcohol that has one carbon group bonded to the carbon atom with the —OH group.

reducing agent The reactant that loses electrons and is oxidized.

reduction The gain of electrons by a substance.

secondary (2°) alcohol An alcohol that has two carbon groups bonded to the carbon atom with the —OH group.

tertiary (3°) alcohol An alcohol that has three carbon groups bonded to the carbon atom with the —OH group.

voltaic cell A type of cell with two compartments that uses spontaneous oxidation–reduction reactions to produce electrical energy.

CORE CHEMISTRY SKILLS

The chapter section containing each Core Chemistry Skill is shown in parentheses at the end of each heading.

Identifying Oxidized and Reduced Substances (15.1)

- In an oxidation–reduction reaction (abbreviated *redox*), one reactant is oxidized when it loses electrons, and another reactant is reduced when it gains electrons.
- Oxidation is the *loss* of electrons; reduction is the *gain* of electrons.

Example: For the following redox reaction, identify the reactant that is oxidized, and the reactant that is reduced:

$$Fe(s) + Cu^{2+}(aq) \longrightarrow Fe^{2+}(aq) + Cu(s)$$

Answer: $Fe^0(s) \longrightarrow Fe^{2+}(aq) + 2\,e^-$

Fe loses electrons; it is oxidized.

$Cu^{2+}(aq) + 2\,e^- \longrightarrow Cu^0(s)$

Cu^{2+} gains electrons; it is reduced.

Assigning Oxidation Numbers (15.2)

- Oxidation numbers are assigned to atoms or ions in a reaction to determine the substance that is oxidized and the substance that is reduced.
- The rules for assigning oxidation numbers are as follows:
  (1) for a molecule is 0; for a polyatomic ion is its charge
  (2) for an element is 0
  (3) for a monatomic ion is its charge
  (4) for Group 1A (1) metals is +1, Group 2A (2) metals is +2
  (5) for fluorine is −1; for other Group 7A (17) metals is −1, except when combined with O or F
  (6) for oxygen is −2, except in OF_2
  (7) for H in nonmetal compounds is +1; for H with a metal is −1

Example: Assign oxidation numbers to each of the elements in the following:

a. Sn^{4+} **b.** Mn **c.** MnO_2 **d.** $MgCO_3$

Answer: **a.** Sn^{4+} (+4) **b.** Mn (0) **c.** MnO_2 (+4 −2) **d.** $MgCO_3$ (+2 +4 −2)

Using Oxidation Numbers (15.2)

- An atom is oxidized when its oxidation number increases from reactant to product.
- An atom is reduced when its oxidation number decreases from reactant to product.

Example: Assign oxidation numbers to each element and identify which is oxidized and which is reduced.

$$SnO_2(s) + 2H_2(g) \longrightarrow Sn(s) + 2H_2O(l)$$

Answer:
$$\underset{+4\,-2}{SnO_2}(s) + 2\underset{0}{H_2}(g) \longrightarrow \underset{0}{Sn}(s) + 2\underset{+1\,-2}{H_2O}(l)$$

$Sn(+4) \longrightarrow Sn(0)$ Sn is reduced.

$H(0) \longrightarrow H(+1)$ H is oxidized.

Identifying Oxidizing and Reducing Agents (15.2)

- In an oxidation–reduction reaction, the substance that is oxidized is the reducing agent.
- In an oxidation–reduction reaction, the substance that is reduced is the oxidizing agent.

Example: Identify the oxidizing agent and the reducing agent in the following:

$$SnO_2(s) + 2H_2(g) \longrightarrow Sn(s) + 2H_2O(l)$$

Answer: Oxidation numbers are assigned to identify the substance that is oxidized as the reducing agent and the substance that is reduced as the oxidizing agent.

$$\underset{+4\,-2}{SnO_2}(s) + 2\underset{0}{H_2}(g) \longrightarrow \underset{0}{Sn}(s) + 2\underset{+1\,-2}{H_2O}(l)$$

$Sn(+4) \longrightarrow Sn(0)$
Sn is reduced; SnO_2 is the oxidizing agent.

$H(0) \longrightarrow H(+1)$
H is oxidized; H_2 is the reducing agent.

Using Half-Reactions to Balance Redox Equations (15.3)

- The half-reaction method for balancing equations involves
  (1) separating the oxidation–reduction reaction into two *half-reactions*
  (2) balancing the elements in each except H and O; then balancing O with H_2O and H with H^+
  (3) balancing charge by adding electrons
  (4) multiplying each half-reaction by factors that equalize the loss and gain of electrons
  (5) combining half-reactions and cancelling electrons, and identical ions or molecules

Example: Use the half-reaction method to balance the following oxidation–reduction equation:

$$NO_3^-(aq) + Sn^{2+}(aq) \longrightarrow NO(g) + Sn^{4+}(aq)$$

Answer:

(1) $NO_3^-(aq) \longrightarrow NO(g)$
$Sn^{2+}(aq) \longrightarrow Sn^{4+}(aq)$

(2) $4H^+(aq) + NO_3^-(aq) \longrightarrow NO(g) + 2H_2O(l)$
$Sn^{2+}(aq) \longrightarrow Sn^{4+}(aq)$

(3) $\mathbf{3\,e^-} + 4H^+(aq) + NO_3^-(aq) \longrightarrow NO(g) + 2H_2O(l)$
$Sn^{2+}(aq) \longrightarrow Sn^{4+}(aq) + \mathbf{2\,e^-}$

(4) $\mathbf{2} \times [\mathbf{3\,e^-} + 4H^+(aq) + NO_3^-(aq) \longrightarrow NO(g) + 2H_2O(l)]$
$\mathbf{6\,e^-} + 8H^+(aq) + 2NO_3^-(aq) \longrightarrow 2NO(g) + 4H_2O(l)$
$\mathbf{3} \times [Sn^{2+}(aq) \longrightarrow Sn^{4+}(aq) + \mathbf{2\,e^-}]$
$3Sn^{2+}(aq) \longrightarrow 3Sn^{4+}(aq) + \mathbf{6\,e^-}$

(5) $8H^+(aq) + 2NO_3^-(aq) + 3Sn^{2+}(aq) \longrightarrow 2NO(g) + 3Sn^{4+}(aq) + 4H_2O(l)$

Identifying Spontaneous Reactions (15.4)

- The activity series in Table 15.3 places the metals that are easily oxidized at the top, and the metals that do not oxidize easily at the bottom.
- A metal will oxidize spontaneously when it is combined with the reverse of the half-reaction of any metal below it on the activity series in Table 15.3.

Example: Write a balanced redox equation for the spontaneous reaction for the following half-reactions on the activity series:

$Ca(s) \longrightarrow Ca^{2+}(aq) + 2\,e^-$
$Ni(s) \longrightarrow Ni^{2+}(aq) + 2\,e^-$

Answer: The spontaneous reaction is a combination of the oxidation half-reaction higher on the activity series with the reverse of the half-reaction below it.

$Ca(s) \longrightarrow Ca^{2+}(aq) + 2\,e^-$ Oxidation
$Ni^{2+}(aq) + 2\,e^- \longrightarrow Ni(s)$ Reduction
$Ca(s) + Ni^{2+}(aq) \longrightarrow Ca^{2+}(aq) + Ni(s)$ Spontaneous reaction

UNDERSTANDING THE CONCEPTS

The chapter sections to review are shown in parentheses at the end of each question.

15.45 Classify each of the following as oxidation or reduction: (15.1, 15.2)

a. Electrons are lost.
b. Reaction of an oxidizing agent.
c. $O_2(g) \longrightarrow OH^-(aq)$
d. $Br_2(l) \longrightarrow 2Br^-(aq)$
e. $Sn^{2+}(aq) \longrightarrow Sn^{4+}(aq)$

15.46 Classify each of the following as oxidation or reduction: (15.1, 15.2)

a. Electrons are gained.
b. Reaction of a reducing agent.
c. $Ni(s) \longrightarrow Ni^{2+}(aq)$
d. $MnO_4^-(aq) \longrightarrow MnO_2(s)$
e. $Sn^{4+}(aq) \longrightarrow Sn^{2+}(aq)$

15.47 Assign oxidation numbers to the elements in each of the following: (15.2)

a. VO_2 **b.** Ag_2CrO_4
c. $S_2O_8^{2-}$ **d.** $FeSO_4$

15.48 Assign oxidation numbers to the elements in each of the following: (15.2)

a. $NbCl_3$ **b.** NbO
c. NbO_2 **d.** Nb_2O_5

15.49 Which of the following are oxidation–reduction reactions? (15.2)

a. $Ca(s) + 2H_2O(l) \longrightarrow Ca(OH)_2(aq) + H_2(g)$
b. $CaCO_3(s) \longrightarrow CaO(s) + CO_2(g)$
c. $4Al(s) + 3O_2(g) \longrightarrow 2Al_2O_3(s)$

15.50 Which of the following are oxidation–reduction reactions? (15.2)

a. $BaCl_2(aq) + Na_2SO_4(aq) \longrightarrow BaSO_4(s) + 2NaCl(aq)$
b. $Cl_2(g) + 2NaBr(aq) \longrightarrow Br_2(l) + 2NaCl(aq)$
c. $2KClO_3(s) \longrightarrow 2KCl(s) + 3O_2(g)$

15.51 For this reaction, identify each of the following: (15.2)

$$2Cr_2O_3(s) + 3Si(s) \longrightarrow 4Cr(s) + 3SiO_2(s)$$

a. the substance reduced
b. the substance oxidized
c. the oxidizing agent
d. the reducing agent

Chromium(III) oxide and silicon undergo an oxidation–reduction reaction.

15.52 For this reaction, identify each of the following: (15.2)

$$C_2H_4(g) + 3O_2(g) \xrightarrow{\Delta} 2CO_2(g) + 2H_2O(g)$$

a. the substance reduced
b. the substance oxidized
c. the oxidizing agent
d. the reducing agent

15.53 Balance each of the following half-reactions in acidic solution: (15.3)

a. $Zn(s) \longrightarrow Zn^{2+}(aq)$
b. $SnO_2^{2-}(aq) \longrightarrow SnO_3^{2-}(aq)$
c. $SO_3^{2-}(aq) \longrightarrow SO_4^{2-}(aq)$
d. $NO_3^-(aq) \longrightarrow NO(g)$

15.54 Balance each of the following half-reactions in acidic solution: (15.3)

a. $I_2(s) \longrightarrow I^-(aq)$
b. $MnO_4^-(aq) \longrightarrow Mn^{2+}(aq)$
c. $Br_2(l) \longrightarrow BrO_3^-(aq)$
d. $ClO_3^-(aq) \longrightarrow ClO_4^-(aq)$

15.55 Consider the following voltaic cell: (15.4)

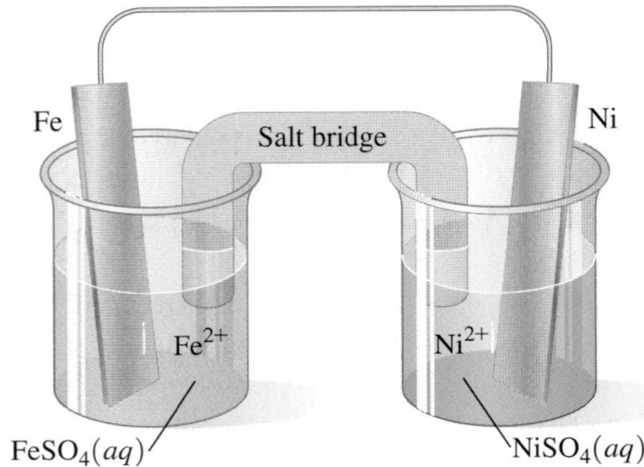

a. What is the oxidation half-reaction?
b. What is the reduction half-reaction?
c. What metal is the anode?
d. What metal is the cathode?
e. What is the direction of electron flow?
f. What is the overall reaction that takes place?
g. Write the shorthand cell notation.

15.56 Consider the following voltaic cell: (15.4)

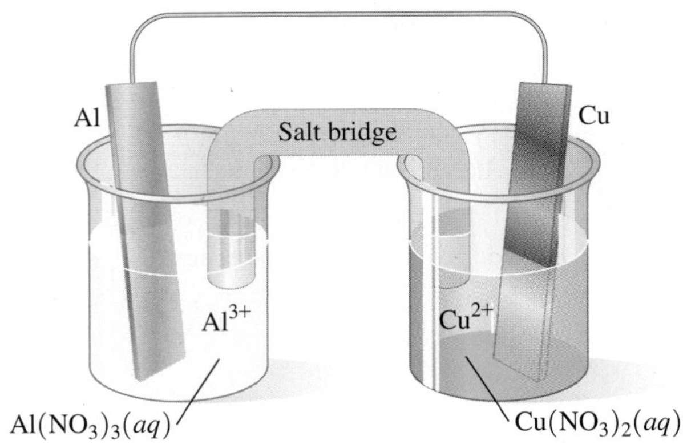

a. What is the oxidation half-reaction?
b. What is the reduction half-reaction?
c. What metal is the anode?
d. What metal is the cathode?
e. What is the direction of electron flow?
f. What is the overall reaction that takes place?
g. Write the shorthand cell notation.

15.57 Classify each of the following as a primary, secondary, or tertiary alcohol: (15.6)

a. $CH_3-CH(CH_3)-CH_2-OH$

b. $CH_3-C(CH_3)_2-CH_2-CH(OH)-CH_3$

c. CH_3-OH

15.58 Classify each of the following as a primary, secondary, or tertiary alcohol: (15.6)

a. $CH_3-CH(CH_2-OH)-CH_2-CH_3$

b. $CH_3-C(OH)(CH_3)-CH_2-CH(CH_3)-CH_3$

c. CH_3-CH_2-OH

15.59 Draw the condensed structural formula for the aldehyde or ketone product of each of the following reactions: (15.6)

a. $CH_3-CH(CH_3)-CH_2-OH \xrightarrow{[O]}$

b. $CH_3-CH_2-CH(OH)-CH_3 \xrightarrow{[O]}$

15.60 Draw the condensed structural formula for the aldehyde or ketone product of each of the following reactions: (15.6)

a. $CH_3-CH(CH_3)-CH(OH)-CH_3 \xrightarrow{[O]}$

b. $CH_3-CH_2-CH_2-CH(OH)-CH_3 \xrightarrow{[O]}$

ADDITIONAL QUESTIONS AND PROBLEMS

15.61 Which of the following are oxidation–reduction reactions? (15.1, 15.2)
a. $AgNO_3(aq) + NaCl(aq) \longrightarrow AgCl(s) + NaNO_3(aq)$
b. $6Li(s) + N_2(g) \longrightarrow 2Li_3N(s)$
c. $Ni(s) + Pb(NO_3)_2(aq) \longrightarrow Ni(NO_3)_2(aq) + Pb(s)$
d. $2K(s) + 2H_2O(l) \longrightarrow 2KOH(aq) + H_2(g)$

15.62 Which of the following are oxidation–reduction reactions? (15.1, 15.2)
a. $Ca(s) + F_2(g) \longrightarrow CaF_2(s)$
b. $Fe(s) + 2HCl(aq) \longrightarrow FeCl_2(aq) + H_2(g)$
c. $2NaCl(aq) + Pb(NO_3)_2(aq) \longrightarrow PbCl_2(s) + 2NaNO_3(aq)$
d. $2CuCl(aq) \longrightarrow Cu(s) + CuCl_2(aq)$

15.63 In the mitochondria of human cells, energy is provided by the oxidation and reduction of the iron ions in the cytochromes. Identify each of the following reactions as an oxidation or reduction: (15.1, 15.2)
a. $Fe^{3+} + e^- \longrightarrow Fe^{2+}$　**b.** $Fe^{2+} \longrightarrow Fe^{3+} + e^-$

15.64 Chlorine (Cl_2) is used as a germicide to kill microbes in swimming pools. If the product is Cl^-, was the elemental chlorine oxidized or reduced? (15.1, 15.2)

15.65 Assign oxidation numbers to all the elements in each of the following: (15.2)
a. Co_2O_3　**b.** $KMnO_4$
c. $SbCl_5$　**d.** ClO_3^-
e. PO_4^{3-}

15.66 Assign oxidation numbers to all the elements in each of the following: (15.2)
a. PO_3^{2-}　**b.** NH_4^+
c. $Fe(OH)_2$　**d.** HNO_3
e. H_2CO

15.67 Assign oxidation numbers to all the elements in each of the following reactions, and identify the reactant that is oxidized, the reactant that is reduced, the oxidizing agent, and the reducing agent: (15.2)
a. $2FeCl_2(aq) + Cl_2(g) \longrightarrow 2FeCl_3(aq)$
b. $2H_2S(g) + 3O_2(g) \longrightarrow 2H_2O(l) + 2SO_2(g)$
c. $P_2O_5(s) + 5C(s) \longrightarrow 2P(s) + 5CO(g)$

15.68 Assign oxidation numbers to all the elements in each of the following reactions, and identify the reactant that is oxidized, the reactant that is reduced, the oxidizing agent, and the reducing agent: (15.2)
a. $4Al(s) + 3O_2(g) \longrightarrow 2Al_2O_3(s)$
b. $I_2O_5(s) + 5CO(g) \longrightarrow I_2(g) + 5CO_2(g)$
c. $2Cr_2O_3(s) + 3C(s) \longrightarrow 4Cr(s) + 3CO_2(g)$

15.69 Write the balanced half-reactions and a balanced redox equation for each of the following reactions in acidic solution: (15.3)
a. $Zn(s) + NO_3^-(aq) \longrightarrow Zn^{2+}(aq) + NO_2(g)$
b. $MnO_4^-(aq) + SO_3^{2-}(aq) \longrightarrow Mn^{2+}(aq) + SO_4^{2-}(aq)$
c. $ClO_3^-(aq) + I^-(aq) \longrightarrow Cl^-(aq) + I_2(s)$
d. $Cr_2O_7^{2-}(aq) + C_2O_4^{2-}(aq) \longrightarrow Cr^{3+}(aq) + CO_2(g)$

15.70 Write the balanced half-reactions and a balanced redox equation for each of the following reactions in acidic solution: (15.3)
a. $Sn^{2+}(aq) + IO_4^-(aq) \longrightarrow Sn^{4+}(aq) + I^-(aq)$
b. $S_2O_3^{2-}(aq) + I_2(s) \longrightarrow S_4O_6^{2-}(aq) + I^-(aq)$
c. $Mg(s) + VO_4^{3-}(aq) \longrightarrow Mg^{2+}(aq) + V^{2+}(aq)$
d. $Al(s) + Cr_2O_7^{2-}(aq) \longrightarrow Al^{3+}(aq) + Cr^{3+}(aq)$

15.71 Use the activity series in Table 15.3 to predict whether each of the following reactions will occur spontaneously: (15.4)
a. $2Cr(s) + 3Ni^{2+}(aq) \longrightarrow 2Cr^{3+}(aq) + 3Ni(s)$
b. $Cu(s) + Zn^{2+}(aq) \longrightarrow Cu^{2+}(aq) + Zn(s)$
c. $Zn(s) + Pb^{2+}(aq) \longrightarrow Zn^{2+}(aq) + Pb(s)$

15.72 Use the activity series in Table 15.3 to predict whether each of the following reactions will occur spontaneously: (15.4)
a. $Zn(s) + Mg^{2+}(aq) \longrightarrow Zn^{2+}(aq) + Mg(s)$
b. $3Na(s) + Al^{3+}(aq) \longrightarrow 3Na^+(aq) + Al(s)$
c. $Mg(s) + Ni^{2+}(aq) \longrightarrow Mg^{2+}(aq) + Ni(s)$

15.73 In a voltaic cell, one half-cell consists of nickel metal in a Ni^{2+} solution, and the other half-cell consists of magnesium metal in a Mg^{2+} solution. Identify each of the following: (15.4)

a. the anode
b. the cathode
c. the half-reaction at the anode
d. the half-reaction at the cathode
e. the overall reaction
f. the shorthand cell notation

15.74 In a voltaic cell, one half-cell consists of a zinc metal in a Zn^{2+} solution, and the other half-cell consists of a copper metal in a Cu^{2+} solution. Identify each of the following: (15.4)

a. the anode
b. the cathode
c. the half-reaction at the anode
d. the half-reaction at the cathode
e. the overall reaction
f. the shorthand cell notation

15.75 Use the activity series in Table 15.3 to determine which of the following ions will be reduced when an iron strip is placed in an aqueous solution of that ion: (15.4)

a. $Ca^{2+}(aq)$
b. $Ag^{+}(aq)$
c. $Ni^{2+}(aq)$
d. $Al^{3+}(aq)$
e. $Pb^{2+}(aq)$

15.76 Use the activity series in Table 15.3 to determine which of the following ions will be reduced when an aluminum strip is placed in an aqueous solution of that ion: (15.4)

a. $Fe^{2+}(aq)$
b. $Au^{3+}(aq)$
c. $Mg^{2+}(aq)$
d. $H^{+}(aq)$
e. $Pb^{2+}(aq)$

15.77 In a lead storage battery, the following unbalanced half-reaction takes place: (15.4)

$$Pb(s) + SO_4^{2-}(aq) \longrightarrow PbSO_4(s)$$

a. Balance the half-reaction.
b. Is $Pb(s)$ oxidized or reduced?
c. Indicate whether the half-reaction takes place at the anode or cathode.

15.78 In an acidic dry-cell battery, the following unbalanced half-reaction takes place in acidic solution: (15.4)

$$MnO_2(s) \longrightarrow Mn_2O_3(s)$$

a. Balance the half-reaction.
b. Is $MnO_2(s)$ oxidized or reduced?
c. Indicate whether the half-reaction takes place at the anode or cathode.

15.79 Steel bolts made for sailboats are coated with zinc. Add the necessary components (electrodes, wires, batteries) to this diagram of an electrolytic cell with a zinc nitrate solution to show how it could be used to zinc plate a steel bolt. (15.4, 15.5)

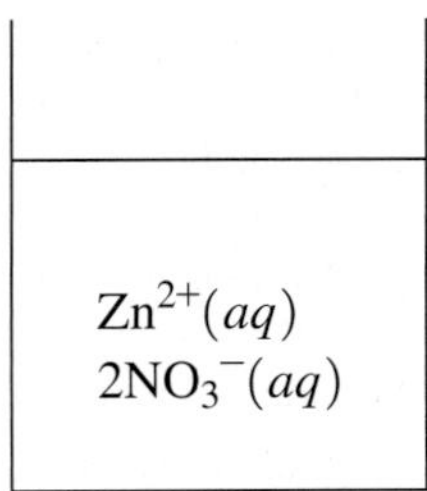

a. What is the anode?
b. What is the cathode?
c. What is the half-reaction that takes place at the anode?
d. What is the half-reaction that takes place at the cathode?
e. If steel is mostly iron, what is the purpose of the zinc coating?

15.80 Copper cooking pans are stainless steel pans plated with a layer of copper. Add the necessary components (electrodes, wires, batteries) to this diagram of an electrolytic cell with a copper(II) nitrate solution to show how it could be used to copper plate a stainless steel (iron) pan. (15.4, 15.5)

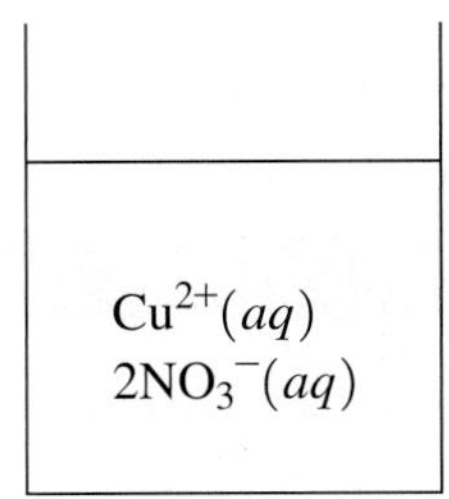

a. What is the anode?
b. What is the cathode?
c. What is the half-reaction that takes place at the anode?
d. What is the half-reaction that takes place at the cathode?

15.81 Draw the condensed structural formula for the aldehyde or ketone formed when each of the following is oxidized: (15.6)

a. $CH_3—CH_2—CH_2—OH$

b. $CH_3—CH(OH)—CH_2—CH_2—CH_3$ (OH on the second carbon)

c. $CH_3—CH_2—CH_2—CH_2—OH$

15.82 Draw the condensed structural formula for the aldehyde or ketone formed when each of the following is oxidized: (15.6)

a. $CH_3—CH_2—CH(OH)—CH_2—OH$ (OH on the third carbon)

b. $CH_3—CH(OH)—CH_3$ (OH on the central carbon)

c. $CH_3—CH(CH_3)—CH_2—CH_2—OH$ (CH_3 on the second carbon)

CHALLENGE QUESTIONS

15.83 Determine the oxidation number of Br in each of the following: (15.2)

a. Br_2
b. $HBrO_2$
c. BrO_3^{-}
d. $NaBrO_4$

15.84 Determine the oxidation number of Cr in each of the following: (15.2)

a. CrO
b. $HCrO_4^{-}$
c. CrO_3^{-}
d. CrF_4

15.85 Use half-reactions to balance the following equation in acidic solution: (15.3)

$$Cr_2O_7^{2-}(aq) + NO_2^-(aq) \longrightarrow Cr^{3+}(aq) + NO_3^-(aq)$$

15.86 Use half-reactions to balance the following equation in acidic solution: (15.3)

$$Mn(s) + Cr^{3+}(aq) \longrightarrow Mn^{2+}(aq) + Cr(s)$$

15.87 The following unbalanced reaction takes place in acidic solution: (11.7, 11.9, 12.6, 15.3)

$$Ag(s) + NO_3^-(aq) \longrightarrow Ag^+(aq) + NO(g)$$

a. Write the balanced equation.
b. How many liters of $NO(g)$ are produced at STP when 15.0 g of silver reacts with excess nitric acid?

15.88 The following unbalanced reaction takes place in acidic solution: (12.6, 15.3)

$$MnO_4^-(aq) + Fe^{2+}(aq) \longrightarrow Mn^{2+}(aq) + Fe^{3+}(aq)$$

a. Write the balanced equation.
b. How many milliliters of a 0.150 M $KMnO_4$ solution are needed to react with 25.0 mL of a 0.400 M $FeSO_4$ solution?

15.89 A concentrated nitric acid solution is used to dissolve copper(II) sulfide. (12.6, 15.3)

$$CuS(s) + HNO_3(aq) \longrightarrow CuSO_4(aq) + NO(g) + H_2O(l)$$

a. Write the balanced equation.
b. How many milliliters of a 16.0 M HNO_3 solution are needed to dissolve 24.8 g of CuS?

15.90 The following unbalanced reaction takes place in acidic solution: (12.6, 15.3)

$$Cr_2O_7^{2-}(aq) + Fe^{2+}(aq) \longrightarrow Cr^{3+}(aq) + Fe^{3+}(aq)$$

a. Write the balanced equation.
b. How many milliliters of a 0.211 M $K_2Cr_2O_7$ solution are needed to react with 5.00 g of $FeSO_4$?

15.91 Balance the equation for the reaction that takes place in basic solution. (15.3)

$$Br^-(aq) + MnO_4^-(aq) \longrightarrow BrO_3^-(aq) + MnO_2(s)$$

15.92 Balance the equation for the reaction that takes place in basic solution. (15.3)

$$CN^-(aq) + IO_3^-(aq) \longrightarrow CNO^-(aq) + I^-(aq)$$

15.93 Using the activity series in Table 15.3, indicate whether each of the following reactions is spontaneous: (15.4)
a. $Zn(s) + Ca^{2+}(aq) \longrightarrow Zn^{2+}(aq) + Ca(s)$
b. $2Al(s) + 3Sn^{2+}(aq) \longrightarrow 2Al^{3+}(aq) + 3Sn(s)$
c. $Mg(s) + 2H^+(aq) \longrightarrow Mg^{2+}(aq) + H_2(g)$

15.94 Using the activity series in Table 15.3, indicate whether each of the following reactions is spontaneous: (15.4)
a. $Cu(s) + Ni^{2+}(aq) \longrightarrow Cu^{2+}(aq) + Ni(s)$
b. $2Cr(s) + 3Fe^{2+}(aq) \longrightarrow 2Cr^{3+}(aq) + 3Fe(s)$
c. $Fe(s) + Mg^{2+}(aq) \longrightarrow Fe^{2+}(aq) + Mg(s)$

15.95 Draw a diagram of a voltaic cell for $Ni(s)\,|\,Ni^{2+}(aq)\,\|\,Ag^+(aq)\,|\,Ag(s)$. (15.4)
a. What is the anode?
b. What is the cathode?
c. What is the half-reaction that takes place at the anode?
d. What is the half-reaction that takes place at the cathode?
e. What is the overall reaction for the cell?

15.96 Draw a diagram of a voltaic cell for $Mg(s)\,|\,Mg^{2+}(aq)\,\|\,Al^{3+}(aq)\,|\,Al(s)$. (15.4)
a. What is the anode?
b. What is the cathode?
c. What is the half-reaction that takes place at the anode?
d. What is the half-reaction that takes place at the cathode?
e. What is the overall reaction for the cell?

ANSWERS

Answers to Study Checks

15.1 a. Because H has an oxidation number of +1, and O is −2, P will have an oxidation number of +5 to maintain a neutral charge.

H_3PO_4
+1+5−2

b. Because O has an oxidation number of −2, Mn must be +7 to give an overall charge of −1.

MnO_4^-
+7 −2

15.2 The oxidation number of Al increases from 0 to +3; Al is oxidized. The oxidation number of Sn^{2+} decreases from +2 to 0; Sn^{2+} is reduced.

15.3 $Zn(s) + 2Fe^{3+}(aq) \longrightarrow Zn^{2+}(aq) + 2Fe^{2+}(aq)$

15.4 $12H^+(aq) + 10Fe^{2+}(aq) + 2IO_3^-(aq) \longrightarrow 10Fe^{3+}(aq) + I_2(s) + 6H_2O(l)$

15.5 $N_2O(g) + 2ClO^-(aq) + 2OH^-(aq) \longrightarrow 2Cl^-(aq) + 2NO_2^-(aq) + H_2O(l)$

15.6 Anode reaction: $Co(s) \longrightarrow Co^{2+}(aq) + 2e^-$
Cathode reaction: $Cu^{2+}(aq) + 2e^- \longrightarrow Cu(s)$
Overall cell reaction: $Co(s) + Cu^{2+}(aq) \longrightarrow Co^{2+}(aq) + Cu(s)$

15.7 Since Fe is below Cr in the activity series, the plating of Cr^{3+} onto Fe is not spontaneous. Energy is needed to make the reaction proceed.

15.8
```
       CH3  CH3         O
       |    |           ||
CH3 — CH — CH — CH2 — C — H
```

Answers to Selected Questions and Problems

15.1 a. Na^+ gains electrons; this is a reduction.
b. Ni loses electrons; this is an oxidation.
c. Cr^{3+} gains electrons; this is a reduction.
d. H^+ gains electrons; this is a reduction.

15.3 a. Zn loses electrons and is oxidized. Cl_2 gains electrons and is reduced.
b. Br^- (in NaBr) loses electrons and is oxidized. Cl_2 gains electrons and is reduced.
c. Pb loses electrons and is oxidized. O_2 gains electrons and is reduced.
d. Sn^{2+} loses electrons and is oxidized. Fe^{3+} gains electrons and is reduced.

15.5 a. 0 **b.** 0 **c.** +2 **d.** −1

15.7 a. K is +1, Cl is −1. **b.** Mn is +4, O is −2.
c. N is +2, O is −2. **d.** Mn is +3, O is −2.

15.9 a. Li is +1, P is +5, and O is −2.
b. S is +4, O is −2.
c. Cr is +3, S is −2.
d. N is +5, O is −2.

15.11 a. H is +1, S is +6, and O is −2.
b. H is +1, P is +3, and O is −2.
c. Cr is +6, O is −2.
d. Na is +1, C is +4, and O is −2.

15.13 a. +5 **b.** −2 **c.** +5 **d.** +6

15.15 a. The substance that is oxidized is the reducing agent.
b. The substance that gains electrons is reduced and is the oxidizing agent.

15.17 a. Li is oxidized; Li is the reducing agent. Cl (in Cl_2) is reduced; Cl_2 is the oxidizing agent.
b. Br^- (in NaBr) is oxidized; NaBr is the reducing agent. Cl (in Cl_2) is reduced; Cl_2 is the oxidizing agent.
c. Pb is oxidized; Pb is the reducing agent. O (in O_2) is reduced; O_2 is the oxidizing agent.
d. Al is oxidized; Al is the reducing agent. Ag^+ is reduced; Ag^+ is the oxidizing agent.

15.19 a. S^{2-} (in NiS) is oxidized; NiS is the reducing agent. O (in O_2) is reduced; O_2 is the oxidizing agent.
b. Sn^{2+} is oxidized; Sn^{2+} is the reducing agent. Fe^{3+} is reduced; Fe^{3+} is the oxidizing agent.
c. C (in CH_4) is oxidized; CH_4 is the reducing agent. O (in O_2) is reduced; O_2 is the oxidizing agent.
d. Si is oxidized; Si is the reducing agent. Cr^{3+} (in Cr_2O_3) is reduced; Cr_2O_3 is the oxidizing agent.

15.21 a. $Sn^{2+}(aq) \longrightarrow Sn^{4+}(aq) + 2\,e^-$
b. $Mn^{2+}(aq) + 4H_2O(l) \longrightarrow MnO_4^-(aq) + 8H^+(aq) + 5\,e^-$
c. $NO_2^-(aq) + H_2O(l) \longrightarrow NO_3^-(aq) + 2H^+(aq) + 2\,e^-$
d. $e^- + 2H^+(aq) + ClO_3^-(aq) \longrightarrow ClO_2(aq) + H_2O(l)$

15.23 a. $2H^+(aq) + Ag(s) + NO_3^-(aq) \longrightarrow Ag^+(aq) + NO_2(g) + H_2O(l)$
b. $4H^+(aq) + 4NO_3^-(aq) + 3S(s) \longrightarrow 4NO(g) + 3SO_2(g) + 2H_2O(l)$
c. $2S_2O_3^{2-}(aq) + Cu^{2+}(aq) \longrightarrow S_4O_6^{2-}(aq) + Cu(s)$

15.25 a. $2Fe(s) + 2CrO_4^{2-}(aq) + 2H_2O(l) \longrightarrow Fe_2O_3(s) + Cr_2O_3(s) + 4OH^-(aq)$
b. $3CN^-(aq) + 2MnO_4^-(aq) + H_2O(l) \longrightarrow 3CNO^-(aq) + 2MnO_2(s) + 2OH^-(aq)$

15.27 a. Since Au is below H_2 in the activity series, the reaction will not be spontaneous.
b. Since Fe is above Ni in the activity series, the reaction will be spontaneous.
c. Since Ag is below Cu in the activity series, the reaction will not be spontaneous.

15.29 a. Anode reaction: $Pb(s) \longrightarrow Pb^{2+}(aq) + 2\,e^-$
Cathode reaction: $Cu^{2+}(aq) + 2\,e^- \longrightarrow Cu(s)$
Overall cell reaction: $Pb(s) + Cu^{2+}(aq) \longrightarrow Pb^{2+}(aq) + Cu(s)$
b. Anode reaction: $Cr(s) \longrightarrow Cr^{2+}(aq) + 2\,e^-$
Cathode reaction: $Ag^+(aq) + e^- \longrightarrow Ag(s)$
Overall cell reaction: $Cr(s) + 2Ag^+(aq) \longrightarrow Cr^{2+}(aq) + 2Ag(s)$

15.31 a. The anode is a Cd metal electrode in a Cd^{2+} solution. The anode reaction is

$$Cd(s) \longrightarrow Cd^{2+}(aq) + 2\,e^-$$

The cathode is a Sn metal electrode in a Sn^{2+} solution. The cathode reaction is

$$Sn^{2+}(aq) + 2\,e^- \longrightarrow Sn(s)$$

The shorthand notation for this cell is

$$Cd(s)\,|\,Cd^{2+}(aq)\,\|\,Sn^{2+}(aq)\,|\,Sn(s)$$

b. The anode is a Zn metal electrode in a Zn^{2+} solution. The anode reaction is

$$Zn(s) \longrightarrow Zn^{2+}(aq) + 2\,e^-$$

The cathode is a C (graphite) electrode, where Cl_2 gas is reduced to Cl^-. The cathode reaction is

$$Cl_2(g) + 2\,e^- \longrightarrow 2Cl^-(aq)$$

The shorthand notation for this cell is

$$Zn(s)\,|\,Zn^{2+}(aq)\,\|\,Cl_2(g), Cl^-(aq)\,|\,C\ (graphite)$$

15.33 a. The half-reaction is an oxidation.
b. Cd metal is oxidized.
c. Oxidation takes place at the anode.

15.35 a. The half-reaction is an oxidation.
b. Zn metal is oxidized.
c. Oxidation takes place at the anode.

15.37 a. $Sn^{2+}(aq) + 2\,e^- \longrightarrow Sn(s)$
b. The reduction of Sn^{2+} to Sn occurs at the cathode, which is the iron can.
c. The oxidation of Sn to Sn^{2+} occurs at the anode, which is the tin bar.

15.39 Since Fe is above Sn in the activity series, if the Fe is exposed to air and water, Fe will be oxidized and rust will form. To protect iron, Sn would have to be more active than Fe and it is not.

15.41 a. primary **b.** primary **c.** tertiary

15.43 a. $CH_3-CH_2-CH_2-CH_2-\overset{\overset{\displaystyle O}{\|}}{C}-H$
b. none
c. $CH_3-\overset{\overset{\displaystyle O}{\|}}{C}-CH_2-\overset{\overset{\displaystyle CH_3}{|}}{CH}-CH_3$

15.45 a. oxidation **b.** reduction
c. reduction **d.** reduction
e. oxidation

15.47 a. V = +4, O = −2
b. Ag = +1, Cr = +6, O = −2
c. S = +7, O = −2
d. Fe = +2, S = +6, O = −2

15.49 Reactions **a** and **c** involve loss and gain of electrons; **a** and **c** are oxidation–reduction reactions.

15.51 a. Cr in Cr_2O_3 is reduced.
b. Si is oxidized.
c. Cr_2O_3 is the oxidizing agent.
d. Si is the reducing agent.

15.53 a. $Zn(s) \longrightarrow Zn^{2+}(aq) + 2\,e^-$
b. $SnO_2^{2-}(aq) + H_2O(l) \longrightarrow SnO_3^{2-}(aq) + 2H^+(aq) + 2\,e^-$
c. $SO_3^{2-}(aq) + H_2O(l) \longrightarrow SO_4^{2-}(aq) + 2H^+(aq) + 2\,e^-$
d. $3\,e^- + 4H^+(aq) + NO_3^-(aq) \longrightarrow NO(g) + 2H_2O(l)$

15.55 a. $Fe(s) \longrightarrow Fe^{2+}(aq) + 2\,e^-$
b. $Ni^{2+}(aq) + 2\,e^- \longrightarrow Ni(s)$
c. Fe is the anode.
d. Ni is the cathode.
e. The electrons flow from Fe to Ni.
f. $Fe(s) + Ni^{2+}(aq) \longrightarrow Fe^{2+}(aq) + Ni(s)$
g. $Fe(s)\,|\,Fe^{2+}(aq)\,\|\,Ni^{2+}(aq)\,|\,Ni(s)$

15.57 a. primary **b.** secondary **c.** primary

15.59 a.
$$\begin{array}{c} \quad\;\; CH_3\;\; O \\ \quad\;\; |\quad\;\; \| \\ CH_3-CH-C-H \end{array}$$

b.
$$\begin{array}{c} \qquad\qquad O \\ \qquad\qquad \| \\ CH_3-CH_2-C-CH_3 \end{array}$$

15.61 Reactions **b**, **c**, and **d** all involve loss and gain of electrons; **b**, **c**, and **d** are oxidation–reduction reactions.

15.63 a. Fe^{3+} is gaining electrons; this is a reduction.
b. Fe^{2+} is losing electrons; this is an oxidation.

15.65 a. Co = +3, O = −2
b. K = +1, Mn = +7, O = −2
c. Sb = +5, Cl = −1
d. Cl = +5, O = −2
e. P = +5, O = −2

15.67 a. $\underset{+2\,-1}{2FeCl_2(aq)} + \underset{0}{Cl_2(g)} \longrightarrow \underset{+3\,-1}{2FeCl_3(aq)}$

Fe in $FeCl_2$ is oxidized; $FeCl_2$ is the reducing agent.
Cl in Cl_2 is reduced; Cl_2 is the oxidizing agent.

b. $\underset{+1\,-2}{2H_2S(g)} + \underset{0}{3O_2(g)} \longrightarrow \underset{+1\,-2}{2H_2O(l)} + \underset{+4\,-2}{2SO_2(g)}$

S in H_2S is oxidized; H_2S is the reducing agent.
O in O_2 is reduced; O_2 is the oxidizing agent.

c. $\underset{+5\,-2}{P_2O_5(s)} + \underset{0}{5C(s)} \longrightarrow \underset{0}{2P(s)} + \underset{+2\,-2}{5CO(g)}$

C is oxidized; C is the reducing agent.
P in P_2O_5 is reduced; P_2O_5 is the oxidizing agent.

15.69 a. $Zn(s) \longrightarrow Zn^{2+}(aq) + 2\,e^-$;
$e^- + 2H^+(aq) + NO_3^-(aq) \longrightarrow NO_2(g) + H_2O(l)$

Overall:

$4H^+(aq) + Zn(s) + 2NO_3^-(aq) \longrightarrow Zn^{2+}(aq) + 2NO_2(g) + 2H_2O(l)$

b. $5\,e^- + 8H^+(aq) + MnO_4^-(aq) \longrightarrow Mn^{2+}(aq) + 4H_2O(l)$;
$SO_3^{2-}(aq) + H_2O(l) \longrightarrow SO_4^{2-}(aq) + 2H^+(aq) + 2\,e^-$

Overall:

$6H^+(aq) + 2MnO_4^-(aq) + 5SO_3^{2-}(aq) \longrightarrow 2Mn^{2+}(aq) + 5SO_4^{2-}(aq) + 3H_2O(l)$

c. $2I^-(aq) \longrightarrow I_2(s) + 2\,e^-$;
$6\,e^- + 6H^+(aq) + ClO_3^-(aq) \longrightarrow Cl^-(aq) + 3H_2O(l)$

Overall:

$6H^+(aq) + ClO_3^-(aq) + 6I^-(aq) \longrightarrow Cl^-(aq) + 3I_2(s) + 3H_2O(l)$

d. $C_2O_4^{2-}(aq) \longrightarrow 2CO_2(g) + 2\,e^-$;
$6\,e^- + 14H^+(aq) + Cr_2O_7^{2-}(aq) \longrightarrow 2Cr^{3+}(aq) + 7H_2O(l)$

Overall:

$14H^+(aq) + Cr_2O_7^{2-}(aq) + 3C_2O_4^{2-}(aq) \longrightarrow 2Cr^{3+}(aq) + 6CO_2(g) + 7H_2O(l)$

15.71 a. Since Cr is above Ni in the activity series, the reaction will be spontaneous.
b. Since Cu is below Zn in the activity series, the reaction will not be spontaneous.
c. Since Zn is above Pb in the activity series, the reaction will be spontaneous.

15.73 a. The anode is Mg.
b. The cathode is Ni.
c. The half-reaction at the anode is

$Mg(s) \longrightarrow Mg^{2+}(aq) + 2\,e^-$

d. The half-reaction at the cathode is

$Ni^{2+}(aq) + 2\,e^- \longrightarrow Ni(s)$

e. The overall reaction is

$Mg(s) + Ni^{2+}(aq) \longrightarrow Mg^{2+}(aq) + Ni(s)$

f. The shorthand cell notation is

$Mg(s)\,|\,Mg^{2+}(aq)\,\|\,Ni^{2+}(aq)\,|\,Ni(s)$

15.75 a. $Ca^{2+}(aq)$ will not be reduced by an iron strip.
b. $Ag^+(aq)$ will be reduced by an iron strip.
c. $Ni^{2+}(aq)$ will be reduced by an iron strip.
d. $Al^{3+}(aq)$ will not be reduced by an iron strip.
e. $Pb^{2+}(aq)$ will be reduced by an iron strip.

15.77 a. $Pb(s) + SO_4^{2-}(aq) \longrightarrow PbSO_4(s) + 2\,e^-$
b. $Pb(s)$ is oxidized.
c. The half-reaction takes place at the anode.

15.79

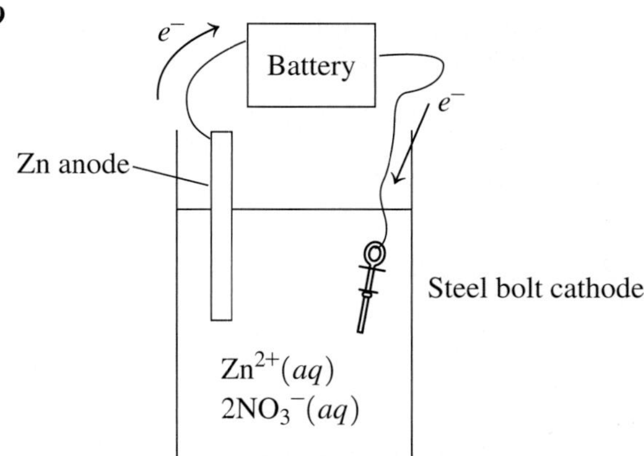

a. The anode is a bar of zinc.
b. The cathode is the steel bolt.
c. The half-reaction at the anode is
$Zn(s) \longrightarrow Zn^{2+}(aq) + 2\,e^-$
d. The half-reaction at the cathode is
$Zn^{2+}(aq) + 2\,e^- \longrightarrow Zn(s)$
e. The purpose of the zinc coating is to prevent rusting of the bolt by H_2O and O_2.

15.81 a. $CH_3-CH_2-\overset{\overset{\displaystyle O}{\|}}{C}-H$

b. $CH_3-\overset{\overset{\displaystyle O}{\|}}{C}-CH_2-CH_2-CH_3$

c. $CH_3-CH_2-CH_2-\overset{\overset{\displaystyle O}{\|}}{C}-H$

15.83 a. 0 **b.** +3 **c.** +5 **d.** +7

15.85 $8H^+(aq) + Cr_2O_7^{2-}(aq) + 3NO_2^-(aq) \longrightarrow 2Cr^{3+}(aq) + 3NO_3^-(aq) + 4H_2O(l)$

15.87 a. $4H^+(aq) + 3Ag(s) + NO_3^-(aq) \longrightarrow 3Ag^+(aq) + NO(g) + 2H_2O(l)$

b. 1.04 L of $NO(g)$ are produced at STP.

15.89 a. $3CuS(s) + 8HNO_3(aq) \longrightarrow 3CuSO_4(aq) + 8NO(g) + 4H_2O(l)$

b. 43.2 mL of HNO_3 solution

15.91 $H_2O(l) + Br^-(aq) + 2MnO_4^-(aq) \longrightarrow BrO_3^-(aq) + 2MnO_2(s) + 2OH^-(aq)$

15.93 a. Since Zn is below Ca in the activity series, the reaction will not be spontaneous.

b. Since Al is above Sn in the activity series, the reaction will be spontaneous.

c. Since Mg is above H_2 in the activity series, the reaction will be spontaneous.

15.95

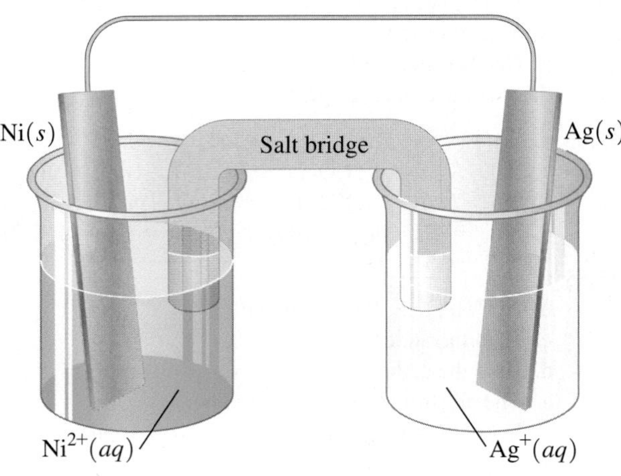

a. $Ni(s)$ is the anode.

b. $Ag(s)$ is the cathode.

c. The half-reaction at the anode is
$Ni(s) \longrightarrow Ni^{2+}(aq) + 2\,e^-$

d. The half-reaction at the cathode is
$Ag^+(aq) + e^- \longrightarrow Ag(s)$

e. The overall cell reaction is
$Ni(s) + 2Ag^+(aq) \longrightarrow Ni^{2+}(aq) + 2Ag(s)$

Nuclear Chemistry 16

LOOKING AHEAD

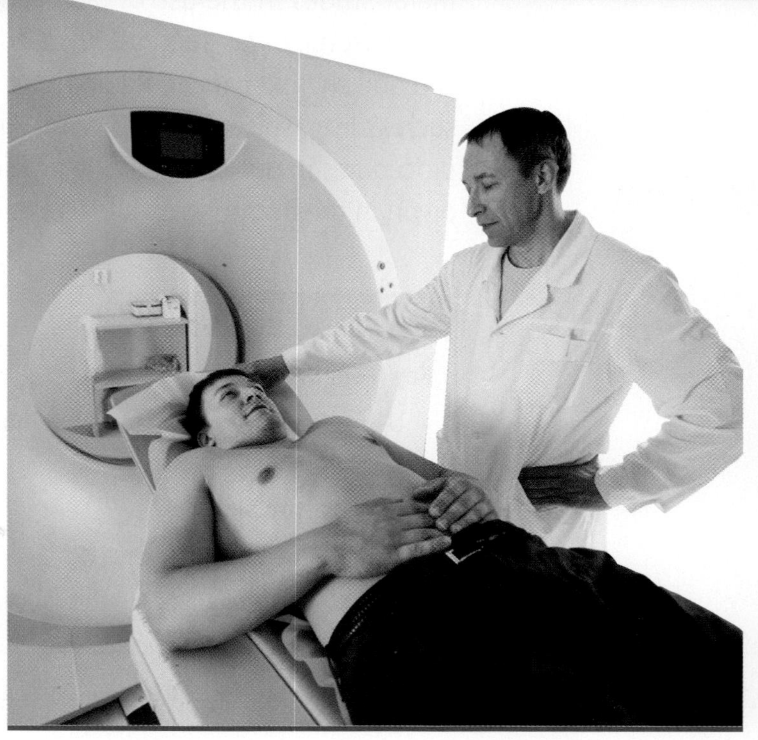

Luke has been experiencing weight loss, loss of appetite, vomiting, and some abdominal pain. Luke visits his doctor, who suspects a problem with his liver. The doctor orders blood work to be completed, and also refers Luke to a radiologist for a CT scan. Computed tomography, more commonly known as CT, uses X-rays to obtain a series of two-dimensional images and is commonly used for the diagnosis of abdominal diseases.

Dr. Berns, a radiologist, begins by explaining the procedure for the CT scan to Luke and asking him if he has any allergies. Luke indicates that he has none, and Dr. Berns places an IV in Luke's arm. Dr. Berns then positions Luke into the scanner, and an initial scan of Luke's liver is taken. Dr. Berns then injects the first dose of contrast into Luke's bloodstream and a contrast scan is taken. From the CT scans, it is clear that a change in the liver tissue has occurred, possibly due to hepatitis or an infection.

The liver has many functions and is critical to metabolism. The liver produces bile, consisting of bile salts and other chemicals, which is required for the digestion of lipids. The liver is also responsible for the conversion of waste products from protein metabolism into urea, which is eliminated in the urine.

Career: Radiologist

Radiologists specialize in the use of imaging techniques to diagnose and treat medical problems. They utilize techniques such as computed tomography (CT), magnetic resonance imaging (MRI), and positron emission tomography (PET). A radiologist may use CT, MRI, or a radioactive isotope to determine the size and location of a tumor within the body. Radiologists prepare a patient by explaining the procedure and properly positioning the patient within the scanning apparatus. A patient may be given radioactive tracers such as technetium-99m, iodine-131, gallium-67, and thallium-201 that emit gamma radiation, which is detected and used to develop an image of the kidneys or thyroid or to follow the blood flow in the heart muscle. Radiologists must be knowledgeable about radiation exposure to limit the amount of radiation to which patients are exposed.

With the production of artificial radioactive substances in 1934, the field of nuclear medicine was established. In 1937, the first radioactive isotope was used to treat a person with leukemia at the University of California at Berkeley. Major strides in the use of radioactivity in medicine occurred in 1946, when a radioactive iodine isotope was successfully used to diagnose thyroid function and to treat hyperthyroidism and thyroid cancer. Radioactive substances are now used to produce images of organs, such as liver, spleen, thyroid gland, kidneys, and the brain, and to detect heart disease. Today, procedures in nuclear medicine provide information about the function and structure of every organ in the body, which allows the nuclear physician to diagnose and treat diseases early.

CHAPTER READINESS*

Key Math Skills

- Using Positive and Negative Numbers in Calculations (1.4B)
- Solving Equations (1.4D)
- Interpreting a Line Graph (1.4E)

Core Chemistry Skills

- Using Conversion Factors (2.7)
- Counting Protons and Neutrons (4.4)
- Writing Atomic Symbols for Isotopes (4.5)
- Balancing a Chemical Equation (8.2)

*These Key Math Skills and Core Chemistry Skills from previous chapters are listed here for your review as you proceed to the new material in this chapter.

LEARNING GOAL

Describe alpha, beta, positron, and gamma radiation.

16.1 Natural Radioactivity

Most naturally occurring isotopes of elements up to atomic number 19 have stable nuclei. Elements with atomic numbers 20 and higher usually have one or more isotopes that have unstable nuclei in which the nuclear forces cannot offset the repulsions between the protons. An unstable nucleus is *radioactive*, which means that it spontaneously emits small particles of energy called **radiation** to become more stable. Radiation may take the form of alpha (α) and beta (β) particles, positrons (β^+), or pure energy such as gamma (γ) rays. An isotope of an element that emits radiation is called a **radioisotope**. For most types of radiation, there is a change in the number of protons in the nucleus, which means that an atom is converted into an atom of a different element. This kind of nuclear change was not evident to Dalton when he made his predictions about atoms. Elements with atomic numbers of 93 and higher are produced artificially in nuclear laboratories and consist only of radioactive isotopes.

The atomic symbols for the different isotopes are written with the mass number in the upper left corner and the atomic number in the lower left corner. The mass number is the sum of the number of protons and neutrons in the nucleus, and the atomic number is equal to the number of protons. For example, a radioactive isotope of iodine used in the diagnosis and treatment of thyroid conditions has a mass number of 131 and an atomic number of 53.

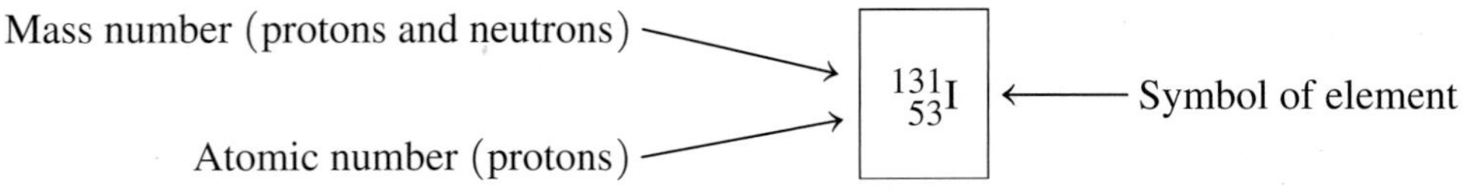

Radioactive isotopes are identified by writing the mass number after the element's name or symbol. Thus, in this example, the isotope is called iodine-131 or I-131. Table 16.1 compares some stable, nonradioactive isotopes with some radioactive isotopes.

TABLE 16.1 Stable and Radioactive Isotopes of Some Elements

Magnesium	Iodine	Uranium
Stable Isotopes		
$^{24}_{12}Mg$	$^{127}_{53}I$	None
Magnesium-24	Iodine-127	
Radioactive Isotopes		
$^{23}_{12}Mg$	$^{125}_{53}I$	$^{235}_{92}U$
Magnesium-23	Iodine-125	Uranium-235
$^{27}_{12}Mg$	$^{131}_{53}I$	$^{238}_{92}U$
Magnesium-27	Iodine-131	Uranium-238

Types of Radiation

By emitting radiation, an unstable nucleus forms a more stable, lower energy nucleus. One type of radiation consists of *alpha particles*. An **alpha particle** is identical to a helium (He) nucleus, which has 2 protons and 2 neutrons. An alpha particle has a mass number of 4, an atomic number of 2, and a charge of 2+. The symbol for an alpha particle is the Greek letter alpha (α) or the symbol of a helium nucleus except that the 2+ charge is omitted.

Another type of radiation occurs when a radioisotope emits a *beta particle*. A **beta particle**, which is a high-energy electron, has a charge of 1−, and because its mass is so much less than the mass of a proton, it has a mass number of 0. It is represented by the Greek letter beta (β) or by the symbol for the electron including the mass number and the charge, $(^{0}_{-1}e)$. A beta particle is formed when a neutron in an unstable nucleus changes into a proton.

A **positron**, similar to a beta particle, has a positive (1+) charge with a mass number of 0. It is represented by the Greek letter beta with a 1+ charge, β^+, or by the symbol of an electron, which includes the mass number and the charge, $^{0}_{+1}e$. A positron is produced by an unstable nucleus when a proton is transformed into a neutron and a positron.

A positron is an example of *antimatter*, a term physicists use to describe a particle that is the exact opposite of another particle, in this case, an electron. When an electron and a positron collide, their minute masses are completely converted to energy in the form of *gamma rays.*

$$^{0}_{-1}e + ^{0}_{+1}e \rightarrow 2\,^{0}_{0}\gamma$$

Gamma rays are high-energy radiation, released when an unstable nucleus undergoes a rearrangement of its particles to give a more stable, lower energy nucleus. Gamma rays are often emitted along with other types of radiation. A gamma ray is written as the Greek letter gamma (γ). Because gamma rays are energy only, zeros are used to show that a gamma ray has no mass or charge.

Table 16.2 summarizes the types of radiation we will use in nuclear equations.

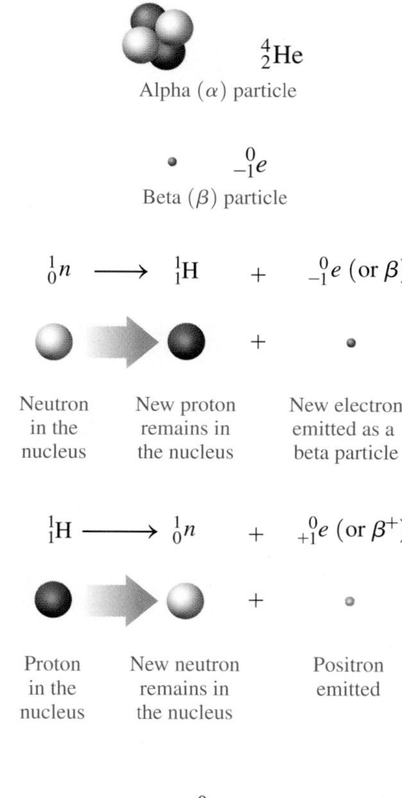

TABLE 16.2 Some Forms of Radiation

Type of Radiation	Symbol		Change in Nucleus	Mass Number	Charge
Alpha Particle	α	$^{4}_{2}He$	Two protons and two neutrons are emitted as an alpha particle.	4	2+
Beta Particle	β	$^{0}_{-1}e$	A neutron changes to a proton and an electron is emitted.	0	1−
Positron	β^+	$^{0}_{+1}e$	A proton changes to a neutron and a positron is emitted.	0	1+
Gamma Ray	γ	$^{0}_{0}\gamma$	Energy is lost to stabilize the nucleus.	0	0
Proton	p	$^{1}_{1}H$	A proton is emitted.	1	1+
Neutron	n	$^{1}_{0}n$	A neutron is emitted.	1	0

CONCEPT CHECK 16.1 Radiation Particles

Identify and write the symbol for each of the following types of radiation:

a. contains two protons and two neutrons
b. has a mass number of 0 and a 1− charge

ANSWER

a. An alpha (α) particle, ${}^{4}_{2}\text{He}$, has two protons and two neutrons.
b. A beta (β) particle, ${}^{0}_{-1}e$, is like an electron with a mass number of 0 and a 1− charge.

Biological Effects of Radiation

When radiation strikes molecules in its path, electrons may be knocked away, forming unstable ions. If this *ionizing radiation* passes through the human body, it may interact with water molecules, removing electrons and producing H_2O^+, which can cause undesirable chemical reactions.

The cells most sensitive to radiation are the ones undergoing rapid division—those of the bone marrow, skin, reproductive organs, and intestinal lining, as well as all cells of growing children. Damaged cells may lose their ability to produce necessary materials. For example, if radiation damages cells of the bone marrow, red blood cells may no longer be produced. If sperm cells, ova, or the cells of a fetus are damaged, birth defects may result. In contrast, cells of the nerves, muscles, liver, and adult bones are much less sensitive to radiation because they undergo little or no cellular division.

Cancer cells are another example of rapidly dividing cells. Because cancer cells are highly sensitive to radiation, large doses of radiation are used to destroy them. The normal tissue that surrounds cancer cells divides at a slower rate and suffers less damage from radiation. However, radiation may cause malignant tumors, leukemia, anemia, and genetic mutations.

Radiation Protection

Radiologists, chemists, doctors, and nurses who work with radioactive isotopes must use proper radiation protection. Proper *shielding* is necessary to prevent exposure. Alpha particles, which have the largest mass and charge of the radiation particles, travel only a few centimeters in the air before they collide with air molecules, acquire electrons, and become helium atoms. A piece of paper, clothing, and our skin are protection against alpha particles. Lab coats and gloves will also provide sufficient shielding. However, if alpha emitters are ingested or inhaled, the alpha particles they give off can cause serious internal damage.

Beta particles have a very small mass and move much faster and farther than alpha particles, traveling as much as several meters through air. They can pass through paper and penetrate as far as 4–5 mm into body tissue. External exposure to beta particles can burn the surface of the skin, but they do not travel far enough to reach the internal organs. Heavy clothing such as lab coats and gloves are needed to protect the skin from beta particles.

Gamma rays travel great distances through the air and pass through many materials, including body tissues. Because gamma rays penetrate so deeply, exposure to gamma rays can be extremely hazardous. Only very dense shielding, such as lead or concrete, will stop them. Syringes used for injections of radioactive materials use shielding made of lead or heavy-weight materials such as tungsten and plastic composites.

When working with radioactive materials, medical personnel wear protective clothing and gloves and stand behind a shield (see Figure 16.1). Long tongs may be used to pick up vials of radioactive material, keeping them away from the hands and body. Table 16.3 summarizes the shielding materials required for the various types of radiation.

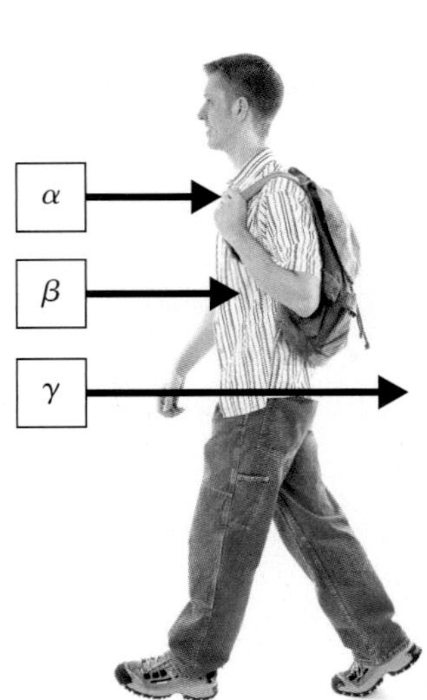

Different types of radiation penetrate the body to different depths.

If you work in an environment where radioactive materials are present, such as a nuclear medicine facility, try to keep the time you spend in a radioactive area to a minimum. Remaining in a radioactive area twice as long exposes you to twice as much radiation.

Keep your distance! The greater the distance from the radioactive source, the lower the intensity of radiation received. By doubling your distance from the radiation source, the intensity of radiation drops to $\left(\frac{1}{2}\right)^2$, or one-fourth of its previous value.

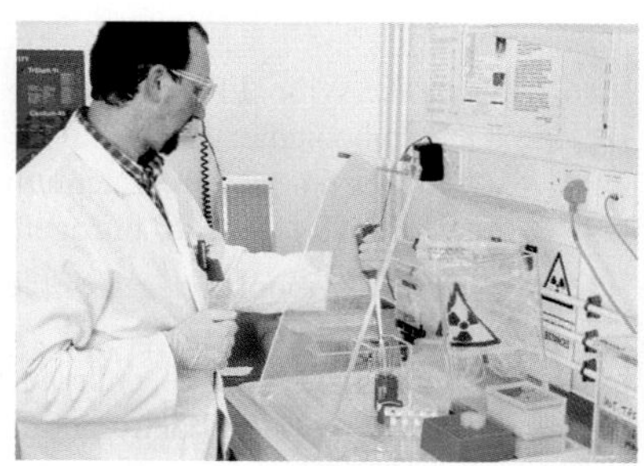

FIGURE 16.1 A person working with radioisotopes wears protective clothing and gloves and stands behind a shield.

Q What types of radiation does a lead shield block?

TABLE 16.3 Properties of Radiation and Shielding Required

Property	Alpha (α) Particle	Beta (β) Particle	Gamma (γ) Ray
Travel Distance in Air	2–4 cm	200–300 cm	500 m
Tissue Depth	0.05 mm	4–5 mm	50 cm or more
Shielding	Paper, clothing	Heavy clothing, lab coats, gloves	Lead, thick concrete
Typical Source	Radium-226	Carbon-14	Technetium-99m

SAMPLE PROBLEM 16.1 Radiation Protection

How does the type of shielding for alpha radiation differ from that used for gamma radiation?

SOLUTION

Alpha radiation is blocked by paper and clothing. However, lead or concrete is needed to block gamma radiation.

STUDY CHECK 16.1

Besides shielding, what other methods help reduce exposure to radiation?

QUESTIONS AND PROBLEMS

16.1 Natural Radioactivity

LEARNING GOAL: *Describe alpha, beta, positron, and gamma radiation.*

16.1 Identify the type of particle or radiation for each of the following:

a. ${}^{4}_{2}\text{He}$ **b.** ${}^{0}_{+1}e$ **c.** ${}^{0}_{0}\gamma$

16.2 Identify the type of particle or radiation for each of the following:

a. ${}^{0}_{-1}e$ **b.** ${}^{1}_{1}\text{H}$ **c.** ${}^{1}_{0}n$

16.3 Naturally occurring potassium consists of three isotopes: potassium-39, potassium-40, and potassium-41.

a. Write the atomic symbol for each isotope.

b. In what ways are the isotopes similar, and in what ways do they differ?

16.4 Naturally occurring iodine is iodine-127. Medically, radioactive isotopes of iodine-125 and iodine-130 are used.

a. Write the atomic symbol for each isotope.

b. In what ways are the isotopes similar, and in what ways do they differ?

16.5 Supply the missing information in the following table:

Medical Use	Atomic Symbol	Mass Number	Number of Protons	Number of Neutrons
Heart imaging	${}^{201}_{81}\text{Tl}$			
Radiation therapy		60	27	
Abdominal scan			31	36
Hyperthyroidism	${}^{131}_{53}\text{I}$			
Leukemia treatment		32		17

16.6 Supply the missing information in the following table:

Medical Use	Atomic Symbol	Mass Number	Number of Protons	Number of Neutrons
Cancer treatment	${}^{131}_{55}\text{Cs}$			
Brain scan			43	56
Blood flow		141	58	
Bone scan		85		47
Lung function	${}^{133}_{54}\text{Xe}$			

16.7 Write the symbol for each of the following isotopes used in nuclear medicine:

a. copper-64 **b.** selenium-75
c. sodium-24 **d.** nitrogen-15

16.8 Write the symbol for each of the following isotopes used in nuclear medicine:

a. indium-111 **b.** palladium-103
c. barium-131 **d.** rubidium-82

16.9 Identify each of the following:

a. ${}^{0}_{-1}X$ **b.** ${}^{4}_{2}X$ **c.** ${}^{1}_{0}X$
d. ${}^{38}_{18}X$ **e.** ${}^{14}_{6}X$

16.10 Identify each of the following:

a. ${}^{1}_{1}X$ **b.** ${}^{81}_{35}X$ **c.** ${}^{0}_{0}X$
d. ${}^{59}_{26}X$ **e.** ${}^{0}_{+1}X$

16.11 Match the type of radiation (**1–3**) with each of the following statements:

1. alpha particle
2. beta particle
3. gamma radiation

a. does not penetrate skin
b. shielding protection includes lead or thick concrete
c. can be very harmful if ingested

16.12 Match the type of radiation (**1–3**) with each of the following statements:

1. alpha particle
2. beta particle
3. gamma radiation

a. penetrates farthest into skin and body tissues
b. shielding protection includes lab coats and gloves
c. travels only a short distance in air

LEARNING GOAL

Write a balanced nuclear equation showing mass numbers and atomic numbers for radioactive decay.

CORE CHEMISTRY SKILL

Writing Nuclear Equations

16.2 Nuclear Reactions

In a process called **radioactive decay**, a nucleus spontaneously breaks down by emitting radiation. This process is shown by writing a *nuclear equation* with the atomic symbols of the original radioactive nucleus on the left, an arrow, and the new nucleus and the type of radiation emitted on the right.

$$\text{Radioactive nucleus} \longrightarrow \text{new nucleus} + \text{radiation } (\alpha, \beta, \beta^{+}, \gamma)$$

In a nuclear equation, the sum of the mass numbers and the sum of the atomic numbers on one side of the arrow must equal the sum of the mass numbers and the sum of the atomic numbers on the other side.

Alpha Decay

An unstable nucleus may emit an alpha particle, which consists of 2 protons and 2 neutrons. Thus, the mass number of the radioactive nucleus decreases by 4, and its atomic number decreases by 2. For example, when uranium-238 emits an alpha particle, the new nucleus that forms has a mass number of 234. Compared to uranium with 92 protons, the new nucleus has 90 protons, which is thorium.

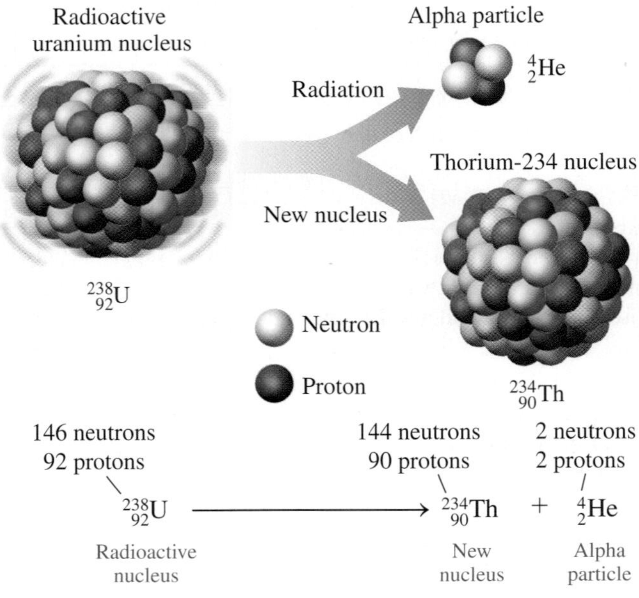

In alpha decay, the mass number of the new nucleus decreases by 4 and its atomic number decreases by 2.

CONCEPT CHECK 16.2 Alpha Decay

When francium-221 undergoes decay, an alpha particle is emitted.

a. Does the new nucleus have a larger or smaller mass number? By how much?
b. Does the new nucleus have a larger or smaller atomic number? By how much?

ANSWER

a. The loss of an alpha particle will give the new nucleus a smaller mass number. Because an alpha particle is a helium nucleus, ${}^{4}_{2}\text{He}$, the mass number of the new nucleus will decrease by four from 221 to 217.
b. The loss of an alpha particle will give the new nucleus a smaller atomic number. Because an alpha particle is a helium nucleus, ${}^{4}_{2}\text{He}$, the atomic number of the new nucleus will decrease by two from 87 to 85.

A smoke detector sounds an alarm when smoke enters its ionization chamber.

We can look at writing a balanced nuclear equation for americium-241, which undergoes alpha decay as shown in Sample Problem 16.2.

SAMPLE PROBLEM 16.2 Writing an Equation for Alpha Decay

Smoke detectors that are used in homes and apartments contain americium-241, which undergoes alpha decay. When alpha particles collide with air molecules, charged particles are produced that generate an electrical current. If smoke particles enter the detector, they interfere with the formation of charged particles in the air, and the electric current is interrupted. This causes the alarm to sound and warns the occupants of the danger of fire. Complete the following nuclear equation for the decay of americium-241:

$${}^{241}_{95}\text{Am} \longrightarrow ? + {}^{4}_{2}\text{He}$$

SOLUTION

Step 1 **Write the incomplete nuclear equation.**

$${}^{241}_{95}\text{Am} \longrightarrow ? + {}^{4}_{2}\text{He}$$

Step 2 **Determine the missing mass number.** In the equation, the mass number of americium, 241, is equal to the sum of the mass numbers of the new nucleus and an alpha particle.

$$241 = ? + 4$$
$$241 - 4 = ?$$
$$241 - 4 = 237 \text{ (mass number of new nucleus)}$$

Step 3 **Determine the missing atomic number.** The atomic number of americium, 95, must equal the sum of the atomic numbers of the new nucleus and an alpha particle.

$$95 = ? + 2$$
$$95 - 2 = ?$$
$$95 - 2 = 93 \text{ (atomic number of new nucleus)}$$

Step 4 **Determine the symbol of the new nucleus.** On the periodic table, the element that has atomic number 93 is neptunium, Np. The nucleus of this isotope of Np is written as ${}^{237}_{93}\text{Np}$.

Step 5 **Complete the nuclear equation.**

$${}^{241}_{95}\text{Am} \longrightarrow {}^{237}_{93}\text{Np} + {}^{4}_{2}\text{He}$$

Guide to Completing a Nuclear Equation

1. Write the incomplete nuclear equation.
2. Determine the missing mass number.
3. Determine the missing atomic number.
4. Determine the symbol of the new nucleus.
5. Complete the nuclear equation.

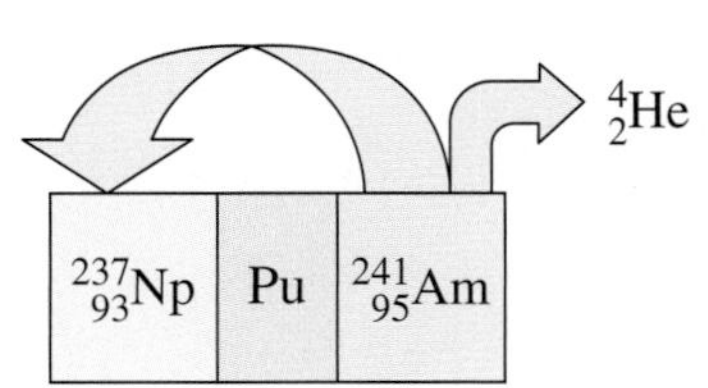

STUDY CHECK 16.2

Write the balanced nuclear equation for the alpha decay of Po-214.

Chemistry Link to the Environment

RADON IN OUR HOMES

The presence of radon gas has become a much publicized environmental and health issue because of the radiation danger it poses. Radioactive isotopes such as radium-226 are naturally present in many types of rocks and soils. Radium-226 emits an alpha particle and is converted into radon gas, which diffuses out of the rocks and soil.

$$^{226}_{88}\text{Ra} \longrightarrow {}^{222}_{86}\text{Rn} + {}^{4}_{2}\text{He}$$

Outdoors, radon gas poses little danger because it disperses in the air. However, if the radioactive source is under a house or building, the radon gas can enter the house through cracks in the foundation or other openings. Those who live or work there may inhale the radon. Inside the lungs, radon-222 emits alpha particles to form polonium-218, which is known to cause lung cancer.

$$^{222}_{86}\text{Rn} \longrightarrow {}^{218}_{84}\text{Po} + {}^{4}_{2}\text{He}$$

The Environmental Protection Agency (EPA) recommends that the maximum level of radon not exceed 4 picocuries (pCi) per liter of air in a home. One picocurie (pCi) is equal to 10^{-12} curies (Ci); curies are described in Section 16.3. In California, 1% of all the houses surveyed exceeded the EPA's recommended maximum radon level.

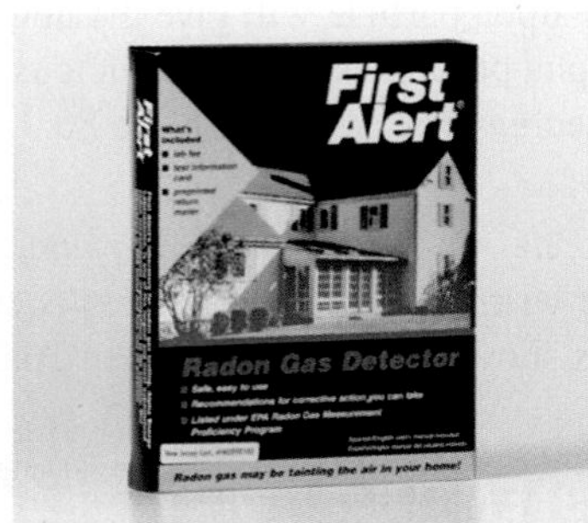

A radon gas detector is used to determine radon levels in buildings.

Beta Decay

The formation of a beta particle is the result of the breakdown of a neutron into a proton and an electron (beta particle). Because the proton remains in the nucleus, the number of protons increases by one, while the number of neutrons decreases by one. Thus, in a nuclear equation for beta decay, the mass number of the radioactive nucleus and the mass number of the new nucleus are the same. However, the atomic number of the new nucleus increases by one, which makes it a nucleus of a different element (*transmutation*). For example, the beta decay of a carbon-14 nucleus produces a nitrogen-14 nucleus.

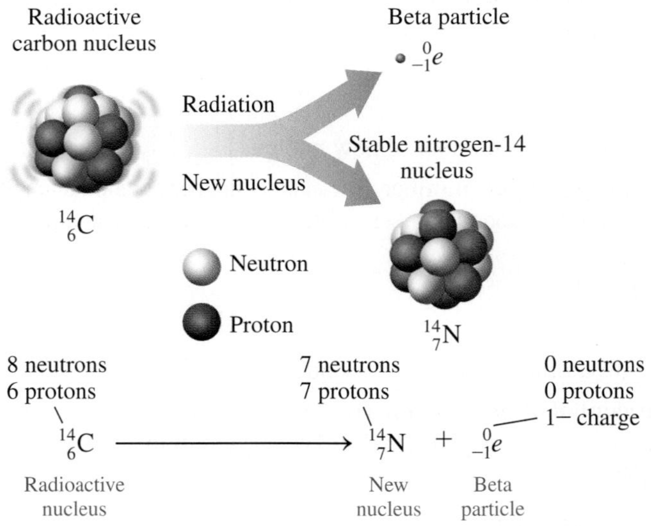

In beta decay, the mass number of the new nucleus remains the same and its atomic number increases by 1.

SAMPLE PROBLEM 16.3 Writing an Equation for Beta Decay

Write the balanced nuclear equation for the beta decay of cobalt-60.

SOLUTION

Step 1 **Write the incomplete nuclear equation.**

$${}^{60}_{27}\text{Co} \longrightarrow ? + {}^{0}_{-1}e$$

Step 2 **Determine the missing mass number.** In the equation, the mass number of cobalt, 60, is equal to the sum of the mass numbers of the new nucleus and the beta particle.

$$60 \quad = ? + 0$$

$$60 - 0 = ?$$

$$60 - 0 = 60 \text{ (mass number of new nucleus)}$$

Step 3 **Determine the missing atomic number.** The atomic number of cobalt, 27, must equal the sum of the atomic numbers of the new nucleus and the beta particle.

$$27 \quad = ? - 1$$

$$27 + 1 = ?$$

$$27 + 1 = 28 \text{ (atomic number of new nucleus)}$$

Step 4 **Determine the symbol of the new nucleus.** On the periodic table, the element that has atomic number 28 is nickel (Ni). The nucleus of this isotope of Ni is written as ${}^{60}_{28}\text{Ni}$.

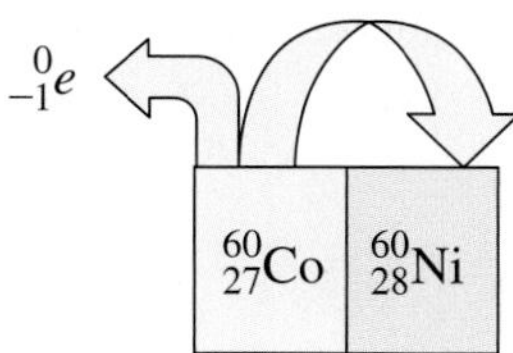

Step 5 **Complete the nuclear equation.**

$${}^{60}_{27}\text{Co} \longrightarrow {}^{60}_{28}\text{Ni} + {}^{0}_{-1}e$$

STUDY CHECK 16.3

Write the balanced nuclear equation for the beta decay of chromium-51.

Positron Emission

In positron emission, a proton in an unstable nucleus is converted to a neutron and a positron. The neutron remains in the nucleus, but the positron is emitted from the nucleus. In a nuclear equation for positron emission, the mass number of the radioactive nucleus and the mass number of the new nucleus are the same. However, the atomic number of the new nucleus decreases by one indicating a change of one element into another (*transmutation*). For example, an aluminum-24 nucleus undergoes positron emission to produce a magnesium-24 nucleus. The atomic number of magnesium (12) and the charge of the positron (1+) give the atomic number of aluminum (13).

$${}^{24}_{13}\text{Al} \longrightarrow {}^{24}_{12}\text{Mg} + {}^{0}_{+1}e$$

SAMPLE PROBLEM 16.4 Writing an Equation for Positron Emission

Write the balanced nuclear equation for manganese-49, which decays by emitting a positron.

SOLUTION

Step 1 **Write the incomplete nuclear equation.**

$${}^{49}_{25}\text{Mn} \longrightarrow ? + {}^{0}_{+1}e$$

Step 2 **Determine the missing mass number.** In the equation, the mass number of the manganese, 49, is equal to the sum of the mass numbers of the new nucleus and the positron.

$$49 = ? + 0$$
$$49 - 0 = ?$$
$$49 - 0 = 49 \text{ (mass number of new nucleus)}$$

Step 3 **Determine the missing atomic number.** The atomic number of manganese, 25, must equal the sum of the atomic numbers of the new nucleus and the positron.

$$25 = ? + 1$$
$$25 - 1 = ?$$
$$25 - 1 = 24 \text{ (atomic number of new nucleus)}$$

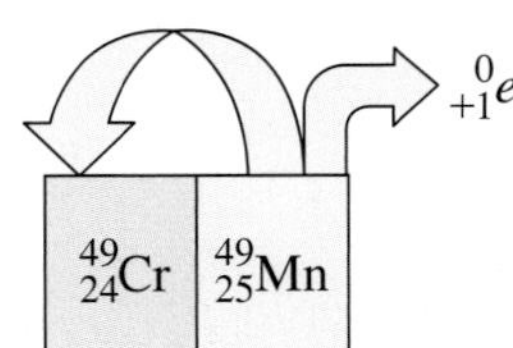

Step 4 **Determine the symbol of the new nucleus.** On the periodic table, the element that has atomic number 24 is chromium (Cr). The nucleus of this isotope of Cr is written as $^{49}_{24}Cr$.

Step 5 **Complete the nuclear equation.**

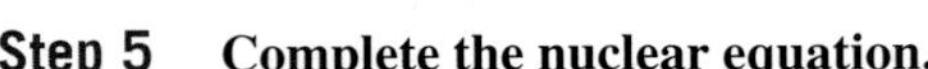

$$^{49}_{25}Mn \longrightarrow\ ^{49}_{24}Cr + \ ^{0}_{+1}e$$

STUDY CHECK 16.4

Write the balanced nuclear equation for xenon-118, which undergoes positron emission.

Radiation Source	Radiation		New Nucleus
Alpha emitter	$^{4}_{2}He$	+	New element Mass number − 4 Atomic number − 2
Beta emitter	$^{0}_{-1}e$	+	New element Mass number same Atomic number + 1
Positron emitter	$^{0}_{+1}e$	+	New element Mass number same Atomic number − 1
Gamma emitter	$^{0}_{0}\gamma$	+	Stable nucleus of the same element Mass number same Atomic number same

FIGURE 16.2 When the nuclei of alpha, beta, positron, and gamma emitters emit radiation, new, more stable nuclei are produced.

Q What changes occur in the number of protons and neutrons when an alpha emitter gives off radiation?

Gamma Emission

Pure gamma emitters are rare, although gamma radiation accompanies most alpha and beta radiation. In radiology, one of the most commonly used gamma emitters is technetium (Tc). The unstable isotope of technetium is written as the *metastable* (symbol m) isotope technetium-99m, Tc-99m, or $^{99m}_{43}Tc$. By emitting energy in the form of gamma rays, the nucleus becomes more stable.

$$^{99m}_{43}Tc \longrightarrow\ ^{99}_{43}Tc + \ ^{0}_{0}\gamma$$

Figure 16.2 summarizes the changes in the nucleus for alpha, beta, positron, and gamma radiation.

Producing Radioactive Isotopes

Today, many radioisotopes are produced in small amounts by converting stable, nonradioactive isotopes into radioactive ones. In a process called *transmutation*, a stable nucleus is bombarded by high-speed particles such as alpha particles, protons, neutrons, and small nuclei. When one of these particles is absorbed, the stable nucleus is converted to a radioactive isotope and usually some type of radiation particle.

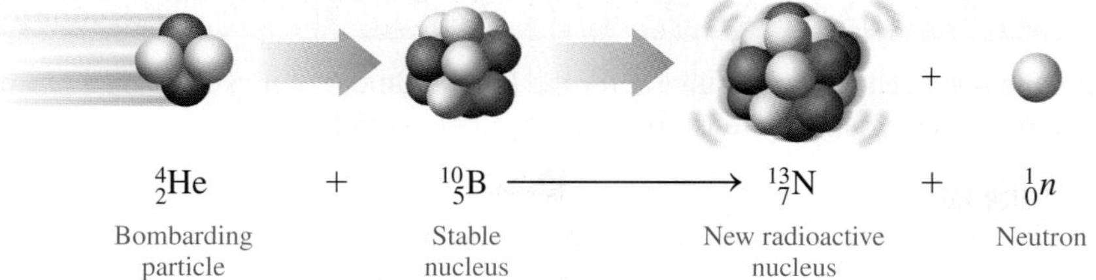

$$^{4}_{2}He + ^{10}_{5}B \longrightarrow ^{13}_{7}N + ^{1}_{0}n$$

Bombarding particle | Stable nucleus | New radioactive nucleus | Neutron

When nonradioactive B-10 is bombarded by an alpha particle, the products are radioactive N-13 and a neutron.

All elements that have an atomic number greater than 92 have been produced by bombardment. Most have been produced in only small amounts and exist for only a short time, making it difficult to study their properties. For example, when californium-249 is bombarded with nitrogen-15, the radioactive element dubnium-260 and four neutrons are produced.

$$^{15}_{7}N + ^{249}_{98}Cf \longrightarrow ^{260}_{105}Db + 4\,^{1}_{0}n$$

Technetium-99m is a radioisotope used in nuclear medicine for several diagnostic procedures, including the detection of brain tumors and examinations of the liver and spleen. The source of technetium-99m is molybdenum-99, which is produced in a nuclear reactor by neutron bombardment of molybdenum-98.

$$^{1}_{0}n + ^{98}_{42}Mo \longrightarrow ^{99}_{42}Mo$$

Many radiology laboratories have small generators containing molybdenum-99, which decays to the technetium-99m radioisotope.

$$^{99}_{42}Mo \longrightarrow ^{99m}_{43}Tc + ^{0}_{-1}e$$

The technetium-99m radioisotope decays by emitting gamma rays. Gamma emission is desirable for diagnostic work because the gamma rays pass through the body to the detection equipment.

$$^{99m}_{43}Tc \longrightarrow ^{99}_{43}Tc + ^{0}_{0}\gamma$$

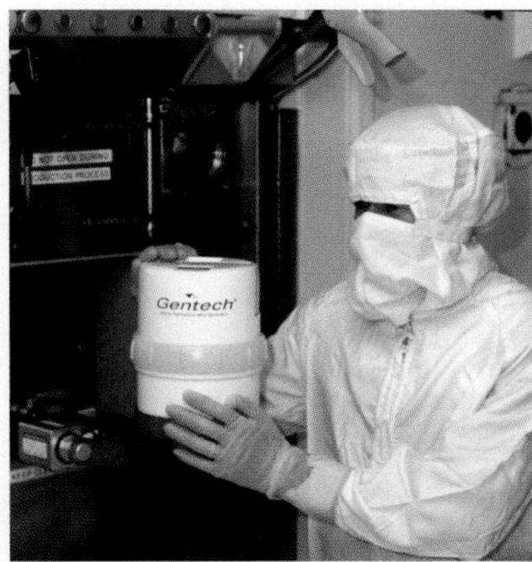

A generator is used to prepare technetium-99m.

CONCEPT CHECK 16.3 Writing an Equation for an Isotope Produced by Bombardment

Sulfur-32 is bombarded with a neutron to produce a radioactive isotope and an alpha particle. What is the symbol for the new isotope?

$$^{1}_{0}n + ^{32}_{16}S \longrightarrow ? + ^{4}_{2}He$$

ANSWER

To determine the new isotope, we need to calculate its mass number and atomic number. On the left side of the equation, the sum of the mass numbers of one neutron, 1, and the sulfur isotope, 32, gives a total of 33. On the right side, the sum of the mass number of the new isotope and that of the alpha particle, 4, must equal 33. Thus, the new isotope has a mass number of 29.

$$^{1}_{0}n + ^{32}_{16}S \longrightarrow ^{29}_{?}? + ^{4}_{2}He$$

On the left side of the equation, the sum of the atomic numbers of a neutron, 0, and the sulfur, 16, gives a total of 16. On the right side, the sum of the atomic number of the new isotope and the atomic number of the alpha particle, 2, must equal 16. Thus, the new isotope has an atomic number of 14. On the periodic table, the element that has atomic number 14 is silicon. Thus, the symbol for the new isotope is $^{29}_{14}Si$.

$$^{1}_{0}n + ^{32}_{16}S \longrightarrow ^{29}_{14}Si + ^{4}_{2}He$$

SAMPLE PROBLEM 16.5 Writing an Equation for Isotope Production

Write the balanced nuclear equation for the bombardment of nickel-58 by a proton, ${}^{1}_{1}H$, which produces a radioactive isotope and an alpha particle.

SOLUTION

Step 1 **Write the incomplete nuclear equation.**

$${}^{1}_{1}H + {}^{58}_{28}Ni \longrightarrow ? + {}^{4}_{2}He$$

Step 2 **Determine the missing mass number.** In the equation, the sum of the mass numbers of the proton, 1, and the nickel, 58, must equal the sum of the mass numbers of the new nucleus and the alpha particle, 4.

$$1 + 58 = ? + 4$$
$$59 - 4 = ?$$
$$59 - 4 = 55 \text{ (mass number of new nucleus)}$$

Step 3 **Determine the missing atomic number.** The sum of the atomic numbers of the proton, 1, and of the nickel, 28, must equal the sum of the atomic numbers of the new nucleus and the alpha particle, 2.

$$1 + 28 = ? + 2$$
$$29 - 2 = ?$$

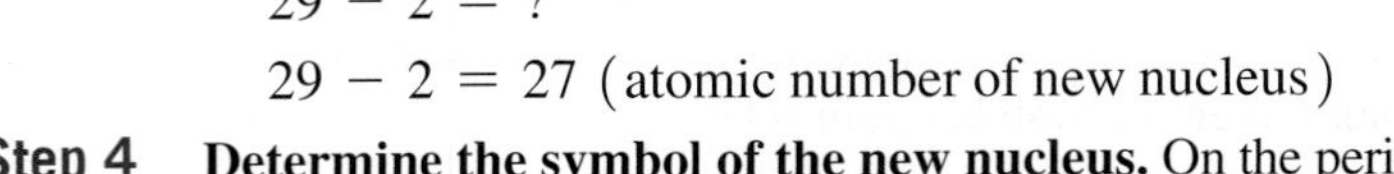

$$29 - 2 = 27 \text{ (atomic number of new nucleus)}$$

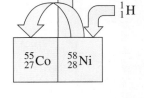

Step 4 **Determine the symbol of the new nucleus.** On the periodic table, the element that has atomic number 27 is cobalt, Co. The nucleus of this isotope of Co is written as ${}^{55}_{27}Co$.

Step 5 **Complete the nuclear equation.**

$${}^{1}_{1}H + {}^{58}_{28}Ni \longrightarrow {}^{55}_{27}Co + {}^{4}_{2}He$$

STUDY CHECK 16.5

The first radioactive isotope was produced in 1934 by the bombardment of aluminum-27 by an alpha particle to produce a radioactive isotope and one neutron. What is the balanced nuclear equation for this transmutation?

QUESTIONS AND PROBLEMS

16.2 Nuclear Reactions

LEARNING GOAL: *Write a balanced nuclear equation showing mass numbers and atomic numbers for radioactive decay.*

16.13 Write a balanced nuclear equation for the alpha decay of each of the following radioactive isotopes:

a. ${}^{208}_{84}Po$
b. ${}^{232}_{90}Th$
c. ${}^{251}_{102}No$
d. radon-220

16.14 Write a balanced nuclear equation for the alpha decay of each of the following radioactive isotopes:

a. curium-243
b. ${}^{252}_{99}Es$
c. ${}^{251}_{98}Cf$
d. ${}^{261}_{107}Bh$

16.15 Write a balanced nuclear equation for the beta decay of each of the following radioactive isotopes:

a. ${}^{25}_{11}Na$
b. ${}^{20}_{8}O$
c. strontium-92
d. iron-60

16.16 Write a balanced nuclear equation for the beta decay of each of the following radioactive isotopes:

a. ${}^{44}_{19}K$
b. iron-59
c. potassium-42
d. ${}^{141}_{56}Ba$

16.17 Write a balanced nuclear equation for the positron emission of each of the following radioactive isotopes:

a. silicon-26

b. cobalt-54

c. $^{77}_{37}Rb$

d. $^{93}_{45}Rh$

16.18 Write a balanced nuclear equation for the positron emission of each of the following radioactive isotopes:

a. boron-8

b. $^{15}_{8}O$

c. $^{40}_{19}K$

d. nitrogen-13

16.19 Complete each of the following nuclear equations and describe the type of radiation:

a. $^{28}_{13}Al \longrightarrow ? + ^{0}_{-1}e$

b. $^{180m}_{73}Ta \longrightarrow ^{180}_{73}Ta + ?$

c. $^{66}_{29}Cu \longrightarrow ^{66}_{30}Zn + ?$

d. $? \longrightarrow ^{234}_{90}Th + ^{4}_{2}He$

e. $^{188}_{80}Hg \longrightarrow ? + ^{0}_{+1}e$

16.20 Complete each of the following nuclear equations and describe the type of radiation:

a. $^{11}_{6}C \longrightarrow ^{11}_{5}B + ?$

b. $^{35}_{16}S \longrightarrow ? + ^{0}_{-1}e$

c. $? \longrightarrow ^{90}_{39}Y + ^{0}_{-1}e$

d. $^{210}_{83}Bi \longrightarrow ? + ^{4}_{2}He$

e. $? \longrightarrow ^{89}_{39}Y + ^{0}_{+1}e$

16.21 Complete each of the following bombardment reactions:

a. $^{1}_{0}n + ^{9}_{4}Be \longrightarrow ?$

b. $^{1}_{0}n + ^{131}_{52}Te \longrightarrow ? + ^{0}_{-1}e$

c. $^{1}_{0}n + ? \longrightarrow ^{24}_{11}Na + ^{4}_{2}He$

d. $^{4}_{2}He + ^{27}_{13}Al \longrightarrow ? + ^{1}_{0}n$

16.22 Complete each of the following bombardment reactions:

a. $? + ^{40}_{18}Ar \longrightarrow ^{43}_{19}K + ^{1}_{1}H$

b. $^{1}_{0}n + ^{238}_{92}U \longrightarrow ?$

c. $^{1}_{0}n + ? \longrightarrow ^{14}_{6}C + ^{1}_{1}H$

d. $? + ^{64}_{28}Ni \longrightarrow ^{272}_{111}Rg + ^{1}_{0}n$

16.3 Radiation Measurement

LEARNING GOAL

Describe the detection and measurement of radiation.

One of the most common instruments for detecting beta and gamma radiation is the Geiger counter. It consists of a metal tube filled with a gas such as argon. When radiation enters a window on the end of the tube, it forms charged particles in the gas, which produce an electrical current. Each burst of current is amplified to give a click and a reading on a meter.

$$Ar + \text{radiation} \longrightarrow Ar^{+} + e^{-}$$

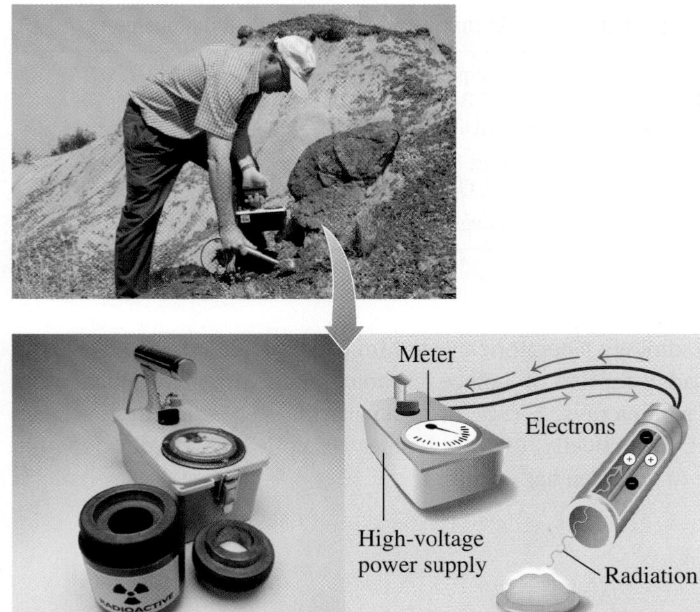

A radiation technician uses a Geiger counter to check radiation levels.

Measuring Radiation

Radiation is measured in several different ways. When a radiology laboratory obtains a radioisotope, the *activity* of the sample is measured in terms of the number of nuclear disintegrations per second. The **curie (Ci)**, the original unit of activity, was defined as the number of disintegrations that occurs in 1 sec for 1 g of radium, which is equal to 3.7×10^{10} disintegrations/s. The unit was named for the Polish scientist Marie Curie, who along with her husband, Pierre, discovered the radioactive elements radium and polonium. The SI unit of radiation activity is the **becquerel (Bq)**, which is 1 disintegration/s.

The **rad (radiation absorbed dose)** is a unit that measures the amount of radiation absorbed by a gram of material such as body tissue. The SI unit for absorbed dose is the **gray (Gy)**, which is defined as the joules of energy absorbed by 1 kilogram of body tissue. The gray is equal to 100 rad.

The **rem (radiation equivalent in humans)** is a unit that measures the biological effects of different kinds of radiation. Although alpha particles do not penetrate the skin, if they should enter the body by some other route, they can cause extensive damage within a short distance in tissue. High-energy radiation, such as beta particles, high-energy protons, and neutrons that travel into tissue, cause more damage. Gamma rays are damaging because they travel a long way through body tissue.

To determine the **equivalent dose** or rem dose, the absorbed dose (rads) is multiplied by a factor that adjusts for biological damage caused by a particular form of radiation. For beta and gamma radiation the factor is 1, so the biological damage in rems is the same as the absorbed radiation (rads). For high-energy protons and neutrons, the factor is about 10, and for alpha particles it is 20.

$$\text{Biological damage (rem)} = \text{Absorbed dose (rad)} \times \text{Factor}$$

Often, the measurement for an equivalent dose will be in units of millirems (mrem). One rem is equal to 1000 mrem. The SI unit is the **sievert (Sv)**. One sievert is equal to 100 rem. Table 16.4 summarizes the units used to measure radiation.

TABLE 16.4 Units of Radiation Measurement

Measurement	Common Unit	SI Unit	Relationship
Activity	curie (Ci) 1 Ci = 3.7×10^{10} disintegrations/s	becquerel (Bq) 1 Bq = 1 disintegration/s	1 Ci = 3.7×10^{10} Bq
Absorbed Dose	rad	gray (Gy) 1 Gy = 1 J/kg of tissue	1 Gy = 100 rad
Biological Damage	rem	sievert (Sv)	1 Sv = 100 rem

A film badge measures radiation exposure.

People who work in radiology laboratories wear film badges to determine their exposure to radiation. A film badge consists of a piece of photographic film in a container that is attached to clothing. If gamma rays, X-rays, or beta particles strike the film, it appears darker upon development. Periodically, the film badges are collected and developed to determine if any exposure to radiation has occurred.

Chemistry Link to the Environment

RADIATION AND FOOD

Food-borne illnesses caused by pathogenic bacteria such as *Salmonella*, *Listeria*, and *Escherichia coli* have become a major health concern in the United States. The Centers for Disease Control and Prevention estimates that each year, *E. coli* in contaminated foods infects 20 000 people in the United States and that 500 people die. *E. coli* has been responsible for outbreaks of illness from contaminated ground beef, fruit juices, lettuce, and alfalfa sprouts.

The Food and Drug Administration (FDA) has approved the use of 0.3 kGy to 1 kGy of radiation produced by cobalt-60 or cesium-137 for the treatment of foods. The irradiation technology is much like that used to sterilize medical supplies. Cobalt pellets are placed in stainless steel tubes, which are arranged in racks. When food moves through the series of racks, the gamma rays pass through the food and kill the bacteria.

It is important for consumers to understand that when food is irradiated, it never comes in contact with the radioactive source. The gamma rays pass through the food to kill bacteria, but that does not make the food radioactive. The radiation kills bacteria because it stops their ability to divide and grow. We cook or heat food thoroughly for the same purpose. Radiation, as well as heat, has little effect on the food itself because its cells are no longer dividing or growing. Thus irradiated food is not harmed, although a small amount of vitamin B_1 and C may be lost.

Currently, tomatoes, blueberries, strawberries, and mushrooms are being irradiated to allow them to be harvested when completely ripe and extend their shelf life (see Figure 16.3). The FDA has also approved the irradiation of pork, poultry, and beef in order to decrease potential infections and to extend shelf life. Currently, irradiated vegetable and meat products are available in retail markets in more than 40 countries. In the United States, irradiated foods such as tropical fruits, spinach, and ground meats are found in some stores. *Apollo* 17 astronauts ate irradiated foods on the moon, and some U.S. hospitals and nursing homes now use irradiated poultry to reduce the possibility of salmonella infections among residents. The extended shelf life of irradiated food also makes it useful for campers and military personnel. Soon, consumers concerned about food safety will have a choice of irradiated meats, fruits, and vegetables at the market.

(a)

(b)

FIGURE 16.3 **(a)** The FDA requires this symbol to appear on irradiated retail foods. **(b)** After two weeks, the irradiated strawberries on the right show no spoilage. Mold is growing on the nonirradiated ones on the left.

Q Why are irradiated foods used on spaceships and in nursing homes?

CONCEPT CHECK 16.4 Radiation Measurement

One treatment for bone pain involves intravenous administration of the radioisotope phosphorus-32, which is incorporated into bone. A typical dose of 7 mCi can produce up to 450 rad in the bone. What is the difference between the units of mCi and rad?

ANSWER

The millicuries (mCi) indicate the activity of the P-32 in terms of nuclei that break down in 1 second. The radiation absorbed dose (rad) is a measure of amount of radiation absorbed by the bone.

Exposure to Radiation

Every day, we are exposed to low levels of radiation from naturally occurring radioactive isotopes in the buildings where we live and work, in our food and water, and in the air we breathe. For example, potassium-40, a naturally occurring radioactive

TABLE 16.5 Average Annual Radiation Received by a Person in the United States

Source	Dose (mrem)
Natural	
Ground	20
Air, water, food	30
Cosmic rays	40
Wood, concrete, brick	50
Medical	
Chest X-ray	20
Dental X-ray	20
Mammogram	40
Hip X-ray	60
Lumbar spine X-ray	70
Upper gastrointestinal tract X-ray	200
Other	
Nuclear power plants	0.1
Television	20
Air travel	10
Radon	200*

*Varies widely.

isotope, is present in any potassium-containing food. Other naturally occurring radioisotopes in air and food are carbon-14, radon-222, strontium-90, and iodine-131. The average person in the United States is exposed to about 360 mrem of radiation annually. Medical sources of radiation, including dental, hip, spine, and chest X-rays and mammograms, add to our radiation exposure. Table 16.5 lists some common sources of radiation.

Another source of background radiation is cosmic radiation produced in space by the Sun. People who live at high altitudes or travel by airplane receive a greater amount of cosmic radiation because there are fewer molecules in the atmosphere to absorb the radiation. For example, a person living in Denver receives about twice the cosmic radiation as a person living in Los Angeles. A person living close to a nuclear power plant normally does not receive much additional radiation, perhaps 0.1 mrem in one year. (One rem equals 1000 mrem.) However, in the accident at the Chernobyl nuclear power plant in 1986 in Ukraine, it is estimated that people in a nearby town received as much as 1 rem/h.

Radiation Sickness

The larger the dose of radiation received at one time, the greater the effect on the body. Exposure to radiation of less than 25 rem usually cannot be detected. Whole-body exposure of 100 rem produces a temporary decrease in the number of white blood cells. If the exposure to radiation is greater than 100 rem, a person may suffer the symptoms of radiation sickness: nausea, vomiting, fatigue, and a reduction in white-cell count. A whole-body dosage greater than 300 rem can decrease the white-cell count to zero. The person suffers diarrhea, hair loss, and infection. Exposure to radiation of 500 rem is expected to cause death in 50% of the people receiving that dose. This amount of radiation to the whole body is called the *lethal dose for one-half the population*, or the LD_{50}. The LD_{50} varies for different life forms, as Table 16.6 shows. Whole-body radiation of 600 rem or greater would be fatal to all humans within a few weeks.

TABLE 16.6 Lethal Doses of Radiation for Some Life Forms

Life Form	LD_{50} (rem)
Insect	100 000
Bacterium	50 000
Rat	800
Human	500
Dog	300

QUESTIONS AND PROBLEMS

16.3 Radiation Measurement

LEARNING GOAL: *Describe the detection and measurement of radiation.*

16.23 Match each property (**1–3**) with its unit of measurement.
1. activity
2. absorbed dose
3. biological damage

a. rad **b.** mrem
c. mCi **d.** Gy

16.24 Match each property (**1–3**) with its unit of measurement.
1. activity
2. absorbed dose
3. biological damage

a. mrad **b.** gray
c. becquerel **d.** Sv

16.25 Two technicians in a nuclear laboratory were accidentally exposed to radiation. If one was exposed to 8 mGy and the other to 5 rad, which technician received more radiation?

16.26 Two samples of a radioisotope were spilled in a nuclear laboratory. The activity of one sample was 8 kBq and the other 15 mCi. Which sample produced the higher amount of radiation?

16.27 a. The recommended dosage of iodine-131 is 4.20 μCi/kg of body mass. How many microcuries of iodine-131 are needed for a 70.0-kg person with hyperthyroidism?
b. A person receives 50 rad of gamma radiation. What is that amount in grays?

16.28 a. The dosage of technetium-99m for a lung scan is 20. μCi/kg of body mass. How many millicuries of technetium-99m should be given to a 50.0-kg person ($1 \text{ mCi} = 1000\ \mu\text{Ci}$)?
b. Suppose a person absorbed 50 mrad of alpha radiation. What would be the equivalent dose in millirems?

16.4 Half-Life of a Radioisotope

LEARNING GOAL

Given the half-life of a radioisotope, calculate the amount of radioisotope remaining after one or more half-lives.

The **half-life** of a radioisotope is the amount of time it takes for one-half of a sample to decay. For example, $^{131}_{53}I$ has a half-life of 8.0 days. As $^{131}_{53}I$ decays, it produces the nonradioactive isotope $^{131}_{54}Xe$ and a beta particle.

$$^{131}_{53}I \longrightarrow \, ^{131}_{54}Xe + \, ^{0}_{-1}e$$

Suppose we have a sample that initially contains 20. mg of $^{131}_{53}I$. In 8.0 days, one-half (10. mg) of all the I-131 nuclei in the sample will decay, which leaves 10. mg of I-131. After 16 days (two half-lives), 5.0 mg of the remaining I-131 decays, which leaves 5.0 mg of I-131. After 24 days, (three half-lives), 2.5 mg of the remaining I-131 decays, which leaves 2.5 mg of I-131 nuclei still capable of producing radiation.

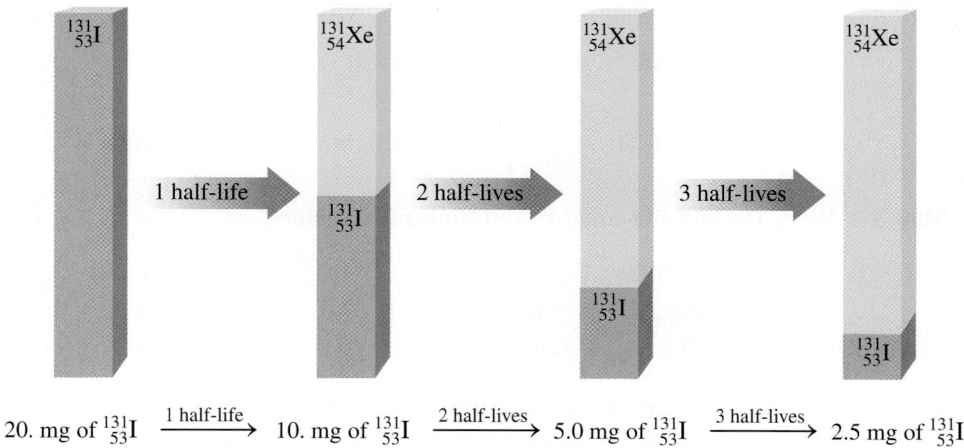

$$20.\ \text{mg of } ^{131}_{53}I \xrightarrow{\text{1 half-life}} 10.\ \text{mg of } ^{131}_{53}I \xrightarrow{\text{2 half-lives}} 5.0\ \text{mg of } ^{131}_{53}I \xrightarrow{\text{3 half-lives}} 2.5\ \text{mg of } ^{131}_{53}I$$

A **decay curve** is a diagram of the decay of a radioactive isotope. Figure 16.4 shows such a curve for the $^{131}_{53}I$ we have discussed.

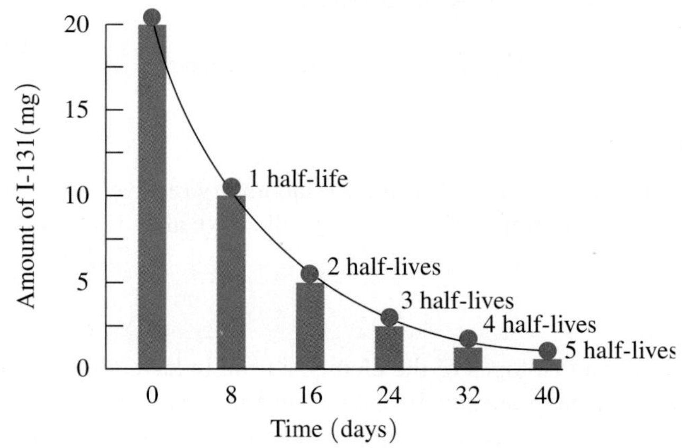

FIGURE 16.4 The decay curve for iodine-131 shows that one-half of the radioactive sample decays and one-half remains radioactive after each half-life of 8.0 days.

Q How many milligrams of the 20.-mg sample remain radioactive after 2 half-lives?

CONCEPT CHECK 16.5 Half-Lives

Iridium-192, used to treat breast cancer, has a half-life of 74 days. What is the activity of the Ir-192 after 74 days if the activity of the initial sample of Ir-192 is 8×10^4 Bq?

ANSWER

In 74 days, which is one half-life of iridium-192, one-half of all of the iridium-192 atoms will decay. Thus, after 74 days, the activity is half of the initial activity, which is 4×10^4 Bq.

CORE CHEMISTRY SKILL 

Using Half-Lives

SAMPLE PROBLEM 16.6 Using Half-Lives of a Radioisotope

Phosphorus-32, a radioisotope used in the treatment of leukemia, has a half-life of 14.3 days. If a sample contains 8.0 mg of phosphorus-32, how many milligrams of phosphorus-32 remain after 42.9 days?

Guide to Using Half-Lives

1. State the given and needed quantities.
2. Write a plan to calculate the unknown quantity.
3. Write the half-life equality and conversion factors.
4. Set up the problem to calculate the needed quantity.

SOLUTION

Step 1 State the given and needed quantities.

	Given	Need
Analyze the Problem	8.0 mg of P-32, 42.9 days elapsed, half-life = 14.3 days	milligrams of P-32 remaining

Step 2 Write a plan to calculate the unknown quantity.

days → Half-life → number of half-lives

milligrams of $^{32}_{15}P$ → Number of half-lives → milligrams of $^{32}_{15}P$ remaining

Step 3 Write the half-life equality and conversion factors.

$$1 \text{ half-life} = 14.3 \text{ days}$$
$$\frac{14.3 \text{ days}}{1 \text{ half-life}} \text{ and } \frac{1 \text{ half-life}}{14.3 \text{ days}}$$

Step 4 Set up the problem to calculate the needed quantity. First we determine the number of half-lives in the amount of time that has elapsed.

$$\text{number of half-lives} = 42.9 \cancel{\text{days}} \times \frac{1 \text{ half-life}}{14.3 \cancel{\text{days}}} = 3.00 \text{ half-lives}$$

Now we can determine how much of the sample decays in 3 half-lives and how many grams of the phosphorus remain.

$$8.0 \text{ mg of } ^{32}_{15}P \xrightarrow{\text{1 half-life}} 4.0 \text{ mg of } ^{32}_{15}P \xrightarrow{\text{2 half-lives}} 2.0 \text{ mg of } ^{32}_{15}P \xrightarrow{\text{3 half-lives}} 1.0 \text{ mg of } ^{32}_{15}P$$

STUDY CHECK 16.6

Iron-59 has a half-life of 44 days. If a nuclear laboratory receives a sample of 8 μg of iron-59, how many micrograms of iron-59 are still active after 176 days?

Naturally occurring isotopes of the elements usually have long half-lives, as shown in Table 16.7. They disintegrate slowly and produce radiation over a long period of time, even hundreds or millions of years. In contrast, the radioisotopes used in nuclear medicine have much shorter half-lives. They disintegrate rapidly and produce almost all their radiation in a short period of time. For example, technetium-99m emits half of its radiation in the first six hours. This means that a small amount of the radioisotope given to a patient is essentially gone within two days. The decay products of technetium-99m are totally eliminated by the body.

TABLE 16.7 Half-Lives of Some Radioisotopes

Element	Radioisotope	Half-Life	Type of Radiation
Naturally Occurring Radioisotopes			
Carbon-14	${}^{14}_{6}C$	5730 y	Beta
Potassium-40	${}^{40}_{19}K$	1.3×10^9 y	Beta, gamma
Radium-226	${}^{226}_{88}Ra$	1600 y	Alpha
Strontium-90	${}^{90}_{38}Sr$	38.1 y	Alpha
Uranium-238	${}^{238}_{92}U$	4.5×10^9 y	Alpha
Some Medical Radioisotopes			
Chromium-51	${}^{51}_{24}Cr$	28 d	Gamma
Iodine-131	${}^{131}_{53}I$	8.0 d	Gamma
Iridium-192	${}^{192}_{77}Ir$	74 d	Beta, gamma
Iron-59	${}^{59}_{26}Fe$	44 d	Beta, gamma
Radon-222	${}^{222}_{86}Rn$	3.8 d	Alpha
Technetium-99m	${}^{99m}_{43}Tc$	6.0 h	Beta, gamma

Chemistry Link to the Environment

DATING ANCIENT OBJECTS

Radiological dating is a technique used by geologists, archaeologists, and historians to determine the age of ancient objects. The age of an object derived from plants or animals (such as wood, fiber, natural pigments, bone, and cotton or woolen clothing) is determined by measuring the amount of carbon-14, a naturally occurring radioactive form of carbon. In 1960, Willard Libby received the Nobel Prize for the work he did developing carbon-14 dating techniques during the 1940s. Carbon-14 is produced in the upper atmosphere by the bombardment of ${}^{14}_{7}N$ by high-energy neutrons from cosmic rays.

$$ {}^{1}_{0}n + {}^{14}_{7}N \longrightarrow {}^{14}_{6}C + {}^{1}_{1}H $$

Neutron from cosmic rays; Nitrogen in atmosphere; Radioactive carbon-14; Proton

The carbon-14 reacts with oxygen to form radioactive carbon dioxide, ${}^{14}_{6}CO_2$. Living plants continuously absorb carbon dioxide, which incorporates carbon-14 into the plant material. The uptake of carbon-14 stops when the plant dies.

$$ {}^{14}_{6}C \longrightarrow {}^{14}_{7}N + {}^{0}_{-1}e $$

The age of the Dead Sea Scrolls was determined using carbon-14.

As the carbon-14 decays, the amount of radioactive carbon-14 in the plant material steadily decreases. In a process called *carbon dating*, scientists use the half-life of carbon-14 (5730 y) to calculate the length of time since the plant died. For example, a wooden beam found in an ancient dwelling might have one-half of the carbon-14 found in living plants today. Because one half-life of carbon-14 is 5730 y, the dwelling was constructed about 5730 y ago. Carbon-14 dating was used to determine that the Dead Sea Scrolls are about 2000 y old.

A radiological dating method used for determining the age of much older items is based on the radioisotope uranium-238, which decays through a series of reactions to lead-206. The uranium-238 isotope has an incredibly long half-life, about 4×10^9 (4 billion) years. Measurements of the amounts of uranium-238 and lead-206 enable geologists to determine the age of rock samples. The older rocks will have a higher percentage of lead-206 because more of the uranium-238 has decayed. The age of rocks brought back from the Moon by the *Apollo* missions, for example, was determined using uranium-238. They were found to be about 4×10^9 y old, approximately the same age calculated for Earth.

SAMPLE PROBLEM 16.7 Dating Using Half-Lives

The age of a bone sample from a skeleton can be determined by carbon dating.

Carbon material in the bones of humans and animals assimilates carbon until death. Using radiocarbon dating, the number of half-lives of carbon-14 from a bone sample determine the age of the bone. Suppose a sample is obtained from a prehistoric animal and used for radiocarbon dating. We can calculate the age of the bone or the years elapsed since the animal died by using the half-life of carbon-14, which is 5730 years. If the sample shows that four half-lives have passed, how much time has elapsed since the animal died?

SOLUTION

Step 1 State the given and needed quantities.

	Given	Need
Analyze the Problem	1 half-life of C-14 = 5730 y, 4 half-lives elapsed	years elapsed

Step 2 Write a plan to calculate the unknown quantity.

4 half-lives → Half-life → years elapsed

Step 3 Write the half-life equality and conversion factors.

$$1 \text{ half-life} = 5730 \text{ y}$$

$$\frac{5730 \text{ y}}{1 \text{ half-life}} \quad \text{and} \quad \frac{1 \text{ half-life}}{5730 \text{ y}}$$

Step 4 Set up the problem to calculate the needed quantity.

$$\text{Years elapsed} = 4.0 \cancel{\text{half-lives}} \times \frac{5730 \text{ y}}{1 \cancel{\text{half-life}}} = 23\,000 \text{ y}$$

We would estimate that the animal lived 23 000 years ago.

STUDY CHECK 16.7

Suppose that a piece of wood found in a tomb had $\frac{1}{8}$ of its original carbon-14 activity. About how many years ago was the wood part of a living tree?

QUESTIONS AND PROBLEMS

16.4 Half-Life of a Radioisotope

LEARNING GOAL: *Given the half-life of a radioisotope, calculate the amount of radioisotope remaining after one or more half-lives.*

16.29 For each of the following, indicate if the number of half-lives elapsed is:

1. one half-life **2.** two half-lives **3.** three half-lives

a. a sample of Pd-103 with a half-life of 17 days after 34 days
b. a sample of C-11 with a half-life of 20 min after 20 min
c. a sample of At-211 with a half-life of 7 h after 21 h

16.30 For each of the following, indicate if the number of half-lives elapsed is:

1. one half-life **2.** two half-lives **3.** three half-lives

a. a sample of Ce-141 with a half-life of 32.5 days after 32.5 days
b. a sample of F-18 with a half-life of 110 min after 330 min
c. a sample of Au-198 with a half-life of 2.7 days after 5.4 days

16.31 Technetium-99m is an ideal radioisotope for scanning organs because it has a half-life of 6.0 h and is a pure gamma emitter. Suppose that 80.0 mg were prepared in the technetium generator this morning. How many milligrams of technetium-99m would remain after the following intervals?

a. one half-life **b.** two half-lives
c. 18 h **d.** 24 h

16.32 A sample of sodium-24 with an activity of 12 mCi is used to study the rate of blood flow in the circulatory system. If sodium-24 has a half-life of 15 h, what is the activity after each of the following intervals?

a. one half-life **b.** 30 h
c. three half-lives **d.** 2.5 days

16.33 Strontium-85, used for bone scans, has a half-life of 65 days.

a. How long will it take for the radiation level of strontium-85 to drop to one-fourth of its original level?
b. How long will it take for the radiation level of strontium-85 to drop to one-eighth of its original level?

16.34 Fluorine-18, which has a half-life of 110 min, is used in PET scans.

a. If 100. mg of fluorine-18 is shipped at 8:00 A.M., how many milligrams of the radioisotope are still active after 110 minutes?
b. If 100. mg of fluorine-18 is shipped at 8:00 A.M., how many milligrams of the radioisotope are still active when the sample arrives at the radiology laboratory at 1:30 P.M.?

16.5 Medical Applications Using Radioactivity

LEARNING GOAL

Describe the use of radioisotopes in medicine.

To determine the condition of an organ in the body, a radiologist may use a radioisotope that concentrates in that organ. The cells in the body do not differentiate between a non-radioactive atom and a radioactive one, so these radioisotopes are easily incorporated. Then the radioactive atoms are detected because they emit radiation. Some radioisotopes used in nuclear medicine are listed in Table 16.8.

TABLE 16.8 Medical Applications of Radioisotopes

Isotope	Half-Life	Radiation	Medical Application
Au-198	2.7 d	Beta	Liver imaging; treatment of abdominal carcinoma
Ce-141	32.5 d	Gamma	Gastrointestinal tract diagnosis; measuring blood flow to the heart
Cs-131	9.7 d	Gamma	Prostrate brachytherapy
F-18	110 min	Positron	Positron emission tomography (PET)
Ga-67	78 h	Gamma	Abdominal imaging; tumor detection
Ga-68	68 min	Gamma	Detection of pancreatic cancer
I-123	13.2 h	Gamma	Treatment of thyroid, brain, and prostate cancer
I-131	8.0 d	Beta	Treatment of Graves' disease, goiter, hyperthyroidism, thyroid and prostate cancer
Ir-192	74 d	Gamma	Treatment of breast and prostate cancer
P-32	14.3 d	Beta	Treatment of leukemia, excess red blood cells, pancreatic cancer
Pd-103	17 d	Gamma	Prostate brachytherapy
Sr-85	65 d	Gamma	Detection of bone lesions; brain scans
Tc-99m	6 h	Gamma	Imaging of skeleton and heart muscle, brain, liver, heart, lungs, bone, spleen, kidney, and thyroid; most widely used radioisotope in nuclear medicine
Y-90	2.7 d	Beta	Treatment of liver cancer

Scans with Radioisotopes

After a person receives a radioisotope, the radiologist determines the level and location of radioactivity emitted by the radioisotope. An apparatus called a *scanner* is used to produce an image of the organ. The scanner moves slowly across the body above the region where the organ containing the radioisotope is located. The gamma rays emitted from the radioisotope in the organ can be used to expose a photographic plate, producing a *scan* of the organ. On a scan, an area of decreased or increased radiation can indicate conditions such as a disease of the organ, a tumor, a blood clot, or edema.

A common method of determining thyroid function is the use of *radioactive iodine uptake* (RAIU). Taken orally, the radioisotope iodine-131 mixes with the iodine already present in the thyroid. Twenty-four hours later, the amount of iodine taken up by the thyroid is determined. A detection tube held up to the area of the thyroid gland detects the radiation coming from the iodine-131 that has located there (see Figure 16.5).

A person with a hyperactive thyroid will have a higher than normal level of radioactive iodine, whereas a person with a hypoactive thyroid will have lower values. If a person has hyperthyroidism, treatment is begun to lower the activity of the thyroid. One treatment involves giving a therapeutic dosage of radioactive iodine, which has a higher radiation level than the diagnostic dose. The radioactive iodine goes to the

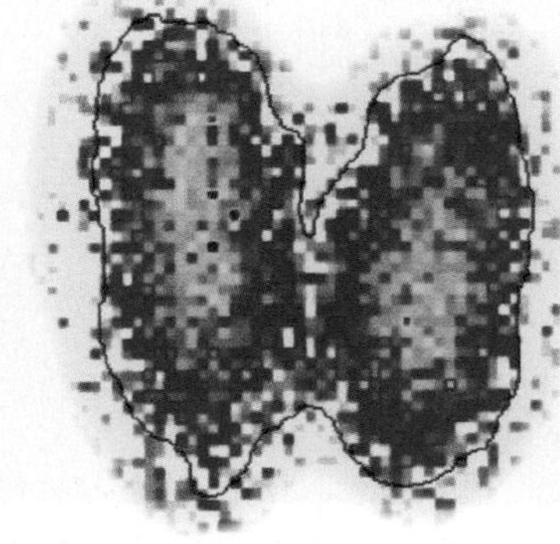

(a) (b)

FIGURE 16.5 **(a)** A scanner is used to detect radiation from a radioisotope that has accumulated in an organ. **(b)** A scan of the thyroid shows the accumulation of radioactive iodine-131 in the thyroid.

Q What type of radiation would move through body tissues to create a scan?

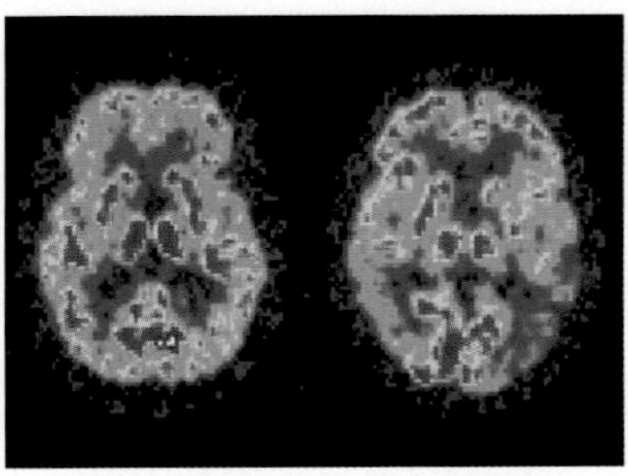

FIGURE 16.6 These PET scans of the brain show a normal brain on the left and a brain affected by Alzheimer's disease on the right.

Q When positrons collide with electrons, what type of radiation is produced that gives an image of an organ?

thyroid where its radiation destroys some of the thyroid cells. The thyroid produces less thyroid hormone, bringing the hyperthyroid condition under control.

Positron Emission Tomography (PET)

Positron emitters with short half-lives such as carbon-11, oxygen-15, nitrogen-13, and fluorine-18 are used in an imaging method called *positron emission tomography* (PET). A positron-emitting isotope such as fluorine-18 combined with substances in the body such as glucose is used to study brain function, metabolism, and blood flow.

$$^{18}_{9}F \longrightarrow ^{18}_{8}O + ^{0}_{+1}e$$

As positrons are emitted, they combine with electrons to produce gamma rays that are detected by computerized equipment to create a three-dimensional image of the organ (see Figure 16.6).

SAMPLE PROBLEM 16.8 Medical Applications of Radioactivity

In the treatment of abdominal carcinoma, a person is treated with seeds of gold-198, which is a beta emitter. Write the nuclear equation for the beta decay of gold-198.

SOLUTION

We can write the incomplete nuclear equation starting with gold-198.

$$^{198}_{79}Au \longrightarrow ? + ^{0}_{-1}e$$

In beta decay, the mass number, 198, does not change, but the atomic number of the new nucleus increases by one. The new atomic number is 80, which is mercury, Hg.

$$^{198}_{79}Au \longrightarrow ^{198}_{80}Hg + ^{0}_{-1}e$$

STUDY CHECK 16.8

In an experimental treatment, a person is given boron-10, which is taken up by malignant tumors. When bombarded with neutrons, boron-10 decays by emitting alpha particles that destroy the surrounding tumor cells. Write the balanced equation for the nuclear reaction for this experimental procedure.

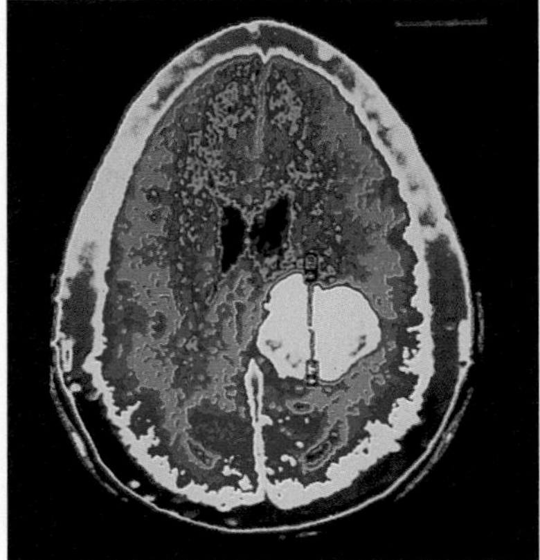

A CT scan shows a tumor (yellow) in the brain.

Computed Tomography (CT)

Another imaging method used to scan organs such as the brain, lungs, and heart is *computed tomography* (CT). A computer monitors the absorption of 30 000 X-ray beams directed at successive layers of the target organ. Based on the densities of the tissues and fluids in the organ, the differences in absorption of the X-rays provide a series of images of the organ. This technique is successful in the identification of hemorrhages, tumors, and atrophy.

Magnetic Resonance Imaging (MRI)

Magnetic resonance imaging (MRI) is a powerful imaging technique that does not involve X-ray radiation. It is the least invasive imaging method available. MRI is based on the absorption of energy when the protons in hydrogen atoms are excited by a strong magnetic field. Hydrogen atoms make up 63% of all the atoms in the body. In the hydrogen nuclei, the protons act like tiny bar magnets. With no external field, the protons have random orientations. However, when placed within a strong magnetic field, the protons align with the field. A proton aligned with the field has a lower energy than one that is aligned against the field. As the MRI scan proceeds, radiofrequency pulses of energy are applied and the hydrogen nuclei resonate at a certain frequency. Then the radio waves are quickly turned off and the protons slowly return to their natural alignment within the magnetic field, and resonate at a different frequency. They release the energy absorbed from the radio wave pulses. The difference in energy between the two states is released as photons, which produce the electromagnetic signal that the scanner detects. These signals are sent to a computer system, where a color image of the body is generated. Because hydrogen atoms in the body are in different chemical environments, different energies are absorbed. MRI is particularly useful in obtaining images of soft tissues, which contain large amounts of hydrogen atoms in the form of water.

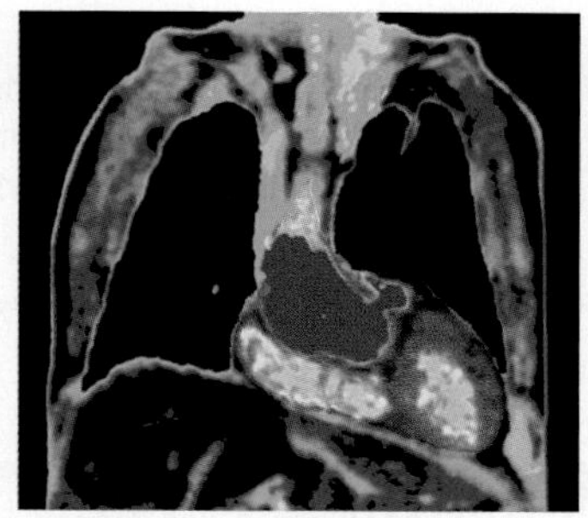

An MRI scan provides images of the heart and lungs.

Chemistry Link to Health

BRACHYTHERAPY

The process called *brachytherapy*, or seed implantation, is an internal form of radiation therapy. The prefix *brachy* is from the Greek word for short distance. With internal radiation, a high dose of radiation is delivered to a cancerous area, while normal tissue sustains minimal damage. Because higher doses are used, fewer treatments of shorter duration are needed. Conventional external treatment delivers a lower dose per treatment, but requires six to eight weeks of treatments.

Permanent Brachytherapy

One of the most common forms of cancer in males is prostate cancer. In addition to surgery and chemotherapy, one treatment option is to place 40 or more titanium capsules, or "seeds," in the malignant area. Each seed, which is the size of a grain of rice, contains radioactive iodine-125, palladium-103, or cesium-131, which decays by gamma emission. The radiation from the seeds destroys the cancer by interfering with the reproduction of cancer cells with minimal damage to adjacent normal tissues. Ninety percent (90%) of the radioisotopes decay within a few months because they have short half-lives.

Isotope	I-125	Pd-103	Cs-131
Radiation	Gamma	Gamma	Gamma
Half-life	60 days	17 days	10 days
Time required to deliver 90% of radiation	7 months	2 months	1 month

Almost no radiation passes out of the patient's body. The amount of radiation received by a family member is no greater than that received on a long plane flight. Because the radioisotopes decay to products that are not radioactive, the inert titanium capsules can be left in the body.

Temporary Brachytherapy

In another type of treatment for prostate cancer, long needles containing iridium-192 are placed in the tumor. However, the needles are removed after 5 to 10 min, depending on the activity of the iridium isotope. Compared to permanent brachytherapy, temporary brachytherapy can deliver a higher dose of radiation over a shorter time. The procedure may be repeated in a few days.

Brachytherapy is also used following breast cancer lumpectomy. An iridium-192 isotope is inserted into the catheter implanted in the space left by the removal of the tumor. The isotope is removed after 5 to 10 min, depending on the activity of the iridium source. Radiation is delivered primarily to the tissue surrounding the cavity that contained the tumor and where the cancer is most likely to recur. The procedure is repeated twice a day for five days to give an absorbed dose of 34 Gy (3400 rad). The catheter is removed, and no radioactive material remains in the body.

In conventional external beam therapy for breast cancer, a patient is given 2 Gy once a day for six to seven weeks, which gives a total absorbed dose of about 80 Gy or 8000 rad. The external beam therapy irradiates the entire breast, including the tumor cavity.

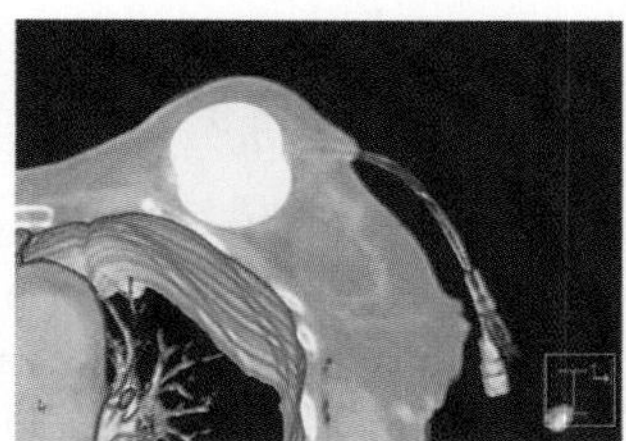

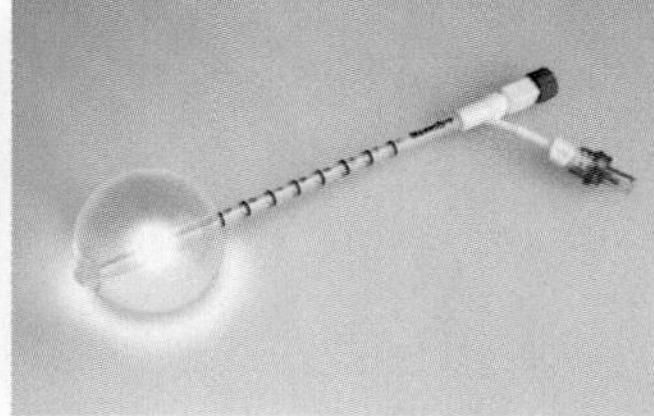

A catheter placed temporarily in the breast for radiation from Ir-192.

QUESTIONS AND PROBLEMS

16.5 Medical Applications Using Radioactivity

LEARNING GOAL: *Describe the use of radioisotopes in medicine.*

16.35 Bone and bony structures contain calcium and phosphorus.

a. Why would the radioisotopes calcium-47 and phosphorus-32 be used in the diagnosis and treatment of bone diseases?

b. During nuclear tests, scientists were concerned that strontium-85, a radioactive product, would be harmful to the growth of bone in children. Explain.

16.36 a. Technetium-99m emits only gamma radiation. Why would this type of radiation be used in diagnostic imaging rather than an isotope that also emits beta or alpha radiation?

b. A person with *polycythemia vera* (excess production of red blood cells) receives radioactive phosphorus-32. Why would this treatment reduce the production of red blood cells in the bone marrow of the patient?

16.37 In a diagnostic test for leukemia, a person receives 4.0 mL of a solution containing selenium-75. If the activity of the selenium-75 is 45 μCi/mL, what dose, in microcuries, does the patient receive?

16.38 A vial contains radioactive iodine-131 with an activity of 2.0 mCi/mL. If a thyroid test requires 3.0 mCi in an "atomic cocktail," how many milliliters are used to prepare the iodine-131 solution?

LEARNING GOAL

Describe the processes of nuclear fission and fusion.

16.6 Nuclear Fission and Fusion

During the 1930s, scientists bombarding uranium-235 with neutrons discovered that the U-235 nucleus splits into two smaller nuclei and produces a great amount of energy. This was the discovery of nuclear **fission**. The energy generated by splitting the atom was called *atomic energy*. A typical equation for nuclear fission is:

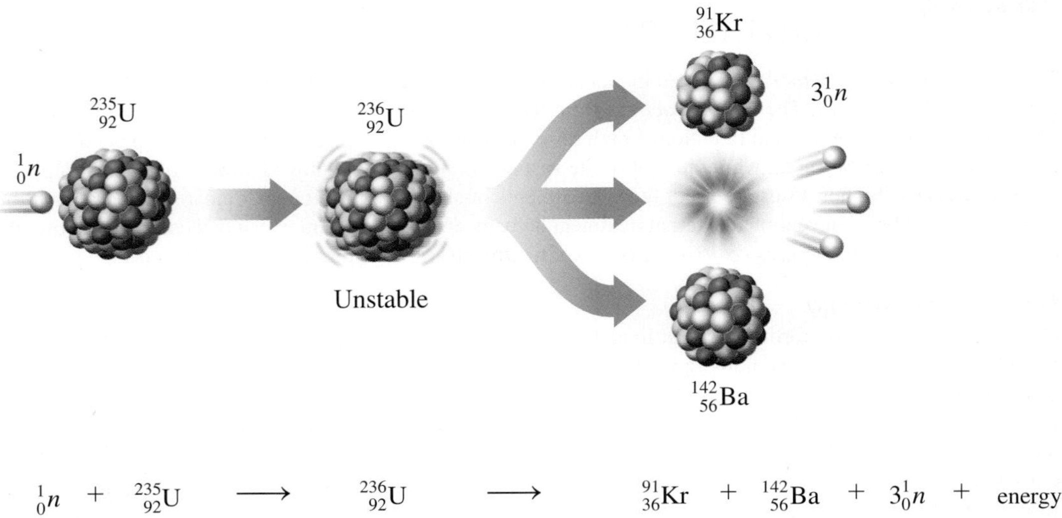

$$^{1}_{0}n + ^{235}_{92}U \longrightarrow ^{236}_{92}U \longrightarrow ^{91}_{36}Kr + ^{142}_{56}Ba + 3^{1}_{0}n + \text{energy}$$

If we could determine the mass of the products krypton, barium, and 3 neutrons, with great accuracy, we would find that their total mass is slightly less than the mass of the starting materials. The missing mass has been converted into an enormous amount of energy, consistent with the famous equation derived by Albert Einstein.

$$E = mc^2$$

where E is the energy released, m is the mass lost, and c is the speed of light, 3×10^8 m/s. Even though the mass loss is very small, when it is multiplied by the speed of light squared, the result is a large value for the energy released. The fission of 1 g of uranium-235 produces about as much energy as the burning of 3 tons of coal.

Chain Reaction

Fission begins when a neutron collides with the nucleus of a uranium atom. The resulting nucleus is unstable and splits into smaller nuclei. This fission process also releases several neutrons and large amounts of gamma radiation and energy. The neutrons emitted have high energies and bombard other uranium-235 nuclei. In a **chain reaction**, there is a rapid increase in the number of high-energy neutrons available to react with more uranium. To sustain a nuclear chain reaction, sufficient quantities of uranium-235 must be brought together to provide a *critical mass* in which almost all the neutrons immediately collide with more uranium-235 nuclei. So much heat and energy build up that an atomic explosion can occur (see Figure 16.7).

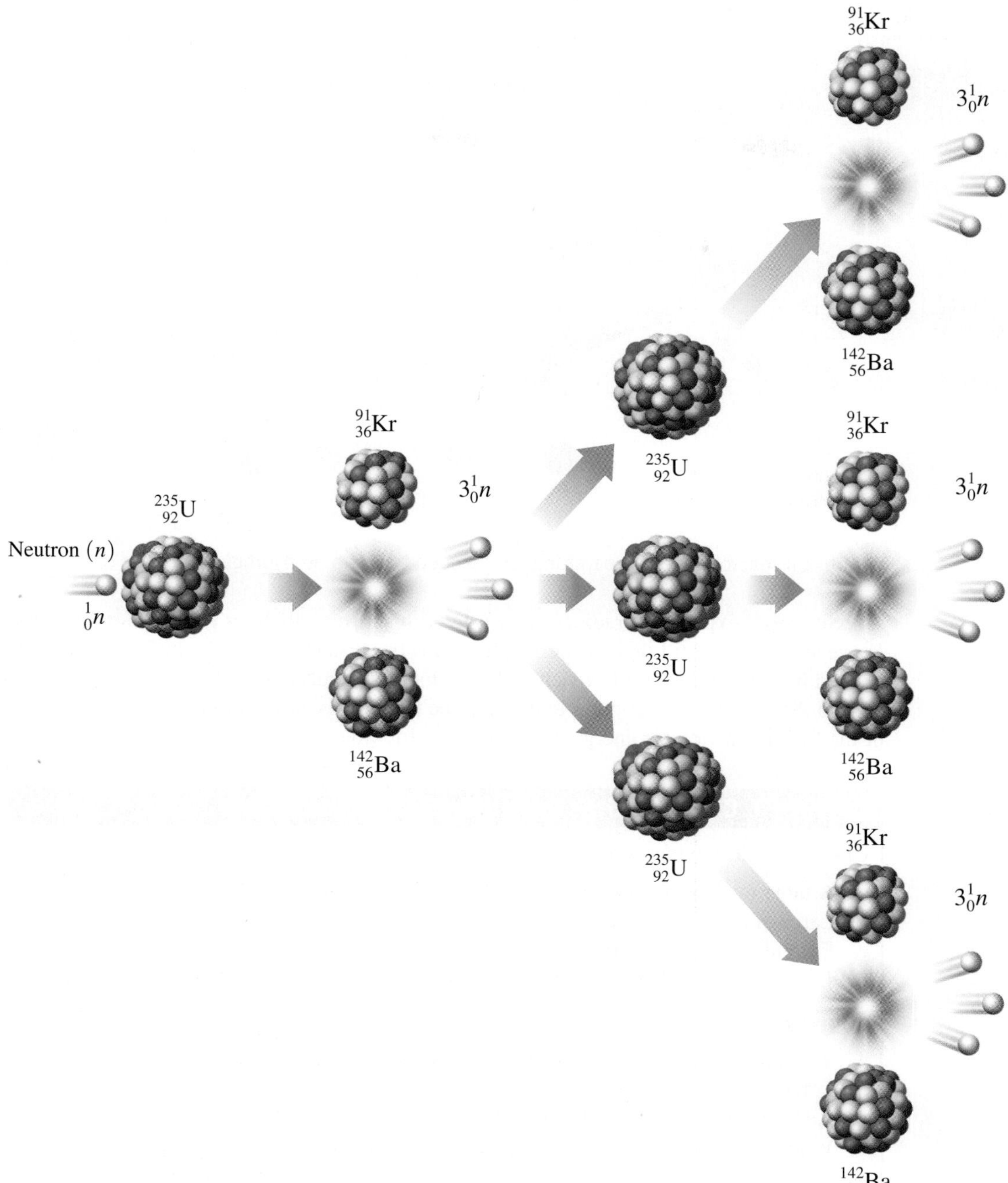

FIGURE 16.7 In a nuclear chain reaction, the fission of each uranium-235 atom produces three neutrons that cause the nuclear fission of more and more uranium-235 atoms.

Q Why is the fission of uranium-235 called a chain reaction?

Nuclear Fusion

In **fusion**, two small nuclei combine to form a larger nucleus. Mass is lost, and a tremendous amount of energy is released, even more than the energy released from nuclear fission. However, a fusion reaction requires a temperature of 100 000 000 °C to overcome the repulsion of the hydrogen nuclei and cause them to undergo fusion. Fusion reactions occur continuously in the Sun and other stars, providing us with heat and light. The huge amounts of energy produced by our Sun come from the fusion of 6×10^{11} kg of hydrogen every second. In a fusion reaction, isotopes of hydrogen combine to form helium and large amounts of energy.

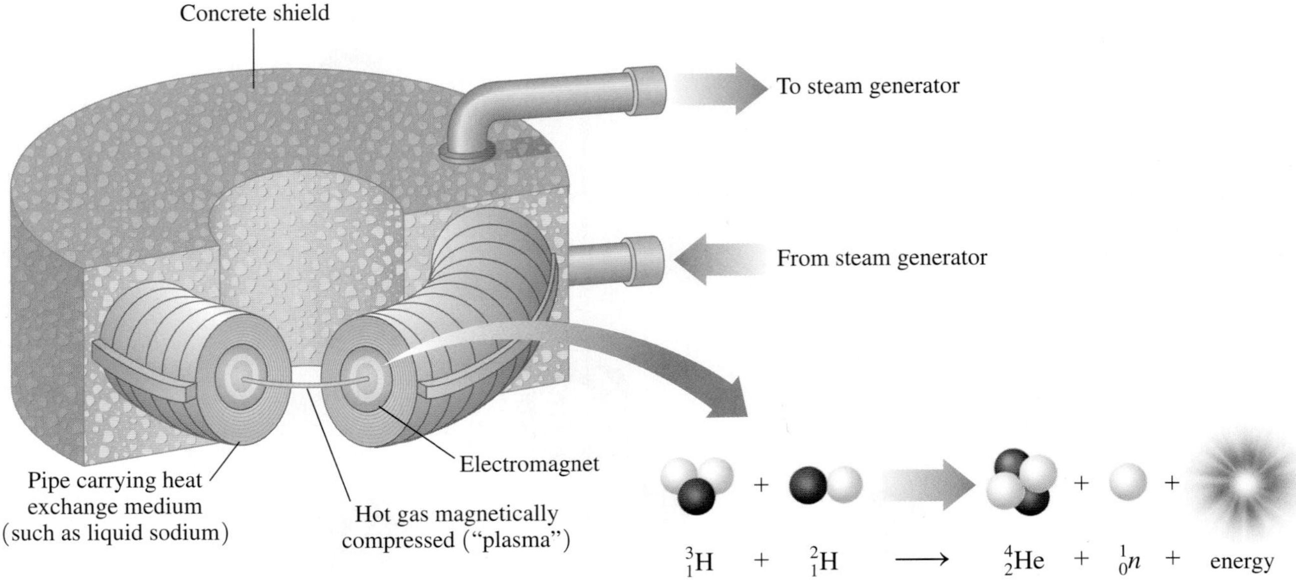

In a fusion reactor, high temperatures are needed to combine hydrogen atoms.

Scientists expect less radioactive waste with shorter half-lives from fusion reactors. However, fusion is still in the experimental stage because the extremely high temperatures needed have been difficult to reach and even more difficult to maintain. Research groups around the world are attempting to develop the technology needed to make the harnessing of the fusion reaction for energy a reality in our lifetime.

CONCEPT CHECK 16.6 Identifying Fission and Fusion

Classify the following as pertaining to fission, fusion, or both:

a. A large nucleus breaks apart to produce smaller nuclei.
b. Large amounts of energy are released.
c. Extremely high temperatures are needed for reaction.
d. $^{3}_{1}H + ^{2}_{1}H \longrightarrow ^{4}_{2}He + ^{1}_{0}n +$ energy

ANSWER

a. When a large nucleus breaks apart to produce smaller nuclei, the process is fission.
b. Large amounts of energy are generated in both the fusion and fission processes.
c. An extremely high temperature is required for fusion.
d. When small nuclei combine to release energy, the process is fusion.

QUESTIONS AND PROBLEMS

16.6 Nuclear Fission and Fusion

LEARNING GOAL: *Describe the processes of nuclear fission and fusion.*

16.39 What is nuclear fission?

16.40 How does a chain reaction occur in nuclear fission?

16.41 Complete the following fission reaction:

$$^{1}_{0}n + ^{235}_{92}U \longrightarrow ^{131}_{50}Sn + ? + 2^{1}_{0}n + \text{energy}$$

16.42 In another fission reaction, uranium-235 bombarded with a neutron produces strontium-94, another small nucleus, and three neutrons. Write the balanced nuclear equation for the fission reaction.

16.43 Indicate whether each of the following is characteristic of the fission or fusion process, or both:
a. Neutrons bombard a nucleus.
b. The nuclear process occurs in the Sun.
c. A large nucleus splits into smaller nuclei.
d. Small nuclei combine to form larger nuclei.

16.44 Indicate whether each of the following is characteristic of the fission or fusion process, or both:
a. Very high temperatures are required to initiate the reaction.
b. Less radioactive waste is produced.
c. Hydrogen nuclei are the reactants.
d. Large amounts of energy are released when the nuclear reaction occurs.

Chemistry Link to the Environment

NUCLEAR POWER PLANTS

In a nuclear power plant, the quantity of uranium-235 is held below a critical mass, so it cannot sustain a chain reaction. The fission reactions are slowed by placing control rods, which absorb some of the fast-moving neutrons, among the uranium samples. In this way, less fission occurs, and there is a slower, controlled production of energy. The heat from the controlled fission is used to produce steam. The steam drives a generator, which produces electricity. Approximately 10% of the electrical energy produced in the United States is generated in nuclear power plants.

Although nuclear power plants help meet some of our energy needs, there are some problems associated with nuclear power. One of the most serious problems is the production of radioactive by-products that have very long half-lives, such as plutonium-239 with a half-life of 24 000 y. It is essential that these waste products be stored safely in a place where they do not contaminate the environment. Several countries are now in the process of selecting areas where nuclear waste can be placed in caverns 1000 m below the surface of the Earth. In the United States, a current proposed repository site for nuclear waste is Yucca Mountain, Nevada.

Nuclear power plants supply about 10% of electricity in the United States.

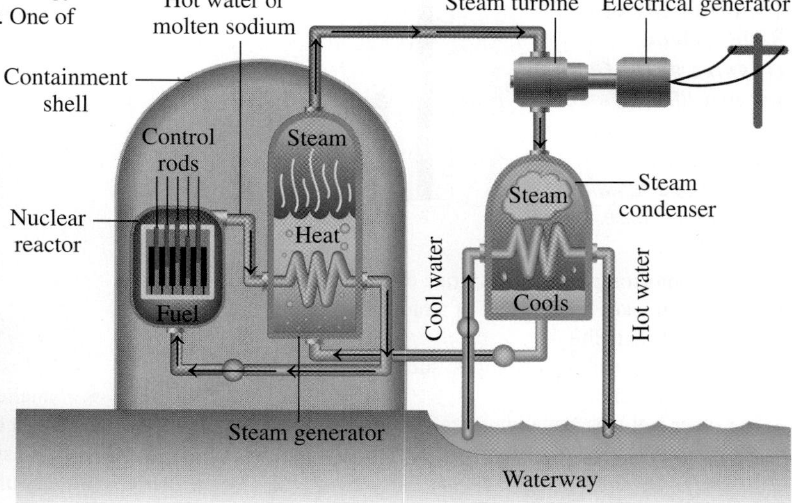

Heat from nuclear fission is used to generate electricity.

CHAPTER REVIEW

16.1 Natural Radioactivity

LEARNING GOAL: *Describe alpha, beta, positron, and gamma radiation.*

Alpha (α) particle

- Radioactive isotopes have unstable nuclei that break down (decay), spontaneously emitting alpha (α), beta (β), positron (β^+), and gamma (γ) radiation.
- Because radiation can damage the cells in the body, proper protection must be used: shielding, limiting the time of exposure, and distance.

16.2 Nuclear Reactions

LEARNING GOAL: *Write a balanced nuclear equation showing mass numbers and atomic numbers for radioactive decay.*

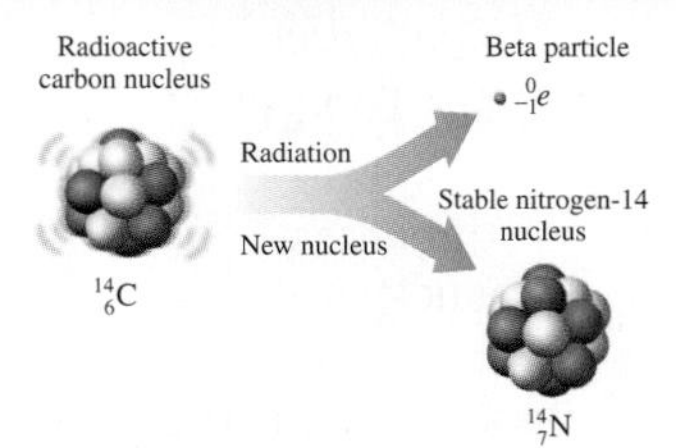

- A balanced nuclear equation is used to represent the changes that take place in the nuclei of the reactants and products.
- The new isotopes and the type of radiation emitted can be determined from the symbols that show the mass numbers and atomic numbers of the isotopes in the nuclear equation.
- A radioisotope is produced artificially when a nonradioactive isotope is bombarded by a small particle.

16.3 Radiation Measurement

LEARNING GOAL: *Describe the detection and measurement of radiation.*

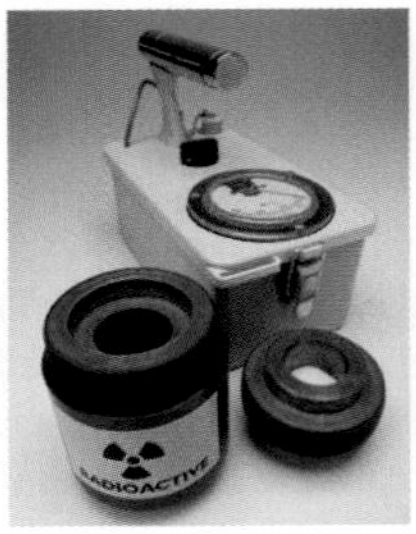

- In a Geiger counter, radiation produces charged particles in the gas contained in a tube, which generates an electrical current.
- The curie (Ci) and the becquerel (Bq) measure the activity, which is the number of nuclear transformations per second.
- The amount of radiation absorbed by a substance is measured in rads or the gray (Gy).
- The rem and the sievert (Sv) are units used to determine the biological damage from the different types of radiation.

16.4 Half-Life of a Radioisotope

LEARNING GOAL: *Given the half-life of a radioisotope, calculate the amount of radioisotope remaining after one or more half-lives.*

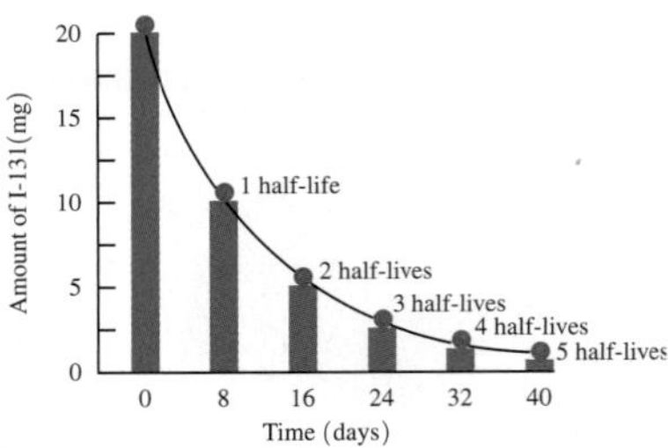

- Every radioisotope has its own rate of emitting radiation.
- The time it takes for one-half of a radioactive sample to decay is called its half-life.
- For many medical radioisotopes, such as Tc-99m and I-131, half-lives are short.
- For other isotopes, usually naturally occurring ones such as C-14, Ra-226, and U-238, half-lives are extremely long.

16.5 Medical Applications Using Radioactivity

LEARNING GOAL: *Describe the use of radioisotopes in medicine.*

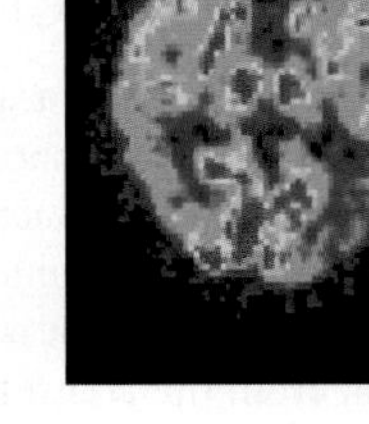

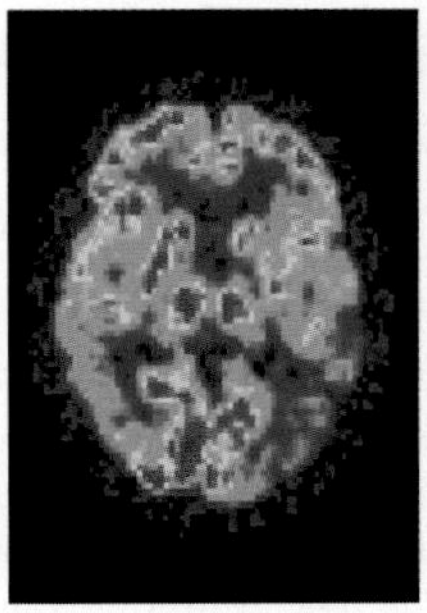

- In nuclear medicine, radioisotopes that go to specific sites in the body are given to the patient.
- By detecting the radiation they emit, an evaluation can be made about the location and extent of an injury, disease, tumor, or the level of function of a particular organ.
- Higher levels of radiation are used to treat or destroy tumors.

16.6 Nuclear Fission and Fusion

LEARNING GOAL: *Describe the processes of nuclear fission and fusion.*

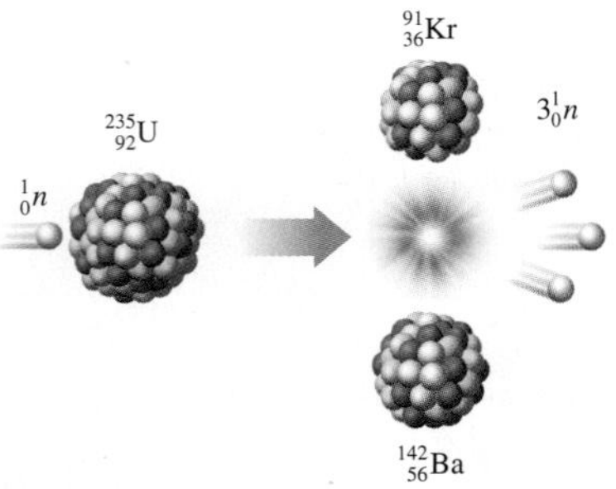

- In fission, the bombardment of a large nucleus breaks it apart into smaller nuclei, releasing one or more types of radiation and a great amount of energy.
- In fusion, small nuclei combine to form larger nuclei while great amounts of energy are released.

CONCEPT MAP

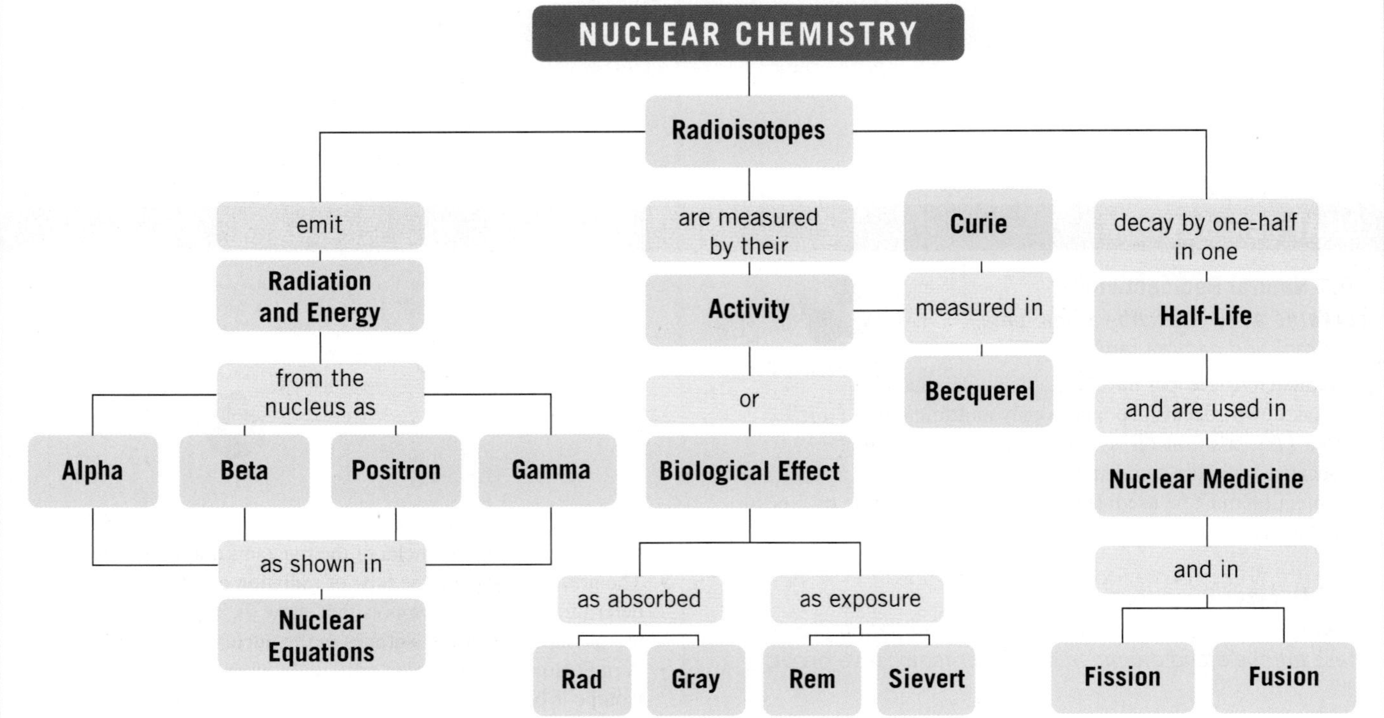

NUCLEAR CHEMISTRY

Radioisotopes

emit **Radiation and Energy** from the nucleus as **Alpha**, **Beta**, **Positron**, **Gamma** as shown in **Nuclear Equations**

are measured by their **Activity** measured in **Curie**, **Becquerel**; or **Biological Effect** as absorbed **Rad**, **Gray**; as exposure **Rem**, **Sievert**

decay by one-half in one **Half-Life** and are used in **Nuclear Medicine** and in **Fission**, **Fusion**

KEY TERMS

alpha particle A nuclear particle identical to a helium nucleus, symbol α or ${}^{4}_{2}He$.

becquerel (Bq) A unit of activity of a radioactive sample equal to one disintegration per second.

beta particle A particle identical to an electron, symbol, ${}^{\ 0}_{-1}e$ or β, that forms in the nucleus when a neutron changes to a proton and an electron.

chain reaction A fission reaction that will continue once it has been initiated by a high-energy neutron bombarding a heavy nucleus such as uranium-235.

curie (Ci) A unit of activity of a radioactive sample equal to 3.7×10^{10} disintegrations/s.

decay curve A diagram of the decay of a radioactive element.

equivalent dose The measure of biological damage from an absorbed dose that has been adjusted for the type of radiation.

fission A process in which large nuclei are split into smaller pieces, releasing large amounts of energy.

fusion A reaction in which large amounts of energy are released when small nuclei combine to form larger nuclei.

gamma ray High-energy radiation, symbol ${}^{0}_{0}\gamma$, emitted by an unstable nucleus.

gray (Gy) A unit of absorbed dose equal to 100 rad.

half-life The length of time it takes for one-half of a radioactive sample to decay.

positron A particle of radiation with no mass and a positive charge, symbol β^{+} or ${}^{\ 0}_{+1}e$, produced when a proton is transformed into a neutron and a positron.

rad (radiation absorbed dose) A measure of an amount of radiation absorbed by the body.

radiation Energy or particles released by radioactive atoms.

radioactive decay The process by which an unstable nucleus breaks down with the release of high-energy radiation.

radioisotope A radioactive atom of an element.

rem (radiation equivalent in humans) A measure of the biological damage caused by the various kinds of radiation (rad $\times$ radiation biological factor).

sievert (Sv) A unit of biological damage (equivalent dose) equal to 100 rem.

CORE CHEMISTRY SKILLS

The chapter section containing each Core Chemistry Skill is shown in parentheses at the end of each heading.

Writing Nuclear Equations (16.2)

- A nuclear equation is written with the atomic symbols of the original radioactive nucleus on the left, an arrow, and the new nucleus and the type of radiation emitted on the right.
- The sum of the mass numbers and the sum of the atomic numbers on one side of the arrow must equal the sum of the mass numbers and the sum of the atomic numbers on the other side.
- When an alpha particle is emitted, the mass number of the new nucleus decreases by 4, and its atomic number decreases by 2.
- When a beta particle is emitted, there is no change in the mass number of the new nucleus, but its atomic number increases by one.
- When a positron is emitted, there is no change in the mass number of the new nucleus, but its atomic number decreases by one.
- In gamma emission, there is no change in the mass number or the atomic number of the new nucleus.

Example: **a.** Write a balanced nuclear equation for the alpha decay of Po-210.

b. Write a balanced nuclear equation for the beta decay of Co-60.

Answer: **a.** When an alpha particle is emitted, we calculate the decrease of 4 in the mass number of polonium, and a decrease of 2 in its atomic number.

$${}^{210}_{84}Po \longrightarrow {}^{206}_{82}? + {}^{4}_{2}He$$

Because lead has atomic number 82, the new nucleus must be an isotope of lead.

$${}^{210}_{84}Po \longrightarrow {}^{206}_{82}Pb + {}^{4}_{2}He$$

b. When a beta particle is emitted, there is no change in the mass number (60) of cobalt, but there is an increase of 1 in its atomic number.

$${}^{60}_{27}Co \longrightarrow {}^{60}_{28}? + {}^{\ 0}_{-1}e$$

Because nickel has atomic number 28, the new nucleus must be an isotope of nickel.

$${}^{60}_{27}Co \longrightarrow {}^{60}_{28}Ni + {}^{\ 0}_{-1}e$$

Using Half-Lives (16.4)

- The half-life of a radioisotope is the amount of time it takes for one-half of a sample to decay.
- The remaining amount of a radioisotope is calculated by dividing its quantity or activity by one-half for each half-life that has elapsed.

Example: Co-60 has a half-life of 5.3 years. If the initial sample of Co-60 has an activity of 1200 Ci, what is its activity after 15.9 years?

Answer:

Years	Number of Half-Lives	Co-60 (Activity)
0	0	1200 Ci
5.3	1	600 Ci
10.6	2	300 Ci
15.9	3	150 Ci

In 15.9 y, three half-lives have passed. Thus the activity was reduced from 1200 Ci to 150 Ci.

$$1200\text{ Ci} \xrightarrow{\text{1 half-life}} 600\text{ Ci} \xrightarrow{\text{2 half-lives}} 300\text{ Ci} \xrightarrow{\text{3 half-lives}} 150\text{ Ci}$$

UNDERSTANDING THE CONCEPTS

The chapter sections to review are shown in parentheses at the end of each question.

In Problems 16.45 to 16.48, a nucleus is shown with protons and neutrons.

16.45 Draw the new nucleus when this isotope emits a positron to complete the following figure: (16.2)

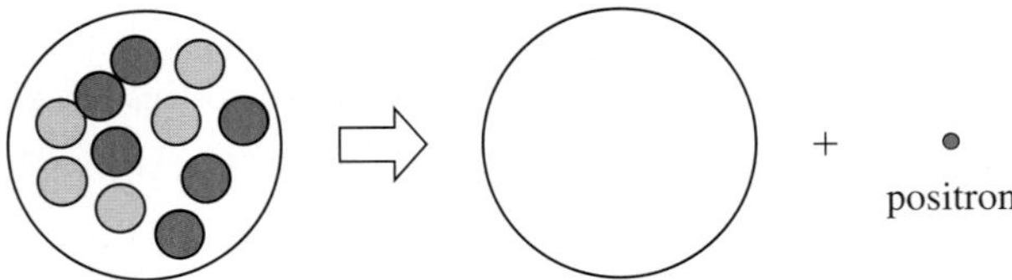

16.46 Draw the nucleus that emits a beta particle to complete the following figure: (16.2)

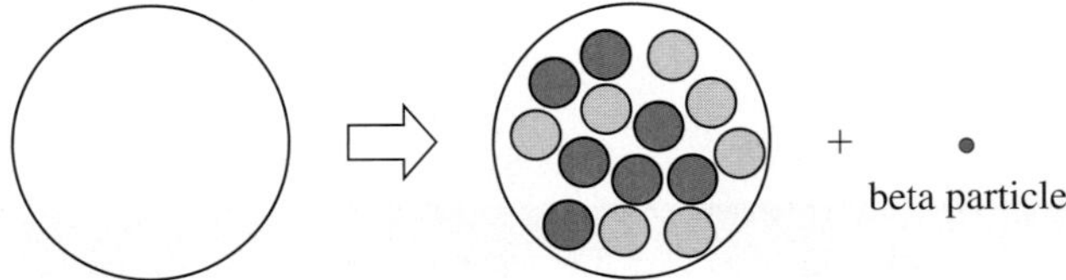

16.47 Draw the nucleus of the isotope that is bombarded in the following figure: (16.2)

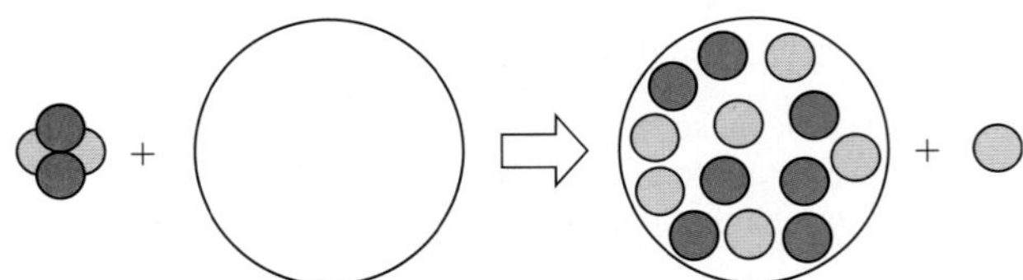

16.48 Complete the following bombardment reaction by drawing the nucleus of the new isotope that is produced in the following figure: (16.2)

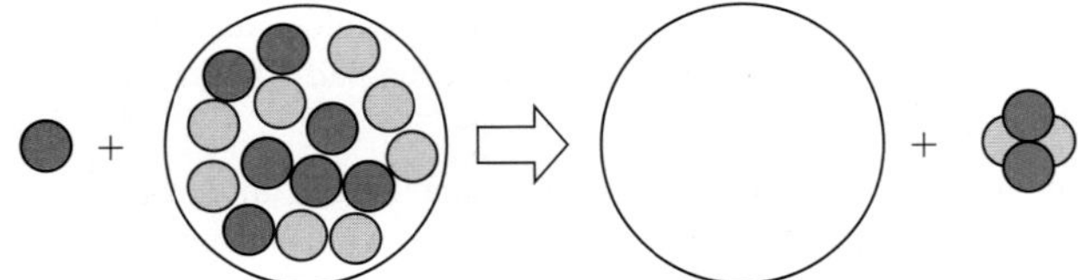

16.49 Carbon dating of small bits of charcoal used in cave paintings has determined that some of the paintings are from 10 000 to 30 000 y old. Carbon-14 has a half-life of 5730 y. In a 1 μg-sample of carbon from a live tree, the activity of carbon-14 is 6.4 μCi. If researchers determine that 1 μg of charcoal from a prehistoric cave painting in France has an activity of 0.80 μCi, what is the age of the painting? (16.4)

The technique of carbon dating is used to determine the age of ancient cave paintings.

16.50 Use the following decay curve for iodine-131 to answer Questions **a–c**: (16.4)

a. Complete the values for the mass of radioactive iodine-131 on the vertical axis.

b. Complete the number of days on the horizontal axis.

c. What is the half-life, in days, of iodine-131?

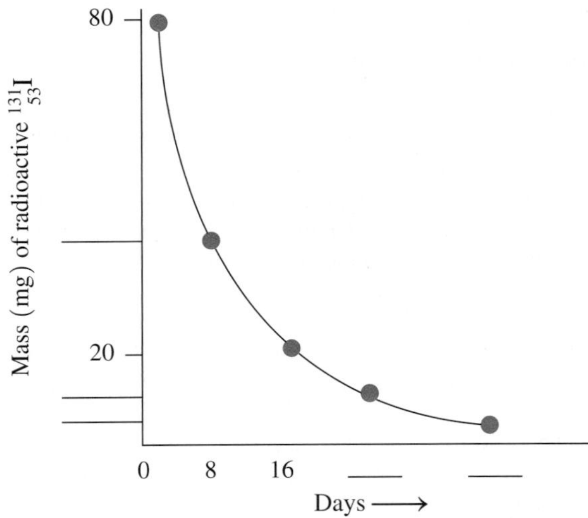

ADDITIONAL QUESTIONS AND PROBLEMS

16.51 Give the number of protons and number of neutrons in the nucleus of each the following: (16.1)

a. sodium-25 **b.** nickel-61
c. rubidium-84 **d.** silver-110

16.52 Give the number of protons and number of neutrons in the nucleus of each of the following: (16.1)

a. boron-10 **b.** zinc-72
c. iron-59 **d.** gold-198

16.53 Identify each of the following as alpha decay, beta decay, positron emission, or gamma emission: (16.1, 16.2)

a. $^{27m}_{13}Al \longrightarrow ^{27}_{13}Al + ^{0}_{0}\gamma$

b. $^{8}_{5}B \longrightarrow ^{8}_{4}Be + ^{0}_{+1}e$

c. $^{220}_{86}Rn \longrightarrow ^{216}_{84}Po + ^{4}_{2}He$

16.54 Identify each of the following as alpha decay, beta decay, positron emission, or gamma emission: (16.1, 16.2)

a. $^{127}_{55}Cs \longrightarrow ^{127}_{54}Xe + ^{0}_{+1}e$

b. $^{90}_{38}Sr \longrightarrow ^{90}_{39}Y + ^{0}_{-1}e$

c. $^{218}_{85}At \longrightarrow ^{214}_{83}Bi + ^{4}_{2}He$

16.55 Write the balanced nuclear equation for each of the following: (16.1, 16.2)

a. Th-225 (α decay) **b.** Bi-210 (α decay)
c. cesium-137 (β decay) **d.** tin-126 (β decay)
e. F-18 (β^{+} emission)

16.56 Write the balanced nuclear equation for each of the following: (16.1, 16.2)

a. potassium-40 (β decay) **b.** sulfur-35 (β decay)
c. platinum-190 (α decay) **d.** Ra-210 (α decay)
e. In-113m (γ emission)

16.57 Complete each of the following nuclear equations: (16.2)

a. ${}^{4}_{2}He + {}^{14}_{7}N \longrightarrow ? + {}^{1}_{1}H$
b. ${}^{4}_{2}He + {}^{27}_{13}Al \longrightarrow {}^{30}_{14}Si + ?$
c. ${}^{1}_{0}n + {}^{235}_{92}U \longrightarrow {}^{90}_{38}Sr + 3{}^{1}_{0}n + ?$
d. ${}^{23m}_{12}Mg \longrightarrow ? + {}^{0}_{0}\gamma$

16.58 Complete each of the following nuclear equations: (16.2)

a. $? + {}^{59}_{27}Co \longrightarrow {}^{56}_{25}Mn + {}^{4}_{2}He$
b. $? \longrightarrow {}^{14}_{7}N + {}^{0}_{-1}e$
c. ${}^{0}_{-1}e + {}^{76}_{36}Kr \longrightarrow ?$
d. ${}^{4}_{2}He + {}^{241}_{95}Am \longrightarrow ? + 2{}^{1}_{0}n$

16.59 Write the balanced nuclear equation for each of the following: (16.2)

a. When two oxygen-16 atoms collide, one of the products is an alpha particle.
b. When californium-249 is bombarded by oxygen-18, a new element, seaborgium-263, and four neutrons are produced.
c. Radon-222 undergoes alpha decay.
d. An atom of strontium-80 emits a positron.

16.60 Write the balanced nuclear equation for each of the following: (16.2)

a. Polonium-210 decays to give lead-206.
b. Bismuth-211 emits an alpha particle.
c. A radioisotope emits a positron to form titanium-48.
d. An atom of germanium-69 emits a positron.

16.61 The activity of K-40 in a 70.-kg human body is estimated to be 120 nCi. What is this activity in becquerels? (16.3)

16.62 The activity of C-14 in a 70.-kg human body is estimated to be 3.7 kBq. What is this activity in microcuries? (16.3)

16.63 If the amount of radioactive phosphorus-32 in a sample decreases from 1.2 mg to 0.30 mg in 28.6 days, what is the half-life of phosphorus-32? (16.4)

16.64 If the amount of radioactive iodine-123 in a sample decreases from 0.4 mg to 0.1 mg in 26.4 h, what is the half-life of iodine-123? (16.4)

16.65 Calcium-47, a beta emitter, has a half-life of 4.5 days. (16.2, 16.4)

a. Write the balanced nuclear equation for the beta decay of calcium-47.
b. How many milligrams of a 16-mg sample of calcium-47 remain after 18 days?
c. How many days have passed if 4.8 mg of calcium-47 decayed to 1.2 mg of calcium-47?

16.66 Cesium-137, a beta emitter, has a half-life of 30 y. (16.2, 16.4)

a. Write the balanced nuclear equation for the beta decay of cesium-137.
b. How many milligrams of a 16-mg sample of cesium-137 remain after 90 y?
c. How many years are required for 28 mg of cesium-137 to decay to 3.5 mg of cesium-137?

16.67 A 120-mg sample of technetium-99m is used for a diagnostic test. If technetium-99m has a half-life of 6.0 h, how many milligrams of the technetium-99m sample remains active 24 h after the test? (16.4)

16.68 The half-life of oxygen-15 is 124 s. If a sample of oxygen-15 has an activity of 4000 Bq, how many minutes will elapse before it has an activity of 500 Bq? (16.4)

16.69 What is the difference between fission and fusion? (16.6)

16.70 a. What are the products in the fission of uranium-235 that make possible a nuclear chain reaction? (16.6)
b. What is the purpose of placing control rods among uranium samples in a nuclear reactor?

16.71 Where does fusion occur naturally? (16.6)

16.72 Why are scientists continuing to try to build a fusion reactor even though the very high temperatures it requires have been difficult to reach and maintain? (16.6)

CHALLENGE QUESTIONS

16.73 Write the balanced equation for each of the following radioactive emissions: (16.2)

a. an alpha particle from Hg-180
b. a beta particle from Au-198
c. a positron from Rb-82

16.74 Write the balanced equation for each of the following radioactive emissions: (16.2)

a. an alpha particle from Gd-148
b. a beta particle from Sr-90
c. a positron from Al-25

16.75 All the elements beyond uranium, the transuranium elements, have been prepared by bombardment and are not naturally occurring elements. The first transuranium element neptunium, Np, was prepared by bombarding U-238 with neutrons to form a neptunium atom and a beta particle. Complete the following equation: (16.2)

$${}^{1}_{0}n + {}^{238}_{92}U \longrightarrow ? + ?$$

16.76 One of the most recent transuranium elements ununoctinum-294 (Uuo-294), atomic number 118, was prepared by bombarding californium-249 with another isotope. Complete the following equation for the preparation of this new element: (16.2)

$$? + {}^{249}_{98}Cf \longrightarrow {}^{294}_{118}Uuo + 3{}^{1}_{0}n$$

16.77 A nuclear technician was accidentally exposed to potassium-42 while doing brain scans for possible tumors. The error was not discovered until 36 h later when the activity of the potassium-42 sample was 2.0 μCi. If potassium-42 has a half-life of 12 h, what was the activity of the sample at the time the technician was exposed? (16.3, 16.4)

16.78 A wooden object from the site of an ancient temple has a carbon-14 activity of 10 counts/min compared with a reference piece of wood cut today that has an activity of 40 counts/min. If the half-life for carbon-14 is 5730 y, what is the age of the ancient wood object? (16.3, 16.4)

16.79 The half-life for the radioactive decay of calcium-47 is 4.5 d. If a sample has an activity of 1.0 μCi after 27 d, what was the initial activity, in microcuries, of the sample? (16.3, 16.4)

16.80 The half-life for the radioactive decay of Ce-141 is 32.5 days. If a sample has an activity of 4.0 μCi after 130 d have elapsed, what was the initial activity, in microcuries, of the sample? (16.3, 16.4)

16.81 A 64-μCi sample of Tl-201 decays to 4.0 μCi in 12 days. What is the half-life, in days, of Tl-201? (16.3, 16.4)

16.82 A 16-μg sample of sodium-24 decays to 2.0 μg in 45 h. What is the half-life, in hours, of sodium-24? (16.4)

16.83 Element 114 was recently named flerovium, symbol Fl. The reaction for its synthesis involves bombarding Pu-244 with Ca-48. Write the nuclear equation for the synthesis of flerovium.

16.84 Element 116 was recently named livermorium, symbol Lv. The reaction for its synthesis involves bombarding Cm-248 with Ca-48. Write the nuclear equation for the synthesis of livermorium.

ANSWERS

Answers to Study Checks

16.1 Limiting the time one spends near a radioactive source and staying as far away as possible will reduce exposure to radiation.

16.2 $^{214}_{84}\text{Po} \longrightarrow \, ^{210}_{82}\text{Pb} + \, ^{4}_{2}\text{He}$

16.3 $^{51}_{24}\text{Cr} \longrightarrow \, ^{51}_{25}\text{Mn} + \, ^{0}_{-1}e$

16.4 $^{118}_{54}\text{Xe} \longrightarrow \, ^{118}_{53}\text{I} + \, ^{0}_{+1}e$

16.5 $^{4}_{2}\text{He} + \, ^{27}_{13}\text{Al} \longrightarrow \, ^{30}_{15}\text{P} + \, ^{1}_{0}n$

16.6 2.0 μg of iron-59

16.7 17 200 years

16.8 $^{1}_{0}n + \, ^{10}_{5}\text{B} \longrightarrow \, ^{7}_{3}\text{Li} + \, ^{4}_{2}\text{He}$

Answers to Selected Questions and Problems

16.1 **a.** alpha particle
b. positron
c. gamma radiation

16.3 **a.** $^{39}_{19}\text{K}$, $^{40}_{19}\text{K}$, $^{41}_{19}\text{K}$
b. They all have 19 protons and 19 electrons, but they differ in the number of neutrons.

16.5

Medical Use	Atomic Symbol	Mass Number	Number of Protons	Number of Neutrons
Heart imaging	$^{201}_{81}\text{Tl}$	201	81	120
Radiation therapy	$^{60}_{27}\text{Co}$	60	27	33
Abdominal scan	$^{67}_{31}\text{Ga}$	67	31	36
Hyperthyroidism	$^{131}_{53}\text{I}$	131	53	78
Leukemia treatment	$^{32}_{15}\text{P}$	32	15	17

16.7 **a.** $^{64}_{29}\text{Cu}$ **b.** $^{75}_{34}\text{Se}$
c. $^{24}_{11}\text{Na}$ **d.** $^{15}_{7}\text{N}$

16.9 **a.** β or $^{0}_{-1}e$ **b.** α or $^{4}_{2}\text{He}$
c. n or $^{1}_{0}n$ **d.** $^{38}_{18}\text{Ar}$
e. $^{14}_{6}\text{C}$

16.11 **a.** **1.** alpha particle
b. **3.** gamma radiation
c. **1.** alpha particle

16.13 **a.** $^{208}_{84}\text{Po} \longrightarrow \, ^{204}_{82}\text{Pb} + \, ^{4}_{2}\text{He}$
b. $^{232}_{90}\text{Th} \longrightarrow \, ^{228}_{88}\text{Ra} + \, ^{4}_{2}\text{He}$
c. $^{251}_{102}\text{No} \longrightarrow \, ^{247}_{100}\text{Fm} + \, ^{4}_{2}\text{He}$
d. $^{220}_{86}\text{Rn} \longrightarrow \, ^{216}_{84}\text{Po} + \, ^{4}_{2}\text{He}$

16.15 **a.** $^{25}_{11}\text{Na} \longrightarrow \, ^{25}_{12}\text{Mg} + \, ^{0}_{-1}e$
b. $^{20}_{8}\text{O} \longrightarrow \, ^{20}_{9}\text{F} + \, ^{0}_{-1}e$
c. $^{92}_{38}\text{Sr} \longrightarrow \, ^{92}_{39}\text{Y} + \, ^{0}_{-1}e$
d. $^{60}_{26}\text{Fe} \longrightarrow \, ^{60}_{27}\text{Co} + \, ^{0}_{-1}e$

16.17 **a.** $^{26}_{14}\text{Si} \longrightarrow \, ^{26}_{13}\text{Al} + \, ^{0}_{+1}e$
b. $^{54}_{27}\text{Co} \longrightarrow \, ^{54}_{26}\text{Fe} + \, ^{0}_{+1}e$
c. $^{77}_{37}\text{Rb} \longrightarrow \, ^{77}_{36}\text{Kr} + \, ^{0}_{+1}e$
d. $^{93}_{45}\text{Rh} \longrightarrow \, ^{93}_{44}\text{Ru} + \, ^{0}_{+1}e$

16.19 **a.** $^{28}_{14}\text{Si}$, beta decay
b. $^{0}_{0}\gamma$, gamma emission
c. $^{0}_{-1}e$, beta decay
d. $^{238}_{92}\text{U}$, alpha decay
e. $^{188}_{79}\text{Au}$, positron emission

16.21 **a.** $^{10}_{4}\text{Be}$ **b.** $^{132}_{53}\text{I}$
c. $^{27}_{13}\text{Al}$ **d.** $^{30}_{15}\text{P}$

16.23 **a.** **2.** absorbed dose **b.** **3.** biological damage
c. **1.** activity **d.** **2.** absorbed dose

16.25 The technician exposed to 5 rad received the higher amount of radiation.

16.27 **a.** 294 μCi **b.** 0.5 Gy

16.29 **a.** two half-lives
b. one half-life
c. three half-lives

16.31 **a.** 40.0 mg **b.** 20.0 mg
c. 10.0 mg **d.** 5.00 mg

16.33 **a.** 130 days **b.** 195 days

16.35 **a.** Since the elements Ca and P are part of the bone, the radioactive isotopes of Ca and P will become part of the bony structures of the body, where their radiation can be used to diagnose or treat bone diseases.
b. Strontium (Sr) acts much like calcium (Ca) because both are Group 2A (2) elements. The body will accumulate radioactive strontium in bones in the same way that it incorporates calcium. Radioactive strontium is harmful to children because the radiation it produces causes more damage in cells that are dividing rapidly.

16.37 180 μCi

16.39 Nuclear fission is the splitting of a large atom into smaller fragments with the release of large amounts of energy.

16.41 $^{103}_{42}\text{Mo}$

16.43 **a.** fission **b.** fusion
c. fission **d.** fusion

16.45

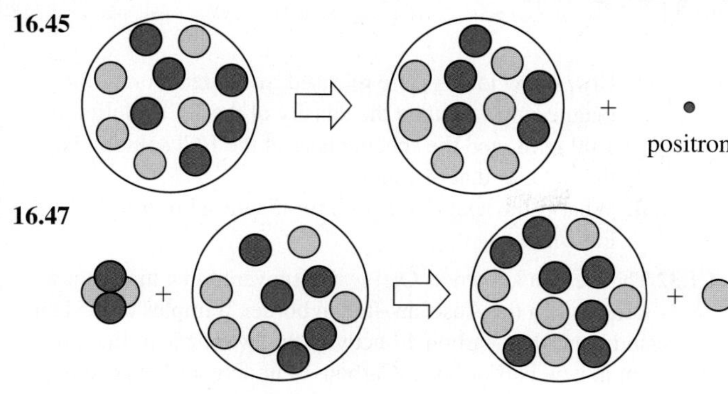

16.47

16.49 17 200 years old

16.51 **a.** 11 protons and 14 neutrons
b. 28 protons and 33 neutrons
c. 37 protons and 47 neutrons
d. 47 protons and 63 neutrons

16.53 **a.** gamma emission
b. positron emission
c. alpha decay

16.55 **a.** ${}^{225}_{90}\mathrm{Th} \longrightarrow {}^{221}_{88}\mathrm{Ra} + {}^{4}_{2}\mathrm{He}$
b. ${}^{210}_{83}\mathrm{Bi} \longrightarrow {}^{206}_{81}\mathrm{Tl} + {}^{4}_{2}\mathrm{He}$
c. ${}^{137}_{55}\mathrm{Cs} \longrightarrow {}^{137}_{56}\mathrm{Ba} + {}^{0}_{-1}e$
d. ${}^{126}_{50}\mathrm{Sn} \longrightarrow {}^{126}_{51}\mathrm{Sb} + {}^{0}_{-1}e$
e. ${}^{18}_{9}\mathrm{F} \longrightarrow {}^{18}_{8}\mathrm{O} + {}^{0}_{+1}e$

16.57 **a.** ${}^{17}_{8}\mathrm{O}$ **b.** ${}^{1}_{1}\mathrm{H}$
c. ${}^{143}_{54}\mathrm{Xe}$ **d.** ${}^{23}_{12}\mathrm{Mg}$

16.59 **a.** ${}^{16}_{8}\mathrm{O} + {}^{16}_{8}\mathrm{O} \longrightarrow {}^{28}_{14}\mathrm{Si} + {}^{4}_{2}\mathrm{He}$
b. ${}^{18}_{8}\mathrm{O} + {}^{249}_{98}\mathrm{Cf} \longrightarrow {}^{263}_{106}\mathrm{Sg} + 4{}^{1}_{0}n$
c. ${}^{222}_{86}\mathrm{Rn} \longrightarrow {}^{218}_{84}\mathrm{Po} + {}^{4}_{2}\mathrm{He}$
d. ${}^{80}_{38}\mathrm{Sr} \longrightarrow {}^{80}_{37}\mathrm{Rb} + {}^{0}_{+1}e$

16.61 4.4×10^{3} Bq

16.63 14.3 d

16.65 **a.** ${}^{47}_{20}\mathrm{Ca} \longrightarrow {}^{47}_{21}\mathrm{Sc} + {}^{0}_{-1}e$
b. 1.0 mg of Ca-47
c. 9.0 d

16.67 7.5 mg of Tc-99m

16.69 In the fission process, an atom splits into smaller nuclei. In fusion, small nuclei combine (fuse) to form a larger nucleus.

16.71 Fusion occurs naturally in the Sun and other stars.

16.73 **a.** ${}^{180}_{80}\mathrm{Hg} \longrightarrow {}^{176}_{78}\mathrm{Pt} + {}^{4}_{2}\mathrm{He}$
b. ${}^{198}_{79}\mathrm{Au} \longrightarrow {}^{198}_{80}\mathrm{Hg} + {}^{0}_{-1}e$
c. ${}^{82}_{37}\mathrm{Rb} \longrightarrow {}^{82}_{36}\mathrm{Kr} + {}^{0}_{+1}e$

16.75 ${}^{1}_{0}n + {}^{238}_{92}\mathrm{U} \longrightarrow {}^{238}_{93}\mathrm{Np} + {}^{0}_{-1}e$

16.77 16 μCi

16.79 64 μCi

16.81 3.0 days

16.83 ${}^{48}_{20}\mathrm{Ca} + {}^{244}_{94}\mathrm{Pu} \longrightarrow {}^{292}_{114}\mathrm{Fl}$

Combining Ideas from Chapters 15 and 16

CI.29 Consider the reaction of sodium oxalate ($Na_2C_2O_4$) and potassium permanganate ($KMnO_4$) in acidic solution. The unbalanced equation is the following: (9.1, 9.2, 12.4, 12.5, 15.3)

$$MnO_4^-(aq) + C_2O_4^{2-}(aq) \longrightarrow Mn^{2+}(aq) + CO_2(g)$$

In an oxidation–reduction titration, the $KMnO_4$ from the buret reacts with $Na_2C_2O_4$.

a. What is the balanced oxidation half-reaction?
b. What is the balanced reduction half-reaction?
c. What is the balanced ionic equation for the reaction?
d. If 24.6 mL of a $KMnO_4$ solution is needed to titrate a solution containing 0.758 g of sodium oxalate ($Na_2C_2O_4$), what is the molarity of the $KMnO_4$ solution?

CI.30 A strip of magnesium metal dissolves rapidly in 6.00 mL of a 0.150 M HCl solution, producing hydrogen gas and magnesium chloride. (9.1, 9.2, 12.4, 12.5, 14.6, 15.2, 15.3)

$$Mg(s) + HCl(aq) \longrightarrow H_2(g) + MgCl_2(aq) \text{ Unbalanced}$$

Magnesium metal reacts vigorously with hydrochloric acid.

a. Assign oxidation numbers to all of the elements in the reactants and products.
b. What is the balanced equation for the reaction?
c. What is the oxidizing agent?
d. What is the reducing agent?
e. What is the pH of the 0.150 M HCl solution?
f. How many grams of magnesium can dissolve in the HCl solution?

CI.31 A piece of magnesium with a mass of 0.121 g is added to 50.0 mL of a 1.00 M HCl solution at a temperature of 22 °C. When the magnesium dissolves, the solution reaches a temperature of 33 °C. For the equation, see your answer to Problem CI.30 b. (9.1, 9.2, 9.3, 9.4, 9.5, 12.4, 12.5)

a. What is the limiting reactant?
b. What volume, in milliliters, of hydrogen gas would be produced at 33 °C when the pressure is 750. mmHg?
c. How many joules were released by the reaction of the magnesium? Assume the density of the HCl solution is 1.00 g/mL and the specific heat of the HCl solution is the same as that of water.
d. What is the heat of reaction for magnesium in J/g? in kJ/mol?

CI.32 The iceman known as Ötzi was discovered in a high mountain pass on the Austrian–Italian border. Samples of his hair and bones had carbon-14 activity that was 50% of that present in new hair or bone. Carbon-14 undergoes beta decay and has a half-life of 5730 y. (16.2, 16.4)

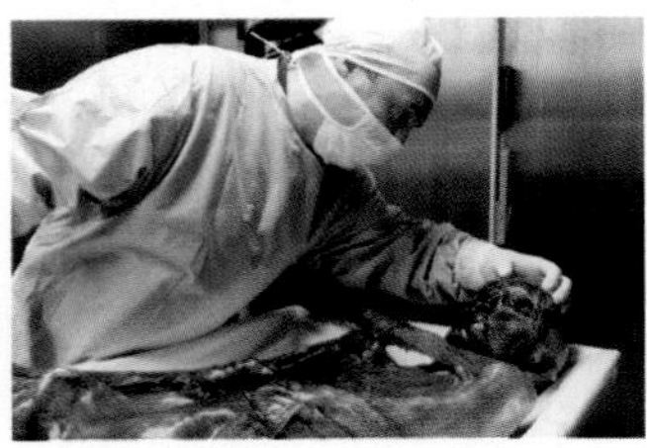

The mummified remains of Ötzi were discovered in 1991.

a. How long ago did Ötzi live?
b. Write a balanced nuclear equation for the decay of carbon-14.

CI.33 Some of the isotopes of silicon are listed in the following table: (4.5, 5.4, 10.2, 16.2, 16.4)

Isotope	% Natural Abundance	Atomic Mass	Half-Life (radioactive)	Radiation
$^{27}_{14}Si$		26.987	4.9 s	Positron
$^{28}_{14}Si$	92.23	27.977	Stable	None
$^{29}_{14}Si$	4.683	28.976	Stable	None
$^{30}_{14}Si$	3.087	29.974	Stable	None
$^{31}_{14}Si$		30.975	2.6 h	Beta

a. In the following table, indicate the number of protons, neutrons, and electrons for each isotope listed:

Isotope	Number of Protons	Number of Neutrons	Number of Electrons
$^{27}_{14}Si$			
$^{28}_{14}Si$			
$^{29}_{14}Si$			
$^{30}_{14}Si$			
$^{31}_{14}Si$			

b. What are the electron configuration and the abbreviated electron configuration of silicon?
c. Calculate the atomic mass for silicon using the isotopes that have a natural abundance.
d. Write the balanced nuclear equations for the positron emission of Si-27 and the beta decay of Si-31.
e. Draw the electron-dot formula and predict the shape of $SiCl_4$.
f. How many hours are needed for a sample of Si-31 with an activity of 16 μCi to decay to 2.0 μCi?

CI.34 K^+ is an electrolyte required by the human body and found in many foods as well as salt substitutes. One of the isotopes of potassium is potassium-40, which has a natural abundance of 0.012% and a half-life of 1.30×10^9 y. The isotope potassium-40 decays to calcium-40 or to argon-40. A typical activity for potassium-40 is 7.0 μCi per gram. (16.2, 16.3, 16.4)

Potassium chloride is used as a salt substitute.

a. Write a balanced nuclear equation for each type of decay.
b. Identify the particle emitted for each type of decay.
c. How many K^+ ions are in 3.5 oz of KCl?
d. What is the activity of 25 g of KCl in becquerels?

CI.35 Uranium-238 decays in a series of nuclear changes until stable lead-206 is produced. Complete the following nuclear equations that are part of the uranium-238 decay series: (16.2, 16.3, 16.4)

a. $^{238}_{92}U \longrightarrow {}^{234}_{90}Th + ?$
b. $^{234}_{90}Th \longrightarrow ? + {}^{0}_{-1}e$
c. $? \longrightarrow {}^{222}_{86}Rn + {}^{4}_{2}He$

CI.36 Of much concern to environmentalists is radon-222, which is a radioactive noble gas that can seep from the ground into basements of homes and buildings. Radon-222 is a product of the decay of radium-226 that occurs naturally in rocks and soil in much of the United States. Radon-222, which has a half-life of 3.8 days, decays by emitting an alpha particle. Radon-222, which is a gas, can be inhaled into the lungs where it is strongly associated with lung cancer. Radon levels in a home can be measured with a home radon-detection kit. Environmental agencies have set the maximum level of radon-222 in a home at 4 picocuries per liter (pCi/L) of air. (16.2, 16.3, 16.4)

a. Write the balanced nuclear equation for the decay of Ra-226.
b. Write the balanced nuclear equation for the decay of Rn-222.
c. If a room contains 24 000 atoms of radon-222, how many atoms of radon-222 remain after 15.2 days?
d. Suppose a room has a volume of 72 000 L (7.2×10^4 L). If the radon level is the maximum allowed (4 pCi/L), how many alpha particles are emitted from Rn-222 in one day? (1 Ci = 3.7×10^{10} disintegrations per second)

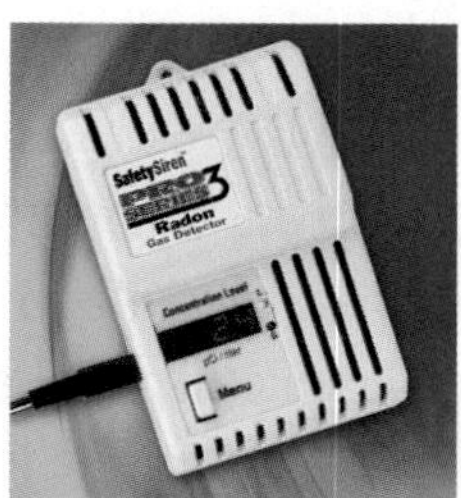

A home detection kit is used to measure the level of radon-222.

ANSWERS

CI.29 a. $C_2O_4^{2-}(aq) \longrightarrow 2CO_2(g) + 2\,e^-$
b. $5\,e^- + 8H^+(aq) + MnO_4^-(aq) \longrightarrow Mn^{2+}(aq) + 4H_2O(l)$
c. $16H^+(aq) + 2MnO_4^-(aq) + 5C_2O_4^{2-}(aq) \longrightarrow 10CO_2(g) + 2Mn^{2+}(aq) + 8H_2O(l)$
d. 0.0920 M $KMnO_4$ solution

CI.31 a. Mg is the limiting reactant.
b. 127 mL of $H_2(g)$
c. 2.3×10^3 J
d. 1.9×10^4 J/g; 462 kJ/mol

CI.33 a.

Isotope	Number of Protons	Number of Neutrons	Number of Electrons
$^{27}_{14}Si$	14	13	14
$^{28}_{14}Si$	14	14	14
$^{29}_{14}Si$	14	15	14
$^{30}_{14}Si$	14	16	14
$^{31}_{14}Si$	14	17	14

b. $1s^22s^22p^63s^23p^2$; $[Ne]3s^23p^2$
c. 28.09 amu
d. $^{27}_{14}Si \longrightarrow {}^{27}_{13}Al + {}^{0}_{+1}e$
$^{31}_{14}Si \longrightarrow {}^{31}_{15}P + {}^{0}_{-1}e$
e.

```
      :Cl:
       |
  :Cl—Si—Cl:
       |
      :Cl:
```

Tetrahedral
f. 7.8 h

CI.35 a. $^{238}_{92}U \longrightarrow {}^{234}_{90}Th + {}^{4}_{2}He$
b. $^{234}_{90}Th \longrightarrow {}^{234}_{91}Pa + {}^{0}_{-1}e$
c. $^{226}_{88}Ra \longrightarrow {}^{222}_{86}Rn + {}^{4}_{2}He$

17 Organic Chemistry

LOOKING AHEAD

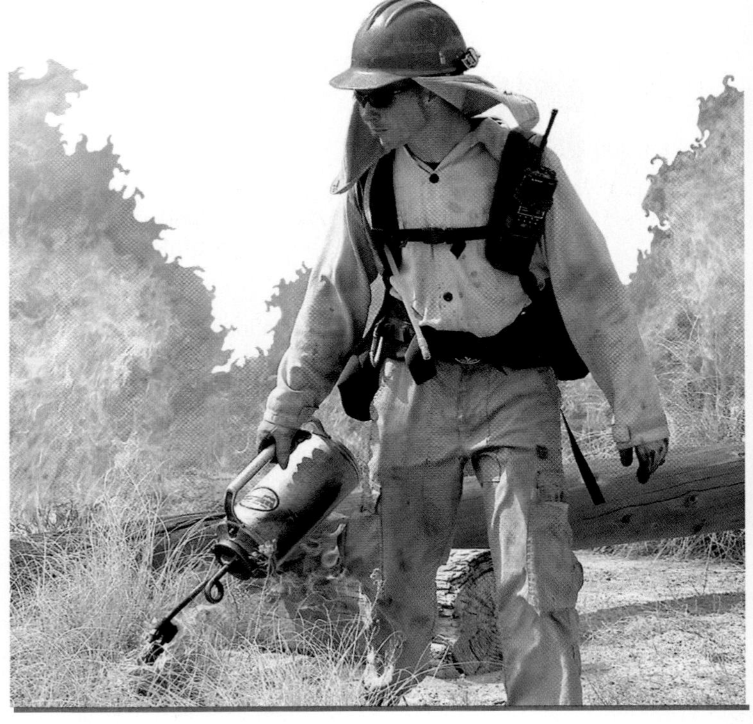

A wildfire started near Rocky Mountain National Park from a lightning strike. Due to a lack of rain, there was considerable dry timber and grasses to provide fuel for the fire. The local firefighters decided to begin a backfire, which is deliberately set in the path of the wildfire as it consumes the dry timber and grasses, and thus, stops or confines the fire. Jack put on his fire-resistant pants, jacket, and face protection. Jack then started the backfire by using a drip torch containing a mixture of diesel and gasoline.

Gasoline and diesel consist of organic molecules called alkanes. Alkanes, or hydrocarbons, are chains of carbon and hydrogen atoms, and are considered to be the backbone of organic chemistry. The alkanes present in gasoline consist of a mixture of 5–8 carbon atoms in a chain, while diesel typically consists of a mixture of 11–20 carbon atoms. Because alkanes undergo combustion reactions, they can be used as a fuel source to start a backfire.

Career: Firefighter

Firefighters are first responders to fires, traffic accidents, and other emergency situations. They are required to have an emergency medical technician or paramedic certification in order to be able to treat seriously injured people. By combining the skills of a firefighter and a paramedic, they increase the survival rates of the injured. The physical demands of firefighters are extremely high as they fight, extinguish, and prevent fires while wearing heavy protective clothing and gear. They also train for and participate in firefighting drills, and maintain fire equipment so that it is always working and ready. Firefighters must also be knowledgeable about fire codes, arson, and the handling and disposal of hazardous materials. Since firefighters also provide emergency care for sick and injured people, they need to be aware of emergency medical and rescue procedures, as well as the proper methods for controlling the spread of infectious disease.

Organic chemistry is the chemistry of compounds that are based on carbon. We use many organic compounds every day in products such as fuels, clothing, drugs, and cosmetics. The foods in our diets are composed of organic compounds such as carbohydrates, fats, and proteins that undergo digestion and metabolism to give us energy and small organic compounds that are used to build and repair the cells of our bodies.

Alcohols, which contain the hydroxyl ($-$OH) group, are commonly found in biomolecules such as sugars and starches, as well as in steroids. Aldehydes and ketones, which contain a carbonyl (C$=$O) group, contribute to the odors we associate with flavorings, fruits, flowers, and perfumes. Carboxylic acids are weak acids that give the sour taste to vinegar, lemon, and grapefruit. When a carboxylic acid combines with an alcohol, an ester and water are produced. Amines and amides are nitrogen-containing organic compounds that are components of amino acids, proteins, and nucleic acids (DNA and RNA). Many amines are used in medicine as decongestants, anesthetics, and sedatives. Alkaloids, such as caffeine, nicotine, heroin, and Oxycontin which have strong physiological activity, are obtained from plants.

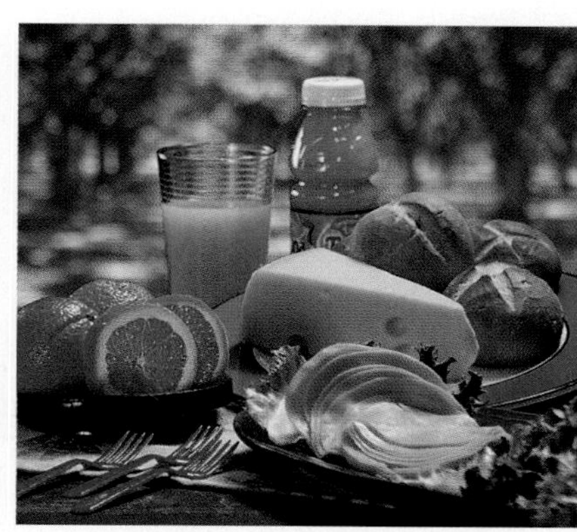

Foods in the diet provide energy and materials for the cells of the body.

CHAPTER READINESS*

Core Chemistry Skills

- Naming and Drawing Alkanes (6.7)
- Balancing Combustion Reactions (8.3)
- Identifying Functional Groups (8.4)
- Identifying Oxidized and Reduced Substances (15.1)

*These Core Chemistry Skills from previous chapters are listed here for your review as you proceed to the new material in this chapter.

17.1 Alkanes and Naming Substituents

LEARNING GOAL

Write the IUPAC names and draw the condensed structural formulas for alkanes with substituents.

At the beginning of the nineteenth century, scientists classified chemical compounds as inorganic or organic. An inorganic compound was a substance that was composed of minerals, and an organic compound was a substance that came from an organism, thus the use of the word *organic*. It was thought that some type of "vital force," which could only be found in living cells, was required to synthesize an organic compound. This perception was shown to be incorrect in 1828, when the German chemist Friedrich Wöhler synthesized urea, a product of protein metabolism, by heating an inorganic compound, ammonium cyanate. Organic compounds contain carbon and hydrogen and sometimes oxygen and other nonmetallic elements.

$$\underset{\text{Ammonium cyanate (inorganic)}}{NH_4CNO} \xrightarrow{\text{Heat}} \underset{\text{Urea (organic)}}{H_2N-\overset{\overset{\large O}{\|}}{C}-NH_2}$$

The carbon atom in the simplest organic compound, methane (CH_4), has four valence electrons that are shared with four hydrogen atoms to form an octet. In the electron-dot formula, four single bonds represent the shared pairs of electrons. An expanded structural formula is drawn to show the bonds between the atoms.

$$\cdot\dot{\underset{\cdot}{C}}\cdot + 4H\cdot \longrightarrow H:\underset{\underset{H}{..}}{\overset{\overset{H}{..}}{C}}:H \;=\; H-\underset{\underset{H}{|}}{\overset{\overset{H}{|}}{C}}-H$$

Methane

Alkanes

The alkanes are organic compounds that contain carbon and hydrogen atoms connected by single bonds. The alkanes ethane, propane, and butane contain two, three, and four carbon atoms connected in a row or a *continuous chain*. These names are part of the *IUPAC* (*International Union of Pure and Applied Chemistry*) *system*. Alkanes with five or more carbon atoms in a chain are named using Greek prefixes: *pent* (5), *hex* (6), *hept* (7), *oct* (8), *non* (9), and *dec* (10) (see Table 17.1).

TABLE 17.1 IUPAC Names, Molecular Formulas, and Condensed Structural Formulas of the First Ten Alkanes

Number of Carbon Atoms	Prefix	Name	Molecular Formula	Condensed Structural Formula
1	Meth	Methane	CH_4	CH_4
2	Eth	Ethane	C_2H_6	CH_3-CH_3
3	Prop	Propane	C_3H_8	$CH_3-CH_2-CH_3$
4	But	Butane	C_4H_{10}	$CH_3-CH_2-CH_2-CH_3$
5	Pent	Pentane	C_5H_{12}	$CH_3-CH_2-CH_2-CH_2-CH_3$
6	Hex	Hexane	C_6H_{14}	$CH_3-CH_2-CH_2-CH_2-CH_2-CH_3$
7	Hept	Heptane	C_7H_{16}	$CH_3-CH_2-CH_2-CH_2-CH_2-CH_2-CH_3$
8	Oct	Octane	C_8H_{18}	$CH_3-CH_2-CH_2-CH_2-CH_2-CH_2-CH_2-CH_3$
9	Non	Nonane	C_9H_{20}	$CH_3-CH_2-CH_2-CH_2-CH_2-CH_2-CH_2-CH_2-CH_3$
10	Dec	Decane	$C_{10}H_{22}$	$CH_3-CH_2-CH_2-CH_2-CH_2-CH_2-CH_2-CH_2-CH_2-CH_3$

The smaller alkanes from 1–4 carbon atoms are gases at room temperature and used as heating fuels. The alkanes with 5–8 carbon atoms are liquids at room temperature and found in fuels such as gasoline. The molecular formula gives the total number of each kind of atom, but does not indicate the arrangement of the atoms in the molecule. Table 17.2 shows the molecular, expanded, and condensed structural formulas for alkanes with one, two, and three carbon atoms.

In chains of three carbon atoms or more, however, the carbon atoms do not actually lie in a straight line but in a zigzag pattern.

TABLE 17.2 Drawing Structural Formulas for Some Alkanes

Alkane	Methane	Ethane	Propane
Molecular Formula	CH_4	C_2H_6	C_3H_8
Expanded Structural Formula	$H-\underset{\underset{H}{\mid}}{\overset{\overset{H}{\mid}}{C}}-H$	$H-\underset{\underset{H}{\mid}}{\overset{\overset{H}{\mid}}{C}}-\underset{\underset{H}{\mid}}{\overset{\overset{H}{\mid}}{C}}-H$	$H-\underset{\underset{H}{\mid}}{\overset{\overset{H}{\mid}}{C}}-\underset{\underset{H}{\mid}}{\overset{\overset{H}{\mid}}{C}}-\underset{\underset{H}{\mid}}{\overset{\overset{H}{\mid}}{C}}-H$
Condensed Structural Formulas	CH_4	CH_3-CH_3	$CH_3-CH_2-CH_3$ or $CH_3\diagup CH_2 \diagdown CH_3$

CONCEPT CHECK 17.1 Drawing Structural Formulas for Alkanes

Draw the condensed structural and skeletal formula for octane.

ANSWER

In a condensed structural formula, each carbon atom and its hydrogen atoms are written as

$$CH_3—,\ —CH_2—,\ \text{or}\ —\overset{|}{C}H—$$

To draw the condensed structural formula for octane, we need a carbon chain with eight carbon atoms.

$$C—C—C—C—C—C—C—C$$

All the carbon atoms need four bonds. The carbon atoms at the beginning and end of the chain have one bond to a carbon atom and need three hydrogen atoms.

$$CH_3—C—C—C—C—C—C—CH_3$$

All of the carbon atoms in the middle of the carbon chain of octane have two bonds to two carbons and need two hydrogen atoms.

$$CH_3—CH_2—CH_2—CH_2—CH_2—CH_2—CH_2—CH_3$$

The skeletal formula shows the carbon skeleton as a zigzag line where the ends and corners represent C atoms and the number of H atoms is understood.

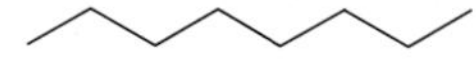

Alkane Name Hexane
Molecular Formula C_6H_{14}
Ball-and-Stick Model

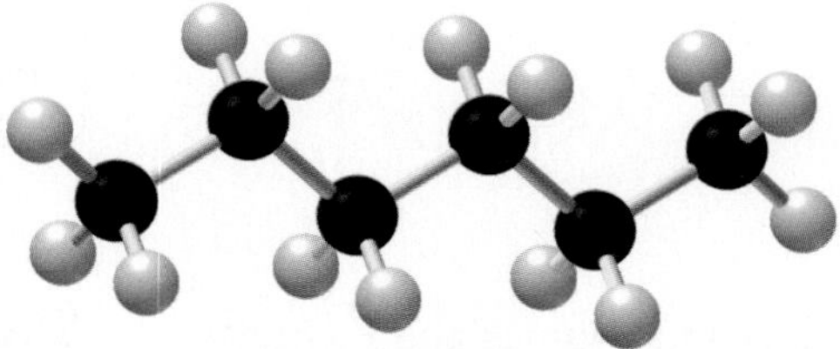

Expanded Structural Formula

```
    H   H   H   H   H   H
    |   |   |   |   |   |
H — C — C — C — C — C — C — H
    |   |   |   |   |   |
    H   H   H   H   H   H
```

Condensed Structural Formulas

```
      CH2     CH2     CH3
     /   \   /   \   /
  CH3     CH2     CH2
```

$$CH_3—CH_2—CH_2—CH_2—CH_2—CH_3$$

Skeletal Formula

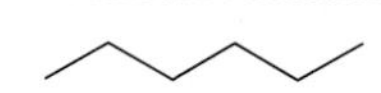

From the ball-and-stick model of hexane, we can write a molecular formula, C_6H_{14}, and draw its expanded structural formula, condensed structural formula, and skeletal formula.

Alkanes with Substituents

When an alkane has four or more carbon atoms, the atoms can be arranged so that a side group called a **branch or substituent** is attached to a carbon chain. For example, there are different ball-and-stick models for two compounds that have the molecular formula C_4H_{10}. One model is shown as a chain of four carbon atoms. In the other model, a carbon atom is attached as a branch or substituent to a carbon in a chain of three atoms (see Figure 17.1). An alkane with at least one branch is called a **branched alkane**. When two compounds have the same molecular formula but different arrangements of atoms, they are called **isomers**.

In another example, we can draw three different structural isomers that have the molecular formula C_5H_{12}. One is the continuous or *straight* chain of five carbon atoms. The second one has a methyl group attached to a four-carbon chain. The third one has two methyl groups attached to a three-carbon chain. Thus, three compounds with the same molecular formula have the same atoms arranged in different bonding patterns.

Isomers of C_5H_{12}

```
                                          CH3                    CH3
                                          |                      |
CH3—CH2—CH2—CH2—CH3              CH3—CH—CH2—CH3          CH3—C—CH3
                                                                 |
                                                                 CH3
```

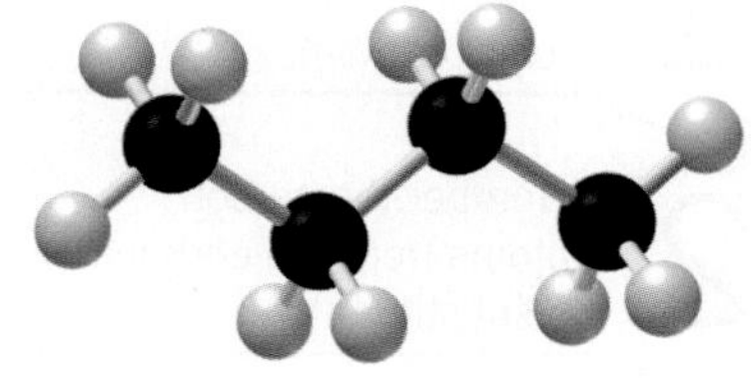

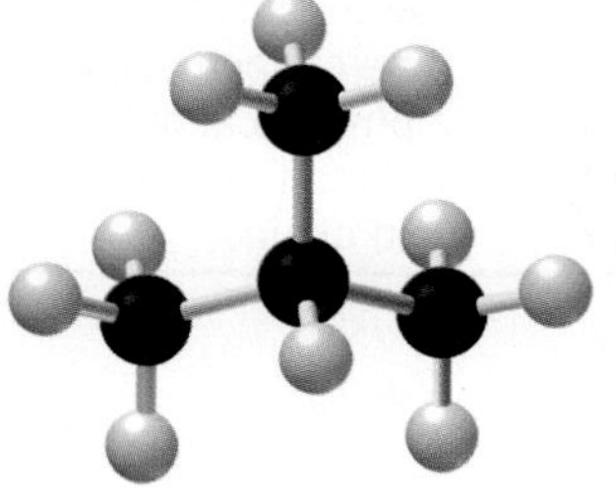

FIGURE 17.1 The isomers of C_4H_{10} have the same number and type of atoms but are bonded in a different order.

Q What makes these molecules isomers?

CONCEPT CHECK 17.2 Structural Isomers

Indicate whether the following condensed structural formulas represent structural isomers or the same molecule:

```
     CH3                    CH3         CH3
     |                      |           |
CH3—CH—CH2—CH3    and      CH2—CH2—CH2
```

ANSWER

Both condensed structural formulas contain five carbon atoms with a molecular formula C_5H_{12}. However, the one on the left has a carbon chain of four carbon atoms with a $-CH_3$ substituent attached to carbon 2. The one on the right has five carbon atoms in a continuous chain with no attached substituents. Thus, they represent structural isomers.

Substituents in Alkanes

In the IUPAC names for alkanes, a carbon branch is named as an **alkyl group**, which is an alkane that is missing one hydrogen atom. The alkyl group is named by replacing the *ane* ending of the alkane name with *yl*. Alkyl groups cannot exist by themselves; they must be attached to a carbon chain. When a halogen atom is attached to a carbon chain, it is named as a *halo* group: fluoro (F), chloro (Cl), bromo (Br), or iodo (I). Some of the common groups attached to carbon chains are illustrated in Table 17.3.

TABLE 17.3 Names and Formulas of Some Common Substituents

Substituent	Name
CH_3-	Methyl
CH_3-CH_2-	Ethyl
$CH_3-CH_2-CH_2-$	Propyl
$CH_3-\overset{\vert}{C}H-CH_3$	Isopropyl
$F-, Cl-, Br-, I-$	Fluoro, chloro, bromo, iodo

Naming Alkanes with Substituents

In the IUPAC system of naming, the longest carbon chain is numbered to give the location of one or more substituents attached to it. Let's take a look at how we use the IUPAC system to name the alkane shown in Sample Problem 17.1.

SAMPLE PROBLEM 17.1 Writing IUPAC Names

Give the IUPAC name for the following:

```
      CH3                 Br
      |                   |
CH3—CH—CH2—CH2—C—CH3
                          |
                          CH3
```

Guide to Naming Alkanes

1 Write the alkane name of the longest chain of carbon atoms.

2 Number the carbon atoms from the end nearer a substituent.

3 Give the location and name of each substituent (alphabetical order) as a prefix to the name of the main chain.

SOLUTION

Step 1 **Write the alkane name of the longest chain of carbon atoms.** In this alkane, the longest chain has six carbon atoms, which is *hexane*.

```
      CH3                 Br
      |                   |
CH3—CH—CH2—CH2—C—CH3          hexane
                          |
                          CH3
```

Step 2 **Number the carbon atoms from the end nearer a substituent.** When there are two or more substituents, the main chain is numbered in the direction that gives the lower set of numbers. Carbon 1 on the chain will be the carbon closer to the $-Br$ and methyl ($-CH_3$) substituents.

```
      CH3                 Br
      |                   |
CH3—CH—CH2—CH2—C—CH3          hexane
                          |
                          CH3
 6    5    4    3    2   1
```

Step 3 **Give the location and name of each substituent (alphabetical order) as a prefix to the name of the main chain.** The substituents, which are bromo and methyl groups, are listed in alphabetical order (bromo first, then methyl). A hyphen is placed between the number on the carbon chain and the substituent name. When there are two or more of the same substituent, a prefix (*di*, *tri*, *tetra*) is used in front of the name. Then commas are used to separate the numbers that designate the locations of the same substituent.

$$\begin{array}{ccccccccccc} & & CH_3 & & & & Br & & \\ & & | & & & & | & & \\ CH_3 & — & CH & — & CH_2 & — CH_2 — & C & — & CH_3 \\ & & & & & & | & & \\ & & & & & & CH_3 & & \\ 6 & & 5 & & 4 & 3 & 2 & & 1 \end{array}$$

2-bromo-2,5-dimethylhexane

STUDY CHECK 17.1

Give the IUPAC name for the following compound:

$$\begin{array}{ccccccc} & & CH_3 & & CH_3 & & \\ & & | & & | & & \\ CH_3—CH_2— & & CH & —CH_2— & CH & —CH_2— & Cl \end{array}$$

Drawing Condensed Structural Formulas for Alkanes

The IUPAC name gives all the information needed to draw the condensed structural formula for an alkane. Suppose you are asked to draw the condensed structural formula for 2,3-dimethylbutane. The alkane name gives the number of carbon atoms in the longest chain. The names in the beginning indicate the substituents and where they are attached. We can break down the name in the following way:

2,3-dimethylbutane

2,3-	di	methyl	but	ane
Substituents on carbons 2 and 3	Two identical groups	$CH_3—$ alkyl groups	4 C atoms in the main chain	Single C—C bonds

In Sample Problem 17.2, we utilize the IUPAC name to draw the structural formulas for an alkane.

SAMPLE PROBLEM 17.2 Drawing Structural Formulas from IUPAC Names

Draw the condensed structural formula and skeletal formula for 2,3-dimethylbutane.

SOLUTION

Step 1 **Draw the main chain of carbon atoms.** For butane, we draw a chain of four carbon atoms. For the skeletal formula, we show bond lines.

C—C—C—C

Step 2 **Number the chain and place the substituents on the carbons indicated by the numbers.** The first part of the name indicates two methyl groups ($CH_3—$), one on carbon 2 and one on carbon 3. In the skeletal formula, the methyl groups are drawn as vertical lines on carbon 2 and 3.

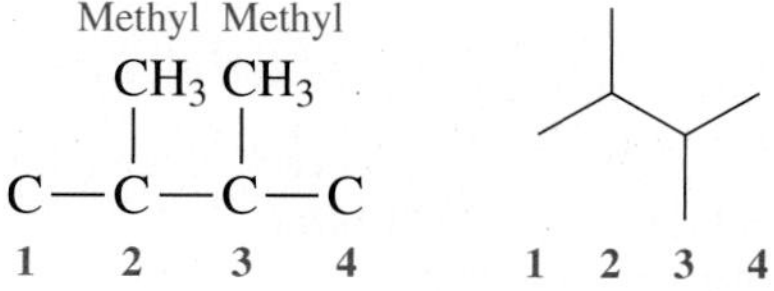

1 2 3 4

Guide to Drawing Alkane Formulas

1. Draw the main chain of carbon atoms.
2. Number the chain and place the substituents on the carbons indicated by the numbers.
3. Add the correct number of hydrogen atoms to give four bonds to each C atom.

Step 3 **Add the correct number of hydrogen atoms to give four bonds to each C atom.**

$$\begin{array}{c} \quad CH_3 \quad CH_3 \\ \quad | \qquad\ \ | \\ CH_3-CH-CH-CH_3 \end{array}$$

2,3-Dimethylbutane

STUDY CHECK 17.2

Draw the condensed structural formula and skeletal formula for 2,4-dibromopentane.

QUESTIONS AND PROBLEMS

17.1 Alkanes and Naming Substituents

LEARNING GOAL: *Write the IUPAC names and draw the condensed structural formulas for alkanes with substituents.*

17.1 Give the IUPAC name for each of the following alkanes:

a. $CH_2(CH_3)-CH_2-CH_2(CH_3)$

b.

17.2 Give the IUPAC name for each of the following alkanes:

a. $CH_3-CH_2-CH_2-CH_3$

b.

17.3 Indicate whether each of the following pairs of formulas represents structural isomers or the same molecule:

a. $CH_3-CH(CH_3)-CH_3$ and $CH(CH_3)(CH_3)-CH_3$

b. $CH_2(CH_3)-CH(CH_3)-CH_2-CH_3$ and $CH_3-CH(CH_3)-CH(CH_3)-CH_3$

c. and

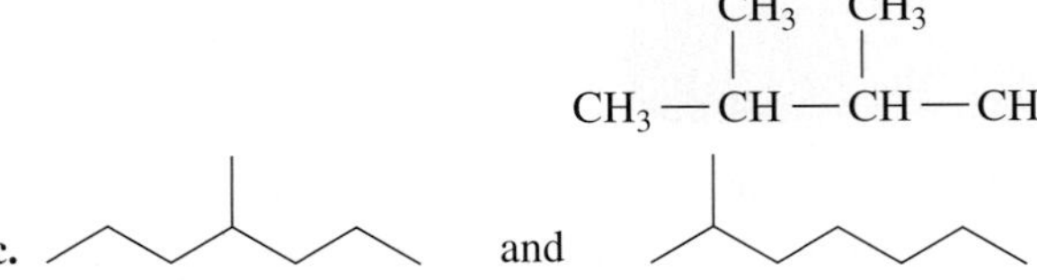

17.4 Indicate whether each of the following pairs of formulas represents structural isomers or the same molecule:

a. $CH_3-C(CH_3)_2-CH_3$ and $CH(CH_3)(CH_3)-CH_2-CH_3$

b. $CH_3-CH(CH_3)-CH(CH_3)-CH_2(CH_3)$ and $CH_3-CH(CH_3)-CH_2-CH(CH_3)-CH_3$

c. and

17.5 Give the IUPAC name for each of the following:

a. $CH_3-CH(F)-CH_2-CH_3$

b. $CH_3-C(CH_3)_2-CH_3$

c. Cl

17.6 Give the IUPAC name for each of the following:

a. $CH_3-CH(CH_3)-CH_2-CH_2-CH_2-Br$

b. $CH_3-CH(CH_3)-CH(CH_3)-CH_2-CH_2-CH_3$

c. Br Cl

17.7 Draw the condensed structural formula for each of the following:

a. 2-methylbutane

b. 3,3-dichloropentane

c. 2,3,5-trimethylhexane

17.8 Draw the condensed structural formula for each of the following:

a. 3-iodopentane

b. 3-ethyl-2-methylpentane

c. 2,2,3,5-tetrabromohexane

17.9 Draw the skeletal formula for each of the following:

a. 2-chloro-2-methylhexane

b. 2,3-dimethylheptane

c. 3-chloro-2-methylpentane

17.10 Draw the skeletal formula for each of the following:

a. 1,5-dibromo-3-methylheptane

b. 1,1,5-trichloropentane

c. 2,2,3-trimethylheptane

17.2 Alkenes, Alkynes, and Polymers

LEARNING GOAL

Write the IUPAC names and formulas for alkenes and alkynes; draw the condensed structural formulas for the monomers that form a polymer.

Alkenes and alkynes are unsaturated hydrocarbons because they contain *double* and *triple* bonds, respectively. An *alkene* contains at least one double bond between carbons. The double bond forms when two adjacent carbon atoms share two pairs of valence electrons. The simplest alkene is ethene, C_2H_4, which is often called by its common name, ethylene. In ethene, each carbon atom is attached to two H atoms and the other carbon atom in the double bond. The resulting molecule has a flat geometry because the carbon and hydrogen atoms all lie in the same plane (see Figure 17.2). In an *alkyne*, a triple bond occurs when two carbon atoms share three pairs of valence electrons.

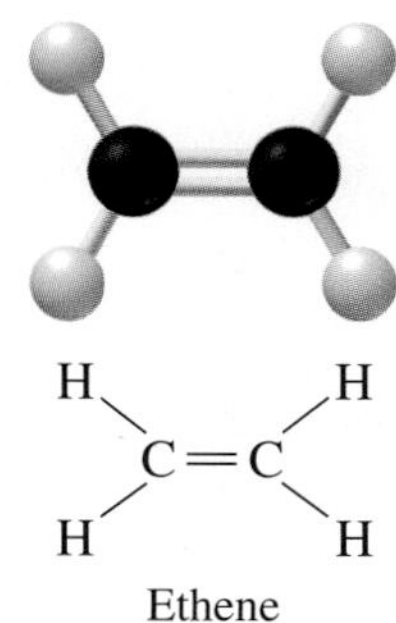

Ethene

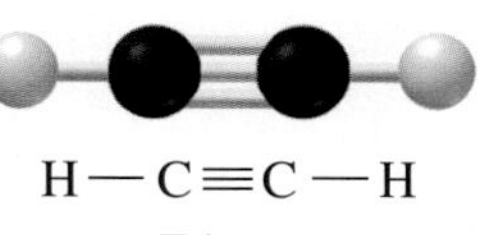

$H-C\equiv C-H$

Ethyne

FIGURE 17.2 Ball-and-stick models of ethene and ethyne show the functional groups of double or triple bonds.

Q Why are these compounds called unsaturated hydrocarbons?

Naming Alkenes and Alkynes

The IUPAC names for alkenes and alkynes are similar to those of alkanes. The IUPAC name of the simplest alkyne is ethyne, although it is often called by the common name, acetylene (see Table 17.4). When naming alkenes and alkynes, the longest carbon chain must contain the double or triple bond.

TABLE 17.4 Comparison of Alkanes, Alkenes, and Alkynes

Alkane	Alkene	Alkyne
CH_3-CH_3 Ethane	$H_2C=CH_2$ Ethene (ethylene)	$HC\equiv CH$ Ethyne (acetylene)
$CH_3-CH_2-CH_3$ Propane	$CH_3-CH=CH_2$ Propene (propylene)	$CH_3-C\equiv CH$ Propyne
Propane (line-angle)	Propene (line-angle)	Propyne (line-angle)

Examples of naming an alkene and an alkyne are shown in Sample Problem 17.3.

SAMPLE PROBLEM 17.3 Naming Alkenes and Alkynes

Write the IUPAC name for each of the following:

a. $CH_3-\underset{|}{\overset{CH_3}{CH}}-CH=CH-CH_3$ (the CH_3 branch is on the second carbon)

b. $CH_3-CH_2-C\equiv C-CH_2-CH_3$

SOLUTION

a.

Analyze the Problem	Functional Group	Family	IUPAC Naming
	double bond	alkene	replace the *ane* of the alkane name with *ene*

Step 1 **Name the longest carbon chain that contains the double or triple bond.** There are five carbon atoms in the longest carbon chain containing the double bond. Replacing the corresponding alkane ending with *ene* gives pentene.

$CH_3-\overset{CH_3}{\overset{|}{CH}}-CH=CH-CH_3$ pentene

Guide to Naming Alkenes and Alkynes

1. Name the longest carbon chain that contains the double or triple bond.
2. Number the carbon chain from the end nearer the double or triple bond.
3. Give the location and name of each substituent (alphabetical order) as a prefix to the alkene or alkyne name.

Step 2 **Number the carbon chain from the end nearer the double or triple bond.** The number of the first carbon in the double bond is used to give the location of the double bond. Alkenes or alkynes with two or three carbons do not need numbers. For example, the double bond in ethene or propene must be between carbon 1 and carbon 2.

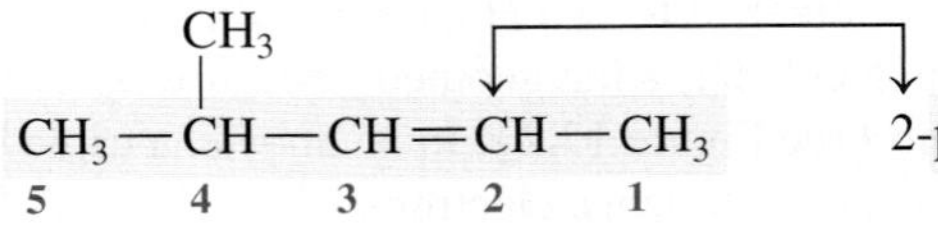

$$\underset{5}{CH_3}-\underset{4}{\overset{\overset{CH_3}{|}}{CH}}-\underset{3}{CH}=\underset{2}{CH}-\underset{1}{CH_3} \qquad \text{2-pentene}$$

Step 3 **Give the location and name of each substituent (alphabetical order) as a prefix to the alkene or alkyne name.** The methyl group is located on carbon 4.

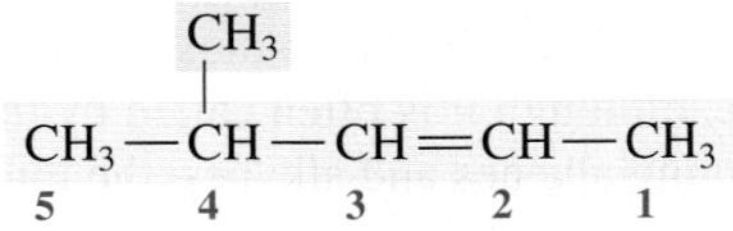

$$\underset{5}{CH_3}-\underset{4}{\overset{\overset{CH_3}{|}}{CH}}-\underset{3}{CH}=\underset{2}{CH}-\underset{1}{CH_3} \qquad \text{4-methyl-2-pentene}$$

b.

Analyze the Problem	Functional Group	Family	IUPAC Naming
	triple bond	alkyne	replace the *ane* of the alkane name with *yne*

Step 1 **Name the longest carbon chain that contains the double or triple bond.** There are six carbon atoms in the longest chain containing the triple bond. Replacing the corresponding alkane ending with *yne* gives hexyne.

$$CH_3-CH_2-C\equiv C-CH_2-CH_3 \qquad \text{hexyne}$$

Step 2 **Number the carbon chain from the end nearer the double or triple bond.** The number of the first carbon in the triple bond is used to give the location of the triple bond.

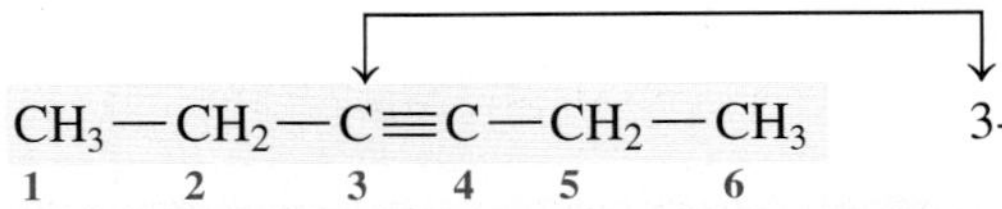

$$\underset{1}{CH_3}-\underset{2}{CH_2}-\underset{3}{C}\equiv\underset{4}{C}-\underset{5}{CH_2}-\underset{6}{CH_3} \qquad \text{3-hexyne}$$

Step 3 **Give the location and name of each substituent (alphabetical order) as a prefix to the alkene or alkyne name.** There are no substituents in this formula.

STUDY CHECK 17.3

Draw the condensed structural formula for each of the following:

a. 2-pentyne **b.** 3-methyl-1-pentene

Polymers

A **polymer** is a large molecule that consists of small repeating units called **monomers**. In the past hundred years, the plastics industry has made synthetic polymers that are in many of the materials we use every day, such as carpeting, plastic wrap, nonstick pans, plastic cups, and rain gear. In medicine, synthetic polymers are used to replace diseased or damaged body parts such as hip joints, teeth, heart valves, and blood vessels (see Figure 17.3). There are about 100 billion kg of plastics produced every year, which is about 15 kg for every person on Earth.

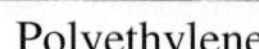
Polyethylene

Polyvinyl chloride

Polypropylene

Polytetrafluoroethylene (Teflon®)

Polydichloroethylene (Saran™)

Polystyrene

FIGURE 17.3 Synthetic polymers provide a wide variety of items that we use every day.

Q What are some alkenes used to make the polymers in these plastic items?

Many of the synthetic polymers are made by reactions of small alkene monomers. Polymerization reactions require high temperature, a catalyst, and high pressure (over 1000 atm). A polymer grows longer as each monomer is added at the end of the chain and contains as many as 1000 monomers. Polyethylene, a polymer made from ethylene monomers, is used in plastic bottles, film, and plastic dinnerware. More polyethylene is produced worldwide than any other polymer.

$$\underbrace{H_2C{=}CH_2 + H_2C{=}CH_2 + H_2C{=}CH_2}_{\text{Ethene (ethylene) monomers}} \longrightarrow \underbrace{-CH_2-CH_2-\overbrace{\left[CH_2-CH_2\right]_{many}}^{\text{Monomer unit repeats}}-CH_2-CH_2-}_{\text{Polyethylene section}}$$

Table 17.5 lists several alkene monomers that are used to produce common synthetic polymers. The alkane nature of these synthetic polymers makes them unreactive. Thus, they do not decompose easily (they are not biodegradable). As a result, they have become significant contributors to pollution, on land and in the oceans. Efforts are being made to make them more degradable.

You can identify the type of polymer used to manufacture a plastic item by looking for the recycling symbol (arrows in a triangle) found on the label or on the bottom of the plastic container. For example, either the number 5 or the letters PP inside the triangle is a code for a polypropylene plastic. Many cities now maintain recycling programs that reduce the amount of plastic materials that are transported to landfills.

1 **PETE**	2 **HDPE**	3 **PVC**	4 **LDPE**	5 **PP**	6 **PS**	7 **O**
Polyethylene terephthalate	High-density polyethylene	Polyvinyl chloride	Low-density polyethylene	Polypropylene	Polystyrene	Other

The recycling symbol indicates the type of polymer.

TABLE 17.5 Some Alkenes and Their Polymers

Monomer	Polymer Section	Common Uses
$H_2C{=}CH_2$ Ethene (ethylene)	$-\overset{H}{\underset{H}{C}}-\overset{H}{\underset{H}{C}}-\overset{H}{\underset{H}{C}}-\overset{H}{\underset{H}{C}}-\overset{H}{\underset{H}{C}}-\overset{H}{\underset{H}{C}}-$ Polyethylene	Plastic bottles, film, insulation materials
$H_2C{=}\overset{Cl}{CH}$ Chloroethene (vinyl chloride)	$-\overset{H}{\underset{H}{C}}-\overset{Cl}{\underset{H}{C}}-\overset{H}{\underset{H}{C}}-\overset{Cl}{\underset{H}{C}}-\overset{H}{\underset{H}{C}}-\overset{Cl}{\underset{H}{C}}-$ Polyvinyl chloride (PVC)	Plastic pipes and tubing, garden hoses, garbage bags
$H_2C{=}\overset{CH_3}{CH}$ Propene (propylene)	$-\overset{H}{\underset{H}{C}}-\overset{CH_3}{\underset{H}{C}}-\overset{H}{\underset{H}{C}}-\overset{CH_3}{\underset{H}{C}}-\overset{H}{\underset{H}{C}}-\overset{CH_3}{\underset{H}{C}}-$ Polypropylene	Ski and hiking clothing, carpets, artificial joints
$F-\overset{F}{C}{=}\overset{F}{C}-F$ Tetrafluoroethene	$-\overset{F}{\underset{F}{C}}-\overset{F}{\underset{F}{C}}-\overset{F}{\underset{F}{C}}-\overset{F}{\underset{F}{C}}-\overset{F}{\underset{F}{C}}-\overset{F}{\underset{F}{C}}-$ Polytetrafluoroethylene (Teflon)	Nonstick coatings
$H_2C{=}\overset{Cl}{C}-Cl$ 1,1-Dichloroethene	$-\overset{H}{\underset{H}{C}}-\overset{Cl}{\underset{Cl}{C}}-\overset{H}{\underset{H}{C}}-\overset{Cl}{\underset{Cl}{C}}-\overset{H}{\underset{H}{C}}-\overset{Cl}{\underset{Cl}{C}}-$	Plastic film and wrap
$H_2C{=}\overset{C_6H_5}{CH}$ Phenylethene (styrene)	$-CH_2-\overset{C_6H_5}{CH}-CH_2-\overset{C_6H_5}{CH}-CH_2-\overset{C_6H_5}{CH}-$ Polystyrene	Plastic coffee cups and cartons, insulation

SAMPLE PROBLEM 17.4 Polymers

Give the name and draw the condensed structural formula for the starting monomers for each of the following polymers:

a. polypropylene

b. Saran $-\overset{H}{\underset{H}{C}}-\overset{Cl}{\underset{Cl}{C}}-\overset{H}{\underset{H}{C}}-\overset{Cl}{\underset{Cl}{C}}-\overset{H}{\underset{H}{C}}-\overset{Cl}{\underset{Cl}{C}}-$

SOLUTION

a. propene (propylene) $H_2C{=}\overset{CH_3}{CH}$

b. 1,1-dichloroethene $H_2C{=}\overset{Cl}{C}-Cl$

STUDY CHECK 17.4

Draw the condensed structural formula for the monomer used in the manufacturing of PVC.

Tables, benches, trash receptacles, and pipes used for irrigation systems are made from recycled plastics.

QUESTIONS AND PROBLEMS

17.2 Alkenes, Alkynes, and Polymers

LEARNING GOAL: *Write the IUPAC names and formulas for alkenes and alkynes; draw the condensed structural formulas for the monomers that form a polymer.*

17.11 Identify each of the following as an alkane, alkene, or alkyne:

a. $CH_3—CH=CH_2$

b. $CH_3—CH_2—C \equiv CH$

c.

17.12 Identify each of the following as an alkane, alkene, or alkyne:

a.

b. $CH_3—C(CH_3)=C(CH_3)—CH_3$

c. $CH_3—CH_2—CH(CH_3)—CH_3$

17.13 Give the IUPAC name for each of the following:

a. $H_2C=CH_2$

b. $CH_3—C(CH_3)=CH_2$

c. $CH_3—CH_2—C \equiv C—CH_3$

17.14 Give the IUPAC name for each of the following:

a. $H_2C=CH—CH_2—CH_3$

b. $CH_3—C \equiv C—CH_2—CH(CH_3)—CH_3$

c. $CH_3—CH_2—CH=CH—CH_3$

17.15 Draw the condensed structural formula for each of the following compounds:

a. propene **b.** 1-hexyne

c. 2-methyl-1-butene

17.16 Draw the condensed structural formula for each of the following compounds:

a. 1-pentene **b.** 3-methyl-1-butyne

c. 3,4-dimethyl-1-pentene

17.17 What is a polymer?

17.18 What is a monomer?

17.19 Write an equation that represents the formation of a part of the polypropylene polymer using three of its monomer units.

17.20 Write an equation that represents the formation of a part of the polystyrene polymer using three of its monomer units.

17.3 Aromatic Compounds

LEARNING GOAL

Describe the bonding in benzene; name aromatic compounds and draw their condensed structural formulas.

In 1825, Michael Faraday isolated a hydrocarbon called *benzene*, which had the molecular formula C_6H_6. A molecule of **benzene** consists of a ring of six carbon atoms with one hydrogen atom attached to each carbon. Because many compounds containing benzene had fragrant odors, the family of benzene compounds became known as **aromatic compounds**.

In benzene, each carbon atom uses three valence electrons to bond to the hydrogen atom and two adjacent carbons. That leaves one valence electron, which scientists first thought was shared in a double bond with an adjacent carbon. In 1865, August Kekulé proposed that the carbon atoms in benzene were arranged in a flat ring with alternating single and double bonds between the carbon atoms. There are two possible structural representations of benzene due to resonance in which the double bonds can form between two different carbon atoms.

Today, we know that the six electrons are shared equally among the six carbon atoms and that all the carbon–carbon bonds in benzene are identical due to resonance. This unique feature of benzene makes it especially stable. Benzene is most often represented as a skeletal formula, which shows a hexagon with a circle in the center. Some of the ways to represent benzene are shown as follows:

H H H H H H ⟷ H H H H H H   H H H H H H

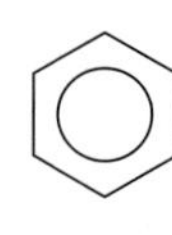

Structural representations for benzene

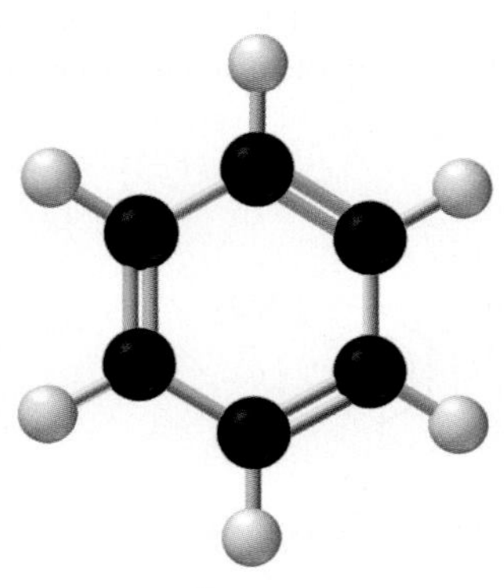

Benzene

Naming Aromatic Compounds

Many compounds containing benzene have been important in chemistry for many years and still use their common names. Names such as toluene, aniline, and phenol are allowed by IUPAC rules.

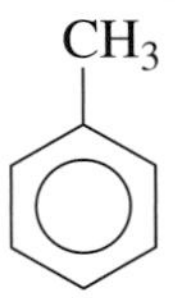

CH_3 NH_2 OH

Toluene (methylbenzene) 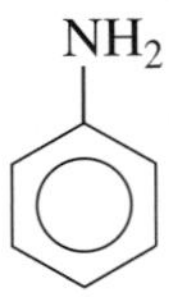 Aniline (aminobenzene) 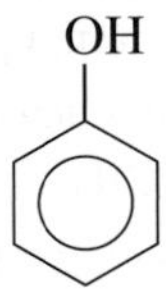 Phenol (hydroxybenzene)

When benzene has only one substituent, the ring is not numbered. When there are two substituents, the benzene ring is numbered to give the lowest numbers to the substituents. When a common name can be used such as toluene, aniline, or phenol, the carbon atom attached to the methyl, amine, or hydroxyl group, is numbered as carbon 1.

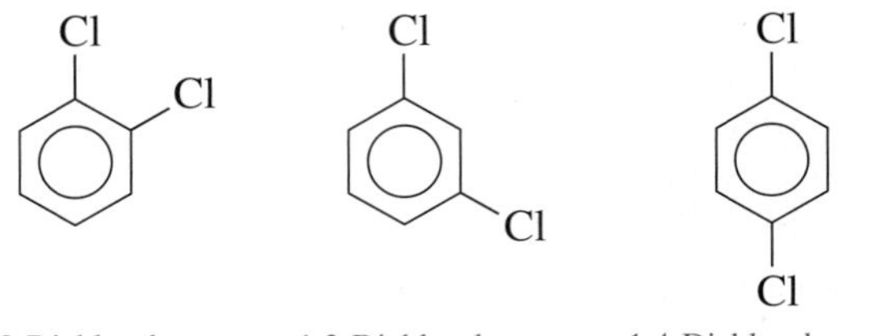

1,2-Dichlorobenzene 1,3-Dichlorobenzene 1,4-Dichlorobenzene

The substituents are named alphabetically. A prefix (*di*, *tri*, *tetra*) is used to indicate two or more of the same substituents.

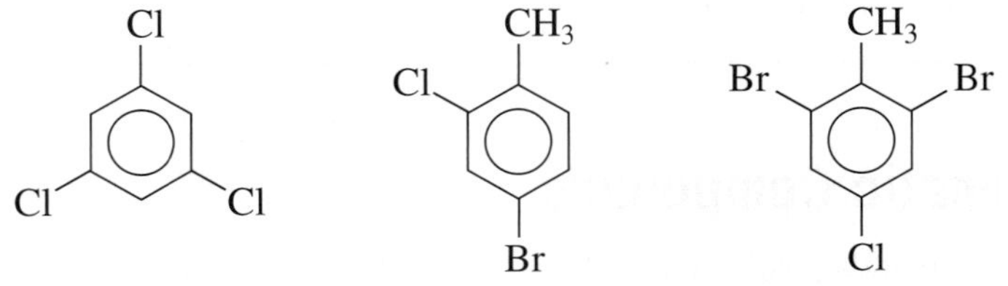

1,3,5-Trichlorobenzene 4-Bromo-2-chlorotoluene 2,6-Dibromo-4-chlorotoluene

Chemistry Link to the Environment

SOME COMMON AROMATIC COMPOUNDS

Aromatic compounds are common in nature and in medicine. Toluene is used as a reactant to make drugs, dyes, and explosives such as TNT (trinitrotoluene). The benzene ring is found in some amino acids (the building blocks of proteins), pain relievers such as aspirin, acetaminophen, and ibuprofen; and flavorings such as vanillin.

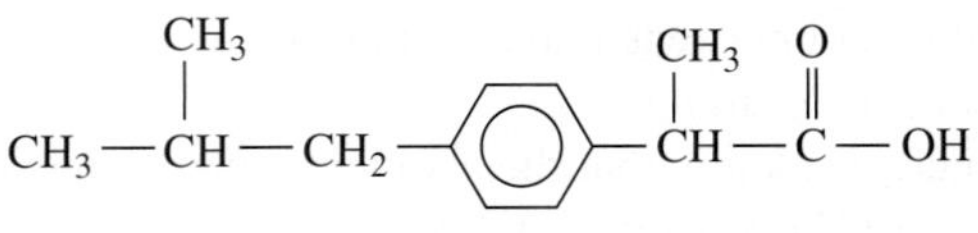

Ibuprofen

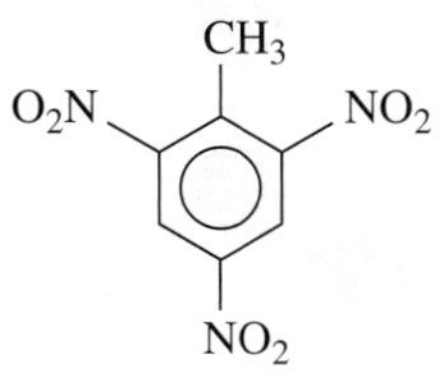

TNT (2,4,6-trinitrotoluene) 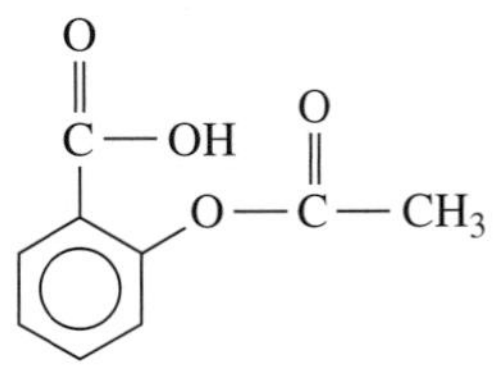 Aspirin 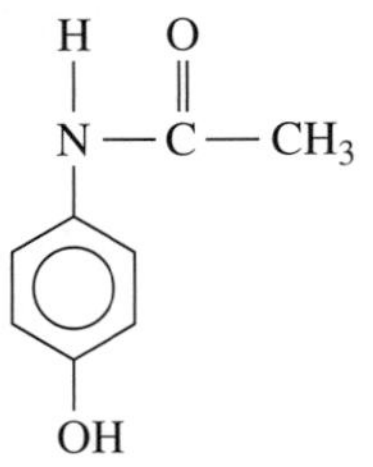 Acetaminophen 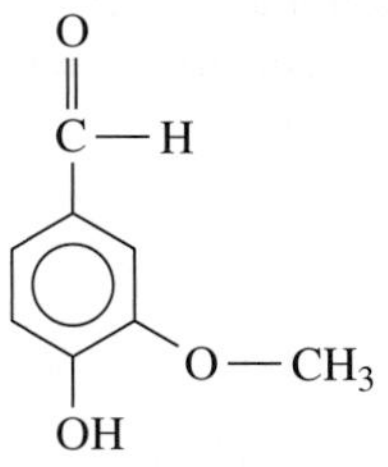 Vanillin

SAMPLE PROBLEM 17.5 Naming Aromatic Compounds

Give the IUPAC name for each of the following aromatic compounds:

a. 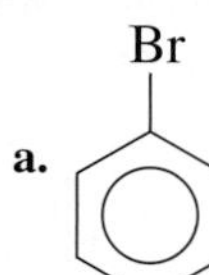

b. 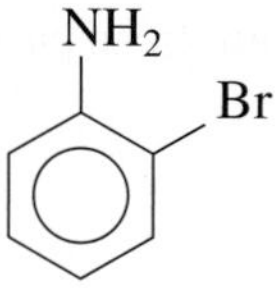 NH_2, Br

SOLUTION

a. **Step 1 Write the name of the aromatic compound.** benzene

Step 2 If there are two or more substituents, number the aromatic ring starting from the substituent. When there is only one substituent, the benzene ring is not numbered.

Step 3 Name a substituent as a prefix. bromobenzene

b. **Step 1 Write the name of the aromatic compound.** This aromatic compound contains a benzene ring with an amine group. aniline

Step 2 If there are two or more substituents, number the aromatic ring starting from the substituent. The benzene ring is numbered to give the lower number when counting the carbon with the amine group as 1. The bromine atom is on carbon 2.

Step 3 Name a substituent as a prefix. 2-bromoaniline

STUDY CHECK 17.5

Give the IUPAC name for the following compound:

CH_3, Cl

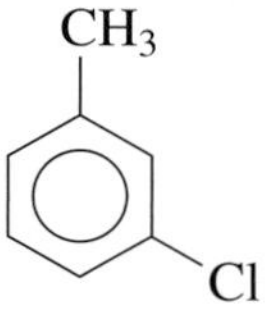

Guide to Naming Aromatic Compounds

1. Write the name of the aromatic compound.
2. If there are two or more substituents, number the aromatic ring starting from the substituent.
3. Name a substituent as a prefix.

QUESTIONS AND PROBLEMS

17.3 Aromatic Compounds

LEARNING GOAL: *Describe the bonding in benzene; name aromatic compounds and draw their condensed structural formulas.*

17.21 Give the IUPAC name for each of the following:

a. 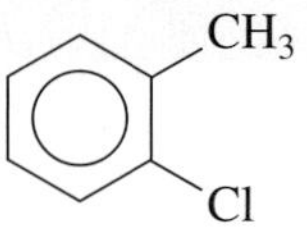 CH_3, Cl

b. 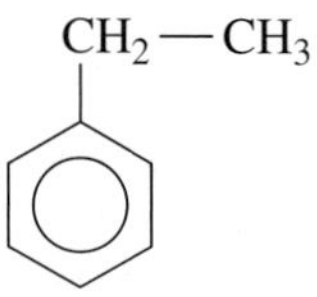 $CH_2—CH_3$

c. 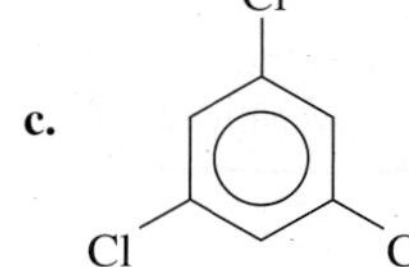

17.22 Give the IUPAC name for each of the following:

a. 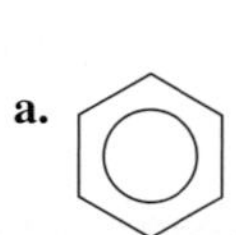

b. 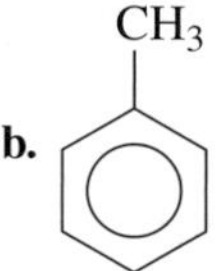

c. 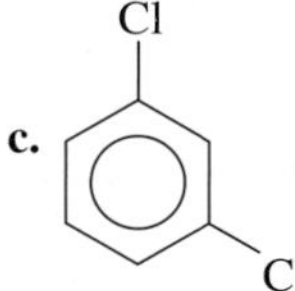

17.23 Draw the condensed structural formula for each of the following compounds:

a. toluene
b. 1-chloro-4-fluorobenzene
c. 4-ethyltoluene

17.24 Draw the condensed structural formula for each of the following compounds:

a. 1,3-dibromo-5-chlorobenzene
b. 2,4-dichlorotoluene
c. propylbenzene

LEARNING GOAL

Write the IUPAC and common names for alcohols, phenols, and ethers; draw the condensed structural formulas when given their names.

17.4 Alcohols, Phenols, and Ethers

In an *alcohol*, a hydroxyl (—OH) group is bonded to the hydrocarbon chain of an alkane. In a *phenol*, the hydroxyl group is attached to a benzene ring. Molecules of alcohols and phenols have a bent shape around the oxygen atom. In an *ether*, an oxygen atom is attached to two carbon atoms (see Figure 17.4).

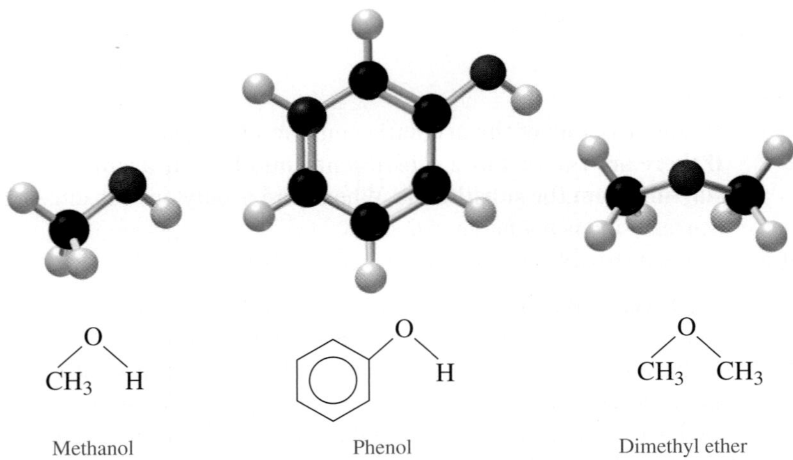

FIGURE 17.4 An alcohol or a phenol has a hydrogen atom replaced by a hydroxyl (—OH) group; an ether contains an oxygen atom (—O—) bonded to two carbon groups.

Q How are the structures of alcohols and phenols similar?

Naming Alcohols

In the IUPAC system, an alcohol is named by replacing the final *e* in the corresponding alkane name with *ol*. The common name of a simple alcohol uses the name of the alkyl group followed by *alcohol*.

$CH_3—OH$
Methanol
(methyl alcohol)

$CH_3—CH_2—OH$
Ethanol
(ethyl alcohol)

Alcohols with one or two carbon atoms do not require a number for the hydroxyl group. When an alcohol consists of a chain with three or more carbon atoms, the chain is numbered to give the position of the —OH group and any substituents on the chain.

$$\underset{3}{CH_3}—\underset{2}{CH_2}—\underset{1}{CH_2}—OH$$
1-Propanol
(propyl alcohol)

$$\underset{1}{CH_3}—\underset{2}{\overset{\overset{OH}{|}}{CH}}—\underset{3}{CH_3}$$
2-Propanol
(isopropyl alcohol)

SAMPLE PROBLEM 17.6 Naming Alcohols

Give the IUPAC name for the following compound:

$$CH_3—\overset{\overset{CH_3}{|}}{CH}—CH_2—\overset{\overset{OH}{|}}{CH}—CH_3$$

SOLUTION

	Functional Group	Family	IUPAC Naming
Analyze the Problem	hydroxyl group	alcohol	replace the *e* in the alkane name with *ol*

Step 1 **Name the longest carbon chain attached to the —OH group by replacing the *e* in the alkane name with *ol*. Name an aromatic alcohol as a *phenol*.** The parent chain is pentane; the alcohol is named pentanol.

$$CH_3-\underset{}{\overset{CH_3}{\overset{|}{C}H}}-CH_2-\overset{OH}{\overset{|}{C}H}-CH_3 \quad \text{pentanol}$$

Step 2 **Number the chain from the end nearer the —OH group.** The carbon chain is numbered from right to left to give the position of the —OH group on carbon 2, which is shown as a prefix in the name 2-pentanol.

$$\underset{5}{CH_3}-\underset{4}{\overset{CH_3}{\overset{|}{C}H}}-\underset{3}{CH_2}-\underset{2}{\overset{OH}{\overset{|}{C}H}}-\underset{1}{CH_3} \quad \text{2-pentanol}$$

Step 3 **Give the location and name of each substituent relative to the —OH group.** With a methyl group on carbon 4, the compound is named 4-methyl-2-pentanol.

$$\underset{5}{CH_3}-\underset{4}{\overset{CH_3}{\overset{|}{C}H}}-\underset{3}{CH_2}-\underset{2}{\overset{OH}{\overset{|}{C}H}}-\underset{1}{CH_3} \quad \text{4-methyl-2-pentanol}$$

Guide to Naming Alcohols

1. Name the longest carbon chain attached to the —OH group by replacing the *e* in the alkane name with *ol*. Name an aromatic alcohol as a *phenol*.
2. Number the chain from the end nearer the —OH group.
3. Give the location and name of each substituent relative to the —OH group.

STUDY CHECK 17.6

Give the IUPAC name for the following:

$$CH_3-\overset{Cl}{\overset{|}{C}H}-CH_2-CH_2-OH$$

Chemistry Link to Health

SOME IMPORTANT ALCOHOLS AND PHENOLS

Methanol (*methyl alcohol*), the simplest alcohol, is found in many solvents and paint removers. If ingested, methanol is oxidized to formaldehyde, which can cause headaches, blindness, and death. Methanol is used to make plastics, medicines, and fuels. In car racing, it is used as a fuel because it is less flammable and has a higher octane rating than does gasoline.

1,2,3-Propanetriol (*glycerol* or *glycerin*), a trihydroxy alcohol, is a viscous liquid obtained from oils and fats during the production of soaps. The presence of several polar —OH groups makes it strongly attracted to water, a feature that makes glycerin useful as a skin softener in products such as skin lotions, cosmetics, shaving creams, and liquid soaps.

$$HO-CH_2-\overset{OH}{\overset{|}{C}H}-CH_2-OH$$

1,2,3-Propanetriol (glycerol)

1,2-Ethanediol (*ethylene glycol*) is used as an antifreeze in heating and cooling systems. It is also a solvent for paints, inks, and plastics, and it is used in the production of synthetic fibers such as Dacron. If ingested, it is extremely toxic. In the body, it is oxidized to oxalic acid, which forms insoluble salts in the kidneys that cause renal damage, convulsions, and death. Because its sweet taste is attractive to pets and children, ethylene glycol solutions must be carefully stored.

$$HO-CH_2-CH_2-OH \xrightarrow{[O]} HO-\overset{O}{\overset{\|}{C}}-\overset{O}{\overset{\|}{C}}-OH$$

1,2-Ethanediol (ethylene glycol) — Oxalic acid

Antifreeze raises the boiling point and decreases the freezing point of water in a radiator.

Phenols are found in several of the essential oils of plants, which produce the odor or flavor of the plant. Eugenol is found in cloves, vanillin in vanilla bean, isoeugenol in nutmeg, and thymol in thyme and mint. Thymol has a pleasant, minty taste and is used in mouthwashes and by dentists to disinfect a cavity before adding a filling compound.

Bisphenol A (BPA) is used to make polycarbonate, a clear plastic that is used to manufacture beverage bottles, including baby bottles. Washing polycarbonate bottles with certain detergents or at high temperatures disrupts the polymer, causing small amounts of BPA to leach from the bottles. Because BPA is an estrogen mimic, there are concerns about the harmful effects from low levels of BPA. In 2008, Canada banned the use of polycarbonate baby bottles, which are now labeled "BPA free." Plastic bottles and containers made of polycarbonate have the recycling symbol "7."

CH_3

HO—⟨benzene ring⟩—C—⟨benzene ring⟩—OH

CH_3

Bisphenol A (BPA)

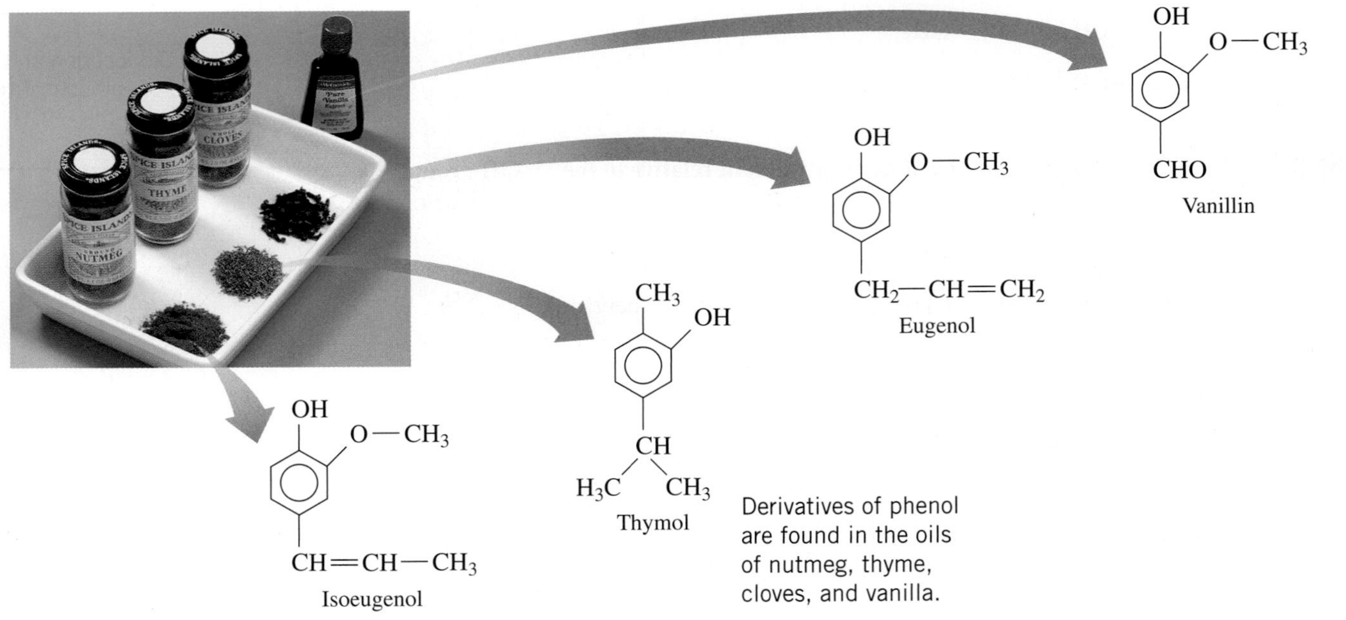

Derivatives of phenol are found in the oils of nutmeg, thyme, cloves, and vanilla.

Naming Ethers

An *ether* consists of an oxygen atom that is attached by single bonds to two carbon groups that are alkyl or aromatic groups. In the common name of an ether, the names of the alkyl or aromatic groups attached to the oxygen atom are written in alphabetical order, followed by the word *ether*.

Methyl group ↓ Propyl group ↓

$$\boxed{CH_3}-O-\boxed{CH_2-CH_2-CH_3}$$

Common name: methyl propyl ether

CONCEPT CHECK 17.3 Common Names of Ethers

Give the common name for the following:

$$CH_3-CH_2-O-CH_2-CH_2-CH_2-CH_3$$

ANSWER

The groups attached to the oxygen are an ethyl group and a butyl group. The common name is butyl ethyl ether.

QUESTIONS AND PROBLEMS

17.4 Alcohols, Phenols, and Ethers

LEARNING GOAL: *Write the IUPAC and common names for alcohols, phenols, and ethers; draw the condensed structural formulas when given their names.*

17.25 Give the IUPAC name for each of the following:

a. $CH_3—CH_2—OH$

b. OH (skeletal structure)

c. OH (benzene ring)

17.26 Give the IUPAC name for each of the following:

a. OH (skeletal structure)

b.
$$CH_3—CH_2—\underset{}{\overset{CH_3}{\overset{|}{CH}}}—\overset{CH_3}{\overset{|}{CH}}—CH_2—OH$$

c. OH (benzene ring) $CH_2—CH_3$

17.27 Draw the condensed structural formula for each of the following:

a. 1-propanol
b. methyl alcohol
c. 3-pentanol
d. 2-methyl-2-butanol

17.28 Draw the condensed structural formula for each of the following:

a. ethyl alcohol
b. 3-methyl-1-butanol
c. 2,4-dichloro-3-hexanol
d. propyl alcohol

17.29 Give the common name for each of the following:

a. $CH_3—O—CH_2—CH_3$

b. $CH_3—CH_2—CH_2—O—CH_2—CH_2—CH_3$

c. O (skeletal structure)

17.30 Give the common name for each of the following:

a. $CH_3—CH_2—O—CH_2—CH_2—CH_3$

b. O (benzene ring)

c. $CH_3—O—CH_3$

17.5 Aldehydes and Ketones

LEARNING GOAL

Write the IUPAC and common names for aldehydes and ketones; draw the condensed structural formulas when given their names.

The *carbonyl* (C=O) *group* has a carbon–oxygen double bond with two groups of atoms attached to the carbon atom at angles of 120°. Because the oxygen atom in the carbonyl group is much more electronegative than the carbon atom, the carbonyl group has a dipole with a partial negative charge (δ^-) on the oxygen and a partial positive charge (δ^+) on the carbon.

In an *aldehyde*, the carbon of the carbonyl group is bonded to at least one hydrogen atom. That carbon may also be bonded to another hydrogen, a carbon atom in an alkyl group, or an aromatic ring (see Figure 17.5). In a *ketone*, the carbon of the carbonyl group is bonded to two alkyl groups or aromatic rings.

Naming Aldehydes

In the IUPAC system, an aldehyde is named by replacing the *e* in the corresponding alkane name with *al*. No number is needed for the aldehyde group because it always appears at the beginning of the chain. However, the aldehydes with carbon chains

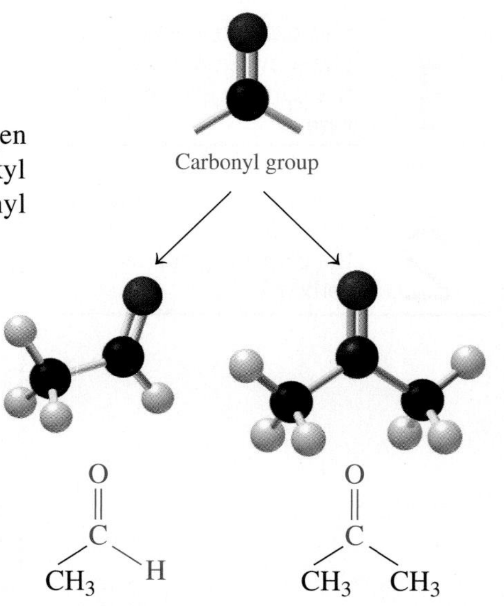

FIGURE 17.5 The carbonyl group is found in aldehydes and ketones.

Q If aldehydes and ketones both contain a carbonyl group, how can you differentiate between compounds from each family?

of one to four carbon atoms are often referred to by their common names, which end in *aldehyde*. The roots (*form*, *acet*, *propion*, and *butyr*) of these common names are derived from Latin or Greek words (see Figure 17.6).

The aldehyde of benzene is named benzaldehyde.

Benzaldehyde

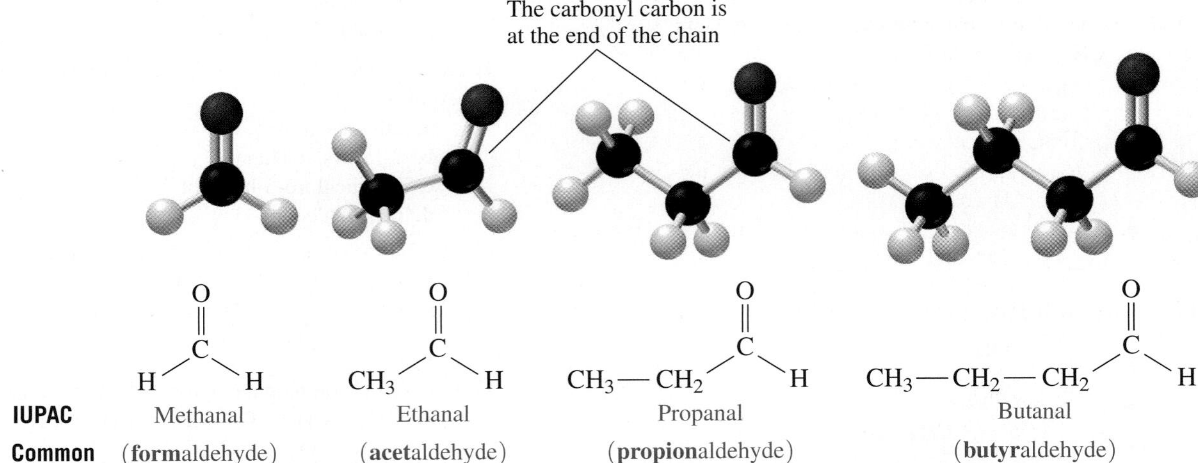

IUPAC	Methanal	Ethanal	Propanal	Butanal
Common	(**form**aldehyde)	(**acet**aldehyde)	(**propion**aldehyde)	(**butyr**aldehyde)

FIGURE 17.6 In the structures of aldehydes, the carbonyl group is always the end carbon.

Q Why is the carbon in the carbonyl group in aldehydes always at the end of the chain?

SAMPLE PROBLEM 17.7 Naming Aldehydes

Give the IUPAC name for the following:

$$CH_3-CH_2-\underset{\displaystyle |}{\overset{CH_3}{CH}}-CH_2-\overset{\displaystyle O}{\overset{\|}{C}}-H$$

SOLUTION

	Functional Group	Family	IUPAC Naming
Analyze the Problem	carbonyl group (carbon 1)	aldehyde	replace the *e* in the alkane name with *al*

Guide to Naming Aldehydes

1. Name the longest carbon chain by replacing the *e* in the alkane name with *al*.
2. Name and number the substituents by counting the carbonyl group as carbon 1.

Step 1 **Name the longest carbon chain by replacing the *e* in the alkane name with *al*.** The longest carbon chain containing the carbonyl group has five carbon atoms.

$$CH_3-CH_2-\overset{CH_3}{\overset{|}{CH}}-CH_2-\overset{O}{\overset{\|}{C}}-H \qquad \text{pentanal}$$

Step 2 **Name and number the substituents by counting the carbonyl group as carbon 1.** The substituent, which is the $-CH_3$ group on carbon 3, is methyl.

$$\underset{5}{CH_3}-\underset{4}{CH_2}-\underset{3}{\overset{CH_3}{\overset{|}{CH}}}-\underset{2}{CH_2}-\underset{1}{\overset{O}{\overset{\|}{C}}}-H \qquad \text{3-methylpentanal}$$

STUDY CHECK 17.7

What are the IUPAC and common names of the aldehyde with three carbon atoms?

Chemistry Link to the Environment

VANILLA

Vanilla has been used as a flavoring for over a thousand years. After drinking a beverage made from powdered vanilla and cocoa beans with Emperor Montezuma in Mexico, the Spanish conquistador Hernán Cortés took vanilla back to Europe where it became popular for flavoring and for scenting perfumes and tobacco. Thomas Jefferson introduced vanilla to the United States during the late 1700s. Today much of the vanilla we use in the world is grown in Mexico, Madagascar, Réunion, Seychelles, Tahiti, Sri Lanka, Java, the Philippines, and Africa.

The vanilla plant is a member of the orchid family and thrives under tropical conditions. There are many species of *Vanilla*, but *Vanilla planifolia* (or *V. fragrans*) is considered to produce the best flavor. The vanilla plant grows like a vine, which can attain a length of 100 feet. Its flowers are hand-pollinated to produce a green fruit that is picked in 8 or 9 months. The fruit is sun-dried so that it becomes a long, dark brown pod, which is called a "vanilla bean" because it looks like a string bean. The flavor and fragrance of the vanilla bean comes from the tiny black seeds found inside the dried bean.

The seeds and pod are used to flavor desserts such as custards and ice cream. The extract of vanilla is made by chopping up vanilla beans and mixing them with a 35% ethanol–water mixture. The liquid, which contains the aldehyde *vanillin*, is drained from the bean residue and used for flavoring.

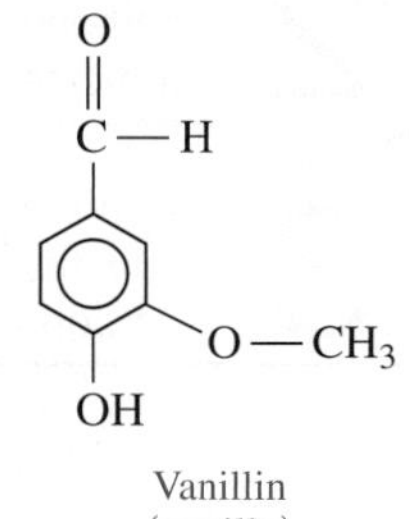

Vanillin (vanilla)

The vanilla bean is the dried fruit of the vanilla plant.

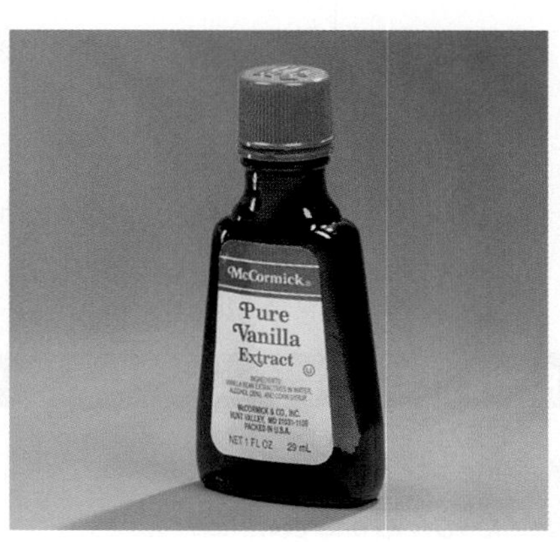

Vanilla flavoring liquid is prepared by soaking vanilla beans in ethanol and water.

Naming Ketones

In the IUPAC system, the name of a ketone is obtained by replacing the *e* in the corresponding alkane name with *one*. However, the common names for unbranched ketones are still in use. Then the alkyl groups bonded on either side of the carbonyl group are listed alphabetically followed by *ketone*. The name of acetone, which is another name for propanone, has also been retained by the IUPAC system. The naming of a ketone is shown in Sample Problem 17.8.

SAMPLE PROBLEM 17.8 Naming Ketones

Give the IUPAC name for the following ketone:

$$\begin{array}{c} \quad\; CH_3 \qquad\quad\;\; O \\ \quad\;\; | \qquad\qquad\;\; \| \\ CH_3—CH—CH_2—C—CH_3 \end{array}$$

SOLUTION

	Functional Group	Family	IUPAC Naming
Analyze the Problem	carbonyl group bonded to two carbon atoms within a chain	ketone	replace the *e* in the alkane name with *one* and count from the end nearer the carbonyl group to number any substituent

Guide to Naming Ketones

1 Name the longest carbon chain by replacing the *e* in the alkane name with *one*.

2 Number the carbon chain from the end nearer the carbonyl group, and indicate its location.

3 Name and number any substituents on the carbon chain.

Step 1 **Name the longest carbon chain by replacing the *e* in the alkane name with *one*.**

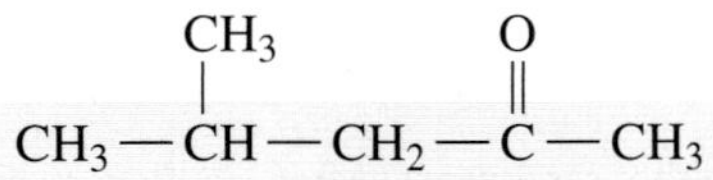

$$CH_3-\overset{\displaystyle CH_3}{\overset{|}{C}H}-CH_2-\overset{\displaystyle O}{\overset{\|}{C}}-CH_3 \qquad \text{pentanone}$$

Step 2 **Number the carbon chain from the end nearer the carbonyl group, and indicate its location.**

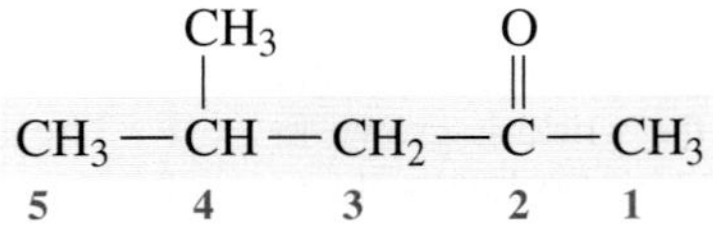

$$\underset{5}{CH_3}-\underset{4}{\overset{\displaystyle CH_3}{\overset{|}{C}H}}-\underset{3}{CH_2}-\underset{2}{\overset{\displaystyle O}{\overset{\|}{C}}}-\underset{1}{CH_3} \qquad \text{2-pentanone}$$

Step 3 **Name and number any substituents on the carbon chain.** Counting from the end nearer the carbonyl group places the methyl group on carbon 4.

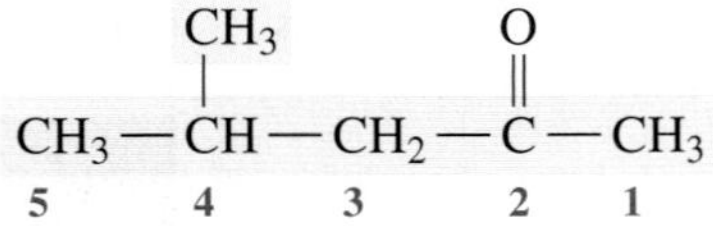

$$\underset{5}{CH_3}-\underset{4}{\overset{\displaystyle CH_3}{\overset{|}{C}H}}-\underset{3}{CH_2}-\underset{2}{\overset{\displaystyle O}{\overset{\|}{C}}}-\underset{1}{CH_3} \qquad \text{4-methyl-2-pentanone}$$

STUDY CHECK 17.8

What is the common name of 3-hexanone?

QUESTIONS AND PROBLEMS

17.5 Aldehydes and Ketones

LEARNING GOAL: *Write the IUPAC and common names for aldehydes and ketones; draw the condensed structural formulas when given their names.*

17.31 Give the common name for each of the following:

a. 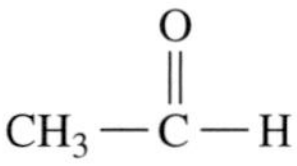 $CH_3-\overset{\displaystyle O}{\overset{\|}{C}}-H$

b. (skeletal structure with O)

c. $H-\overset{\displaystyle O}{\overset{\|}{C}}-H$

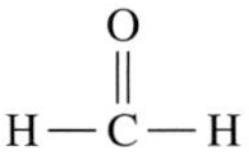

17.32 Give the common name for each of the following:

a. 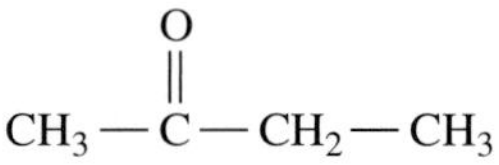 $CH_3-\overset{\displaystyle O}{\overset{\|}{C}}-CH_2-CH_3$

b. (skeletal structure with O)

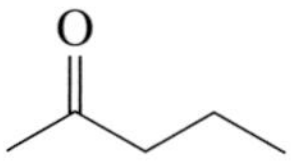

c. $CH_3-CH_2-\overset{\displaystyle O}{\overset{\|}{C}}-H$

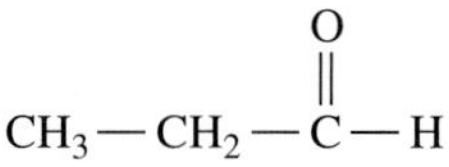

17.33 Give the IUPAC name for each of the following:

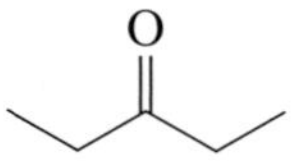

a. 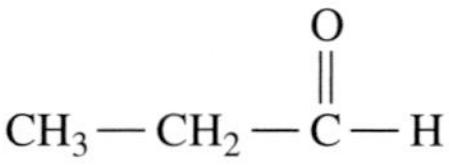 $CH_3-CH_2-\overset{\displaystyle O}{\overset{\|}{C}}-H$

b. (skeletal structure with O)

c. (benzene ring with $\overset{\displaystyle O}{\overset{\|}{C}}-H$)

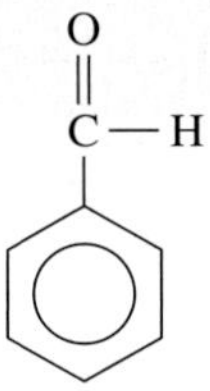

17.34 Give the IUPAC name for each of the following:

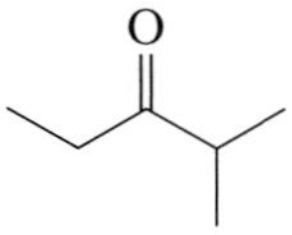

a. 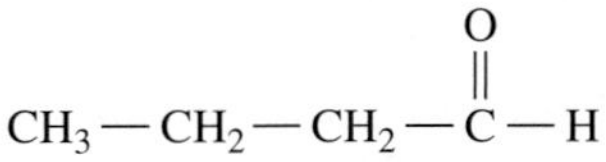 $CH_3-CH_2-CH_2-\overset{\displaystyle O}{\overset{\|}{C}}-H$

b. (skeletal structure with O)

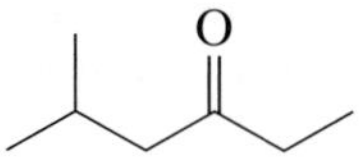

c. (benzene ring with $\overset{\displaystyle O}{\overset{\|}{C}}-H$ and Cl)

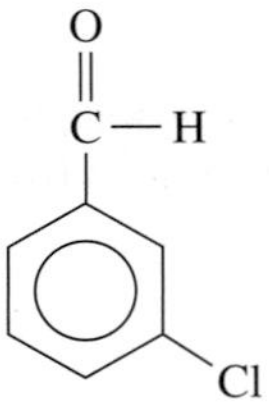

17.35 Draw the condensed structural formula for each of the following:

a. acetaldehyde

b. 2-pentanone

c. butyl methyl ketone

17.36 Draw the condensed structural formula for each of the following:

a. propionaldehyde

b. 3,4-dimethylhexanal

c. 4-bromobutanone

17.6 Carboxylic Acids and Esters

LEARNING GOAL

Write the IUPAC and common names for carboxylic acids and esters; draw the condensed structural formulas when given their names.

In a *carboxylic acid*, the carbon atom of a carbonyl group on the first carbon is attached to a hydroxyl (—OH) group, which forms a **carboxyl group**. Some ways to represent the carboxyl group in propanoic acid follow.

Carbonyl group

$$-\overset{\boxed{O}}{\overset{\|}{\boxed{C}}}-\boxed{OH}$$ *Hydroxyl group*

Carboxyl group

$$CH_3-CH_2-\overset{O}{\overset{\|}{C}}-OH \qquad \text{(skeletal formula with O and OH)} \qquad CH_3-CH_2-COOH$$

Propanoic acid
(propionic acid)

IUPAC Names of Carboxylic Acids

The IUPAC names of carboxylic acids replace the *e* in the corresponding alkane name with *oic acid*. If there are substituents, the carbon chain is numbered beginning with the carboxyl carbon.

$$H-\overset{O}{\overset{\|}{C}}-OH \qquad CH_3-\overset{CH_3}{\overset{|}{CH}}-\overset{O}{\overset{\|}{C}}-OH \qquad CH_3-\overset{OH}{\overset{|}{CH}}-CH_2-\overset{O}{\overset{\|}{C}}-OH$$

Methanoic acid — 2-Methylpropanoic acid — 3-Hydroxybutanoic acid

The sour taste of vinegar is due to ethanoic acid (acetic acid).

As with the aldehydes, carboxylic acids with one to four carbon atoms have common names, which are derived from their natural sources. The common names use the prefixes of *form*, *acet*, *propion*, and *butyr*; these common names are derived from Latin or Greek words (see Table 17.6).

TABLE 17.6 IUPAC and Common Names of Selected Carboxylic Acids

Condensed Structural Formula	IUPAC Name	Common Name	Ball-and-Stick Model
$H-\overset{O}{\overset{\|}{C}}-OH$	Methanoic acid	Formic acid	
$CH_3-\overset{O}{\overset{\|}{C}}-OH$	Ethanoic acid	Acetic acid	
$CH_3-CH_2-\overset{O}{\overset{\|}{C}}-OH$	Propanoic acid	Propionic acid	
$CH_3-CH_2-CH_2-\overset{O}{\overset{\|}{C}}-OH$	Butanoic acid	Butyric acid	

The name of the carboxylic acid of benzene is benzoic acid. The carbon of the carboxyl group is bonded to carbon 1 in the ring, and the ring is numbered to give the lowest numbers for any substituents.

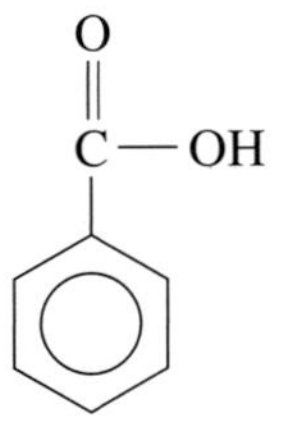

Benzoic acid

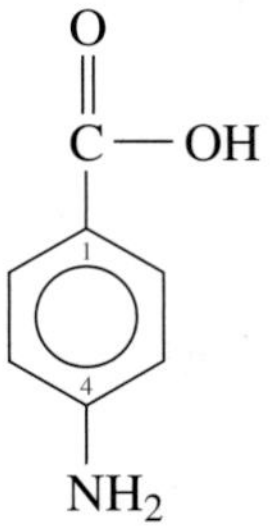

4-Aminobenzoic acid (*p*-aminobenzoic acid; PABA)

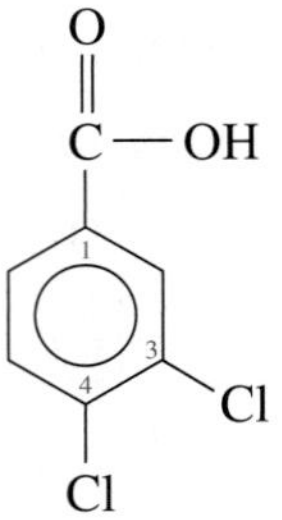

3,4-Dichlorobenzoic acid

SAMPLE PROBLEM 17.9 Naming Carboxylic Acids

Give the IUPAC name for each of the following carboxylic acids:

a.

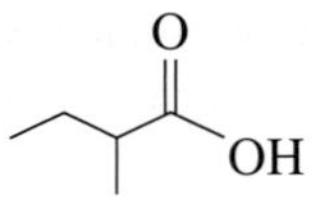

b.

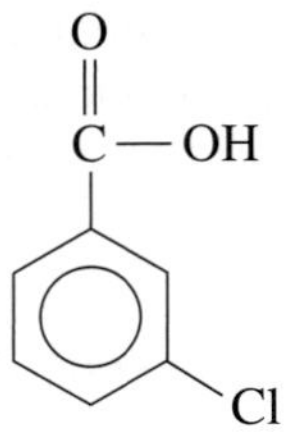

SOLUTION

	Family	IUPAC Naming
Analyze the Problem	carboxylic acid	replace the *e* in the alkane name with *oic acid* and count from carbon 1 of the carboxyl group for any substituents

Guide to Naming Carboxylic Acids

1 Identify the longest carbon chain and replace the *e* in the alkane name with *oic acid*.

2 Give the location and name of each substituent by counting the carboxyl carbon as 1.

a. Step 1 **Identify the longest carbon chain and replace the *e* in the alkane name with *oic acid*.** A carboxylic acid with four carbon atoms is named butanoic acid.

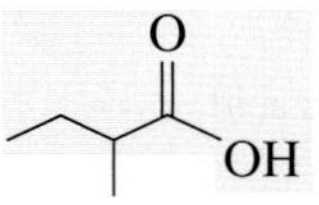

butanoic acid

Step 2 **Give the location and name of each substituent by counting the carboxyl carbon as 1.** This carboxylic acid has a methyl group on the second carbon from the carboxyl end. The IUPAC name is 2-methylbutanoic acid.

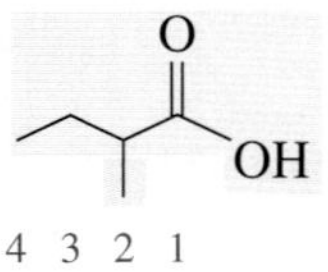

2-methylbutanoic acid

b. Step 1 **Identify the carbon chain containing the carboxyl group and replace the *e* in the alkane name with *oic acid*.** The carboxylic acid of benzene is named benzoic acid.

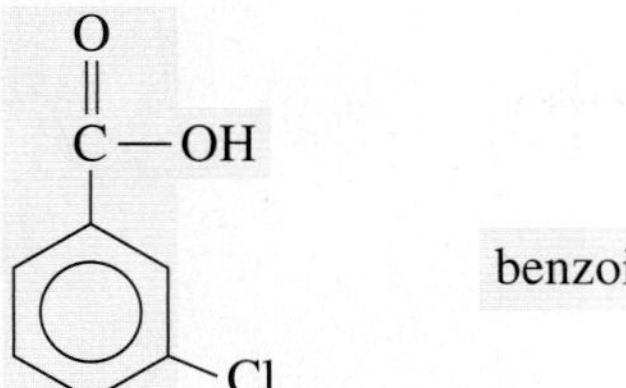

benzoic acid

Step 2 **Give the location and name of each substituent by counting the carboxyl carbon as 1.** The Cl atom is on carbon 3 when we count the carbon attached to the carboxyl group as carbon 1.

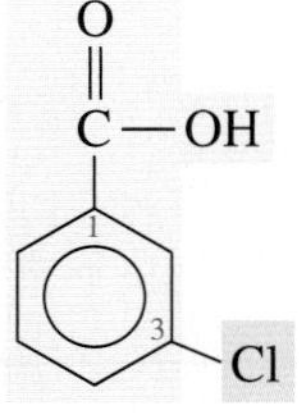

3-chlorobenzoic acid

STUDY CHECK 17.9

Draw the condensed structural formula for pentanoic acid.

Chemistry Link to Health

CARBOXYLIC ACIDS IN METABOLISM

Several carboxylic acids are part of the metabolic processes within our cells. For example, during glycolysis, a molecule of glucose is broken down into two molecules of pyruvic acid, or actually, its carboxylate ion, pyruvate. During strenuous exercise when oxygen levels are low (anaerobic), pyruvic acid is reduced to give lactic acid or the lactate ion.

$$\underset{\text{Pyruvic acid}}{CH_3-\overset{\overset{O}{\|}}{C}-\overset{\overset{O}{\|}}{C}-OH} + 2H \xrightarrow{\text{Reduction}} \underset{\text{Lactic acid}}{CH_3-\overset{\overset{OH}{|}}{CH}-\overset{\overset{O}{\|}}{C}-OH}$$

During exercise, pyruvic acid is converted to lactic acid in the muscles.

In the *citric acid cycle*, also called the Krebs cycle, di- and tricarboxylic acids are oxidized and decarboxylated (loss of CO_2) to produce energy for the cells of the body. These carboxylic acids are normally referred to by their common names. At the start of the citric acid cycle, citric acid with six carbons is converted to five-carbon α-ketoglutaric acid. Citric acid is also the acid that gives the sour taste to citrus fruits such as lemons and grapefruits.

$$\underset{\text{Citric acid}}{\begin{array}{c} COOH \\ | \\ CH_2 \\ | \\ HO-C-COOH \\ | \\ CH_2 \\ | \\ COOH \end{array}} \xrightarrow{[O]} \underset{\alpha\text{-Ketoglutaric acid}}{\begin{array}{c} COOH \\ | \\ CH_2 \\ | \\ CH_2 \\ | \\ C{=}O \\ | \\ COOH \end{array}} + CO_2$$

The citric acid cycle continues as α-ketoglutaric acid loses CO_2 to give a four-carbon succinic acid. Then a series of reactions converts succinic acid to oxaloacetic acid. We see that some of the functional groups we have studied along with reactions such as hydration and oxidation are part of the metabolic processes that take place in our cells.

$$\underset{\text{Succinic acid}}{\begin{array}{c}\text{COOH}\\|\\\text{CH}_2\\|\\\text{CH}_2\\|\\\text{COOH}\end{array}} \xrightarrow{[O]} \underset{\text{Fumaric acid}}{\begin{array}{c}\text{COOH}\\|\\\text{C—H}\\\|\\\text{H—C}\\|\\\text{COOH}\end{array}} \xrightarrow{H_2O} \underset{\text{Malic acid}}{\begin{array}{c}\text{COOH}\\|\\\text{HO—C—H}\\|\\\text{CH}_2\\|\\\text{COOH}\end{array}} \xrightarrow{[O]} \underset{\text{Oxaloacetic acid}}{\begin{array}{c}\text{COOH}\\|\\\text{C=O}\\|\\\text{CH}_2\\|\\\text{COOH}\end{array}}$$

At the pH of the aqueous environment in the cells, the carboxylic acids are ionized, which means it is actually the carboxylate ions that take part in the reactions of the citric acid cycle. For example, in water, succinic acid is in equilibrium with its carboxylate ion, succinate.

$$\underset{\text{Succinic acid}}{\begin{array}{c}\text{COOH}\\|\\\text{CH}_2\\|\\\text{CH}_2\\|\\\text{COOH}\end{array}} + 2H_2O \rightleftharpoons \underset{\text{Succinate ion}}{\begin{array}{c}\text{COO}^-\\|\\\text{CH}_2\\|\\\text{CH}_2\\|\\\text{COO}^-\end{array}} + 2H_3O^+$$

Citric acid gives the sour taste to citrus fruits.

Esters

A carboxylic acid reacts with an alcohol to form an *ester*. In an ester, the —H of the carboxylic acid is replaced by an alkyl group. Aspirin is an ester as well as a carboxylic acid. Fats and oils in our diets contain esters of glycerol and fatty acids, which are long-chain carboxylic acids. The aromas and flavors of many fruits including bananas, oranges, and strawberries are due to esters.

Carboxylic Acid | **Ester**

$$\underset{\substack{\text{Ethanoic acid}\\\text{(acetic acid)}}}{CH_3—\overset{\overset{\large O}{\|}}{C}—O—H} \qquad \underset{\substack{\text{Methyl ethanoate}\\\text{(methyl acetate)}}}{CH_3—\overset{\overset{\large O}{\|}}{C}—O—CH_3}$$

Esterification

In a reaction called **esterification**, an ester is produced when a carboxylic acid and an alcohol are heated with a strong acid catalyst (usually H_2SO_4). An excess of the alcohol reactant is used to shift the equilibrium in the direction of the formation of the ester product. In this esterification reaction, the —OH removed from the carboxylic acid and the —H removed from the alcohol combine to form water.

$$\underset{\substack{\text{Ethanoic acid}\\\text{(acetic acid)}}}{CH_3—\overset{\overset{\large O}{\|}}{C}—O—H} + \underset{\substack{\text{Methanol}\\\text{(methyl alcohol)}}}{H—O—CH_3} \underset{}{\overset{H^+,\ \text{heat}}{\rightleftharpoons}} \underset{\substack{\text{Methyl ethanoate}\\\text{(methyl acetate)}}}{CH_3—\overset{\overset{\large O}{\|}}{C}—O—CH_3} + H—O—H$$

SAMPLE PROBLEM 17.10 Writing Esterification Equations

The ester that is present in pineapples can be synthesized from butanoic acid and methanol. What is the chemical equation for the formation of this ester?

SOLUTION

Analyze the Problem	Reaction	Reactants	Products
	esterification	carboxylic acid and alcohol	ester + H_2O

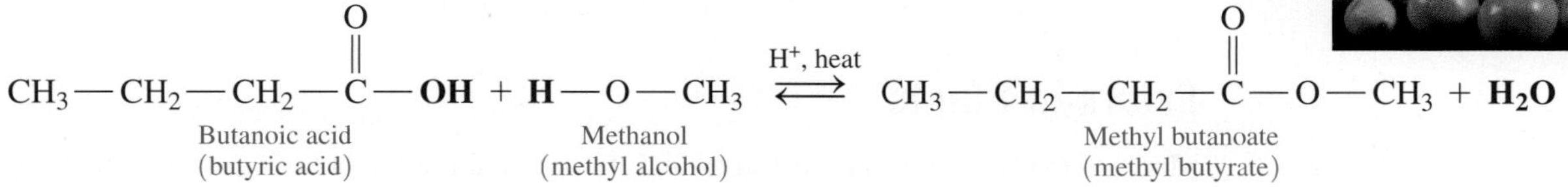

STUDY CHECK 17.10

What are the IUPAC names of the carboxylic acid and alcohol that are needed to form the following ester, which has the odor of apples? (*Hint*: Separate the O and C=O of the ester group and add H— and —OH to give the original alcohol and carboxylic acid.)

$$CH_3-CH_2-\overset{\overset{\displaystyle O}{\|}}{C}-O-CH_2-CH_2-CH_2-CH_2-CH_3$$

Naming Esters

The name of an ester consists of two words that are derived from the names of the alcohol and the acid in that ester. The first word indicates the *alkyl* part from the alcohol. The second word is the *carboxylate* part from the carboxylic acid. The IUPAC names of esters use the IUPAC names for the carbon chain of the acid, while the common names of esters use the common names of the acids. Let's take a look at the following ester, which has a fruity odor. We start by separating the ester bond into two parts, which gives us the alkyl of the alcohol and the carboxylate of the acid. Then we name the ester as an alkyl carboxylate (see Figure 17.7).

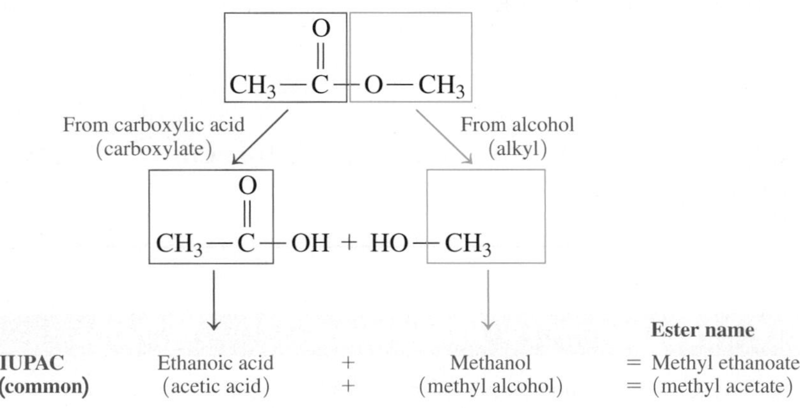

FIGURE 17.7 The ester methyl ethanoate (methyl acetate) is made from methyl alcohol and ethanoic acid (acetic acid).

Q What change is made in the name of the carboxylic acid used to make the ester?

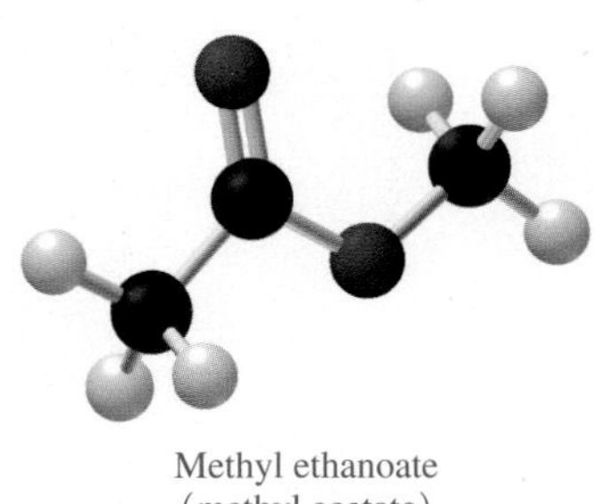

Methyl ethanoate
(methyl acetate)

CONCEPT CHECK 17.4 Naming Esters

The odor and flavor of oranges is the ester from octanol and ethanoic acid. What is the IUPAC name of this ester?

ANSWER

The first part of an ester name comes from the alkyl part of octanol, which would be *octyl*. The second part is obtained from the name of the carboxylic acid by replacing *ic acid* with *ate*. The name of the ester for orange flavor is octyl ethanoate.

Esters in Plants

Many of the fragrances of perfumes and flowers and the flavors of fruits are due to esters. Small esters are volatile, so we can smell them, and soluble in water, so we can taste them. Several of these are listed in Table 17.7.

TABLE 17.7 Some Esters in Fruits and Flavorings

Condensed Structural Formula and Name	Flavor/Odor
$CH_3-\overset{\overset{\displaystyle O}{\Vert}}{C}-O-CH_2-CH_2-CH_3$ Propyl ethanoate (propyl acetate)	Pears
$CH_3-\overset{\overset{\displaystyle O}{\Vert}}{C}-O-CH_2-CH_2-CH_2-CH_2-CH_3$ Pentyl ethanoate (pentyl acetate)	Bananas
$CH_3-\overset{\overset{\displaystyle O}{\Vert}}{C}-O-CH_2-CH_2-CH_2-CH_2-CH_2-CH_2-CH_2-CH_3$ Octyl ethanoate (octyl acetate)	Oranges
$CH_3-CH_2-CH_2-\overset{\overset{\displaystyle O}{\Vert}}{C}-O-CH_2-CH_3$ Ethyl butanoate (ethyl butyrate)	Pineapples
$CH_3-CH_2-CH_2-\overset{\overset{\displaystyle O}{\Vert}}{C}-O-CH_2-CH_2-CH_2-CH_2-CH_3$ Pentyl butanoate (pentyl butyrate)	Apricots

SAMPLE PROBLEM 17.11 Naming Esters

Write the IUPAC and common names of the following ester:

$$CH_3-CH_2-\overset{\overset{\displaystyle O}{\Vert}}{C}-O-CH_2-CH_2-CH_3$$

SOLUTION

Analyze the Problem	Family	IUPAC Naming
	ester	write the alkyl name for the carbon chain of the alcohol, and change the *ic acid* in the acid name to *ate*

Step 1 **Write the name of the carbon chain from the alcohol as an *alkyl* group.** The alcohol that is used for the ester is propanol, which is named as the alkyl group propyl.

$$CH_3-CH_2-\overset{\overset{\displaystyle O}{\|}}{C}-O-CH_2-CH_2-CH_3 \qquad \text{propyl}$$

Step 2 **Change the *ic acid* in the acid name to *ate*.** The carboxylic acid with three carbon atoms is propanoic acid. Replacing the *ic acid* with *ate* gives the IUPAC name propyl propanoate. The common name of propionic acid gives the common name for the ester of propyl propionate.

$$CH_3-CH_2-\overset{\overset{\displaystyle O}{\|}}{C}-O-CH_2-CH_2-CH_3 \qquad \text{propyl propanoate}$$

(propyl propionate)

STUDY CHECK 17.11

Draw the condensed structural formula for ethyl heptanoate that gives the odor and flavor to grapes.

Guide to Naming Esters

1. Write the name of the carbon chain from the alcohol as an *alkyl* group.
2. Change the *ic acid* in the acid name to *ate.*

The odor of grapes is due to ethyl heptanoate.

QUESTIONS AND PROBLEMS

17.6 Carboxylic Acids and Esters

LEARNING GOAL: *Write the IUPAC and common names for carboxylic acids and esters; draw the condensed structural formulas when given their names.*

17.37 Give the IUPAC and common name (if any) for each of the following carboxylic acids:

a. $CH_3-\overset{\overset{\displaystyle O}{\|}}{C}-OH$

b. $CH_3-CH_2-\overset{\overset{\displaystyle O}{\|}}{C}-OH$

c. 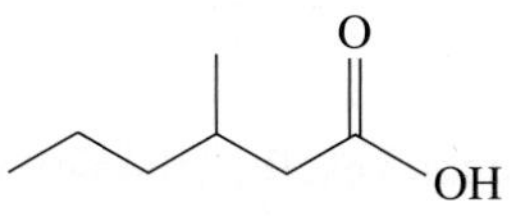 (skeletal structure) O, OH

d.

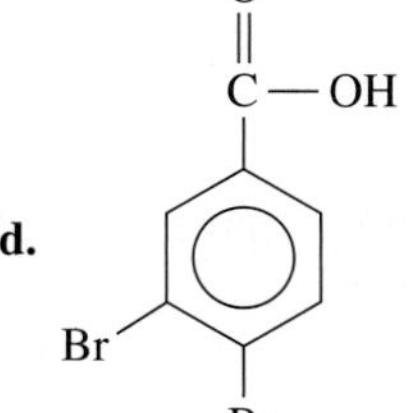

17.38 Give the IUPAC and common name (if any) for each of the following carboxylic acids:

a. $H-\overset{\overset{\displaystyle O}{\|}}{C}-OH$

b. 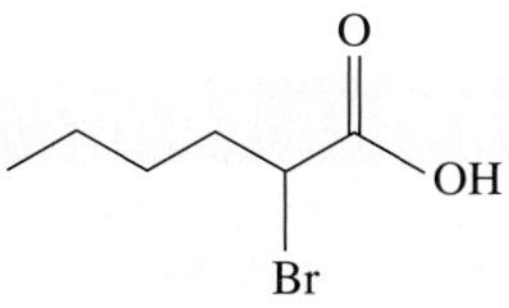 (skeletal structure) O, OH, Br

c. 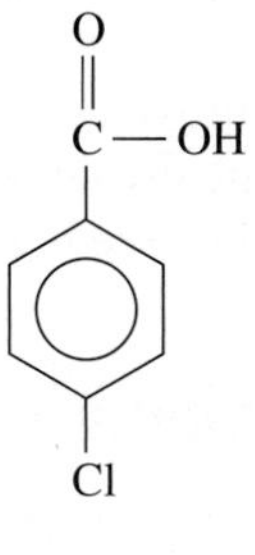 (benzene ring with $\overset{\overset{\displaystyle O}{\|}}{C}-OH$ and Cl)

d. $CH_3-CH_2-\overset{\overset{\displaystyle CH_3}{|}}{CH}-\overset{\overset{\displaystyle O}{\|}}{C}-OH$

17.39 Draw the condensed structural formula for each of the following carboxylic acids:
a. propionic acid **b.** benzoic acid
c. 2-chloroethanoic acid **d.** 3-hydroxypropanoic acid

17.40 Draw the condensed structural formula for each of the following carboxylic acids:
a. 2-methylhexanoic acid **b.** 3-ethylbenzoic acid
c. 2-hydroxyacetic acid **d.** 2,4-dibromobutanoic acid

17.41 Draw the condensed structural formula for the ester formed when each of the following reacts with methyl alcohol:
a. acetic acid **b.** pentanoic acid

17.42 Draw the condensed structural formula for the ester formed when each of the following reacts with ethyl alcohol:
a. formic acid **b.** propionic acid

17.43 Draw the condensed structural formula for the ester formed when the following carboxylic acids and alcohols react:

a. $CH_3-CH_2-\overset{\overset{O}{\|}}{C}-OH + HO-CH_2-CH_2-CH_3 \xrightleftharpoons{H^+, \text{heat}}$

b. $CH_3-CH_2-CH_2-CH_2-\overset{\overset{O}{\|}}{C}-OH + HO-\overset{\overset{CH_3}{|}}{CH}-CH_3 \xrightleftharpoons{H^+, \text{heat}}$

17.44 Draw the condensed structural formula for the ester formed when the following carboxylic acids and alcohols react:

a. $CH_3-CH_2-\overset{\overset{O}{\|}}{C}-OH + HO-CH_3 \xrightleftharpoons{H^+, \text{heat}}$

b. $C_6H_5-\overset{\overset{O}{\|}}{C}-OH + HO-CH_2-CH_2-CH_2-CH_3 \xrightleftharpoons{H^+, \text{heat}}$ (benzene ring attached to C)

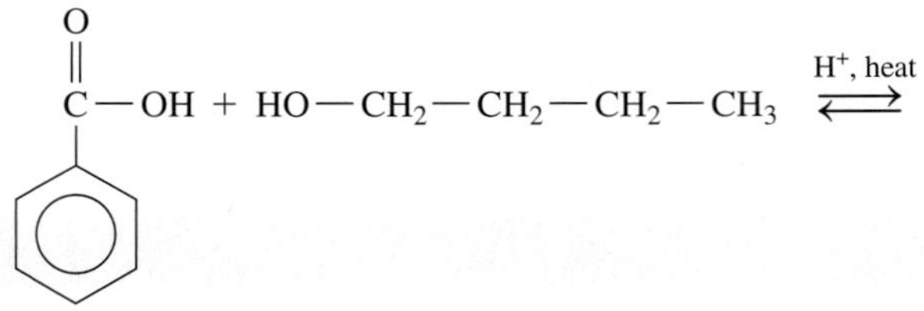

17.45 Write the IUPAC name for each of the following:

a. $H-\overset{\overset{O}{\|}}{C}-O-CH_3$

b. $CH_3-\overset{\overset{O}{\|}}{C}-O-CH_3$

c. $CH_3-CH_2-\overset{\overset{O}{\|}}{C}-O-CH_2-CH_3$

17.46 Write the IUPAC name for each of the following:

a. $CH_3-CH_2-CH_2-\overset{\overset{O}{\|}}{C}-O-CH_2-CH_3$

b. $CH_3-CH_2-CH_2-CH_2-CH_2-\overset{\overset{O}{\|}}{C}-O-CH_3$

c. $CH_3-CH_2-CH_2-\overset{\overset{O}{\|}}{C}-O-CH_3$

17.47 Draw the condensed structural formula for each of the following:
a. methyl acetate **b.** butyl formate
c. ethyl pentanoate **d.** propyl propanoate

17.48 Draw the condensed structural formula for each of the following:
a. hexyl acetate **b.** ethyl formate
c. ethyl hexanoate **d.** methyl benzoate

LEARNING GOAL

Write the common names for amines and the IUPAC and common names for amides; draw the condensed structural formulas when given their names.

17.7 Amines and Amides

Amines are derivatives of ammonia (NH_3) in which one or more hydrogen atoms are replaced with alkyl or aromatic groups. In methylamine, a methyl group replaces one hydrogen atom in ammonia. The bonding of two methyl groups gives dimethylamine. In trimethylamine, methyl groups replace all three hydrogen atoms attached to the nitrogen atom (see Figure 17.8).

Naming Amines

Several systems are used for naming amines. For simple amines, the common names are often used. In the common name, the alkyl groups bonded to the nitrogen atom are listed in alphabetical order. The prefixes *di* and *tri* are used to indicate two and three identical substituents.

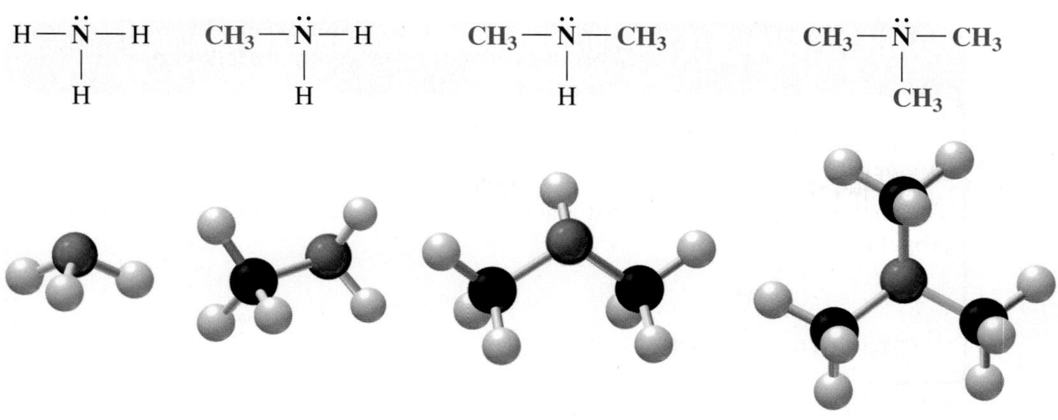

Ammonia Methylamine Dimethylamine Trimethylamine

FIGURE 17.8 Amines have one or more carbon atoms bonded to the N atom.

Q How many carbon atoms are bonded to the nitrogen atom in dimethylamine?

Aromatic Amines

The aromatic amines use the name *aniline*, which is approved by IUPAC.

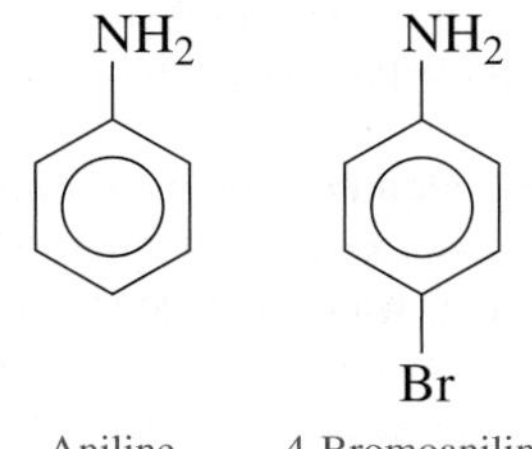

Aniline 4-Bromoaniline

Aniline is used to make many dyes, which give color to wool, cotton, and silk fibers, as well as blue jeans. It is also used to make the polymer polyurethane and in the synthesis of the pain reliever acetaminophen.

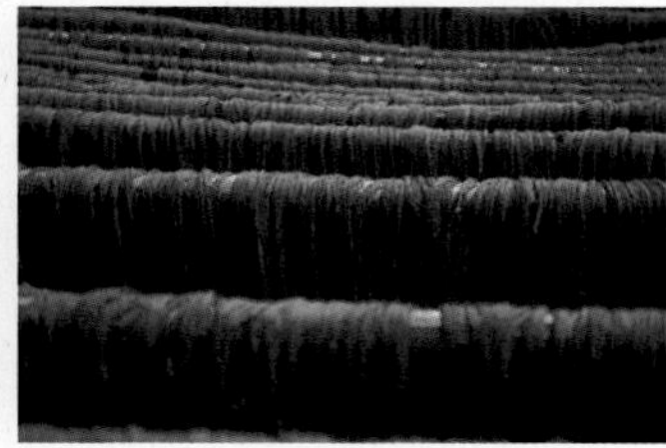

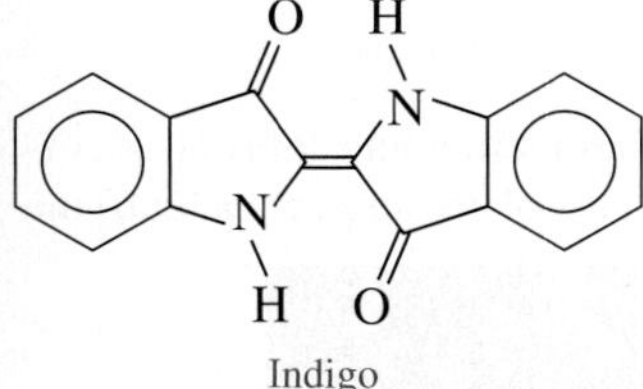

Indigo

Indigo used in blue dyes can be obtained from tropical plants such as *Indigofera tinctoria*.

CONCEPT CHECK 17.5 Naming Amines

Give the common name for each of the following amines:

a. $CH_3—CH_2—NH_2$ **b.** $CH_3—N(CH_3)—CH_3$ **c.** (benzene ring with NH_2)

ANSWER

a. This amine has one ethyl group attached to the nitrogen atom; its name is ethylamine.

b. The common name for an amine with three methyl groups attached to the nitrogen atom is trimethylamine.

c. This aromatic amine is aniline.

CONCEPT CHECK 17.6 Drawing Condensed Structural Formulas for Amines

Draw the condensed structural formula for ethylpropylamine.

ANSWER

The common name indicates that a nitrogen atom is attached to an ethyl group and a propyl group.

$$CH_3-CH_2-\underset{}{\overset{\displaystyle H}{\overset{|}{N}}}-CH_2-CH_2-CH_3$$

Chemistry Link to the Environment

ALKALOIDS: AMINES IN PLANTS

Alkaloids are physiologically active nitrogen-containing compounds produced by plants. The term *alkaloid* refers to the "alkali-like" or basic characteristics we have seen for amines. Certain alkaloids are used in anesthetics, in antidepressants, and as stimulants, and many are habit forming.

As a stimulant, nicotine increases the level of adrenaline in the blood, which increases the heart rate and blood pressure. Nicotine is addictive because it activates pleasure centers in the brain. Coniine, which is obtained from hemlock, is extremely toxic.

Nicotine

Coniine

Caffeine is a central nervous system stimulant. Present in coffee, tea, soft drinks, energy drinks, chocolate, and cocoa, caffeine increases alertness, but it may cause nervousness and insomnia. Caffeine is also used in certain pain relievers to counteract the drowsiness caused by an antihistamine.

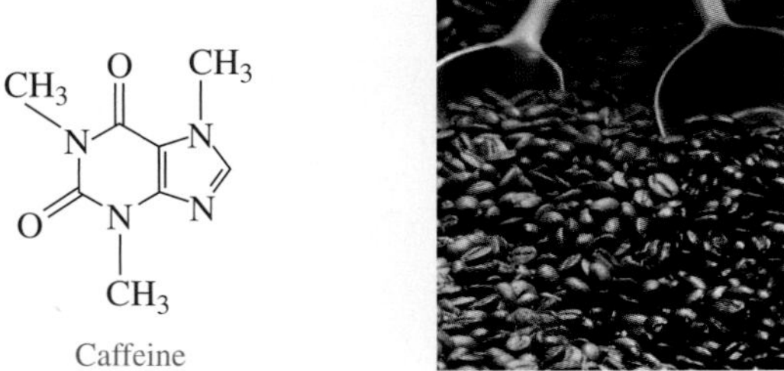

Caffeine is a stimulant found in coffee, tea, energy drinks, and chocolate.

Several alkaloids are used in medicine. Quinine, obtained from the bark of the cinchona tree, has been used in the treatment of malaria since the 1600s. Atropine from nightshade (belladonna) is used in low concentrations to accelerate slow heart rates and as an anesthetic for eye examinations.

Quinine

Atropine

For many centuries morphine and codeine, alkaloids found in the oriental poppy plant, have been used as effective painkillers. Codeine, which is structurally similar to morphine, is used in some prescription painkillers and cough syrups. Heroin, obtained by a chemical modification of morphine, is strongly addicting and is not used medically. The structure of the prescription drug OxyContin® (oxycodone) used to relieve severe pain is similar to heroin. Today, there are an increasing number of deaths from OxyContin® abuse because its physiological effects are also similar to those of heroin.

Morphine

Codeine

Heroin

OxyContin®

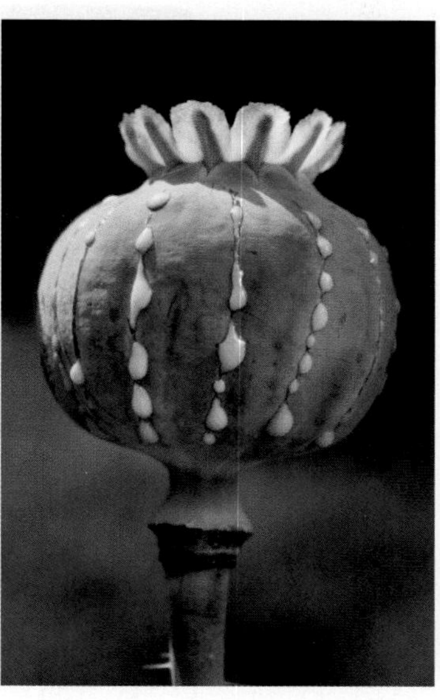

The green, unripe poppy seed capsule contains a sap (opium) that is the source of the alkaloids morphine and codeine.

Amides

Amides are derivatives of carboxylic acids in which a nitrogen group replaces the hydroxyl group (see Figure 17.9).

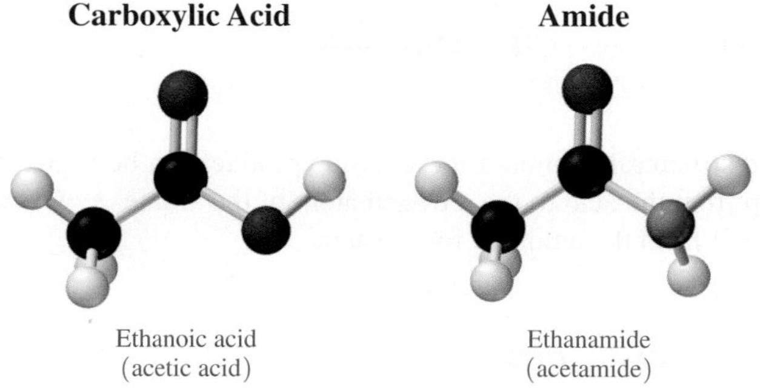

FIGURE 17.9 Amides are derivatives of carboxylic acids in which an amino group replaces the hydroxyl (—OH) group.

Q What is the amide of pentanoic acid?

Amidation

An amide is produced in a reaction called **amidation**, in which a carboxylic acid reacts with ammonia or an amine. A molecule of water is eliminated, and the fragments of the carboxylic acid and amine molecules join to form the amide, much like the formation of esters.

Amide bond

$$CH_3-CH_2-\overset{\overset{\large O}{\|}}{C}-\mathbf{OH} + \mathbf{H}-\overset{\overset{\large H}{|}}{N}-H \xrightarrow{\text{Heat}} CH_3-CH_2-\overset{\overset{\large O}{\|}}{C}-\overset{\overset{\large H}{|}}{N}-H + \mathbf{H_2O}$$

Propanoic acid (propionic acid) — Ammonia — Propanamide (propionamide)

$$CH_3-CH_2-\overset{\overset{\large O}{\|}}{C}-\mathbf{OH} + \mathbf{H}-\overset{\overset{\large H}{|}}{N}-CH_3 \xrightarrow{\text{Heat}} CH_3-CH_2-\overset{\overset{\large O}{\|}}{C}-\overset{\overset{\large H}{|}}{N}-CH_3 + \mathbf{H_2O}$$

Propanoic acid (propionic acid) — Methylamine — *N*-Methylpropanamide (*N*-methylpropionamide)

CONCEPT CHECK 17.7 Amidation

Draw the condensed structural formula for the amide product in the following reaction:

$$C_6H_5-\overset{\overset{\displaystyle O}{\|}}{C}-OH + NH_3 \xrightarrow{\text{Heat}}$$

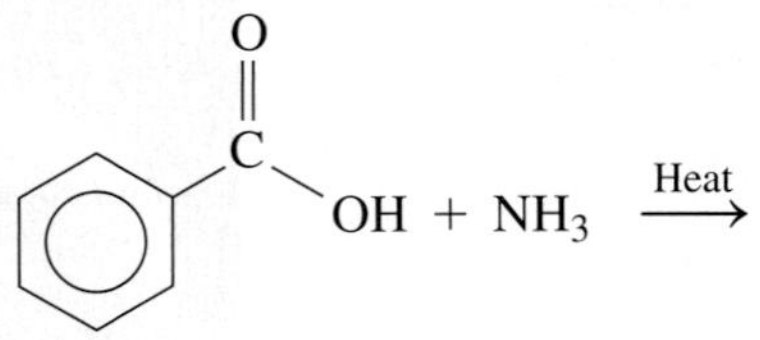

ANSWER

The condensed structural formula for the amide product is drawn by attaching the carbonyl group from the acid to the nitrogen atom of ammonia. The —OH group is removed from the acid and —H from ammonia to form water.

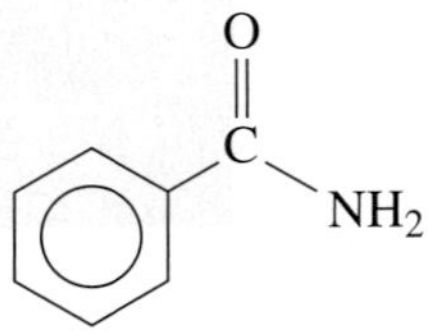

$$C_6H_5-\overset{\overset{\displaystyle O}{\|}}{C}-NH_2$$

SAMPLE PROBLEM 17.12 Formation of Amides

Draw the condensed structural formula for the amide product in the following reaction:

$$CH_3-\overset{\overset{\displaystyle O}{\|}}{C}-OH + H_2N-CH_2-CH_3 \xrightarrow{\text{Heat}}$$

SOLUTION

The condensed structural formula for the amide product can be drawn by attaching the carbonyl group from the acid to the nitrogen atom of the amine. —OH is removed from the acid and —H from the amine to form water.

$$CH_3-\overset{\overset{\displaystyle O}{\|}}{C}-\overset{\overset{\displaystyle H}{|}}{N}-CH_2-CH_3$$

STUDY CHECK 17.12

What are the condensed structural formulas of the carboxylic acid and amine needed to prepare the following amide?

$$H-\overset{\overset{\displaystyle O}{\|}}{C}-\overset{\overset{\displaystyle CH_3}{|}}{N}-CH_3$$

Naming Amides

In both the IUPAC and common names, amides are named by dropping the *ic acid* or *oic acid* from the carboxylic acid name (IUPAC or common), and adding the suffix *amide*. We can diagram the name of an amide in the following way:

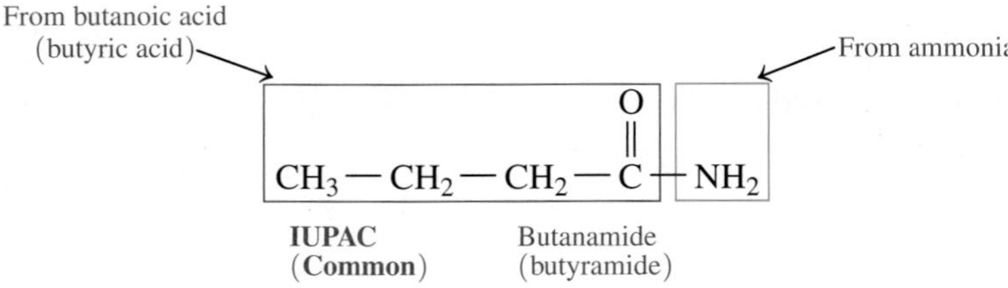

$$\underset{\text{Methanamide (formamide)}}{H-\overset{\overset{\large O}{\|}}{C}-NH_2} \qquad \underset{\text{Ethanamide (acetamide)}}{CH_3-\overset{\overset{\large O}{\|}}{C}-NH_2} \qquad \underset{\text{Benzamide}}{C_6H_5-\overset{\overset{\large O}{\|}}{C}-NH_2}$$

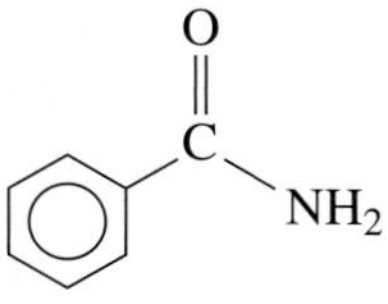

Methanamide (formamide) Ethanamide (acetamide) Benzamide

SAMPLE PROBLEM 17.13 Naming Amides

Give the IUPAC and common names for

$$CH_3-CH_2-\overset{\overset{\large O}{\|}}{C}-NH_3$$

SOLUTION

The IUPAC name of the carboxylic acid is propanoic acid; the common name is propionic acid. Replacing the *oic acid* or *ic acid* ending with *amide* gives the IUPAC name of propanamide and common name of propionamide.

STUDY CHECK 17.13

Draw the condensed structural formula for benzamide.

QUESTIONS AND PROBLEMS

17.7 Amines and Amides

LEARNING GOAL: *Write the common names for amines and the IUPAC and common names for amides; draw the condensed structural formulas when given their names.*

17.49 Write the common name for each of the following:

a. CH_3-NH_2

b. $CH_3-\overset{\overset{\large H}{|}}{N}-CH_2-CH_2-CH_3$

c. $CH_3-CH_2-\overset{\overset{\large CH_3}{|}}{N}-CH_2-CH_3$

17.50 Write the common name for each of the following:

a. $CH_3-CH_2-CH_2-NH_2$

b. $CH_3-\overset{\overset{\large H}{|}}{N}-CH_2-CH_3$

c. $CH_3-CH_2-CH_2-CH_2-NH_2$

17.51 Draw the condensed structural formula for the amide formed in each of the following reactions:

a. $CH_3-\overset{\overset{\large O}{\|}}{C}-OH + NH_3 \xrightarrow{\text{Heat}}$

b. $CH_3-\overset{\overset{\large O}{\|}}{C}-OH + H_2N-CH_2-CH_3 \xrightarrow{\text{Heat}}$

c. 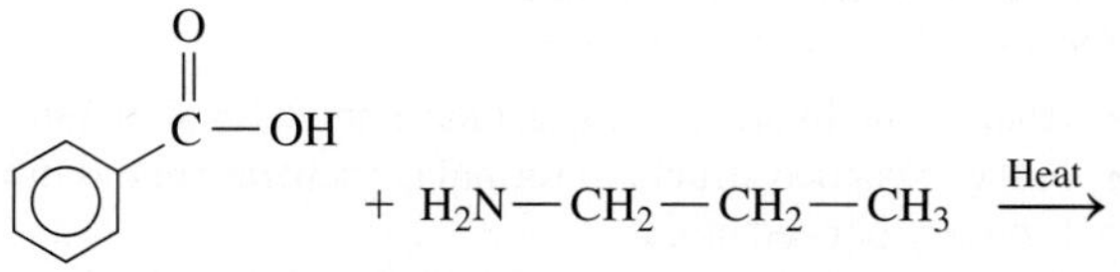 $C_6H_5-\overset{\overset{\large O}{\|}}{C}-OH + H_2N-CH_2-CH_2-CH_3 \xrightarrow{\text{Heat}}$

17.52 Draw the condensed structural formula for the amide formed in each of the following reactions:

a. $CH_3-CH_2-CH_2-CH_2-\overset{\overset{\large O}{\|}}{C}-OH + NH_3 \xrightarrow{\text{Heat}}$

b. $CH_3-\overset{\overset{\large CH_3}{|}}{CH}-\overset{\overset{\large O}{\|}}{C}-OH + H_2N-CH_2-CH_3 \xrightarrow{\text{Heat}}$

c. 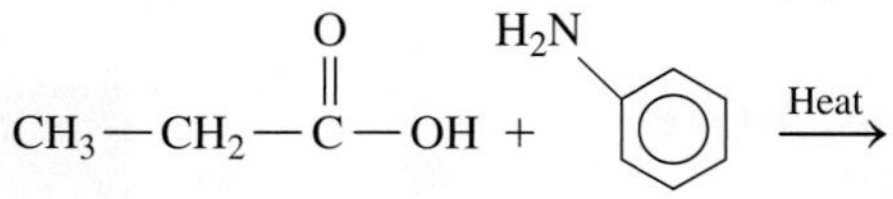 $CH_3-CH_2-\overset{\overset{\large O}{\|}}{C}-OH + H_2N-C_6H_5 \xrightarrow{\text{Heat}}$

17.53 Give the IUPAC and common name (if any) for each of the following amides:

a. $CH_3-\overset{\overset{O}{\|}}{C}-NH_2$

b. $CH_3-CH_2-\overset{\overset{Cl}{|}}{CH}-\overset{\overset{O}{\|}}{C}-NH_2$

c. $H-\overset{\overset{O}{\|}}{C}-NH_2$

17.54 Give the IUPAC and common name (if any) for each of the following amides:

a. $CH_3-\overset{\overset{Br}{|}}{CH}-\overset{\overset{O}{\|}}{C}-NH_2$

b. $CH_3-CH_2-CH_2-CH_2-CH_2-\overset{\overset{O}{\|}}{C}-NH_2$

c. (benzene ring with CH_3 substituent)$-\overset{\overset{O}{\|}}{C}-NH_2$

17.55 Draw the condensed structural formula for each of the following amides:

a. propionamide

b. 2-methylpentanamide

c. methanamide

17.56 Draw the condensed structural formula for each of the following amides:

a. formamide

b. benzamide

c. 3-methylbutanamide

CHAPTER REVIEW

17.1 Alkanes and Naming Substituents

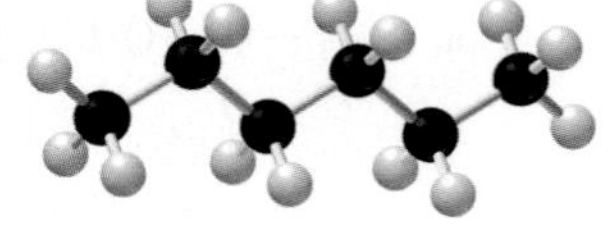

LEARNING GOAL: *Write the IUPAC names and draw the condensed structural formulas for alkanes with substituents.*

- Alkanes are hydrocarbons that have only C—C single bonds.
- In the expanded structural formula, a separate line is drawn for every bonded atom.
- A condensed structural formula depicts groups composed of each carbon atom and its attached hydrogen atoms.
- A skeletal formula represents the carbon skeleton as ends and corners of a zigzag line or geometric figure.
- The IUPAC system is used to name organic compounds by indicating the number of carbon atoms.
- Substituents such as alkyl groups and halogen atoms (named as fluoro, chloro, bromo, or iodo) can replace hydrogen atoms on the main chain.

17.2 Alkenes, Alkynes, and Polymers

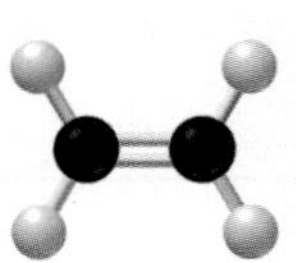

LEARNING GOAL: *Write the IUPAC names and formulas for alkenes and alkynes; draw the condensed structural formulas for the monomers that form a polymer.*

- Alkenes are unsaturated hydrocarbons that contain carbon–carbon double bonds (C=C).
- Alkynes contain a triple bond (C≡C).
- The IUPAC names of alkenes end with *ene*; alkyne names end with *yne*.
- The main chain is numbered from the end nearer the double or triple bond.
- Polymers are long-chain molecules that consist of many repeating units of smaller carbon molecules called monomers.

17.3 Aromatic Compounds

LEARNING GOAL: *Describe the bonding in benzene; name aromatic compounds and draw their condensed structural formulas.*

- Most aromatic compounds contain benzene, C_6H_6, a cyclic structure containing six carbon atoms and six hydrogen atoms.
- The structure of benzene is represented as a hexagon with a circle in the center.
- Aromatic compounds are named using the IUPAC name benzene, although common names such as toluene are retained.
- When the benzene ring is numbered, the substituents are listed in alphabetical order.

17.4 Alcohols, Phenols, and Ethers

LEARNING GOAL: *Write the IUPAC and common names for alcohols, phenols, and ethers; draw the condensed structural formulas when given their names.*

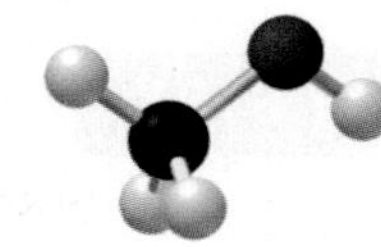

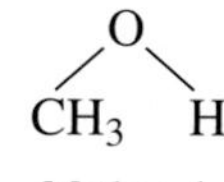

Methanol

- The functional group of an alcohol is the hydroxyl (—OH) group bonded to a carbon chain.
- In a phenol, the hydroxyl group is bonded to an aromatic ring.
- In the IUPAC system, the names of alcohols have *ol* endings, and the location of the —OH group is given by numbering the carbon chain.
- In an ether, an oxygen atom (—O—) is connected by single bonds to two alkyl or aromatic groups.
- In the common names of ethers, the alkyl groups are listed alphabetically followed by the name *ether*.

17.5 Aldehydes and Ketones

LEARNING GOAL: *Write the IUPAC and common names for aldehydes and ketones; draw the condensed structural formulas when given their names.*

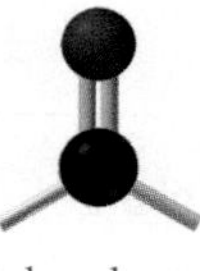

Carbonyl group

- Aldehydes and ketones contain a carbonyl (C=O) group, which is strongly polar.
- In aldehydes, the carbonyl group appears at the end of the carbon chain attached to at least one hydrogen atom.
- In ketones, the carbonyl group occurs between two alkyl or aromatic groups.

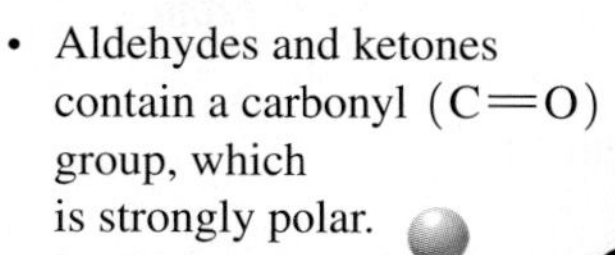

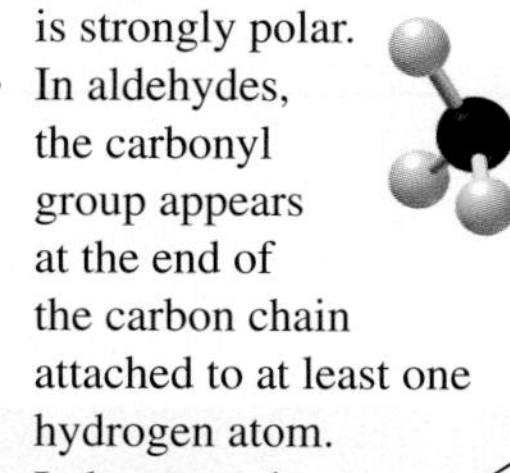

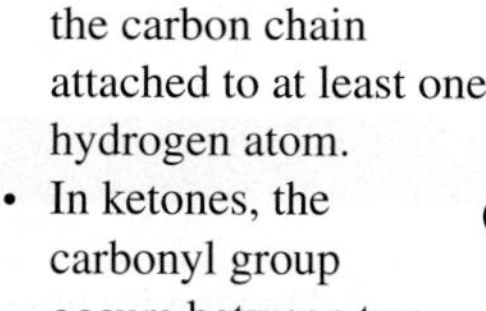

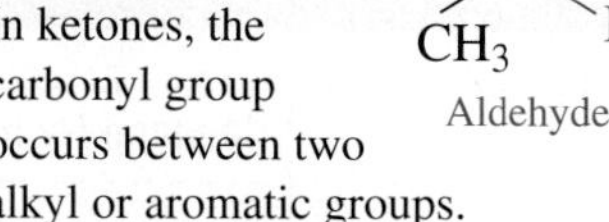

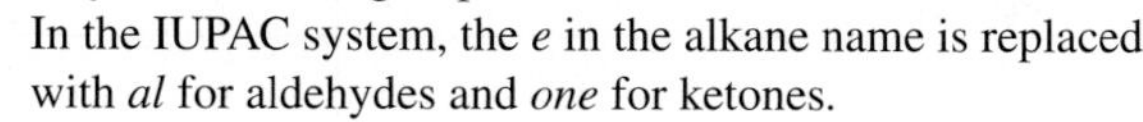

Aldehyde Ketone

- In the IUPAC system, the *e* in the alkane name is replaced with *al* for aldehydes and *one* for ketones.
- For ketones with more than four carbon atoms in the main chain, the carbonyl group is numbered to show its location.
- Many of the simple aldehydes and ketones use common names.

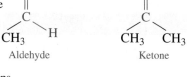

17.6 Carboxylic Acids and Esters

LEARNING GOAL: *Write the IUPAC and common names for carboxylic acids and esters; draw the condensed structural formulas when given their names.*

- A carboxylic acid contains the carboxyl functional group, which is a hydroxyl group connected to a carbonyl group.
- The IUPAC name of a carboxylic acid is obtained by replacing the *e* in the alkane name with *oic acid.*
- The common names of carboxylic acids with one to four carbon atoms are: formic acid, acetic acid, propionic acid, and butyric acid.
- In an ester, an alkyl or aromatic group replaces the H of the hydroxyl group of a carboxylic acid.
- In the presence of a strong acid, a carboxylic acid reacts with an alcohol to produce an ester. A molecule of water is removed: —OH from the carboxylic acid and —H from the alcohol molecule.
- The names of esters consist of two words, the alkyl group from the alcohol and the name of the carboxylate obtained by replacing the *ic acid* ending with *ate*.

17.7 Amines and Amides

LEARNING GOAL: *Write the common names for amines and the IUPAC and common names for amides; draw the condensed structural formulas when given their names.*

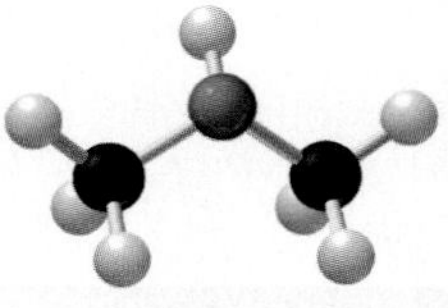

Dimethylamine

- A nitrogen atom attached to alkyl or aromatic groups forms an amine.
- In the common names of simple amines, the alkyl groups are listed alphabetically followed by the suffix *amine.*
- Amides are derivatives of carboxylic acids in which the hydroxyl group is replaced by $—NH_2$. Amides are named by replacing the *ic acid* or *oic acid* ending with *amide*.

CONCEPT MAP

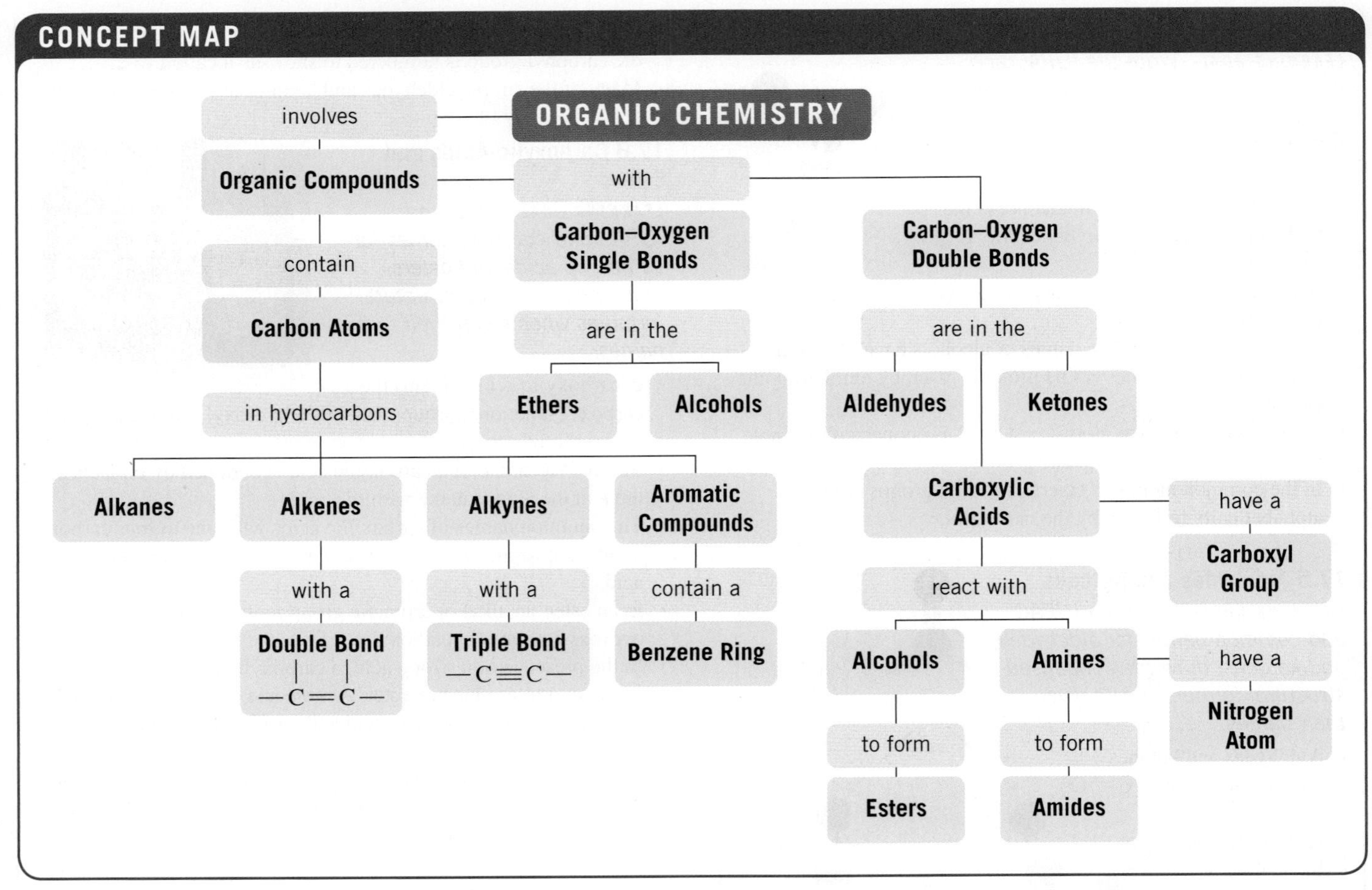

SUMMARY OF NAMING

Condensed Structural Formula	Family	IUPAC Name	Common Name
$CH_3—CH_2—CH_3$	Alkane	Propane	
$CH_3—CH(CH_3)—CH_3$	Alkane with a substituent	Methylpropane	
$CH_3—CH_2—CH_2—Cl$	Haloalkane	1-Chloropropane	Propyl chloride
$CH_3—CH=CH_2$	Alkene	Propene	Propylene
$CH_3—C≡CH$	Alkyne	Propyne	
	Aromatic	Benzene	
CH_3	Aromatic with a substituent	Methylbenzene or toluene	
$CH_3—OH$	Alcohol	Methanol	Methyl alcohol
—OH	Phenol	Phenol	
$CH_3—O—CH_3$	Ether		Dimethyl ether

Condensed Structural Formula	Family	IUPAC Name	Common Name
$H-\overset{\overset{\displaystyle O}{\parallel}}{C}-H$	Aldehyde	Methanal	Formaldehyde
$CH_3-\overset{\overset{\displaystyle O}{\parallel}}{C}-CH_3$	Ketone	Propanone	Acetone; dimethyl ketone
$CH_3-\overset{\overset{\displaystyle O}{\parallel}}{C}-OH$	Carboxylic acid	Ethanoic acid	Acetic acid
$CH_3-\overset{\overset{\displaystyle O}{\parallel}}{C}-O-CH_3$	Ester	Methyl ethanoate	Methyl acetate
$CH_3-CH_2-NH_2$	Amine		Ethylamine
$CH_3-\overset{\overset{\displaystyle O}{\parallel}}{C}-NH_2$	Amide	Ethanamide	Acetamide

SUMMARY OF REACTIONS

Esterification: Carboxylic Acid and an Alcohol

$$\underset{\text{Ethanoic acid (acetic acid)}}{CH_3-\overset{\overset{\displaystyle O}{\parallel}}{C}-OH} + \underset{\text{Methanol (methyl alcohol)}}{HO-CH_3} \xrightleftharpoons{H^+,\ \text{heat}} \underset{\text{Methyl ethanoate (methyl acetate)}}{CH_3-\overset{\overset{\displaystyle O}{\parallel}}{C}-O-CH_3} + H_2O$$

Amidation: Carboxylic Acid and an Amine

$$\underset{\text{Propanoic acid (propionic acid)}}{CH_3-CH_2-\overset{\overset{\displaystyle O}{\parallel}}{C}-OH} + \underset{\text{Ammonia}}{H-\overset{\overset{\displaystyle H}{|}}{N}-H} \xrightarrow{\text{Heat}} \underset{\text{Propanamide (propionamide)}}{CH_3-CH_2-\overset{\overset{\displaystyle O}{\parallel}}{C}-\overset{\overset{\displaystyle H}{|}}{N}-H} + H_2O$$

KEY TERMS

alkyl group An alkane minus one hydrogen atom. Alkyl groups are named like the corresponding alkanes except a *yl* ending replaces *ane*.

amidation The formation of an amide from a carboxylic acid and an amine with the elimination of a molecule of water.

aromatic compounds Compounds that contain the ring structure of benzene.

benzene A ring of six carbon atoms each of which is attached to one hydrogen atom, C_6H_6.

branch A carbon group bonded to the main carbon chain.

branched alkane An alkane containing a hydrocarbon substituent bonded to the main chain.

carboxyl group A functional group found in carboxylic acids composed of carbonyl and hydroxyl groups.

$$-\overset{\overset{\displaystyle O}{\parallel}}{C}-OH \quad \text{Carboxyl group}$$

esterification The formation of an ester from a carboxylic acid and an alcohol with the elimination of a molecule of water in the presence of a strong acid catalyst.

isomers Organic compounds in which identical molecular formulas have different arrangements of atoms.

monomer The small organic molecule that is repeated many times in a polymer.

polymer A very large molecule that is composed of many small, repeating structural units that are identical.

substituent Groups of atoms such as an alkyl group or a halogen bonded to the main chain or ring of carbon atoms.

UNDERSTANDING THE CONCEPTS

The chapter sections to review are shown in parentheses at the end of each question.

17.57 Draw the structure of a section of Teflon that contains four monomers. The monomer of Teflon is 1,1,2,2-tetrafluoroethene. (17.2)

Teflon is used as a nonstick coating on cooking pans.

17.58 A garden hose is made of polyvinyl chloride (PVC) using the monomer chloroethene (vinyl chloride). Draw the condensed structural formula for a section of PVC that contains four monomers. (17.2)

A plastic garden hose is made of PVC.

17.59 Citronellal, found in oil of citronella, lemon, and lemon grass, is used in perfumes and as an insect repellent. (17.2, 17.5)

An insect-repelling candle contains citronellal, which is found in natural sources.

Citronellal has the following structure:

$$\begin{array}{c} \quad CH_3 \qquad\qquad\qquad\qquad\qquad CH_3 \qquad\qquad O \\ \quad | \qquad\qquad\qquad\qquad\qquad\quad | \qquad\qquad\quad \| \\ CH_3-C=CH-CH_2-CH_2-CH-CH_2-C-H \end{array}$$

a. Complete the IUPAC name for citronellal: ___, ___-di________-___-octenal.
b. What does the *en* in octenal signify?
c. What does the *al* in octenal signify?

17.60 Draw the condensed structural formula for each of the following: (17.5)
a. 2-heptanone, an alarm pheromone of bees
b. 2,6-dimethyl-3-heptanone, a communication pheromone of bees

Bees emit chemicals called pheromones to communicate.

ADDITIONAL QUESTIONS AND PROBLEMS

17.61 Draw the condensed structural formula for each of the following: (17.1, 17.2)
a. 3-ethylhexane
b. 2-pentene
c. 2-hexyne

17.62 Draw the condensed structural formula for each of the following: (17.1, 17.2)
a. 1-chloro-2-butyne
b. 2,3-dimethylpentane
c. 3-hexene

17.63 Give the IUPAC name for each of the following: (17.1, 17.2)

a.
$$\begin{array}{c} CH_3 \\ | \\ CH_3-CH_2-C-CH_3 \\ | \\ CH_3 \end{array}$$

b. $CH_3-CH_2-C\equiv CH$

c. $CH_3-CH=CH-CH_2-CH_3$

17.64 Give the IUPAC name for each of the following: (17.1, 17.2)

CH_3
|
a. 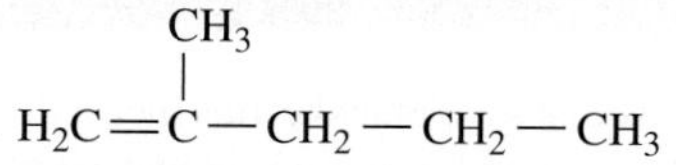 $H_2C{=}C{-}CH_2{-}CH_2{-}CH_3$

b. $CH_3{-}CH_2{-}Cl$

$CH_3{-}CH_2$ (on C3), Br (on C5)
c. 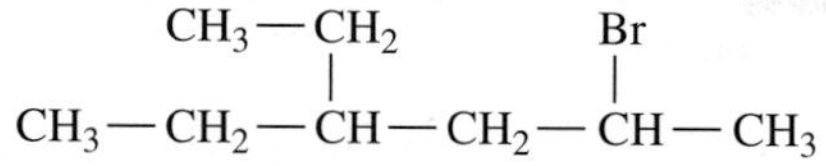 $CH_3{-}CH_2{-}CH{-}CH_2{-}CH{-}CH_3$

17.65 Name each of the following: (17.3)

a. 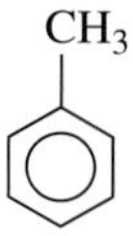 benzene ring with CH_3

b. 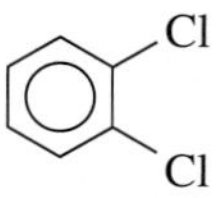 benzene ring with Cl, Cl (adjacent)

c. 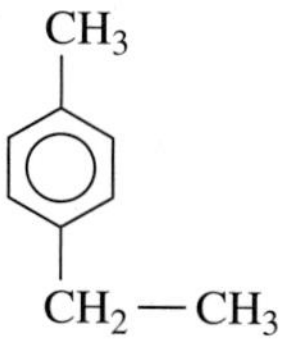 benzene ring with CH_3 and, para, $CH_2{-}CH_3$

17.66 Draw the condensed structural formula for each of the following: (17.3)
a. ethylbenzene
b. 4-chlorotoluene
c. 1,2,4-trimethylbenzene

17.67 Draw the condensed structural formula for each of the following: (17.3, 17.5)
a. 4-chlorophenol
b. 2-methyl-3-pentanol
c. 3-pentanone

17.68 Draw the condensed structural formula for each of the following: (17.4)
a. 3-hexanol
b. 2-pentanol
c. ethyl propyl ether

17.69 Give the IUPAC name for each of the following: (17.5)

a. 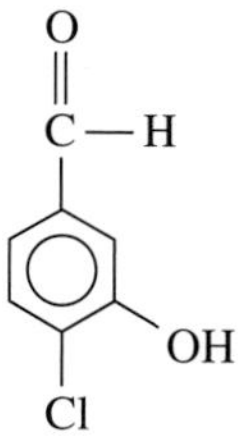 benzene ring with $\overset{\displaystyle O}{\overset{\|}{C}}{-}H$, OH, and Cl

b. $Cl{-}CH_2{-}CH_2{-}\overset{\displaystyle O}{\overset{\|}{C}}{-}H$

c. $CH_3{-}\underset{}{\overset{\displaystyle Cl}{\overset{|}{CH}}}{-}\overset{\displaystyle O}{\overset{\|}{C}}{-}CH_2{-}CH_3$

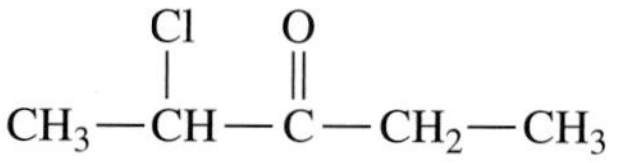

17.70 Give the IUPAC name for each of the following: (17.5)

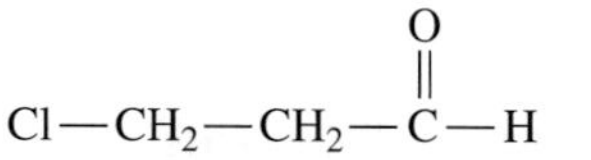

a. 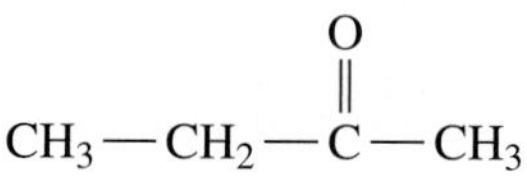 $CH_3{-}CH_2{-}\overset{\displaystyle O}{\overset{\|}{C}}{-}CH_3$

b. benzene ring with $\overset{\displaystyle O}{\overset{\|}{C}}{-}H$, Cl, Cl

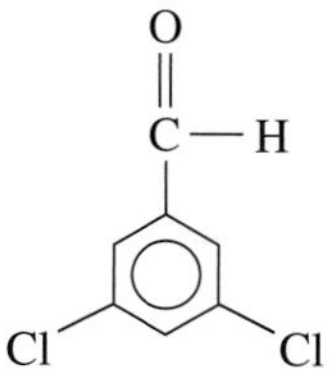

c. $CH_3{-}\overset{\displaystyle CH_3}{\overset{|}{CH}}{-}\overset{\displaystyle OH}{\overset{|}{CH}}{-}CH_2{-}\overset{\displaystyle O}{\overset{\|}{C}}{-}H$

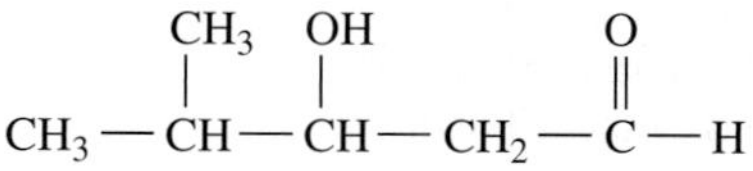

17.71 Draw the condensed structural formula for each of the following: (17.5)
a. 4-chlorobenzaldehyde
b. 3-chloropropionaldehyde
c. ethyl methyl ketone

17.72 Draw the condensed structural formula for each of the following: (17.5)
a. butyraldehyde
b. 2-bromobutanal
c. 3,5-dimethylhexanal

17.73 Give the IUPAC name for each of the following: (17.6)

a. 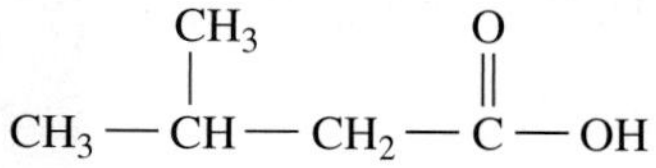 $CH_3{-}\overset{\displaystyle CH_3}{\overset{|}{CH}}{-}CH_2{-}\overset{\displaystyle O}{\overset{\|}{C}}{-}OH$

b. benzene ring with $\overset{\displaystyle O}{\overset{\|}{C}}{-}O{-}CH_3$

c. $CH_3{-}CH_2{-}\overset{\displaystyle O}{\overset{\|}{C}}{-}O{-}CH_2{-}CH_3$

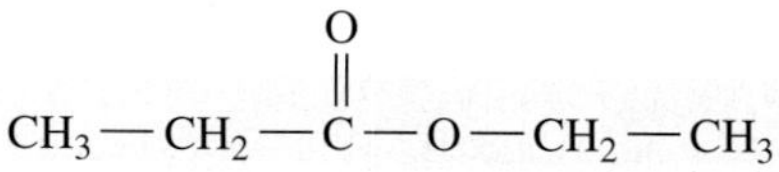

17.74 Give the IUPAC name for each of the following: (17.6)

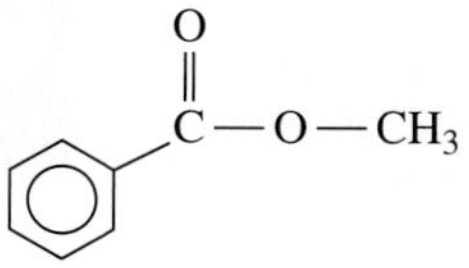

a. 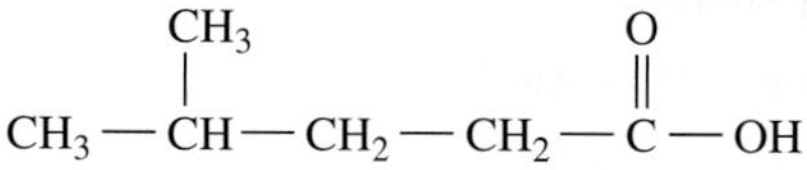 $CH_3{-}\overset{\displaystyle CH_3}{\overset{|}{CH}}{-}CH_2{-}CH_2{-}\overset{\displaystyle O}{\overset{\|}{C}}{-}OH$

b. benzene ring with $\overset{\displaystyle O}{\overset{\|}{C}}{-}OH$, Cl, Cl

c. benzene ring with $\overset{\displaystyle O}{\overset{\|}{C}}{-}O{-}CH_2{-}CH_3$

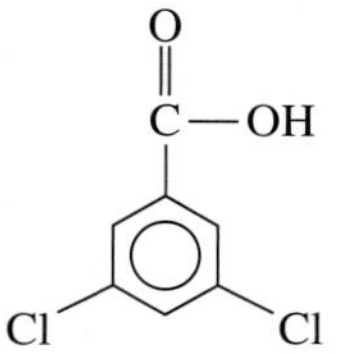

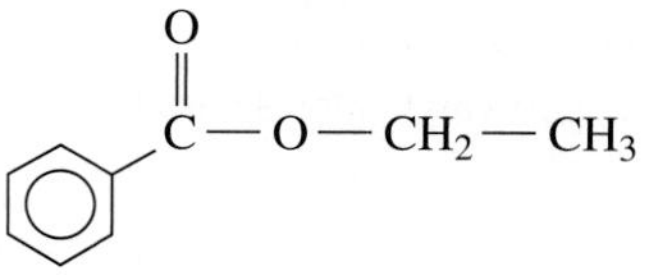

17.75 Draw the condensed structural formula for each of the following: (17.7)
a. ethylamine
b. dimethylamine
c. triethylamine

17.76 Give the IUPAC name for each of the following amides: (17.7)

a. 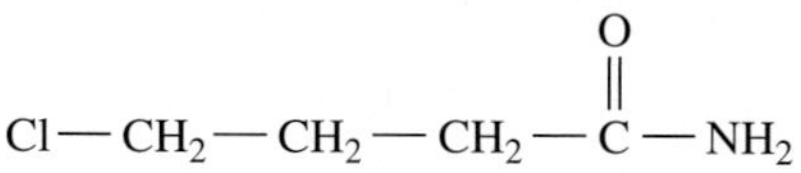 $Cl{-}CH_2{-}CH_2{-}CH_2{-}\overset{\displaystyle O}{\overset{\|}{C}}{-}NH_2$

b. $CH_3{-}CH_2{-}\overset{\displaystyle O}{\overset{\|}{C}}{-}NH_2$

c. $CH_3{-}CH_2{-}\overset{\displaystyle Br}{\overset{|}{CH}}{-}CH_2{-}CH_2{-}\overset{\displaystyle O}{\overset{\|}{C}}{-}NH_2$

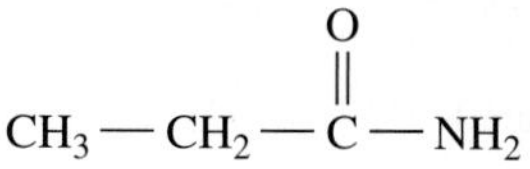

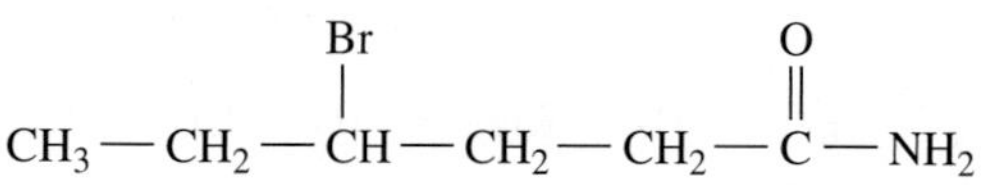

CHALLENGE QUESTIONS

17.77 Draw the condensed structural formulas and give the IUPAC names for all eight alcohols that have the molecular formula $C_5H_{12}O$. (17.4)

17.78 There are four amine isomers with the molecular formula C_3H_9N. Draw their condensed structural formulas. (17.7)

17.79 The insect repellent DEET can be made from an amidation reaction of 3-methylbenzoic acid and diethylamine. Draw the condensed structural formula for DEET. (17.7)

Many insect repellents contain DEET, which is an amide.

17.80 One of the compounds that give blackberries their odor and flavor can be made by heating hexanoic acid and 1-propanol with an acid catalyst. Draw the condensed structural formula for this compound. (17.6)

ANSWERS

Answers to Study Checks

17.1 1-chloro-2,4-dimethylhexane

17.2 $CH_3-\overset{\text{Br}}{\overset{|}{CH}}-CH_2-\overset{\text{Br}}{\overset{|}{CH}}-CH_3$

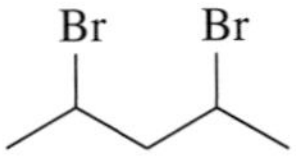

Br Br

17.3 a. $CH_3-C{\equiv}C-CH_2-CH_3$

b. $H_2C{=}CH-\overset{CH_3}{\overset{|}{CH}}-CH_2-CH_3$

17.4 The monomer of PVC, polyvinyl chloride, is chloroethene.

$H_2C{=}\overset{\text{Cl}}{\overset{|}{CH}}$

17.5 3-chlorotoluene

17.6 3-chloro-1-butanol

17.7 propanal (IUPAC), propionaldehyde (common)

17.8 ethyl propyl ketone

17.9 $CH_3-CH_2-CH_2-CH_2-\overset{\text{O}}{\overset{\|}{C}}-OH$

17.10 propanoic acid and 1-pentanol

17.11 $CH_3-CH_2-CH_2-CH_2-CH_2-CH_2-\overset{\text{O}}{\overset{\|}{C}}-O-CH_2-CH_3$

17.12 $H-\overset{\text{O}}{\overset{\|}{C}}-OH$ and $H-\overset{CH_3}{\overset{|}{N}}-CH_3$

17.13 $C_6H_5-\overset{\text{O}}{\overset{\|}{C}}-NH_2$

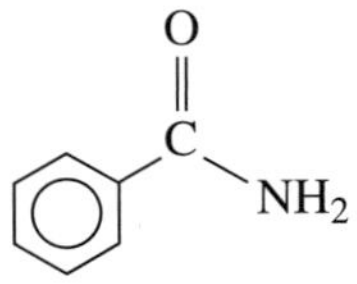

Answers to Selected Questions and Problems

17.1 a. pentane **b.** heptane

17.3 a. same molecule
b. isomers of C_6H_{14}
c. isomers of C_8H_{18}

17.5 a. 2-fluorobutane
b. 2,2-dimethylpropane
c. 2-chloro-3-methylpentane

17.7 a. $CH_3-\overset{CH_3}{\overset{|}{CH}}-CH_2-CH_3$

b. $CH_3-CH_2-\underset{\text{Cl}}{\underset{|}{\overset{\text{Cl}}{\overset{|}{C}}}}-CH_2-CH_3$

c. $CH_3-\overset{CH_3}{\overset{|}{CH}}-\overset{CH_3}{\overset{|}{CH}}-CH_2-\overset{CH_3}{\overset{|}{CH}}-CH_3$

17.9 a. Cl

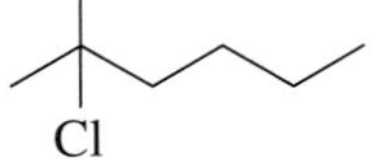

b.

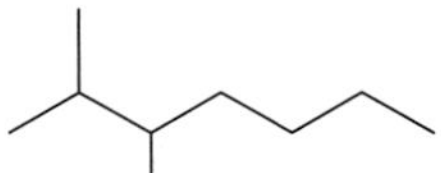

c. Cl

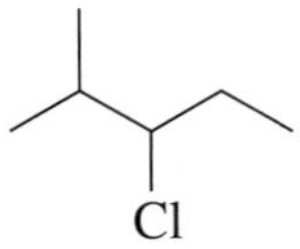

17.11 a. An alkene has a double bond.
b. An alkyne has a triple bond.
c. An alkene has a double bond.

17.13 a. ethene
b. 2-methylpropene
c. 2-pentyne

17.15 **a.** $CH_3-CH{=}CH_2$
b. $HC{\equiv}C-CH_2-CH_2-CH_2-CH_3$
c. $H_2C{=}\overset{\overset{CH_3}{|}}{C}-CH_2-CH_3$

17.17 A polymer is a very large molecule composed of small units that are repeated many times.

17.19 $3\ H_2C{=}\overset{\overset{CH_3}{|}}{CH} \longrightarrow -\underset{\underset{H}{|}}{\overset{\overset{H}{|}}{C}}-\underset{\underset{H}{|}}{\overset{\overset{CH_3}{|}}{C}}-\underset{\underset{H}{|}}{\overset{\overset{H}{|}}{C}}-\underset{\underset{H}{|}}{\overset{\overset{CH_3}{|}}{C}}-\underset{\underset{H}{|}}{\overset{\overset{H}{|}}{C}}-\underset{\underset{H}{|}}{\overset{\overset{CH_3}{|}}{C}}-$

17.21 **a.** 2-chlorotoluene
b. ethylbenzene
c. 1,3,5-trichlorobenzene

17.23 **a.** CH_3 (on benzene ring) **b.** Cl (on benzene ring), F (para) **c.** CH_3 (on benzene ring), CH_2-CH_3 (para)

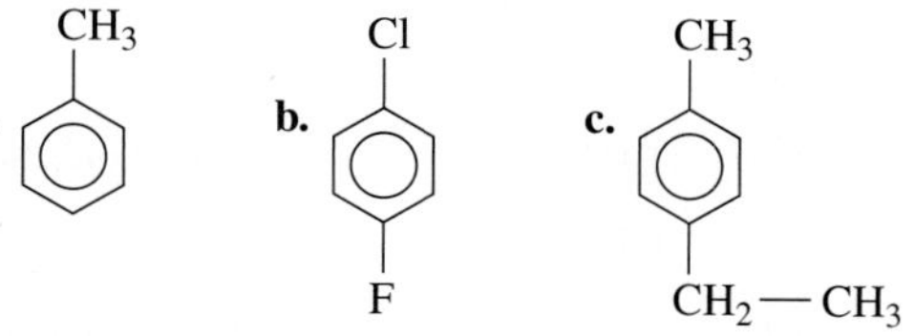

17.25 **a.** ethanol **b.** 2-butanol **c.** phenol

17.27 **a.** $CH_3-CH_2-CH_2-OH$
b. CH_3-OH
c. $CH_3-CH_2-\overset{\overset{OH}{|}}{CH}-CH_2-CH_3$
d. $CH_3-\underset{\underset{CH_3}{|}}{\overset{\overset{OH}{|}}{C}}-CH_2-CH_3$

17.29 **a.** ethyl methyl ether **b.** dipropyl ether
c. methyl propyl ether

17.31 **a.** acetaldehyde **b.** methyl propyl ketone
c. formaldehyde

17.33 **a.** propanal **b.** 2-methyl-3-pentanone
c. benzaldehyde

17.35 **a.** $CH_3-\overset{\overset{O}{\|}}{C}-H$
b. $CH_3-\overset{\overset{O}{\|}}{C}-CH_2-CH_2-CH_3$
c. $CH_3-\overset{\overset{O}{\|}}{C}-CH_2-CH_2-CH_2-CH_3$

17.37 **a.** ethanoic acid (acetic acid)
b. propanoic acid (propionic acid)
c. 3-methylhexanoic acid
d. 3,4-dibromobenzoic acid

17.39 **a.** $CH_3-CH_2-\overset{\overset{O}{\|}}{C}-OH$ **b.** $\overset{\overset{O}{\|}}{C}-OH$ (on benzene ring)
c. $Cl-CH_2-\overset{\overset{O}{\|}}{C}-OH$
d. $HO-CH_2-CH_2-\overset{\overset{O}{\|}}{C}-OH$

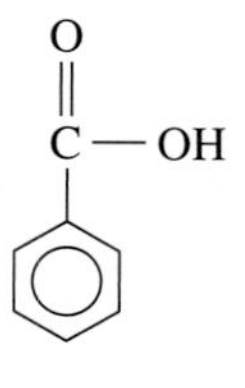

17.41 **a.** $CH_3-\overset{\overset{O}{\|}}{C}-O-CH_3$
b. $CH_3-CH_2-CH_2-CH_2-\overset{\overset{O}{\|}}{C}-O-CH_3$

17.43 **a.** $CH_3-CH_2-\overset{\overset{O}{\|}}{C}-O-CH_2-CH_2-CH_3$
b. $CH_3-CH_2-CH_2-CH_2-\overset{\overset{O}{\|}}{C}-O-\overset{\overset{CH_3}{|}}{CH}-CH_3$

17.45 **a.** methyl methanoate **b.** methyl ethanoate
c. ethyl propanoate

17.47 **a.** $CH_3-\overset{\overset{O}{\|}}{C}-O-CH_3$
b. $H-\overset{\overset{O}{\|}}{C}-O-CH_2-CH_2-CH_2-CH_3$
c. $CH_3-CH_2-CH_2-CH_2-\overset{\overset{O}{\|}}{C}-O-CH_2-CH_3$
d. $CH_3-CH_2-\overset{\overset{O}{\|}}{C}-O-CH_2-CH_2-CH_3$

17.49 **a.** methylamine **b.** methylpropylamine
c. diethylmethylamine

17.51 **a.** $CH_3-\overset{\overset{O}{\|}}{C}-NH_2$
b. $CH_3-\overset{\overset{O}{\|}}{C}-\overset{\overset{H}{|}}{N}-CH_2-CH_3$
c. (benzene ring)$-\overset{\overset{O}{\|}}{C}-\overset{\overset{H}{|}}{N}-CH_2-CH_2-CH_3$

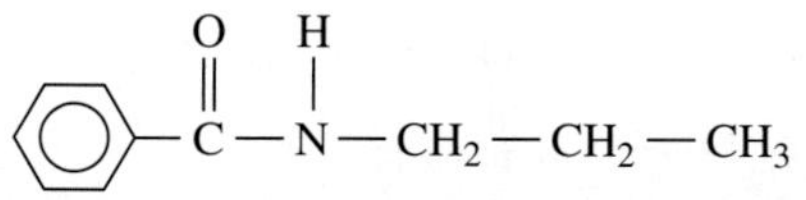

17.53 **a.** ethanamide (acetamide) **b.** 2-chlorobutanamide
c. methanamide (formamide)

17.55 **a.** $CH_3-CH_2-\overset{\overset{O}{\|}}{C}-NH_2$
b. $CH_3-CH_2-CH_2-\overset{\overset{CH_3}{|}}{CH}-\overset{\overset{O}{\|}}{C}-NH_2$
c. $H-\overset{\overset{O}{\|}}{C}-NH_2$

17.57 $-\overset{F}{\underset{F}{C}}-\overset{F}{\underset{F}{C}}-\overset{F}{\underset{F}{C}}-\overset{F}{\underset{F}{C}}-\overset{F}{\underset{F}{C}}-\overset{F}{\underset{F}{C}}-\overset{F}{\underset{F}{C}}-\overset{F}{\underset{F}{C}}-$

17.59 **a.** 3,7-dimethyl-6-octenal
b. The *en* signifies that a double bond is present.
c. The *al* signifies that an aldehyde is present.

17.61 **a.** $CH_3-CH_2-\overset{CH_2-CH_3}{CH}-CH_2-CH_2-CH_3$
b. $CH_3-CH{=}CH-CH_2-CH_3$
c. $CH_3-C{\equiv}C-CH_2-CH_2-CH_3$

17.63 **a.** 2,2-dimethylbutane **b.** 1-butyne
c. 2-pentene

17.65 **a.** toluene **b.** 1,2-dichlorobenzene
c. 4-ethyltoluene

17.67 **a.** (benzene ring with OH and Cl in para positions: 4-chlorophenol)
b. $CH_3-\overset{CH_3}{CH}-\overset{OH}{CH}-CH_2-CH_3$
c. $CH_3-CH_2-\overset{O}{\overset{\|}{C}}-CH_2-CH_3$

17.69 **a.** 4-chloro-3-hydroxybenzaldehyde
b. 3-chloropropanal
c. 2-chloro-3-pentanone

17.71 **a.** (benzene ring with $-\overset{O}{\overset{\|}{C}}-H$ and Cl in para positions)
b. $Cl-CH_2-CH_2-\overset{O}{\overset{\|}{C}}-H$
c. $CH_3-CH_2-\overset{O}{\overset{\|}{C}}-CH_3$

17.73 **a.** 3-methylbutanoic acid
b. methyl benzoate
c. ethyl propanoate

17.75 **a.** $CH_3-CH_2-NH_2$ **b.** $CH_3-NH-CH_3$
c. $CH_3-CH_2-\overset{CH_2-CH_3}{N}-CH_2-CH_3$

17.77

Structure	Name
$CH_3-CH_2-CH_2-CH_2-CH_2-OH$	1-pentanol
$CH_3-\overset{OH}{CH}-CH_2-CH_2-CH_3$	2-pentanol
$CH_3-CH_2-\overset{OH}{CH}-CH_2-CH_3$	3-pentanol
$HO-CH_2-\overset{CH_3}{CH}-CH_2-CH_3$	2-methyl-1-butanol
$HO-CH_2-CH_2-\overset{CH_3}{CH}-CH_3$	3-methyl-1-butanol
$CH_3-\overset{CH_3}{\underset{OH}{C}}-CH_2-CH_3$	2-methyl-2-butanol
$CH_3-\overset{OH}{CH}-\overset{CH_3}{CH}-CH_3$	3-methyl-2-butanol
$CH_3-\overset{CH_3}{\underset{CH_3}{C}}-CH_2-OH$	2,2-dimethylpropanol

17.79 (benzene ring with CH_3 and, in meta position, $-\overset{O}{\overset{\|}{C}}-N(CH_2-CH_3)_2$)

Biochemistry 18

LOOKING AHEAD

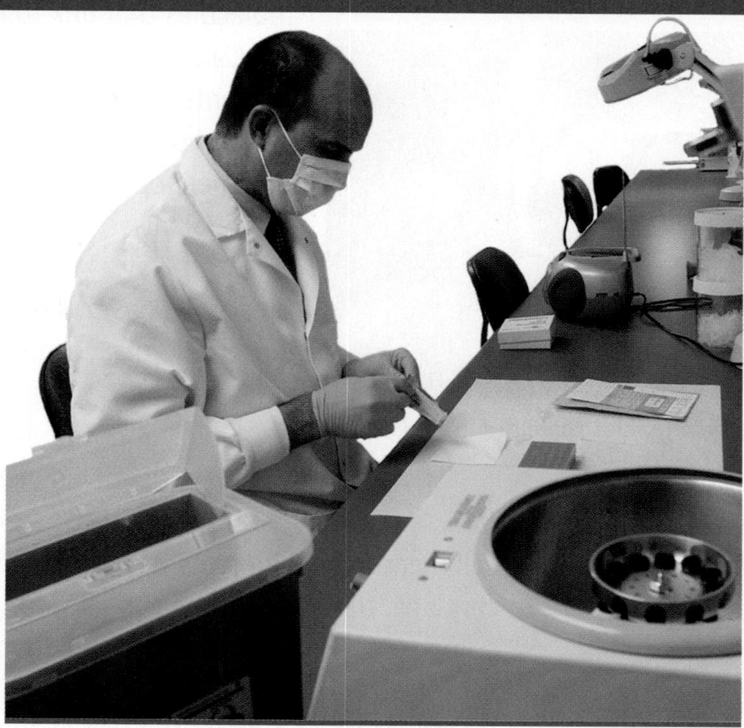

A burglary was being committed when a young couple, Aaron and Debra, arrived home. Aaron was shot in the leg, the criminals fled, and Debra called 911. Aaron was taken to the hospital and luckily, he survived. The police arrived to investigate the crime and file a report, while a crime scene investigator collected evidence that included several strands of hair. The hair samples were sent to a crime lab, where Ron, a forensic toxicologist, begins the process of analyzing the samples.

Ron examines the hair samples under a microscope to determine if they are human, or if the hair came from a pet such as a dog or cat. Ron concludes that the hair is human and then begins to determine what part of the body the hair came from and if it could specify the person's race, whether it was dyed, and if the hair fell out or was pulled out. After this analysis, Ron extracts the hair DNA to build a DNA profile, which will help identify the criminals while strengthening the evidence for a potential court case.

Hair is a structural protein that is comprised of long strings of amino acids called polypeptides. Amino acids are the building blocks of all proteins, and there are 20 common amino acids. Each of these amino acids has a similar structure except for a unique side chain called an R group. The R group identifies each of the 20 amino acids. DNA codes for the exact sequence of the amino acids in the protein, and if there is a different DNA sequence, there will be a different protein.

Career: Forensic Toxicologist

Forensic toxicologists perform two main roles: the first is to examine and analyze evidence associated with a criminal investigation. The evidence varies depending on the crime, as it may involve trace evidence such as gunshot residue, paint residue, illicit drugs, bullet casings, firearms, bodily fluids, hair or fiber samples, fingerprints, footprints, or any documents associated with the crime. This analysis requires forensic toxicologists to use a variety of sophisticated instruments to perform measurements and tests, carefully record the findings, and preserve the criminal evidence. The second role requires a forensic toxicologist to prepare detailed reports of his or her findings and to testify as an expert witness in trials or hearings. Their work is critical in apprehending and convicting criminals.

In *biochemistry*, we study the structures and reactions of chemicals that occur in living systems. In this chapter, we will focus on four important types of biomolecules: carbohydrates, lipids, proteins, and nucleic acids. Each of these consists of small molecules that link together to form large molecules.

Carbohydrates contained in foods such as pasta and bread provide energy for the body.

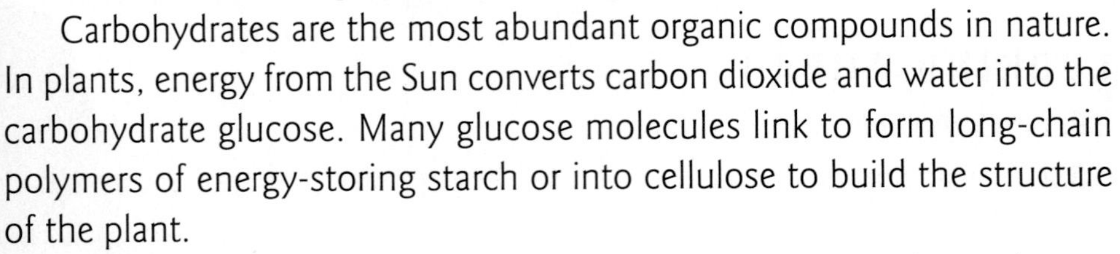

Carbohydrates are the most abundant organic compounds in nature. In plants, energy from the Sun converts carbon dioxide and water into the carbohydrate glucose. Many glucose molecules link to form long-chain polymers of energy-storing starch or into cellulose to build the structure of the plant.

Each day, you may enjoy the polysaccharides called starches in bread and pasta. The table sugar used to sweeten cereal, tea, or coffee is sucrose, a disaccharide that consists of two simple sugars, glucose and fructose.

Lipids and proteins are also important nutrients that we obtain from food. Lipids include the fats and oils in our diets, steroid hormones, and cholesterol. In the body, lipids store energy, insulate organs, and build cell membranes. Proteins have many functions in the body including building muscle and cartilage, transporting oxygen in blood, and directing biological reactions. All proteins are composed of building blocks called amino acids.

Nucleic acids are molecules in our cells that store information for cellular growth and reproduction and direct the use of this information. Deoxyribonucleic acid (DNA) contains the directions for making proteins, whereas ribonucleic acids (RNA) are used to decode this information for the production of proteins.

LEARNING GOAL

Classify a carbohydrate as an aldose or a ketose; draw the open-chain and Haworth structures for glucose, galactose, and fructose.

18.1 Carbohydrates

Carbohydrates such as table sugar, lactose in milk, and cellulose are all made of carbon, hydrogen, and oxygen. Simple sugars, which have formulas of $C_n(H_2O)_n$, were once thought to be hydrates of carbon, thus the name *carbohydrate.* In a series of reactions called *photosynthesis*, energy from the Sun is used to combine the carbon atoms from carbon dioxide (CO_2) and the hydrogen and oxygen atoms of water into the carbohydrate glucose.

$$6CO_2 + 6H_2O + \text{energy} \underset{\text{Respiration}}{\overset{\text{Photosynthesis}}{\rightleftharpoons}} \underset{\text{Glucose}}{C_6H_{12}O_6} + 6O_2$$

In our body, glucose is oxidized in a series of metabolic reactions known as *respiration*, which releases chemical energy to do work in the cells. Carbon dioxide and water are produced and returned to the atmosphere. The combination of photosynthesis and respiration is the *carbon cycle*, in which energy from the Sun is stored in plants by photosynthesis and made available to us when the carbohydrates in our diets are metabolized (see Figure 18.1).

Monosaccharides

The simplest carbohydrates are the **monosaccharides**. A monosaccharide cannot be split into smaller carbohydrates. A monosaccharide has a chain of three to six carbon atoms, one in a carbonyl group and all the others attached to hydroxyl (—OH) groups. In an **aldose**, the carbonyl group is on the first carbon (—CHO); a **ketose** contains the carbonyl group on the second carbon atom as a ketone (C=O).

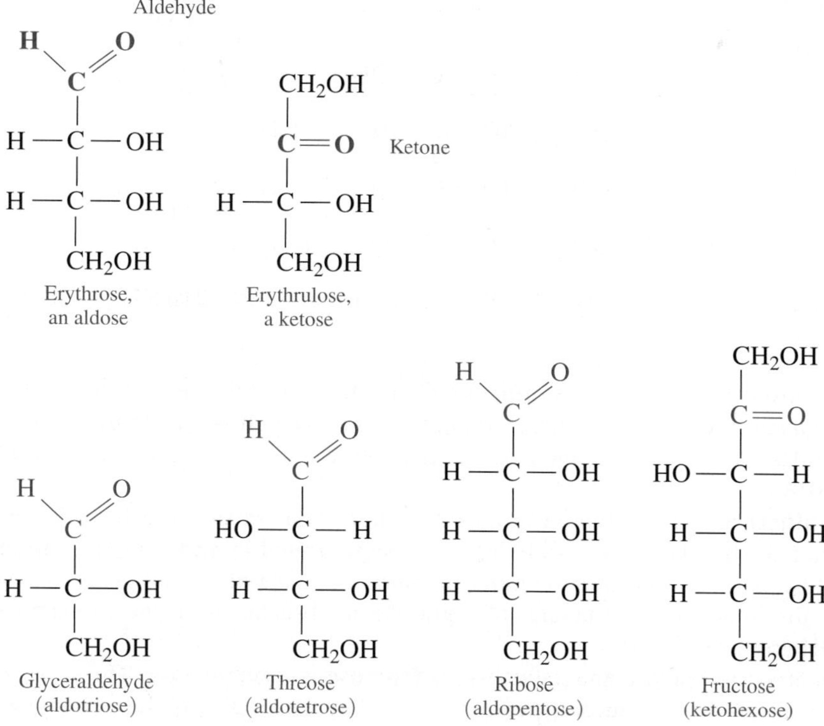

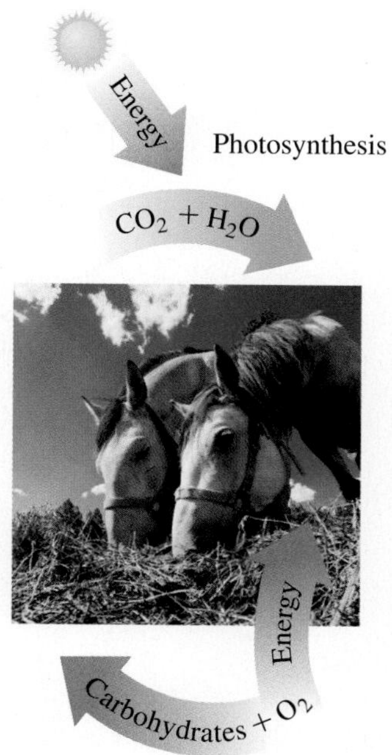

FIGURE 18.1 During photosynthesis, energy from the Sun combines CO_2 and H_2O to form glucose, $C_6H_{12}O_6$, and O_2. During respiration in the body, carbohydrates are oxidized to CO_2 and H_2O, while energy is produced.

Q What are the reactants and products of respiration?

CONCEPT CHECK 18.1 Monosaccharides

Classify each of the following monosaccharides to indicate their carbonyl group and number of carbon atoms:

a.

```
     CH2OH
     |
     C=O
     |
  H—C—OH
     |
  H—C—OH
     |
     CH2OH
```

Ribulose

b.

```
   H    O
    \\ //
      C
      |
   H—C—OH
      |
  HO—C—H
      |
   H—C—OH
      |
   H—C—OH
      |
      CH2OH
```

Glucose

ANSWER

a. Ribulose has five carbon atoms (pentose) and a ketone group; ribulose is a ketopentose.

b. Glucose has six carbon atoms (hexose) and an aldehyde group; glucose is an aldohexose.

Open-Chain Structures of Some Important Monosaccharides

The hexoses glucose, galactose, and fructose are the most important monosaccharides. They are all hexoses with the molecular formula $C_6H_{12}O_6$. In nature and the cells of the body, their most common form is the D isomer, which has the —OH group attached to carbon 5 on the right side of the chain.

D-Glucose	D-Galactose	D-Fructose
H–C_1=O	H–C_1=O	$_1CH_2OH$
H—C_2—OH	H—C_2—OH	C_2=O
HO—C_3—H	HO—C_3—H	HO—C_3—H
H—C_4—**OH**	**HO**—C_4—H	H—C_4—OH
H—C_5—OH	H—C_5—OH	H—C_5—OH
$_6CH_2OH$	$_6CH_2OH$	$_6CH_2OH$

The most common hexose, **D-glucose**, $C_6H_{12}O_6$, also known as dextrose and blood sugar, is found in fruits, vegetables, corn syrup, and honey. It is a building block of the disaccharides sucrose, lactose, and maltose, and polysaccharides such as starch, cellulose, and glycogen.

D-Galactose is an aldohexose that does not occur in the free form in nature. It is obtained from the disaccharide lactose, a sugar found in milk and milk products. D-Galactose is important in the cellular membranes of the brain and nervous system. The only difference in the structures of D-glucose and D-galactose is the arrangement of the —OH group on carbon 4.

In contrast to glucose and galactose, **D-fructose** is a ketohexose. The structure of D-fructose differs from D-glucose at carbons 1 and 2 by the location of the carbonyl group. D-Fructose is the sweetest of the carbohydrates, twice as sweet as sucrose (table sugar). This makes D-fructose popular with dieters because less D-fructose and, therefore, fewer calories are needed to provide a pleasant taste. D-Fructose is found in fruit juices and honey.

Chemistry Link to Health

HYPERGLYCEMIA AND HYPOGLYCEMIA

A doctor may order a glucose tolerance test to evaluate the body's ability to return to normal blood glucose concentrations of 70–90 mg/dL (1 dL = 100 mL) of blood in response to the ingestion of a specified amount of glucose. The patient fasts for 12 hours and then drinks a solution containing glucose. If the blood glucose exceeds 200 mg/dL and remains high, hyperglycemia may be indicated. The term *glyc* or *gluco* refers to "sugar." The prefix *hyper* means above or over, and *hypo* is below or under. Thus the blood sugar level in *hyperglycemia* is above normal and below normal in *hypoglycemia*.

An example of a disease that can cause hyperglycemia is diabetes mellitus, which occurs when the pancreas is unable to produce sufficient quantities of insulin. As a result, glucose levels in the body fluids can rise as high as 350 mg/dL. Symptoms of diabetes include thirst, excessive urination, increased appetite, and weight loss. In older persons, diabetes is sometimes a consequence of excessive weight gain.

When a person is hypoglycemic, the blood glucose level rises and then decreases rapidly to levels as low as 40 mg/dL. In some cases, hypoglycemia is caused by overproduction of insulin by the pancreas. Low blood glucose can cause dizziness, general weakness, and muscle tremors. A diet may be prescribed that consists of several small meals high in protein and low in carbohydrate. Some hypoglycemic patients are finding success with diets that include more complex carbohydrates rather than simple sugars.

A glucose solution is given to determine blood glucose levels.

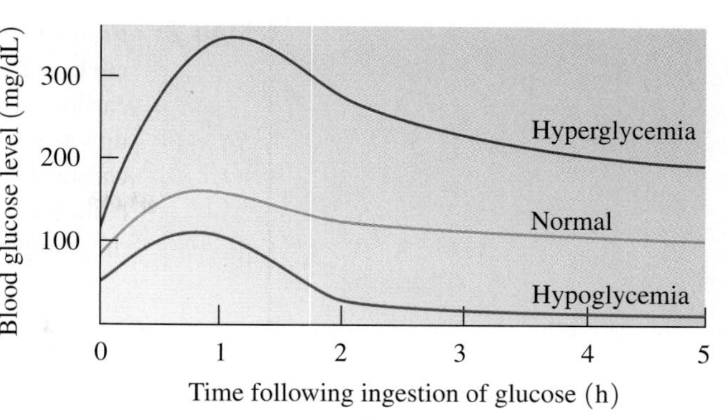

Haworth Structures of Monosaccharides

Up until now, we have drawn the structures for monosaccharides such as D-glucose as open chains. However, the most stable form of hexoses is a six-atom ring, known as a *Haworth structure*. We can draw the Haworth structure for D-glucose as shown in Sample Problem 18.1.

SAMPLE PROBLEM 18.1 Drawing the Haworth Structure for D-Glucose

D-Glucose has the following open-chain structure. Draw the Haworth structure for D-glucose.

H O
C
H—C—OH
HO—C—H
H—C—OH
H—C—OH
CH_2OH

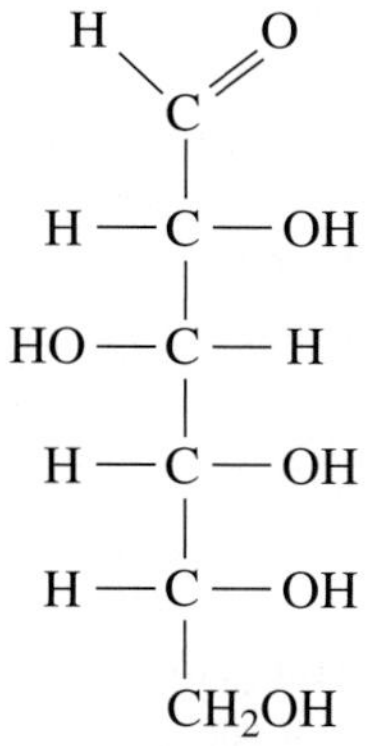

D-Glucose

SOLUTION

Step 1 **Turn the open-chain structure clockwise by 90°.** The —H and —OH groups on the right of the vertical carbon chain are now below the horizontal carbon chain. Those on the left of the open chain are now above the horizontal carbon chain.

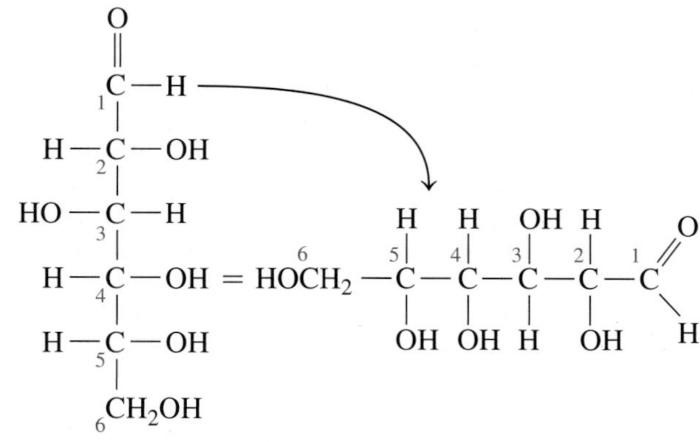

Guide to Drawing Haworth Structures

1 Turn the open-chain structure clockwise by 90°.

2 Fold the horizontal carbon chain into a hexagon and bond the O on carbon 5 to the carbonyl group to form the Haworth structure.

3 Complete the Haworth structure by drawing the —OH group on carbon 1 below the ring to give the α form, or above the ring to give the β form.

Step 2 **Fold the horizontal carbon chain into a hexagon and bond the O on carbon 5 to the carbonyl group to form the Haworth structure.** With carbons 2 and 3 as the base of the hexagon, move the remaining carbons upward. Draw the reacting —OH group on carbon 5 next to the carbonyl carbon 1. Draw carbon 6 in the $—CH_2OH$ group above carbon 5. To complete the Haworth structure, draw a bond between the oxygen of the —OH group on carbon 5 to the carbonyl carbon.

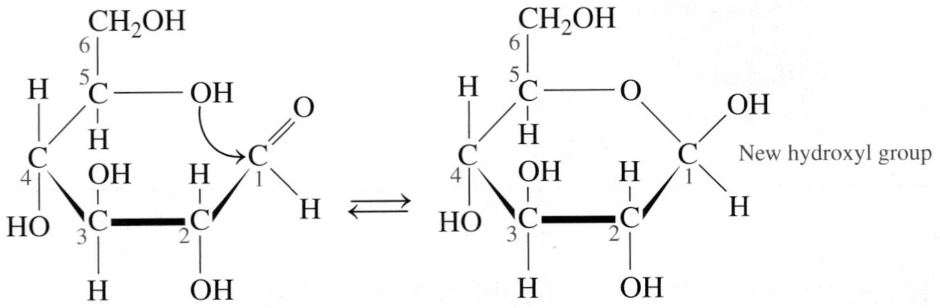

Carbon-5 oxygen bonds to carbonyl

Haworth structure

New hydroxyl group

Step 3 **Complete the Haworth structure by drawing the —OH group on carbon 1 below the ring to give the α form, or above the ring to give the β form.** Because the new —OH group can form above or below the plane of the Haworth structure, there are two forms of D-glucose, which differ only by the position of the —OH group at carbon 1. In the α (alpha) form, the —OH group is drawn below the plane of the ring. In the β (beta) form, the —OH group is drawn above the plane of the ring. By convention, the carbon atoms in the ring are drawn as corners using their skeletal formula.

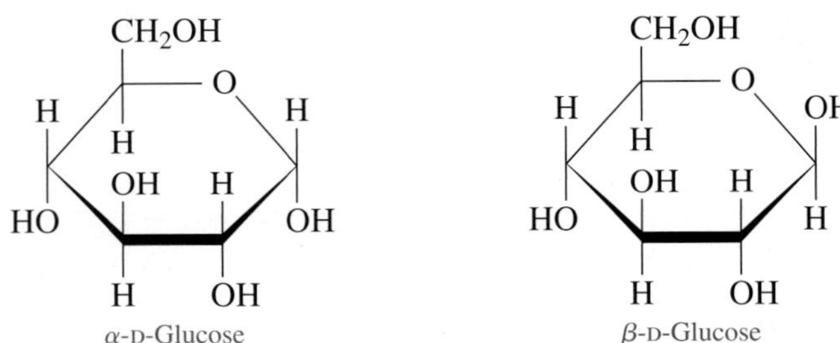

α-D-Glucose

β-D-Glucose

STUDY CHECK 18.1

D-Galactose is an aldohexose like D-glucose, differing only in the arrangement of the —OH group on carbon 4. Draw the Haworth structure for α-D-galactose.

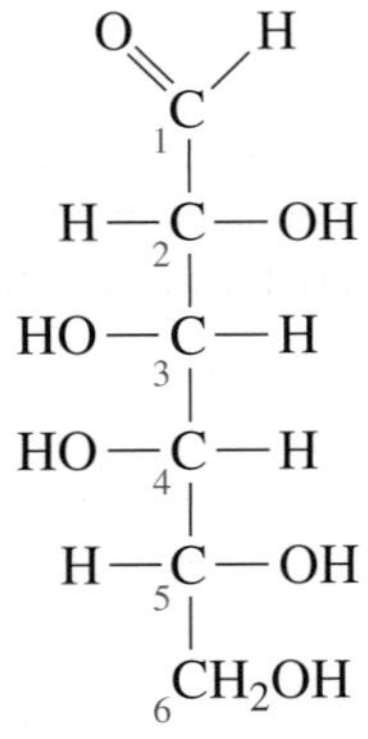

D-Galactose

In contrast to D-glucose and D-galactose, D-fructose is a ketohexose. It forms the five-atom ring when the hydroxyl group on carbon 5 reacts with the carbon of the ketone group. The new hydroxyl group is on carbon 2.

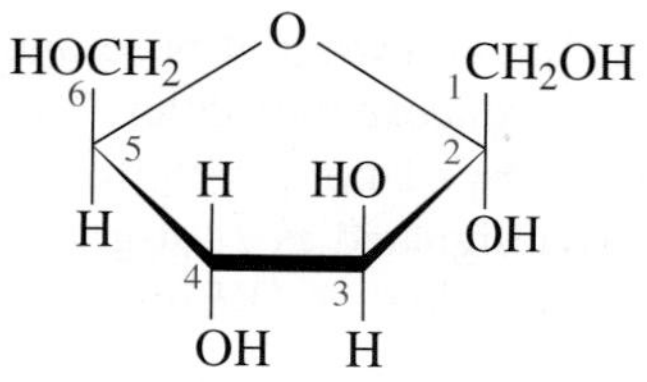

HOCH$_2$ (6), O, CH$_2$OH (1); 5: H; 2: OH; H HO; 4: OH; 3: H

α-D-Fructose

QUESTIONS AND PROBLEMS

18.1 Carbohydrates

LEARNING GOAL: *Classify a carbohydrate as an aldose or a ketose; draw the open-chain and Haworth structures for glucose, galactose, and fructose.*

18.1 What functional groups are found in all monosaccharides?

18.2 What is the difference between an aldose and a ketose?

18.3 What are the functional groups and number of carbons in a ketopentose?

18.4 What are the functional groups and number of carbons in an aldohexose?

18.5 Classify each of the following monosaccharides as an aldopentose, aldohexose, ketopentose, or ketohexose:

a.

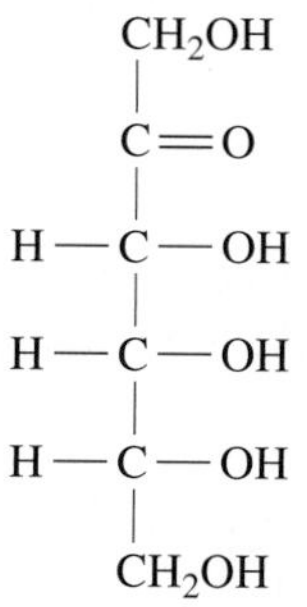

```
     CH2OH
      |
      C=O
      |
  H—C—OH
      |
  H—C—OH
      |
  H—C—OH
      |
     CH2OH
```

Psicose

b.

```
  H    O
   \  //
     C
     |
 HO—C—H
     |
 HO—C—H
     |
  H—C—OH
     |
    CH2OH
```

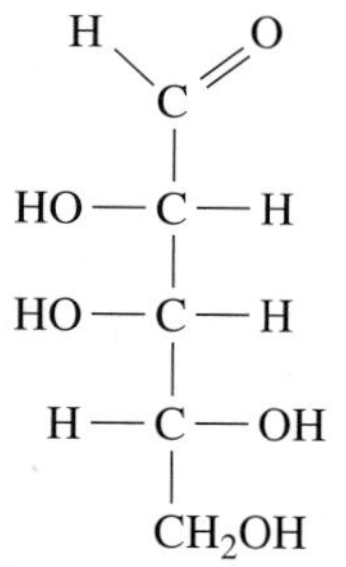

Lyxose

18.6 Classify each of the following monosaccharides as an aldopentose, aldohexose, ketopentose, or ketohexose:

a.

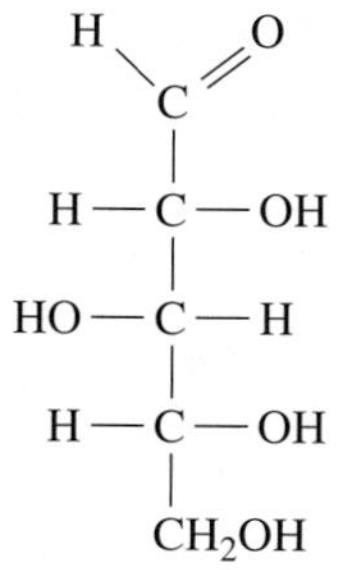

```
  H    O
   \  //
     C
     |
  H—C—OH
     |
 HO—C—H
     |
  H—C—OH
     |
    CH2OH
```

Xylose

b.

```
     CH2OH
      |
      C=O
      |
 HO—C—H
      |
 HO—C—H
      |
  H—C—OH
      |
     CH2OH
```

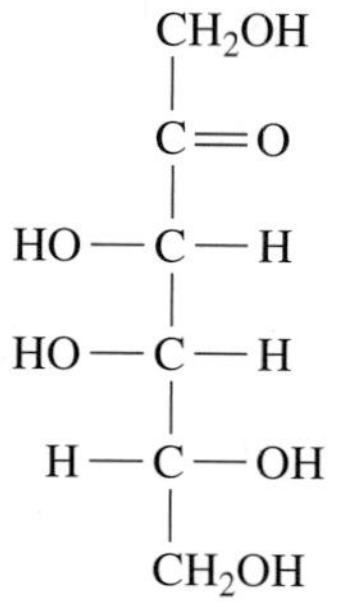

Tagatose

18.7 How does the open-chain structure of D-galactose differ from that of D-glucose?

18.8 How does the open-chain structure of D-fructose differ from that of D-glucose?

18.9 What are the kind and number of atoms in the ring portion of the Haworth structure of D-glucose?

18.10 What are the kind and number of atoms in the ring portion of the Haworth structure of D-fructose?

18.11 Identify each of the following Haworth structures as the α or β form:

a. HOCH$_2$, O, CH$_2$OH; H, OH; H HO; OH H

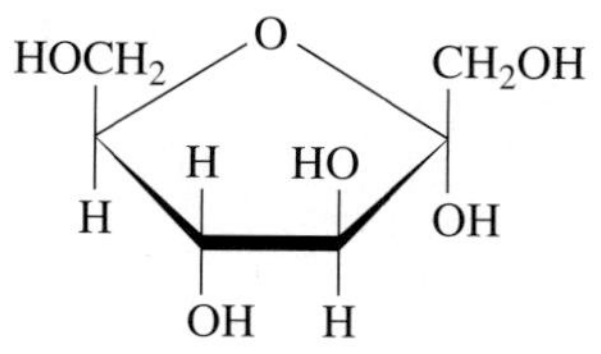

b.

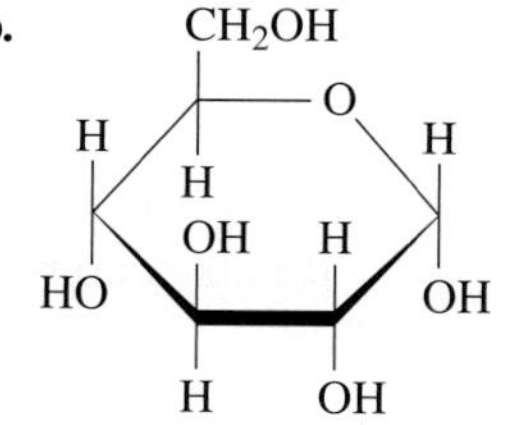

18.12 Identify each of the following Haworth structures as the α or β form:

a. CH$_2$OH; O; HO, OH; H; OH H; H, H; H OH

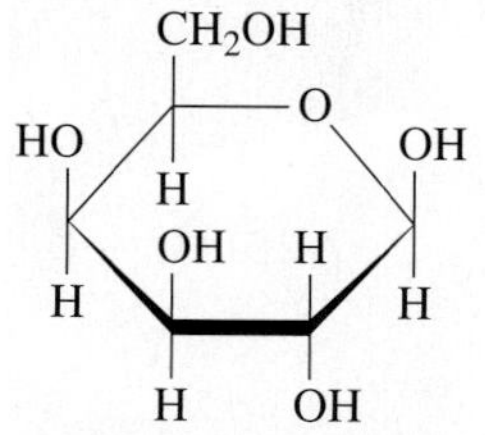

b. CH$_2$OH; O; HO, H; H; OH H; H, OH; H OH

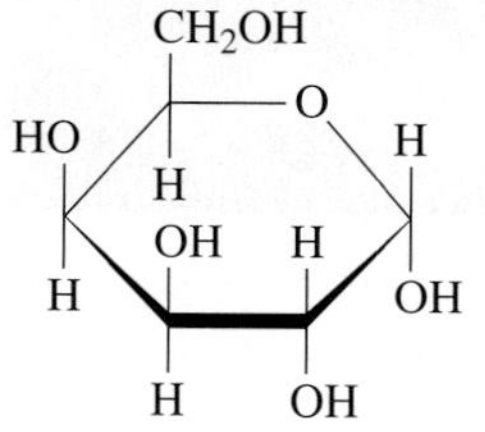

LEARNING GOAL

Describe the monosaccharide units and linkages in disaccharides and polysaccharides.

18.2 Disaccharides and Polysaccharides

A **disaccharide** is composed of two monosaccharides linked together. The most common disaccharides are maltose, lactose, and sucrose.

Maltose, or malt sugar, used in cereals, candies, and the brewing of beverages, is a disaccharide. Maltose has a *glycosidic bond* between two glucose molecules. To form maltose, the —OH group on carbon 1 in the first glucose forms a bond with the —OH group on carbon 4 in a second glucose molecule, which is designated as a 1,4-glycosidic bond. Because the second glucose molecule in maltose has a free —OH on carbon 1, there are α and β forms of maltose.

α Form

α-D-Glucose + α-D-Glucose → α-Maltose + H_2O

α-1,4-Glycosidic bond

α-Maltose, a disaccharide

Lactose, milk sugar, is a disaccharide found in milk and milk products (see Figure 18.2). It makes up 6–8% of human milk and about 4–5% of cow's milk. Some people do not

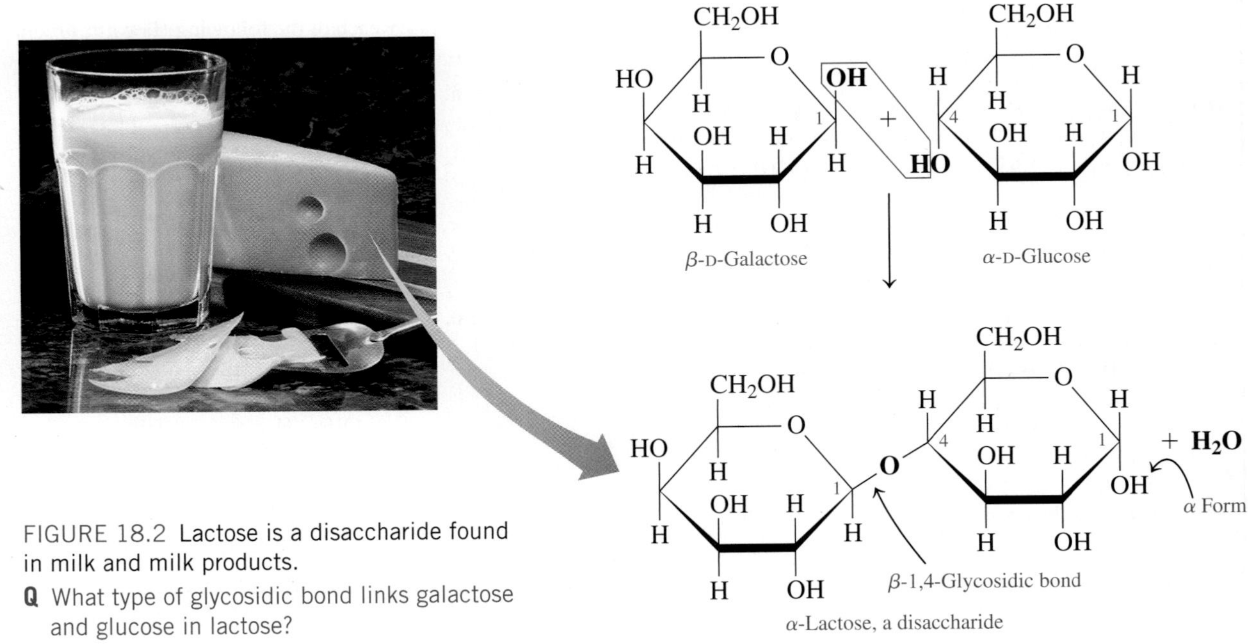

FIGURE 18.2 Lactose is a disaccharide found in milk and milk products.

Q What type of glycosidic bond links galactose and glucose in lactose?

produce sufficient quantities of the enzyme needed to break down lactose, and the sugar remains undigested, causing abdominal cramps and diarrhea. In some commercial milk products, an enzyme called lactase is added to break down lactose. The bond in lactose is a β-1,4-glycosidic bond because the β form of galactose links to the hydroxyl group on carbon 4 of glucose.

Sucrose, ordinary table sugar, is the most abundant disaccharide in the world. Most of the sucrose for table sugar comes from sugar cane (20% by mass) or sugar beets (15% by mass) (see Figure 18.3). Both the raw and refined forms of sugar are sucrose. Some estimates indicate that each person in the United States consumes an average of 68 kg (150 lb) of sucrose every year either by itself or in a variety of food products. Sucrose consists of an α-D-glucose and a β-D-fructose molecule joined by a bond called an α,β-1,2-glycosidic bond (see Figure 18.3).

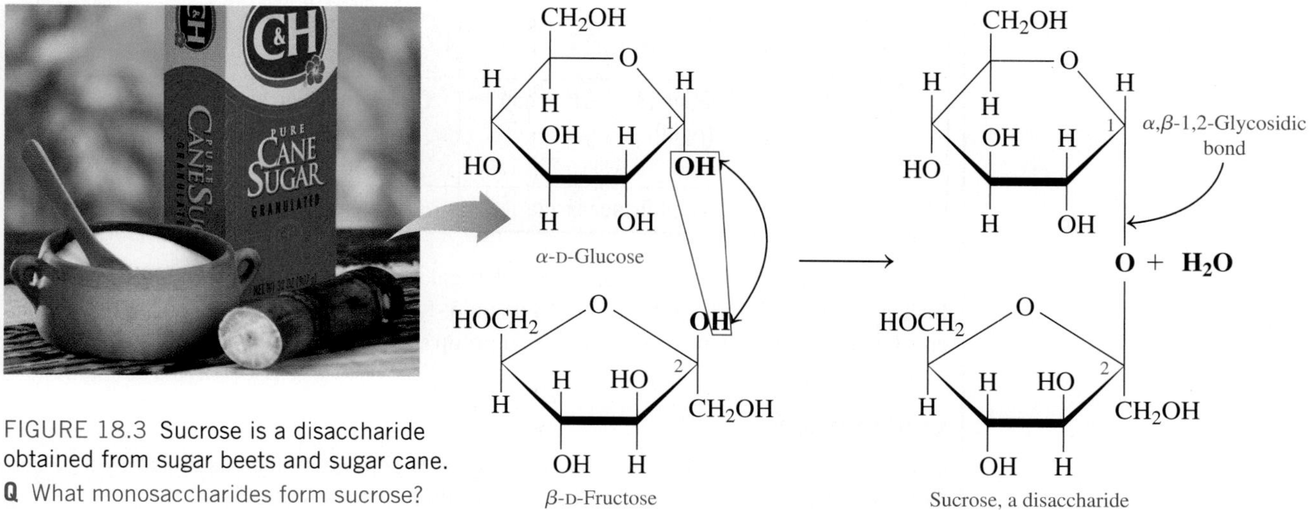

FIGURE 18.3 Sucrose is a disaccharide obtained from sugar beets and sugar cane.
Q What monosaccharides form sucrose?

SAMPLE PROBLEM 18.2 Glycosidic Bonds in Disaccharides

Melibiose is a disaccharide that is 30 times sweeter than sucrose.

Melibiose

a. What are the monosaccharide units in melibiose?
b. What type of glycosidic bond links the monosaccharides?
c. Identify the structure as α- or β-melibiose.

SOLUTION

Analyze the Problem	**First Monosaccharide (left)**	When the —OH group on carbon 4 is drawn above the plane of the ring, it is D-galactose. When the —OH group on carbon 1 is drawn below the plane of the ring, it is the α form of D-galactose.
	Second Monosaccharide (right)	When the —OH group on carbon 4 is drawn below the plane of the ring, it is D-glucose.
	Type of Glycosidic Bond	The —OH group at carbon 1 comes from α-D-galactose to the —OH group on carbon 6 of glucose, which makes it an α-1,6-glycosidic bond.
	Position of —OH Group (right)	The —OH group on carbon 1 of glucose is drawn below the plane of the ring, which is the α form of melibiose.
	Name of Disaccharide	α-Melibiose

a. The monosaccharide on the left side is α-D-galactose; on the right is α-D-glucose.
b. The monosaccharide units are linked by an α-1,6-glycosidic bond.
c. The downward position of the hydroxyl group on carbon 1 of the glucose makes it α-melibiose.

STUDY CHECK 18.2

Cellobiose is a disaccharide composed of two β-D-glucose molecules linked by a β-1,4-glycosidic bond. Draw the Haworth structure for β-D-cellobiose.

Chemistry Link to Health

HOW SWEET IS MY SWEETENER?

Although many of the monosaccharides and disaccharides taste sweet, they differ considerably in their degree of sweetness. Dietetic foods contain sweeteners that are noncarbohydrate or carbohydrates that are sweeter than sucrose. Some examples of sweeteners compared with sucrose are shown in Table 18.1.

Sucralose is made from sucrose by replacing some of the hydroxyl groups with chlorine atoms.

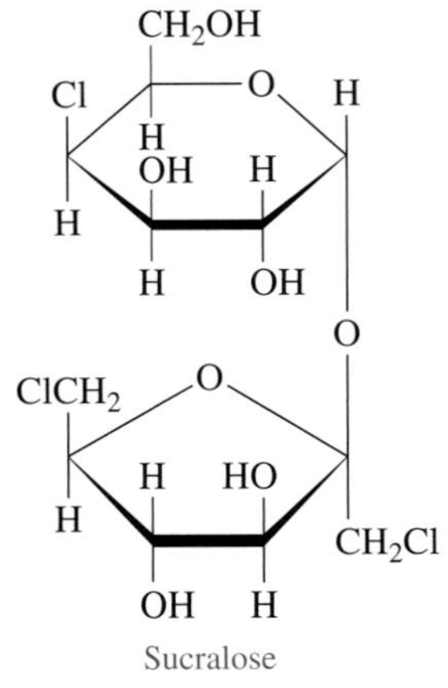

Sucralose

TABLE 18.1 Relative Sweetness of Sugars and Artificial Sweeteners

	Sweetness Relative to Sucrose
Monosaccharides	
Galactose	30
Glucose	75
Fructose	175
Disaccharides	
Lactose	16
Maltose	33
Sucrose	100 = reference standard
Artificial Sweeteners	
Aspartame	18 000
Saccharin	45 000
Sucralose	60 000
Neotame	1 000 000

Aspartame, which is marketed as NutraSweet and Equal, is used in a large number of sugar-free products. It is a noncarbohydrate sweetener made of aspartic acid and a methyl ester of phenylalanine. It does have some caloric value, but it is so sweet that only a very small quantity is needed. However, phenylalanine, one of the breakdown products, poses a danger to anyone who cannot metabolize it properly, a condition called *phenylketonuria* (PKU).

$$H_3\overset{+}{N}-CH(CH_2-COO^-)-C(=O)-N(H)-CH(CH_2-C_6H_5)-C(=O)-O-CH_3$$

Methyl ester

From aspartic acid — From phenylalanine

Aspartame (NutraSweet)

Another artificial sweetener, Neotame, is a modification of the aspartame structure. The addition of a large alkyl group to the amine group prevents enzymes from breaking the amide bond between aspartic acid and phenylalanine. Thus, phenylalanine is not produced when Neotame is used as a sweetener. Very small amounts of Neotame are needed because it is about 10 000 times sweeter than sucrose.

$$CH_3-C(CH_3)_2-CH_2-CH_2-N(H)-CH(CH_2-COO^-)-C(=O)-N(H)-CH(CH_2-C_6H_5)-C(=O)-O-CH_3$$

Large alkyl group to modify Aspartame

Neotame

Saccharin, which is marketed as Sweet'N Low, has been used as a noncarbohydrate artificial sweetener for the past 25 years. The use of saccharin has been banned in Canada because studies indicate that it may cause bladder tumors. However, it is still approved for use by the FDA in the United States.

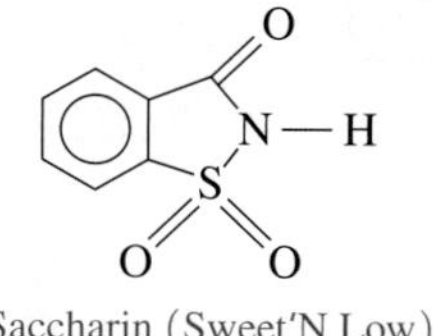

Saccharin (Sweet'N Low)

Artificial sweeteners are used as sugar substitutes.

Polysaccharides

A **polysaccharide** is a polymer of many monosaccharides joined together. Four biologically important polysaccharides—amylose, amylopectin, glycogen, and cellulose—are all polymers of D-glucose that differ only in the type of glycosidic bonds and the amount of branching in the molecule.

Starch, a storage form of glucose in plants, is found as insoluble granules in rice, wheat, potatoes, beans, and cereals. Starch is composed of two kinds of polysaccharides, *amylose* and *amylopectin*. **Amylose**, which makes up about 20% of starch, consists of α-glucose molecules connected by α-1,4-glycosidic bonds in a continuous chain. A typical polymer of amylose may contain from 250 to 4000 α-D-glucose molecules. Sometimes called a straight-chain polymer, polymers of amylose are actually coiled in helical fashion.

Amylopectin, which makes up as much as 80% of plant starch, is a branched-chain polysaccharide. Like amylose, the glucose molecules are connected by α-1,4-glycosidic bonds. However, at about every 25 glucose units, there is a branch of glucose molecules attached by an α-1,6-glycosidic bond between carbon 1 of the branch and carbon 6 in the main chain (see Figure 18.4).

Starches hydrolyze easily in water and acid to give smaller saccharides called *dextrins*, which then hydrolyze to maltose and finally glucose. In our bodies, these complex carbohydrates are digested by the enzymes amylase (in saliva) and maltase. The glucose obtained provides about 50% of our nutritional calories.

$$\text{Amylose, amylopectin} \xrightarrow{H^+ \text{ or amylase}} \text{dextrins} \xrightarrow{H^+ \text{ or amylase}} \text{maltose} \xrightarrow{H^+ \text{ or maltase}} \text{many glucose units}$$

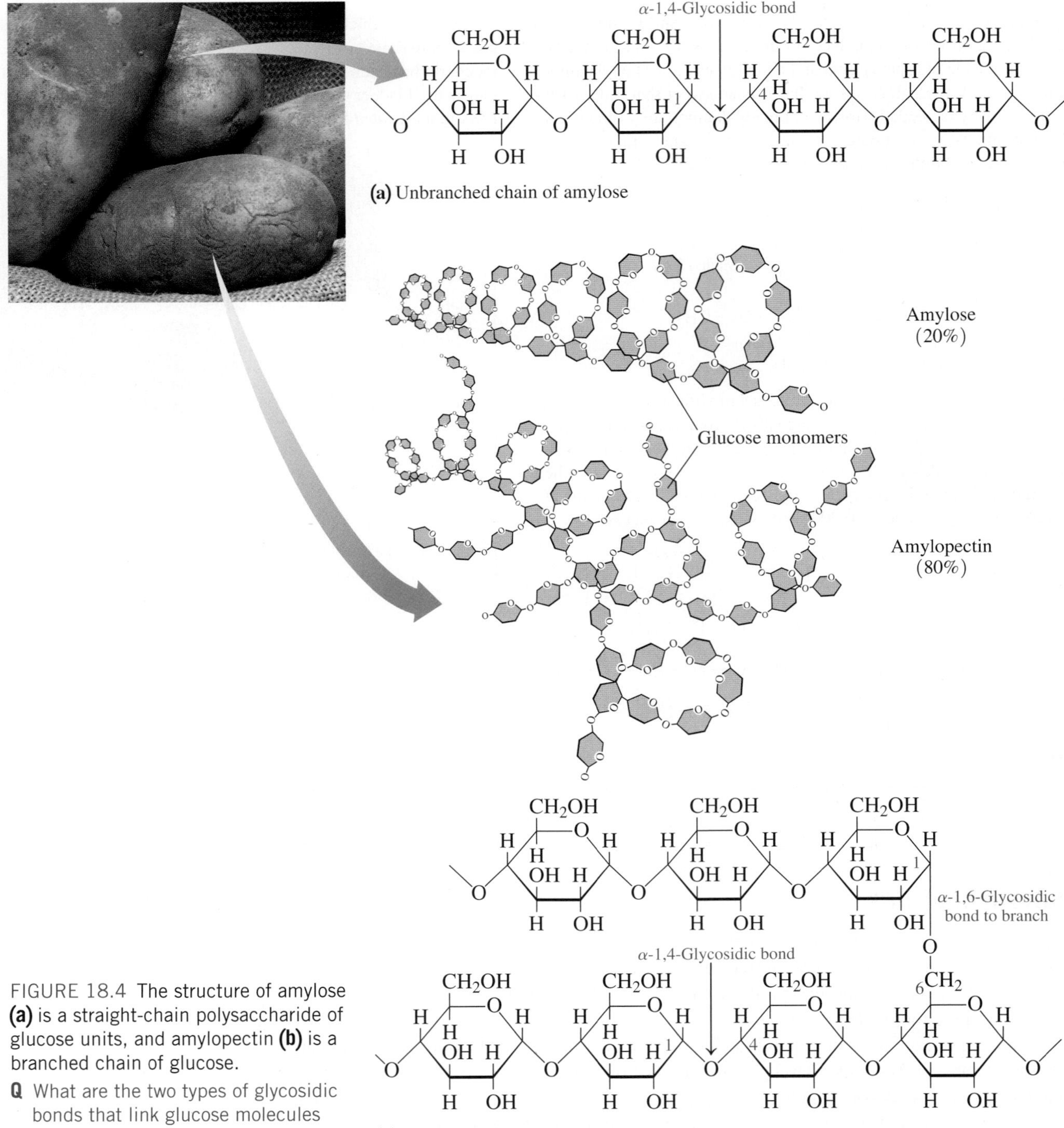

FIGURE 18.4 The structure of amylose **(a)** is a straight-chain polysaccharide of glucose units, and amylopectin **(b)** is a branched chain of glucose.

Q What are the two types of glycosidic bonds that link glucose molecules in amylopectin?

Glycogen, or animal starch, is a polymer of glucose that is stored in the liver and muscle of animals. It is used in our cells at a rate that maintains the blood level of glucose and provides energy between meals. The structure of glycogen is very similar to that of amylopectin except that glycogen is more highly branched.

Cellulose is the major structural material of wood and plants. Cotton is almost pure cellulose. In cellulose, glucose molecules form a long unbranched chain similar to that of amylose. However, the glucose units in cellulose are linked by β-1,4-glycosidic bonds (see Figure 18.5).

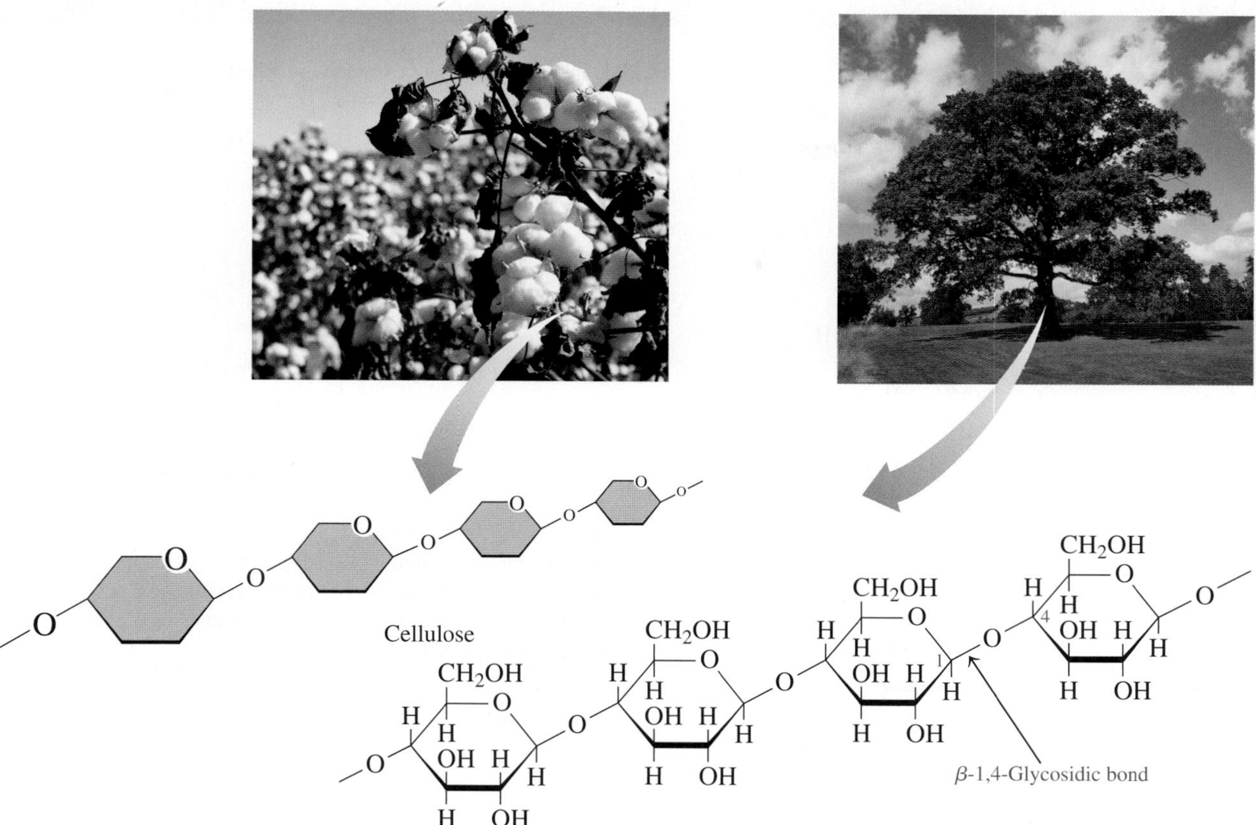

FIGURE 18.5 The polysaccharide cellulose is composed of glucose units linked by β-1,4-glycosidic bonds.

Q Why are humans unable to digest cellulose?

Humans have enzymes in saliva and pancreatic juices that break apart the α-1,4-glycosidic bonds of starches but not the β-1,4-glycosidic bonds of cellulose. Thus, humans cannot digest cellulose. Animals such as horses, cows, and goats can obtain glucose from cellulose because their digestive systems contain bacteria that provide enzymes to break apart β-1,4-glycosidic bonds.

SAMPLE PROBLEM 18.3 Structures of Polysaccharides

Identify the polysaccharide described by each of the following:

a. a polysaccharide that is stored in the liver and muscle tissues
b. an unbranched polysaccharide containing β-1,4-glycosidic bonds
c. a starch containing α-1,4- and α-1,6-glycosidic bonds

SOLUTION

a. glycogen **b.** cellulose **c.** amylopectin, glycogen

STUDY CHECK 18.3

Cellulose and amylose are both unbranched glucose polymers. How do they differ?

QUESTIONS AND PROBLEMS

18.2 Disaccharides and Polysaccharides

LEARNING GOAL: *Describe the monosaccharide units and linkages in disaccharides and polysaccharides.*

18.13 For each of the following, state the monosaccharide units, the type of glycosidic bond, and the name of the disaccharide, including the α or β form:

a.

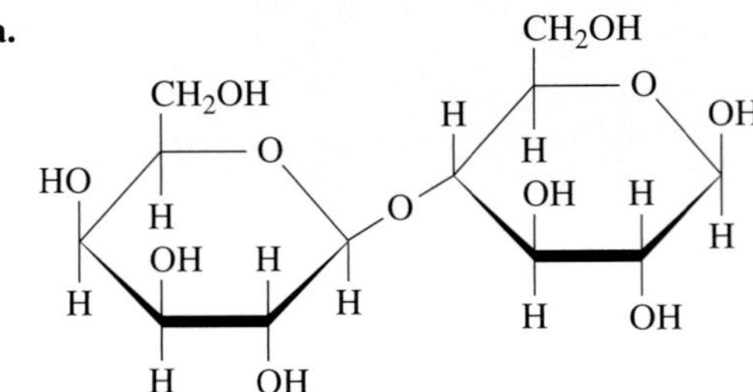

b.

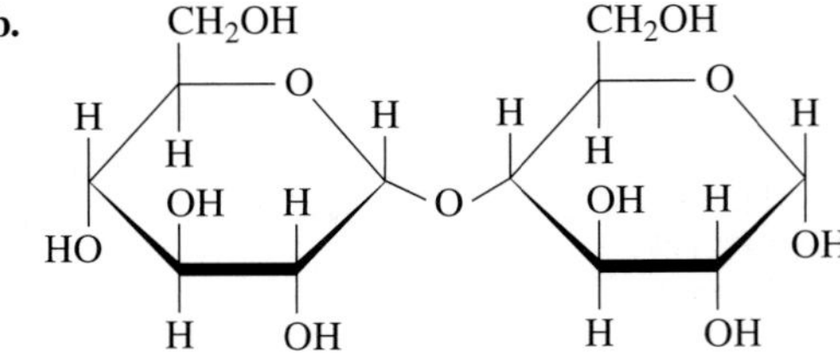

18.14 For each of the following, state the monosaccharide units, the type of glycosidic bond, and the name of the disaccharide, including the α or β form:

a.

b.

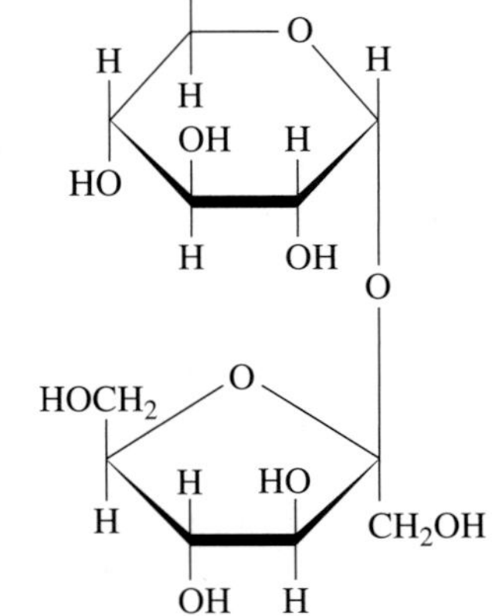

18.15 Isomaltose, obtained from the breakdown of starch, has the following Haworth structure:

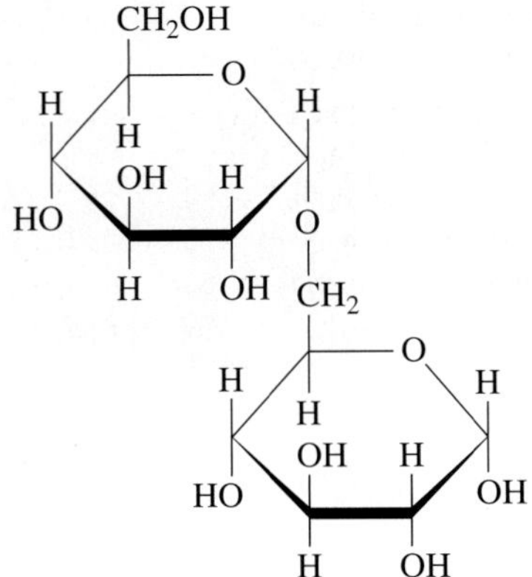

a. Is isomaltose a mono-, di-, or polysaccharide?
b. What are the monosaccharides in isomaltose?
c. What is the glycosidic link in isomaltose?
d. Is this the α or β form of isomaltose?

18.16 Sophorose, found in certain types of beans, has the following Haworth structure:

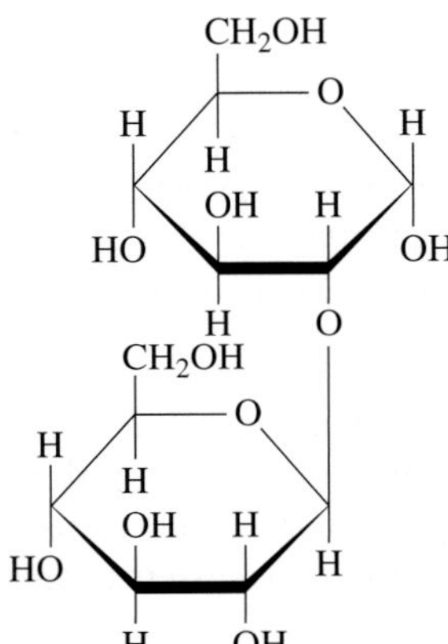

a. Is sophorose a mono-, di-, or polysaccharide?
b. What are the monosaccharides in sophorose?
c. What is the glycosidic link in sophorose?
d. Is this the α or β form of sophorose?

18.17 Identify the disaccharide that fits each of the following descriptions:
a. ordinary table sugar
b. found in milk and milk products
c. also called malt sugar
d. contains galactose and glucose

18.18 Identify the disaccharide that fits each of the following descriptions:
- **a.** used in brewing
- **b.** composed of two glucose units
- **c.** also called milk sugar
- **d.** contains glucose and fructose

18.19 Give the name of one or more polysaccharides that matches each of the following descriptions:
- **a.** not digestible by humans
- **b.** the storage form of carbohydrates in plants
- **c.** contains only α-1,4-glycosidic bonds
- **d.** the most highly branched polysaccharide

18.20 Give the name of one or more polysaccharides that matches each of the following descriptions:
- **a.** the storage form of carbohydrates in animals
- **b.** contains only β-1,4-glycosidic bonds
- **c.** contains both α-1,4- and α-1,6-glycosidic bonds
- **d.** produces maltose during digestion

18.3 Lipids

LEARNING GOAL

Describe some properties of lipids.

Lipids are a family of biomolecules that have the common property of being soluble in organic solvents but not very soluble in water. The word *lipid* comes from the Greek word *lipos*, meaning "fat" or "lard." Within the lipid family, there are certain structures that distinguish the different types of lipids. Lipids that contain *fatty acids* include waxes and triacylglycerols, commonly known as fats and oils, which are esters of glycerol and fatty acids. Lipids that are *steroids* do not contain fatty acids but are characterized by the steroid nucleus of four fused carbon rings.

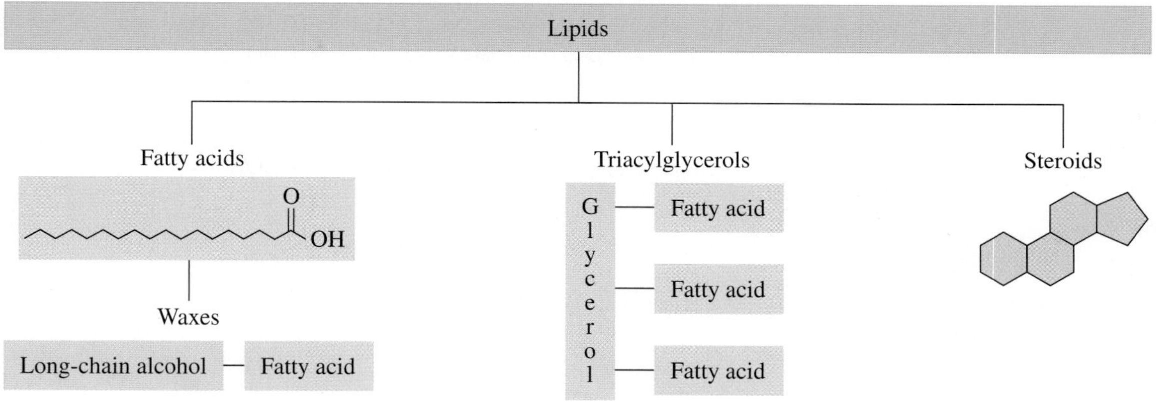

Lipids are naturally occurring compounds in cells and tissues, which are soluble in organic solvents and not in water.

Fatty Acids

A **fatty acid** contains a long unbranched carbon chain with a carboxylic acid group at one end. The long carbon chain makes fatty acids insoluble in water. An example is lauric acid, a 12-carbon acid found in coconut oil, which has a structure that can be written in several forms as follows:

$$CH_3{-}(CH_2)_{10}{-}\overset{\overset{\displaystyle O}{\|}}{C}{-}OH \qquad CH_3{-}(CH_2)_{10}{-}COOH$$

$$CH_3{-}CH_2{-}CH_2{-}CH_2{-}CH_2{-}CH_2{-}CH_2{-}CH_2{-}CH_2{-}CH_2{-}CH_2{-}C{\overset{\displaystyle //O}{\underset{\displaystyle \backslash OH}{}}}$$

Condensed structural formulas

O

OH

Skeletal formula

Saturated fatty acids, such as lauric acid, contain only single bonds between carbons. *Monounsaturated fatty acids* have one double bond in the carbon chain, and *polyunsaturated fatty acids* have two or more double bonds. Table 18.2 lists some of the typical fatty acids in lipids.

TABLE 18.2 Structures and Melting Points of Common Fatty Acids

Name	Carbon Atoms	Source	Melting Point (°C)	Structures
Saturated Fatty Acids				
Lauric acid	12	Coconut	44	$CH_3—(CH_2)_{10}—COOH$
Myristic acid	14	Nutmeg	55	$CH_3—(CH_2)_{12}—COOH$
Palmitic acid	16	Palm	63	$CH_3—(CH_2)_{14}—COOH$
Stearic acid	18	Animal fat	69	$CH_3—(CH_2)_{16}—COOH$
Monounsaturated Fatty Acids				
Palmitoleic acid	16	Butter	0	$CH_3—(CH_2)_5—CH=CH—(CH_2)_7—COOH$
Oleic acid	18	Olive, pecan, grapeseed	14	$CH_3—(CH_2)_7—CH=CH—(CH_2)_7—COOH$
Polyunsaturated Fatty Acids				
Linoleic acid	18	Soybeans, sunflowers	−5	$CH_3—(CH_2)_4—CH=CH—CH_2—CH=CH—(CH_2)_7—COOH$
Linolenic acid	18	Corn	−11	$CH_3—(CH_2—CH=CH)_3—(CH_2)_7—COOH$

Compounds with double bonds can be drawn as two structures known as *cis* and *trans* isomers. In butene, which has a double bond, the cis isomer has the carbon groups on the same side of the double bond, but the trans isomer has the carbon groups on opposite sides of the double bond.

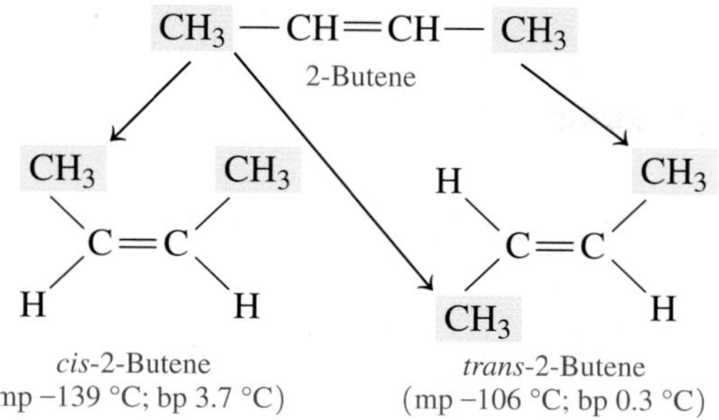

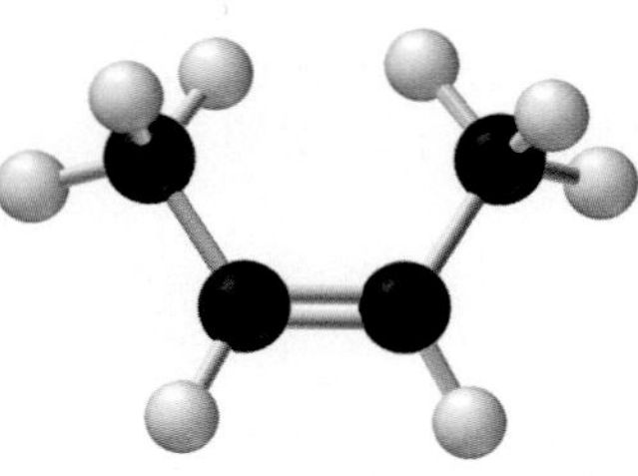
cis-2-Butene

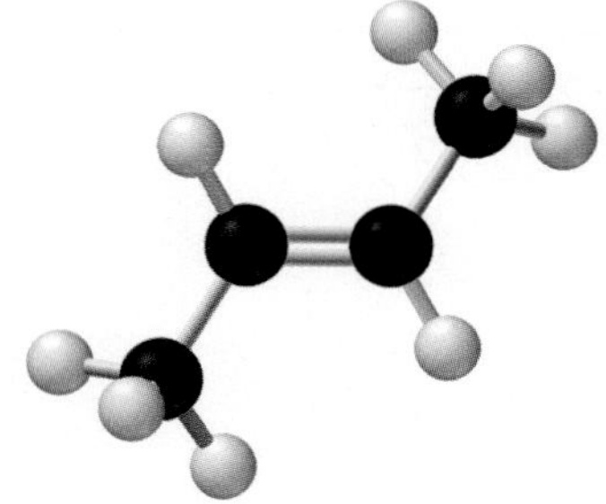
trans-2-Butene

We can draw the unsaturated fatty acid oleic acid as cis and trans isomers using its skeletal formula. The cis structure is the most prevalent isomer found in naturally occurring unsaturated fatty acids. In the *cis*-oleic acid isomer, the carbon has a "kink" at the double bond site. In contrast, *trans*-oleic acid has a regular, linear order of atoms. Saturated fatty acids fit close together in a regular pattern, which allows strong attractions to occur between the carbon chains. However, unsaturated fatty acids have irregular shape, which leads to fewer interactions between carbon chains. Thus, saturated fatty acids have high melting points because more energy is required to separate the fatty acid molecules (see Table 18.2).

cis-Oleic acid
cis double bond

trans-Oleic acid
trans double bond

Almost all naturally occurring unsaturated fatty acids have one or more cis double bonds.

CONCEPT CHECK 18.2 Fatty Acids

Using Table 18.2, identify the following:

a. the 18-carbon saturated fatty acid
b. a monounsaturated fatty acid found in olives
c. an 18-carbon fatty acid with three double bonds

ANSWER

a. Stearic acid is the saturated 18-carbon fatty acid.
b. Oleic acid is a monounsaturated (one double bond) fatty acid found in olives.
c. Linolenic acid is an 18-carbon fatty acid with three double bonds.

SAMPLE PROBLEM 18.4 Structures and Properties of Fatty Acids

Consider the condensed structural formula for oleic acid.

$$CH_3-(CH_2)_7-CH=CH-(CH_2)_7-\overset{\overset{\displaystyle O}{\|}}{C}-OH$$

a. Why is this substance an acid?
b. How many carbon atoms are in oleic acid?
c. Is the fatty acid saturated, monounsaturated, or polyunsaturated?
d. Would it be soluble in water?

SOLUTION

a. Oleic acid contains a carboxylic acid group.
b. It contains 18 carbon atoms.
c. It is a monounsaturated fatty acid.
d. No; its long hydrocarbon chain makes it insoluble in water.

STUDY CHECK 18.4

Palmitoleic acid is a fatty acid with the following condensed structural formula:

$$CH_3-(CH_2)_5-CH=CH-(CH_2)_7-\overset{\displaystyle O}{\overset{\|}{C}}-OH$$

a. How many carbon atoms are in palmitoleic acid?
b. Is the fatty acid saturated, monounsaturated, or polyunsaturated?
c. Would it be soluble in water?

Waxes

Waxes are found in many plants and animals. A wax is an ester of a long-chain fatty acid and a long-chain alcohol. The formulas of some common waxes are given in Table 18.3. Beeswax obtained from honeycombs and carnauba wax from palm trees are used to give a protective coating to furniture, cars, and floors. Jojoba wax is used in making candles and cosmetics such as lipstick. Lanolin, a mixture of waxes obtained from wool, is used in hand and facial lotions to aid retention of water, which softens the skin.

Honeycomb (beeswax) is an ester of a saturated fatty acid and a long-chain alcohol.

TABLE 18.3 Some Typical Waxes

Type	Condensed Structural Formula	Source	Uses
Beeswax	$CH_3-(CH_2)_{14}-\overset{\displaystyle O}{\overset{\|}{C}}-O-(CH_2)_{29}-CH_3$	Honeycomb	Candles, shoe polish, wax paper
Carnauba wax	$CH_3-(CH_2)_{24}-\overset{\displaystyle O}{\overset{\|}{C}}-O-(CH_2)_{29}-CH_3$	Brazilian palm tree	Waxes for furniture, cars, floors, shoes
Jojoba wax	$CH_3-(CH_2)_{18}-\overset{\displaystyle O}{\overset{\|}{C}}-O-(CH_2)_{19}-CH_3$	Jojoba bush	Candles, soaps, cosmetics

Fats and Oils: Triacylglycerols

In the body, fatty acids are stored as fats and oils known as **triacylglycerols**. These substances, also called *triglycerides*, are triesters of glycerol (a trihydroxy alcohol) and fatty acids. In a triacylglycerol, three hydroxyl groups on glycerol form ester bonds with the carboxyl groups of three fatty acids. For example, glycerol and three molecules of stearic acid form glyceryl tristearate (tristearin).

$CH_2-O-C(=O)$ (chain)
$CH-O-C(=O)$ (chain)
$CH_2-O-C(=O)$ (chain)

Triacylglycerol

Glycerol — Fatty acid
— Fatty acid
— Fatty acid

$$
\begin{array}{l}
\mathrm{CH_2{-}O{-}H} + \mathrm{HO{-}\overset{\overset{\large O}{\|}}{C}{-}(CH_2)_{16}{-}CH_3} \\
\quad | \\
\mathrm{CH{-}O{-}H} + \mathrm{HO{-}\overset{\overset{\large O}{\|}}{C}{-}(CH_2)_{16}{-}CH_3} \\
\quad | \\
\mathrm{CH_2{-}O{-}H} + \mathrm{HO{-}\overset{\overset{\large O}{\|}}{C}{-}(CH_2)_{16}{-}CH_3} \\
\text{Glycerol} \qquad \text{3 Stearic acid molecules}
\end{array}
\longrightarrow
\begin{array}{l}
\mathrm{CH_2{-}O{-}\overset{\overset{\large O}{\|}}{C}{-}(CH_2)_{16}{-}CH_3} \quad \leftarrow \text{Ester bond} \\
\quad | \\
\mathrm{CH{-}O{-}\overset{\overset{\large O}{\|}}{C}{-}(CH_2)_{16}{-}CH_3} + 3H_2O \\
\quad | \\
\mathrm{CH_2{-}O{-}\overset{\overset{\large O}{\|}}{C}{-}(CH_2)_{16}{-}CH_3} \\
\text{Glyceryl tristearate (tristearin, a fat)}
\end{array}
$$

Triacylglycerols are the major form of energy storage for animals. Animals that hibernate eat large quantities of plants, seeds, and nuts that contain large amounts of fats and oils. Prior to hibernation, these animals, such as polar bears, gain as much as 14 kg a week. As the external temperature drops, the animal goes into hibernation. The body temperature drops to nearly freezing, and there is a dramatic reduction in cellular activity, respiration, and heart rate. Animals that live in extremely cold climates will hibernate for 4–7 months. During this time, stored fat is the only source of energy.

Prior to hibernation, a polar bear eats food with a high content of fats and oils.

SAMPLE PROBLEM 18.5 Drawing Structures for a Triacylglycerol

Draw the condensed structural formula for glyceryl trioleate (triolein), a triacylglycerol that uses oleic acid.

SOLUTION

Analyze the Problem	Name of Lipid	Type of Lipid	Type of Alcohol	Fatty Acids	Type of Bonds
	glyceryl trioleate (triolein)	triacylglycerol	glycerol	three oleic acids	ester

$$
\begin{array}{l}
\mathrm{CH_2{-}O{-}\overset{\overset{\large O}{\|}}{C}{-}(CH_2)_7{-}CH{=}CH{-}(CH_2)_7{-}CH_3} \\
\quad | \\
\mathrm{CH{-}O{-}\overset{\overset{\large O}{\|}}{C}{-}(CH_2)_7{-}CH{=}CH{-}(CH_2)_7{-}CH_3} \\
\quad | \\
\mathrm{CH_2{-}O{-}\overset{\overset{\large O}{\|}}{C}{-}(CH_2)_7{-}CH{=}CH{-}(CH_2)_7{-}CH_3}
\end{array}
$$

Glyceryl trioleate (triolein)

STUDY CHECK 18.5

Draw the condensed structural formula for the triacylglycerol containing three molecules of myristic acid.

Melting Points of Fats and Oils

A **fat** is a triacylglycerol that is solid at room temperature, such as fats in meat, whole milk, butter, and cheese. An **oil** is a triacylglycerol that is usually liquid at room temperature and is usually obtained from a plant source (see Figure 18.6).

The amounts of saturated, monounsaturated, and polyunsaturated fatty acids in some typical fats and oils are shown in Figure 18.7. Saturated fatty acids have higher melting points than unsaturated fatty acids because they pack together more tightly. Animal fats usually contain more saturated fatty acids than do vegetable oils. Therefore the melting points of animal fats are higher than those of vegetable oils.

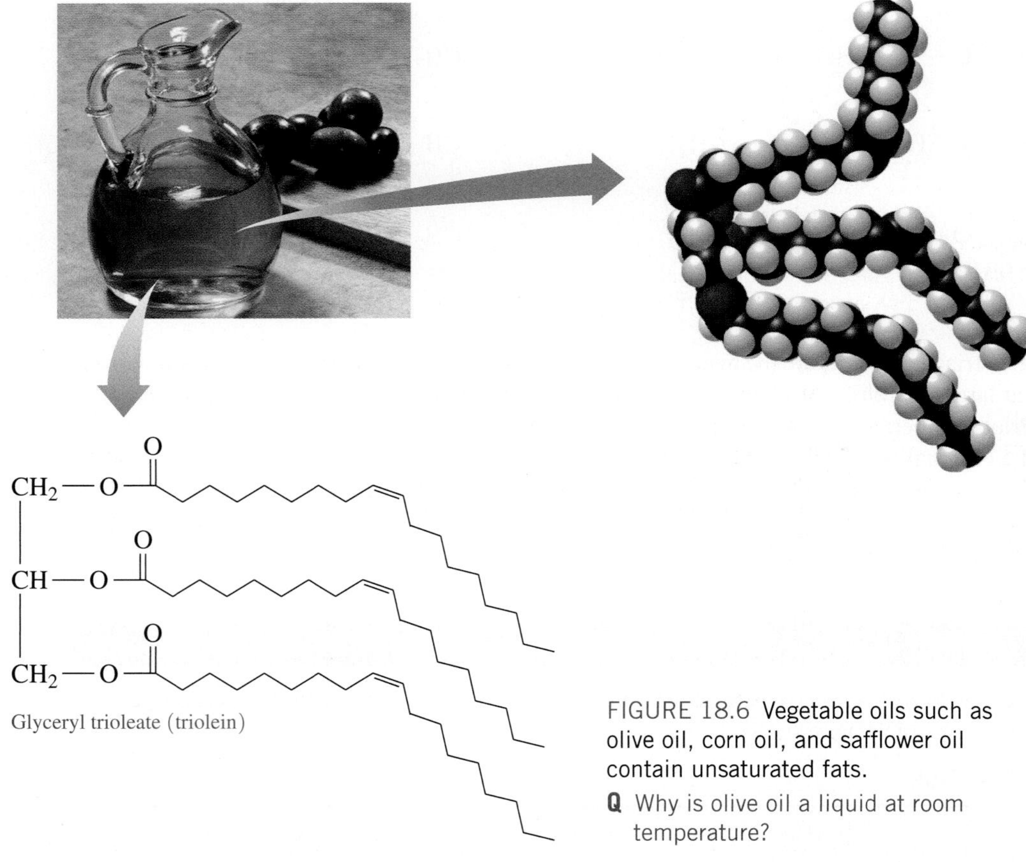

FIGURE 18.6 Vegetable oils such as olive oil, corn oil, and safflower oil contain unsaturated fats.

Q Why is olive oil a liquid at room temperature?

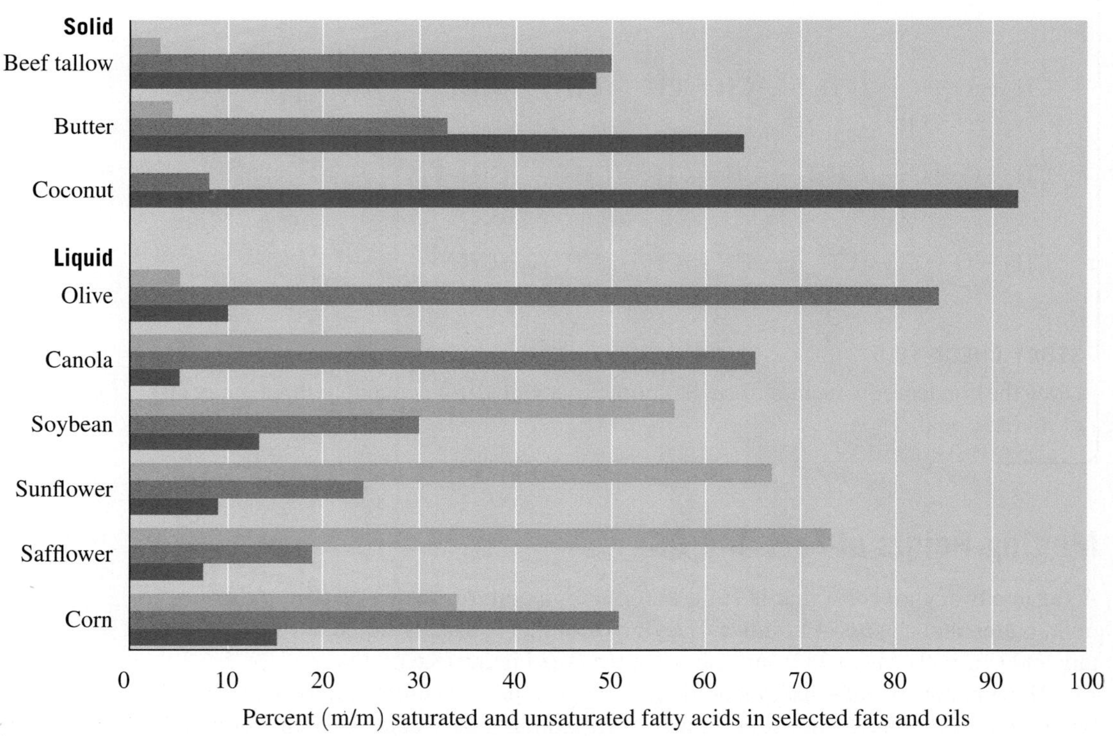

FIGURE 18.7 Vegetable oils have low melting points because they have a higher percentage of unsaturated fatty acids than do animal fats.

Q Why is the melting point of butter higher than that of olive or canola oil?

Chemistry Link to Health

OLESTRA: A FAT SUBSTITUTE

In 1968, food scientists designed an artificial fat called *olestra* as an intended source of nutrition for premature babies. However, olestra could not be digested and was never used for that purpose. Later, scientists realized that olestra had the flavor and texture of a fat without the calories.

Olestra (also known by the brand name Olean) is manufactured by obtaining the fatty acids from the fats in cottonseed or soybean oils and bonding the fatty acids with the hydroxyl groups on sucrose. Chemically, olestra is composed of six to eight long-chain fatty acids attached by ester links to a sucrose molecule rather than to a glycerol molecule. This structure makes olestra a very large molecule that cannot be absorbed through the intestinal walls. The enzymes and bacteria in the intestinal tract are unable to break down the olestra molecule, and it travels through the intestinal tract undigested.

The large molecule of olestra also combines with fat-soluble vitamins (A, D, E, and K) before they can be absorbed through the intestinal wall. Once the olestra combines with these molecules, they pass through the intestinal tract without being absorbed. The FDA now requires manufacturers to add the four vitamins to olestra products. There have been reports of some adverse reactions, including diarrhea, abdominal cramps, and anal leakage, indicating that olestra may act as a laxative in some people. However, the manufacturers contend there is no direct proof that olestra is the cause of those effects.

Snack foods made with olestra, such as potato chips, tortilla chips, crackers, and fried snacks, are found in supermarkets nationwide. It remains to be seen whether olestra will have any significant effect on reducing the problem of obesity.

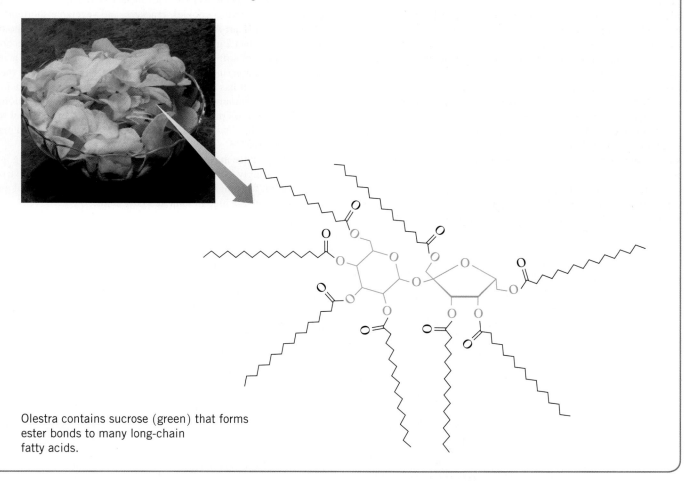

Olestra contains sucrose (green) that forms ester bonds to many long-chain fatty acids.

Reactions of Triacylglycerols

The double bonds in unsaturated fatty acids will react with hydrogen to produce saturated fatty acids. For example, when hydrogen is added to glyceryl trioleate (triolein) using a nickel catalyst, the product is the saturated fat glyceryl tristearate (tristearin).

$$\begin{array}{l} CH_2-O-\overset{\overset{\displaystyle O}{\|}}{C}-(CH_2)_7-CH{=}CH-(CH_2)_7-CH_3 \\ | \\ CH-O-\overset{\overset{\displaystyle O}{\|}}{C}-(CH_2)_7-CH{=}CH-(CH_2)_7-CH_3 \\ | \\ CH_2-O-\overset{\overset{\displaystyle O}{\|}}{C}-(CH_2)_7-CH{=}CH-(CH_2)_7-CH_3 \end{array} + 3H_2 \xrightarrow{Ni} \begin{array}{l} CH_2-O-\overset{\overset{\displaystyle O}{\|}}{C}-(CH_2)_{16}-CH_3 \\ | \\ CH-O-\overset{\overset{\displaystyle O}{\|}}{C}-(CH_2)_{16}-CH_3 \\ | \\ CH_2-O-\overset{\overset{\displaystyle O}{\|}}{C}-(CH_2)_{16}-CH_3 \end{array}$$

Glyceryl trioleate (triolein) — Glyceryl tristearate (tristearin)

Chemistry Link to Health

TRANS FATTY ACIDS AND HYDROGENATION

During the early 1900s, margarine became a popular replacement for highly saturated fats such as butter and lard. Margarine is produced by partially hydrogenating the unsaturated fats in vegetable oils such as safflower oil, corn oil, canola oil, cottonseed oil, and sunflower oil.

During the hydrogenation process, double bonds in the unsaturated fats are converted to single bonds. However, a small number of the cis double bonds are converted to trans double bonds. If the label on a product states that the oils have been "partially hydrogenated," that product will also contain trans fatty acids.

During the 1980s, research indicated that trans fatty acids have an effect on blood cholesterol similar to that of saturated fats, although study results vary. Several studies reported that trans fatty acids raise the levels of LDL-cholesterol, low-density lipoproteins containing cholesterol that can accumulate in the arteries. Some studies also report that trans fatty acids lower HDL-cholesterol, high-density lipoproteins that carry cholesterol to the liver to be excreted.

Foods containing trans fatty acids include baked goods, stick margarine, soft margarine, cookies, crackers, and vegetable shortening. The American Heart Association recommends that margarine should have no more than 2 g of saturated fat per tablespoon. It also recommends the use of soft margarine, which is lower in trans fatty acids because soft margarine is only slightly hydrogenated, and diet margarine because it has less fat and therefore fewer trans fatty acids. Currently, the amount of trans fats is included on the Nutritional Facts label on food products. In the United States, a food label for a product that has less than 0.5 g of trans fat in one serving can read "0 g of trans fat."

The best advice may be to reduce total fat in the diet by using fats and oils sparingly, cooking with little or no fat, substituting olive oil or canola oil for other oils, and limiting the use of coconut oil and palm oil, which are high in saturated fatty acids.

Undesired side product (*trans*-oleic acid) — Desired saturated product (stearic acid)

Saponification occurs when a fat is heated with a strong base such as sodium hydroxide to give glycerol and the sodium salts of the fatty acids, which are soaps. When NaOH is used, a solid soap is produced that can be molded into a desired shape; KOH produces a softer, liquid soap. Oils that are polyunsaturated produce softer soaps. Names like "coconut soap" or "avocado shampoo" tell you the sources of the oil used in the reaction.

$$\text{Fat or oil} + \text{strong base} \longrightarrow \text{glycerol} + \text{salts of fatty acids (soaps)}$$

$$\begin{array}{l} CH_2{-}O{-}\overset{O}{\overset{\|}{C}}{-}(CH_2)_{14}{-}CH_3 \\ | \\ CH{-}O{-}\overset{O}{\overset{\|}{C}}{-}(CH_2)_{14}{-}CH_3 \\ | \\ CH_2{-}O{-}\overset{O}{\overset{\|}{C}}{-}(CH_2)_{14}{-}CH_3 \end{array} + \mathbf{3NaOH} \longrightarrow \begin{array}{l} CH_2{-}\mathbf{OH} \\ | \\ CH{-}\mathbf{OH} \\ | \\ CH_2{-}\mathbf{OH} \end{array} + \begin{array}{l} \mathbf{Na^{+}\,{}^{-}O}{-}\overset{O}{\overset{\|}{C}}{-}(CH_2)_{14}{-}CH_3 \\ \mathbf{Na^{+}\,{}^{-}O}{-}\overset{O}{\overset{\|}{C}}{-}(CH_2)_{14}{-}CH_3 \\ \mathbf{Na^{+}\,{}^{-}O}{-}\overset{O}{\overset{\|}{C}}{-}(CH_2)_{14}{-}CH_3 \end{array}$$

Glyceryl tripalmitate (tripalmitin) — Glycerol — 3 Sodium palmitate (soap)

Steroids: Cholesterol and Steroid Hormones

Steroids are compounds containing the steroid nucleus, which consists of four carbon rings fused together. Although they are lipids, steroids do not contain fatty acids.

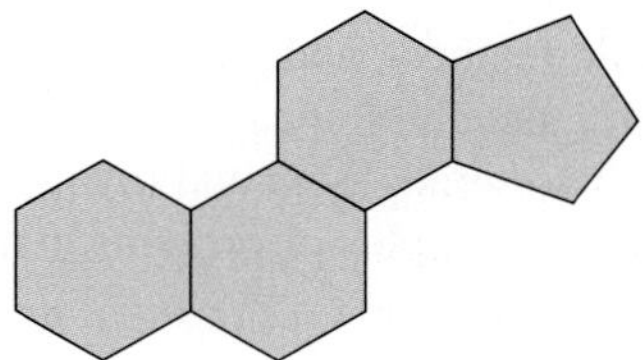

Steroid nucleus

Attaching other atoms and groups of atoms to the steroid nucleus forms a wide variety of steroid compounds. **Cholesterol**, which is one of the most important and abundant steroids in the body, is a *sterol* because it contains an oxygen atom as a hydroxyl (—OH) group. Like many steroids, cholesterol has methyl groups, a double bond, and a carbon side chain. In other steroids, the hydroxyl group is replaced by a carbonyl (C=O) group. Cholesterol is obtained from eating meats, milk, and eggs, and it is also synthesized by the liver from fats, carbohydrates, and proteins. There is no cholesterol in vegetable and plant products. High levels of cholesterol are also associated with the accumulation of lipid deposits (plaque) that line and narrow the coronary arteries (see Figure 18.8).

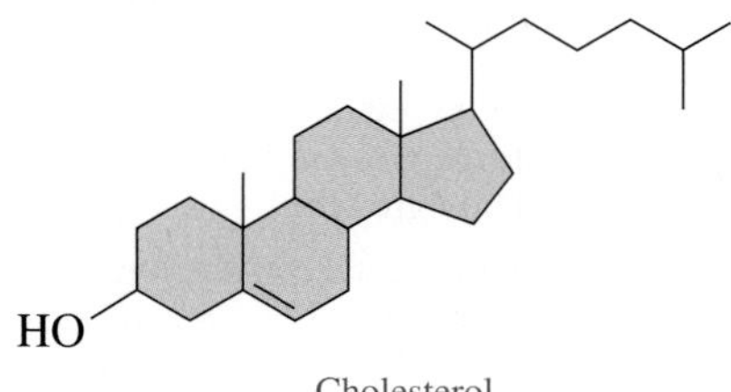

Cholesterol

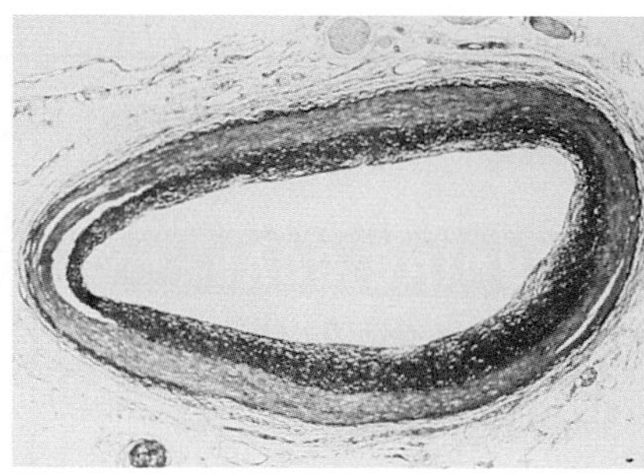

(a)

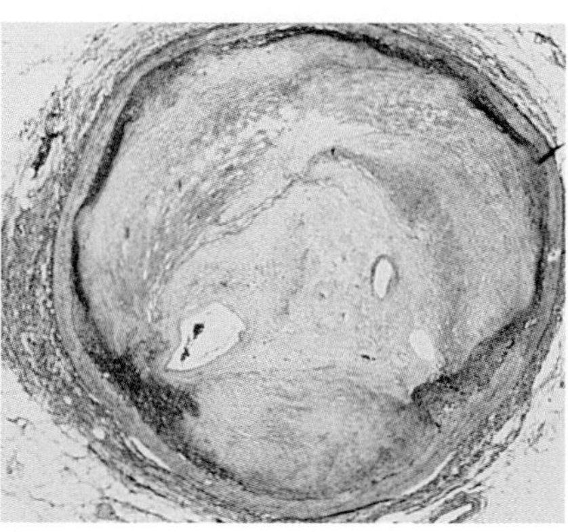

(b)

FIGURE 18.8 Excess cholesterol forms plaque that can block an artery, resulting in a heart attack. **(a)** A normal, open artery shows no buildup of plaque. **(b)** An artery that is almost completely clogged by atherosclerotic plaque.

Q What property of cholesterol would cause it to form deposits along the coronary arteries?

QUESTIONS AND PROBLEMS

18.3 Lipids

LEARNING GOAL: *Describe some properties of lipids.*

18.21 Classify each of the following fatty acids as saturated, monounsaturated, or polyunsaturated (see Table 18.2):
a. lauric acid **b.** linolenic acid **c.** stearic acid

18.22 Classify each of the following fatty acids as saturated, monounsaturated, or polyunsaturated (see Table 18.2):
a. linoleic acid **b.** palmitoleic acid **c.** myristic acid

18.23 Draw the condensed structural formula for glyceryl trimyristate (trimyristin).

18.24 Draw the condensed structural formula for glyceryl trilaurate (trilaurin).

18.25 Safflower oil is called a polyunsaturated oil, whereas olive oil is a monounsaturated oil. Explain.

18.26 Why does olive oil have a lower melting point than butter fat?

18.27 A label on a container of margarine states that it contains partially hydrogenated corn oil.
  a. How has the liquid corn oil been changed?
  b. Why is the margarine product solid?

18.28 Draw the condensed structural formula for the product of the hydrogenation of the following triacylglycerol:

$$
\begin{array}{l}
CH_2-O-\overset{\displaystyle O}{\overset{\|}{C}}-(CH_2)_{16}-CH_3 \\
| \\
CH-O-\overset{\displaystyle O}{\overset{\|}{C}}-(CH_2)_7-CH{=}CH-(CH_2)_7-CH_3 \\
| \\
CH_2-O-\overset{\displaystyle O}{\overset{\|}{C}}-(CH_2)_{16}-CH_3
\end{array}
$$

18.29 Draw the structure for the steroid nucleus.

18.30 What are the functional groups on the cholesterol molecule?

LEARNING GOAL

Describe protein functions, and draw structures for amino acids and dipeptides.

18.4 Proteins

Proteins perform different functions in the body. Some proteins form structural components such as cartilage, muscles, hair, and nails. Wool, silk, feathers, and horns in animals are made of proteins. Proteins that function as enzymes regulate biological reactions such as digestion and cellular metabolism. Other proteins, such as hemoglobin and myoglobin, transport oxygen in the blood and muscle. Table 18.4 gives examples of proteins that are classified by their functions in biological systems.

The horns of animals are made of proteins.

TABLE 18.4 Classification of Some Proteins and Their Functions

Class of Protein	Function	Examples
Structural	Provide structural components	*Collagen* is in tendons and cartilage. *Keratin* is in hair, skin, wool, and nails.
Contractile	Move muscles	*Myosin* and *actin* contract muscle fibers.
Transport	Carry essential substances throughout the body	*Hemoglobin* transports oxygen. *Lipoproteins* transport lipids.
Storage	Store nutrients	*Casein* stores protein in milk. *Ferritin* stores iron in the spleen and liver.
Hormone	Regulate body metabolism and nervous system	*Insulin* regulates blood glucose level. *Growth hormone* regulates body growth.
Enzyme	Catalyze biochemical reactions in the cells	*Sucrase* catalyzes the hydrolysis of sucrose. *Trypsin* catalyzes the hydrolysis of proteins.
Protection	Recognize and destroy foreign substances	*Immunoglobulins* stimulate immune responses.

Amino Acids

Proteins are composed of molecular building blocks called *amino acids*. Every **amino acid**, which is ionized in biological environments, has a central alpha carbon atom (α-carbon) bonded to an ammonium ($-NH_3^+$) group, a carboxylate ($-COO^-$) group, a hydrogen atom, and an R group. The differences in the 20 α-amino acids present in human proteins are due to the unique characteristics of the R groups.

Ionized Structure of Alanine, an α-Amino Acid

We classify amino acids according to their R groups, which determine their properties in aqueous solution. The **nonpolar amino acids** have hydrogen, alkyl, or aromatic R groups, which make them *hydrophobic* ("water fearing"). A **polar amino acid** interacts with water because it has a polar R group, which is *hydrophilic* ("water loving"). *Neutral polar amino acids* contain hydroxyl ($-OH$), thiol ($-SH$), or amide ($-CONH_2$) groups. The *acidic polar amino acids* contain a carboxylate group ($-COO^-$). The *basic polar amino acids* have amine R groups. The ionized structures and common names of the 20 α-amino acids commonly found in proteins with their R groups highlighted in tan, and their three-letter and one-letter abbreviations, are listed in Table 18.5.

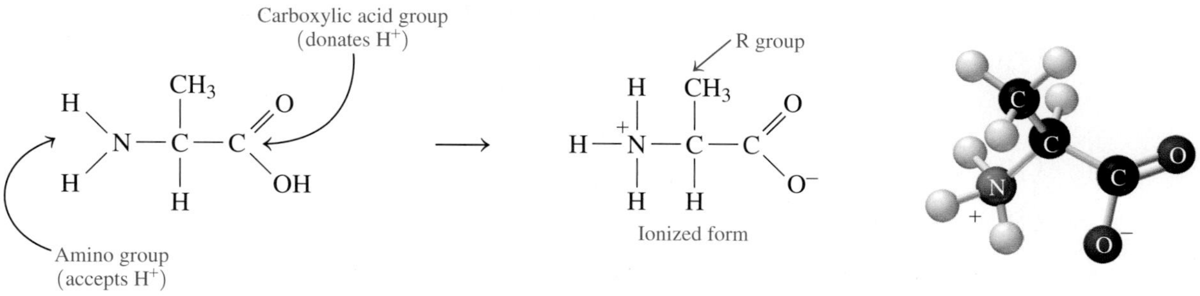

Carboxylic acid group (donates H^+)

R group

Ionized form

Amino group (accepts H^+)

In biological systems, amino acids are ionized.

A summary of the classification of amino acids follows:

Type of Amino Acid	Type of R Groups	Polarity	Water
Nonpolar	Nonpolar	Nonpolar	Hydrophobic
Polar, neutral	Contain O and S atoms, but no charge	Polar	Hydrophilic
Polar, acidic	Contain carboxyl groups, negative charge	Polar	Hydrophilic
Polar, basic	Contain amino groups, positive charge	Polar	Hydrophilic

CONCEPT CHECK 18.3 Polarity of Amino Acids

Classify each of the following amino acids as nonpolar or polar. If polar, indicate if the R group is neutral, acidic, or basic. Indicate if each would be hydrophobic or hydrophilic.

a. valine **b.** asparagine **c.** histidine

ANSWER

a. The R group in valine consists of several C atoms and H atoms, which makes valine a nonpolar amino acid that is hydrophobic.

b. The R group in asparagine contains C atoms, H atoms, and an amide group, which makes asparagine a polar amino acid that is neutral and hydrophilic.

c. The R group in histidine contains C atoms, H atoms, and a ring containing a N^+, which makes histidine a polar amino acid that is basic and hydrophilic.

TABLE 18.5 Structures, Names, and Abbreviations of 20 Common Amino Acids at Physiological pH (7.4)

Nonpolar Amino Acids (Hydrophobic)

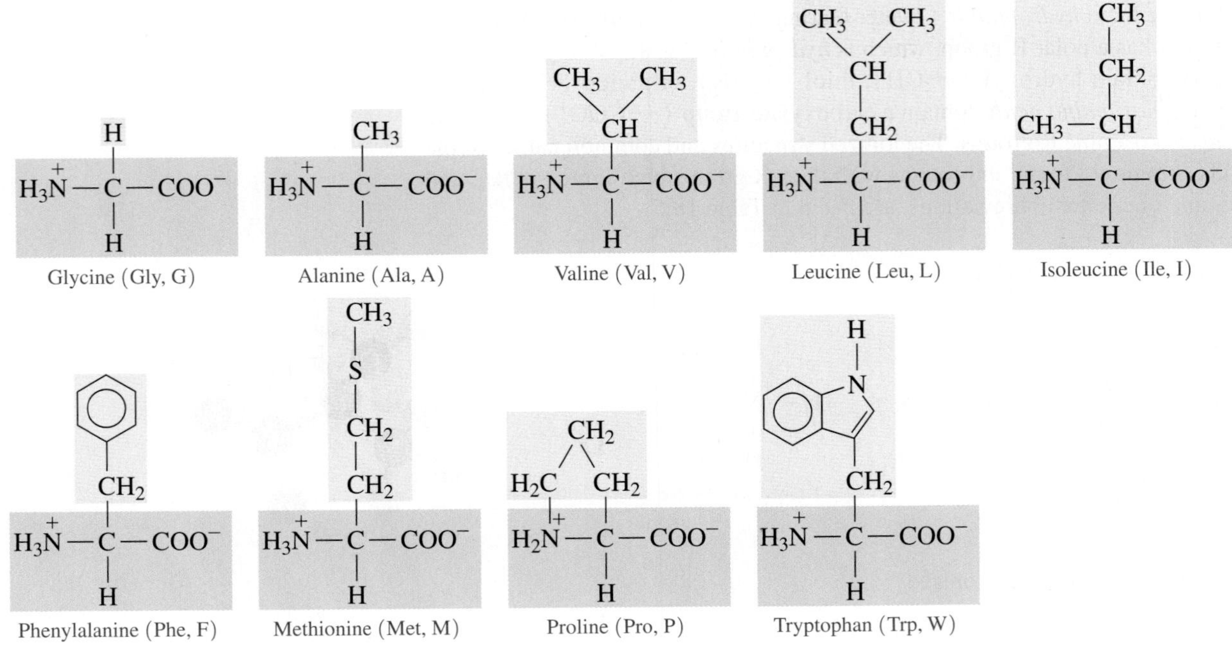

Polar Amino Acids (Hydrophilic)

Amino Acids with Neutral R Groups

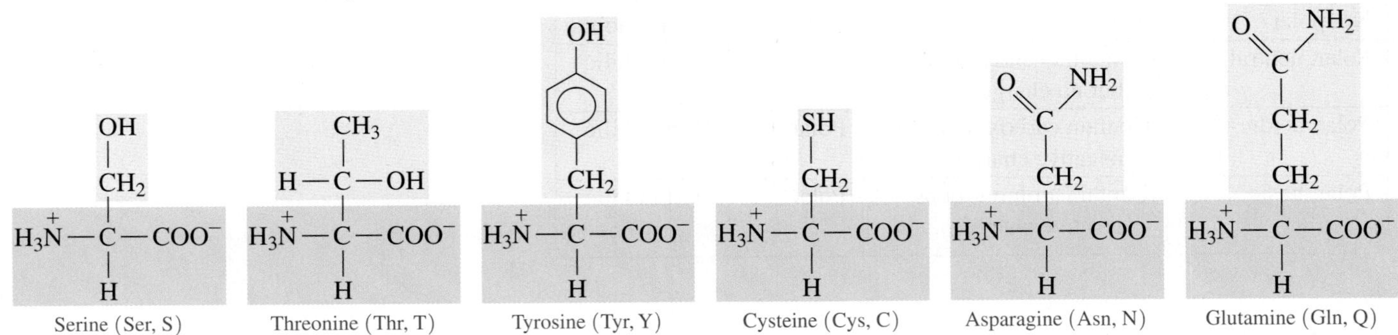

Amino Acids with Charged R Groups

Acidic (negative charge)

Basic (positive charge)

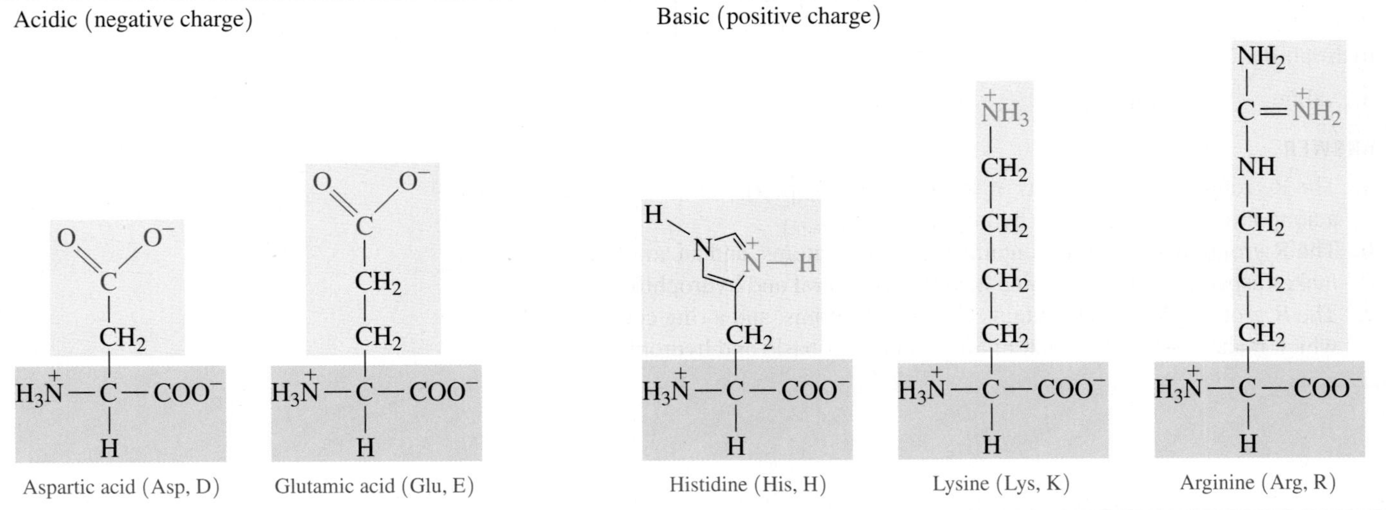

SAMPLE PROBLEM 18.6 Structural Formulas of Amino Acids

Draw the condensed structural formula and give the abbreviations for serine.

serine (R = $-CH_2-OH$)

SOLUTION

The structure of a specific amino acid is drawn by attaching the side group (R) to the central carbon atom of the general structure of an amino acid.

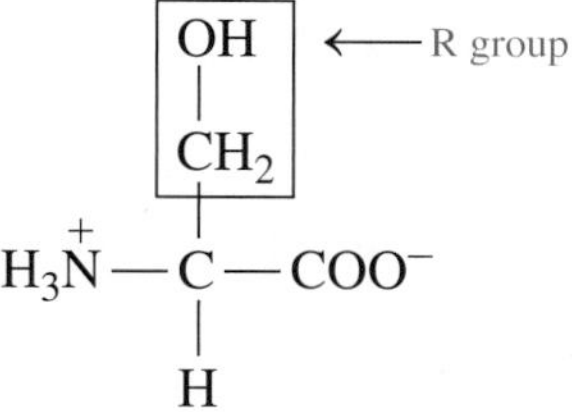

The abbreviations for serine are Ser and S.

STUDY CHECK 18.6

Classify serine in Sample Problem 18.6 as polar or nonpolar and hydrophobic or hydrophilic.

Chemistry Link to Health

ESSENTIAL AMINO ACIDS

Of the 20 amino acids used to build the proteins in the body, only 11 can be synthesized in the body. The other 9 amino acids, listed in Table 18.6, are *essential amino acids* that cannot be synthesized and must be obtained from the proteins in the diet.

Complete proteins, which contain all of the essential amino acids, are found in animal products such as eggs, milk, meat, fish, and poultry. However, gelatin and plant proteins such as grains, beans, and nuts are *incomplete proteins* because they are deficient in one or more of the essential amino acids. Diets that rely on plant foods for protein must contain a variety of protein sources to obtain all the essential amino acids. For example, a diet of rice and beans contains all the essential amino acids because they are *complementary proteins*. Rice contains the methionine and tryptophan deficient in beans, while beans contain the lysine that is lacking in rice (see Table 18.7).

TABLE 18.6 Essential Amino Acids for Adults

Histidine (His)	Phenylalanine (Phe)
Isoleucine (Ile)	Threonine (Thr)
Leucine (Leu)	Tryptophan (Trp)
Lysine (Lys)	Valine (Val)
Methionine (Met)	

TABLE 18.7 Amino Acid Deficiency in Selected Vegetables and Grains

Food Source	Amino Acids Missing
Eggs, milk, meat, fish, poultry	None
Wheat, rice, oats	Lysine
Corn	Lysine, tryptophan
Beans	Methionine, tryptophan
Peas	Methionine
Almonds, walnuts	Lysine, tryptophan
Soy	Low in methionine

Complete proteins such as eggs, milk, meat, and fish contain all of the essential amino acids. Incomplete proteins from plants such as grains, beans, and nuts are deficient in one or more essential amino acids.

Peptides

A *peptide bond* is an amide bond that forms when the $-COO^-$ group of one amino acid reacts with the $-NH_3^+$ group of the next amino acid. We can write the formation of the dipeptide glycylalanine (Gly-Ala, GA) between glycine and alanine. With a free

$—NH_3^+$ group on the left, glycine is the N-terminal amino acid. The C-terminal amino acid is alanine on the right, which has a free $—COO^-$ group. In the name of a peptide, each amino acid beginning from the N-terminal end has the *ine* (or *ic* acid) replaced by *yl*. The last amino acid at the C-terminal end of the peptide uses its full name.

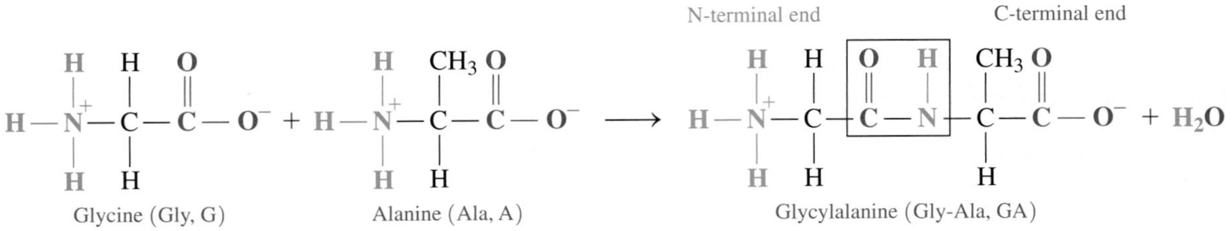

N-terminal end C-terminal end

$$H_3\overset{+}{N}—CH_2—COO^- + H_3\overset{+}{N}—CH(CH_3)—COO^- \longrightarrow H_3\overset{+}{N}—CH_2—\boxed{C(=O)—NH}—CH(CH_3)—COO^- + H_2O$$

Glycine (Gly, G) Alanine (Ala, A) Glycylalanine (Gly-Ala, GA)

A peptide bond between the ionized structures of glycine and alanine as forms the dipeptide glycylalanine.

CONCEPT CHECK 18.4 Structure and Names of Peptides

Consider the dipeptide Val-Thr, VT:

a. What amino acid is the N-terminal amino acid?
b. What amino acid is the C-terminal amino acid?
c. How are the amino acids connected?
d. Give the name of the dipeptide.

ANSWER

a. Valine, the first amino acid in the peptide name, would be the N-terminal amino acid and written on the left with a free $—NH_3^+$ group.
b. Threonine, the last amino acid in the peptide name, would be the C-terminal amino acid and written on the right with a free $—COO^-$ group.
c. The O is removed from the carboxylate group of valine and two H atoms are removed from the ammonium ion in threonine to form water. The C=O part of valine and the N—H part of threonine are joined, which gives a peptide (amide) bond in the dipeptide.
d. In the name of a peptide, the ending *ine* of valine is change to *yl*, which is *valyl*. The last amino acid, threonine, does not change its name. Thus, the dipeptide is named valylthreonine.

QUESTIONS AND PROBLEMS

18.4 Proteins

LEARNING GOAL: *Describe protein functions, and draw structures for amino acids and dipeptides.*

18.31 Describe the functional groups found in all α-amino acids.

18.32 How does the polarity of the R group in leucine compare to that of serine?

18.33 Draw the ionized form for each of the following amino acids:
a. glycine **b.** threonine **c.** phenylalanine

18.34 Draw the ionized form for each of the following amino acids:
a. tyrosine **b.** leucine **c.** methionine

18.35 Classify each of the amino acids in Problem 18.33 as nonpolar or polar. If polar, indicate if the R group is neutral, acidic, or basic. Indicate if each would be hydrophobic or hydrophilic.

18.36 Classify each of the amino acids in Problem 18.34 as nonpolar or polar. If polar, indicate if the R group is neutral, acidic, or basic. Indicate if each would be hydrophobic or hydrophilic.

18.37 Give the name of the amino acid represented by each of the following abbreviations:
a. Ala **b.** V
c. Lys **d.** C

18.38 Give the name of the amino acid represented by each of the following abbreviations:
a. Trp **b.** M
c. Pro **d.** G

18.39 Draw the condensed structural formula for each of the following peptides:
a. Ala-Cys **b.** Ser-Phe **c.** Gly-Ala-Val

18.40 Draw the condensed structural formula for each of the following peptides:
a. Met-Asp **b.** Thr-Trp **c.** Leu-Glu-Lys

18.5 Protein Structure

LEARNING GOAL

Identify the levels of structure of a protein.

A **protein** is a polypeptide of 50 or more amino acids that has biological activity. Each protein in our cells has a unique sequence of amino acids that determines its three-dimensional structure and biological function.

Primary Structure

The **primary structure** of a protein is the particular sequence of amino acids held together by peptide bonds. The first protein to have its primary structure determined was insulin, which was accomplished by Frederick Sanger in 1953. Since that time, scientists have determined the amino acid sequences of thousands of proteins. Insulin is a hormone that regulates the glucose level in the blood. In the primary structure of human insulin, there are two polypeptide chains. In chain A, there are 21 amino acids, and in chain B there are 30 amino acids. The polypeptide chains are held together by *disulfide bonds* formed by the thiol groups of the cysteine amino acids in each of the chains (see Figure 18.9). Today, human insulin with this exact same structure is produced in large quantities through genetic engineering for the treatment of diabetes.

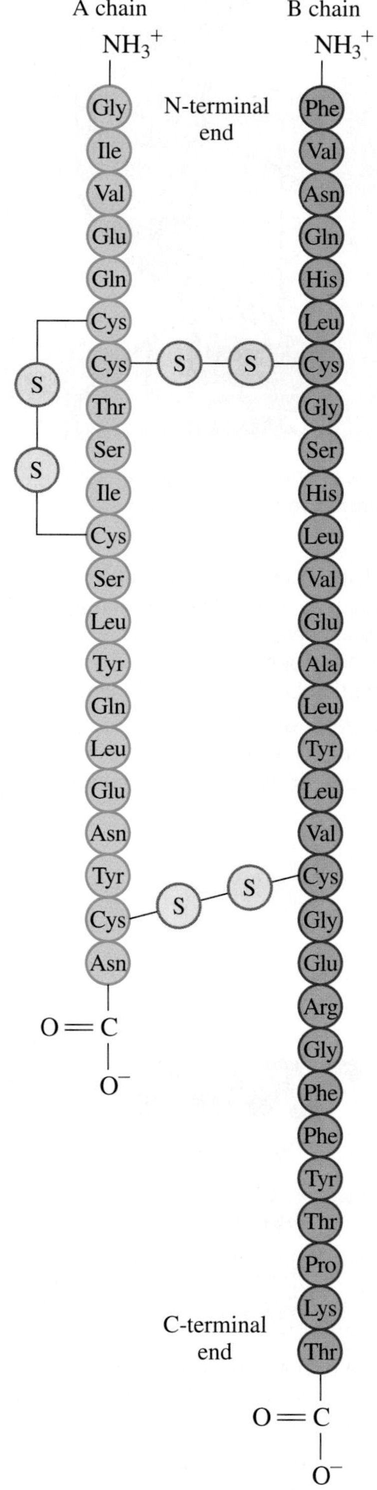

FIGURE 18.9 The sequence of amino acids in human insulin is the primary structure.

Q What kinds of bonds occur in the primary structure of a protein?

CONCEPT CHECK 18.5 Primary Structure

What are the three-letter and one-letter abbreviations of the possible tetrapeptides containing two valines, one proline, and one histidine if the C-terminal amino acid is proline?

ANSWER

The C-terminal amino acid of proline in the possible tetrapeptides would be preceded by three different sequences of two valines and one histidine: Val-Val-His-Pro (VVHP), Val-His-Val-Pro (VHVP), and His-Val-Val-Pro (HVVP).

Secondary Structure

The **secondary structure** of a protein describes the type of structure that forms when amino acids form hydrogen bonds within a polypeptide or between polypeptides.

In an alpha helix (α helix), hydrogen bonds form between each N—H group and the oxygen of a C=O group in the next turn of the α helix (see Figure 18.10). Because there are many hydrogen bonds along the peptide, it has a helical or coiled shape.

In another secondary structure known as the *beta-pleated sheet* (*β-pleated sheet*), hydrogen bonds hold polypeptide chains together side by side. The hydrogen bonds holding the sheets tightly in place account for the strength and durability of proteins such as silk (see Figure 18.11).

Collagen, the most abundant protein, makes up as much as one-third of all the protein in vertebrates. It is found in connective tissue, blood vessels, skin, tendons, ligaments, the cornea of the eye, and cartilage. The strong structure of collagen is a result of three polypeptides woven together like a braid to form a *triple helix*. When several triple helixes wrap together, they form the fibrils that make up connective tissues and tendons. In a young person, collagen is elastic. As a person ages, additional bonds form between the fibrils, which make collagen less elastic. Cartilage and tendons become more brittle, and wrinkles are seen in the skin.

The shape of an alpha helix is similar to that of a spiral staircase.

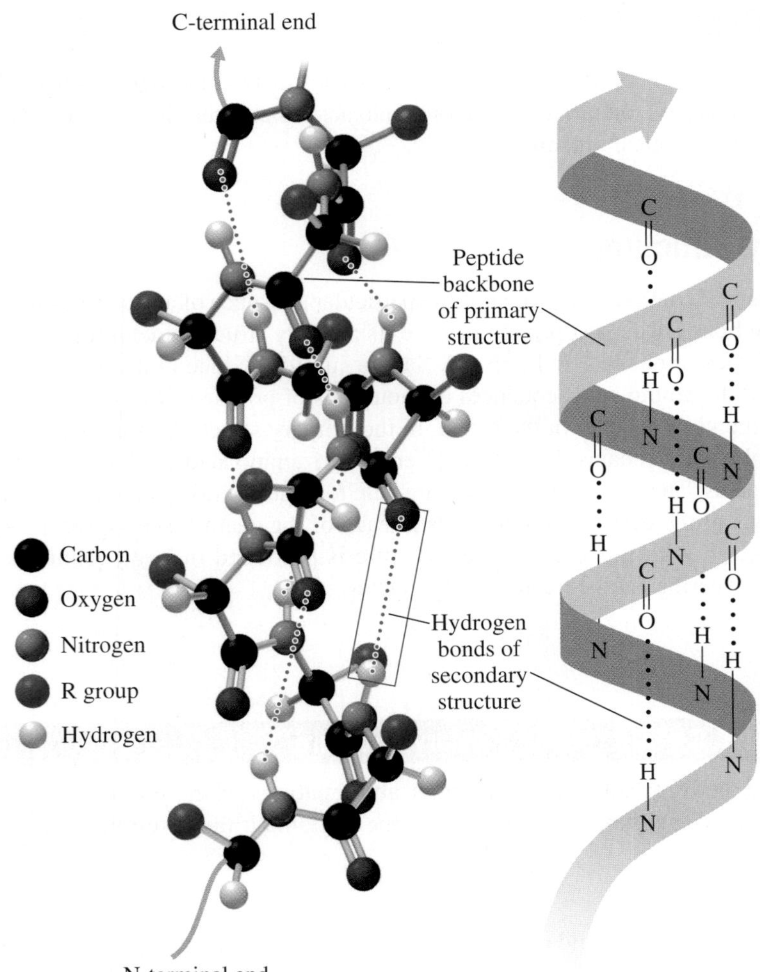

FIGURE 18.10 The α (alpha) helix acquires a coiled shape from hydrogen bonds between the N—H of the peptide bond in one loop and the C=O of the peptide bond in the next loop.

Q What are partial charges of the H in N—H and the O in C=O that permit hydrogen bonds to form?

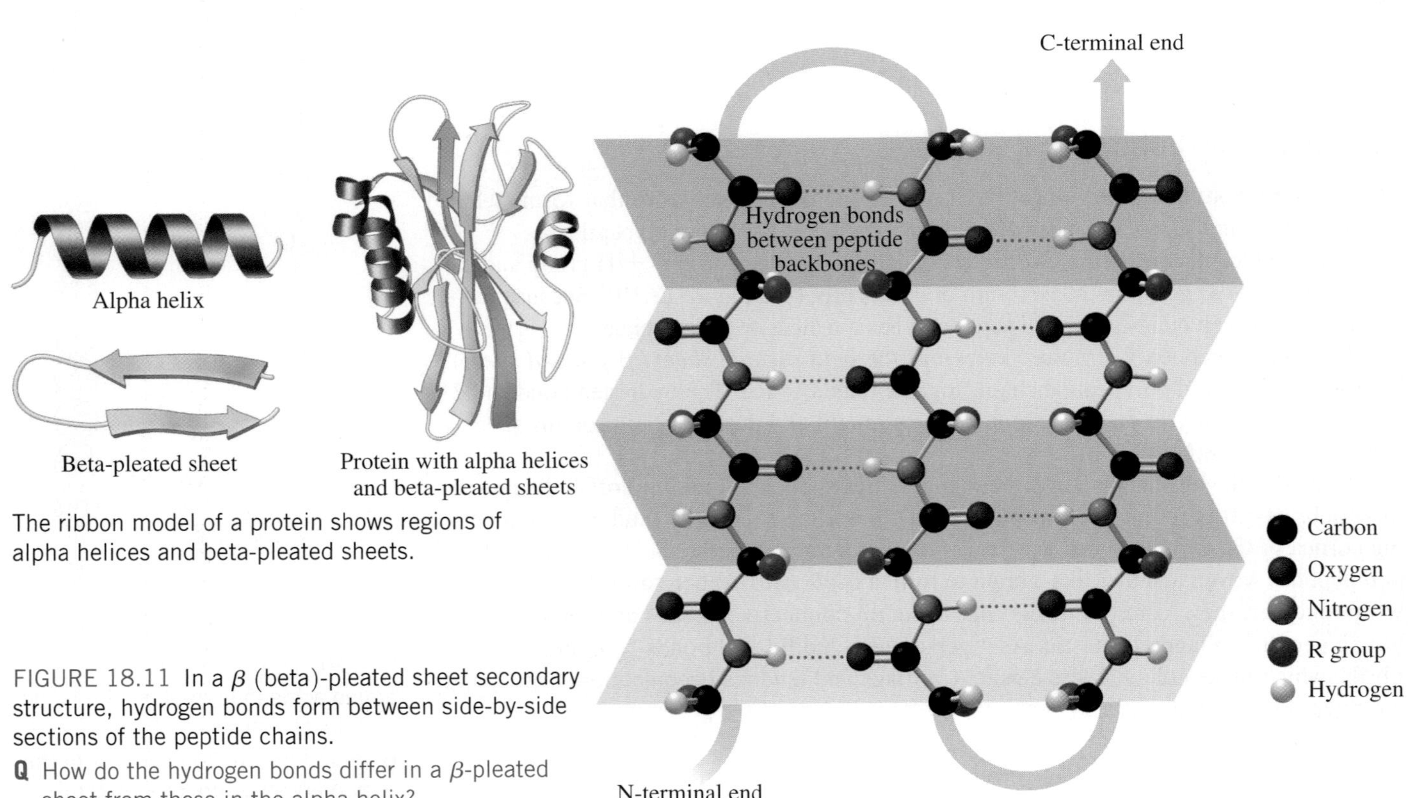

The ribbon model of a protein shows regions of alpha helices and beta-pleated sheets.

FIGURE 18.11 In a β (beta)-pleated sheet secondary structure, hydrogen bonds form between side-by-side sections of the peptide chains.

Q How do the hydrogen bonds differ in a β-pleated sheet from those in the alpha helix?

CONCEPT CHECK 18.6 Identifying Secondary Structures

Indicate the secondary structure (α helix, β-pleated sheet, or triple helix) described in each of the following:

a. a structure that has hydrogen bonds between adjacent polypeptide chains
b. three α-helical polypeptides woven together
c. a peptide chain with a coiled or corkscrew shape that is held in place by hydrogen bonds

ANSWER

a. β-pleated sheet
b. triple helix
c. α helix

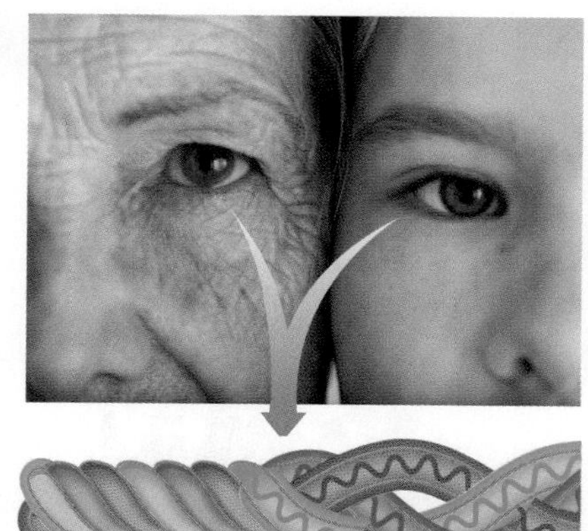

Collagen fibers are triple helixes of polypeptide chains held together by hydrogen bonds.

Tertiary Structure

The **tertiary structure** of a protein involves attractions and repulsions between the R groups of the amino acids in the polypeptide chain. It is the unique three-dimensional shape of the *tertiary structure* that determines the biological function of the molecule. Table 18.8 lists the interactions that stabilize the tertiary structures of proteins.

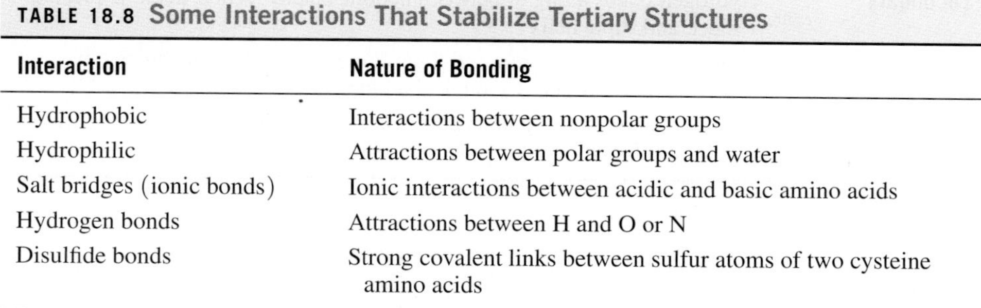

TABLE 18.8 Some Interactions That Stabilize Tertiary Structures

Interaction	Nature of Bonding
Hydrophobic	Interactions between nonpolar groups
Hydrophilic	Attractions between polar groups and water
Salt bridges (ionic bonds)	Ionic interactions between acidic and basic amino acids
Hydrogen bonds	Attractions between H and O or N
Disulfide bonds	Strong covalent links between sulfur atoms of two cysteine amino acids

CONCEPT CHECK 18.7 Tertiary Structural Level

In a tertiary structure of a protein, identify the type of interaction that occurs between

a. lysine and aspartic acid
b. phenylalanine and proline

ANSWER

a. An ionic bond called a salt bridge occurs between the $-NH_3^+$ in the R group of the basic amino acid lysine and the $-COO^-$ in the R group of aspartic acid.
b. A hydrophobic interaction occurs between two nonpolar R groups.

SAMPLE PROBLEM 18.7 Interactions That Stabilize Tertiary Structures

What type of interaction would you expect between the R groups of the following amino acids?

a. cysteine and cysteine
b. glutamic acid and lysine

SOLUTION

a. Because the cysteine contains $-SH$, a disulfide bond will form.
b. An ionic bond (salt bridge) can form by the interaction of the $-COO^-$ in the R group of glutamic acid and the $-NH_3^+$ in the R group of lysine.

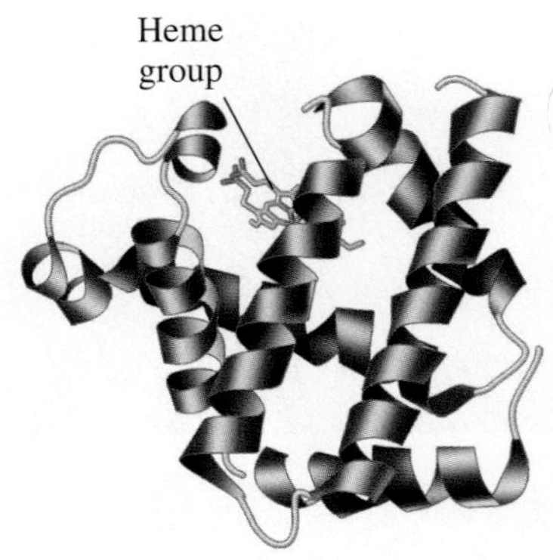

FIGURE 18.12 The ribbon model represents the tertiary structure of the polypeptide chain of myoglobin, which is a globular protein that contains a heme pocket that binds oxygen.

Q Would hydrophilic amino acids be found on the outside or inside of the myoglobin structure?

STUDY CHECK 18.7

What type of interaction would you expect between valine and leucine in the tertiary structure of a protein?

Myoglobin, a single polypeptide chain of 153 amino acids, stores oxygen in skeletal muscle. It forms a compact tertiary structure that contains a pocket of amino acids and a heme group that binds and stores one oxygen (O_2) molecule (see Figure 18.12).

Quaternary Structure

When a biologically active protein consists of two or more polypeptide subunits, the structural level is referred to as a **quaternary structure**. Hemoglobin, a protein that transports oxygen in blood, consists of four polypeptide chains or subunits. The subunits are held together in the quaternary structure by the same kinds of interactions that stabilize the tertiary structures. In the hemoglobin molecule, the quaternary structure of hemoglobin can bind and transport four molecules of oxygen. Table 18.9 and Figure 18.13 summarize the structural levels of proteins.

TABLE 18.9 Summary of Structural Levels in Proteins

Structural Level	Characteristics
Primary	The sequence of amino acids held together by peptide bonds
Secondary	Hydrogen bonds along or between peptide chains form α helix, β-pleated sheet, and triple helix
Tertiary	A protein folds into a compact, three-dimensional shape stabilized by interactions between R groups of amino acids
Quaternary	Two or more protein subunits combine to form a biologically active protein stabilized by the same interactions as in the tertiary structure

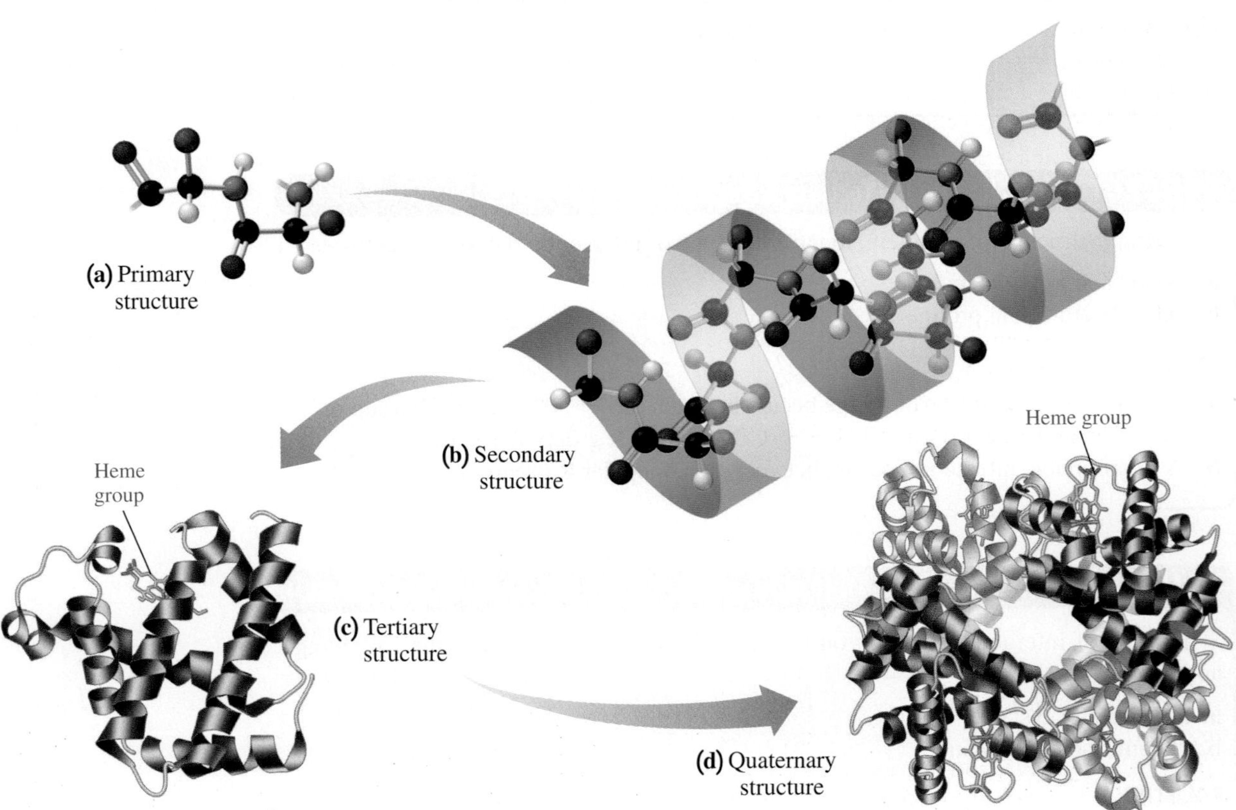

FIGURE 18.13 The quaternary structure of hemoglobin consists of four polypeptide subunits, each containing a heme group that binds an oxygen molecule.

Q What is the difference between a tertiary structure and a quaternary structure?

SAMPLE PROBLEM 18.8 Identifying Protein Structure

Indicate whether the following conditions are present in the primary, secondary, tertiary, and quaternary structures of proteins:

a. disulfide bonds between portions of a protein chain
b. sequence of amino acids held together by peptide bonds
c. hydrophobic interactions

SOLUTION

a. Disulfide bonds help to stabilize the tertiary and quaternary structures of proteins.
b. Peptide bonds form between amino acids in the primary structure of a protein.
c. Hydrophobic interactions between two nonpolar R groups occur in the tertiary and quaternary structures of proteins.

STUDY CHECK 18.8

What structural level is represented by the grouping of two subunits in insulin?

QUESTIONS AND PROBLEMS

18.5 Protein Structure

LEARNING GOAL: *Identify the levels of structure of a protein.*

18.41 Two peptides each contain one molecule of valine and two molecules of serine. What are their possible primary structures?

18.42 What are three different types of secondary protein structure?

18.43 What is the difference in bonding between an α helix and a β-pleated sheet?

18.44 How is the secondary structure of a β-pleated sheet different from that of a triple helix?

18.45 What type of interaction would you expect between the following amino acids in a tertiary structure?
a. two cysteine residues
b. serine and aspartic acid
c. two leucine residues

18.46 In myoglobin, about one-half of the 153 amino acids have nonpolar R groups.
a. Where would you expect those amino acids to be located in the tertiary structure?
b. Where would you expect the polar R groups to be?

18.47 A portion of a polypeptide chain contains the following sequence of amino acid residues:

-Leu-Val-Cys-Asp-

a. Which amino acid(s) can form a disulfide bond?
b. Which amino acid(s) are likely to be found on the inside of the protein structure? Why?
c. Which amino acid(s) would be found on the outside of the protein? Why?
d. How does the primary structure of a protein affect its tertiary structure?

18.48 State whether the following statements apply to primary, secondary, tertiary, or quaternary protein structure:
a. R groups interact to form disulfide bonds or ionic bonds.
b. Peptide bonds connect amino acids in a polypeptide chain.
c. Several polypeptides are held together by hydrogen bonds between adjacent chains.
d. Hydrogen bonds occur between the O atoms of carbonyl groups and the H atoms bonded to the N atoms in the amide groups to give a coiled shape.
e. Hydrophobic R groups seeking a nonpolar environment move toward the inside of the folded protein.
f. Protein chains of collagen form a triple helix.
g. An active protein contains four tertiary subunits.

18.6 Proteins as Enzymes

LEARNING GOAL

Describe the role of an enzyme in an enzyme-catalyzed reaction.

An **enzyme** has a unique three-dimensional shape that recognizes and binds a small group of reacting molecules called *substrates*. In a catalyzed reaction, an enzyme must first bind to a substrate in a way that favors catalysis.

A typical enzyme is much larger than its substrate. However, within its large tertiary structure, there is a region called the **active site** that binds a substrate or substrates and catalyzes the reaction. This active site is often a small pocket that closely fits the structure of the substrate (see Figure 18.14).

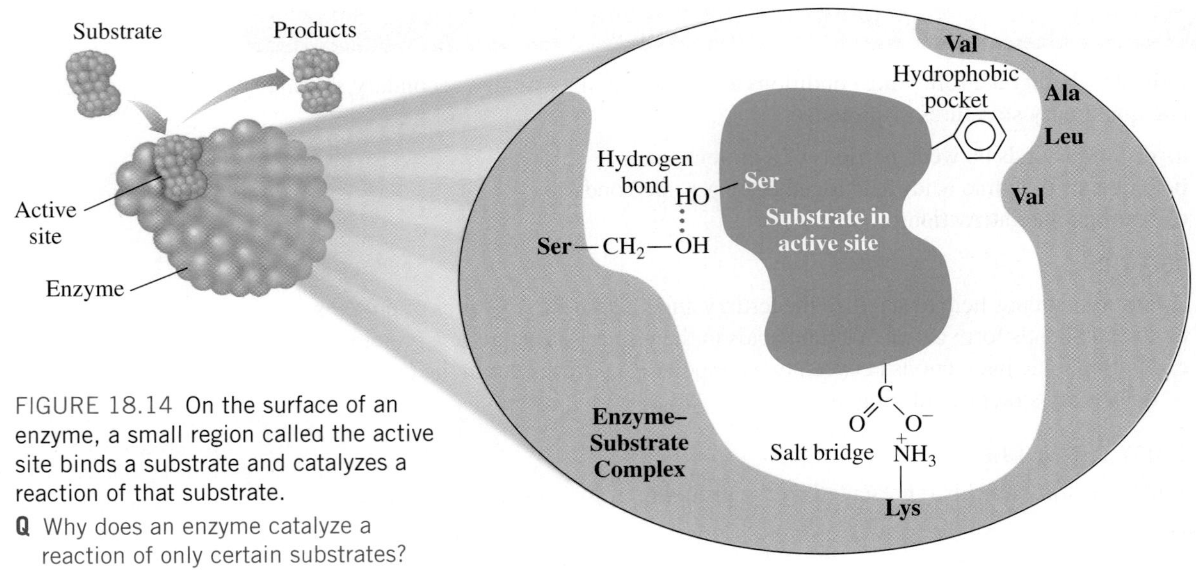

FIGURE 18.14 On the surface of an enzyme, a small region called the active site binds a substrate and catalyzes a reaction of that substrate.

Q Why does an enzyme catalyze a reaction of only certain substrates?

Enzyme-Catalyzed Reaction

The combination of an enzyme (E) and a substrate (S) within the active site forms an *enzyme–substrate* (ES) *complex* that provides an alternative pathway for the reaction with lower activation energy. Within the active site, the amino acid R groups catalyze the reaction to give an *enzyme–product* (EP) *complex*. Then the products are released, and the enzyme is available to bind to another substrate molecule.

$$\mathbf{E + S} \rightleftharpoons \mathbf{ES\ complex} \longrightarrow \mathbf{EP\ complex} \longrightarrow \mathbf{E + P}$$

Enzyme and Substrate — Enzyme–Substrate Complex — Enzyme–Product Complex — Enzyme and Product

Models of Enzyme Action

An early theory of enzyme action, called the **lock-and-key model**, described the active site as having a rigid, inflexible shape. According to the lock-and-key model, the shape of the active site was analogous to a lock, and its substrate was the key that specifically fit that lock. However, this model was a static one that did not allow for the flexibility of the tertiary shape of an enzyme and the way we now know that the active site can adjust to the shape of a substrate.

In the dynamic model of enzyme action, called the **induced-fit model**, the flexibility of the active site allows it to adapt to the shape of the substrate. At the same time, the shape of the substrate is modified to better fit the geometry of the active site. As a result, the fit of both the active site and the substrate provides the best alignment for the catalysis of the reaction of the substrate. In the induced-fit model, substrate and enzyme work together to acquire a geometrical arrangement that lowers the activation energy.

In the hydrolysis of the disaccharide sucrose by the enzyme sucrase, a molecule of sucrose binds to the active site of sucrase. As the sucrose binds to the enzyme, both the active site and the substrate sucrose change shape. In this ES complex, the glycosidic bond of sucrose is in a position that is favorable for hydrolysis, which is the splitting by water of a large molecule into smaller parts. The R groups on the amino acid in the active site then catalyze the hydrolysis of sucrose, which produces the monosaccharides glucose and fructose. Because the structures of the products are no longer attracted to the active site, they are released, which allows sucrase to react with another sucrose (see Figure 18.15).

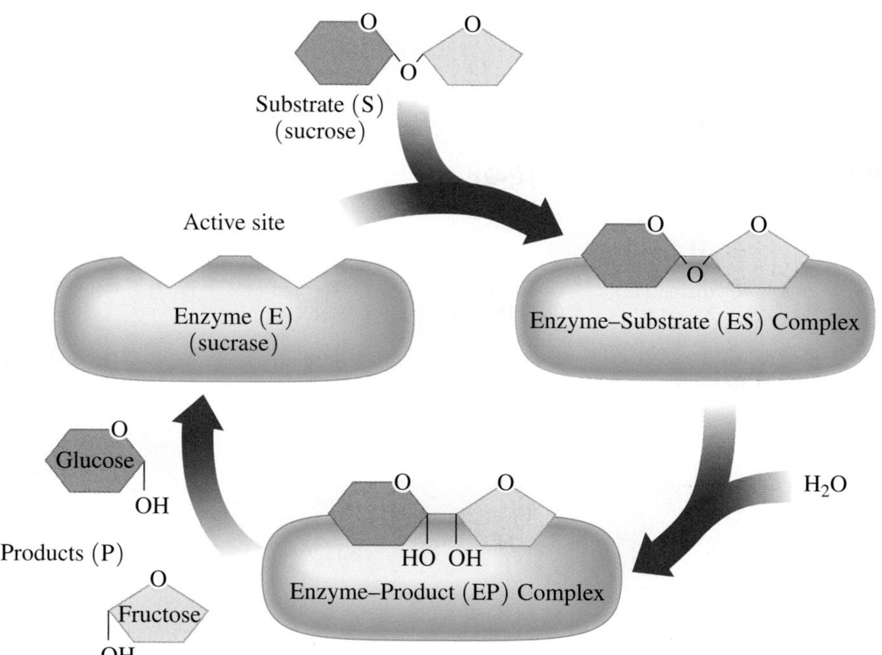

FIGURE 18.15 In the induced-fit model, a flexible active site and substrate both adjust to provide the best fit for the reaction. Sucrose binds to the active site to align the glycosidic bond for hydrolysis. The monosaccharide products are released, and the enzyme binds to another sucrose.

Q Why does the enzyme-catalyzed hydrolysis of sucrose go faster than the hydrolysis of sucrose in the chemistry laboratory?

QUESTIONS AND PROBLEMS

18.6 Proteins as Enzymes

LEARNING GOAL: *Describe the role of an enzyme in an enzyme-catalyzed reaction.*

18.49 Match the terms, (1) enzyme, (2) enzyme–substrate complex, and (3) substrate, with each of the following:
- **a.** has a tertiary structure that recognizes the substrate
- **b.** has a structure that fits the active site of an enzyme
- **c.** the combination of an enzyme with the substrate

18.50 Match the terms, (1) active site, (2) lock-and-key model, and (3) induced-fit model, with each of the following:
- **a.** the portion of an enzyme where catalytic activity occurs
- **b.** an active site that adapts to the shape of a substrate
- **c.** an active site that has a rigid shape

18.51 a. Write an equation that represents an enzyme-catalyzed reaction.
- **b.** How is the active site different from the whole enzyme structure?

18.52 a. Why does an enzyme speed up the reaction of a substrate?
- **b.** After the products have formed, what happens to the enzyme?

18.7 Nucleic Acids

LEARNING GOAL

Describe the structure of the nucleic acids in DNA and RNA.

There are two closely related types of nucleic acids: deoxyribonucleic acid **(DNA)** and ribonucleic acid **(RNA)**. Both are polymers of repeating monomer units known as *nucleotides*. A DNA molecule may contain several million nucleotides; smaller RNA molecules may contain up to several thousand. Each nucleotide has three components: a base, a five-carbon sugar, and a phosphate group (see Figure 18.16).

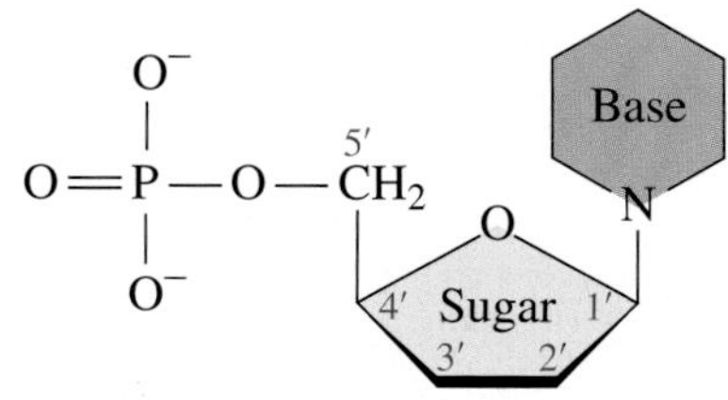

FIGURE 18.16 A diagram of the general structure of a nucleotide found in nucleic acids.

Q In a nucleotide, what types of groups are bonded to a five-carbon sugar?

Bases

The *bases* in nucleic acids are derivatives of *pyrimidine* or *purine*. In DNA, the purine bases are adenine (A) and guanine (G), and the pyrimidine bases are cytosine (C) and thymine (T). In RNA, thymine (T) is replaced by uracil (U); adenine (A), guanine (G), and cytosine (C) are the same as in DNA (see Figure 18.17).

Pyrimidine

Purine

Pyrimidines

Cytosine (C)
(DNA and RNA)

Thymine (T)
(DNA only)

Uracil (U)
(RNA only)

Purines

Adenine (A)
(DNA and RNA)

Guanine (G)
(DNA and RNA)

FIGURE 18.17 DNA contains the bases A, G, C, and T; RNA contains A, G, C, and U.

Q Which bases are found in DNA?

Pentose Sugars in RNA and DNA

Ribose in RNA

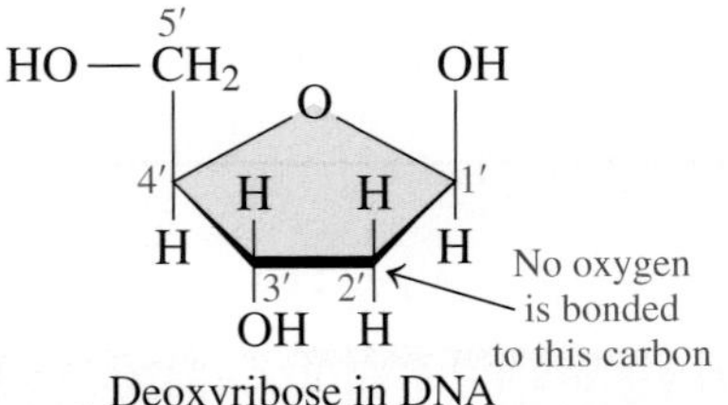

Deoxyribose in DNA

FIGURE 18.18 The five-carbon pentose sugar found in RNA is ribose and deoxyribose in DNA.

Q What is the difference between ribose and deoxyribose?

Ribose and Deoxyribose Sugars

In RNA, the five-carbon sugar is *ribose*, which gives the letter R in the abbreviation RNA. The atoms in the pentose sugars are numbered with primes (1′, 2′, 3′, 4′, and 5′) to differentiate them from the atoms in the bases. In DNA, the five-carbon sugar is *deoxyribose*, which is similar to ribose except that there is no hydroxyl (—OH) group on C2′. The *deoxy* prefix means "without oxygen" and provides the D in DNA (see Figure 18.18).

Nucleosides and Nucleotides

A **nucleoside** is produced when a pyrimidine or purine forms a glycosidic bond to C1′ of a sugar, either ribose or deoxyribose. For example, adenine, a purine, and ribose form a nucleoside called adenosine.

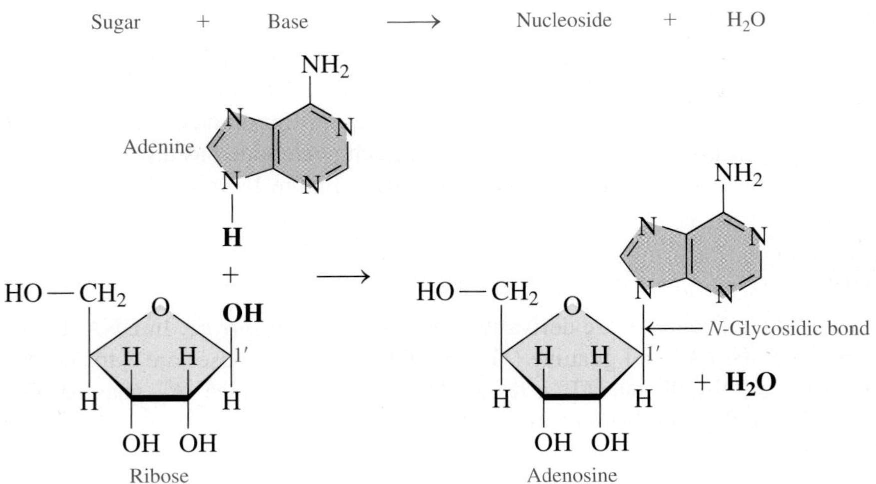

A base forms an *N*-glycosidic bond with ribose or deoxyribose to form a nucleoside.

Nucleotides are produced when the C5′—OH group of ribose or deoxyribose in a nucleoside forms a phosphate ester. All the nucleotides in RNA and DNA are shown in Figure 18.19.

Adenosine-5′-monophosphate (AMP)
Deoxyadenosine-5′-monophosphate (dAMP)

Guanosine-5′-monophosphate (GMP)
Deoxyguanosine-5′-monophosphate (dGMP)

Cytidine-5′-monophosphate (CMP)
Deoxycytidine-5′-monophosphate (dCMP)

Uridine-5′-monophosphate (UMP)

Deoxythymidine-5′-monophosphate (dTMP)

FIGURE 18.19 The nucleotides of RNA are similar to those of DNA, except in DNA (shown in magenta) the sugar is deoxyribose and deoxythymidine replaces uridine.

Q What are two differences in the nucleotides of RNA and DNA?

The name of a nucleoside that contains a purine ends with *osine*, whereas a nucleoside that contains a pyrimidine ends with *idine*. The names of nucleosides of DNA add *deoxy* to the beginning of their names. The corresponding nucleotides in RNA and DNA are named by adding 5′-monophosphate. Although the letters A, G, C, U, and T represent the bases, they are often used in the abbreviations of the respective nucleotides.

Structure of Nucleic Acids

The **nucleic acids** are polymers of many nucleotides in which the 3′-hydroxyl group of the sugar in one nucleotide bonds to the phosphate group on the C5′-carbon atom in the sugar of the next nucleotide. This link between the sugars in adjacent nucleotides is referred to as a **phosphodiester bond**. As more nucleotides are added, a backbone forms that consists of alternating sugar and phosphate groups.

In any nucleic acid, the sugar at one end has a free 5′-phosphate group, and the sugar at the other end has a free 3′-hydroxyl group. A nucleic acid sequence is read from the free 5′-phosphate to the free 3′-hydroxyl using only the letters of the bases. For example, the nucleotide sequence in the section of RNA shown in Figure 18.20 is —A C G U—.

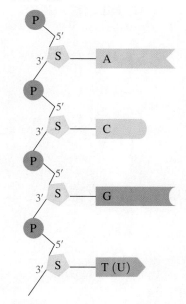

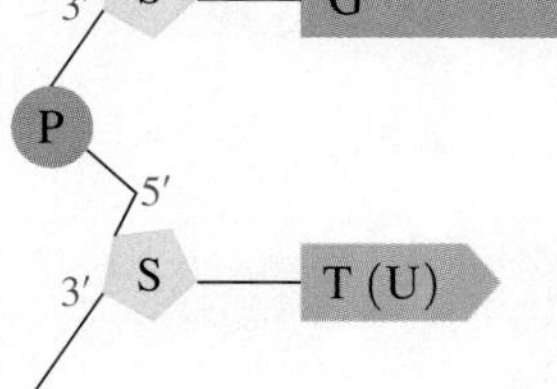

In the primary structure of nucleic acids, each sugar (S) in a sugar–phosphate backbone is attached to a base (A, C, G, or T(U)).

RNA (ribonucleic acid)

Free 5′-end

Adenine (A)

Cytosine (C)

Guanine (G)

Uracil (U)

3′–5′-Phosphodiester bond

Free 3′-end

FIGURE 18.20 In the primary structure of an RNA, the nucleotides are linked by 3′–5′ phosphodiester bonds.

Q What is the abbreviation for the sequence of nucleotides in this RNA section?

The double helix is the characteristic shape of DNA molecules.

DNA Double Helix: A Secondary Structure

In 1953, James Watson and Francis Crick proposed that DNA was a **double helix** that consists of two polynucleotide strands winding about each other like a spiral staircase. The sugar–phosphate backbones are analogous to the outside railings, with the bases arranged like steps along the inside.

Complementary Base Pairs

Each of the bases along one polynucleotide strand forms hydrogen bonds to a specific base on the opposite DNA strand. Adenine only bonds to thymine, and guanine only bonds to cytosine (see Figure 18.21). The pairs A—T and G—C are called **complementary base pairs**. The specific pairing of the bases occurs because adenine and thymine form two hydrogen bonds, while cytosine and guanine form three hydrogen bonds.

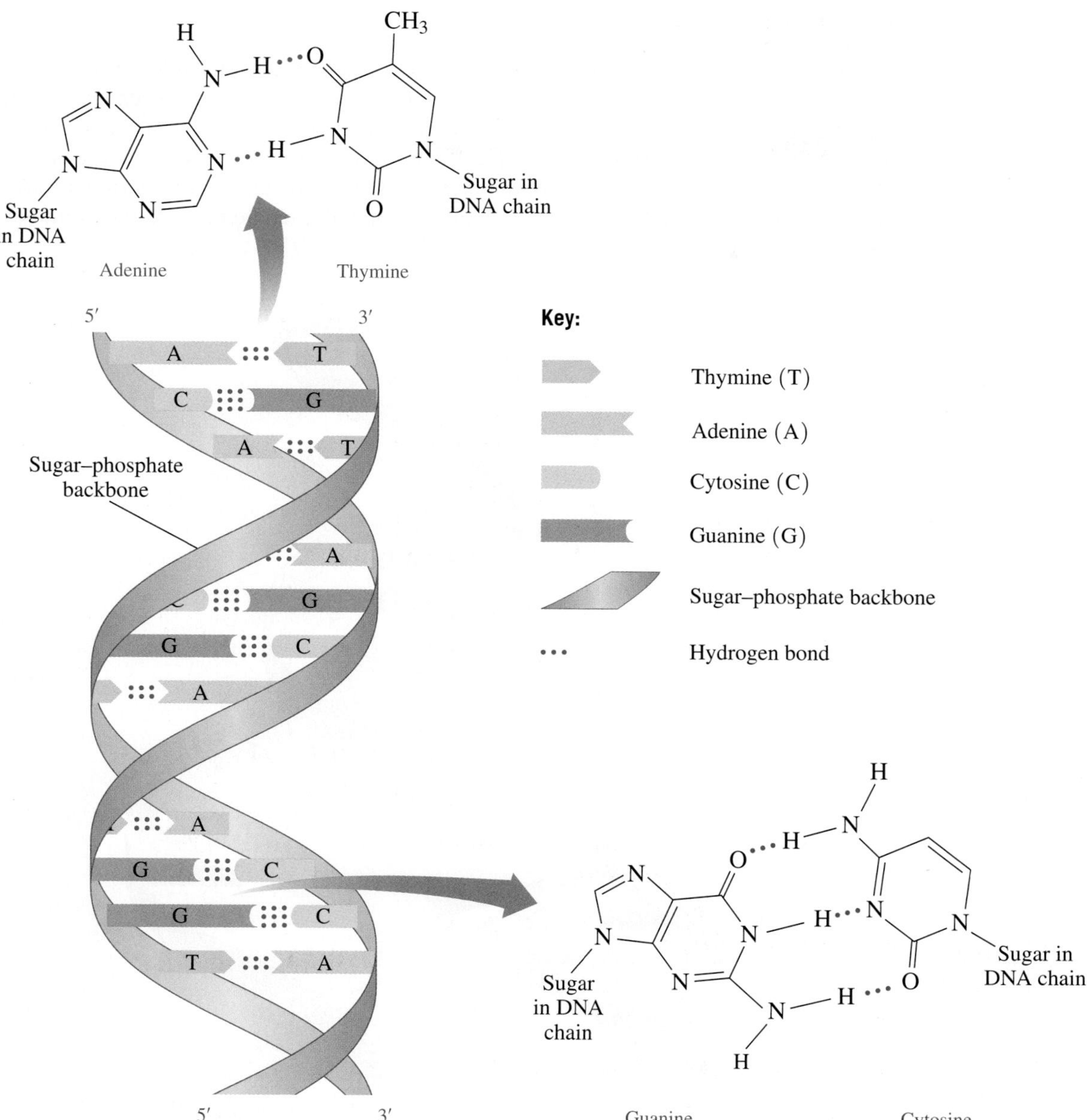

FIGURE 18.21 Hydrogen bonds between complementary base pairs hold the polynucleotide strands together in the double helix of DNA.

Q Why are G—C base pairs more stable than A—T base pairs?

SAMPLE PROBLEM 18.9 Complementary Base Pairs

Write the complementary base sequence for the following segment of a strand of DNA:

—A C G A T C T—

SOLUTION

In the complementary strand of DNA, the base A pairs with T, and G pairs with C.

Given segment of DNA: —A C G A T C T—

Complementary segment: —T G C T A G A—

STUDY CHECK 18.9

Write the complementary base sequence for the following segment of a strand of DNA:

—G G T T A A C C —

DNA Replication

In DNA **replication**, the strands in the parent DNA separate, which allows the synthesis of complementary strands of DNA. The replication process begins when an enzyme catalyzes the unwinding of a portion of the double helix by breaking the hydrogen bonds between the complementary bases. These single strands or *parent DNA* now act as templates for the synthesis of new complementary strands of DNA (see Figure 18.22). Within the nucleus, nucleotides for each base form hydrogen bonds with their complementary bases.

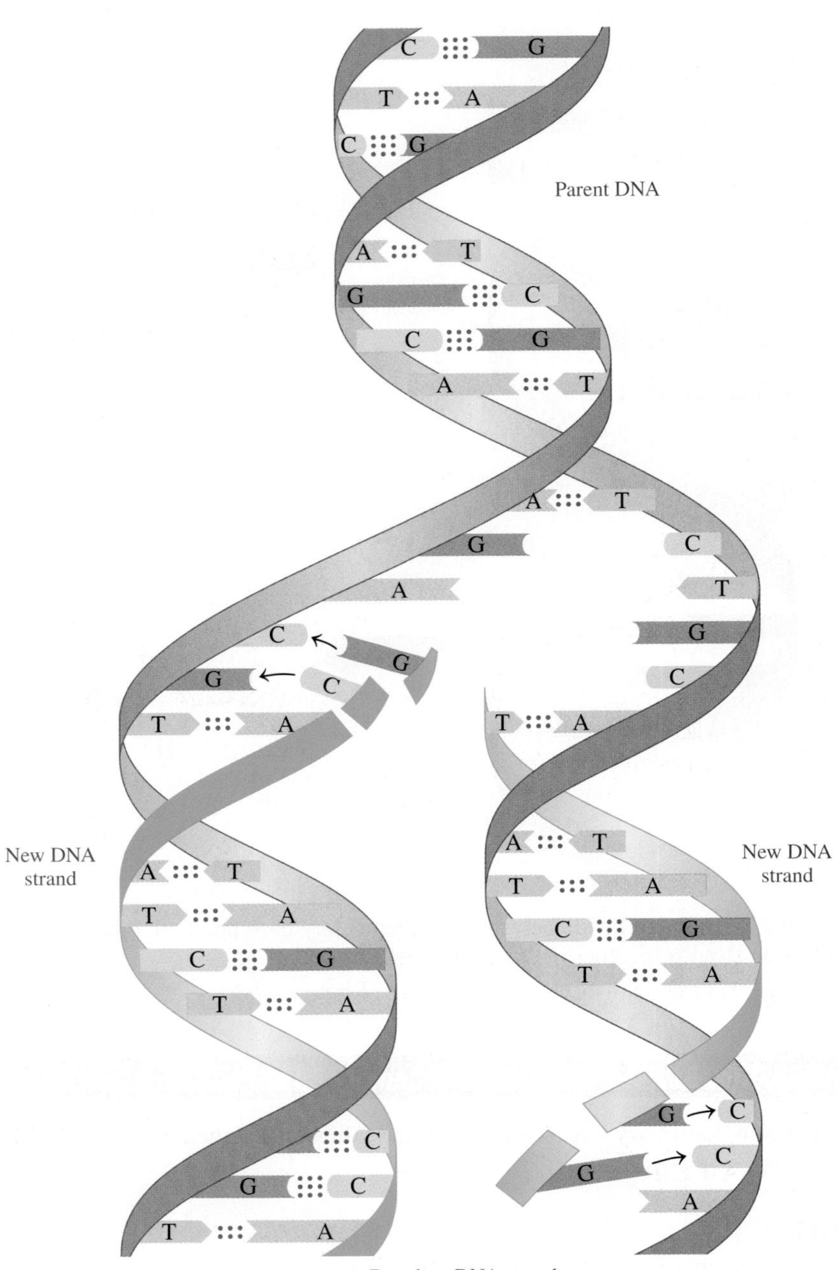

FIGURE 18.22 In DNA replication, the separate strands of the parent DNA are the templates for the synthesis of complementary strands, which produces two exact copies of DNA.

Q How many strands of the parent DNA are in each of the new double-stranded copies of DNA?

Eventually, the entire double helix of the parent DNA is copied. In each new DNA molecule, one strand of the double helix is from the original DNA and one is a newly synthesized strand. This process produces two new DNAs called *daughter DNA* that are identical to each other and exact copies of the original parent DNA. In DNA replication, complementary base pairing ensures the correct placements of bases in the new DNA strands.

QUESTIONS AND PROBLEMS

18.7 Nucleic Acids

LEARNING GOAL: *Describe the structure of the nucleic acids in DNA and RNA.*

18.53 Identify the following base as present in RNA, DNA, or both:
- **a.** thymine
- **b.** NH_2 (structure: N, N, O, H)

18.54 Identify the following base as present in RNA, DNA, or both:
- **a.** guanine
- **b.** NH_2 (structure: N, N, N, N, H)

18.55 How are the two strands of nucleic acid in DNA held together?

18.56 What is meant by complementary base pairing?

18.57 Complete the base sequence in a second DNA strand if a portion of one strand has the following base sequence:
- **a.** —A A A A A A—
- **b.** —G G G G G G—
- **c.** —A G T C C A G G T—
- **d.** —C T G T A T A C G T T—

18.58 Complete the base sequence in a second DNA strand if a portion of one strand has the following base sequence:
- **a.** —T T T T T T—
- **b.** —C C C C C C C C C—
- **c.** —A T G G C A—
- **d.** —A T A T G C G C T A—

18.59 What process ensures that the replication of DNA produces identical copies?

18.60 What is daughter DNA?

18.8 Protein Synthesis

LEARNING GOAL

Describe the synthesis of protein from mRNA.

Ribonucleic acid, RNA, which makes up most of the nucleic acid in the cell, is involved with transmitting the genetic information needed to operate the cell. Similar to DNA, RNA molecules are polymers of nucleotides. However, RNA differs from DNA in several important ways.

1. The sugar in RNA is ribose rather than the deoxyribose found in DNA.
2. The base uracil replaces thymine.
3. RNA molecules are single-stranded nucleic acids.
4. RNA molecules are much smaller than DNA molecules.

Types of RNA

There are three major types of RNA in the cells: *messenger RNA*, *ribosomal RNA*, and *transfer RNA*, which are classified according to their location and function, as shown in Table 18.10.

TABLE 18.10 Types of RNA Molecules in Humans

Type	Abbreviation	Function in the Cell	Percentage of Total RNA
Ribosomal RNA	rRNA	Major component of the ribosomes	80
Messenger RNA	mRNA	Carries information for protein synthesis from the DNA in the nucleus to the ribosomes	5
Transfer RNA	tRNA	Brings amino acids to the ribosomes for protein synthesis	15

In replication, the genetic information in DNA is reproduced by making identical copies of DNA. In **transcription**, the information contained in DNA is transferred to mRNA molecules. In **translation**, the genetic information now present in the mRNA is used to build the sequence of amino acids of the desired protein (see Figure 18.23).

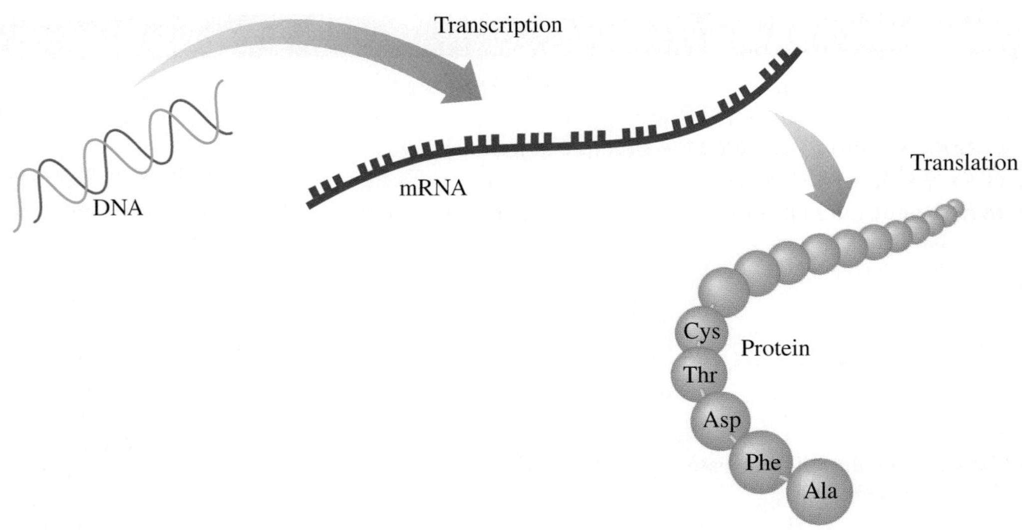

FIGURE 18.23 The genetic information in DNA is replicated in cell division and used to produce messenger RNAs. The mRNAs are converted into amino acids for protein synthesis.

Q What is the difference between transcription and translation?

Transcription begins when the section of DNA to be copied unwinds. One strand of DNA acts as a template as bonds are formed to each complementary base: C is paired with G, T pairs with A, and A pairs with U (not T).

SAMPLE PROBLEM 18.10 RNA Synthesis

The sequence of bases in a segment of the DNA template for mRNA is —C G A T C A—. What corresponding mRNA is produced?

SOLUTION

To form the corresponding section of mRNA, each base in the DNA template is paired with its complementary base: G with C, C with G, T with A, and A with U.

DNA template: —C G A T C A—

↓ ↓ ↓ ↓ ↓ ↓

Complementary base sequence in mRNA: —G C U A G U—

STUDY CHECK 18.10

What is the DNA template that codes for the mRNA segment with the nucleotide sequence —G G G U U U A A A—?

The Genetic Code

The **genetic code** consists of a series of three nucleotides (triplet) in mRNA, called a **codon**. Each codon specifies an amino acid and its sequence in a protein. Early work on protein synthesis showed that repeating triplets of uracil, UUU, produced a polypeptide that contained only phenylalanine. Therefore, a sequence of —UUU UUU UUU— codes for three phenylalanines.

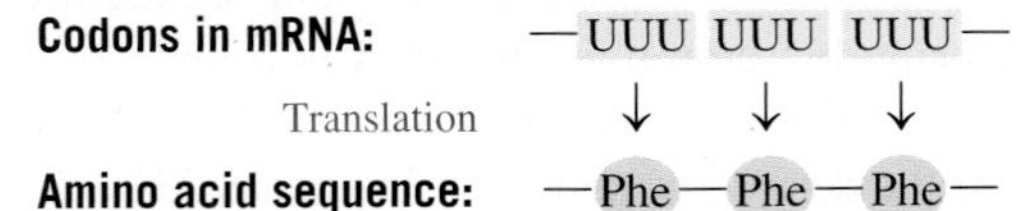

Codons have now been determined for all 20 amino acids. A total of 64 codons is possible from the triplet combinations of A, G, C, and U (see Table 18.11). Three of these, UGA, UAA, and UAG, are stop signals that code for the termination of protein synthesis. All the other codons specify amino acids; one amino acid can have several codons. For example, glycine has four codons: GGU, GGC, GGA, and GGG. The triplet AUG has two roles in protein synthesis. At the beginning of an mRNA, the codon AUG signals the start of protein synthesis. In the middle of a series of codons, AUG codes for the amino acid methionine.

TABLE 18.11 mRNA Codons: The Genetic Code for Amino Acids

First Base	Second Base: U	Second Base: C	Second Base: A	Second Base: G	Third Base
U	UUU Phe	UCU Ser	UAU Tyr	UGU Cys	U
U	UUC Phe	UCC Ser	UAC Tyr	UGC Cys	C
U	UUA Leu	UCA Ser	UAA STOP[b]	UGA STOP[b]	A
U	UUG Leu	UCG Ser	UAG STOP[b]	UGG Trp	G
C	CUU Leu	CCU Pro	CAU His	CGU Arg	U
C	CUC Leu	CCC Pro	CAC His	CGC Arg	C
C	CUA Leu	CCA Pro	CAA Gln	CGA Arg	A
C	CUG Leu	CCG Pro	CAG Gln	CGG Arg	G
A	AUU Ile	ACU Thr	AAU Asn	AGU Ser	U
A	AUC Ile	ACC Thr	AAC Asn	AGC Ser	C
A	AUA Ile	ACA Thr	AAA Lys	AGA Arg	A
A	AUG START[a]/Met	ACG Thr	AAG Lys	AGG Arg	G
G	GUU Val	GCU Ala	GAU Asp	GGU Gly	U
G	GUC Val	GCC Ala	GAC Asp	GGC Gly	C
G	GUA Val	GCA Ala	GAA Glu	GGA Gly	A
G	GUG Val	GCG Ala	GAG Glu	GGG Gly	G

START[a] codon signals the initiation of a peptide chain.
STOP[b] codons signal the end of a peptide chain.

Protein Synthesis: Translation

Once the mRNA is synthesized, it migrates out of the nucleus into the cytoplasm to the ribosomes. At the ribosomes, the *translation* process converts the codons on mRNA into amino acids to make a protein.

Protein synthesis begins when the mRNA combines with a ribosome. There, tRNA molecules, which carry amino acids, align with mRNA, and a peptide bond forms between the amino acids. After the first tRNA detaches from the ribosome, the ribosome shifts to the next codon on the mRNA. Each time the ribosome shifts and the next tRNA aligns with the mRNA, a peptide bond joins the new amino acid to the growing polypeptide chain. After all the amino acids for a particular protein have been linked together by peptide bonds, the ribosome encounters a stop codon. Because there are no tRNAs to complement the termination codon, protein synthesis ends and the completed polypeptide chain is released from the ribosome. Then interactions between the amino acids in the chain form the protein into the three-dimensional structure that makes the polypeptide into a biologically active protein (see Figure 18.24).

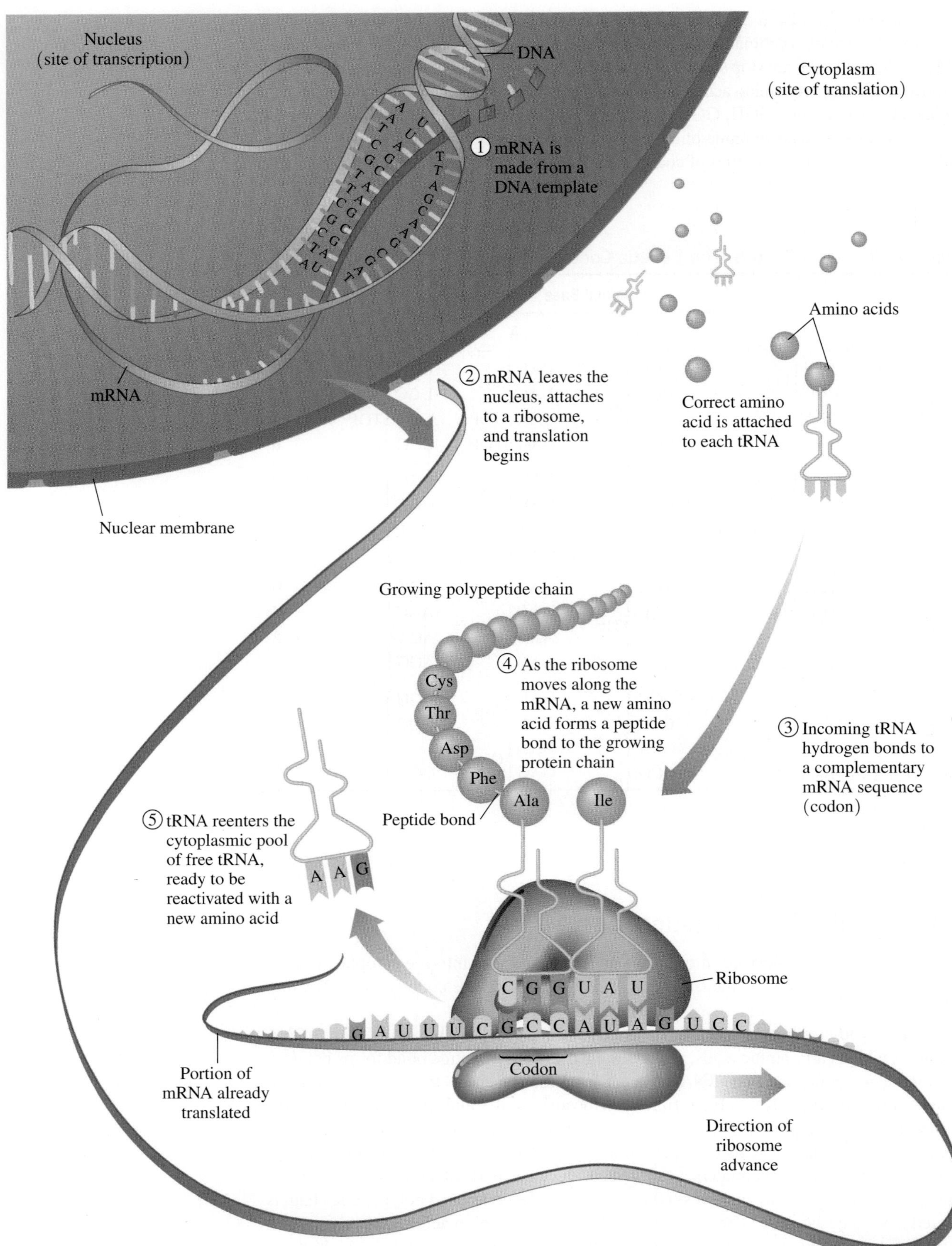

FIGURE 18.24 In the translation process, the mRNA synthesized by transcription attaches to a ribosome, and tRNAs pick up their amino acids and place them in a growing peptide chain.

Q How is the correct amino acid placed in the peptide chain?

CONCEPT CHECK 18.8 The Genetic Code

Indicate the nucleotides in mRNA that code for the following:

a. the amino acid phenylalanine
b. the amino acid proline
c. the start of polypeptide synthesis

ANSWER

a. In mRNA, the codons for the amino acid phenylalanine (Phe) are UUU and UUC.
b. In mRNA, the codons for the amino acid proline (Pro) are CCU, CCC, CCA, and CCG.
c. In mRNA, the codon AUG signals the start of polypeptide synthesis.

SAMPLE PROBLEM 18.11 Protein Synthesis: Translation

What order of amino acids would you expect in a peptide for the mRNA sequence of —UCA AAA GCC CUU—?

SOLUTION

Each of the codons specifies a particular amino acid. Using Table 18.11, we write the codons and the amino acids in the peptide.

	Codon (Three-Base Sequence)	Amino Acid
Analyze the Problem	UCA	serine (Ser)
	AAA	lysine (Lys)
	GCC	alanine (Ala)
	CUU	leucine (Leu)

mRNA codons: —UCA AAA GCC CUU—

↓ ↓ ↓ ↓

Amino acid sequence: —Ser—Lys—Ala—Leu—

STUDY CHECK 18.11

Where would protein synthesis stop in the following series of bases in an mRNA?
—GGG AGC AGU UAG GUU—

QUESTIONS AND PROBLEMS

18.8 Protein Synthesis

LEARNING GOAL: *Describe the synthesis of protein from mRNA.*

18.61 What are the three different types of RNA?

18.62 What are the functions of each type of RNA?

18.63 What is meant by the term *transcription*?

18.64 What bases in mRNA are used to complement the bases A, T, G, and C in DNA?

18.65 Write the corresponding section of mRNA produced from the following section of DNA template:

—C C G A A G G T T C A C—

18.66 Write the corresponding section of mRNA produced from the following section of DNA template:

—T A C G G A A G C T A—

18.67 What amino acid is coded for by each of the following codons?

a. CUG
b. UCC
c. GGU
d. AGG

18.68 What amino acid is coded for by each of the following codons?

a. AAG
b. GUC
c. CGG
d. GCA

CHAPTER REVIEW

18.1 Carbohydrates

LEARNING GOAL: *Classify a carbohydrate as an aldose or a ketose; draw the open-chain and Haworth structures for glucose, galactose, and fructose.*

H—C=O (CHO)
H—C—OH
HO—C—H
H—C—OH
H—C—OH
CH_2OH

- Carbohydrates are composed of carbon, hydrogen, and oxygen.
- Monosaccharides are polyhydroxy aldehydes (aldoses) or ketones (ketoses).
- Monosaccharides are also classified by their number of carbon atoms: *triose*, *tetrose*, *pentose*, or *hexose*. Important monosaccharides are glucose, galactose, and fructose.
- The predominant form of monosaccharides is the cyclic form of five or six atoms.
- The Haworth structure forms by a reaction between a —OH group (usually the one on carbon 5 in hexoses) with the carbon atom of the carbonyl group in the same molecule.

18.2 Disaccharides and Polysaccharides

LEARNING GOAL: *Describe the monosaccharide units and linkages in disaccharides and polysaccharides.*

- Disaccharides are two monosaccharide units joined together by a glycosidic bond.
- In the most common disaccharides maltose, lactose, and sucrose, there is at least one glucose molecule.
- Polysaccharides are polymers of monosaccharide units. Amylose is an unbranched polymer of glucose, and amylopectin is a branched polymer of glucose. Glycogen, the storage form of glucose in animals, is similar to amylopectin with more branching. Cellulose is also a polymer of glucose, but in cellulose the glycosidic bonds are β bonds rather than α bonds.

18.3 Lipids

LEARNING GOAL: *Describe some properties of lipids.*

- Lipids are nonpolar compounds that are not soluble in water.
- Classes of lipids include fats, oils, and steroids.
- Fatty acids are long-chain carboxylic acids that may be saturated or unsaturated.
- Triacylglycerols are esters of glycerol with three fatty acids.
- Animal fats contain more saturated fatty acids and have higher melting points than most vegetable oils.
- The hydrogenation of unsaturated fatty acids converts double bonds to single bonds.
- In saponification, a fat heated with a strong base produces glycerol and the salts of the fatty acids (soaps).

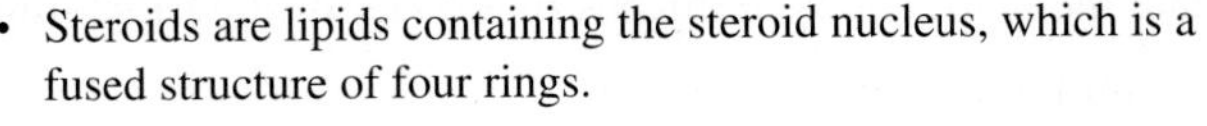

- Steroids are lipids containing the steroid nucleus, which is a fused structure of four rings.

18.4 Proteins

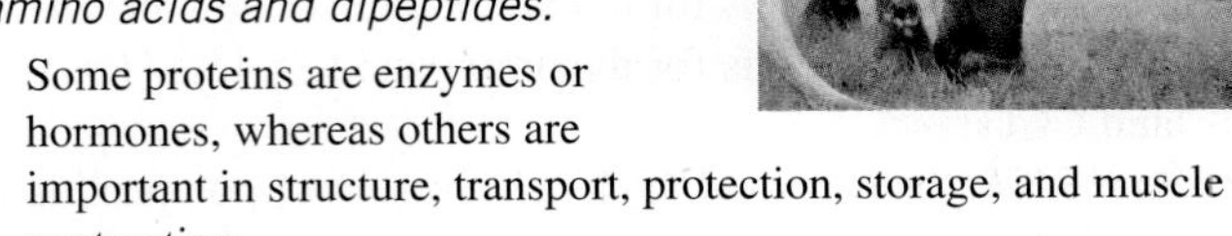

LEARNING GOAL: *Describe protein functions, and draw structures for amino acids and dipeptides.*

- Some proteins are enzymes or hormones, whereas others are important in structure, transport, protection, storage, and muscle contraction.
- A group of 20 amino acids provides the molecular building blocks of proteins.
- Attached to the central (alpha) carbon of each amino acid is an ammonium group, a carboxylate group, and a unique R group.
- Peptides form when the C-terminal of one amino acid bonds with the N-terminal of a second amino acid. Long chains of amino acids are called proteins.

18.5 Protein Structure

LEARNING GOAL: *Identify the levels of structure of a protein.*

Heme group

- The primary structure of a protein is its sequence of amino acids.
- In the secondary structure, hydrogen bonds between peptide groups produce a characteristic shape such as an α helix, a β-pleated sheet, or a triple helix.
- A tertiary structure is stabilized by interactions between R groups of amino acids in one region of the polypeptide chain with R groups in different regions of the protein.
- In a quaternary structure, two or more tertiary subunits combine for biological activity.

18.6 Proteins as Enzymes

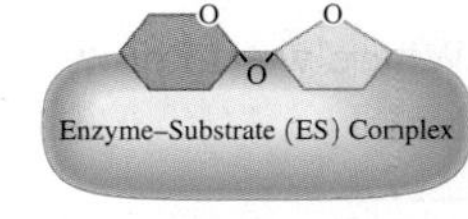

LEARNING GOAL: *Describe the role of an enzyme in an enzyme-catalyzed reaction.*

- Enzymes are proteins that act as biological catalysts by accelerating the rate of cellular reactions.
- Within the tertiary structure of an enzyme, a small pocket called the active site binds the substrates.
- In the lock-and-key model, a substrate precisely fits the shape of the active site.
- In the induced-fit model, substrates induce the active site to change structure to give an optimal fit by the substrate. In the enzyme–substrate complex, catalysis takes place when the amino acid R groups react with a substrate.
- The products are released, and the enzyme is available to bind another substrate molecule.

18.7 Nucleic Acids

LEARNING GOAL: *Describe the structure of the nucleic acids in DNA and RNA.*

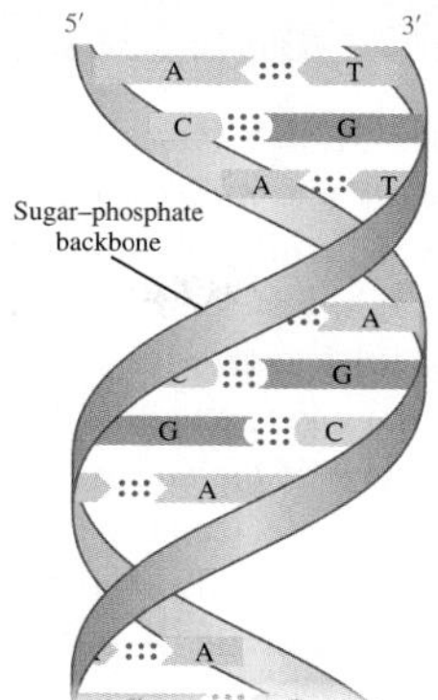

- Nucleic acids, such as deoxyribonucleic acid (DNA) and ribonucleic acid (RNA), are polymers of nucleotides.
- A nucleotide is a combination of a base, a pentose sugar, and a phosphate group.
- In DNA, the sugar is deoxyribose and the base can be adenine, thymine, guanine, or cytosine. In RNA, the sugar is ribose and uracil replaces thymine.
- Each nucleic acid has its own unique sequence of bases.
- A DNA molecule consists of two strands of nucleotides that are wound around each other like a spiral staircase.
- The two strands are held together by hydrogen bonds between complementary base pairs: A with T, and G with C.

18.8 Protein Synthesis

LEARNING GOAL: *Describe the synthesis of protein from mRNA.*

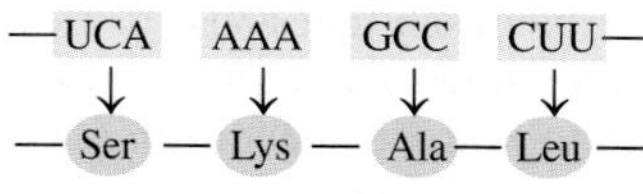

- The bases in the mRNA are complementary to the DNA, except A in DNA is paired with U in RNA.
- The genetic code consists of a series of codons, which are sequences of three bases that specify the order of amino acids in a protein.
- Proteins are synthesized at the ribosomes.
- During translation, tRNAs bring the appropriate amino acids to the mRNA at the ribosome and peptide bonds form.
- When the polypeptide is released, it takes on its secondary and tertiary structures and becomes a functional protein in the cell.

CONCEPT MAP

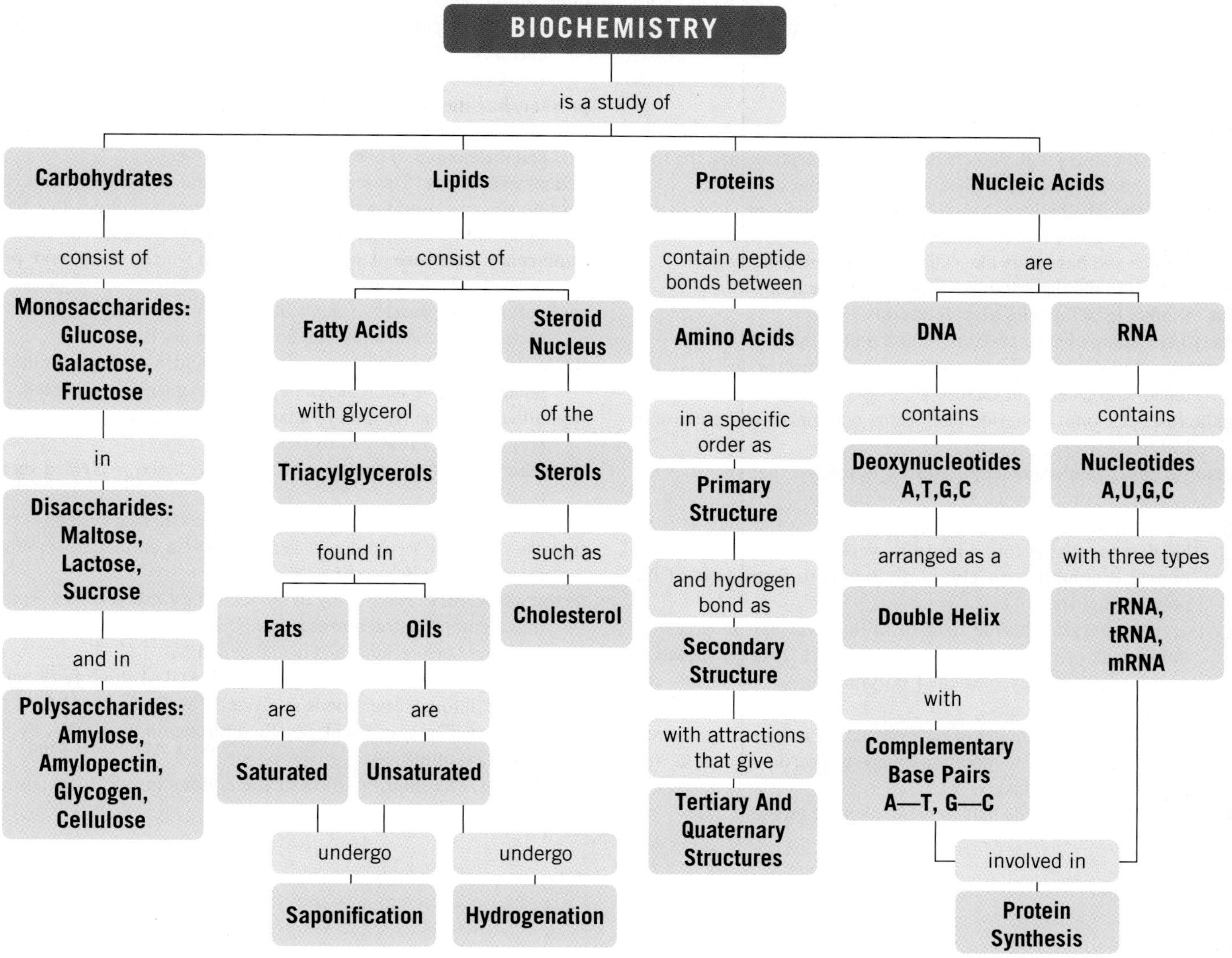

BIOCHEMISTRY

is a study of

- **Carbohydrates**
  - consist of
  - **Monosaccharides: Glucose, Galactose, Fructose**
  - in
  - **Disaccharides: Maltose, Lactose, Sucrose**
  - and in
  - **Polysaccharides: Amylose, Amylopectin, Glycogen, Cellulose**
- **Lipids**
  - consist of
  - **Fatty Acids**
    - with glycerol
    - **Triacylglycerols**
    - found in
    - **Fats** — are — **Saturated**
    - **Oils** — are — **Unsaturated**
    - undergo — **Saponification**
    - undergo — **Hydrogenation**
  - **Steroid Nucleus**
    - of the
    - **Sterols**
    - such as
    - **Cholesterol**
- **Proteins**
  - contain peptide bonds between
  - **Amino Acids**
  - in a specific order as
  - **Primary Structure**
  - and hydrogen bond as
  - **Secondary Structure**
  - with attractions that give
  - **Tertiary And Quaternary Structures**
- **Nucleic Acids**
  - are
  - **DNA**
    - contains
    - **Deoxynucleotides A,T,G,C**
    - arranged as a
    - **Double Helix**
    - with
    - **Complementary Base Pairs A—T, G—C**
  - **RNA**
    - contains
    - **Nucleotides A,U,G,C**
    - with three types
    - **rRNA, tRNA, mRNA**
  - involved in
  - **Protein Synthesis**

KEY TERMS

active site A pocket in a part of the tertiary enzyme structure that binds substrate and catalyzes a reaction.

aldose A monosaccharide that contains an aldehyde group.

amino acid The building block of proteins, consisting of an ammonium group, a carboxylate group, and a unique R group attached to the alpha carbon.

amylopectin A branched-chain polymer of starch composed of glucose units joined by α-1,4- and α-1,6-glycosidic bonds.

amylose An unbranched polymer of starch composed of glucose units joined by α-1,4-glycosidic bonds.

carbohydrate A simple or complex sugar composed of carbon, hydrogen, and oxygen.

cellulose An unbranched polysaccharide composed of glucose units linked by β-1,4-glycosidic bonds that cannot be hydrolyzed by the human digestive system.

cholesterol The most prevalent of the steroid compounds found in cellular membranes.

codon A sequence of three bases in mRNA that specifies a certain amino acid to be placed in a protein. A few codons signal the start or stop of protein synthesis.

complementary base pairs In DNA, adenine is always paired with thymine (A—T or T—A), and guanine is always paired with cytosine (G—C or C—G). In forming RNA, adenine is paired with uracil (A—U).

disaccharide A carbohydrate composed of two monosaccharides joined by a glycosidic bond.

DNA Deoxyribonucleic acid; the genetic material of all cells containing nucleotides with deoxyribose sugar, phosphate, and the four bases adenine, thymine, guanine, and cytosine.

double helix The helical shape of the double chain of DNA that is like a spiral staircase with a sugar–phosphate backbone on the outside and base pairs like stair steps on the inside.

enzyme A protein that catalyzes a biological reaction.

fat Another term for solid triacylglycerols.

fatty acid Long-chain carboxylic acid found in fats and oils.

fructose A monosaccharide found in honey and fruit juices; it is combined with glucose in sucrose.

galactose A monosaccharide that occurs combined with glucose in lactose.

genetic code The sequence of codons in mRNA that specifies the amino acid order for the synthesis of protein.

glucose The most prevalent monosaccharide in the diet. It is an aldohexose that is found in fruits, vegetables, corn syrup, and honey. It combines in glycosidic bonds to form most of the polysaccharides.

glycogen A polysaccharide formed in the liver and muscles for the storage of glucose as an energy reserve. It is composed of glucose in a highly branched polymer joined by α-1,4- and α-1,6-glycosidic bonds.

induced-fit model A model of enzyme action in which a substrate induces an enzyme to modify its shape to give an optimal fit with the substrate structure.

ketose A monosaccharide that contains a ketone group.

lactose A disaccharide consisting of glucose and galactose found in milk and milk products.

lipids A family of compounds that is nonpolar in nature and not soluble in water; includes fats, waxes, and steroids.

lock-and-key model A model of an enzyme in which the substrate, like a key, exactly fits the shape of the lock, which is the specific shape of the active site.

maltose A disaccharide consisting of two glucose units; it is obtained from the hydrolysis of starch.

monosaccharide A polyhydroxy compound that contains an aldehyde or a ketone group.

nonpolar amino acids Amino acids that are not soluble in water because they contain a nonpolar R group.

nucleic acids Large molecules composed of nucleotides, found as a double helix in DNA and as the single strands of RNA.

nucleoside The combination of a pentose sugar and a base.

nucleotides Building blocks of a nucleic acid consisting of a base, a pentose sugar (ribose or deoxyribose), and a phosphate group.

oil Another term for a liquid triacylglycerol.

phosphodiester bond The phosphate link that joins the hydroxyl group in one nucleotide to the phosphate group on the next nucleotide.

polar amino acids Amino acids that are soluble in water because their R group is polar: hydroxyl (—OH), sulfur group (—SH), carbonyl (C=O), ammonium ($-NH_3^+$), or carboxylate ($-COO^-$).

polysaccharides Polymers of many monosaccharide units, usually glucose. Polysaccharides differ in the types of glycosidic bonds and the amount of branching in the polymer.

primary structure The sequence of the amino acids in a protein.

protein A term used for biologically active polypeptides that have many amino acids linked together by peptide bonds.

quaternary structure A protein structure in which two or more protein subunits form an active protein.

replication The process of duplicating DNA by pairing the bases on each parent strand with their complementary bases.

RNA Ribonucleic acid, a type of nucleic acid, is a single strand of nucleotides containing adenine, cytosine, guanine, and uracil.

saponification The reaction of a fat with a strong base to form glycerol and salts of fatty acids (soaps).

secondary structure The formation of an α helix, β-pleated sheet, or triple helix.

steroids Types of lipid composed of a multicyclic ring system.

sucrose A disaccharide composed of glucose and fructose; commonly called table sugar or "sugar."

tertiary structure The folding of the secondary structure of a protein into a compact structure that is stabilized by the interactions of R groups such as ionic and disulfide bonds.

triacylglycerols A family of lipids composed of three fatty acids bonded through ester bonds to glycerol, a trihydroxy alcohol.

transcription The transfer of genetic information from DNA by the formation of mRNA.

translation The interpretation of the codons in mRNA as amino acids in a peptide.

UNDERSTANDING THE CONCEPTS

The chapter sections to review are shown in parentheses at the end of each question.

18.69 Melezitose is a saccharide with the following structure: (18.1, 18.2)

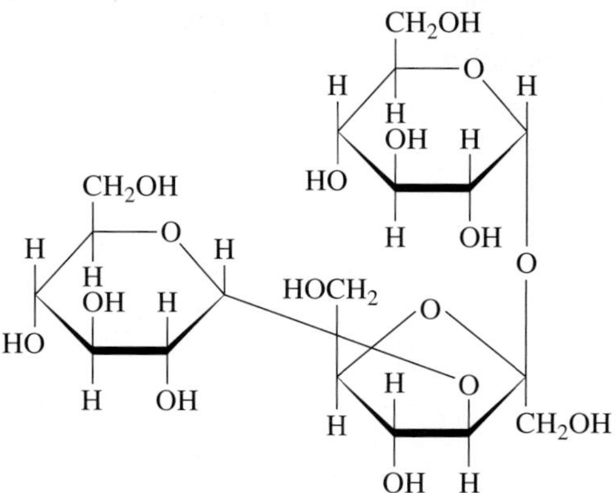

a. Is melezitose a mono-, di-, tri-, or polysaccharide?

b. What ketohexose and aldohexose are used to produce melezitose?

18.70 What are the disaccharides and polysaccharides present in each of the following? (18.1, 18.2)

(a) (b) (c) (d)

18.71 Palmitic acid is obtained from palm oil as glyceryl tripalmitate. Draw the condensed structural formula for glyceryl tripalmitate. (18.3)

Palm fruit from palm trees are a source of palm oil.

18.72 Identify each of the following as a saturated, monounsaturated, or polyunsaturated fatty acid: (18.3)

a. $CH_3-(CH_2)_4-(CH{=}CH-CH_2)_2-(CH_2)_6-COOH$

b. linolenic acid

c. $CH_3-(CH_2)_{14}-COOH$

d. $CH_3-(CH_2)_7-CH{=}CH-(CH_2)_7-COOH$

Salmon is a good source of unsaturated fatty acids.

18.73 Sunflower oil can be used to make margarine. A triacylglycerol in sunflower oil contains two linoleic acids and one oleic acid. (18.3)

Sunflower oil is obtained from the seeds of the sunflower.

a. Draw the condensed structural formulas for two isomers for the triacylglycerol in sunflower oil.

b. Using one of the isomers, write the reaction that would be used when sunflower oil is used to make solid margarine.

18.74 One of the compounds in jojoba wax used to make candles consists of an 18-carbon saturated fatty acid and a 22-carbon saturated alcohol. Draw the condensed structural formula for this compound. (18.3)

Candles contain jojoba wax.

18.75 Seeds and vegetables are often deficient in one or more essential amino acids. The table below shows which essential amino acids are present in each food. (18.4)

Source	Lysine	Tryptophan	Methionine
Oatmeal	No	Yes	Yes
Rice	No	Yes	Yes
Garbanzo beans	Yes	No	Yes
Lima beans	Yes	No	No
Cornmeal	No	No	Yes

Use the table to decide if each food combination provides all the essential amino acids: lysine, tryptophan, and methionine.

a. rice and garbanzo beans
b. lima beans and cornmeal
c. a salad of garbanzo beans and lima beans

18.76 Use the table in Problem 18.75 to decide if each food combination provides all the essential amino acids: lysine, tryptophan, and methionine. (18.4)

Oatmeal is deficient in the essential amino acid lysine.

a. rice and lima beans
b. rice and oatmeal
c. oatmeal and lima beans

18.77 For each of the following pairs of R groups, identify the amino acids and the type of interaction that forms between them: (18.4, 18.5)

a. $-CH_2-C(=O)-NH_2$ and $HO-CH_2-$

b. $-CH_2-C(=O)-O^-$ and $H_3\overset{+}{N}-(CH_2)_4-$

18.78 For each of the following pairs of R groups, identify the amino acids and the type of interaction that forms between them: (18.4, 18.5)

a. $-CH_2-SH$ and $HS-CH_2-$

b. $-CH_2-CH(CH_3)-CH_3$ and CH_3-

The proteins in hair contain many cysteine R groups.

18.79 Answer the following questions for the given section of DNA: (18.4, 18.5, 18.8)

a. Complete the bases in the parent and new strands.

Parent strand:		A	T			G	T		
New strand:	C			G	G			C	C

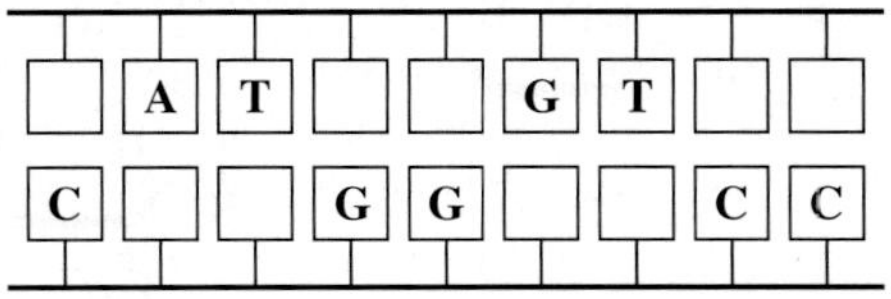

b. Using the new strand as a template, write the mRNA sequence.

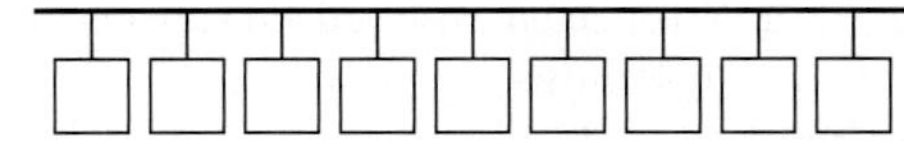

c. Write the 3-letter symbols of the amino acids that would go into the peptide from the mRNA you wrote in part **b**.

18.80 Answer the following questions for the given section of DNA: (18.4, 18.5, 18.8)

a. Complete the bases in the parent and new strands.

Parent strand:	A		G	T				C	T
New strand:		C			G	C	G		

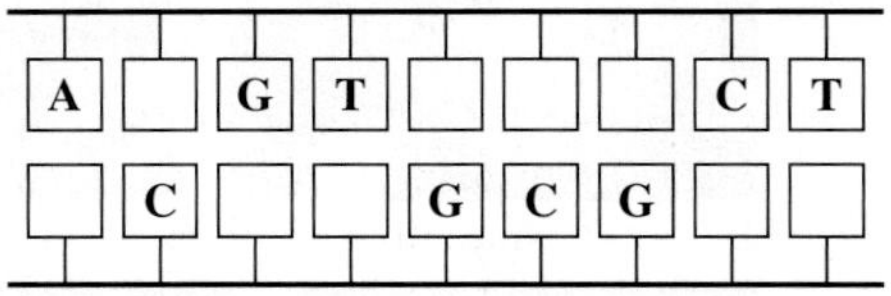

b. Using the new strand as a template, write the mRNA sequence.

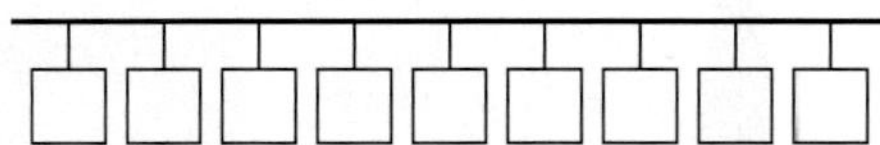

c. Write the 3-letter symbols of the amino acids that would go into the peptide from the mRNA you wrote in part **b**.

ADDITIONAL QUESTIONS AND PROBLEMS

18.81 What are the structural differences in D-glucose and D-galactose? (18.1)

18.82 What are the structural differences in D-glucose and D-fructose? (18.1)

18.83 Draw the Haworth structure for α-D- and β-D-gulose, whose open-chain structure is shown at right. (18.1)

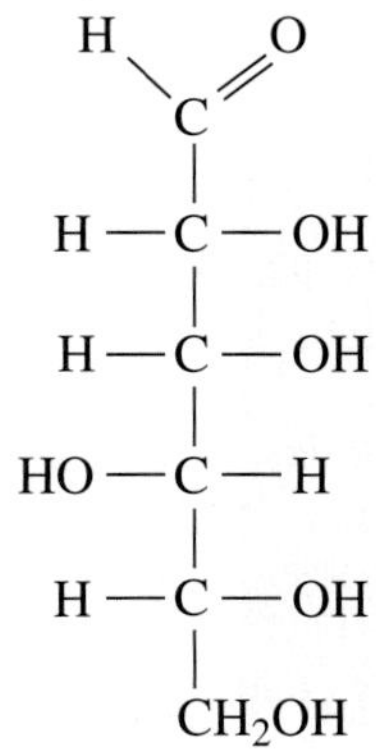

$$
\begin{array}{c}
H\diagdown\ \ \diagup\!\!\!/O \\
C \\
| \\
H-C-OH \\
| \\
H-C-OH \\
| \\
HO-C-H \\
| \\
H-C-OH \\
| \\
CH_2OH
\end{array}
$$

D-Gulose

18.84 From the compounds shown, select those that match the following: (18.1)
a. an aldohexose **b.** an aldopentose **c.** a ketohexose

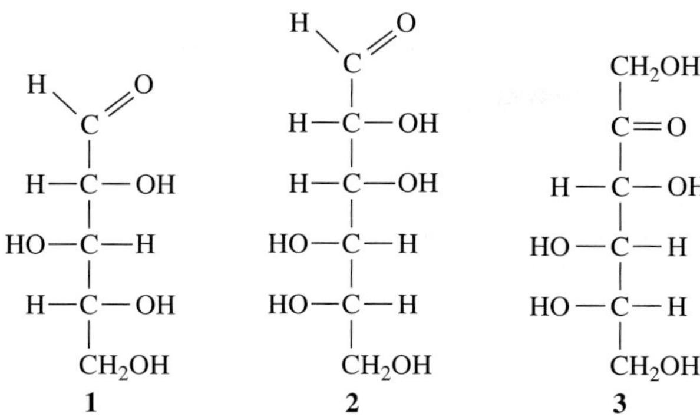

18.85 Gentiobiose, a carbohydrate found in saffron, contains two glucose molecules linked by a β-1,6-glycosidic bond. Draw the Haworth structure for α-gentiobiose. (18.1, 18.2)

18.86 β-Cellobiose is a disaccharide obtained from the hydrolysis of cellulose. It is similar to maltose except it has a β-1,4-glycosidic bond. Draw the Haworth structure for β-cellobiose. (18.1, 18.2)

18.87 Draw the condensed structural formula for Ser-Lys-Asp at physiological pH. (18.4)

18.88 Draw the condensed structural formula for Val-Ala-Leu at physiological pH. (18.4)

18.89 Identify the base and sugar in each of the following nucleosides: (18.7)
a. deoxythymidine **b.** adenosine
c. cytidine **d.** deoxyguanosine

18.90 Identify the base and sugar in each of the following nucleotides: (18.7)
a. CMP **b.** dAMP
c. dGMP **d.** UMP

18.91 Write the complementary base sequence for each of the following parent DNA segments: (18.4, 18.5, 18.8)
a. —G A C T T A G G C—
b. —T G C A A A C T A G C T—
c. —A T C G A T C G A T C G—

18.92 Write the complementary base sequence for each of the following parent DNA segments: (18.4, 18.5, 18.8)
a. —T T A C G G A C C G C—
b. —A T A G C C C T T A C T G G—
c. —G G C C T A C C T T A A C G—

18.93 Match the following statements with rRNA, mRNA, or tRNA: (18.8)
a. carries genetic information from the nucleus to the ribosomes
b. acts as a template for protein synthesis

18.94 Match the following statements with rRNA, mRNA, or tRNA: (18.8)
a. found in the ribosome
b. brings amino acids to the ribosomes for protein synthesis

CHALLENGE QUESTIONS

18.95 Raffinose is a trisaccharide found in green vegetables such as cabbage, asparagus, and broccoli. It is composed of three different monosaccharides. Identify the monosaccharides in raffinose. (18.1, 18.2)

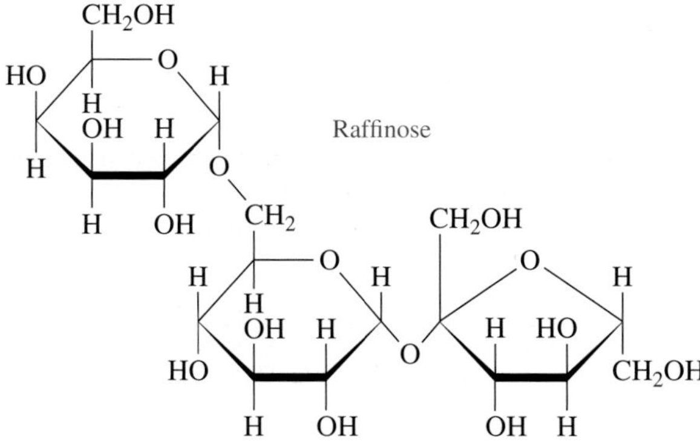

18.96 The disaccharide trehalose found in mushrooms is composed of two α-D-glucose molecules joined by an α,α-1,1-glycosidic bond. Draw the Haworth structure for trehalose. (18.1, 18.2)

18.97 What are some differences between each of the following pairs? (18.4, 18.5)
a. secondary and tertiary protein structures
b. essential and nonessential amino acids
c. polar and nonpolar amino acids
d. di- and tripeptides
e. an ionic bond (salt bridge) and a disulfide bond
f. α helix and β-pleated sheet
g. tertiary and quaternary structures of proteins

18.98 What type of interaction would you expect between the following amino acids in a tertiary structure? (18.4, 18.5)
a. threonine and asparagine
b. valine and alanine
c. arginine and aspartic acid

18.99 The following is a segment in a DNA template strand: (18.4, 18.5, 18.8)

—GCT TTT CAA AAA—

a. What is the corresponding mRNA section?
b. What amino acids will be placed in the peptide chain?

18.100 The following is a segment in a DNA template strand: (18.4, 18.5, 18.8)

—TGT GGG GTT ATT—

a. What is the corresponding mRNA section?
b. What amino acids will be placed in the peptide chain?

18.101 Endorphins are polypeptides that reduce pain. What is the amino acid order for the following mRNA that codes for a pentapeptide that is an endorphin called leucine enkephalin? (18.4, 18.5, 18.8)

—AUG UAC GGU GGA UUU CUA UAA—

18.102 Endorphins are polypeptides that reduce pain. What is the amino acid order for the following mRNA that codes for a pentapeptide that is an endorphin called methionine enkephalin? (18.4, 18.5, 18.8)

—AUG UAC GGU GGA UUU AUG UAA—

ANSWERS

Answers to Study Checks

18.1 CH_2OH O HO H H OH H H OH H OH

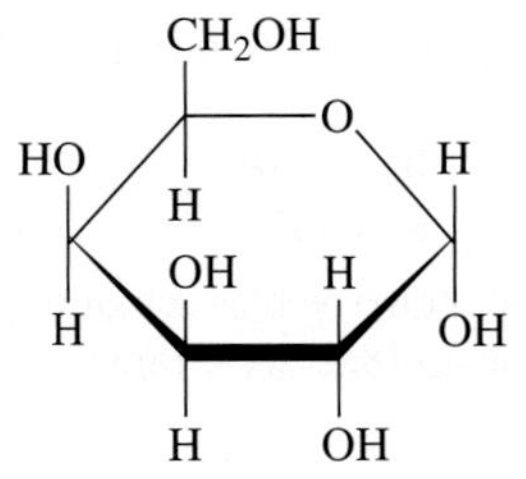

18.2 CH_2OH O H H OH H HO H H OH O CH_2OH O H OH H OH H H H OH

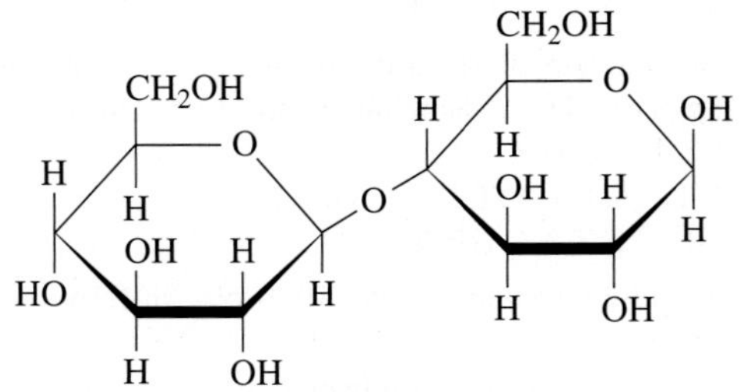

18.3 Cellulose contains glucose units connected by β-1,4-glycosidic bonds, whereas the glucose units in amylose are connected by α-1,4-glycosidic bonds.

18.4 **a.** 16
b. monounsaturated
c. No, its long hydrocarbon chain makes it insoluble in water.

18.5

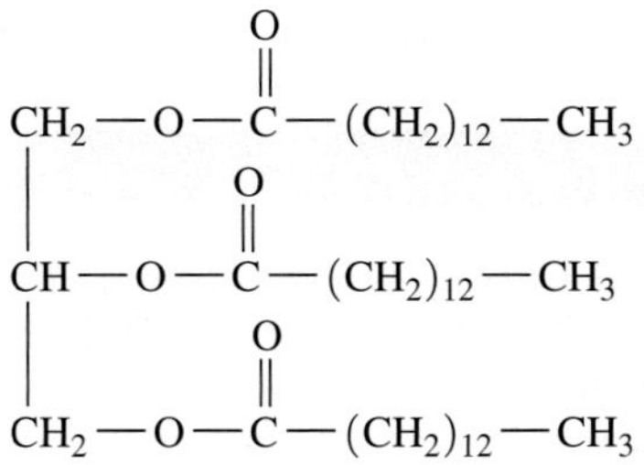

$$\begin{array}{l} CH_2-O-\overset{O}{\overset{\|}{C}}-(CH_2)_{12}-CH_3 \\ | \\ CH-O-\overset{O}{\overset{\|}{C}}-(CH_2)_{12}-CH_3 \\ | \\ CH_2-O-\overset{O}{\overset{\|}{C}}-(CH_2)_{12}-CH_3 \end{array}$$

18.6 polar, hydrophilic

18.7 Both are nonpolar and would have hydrophobic interactions.

18.8 quaternary

18.9 —C C A A T T G G—

18.10 —C C C A A A T T T—

18.11 at —UAG—

Answers to Selected Questions and Problems

18.1 Hydroxyl groups are found in all monosaccharides along with a carbonyl on the first or second carbon.

18.3 A ketopentose contains hydroxyl and ketone functional groups and has five carbon atoms.

18.5 **a.** ketohexose **b.** aldopentose

18.7 In galactose, the hydroxyl on carbon 4 extends to the left. In glucose, this hydroxyl goes to the right.

18.9 In the ring portion of the Haworth structure of glucose, there are five carbon atoms and an oxygen.

18.11 **a.** α form **b.** α form

18.13 **a.** one molecule of glucose and one molecule of galactose; β-1,4-glycosidic bond; β-lactose
b. two molecules of glucose; α-1,4-glycosidic bond; α-maltose

18.15 **a.** disaccharide
b. two molecules of α-glucose
c. α-1,6-glycosidic bond
d. α

18.17 **a.** sucrose **b.** lactose
c. maltose **d.** lactose

18.19 **a.** cellulose **b.** amylose, amylopectin
c. amylose **d.** glycogen

18.21 **a.** saturated **b.** polyunsaturated
c. saturated

18.23

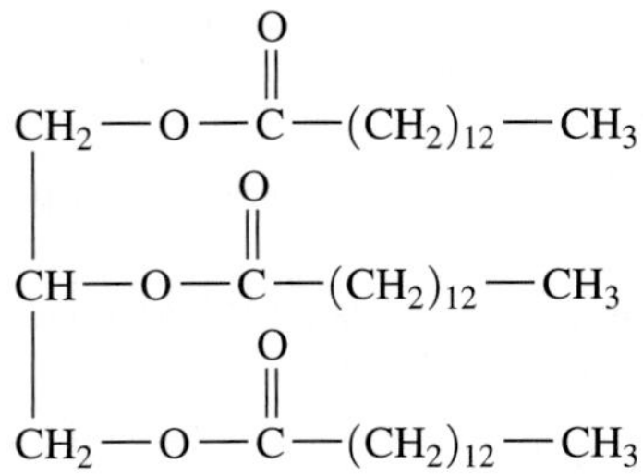

$$\begin{array}{l} CH_2-O-\overset{O}{\overset{\|}{C}}-(CH_2)_{12}-CH_3 \\ | \\ CH-O-\overset{O}{\overset{\|}{C}}-(CH_2)_{12}-CH_3 \\ | \\ CH_2-O-\overset{O}{\overset{\|}{C}}-(CH_2)_{12}-CH_3 \end{array}$$

18.25 Safflower oil contains fatty acids with two or three double bonds; olive oil contains a large amount of oleic acid, which has only one (monounsaturated) double bond.

18.27 **a.** Some of the double bonds in the unsaturated fatty acids have been converted to single bonds by the addition of hydrogen.
b. It is mostly saturated fatty acids.

18.29

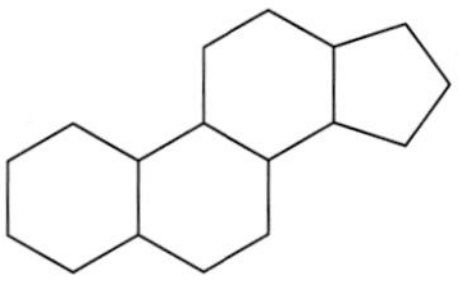

18.31 All amino acids contain a carboxylate group and an ammonium group on the α-carbon.

18.33 **a.** $H_3\overset{+}{N}-\underset{H}{\overset{H}{C}}-COO^-$ **b.** $H_3\overset{+}{N}-\underset{H}{C}(-CH(OH)CH_3)-COO^-$

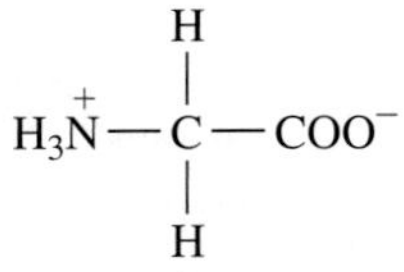

c. $H_3\overset{+}{N}-\underset{H}{C}(-CH_2-C_6H_5)-COO^-$

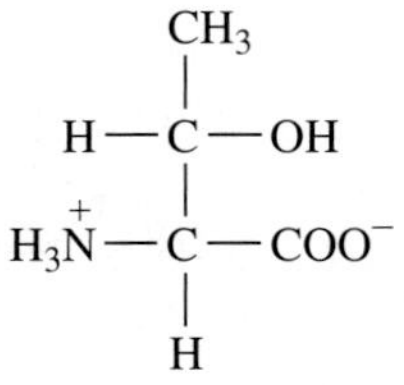

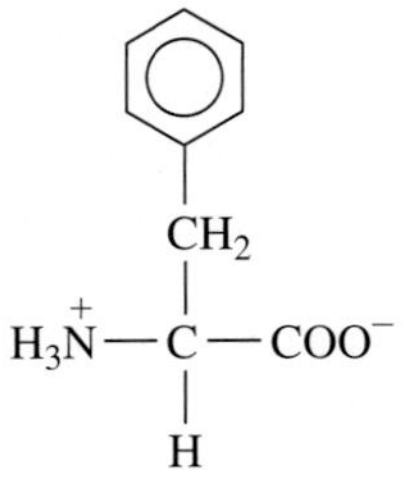

18.35 **a.** nonpolar, hydrophobic
b. polar, neutral, hydrophilic
c. nonpolar, hydrophobic

18.37 **a.** alanine **b.** valine
c. lysine **d.** cysteine

18.39 **a.**

```
                               SH
                               |
            CH3  O    H    CH2  O
            |    ||   |    |    ||
   H3N+ —   C  — C  — N  — C  — C — O−
            |                 |
            H                 H
```

b.

```
            OH            (benzene ring)
            |                 |
            CH2  O    H    CH2  O
            |    ||   |    |    ||
   H3N+ —   C  — C  — N  — C  — C — O−
            |              |
            H              H
```

c.

```
                                            CH3 CH3
                                              \ /
            H    O    H    CH3  O    H        CH  O
            |    ||   |    |    ||   |        |   ||
   H3N+ —   C  — C  — N  — C  — C  — N  —  C  — C — O−
            |              |               |
            H              H               H
```

18.41 Val-Ser-Ser, Ser-Val-Ser, or Ser-Ser-Val

18.43 In the α helix, hydrogen bonds form between the oxygen atom in the carbonyl group and hydrogen in the amide group in the next turn of the chain. In the β-pleated sheet, side-by-side hydrogen bonds occur between parallel peptides or across sections of a long polypeptide chain.

18.45 **a.** disulfide bond **b.** hydrogen bond
c. hydrophobic interaction

18.47 **a.** cysteine
b. Leucine and valine will be found on the inside of the protein because they are hydrophobic.
c. The cysteine and aspartic acid would be on the outside of the protein because they are polar.
d. The order of the amino acids (the primary structure) provides the R groups, whose interactions determine the tertiary structure of the protein.

18.49 **a.** (1) enzyme **b.** (3) substrate
c. (2) enzyme–substrate complex

18.51 **a.** $E + S \rightleftarrows ES \longrightarrow EP \longrightarrow E + P$
b. The active site is a region or pocket within the tertiary structure of an enzyme that accepts the substrate, aligns the substrate for reaction, and catalyzes the reaction.

18.53 **a.** DNA **b.** both DNA and RNA

18.55 The two DNA strands are held together by hydrogen bonds between the complementary bases in each strand.

18.57 **a.** —T T T T T T—
b. —C C C C C C—
c. —T C A G G T C C A—
d. —G A C A T A T G C A A—

18.59 The DNA strands separate to allow each of the bases to pair with its complementary base, which produces two exact copies of the original DNA.

18.61 ribosomal RNA, messenger RNA, and transfer RNA

18.63 In transcription, the sequence of nucleotides on a DNA template (one strand) is used to produce the base sequences of a messenger RNA.

18.65 —G G C U U C C A A G U G—

18.67 **a.** leucine (Leu) **b.** serine (Ser)
c. glycine (Gly) **d.** arginine (Arg)

18.69 **a.** Melezitose is a trisaccharide.
b. Melezitose contains two glucose molecules and a fructose molecule.

18.71

```
           O
           ||
CH2—O—C—(CH2)14—CH3
|          O
|          ||
CH—O—C—(CH2)14—CH3          Glyceryl tripalmitate
|          O
|          ||
CH2—O—C—(CH2)14—CH3
```

18.73 **a.**

```
           O
           ||
CH2—O—C—(CH2)7—CH=CH—CH2—CH=CH—(CH2)4—CH3
|          O
|          ||
CH—O—C—(CH2)7—CH=CH—(CH2)7—CH3
|          O
|          ||
CH2—O—C—(CH2)7—CH=CH—CH2—CH=CH—(CH2)4—CH3
```

```
           O
           ||
CH2—O—C—(CH2)7—CH=CH—CH2—CH=CH—(CH2)4—CH3
|          O
|          ||
CH—O—C—(CH2)7—CH=CH—CH2—CH=CH—(CH2)4—CH3
|          O
|          ||
CH2—O—C—(CH2)7—CH=CH—(CH2)7—CH3
```

b.

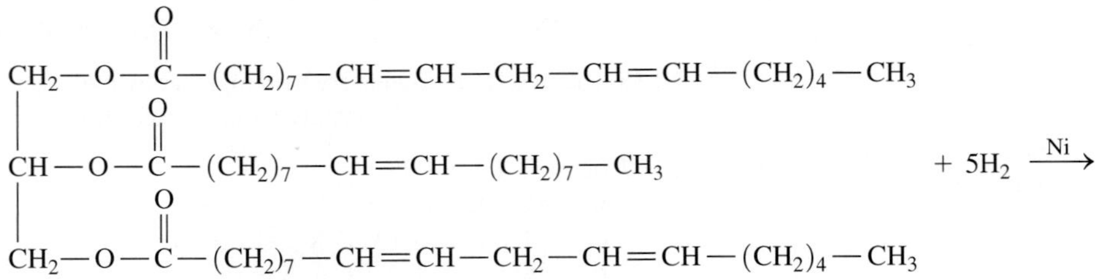

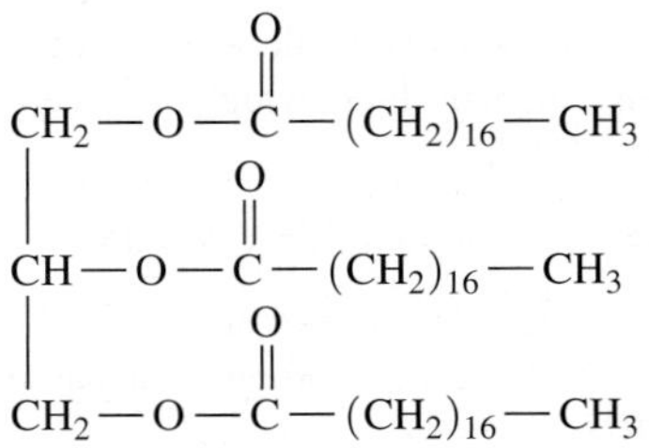

18.75 **a.** yes **b.** no **c.** no

18.77 **a.** asparagine and serine; hydrogen bond
b. aspartic acid and lysine; salt bridge

18.79 **a.**

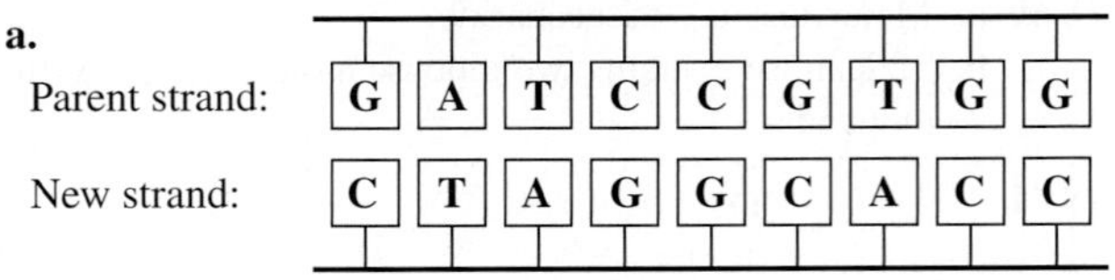

b.

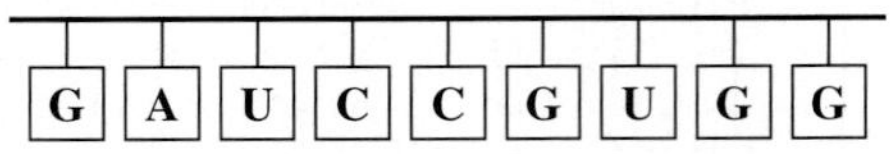

c. Asp-Pro-Trp

18.81 They differ only at carbon 4 where the —OH group in glucose is on the right side and in galactose it is on the left side.

18.83

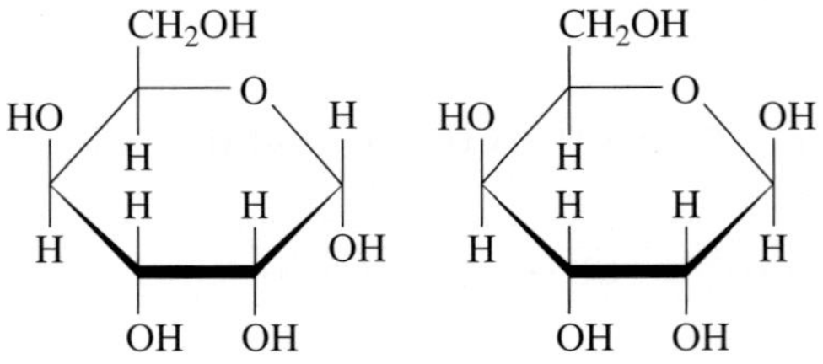

α-D-Gulose β-D-Gulose

18.85

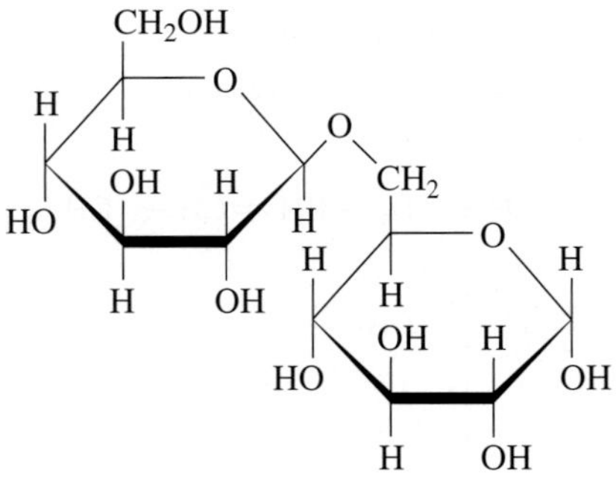

18.87

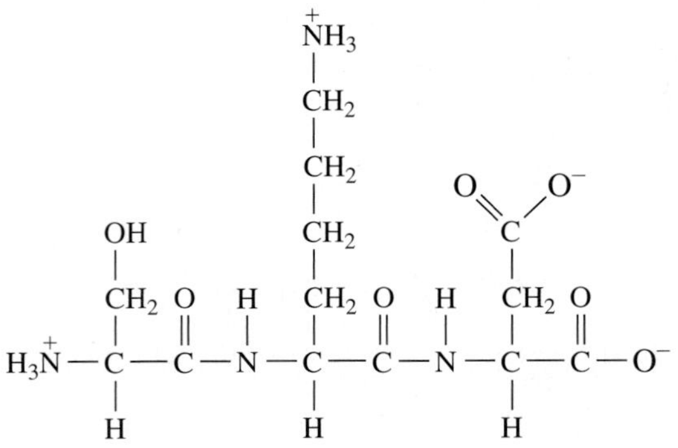

18.89 **a.** thymine and deoxyribose
b. adenine and ribose
c. cytosine and ribose
d. guanine and deoxyribose

18.91 **a.** —C T G A A T C C G—
b. —A C G T T T G A T G A—
c. —T A G C T A G C T A G C—

18.93 **a.** mRNA **b.** mRNA

18.95 galactose, glucose, and fructose

18.97 **a.** The secondary structure of a protein depends on hydrogen bonds to form a helix or a pleated sheet. The tertiary structure is determined by the interaction of R groups, which determine the three-dimensional structure of the protein.
b. Nonessential amino acids are synthesized by the body, but essential amino acids must be supplied by the diet.
c. Polar amino acids have hydrophilic side groups; nonpolar amino acids have hydrophobic side groups.
d. Dipeptides contain two amino acids; tripeptides contain three.
e. An ionic bond is an interaction between a basic and an acidic side group; a disulfide bond links the —SH groups of two cysteines.
f. The alpha helix is the secondary shape like a spiral staircase or corkscrew. The beta-pleated sheet is a secondary structure that is formed by many peptide chains side by side.
g. The tertiary structure of a protein is its three-dimensional structure. In the quaternary structure, two or more peptide subunits interact to form a biologically active protein.

18.99 **a.** —CGA AAA GUU UUU—
b. -Arg-Lys-Val-Phe-

18.101 START-Tyr-Gly-Gly-Phe-Leu-STOP

Combining Ideas from Chapters 17 and 18

CI.37 A compound called butylated hydroxytoluene, or BHT, with a molecular formula $C_{15}H_{24}O$, is added to preserve foods such as cereal. As an antioxidant, BHT reacts with oxygen in the cereal container, which protects the food from spoilage. (2.6, 2.7, 8.4, 17.3, 17.4)

CH_3 OH CH_3
CH_3-C … $C-CH_3$
CH_3 CH_3
CH_3

BHT is an antioxidant added to preserve foods such as cereal.

a. What functional group is present in BHT?
b. Why is BHT referred to as an "antioxidant"?
c. The FDA (Food and Drug Administration) allows a maximum of 50. ppm of BHT added to cereal. How many milligrams of BHT could be added to a box of cereal that contains 15 oz of dry cereal?

CI.38 A compound with the formula C_4H_8O is synthesized by oxidation of 2-methyl-1-propanol. (8.4, 8.5, 17.4, 17.5)
a. Draw the condensed structural formula for the compound.
b. Write the IUPAC name of the product.

CI.39 Acetylene gas (ethyne) reacts with oxygen and burns at high temperature in an acetylene torch. (7.1, 8.3, 8.4, 8.5, 9.1, 11.7, 11.9)
a. Write the balanced equation for the complete combustion of acetylene.

An acetylene torch is used to weld and cut metals.

b. How many grams of oxygen are needed to react with 8.5 L of acetylene at STP?
c. How many liters of CO_2 (at STP) are produced when 30.0 g of acetylene undergoes combustion?

CI.40 Olive oil contains a high percentage of glyceryl trioleate (triolein). (8.4, 11.9, 18.3)
a. Draw the condensed structural formula for glyceryl trioleate (triolein).
b. How many liters of H_2 gas at STP are needed to completely react with the double bonds in 100. g of triolein?
c. How many milliliters of a 6.00 M NaOH solution are needed to completely saponify 100. g of triolein?

One of the triacylglycerols in olive oil is glyceryl trioleate (triolein).

CI.41 A sink drain can become clogged with solid fat such as glyceryl tristearate (tristearin). (8.2, 12.6, 18.3)
a. How would adding lye (NaOH) to the sink drain remove the blockage?
b. Write a balanced equation for the reaction that occurs.
c. How many milliliters of a 0.500 M NaOH solution are needed to completely saponify 10.0 g of tristearin?

A sink drain can become clogged with saturated fats.

CI.42 In response to signals from the nervous system, the hypothalamus secretes a polypeptide hormone known as gonadotropin-releasing factor (GnRF), which stimulates the pituitary gland to release other hormones into the bloodstream.

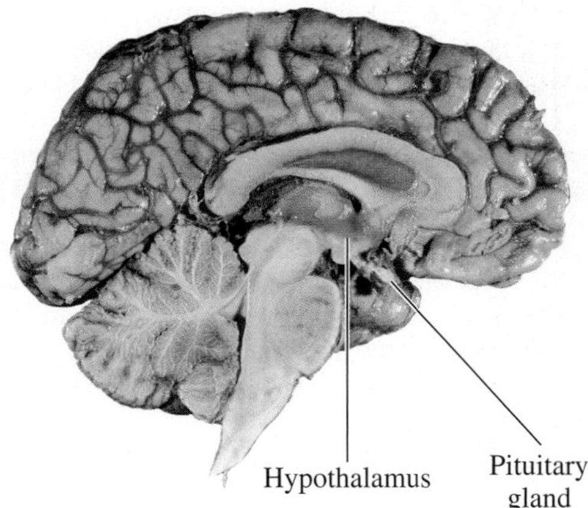

Gonadotropin-releasing factor (GnRF) is secreted by the hypothalamus.

Two of the hormones are known as gonadotropins, which are the luteinizing hormone (LH) in males, and the follicle-stimulating hormone (FSH) in females. GnRF is a decapeptide with the following primary structure: Glu-His-Trp-Ser-Tyr-Gly-Leu-Arg-Pro-Gly. (18.4, 18.5)
a. What is the N-terminal amino acid in GnRF?
b. What is the C-terminal amino acid in GnRF?
c. Which amino acids in GnRF are nonpolar?
d. Draw the condensed structural formulas at physiological pH for the acidic and basic amino acids in GnRF.
e. Draw the condensed structural formulas for the primary structure of the first three amino acids starting from the N-terminal amino acid of GnRF at physiological pH.

CI.43 The plastic known as PETE (**poly**ethylene**te**rephthalate) is a polymer of terephthalic acid and ethylene glycol. PETE is used to make plastic soft drink bottles and containers for salad dressings, shampoos, and dishwashing liquids. Today, PETE is the most widely recycled of all the plastics; in a single year, 2.4×10^9 lb of PETE are recycled. After PETE is separated from other plastics, it can be used in polyester fabric, fill for sleeping bags, door mats, and tennis ball containers. The density of PETE is 1.38 g/mL. (2.6, 2.7, 8.4, 17.6)

$$HO-\overset{\overset{O}{\|}}{C}-C_6H_4-\overset{\overset{O}{\|}}{C}-OH \qquad HO-CH_2-CH_2-OH$$

Terephthalic acid — Ethylene glycol

Plastic bottles made of PETE are ready to be recycled.

a. Draw the condensed structural formula for the ester formed from one molecule of terephthalic acid and one molecule of ethylene glycol.

b. Draw the condensed structural formula for the product formed when a second molecule of ethylene glycol reacts with the ester you drew for the answer in part **a**.

c. How many kilograms of PETE are recycled in one year?

d. What volume, in liters, of PETE is recycled in one year?

e. Suppose a landfill with an area of a football field and a depth of 5.0 m holds 2.7×10^7 L of recycled PETE. If all of the PETE that is recycled in a year were placed instead in landfills, how many would it fill?

CI.44 Thalassemia is an inherited genetic mutation that limits the production of the beta chain needed for the formation of hemoglobin. If low levels of the beta chain are produced, there is a shortage of red blood cells (anemia). As a result, the body does not have sufficient amounts of oxygen. In one form of thalassemia, a single nucleotide is deleted in the DNA that codes for the beta chain. This mutation involves the deletion of thymine (T) from section 91 (bold) in the following segment of normal DNA: (18.4, 18.5, 18.8)

89 90 91 92 93 94
—AGT GAG **CTG** CAC TGT GAC A. . . .
(Normal DNA segment)

a. Write the complementary strand for this normal DNA segment.

b. Write the mRNA sequence using the complementary strand in part **a**.

c. What amino acids are placed in the beta chain using the portion of mRNA in part **b**?

d. What is the order of nucleotides in the mutation?

e. Write the complementary strand for the mutant DNA section.

f. Write the mRNA sequence using the complementary strand in part **e**.

g. What amino acids are placed in the beta chain by the mutation?

h. How might the properties of this segment of the beta chain be different from the properties of the normal protein?

i. How might the level of structure in hemoglobin be affected if beta chains are not produced?

ANSWERS

CI.37 a. The —OH group in BHT is bonded to a carbon atom in an aromatic ring, which means BHT has a phenol functional group.

b. BHT is referred to as an "antioxidant" because it reacts with oxygen in the food container, rather than the food, thus preventing or retarding spoilage of the food.

c. 21 mg of BHT

CI.39 a. acetylene $HC \equiv CH$ or C_2H_2

$$2C_2H_2(g) + 5O_2(g) \xrightarrow{\Delta} 4CO_2(g) + 2H_2O(g) + \text{energy}$$

b. 30. g of O_2

c. 51.6 L of CO_2

CI.41 a. Adding NaOH will saponify the glyceryl tristearate (fat), breaking it up into fatty acid salts and glycerol, which are soluble and will wash down the drain.

b.

$$\begin{array}{l} CH_2-O-\overset{\overset{O}{\|}}{C}-(CH_2)_{16}-CH_3 \\ | \\ CH-O-\overset{\overset{O}{\|}}{C}-(CH_2)_{16}-CH_3 + 3NaOH \longrightarrow \\ | \\ CH_2-O-\overset{\overset{O}{\|}}{C}-(CH_2)_{16}-CH_3 \end{array}$$

$$\begin{array}{l} CH_2-OH \\ | \\ CH-OH + 3Na^+\,^-O-\overset{\overset{O}{\|}}{C}-(CH_2)_{16}-CH_3 \\ | \\ CH_2-OH \end{array}$$

c. 67.3 mL of a 0.500 M NaOH solution

CI.43 a. $HO-\overset{\overset{O}{\|}}{C}-C_6H_4-\overset{\overset{O}{\|}}{C}-O-CH_2-CH_2-OH$

b. $HO-CH_2-CH_2-O-\overset{\overset{O}{\|}}{C}-C_6H_4-\overset{\overset{O}{\|}}{C}-O-CH_2-CH_2-OH$

c. 1.1×10^9 kg of PETE

d. 8.0×10^8 L of PETE

e. 30. landfills

Credits

Covers

Front Kenneth Libbrecht / Photo Researchers, Inc.
Back Rene Jansa / Shutterstock

Front Matter

p. xxii Natural History Museum of Los Angeles

Chapter 1

p. 1 nyaivanova / Shutterstock
p. 2 Patrick Clark / Getty Images
p. 3 *top:* USGS National Center
p. 3 *bottom:* Pearson Education
p. 4 *top, left:* Jan van der Straet / Superstock
p. 4 *top, right:* The Print Collector / Alamy
p. 4 *bottom:* Pearson Education / Eric Schrader
p. 5 epstock / Shutterstock
p. 6 *top:* J.R. Eyerman / Time & Life Pictures / Getty Images
p. 6 *bottom:* Argonne National Laboratory
p. 7 *top, left:* Robynrg / Shutterstock
p. 7 *top, right:* iStockphoto
p. 7 *middle:* Pearson Education
p. 7 *bottom:* iStockphoto
p. 8 *left:* U.S. Department of Agriculture
p. 8 *right, top:* Maxfocus / Shutterstock
p. 8 *right, bottom:* Denton Rumsey / Shutterstock
p. 9 evgenyb / iStockphoto
p. 10 track5 / Shutterstock
p. 11 Design Pics Inc / Alamy Images
p. 14 Joe Gough / Fotolia
p. 15 Dorling Kindersley
p. 16 VIPDesign / Fotolia
p. 18 *left, top:* Pearson Education
p. 18 *left, bottom:* Argonne National Laboratory
p. 18 *right, top:* track5 / iStockphoto
p. 18 *right, bottom:* VIPDesign / Fotolia
p. 20 coolgraphic / iStockphoto
p. 21 U.S. Marine Corps / Lance Corporal Kelsey J. Green

Chapter 2

p. 24 AVAVA / Shutterstock
p. 25 *top:* Rod Ferris / Shutterstock
p. 25 *bottom:* pastorscott / iStockphoto
p. 26 AndreasReh / iStockphoto
p. 27 *top, left:* Pearson Education
p. 27 *top, right:* National Institute of Standards and Technology
p. 27 *middle:* Richard Megna / Fundamental Photographs
p. 27 *bottom:* Pearson Education
p. 28 Pearson Education
p. 29 *left:* Jason Stitt / Shutterstock
p. 29 *right:* Photo Researchers, Inc.
p. 30 Science Photo Library / Alamy Images
p. 33 Kameleon007 / iStockphoto
p. 35 Radu Razvan / Shutterstock
p. 36 emin kuliyev / Shutterstock
p. 40 *top:* Alias Studiot Oy / Shutterstock
p. 40 *middle:* Monkey Business Images / Shutterstock
p. 40 *bottom:* Pearson Education
p. 41 *top:* U.S. Navy / Jake Berenguer
p. 41 *bottom:* Timothy Stirling / Fotolia
p. 42 Pearson Education
p. 44 Pearson Education / Eric Schrader
p. 45 Pearson Education / Eric Schrader
p. 46 Pearson Education
p. 47 *top:* Pearson Education
p. 47 *bottom:* carlosalvarez / iStockphoto
p. 51 Stocktrek / Getty Images
p. 52 Associated Press / Kirsty Wigglesworth
p. 54 *top:* Aprescindere / Dreamstime
p. 54 *bottom:* Pearson Education
p. 56 Roza / Dreamstime
p. 57 *top, all:* Pearson Education
p. 57 *bottom:* DJMattaar / iStockphoto
p. 58 Pearson Education
p. 59 *top:* GoodMood Photo / Fotolia
p. 59 *bottom, left:* Prof. P. La Motta, Dept. Anatomy, University La Sapienza, Rome / Photo Researchers, Inc.
p. 59 *bottom, middle:* Prof. La Motta, Dept. Anatomy, Univ. La Sapienza, Rome / Photo Researchers, Inc.
p. 59 *bottom, right:* Phanie / Photo Researchers, Inc.
p. 60 Dallas Events Inc. / Shutterstock
p. 61 *left, top:* Pearson Education
p. 61 *left, 2nd from top:* Jason Stitt / Shutterstock
p. 61 *2nd from left, 2nd from top:* Photo Researchers, Inc.
p. 61 *left, bottom:* emin kuliyev / Shutterstock
p. 61 *right, top:* Pearson Education / Eric Schrader
p. 61 *right, bottom:* Pearson Education
p. 65 romans14 / Fotolia
p. 66 Cristian Ciureanu / Alamy Images

Chapter 3

p. 69 Network Photographer / Alamy Images
p. 71 *top, left:* anthonysp / iStockphoto
p. 71 *top, right:* Bomshtein / Shutterstock
p. 71 *middle, left:* Pearson Education
p. 71 *middle, right:* Pearson Education / Eric Schrader
p. 71 *bottom, left:* Richard Megna / Fundamental Photographs
p. 71 *bottom, right:* Pearson Education
p. 72 *top, left:* ODonnell Photograf / iStockphoto
p. 72 *top, 2nd from left:* Pearson Education
p. 72 *top, 2nd from right:* Lagui / Shutterstock
p. 72 *top, right:* Pearson Education
p. 72 *middle:* Dave King / Dorling Kindersley Media Library
p. 72 *bottom:* David Murray and Jules Selmes / Dorling Kindersley Media Library
p. 73 *top, left:* Richard Megna / Fundamental Photographs
p. 73 *top, right:* Pearson Education / Eric Schrader
p. 73 *bottom:* Nicolas Dupont / Fotolia
p. 74 *top:* Pearson Education
p. 74 *bottom:* Siede Preis / Getty Images
p. 75 *left:* Justinb / Fotolia
p. 75 *right:* Lisay / iStockphoto
p. 76 *top:* Elena Elisseeva / Shutterstock
p. 76 *middle, left:* John A. Rizzo / Getty Images
p. 76 *middle, center:* Getty Images
p. 76 *middle, right:* Mark Downey / Getty Images
p. 76 *2nd from bottom:* Ray Roberts / Alamy
p. 76 *bottom:* Creativ Studio Heinemann / Alamy
p. 77 Rafa Irusta / Shutterstock
p. 80 Gala_K / Fotolia
p. 81 Digital Vision / Alamy Images
p. 83 JenniferPhotographyImaging / iStockphoto
p. 84 WendellandCarolyn / iStockphoto
p. 86 Celso Pupo / Fotolia
p. 88 *top:* Joe_Potato / iStockphoto
p. 88 *bottom:* Roman Sigaev / Shutterstock
p. 90 NASA / John F. Kennedy Space Center
p. 92 Pearson Education
p. 94 Stockbyte / Getty Images
p. 95 *left, top:* Richard Megna / Fundamental Photographs
p. 95 *left, bottom:* Justinb / Fotolia
p. 95 *right, top:* JenniferPhotographyImaging / iStockphoto
p. 95 *right, bottom:* Joe_Potato / iStockphoto
p. 98 *top, left:* Pearson Education
p. 98 *top, 2nd from left:* Masterfile USA Corporation
p. 98 *top, 2nd from right:* Spencer Jones / Getty Images
p. 98 *top, right:* FuatKose / iStockphoto
p. 98 *bottom:* starfotograf / iStockphoto
p. 99 Khoroshunova Olga / Shutterstock
p. 102 *top:* Olga A / Shutterstock

p. 102 *bottom:* Shalom Ormsby / Getty Images
p. 103 *top:* Pearson Education / Eric Schrader
p. 103 *middle:* Masterfile USA Corporation
p. 103 *bottom:* David Reilly / Shutterstock

Chapter 4

p. 104 Martin Harvey / Alamy
p. 106 *left:* gabyjalbert / iStockphoto
p. 106 *right:* Atiketta Sangasaeng / Shutterstock
p. 107 *all:* Pearson Education
p. 108 Mary Ann Sullivan
p. 110 *all:* Pearson Education
p. 111 Polushkin Ivan Nikolaevich / Shutterstock
p. 112 Pearson Education
p. 115 *top:* Pearson Prentice Hall, Inc.-High School
p. 115 *bottom:* IBM Research Division
p. 117 Pearson Education
p. 119 *left:* Eric Schrader / Fundamental Photographs
p. 119 *right:* Pearson Education
p. 123 *top:* Pearson Education
p. 123 *bottom:* tarasov / Shutterstock
p. 126 Pearson Education
p. 129 craftvision / iStockphoto

Chapter 5

p. 133 Sandia National Labs - US Department of Energy
p. 134 kodachrome25 / iStockphoto
p. 137 *top:* Cindy Minear / Shutterstock
p. 137 *bottom:* Pearson Education
p. 138 *top:* lior2 / iStockphoto.com
p. 138 *2nd from top:* roza / Fotolia
p. 138 *2nd from bottom:* Piotr Rzeszutek / Shutterstock
p. 138 *bottom:* Andrew Syred / Photo Researchers, Inc.
p. 139 *all:* Pearson Education
p. 140 Thorsten Rust / Shutterstock
p. 144 olly / Fotolia
p. 148 Pearson Education
p. 161 *top:* iStockphoto
p. 161 *bottom:* lior2 / iStockphoto.com
p. 165 NASA Earth Observing System

Chapter 6

p. 168 Don Hammond / Alamy
p. 169 buckarooh / iStockphoto
p. 170 2009 / Alamy
p. 174 Pearson Education
p. 176 *top, left:* Richard Megna / Fundamental Photographs
p. 176 *top, right:* Pearson Education
p. 176 *middle:* Pearson Education
p. 176 *bottom:* Pearson Education
p. 178 Pearson Education / Eric Schrader
p. 180 Gary Blakeley / Shutterstock
p. 181 Mark Huls / Fotolia
p. 182 *all:* Pearson Education
p. 184 *top:* ITAR-TASS / Vladimir Smirnov / Newscom
p. 184 *bottom:* Kurhan / Fotolia
p. 185 Kameel4u / Shutterstock
p. 193 Pearson Education
p. 194 *left:* lillis photography / iStockphoto
p. 194 *right:* Pearson Education
p. 197 Pearson Education
p. 198 Getty Images
p. 199 *left, top:* Pearson Education
p. 199 *left, 2nd from top:* Pearson Education
p. 199 *right:* Pearson Education
p. 199 *bottom:* Kameel4u / Shutterstock
p. 202 *left:* AlsoSalt
p. 202 *right:* Jason Nemeth / iStockphoto

Chapter 7

p. 207 Nagy Melinda / Shutterstock
p. 209 *left:* Pearson Education
p. 209 *right:* lissart / iStockphoto
p. 210 Reika / Shutterstock
p. 211 Pearson Education
p. 213 Pearson Education
p. 214 *top:* Polushkin Ivan Nikolaevich / Shutterstock
p. 214 *bottom, all:* Pearson Education
p. 215 ruzanna / Shutterstock
p. 216 Pearson Education / Eric Schrader
p. 218 Pearson Education
p. 219 Tamara Kulikova / iStockphoto
p. 220 Mike Hill / iStockphoto
p. 221 Pearson Education
p. 222 pamspix / iStockphoto
p. 224 *top:* Jeffrey Heyden / iStockphoto
p. 224 *bottom:* magicinfoto / iStockphoto
p. 228 HammerINK / NotNeutral.com
p. 229 *top:* Pichugin Dmitry / Shutterstock
p. 229 *bottom, left:* lissart / iStockphoto
p. 229 *bottom, right:* Pearson Education
p. 230 *left:* Pearson Education
p. 230 *right:* HammerINK / NotNeutral .com
p. 231 *left:* Gabriele Rohde / Fotolia
p. 231 *right:* Ljupco Smokovski / Fotolia
p. 232 *all:* Pearson Education
p. 234 *left, top:* goldenangel / Shutterstock
p. 234 *left, middle:* Pearson Education
p. 234 *left, bottom:* Foodcollection / Getty Images
p. 234 *right, top:* Photodisc Blue / Getty Images
p. 234 *right, bottom:* FreshPaint / Shutterstock
p. 237 *left, top:* flydragon / Shutterstock
p. 237 *left, bottom:* attem / Shutterstock
p. 237 *right, top:* molekuul.be / Shutterstock
p. 237 *right, middle:* Photolibrary
p. 237 *right, bottom:* Public Domain / Moriori
p. 238 IS293 / Alamy

Chapter 8

p. 239 Javier Larrea / AGE Fotostock
p. 240 Pearson Education
p. 241 *all:* Pearson Education
p. 244 Pearson Education
p. 245 Richard Megna / Fundamental Photographs
p. 248 *all:* Pearson Education
p. 249 Patrick Clark / Getty Images
p. 250 *all:* Pearson Education
p. 251 *top:* Sergiy Zavgorodny / Shutterstock
p. 251 *bottom:* HansChris / iStockphoto
p. 254 *top:* Pearson Education
p. 254 *bottom:* Tim Hall / Getty Images
p. 255 Nigel Cattlin / Alamy
p. 256 *top:* Dirk Richter / iStockphoto
p. 256 *bottom:* Medical-on-Line / Alamy
p. 257 *top:* Dorling Kindersley Media Library
p. 257 *bottom:* Antagain / iStockphoto
p. 258 *top:* zpyder / Shutterstock
p. 258 *bottom:* Pearson Education
p. 259 *top:* Pearson Education
p. 259 *middle:* Pearson Education
p. 259 *bottom:* robophobic / Shutterstock
p. 261 Jcjgphotography / Dreamstime
p. 263 *top:* Valentyn Volkov / Shutterstock
p. 263 *bottom:* Pearson Education
p. 265 *top:* Jupiterimages
p. 265 *bottom:* John Pitcher / iStockphoto
p. 266 *all:* Pearson Education
p. 268 evemilla / iStockphoto
p. 270 Pearson Education
p. 272 Richard Megna / Fundamental Photographs
p. 274 *top:* SK Designs / iStockphoto
p. 274 *2nd from top:* C Squared Studios / Getty
p. 274 *2nd from bottom:* Multiart / Shutterstock
p. 274 *bottom:* stanislaff / iStockphoto
p. 275 *left, top:* Pearson Education
p. 275 *left, bottom:* Pearson Education
p. 275 *right, top:* DenisNata / Shutterstock

Chapter 9

p. 279 BartCo / iStockphoto
p. 281 *all:* Pearson Education
p. 282 *all:* Pearson Education
p. 283 Clark Brennan / Alamy
p. 285 Thinkstock Images / Getty Images
p. 288 *top, all:* Pearson Education
p. 288 *bottom:* Brian A Jackson / Shutterstock
p. 290 Klaus Schräder / Alamy
p. 293 NASA Earth Observing System
p. 297 Pearson Education
p. 298 *top:* Richard Megna / Fundamental Photographs
p. 298 *left, bottom, all:* Pearson Education
p. 298 *right, 2nd from bottom:* Thinkstock Images / Getty Images
p. 298 *right, bottom:* Klaus Schräder / Alamy
p. 299 NASA Earth Observing System

Chapter 10

p. 306 B Boissonnet / AGE Fotostock
p. 311 NASA
p. 331 *all:* Pearson Education
p. 333 *left:* John A. Rizzo / Getty Images
p. 333 *middle:* John A. Rizzo / Getty Images
p. 333 *right:* Mark Downey / Getty Images
p. 336 *left:* Pearson Education

p. 336 *middle:* Helene Canada / iStockphoto
p. 336 *right:* johnnyscriv / iStockphoto
p. 337 © Patrick Kociniak / Vibe Images / Alamy
p. 342 *top:* Alessandro Trovati / Associated Press
p. 342 *bottom:* Mark Dahners / Associated Press
p. 348 *left:* a-wrangler / iStockphoto
p. 348 *right, top:* Pearson Education / Eric Schrader
p. 348 *right, bottom:* Kiichiro Sato / Associated Press
p. 349 *top:* Jane Norton / iStockphoto
p. 349 *bottom:* gvictoria / iStockphoto
p. 350 Pearson Education / Eric Schrader

Chapter 11

p. 351 Adam Gault / Alamy
p. 354 NASA
p. 355 Pearson Education
p. 357 Andrzej Gibasiewicz / Shutterstock
p. 360 Pearson Education
p. 363 Larry Brownstein / Getty Images
p. 368 *all:* Pearson Education
p. 370 T. O'Keefe / Getty Images
p. 372 iStockphoto
p. 373 Getty Images
p. 375 Yuri Bathan / iStockphoto
p. 379 Eric Schrader / Fundamental Photographs
p. 384 IS098SU4V / Alamy
p. 385 *top:* T. O'Keefe / Getty Images
p. 385 *bottom:* Yuri Bathan / iStockphoto
p. 386 Eric Schrader / Fundamental Photographs
p. 389 Library of Congress

Chapter 12

p. 392 AJPhoto / Photo Researchers, Inc.
p. 394 *all:* Pearson Education
p. 395 *top:* Pearson Education
p. 395 *bottom:* Jupiter Images
p. 396 *all:* Pearson Education
p. 398 *all:* Pearson Education
p. 400 *all:* Pearson Education
p. 401 Pearson Education
p. 402 *all:* Pearson Education
p. 403 *top:* CNRI / Science Photo Library/ Photo Researchers, Inc.
p. 403 *bottom, left:* NMSB / Custom Medical Stock
p. 403 *bottom, right:* CMSP / Newscom
p. 404 *all:* Pearson Education
p. 406 *all:* Pearson Education
p. 407 *all:* Pearson Education
p. 411 *all:* Pearson Education
p. 412 *all:* Pearson Education
p. 414 Pearson Education
p. 415 Pearson Education
p. 420 *top:* Jane Norton / iStockphoto
p. 420 *bottom:* argonaut / Shutterstock
p. 423 Florida Images / Alamy
p. 425 *top:* Thinkstock Images / Getty Images
p. 425 *bottom, all:* Sam Singer
p. 426 Dorling Kindersley
p. 427 Picsfive / Shutterstock
p. 428 *all:* Pearson Education
p. 429 Pearson Education
p. 432 *top:* Professor25 / iStockphoto
p. 432 *bottom:* Corbis

Chapter 13

p. 437 PhotoStock-Israel / Photo Researchers, Inc.
p. 438 *all:* Pearson Education
p. 440 Pearson Education
p. 441 Pearson Education
p. 447 Gudellaphoto / Fotolia
p. 458 incamerastock / Alamy
p. 460 *top:* Jack Star / Getty Images
p. 460 *bottom:* Sean Thompson / Getty Images
p. 461 Scimat / Photo Researchers, Inc.
p. 462 Verkhovynets Taras / Shutterstock
p. 463 Dorling Kindersley
p. 466 Dorling Kindersley
p. 466 *left:* Gudellaphoto / Fotolia
p. 466 *right:* incamerastock / Alamy

Chapter 14

p. 473 Gina Sanders / Shutterstock
p. 474 magicinfoto / iStockphoto
p. 476 jamesbenet / iStockphoto
p. 477 *top, left:* Richard Megna / Fundamental Photographs
p. 477 *top, right:* Kul Bhatia / Photo Researchers, Inc.
p. 477 *bottom:* David Wei / Alamy
p. 478 Kesu / Shutterstock
p. 482 Pearson Education
p. 483 *top:* Pearson Education
p. 483 *bottom:* Richard Megna / Fundamental Photographs
p. 484 Pearson Education
p. 492 *all:* Pearson Education
p. 493 *top, all:* Pearson Education
p. 493 *bottom:* Joerg Beuge / Shutterstock
p. 494 *top:* Wayne Hutchinson / Alamy
p. 494 *bottom:* Pearson Education
p. 499 Richard Megna / Fundamental Photographs
p. 500 Pearson Education / Eric Schrader
p. 501 *left:* Kristen Brochmann / Fundamental Photographs
p. 501 *right:* Michael Fernahl / iStockphoto
p. 502 Pearson Science / Renn Sminkey
p. 503 *all:* Pearson Education
p. 510 Pearson Education
p. 511 *left:* Pearson Education
p. 511 *right, bottom:* Pearson Education
p. 511 *right, top:* Richard Megna / Fundamental Photographs
p. 514 geotrac / iStockphoto
p. 516 Universal Images Group / SuperStock
p. 519 *top:* Center for Liquefied Natural Gas
p. 519 *middle, left:* Patsy Michaud / Shutterstock
p. 519 *middle, middle:* Isifa Image Service / Alamy
p. 519 *middle, right:* MvH / iStockphoto
p. 519 *bottom:* a-wrangler / iStockphoto
p. 520 *left, top:* Richard Megna / Fundamental Photographs
p. 520 *left, bottom:* Charles D. Winters / Photo Researchers, Inc.
p. 520 *right:* Pearson Education

Chapter 15

p. 521 Craig Holmes Premium / Alamy
p. 522 *top:* Mitch Hrdlicka / Getty Images
p. 522 *bottom:* Oleg - F / Shutterstock
p. 524 *all:* Pearson Education
p. 528 Andrew Lambert / Photo Researchers, Inc.
p. 531 Richard Megna / Fundamental Photographs
p. 534 Pearson Education
p. 538 terekhov igor / Shutterstock
p. 539 *top:* Eric Schrader / Pearson Education
p. 539 *bottom:* Creative Digital Visions / Pearson Education
p. 540 *top:* Pearson Education
p. 540 *bottom:* Stinkyt / iStockphoto
p. 542 NASA Earth Observing System
p. 544 *top:* Corbis
p. 544 *middle:* Jim Barber / Shutterstock
p. 544 *bottom:* artproem / Shutterstock
p. 548 *top:* SLOFotomedia / iStockphoto
p. 548 *bottom, left:* Mitch Hrdlicka / Getty Images
p. 548 *bottom, right:* Andrew Lambert / Photo Researchers, Inc.
p. 549 *top, left:* Richard Megna / Fundamental Photographs
p. 549 *top, right:* Jim Barber / Shutterstock
p. 549 *bottom:* Pearson Education
p. 552 *left:* Andy Crawford and Tim Ridley / Dorling Kindersley
p. 552 *right:* Andrew Lambert / Photo Researchers, Inc.

Chapter 16

p. 559 Konstantin Sutyagin / Shutterstock
p. 562 joshblake / iStockphoto
p. 563 Health Protection Agency / Photo Researchers, Inc.
p. 565 Uberphotos / iStockphoto
p. 566 Pearson Education
p. 569 Pearson Education
p. 571 *top:* James McPherson / Associated Press
p. 571 *bottom:* Don Farrall / Getty Images
p. 572 Neil Stanford
p. 573 Pearson Education
p. 577 Library of Congress
p. 578 Jihad Siqlawi / Newscom
p. 579 *left:* PHANIE / Photo Researchers, Inc.
p. 579 *right:* Pasieka / Photo Researchers, Inc.
p. 580 *top:* Lawrence Berkeley National Library / Getty Images
p. 580 *bottom:* Getty Images
p. 581 *top:* GJLP / Photo Researchers, Inc.
p. 581 *bottom, all:* Cytyc Hologic Corporation
p. 585 foto-rolf / iStockphoto
p. 586 *left:* Don Farrall / Getty Images

p. 586 *right:* Lawrence Berkeley National Library / Getty Images
p. 588 Peter Buckley / Pearson Education
p. 592 *top, left:* Andrew Lambert Photography / SPL / Photo Researchers, Inc.
p. 592 *top, right:* Augustin Ochenreite / Associated Press
p. 592 *bottom:* Richard Megna / Fundamental Photographs
p. 593 *left:* AlsoSalt
p. 593 *right:* Family Safety Products Inc.

Chapter 17

p. 594 Andrew Poertner / Associated Press
p. 595 Pearson Education
p. 603 *all:* Pearson Education
p. 604 blackred / iStockphoto
p. 609 Pearson Education
p. 610 Pearson Education
p. 613 *all:* Pearson Education
p. 615 Pearson Education
p. 617 REUTERS / Jose Manuel Ribeiro
p. 618 Pearson Education
p. 619 Pearson Education
p. 621 Lynn Watson / Shutterstock
p. 623 *left:* blickwinkel / Alamy
p. 623 *right:* Imagestate Media Partners / Alamy
p. 624 Pearson Education
p. 625 Arterra Picture Library / Alamy
p. 628 Pearson Education
p. 629 Pearson Education
p. 632 *left, top:* DuPont & Company
p. 632 *left, middle:* Siede Preis / Getty Images
p. 632 *left, bottom:* Pearson Education
p. 632 *right:* Frank Greenaway / Dorling Kindersley
p. 634 Pearson Education

Chapter 18

p. 637 Chris Martinez / Newscom
p. 638 Pearson Education
p. 639 AZP Worldwide / Shutterstock
p. 641 Addison Wesley Longman, Inc. / San Francisco
p. 644 Pearson Education
p. 645 Pearson Education
p. 647 Pearson Education
p. 648 Pearson Education
p. 649 *left:* Danny E Hooks / Shutterstock
p. 649 *right:* David Toase / Getty Images
p. 654 Tischenko Irina / Shutterstock
p. 655 John Pitcher / iStockphoto
p. 656 Pearson Education
p. 657 Pearson Education
p. 659 *all:* National Heart, Lung, and Blood Institute
p. 660 DHuss / iStockphoto
p. 663 Pearson Education
p. 666 Niar / Shutterstock
p. 667 PhotoAlto / Alamy
p. 674 Pearson Education
p. 682 *left, top:* Pearson Education
p. 682 *left, bottom:* John Pitcher / iStockphoto
p. 682 *right:* DHuss / iStockphoto
p. 685 *left, top:* Pearson Education
p. 685 *2nd from left, top:* Katherine Welles / Shutterstock
p. 685 *left, 2nd from top:* Pearson Education
p. 685 *2nd from left, 2nd from top:* Pearson Education
p. 685 *left, bottom:* Light Creation Photography / iStockphoto
p. 685 *right, top:* Pearson Education
p. 685 *right, middle:* Elena Schweitzer / iStockphoto
p. 685 *right, bottom:* Maternal Memories Photography / iStockphoto
p. 686 *left:* Pearson Education
p. 686 *right:* Miep van Damm / Pearson Education
p. 691 *left, top:* gem photography / iStockphoto
p. 691 *left, bottom:* Charles D. Winters / Photo Researchers, Inc.
p. 691 *right, top:* Pearson Education
p. 691 *right, middle:* Lauree Feldmen/ Getty Images
p. 691 *right, bottom:* Martin M. Rotker / Photo Researchers, Inc.
p. 692 David Zaitz / Alamy

Glossary/Index

t = table
Italic number = figure

A

Abbreviated electron configuration, 147
Absolute zero, 79, 81t
Acetaldehyde, 226t, 547
Acetic acid, 226t, 332t, 476
  buffers, *505*, 506
Acetone, 258, 332t
Acetylene (ethyne), 254, 601
Acetylsalicylic acid (aspirin), 47t, 259
Acid A substance that dissolves in water and produces hydrogen ions (H^+), according to the Arrhenius theory. All acids are hydrogen ion donors, according to the Brønsted–Lowry theory, 473–518
  bases and (neutralization), 500–501
  Brønsted–Lowry, 478
  characteristics of, 477t, 487t
  conjugate acid–base pair, 479–481
  diprotic, 482–484
  naming, 475t, 475–477
  reactions of, 499–503
  stomach, 498
  strength of, 481–486
  strong, 481–482, 482t, *483*, 487t
  titration, *503*, 503–504
  weak, 481–482, 482t, *483*
Acid–base titration, *503*, 503–504
Acid dissociation constant (K_a) The product of the concentrations of the ions from the dissociation of a weak acid divided by the concentration of the weak acid, 486–488, 487t
Acidic amino acid An amino acid that has an R group with a carboxylate ($—COO^-$) group, 661
Acidic solution, *490*
  balancing oxidation–reduction equations in, 530–532
  examples of, 490t
  pH of, *492*
  stomach acid, 498
Acidosis A condition in which the blood has a lower pH than normal, 509, 509t
Acid rain, 500–501
Activation energy The energy that must be provided by a collision to break apart the bonds of the reacting molecules, 439–440, *440*
Active learning, 10, 10t
Active site A pocket in a part of the tertiary enzyme structure that binds substrate and catalyzes a reaction, 669, *670*
Activity series A table of half-reactions with the metals that oxidize most easily at the top, and the metals that do not oxidize easily at the bottom, 534, 534t
Actual yield The actual amount of product produced by a reaction, 292
Addition (mathematical)
  negative numbers, 13
  positive numbers, 13
  significant figures and, 36–37
Adenine (A), 671–672, *672*
Adenosine-5′-monophosphate (AMP), 672, *673*
Air
  as gas mixture, 381, 393
  typical composition, 381t
Alanine, 267t, 268, 327, 661, 662t
Alchemists, 4
Alcohol An organic compound that contains the hydroxyl (—OH) group bonded to a carbon atom, 256–257, 261t, 608–611
  ball-and-stick model, *608*
  classification of, 545–547
  classifying, 261t, 608–609
  combustion of, 257
  functional group, 261t
  hydroxyl groups in, 256–257, 608
  important, 609–610
  naming, 608–609
  oxidation of, 545–547
Aldehyde A class of organic compounds that contains a carbonyl (C=O) group bonded to at least one hydrogen atom, 257–258, 261t
  naming, 611–612
Aldohexose, 640
Aldose A monosaccharide that contains an aldehyde group, 639
Alkali metal Elements of Group 1A (1) except hydrogen; these are soft, shiny metals, 110, *110*
Alkaline battery, 539
Alkaline earth metals Group 2A (2) elements, 110
Alkaloid An amine having physiological activity that is produced in plants, 624–625
Alkalosis, 509, 509t
Alkanes Hydrocarbons containing only single bonds between carbon atoms, 195–198
  ball-and-stick model, *597*
  boiling point of, 326t
  branch, substituents in, 595–600, 598t
  comparing name, 601t
  condensed structural formulas for, 599–600
  cycloalkanes, 594, 596t
  mass of, 326t
  naming, 195–196, 196t, 598–599
  properties of, 197
  structural formulas, 195–197, *197*, 596t
  substituents used in naming, 598–599
Alkenes A type of hydrocarbon that contains carbon–carbon double bonds (C=C), 254
  double bond, 254–255, 261t, 601–605
  hydrogenation of, 255
  identifying, 601–602
  naming, 601t, 601–602, 606–607
  polymers, 602–605, *603*, 604t
  structure, 254, *254*, *601*
Alkyl group An alkane minus one hydrogen atom. Alkyl groups are named like the corresponding alkanes except a *yl* ending replaces *ane*, 598
Alkynes Hydrocarbons that contain carbon–carbon triple bonds (C≡C), 601–605
  identifying, 601–602
  naming, 601t, 601–602, 606–607
  structure, 601, *601*
α (alpha) helix A secondary level of protein structure, in which hydrogen bonds connect the N—H of one peptide bond with the C=O of a peptide bond farther down the chain to form a coiled or corkscrew structure, 665, *666*
Alpha decay, 564–566
Alpha particle A nuclear particle identical to a helium nucleus, symbol α or ${}^4_2He$, 561, 561t
  protecting from, 562, 563t
Altitude
  atmospheric pressure and, 357t
  boiling point and, 367, *368*
  high, 457–458
  oxygen–hemoglobin equilibrium and, 457–458
Aluminum, *107*, 540
Amethyst, *74*
Amidation The formation of an amide from a carboxylic acid and an amine with the elimination of a molecule of water, 625–626, 631
Amide An organic compound in which a carbon containing the carbonyl group is attached to a nitrogen group, 261, 262t, 625–627
Amine An organic compound that contains a nitrogen atom bonded to one or more carbon atoms, 260–261, 262t
  aromatic, 623
  biogenic, 260–261
  definition of, 622
  in health and medicine, 260–261
  naming of, 622–623
Amino acid The building block of proteins, consisting of an amino group, a carboxylic acid group, and a unique side group attached to the alpha carbon, 660–664
  basic, 661
  codons for, 678–679
  definition of, 266
  essential, 663
  genetic code and, 678–679
  N- and C-terminal, 664
  polar and nonpolar, 661, 662t
  in proteins, 662t
  protein synthesis (translation), 679, *680*
  structure of, 267, 327, 660, 662t
  types of, 267t
Ammonia, 332t, *623*
Ammonium ion, 183t

AMP (adenosine-5′-monophosphate), 672, *673*
Amphetamines, 261
Amphoteric Substances that act as either an acid or a base in water, 480
Amylase, 647
Amylopectin A branched-chain polymer of starch composed of glucose units joined by α-1,4- and α-1,6-glycosidic bonds, 647, *648*
Amylose An unbranched polymer of starch composed of glucose units joined by α-1,4-glycosidic bonds, *538*, 647
Aniline, 606, 623
Anion A negatively charged ion, 171
Anode The electrode where oxidation takes place, 536, 538, 540
Antabuse, 548
Antacids, *241*, 502–503, 503t
Anthracene, 256
Antihistamine, 624
Antimatter, 561
Aqueous solution, 396, 399t
Area, 35
Arginine, 662t
Argon (Ar), 148
Aromatic amines, 623
Aromatic compounds Compounds that contain the ring structure of benzene, 255–256, 261t–262t, 605–607
  naming, 606–607
Arrhenius, Svante, 475
Arrhenius theory, 475, 477t
Arsenic (As), 113t
Artery, 355
Artificial kidney, 426–427
Artificial sweeteners, 646t, 646–647
Ascorbic acid, 224
Asparagine, 327, 662t
Aspartame, 268, 646t, 647
Aspartic acid, 327, 662t
Aspirin, 47t, 168
Atherosclerosis, 265
Atmosphere (atm) A unit equal to the pressure exerted by a column of mercury 760 mm high, *354*, 356, 357t
Atmospheric pressure The pressure exerted by the atmosphere, 353, 381
  altitude and, 357t
Atom The smallest particle of an element that retains the characteristics of the element, 115–118
  composition of, representative, 120t
  electrical charges in, 115–116
  isotopes, 122–126
  mass of, 117–118, 122–126
  particles in (subatomic), 115, 117t
  sizes of, 170–171
  structure of, 116–117, *117*
Atomic energy, 582
Atomic mass The weighted average mass of all the naturally occurring isotopes of an element, 122–126
  calculating, 124–125
  of common elements, 124t
  isotopes and, 122–126
Atomic mass unit (amu) A small mass unit used to describe the mass of very small particles such as atoms and subatomic particles; 1 amu is equal to one-twelfth the mass of a carbon-12 atom, 117, 117t
Atomic number A number that is equal to the number of protons in an atom, 118–121, 120t
Atomic radius, 156–158
Atomic size The distance between the outermost electrons and the nucleus, 156–158, *157*, 159t
Atomic spectrum A series of lines specific for each element produced by photons emitted by electrons dropping to lower energy levels, 138–139, *139*
Atomic symbol An abbreviation for an isotope, which shows the mass number in the upper-left corner and the atomic number in the lower-left corner, 122, 122t
Atomic theory, 115
Atropine, 624
Attractive force, 74
  in compounds, 324–328, 325t
  melting points and, 326–328
  types of, 324–328, 325t
Autoclave, *368*
Avogadro, Amedeo, 208
Avogadro's law A gas law stating that the volume of gas is directly related to the number of moles when temperature and pressure do not change, *371*, 371–374
Avogadro's number The number of items in a mole, equal to 6.022×10^{23}, 208–210, 209t

B

Background radiation, 573–574, 574t
Baking soda, 47t
Balanced equation The final form of a chemical equation that shows the same number of atoms of each element in the reactants and products, 242–247
Ball-and-stick model, *258*, *309*
  alcohols, *608*
  branched alkanes, 597
  ethane, *195*
  ethene (ethylene), *601*
  ethyne (acetylene), *601*
  hexane, *197*
  methane, *195*
Barium sulfate, 403, *403*
Barometer, *356*, 356–357
Base (chemical) A substance that dissolves in water and produces hydroxide ions (OH^-) according to the Arrhenius theory. All bases are hydrogen ion acceptors, according to the Brønsted–Lowry theory, 473–518
  acids and (neutralization), 500–501
  Brønsted–Lowry, 478
  characteristics of, 477t
  conjugate acid–base pair, 479–481
  naming, 477–478
  reactions of, 499–503
  strength of, 481–486
  strong, 484
  weak, 484
Base (nucleic acid) Nitrogen-containing compounds found in DNA and RNA: adenosine (A), thymine (T), cytosine (C), guanine (G), and uracil (U), 671–672
  complementary base pairs, 674, *675*
Base dissociation constant (K_b) The product of the concentrations of the ions from the dissociation of a weak base divided by the concentration of the weak base, 487
Basic amino acid An amino acid that contains an R group with an ammonium ($-NH_3^+$) ion, 661
Basic solution, *490*
  balancing oxidation–reduction equations in, 532–533
  examples of, 490t
  pH of, *492*
Batteries, 538–539
Becquerel (Bq) A unit of activity of a radioactive sample equal to one disintegration per second, 572, 572t
Beeswax, 654, 654t
Belladonna, 624
Bends, scuba diving and, 384
Bent The shape of a molecule with two bonded atoms and one lone pair or two lone pairs, 315–316, 316t
Benzamide, 627
Benzedrine, 260
Benzene A ring of six carbon atoms each of which is attached to one hydrogen atom (C_6H_6), 605
  in aromatics, 255, 605–607
Benzoic acid, 616
Benzo[*a*]pyrene, 256
Beryllium (Be), 110
β (beta)-pleated sheet A secondary level of protein structure that consists of hydrogen bonds between peptide links in parallel polypeptide chains, 665, *666*
Beta decay, 566–567
Beta particle A particle identical to an electron with symbol ${}^{0}_{-1}e$ or β, that forms in the nucleus when a neutron changes to a proton and an electron, 561, 561t
  beta decay, 566–567
  protecting from, 562, 563t
Biogenic amines, 260–261
Bisphenol A (BPA), 610
Blimp, helium, 170
Block elements, *150*, 150–151
Blood
  buffers in, 508–509, 509t
  partial pressures of gases in, 383t
  plasma, 395
Blood alcohol concentration, 548
Blood clotting, 113t
Blood gas, 383t, 383–384
Blood glucose, 640
Blood pressure, measuring, 355
Blood sugar. *See* Glucose
Body, human. *See* Human body
Body fat, 45–46, *46*
Body temperature, 460
Boiling The formation of bubbles of gas throughout a liquid, 331, *331*
Boiling point The temperature at which a substance exists as a liquid and gas; liquid changes to gas (boils), and gas changes to liquid (condenses), 331
  of alkanes, 326t
  Celsius (°C) scale, 78
  elevation of, molality used to calculate, 421–422
  Fahrenheit (°F) scale, 78

D

temperature change and, 441, 441t, 458–459, 459t
volume (pressure) change and, 456–458, 459t
Equilibrium constant expression The ratio of the concentrations of products to the concentrations of reactants, with each component raised to an exponent equal to the coefficient of that compound in the balanced chemical equation, 447–448
Equilibrium constant (K_c) The numerical value obtained by substituting the equilibrium concentrations of the components into the equilibrium constant expression, 447–448
calculating, 449t, 449–451
large, 451, *451*, 452t
small, 451–452, 452t, *452*
using, 451–454
Equivalent dose The measure of biological damage from an absorbed dose that has been adjusted for the type of radiation, 572
Erythrose, 226t
Essential amino acid Amino acids that must be supplied by the diet because they are not synthesized by the body, 663
Ester An organic compound that contains a carboxyl (—COO—) group with an oxygen atom bonded to carbon, 259, 261t
formation of, 618
fruit and flavoring, 259, 620t
naming of, 619–620
in plants, 620–621
Ester bond, 654
Esterification The formation of an ester from a carboxylic acid and an alcohol with the elimination of a molecule of water in the presence of a strong acid catalyst, 618–619, 631
Ethanamide, 625, 627
Ethane, *195*, 326t, 596t
Ethanediol (ethylene glycol), 609
Ethanoic acid, 476, 615t, 618–619, 625
Ethanol (ethyl alcohol)
description of, 256
in hand sanitizers, 257
heat of fusion for, 332t
heat of vaporization for, 332t
oxidation of, 547–548
value, 47t
See also Alcohol
Ethene (ethylene), 254, *254*, 601, *601*, 604t
Ether A class of organic compounds that contains an oxygen atom bonded to two carbon atoms (—O—), 259, 608, 610–611
Ethyl alcohol, 256
Ethyl butanoate, 620t
Ethylene (ethene), 254, *254*, 601, *601*, 604t
Ethylene glycol, 609
Ethyl heptanoate, *621*
Ethyne (acetylene), 601, *601*
Eugenol, 609–610
Evaporation The formation of a gas (vapor) by the escape of high-energy molecules from the surface of a liquid, 331, *331*
Exact number A number obtained by counting or definition, 33–34, 34t
Excess reactant The reactant that remains when the limiting reactant is used up in a reaction, 288
Exercise physiologist, 239
Exhalation, 361
Exothermic reaction A reaction wherein the energy of the products is lower than that of the reactants, 295
equilibrium shifting from temperature change, 458–459, 459t
in hot pack, 297
Expanded structural formula A type of structural formula that shows the arrangement of the atoms by showing each bond between carbon atoms or between carbon and hydrogen, 195, 197
butane, 197
hexane, *197*
Experiment A procedure that tests the validity of a hypothesis, 6
EXP function key, 30
Expiration, 361

F

Fahrenheit (°F) temperature scale, 15, 78–85
boiling and freezing point of water, 78, 81t
comparison of temperature scales, 78–80, 81t
converting to Celsius temperature, 79
Faraday, Michael, 255, 605
Farming, 104
Fat Another term for solid triacylglycerols, 654–659
energy content, 93t
hibernation and, 655
hydrogenation, 658, *658*
melting point, 655–656, *656*
saponification, 658–659
saturated, 658
source of energy during hibernation, 655
substitute (Olestra), 657
Fatty acid Long-chain carboxylic acid found in fats and oils, 651–654
description of, 264
melting points, 652t
monounsaturated, 652, 652t
polyunsaturated, 652, 652t
properties of, 651–654
saturated, 652, 652t, 658
sources of, 264t
structure of, 264t
structures, 652t
trans, 658
***f* block** The 14 elements in the rows at the bottom of the periodic table in which electrons fill the seven 4*f* and 5*f* orbitals, *150*, 151
Femto (f), 39t
Ferritin, 660t
Fertilizers, 104, 221
Fibril, collagen, 667
"Fight-or-flight," 260
Film badges, 572, *572*
Filtration, 73
Firefighter, 594
Fish, mercury level in, 108
Fish oils, omega-3 fatty acids in, 264–265
Fission A process in which large nuclei are split into smaller pieces, releasing large amounts of energy, 582, *583*
Flammability
inorganic compound, 194t
organic compound, 194t
Food
energy values of, 91–93
irradiating, 573
mercury content, 108
nutrition labeling, *92*
water percentage, 395t
Force
attractive, 324–328, 325t
dispersion, 325, 325t
See also Pressure
Forensic scientist, 1
Forensic toxicologist, 637
Formaldehyde, 258
Formic acid, 476
Formula The group of symbols and subscripts that represent the atoms or ions in a compound, 175–178
See also Condensed structural formula; Expanded structural formula
Formula unit The group of ions represented by the formula of an ionic compound, 177, 209
Forward reaction, 443–444, *445*
Fossil fuel, 56, 364
Fractional distillation, 198
Freeze-dried foods, 336
Freezer burn, 336
Freezing A change of state from liquid to solid, 329
Freezing point (fp) The temperature at which a liquid changes to a solid (freezes) and a solid changes to a liquid (melts), 329
Celsius (°C) scale, 78, 81t
Fahrenheit (°F) scale, 78, 81t
Kelvin (K) scale, 79, 81t
lowering of, molality used to calculate, 421–422
solutes used to lower, 419–420, 422t
Frequency The number of times the crests of a wave pass a point in 1 s, 135, 137
Fructose A monosaccharide found in honey and fruit juices; it is combined with glucose in sucrose, 263, 640
Fruits
esters in, 620t
ripening, *254*
Fuel cells, 542
Fumaric acid, 618
Functional group A group of atoms that determines the physical and chemical properties and naming of a class of organic compounds, 253–263, 254t
Fusion A reaction in which large amounts of energy are released when small nuclei combine to form larger nuclei, 583–584

G

Galactose A monosaccharide that occurs combined with glucose in lactose, 640
Gallium-67, 579t
Gallium-68, 579t
Galvanization, 541
Gamma emission, 568
Gamma ray High-energy radiation, symbol γ, or ${}^{0}_{0}\gamma$, emitted by an unstable nucleus, 561, 561t
killing bacteria in food with, 573
protecting from, 562, 563t

Nucleus (*Continued*)
fusion, 582
splitting, 582
Numerator, 42
NutraSweet, 647
Nutrient labeling, *92*
Nutrition, 91–94
caloric value of foods, 91–93, 93t
Nutrition Facts label, *92*

O

Observation Information determined by noting and recording a natural phenomenon, 6
Octet rule Representative elements react with other elements to produce a noble-gas configuration with eight valence electrons, 170
exceptions, 313–314
Octyl ethanoate, 620t
Oil Another term for a liquid triacylglycerol, 265
hydrogenation, 658, *658*
melting point, 655–656, *656*
polyunsaturated, 655
vegetable, 658
See also Crude oil
Oil spills, 56–57
Oleic acid, 264t, 266, 652t, 653
Olestra, 657
Omega-3 fatty acids in fish oils, 264–265
Opium, 624
Orbital The region around the nucleus where electrons of certain energy are more likely to be found: *s* orbitals are spherical; *p* orbitals have two lobes, *142*
shape of, 142–144
Orbital capacity, 144
Orbital diagram A diagram that shows the distribution of electrons in the orbitals of the energy levels, 145–146, *146–147*
Period 1, 147
Period 2, 147
Period 3, 148
Organic compounds Compounds of carbon that have covalent bonds with properties that include low melting and boiling points, insolubility in water, and flammability, 169, 193–195
alkanes, 195–198
bonding, 194t, 194–195
classification of, 261t–262t
covalent bonds, 254t
functional groups, 253–263, 254t
naming, 195–196, 196t, *197*
properties of, 194t
tetrahedral structure of carbon, 195
Osmosis The flow of a solvent, usually water, through a semipermeable membrane into a solution of higher solute concentration, 423–424
Osmotic pressure The pressure that prevents the flow of water into the more concentrated solution, 423–424
Osteoporosis, 59
Overweight, 69
Oxaloacetic acid, 618
Oxidation The loss of electrons by a substance, 523
of alcohols, 545–547
definition of, 523–524
of ethanol, 547–548
of primary alcohol, 546
of secondary alcohol, 546
Oxidation number A number equal to zero in an element or the charge of a monatomic ion; in molecular compounds and polyatomic ions, oxidation numbers are assigned using a set of rules, 525t, 525–529
assigning of, 525–527
oxidation–reduction identified using, 527–528
Oxidation–reduction reaction A reaction in which electrons are transferred from one reactant to another, 523–524
balancing of, 529–533
definition of, 522
electrical energy and, 534–544
half-reactions used to balance, 529–533
oxidation numbers used to identify, 527–528
Oxidizing agent The reactant that gains electrons and is reduced, 528
Oxycodone (OxyContin), 624–625
Oxygen (O)
density of, 55t
function of, 113t
hydroxyl group, 608
partial pressure in blood and tissue, 383, 383t
Oxygen–hemoglobin equilibrium, 457–458
Ozone, 311–312

P

Pain relievers, 624
Palladium-103, 579t, 581
Palmitic acid, 264t, 652t
Palmitoleic acid, 652t
Paracelsus, 4, 47
Paraffins, 197
Partial pressure The pressure exerted by a single gas in a gas mixture, 380–383, 383t
Pascal (Pa), 356t
Pauli exclusion principle, 144
***p* block** The elements in Groups 3A (13) to 8A (18) in which electrons fill the *p* orbitals, 150, *150*
Pentose sugars, 672
Pentyl butanoate, 620t
Pentyl ethanoate, 620t
Peptide, 267–268
Peptide bond The amide bond in peptides that joins the carboxylate group of one amino acid with the ammonium group in the next amino acid, 267, 663–664
Peptide chain, *665*
Percentage, 14, 45–46
Percent concentration, 406–408, 409t
Percent yield The ratio of the actual yield for a reaction to the theoretical yield possible for the reaction, 292–294
Period A horizontal row of elements in the periodic table, 109
Periodic properties, 154–161
Periodic table An arrangement of elements by increasing atomic number such that elements having similar chemical behavior are grouped in vertical columns, 108–114, *109*
electron configurations and, *150*, 150–154
periods and groups in, 109–110, *109–110*
trends in, 154–161
Per (prefix), 183
Pesticides, 8, 47t
Peta (P), 39t
PETE (polyethylene terephthalate), 603
pH A measure of the $[H_3O^+]$ in a solution; $pH = -\log[H_3O^+]$, 491–499, *493*
calculating, 493–496, 506–508
indicators, 503
scale, *492*
Phenol An organic compound that has a hydroxyl ($-OH$) group attached to a benzene ring, 606, 608, *608*
plant sources of, 609
structure of, 606
types of, 609–610
Phenolphthalein, 503
Phenylalanine, 267t, 647, 662t
Phenylketonuria (PKU), 268, 647
Pheromones, 255
pH meter, *493*
Phosphodiester bond The phosphate link that joins the hydroxyl group in one nucleotide to the phosphate group on the next nucleotide, 673
Phosphorus (P), 104, 113t, 183t
Phosphorus-32, 579t
Photochemical smog, 249
Photon The smallest particle of light, 138
Photosynthesis, 638, *638–639*
Physical change A change in which the physical properties of a substance change without any change in its identity, 76, 76t
Physical properties The properties that can be observed or measured without affecting the identity of a substance, 75t, 76, 77t
Pico (p), 39t
PKU (phenylketonuria), 647
Place values, 12–18
Plaque, 659, *659*
Plasma, 395
Plastics, 603–604
recycling, 603
pOH A measure of the $[OH^-]$ in a solution; $pOH = -\log[OH^-]$, 496–497
Polar amino acid Amino acids that are soluble in water because their R group is polar: hydroxyl ($-OH$), sulfur group ($-SH$), carbonyl ($C{=}O$), ammonium ($-NH_3^+$), or carboxylate ($-COO^-$), 661, 662t
Polar covalent bond A covalent bond in which the electrons are shared unequally, *320*
Polarity A measure of the unequal sharing of electrons, indicated by the difference in electronegativities, 320–324
Polar molecule One end of a molecule is more negatively charged than the other end, 322–323
Polar solute, 396
Polar solvent, 395
Polyatomic ion A group of covalently bonded atoms that has an overall electrical charge, 182–187
bones and teeth, 184
compounds containing, 184, 185t
naming, 183, 183t, 185–187
products containing, *182*

writing formula, 183–185
Polycyclic aromatic hydrocarbons (PAHs), 256
Polydichloroethylene (Saran), *603*, 604t
Polyethylene, 603, *603*, 604t
Polyethylene terephthalate (PETE), 603
Polymer A very large molecule that is composed of many small, repeating structural units that are identical, 601, *603*
alkene, *601*, 602–605, *603*, 604t
definition of, 602
recycling, 603, *603*
synthetic, 602–603, *603*
Polypropylene, 603, *603*, 604t
Polysaccharide Polymers of many monosaccharide units, usually glucose. Polysaccharides differ in the types of glycosidic bonds and the amount of branching in the polymer, 647–651
cellulose, 647–649, *649*
chemical structure of, 264
definition of, 263–264
digesting, 649
Polystyrene, 603, *603*, 604t
Polytetrafluoroethylene (Teflon), *603*, 604t
Polyunsaturated fatty acid A fatty acid that contains two or more double bonds, 652
melting point and structure, 652t
Polyvinyl chloride (PVC), 603, *603*, 604t
p orbitals, 143
Positive ion, 170–171, 179t–180t, 179–181
Positive numbers, 13
Positron A particle with no mass and a positive charge, symbol β^+ or ${}^{0}_{+1}e$, produced when a proton is transformed into a neutron and a positron, 561, 561t
Positron emission, 567–568
Positron emission tomography (PET), 580
Potassium (K)
alkali metal, 110, *110*
as fertilizer, 104
function of, 113t
ion in the body, 174t
Potassium-40, 577t
Potential energy A type of energy related to position or composition of a substance, 83
Pound, 27
conversion factor, 43–44
Power of ten, 29t, 29–30
Power plant, nuclear, 585
Chernobyl, 574
Prefix The part of the name of a metric unit that precedes the base unit and specifies the size of the measurement. All prefixes are related on a decimal scale, 38–42, 39t, 606
Pressure The force exerted by gas particles that hit the walls of a container, *353*, 353–354, *353–354*
altitude and, 357t
atmospheric, 353, *356*, 356–357
blood, measuring, 355
in breathing, 361
change, equilibrium and, 456–457, *457*
gas, 353–354, 355t, 356–358
gradient, 361
measuring, 356, 356t, *356*
osmotic, 423–424
partial, 380–383, 383t
solubility and (Henry's law), 401–402
standard (STP), *372*, 372–374
temperature and (Gay-Lussac's law), *366*, 366–369
vapor, 367t, 367–368
volume and (Boyle's law), 358–362
Primary (1°) alcohol An alcohol that has one carbon group bonded to the carbon atom with the —OH group, 545–546
Primary structure The sequence of amino acids in a protein, 665, 668t, *673*, 673–674
Principal quantum number (n) The number ($n = 1, n = 2 \ldots$) assigned to an energy level, 139
Prism, light passing through, *134*
Problem solving, 48–54
cancellation of units, 49
Guide to Problem Solving (GPS), 50
using two or more conversion factors, 50–51
Products The substances formed as a result of a chemical reaction, 240, 242
Proline, 662t
Propane, 193, *194*, 326t, 596t
Propanetriol (glycerol, glycerin), 609
Propanoic acid, 476, 615t
Propionic acid, 476
Propyl ethanoate, 620t
Prostate cancer, 581
Protein A biologically active compound that is a polymer of amino acids; A term used for biologically active polypeptides that have many amino acids linked together by peptide bonds, 660–671
classification of, 675t
composition of, 327
definition of, 266, 665
energy content, 93t
as enzymes, 669–671
primary structure, 665
secondary structure, 665–667, *666*
shapes of, 327–328
structure, summary of, 668t
20 amino acids in, 662t
Protein synthesis, 679, *680*
translation, 679, *680*
Proton A positively charged subatomic particle having a mass of 1 amu and found in the nucleus of an atom; its symbol is p or p^+, 115–116, *116*, 117t, *117*, 561t
psi (pound per square inch), 356, 356t
Pure substance A type of matter composed of elements or compounds that has a definite composition, 70
Purine, 671–672, *672*
Pyrimidine, 671–672, *672*
Pyruvic acid, 617

Q

Quart, 27
Quaternary structure A protein structure in which two or more protein subunits form an active protein, 668, 668t
Quinine, 624

R

Rad (radiation absorbed dose) A measure of an amount of radiation absorbed by the body, 572, 572t
Radiation Energy or particles released by radioactive atoms, 560
average annual per person, 574t
background, 573–574, 574t
biological effects of, 562
common forms, 574t
doses in medical procedures, *579*
exposure, 573–574, 574t
food and, 573
lethal dosage, 574, 574t
measuring, 571–574, 572t
medical applications, 579–582
protecting from, 562–563
sickness, 574
treating food, 573
types of, 561
Radiation therapy The use of high doses of radiation to destroy harmful tissues in the body, *579*, 580–581
Radioactive The process by which an unstable nucleus breaks down with the release of high-energy radiation, 560
Radioactive decay The process by which an unstable nucleus breaks down with the release of high-energy radiation, 564–571
Radioactive iodine, 560
Radioactive iodine uptake (RAIU), 579
Radioactive isotope, 560–564, 561t
producing, 568–569
Radioactive waste, 585
Radioactivity, 579–582
Radioisotope A radioactive atom of an element, 560–564, 561t
half-life, 575–578, 579t
medical applications, 577t, 579t, *579*, 579–582
scans with, *579*, 579–580, *581*
Radiologist, 559
Radio waves, 135
Radium-226, 577t
Radon (Rn), 111, 566
Radon-222, 577t
Rate of reaction The speed at which reactants form product(s), *438*, 439–443
factors affecting, 441t, 441–442
formula, 440
Reactants The initial substances that undergo change in a chemical reaction, 240, 242
excess, 288
increasing concentration, 441, 441t, *441*
limiting, 288–292
mole–mole factor calculation, 285–287
Reaction
catalysts and, 441, 441t, *670*
direction of, 485
heat of, 295–297
See also Chemical reaction; Rate of reaction
Recycling
plastics, 603, *603*
plastics, symbols for, 603
Red blood cells, 562
Redox. *See* Oxidation–reduction reaction
Reducing agent The reactant that loses electrons and is oxidized, 528
Reduction The gain of electrons by a substance, 522–524
Registered nurse, 24
Rem (radiation equivalent in humans) A measure of the biological damage caused by the various kinds of radiation (rad × radiation biological factor), 572, 572t

T

Metric and SI Units and Some Useful Conversion Factors

Length	SI Unit Meter (m)	Volume	SI Unit Cubic Meter (m^3)	Mass	SI Unit Kilogram (kg)
1 meter (m) = 100 centimeters (cm)		1 liter (L) = 1000 milliliters (mL)		1 kilogram (kg) = 1000 grams (g)	
1 meter (m) = 1000 millimeters (mm)		1 mL = 1 cm^3		1 g = 1000 milligrams (mg)	
1 cm = 10 mm		1 L = 1.057 quart (qt)		1 kg = 2.205 lb	
1 kilometer (km) = 0.6214 mile (mi)		1 qt = 946.3 mL		1 lb = 453.6 g	
1 inch (in.) = 2.54 cm (exact)				1 mol = 6.022×10^{23} particles	
				Water	
				density = 1.00 g/mL (at 4 °C)	

Temperature	SI Unit Kelvin (K)	Pressure	SI Unit Pascal (Pa)	Energy	SI Unit Joule (J)
$°F = 1.8(°C) + 32$		1 atm = 760 mmHg		1 calorie (cal) = 4.184 J	
$°C = \frac{(°F - 32)}{1.8}$		1 atm = 101.325 kPa		1 kcal = 1000 cal	
$K = °C + 273$		1 atm = 760 torr		**Water**	
		1 mol of gas (STP) = 22.4 L		Heat of fusion = 334 J/g; 80. cal/g	
		R = 0.0821 L · atm/mol · K		Heat of vaporization = 2260 J/g; 540 cal/g	
		R = 62.4 L · mmHg/mol · K		Specific heat (*SH*) = 4.184 J/g °C	

Prefixes for Metric (SI) Units

Prefix	Symbol	Power of Ten
Values Greater than 1		
peta	P	10^{15}
tera	T	10^{12}
giga	G	10^{9}
mega	M	10^{6}
kilo	k	10^{3}
Values Less than 1		
deci	d	10^{-1}
centi	c	10^{-2}
milli	m	10^{-3}
micro	μ	10^{-6}
nano	n	10^{-9}
pico	p	10^{-12}
femto	f	10^{-15}

Formulas and Molar Masses of Some Typical Compounds

Name	Formula	Molar Mass (g/mol)	Name	Formula	Molar Mass (g/mol)
Ammonia	NH_3	17.03	Hydrogen chloride	HCl	36.46
Ammonium chloride	NH_4Cl	53.49	Iron(III) oxide	Fe_2O_3	159.70
Ammonium sulfate	$(NH_4)_2SO_4$	132.15	Magnesium oxide	MgO	40.31
Bromine	Br_2	159.80	Methane	CH_4	16.04
Butane	C_4H_{10}	58.12	Nitrogen	N_2	28.02
Calcium carbonate	$CaCO_3$	100.09	Oxygen	O_2	32.00
Calcium chloride	$CaCl_2$	110.98	Potassium carbonate	K_2CO_3	138.21
Calcium hydroxide	$Ca(OH)_2$	74.10	Potassium nitrate	KNO_3	101.11
Calcium oxide	CaO	56.08	Propane	C_3H_8	44.09
Carbon dioxide	CO_2	44.01	Sodium chloride	NaCl	58.44
Chlorine	Cl_2	70.90	Sodium hydroxide	NaOH	40.00
Copper(II) sulfide	CuS	95.62	Sulfur trioxide	SO_3	80.07
Hydrogen	H_2	2.016	Water	H_2O	18.02